AN INDEX
TO BOOK REVIEWS
IN THE HUMANITIES

VOLUME 23
1982

PHILLIP THOMSON
WILLIAMSTON, MICHIGAN

This volume of the INDEX contains data collected up to 31 December 1982.

This is an index to book reviews in humanities periodicals. Beginning with volume 12 of this Index (dated 1971), the former policy of selectively indexing reviews of books in certain subject categories only was dropped in favor of a policy of indexing all reviews in the periodicals indexed, with the one exception of children's books — the reviews of which will not be indexed.

The form of the entries used is as follows:

> Author. Title.
> Reviewer. Identifying Legend.

The author's name used is the name that appears on the title-page of the book being reviewed, as well as we are able to determine, even though this name is known to be a pseudonym. The title only is shown; subtitles are included only where they are necessary to identify a book in a series. The identifying legend consists of the periodical, each of which has a code number, and the date and page number of the periodical where the review is to be found. PMLA abbreviations are also shown (when a periodical has such an abbreviation, but such abbreviations are limited to four letters) immediately following the code number of the periodical. To learn the name of the periodical in which the review appears, it is necessary to refer to the code number to the numerically-arranged list of periodicals beginning on page iii. This list also shows the volume and number of the periodical issues indexed.

Reviews are indexed as they appear and no attempt is made to hold the title until all the reviews are published. For this reason it is necessary to refer to previous and subsequent volumes of this Index to be sure that the complete roster of reviews of any title is seen. As an aid to the user, an asterisk (*) has been added immediately following any title that was also indexed in Volume 22 (1981) of this Index.

Authors with hyphenated surnames are indexed under the name before the hyphen, and the name following the hyphen is not cross-indexed. Authors with more than one surname, but where the names are not hyphenated, are indexed under the first of the names and the last name is cross-indexed. When alphabetizing surnames containing umlauts, the umlauts are ignored. Editors are always shown in the author-title entry, and they are cross-indexed (except where the editor's surname is the same as that of the author). Translators are shown only when they are necessary to identify the book being reviewed (as in the classics), and they are not cross-indexed unless the book being reviewed has no author or editor. Certain reference works and anonymous works that are known primarily by their title are indexed under that title and their editors are cross-indexed.

A list of abbreviations used is shown on page ii.

ABBREVIATIONS

```
Anon.........Anonymous
Apr..........April
Aug..........August
Bk...........Book
Comp(s) .....Compiler(s)
Cont.........Continued
Dec..........December
Ed(s)........Editor(s) [or] Edition(s)
Fasc.........Fascicule
Feb..........February
Jan..........January
Jul..........July
Jun..........June
Mar..........March
No...........Number
Nov..........November
Oct..........October
Prev.........Previous volume of this Index
Pt...........Part
Rev..........Revised
Sep..........September
Ser..........Series
Supp.........Supplement
Trans........Translator(s)
Vol..........Volume
* (asterisk)....This title was also shown
                in the volume of this Index
                immediately preceding this
                one
```

The periodicals in which the reviews appear are identified in this Index by a number. To supplement this number, and to promote ready identification, PMLA abbreviations are also given following this number. Every attempt will be made to index those issues shown here as "missing" in a later volume of this Index.
The following is a list of the periodicals indexed in volume 23:

2(AfrA) - African Arts. Los Angeles.
    Nov80 thru Aug81 (vol 14 complete)
9(AlaR) - Alabama Review. University, Alabama.
    Jan81 thru Oct81 (vol 34 complete)
14 - American Archivist. Chicago.
    Winter80 thru Fall81 (vols 43 and 44 complete)
16 - American Art Journal. New York.
    Winter81 thru Autumn81 (vol 13 complete)
18 - American Film. Washington.
    Oct80 thru Sep81 (vol 6 complete)
24 - American Journal of Philology. Baltimore.
    Spring81 thru Winter81 (vol 102 complete)
26(ALR) - American Literary Realism, 1870-1910. Arlington.
    Spring81 and Autumn81 (vol 14 complete)
27(AL) - American Literature. Durham.
    Mar81 thru Jan82 (vol 53 complete)
29 - The American Poetry Review. Philadelphia.
    Jan-Feb82 thru Nov-Dec82 (vol 11 complete)
35(AS) - American Speech. University, Alabama.
    Spring-Summer77 and Fall-Winter77, Spring81 thru Winter81 (vols 52 and 56 complete)
37 - The Américas. Washington.
    Jan81 thru Nov-Dec81 (vol 33 complete)
38 - Anglia. Tübingen.
    Band 99 complete
39 - Apollo. London.
    Jan81 thru Dec81 (vols 113 and 114 complete)
42(AR) - Antioch Review. Yellow Springs.
    Winter81 thru Fall81 (vol 39 complete)
43 - Architectura. Munich.
    Band 10 and Band 11 complete
45 - Architectural Record. New York.
    Jan81 thru Oct 81 and Dec81 (vol 169 no 1-13 and no 16) [Nov81 issue missing]
46 - Architectural Review. London.
    Jan81 thru Apr81, Jun81, Jul81 thru Dec81 (vol 169 no 1007-1010, vol 169 no 1012, vol 170 complete) [May 81 issue missing]
48 - Archivo Español de Arte. Madrid.
    Jan-Mar81 thru Oct-Dec81 (vol 54 complete) [entire vol 53 is missing]

49 - Ariel. Calgary.
    Jan81 thru Oct81 (vol 12 complete)
50(ArQ) - Arizona Quarterly. Tucson.
    Spring81 thru Winter81 (vol 37 complete)
52 - Arcadia. Berlin.
    Band 15 complete
53(AGP) - Archiv für Geschichte der Philosophie. Berlin.
    Band 62 and Band 63 complete
54 - Art Bulletin. New York.
    Mar81 thru Dec81 (vol 63 complete)
55 - Art News. New York.
    Jan81 thru Dec81 (vol 80 complete)
57 - Artibus Asiae. Ascona.
    Vol 42 complete
59 - Art History. Henley-on-Thames.
    Mar81 thru Dec81 (vol 4 complete)
60 - Arts of Asia. Hong Kong.
    Jan-Feb81 thru Nov-Dec81 (vol 11 complete)
61 - Atlantic Monthly. Boston.
    Jan82 thru Dec82 (vols 249 and 250 complete)
62 - Artforum. New York.
    Sep80 thru Summer82 (vols 19 and 20 complete)
63 - Australasian Journal of Philosophy. Canberra.
    Mar81 thru Dec81 (vol 59 complete)
67 - AUMLA [Journal of the Australasian Universities Language and Literature Assn.] Hobart.
    May81 and Nov81 (no 55 and no 56)
69 - Africa. Manchester.
    Vol 50 complete
70(AN&Q) - American Notes & Queries. Owingsville.
    Sep80 thru Nov/Dec80 (vol 19 no 1-3)
71(ALS) - Australian Literary Studies. St. Lucia.
    May81 and Oct81 (vol 10 no 1 and 2)
72 - Archiv für das Studium der neueren Sprachen und Literaturen. Braunschweig.
    Band 217 complete
73 - Art Magazine. Toronto.
    Sep/Oct80 thru May/Jun81 (vol 12 complete)
75 - Babel. Budapest.
    1/1980 thru 4/1980 (vol 26 complete)
77 - Biography. Honolulu.
    Winter81 thru Fall81 (vol 4 complete)
78(BC) - Book Collector. London.
    Spring81 thru Winter81 (vol 30 complete)
81 - Boundary 2. Binghamton.
    Fall79 and Spring80 thru Spring-Fall81 (vol 8 no 1 and 3, vol 9 no 1 thru vol 10 no 1) [vol 8 no 2 is missing; double issue Spring-Fall81 is vol 9 no 3 and vol 10 no 1]
83 - The British Journal for Eighteenth-Century Studies. Southampton.
    Spring81 and Autumn81 (vol 4 complete)
84 - The British Journal for the Philosophy of Science. Aberdeen.
    Mar81 thru Dec81 (vol 32 complete)

85(SBHC) - Studies in Browning and His
Circle. Waco.
  Spring81 and Fall81 (vol 9 complete)
86(BHS) - Bulletin of Hispanic Studies.
Liverpool.
  Jan81 thru Oct81 (vol 58 complete)
89(BJA) - The British Journal of Aesthetics. London.
  Winter81 thru Autumn81 (vol 21
  complete)
90 - Burlington Magazine. London.
  Jan81 thru Aug81, Oct81 thru Dec81
  (vol 123, no 934-941, no 943-945)
  [Sep81 issue missing]
95(CLAJ) - CLA Journal. Atlanta.
  Sep80 thru Jun81 (vol 24 complete)
97(CQ) - The Cambridge Quarterly. Cambridge, England.
  Vol 10 complete
98 - Critique. Paris.
  Jan80 thru Dec81 (vols 36 and 37
  complete)
99 - Canadian Forum. Toronto.
  Nov81 thru Mar82 (vol 61 no 713-
  716)
102(CanL) - Canadian Literature. Van-
couver.
  Spring80 thru Autumn81 (no 84 thru
  no 90)
104(CASS) - Canadian-American Slavic
Studies/Revue canadienne-américaine
d'études slaves. Tempe.
  Spring81 thru Winter81 (vol 15
  complete)
105 - Canadian Poetry. London, Ontario.
  Spring/Summer81 and Fall/Winter81
  (no 8 and 9)
106 - The Canadian Review of American
Studies. Winnipeg.
  Spring81 thru Winter81 (vol 12
  complete)
107(CRCL) - Canadian Review of Comparative Literature/Revue Canadienne de
Littérature Comparée. Downsview.
  Winter81 and Spring81 (vol 8 no
  1 and 2)
108 - Canadian Theatre Review. Downsview.
  Fall80 thru Fall81 (no 28 thru no
  32)
111 - Cambridge Review. London.
  7Nov80 thru 1Jun81 (vol 102, no
  2258-2263) [entire vol 101 is
  missing]
112 - Celtica. Dublin.
  Vol 14
114(ChiR) - Chicago Review.
  Summer80 thru Spring81 (vol 32
  complete)
121(CJ) - Classical Journal. Greenville.
  Oct/Nov81 thru Apr/May82 (vol 77
  complete)
122 - Classical Philology. Chicago.
  Jan81 thru Oct81 (vol 76 complete)
123 - Classical Review. London.
  Vol 31 complete
124 - Classical World. Pittsburgh.
  Sep/Oct81 thru Jul/Aug82 (vol 75
  complete)
125 - Clio. Ft. Wayne.
  Fall80 thru Summer81 (vol 10 complete)

127 - Art Journal. New York.
  Fall/Winter80 and Spring81 thru
  Winter81 (vols 40 and 41 complete)
128(CE) - College English. Champaign.
  Jan81 thru Dec81 (vol 43 complete)
130 - Comparative Drama. Kalamazoo.
  Spring81 thru Winter81/82 (vol 15
  complete)
131(CL) - Comparative Literature. Eugene.
  Winter81 thru Fall81 (vol 33 complete)
133 - Colloquia Germanica. Lexington.
  Band 14 complete
134(CP) - Concerning Poetry. Bellingham.
  Spring81 and Fall81 (vol 14 complete)
135 - Connoisseur. New York.
  Jan81 thru Dec81 (vols 206-208
  complete)
136 - Conradiana. Lubbock.
  Vol 13 complete
139 - American Craft. New York.
  Feb/Mar81 thru Dec81/Jan82 (vol
  41 complete)
140(CR) - The Critical Review. Melbourne.
  No 23 [no reviews indexed]
141 - Criticism. Detroit.
  Winter81 thru Fall81 (vol 23 complete)
142 - Philosophy and Social Criticism.
Dordrecht.
  Spring80 thru Fall/Winter80 (vol
  7 complete)
145(Crit) - Critique. Washington.
  Vols 22 and 23 complete
148 - Critical Quarterly. Manchester.
  Spring81 thru Winter81 (vol 23
  complete)
149(CLS) - Comparative Literature Studies.
Champaign.
  Mar81 thru Dec81 (vol 18 complete)
150(DR) - Dalhousie Review. Halifax.
  Spring81 thru Winter81/82 (vol 61
  complete)
151 - Dance Magazine. New York.
  Jul81 thru Dec81 (vol 55 no 7-12)
  [Jan81 thru Jun81 issues missing]
152(UDQ) - The Denver Quarterly.
  Spring81 and Summer81 (vol 16
  no 1 and 2)
153 - Diacritics. Baltimore.
  Spring81 thru Winter81 (vol 11
  complete)
154 - Dialogue. Ottawa.
  Mar81 thru Dec81 (vol 20 complete)
155 - The Dickensian. London.
  Spring81 thru Autumn81 (vol 77
  complete)
157 - Drama/The Quarterly Theatre Review.
London.
  Oct80 thru Winter81 (no 138-142)
161(DUJ) - Durham University Journal.
  Dec80 and Jun81 (vol 73 complete)
165(EAL) - Early American Literature.
Amherst.
  Winter81/82 thru Fall82 (vol 16
  no 3, vol 17 no 1 and 2)
167 - Erkenntnis. Dordrecht.
  Mar81 thru Nov81 (vol 16 complete)
168(ECW) - Essays on Canadian Writing.
Downsview.
  Spring81 and Summer81 (no 21 and
  22) [no reviews indexed]

172(Edda) - Edda. Oslo.
  1981/1 thru 1981/6 (vol 81 complete)
173(ECS) - Eighteenth-Century Studies. Columbus.
  Fall80 thru Summer81 (vol 14 complete)
174(Éire) - Éire-Ireland. St. Paul.
  Spring81 thru Winter81 (vol 16 complete)
175 - English. London.
  Spring81 thru Autumn81 (vol 30 complete)
177(ELT) - English Literature in Transition. Tempe.
  Vol 24 complete
178 - English Studies in Canada. Fredericton.
  Spring81 thru Dec81 (vol 7 complete)
179(ES) - English Studies. Lisse.
  Feb81 thru Dec81 (vol 62 complete)
183(ESQ) - ESQ: A Journal of the American Renaissance. Pullman.
  Vol 27 complete
184(EIC) - Essays in Criticism. Oxford.
  Oct80 thru Oct81 (vol 30 no 4, vol 31 complete)
185 - Ethics. Chicago.
  Oct80 thru Jul82 (vols 91 and 92 complete)
186(ETC.) - Etc. San Francisco.
  Spring81 thru Winter81 (vol 38 complete)
187 - Ethnomusicology. Ann Arbor.
  Jan82 thru Sep82 (vol 26 complete)
188(ECr) - L'Esprit Créateur. Baton Rouge.
  Spring81 thru Winter81 (vol 21 complete)
189(EA) - Etudes Anglaises. Paris.
  Jan-Mar81 thru Oct-Dec81 (vol 34 complete)
190 - Euphorion. Heidelberg.
  Band 74 and Band 75 complete [no reviews indexed]
191(ELN) - English Language Notes. Boulder.
  Sep80 thru Jun81 (vol 18 complete)
193(ELit) - Études Littéraires. Montreal.
  Apr81 thru Dec81 (vol 14 complete)
196 - Fabula. Berlin.
  Band 21 and Band 22 complete
200 - Films in Review. New York.
  Jan81 thru Dec81 (vol 32 complete)
203 - Folklore. London.
  Vol 91 and vol 92 complete
204(FdL) - Forum der Letteren. Muiderberg.
  Mar81 thru Dec81 (vol 22 complete)
205(FMLS) - Forum for Modern Language Studies. St. Andrews.
  Jan80 thru Oct81 (vols 16 and 17 complete)
207(FR) - French Review. Champaign.
  Oct80 thru May82 (vols 54 and 55 complete)
208(FS) - French Studies. London.
  Jan81 thru Oct81 (vol 35 complete)
209(FM) - Le Français Moderne. Paris.
  Jan81 thru Oct81 (vol 49 complete)
210(FrF) - French Forum. Lexington.
  Jan81 thru Sep81 (vol 6 complete)
214 - Gambit. London.
  Vol 10 no 37

215(GL) - General Linguistics. University Park.
  Spring81 thru Winter81 (vol 21 complete)
219(GaR) - Georgia Review. Athens, Georgia.
  Spring81 thru Winter81 (vol 35 complete)
220(GL&L) - German Life and Letters. Oxford.
  Oct81 thru Jul82 (vol 35 complete)
221(GQ) - German Quarterly. Cherry Hill.
  Jan81 thru Nov81 (vol 54 complete)
222(GR) - Germanic Review. Washington.
  Winter81 thru Fall81 (vol 41 complete)
224(GRM) - Germanisch-Romanische Monatsschrift. Heidelberg.
  Band 30 and Band 31 complete
227(GCFI) - Giornale Critico della Filosofia Italiana. Firenze.
  Jan-Apr81 thru Sep-Dec81 (5th ser, vol 1 complete)
228(GSLI) - Giornale storico della letteratura italiana. Torino.
  Vol 156 fasc 495, vols 157 and 158 complete
231 - Harper's Magazine. New York.
  Jan82 thru Dec82 (vols 264 and 265 complete)
234 - The Hemingway Review [ex-Hemingway Notes]. Ada.
  Fall81 and Spring82 (vol 1 complete)
236 - The Hiram Poetry Review. Hiram.
  Spring-Summer81 and Fall-Winter82 (no 30 and 31)
238 - Hispania. University, Miss.
  Mar81 thru Dec81 (vol 64 complete)
240(HR) - Hispanic Review. Philadelphia.
  Winter81 thru Autumn81 (vol 49 complete)
241 - Hispanófila. Chapel Hill.
  Jan81 thru Sep81 (no 71 thru no 73)
244(HJAS) - Harvard Journal of Asiatic Studies. Cambridge, Mass.
  Jun81 and Dec81 (vol 41 complete)
249(HudR) - Hudson Review. New York.
  Spring81 thru Winter81/82 (vol 34 complete)
256 - Humanities in Society. Los Angeles.
  Fall80 thru Fall81 (vol 3 no 4 and vol 4 complete)
257(IRAL) - IRAL: International Review of Applied Linguistics in Language Teaching. Heidelberg.
  Feb81 thru Dec81 (vol 19 complete)
258 - International Philosophical Quarterly. New York and Heverlee-Leuven.
  Mar81 thru Dec81 (vol 21 complete)
259(IIJ) - Indo-Iranian Journal. Dordrecht.
  Jan81 thru Oct81 (vol 23 complete) [entire vol 22 is missing]
260(IF) - Indogermanische Forschungen. Berlin.
  Band 85
261 - Indian Linguistics. Poona.
  Mar79 thru Sep/Dec80 (vols 40 and 41 complete)
262 - Inquiry. Oslo.
  Mar81 thru Dec81 (vol 24 complete)

263(RIB) - Revista Interamericana de Bib-
liografía/Inter-American Review of
Bibliography. Washington.
    Vol 31 complete
268(IFR) - The International Fiction
Review. Fredericton.
    Winter82 and Summer82 (vol 9 com-
plete)
269(IJAL) - International Journal of American Linguistics. Chicago.
    Jan81 thru Oct81 (vol 47 complete)
271 - The Iowa Review. Iowa City.
    Winter81 thru Fall81 (vol 12 com-
plete)
273(IC) - Islamic Culture. Hyderabad.
    Jan80 thru Oct81 (vols 54 and 55
complete)
276 - Italica. New York.
    Spring81 thru Winter81 (vol 58
complete)
277(ITL) - ITL, a Review of Applied Linguistics. Leuven.
    No 47 and no 48
279 - International Journal of Slavic Linguistics and Poetics. Columbus.
    Vols 23 and 24
283 - Jabberwocky - The Journal of the
Lewis Carroll Society. Burton-on-
Trent.
    Winter80/81 and Spring81 (vol 10
no 1 and 2)
284 - The Henry James Review. Baton Rouge.
    Fall81 thru Spring82 (vol 3 com-
plete)
285(JapQ) - Japan Quarterly. Tokyo.
    Jan-Mar81 thru Oct-Dec81 (vol 28
complete)
287 - Jewish Frontier. New York.
    Jan81 thru May81, Aug-Sep81 thru
Nov81 (vol 48 no 1-5 and vol 48
no 7-9) [Jun-Jul81 issue missing]
289 - The Journal of Aesthetic Education.
Urbana.
    Jan81 thru Oct81 (vol 15 complete)
290(JAAC) - Journal of Aesthetics and Art
Criticism. Greenvale.
    Fall81 thru Summer82 (vol 40 com-
plete)
292(JAF) - Journal of American Folklore.
Washington.
    Jan-Mar81 thru Oct-Dec81 (vol 94
complete)
293(JASt) - Journal of Asian Studies. Ann
Arbor.
    Nov80 thru Aug81 (vol 40 complete)
294 - Journal of Arabic Literature. Leiden.
    Vol 11 and vol 12
295(JML) - Journal of Modern Literature.
Philadelphia.
    Vol 8 complete
296(JCF) - Journal of Canadian Fiction.
Guelph.
    No 30 and no 31/32
297(JL) - Journal of Linguistics. Cambridge, England.
    Mar81 and Sep81 (vol 17 complete)
298 - Journal of Canadian Studies/Revue
d'études canadiennes. Peterborough.
    Spring81 thru Fall-Winter81 (vol
16 complete)
300 - Journal of English Linguistics.
Bellingham.
    Mar81 (vol 15)

301(JEGP) - Journal of English and Germanic Philology. Champaign.
    Jan81 thru Oct81 (vol 80 complete)
302 - Journal of Oriental Studies. Hong
Kong. [entries in this periodical
wholly in Chinese are not indexed]
    Vol 18
303(JoHS) - Journal of Hellenic Studies.
London.
    Vol 101
304(JHP) - Journal of Hispanic Philology.
Tallahassee.
    Spring81 thru Winter82 (vol 5 no 3,
vol 6 no 1 and 2)
305(JIL) - The Journal of Irish Literature. Newark, Delaware.
    Jan81 thru Sep81 (vol 10 complete)
307 - Journal of Literary Semantics.
Heidelberg.
    Apr81 and Oct81 (vol 10 complete)
    [Oct80 issue missing]
308 - Journal of Music Theory. New Haven.
    Spring81 and Fall81 (vol 25 com-
plete)
311(JP) - Journal of Philosophy. New York.
    Jan81 thru Dec81 (vol 78 complete)
313 - Journal of Roman Studies. London.
    Vol 71
314 - Journal of South Asian Literature.
East Lansing.
    Winter-Spring81 and Summer-Fall81
(vol 16 complete)
316 - Journal of Symbolic Logic. Providence.
    Mar81 thru Dec81 (vol 46 complete)
317 - Journal of the American Musicological Society. Richmond.
    Spring81 thru Fall81 (vol 34 com-
plete)
318(JAOS) - Journal of the American Oriental Society. New Haven.
    Jan-Mar80 thru Oct-Dec80 (vol 100
complete)
319 - Journal of the History of Philosophy. San Diego.
    Jan81 thru Oct81 (vol 19 complete)
320(CJL) - Canadian Journal of Linguistics. Toronto.
    Spring81 and Fall81 (vol 26 com-
plete)
321 - The Journal of Value Inquiry. The
Hague.
    Vol 15 complete
322(JHI) - Journal of the History of Ideas.
Philadelphia.
    Jan-Mar81 thru Oct-Dec81 (vol 42
complete) [no reviews indexed]
323 - The Journal of the British Society
for Phenomenology. Manchester.
    Jan81 thru Oct81 (vol 12 complete)
324 - Journal of the Royal Society of Arts.
London.
    Dec81 thru Nov82 (vol 130 complete)
325 - Journal of the Society of Archivists.
London.
    Apr81 and Oct81 (vol 6 no 7 and 8)
329(JJQ) - James Joyce Quarterly. Tulsa.
    Fall80 thru Summer81 (vol 18 com-
plete)
340(KSJ) - Keats-Shelley Journal. New York.
    Vol 30

341 - Konsthistorisk Tidskrift. Stockholm.
Vol 50 no 1-3
342 - Kant-Studien. Berlin.
Band 71 and Band 72 complete
344 - The Kenyon Review. Gambier.
Winter82 thru Fall82 (vol 4 complete) [no reviews indexed]
345(KRQ) - Kentucky Romance Quarterly.
Lexington.
Vol 28 complete
349 - Language and Style. Flushing.
Winter81 thru Fall81 (vol 14 complete)
350 - Language. Baltimore.
Mar81 thru Dec82 (vols 57 and 58
complete)
351(LL) - Language Learning. Ann Arbor.
Jun81 and Dec81 (vol 31 complete)
353 - Linguistics. The Hague.
Vol 18 complete
354 - The Library. London.
Mar81 thru Dec81 (vol 3 complete)
355(LSoc) - Language in Society. Cambridge, England.
Apr81 thru Dec81 (vol 10 complete)
356(LR) - Les Lettres Romanes. Louvain.
Feb-May81 thru Nov81 (vol 35 complete)
360(LP) - Lingua Posnaniensis. Poznań.
Vol 23 [no reviews indexed]
361 - Lingua. Amsterdam.
Jan81 thru Dec81 (vols 53-55 complete)
362 - The Listener. London.
7Jan82 thru 30Sep82, 14Oct82 thru
23and30Dec82 (vol 107 complete,
vol 108, no 2767-2780 and no 2782-
2792) [7Oct82 issue missing]
363(LitR) - The Literary Review. Madison.
Fall81, Spring82 and Summer82 (vol
25 no 1, 3 and 4) [Winter82 issue
missing]
364 - London Magazine.
Apr/May81 thru Mar82 (vol 21 complete)
365 - Literary Research Newsletter.
Brockport.
Fall81 thru Spring&Summer82 (vol
6 no 4, vol 7 no 1 and 2/3)
366 - Literature and History. London.
Spring81 and Autumn81 (vol 7 complete)
368 - Landfall. Christchurch.
Sep73 and Dec73, Mar81 thru Dec81
(vol 27 no 3 and 4, vol 35 complete)
377 - Manuscripta. St. Louis.
Mar81 and Jul81 (vol 25 no 1 and 2)
381 - Meanjin Quarterly. Parkville.
Apr81 (vol 40 no 1)
382(MAE) - Medium Aevum. Oxford.
1981/1 and 1981/2 (vol 50 complete)
385(MQR) - Michigan Quarterly Review.
Ann Arbor.
Winter82 thru Fall82 (vol 21 complete)
390 - Midstream. New York.
Jan81 thru Dec81 (vol 27 complete)
392 - The Mississippi Quarterly. Mississippi State.
Winter80/81 thru Fall81 (vol 34
complete)

393(Mind) - Mind. Oxford.
Jan81 thru Oct81 (vol 90 complete)
394 - Mnemosyne. Leiden.
Vol 34 complete
395(MFS) - Modern Fiction Studies. West
Lafayette.
Spring80 thru Winter80/81 (vol 26
complete)
396(ModA) - Modern Age. Bryn Mawr.
Winter81 thru Fall81 (vol 25 complete)
397(MD) - Modern Drama. Toronto.
Mar81 thru Dec81 (vol 24 complete)
398(MPS) - Modern Poetry Studies. Buffalo.
Vol 11 no 1 and 2
399(MLJ) - Modern Language Journal. Madison.
Spring81 thru Winter81 (vol 65
complete)
400(MLN) - MLN [Modern Language Notes].
Baltimore.
Jan81 thru Dec81 (vol 96 complete)
401(MLQ) - Modern Language Quarterly.
Seattle.
Mar81 thru Dec81 (vol 42 complete)
402(MLR) - Modern Language Review. London.
Jan81 thru Oct81 (vol 76 complete)
405(MP) - Modern Philology. Chicago.
Aug81 thru May82 (vol 79 complete)
406 - Monatshefte. Madison.
Spring81 thru Winter81 (vol 73 complete)
407(MN) - Monumenta Nipponica. Tokyo.
Spring81 thru Winter81 (vol 36
complete)
408 - Mosaic. Winnipeg.
Winter81 thru Fall81 (vol 14 complete) [no reviews indexed]
412 - Music Review. Cambridge, England.
Feb80 thru Nov80 (vol 41 complete)
414(MusQ) - Musical Quarterly. New York.
Jan81 thru Oct81 (vol 67 complete)
415 - Musical Times. London.
Jan81 thru Dec81 (vol 122 complete)
418(MR) - Massachusetts Review. Amherst.
Spring81 thru Winter81 (vol 22 complete)
424 - Names. Saranac Lake.
Mar80 thru Dec81 (vols 28 and 29
complete)
432(NEQ) - New England Quarterly. Boston.
Mar81 thru Dec81 (vol 54 complete)
433 - Neophilologus. Groningen.
Jan81 thru Oct81 (vol 65 complete)
[no reviews indexed]
434 - New England Review. Lyme.
Autumn81 thru Summer82 (vol 4 complete)
435 - New Orleans Review. New Orleans.
Winter81 thru Fall81 (vol 8 complete)
436(NewL) - New Letters. Kansas City.
Fall81 thru Spring/Summer82 (vol
48 complete)
437 - New Universities Quarterly. Oxford.
Winter80/81 thru Autumn81 (vol 35
complete)
439(NM) - Neuphilologische Mitteilungen.
Helsinki.
1980/1 thru 1981/4 (vols 81 and
82 complete)

441 - New York Times Book Review.
    3Jan82 thru 26Dec82 (vol 87 complete)
442(NY) - New Yorker.
    4Jan82 thru 27Dec82 (vol 57 no 46-52, vol 58 no 1-45) [vol 58 begins with the 22Feb82 issue]
445(NCF) - Nineteenth-Century Fiction. Berkeley.
    Jun80 thru Mar82 (vols 35 and 36 complete)
446(NCFS) - Nineteenth-Century French Studies. Fredonia.
    Fall-Winter80/81 thru Spring-Summer82 (vols 9 and 10 complete)
447(N&Q) - Notes and Queries. London.
    Feb80 thru Dec80 (vol 27 complete)
448 - Northwest Review. Eugene.
    Vol 19 complete
449 - Noûs. Bloomington.
    Mar81 thru Nov81 (vol 15 complete)
450(NRF) - La Nouvelle Revue Française. Paris.
    Jan81 thru Dec81 (vols 57 and 58 complete)
451 - 19th Century Music. Berkeley.
    Summer81 thru Spring82 (vol 5 complete)
453(NYRB) - The New York Review of Books.
    21Jan82 thru 16Dec82 (vol 28 no 21/22, vol 29 no 1-20)
454 - Novel. Providence.
    Fall81 thru Spring82 (vol 15 complete)
459 - Obsidian. Detroit.
    Spring-Summer80 and Winter80 (vol 6 complete)
460(OhR) - The Ohio Review. Athens, Ohio.
    No 28 and no 29
461 - The Ontario Review. Princeton.
    Spring-Summer81 and Fall-Winter 81/82 (no 14 and 15)
462(OL) - Orbis Litterarum. Copenhagen.
    Vol 35 and vol 36 complete
463 - Oriental Art. Richmond, Surrey.
    Spring81 thru Winter81/82 (vol 27 complete)
468 - Paideuma. Orono.
    Spring81 thru Winter81 (vol 10 complete)
471 - Pantheon. München.
    Jan/Feb/Mar81 thru Oct/Nov/Dec81 (vol 39 complete)
472 - Parnassus: Poetry in Review. New York.
    Spring/Summer81 thru Spring/Summer 82 (vol 9 complete and vol 10 no 1)
473(PR) - Partisan Review. Boston.
    1/1981 thru 4/1981 (vol 48 complete)
474(PIL) - Papers in Linguistics. Edmonton.
    Vol 13 complete [no reviews indexed]
475 - Papers on French Seventeenth Century Literature. Tübingen.
    No 13, 14 and 15
476 - Performing Arts Review. Washington.
    Vol 11
478 - Philosophy and Literature. Baltimore.
    Spring81 and Fall81 (vol 5 complete)

479(PhQ) - Philosophical Quarterly. Edinburgh.
    Jan81 thru Oct81 (vol 31 complete)
480(P&R) - Philosophy and Rhetoric. University Park.
    Winter81 thru Fall81 (vol 14 complete)
481(PQ) - Philological Quarterly. Iowa City.
    Winter80 thru Fall80 (vol 59 complete)
482(PhR) - Philosophical Review. Ithaca.
    Jan81 thru Oct81 (vol 90 complete)
483 - Philosophy. Cambridge, England.
    Jan81 thru Jul81 (vol 56 no 215-217)
484(PPR) - Philosophy and Phenomenological Research. Providence.
    Sep81 thru Jun82 (vol 42 complete)
485(PE&W) - Philosophy East and West. Honolulu.
    Jan81 thru Oct81 (vol 31 complete)
486 - Philosophy of Science. East Lansing.
    Mar81 thru Dec81 (vol 48 complete)
487 - Phoenix. Toronto.
    Spring81 thru Winter81 (vol 35 complete)
488 - Philosophy of the Social Sciences. Waterloo.
    Mar80 thru Dec81 (vols 10 and 11 complete)
489(PJGG) - Philosophisches Jahrbuch. Freiburg.
    Band 88 complete
490 - Poetica. Amsterdam.
    Band 12 complete
491 - Poetry. Chicago.
    Oct81 thru Mar82 (vol 139 complete)
492 - Poetics. Amsterdam.
    Feb81 thru Dec81 (vol 10 complete) [no reviews indexed]
493 - Poetry Review. London.
    Jun81 and Sep81 (vol 71 no 1 and no 2/3)
494 - Poetics Today. Cambridge, Mass.
    Autumn79 thru Summer-Autumn81 (vols 1 and 2 complete)
495(PoeS) - Poe Studies. Pullman.
    Jun81 and Dec81 (vol 14 complete)
497(PolR) - Polish Review. New York.
    Vol 26 complete
502(PrS) - Prairie Schooner. Lincoln.
    Spring-Summer81 thru Winter81/82 (vol 55 complete)
503 - The Private Library. Pinner.
    Spring81 thru Winter81 (vol 4 complete)
505 - Progressive Architecture. New York.
    Jan81 thru Dec81 (vol 62 complete)
506(PSt) - Prose Studies. London.
    May81 thru Dec81 (vol 4 complete)
513 - Perspectives of New Music. Annandale-on-Hudson.
    Fall-Winter80/Spring-Summer81 (vol 19 no 1/2)
517(PBSA) - Papers of the Bibliographical Society of America. New York.
    Jan-Mar81 thru Oct-Dec81 (vol 75 complete) [Oct-Dec80 issue missing]
518 - Philosophical Books. Oxford.
    Jan81 thru Oct81 (vol 22 complete)

526 - Quarry. Kingston.
Winter81 thru Autumn81 (vol 30
complete)

529(QQ) - Queen's Quarterly. Kingston.
Spring81 thru Winter81 (vol 88
complete)

535(RHL) - Revue d'Histoire Littéraire
de la France. Paris.
Jan-Feb81 thru Nov-Dec81 (vol 81
complete)

539 - Renaissance and Reformation/Renais-
sance et Réforme. Mississauga.
Feb82 thru Nov82 (vol 6 complete)

541(RES) - Review of English Studies.
London.
Feb81 thru Nov81 (vol 32 complete)

542 - Revue Philosophique de la France et
de l'Étranger. Paris.
Jan-Mar81 thru Oct-Dec81 (vol 171
complete)

543 - Review of Metaphysics. Washington.
Sep80 thru Jun81 (vol 34 complete)

545(RPh) - Romance Philology. Berkeley.
Aug80 thru May81 (vol 34 complete)

546(RR) - Romanic Review. New York.
Jan81 thru Nov81 (vol 72 complete)

549(RLC) - Revue de Littérature Comparée.
Paris.
Jan-Mar81 thru Jul-Dec81 (vol 55
complete)

550(RusR) - Russian Review. Stanford.
Jan81 thru Oct81 (vol 40 complete)

551(RenQ) - Renaissance Quarterly. New
York.
Spring80 thru Winter80 (vol 33
complete)

552(REH) - Revista de estudios hispánicos.
University, Alabama.
Jan81 thru Oct81 (vol 15 complete)

555 - Revue de Philologie. Paris.
Vol 54 complete

557(RSH) - Revue des Sciences Humaines.
Lille.
Jan-Mar81 thru Oct-Dec81 (no 181-
184) [no reviews indexed]

558(RLJ) - Russian Language Journal. East
Lansing.
Winter81 and Spring-Fall81 (vol
35 complete)

559 - Russian Linguistics. Dordrecht.
Jun80 thru Aug81 (vol 5 complete)

560 - Salmagundi. Saratoga Springs.
Spring-Summer81 thru Winter82
(no 52/53 thru no 55)

562(Scan) - Scandinavica. Norwich.
May81 and Nov81 (vol 20 complete)

563(SS) - Scandinavian Studies. Lawrence.
Winter81 thru Autumn81 (vol 53 complete)

565 - Stand. Newcastle upon Tyne.
Vol 22 complete

566 - The Scriblerian. Philadelphia.
Autumn80 thru Spring82 (vols 13
and 14 complete)

567 - Semiotica. The Hague.
Vol 33 thru vol 36 complete

568(SCN) - Seventeenth-Century News.
University Park.
Spring81 thru Winter81 (vol 39 com-
plete)

569(SR) - Sewanee Review. Sewanee.
Winter81 thru Fall81 (vol 89 complete)

570(SQ) - Shakespeare Quarterly. Washington.
Spring81 thru Winter81 (vol 32 complete)

571(ScLJ) - Scottish Literary Journal.
Aberdeen.
May80 thru Winter81 (vols 7 and 8
complete plus supps 12-15)

572 - Shaw: The Annual of Bernard Shaw
Studies. University Park.
Vol 1 and vol 2

573(SSF) - Studies in Short Fiction. New-
berry.
Winter81 thru Fall81 (vol 18 complete)

574(SEEJ) - Slavic and East European Journal. Tucson.
Spring81 thru Winter81 (vol 25
complete)

575(SEER) - Slavonic and East European
Review. London.
Jan81 thru Oct81 (vol 59 complete)

576 - Journal of the Society of Architectural Historians. Philadelphia.
Mar81 thru Dec81 (vol 40 complete)

577(SHR) - Southern Humanities Review.
Auburn.
Winter81 thru Fall81 (vol 15 com-
plete)

578 - Southern Literary Journal. Chapel
Hill.
Spring82 and Fall82 (vol 14 no 2
and vol 15 no 1)

579(SAQ) - South Atlantic Quarterly. Durham.
Winter81 thru Autumn81 (vol 80
complete)

580(SCR) - The South Carolina Review.
Clemson.
Fall80 thru Spring82 (vols 13 and
14 complete)

581 - Southerly. Sydney.
Sep80 thru Dec81 (vol 40 no 3,
vol 41 complete)

583 - Southern Speech Communication Journal. Knoxville.
Fall80 thru Summer82 (vols 46 and
47 complete)

584(SWR) - Southwest Review. Dallas.
Winter81 thru Autumn81 (vol 66
complete)

585(SoQ) - The Southern Quarterly.
Hattiesburg.
Fall80 thru Spring-Summer81 (vol
19 complete)

586(SoRA) - Southern Review. Adelaide.
Mar80 and Jul80 (vol 13 no 1 and
2) [no reviews indexed]

587(SAF) - Studies in American Fiction.
Boston.
Spring81 and Autumn81 (vol 9 com-
plete)

588(SSL) - Studies in Scottish Literature.
Columbia.
Vol 16

589 - Speculum. Cambridge, Mass.
Jan81 thru Oct81 (vol 56 complete)

591(SIR) - Studies in Romanticism. Boston.
Spring81 thru Winter81 (vol 20
complete)

593 - Symposium. Washington.
Summer80 thru Winter81/82 (vol 34
no 2-4, vol 35 complete)

594 - Studies in the Novel. Denton.
Spring-Summer81 thru Winter81 (vol 13 complete)

596(SL) - Studia Linguistica. Lund.
Vol 35 no 1/2 [no reviews indexed]

597(SN) - Studia Neophilologica. Stockholm.
Vol 53 complete

598(SoR) - The Southern Review. Baton Rouge.
Winter82 thru Fall82 (vol 18 complete)

599 - Style. Fayetteville.
Winter81 thru Fall81 (vol 15 complete)

600 - Simiolus. Utrecht.
Vol 12 no 1 and 2/3

601 - Southern Poetry Review. Charlotte.
Spring81 and Fall81 (vol 21 complete)

602 - Sprachkunst. Vienna.
Vol 12 complete

603 - Studies in Language. Amsterdam.
Vol 5 complete

604 - Spenser Newsletter. Pittsburgh.
Winter81 thru Fall81 (vol 12 complete)

607 - Tempo. London.
Mar81 thru Dec81 (no 136-139)

608 - TESOL Quarterly. Washington.
Mar82 thru Dec82 (vol 16 complete)

609 - Theater. New Haven.
Spring82 and Summer/Fall82 (vol 13 no 2 and 3) [vol 13 no 1 is missing]

610 - Theatre Research International. London.
Winter80/81 thru Autumn81 (vol 6 complete)

611(TN) - Theatre Notebook. London.
Vol 35 complete

612(ThS) - Theatre Survey. Albany.
May81 and Nov81 (vol 22 complete)

613 - Thought. Bronx.
Mar81 thru Dec81 (vol 56 complete)

614 - The Textile Booklist. Lopez Island.
Winter81 thru Fall82 (vols 6 and 7 complete)

617(TLS) - The Times Literary Supplement. London.
1Jan82 thru 31Dec82 (no 4109-4161)

627(UTQ) - University of Toronto Quarterly.
Fall80 thru Summer81 (vol 50 complete) [in Summer issue, only the "Humanities" section is indexed]

628(UWR) - University of Windsor Review.
Fall-Winter81 and Spring-Summer82 (vol 16 complete)

636(VP) - Victorian Poetry. Morgantown.
Spring81 thru Winter81 (vol 19 complete)

637(VS) - Victorian Studies. Bloomington.
Autumn80 thru Summer81 (vol 24 complete)

639(VQR) - Virginia Quarterly Review. Charlottesville.
Winter81 thru Autumn81 (vol 57 complete)

646(WWR) - Walt Whitman Review. Detroit.
Mar81 thru Dec81 (vol 27 complete)

648(WCR) - West Coast Review. Burnaby.
Jun80 thru vol 15 no 4 (vol 15 complete)

649(WAL) - Western American Literature. Logan.
Winter81 thru Winter82 (vol 15 no 4, vol 16 complete)

650(WF) - Western Folklore. Los Angeles.
Jan81 thru Oct81 (vol 40 complete)

651(WHR) - Western Humanities Review. Salt Lake City.
Spring81 thru Winter81 (vol 35 complete)

654(WB) - Weimarer Beiträge. Berlin.
1/1981 thru 12/1981 (vol 27 complete)

656(WMQ) - William and Mary Quarterly. Williamsburg.
Jan81 thru Oct81 (vol 38 complete)

658 - Winterthur Portfolio. Chicago.
Spring81 thru Winter81 (vol 16 complete)

659(ConL) - Contemporary Literature. Madison.
Winter82 thru Fall82 (vol 23 complete)

660(Word) - Word. New York.
Apr80 thru Dec80 (vol 31 complete)

661(WC) - The Wordsworth Circle. Philadelphia.
Winter81 thru Autumn81 (vol 12 complete)

676(YR) - Yale Review. New Haven.
Autumn81 thru Summer82 (vol 71 complete)

677(YES) - The Yearbook of English Studies. London.
Vol 11

678(YCGL) - Yearbook of Comparative and General Literature. Bloomington.
No 29

679 - Zeitschrift für allgemeine Wissenschaftstheorie. Wiesbaden.
Band 11 and Band 12 complete

680(ZDP) - Zeitschrift für deutsche Philologie. Berlin.
Band 99 and Band 100 complete

682(ZPSK) - Zeitschrift für Phonetik, Sprachwissenschaft und Kommunikationsforschung. Berlin.
Band 32 Heft 2 and Band 33 complete

683 - Zeitschrift für Kunstgeschichte. München.
Band 43 and Band 44 complete

684(ZDA) - Zeitschrift für deutsches Altertum und deutsche Literatur [Anzeiger section]. Wiesbaden.
Band 109 and Band 110 complete

685(ZDL) - Zeitschrift für Dialektologie und Linguistik. Wiesbaden.
1/1981 (vol 48 no 1)

688(ZSP) - Zeitschrift für slavische Philologie. Heidelberg.
Band 41 Heft 2 and Band 42 Heft 1 and 2

Each year we are unable (for one reason
or another) to index the reviews appearing
in all of the periodicals scanned. The
following is a list of the periodicals
whose reviews were not included in this
volume of the Index. Every attempt will
be made to index these reviews in the next
volume of the Index:

31(ASch) - American Scholar. Washington.
88 - Blake, An Illustrated Quarterly.
   Albuquerque.
96 - Artscanada. Toronto.
113 - Centrum. Minneapolis.
116 - Chinese Literature: Essays, Articles,
   Reviews. Madison.
137 - CV/II: Contemporary Verse Two.
   Winnipeg.
180(ESA) - English Studies in Africa.
   Johannesburg.
181 - Epoch. Ithaca.
192(EP) - Les Études Philosophiques. Paris.
194(EC) - Études Celtiques. Paris.
198 - The Fiddlehead. Fredericton.
299 - Journal of Beckett Studies. London.
391 - Milton Quarterly. Athens, Ohio.
410(M&L) - Music & Letters. London.
498 - Popular Music and Society. Bowling
   Green.
519(PhS) - Philosophical Studies. Dordrecht.
547(RF) - Romanische Forschungen. Frankfurt am Main.
548(RCSF) - Rivista critica di storia
   della filosofia. Firenze.
553(RLiR) - Revue de Linguistique Romane.
   Strasbourg.
554 - Romania. Paris.
561(SFS) - Science-Fiction Studies. Montréal.
564 - Seminar. Toronto.
582(SFQ) - Southern Folklore Quarterly.
   Gainesville.
590 - Spirit. South Orange.
592 - Studio International. London.
595(ScS) - Scottish Studies. Edinburgh.
615(TJ) - Theatre Journal. Washington.
662(W&L) - Women & Literature. New Brunswick.
686(ZGL) - Zeitschrift für germanistische
   Linguistik. Berlin.
687 - Zeitschrift für philosophische Forschung. Meisenheim/Glan.

Aagaard-Mogensen, L. and G. Hermerén, eds. Contemporary Aesthetics in Scandinavia.
  C. Lyas, 89(BJA):Summer81-268
  J. Olen, 290(JAAC):Winter81-224
Aalto, P. Classical Studies in Finland 1828-1918.
  E.J. Kenney, 123:Vol131No2-330
Aaron, J. Second Sight.
  A. Williamson, 441:10Oct82-30
Aaronson, D. and R.W. Rieber, eds. Psycholinguistic Research.
  D.G. MacKay and J. Dwyer, 350:Mar81-250
Aarsleff, H. From Locke to Saussure.
  I. Hacking, 453(NYRB):10Jun82-36
  R. Posner, 617(TLS):9Jul82-734
Abbey, E. Down the River.
  T. Cahill, 441:30May82-6
Abbey, E. Good News.
  J.A. Herndon, 649(WAL):Summer81-143
Abbey, L. Braindances.
  D. Barbour, 648(WCR):Vol 15No3-44
Abbey, L. Destroyer and Preserver.*
  B.A. Hirsch, 301(JEGP):Jul81-425
  J.E. Hogle, 661(WC):Summer81-183
  D. Hughes, 591(SIR):Summer81-262
  F.W. Shilstone, 580(SCR):Fall81-127
  L.J. Swingle, 340(KSJ):Vol30-194
Abbi, A. Semantic Grammar of Hindi.
  M.C. Shapiro, 350:Jun82-487
Abbott, J.H. In the Belly of the Beast.*
  J. McCarthy, 617(TLS):22Jan82-74
Abbott, L.K., Jr. The Heart Never Fits Its Wanting.*
  E. Friedman, 461:Fall-Winter81/82-93
  T. Hoeksema, 435:Summer81-212
  W. Marling, 584(SWR):Summer81-335
Abbott, N. Studies in Arabic Literary Papyri. (Vol 3)
  R.G. Khoury, 318(JAOS):Jul/Sep80-335
Abbs, P. English Within the Arts.
  C. Rawson, 617(TLS):10Dec82-1371
Abdullah, M.M. - see under Morsy Abdullah, M.
Abegg, M. Apropos Patterns for Embroidery, Lace and Woven Textiles.
  S. Müller-Christensen, 471:Jan/Feb/Mar81-92
Abel, A.S. Towards a Constitutional Charter for Canada.
  V. Lyon, 298:Summer81-122
Abel, D. Guide to the Wines of the United States.
  W. and C. Cowen, 639(VQR):Spring81-73
Abel, G. Stoizismus und frühe Neuzeit.
  P.O. Kristeller, 551(RenQ):Summer80-235
Abelard, P. A Dialogue of a Philosopher with a Jew and a Christian. (P.J. Payer, trans)
  D. Luscombe, 382(MAE):1981/2-315
Abelein, W. Henrik Steffens' politische Schriften.*
  H. Moenkemeyer, 563(SS):Winter81-104
Abell, G.O. and B. Singer, eds. Science and the Paranormal.
  T. Ferris, 441:14Feb82-16
Abellán, J.L. - see de Valdés, A.
Abernethy, F.E., ed. Built in Texas.
  D. Tebbetts, 292(JAF):Jul-Sep81-378
Abernethy, V., ed. Frontiers in Medical Ethics.
  J.C.M., 185:Apr82-593

Abi-Saab, G. The United Nations Operation in the Congo 1960-1964.
  D.P. Biebuyck, 69:Vol50No1-101
Abimbola, 'W. Ifā.
  K. Barber, 69:Vol50No1-105
Abish, W. How German Is It.*
  M. Hofmann, 617(TLS):2Apr82-395
  G. Kearns, 249(HudR):Summer81-303
  J. Klinkowitz, 219(GaR):Summer81-416
  639(VQR):Spring81-59
Ableman, P. Anatomy of Nakedness.
  M. Church, 617(TLS):29Oct82-1185
Abouchar, A. Economic Evaluation of Soviet Socialism.*
  D.A. Dyker, 575(SEER):Jan81-146
About, P-J. - see Plato
Abraham, C. Tristan L'Hermite.
  H.B. McDermott, 207(FR):Apr82-674
Abraham, W., ed. Valence, Semantic Case and Grammatical Relations.
  A.R. Tellier, 189(EA):Jul-Sep81-331
Abraham, W., with J.F. Brand - see Klappenbach, R.
Abraham, W.J. Divine Revelation and the Limits of Historical Criticism.
  J. Barr, 617(TLS):24Dec82-1422
Abrahamian, E. Iran between Two Revolutions.
  S. Bakhash, 453(NYRB):18Nov82-19
  E. Kedourie, 617(TLS):3Dec82-1327
Abrahams, P. The Fury of Rachel Monette.
  T.J. Binyon, 617(TLS):22Jan82-77
Abrahams, W., ed. Prize Stories 1980: The O. Henry Awards. Prize Stories 1981: The O. Henry Awards.
  B. Allen, 434:Spring82-478
Abrahams, W., ed. Prize Stories 1982: The O. Henry Awards.
  N. Perrin, 441:2May82-11
Abrahams, W., ed. Prize Stories of the Seventies from the O. Henry Awards.
  B. Allen, 434:Spring82-478
  639(VQR):Summer81-100
Abram, M.B. The Day is Short.
  W. Goodman, 441:31Oct82-16
Abrams, P. Historical Sociology.
  F. Parkin, 617(TLS):23Jul82-801
Abrams, P. and E.A. Wrigley, eds. Towns in Societies.
  J. Rykwert, 576:May81-172
Abrams, R. Foundations of Political Analysis.
  G.M., 185:Jan81-349
Abse, D. Way Out in the Centre.*
  P. Bland, 364:Oct81-79
Abse, J. John Ruskin.*
  V.A. Burd, 637(VS):Spring81-386
  V. Powell, 39:Jan81-62
Absher, T. Forms of Praise.
  K. Callaway, 472:Spring/Summer82-185
Abzug, R.H. Passionate Liberator.
  B. Fladeland, 579(SAQ):Autumn81-486
Accarie, M. Étude sur le sens moral de la Passion de Jean Michel.
  C. Foxton, 402(MLR):Oct81-957
Accarie, M. Le théâtre sacré de la fin du moyen âge.
  T.B. Lynn, 207(FR):May81-864
  G.R. Muller, 589:Jul81-582
  G.A. Runnalls, 382(MAE):1981/1-161

Achten, G. Das christliche Gebetbuch im
  Mittelalter.
    P. Ochsenbein, 684(ZDA):Band110Heft2-
    75
Achugar, H. Ideología y estructuras nar-
  rativas en José Donoso.*
    D.W. Foster, 238:Sep81-483
    205(FMLS):Apr80-186
Acker, K. The Persian Poems by Janey
  Smith.
    D. Blau, 62:Jan82-73
Ackerley, J.R. My Sister and Myself. (F.
  King, ed)
    V. Glendinning, 617(TLS):30Apr82-478
    N. Mosley, 362:1Apr82-22
Ackerman, B.A. Social Justice in the
  Liberal State.*
    B. Agger, 256:Winter81-7
    E.A. Fowler, 256:Winter81-57
    M. Mosher, 256:Winter81-31
Ackerman, B.A. and W.T. Hassler. Clean
  Coal/Dirty Air.
    J. Naughton, 617(TLS):8Jan82-36
Ackerman, E.B. Village on the Seine.
    M. Anderson, 208(FS):Jul81-353
    M.G. Hydak, 207(FR):Dec80-373
Ackermann, E. Lukrez und der Mythos.
    E.J. Kenney, 123:Vol31No1-19
Ackermann, H.C. Narrative Stone Reliefs
  From Gandhāra in the Victoria and Albert
  Museum in London.
    R. Morris, 57:Vol42No2/3-236
Ackrill, J.L. Aristotle the Philosopher.
    J. Lear, 617(TLS):12Mar82-285
Ackroyd, J. - see Hakuseki, A.
Ackroyd, P. The Great Fire of London.
    K.C. O'Brien, 362:28Jan82-24
    G. Strawson, 617(TLS):29Jan82-105
Ackroyd, P. Ezra Pound and His World.*
    K. Oderman, 584(SWR):Summer81-337
    W.H. Pritchard, 249(HudR):Autumn81-418
    27(AL):Nov81-568
"Actas do I Congresso Internacional de
  Estudos Pessoanos (Porto, 1978)."
    J.M. Parker, 86(BHS):Jul81-272
"Actes du deuxième colloque international
  de linguistique fonctionelle (Clemont-
  Ferrand, 22-25 juillet 1976)."
    G. Ineichen, 260(IF):Band85-304
"Actes du IIe colloque international de
  sinologie."
    T.N. Foss, 293(JASt):May81-574
"Actes du 97e Congrès des Sociétés Savan-
  tes, Nantes 1972: Section d'histoire
  moderne et contemporaine." (Vol 1)
    T.M. Adams, 173(ECS):Fall80-174
Acton, E. Alexander Herzen and the Role
  of the Intellectual Revolutionary.*
    A. Gleason, 104(CASS):Winter81-581
    205(FMLS):Jan80-79
Acton, H. The Soul's Gymnasium.
    A. Hollinghurst, 617(TLS):26Feb82-214
    J. Mellors, 362:15Apr82-23
    442(NY):15Nov82-203
Acuaviva, A.O. - see under Orozco Acuaviva,
  A.
Aczél, T. Illuminations.*
    G. Gömöri, 617(TLS):12Mar82-276
Adalbero of Laon. Adalbéron de Laon:
  Poème au roi Robert. (C. Carozzi, ed
  and trans)
    J.J. Contreni, 589:Apr81-337

Adam, H. Gone Sailing.
    P. Schjeldahl, 472:Spring/Summer81-284
Adam, J. Wage Control and Inflation in
  the Soviet Bloc Countries.
    A. McAuley, 575(SEER):Jan81-145
Adam, N.R. Die russische Koreaforschung.
    H. Walravens, 318(JAOS):Apr/Jun80-213
Adam, W. Vitruvius Scoticus.
    I.R.M. Mowat, 46:Apr81-255
Adam, W. Die "wandelunge."
    D.H. Green, 402(MLR):Apr81-497
Adams, A. To See You Again.
    B. De Mott, 441:11Apr82-7
Adams, A.B. The Disputed Lands.
    J.K. Putnam, 649(WAL):Fall81-244
Adams, C. English Speech Rhythm and the
  Foreign Learner.*
    205(FMLS):Apr80-186
Adams, C. Ordinary Lives: A Hundred Years
  Ago.
    S. Brook, 617(TLS):13Aug82-889
Adams, D. Life, the Universe and Every-
  thing.
    R. Brown, 617(TLS):24Sep82-1032
Adams, E.W. The Logic of Conditionals.
    D. Nute and W. Mitcheltree, 449:Sep81-
    432
Adams, J.N. The Latin Sexual Vocabulary.
    P. Howell, 617(TLS):17Dec82-1386
Adams, J.Q. Diary of John Quincy Adams.
  (Vols 1 and 2) (D.G. Allen and others,
  eds)
    P. Shaw, 617(TLS):29Oct82-1194
Adams, J.S. Citizen Inspectors in the
  Soviet Union.
    W.E. Butler, 575(SEER):Jan81-144
Adams, P. and S. Knockback.
    A. Ryan, 362:9Dec82-26
Adams, P.G. - see Thomson, J.
Adams, R. and R. Lockley. Voyage Through
  the Antarctic.
    P-L. Adams, 61:Dec82-106
Adams, R.M. Afterjoyce.*
    C. Butler, 447(N&Q):Jun80-279
Adams, R.M. The Lost Museum.*
    639(VQR):Spring81-67
Adams, R.M. - see Jonson, B.
Adams, T.B. A New Nation.
    P-L. Adams, 61:Mar82-88
Adams, T.R. The American Controversy.
    J.D. Haskell, Jr., 656(WMQ):Jul81-531
    78(BC):Winter81-447
Adams, T.R. American Independence.
    78(BC):Winter81-447
Adams, W.H. The French Garden 1500-1800.*
  (French title: Le jardins en France
  (1500-1800).)
    J-R. Mantion, 98:Dec81-1301
Adams, W.P. The First American Constitu-
  tions.
    J.N. Rakove, 656(WMQ):Apr81-297
Adamson, D. Balzac: "Illusions perdues."
    O. Heathcote, 446(NCFS):Spring-Sum-
    mer82-361
Adamson, J. "Othello" as Tragedy.*
    J.A. Bryant, Jr., 130:Fall81-269
    M. Campbell, 67:Nov81-242
    G.F. Parker, 184(EIC):Oct81-346
Adamson, W.L. Hegemony and Revolution.
    A.L., 185:Jan82-391

2

Addison, J. The Freeholder. (J. Leheny, ed)
  J.B., 148:Summer81-92
  E.A. Bloom, 506(PSt):Sep81-206
  B. Tippett, 366:Autumn81-256
  566:Spring81-119
Addiss, S., with K.S. Wong. Obaku.
  B. Sweet, 60:Sep-Oct81-147
Aden, J.M. Pope's Once and Future Kings.*
  D. Fairer, 677(YES):Vol 11-276
  W. Kinsley, 173(ECS):Spring81-348
  D.E. Richardson, 569(SR):Fall81-638
  P. Rogers, 447(N&Q):Oct80-445
Adewoye, O. The Judicial System in Southern Nigeria, 1854-1954.
  J. Howard, 69:Vol50No4-436
Adilman, M.E. Piece Work.
  A. Brooks, 526:Autumn81-160
Adlard, J. Owen Seaman.
  W. Gould, 72:Band217Heft2-435
Adler, H. Soziale Romane im Vormärz.
  J.L. Sammons, 221(GQ):May81-358
Adler, H.J. and D.A. Brusegard, eds. Perspectives Canada III.
  K. Bryden, 529(QQ):Winter81-679
Adler, J.D. and J.J. White, eds. August Stramm.*
  R. Schier, 301(JEGP):Jul81-392
  E. Weidl, 406:Fall81-363
Adler, J.S. War in Melville's Imagination.*
  C.L. Karcher, 405(MP):Nov81 217
  M.R. Stern, 27(AL):Nov81-514
Adler, M. Das Soziologische in Kants Erkenntniskritik. Kant,und der Marxismus.
  R. Malter, 342:Band71Heft3-380
Adler, M.J. How to Think About God.
  V.J.B., 543:Jun81-775
Adler, M.J. A Pragmatic Logic for Commands.
  J. Mey, 350:Dec82-930
  205(FMLS):Jan81-92
Adler, M.K. Sex Differences in Human Speech.
  L.A. Matossian, 355(LSoc):Apr81-120
Adler, S.M. Calvino.
  J. Cannon, 276:Winter81-337
Adler, W. American Quartet.
  N. Callendar, 441:17Oct82-41
Admussen, R.L. The Samuel Beckett Manuscripts.
  J. Pilling, 541(RES):Feb81-115
  D. Sherzer, 395(MFS):Summer80-355
Adorno, T. In Search of Wagner.*
  R. Anderson, 415:Jul81-479
Adorno, T.W. Prisms.
  D.J.R. Bruckner, 441:23May82-15
Adriaansens, H.P.M. Talcott Parsons and the Conceptual Dilemma.
  K.E. Soltan, 185:Jul82-769
Adrienne. Spanish in 32 Lessons.
  R.H. Gilmore, 399(MLJ):Summer81-226
Aebersold, D. Céline, un démystificateur mythomane.
  D. Frizot, 535(RHL):Jul-Oct81-838
Aelfric. Aelfric's Catholic Homilies: The Second Series, Text. (M. Godden, ed)
  T.H. Leinbaugh, 589:Oct81-871
Aers, D. Chaucer, Langland, and the Creative Imagination.*
  J.J. Anderson, 148:Summer81-82

Aeschylus. The "Oresteia" of Aeschylus.* (R. Lowell, trans)
  J. Herington, 472:Fall/Winter81-217
"Africa in Antiquity."
  S. Hale, 2(AfrA):Nov80-29
"African Books in Print." (2nd ed) (H. Zell, ed)
  E. Skurjat, 69:Vol50No4-449
Afterman, A. Purple Adam.
  G. Catalano, 381:Apr81-114
Agassi, J. Towards a Rational Philosophical Anthropology.
  M. Hollis, 488:Jun80-208
  G. Weiler, 488:Jun80-201
Agawa, H. The Reluctant Admiral.
  639(VQR):Winter81-9
Agee, J. Twelve Years.*
  M. Hofmann, 617(TLS):4Jun82-623
  S. Jacobson, 362:14Jan82-22
Aggeler, G. Anthony Burgess.
  C. Holte, 395(MFS):Winter80/81-694
Agler-Beck, G. Der von Kürenberg.*
  N.A. Perrin, 221(GQ):May81-338
Agnello, G. Bibliografia degli scritti di Giuseppe Agnello. (S.L. Agnello and G. Palermo, eds)
  W. Krönig, 683:Band44Heft2-188
Agnew, G. and others. A Dealer's Record.
  D. Sutton, 39:Sep81-144
Agrawal, C. Nānakvānī kā bhāṣīy tathā dārśanik nirūpan.
  H.C. Patyal, 261:Sep/Dec80-196
Agricola, C. and E. Wörter und Gegenwörter.
  U. Schröter, 682(ZPSK):Band33Heft6-737
Aguayo, J., ed and trans. Sistema de clasificación decimal.
  M. Solares, 263(RIB):Vol31No4-543
Aguinaga, C.B., J. Rodriguez Puertolas and I.M. Zavala - see under Blanco Aguinaga, C., J. Rodriguez Puertolas and I.M. Zavala
Aguirre, J.M. - see Manrique, J.
Agulhon, M. Marianne into Battle.*
  B.T. Cooper, 446(NCFS):Spring-Summer82-370
Agulhon, M. La République au village. (2nd ed)
  B. Rigby, 208(FS):Apr81-213
Agulhon, M. - see Renouvier, C.
Agulló y Cobo, M. Más noticias sobre pintores madrileños de los siglos XVI al XVIII.*
  D. Angulo Íñiguez, 48:Apr-Jun81-227
Agustín, J. Three Lectures. (J. Kirk and D. Schmidt, eds)
  P.R. Beardsell, 86(BHS):Apr81-164
  205(FMLS):Jan80-79
Ahmad, B. Muhammad and the Jews.
  S. Vahiduddin, 273(IC):Jan80-53
Ahmad, K. and Z.I. Ansari, eds. Islamic Perspectives.*
  S.A. Akbarabadi, 273(IC):Apr81-135
Ahmad, R. Masdūd rāhoṇ ke musāfir.
  L. Wentink, 314:Summer-Fall81-240
Ahmed, I., ed. Caste and Social Stratification Among Muslims in India. (2nd ed)
  D.M. Neuman, 293(JASt):Feb81-400
Ahsan, M.M. Social Life under the Abbasids, 170-289 A.H./786-902 A.D.
  M.S. Khan, 273(IC):Jan80-57
Ai. Killing Floor.
  S.M. Gilbert, 491:Oct81-35

Aidoo, A.A. Our Sister Killjoy, or Reflections from a Black-Eyed Squint.
R. Bishop, 459:Spring-Summer80-251
Aiken, J. The Way to Write for Children.
G. Trease, 617(TLS):17Sep82-1000
Aiken, W. and H. La Follette, eds. Whose Child?
P.H.J., 185:Oct81-188
Aili, H. The Prose Rhythm of Sallust and Livy.*
H.C. Gotoff, 122:Oct81-335
Ainsztein, R. The Warsaw Ghetto Revolt.
M.W. Kiel, 287:Apr81-26
Aird, C. Last Respects.
T.J. Binyon, 617(TLS):29Oct82-1196
Aitken, A.J. and T. McArthur, eds. Languages of Scotland.
A. Davies, 399(MLJ):Summer81-239
N.C. Dorian, 350:Mar81-196
K.C. Phillipps, 571(ScLJ):Summer80-77
S. Romaine, 297(JL):Sep81-364
Aitken, A.J., M.P. McDiarmid and D.S. Thomson, eds. Bards and Makars.*
W. Scheps, 588(SSL):Vol 16-247
K. Wittig, 38:Band99Heft1/2-237
Aitzetmüller, R. Belegstellenverzeichnis der altkirchenslavischen Verbalformen.*
C. Koch, 688(ZSP):Band41Heft2-407
Ajami, F. The Arab Predicament.
E. Mortimer, 617(TLS):10Sep82-963
"Akademičeskie školy v russkom literaturovedenii."
W. Busch, 688(ZSP):Band42Heft1-167
Akenson, D. The Lazar House Notebooks.
E. Crawley, 529(QQ):Autumn81-561
Akenson, D.H. Between Two Revolutions.*
S.H. Palmer, 174(Éire):Spring81-119
Akerman, S. Le Mythe de Bérénice.
H.C. Knutson, 475:No14Pt1-143
Akhavi, S. Religion and Politics in Contemporary Iran.
W.L. Cleveland, 529(QQ):Summer81-273
Akhmanova, A. Linguostylistics.
W. Kühlwein, 277(ITL):No47-69
Akhmatova, A. [A. Axmatova] O Puškine.
N. Perlina, 558(RLJ):Winter81-213
Akkerman, F., H.G. Hubbeling and A.G. Westerbrink - see de Spinoza, B.
Akmajian, A., R.A. Demers and R.M. Harnish. Linguistics.
D.R. Ladd, 350:Dec82-890
Akurgal, E., ed. The Art and Architecture of Turkey.
M. Levey, 39:Jul81-67
Al, B.P.F. La notion de grammaticalité en grammaire générative-transformationnelle.
R. Posner, 545(RPh):Aug80-95
Alan of Lille. De Planctu naturae. (N.M. Haring, ed) The Plaint of Nature. (J.J. Sheridan, trans)
J. Ziolkowski, 382(MAE):1981/2-312
de Alarcón, J.R. - see under Ruiz de Alarcón, J.
de Alarcón, P.A. La Pródiga. (A. Navarro González, ed)
L.H. Klibbe, 552(REH):May81-312
Alarcos Llorach, E. Ensayos y Estudios Literarios.
C. González, 241:Jan81-73
Alatis, J.E. and G.R. Tucker, eds. Language in Public Life.
G. Kress, 355(LSoc):Apr81-73
M.R. Webb, 399(MLJ):Autumn81-332

Alazraki, J. and I. Ivask, eds. The Final Island.*
J.D. Bruce-Novoa, 552(REH):May81-313
Alba, M.S. - see under Sito Alba, M.
Albanese, R., Jr. Initiation aux problèmes socioculturels de la France au XVIIe siècle.
H.G. Hall, 208(FS):Apr81-202
Albeck, G. - see Grundtvig, N.F.S.
Alber, C.J. - see Semanov, V.I.
Albersmeier, F-J., ed. Texte zur Theorie des Films.
R.C. Reimer, 406:Winter81-442
Albert, G. Matters of Chance.
B. Caplan, 441:28Nov82-12
Albert, R.S. and others, eds. A Franco-American Overview.
A.B. Chartier, 207(FR):May82-932
Albert, S. and E.C. Luck, eds. On the Endings of Wars.
M.A.K., 185:Jul81-699
Alberti, G.B. Problemi di critica testuale.
J. Soubiran, 555:Vol54fasc2-366
Alberts, W. Einfache Verbformen und verbale Gefüge in zwei Augsburger Chroniken des 15. Jahrhunderts.*
G. Brandt, 682(ZPSK):Band33Heft2-241
Alblas, J.B.H. and R. Todd, eds. From Caxton to Beckett.
G. Bourcier, 189(EA):Oct-Dec81-458
Albrecht, J. Linguistik und Übersetzung.
H. and R. Kahane, 545(RPh):Feb81(supp)-9
Albrecht, M. Kants Antinomie der praktischen Vernunft.
L. Guillermit, 542:Jul-Sep81-375
Albright, D. Personality and Impersonality.*
H.T. Moore, 402(MLR):Oct81-940
Albright, D.E., ed. Communism in Africa.
A.Z. Rubinstein, 550(RusR):Jan81-78
Albritton, C.C., Jr. The Abyss of Time.
C.J. Schneer, 584(SWR):Autumn81-vi
Alcolea, S. Pintura de la Universidad de Barcelona.
I. Mateo Gómez, 48:Oct-Dec81-463
Alden, D. Marcel Proust's Grasset Proofs.
B. Brun, 535(RHL):Mar-Apr81-324
A. Finch, 208(FS):Apr81-223
D. Sherzer, 395(MFS):Summer80-355
Alden, D.W. and R.A. Brooks. A Critical Bibliography of French Literature. (Pt 6)
C.S. Brosman, 207(FR):Dec80-347
Alden, J., with D.C. Landis, eds. European Americana. (Vol 1)
78(BC):Winter81-447
354:Jun81-179
Alderman, H. Nietzsche's Gift.
W.B.A., 543:Sep80-123
G.J. Stack, 319:Apr81-270
Alderson, B. - see Darton, F.J.H.
Aldhelm. The Prose Works. (M. Lapidge and M. Herren, trans)
M.M. Gatch, 487:Winter81-387
J.D. Pheifer, 447(N&Q):Dec80-539
Aldiss, B. Helliconia Spring.
C. Greenland, 617(TLS):5Mar82-245
G. Mortimer, 364:Mar82-82
Aldred, C. Egyptian Art.
62:Feb81-71

Aldridge, T.M. Registers and Records. (3rd ed)
 F. Strong, 325:Apr81-441
Aleichem, S. Marienbad.
 P-L. Adams, 61:Oct82-105
 442(NY):20Sep82-151
Alekseyev, M.P. Russko-Angliyskiye litera-turnyye svyazi (XVIII vek — pervaya polovina XIX veka).
 H. Gifford, 617(TLS):10Dec82-1368
Alekseyev, M.P., V.V. Zakharov and B.B. Tomashevsky, eds. Angliyskaya poeziya v russkikh perevodakh: XIV-XIX veka.
 H. Gifford, 617(TLS):13Aug82-891
Aleramo, S. A Woman.
 639(VQR):Summer81-102
Alexander, C.C. Here the Country Lies.*
 W.B. Rhoads, 576:Oct81-258
 B.T. Spencer, 27(AL):Nov81-554
Alexander, E. The Resonance of Dust.
 A.H. Rosenfeld, 390:Mar81-56
Alexander, J.H. The Reception of Scott's Poetry by his Correspondents: 1796-1817.
 D. Roper, 677(YES):Vol 11-296
 K. Sutherland, 571(ScLJ):Summer80-98
Alexander, J.H. Two Studies in Romantic Reviewing.
 D. Roper, 677(YES):Vol 11-296
Alexander, J.J.G. Insular Manuscripts, 6th to the 9th Century.
 H.L. Kessler, 589:Apr81-338
Alexander, J.J.G. Italian Renaissance Illuminations.
 78(BC):Spring81-14
Alexander, J.J.G. Wallace Collection, Catalogue of Illuminated Manuscript Cuttings.
 B. Scott, 39:Oct81-274
Alexander, J.K. Render Them Submissive.
 R.A. Ryerson, 656(WMQ):Apr81-305
Alexander, J.T. Bubonic Plague in Early Modern Russia.*
 P.H. Clendenning, 550(RusR):Apr81-185
Alexander, M. The Poetic Achievement of Ezra Pound.*
 R. Bush, 301(JEGP):Apr81-284
 E. Creene, 529(QQ):Winter81-774
 P. Stevens, 106:Winter81-355
Alexander, P. Roy Campbell.
 V. Glendinning, 617(TLS):28May82-580
 D. Wright, 362:18Mar82-22
Alexander, R.D. Darwinism and Human Affairs.
 T. Ball, 185:Oct81-161
 F.N. Egerton, 125:Fall80-118
 M. Ruse, 486:Dec81-627
Alexander, S. Marc Chagall.
 E. Roditi, 390:Aug/Sep81-62
Alexander, W. Johnny Gibb of Gushetneuk.
 D. Buchan, 571(ScLJ):Winter81-122
Alexandre-Gras, D. Le "Canzoniere" de Boiardo, du pétrarquisme à l'inspiration personnelle.
 E. Bigi, 228(GSLI):Vol 158fasc504-603
Alexandrescu, P. Histria. (Vol 4)
 R.M. Cook, 303(JoHS):Vol 101-214
Alexandrian. Le Socialisme romantique.
 M. Bossis, 535(RHL):Jul-Oct81-797
Alexis, J.S. Compère Général Soleil.
 J. Kirkup, 617(TLS):9Jul82-750
Alfaenger, P.K. Le Théâtre.
 C.F. Coates, 207(FR):Dec81-282

Alfieri, V. Parere sulle tragedie e altre prose critiche. (M. Pagliai, ed)
 A. Di Benedetto, 228(GSLI):Vol 157-fasc498-301
Alfonso X el Sabio. Cantigas de Santa Maria.*
 K. Kulp-Hill, 345(KRQ):Vol128No2-213
Alfonso X el Sabio. Lapidario. (S. Rod-ríguez M. Montalvo, ed)
 A.J. Cárdenas, 304(JHP):Winter82-157
Alfonso, P. Disciplina clericalis. (M.J. Lacarra, ed; E. Ducay, trans)
 D.W. Lomax, 86(BHS):Apr81-161
Alford, N. The Rhymers' Club.*
 K. Beckson, 636(VP):Winter81-397
Algar, H. - see Iman Khomeini
Algeo, J. - see Pyles, T.
Ali, M.J. Scheherazade in England.
 J.R. King, 150(DR):Winter81/82-756
Ali Bouacha, A., ed. La Pédagogie du fran-çais langue étrangère.
 B. Ebling 2d, 207(FR):Dec80-353
Alighieri, D. - see under Dante Alighieri
Alinder, J. - see "Wright Morris: Photo-graphs and Words"
Alinei, M. Spogli elletronici dell'-Italiano del Origini e del Duecento. (1st Scr, Vols 1 and 2)
 G.C. Lepschy, 353:Vol 18No3/4-375
Alkire, L.G., Jr., ed. Periodical Title Abbreviations: By Abbreviation. (3rd ed) (Vol 1)
 K.B. Harder, 424:Dec80-293
Alkire, L.G., Jr., ed. Periodical Title Abbreviations. (3rd ed) (Vol 2)
 K.B. Harder, 424:Dec81-314
Alkon, P.K. Defoe and Fictional Time.*
 M. Byrd, 402(MLR):Jan81-164
Allan, D.G.C. and R.E. Schofield. Stephen Hales.*
 H.A. Leventhal, 656(WMQ):Oct81-744
 H.A. Waldron, 83:Spring81-109
Allan, M. William Robinson 1838-1935.
 J. Buxton, 617(TLS):26Nov82-1321
Allan, S. and A.P. Cohen, eds. Legend, Lore and Religion in China.
 D.K. Jordan, 293(JASt):May81-570
Allard, J. Zola: le chiffre du texte.*
 C.B. Jennings, 188(ECr):Spring81-109
 C.B. Jennings, 627(UTQ):Spring81-323
Allard, L. Mademoiselle Hortense ou l'école du septième rang.
 E.R. Babby, 207(FR):May82-919
Allardt, E. Implications of the Ethnic Revival in Modern, Industrialized Society.
 J.A. Fishman, 355(LSoc):Aug81-288
Allbeury, T. All Our Tomorrows.
 T.J. Binyon, 617(TLS):10Dec82-1378
Allbeury, T. The Other Side of Silence.*
 N. Callendar, 441:24Jan82-34
Allbeury, T. Shadow of Shadows.
 T.J. Binyon, 617(TLS):16Apr82-446
 M. Laski, 362:29Apr82-27
Allchin, F.R. and N. Hammond, eds. The Archaeology of Afghanistan.
 R.N. Frye, 293(JASt):Aug81-809
Alldritt, K. Elgar on the Journey to Han-ley.
 I.P., 412:Feb80-70
Alldritt, K. The Lover Next Door.
 P. Lewis, 565:Vol22No3-55

Allemand, A. L'oeuvre romanesque de
Nathalie Sarraute.
  G.R. Besser, 207(FR):Oct81-147
  V. Gillion-Delfosse, 356(LR):Nov81-371
  A. Jefferson, 402(MLR):Oct81-977
Allen, C. Raj.
  J-F. Jarrige, 98:Feb-Mar81-309
Allen, D., ed. Allen Ginsberg: Composed
on the Tongue.
  D. Pinckney, 472:Spring/Summer82-99
Allen, D. - see Creeley, R.
Allen, D. - see Dorn, E.
Allen, D. - see Spicer, J.
Allen, D.G. and others - see Adams, J.Q.
Allen, G. Charles Moore.
  L. Knobel, 46:Mar81-191
  E. McCoy, 505:Oct81-142
Allen, G.C. Japan's Economic Policy.
  Shimura Kaichi, 285(JapQ):Apr-Jun81-
  287
Allen, G.W. Waldo Emerson.*
  J. Ditsky, 628(UWR):Spring-Summer82-
  117
  A. Kazin, 453(NYRB):21Jan82-3
Allen, J. December Flower.
  J. Astor, 362:15Jul82-23
  P. Craig, 617(TLS):28May82-593
Allen, J.D. and T.H. Wilson. Swahili
Houses and Tombs on the Coast of Kenya.
  B. Riley, 2(AfrA):May81-85
Allen, J.J. Don Quixote: Hero or Fool?
(Pt 2)
  J.G. Weiger, 400(MLN):Mar81-449
  E. Williamson, 402(MLR):Jan81-220
Allen, J.M. Candles and Carnival Lights.
  R. Astro, 395(MFS):Summer80-325
  J. Tavernier-Courbin, 106:Winter81-397
Allen, J.S. Popular French Romanticism.*
  B.T. Cooper, 446(NCFS):Fall-Win-
  ter81/82-175
  R.T. Denommé, 207(FR):Mar82-575
  639(VQR):Summer81-85
Allen, L. and D. The Allen Press Bibliog-
raphy.
  G.F. Ritchie, 503:Summer81-86
Allen, M. Selling Dreams.
  B. Harrison, 617(TLS):26Mar82-358
Allen, M. Spence at Marlby Manor.
  N. Callendar, 441:7Nov82-39
Allen, M.V. The Achievement of Margaret
Fuller.*
  M.O. Urbanski, 432(NEQ):Jun81-286
Allen, P. The Cambridge Apostles: The
Early Years.*
  R. Mason, 447(N&Q):Jun80-254
Allen, P. Vladimir Soloviev: Russian
Mystic.
  S. Levitzky, 396(ModA):Spring81-213
Allen, R. The Arabic Novel.
  R. Ostle, 617(TLS):10Sep82-978
Allen, R., S. Luxton and M. Teicher. Late
Romantics.
  L. Mathews, 628(UWR):Fall-Winter81-119
Allen, R.F. German Expressionist Poetry.
  E. Krispyn, 406:Winter81-476
Allen, R.R. - see "The Eighteenth Century:
A Current Bibliography"
Allen, S. Arrow in the Dark.
  T.J. Binyon, 617(TLS):31Dec82-1448
Allen, S. The Talk Show Murders.
  N. Callendar, 441:4Apr82-29

Allen, W. As I Walked Down New Grub
Street.*
  F. Tuohy, 364:Dec81/Jan82-112
  442(NY):12Apr82-154
Allen, W. Four Films of Woody Allen.
  J. Atlas, 61:Dec82-102
Allen, W. The Short Story in English.*
  B. Allen, 569(SR):Summer81-cii
  C. van Boheemen-Saaf, 204(FdL):Jun81-
  224
Allen, W. Side Effects.
  E. King, 287:May81-24
Allen, W.S. Accent and Rhythm.
  C.J. Ruijgh, 394:Vol34fasc3/4-399
Allender, M. and A. Tennant. The Guada-
lupe Mountains of Texas.
  L. Milazzo, 584(SWR):Spring81-v
Allerton, D.J. Essentials of Grammatical
Theory.*
  G. Horrocks, 307:Apr81-50
Allett, J. New Liberalism.
  S. Collini, 617(TLS):13Aug82-872
Alleyne, M.C. Comparative Afro-American.
  M. Sebba, 361:Aug81-361
Allison, L. Condition of England.
  C. Brown, 617(TLS):12Mar82-284
Allman, E.J. Player-King and Adversary.*
  M. Novy, 405(MP):Feb82-321
  J.A. Porter, 579(SAQ):Autumn81-493
Allodi, M. Printmaking in Canada/Les
Débuts de l'Estampe Imprimée au Canada.
  M. Bell, 529(QQ):Summer81-354
Allott, M., ed. Essays on Shelley.
  I. McGilchrist, 617(TLS):5Nov82-1213
Allott, T. - see Hardy, A.
Allwood, J., L-G. Andersson and Ö. Dahl.
Logic In Linguistics.
  R.W. Thomason, 350:Jun82-492
Allworth, E., ed. Ethnic Russia in the
USSR.
  I. Kreindler, 550(RusR):Jan81-72
Almagor, U. Pastoral Partners.
  V. Luling, 69:Vol50No4-444
de Almeida, A.W.B. - see under Berno de
Almeida, A.W.
de Almeida, H. Byron and Joyce Through
Homer.
  R. Brown, 617(TLS):15Jan82-56
  M. Seidel, 676(YR):Summer82-604
de Almela, D.R. - see under Rodríguez de
Almela, D.
Almendros, N. Un Homme à la caméra.
  J. Van Baelen, 207(FR):Apr82-699
Almon, B. Blue Sunrise.
  S. Hamill, 649(WAL):Spring81-69
  G. McWhirter, 102(CanL):Autumn81-160
Alonso, H.C. - see under Casado Alonso, H.
Alonso Hernández, J.L. Léxico del margi-
nalismo del Siglo de Oro.
  S.N. Dworkin, 545(RPh):Feb81(supp)-339
Alpers, A. The Life of Katherine Mans-
field.*
  D.B. Kesterson, 573(SSF):Summer81-327
  M. Magalaner, 651(WHR):Spring81-88
  R. Morton, 529(QQ):Spring81-157
  G.W., 102(CanL):Autumn81-167
  A.K. Weatherhead, 395(MFS):Winter80/81-
  710
  295(JML):Vol8No3/4-565
Alpers, P. The Singer of the "Eclogues."*
  P.L. Smith, 487:Fall81-291
Alpert, J. Growing Up Underground.*
  M. Kempton, 453(NYRB):21Jan82-48

6

Alsop, J. F.D.R.
  D. Adams, 617(TLS):16Jul82-763
  J. Grigg, 362:4Feb82-24
  M. Kempton, 453(NYRB):15Apr82-3
  442(NY):1Feb82-133
Alsop, J. The Rare Art Traditions.
  E.H. Gombrich, 453(NYRB):2Dec82-39
  J.R. Mellow, 441:7Nov82-11
Alsop, S.M. Yankees at the Court.
  W. Goodman, 441:30May82-10
Alstermark, H. Das Arzneibuch des Johan
  van Segen.
  B.D. Haage, 680(ZDP):Band99Heft1-149
Alt, A.T. - see Storm, T. and E. Esmarch
Altbauer, M. Der Älteste Serbische
  Psalter.
  T.F. Magner, 574(SEEJ):Winter81-107
Alten, S.R. Audio in Media.
  A. Ray, 583:Winter82-234
Alter, J. Dorothy Johnson.
  A. Frietzsche, 649(WAL):Fall81-231
Alter, R. The Art of Biblical Narrative.*
  J.M. Cameron, 453(NYRB):15Apr82-28
  D. Lodge, 617(TLS):5Nov82-1207
Alter, R., with C. Cosman. A Lion for
  Love.*
  G.M. Rosa, 207(FR):Feb82-412
Alter, R., with C. Cosman. Stendhal.
  K.C. McWatters, 208(FS):Jan81-77
Althaus, H.P., H. Henne and H.E. Wiegand.
  Lexikon der germanistischen Linguistik.
  (2nd ed)
  E.A. Ebbinghaus, 215(GL):Spring81-29
Altieri, C. Act and Quality.
  W. Martin, 401(MLQ):Dec81-404
Altieri, C. Enlarging the Temple.*
  M. Perloff, 295(JML):Vol18No3/4-424
Altman, H.B. and C.V. James, eds. Foreign
  Language Teaching.
  W.F. Smith, 399(MLJ):Winter81-412
Altman, J.B. The Tudor Play of Mind.*
  R. Todd, 179(ES):Oct81-482
Altmann, G. Statistik für Linguisten.
  A.J. Naro, 350:Jun82-493
"Altro Polo." (Vol 1) (S. Trambaiolo and
  N. Newbigin, eds)
  J.A. Scott, 67:May81-128
Alvar, M. - see Rohlfs, G.
Alvarez, A. Life After Marriage.
  P. Beer, 362:10Jun82-23
  R. Dinnage, 617(TLS):2Jul82-714
  D. Johnson, 453(NYRB):12Aug82-9
  P. Lopate, 441:31Jan82-10
Álvarez, N.E. La obra literaria de Jorge
  Mañach.
  L. Monguió, 345(KRQ):Vol28No2-209
Amacher, R.E. and V. Lange, eds. New Per-
  spectives in German Literary Criticism.
  B. Bassoff, 577(SHR):Summer81-262
  W.W. Holdheim, 131(CL):Winter81-83
Amado, J. The Swallow and the Tom Cat.
  P-L. Adams, 61:Nov82-171
Amado, J. Tereza Batista.
  R. Blythe, 362:25Nov82-28
  S. Brook, 617(TLS):12Nov82-1254
Amalrik, A. Journal d'un provocateur.
  J-P. Barou, 98:Jan81-67
Amalrik, A. Notes of a Revolutionary.
  A. Austin, 441:11Jul82-11
Amann, J.J. Das Symbol Kafka.
  B. Goldstein, 406:Spring81-67
Amanuddin, S. The King Who Sold His Wife.
  A.L. Weir, 314:Summer-Fall81-226

Amaral, A. Will James.*
  J.R. Nicholl, 649(WAL):Fall81-253
Amborn, H., G. Minker and H-J. Sasse. Das
  Dullay.
  M.L. Bender, 350:Sep82-730
Ambroise, C. Le Chrétien devant la mort.
  G. Sartoris, 450(NRF):Apr81-139
Ambrose, A. and M. MacDonald. Wittgen-
  stein's Lectures: Cambridge 1932-1935.
  (A. Ambrose, ed)
  P.M.S. Hacker, 482(PhR):Jul81-444
Amburger, E. Ingermanland.
  D. Kirby, 575(SEER):Oct81-607
Amelung, P. Der Frühdruck im deutschen
  Südwesten, 1473-1500.* (Vol 1)
  B.M. Rosenthal, 517(PBSA):Apr-Jun81-
  222
"The American Image."
  J.C. Maddox, 14:Spring80-220
"The American Renaissance: 1876-1917."
  R.J. Betts, 658:Spring81-117
Ameriks, K. Kant's Theory of Mind.
  F. Schier, 617(TLS):29Oct82-1198
Ames-Lewis, F. Drawing in Early Renais-
  sance Italy.
  K. Andrews, 617(TLS):19Mar82-318
  F. Russell, 324:Sep82-679
"Ami and Amile." (S. Danon and S.N. Rosen-
  berg, trans)
  D.A. Fein, 207(FR):Feb82-402
Amiet, P. and others. Art in the Ancient
  World.*
  E.C. Pemberton, 124:May-Jun82-309
Amigues, S. Les subordonnées finales par
  "hópōs" en attique classique.*
  C. Justus, 350:Jun82-483
Amin, A. My Life.
  P. Cachia, 318(JAOS):Jul/Sep80-342
Amis, M. Invasion of the Space Invaders.
  D. Trotter, 617(TLS):26Nov82-1290
Amis, M. Other People.*
  J.R. Banks, 148:Summer81-84
  W. Boyd, 364:Apr/May81-129
Ammeter, A.E. The Bridge, That Summer.*
  (W. Tefs, ed)
  D. Barbour, 648(WCR):Jun80-75
Ammianus Marcellinus. Ammien Marcellin,
  "Histoire."* (Vol 4, Bks 23-25) (J.
  Fontaine, ed and trans)
  P. de Jonge, 394:Vol34fasc1/2-167
Ammon, U. and U. Loewer. Schwäbisch.
  H. Fischer, 680(ZDP):Band99Heft3-467
Ammons, A.R. A Coast of Trees.
  D. Lehman, 472:Fall/Winter81-73
  R. Phillips, 249(HudR):Autumn81-429
Ammons, A.R. Selected Longer Poems.*
  D. Lehman, 472:Fall/Winter81-73
Ammons, A.R. Worldly Hopes.
  M. Kinzie, 29:Sep/Oct82-37
Ammons, E., ed. Critical Essays on Har-
  riet Beecher Stowe.
  L.W. Wagner, 587(SAF):Autumn81-284
Ammons, E. Edith Wharton's Argument with
  America.
  A.R. Beauchamp, 26(ALR):Autumn81-308
  T.K. Lischer, 27(AL):May81-332
  C.G. Wolff, 587(SAF):Spring81-125
Amoia, A.D. Edmond Rostand.*
  W.D. Howarth, 208(FS):Jan81-88
  P.E. Williams, 207(FR):Oct80-170
Amore, R.C., ed. Developments in Buddhist
  Thought.
  D.L. Overmyer, 485(PE&W):Jul81-383

7

Amory, M. - see Waugh, E.
Amos, A.R., Jr. Time, Space, and Value.
  P.G. Hogan, Jr., 577(SHR):Winter81-76
Amossy, R. Les Jeux de l'allusion littér-
  aire dans "Un Beau Ténébreux" de Julien
  Gracq.*
  G. Prince, 400(MLN):May81-947
Ampalavanar, R. The Indian Minority and
  Political Change in Malaya 1945-1957.
  D.J. Duncanson, 617(TLS):3Dec82-1328
Amprimoz, A.L. Other Realities.
  J. Bell, 526:Spring81-65
Amsterdamski, S. Between Experience and
  Metaphysics.
  L. Sklar, 449:Sep81-429
Anand, M.R. Author to Critic. (S. Cowas-
  jee, ed)
  D.B. Shimer, 314:Winter-Spring81-242
Anand, M.R. and K.N. Hutheesing. The Book
  of Indian Beauty. (new ed)
  P. Bach, 614:Winter82-14
Anand, V. The Disputed Crown.
  S. Altinel, 617(TLS):17Dec82-1398
Ananthanarayana, H.S. Four Lectures on
  Pa:nini's Asta:dhya:yi:.
  H. Scharfe, 350:Jun81-493
Ananthanarayana, H.S. A Syntactic Study
  of Old Indo-Aryan.
  D. Disterheft, 350:Jun81-491
Anaya, R.A. and A. Márquez. Cuentos chi-
  canos.
  D. Gerdes, 238:Dec81-642
Ancelet, B.J., ed. Cris sur le Bayou.
  B.C. Freeman, 207(FR):Dec81-297
Anderegg, J. Literaturwissenschaftliche
  Stiltheorie.
  J.M. Ellis, 599:Winter81-32
Anderle, M. Deutsche Lyrik des 19.
  Jahrhunderts.
  B. Bjorklund, 221(GQ):May81-367
  H.M.K. Riley, 133:Band14Heft2-186
Andersch, A. Flucht in Etrurien.
  C. Russ, 617(TLS):5Feb82-147
Andersch, A. Die Kirschen der Freiheit
  and Selected Stories. (C.A.H. Russ, ed)
  E. Glass, 399(MLJ):Autumn81-353
  205(FMLS):Oct80-371
Andersen, C. Studien zur Namengebung in
  Nordfriesland.
  G.B. Droege, 424:Jun80-153
Andersen, H.C. Tales and Stories by Hans
  Christian Andersen.* (P.L. Conroy and
  S.H. Rossel, trans)
  F. Hugus, 563(SS):Summer81-358
Andersen, K.V. African Traditional Archi-
  tecture.
  T.C. Colchester, 69:Vol50No2-208
Andersen, R.W., ed. The Acquisition and
  Use of Spanish and English as First
  and Second Languages.
  R. Otheguy, 399(MLJ):Spring81-104
  T.D. Terrell, 350:Mar81-236
Anderson, A. The Man Who Was H.M. Bateman.
  T. Fitton, 617(TLS):24Dec82-1430
Anderson, C.R. Person, Place, and Thing
  in Henry James's Novels.*
  S. Perosa, 599:Fall81-468
  D.J. Schneider, 580(SCR):Fall80-99
Anderson, D. - see Smith, R.
Anderson, D.G. Abraham Lincoln.
  G.M. Fredrickson, 453(NYRB):15Jul82-13
  W. Goodman, 441:18Jul82-11

Anderson, D.R. American Flower Painting.
  J.V. Turano, 16:Summer81-85
Anderson, E. and M. Kinzie, eds. The
  Little Magazine in America.
  B. Duffey, 27(AL):Nov81-538·
  S. Weiland, 577(SHR):Spring81-166
Anderson, F. and others - see Twain, M.
Anderson, J. The Bluegum Smokes a Long
  Cigar.
  C. Pollnitz, 581:Jun81-221
Anderson, J. Cypresses.
  T.R. Jahns, 460(OhR):No29-132
  T. Swiss, 434:Spring82-489
Anderson, J. The One and Only.
  R. Buckle, 617(TLS):30Jul82-828
Anderson, J. Sir Walter Scott and History.
  C. Lamont, 617(TLS):13Aug82-890
Anderson, J. This Was Harlem.
  D. Bradley, 441:9May82-7
  R.G. O'Meally, 617(TLS):31Dec82-1441
  D. Pinckney, 453(NYRB):7Oct82-29
Anderson, J. Tirra Lirra by the River.*
  C. Hanna, 581:Sep80-360
Anderson, J.I. William Howard Taft.
  J.A. Thompson, 617(TLS):24Sep82-1026
Anderson, J.J., ed. Cleanness.*
  W. Obst, 38:Band99Heft3/4-502
Anderson, J.M. On Case Grammar.
  J.R. Hurford, 297(JL):Sep81-374
  S. Starosta, 350:Sep81-720
Anderson, J.M. and B. Rochet. Historical
  Romance Morphology.*
  S. Fleischman, 350:Jun82-424
Anderson, J.R.L. Late Delivery.
  T.J. Binyon, 617(TLS):16Apr82-446
Anderson, K. Catalogue of Sets of Vocal
  Music.
  R. Andrewes, 415:Oct81-675
Anderson, M. Guatemalan Textiles Today.
  F.H. Pettit, 37:May81-26
Anderson, M. Years That Answer.
  D. Smith, 29:Jan/Feb82-36
Anderson, P. Arguments within English
  Marxism.
  A.L., 185:Oct81-191
Anderson, R.M. Hispanic Costume 1480-
  1530.*
  E. Harris, 90:Jun81-367
Anderson, S., ed. On Streets.*
  G. Simmons, 658:Winter81-354
Anderson, T.C. The Foundation and Struc-
  ture of Sartrean Ethics.*
  J.H. McMahon, 207(FR):May81-878
  A. Manser, 185:Apr81-523
  F.A. Olafson, 482(PhR):Oct81-616
Anderson, T.H. The United States, Great
  Britain, and the Cold War 1944-47.
  V. Rothwell, 617(TLS):26Feb82-225
Anderson, W. and C. Hicks. Cathedrals in
  Britain and Ireland from Early Times to
  the Reign of Henry VIII.
  D. Guinness, 576:May81-154
  D. Watkin, 39:Jan81-61
Anderson Imbert, E. Teoría y técnica del
  cuento.
  E. Pupo-Walker, 238:Sep81-480
Andersson, S-G. Deutsch gestern und heute.
  K. Nyholm, 439(NM):1981/3-354
Andersson, T.M. The Legend of Brynhild.
  C.S. Brown, 569(SR):Summer81-lxviii
  C.B. Hieatt, 651(WHR):Winter81-377
  P.B. Taylor, 563(SS):Spring81-210
  O.J. Zitzelsberger, 222(GR):Fall81-164

8

de Andrade, C.D. - see under Drummond de
Andrade, C.
Andrade, J.C. - see under Carrera Andrade,
J.
Andre, C. and H. Frampton. 12 Dialogues
1962-1963. (B.H.D. Buchloh, ed)
R. Odlin, 472:Fall/Winter81-206
André, J. Les mots à redoublement en
Latin.*
G.M. Messing, 122:Apr81-162
W.P. Schmid, 260(IF):Band85-360
Andreu, P. and F. Grover. Drieu la
Rochelle.
R. Veasey, 402(MLR):Jan81-201
Andreu, P.A.G. - see under Galera Andreu,
P.A.
Andrew, C.M. and A.S. Kanya-Forstner.
France Overseas.
A. Hourani, 617(TLS):22Jan82-89
Andrew, J. Writers and Society During the
Rise of Russian Realism.
C.M. Barrett, 550(RusR):Apr81-218
F. Kitch, 402(MLR):Oct81-1004
T.G. Marullo, 574(SEEJ):Winter81-93
Andrew, L.B. The Early Temples of the Mor-
mons.*
R.L. Bushman, 658:Spring81-100
Andrew, M. and R. Waldron, eds. The Poems
of the "Pearl" Manuscript.*
J.A. Burrow, 677(YES):Vol 11-223
G. Gauvin, 189(EA):Apr-Jun81 212
C.K. Zacher, 589:Apr81-340
Andrew, W. The Gawain-Poet.
M.H. Fleming, 365:Fal181-171
Andrews, B.G. and W.H. Wilde. Australian
Literature to 1900.
L.T. Hergenhan, 71(ALS):May81-137
Andrews, G.R. The Afro-Argentines of
Buenos Aires, 1800-1900.
L.B. Rout, Jr., 263(RIB):Vol31No3-404
Andrews, M. - see Dickens, C.
Andrews, M.A. The Flight of the Condor.
S.D. Smith, 441:5Dec82-65
Andrews, V.C. My Sweet Audrina.
E.R. Lipson, 441:30ct82-13
Andrews, W. Voltaire.*
M. Mudrick, 249(HudR):Winter81/82-525
Andrews, W.L. The Literary Career of
Charles W. Chesnutt.
P.J. Delmar, 26(ALR):Spring81-143
W. Sollors, 27(AL):May81-331
639(VQR):Spring81-69
Andrian, G.W. and J.D. Davies, eds. Prêt
à lire.
W. Wrage, 207(FR):Oct80-212
Andriot, J.L., ed. Township Atlas of the
United States.
E.C. Smith, 424:Mar80-89
Andritch, I. La Soif et autres nouvelles.
J-M. le Sidaner, 450(NRF):Feb81-145
Angeli, G. Il mondo rovesciato.
T. Barolini, 545(RPh):Nov80-262
Angell, J., ed. Lingerie and Sleepwear.
P. Bach, 614:Fal182-18
Angell, R. Late Innings.
M. Harris, 441:23May82-3
W. Sheed, 453(NYRB):23Sep82-45
Angenot, M. Les Champions des Femmes.*
S. Bayne, 475:No14Pt1-146
"Les Angevins de la littérature."
C. Delmas, 535(RHL):Jul-Oct81-846
Angiolillo, P.F. A Criminal as Hero.
M.S. Miller, 173(ECS):Summer81-497

Anglés, J.E.A. - see under Arias Anglés,
J.E.
Lord Anglesey. A History of the British
Cavalry 1816-1919. (Vol 3)
B. Bond, 617(TLS):24Sep82-1043
D. Hunt, 362:16Sep82-28
Anglicus, B. - see under Bartholomaeus
Anglicus
Angrémy, A. and others, comps. Voltaire,
un homme, un siècle.
W.H. Barber, 535(RHL):Mar-Apr81-302
Angulo Iñiguez, D. Murillo.
E. Young, 39:Oct81-255
Anikin, V.P. Russkaja narodnaja skazka.
J.L. Conrad, 574(SEEJ):Summer81-99
Anikst, M.A. and V.S. Turchin. ... v
Okrestnostyakh Moskvy.
J.S.G. Simmons, 78(BC):Summer81-267
"Annales Universitatis Scientiarum Buda-
pestinensis de Rolando Eötvös nominatae."
(Sectio Linguistica III)
G.F. Meier, 682(ZPSK):Band32Heft2-222
Annan, N. - see Stephen, L.
Annas, J. An Introduction to Plato's
"Republic."
C. Janaway, 617(TLS):21May82-565
Annibaldi, C. and M. Monna. Bibliografia
e catalogo delle opere di Goffredo
Petrassi.
C. Bennett, 607:Dec81-47
"Annual Review of Applied Linguistics."
(1980) (R.B. Kaplan, R.L. Jones and
G.R. Tucker, eds)
A. Roca, 608:Sep82-398
"El año cultural español 1979."
C.A. Longhurst, 86(BHS):Apr81-151
Anoyanakis, F. Greek Popular Musical
Instruments.
H. Myers, 415:May81-315
van Anrooij, F. and others, eds. Between
People and Statistics.
R. Van Niel, 293(JASt):Nov80-210
Ansari, M.A. Muslims and the Congress.
(M. Hasan, ed)
K. McPherson, 293(JASt):Aug81-822
Ansart-Dourlen, M. Dénaturation et vio-
lence dans la pensée de Jean-Jacques
Rousseau.
D. Oger, 356(LR):Nov81-359
Ansay, T. and D. Wallace, Jr., eds. Intro-
duction to Turkish Law. (2nd ed)
D.J. Forte, 318(JAOS):Apr/Jun80-147
Anscombe, G.E.M. Collected Philosophical
Papers.
M. Tiles, 617(TLS):30Apr82-492
Anscombe, G.E.M. - see Wittgenstein, L.
Anscombe, G.E.M. and G.H. von Wright - see
Wittgenstein, L.
Anscombe, I. Omega and After.
A. Ross, 364:Feb82-101
R. Shone, 617(TLS):30Apr82-494
Anselment, R.A. "Betwixt Jest and Ear-
nest."
J. Egan, 568(SCN):Spring81-12
A.M. Patterson, 551(RenQ):Winter80-816
P. Sabor, 566:Spring81-121
P.G. Stanwood, 301(JEGP):Apr81-253
205(FMLS):Jan81-92
Anson, R.S. Gone Crazy and Back Again.*
639(VQR):Summer81-91

Antoine, R. Les écrivains français et les
Antilles, des premiers Pères Blancs aux
Surréalistes Noirs.*
   C. Cesbron, 446(NCFS):Spring-Summer81-
   289
   H. Duranton, 535(RHL):Jul-Oct81-847
Anton, B. Romantisches Parodieren.
   K. Peter, 133:Band14Heft2-184
Antón, I.G. - see under García Antón, I.
Antonaci, A. Ricerche sull'aristotelismo
del Rinascimento: Marcantonio Zimara.
(Vol 2)
   C.B. Schmitt, 319:Oct81-506
Antonov-Ovseyenko, A. The Time of Stalin.
   H.E. Salisbury, 441:17Jan82-8
Antrim, L. Louisa, Lady in Waiting. (E.
Longford, ed)
   F. Hardie, 637(VS):Spring81-357
Anttila, R. and W.A. Brewer, comps.
Analogy: A Basic Bibliography.
   P. Baldi, 260(IF):Band85-307
Anwar, M. The Myth of Return.
   P. Jeffery, 293(JASt):Aug81-810
Anzilotti, R., ed. Robert Lowell.*
   R. Asselineau, 189(EA):Jul-Sep81-358
   G. Willis, 106:Spring81-113
Apel, F. Die Zaubergärten der Phantasie.*
   G.J. Holst, 221(GQ):Mar81-247
Apel, K-O. Die Erklären.
   J.M. Connolly, 262:Mar81-123
Apel, K-O. Towards a Transformation of
Philosophy.*
   J.M. Connolly, 393(Mind):Oct81-628
   C. Hookway, 483:Jan81-134
   R.B.S., 185:Jul82-796
Apenes, S.I. Rapport om Petter Dass.*
   N.M. Knutsen, 562(Scan):Nov81-219
Apollinaire, G. Calligrammes. (A.H.
Greet, trans)
   R. Feld, 472:Spring/Summer81-17
   42(AR):Spring81-266
Apollonius. The Syntax of Apollonius
Dyscolus. (F.W. Householder, trans)
   P. Swiggers, 350:Sep82-723
Appel, R. and others, eds. Taalproblemen
van buitenlandse arbeiders en hun
kinderen.
   G.A.T. Koefoed, 204(FdL):Jun81-219
Appelfeld, A. The Age of Wonders.*
   A. Alvarez, 453(NYRB):4Feb82-33
   B. Josipovici, 617(TLS):19Nov82-1269
Appelfeld, A. Badenheim 1939.*
   A.B. Carb, 287:Apr81-25
Appelt, H., with R.M. Herkenrath and W.
Koch, eds. Die Urkunden Friedrichs I.,
1158-1167.
   R.H. Schmandt, 589:Apr81-447
Apple, M., ed. Southwest Fiction.
   C.M. Cardon, 50(ArQ):Winter81-376
Appleby, J.O. Economic Thought and Ideol-
ogy in Seventeenth Century England.
   J.S. Morrill, 161(DUJ):Jun81-243
Appleton, W.W. - see Smith, O.
Applewhite, C. Summer Dreams and the
Kleig Light Gas Company.
   442(NY):3May82-165
Applewhite, J. Following Gravity.
   R.T. Smith, 577(SHR):Fall81-371
Appleyard, D., ed. The Conservation of
European Cities.
   G. Sutherland, 46:Apr81-255

Apter, T.E. Thomas Mann.
   K.M. Hewitt, 447(N&Q):Oct80-475
   E.A. McCormick, 594:Fall81-332
Apter, T.E. Virginia Woolf.*
   N. Bradbury, 541(RES):May81-237
   A.L. McLaughlin, 395(MFS):Summer80-282
Aquila, R.E. Intentionality.
   D. Willard, 319:Jan81-132
Aquin, H. Hamlet's Twin.*
   L. Rogers, 102(CanL):Spring81-104
Aquinas, T. Opera omnia iussu Leonis XIII
P.M. edita. (Vol 43) (H-F. Dondaine, ed)
   S.F. Brown, 589:Jan81-198
"Arabic and Islamic Garland."
   U. Abd-Allāh, 318(JAOS):Apr/Jun80-141
Arac, J. Commissioned Spirits.*
   C. Dahl, 125:Spring81-335
   P.K. Garrett, 637(VS):Winter81-251
   W.L. Reed, 445(NCF):Sep80-236
   E.J. Sundquist, 580(SCR):Fall80-104
Arad, Y. The Partisan.
   M.W. Kiel, 287:Apr81-26
Aradoon, Z. The Belly Dance Costume Book.
   P. Bach, 614:Spring81-16
Aragon, L. Le Mentir-vrai.*
   J-C. Gateau, 450(NRF):Jan81-130
Araluce Cuenca, J.R. El Libro de los
Estados.*
   F. Domínguez, 241:Jan81-76
Arathorn, D.W. Kamal.
   S. Ellin, 441:30May82-19
Arboleda, J.R. - see Bécquer, G.A.
Arbour, R. L'Ere baroque en France (1585-
1643).* (Pt 1)
   E.J. Campion, 207(FR):Apr82-674
   P-L. Vaillancourt, 539:Aug82-203
Arbour, R. L'Ere baroque en France (1585-
1643).* (Pts 2 and 3) [entry in prev
was of Pts 1 and 2]
   E.J. Campion, 207(FR):Apr82-674
   W. Leiner, 475:No14Pt1-157
   P-L. Vaillancourt, 539:Aug82-203
Arce, H. Gary Cooper.
   J. Beaver, 200:Oct81-509
Arcelus Ulibarrena, J.M. Introducción a
la filología española.
   O.T. Myers, 545(RPh):Feb81-342
Archbold, G.J.D.E. A Concordance to the
History of Ammianus Marcellinus.
   R.S. Bagnall, 121(CJ):Feb/Mar82-277
Archer, C. and S. Maxwell, eds. The Nor-
dic Model.
   R.F. Tomasson, 563(SS):Winter81-95
Archer, J. The Prodigal Daughter.
   N. Johnson, 441:11Jul82-14
Archer, J. A Quiver Full of Arrows.*
   M. Mewshaw, 441:28Nov82-12
Archer, M. Early Views of India.
   B. Llewellyn, 135:Jun81-88
   V. Powell, 39:Feb81-127
Arco Magrì, M., ed. Clemente Innografo e
gli inediti canoni cerimoniali.
   É. des Places, 555:Vol54fasc2-365
Ardagh, J. France in the 1980s.
   P. Daudy, 617(TLS):26Nov82-1313
   P. Johnson, 362:8Jul82-22
Ardagh, J. A Tale of Five Cities.*
   42(AR):Spring81-265
Ardao, A. Génesis de la idea y el nombre
de América Latina.
   A. Cordero, 263(RIB):Vol31No3-405

Arden, H. Fools' Plays.*
    J. Alter, 207(FR):Apr81-732
    P.E. Bennett, 402(MLR):Oct81-958
    S. Billington, 382(MAE):1981/1-147
    A.E. Knight, 589:Oct81-840
    K.V. Sinclair, 67:May81-114
    205(FMLS):Oct80-371
Arden, J. Silence Among the Weapons.
    J. Mellors, 362:26Aug82-24
    R. Owen, 617(TLS):27Aug82-920
Arellano, J.E. La colección Squier-
    Zapatera.
    G. Loyola de Artaza, 263(RIB):Vol31No1-
    76
Arén, G. Evangelical Pioneers in Ethiopia.
    W.A. Shack, 69:Vol50No2-211
Arendt, H. La Vie de l'esprit. (Vol 1)
    T. Cordellier, 450(NRF):Dec81-120
Arendt, J.D., D.L. Lange and P.J. Meyers,
    eds. Foreign Language Learning Today
    and Tomorrow.
    R.W. Newman, 207(FR):May82-915
Arenhövel, W. and C. Schreiber, eds.
    Berlin und die Antike.
    H. Plommer, 303(JoHS):Vol 101-234
Argue, V. and others. Devant le micro.
    L. Vines, 207(FR):May81-885
Argyle, G. German Elements in the Fiction
    of George Eliot, Gissing, and Meredith.
    M. Brown, 445(NCF):Jun81-86
    M.K. Flavell, 402(MLR):Oct81-992
Argyle, J. and E. Preston-Whyte, eds.
    Social System and Tradition in Southern
    Africa.
    C. Murray, 69:Vol50No4-429
Argyle, M. and P. Trower. Person to Per-
    son.
    G.W. Beattie, 353:Vol 18No3/4-369
Arias, J. "Guzmán de Alfarache."
    R. Bjornson, 131(CL):Spring81-194
Arias Anglés, J.E. J. Pérez Villaamil.
    D. Angulo Íñiguez, 48:Jul-Sep81-378
Aridjis, H. Exaltation of Light. (E.
    Weinberger, ed and trans)
    H.J.F. de Aguilar, 472:Fall/Winter81-
    277
Ariès, P. The Hour of Our Death.*
    T. Des Pres, 676(YR):Winter82-241
Ariès, P., with M. Winock. Un Historien
    du dimanche.*
    N. Hampson, 208(FS):Apr81-246
Ariosto, L. Commedie. (A. Casella, G.
    Ronchi and E. Varasi, eds)
    F. Lorusso, 228(GSLI):Vol 156fasc495-
    461
Ariotti, P. and P. de Comes. Arletty.
    M.G. Hydak, 207(FR):Oct81-151
Aris, M. - see Davis, S.
Aristophanes. The Knights; Peace; The
    Birds; The Assemblywomen; Wealth. (D.
    Barrett and A.H. Sommerstein, trans)
    N.V. Dunbar, 447(N&Q):Apr80-183
Aristotle. Aristote, "Ethique à Eudème."*
    (V. Décarie, with R. Houde-Sauvé, eds
    and trans)
    J-L. Poirier, 542:Apr-Jun81-265
Aristotle. Aristote: "La Poétique." (R.
    Dupont-Roc and J. Lallot, eds and trans)
    B.R. Rees, 123:Vol31No2-178
Aristotle. Aristotelis "Ars Rhetorica."
    (R. Kassel, ed)
    M.C. Nussbaum, 53(AGP):Band63Heft3-346
Aristotle. Aristotle's "De Motu Animal-
    ium."* (M.C. Nussbaum, ed and trans)
    J. Ackrill, 482(PhR):Oct81-601
    M.F. Burnyeat, 53(AGP):Band63Heft2-184
    H.B. Gottschalk, 24:Spring81-84
    P. Louis, 555:Vol154fasc1-165
    M. Schofield, 303(JoHS):Vol 101-156
Aristotle. Aristotle's Eudemian Ethics,
    Books 1, 2, and 8. (M. Woods, trans)
    A.W. Price, 617(TLS):26Nov82-1322
Aristotle. Aristotle's "Posterior
    Analytics." (J. Barnes, ed and trans)
    T. Ebert, 53(AGP):Band62Heft1-85
Arkell, D. Looking for Laforgue.*
    M. Hannoosh, 188(ECr):Summer81-99
    J.A. Hiddleston, 208(FS):Apr81-217
    M. Wood, 453(NYRB):27May82-40
Arland, M. Mais enfin qui êtes-vous?
    R. André, 450(NRF):Jun81-112
Arlen, M.J. The Camera Age.*
    M. Mayer, 18:Apr81-72
    J. Simpson, 362:4Feb82-24
Arlen, M.J. Thirty Seconds.*
    N. Berry, 364:Jun81-83
Armistead, S.G., with others. El roman-
    cero judeo-español en el Archivo
    Menéndez Pidal (Catálogo-índice de
    romances y canciones).
    S.L. Arora, 292(JAF):Jan-Mar81-107
    M.E. Barrick, 240(HR):Winter81-121
    J.G. Cummins, 86(BHS):Apr81-136
    I.J. Levy, 238:May81-311
Armistead, S.G. and J.H. Silverman. Tres
    calas en el romancero sefardí (Rodas,
    Jerusalén, Estados Unidos).
    L.P. Harvey, 86(BHS):Apr81-138
    S. Petersen, 238:Sep81-476
Armistead, S.G. and J.H. Silverman, with
    O.A. Librowicz. Romances judeo-espa-
    ñoles de Tánger recogidos por Zarita
    Nahón.*
    J.G. Cummins, 86(BHS):Apr81-136
Arms, G. and others - see Howells, W.D.
Arms, G., C. Lohmann and J. Herron - see
    Howells, W.D.
Armstrong, D. and C.H. van Schooneveld,
    eds. Roman Jakobson.
    M. Krampen, 567:Vol33No3/4-261
Armstrong, D.M. The Nature of Mind and
    Other Essays.
    E. Conee, 484(PPR):Jun82-622
Armstrong, J. The Idea of Holiness and
    the Humane Response.
    R. Hayward, 617(TLS):5Feb82-146
Armstrong, J.D. Revolutionary Diplomacy.*
    B.D. Larkin, 293(JASt):Feb81-338
Armstrong, L. Renaissance Miniature
    Painters and Classical Imagery.
    G. Reynolds, 617(TLS):19Mar82-304
Armstrong, R. and J. Shenk. El Salvador.
    R. Bonner, 441:17Oct82-7
Árnason, K. Quantity in Historical Phonol-
    ogy.
    E.M. Kaisse, 350:Mar82-241
    A. Liberman, 215(GL):Winter81-281
Arnaud, N. and H. Bordillon - see Jarry, A.
Arnaud, P. Ann Radcliffe et le fantas-
    tique.
    D.P. Varma, 189(EA):Jan-Mar81-95
Arnaud, P. and J. Raimond. Le Préroman-
    tisme anglais.
    C.J. Rawson, 189(EA):Oct-Dec81-472

Arnauld, A. and C. Lancelot. General and
Rational Grammar. (J. Rieux and B.E.
Rollin, ed and trans)
   N.L. Corbett, 545(RPh):Nov80-233
Arndt, K., G.F. Koch and L.O. Larsson.
Albert Speer, Architektur.
   A.M. Vogt, 576:May81-163
Arndt, W. - see Busch, W.
Arnesen, P.J. The Medieval Japanese
Daimyo.
   M.E. Berry, 407(MN):Summer81-187
   H. Bolitho, 293(JASt):May81-598
   M. Collcutt, 244(HJAS):Dec81-640
Arngart, O., ed. The Proverbs of Alfred.*
   K. Bitterling, 38:Band99Heft3/4-496
   A.G. Rigg, 541(RES):Feb81-68
Arnold, A.J. Modernism and Negritude.
   P.L. Bowles, 617(TLS):14May82-541
Arnold, B. Orpen.*
   J. Darracott, 364:Jun81-87
   A.D. Fraser Jenkins, 135:Jun81-89
Arnold, D. Giovanni Gabrieli and the
Music of the Venetian High Renaissance.
   J. Glixon, 317:Spring81-149
Arnold, J., ed. "Lost from Her Majesties
Back."
   R.L. Shep, 614:Spring81-20
Arnold, M. The Complete Prose Works of
Matthew Arnold.* (Vol 11) (R.H. Super,
ed)
   D. Douglas, 179(ES):Apr81-184
Arnold, T. The Letters of Thomas Arnold
the Younger (1850-1900). (J. Bertram,
ed)
   639(VQR):Winter81-10
Arnson, C. El Salvador.
   R. Bonner, 441:17Oct82-7
Arnstein, W.L. Protestant versus Catholic
in Mid-Victorian England.
   E. Norman, 617(TLS):16Jul82-758
Aron, J-P., ed. Misérable et glorieuse.
   P. Clark, 207(FR):May82-931
Aron, T. L'objet du texte et le texte-
objet.
   M-T. Ligot, 209(FM):Oct81-370
Aroniawenrate - see under Blue Cloud, P.
Aronov, S.I. A Descriptive Catalogue of
the Bension Collection of Sephardic Manu-
scripts and texts.
   A. Schischa, 354:Mar81-65
Aronson, A. Music and the Novel.
   D. Melnick, 395(MFS):Winter80/81-728
Aronson, D.R. The City is Our Farm.
   J. Eades, 69:Vol50No2-229
Aronson, N. Mademoiselle de Scudéry.*
   E.M. Tilton, 568(SCN):Winter81-95
Aronson, R. Jean-Paul Sartre — Philosophy
in the World.
   W.L. McBride, 185:Apr82-561
   L.S. Roudiez, 546(RR):Nov81-504
Arp, J. Collected French Writings. (M.
Jean, ed)
   R. Cardinal, 529(QQ):Spring81-19
Arpin, G.Q. The Poetry of John Berryman.
   S. Fender, 677(YES):Vol 11-365
Arrabal, F. Lettre aux militants commun-
istes espagnols.
   J. Spinale, 207(FR):Feb82-432
Arrabal, F. Théâtre XII.
   J. Spinale, 207(FR):Dec80-359
Arrants, C., with J. Asbjornsen. Sew
Wonderful Silk.
   P. Bach, 614:Summer82-18

Arrighi, G. and others. La scuola gali-
leiana.
   H. Vedrine, 542:Jul-Sep81-348
Arróniz, O. Teatro de evangelización en
Nueva España.
   M. Tietz, 72:Band217Heft2-469
Arroyo, C.M. - see under Morón Arroyo, C.
Arseguel, G. Décharges.
   C. Grivel, 98:Feb80-174
Artaud, A. Oeuvres complètes.* (Vol 15)
   F. Trémolières, 450(NRF):Nov81-118
Artaud, P-Y. and G. Geay. Flûtes au
présent — Present-day Flutes.
   N. O'Loughlin, 415:Jun81-383
Arthur, J., ed. Morality and Moral Contro-
versies.
   D.G.T., 185:Jan82-402
"Artists of Israel 1920-1980."
   385(MQR):Spring82-375
Artmann, H.C. and others, eds. Contempor-
ary Surrealist Prose. (Vol 1)
   C. Bayard, 102(CanL):Winter80-141
   J. Martin, 648(WCR):Vol 15No3-68
Arumaa, P. Urslavische Grammatik.* (Vol
2)
   H. Birnbaum, 279:Vol124-153
Arundell, D. The Critic at the Opera.
   E.T. Harris, 414(MusQ):Apr81-290
Arwas, V. Art Deco.
   62:Jan81-64
Asals, H.A.R. Equivocal Predication.
   R. Selden, 617(TLS):11Jun82-647
Asbell, B. - see Roosevelt, E. and A.
Aschenbrenner, J., with L. Williams. Kath-
erine Dunham.
   J.C. Dje Dje, 187:Sep82-473
Ascher, C. Simone de Beauvoir.
   J. Uglow, 617(TLS):12Feb82-167
   639(VQR):Autumn81-126
Ascherson, N. The Polish August.
   A. Brumberg, 617(TLS):11Jun82-640
   L. Schapiro, 453(NYRB):4Feb82-3
   J. Simpson, 362:7Jan82-26
   F. Tuohy, 364:Mar82-90
   R.M. Watt, 441:25Apr82-11
Ash, J. The Goodbyes.
   D. Davis, 362:16Dec82-23
   M. Imlah, 617(TLS):29Oct82-1200
Ash, T.G. - see under Garton Ash, T.
Ashbery, J. As We Know.*
   G. Kuzma, 502(PrS):Fall81-95
Ashbery, J. Houseboat Days.*
   C. Lambert, 97(CQ):Vol 10No1-84
Ashbery, J. Shadow Train.*
   H. Beaver, 472:Fall/Winter81-54
   D. Gioia, 249(HudR):Winter81/82-587
   B. Morrison, 617(TLS):8Oct82-1105
   S. Yenser, 676(YR):Autumn81-97
   639(VQR):Autumn81-130
Ashbrook, W. Donizetti and his Operas.
   M. Tanner, 617(TLS):24Sep82-1038
Ashby, W. Frank Porter Graham.
   J.W. Pence, Jr., 583:Fall81-92
Ashe, G. A Guidebook to Arthurian
Britain.
   R. Barber, 203:Vol92No2-252
Asher, C. and others. Something to Talk
About in French: Les Vacances.
   205(FMLS):Jan80-80
Ashford, J. The Loss of the Culion.*
   N. Callendar, 441:17Jan82-29

12

Ashhurst, A.W. La literatura hispano-
americana en la crítica española.*
  K. Schwartz, 238:May81-317
  D.L. Shaw, 86(BHS):Apr81-156
Ashley, M. The People of England.
  J. Ridley, 617(TLS):31Dec82-1436
Ashley, M. - see Gaskell, E.C.
Ashmore, H.S. Hearts and Minds.
  C. Sitton, 441:20Jun82-8
Asholt, W. Semantische Strukturen in
"L'Enfant" von Jules Vallès.
  P. Moores, 208(FS):Oct81-460
Ashraf, P.M. Englische Arbeiterliteratur
vom 18. Jahrhundert bis zum ersten Welt-
krieg.
  H. Behrend, 654(WB):5/1981-176
Ashtiyânî, S.J., ed. Anthologie des
philosophes iraniens depuis le XVIIe
siècle jusqu'à nos jours.
  J-C. Foussard, 98:May80-498
Ashton, D. American Art Since 1945.
  P. Overy, 617(TLS):19Mar82-316
Ashton, D. and D.B. Hare. Rosa Bonheur.*
  A. Berman, 55:Dec81-29
Ashton, R. The City and the Court, 1603-
1643.
  P. Zagorin, 551(RenQ):Winter80-798
Ashton, R. The German Idea.
  M. Brown, 445(NCF):Jun81-86
  M.K. Flavell, 402(MLR):Oct81-992
  L.R. Furst, 301(JECP):Jan81-95
  R. Maniquis, 637(VS):Spring81-367
  M. Moran, 89(BJA):Winter81-88
  T.C. Sauer, 133:Band14Heft4-374
  205(FMLS):Oct80-371
Ashton-Warner, S. I Passed This Way.*
  M. Ellmann, 569(SR):Summer81-454
Asimov, I. Extraterrestrial Civilizations.
  E. Argyle, 529(QQ):Spring81-185
Asimov, I. Foundation's Edge.
  G. Jonas, 441:19Dec82-13
Asimov, I. - see Swift, J.
Asimov, I. and J.O. Jeppson, eds. Laugh-
ing Space.
  D.J. Enright, 362:25Nov82-22
de Asis, L. From Bataan to Tokyo. (G.K.
Goodman, ed)
  Tsurumi Yoshiyuki, 285(JapQ):Jan-Mar81-
111
Aslet, C. The Last Country Houses.
  S. Gardiner, 362:25Nov82-21
  A. Saint, 617(TLS):26Nov82-1295
Aspelin, K. "Poesi i sak."
  M.J. Blackwell, 563(SS):Autumn81-499
Aspetsberger, F. Literarisches Leben im
Austrofaschismus.
  E. Schwarz, 301(JEGP):Jul81-396
Aspiz, H. Walt Whitman and the Body Beau-
tiful.
  G.W. Allen, 27(AL):Nov81-549
  M. Hindus, 646(WWR):Jun81-87
  639(VQR):Summer81-83
Aspland, C.W., ed. A Medieval French
Reader.*
  T. Hunt, 402(MLR):Jul81-690
  W.W. Kibler, 207(FR):Oct80-212
  A.E. Knight, 399(MLJ):Spring81-89
  P. Rickard, 382(MAE):1981/1-153
  N.B. Smith, 589:Jan81-93
Asquith, H.H. H.H. Asquith: Letters to
Venetia Stanley. (M. and E. Brock, eds)
  M.B. Carter, 362:4Nov82-22
  S. Koss, 617(TLS):26Nov82-1289

Assaf, U. and Y., eds and trans. Märchen
aus dem Libanon.*
  H-J. Uther, 196:Band21Heft1/2-102
Asselineau, R. The Transcendentalist
Constant in American Literature.
  R. Christiansen, 617(TLS):22Jan82-82
  J.D. Eberwein, 646(WWR):Sep81-136
  K.M. Price, 26(ALR):Autumn81-297
  R.E. Spiller, 27(AL):Nov81-545
Assmann, E., ed. Godeschalcus und Visio
Godeschalci.
  F. Rädle, 684(ZDA):Band110Heft1-19
Assunção, F. El gaucho. Pilchas criollas.
  R. Etchepareborda, 263(RIB):Vol31No2-
271
Aste, M. La narrativa di Luigi Pirandello.
  B. Lawton, 395(MFS):Winter80/81-746
Astengo, D. and F. Contorbia - see
Sbarbaro, C.
Aster, H. - see Layton, I.
Asthana, R.K. Henry James.
  D.S. Maini, 284:Fall81-74
Astley, N., ed. Ten North-East Poets.*
  B. Ruddick, 148:Winter81-71
Astor, S. Dame.
  V. Young, 249(HudR):Spring81-153
Asturias, M.Á. El señor Presidente.
  205(FMLS):Oct80-372
Asturias, M.Á. Viernes de dolores.* (I.H.
Verdugo, ed)
  D.L. Shaw, 86(BHS):Apr81-158
Atha, A. - see St. John, C.
Athanassiadi-Fowden, P. Julian and
Hellenism.
  A. Cameron, 617(TLS):26Feb82-206
Athens, L.H. Violent Criminal Acts and
Actors.
  S.W., 185:Apr81-535
Atherton, S.S. Alan Sillitoe.
  R.D. Sell, 541(RES):Nov81-494
  M. Théry, 189(EA):Apr-Jun81-231
Atik, A. Words in Hock.
  R. Garfitt, 617(TLS):2Apr82-392
Atkin, M. Russia and Iran, 1780-1828.
  D.S.M. Williams, 575(SEER):Jul81-449
Atkins, B.T. and others - see under
"Collins Robert French-English, English-
French Dictionary"
Atkins, G.D. The Faith of John Dryden.
  W. Frost, 566:Spring81-110
  D. Griffin, 401(MLQ):Mar81-93
Atkins, M.E. Palimpsest.
  K. Jeffery, 617(TLS):11Jun82-642
  M. Laski, 362:29Apr82-27
Atkins, P.W. The Creation.
  J.L. Mackie, 617(TLS):5Feb82-126
Atkinson, R.F. Knowledge and Explanation
in History.*
  S. Ajzenstat, 529(QQ):Spring81-171
  G. Graham, 479(PhQ):Jan81-88
  P. Nowell-Smith, 185:Apr81-530
  T. O'Hagan, 393(Mind):Jul81-462
"Atlas Linguarum Europae (ALE)." (Intro-
duction and 1st Questionnaire) (A.
Weijnen, ed-in-chief)
  W. Viereck, 38:Band99Heft1/2-201
Attali, J. L'ordre cannibale.
  F. Roustang, 98:Jan80-25
Attebery, B. The Fantasy Tradition in
American Literature.
  H.N. Smith, 445(NCF):Sep81-193
Attenborough, D. Life on Earth.*
  C.D. May, 441:3Jan82-10

13

Attfield, R. God and the Secular.*
  H.A.D., 543:Mar81-597
"Atti del Convegno internazionale di studi
  Danteschi, a cura del Comune di Ravenna
  e della Società Dantesca Italiana
  (Ravenna, 10-12 Settembre 1971)."
  M. Waller, 589:Jan81-213
Atwood, M. Bodily Harm.
  P-L. Adams, 61:Apr82-110
  F. Davey, 99:Dec81/Jan82-29
  P. Kemp, 617(TLS):11Jun82-643
  J. Leonard, 441:21Mar82-3
  K.C. O'Brien, 362:22Jul82-24
  J.A. Wainwright, 150(DR):Autumn81-581
  442(NY):12Apr82-153
Atwood, M. Dancing Girls and Other
  Stories.
  A. Tyler, 441:19Sep82-3
  442(NY):4Oct82-146
Atwood, M. Life Before Man.*
  G. Woodcock, 102(CanL):Autumn80-136
Atwood, M. Two-headed Poems and Others.*
  L. Weir, 102(CanL):Autumn80-118
Atwood, W.G. The Lioness and the Little
  One.*
  L.S. Herrmann, 446(NCFS):Fall-Win-
    ter81/82-190
  J. Kallberg, 451:Spring82-244
  F.W. Kaye, 502(PrS):Winter81/82-94
Aub, M. Crimes exemplaires.
  J-M. Le Sidaner, 450(NRF):May81-146
Aubailly, J-C., ed. Deux jeux de Carnaval
  de la fin du Moyen Age.
  J. Beck, 545(RPh):Feb81(supp)-304
  A. Hindley, 208(FS):Apr81-185
Aubenque, P., ed. Etudes sur la Méta-
  physique d'Aristote.*
  A. Reix, 542:Apr-Jun81-267
Aubery, P. Anarchiste et décadent.*
  R. Carr, 208(FS):Jul81-352
Auboyer, J. and others. Oriental Art.*
  (J. Hirschen, ed)
  A.C. Soper, 57:Vol42No1-119
Aubral, F. Agonie.
  F.C. St. Aubyn, 207(FR):Dec81-298
Aubrey, J. Monumenta Britannica.* (J.
  Fowles and R. Legg, eds)
  P-L. Adams, 61:Mar82-89
  D.J.R. Bruckner, 441:7Mar82-12
Auburger, L., H. Kloss and H. Rupp, eds.
  Deutsch als Muttersprache in Kanada.
  R. d'Alquen, 406:Winter81-444
Auchincloss, L. Watchfires.
  S. Altinel, 617(TLS):17Dec82-1398
  A. Tyler, 441:2May82-12
  442(NY):24May82-133
Auden, W.H. Forewords and Afterwords. (E.
  Mendelson, ed)
  R. Hindmarsh, 72:Band217Heft2-442
Auden, W.H. Selected Poems of W.H. Auden.*
  (E. Mendelson, ed)
  R.B., 189(EA):Apr-Jun81-240
Auden, W.H. and P.B. Taylor. Norse Poems.
  T.A. Shippey, 617(TLS):26Feb82-205
Audet, N. Quand la voile faseille.
  C.F. Coates, 207(FR):May81-889
von Aue, H. - see under Hartmann von Aue
Auel, J.M. The Valley of Horses.
  S. Isaacs, 441:26Sep82-14
Auerbach, N. Communities of Women.*
  C. Zwarg, 454:Fall81-76
Augé, M. The Anthropological Circle.
  M. Bloch, 617(TLS):12Feb82-164

Augier, P. Quand les grands ducs val-
  saient à Nice.
  A-C. Faitrop, 207(FR):Mar82-576
Aujac, G. - see Dionysius of Halicarnassus
Auletta, K. The Underclass.
  A. Hacker, 453(NYRB):12Aug82-15
  C. Peters, 441:27Jun82-11
Aulotte, R. Montaigne: "L'Apologie de
  Raimond Sebond."
  R. Bernoulli, 535(RHL):Jul-Oct81-754
  C. Dickson, 207(FR):Oct81-135
Aune, B. Kant's Theory of Morals.
  M. Albrecht, 342:Band72Heft3-378
  A. Broadie, 479(PhQ):Apr81-183
  T. Mautner, 63:Jun81-258
  R.B.P., 543:Dec80-369
  H.P. Rickman, 483:Jan81-128
  W. Wick, 185:Jan82-341
Aune, B. Reason and Action.*
  D. Gauthier, 488:Sep80-330
  J.M., 543:Sep80-125
"Aunt Ellen's Crochet Handbook." "Aunt
  Ellen's Knitting Handbook."
  M.Z. Cowan, 614:Fall82-14
Auroux, S. Le Sémiotique des Encyclo-
  pédistes.
  F. Duchesneau, 154:Sep81-587
Ausland, J.C. Norway, Oil and Foreign
  Policy.
  I.N. Means, 563(SS):Winter81-96
Auspitz, K. The Radical Bourgeoisie.
  T. Judt, 617(TLS):22Oct82-1172
Aust, H., ed. Fontane aus heutiger Sicht.
  D.C. Riechel, 399(MLJ):Summer81-233
Austen, J. Jane Austen's "Sir Charles
  Grandison."* (B. Southam, ed)
  J.B., 148:Autumn81-90
Austen, M.E. Love-Act.
  D. Montrose, 617(TLS):21May82-566
Austen-Leigh, J. Stephanie.
  L. Weir, 102(CanL):Spring81-126
Auster, R.D. and M. Silver. The State as
  a Firm.
  W.J. Samuels, 185:Jan81-338
Austin, J.C., with D. Royot. American
  Humor in France.*
  R.G. Collins, 106:Winter81-375
Austin, M. Literary America, 1903-1934.*
  (T.M. Pearce, ed)
  R.S.P., 148:Winter81-93
Austin, N.J.E. Ammianus on Warfare.
  J.M. Alonso-Núñez, 123:Vol131No1-123
Autrand, M. L'Humour de Jules Renard.*
  R. Bourgeois, 535(RHL):Jan-Feb81-157
  N. Thatcher, 208(FS):Apr81-218
Auty, G. The Art of Self-Deception.
  C. Crouch, 437:Spring81-189
Auty, R. and D. Obolensky, eds. An Intro-
  duction to Russian Art and Architecture.*
  T.T. Rice, 575(SEER):Jan81-94
van der Auwera, J., ed. The Semantics of
  Determiners.
  G.N. Carlson, 350:Dec82-901
Avalle-Arce, J.B. - see de Cervantes
  Saavedra, M.
Aveling, H., ed. The Development of Indo-
  nesian Society.
  J. Taylor, 293(JASt):Aug81-852
Avella-Widhalm, G. and others, eds. Lexi-
  kon des Mittelalters I.
  R. Schenda, 196:Band22Heft3/4-357

14

Averill, J.H. Wordsworth and the Poetry of Human Suffering.*
  D.H. Bialostosky, 405(MP):Aug81-92
  W. Galperin, 141:Spring81-185
  F. Garber, 401(MLQ):Dec81-392
Averroës. Three Short Commentaries on Aristotle's "Topics," "Rhetoric," and "Poetics."* (C.E. Butterworth, ed and trans) Commentarium medium in Aristotelis Topica. (C.E. Butterworth and A.A. Haridi, eds)
  A.L. Motzkin, 589:Oct81-842
Avery, S.P. The Diaries 1871-1882 of Samuel P. Avery, Art Dealer. (M.F. Beaufort, H.L. Kleinfield and J.K. Welcher, eds)
  F. Haskell, 90:Apr81-243
  H.W. Morgan, 658:Summer/Autumn81-232
Avery, V. London Spring.
  S. Lermon, 617(TLS):29Oct82-1202
Avianus. Fables. (F. Gaide, ed)
  M.D. Reeve, 123:Vol31No2-209
Avineri, S. Hegels Theorie des modernen Staates.
  K. Hartmann, 489(PJGG):Band88Heft2-412
Avis, W.S. and A.M. Kinloch. Writings on Canadian English, 1792-1975.*
  H. Ulherr, 38:Band99Heft3/4-475
Avison, M. Sunblue.*
  R. Willmot, 102(CanL):Winter80-115
Avotins, I. and M. An Index to the Lives of the Sophists of Philostratus.
  B. Puech, 487:Summer81-195
Avrich, P. An American Anarchist.*
  C. Miller, 77:Summer81-272
Avrich, P. The Modern School Movement.*
  S.G. Weiner, 127:Summer81-189
Awbery, G.M. The Syntax of Welsh.
  A.R. Thomas, 660(Word):Dec80-311
Ax, W. Probleme des Sprachstils als Gegenstand der lateinischen Philologie.
  P.H. Schrijvers, 394:Vol34fasc3/4-432
Axel, J. and K. McCready. Porcelain.
  L. Edelman, 139:Dec81/Jan82-43
Axelrod, S.G. Robert Lowell.*
  R. Pooley, 402(MLR):Oct81-950
  G. Willis, 106:Spring81-113
Axmatova, A. - see under Akhmatova, A.
Axton, M. The Queen's Two Bodies.*
  J. Hurstfield, 402(MLR):Oct81-925
Axton, R. - see Rastell, J.
Ayckbourn, A. Sisterly Feelings. Taking Steps.
  D. Devlin, 157:Autumn81-51
Ayçoberry, P. The Nazi Question.*
  639(VQR):Autumn81-120
Ayer, A.J. Philosophy in the Twentieth Century.
  A. MacIntyre, 441:28Nov82-3
  M. Warnock, 362:30Sep82-24
Ayers, J. Far Eastern Ceramics in the Victoria and Albert Museum.*
  M. Medley, 39:Feb81-130
  W.B.R. Neave-Hill, 463:Summer81-204
Ayers, R.W. - see Milton, J.
Aylen, L. Red Alert: This is a God Warning.
  S. Ellis, 617(TLS):22Jan82-90
Ayling, R. and M.J. Durkan. Sean O'Casey.*
  C.A. Carpenter, 397(MD):Mar81-119
  N. Grene, 677(YES):Vol 11-352

Aylmer, G.E. and J.S. Morrill. The Civil War and Interregnum.
  I. Roy, 325:Oct81-508
Ayme, A. and J. Henric. Paradigme du bleu jaune rouge.
  T. Conley, 153:Winter81-58
Ayres, J. The Shell Book of the Home in Britain.
  R.W. Grant, 324:Mar82-233
Azar, B.S. Understanding and Using English Grammar.
  I. Leki, 608:Dec82-549
Azarpay, G., with others. Sogdian Painting.
  M. Boyce, 617(TLS):7May82-512
Aziz, B.N. Tibetan Frontier Families.*
  M.C. Goldstein, 318(JAOS):Apr/Jun80-214
Aziz, K.K. The British in India.
  B.N. Ramusack, 293(JASt):Nov80-149
Aziz, K.M.A. Kinship in Bangladesh.
  J.P. Thorp, 293(JASt):Nov80-151
Aziz, M. - see James, H.
Aziza, C., C. Olivieri and R. Sctrick. Dictionnaire des symboles et des thèmes littéraires.*
  J. Cruickshank, 208(FS):Oct81-497
Aziza, C., C. Oliviéri and R. Sctrick. Dictionnaire des types et caractères littéraires.
  F.W. Vogler, 207(FR):Mar81-586

B.-Hogue, M. - see under Hogue
Baader, H., ed. Onze études sur l'esprit de la satire.
  A. Blanc, 475:No13Pt1-138
Baader, R., ed. Molière.
  U. Schulz-Buschhaus, 602:Vol 12No2-403
Baader, R. and D. Fricke, eds. Die französische Autorin vom Mittelalter bis zur Gegenwart.
  S. Bayne, 475:No14Pt1-146
  I.W.F. Maclean, 402(MLR):Apr81-456
Babbitt, B., comp. Grand Canyon.
  J. Koenig, 649(WAL):Spring81-80
Babby, L.H. Existential Sentences and Negation in Russian.
  J. Gallant, 350:Mar82-249
  J.M. Kirkwood, 402(MLR):Oct81-1006
Babby, L.H. A Transformational Grammar of Russian Adjectives.
  R. Sussex, 279:Vol23-187
Babcock, D.R. A Gentleman of Strathcona.
  R.D. Francis, 298:Summer81-129
Babinger, F. Mehmed the Conqueror and his Time.* (W.C. Hickman, ed)
  M. Angold, 161(DUJ):Dec80-91
Babington Smith, C. John Masefield.
  D. Hewitt, 447(N&Q):Jun80-260
  R.G. Thomas, 541(RES):Feb81-101
Babitz, E. L.A. Woman.
  P.J. O'Rourke, 441:2May82-12
  442(NY):10May82-168
Bablet, D., ed. Les Voies de la création théâtrale. (Vols 5 and 6)
  L. Rièse, 397(MD):Sep81-388
Bablet, D., ed. Les voies de la création théâtrale. (Vol 7)
  J. Body, 549(RLC):Jul-Dec81-494
  L. Rièse, 397(MD):Sep81-388

Babolin, A. Abraham Joshua Heschel filosofo della religione.
W. Shea, 154:Jun81-395
Babson, M. Death Beside the Seaside.
T.J. Binyon, 617(TLS):29Oct82-1196
Babson, M. Death Warmed Up.
M. Laski, 362:29Apr82-27
Babson, M. Line Up for Murder.
N. Callendar, 441:14Feb82-22
Bacarisse, S., ed. Contemporary Latin American Fiction.
J. Higgins, 86(BHS):Apr81-164
J.M. Kirk, 268(IFR):Winter82-64
Bach, K. and R.M. Harnish. Linguistic Communication and Speech Acts.
D. Hymes, 355(LSoc):Aug81-270
Bach, K.F. and G. Price. Romance Linguistics and the Romance Languages.
C. Schmitt, 72:Band217Heft2-445
Bacharach, A.L. and J.R. Pearce, eds. The Musical Companion. (rev)
C.M.B., 412:Feb80-60
Bachmann, H. Joseph Maria Baernreither (1845-1925).*
F.R. Bridge, 575(SEER):Jul81-455
Bachofen, J.K. Gesammelte Werke. (K. Meuli and others, eds) Du règne de la mère au patriarcat. (A. Turel, ed) Materialen zu Bachofen "Das Mutterrecht." (H-J. Heinrichs, ed) Das Mutterrecht.
H. Weinmann, 98:Jun-Jul81-620
Bacigalupo, M. The Forméd Trace.*
J. Barbarese, 295(JML):Vol8No3/4-591
R. Bush, 141:Winter81-77
J. Espey, 579(SAQ):Autumn81-487
S.M. Gall, 301(JEGP):Apr81-282
J.F. Knapp, 27(AL):Jan82-746
H.N. Schneidau, 405(MP):Nov81-220
Back, M. Die Sassanidischen Staatsinschriften.
C.J. Brunner, 215(GL):Summer81-117
Bäckman, S. Tradition Transformed.
R. Bouyssou, 189(EA):Apr-Jun81-230
H. Marder, 301(JEGP):Jul81-455
J. Stallworthy, 541(RES):Nov81-483
Backus, J.J. Letters from Amelia: 1901-1937.
442(NY):6Sep82-108
Bacot, P. Les Dirigeants du Parti Socialiste.
F. Busi, 207(FR):Oct81-167
J. Howorth, 208(FS):Apr81-247
Bacquet, P. Les Pièces historiques de Shakespeare. (Vol 2)
G. Bullough, 189(EA):Oct-Dec81-463
Bacri, N. Fonctionnement de la négation.
R. Van Deyck, 209(FM):Jan81-74
Badel, P-Y. Le "Roman de la Rose" au XIVe siècle.
C.R. Dahlberg, 589:Oct81-844
J.C. Payen, 382(MAE):1981/1-149
N. Wilkins, 402(MLR):Oct81-957
Badentscher, H. Dramaturgie als Funktion der Ontologie.
A. Arnold, 133:Band14Heft1-90
Badia, G. and others. Les Barbelés de l'exil.
S. Mews, 221(GQ):Mar81-240
Badia, G. and J. Mortier - see Marx, K. and F. Engels
Badian, E. - see Syme, R.
Badinter, E. L'Amour en plus.
N. Aronson, 207(FR):May81-906

Badinter, E. The Myth of Motherhood.
A. Clare, 362:18Feb82-24
R. Dinnage, 617(TLS):9Apr82-401
Badura-Skoda, E. and P. Branscombe, eds. Schubert Studies.
W. Mellers, 617(TLS):17Dec82-1396
de Baena, J.A. Dezir que fizo Juan Alfonso de Baena. (N.F. Martino, ed)
N.G. Round, 86(BHS):Apr81-139
Baensch, O. Johann Heinrich Lamberts Philosophie und seine Stellung zu Kant.
R. Malter, 342:Band72Heft1-116
Baer, G. Fellah and Townsman in the Middle East.
P.J. Vatikiotis, 617(TLS):10Sep82-979
Baéz, E.M. - see under Moreno Baéz, E.
de Báez, Y.J., D. Morán and E. Negrín - see Jiménez de Báez, Y., D. Morán and E. Negrín
Bagchi, A.K. Sanskrit and Modern Medical Vocabulary.
C.G. Kashikar, 261:Dec79-319
Bagley, D. Windfall.
M. Laski, 362:2Dec82-23
Bagliani, A.P. - see under Paravicini Bagliani, A.
Bagnall, R.S., P.J. Sijpesteijn and K.A. Worp. Greek Ostraka.
R. Coles, 123:Vol31No2-325
Bahadur, K.P. - see "The Parrot and the Starling"
Bahamonde, M. Gabriela Mistral en Antofagasta.
T. Cajiao Salas, 263(RIB):Vol31No4-544
Bahro, R. The Alternative in Eastern Europe.) (German title: Die Alternative.)
M. Gagern, 142:Spring80-103
de Baïf, J-A. Le Brave. (S. Maser, ed)
G. Dottin, 535(RHL):Jul-Oct81-752
E.M. Duval, 207(FR):Oct81-133
M. Quainton, 208(FS):Oct81-433
Baigell, M. Dictionary of American Art.
D. Tepfer, 658:Spring81-85
Baigent, M., R. Leigh and H. Lincoln. The Holy Blood and The Holy Grail.
G. Priestland, 362:21January82-21
J. Sumption, 617(TLS):22Jan82-69
Bail, M. Homesickness.
P. Pierce, 381:Apr81-106
Bailbé, J. and J. Lagny - see de Saint-Amant, G.
Bailey, C-J.N. Variation and Linguistic Theory.
A.S. Kaye, 35(AS):Fall81-236
Bailey, D. Making Up.
J. Mellors, 362:15Apr82-23
Bailey, D. Trouble and Strife.
A. Ross, 364:Apr/May81-8
Bailey, D.R.S. - see under Shackleton Bailey, D.R.
Bailey, H.W. Dictionary of Khotan Saka.*
R.E. Emmerick, 259(IIJ):Jan81-66
Bailey, J. Norman Mailer.*
P. Bufithis, 395(MFS):Winter80/81-680
D. Seed, 184(EIC):Jan81-81
G.F. Waller, 106:Winter81-413
Bailey, K.E. Poet and Peasant.
L. Ryken, 599:Fall81-497
Bailey, P. An English Madam.
L. Sage, 617(TLS):5Nov82-1210
H. Wackett, 362:28Oct82-21

16

Bailey, R.W., ed. Early Modern English.
   J. Schäfer, 38:Band99Heft3/4-427
Baillet, M., ed. Qumrân Grotte 4. (Vol 3)
   G. Vermes, 617(TLS):10ct82-1082
Baily, M. Small Net in a Big Sea.
   D.R. Sturtevant, 293(JASt):Feb81-432
Bailyn, B. and J.B. Hench, eds. The Press
   and the American Revolution.
   R.D. Brown, 656(WMQ):Apr81-320
   R. Hamowy, 517(PBSA):Oct-Dec81-490
   C.W. Miller, 432(NEQ):Jun81-274
   78(BC):Winter81-447
Bain, D. Actors and Audience.*
   C. Garton, 122:Apr81-147
   J.C.B. Lowe, 123:Vol31No1-8
Bain, I., ed. The Watercolours and Draw-
   ings of Thomas Bewick and his Workshop
   Apprentices.
   D. Bindman, 617(TLS):220ct82-1168
   D. Chambers, 503:Winter81-177
   W. Gardner, 324:Jul82-500
   135:Nov81-174
Bain, I. - see Bewick, T.
Bain, R., J.M. Flora and L.D. Rubin, Jr.,
   eds. Southern Writers.*
   G.W. Ballenger, 577(SHR):Spring81-183
   T.L. McHaney, 392:Fall81-496
Bainbridge, B. A Weekend with Claude.*
   J. Gies, 441:21Mar82-10
Bainbridge, B. Winter Garden.*
   W. Boyd, 364:Apr/May81-129
Bair, D. Samuel Beckett.*
   J.A. Buttigieg, 81:Fall80-259
Baird, J.D. and C. Ryskamp - see Cowper, W.
Baird, J.L. and J.R. Kane, eds and trans.
   Rossignol.*
   J.C. Laidlaw, 208(FS):Jan81-65
   N. Margolis, 589:Jan81-94
Baird, L.Y. A Bibliography of Chaucer,
   1964-1973.
   T.A. Kirby, 179(ES):Aug81-383
Baizerman, S. and K. Searle. Latin Ameri-
   can Brocades. (rev) Finishes in the
   Ethnic Tradition.
   P. Bach, 614:Spring82-13
Baker, A. The Life of Sir Isaac Pitman.
   D.M. Ottaway, 324:Dec81-62
Baker, C. The Innocent Artists.
   J. Povey, 2(AfrA):Aug81-15
Baker, C. - see Hemingway, E.
Baker, C.L. Introduction to Generative-
   Transformational Syntax.
   C. Adjémian, 399(MLJ):Autumn81-331
   G. Mallinson, 361:Feb-Mar81-227
Baker, D. The Rocket.
   E.L.M. Burns, 529(QQ):Spring81-174
Baker, D.E.U. Changing Political Leader-
   ship in an Indian Province.
   P. Harnetty, 293(JASt):Nov80-153
Baker, D.V. Upstream at the Mill.
   N.S., 617(TLS):26Mar82-363
Baker, E.C. Preece and Those Who Followed.
   M.W. Thring, 324:Feb82-162
Baker, F. - see Wesley, J.
Baker, G.P. and P.M.S. Hacker. Wittgen-
   stein.*
   H.L. Finch, 518:Jul81-140
   S.R., 543:Jun81-776
   S. Shanker, 627(UTQ):Spring81-341
Baker, G.P. and B. McGuinness - see
   Waismann, F.

Baker, H. Persephone's Cave.*
   J.A.S. Evans, 529(QQ):Spring81-87
   J. Redfield, 122:Apr81-142
Baker, H.A., Jr. The Journey Back.
   W.L. Andrews, 27(AL):Mar81-140
   S.L. Blake, 395(MFS):Winter80/81-673
   C.J. Fontenot, Jr., 301(JEGP):Jul81-
   466
   J.O. Perry, 219(GaR):Spring81-170
   E. Sellin, 295(JML):Vol8No3/4-363
Baker, H.D.R. Chinese Family and Kinship.*
   D. Martin, 302:Vol 18-158
Baker, J. Time and Mind in Wordsworth's
   Poetry.*
   J.A. Butler, 661(WC):Summer81-153
   A. McWhir, 627(UTQ):Summer81-122
Baker, J.H. Manual of Law French.
   M. Jones, 325:Oct81-511
Baker, J.H. A Teacher's Guide to Theatre
   for the Young.
   S. Stone-Blackburn, 102(CanL):Summer80-
   107
Baker, P.R. Richard Morris Hunt.*
   M. Kammen, 42(AR):Winter81-126
   H.W. Morgan, 658:Spring81-108
Baker, R. Growing Up.
   R. Lingeman, 441:17Oct82-13
   442(NY):20Dec82-138
Baker, R. Mozart.
   442(NY):12Jul82-104
Baker, S.R. Collaboration et originalité
   chez La Rochefoucauld.
   M.S. Koppisch, 207(FR):Dec81-267
Baker, V.R. The Channels of Mars.
   B. Lovell, 453(NYRB):10Jun82-32
Baker, W. - see Eliot, G.
Bakere, J.A. The Cornish Ordinalia.
   R. Longsworth, 589:Oct81-847
Bakker, B. - see Zola, É.
Bakker, B.H. and others - see Zola, É.
Bakker, B.H., with C. Becker - see Zola, É.
"Bakounine: combats et débats."
   E.H. Carr, 575(SEER):Apr81-317
Bakró-Nagy, M. Die Sprache des Bären-
   kultes im Obugrischen.
   M.D. Birnbaum, 350:Mar81-242
Bal, M. Narratologie.*
   J.M. Cocking, 208(FS):Jan81-101
   A. Jefferson, 494:Autumn79-440
   S.E. Larsen, 462(OL):Vol35No1-83
Bal, W. Afro-Romanica Studia.*
   A. Bollée, 72:Band217Heft2-468
Balachov, N.I., T. Klaniczay and A.D.
   Mikhaïlov, eds. Littérature de la
   Renaissance à la lumière des recherches
   soviétiques et hongroises.
   A. Buck, 52:Band15Heft1-74
   C. Chiappelli, 678(YCGL):No29-40
   W.C. Jordan, 551(RenQ):Spring80-77
Baladié, R. - see Strabo
Balaji, K.P. Abhimanyu.
   J.P. Gemill, 314:Summer-Fall81-239
Balakian, A. The Symbolist Movement.*
   (2nd ed)
   W. Albert, 678(YCGL):No29-37
Balandier, G. Le Pouvoir sur scènes.
   J. Duvignaud, 450(NRF):Mar81-146
Balas, R. and D. Rice. Qu'est-ce qui se
   passe?*
   J.W. Cross, 399(MLJ):Winter81-430

17

Balayé, S. Madame de Staël, lumières et liberté.*
   F.P. Bowman, 446(NCFS):Fall-Winter80/81-128
   J. Gaulmier, 535(RHL):May-Jun81-465
   A. Kappler, 52:Band15Heft3-335
   N. King, 402(MLR):Jan81-190
   T. Logé, 356(LR):Nov81-360
Baldi, P. and R.N. Werth, eds. Readings in Historical Phonology.
   J. Aitchison, 353:Vol 18No5/6-557
   D.H., 355(LSoc):Apr81-145
Baldinger, K. Dictionnaire onomasiologique de l'ancien gascon. (fasc 2/3)
   K.A. Goddard, 208(FS):Oct81-427
Baldridge, M.H. the loneliness of the poet/housewife.
   D. Cooper-Clark, 102(CanL):Autumn80-108
Baldry, H. The Case For The Arts.
   S. Hampshire, 617(TLS):26Feb82-207
Baldwin, A.P. The Theme of Government in "Piers Plowman."
   P. Neuss, 617(TLS):15Jan82-56
Baldwin, H.L. Samuel Beckett's Real Silence.
   R. Selden, 617(TLS):20Aug82-909
Baldwin, R. and R. Paris. The Book of Similies.
   G. Ewart, 362:23Sep82-24
de Baleine, P. Les Danseuses de la France.
   J-P. Ponchie, 207(FR):Apr82-693
Balfour, D. - see Symeon of Thessalonica
Balfour, M. West Germany.
   A.J. Nicholls, 617(TLS):13Aug82-878
Ball, E., with N. Hehn and L. Sanchez. An Apache Odyssey: Indeh.
   G. Ronnow, 649(WAL):Spring81-74
Ball, G.W. The Past Has Another Pattern.
   J. Fallows, 453(NYRB):24Jun82-12
   K. Kyle, 362:2Dec82-21
   D. Yergin, 441:2May82-3
Ball, T., ed. Political Theory and Praxis.
   L.J. Ray, 488:Dec81-494
Ball, V.K. Architecture and Interior Design.
   R. Benhamou, 505:Sep81-260
Ball, W. and T. Martin. Rare Afro-Americana
   L.J. Henry, 14:Fall81-363
Ballantyne, L.M.F.C. Haitian Publications.
   F.J. Malval, 263(RIB):Vol31No4-545
Ballantyne, S. Imaginary Crimes.
   J. Moynahan, 441:21Feb82-1
   442(NY):5Apr82-197
Ballard, J.G. Hello America.*
   W. Boyd, 364:Nov81-83
Ballard, J.G. Myths of the Near Future.
   T. Sutcliffe, 617(TLS):24Sep82-1031
Ballew, S. and others. "Suthin" (it's the opposite of nothin').
   D. Tebbetts, 292(JAF):Jul-Sep81-387
Balliett, W. American Singers.
   M. Harrison, 415:Jun81-387
Balmary, M. L'Homme aux statues.
   J.V. Harari, 400(MLN):May81-877
Balmary, M. Psychoanalyzing Psychoanalysis.
   F. Randall, 441:10Oct82-17
Balmer, H.P. Freiheit statt Teleologie.
   E. Blondel, 542:Oct-Dec81-497

Balogh, L. and L. Király. Az állathangutánzó igék, hivogatók és terelők somogyi nyelvatlasza.
   K. Manherz, 685(ZDL):1/1981-92
Balogh, T. The Irrelevance of Conventional Economics.
   D. Coombes, 362:19Aug82-24
   D.W. Pearce, 617(TLS):27Aug82-930
Balsdon, J.P.V.D. Romans and Aliens.*
   J. Briscoe, 123:Vol31No1-133
   S. Treggiari, 487:Summer81-196
Baltes, M. Die Weltentstehung des platonischen Timaios nach den antiken Interpreten. (Pt 2)
   G.B. Kerferd, 123:Vol31No1-129
Baltzell, E.D. Puritan Boston and Quaker Philadelphia.*
   J.D. Greenstone, 185:Jul82-770
de Balzac, H. L'Envers de l'histoire contemporaine. (S.S. de Sacy, ed)
   C. Smethurst, 208(FS):Oct81-458
de Balzac, H. Rosalie (Albert Savarus). (C. Smethurst, ed)
   M. Le Yaouanc, 535(RHL):Mar-Apr81-308
Bambara, T.C. The Salt Eaters.
   N. Harris, 459:Winter80-101
   C. Rumens, 617(TLS):18Jun82-676
   J.W. Ward, Jr., 435:Summer81-207
Bambas, R.C. The English Language: Its Origin and History.
   J. Shay, 350:Jun82-484
Bambrough, R. Moral Scepticism and Moral Knowledge.*
   R. Attfield, 479(PhQ):Apr81-177
   G.S. Kavka, 482(PhR):Oct81-630
   J.L.M., 185:Jan82-394
   T. Mautner, 63:Sep81-356
   D. Odegard, 154:Dec81-817
Bame, L. Pants Fit for Your Figure.
   P. Bach, 614:Spring81-21
Bamford, J. The Puzzle Palace.
   P. Taubman, 441:19Sep82-9
Bance, A. Theodor Fontane: The Major Novels.
   G. Annan, 617(TLS):17Dec82-1385
Bance, P. Les Fondateurs de la C.G.T. à l'épreuve du droit.
   J-P. Ponchie, 207(FR):Oct81-168
Bancquart, M-C. - see de Maupassant, G.
Bancquart, M-C. - see Sand, G.
Bandelier, A.F. The Discovery of New Mexico by the Franciscan Monk, Friar Marcos de Niza in 1539. (M.T. Rodack, ed and trans)
   L. Milazzo, 584(SWR):Spring81-v
Bandiera, M. I frammenti del I libro degli "Annales" di Q. Ennio.*
   C. Moussy, 555:Vol54fasc1-177
Banerjee, S. Calcutta 200 Years.
   G. Moorhouse, 617(TLS):6Aug82-860
Banfield, A. Unspeakable Sentences.
   E.L. Epstein, 617(TLS):19Nov82-1280
Banham, R. Design by Choice. (P. Sparke, ed)
   J. Glancey, 46:Oct81-259
   M. Pawley, 617(TLS):5Mar82-249
Banim, J. and M. Tales by the O'Hara Family. (1st and 2nd Ser) The Boyne Water. The Croppy. The Anglo-Irish of the Nineteenth Century. The Denounced. The Ghost-Hunter and his Family. The Mayor of Wind-Gap and Canvassing. The Bit
                   [continued]

O'Writin' and Other Tales.
R. Tracy, 445(NCF):Sep80-193
Bankes, G. Moche Pottery from Peru.
A. Cordy-Collins, 2(AfrA):Nov80-81
Banks, J.A. Victorian Values.
B. Harrison, 617(TLS):12Nov82-1252
Banks, R. The New World.
P. Lewis, 565:Vol22No1-60
al-Bannā, H. Five Tracts of Hasan al-
Bannā (1906-1949). (C. Wendell, ed and
trans)
S. Vahiduddin, 273(IC):Apr80-127
Bannister, D. Burning Leaves.
M. Abley, 617(TLS):10Sep82-981
J. Mellors, 362:18Nov82-28
Bannister, D. Sam Chard.
P. Lewis, 565:Vol22No3-55
Banta, M. Failure and Success in America.*
D. Aaron, 677(YES):Vol 11-280
L. Cederstrom, 106:Fall81-235
H. Hill, 395(MFS):Summer80-320
J.C. Rowe, 445(NCF):Jun80-81
Banville, J. The Newton Letter.
A. Brownjohn, 617(TLS):11Jun82-643
K.C. O'Brien, 362:22Jul82-24
Bar-Siman-Tov, Y. The Israeli-Egyptian
War of Attrition, 1969-1970.
639(VQR):Summer81-91
Baragwanath, A.K. 100 Currier and Ives
Favorites.
S. Friesen, 292(JAF):Apr-Jun81-262
Barak, M. Double Cross.
N. Callendar, 441:24Jan82-34
Barak, M. Fractures aux P.C.F.
D. Johnson, 617(TLS):2Jul82-707
Barbeau, J. Le théâtre de la maintenance.
Le jardin de la maison blanche. Une
marquise de Sade et un lézard nommé
King-Kong.
L. Rièse, 108:Spring81-126
Barbeau, M. and M. Hornyansky. The Golden
Phoenix and Other Fairy Tales from
Quebec.
K. Kealy, 102(CanL):Summer81-149
Barber, B. Informed Consent in Medical
Therapy and Research.
J.C.M., 185:Apr82-594
Barber, B.J. and M.W. Beresford. The West
Riding County Council, 1889-1974.
W.B. Stephens, 325:Apr81-436
Barber, C.L. and J.C.P. McCallum. Unem-
ployment and Inflation.
J.R. Seldon, 529(QQ):Spring81-166
Barber, G. - see Contat, N.
Barber, L. The Heyday of Natural History.*
E. Claridge, 364:Jul81-55
Barber, R. 1947 — When All Hell Broke
Loose in Baseball.
W. Sheed, 453(NYRB):23Sep82-45
Barbera, J. and W. McBrien - see Smith, S.
Bàrberi Squarotti, G. - see Tarchetti, I.U.
Barbéris, P. René de Chateaubriand, un
nouveau roman.
T. Logé, 356(LR):Aug81-252
Barbéris, P. Le monde de Balzac.
G. Jacques, 356(LR):Feb-May81-163
Barbey d'Aurevilly, J-A. Un Prêtre marié.
Une Vieille Maîtresse. (J. Petit, ed of
both)
P.J. Yarrow, 208(FS):Oct81-459
Barbier, C.P., ed. Colloque Paul Valéry.
P. Gifford, 402(MLR):Apr81-476
Barbier, M. - see De Vitoria, F.

Barbosa, E.C.C. - see under Corrêa Barbosa,
E.C.
Barbour, D. shore lines.*
J. Giltrow, 102(CanL):Spring81-145
Barbour, D., ed. The Story So Far 5.*
A.J. Harding, 102(CanL):Summer80-149
de la Barca, P.C. - see under Calderón de
la Barca, P.
Barck, C. Wort und Tat bei Homer.
O. Taplin, 123:Vol31No1-103
Bard, M., P. Messaline and M. Newhouse,
eds. And What Are You Going to Do For
Us?
R. Stuart, 108:Summer81-145
Bardèche, M. Balzac.
J.B. Hassel, 446(NCFS):Fall-Win-
ter81/82-142
Bardou, J-P. and others. The Automobile
Revolution.
T.C. Barker, 617(TLS):15Oct82-1133
Baré, J-F. Pouvoir des vivants, langage
des morts.
G. Feeley-Harnik, 69:Vol150No4-446
Bareau, M. - see García, C.
Barcham, T., ed. Anthony Trollope.*
A. Wright, 445(NCF):Dec81-368
Bareham, T. and S. Gatrell. A Bibliogra-
phy of George Crabbe.*
A.J. Sambrook, 677(YES):Vol 11-288
Barelli, Y., J-F. Boudy and J-F. Carenco.
L'Espérance occitane.
F.R.P. Akehurst, 207(FR):Mar81-633
A. Valdman, 207(FR):Oct81-165
Baretti, G. Lettere sparse. (F. Fido, ed)
J.T.S. Wheelock, 276:Spring81-56
Barfoed, N. Don Juan.
N.L. Jensen, 562(Scan):May81-110
Barfoot, J. Abra.
M. Waddington, 102(CanL):Spring80-101
Bargate, V. Tit for Tat.*
P. Craig, 617(TLS):22Oct82-1175
J. Mellors, 364:Jun81-93
Bargen, D.G. The Fiction of Stanley Elkin.
S. Pinsker, 27(AL):Nov81-524
Barich, B. Laughing in the Hills.*
639(VQR):Winter81-10
Barilier, É. Le Rapt.
G. Mackey, 207(FR):Dec81-299
Baring, M. Dear Animated Bust.
J. Jeffs, 617(TLS):7May82-507
Barish, J. The Antitheatrical Prejudice.
N. Davis, 130:Winter81/82-381
N. Dennis, 453(NYRB):18Feb82-35
W.D. King, 609:Spring82-70
T. Murray, 400(MLN):Dec81-1260
Barka, V. Le Prince jaune.
V. Beauvois, 450(NRF):Jun81-139
Barkan, L. - see "Renaissance Drama"
Barker, A.L. Life Stories.*
D.A. Callard, 364:Nov81-90
Barker, C.R. and R.W. Last. Erich Maria
Remarque.
A.F. Bance, 402(MLR):Oct81-1000
Barker, F. and R. Hyde. London: As it
might have been.
H. Hobhouse, 617(TLS):28May82-575
S. Jenkins, 362:27May82-21
Barker, G. Landscape and Society.
L. Barfield, 617(TLS):12Mar82-286
Barker, H. That Good Between Us [and]
Credentials of a Sympathiser.
D. Devlin, 157:Autumn81-51

19

Barker, K. Early Music Hall in Bristol.
  J. Ging, 611(TN):Vol35No1-39
Barkhudarov, L.S. Jazyk i perevod.
  O. Frink, 399(MLJ):Autumn81-348
Barksdale, E.C. Daggers of the Mind.*
  E.J. Brown, 550(RusR):Jan81-80
Barlow, C. The Natural Rubber Industry.
  M-H. Lim, 293(JASt):Nov80-188
Barlow, F. The English Church, 1066-1154.
  A.D. Frankforter, 589:Apr81-342
Barlow, G. Gumbo.*
  P. Stitt, 219(GaR):Fall81-647
Barnard, R. Death and the Princess.
  T.J. Binyon, 617(TLS):2Jul82-725
  M. Laski, 362:29Jul82-27
Barnes, B. Interests and the Growth of
  Knowledge.
  J.W. Grove, 488:Dec81-500
  P.E. Tibbetts, 488:Dec81-503
Barnes, B. T.S. Kuhn and Social Science.
  E. Gellner, 617(TLS):23Apr82-451
Barnes, H.E. Sartre and Flaubert.*
  J. Bayley, 362:4Feb82-22
  V. Brombert, 617(TLS):29Jan82-98
Barnes, J. The American Book of the Dead.
  C. Sutherland, 460(OhR):No29-136
Barnes, J. Before She Met Me.
  M. Abley, 617(TLS):23Apr82-456
  J. Astor, 362:6May82-27
Barnes, J. The Presocratic Philosophers.*
  C.H. Kahn, 311(JP):May81-279
  A.P.D. Mourelatos, 518:Apr81-65
  H.D. Rankin, 303(JoHS):Vol 101-177
Barnes, J. - see Aristotle
Barnes, T.C., T.H. Naylor and C.W. Polzer.
  Northern New Spain.
  S.L. Myres, 14:Summer81-247
Barnetová, V. and others. Russkaja gram-
  matika. (K. Horálek, ed)
  C.E. Townsend, 574(SEEJ):Spring81-136
Barnett, J. The Firing Squad.*
  N. Callendar, 441:14Feb82-22
Barnett, J. Inside the Treasury.
  B. Trend, 617(TLS):16Jul82-755
Barnett, J. Marked for Destruction.
  T.J. Binyon, 617(TLS):31Dec82-1448
Barnett, L.D. Bret Harte.*
  R.W. Etulain, 26(ALR):Autumn81-312
  P.D. Morrow, 649(WAL):Summer81-157
Barnett, L.K. Swift's Poetic Worlds.
  J. Briggs, 617(TLS):17Dec82-1384
Barney, S.A. Allegories of History, Alle-
  gories of Love.*
  C.A. Haeger, 125:Winter81-242
  R.F. Yeager, 594:Winter81-456
Barnhart, C.L. and others, eds. The Sec-
  ond Barnhart Dictionary of New English.
  P-G. Boucé, 189(EA):Jul-Sep81-327
  G. Core, 249(HudR):Autumn81-475
Barnouw, D. Elias Canetti.
  I.M. Goessl, 221(GQ):Mar81-244
Barnstone, W. A Snow Salmon Reached the
  Andes Lake.
  P. Schjeldahl, 472:Spring/Summer81-284
Baroche, C. Pas d'autre intempérie que la
  solitude.
  B.L. Knapp, 207(FR):Mar81-613
Baron, C. - see Neville, G.H.
Baron, D.E. Grammar and Good Taste.
  S.B. Flexner, 441:28Nov82-11

Baron, F., ed. Joachim Camerarius (1500-
  1574).*
  F. Füssel, 52:Band15Heft1-78
  E.H. Rehermann, 196:Band21Heft1/2-106
Baron, M. Wheat Among Bones.*
  H. Thomas, 385(MQR):Winter82-200
Baron, N.S. Speech, Writing, and Sign.
  D.H., 355(LSoc):Dec81-489
Baron, S.H. Muscovite Russia.
  P. Bushkovitch, 550(RusR):Oct81-442
  P. Longworth, 575(SEER):Jul81-435
Barr, A. and P. York. The "Harper's and
  Queen" Official Sloane Ranger Handbook.
  P. Johnson, 362:28Oct82-18
Barr, E. George Wickes 1698-1761, Royal
  Goldsmith.*
  E.L. Clowes, 135:Feb81-167
  M. Ellis, 39:Feb81-129
  C. Oman, 90:Jun81-373
Barr, J.G. Rowdy Tales from Early Alabama.
  (G.W. Hubbs, ed)
  C.S. Watson, 392:Fall81-492
Barraclough, G. Main Trends in History.
  J.W. Zophy, 125:Spring81-349
Barratt, G. Russia in Pacific Waters,
  1715-1825.
  B.C. Cuthbertson, 150(DR):Spring81-159
  R.A. Pierce, 529(QQ):Autumn81-582
Barratt, P. M. Annaei Lucani Belli
  Civilis Liber V.
  R. Mayer, 123:Vol31No1-116
Barreda, P. The Black Protagonist in the
  Cuban Novel.*
  J.F. O'Neill, 395(MFS):Summer80-387
Barrell, J. The Dark Side of the Land-
  scape.
  J. Cook, 59:Mar81-114
  D. Farr, 39:May81-341
  J. Hayes, 324:Apr82-296
  A. Hemingway, 90:May81-316
Barrenechea, A.M. Textos hispano-
  americanos.
  M.L. Bastos, 240(HR):Spring81-251
Barrère, J-B. Le Regard d'Orphée ou
  l'échange poétique.
  S. Nash, 546(RR):Jan81-116
Barreto, L. The Patriot.
  R.J. Oakley, 86(BHS):Jul81-279
Barrett, C. Summer and Winter and Beyond.
  (rev)
  P. Bach, 614:Fall82-21
Barrett, C.K. Essays on Paul. Essays on
  John.
  J.L. Houlden, 617(TLS):5Nov82-1226
Barrett, D.B. World Christian Encyclope-
  dia.
  W.J. Hollenweger, 617(TLS):5Nov82-1224
Barrett, P.H. and H.E. Gruber - see Darwin,
  C.
Barrett, S.R. The Rise and Fall of an
  African Utopia.
  J. Eades, 69:Vol50No1-109
Barrett, W. The Illusion of Technique.
  A. Manser, 393(Mind):Jan81-147
Barrett, W. The Truants.
  H. Kramer, 441:7Feb82-1
Barrett, W. and G. MacBeth. Kings Landing.
  W.N., 102(CanL):Spring81-176
Barroero, L. and others. Ricerche in
  Umbria 2.
  E. Waterhouse, 90:Dec81-752
Barron, G. Groundrush.
  M. Malone, 441:24Oct82-43

Barron, S. and M. Tuchman, eds. The Avant-Garde in Russia, 1910-1930.*
M. Chamot, 39:Sep81-204
C. Cooke, 46:Jul81-63
V. Jirat-Wasiutynski, 529(QQ):Winter81-803
Barron, W.R.J. Trawthe and Treason.
205(FMLS):Jan81-92
Barrón Casanova, E. Un escultor olvidado.
J.E. Arias Anglés, 48:Apr-Jun81-228
Barrow, K. Flora.
G. O'Connor, 617(TLS):29Jan82-112
Barry, D.D. and C. Barner-Barry. Contemporary Soviet Politics.
M. McCauley, 575(SEER):Jan81-134
Barry, D.D., G. Ginsburgs and P.B. Maggs, eds. Soviet Law After Stalin. (Pt 1)
A. Shtromas, 550(RusR):Apr81-211
Barry, D.D., G. Ginsburgs and P.B. Maggs, eds. Soviet Law After Stalin. (Pt 2)
R. Beermann, 575(SEER):Oct81-625
A. Shtromas, 550(RusR):Apr81-211
Barry, N.P. Hayek's Social and Economic Philosophy.
R. Hardin, 185:Jan82-364
Barson, J. La Grammaire à l'oeuvre. (3rd ed)
M. Paschal, 207(FR):May82-916
Barsov, A.A. The Comprehensive Russian Grammar of A.A. Barsov. (L.W. Newman, ed)
B. Comrie, 350:Mar82-249
G.F. Holliday, 399(MLJ):Winter81-439
E. Klenin, 574(SEEJ):Fall81-139
Bartel, H., W. Schröder und G. Seeber. Das Sozialistengesetz 1878-1890.
D. Mühlberg, 654(WB):7/1981-182
Bartelink, G.J.M. Hieronymus: Liber de Optimo Genere Interpretandi (Epistula 57).
J.H.D. Scourfield, 123:Vol31No1-123
Barth, J. Letters.*
J. Mills, 529(QQ):Spring81-145
D.J. Robbins, 448:Vol 19No1/2-218
N. Schmitz, 473(PR):2/1981-320
O. Steele, 271:Winter81-147
Barth, J. Sabbatical.
P.L. Adams, 61:Jun82-100
L. Sage, 617(TLS):23Jul82-781
J. Wolcott, 453(NYRB):10Jun82-14
M. Wood, 441:20Jun82-1
442(NY):7Jun82-144
Barth, J.R. The Symbolic Imagination.
J.D. Pappageorge, 72:Band217Heft2-423
Barth, K. Ethics.
J.M.G., 185:Apr82-585
Barth, R.L. Looking For Peace.
J.M. Young, 150(DR):Summer81-377
Barthelme, D. Sixty Stories.*
R. Ellmann, 453(NYRB):21Jan82-39
Barthes, R. A Barthes Reader. (S. Sontag, ed) The Empire of Signs.
E. White, 441:12Sep82-1
Barthes, R. Camera Lucida.*
S. Charlesworth, 62:Apr82-72
P. Monk, 99:Dec81/Jan82-36
Barthes, R. La Chambre claire.*
S. Varnedoe, 127:Spring81-75
Barthes, R. The Eiffel Tower and Other Mythologies.
42(AR):Fall81-516
Barthes, R. Le Grain de la voix.
J. Stéfan, 450(NRF):Jul-Aug81-199

Bärthlein, K. Zur Geschichte der Philosophie. (Vol 1)
H. Wagner, 53(AGP):Band62Heft2-190
Barthold, B.J. Black Time.*
R. Bone, 268(IFR):Winter82-75
639(VQR):Autumn81-128
Bartholomaeus Anglicus. On the Properties of Soul and Body. (R.J. Long, ed)
T. Lawler, 589:Jan81-214
Bartholomeusz, D. "The Winter's Tale" in Performance in England and America 1611-1976.
S. Wells, 617(TLS):17Dec82-1402
Bartlett, L. William Congreve.*
F.M. Link, 566:Autumn80-48
Bartlett, L. - see Spender, S.
Bartlett, P.B. - see Meredith, G.
Bartlett, R. Gerald of Wales 1146-1223.
G. Jones, 617(TLS):29Oct82-1199
Bartlett, R.P. Human Capital.
J.M. Hartley, 575(SEER):Jan81-102
Bartley, W.W. 3d - see Popper, K.R.
Bartók, B. The Hungarian Folk Song. (B. Suchoff, ed)
A. Cross, 415:Nov81-747
Barton, H.A. Brev från Löftets Land.
A. Swanson, 563(SS):Spring81-225
Barton, J. A Poor Photographer.
C. Hall, 628(UWR):Spring-Summer82-119
Barton, M. - see "British Music Yearbook 1981"
Bartón, P. The Woe Shirt.
S. Dybek, 448:Vol 19No3-165
Bartsch, K. and others, eds. Die Andere Welt.
B. Hannemann, 406:Winter81-470
W.E. Yates, 402(MLR):Jul81-752
Bartz, W.H. Testing Oral Communication in the Foreign Language Classroom.
M.P. Leamon and F.L. Jenks, 399(MLJ):Autumn81-326
de Bary, W.T. and others. The Unfolding of Neo-Confucianism.
Y-S. Yü, 318(JAOS):Apr/Jun80-115
de Bary, W.T. and I. Bloom, eds. Principle and Practicality.
R.H. Minear, 244(HJAS):Jun81-298
Basa, E.M. Sándor Petöfi.
J.V. Rood, 574(SEEJ):Winter81-112
Bascetta, C., ed. Sport e giuochi.
M. Pozzi, 228(GSLI):Vol 157fasc500-616
Basch, F. Les femmes victoriennes.
F. Ducrocq, 98:Feb-Mar81-138
Basheer, V.M. "Me Grandad 'ad an Elephant."
G. Kearns, 249(HudR):Summer81-311
Bashkina, N.N. and others, eds. The United States and Russia: The Beginning of Relations, 1765-1815. (Russian title: Rossiia i SShA: Stanovlenie otnoshenii, 1765-1815.)
E.A.P. Crownhart-Vaughan, 14:Fall81-359
D.M. Griffiths, 656(WMQ):Oct81-725
Basin, H. Un Feu dévore un autre feu.
M. Cardy, 268(IFR):Winter82-50
Basin, Y. Semantic Philosophy of Art.*
E.F. Kaelin, 127:Summer81-183
Baskin, J. In Praise of Practical Fertilizer.
P-L. Adams, 61:Jul82-94
Bass, A. - see Derrida, J.

Bass, E.E., ed. Aldous Huxley.
  J. Meckier, 365:Winter82-34
Basset, L. Les emplois périphrastiques du
  verbe grec "Mellein."
  R. Schmitt, 260(IF):Band85-350
Bassett, W.B. Historic American Buildings
  Survey of New Jersey. (J. Poppeliers,
  ed)
  E.R. McKinstry, 576:Dec81-344
  J. Quinan, 658:Winter81-356
Basso, K.H. Portraits of "the Whiteman."*
  P.V. Kroskrity, 350:Jun81-514
Basson, M.D., ed. Ethics, Humanism, and
  Medicine.
  J.C.M., 185:Apr82-593
Bastet, F.L. and M. de Vos. Proposta per
  una classificazione del terzo stile
  pompeiano.
  R. Ling, 313:Vol71-212
Bastide, F-R. L'Enchanteur et nous.
  M. Mohrt, 450(NRF):May81-123
Bataille, G. Oeuvres Complètes.* (Vol 9)
  (D. Hollier, with D. Lemann, eds)
  R.D.E. Burton, 402(MLR):Jul81-711
Bataille, G.M. and C.L.P. Silet, eds. The
  Pretend Indians.*
  W.A. Bloodworth, Jr., 649(WAL):
  Winter82-323
  W. Galperin, 651(WHR):Winter81-382
Batchelor, D. Children in the Dark.
  J. Astor, 362:8Apr82-23
  S.J. Newman, 617(TLS):2Apr82-370
Batchelor, J. The Edwardian Novelists.
  P. Kemp, 362:25Feb82-24
  H. Lee, 617(TLS):26Mar82-335
Bateman, W.G. Multiple Tabby Weaves.
  (V.I. Harvey, ed)
  P. Bach, 614:Winter82-19
Bater, J.H. The Soviet City.
  C.D. Harris, 550(RusR):Jan81-71
  D.J.B. Shaw, 575(SEER):Jul81-464
Bates, D. The Abyssinian Difficulty.
  R. Pankhurst, 69:Vol50No3-321
Bates, R.H. Markets and States in
  Tropical Africa.
  C. Ehrlich, 617(TLS):26Feb82-210
Batscha, Z. and R. Saage, eds. Friedens-
  utopien.
  W. Steinbeck, 342:Band71Heft1-128
Battaglia, G.B. - see under Bordenache
  Battaglia, G.
Battersby, J.L. Rational Praise and Natu-
  ral Lamentation.
  R.D. Stock, 405(MP):Aug81-89
Battisti, E. Filippo Brunelleschi.
  P. Goldberger, 441:12Dec82-22
  M. Podro, 617(TLS):26Mar82-336
Batts, M.S. The Bibliography of German
  Literature.*
  L. Newman, 402(MLR):Jan81-227
Baude, M. and M-M. Münch, eds. Romantisme
  et Religion.
  R.J. Sealy, 446(NCFS):Fall-Winter81/82-
  130
Baudelaire, C. Les Fleurs du Mal. (R.
  Howard, trans)
  M. Wood, 453(NYRB):2Dec82-16
  P. Zweig, 441:25Jul82-3
Baudelot, C. and others. Qui travaille
  pour qui?
  I. Kaplan, 207(FR):Dec80-377
Baudrillard, J. De la séduction.
  F. Gaillard, 98:Oct80-954

Bauer, H. The Flying Mystique.
  M.J. King, 42(AR):Winter81-124
Bauer, L. and others. American English
  Pronunciation.
  J.T. Jensen, 350:Sep82-728
Bauer, N.S. William Wordsworth.
  P.M. Ball, 677(YES):Vol 11-298
Bauer, P.T. Equality, the Third World,
  and Economic Delusion.*
  A. Sen, 453(NYRB):4Mar82-3
Bauer, W. A Family Album.
  D. Brydon, 102(CanL):Winter80-139
Bauer, W. A Greek-English Lexicon of the
  New Testament and Other Early Christian
  Literature. (2nd ed) (F.W. Gingrich and
  F.W. Danker, eds)
  D.J. Georgacas, 122:Apr81-153
Bauer, W. The Terrible Word.
  J. Giltrow, 102(CanL):Winter80-136
Bauer-Lechner, N. Recollections of Gustav
  Mahler.* (P.R. Franklin, ed)
  P. Banks, 451:Spring82-251
Bäuerle, R., U. Egli and A. von Stechow,
  eds. Semantics from Different Points of
  View.
  K. Allan, 350:Mar81-253
Baum, J.A. Montesquieu and Social Theory.
  J.J. Lafontant, 207(FR):May81-868
Baum, L.F. The Wizard of Oz. (illus-
  trated by M. Hague)
  J. Lahr, 617(TLS):26Nov82-1308
Bauman, Z. Hermeneutics and the Social
  Sciences.
  B. Cooper, 488:Mar81-79
  D.E. Hess, 125:Fall80-109
Baumann, W. Die Literatur des Mittel-
  alters in Böhmen.
  H-J. Behr, 684(ZDA):Band109Heft3-95
Baumbach, J. Chez Charlotte and Emily.
  P. Quartermain, 114(ChiR):Autumn80-65
Baumbach, J. The Return of Service.*
  P. Lewis, 565:Vol22No1-60
Baumgartner, D. Studien zu Individuum und
  Mystik im Tristan Gottfrieds von Strass-
  burg.
  D.H. Green, 402(MLR):Jul81-737
Baumgartner, W. Triumph des Irrealismus.
  P.M. Mitchell, 562(Scan):May81-99
Baumwoll, D. and R.L. Saitz. Advanced
  Reading and Writing.* (2nd ed)
  E. Hamp-Lyons, 608:Jun82-253
Bausch, K-H., W.H.U. Schewe and H-R. Spie-
  gel, eds. Fachsprachen — Terminologie.*
  J. Dückert, 682(ZPSK):Band33Heft5-583
Bauschinger, S. Else Lasker-Schüler.
  D.C.G. Lorenz, 221(GQ):May81-368
  K. Weissenberger, 133:Band14Heft3-275
Bausinger, H. Formen der "Volkspoesie."
  (2nd ed)
  E. Moser-Rath, 196:Band22Heft1/2-109
Bauzon, L.E. Asian Studies in the Philip-
  pines.
  D.V. Hart, 293(JASt):May81-644
Bawcutt, N.W. - see Marlowe, C.
Baxandall, M. The Limewood Sculptors of
  Renaissance Germany.*
  M. Baker, 39:May81-340
  E. Langmuir, 89(BJA):Spring81-172
  T. Puttfarken, 59:Dec81-479
Baxi, U. The Indian Supreme Court and
  Politics.
  S.H. Rudolph, 293(JASt):May81-618

22

Baxter, J.K. Collected Poems. (J.E. Weir, ed)
   T. James, 364:Mar82-20
   H. McNaughton, 368:Mar81-62
   M. Schmidt, 362:1Apr82-23
Baxter, J.K. Ode to Auckland and Other Poems.
   A. Baysting, 368:Dec73-355
Baxter, J.K. Runes.
   R. Jackaman, 368:Sep73-265
Baxter, M. The Memoirs of Millicent Baxter.
   F. McKay, 368:Dec81-474
Bayard, M.J. and others - see Garin, F.
Bayard, P. Balzac et le troc de l'imaginaire.
   D. Bellos, 402(MLR):Jan81-196
   O.N. Heathcote, 446(NCFS):Fall-Winter80/81-134
   P. Mustière, 535(RHL):Mar-Apr81-306
Baybars, T. Pregnant Shadows.
   S. Ellis, 617(TLS):22Jan82-90
Bayer, H. Gralsburg und Minnegrotte.
   D.H. Green, 402(MLR):Jan81-233
Bayer, R. Homosexuality and American Psychiatry.
   A. Clare, 617(TLS):19Feb82-181
Bayes, R.H. Fram.
   P.B. Newman, 601:Spring81-74
Baylé, M. La Trinité de Caen, sa place dans l'histoire de l'architecture et du décor romans.*
   J. Herschman, 54:Dec81-677
Bayles, M.D. Morality and Population Policy.
   H.M.S., 185:Apr82-603
Bayley, J. An Essay on Hardy.*
   S.M. Smith, 677(YES):Vol 11-334
Bayley, J. Shakespeare and Tragedy.*
   D. May, 362:14Jan82-25
   G.F. Parker, 184(EIC):Oct81-346
   M. Seymour-Smith, 157:Winter81-48
Bayley, P. French Pulpit Oratory 1598-1650.
   T.C. Cave, 208(FS):Jan81-70
   L.E. Doucette, 539:Aug82-208
   P. France, 402(MLR):Jul81-697
   W.C. Marceau, 207(FR):Apr81-733
   W.J. Samarin, 355(LSoc):Dec81-448
   205(FMLS):Apr81-198
Bayley, P., ed. Spenser: "The Faerie Queene," A Casebook.*
   A.K.H., 604:Winter81-14
Baym, N. The Shape of Hawthorne's Career.*
   M.J. Colacurcio, 183(ESQ):Vol27No2-108
Baym, N. Woman's Fiction.*
   R. Jackson, 677(YES):Vol 11-316
   C. Zwarg, 454:Fall81-76
Baynac, J. Les Socialistes-Révolutionnaires de mars 1881 à mars 1917.
   A. Blakely, 550(RusR):Apr81-193
Bazin, J. and A. Bensa - see Goody, J.
Beach, M.C. Rajput Painting at Bundi and Kota.
   R. Morris, 463:Summer81-198
"Béaloideas." (Vols 45-47)
   J.A.B. Townsend, 203:Vol192No1-121
Bean, P. Punishment.
   M.D., 185:Jul82-778
Beard, G. Craftsmen and Interior Decoration in England, 1660-1820.*
   A. Rowan, 324:Feb82-165

Beard, G. The Work of Robert Adam.*
   D. Watkin, 39:Jan81-61
Beard, J.F. - see Cooper, J.F.
Beasley, J.C., ed. English Fiction, 1660-1800.*
   C.J. Rawson, 677(YES):Vol 11-268
Beasley, J.C. Novels of the 1740s.
   M. Butler, 617(TLS):12Nov82-1241
Beatie, R.H. Saddles.
   L. Milazzo, 584(SWR):Summer81-v
Beaton, R. Folk Poetry of Modern Greece.
   205(FMLS):Apr81-198
Beattie, A. The Burning House.
   M. Atwood, 441:26Sep82-1
Beattie, A. Falling in Place.*
   N. Schmitz, 473(PR):4/1981-629
Beattie, T. Diamonds.
   M. Laski, 362:2Dec82-23
Beauchamp, A. J'ai tant cherché le Soleil.
   M. Cagnon, 207(FR):Mar81-614
   E-M. Kroller, 102(CanL):Winter80-132
Beauchamp, T.L. and N.E. Bowie, eds. Ethical Theory and Business.
   K.E. Goodpaster, 185:Apr81-525
Beauchamp, T.L. and S. Perlin, eds. Ethical Issues in Death and Dying.
   W.C. Starr, 480(P&R):Spring81-132
Beauchamp, T.L. and A. Rosenberg. Hume and the Problem of Causation.
   D.C. Stove, 617(TLS):19Feb82-182
   S.W., 185:Jul82-804
Beauchamp, T.L. and L. Walters, eds. Contemporary Issues in Bioethics.
   L.J. Shein, 154:Jun81-398
Beauchemin, L. and H. Walter, eds. Phonologie et Société.
   L. Kikuchi, 207(FR):Dec80-383
Beauchemin, Y. Le Matou.
   M. Cagnon, 207(FR):May82-920
Beaufort, M.F., H.L. Kleinfield and J.K. Welcher - see Avery, S.P.
de Beaugrande, R. Factors in a Theory of Poetic Translating.*
   S. Beierlein, 52:Band15Heft2-318
de Beaugrande, R. Text, Discourse, and Process.
   B. Lindemann, 307:Oct81-120
   J. Verschueren, 350:Jun82-463
Beaujot, J-P. and others. Synonymies.
   A.S. Allen, 350:Jun81-490
Beaujour, M. Miroirs d'encre.
   J. Michael, 400(MLN):Dec81-1204
   J. Sturrock, 208(FS):Apr81-238
Beaulieu, V-L. Don Quixote in Nighttown.
   M.A. Peterman, 102(CanL):Spring81-100
Beaulieu, V-L. Les Grands-pères.
   E-M. Kroller, 102(CanL):Spring81-93
Beaulieu, V-L. Race de monde.
   P. Merivale, 102(CanL):Spring81-127
Beaulieu, V-L. La tête de Monsieur Ferron ou les Chians.
   A. Wagner, 108:Spring81-124
Beaulieu, V-L. Una.
   A. Senécal, 207(FR):Mar82-562
Beauman, S. The Royal Shakespeare Company.
   D.A.N. Jones, 362:21Oct82-22
   N. de Jongh, 617(TLS):30Jul82-835
de Beaumarchais, P.A.C. Théâtre. (J-P. de Beaumarchais, ed)
   D.C. Spinelli, 207(FR):Mar82-551

23

Beaumont, F. and J. Fletcher. The Dramat-
ic Works in the Beaumont and Fletcher
Canon.* (F. Bowers, ed)
    M. Mincoff, 447(N&Q):Aug80-366
Beaurline, L.A. Jonson and Elizabethan
Comedy.*
    I. Donaldson, 402(MLR):Apr81-442
    R.L. Heffner, Jr., 131(CL):Spring81-
189
Beausoleil, C. La Surface du paysage.
    P.G. Lewis, 207(FR):Feb81-496
Beaussant, P. François Couperin.
    M. Schneider, 450(NRF):Mar81-160
"Beautiful Lace."
    P. Bach, 614:Summer82-12
de Beauvoir, S. Quand prime le spirituel.*
    C.S. Brosman, 207(FR):May81-890
    S. Reynolds, 402(MLR):Jan81-206
de Beauvoir, S. When Things of the Spirit
Come First.
    G. Annan, 362:29Jul82-24
    D. Bair, 441:7Nov82-12
    A. Duchêne, 617(TLS):30Jul82-814
Beaver, J. - see Reed, V.
Bebbington, D.W. The Nonconformist Con-
science.
    I. Bradley, 617(TLS):19Feb82-196
Becerra, F. and J.S. Ford. A Mexican
Sergeant's Recollections of the Alamo
and San Jacinto.
    L. Milazzo, 584(SWR):Spring81-v
Bechert, H., ed. Buddhism in Ceylon and
Studies on Religious Syncretism in Bud-
dhist Countries.
    C. Hallisey, 318(JAOS):Jan/Mar80-57
Bechert, H. and G. von Simson, eds. Ein-
führung in die Indologie.
    J.W. de Jong, 259(IIJ):Jul81-219
Bechert, H., Daw Khin Khin Su and Daw Tin
Tin Myint, comps. Burmese Manuscripts.
(Pt 1)
    J.W. de Jong, 259(IIJ):Jul81-238
Beck, H. Kulturphilosophie der Technik.
    W. Strombach, 489(PJGG):Band88Heft1-
194
Beck, H-G. Das byzantinische Jahrtausend.
    M.J. Angold, 303(JoHS):Vol 101-228
Beck, J., ed. Le Concil de Basle (1434).*
    L.B. Pascoe, 589:Oct81-922
Beck, J.C. To Windward of the Land.*
    E. Bourguignon, 292(JAF):Apr-Jun81-241
Beck, J.S. Erläuternder Auszug aus den
critischen Schriften des Herrn Prof.
Kant, auf Anrathen desselben. (Vol 3)
    J. Kopper, 342:Band71Heft2-274
Beck, M. Untersuchungen zur geistlichen
Literatur im Kölner Druck des frühen 16.
Jahrhunderts.
    W. Hoffmann, 680(ZDP):Band99Heft3-454
Beck, S.M. Bartlett's Familiar Quotations.
(15th ed)
    G. Core, 249(HudR):Autumn81-475
Becker, C. - see Charpentier, G.
Becker, G.J. D.H. Lawrence.
    D. Kirby, 573(SSF):Winter81-99
Becker, G.J. Realism in Modern Literature.
    D. Festa-McCormick, 399(MLJ):Spring81-
110
Becker, H. Die Neidharte.
    O. Sayce, 402(MLR):Jan81-234
    E. Wenzel, 680(ZDP):Band99Heft3-448

Becker, H.J. Mit geballter Faust.
    H. Mörchen, 680(ZDP):Band99Heft2-298
    H. Müssener, 406:Fall81-362
Becker, J. and C. Oberfeld, eds. Die Men-
schen sind arm, weil sie arm sind.
    K.F. Geiger, 196:Band21Heft3/4-293
Becker, J. and R. Rauter, eds. Die Dritte
Welt im Kinderbuch.
    K.F. Geiger, 196:Band21Heft3/4-293
Becker, J-J. Les Français dans la Grande
Guerre.
    S. Haig, 207(FR):Mar82-577
Becker, M.B. Medieval Italy.
    J.K. Hyde, 617(TLS):5Mar82-262
Becker, M.L. The Mitten Book.
    C. Mouton, 614:Fall81-19
Becker, R.A. Revolution, Reform and the
Politics of American Taxation, 1763-1783.
    H.L. Coles, 83:Autumn81-245
Becker, S. The Blue-Eyed Shan.
    A. Bold, 617(TLS):16Jul82-775
Becker, V. Antique and Twentieth-Century
Jewellery.
    G. Seidmann, 135:Feb81-166
Beckett, J.V. Local Taxation.
    J. Thorp, 325:Oct81-509
Beckett, J.W. The Secret of Shakespeare's
Doublet.
    V.R. Filby, 70:Nov/Dec80-64
Beckett, L., ed. Richard Wagner "Parsi-
fal."
    R. Anderson, 415:Dec81-822
    M. Tanner, 617(TLS):8Jan82-25
Beckett, O. J.F. Herring and Sons.
    135:Nov81-174
Beckett, S. Company.* (French title:
Compagnie.)
    G. Kearns, 249(HudR):Summer81-312
    B.L. Knapp, 207(FR):Oct81-152
    J-J. Mayoux, 98:Nov80-1105
Beckett, S. Mal vu mal dit.
    G. Craig, 617(TLS):27Aug82-921
    B.L. Knapp, 207(FR):Dec81-300
    J. Stéfan, 450(NRF):Sep81-126
Beckett, S. Three Occasional Pieces. Ill
Seen Ill Said.
    G. Craig, 617(TLS):27Aug82-921
Beckman, B.J. Underlying Word Order.
    K. Hunold, 350:Mar81-233
Beckman, J. The Religious Dimension of
Socrates' Thought.
    J. Ferguson, 303(JoHS):Vol 101-181
"Max Beckmann Aquarelle und Zeichnungen
1903-1950."
    P. Selz, 54:Mar81-170
Beckson, K. Henry Harland.*
    N. White, 447(N&Q):Jun80-258
Beckwith, C. and T.O. Saitoti. Maasai.*
    P.J. Imperato, 2(AfrA):May81-11
Bécquer, G.A. Historia de los templos de
España. (J.R. Arboleda, ed)
    R. Brown, 86(BHS):Apr81-147
Bedard, M. Pipe and Pearls.
    D. Handler, 526:Autumn81-169
Beddow, M. The Fiction of Humanity.
    T.J. Reed, 617(TLS):8Oct82-1114
Bédé, J-A. and W.B. Edgerton, eds. Colum-
bia Dictionary of Modern European Litera-
ture. (2nd ed)
    J.A. Muyskens, 399(MLJ):Winter81-423
Bedell, M. The Alcotts.*
    J. Myerson, 27(AL):Nov81-511
    A.R. Welch, 432(NEQ):Dec81-601

Bedford, R.D. The Defence of Truth.
  D.F. Bratchell, 447(N&Q):Oct80-444
  R.L. Brett, 677(YES):Vol 11-253
  J.W. Yolton, 518:Apr81-87
Bedouelle, G. - see under Lefèvre
  d'Étaples, J.
Beeching, J. The Galleys at Lepanto.
  M. Mallett, 617(TLS):10Sep82-960
Beehler, R. Moral Life.*
  O. O'Neill, 482(PhR):Apr81-312
van Beek, W.E.A. Bierbrouwers in de
  Bergen.
  P. van Leynseele, 69:Vol50No2-227
Beekman, E.M. - see Rumphius, G.E.
de Beer, E.S. - see Locke, J.
Beer, F. - see Julian of Norwich
Beer, F.A. Peace Against War.
  639(VQR):Autumn81-134
Beer, J. Wordsworth and the Human Heart.*
  V. Longino, 447(N&Q):Jun80-252
  L. Newlyn, 541(RES):May81-227
Beer, J. Wordsworth in Time.*
  R. Gravil, 72:Band217Heft2-424
  L. Newlyn, 541(RES):May81-227
Beer, P. Selected Poems.*
  T. Eagleton, 565:Vol22No2-73
Beer, S.H. Britain Against Itself.
  P. Johnson, 617(TLS):8Oct82-1093
Beer, W.R. The Unexpected Rebellion.
  P. Stevens, 207(FR):Mar82-580
Beers, H.P. Spanish and Mexican Records
  of the American Southwest.
  J.L. Arbena, 37:Feb81-47
  B. Diekemper, 14:Spring80-217
  R.E. Greenleaf, 263(RIB):Vol131No1 77
Beeton, D.R. and H. Dorner. A Dictionary
  of English Usage in Southern Africa.
  M. Görlach, 38:Band99Heft1/2-196
Beg, M.A.J. Arabic Loan-Words in Malay.
  (2nd ed)
  S.A. Rahman, 273(IC):Apr80-135
"Beginnings, 1700-1800, the Colonial His-
  tory and Architecture of Millburn, New
  Jersey."
  E.R. McKinstry, 576:Dec81-344
Béhar, H. - see Tzara, T.
Behler, D. The Theory of the Novel in
  Early German Romanticism.
  K. Peter, 221(GQ):Nov81-514
Beidelman, T.O. Colonial Evangelism.
  L. Mair, 617(TLS):3Dec82-1346
Beidler, W. - see Williams, H.H.
Beierwaltes, W. Identität und Differenz.
  G.J.P. O'Daly, 123:Vol31No2-304
Beilenson, L.W. Survival and Peace in the
  Nuclear Age.
  K. Glaser, 396(ModA):Winter81-73
Beilharz, R. Balzac.
  J-F. Battail, 597(SN):Vol53No1-200
Beissner, F. Kafkas Darstellung des
  "Traumhaften inneren Lebens."
  B. Goldstein, 406:Spring81-67
"Beiträge zur Geschichte der Literatur und
  Kunst des 18. Jahrhunderts." (Vols 1-3)
  (R. Gruenter, ed)
  W. Schröder, 654(WB):1/1981-165
Beitz, C.R. Political Theory and Inter-
  national Relations.
  T.L.P., 543:Sep80-126
  H. Shue, 185:Jul82-710

Bekker, H. The Poetry of Albrecht von
  Johansdorf.*
  N.A. Perrin, 406:Summer81-228
  O. Sayce, 402(MLR):Jan81-230
Bekker-Nielsen, H. and others, eds. Medie-
  val Narrative.
  C.B. Hieatt, 589:Apr81-344
  M.E. Kalinke, 563(SS):Winter81-77
Bekker-Nielsen, H. and others, eds. Oral
  Tradition — Literary Tradition.*
  P.J. Frankis, 447(N&Q):Jun80-286
Bektaev, K.B. Statistico-informationnaja
  tipologia tjurkskogo teksta.
  H.T. Georgiev, 682(ZPSK):Band33Heft2-
  272
Belanger, A.J. Ruptures et constantes.
  M. Dorsinville, 102(CanL):Spring80-84
Bélanger, M. Migrations.
  G.V. Downes, 102(CanL):Winter80-105
Belaval, Y. Études leibniziennes: De
  Leibniz à Hegel.*
  M.D. Wilson, 53(AGP):Band62Heft2-219
Belinga, T.B-E. Ecrivains, cinéastes et
  artistes camerounais.
  T. Cassirer, 207(FR):Apr81-756
Belinga, T.B-E., J. Chauveau-Rabut and M.
  Kadima-Nzuji. Bibliographie des auteurs
  africains de langue française. (4th ed)
  T. Cassirer, 207(FR):Apr81-756
  R.P. Smith, Jr., 207(FR):Dec80-336
Belisle, L.A., comp. Dictionnaire nord-
  americain de la langue française.
  W.N., 102(CanL):Summer81-187
  T.R. Wooldridge, 627(UTQ):Summer81-195
Belitz, J. Studien zur Parodie in Hein-
  rich Wittenwilers "Ring."
  A.S. Andreánszky, 684(ZDA):Band109
  Heft3-125
  E.C. Lutz, 406:Fall81-345
  B. Plate, 680(ZDP):Band100Heft1-141
Belkin, J.S. and E.R. Caley. Eucharius
  Rösslin the Younger: On Minerals and
  Mineral Products.
  K. Kehr, 685(ZDL):1/1981-102
Belkin, K.L. Corpus Rubenianum Ludwig
  Burchard. (Pt 24)
  C. Brown, 324:May82-365
Bell, A., ed. Lord Cockburn.
  J.H. Alexander, 506(PSt):Dec81-347
  P. Garside, 83:Spring81-111
  R.L.C. Hunter, 571(ScLJ):Summer80-109
Bell, A. Sydney Smith.*
  S. Pickering, 569(SR):Summer81-
  lxxxviii
Bell, A. and J.B. Hooper, eds. Syllables
  and Segments.*
  A. Crompton, 353:Vol 18No11/12-1132
  J.J. McCarthy, 350:Mar82-198
Bell, A.C. The Lieder of Brahms.
  E. Sams, 415:Feb81-107
Bell, A.O., with A. McNeillie - see Woolf,
  V.
Bell, D. Frege's Theory of Judgement.*
  J.B., 543:Dec80-371
  G. Currie, 167:Mar81-183
  M. Helme, 518:Apr81-121
Bell, D. The Winding Passage.
  M. Krupnick, 560:Fall81-106
Bell, D. and L. Tepperman. The Roots of
  Disunity.*
  R. Gibbins, 529(QQ):Winter81-797
Bell, D.H. Being a Man.
  P. Lopate, 441:18Jul82-6

Benet, J. A Meditation.
  A. Josephs, 441:23May82-13
Benet, J. Saúl ante Samuel.
  K. Schwartz, 238:Sep81-478
Benevolo, L. The History of the City.
  R.G. Wilson, 45:Jun81-49
Benfield, D. In for the Kill.
  D. Devlin, 157:Winter81-51
Bengtson, H. Die Flavier.
  J-C. Richard, 555:Vol54fasc2-386
Bengtsson, G. Danish Floral Charted
  Designs.
  P. Bach, 614:Summer81-17
Bénichou, P. Le Temps des prophètes.
  L. Frappier-Mazur, 207(FR):Oct80-164
Benítez, R., ed. Mariano José de Larra.
  J. Escobar, 240(HR):Autumn81-507
Benjamin, W. Correspondance. Sens unique.
  Allemands.
  P. Missac, 98:Apr80-370
Benjamin, W. Moskauer Tagebuch.
  M. Chlumsky, 98:Apr81-436
Benkovitz, M.J. Aubrey Beardsley.*
  J.E. Chamberlin, 249(HudR):Autumn81-
  467
Benner, M. and E. Tengström. On the Inter-
  pretation of Learned Neolatin.
  P. Flobert, 555:Vol54fasc1-202
Bennett, A. Arnold Bennett: Sketches for
  Autobiography. (J. Hepburn, ed)
  42(AR):Winter81-132
Bennett, A. Enjoy.
  D. Devlin, 157:2ndQtr81-55
Bennett, A.G. and R. Berson. Fans in
  Fashion.
  R.L. Shep, 614:Fall82-16
Bennett, A., ed. The Literature of West-
  ern Australia.*
  T. Shapcott, 381:Apr81-83
Bennett, B. Modern Drama and German
  Classicism.*
  L. Abicht, 42(AR):Winter81-127
  J.F. Hyde, Jr., 221(GQ):May81-380
  M. Mueller, 678(YCGL):No29-51
  R.A. Nicholls, 131(CL):Winter81-104
  W. Wittkowski, 301(JEGP):Apr81-303
Bennett, B.T. - see Shelley, M.W.
Bennett, F. A Canterbury Tale.
  J. Owens, 368:Sep81-372
Bennett, P. Talking with Texas Writers.
  T. Kuykendall, 584(SWR):Spring81-222
Bennett, R., ed. This Place.
  G. Catalano, 381:Apr81-114
Bennett, T. Formalism and Marxism.*
  W.E. Cain, 580(SCR):Spring82-129
  C. Norris, 402(MLR):Jan81-143
  S. Trombley, 541(RES):Aug81-365
Bennholdt-Thomsen, A. and A. Guzzoni. Der
  "Asoziale" in der Literatur um 1800.
  W. Koepke, 221(GQ):Mar81-219
de Benoist, A. Les idées à l'endroit.
  Y. Michaud, 98:Jan80-31
Benoist, J-M. Chronique de décomposition
  du P.C.F.
  J. Bouveresse, 98:Jan80-51
Benoist, J-M. La Génération sacrifiée.
  E. de La Rochefoucauld, 161(DUJ):Jun81-
  271
Bénoit, F-P. Les idéologies politiques
  modernes.
  A. Reix, 542:Jul-Sep81-381
Bens, J. Oulipo 1960-1963.
  A. Calame, 450(NRF):Jun81-119

Benseler, D.P., ed. ACTFL Annual Bibliog-
  raphy of Books and Articles on Pedagogy
  in Foreign Languages for the Years 1977
  and 1978.
  H. Reinert, 399(MLJ):Summer81-208
Benseler, D.P. and R.A. Schulz. Intensive
  Foreign Language Courses.
  T.D. Terrell, 399(MLJ):Autumn81-327
Bensko, J. Green Soldiers.
  B. Bennett, 441:14Mar82-12
  H. McNeil, 617(TLS):29Jan82-113
Bensley, C. Progress Report.
  W. Scammell, 617(TLS):2Apr82-393
Bensman, J. and R. Lilienfeld. Between
  Public and Private.
  J.D. Greenstone, 185:Oct81-152
Benson, B.J. and M.M. Dillard. Jean
  Toomer.
  S.B. Garren, 95(CLAJ):Jun81-531
Benson, C.D. The History of Troy in Mid-
  dle English Literature.
  L. Ebin, 589:Oct81-848
Benson, M. An English-Serbo-Croatian Dic-
  tionary.*
  R. Alexander, 350:Mar82-251
Benstock, S. and B. Who's He When He's at
  Home.*
  M. Beja, 301(JECP):Jul81-452
  R.M. Kain, 329(JJQ):Winter81-216
  W.T. O'Malley, 70:Sep80-13
Bentinck, W.C. The Correspondence of Lord
  William Cavendish Bentinck, Governor-
  General of India 1828-1835. (C.H.
  Philips, ed)
  R. Rocher, 318(JAOS):Jul/Sep80-321
Bentley, B. - see Hall, H.
Bentley, E.C. The Complete Clerihews of
  E. Clerihew Bentley.
  A. Quinton, 617(TLS):12Nov82-1239
Bentley, E.C., with others. The First
  Clerihews.
  A. Quinton, 617(TLS):12Nov82-1239
Bentley, G.E., Jr. - see Blake, W.
Bentley, T. Winter Season.
  R. Craft, 453(NYRB):12Aug82-28
  S. Padwe, 441:29Aug82-8
  442(NY):16Aug82-91
Bentley, U. The Natural Order.
  J. Astor, 362:15Jul82-23
  L. Duguid, 617(TLS):2Jul82-725
Benton, R. Ignace Pleyel.*
  J. Sachs, 415:Jan81-31
Benvenisti, D. Rehovot Yerushalayim.
  (2nd ed)
  E.D. Lawson, 424:Mar81-87
Beny, R., with P. Gunn. The Churches of
  Rome.
  J. Rykwert, 617(TLS):26Mar82-336
  135:Dec81-250
Beny, R., with A. Thwaite. Odyssey.
  135:Dec81-250
Beolco il Ruzante, A. La Pastoral; La
  prima Orazione; Una lettera giocosa.
  (G. Padoan, ed)
  E. Bonora, 228(GSLI):Vol 158fasc501-
  112
"Beowulf." (J. Queval, trans)
  T.A. Shippey, 617(TLS):1Jan82-9
"'Beowulf' und die kleineren Denkmäler der
  altenglischen Heldensage Waldere und
  Finnsburg."* (Pts 1 and 2) (G. Nickel,
  ed and trans)
  J.D. Pheifer, 382(MAE):1981/1-118

Ber, C. Lieu des éparts.
R.A. Laden, 207(FR):Feb81-497
Berberova, N. - see Bely, A.
de Berceo, G. El libro de Alixandre.
(D.A. Nelson, ed)
R. Ayerbe-Chaux, 238:Mar81-150
I. Macpherson, 86(BHS):Jul81-258
P. Such, 402(MLR):Jan81-213
de Berceo, G. Signos que aparecerán antes
del Juicio Final, Duelo de la Virgen,
Martirio de San Lorenzo. (A.M. Ramoneda,
ed)
B. Dutton, 304(JHP):Autumn81-77
Bercovitch, S. The American Jeremiad.*
E.B. Lowrie, 568(SCN):Spring81-17
P-Y. Petillon, 98:Dec81-1255
R. Pooley, 677(YES):Vol 11-266
Berend, I.T. and G. Ránki. Underdevelop-
ment and Economic Growth.
I. Deak, 104(CASS):Winter81-613
Berenson, B. and C. Marghieri. Lo spec-
chio doppio.
A.F. Price, 617(TLS):8Oct82-1109
Berenson, E.M. Understanding Persons.*
J.D., 185:Apr82-583
Beresford, M.W. and J.K.S. St. Joseph.
Medieval England. (2nd ed)
F.L. Cheyette, 589:Apr81-447
P.S. Gelling, 447(N&Q):Aug80-357
Berg, C. Jean de Boschère ou le mouvement
de l'attente.
E.T. Dubois, 208(FS):Oct81-473
Berg, J. and J. Loudžil - see Bolzano, B.
Berg, M. The Machinery Question and the
Making of Political Economy 1815-1848.
C. Harvie, 637(VS):Spring81-387
Berg, S. With Akhmatova at the Black
Gates.*
P. Mariani, 472:Spring/Summer82-265
W. Scammell, 617(TLS):28May82-592
Berg-Pan, R. Bertolt Brecht and China.
S.L. Gilman, 221(GQ):Jan81-109
Berger, B. and L. Fry. Hangin' On.
L. Milazzo, 584(SWR):Autumn81-414
Berger, D. Cicero als Erzähler.
H.F. Plett, 490:Band12Heft3/4-526
Berger, D., ed. The Jewish-Christian
Debate in the High Middle Ages.
D.J. Lasker, 589:Jul81-583
Berger, F.R., ed. Freedom of Expression.
T.M.S., Jr., 185:Apr82-601
Berger, H. Mission und Kolonial-Politik.
P. Laburthe-Tolra, 69:Vol150No4-448
Berger, J. About Looking.*
H. Foster, 62:Summer81-88
Berger, J. Pig Earth.
M. Kreyling, 573(SSF):Summer81-334
639(VQR):Winter81-30
Berger, K. Theories of Chromatic and
Enharmonic Music in Late 16th Century
Italy.
I. Fenlon, 415:Feb81-109
Berger, P.L. The Heretical Imperative.
J. Patrick, 396(ModA):Winter81-93
Berger, T. Little Big Man.
R.A. Betts, 145(Crit):Vol123No2-85
Berger, T. Reinhart's Women.*
J. Mellors, 362:21Oct82-23
D. Montrose, 617(TLS):3Sep82-940
Berger, T.R. Fragile Freedoms.
E.Z. Friedenberg, 453(NYRB):4Nov82-37
de Bergerac, S.D. - see under de Cyrano de
Bergerac, S.

Bergeron, L. Dictionnaire de la langue
québécoise.
A. Valdman, 207(FR):Feb82-431
T.R. Wooldridge, 627(UTQ):Summer81-195
Bergfeld, J. - see Wagner, R.
Bergh, B. Palaeography and Textual Criti-
cism.
J. André, 555:Vol154fasc1-176
van den Berghe, P.L. The Ethnic Phenome-
non.
M. Banton, 617(TLS):29Jan82-95
Bergin, T.G. Boccaccio.*
P-L. Adams, 61:Feb82-87
E. Cochrane, 441:10Jan82-11
Bergin, T.G., with others - see Hill, R.C.
and T.G. Bergin
Bergman, I. and A. Burgess. Ingrid
Bergman.
P. Bosworth, 18:Nov80-71
P. Cook, 200:Feb81-117
Bergmann, F. On Being Free.
A. Montefiore, 449:Sep81-393
Bergmann, H. Between Obedience and Free-
dom.*
R. Miles, 677(YES):Vol 11-313
Bergmeister, H-J., ed. Die Historia de
Preliis Alexandri Magni.
C. Minis, 684(ZDA):Band10Heft3-113
Bergner, J.T. The Origin of Formalism in
Social Science.
K.E.S., 185:Apr82-604
Bergonzi, B. Reading the Thirties.*
R. Currie, 447(N&Q):Dec80-570
Berke, R. Bounds Out of Bounds.
I. Salusinszky, 617(TLS):14May82-540
Berkeley, G. Viaggio in Italia.
G. Brykman, 542:Jul-Sep81-364
Berkey, J.C., and others - see Dreiser, T.
Berkowitz, G.M. David Garrick.
H.W. Pedicord, 611(TN):Vol135No3-141
Berkowitz, G.M. Sir John Vanbrugh and
the End of Restoration Comedy.
R.D. Hume, 566:Spring82-124
Berkowski, N.J. Die Romantik in Deutsch-
land.
H. Scholz, 654(WB):2/1981-164
Berland, A. Culture and Conduct in the
Novels of Henry James.*
639(VQR):Autumn81-129
Berlin, I. Against the Current.* (H.
Hardy, ed)
J.P. Diggins, 473(PR):2/1981-289
R. Jacoby, 560:Winter82-232
Berlin, I. The Age of Enlightenment.
F. Doherty, 506(PSt):Dec81-346
Berlin, I. Concepts and Categories.* (H.
Hardy, ed)
E. Grosholz, 480(P&R):Spring81-130
R. Jacoby, 560:Winter82-232
Berlin, I. Personal Impressions.* (H.
Hardy, ed)
R. Jacoby, 560:Winter82-232
529(QQ):Summer81-401
639(VQR):Summer81-99
Berlin, I. Russian Thinkers.* (H. Hardy
and A. Kelly, eds)
R. Jacoby, 560:Winter82-232
Berlioz, M. Rabelais restitué. (Vol 1)
S. Bisarello, 356(LR):Feb-May81-157
Berman, L. Planning a Tragedy.
G. Smith, 441:2May82-3

28

Berman, M. All That Is Solid Melts Into
Air.
  R.M. Adams, 453(NYRB):4Mar82-27
  L. Bersani, 441:14Feb82-9
  G. Graff, 61:Jan82-84
Berman, M. Richmond's Jewry.
  B. Gitenstein, 392:Winter80/81-69
Berman, R.A., with S. Bolozky. Modern
Hebrew Structure.*
  P. Cole, 350:Dec82-916
Berman, S. Easy Street.*
  442(NY):4Jan82-91
Bermel, A. Farce.
  F. Randall, 441:11Apr82-14
Bernal, A.M. and others. Tourisme et
développement régional en Andalousie.
  R.A. Pullan, 86(BHS):Jan81-91
Bernard, B., with V. Lloyd. Photodis-
covery.* (British title: The Sunday
Times Book of Photodiscovery.)
  C. Hagen, 62:Nov81-76
Bernard-Griffiths, S. and P. Viallaneix,
eds. Edgar Quinet, ce juif errant.*
  C. Crossley, 208(FS):Jan81-80
Bernardi, J. - see Saint Gregory of Nazian-
zus
Bernardi, W. Morelly e Dom Deschamps.
  N. Wagner, 535(RHL):Jul-Oct81-782
Bernhard, T. Ein Kind.
  S.N. Plaice, 617(TLS):10ct82-1083
Bernhard, T. Immanuel Kant.
  R.M., 342:Band71Heft1-129
Bernhard, T. L'Origine.
  B. Bayen, 450(NRF):Nov81-142
Bernhard, V., ed. Elites, Masses, and
Modernization in Latin America, 1850-
1930.
  F.E. Mallon, 263(RIB):Vol31No1-78
Bernheim, K.F., R.R.J. Lewine and C.T.
Beale. The Caring Family.
  H. Featherstone, 441:7Mar82-11
Bernier, O. The Eighteenth-Century Woman.
  442(NY):3May82-167
Bernier, O. Pleasure and Privilege.*
  639(VQR):Autumn81-120
Bernior, R.M. The Nepalese Pagoda.
  U. Wiesner, 293(JASt):Aug81-811
Berno de Almeida, A.W. Jorge Amado.
  P.K. Speck, 37:Aug81-37
Bernot, D. and others. Dictionnaire
birman-français. (fasc 1)
  J. Wheatley, 350:Dec81-973
Bernstein, A.H. Tiberius Sempronius
Gracchus.
  M.H. Crawford, 313:Vol71-153
Bernstein, B. Family Matters.
  J. Kaplan, 441:4Jul82-7
Bernstein, C.L. Precarious Enchantment.*
  636(VP):Summer81-200
Bernstein, J. Experiencing Science.
  M. Green, 128(CE):Oct81-569
Bernstein, J. Science Observed.
  R.W. Wilson, 441:28Feb82-7
Bernstein, M.A. The Tale of the Tribe.*
  G.F. Butterick, 468:Winter81-645
  M. Davidson, 405(MP):Feb82-335
  S. Lourdeaux, 27(AL):Nov81-551
  F. Sauzey, 468:Fall81-449
  C.F. Terrell, 659(ConL):Winter82-92
Bernstein, R. From the Center of the
Earth.
  J.K. Fairbank, 453(NYRB):27May82-3
  R. Terrill, 441:30May82-1

Berridge, E. People at Play.
  J. Astor, 362:6May82-27
  P. Craig, 617(TLS):16Apr82-446
Berridge, V. and G. Edwards. Opium and
the People.
  A. Hayter, 617(TLS):5Feb82-128
  A. Phillips, 364:Mar82-77
Berruto, G. L'italiano impopolare.*
  R.A. Hall, Jr., 350:Jun81-495
Berry, G.W.D. - see Lemmon, E.J.
Berry, H., ed. The First Public Play-
house.*
  J. Orrell, 610:Autumn81 216
Berry, J. Cut-Way Feelins, Loving, and
Lucy's Letters.
  T. Dooley, 617(TLS):24Sep82-1041
Berry, M.F. Teaching Linguistically
Handicapped Children.
  D.E. Elliott, 350:Jun81-522
Berry, R. Changing Styles in Shakespeare.
  J.R. Brown, 617(TLS):1Jan82-18
Berry, R.A. and R. Soligo, eds. Economic
Policy and Income Distribution in
Columbia.
  L.H. Davis, 263(RIB):Vol31No2-272
Berry, S. Cricket Wallah.
  A. Ross, 617(TLS):6Aug82-863
Berry, T.E. Plots and Characters in Major
Russian Fiction. (Vol 1)
  A. Woronzoff, 558(RLJ):Spring-Fall81-
  315
Berry, W. The Gift of Good Land.*
  J. Ditsky, 628(UWR):Spring-Summer82-
  105
Berry, W. A Part.*
  J. Ditsky, 628(UWR):Fall-Winter81-134
  S. Lea, 472:Fall/Winter81-131
  G.E. Murray, 249(HudR):Spring81-157
Berryman, C. From Wilderness to Waste-
land.*
  R.C. Davis, 106:Winter81-301
  D. Weber, 445(NCF):Jun81-83
Berryman, C.L. and V.A. Eman, eds. Commu-
nication, Language and Sex.
  K. Arens, 399(MLJ):Winter81-413
Bersani, L. Baudelaire and Freud.*
  (French title: Baudelaire et Freud.)
  B. Bassoff, 577(SHR):Summer81-262
  P. Bayard, 450(NRF):May81-125
  J. Forrester, 208(FS):Apr81-170
  F.G. Henry, 446(NCFS):Fall-Winter80/81-
  139
Bersani, L. The Death of Stéphane Mal-
larmé.
  M. Bishop, 150(DR):Winter81/82-692
  G.D. Martin, 617(TLS):2Apr82-386
Bersianik, L. Maternative.
  P.G. Lewis, 207(FR):Mar82-563
Bersianik, L. Le Pique-nique sur l'Acro-
pole.
  M.J. Green, 207(FR):Mar81-615
  P. Merivale, 102(CanL):Spring81-127
Bertelli, L. and I. Lana, eds. Lessico
politico dell'epica greca arcaica.
  W.J. Verdenius, 394:Vol34fasc3/4-409
Bertelli, S. and P. Innocenti. Bibliogra-
fia Machiavelliana.
  F. Chiappelli, 551(RenQ):Winter80-747
Bertens, J.W. The Fiction of Paul Bowles.
  L.D. Stewart, 395(MFS):Summer80-347

Berthier, P. Barbey d'Aurevilly et
l'imagination.*
    J. Greene, 446(NCFS):Fall-Winter80/81-
    137
Berthoff, W. A Literature Without
Qualities.*
    R. Merrill, 405(MP):Aug81-111
    T. Samet, 569(SR):Spring81-liv
    G.F. Waller, 106:Winter81-413
Bertholle, L. French Cuisine for All.
    W. and C. Cowen, 639(VQR):Spring81-70
Berthoud, J. Joseph Conrad: The Major
Phase.*
    E.K. Hay, 405(MP):Nov81-177
    C. Watts, 447(N&Q):Dec80-560
Berthoud, M. H. & R. Daniel 1822-1846.
    T.A. Lockett, 135:Mar81-242
Berthoud, R. Graham Sutherland.
    F. Spalding, 617(TLS):9Jul82-749
    S. Spender, 362:13May82-24
Berti, E. Aristotele: Dalla dialettica
alla filosofia prima.
    H. Krämer, 53(AGP):Band62Heft2-199
Berti, E. Profilo di Aristotele.
    J. Barnes, 123:Vol31No1-127
    F. Volpi, 489(PJGG):Band88Heft1-209
Bertier, J. and others - see Plotinus
Bertin, C. Marie Bonaparte.
    P. Grosskurth, 453(NYRB):16Dec82-15
Bertinelli, M.G.A. Roma e l'oriente.
    E.W. Gray, 313:Vol71-190
Bertini, F. and others. Commedie latine
del XII e XIII secolo. (Vol 2)
    J.C. McKeown, 123:Vol31No2-328
de Bértola, E. and others. Semiótica de
las artes visuales.
    M. Nadin, 290(JAAC):Summer82-443
Berton, K. Moscow.
    M. Winokur, 574(SEEJ):Spring81-117
Berton, P. Flames Across the Border, 1813-
1814.
    E.J. Miles, 150(DR):Autumn81-597
Berton, P. The Invasion of Canada 1812-
1813.*
    M. Power, 628(UWR):Fall-Winter81-131
    G.W., 102(CanL):Spring81-171
Bertram, C., ed. Prospects of Soviet
Power in the 1980s.
    J.N. Westwood, 575(SEER):Oct81-632
Bertram, J. - see Arnold, T.
Bertrand, A. Gaspard de la nuit. (M.
Milner, ed)
    R. Little, 402(MLR):Jul81-705
Bertrand, C.L., ed. Situations révolution-
naires en Europe, 1917-1922.
    D. Kirby, 575(SEER):Jan81-112
Bertuccioli, G. A Florentine in Manila.
    L. Wright, 302:Vol 18-181
Beschloss, M.R. Kennedy and Roosevelt.
    C.K. McFarland, 432(NEQ):Sep81-424
Besemeres, J.F. Socialist Population
Politics.
    A. Helgeson, 550(RusR):Jul81-349
Bessai, D. and D. Jackel. Figures in a
Ground.*
    T. Goldie, 102(CanL):Autumn81-145
Bessen, J. Ionesco und die Farce.
    A. Meech, 610:Winter80/81-79
Besser, G.R. Nathalie Sarraute.*
    A. Jefferson, 402(MLR):Apr81-482
    A. Otten, 345(KRQ):Vol28No3-323
    K. Racevskis, 207(FR):Feb81-480

Besserman, L.L. The Legend of Job in the
Middle Ages.*
    J.J. Anderson, 382(MAE):1981/1-179
Bessette, G. Mes Romans et moi.*
    L. Mailhot, 102(CanL):Spring81-110
Bessette, G. Le Semestre.
    M. Cagnon, 207(FR):Feb81-499
Bessinger, J.B., Jr., ed. A Concordance
to "The Anglo-Saxon Poetic Records."*
    M. Görlach, 72:Band217Heft2-412
Best, D. Philosophy and Human Movement.*
    C.A. Knapp and M.H. Snoeyenbos, 289:
    Oct81-121
Best, G. Humanity in Warfare.*
    C.R.B., 185:Jul81-698
Best, G. War and Society in Revolutionary
Europe, 1770-1870.
    N. Hampson, 617(TLS):2Jul82-723
Best, N. Where Were You at Waterloo?
    D. Profumo, 617(TLS):8Jan82-35
"Best Radio Plays of 1979."*
    D. Parker, 157:Autumn81-50
Bestall, J.M. and D.V. Fowkes. History of
Chesterfield. (Vol 3)
    T.C. Barker, 325:Apr81-436
Besterman, T. - see de Voltaire, F.M.A.
Bethell, N. The Palestine Triangle.*
    B. Wasserstein, 390:Mar81-53
Bethlenfalvay, M. Les Visages de l'enfant
dans la littérature française du XIXe
siècle.
    C. Alcorn, 207(FR):Mar81-598
    R. Gibson, 208(FS):Jul81-350
    M. O'Nan, 446(NCFS):Fall-Winter81/82-
    131
    B. Vercier, 535(RHL):Mar-Apr81-317
Betjeman, J. Uncollected Poems.
    R. Davies, 362:25Nov82-26
Betken, W.T. The Other Shakespeare: "The
Two Gentlemen of Verona."
    D. Nokes, 617(TLS):6Aug82-857
Bettelheim, B. and K. Zelan. On Learning
to Read.
    J. Bruner, 453(NYRB):1Apr82-19
    H. Gardner, 441:31Jan82-11
    442(NY):25Jan82-103
Betti, F. Storia critica delle Lettere
virgiliane.
    S. Garofalo, 276:Spring81-57
Betts, D. Heading West.*
    B. Gutcheon, 441:17Jan82-12
    442(NY):1Feb82-131
Betts, G.R. Writers in Residence.
    D.K. Jeffrey, 577(SHR):Fall81-377
Betts, J.H. Corpus der Minoischen und
Mykenischen Siegel. (Vol 10)
    J.G. Younger, 303(JoHS):Vol 101-218
Betz, P.F. - see Wordsworth, W.
Beucler, A. De Saint-Pétersbourg à Saint-
Germain-des-Prés.
    P. Bourgeade, 450(NRF):Jan81-128
Beugnot, B., ed. Les Critiques de notre
temps et Anouilh.
    D. Knowles, 208(FS):Apr81-230
Beumann, H. and W. Schröder, eds. As-
pekte der Nationenbildung im Mittelalter.
    H. Thomas, 680(ZDP):Band100Heft1-124
Beutler, C. Die Entstehung des Altarauf-
satzes.*
    J. Schroeder, 471:Jan/Feb/Mar81-91
Beutner, B. Die Bildsprache Franz Kafkas.
    B. Goldstein, 406:Spring81-67

30

Beverley, J.R. Aspects of Góngora's "Soledades."
  J.F.G. Gornall, 86(BHS):Oct81-350
Bevington, D., comp. Shakespeare.
  S. Wells, 570(SQ):Spring81-120
Bevington, D. and J.L. Halio, eds. Shakespeare, Pattern of Excelling Nature.*
  B. Vickers, 570(SQ):Autumn81-402
Bevis, R.W. The Laughing Tradition.*
  B. Corman, 627(UTQ):Summer81-112
  J. Milhous, 130:Winter81/82-385
  W.R., 148:Autumn81-88
Bewick, T. A Memoir of Thomas Bewick Written By Himself. (I. Bain, ed)
  A.D. Burnett, 161(DUJ):Jun81-234
Beyer, E. Ibsen.
  B. Erbe, 610:Spring81-153
  P.M. Mitchell, 301(JEGP):Jul81-401
Beyer, I. Die Tempel von Dreros und Prinias A und die Chronologie der kretischen Kunst des 8. und 7. Jhs. v. Chr.
  A.M. Snodgrass, 123:Vol31No2-316
Beyer, J. Schwank und Moral.
  H. Newstead, 545(RPh):May81-556
Beyers, C. - see Young, F.M.
Beynon, J. Proconsul and Paramountcy in South Africa.
  K. Ingham, 617(TLS):9Apr82-409
Bezzel, I. Erasmusdrucke des 16. Jahrhunderts in bayerischen Bibliotheken.*
  F.J. Worstbrock, 684(ZDA):Band109Heft2-75
"The Bhagavadgītā." (K.W. Bolle, trans)
  R.N. Minor, 293(JASt):May81-620
  A. Sharma, 314:Summer-Fall81-223
"The Bhagavad Gītā." (W. Sargeant, trans)
  A.T. de Nicolas, 485(PE&W):Jan81-98
de Bhaldraithe, T. Innéacs Nua-Ghaeilge.
  B. Ó Cuív, 112:Vol 14-186
Bhaskar, R. The Possibility of Naturalism.
  J.D. Moon, 185:Jan82-351
  P. Pettit, 518:Jan81-57
  J.E. Tiles, 393(Mind):Jul81-452
Bhat, D.N.S. The Referents of Noun Phrases.
  A.D. Grimshaw, 350:Jun81-490
Bhatia, S. India's Nuclear Bomb.
  N.D. Palmer, 293(JASt):Aug81-835
Bhatt, P.M. Scholars' Guide to Washington, D.C.: African Studies.
  A. South, 14:Spring81-161
"Jayanta Bhatta's 'Nyāya-Mañjarī' (The Compendium of Indian Speculative Logic)." (Vol 1) (J.V. Bhattacharya, trans)
  K.H. Potter, 485(PE&W):Apr81-239
Bhattacharya, B. Mahatma Gandhi.
  S.M. Asnani, 314:Summer-Fall81-216
Bhattacharya, B. - see "Songs of Kṛṣṇa"
Bhattacharya, J.V. - see "Jayanta Bhatta's 'Nyāya-Mañjarī' (The Compendium of Indian Speculative Logic)"
Bhêly-Quénum, O. Olympe Bhêly-Quénum présenté par lui-même.
  T.N. Hammond, 207(FR):Mar82-540
Bhutto, Z.A. "If I am Assassinated . . ."
  L. Ziring, 293(JASt):Aug81-812
Bialer, S. Stalin's Successors.*
  639(VQR):Spring81-62
Biard, J. and others. Introduction à la lecture de la Science de la logique de Hegel. (Vol 1)
  A. Reix, 542:Oct-Dec81-477

Biard, J.D. Lexique pour l'explication de texte.
  205(FMLS):Oct81-375
"Bible Chasherick Yn Lught Thie: The Manx Family Bible."
  B. Ó Cuív, 112:Vol 14-175
"Bibliothèque Nationale, Catalogue des incunables." (Vol 2, fasc 1)
  D. McKitterick, 617(TLS):6Aug82-866
Bickerman, E.J. Chronology of the Ancient World. (rev)
  D.M. Lewis, 123:Vol31No2-309
Bickerton, D. Roots of Language.
  J. Bruner and C.F. Feldman, 453(NYRB):24Jun82-34
Bickman, M. The Unsounded Centre.
  L. Buell, 445(NCF):Sep81-212
  J.W. Gargano, 495(PoeS):Jun81-14
  F.L. Morey, 646(WWR):Mar81-45
  M.M. Sealts, Jr., 27(AL):May81-339
  A.M. Woodlief, 577(SHR):Fall81-364
Bieber, K. Simone de Beauvoir.
  P. Newman-Gordon, 399(MLJ):Winter81-426
  Y.A. Patterson, 207(FR):Feb81-478
  C.B. Radford, 208(FS):Apr81-229
  S. Reynolds, 402(MLR):Jan81-206
Biebuyck, D.P. Hero and Chief.*
  J. Knappert, 69:Vol150No2-222
Bieder, M. Narrative Perspective in the Post-Civil War Novels of Francisco Ayala, "Muertes de perro" and "El fondo del vaso."
  T. Mermall, 240(HR):Summer81-373
  N.R. Orringer, 238:Mar81-156
Biederman, C. Search for New Arts.
  H. Osborne, 89(BJA):Winter81-83
Bieler, L., ed and trans. The Patrician Texts in the Book of Armagh.
  J.F. Kelly, 589:Jul81-585
Biemel, W. and others, eds. Die Welt des Menschen — Die Welt der Philosophie.
  K. Hartmann, 53(AGP):Band62Heft3-345
Bier, J. Tilmann Riemenschneider.
  M. Baxandall, 617(TLS):18Jun82-675
Bierbrauer, K. Die Ornamentik frühkarolingischer Handschriften aus Bayern.
  L. Nees, 589:Oct81-850
Bierman, J. Righteous Gentile.*
  C. Schine, 441:10Jan82-12
Biers, W.R. The Archaeology of Greece.*
  C. Houser, 576:Oct81-236
  N. Marinatos, 121(CJ):Apr/May82-373
Bierwisch, M., ed. Psychologische Effekte sprachlicher Strukturkomponenten.
  A. Cutler, 353:Vol 18No5/6-568
van Biesbrock, H-R. Die literarische Mode der Physiologien in Frankreich (1840-1842).
  A. Hegenbarth-Rösgen, 535(RHL):Jan-Feb81-150
Biet-Brighelli-Rispail. Manuel du XIXe siècle.
  J. Stéfan, 450(NRF):Nov81-120
Bietenholz, P.G. - see Erasmus
Bigsby, C.W.E. Joe Orton.
  P. Kemp, 362:22Jul82-20
  C. Rawson, 617(TLS):3Sep82-941
Bigsby, C.W.E. The Second Black Renaissance.*
  B. Jackson, 27(AL):Nov81-526
  J.O. Perry, 219(GaR):Spring81-170

Bihaly, A. The Journal of Andrew Bihaly.
(A. Tuttle, ed)
   D. Bronsen, 390:Apr81-50
Bihari, A., ed. Magyar hiedelemmonda kata-
lógus.
   L. Dégh, 196:Band22Heft3/4-323
Bilan, R.P. The Literary Criticism of F.R.
Leavis.*
   P. Byrne, 506(PSt):Sep81-224
   R.G. Cox, 569(SR):Winter81-118
   D. Jackel, 627(UTQ):Summer81-137
   D. Jarrett, 366:Spring81-131
   R. Wellek, 402(MLR):Jan81-175
Bilik, D.S. Immigrant-Survivors.*
   M. Roshwald, 268(IFR):Winter82-68
Biliński, B. Agoni ginnici.
   H.W. Pleket, 303(JoHS):Vol 101-187
Biliński, B. Prolegomena alle "Vite dei
matematici" di Bernardino Baldi (1587-
1596).
   H. Wagner, 53(AGP):Band62Heft2-215
Bill, E.G.W., comp. The Queen Anne
Churches.
   V. Belcher, 325:Apr81-434
Billcliffe, R. Charles Rennie Mackintosh.*
   D. Irwin, 161(DUJ):Jun81-232
   J. Rykwert, 45:Feb81-55
Billcliffe, R. Mackintosh Watercolours.
   D. Irwin, 161(DUJ):Jun81-232
Billerbeck, M. Der Kyniker Demetrius.
   M. Griffin, 123:Vol31No1-58
Billerbeck, M. - see Epictetus
Billeter, J-F. Li Zhi, philosophe maudit
(1527-1602).* (Vol 1)
   J. Ching, 293(JASt):Nov80-95
   P-Y. Wu, 244(HJAS):Jun81-304
Billings, D.B., Jr. Planters and the Mak-
ing of a "New South."
   R.F. Durden, 579(SAQ):Winter81-112
Billington, J.H. Fire in the Minds of
Men.*
   P.F. Lawler, 396(ModA):Summer81-321
   P. Pomper, 550(RusR):Oct81-451
Billington, R. Occasions of Sin.
   L. Duguid, 617(TLS):29Oct82-1203
Billington, R.A. Land of Savagery, Land
of Promise.*
   A. Pagden, 617(TLS):1Oct82-1081
Bills, S.H. Lillian Hellman.
   J.H. Adler, 392:Fall81-463
   K. Lederer, 397(MD):Sep81-385
Bilson, G. A Darkened House.*
   W.N., 102(CanL):Spring81-173
   S.E.D. Shortt, 529(QQ):Spring81-130
Bimson, J.J. Redating the Exodus and Con-
quest.
   T.L. Thompson, 318(JAOS):Jan/Mar80-66
Binchy, M. Light a Penny Candle.
   K.C. O'Brien, 362:30Sep82-27
Binder, H., ed. Kafka-Handbuch.
   F.J. Baharriell, 406:Spring81-101
   J. Strelka, 133:Band14Heft1-88
Binding, P. Separate Country.
   A. Cheney, 392:Winter80/81-74
Binding, T.J., ed. Firebird 1.
   J. Mellors, 362:15Apr82-23
Bingen, J., G. Cambier and G. Nachtergael,
eds. Le monde grec, pensée, littérature,
histoire, documents.
   A. Reix, 542:Apr-Jun81-251

Bingham, A.J. and V.W. Topazio, eds.
Enlightenment Studies in Honour of
Lester G. Crocker.*
   T.E.D. Braun, 207(FR):Oct81-140
   R. Favre, 535(RHL):Jul-Oct81-786
   P. France, 402(MLR):Jan81-186
Bingham, E.R. and G.A. Love, eds. North-
west Perspectives.
   M. Lewis, 649(WAL):Winter81-297
Bingham, J. Brock and the Defector.
   M. Laski, 362:2Dec82-23
Binneberg, K. - see von Ebner-Eschenbach,
M.
Binney, M. and D. Pearce, eds. Railway
Architecture.
   G. Ehrlich, 576:Dec81-336
Binni, W. La protesta di Leopardi.
   E.G. Caserta, 276:Spring81-61
Binnick, R.I. Modern Mongolian.*
   D. Kilby, 297(JL):Mar81-176
Binnie-Clark, G. Wheat and Woman.
   L. Weir, 102(CanL):Spring81-126
Binyon, T.J. Swan Song.
   K. Jeffery, 617(TLS):22Oct82-1174
Biondi, G.G. Semantica di cupidus.
   J. André, 555:Vol154fasc1-186
Biondi, L. The Italian-American Child.
   D. Radcliff-Umstead, 35(AS):Winter81-
295
Birault, H. Heidegger et l'expérience de
la pensée.
   J-L. Chrétien, 98:Dec80-1139
Birch, C. and J.B. Cobb. The Liberation
of Life.
   S. Clark, 617(TLS):11Jun82-630
Bird, C. The Divining Hand.
   J.C. Beck, 650(WF):Jul81-282
Bird, V. Pressing Problems.
   T.J. Binyon, 617(TLS):31Dec82-1448
Bireley, R. Religion and Politics in the
Age of the Counter-reformation.
   H.G. Koenigsberger, 617(TLS):16Apr82-
445
Birkin, A. The Lost Boys.
   T.A. Dunn, 610:Spring81-156
Birley, A. The People of Roman Britain.
   A.A. Barrett, 487:Fall81-293
Birmingham, D. Central Africa to 1970.
   L. Mair, 617(TLS):17Dec82-1390
Birnbaum, M.D. - see Csáth, G.
Birnbaum, P. The Heights of Power.
   S. Hoffmann, 453(NYRB):12Aug82-37
Birney, E. Fall By Fury and Other Makings.
   M.J. Edwards, 102(CanL):Autumn80-113
Birney, E. Spreading Time. (Bk 1)
   W.J. Keith, 105:Spring/Summer81-90
   E. Morrison, 102(CanL):Autumn81-130
Birrell, A. Benjamin Baltzly.*
   W.N., 102(CanL):Autumn81-192
Birrell, G. The Boundless Present.*
   W. Anthony, 400(MLN):Apr81-674
   G. Vitt-Maucher, 678(YCGL):No29-56
Birstein, A. The Rabbi on Forty-Seventh
Street.
   442(NY):26Apr82-142
Birtwhistle, J. Tidal Models.
   I. Hughes, 493:Sep81-78
Birus, H. Poetische Namengebung.*
   D. Borchmeyer, 680(ZDP):Band100Heft4-
595
   C.O. Sjögren, 406:Spring81-112

Bisanz, A.J. and R. Trousson, eds.
Elemente der Literatur.
M. Beller, 133:Band14Heft4-382
G. Fetzer, 196:Band22Heft3/4-329
Bischoff, B., ed. Mittelalterliche Biblio-
thekskataloge. (Vol 4, Pt 1 comp by C.E.
Ineichen-Eder; Vol 4, Pt 2 comp by G.
Glauche and H. Knaus)
H. Thurn, 684(ZDA):Band109Heft4-155
Bischoff, B. Paläographie des römischen
Altertums und des abendländischen Mittel-
alters.
R. Düchting, 72:Band217Heft1-179
P.W. Tax, 221(GQ):Nov81-496
78(BC):Spring81-7
Bischoff, B., J. Duft and S. Sonderegger,
eds. Die "Abrogans"-Handschrift.*
I. Reiffenstein, 680(ZDP):Band100Heft3-
417
Bischoff, B., J. Duft and S. Sonderegger,
eds. Das älteste deutsche Buch.
W. Wegstein, 684(ZDA):Band110Heft3-108
Bishko, C.J. Studies in Medieval Spanish
Frontier History.
D.W. Lomax, 86(BHS):Jul81-275
Bishop, E. Geography III.* Elizabeth
Bishop: The Complete Poems.
V.E. Smith, 584(SWR):Autumn81-431
Bishop, J.P. and A. Tate. The Republic of
Letters in America. (T.D. Young and J.J.
Hindle, eds)
442(NY):18Jan82-130
Bishop, M. The Best of Bishop. (C.P. Rep-
pert, ed)
639(VQR):Spring81-67
Bishop, M., ed. The Language of Poetry.
205(FMLS):Oct81-378
Bishop, O.B., with B.I. Irwin and C.G.
Miller, comps. Bibliography of Ontario
History, 1867-1976.
529(QQ):Spring81-194
Bishop, R. Folk Painters of America.
W. Gavin, 432(NEQ):Jun81-298
Bishop, R. and P. Coblentz. The World of
Antiques, Art, and Architecture in Vic-
torian America.
U. Dietz, 658:Winter81-367
de Bishoven, A.J., with M. Baes-Dondeyne
and D. De Vos - see under Janssens de
Bishoven, A., with M. Baes-Dondeyne and
D. De Vos
Biskup, M. and I. Janosz-Biskupowa, eds.
Akta Stanów Prus Królewskich. (Vol 6)
H.G. Koenigsberger, 575(SEER):Jul81-
434
Bisky, L. Geheime Verführer.
K. Ziermann, 654(WB):8/1981-185
Bissell, C. The Young Vincent Massey.
J. Eayrs, 150(DR):Summer81-363
Bissett, B. pomes for yoshi.
R. Willmot, 102(CanL):Autumn80-138
Bisztray, G. Marxist Models of Literary
Realism.*
P.M.S. Dawson, 447(N&Q):Jun80-283
Bittner, J. Mass Communication.
A. Ray, 583:Spring82-352
Bittrich, B. - see von Ebner-Eschenbach, M.
Bitzer, L. and T. Rueter. Carter vs. Ford.
B. Balthrop, 583:Fall81-84
Bivon, R. Advanced Russian Grammar. (2nd
ed)
M.I. Levin, 558(RLJ):Spring-Fall81-262

Bjork, K.O. - see "Norwegian-American
Studies"
Björkman, S. Le type "avoir besoin."*
M.S. Breslin, 545(RPh):Feb81(supp)-328
Björkstén, I. Leopardväckning.
K. Petherick, 563(SS):Summer81-367
Bjørneboe, J. Bøker og Mennesker.
D. Buttry, 563(SS):Winter81-114
Bjornson, R. The Picaresque Hero in
European Fiction.*
G. Hainsworth, 208(FS):Apr81-201
de Blacha, N.M.G. - see under Girbal de
Blacha, N.M.
Blache, S.E. The Acquisition of Distinc-
tive Features.
L. Menn, 350:Dec81-953
Black, J.L. Citizens for the Fatherland.*
I. de Madariaga, 575(SEER):Oct81-608
M.J. Okenfuss, 104(CASS):Winter81-577
Black, M. Poetic Drama as Mirror of the
Will.*
R.J. Cormier, 568(SCN):Summer-Fall81-
55
Black, R.D.C. - see Jevons, W.S.
Black, T.M. Straight Talk About American
Education.
P-L. Adams, 61:Nov82-171
Black Bear, B., Sr. and R.D. Theisz.
Songs and Dances of the Lakota.
W.K. Powers, 187:May82-325
Blackaby, F., ed. World Armaments and
Disarmament. The Arms Race and Arms
Control.
C.M. Woodhouse, 617(TLS):24Sep82-1030
Blackburn, A. The Myth of the Picaro.*
M. Allott, 541(RES):May81-211
W. Bache, 395(MFS):Summer80-372
G. Hoffmeister, 221(GQ):Mar81-252
J. López-Morillas, 454:Fall81-87
Blackburn, C. Needlepoint Designs for Tra-
ditional Furniture.
P. Bach, 614:Spring81-21
Blackburn, C. The Pillow Book.
T. Cowan, 614:Fall81-20
Blackburn, I.D. - see under Dölz Blackburn,
I.
Blackburn, P. Against the Silences.
T. Olson, 436(NewL):Winter81/82-108
Blackburn, P., comp and trans. Proensa.*
(G. Economou, ed)
R. Sharman, 208(FS):Oct81-421
Blackburn, T. Bread for the Winter Birds.*
H. Lomas, 364:Aug-Sep81-132
Blackmur, R.P. Henry Adams.* (V.A.
Makowsky, ed)
W.E. Cain, 580(SCR):Spring81-114
R.E. Spiller, 27(AL):Nov81-517
T. Woolf, 219(GaR):Summer81-426
Blackwood, C. The Fate of Mary Rose.*
P. Craig, 617(TLS):220ct82-1175
J. Mellors, 364:Jun81-93
Blaiklock, E.M. Between the Valley and
the Sea. Between the Morning and the
Afternoon.
J. Owens, 368:Sep81-372
Blain, V. - see Surtees, R.S.
Blair, J.A. and R.H. Johnson, eds. Infor-
mal Logic.
M.A. Finocchiaro, 480(P&R):Fall81-251
Blair, J.G. The Confidence Man in Modern
Fiction.*
P. Murphy, 541(RES):Nov81-496

33

Blishen, E. Lizzie Pye.
  R. Blythe, 362:24Jun82-21
  A. Duchêne, 617(TLS):15Oct82-1120
  442(NY):4Oct82-150
Blishen, E. Shaky Relations.*
  442(NY):4Oct82-148
Bliss, A. Spoken English in Ireland, 1600-
1740.*
  R.L. Thomson, 447(N&Q):Dec80-547
Blissett, W., ed. Editing Illustrated
Books.
  W. Whitla, 627(UTQ):Summer81-100
Blissett, W. The Long Conversation.*
  G. Davenport, 441:17Oct82-9
  P. Dickinson, 364:Oct81-104
Bloch, C. The Secrets of the Tribe.
  D. Smith, 29:Jan/Feb82-36
Bloch, E. L'Athéisme dans le christian-
isme.
  P-F. Moreau, 450(NRF):Jun81-127
Bloch, L.S. Finders Keepers.
  S. Isaacs, 441:8Aug82-13
Bloch, M. The Duke of Windsor's War.
  J. Grigg, 617(TLS):5Nov82-1212
Bloch, O., ed. Images au XIXe siècle du
matérialisme du XVIIIe siècle.*
  G. Jourdain, 535(RHL):Jul-Oct81-800
Bloch-Dermant, J. The Art of French Glass
1860-1914.
  62:Feb81-71
Block, I., ed. Perspectives on the Phi-
losophy of Wittgenstein.
  S. Blackburn, 617(TLS):30Apr82-492
Block, J.F. Hyde Park Houses.*
  K. Harrington, 658:Spring81-112
Block, L. The Burglar Who Liked To Quote
Kipling.
  T.J. Binyon, 617(TLS):12Mar82-276
Block, L. The Burglar Who Studied Spinoza.
  T.J. Binyon, 617(TLS):23Jul82-807
Block, L. Eight Million Ways to Die.
  N. Callendar, 441:22Aug82-26
Blocker, H.G. and E.H. Smith, eds. John
Rawls' Theory of Social Justice.
  B.B., 185:Apr81-533
Blockmans, W.P. De Volksvertegenwoordig
ing in Vlaanderen in de Overgang van Mid-
deleeuwen naar Nieuwe Tijden (1384-1506).
  B. Lyon, 589:Jan81-96
Blofeld, J. Taoism — the Road to Immor-
tality.
  D.L. Hall, 485(PE&W):Apr81-248
Blok, A. Selected Poems.
  S. Karlinsky, 441:9May82-8
Blomme, R. Studi per una triplice
esperienza poetica del Dante minore.
  T. Barolini, 545(RPh):Feb81(supp)-361
Blöndal, S. The Varangians of Byzantium.*
  (B.S. Benedikz, ed and trans)
  W.E. Kaegi, Jr., 589:Jan81-99
Bloodworth, D. The Messiah and the Manda-
rins.
  D. Wilson, 617(TLS):3Dec82-1328
Bloom, A. - see Rousseau, J-J.
Bloom, C. Limelight and After.
  N. de Jongh, 617(TLS):7May82-517
Bloom, E.A. and L.D., eds. Addison and
Steele: The Critical Heritage.
  D. Crane, 83:Spring81-95
  S.J. Rogal, 566:Spring81-119
  B. Tippett, 366:Autumn81-256

Bloom, E.A. and L.D. Satire's Persuasive
Voice.*
  J.M. Aden, 569(SR):Summer81-441
  W.B. Carnochan, 301(JEGP):Jan81-141
  J.T. Frazier, 599:Fall81-477
  C.J. Rawson, 541(RES):Nov81-457
Bloom, H. Agon.
  R. Alter, 441:31Jan82-8
  D. Donoghue, 617(TLS):30Jul82-811
Bloom, H. The Breaking of the Vessels.
  D. Donoghue, 617(TLS):30Jul82-811
  M. Mudrick, 231:Aug82-65
Bloom, H. and others. Deconstruction and
Criticism.*
  J. Arac, 81:Spring80-241
  A.C. Goodson, 661(WC):Summer81-200
  D.G. Marshall, 473(PR):2/1981-294
  M. Roberts, 506(PSt):Sep81-198
  C. Woodring, 340(KSJ):Vol30-191
Bloom, H. and A. Munich, eds. Robert
Browning.
  D. St. John, 85(SBHC):Spring81-92
Bloom, L. and others. The Inheritance of
Inequality.
  T.C. Miller, 185:Jul82-767
Bloom, L. and M. Lahey. Language Develop-
ment and Language Disorders.
  A. Chandrasekhar, 261:Mar79-51
Blostein, D.A. - see Marston, J.
Blot, D. and D.M. Davidson. Put It In
Writing.
  B. Kroll, 399(MLJ):Winter81-420
Blotkamp, H. and E. De Jong. S. van Rave-
steyn.
  H. Searing, 576:May81-159
Blotner, J. - see Faulkner, W.
Blottière, A. Saad.
  B. Aresu, 207(FR):Feb82-433
  F. de Martinoir, 450(NRF):Jan81-139
Blount, P.G. George Sand and the Victo-
rian World.*
  R. Ashton, 541(RES):Nov81-461
  P. Thomson, 445(NCF):Jun80-120
Blount, R., Jr. Crackers.
  S. Brown, 569(SR):Summer81-431
Blount, T. The Correspondence of Thomas
Blount (1618-1679).* (T. Bongaerts, ed)
  M. Feingold, 78(BC):Spring81-103
Blücher, K. Studio sulle forme "ho can-
tato, cantai, cantavo, stavo cantando."
  S. Norwood, 545(RPh):Feb81(supp)-336
Bludau, B. Frankreich im Werk Nietzsches.
  E. Blondel, 542:Oct-Dec81-497
Bludau, B., E. Heftrich and H. Koopmann,
eds. Thomas Mann 1875-1975.
  H.R. Vaget, 680(ZDP):Band99Heft2-276
Blue Cloud, P. (Aroniawenrate) White Corn
Sister.
  C. Rawlins, 649(WAL):Summer81-135
Bluestone, B. and B. Harrison. The Dein-
dustrialization of America.
  A.E. Kahn, 441:12Dec82-11
Blüher, K-A. and J. Schmidt-Radefeldt, eds.
Poétique et communication: Paul Valéry.
  C.M. Crow, 208(FS):Apr81-225
Blum, A. Annapurna — A Woman's Place.
  M. Ambler, 649(WAL):Winter81-328
Blum, J., ed. Our Forgotten Past.
  L.R. Poos, 617(TLS):28May82-590
Blumenberg, H. Arbeit am Mythos.
  G. Müller, 680(ZDP):Band100Heft2-314

Blumenthal, A.R. Theater Art of the Medici.
  M. Licht, 576:Oct81-241
Blunden, E. Selected Poems. (R. Marsack, ed)
  A. Motion, 617(TLS):9Jul82-733
Blunt, A. The Drawings of Poussin.*
  B. Wind, 568(SCN):Summer-Fall81-62
Bluteau, G. Meurent les alouettes ...
  G. Provost, 296(JCF):No31/32-235
Bly, R. The Man in the Black Coat Turns.
  M. Perloff, 472:Spring/Summer82-209
  P. Stitt, 441:14Feb82-15
Bly, R., ed. News of the Universe.
  T. Hansen, 460(OhR):No28-124
  D. Kirby, 502(PrS):Fall81-97
Bly, R. Talking All Morning.*
  M. Perloff, 472:Spring/Summer82-209
  J.R. Saucerman, 649(WAL):Summer81-162
Bly, R. This Tree Will Be Here for a Thousand Years.*
  J.R. Saucerman, 649(WAL):Summer81-162
Blyth, A., ed. Remembering Britten.
  C. Shaw, 607:Dec81-45
Blyth, A. Wagner's Ring.
  R. Anderson, 415:May81-310
Blyth, R.H. Haiku. Zen in English Literature and Oriental Classics.
  T. Ferris, 441:14Feb82-18
Blyth, R.H. Zen and Zen Classics. (F. Franck, comp)
  F.H. Cook, 318(JAOS):Apr/Jun80-208
  T. Ferris, 441:14Feb82-18
Blythe, R. From the Headlands.
  D.A.N. Jones, 362:9Dec82-25
  P.J. Kavanagh, 617(TLS):26Nov82-1293
Blythe, R. - see Hardy, T.
Bø, O. Dyret i Hagjen.
  O. Holzapfel, 196:Band22Heft1/2-111
Boal, F.W. and J.N.H. Douglas, eds. Integration and Division.
  P. Arthur, 617(TLS):9Jul82-747
Boardman, J. Greek Sculpture: The Archaic Period.
  N. Leipen, 487:Spring81-92
Boardman, J. and M-L. Vollenweider. Ashmolean Museum: Catalogue of the Engraved Gems and Finger Rings. (Vol 1)
  R. Higgins, 303(JoHS):Vol 101-219
Boase, A. - see de Sponde, J.
Boase, P.H., ed. The Rhetoric of Protest and Reform: 1878-1898.
  B.M. Mulvaney, 583:Spring81-306
Boase, R. The Origin and Meaning of Courtly Love.*
  M.D. Johnston, 481(PQ):Winter80-112
Boase, R. The Troubadour Revival.*
  M.D. Johnston, 481(PQ):Winter80-112
  D. Mackenzie, 86(BHS):Jan81-79
  205(FMLS):Jan80-80
Boase, T.S.R. Giorgio Vasari.*
  S.B. Butters, 90:Oct81-622
Bobango, G.J. The Emergence of the Romanian National State.
  S.D. Spector, 104(CASS):Winter81-621
Bobrow, D.B., S. Chan and J.A. Kringen. Understanding Foreign Policy Decisions.
  A.P.L. Liu, 293(JASt):Nov80-96
Bobrow, L.S. and M.A. Arbib. Discrete Mathematics.
  C.C. Elgot, 316:Dec81-878

Bodde, D. Essays on Chinese Civilization. (C. Le Blanc and D. Borei, eds)
  J. Spence, 441:18Apr82-7
Bode, A. Die Flottenpolitik Katharinas II und die Konflikte mit Schweden und der Türkei (1768-1792).
  M.F. Metcalf, 104(CASS):Winter81-580
Bodell, J. A Soldier's View of Empire. (K. Sinclair, ed)
  R. Stow, 617(TLS):13Aug82-874
Boden, M. Minds and Mechanisms.
  D.M. MacKay, 617(TLS):5Mar82-260
Boden, M.A. Piaget.
  W. Mays, 518:Jul81-143
Bodenheimer, E. Philosophy of Responsibility.
  P.S., 185:Oct81-194
"Bodleian Library MS Fairfax 16."
  H. Kane, 191(ELN):Jun81-291
Boehne, P.J. J.V. Foix.
  J. Dagenais, 238:Dec81-640
Boening, J., ed. The Reception of Classical German Literature in England, 1760-1860.
  F. Stock, 52:Band15Heft1-91
de Boer, T. The Development of Husserl's Thought.
  K. Schuhmann, 489(PJGG):Band88Heft1-215
  M.E.Z., 543:Mar81-605
den Boer, W. Private Morality in Greece and Rome.
  N.R.E. Fisher, 123:Vol131No1-75
den Boer, W. Progress in the Greece of Thucydides.
  R. Ferwerda, 394:Vol34fasc1/2-187
  R.W., 555:Vol54fasc1-159
Boerner, W. Das "Cymbalum mundi" des Bonaventure Des Périers.
  F.M. Weinberg, 207(FR):Apr82-671
Boesch, B. Lehrhafte Literatur.*
  P. Wiehl, 680(ZDP):Band100Heft3-427
Boethius. Godfrey of Fontaine's Abridgement of Boethius the Dane's "Modi significandi sive Quaestiones super Priscianum Maiorem." (A.C.S. McDermott, ed and trans)
  L.G. Kelly, 350:Sep82-723
Boetticher, W. Handschriftlich überlieferte Lautenen- und Gitarrentabulaturen des 15. bis 18. Jahrhunderts.*
  A. Ness, 317:Summer81-339
Bog, I. Der Reichsmerkantilismus.
  J-P. Lefebvre, 98:Dec81-1278
Bogan, L. Journey Around My Room.*
  M. Ellmann, 569(SR):Summer81-454
Bogard, T., R. Moody and W.J. Meserve. The Revels History of Drama in English.* (Vol 8)
  J-M. Bonnet, 179(ES):Aug81-394
Bogarde, D. Voices in the Garden.*
  D. Bodeen, 200:Dec81-636
Bogdanor, V. Devolution.
  A. O'Day, 637(VS):Spring81-384
Bogdanor, V. The People and the Party System.
  I. Bradley, 617(TLS):22Jan82-73
Bogdanovich, P. Fritz Lang in America.
  M. Wood, 453(NYRB):10Jun82-34
Bogel, F.V. Acts of Knowledge.
  D. Griffin, 401(MLQ):Sep81-300
  H. Weber, 566:Autumn81-40

Boggs, R.A., comp. Hartmann von Aue: Lem-
matisierte Konkordanz zum Gesamtwerk.
  R.N. Combridge, 402(MLR):Jul81-733
  D.N. Yeandle, 382(MAE):1981/1-158
Boggs, R.S. and R.J. Dixson. English Step
by Step with Pictures. (rev ed)
  B. Kroll, 399(MLJ):Winter81-420
Bogle, M. Textile Conservation Center
Notes.
  P. Bach, 614:Winter81-18
Boglioni, P., ed. La culture populaire au
moyen âge.
  G. Mermier, 207(FR):Dec80-381
Böhl, F. Aufbau und literarische Formen
des aggadischen Teils im Jelamdenu-
Midrasch.
  M. Bregman, 318(JAOS):Apr/Jun80-169
Bohlin, D.D. Prints and Related Drawings
by the Carracci Family.
  E. Young, 39:Aug81-137
Bohlmann, O. Yeats and Nietzsche.
  F.S.L. Lyons, 617(TLS):31Dec82-1438
Bohm, D. Wholeness and the Implicate
Order.
  C.W. Kilmister, 84:Sep81-303
Böhm, R.G. Vigiliae Tullianae. (Vol 1)
  F.R.D. Goodyear, 123:Vol31No2-294
Böhme, G. Zeit und Zahl.
  H. Hoppe, 53(AGP):Band62Heft3-321
Böhme, G. and others. Die gesellschaft-
liche Orientierung des wissenschaft-
lichen Fortschritts — Starnberger
Studien 1.
  C. Lenhardt, 488:Dec81-509
Böhne, W., ed. Hrabanus Maurus und seine
Schule.
  J.M. McCulloh, 589:Oct81-922
Boime, A. Thomas Couture and the Eclectic
Vision.*
  M.R. Brown, 446(NCFS):Fall-Winter81/82-
167
  C. Gould, 324:Mar82-230
  P. Joannides, 59:Sep81-332
  M. Pointon, 89(BJA):Summer81-272
  C. Rosen and H. Zerner, 453(NYRB):
27May82-49
de Boisdeffre, P. Le Roman français
depuis 1900.
  V. Minogue, 208(FS):Apr81-234
Boissard, J. A New Woman. (French title:
Une Femme neuve.)
  N. Aronson, 207(FR):Apr81-758
  S. Ballantyne, 441:3Oct82-9
Boissel, J. Gobineau.
  A. Smith, 446(NCFS):Spring-Summer82-
382
de Boissière, R. Crown Jewel.*
  D. Durrant, 364:Nov81-85
  D. Pinckney, 453(NYRB):27May82-46
Boissonnas, É. Étude.
  D. Leuwers, 450(NRF):Feb81-98
Boissonnault, P., R. Fafard and V. Gadbois.
La Dissertation.
  C. Moisan, 193(ELit):Dec81-561
Boitani, P. Chaucer and Boccaccio.
  P. Boyde, 382(MAE):1981/1-167
Bojsen, E. and others - see "Sprog i
Norden 1980"
Bok, D. Beyond the Ivory Tower.
  T. Bender, 441:23May82-14
Boland, E. Introducing Eavan Boland.
  D. Smith, 29:Jan/Feb82-36

Boland, M.M. Cleomadés.
  N.L. Corbett, 545(RPh):Nov80-270
Bolchazy, L.J., ed. A Concordance to the
"Utopia" of St. Thomas More and a Fre-
quency Word List.
  A. Crosland, 599:Winter81-49
Bold, A. The Ballad.
  M.E. Brown, 571(ScLJ):Winter81-101
  B.D.H. Miller, 447(N&Q):Dec80-545
Bold, A. This Fine Day.
  C. Craig, 571(ScLJ):Winter81-140
Boldy, S. The Novels of Julio Cortázar.*
  205(FMLS):Oct81-375
Bolelli, T. - see Prati, A.
Bolgar, R.R., ed. Classical Influences on
Western Thought, 1650-1870.*
  R.G. Peterson, 173(ECS):Winter80/81-
202
  K. Simonsuuri, 83:Autumn81-205
Bolger, F.W.P. and E.R. Epperly - see Mont-
gomery, L.M.
Böll, H. The Safety Net.
  D.J. Enright, 453(NYRB):18Mar82-46
  R. Fuller, 362:25Mar82-22
  R. Gilman, 441:31Jan82-3
  M. Swales, 617(TLS):2Apr82-371
  J. Updike, 442(NY):14Jun82-131
Böll, H. Was soll aus dem Jungen bloss
werden?
  M. Butler, 617(TLS):7May82-513
Böll-Johansen, H. Stendhal et le roman.
  S. Haig, 207(FR):Dec80-344
  G. Strickland, 208(FS):Jan81-77
Bollack, J. La pensée du plaisir, Epicure.
  J-L. Poirier, 542:Apr-Jun81-268
Bollc, K.W. - see "The Bhagavadgītā"
Bollée, A. Zur Entstehung der franzö-
sischen Kreolendialekte im Indischen
Ozean.*
  H. and R. Kahane, 545(RPh):Feb81(supp)-
26
Boller, P.F., Jr. Freedom and Fate in
American Thought from Edwards to Dewey.
  J.S. Rubin, 106:Spring81-79
Bolloten, B. The Spanish Revolution.
  A. Kerrigan, 396(ModA):Summer81-326
Bologna, F. Gaspare Traversi nell'
illuminismo europeo.
  E. Waterhouse, 90:Jun81-364
Bolotin, D. Plato's Dialogue on Friend-
ship.
  D.C.L., 543:Jun81-779
  S. Rosen, 480(P&R):Spring81-112
Bolotin, N. Klondike Lost.
  B. Robinson, 649(WAL):Fall81-239
Bolton, D. An Approach to Wittgenstein's
Philosophy.
  S.R., 543:Jun81-780
Bolton, J.L. The Medieval English Econ-
omy, 1150-1500.*
  J.T. Rosenthal, 589:Apr81-348
Bolton, K. Two Sestinas.
  G. Bitcon, 581:Dec81-469
Bolton, R. People Skills.
  H.L. Goodall, Jr., 583:Spring82-348
Bolton, W.F. Alcuin and "Beowulf."*
  M.E. Goldsmith, 447(N&Q):Jun80-246
Bolzano, B. Sozialphilosophische Schrif-
ten. (J. Berg and J. Loudžil, eds)
  H. Oberer, 53(AGP):Band62Heft2-230
Bombal, M.L. New Islands.
  R. De Feo, 441:19Dec82-12
  442(NY):18Oct82-179

Bonacasa, N. Arte romana: Scultura.
   M.A.R. Colledge, 123:Vol31No1-140
Bonali-Fiquet, F. - see de Chandieu, A.
Bonansea, B. God and Atheism.
   P.M., 543:Sep80-128
   J.A. Sadowsky, 258:Dec81-463
Bonaparte, F. The Triptych and the Cross.*
   R.D. Ashton, 541(RES):Feb81-90
   J. Beaty, 445(NCF):Dec81-374
Saint Bonaventure. Disputed Questions on
   the Mystery of the Trinity. (Z. Hayes,
   trans)
   E.H. Cousins, 589:Jul81-587
Bonavia, M.R. Railway Policy Between the
   Wars.
   S. Bailey, 617(TLS):19Feb82-196
Bond, B. British Military Policy between
   the Two World Wars.*
   639(VQR):Summer81-86
Bond, D. Crazy Quilt Stitches.
   M.Z. Cowan, 614:Spring82-12
Bond, D. Embroidery Stitches from Old
   American Quilts.
   P. Bach, 614:Winter81-18
Bond, D.H. and W.R. McLeod, eds. News-
   letters to Newspapers.
   F. Rau, 38:Band99Heft1/2-245
Bond, E. The Worlds, with The Activists
   Papers.
   D. Devlin, 157:1stQtr81-54
   M. Martin, 148:Winter81-49
   D.R., 214:Vol 10No37-112
Bond, G., W. Johnson and S.S. Walker, eds.
   African Christianity.
   J.D.Y. Peel, 69:Vol150No3-323
Bond, M., ed. Works of Art in the House
   of Lords.
   90:Jul81-450
Bondi, S. O Puškine.
   J.T. Shaw, 558(RLJ):Winter81-211
Bonenfant, J. Repère.*
   V. Raoul, 102(CanL):Spring81-106
Bongaerts, T. - see Blount, T.
Bongie, L.L. Diderot's "femme savante."*
   C. Battersby, 319:Jan81-118
Bongie, L.L. - see de Condillac, E.B.
Bongrani, P. - see Visconti, G.
Bonheim, H. The Narrative Modes.
   C. Baldick, 617(TLS):26Nov82-1316
Bonilla, H. Gran Bretaña y el Perú. (Vol
   5)
   R.B. St. John, 37:Apr81-26
Bonington, C. Quest for Adventure.
   D.J.R. Bruckner, 441:12Dec82-13
Bonino, J.M. - see under Míguez Bonino, J.
Bonnefoy, Y. and others. Études sur les
   "Poésies" de Rimbaud.
   A. Guyaux, 535(RHL):Jul-Oct81-826
   R. Little, 402(MLR):Jul81-708
   M. Schaettel, 356(LR):Feb-May81-166
Bonnefoy, Y. and others. Le Lieu et la
   formule.
   R. Cardinal, 402(MLR):Apr81-471
Bonnell, P. and F. Sedwick. German for
   Careers.
   M.W. Conner, 399(MLJ):Winter81-433
Bonnet, H. Le progrès spirituel dans "La
   Recherche" de Marcel Proust. (2nd ed)
   P. Somville, 542:Jan-Mar81-117
Bonnet, H. Roman et poésie.* (2nd ed)
   R. Bales, 208(FS):Oct81-485
   G. Cesbron, 535(RHL):Jul-Oct81-845
   P. Somville, 542:Jan-Mar81-117

Bonney, R. The King's Debts.
   R. Mettam, 617(TLS):7May82-514
Bonney, R. Political Change in France
   under Richelieu and Mazarin 1624-1661.
   J. Lough, 208(FS):Jan81-72
Bonney, W.W. Thorns and Arabesques.*
   S. Raval, 594:Winter81-439
   R. Roussel, 445(NCF):Sep81-249
   295(JML):Vol8No3/4-469
Bonnie, F. Squatter's Rights.
   G. Johnson, 461:Spring-Summer81-92
Bonnier, H. L'Enfant du Mont-Salvat.
   M.E. Birkett, 207(FR):Apr81-759
Bonta, J.P. Architecture and Its Inter-
   pretation.*
   C.F. Otto, 127:Fall/Winter80-423
   R. Wesley, 576:Mar81-83
Bonville, W.J. A Study of the Nature of
   Expression in the Arts.
   D. Novitz, 63:Jun81-246
"The Book of Lech Walesa."
   A. Brumberg, 617(TLS):11Jun82-640
   J. Simpson, 362:4Mar82-21
"The Book of the Rhymers' Club [and] The
   Second Book of the Rhymers' Club."
   K. Beckson, 636(VP):Winter81-397
Booker, C. The Games War.*
   C. Parrott, 364:Jul81-63
"Bookman's Price Index." (Vols 16 and 17)
   (D.F. McGrath, ed)
   R.A. Gekoski, 677(YES):Vol 11-219
"Bookman's Price Index." (Vol 20) (D.F.
   McGrath, ed)
   C.W. Mann, 568(SCN):Spring81-24
Bookspan, M. and R. Yockey. Zubin Mehta.
   N. Goodwin, 415:Jun81-385
Boolos, G. The Unprovability of Consist-
   ency.
   C. Smoryński, 316:Dec81-871
Boone, C. and W. Keutsch. Praxis der
   Interpretation: englische Prosa.
   (2nd ed)
   H.R. Spielmann, 38:Band99Heft1/2-269
Boorman, S.A. and P.R. Levitt. The Genet-
   ics of Altruism.
   R.A., 185:Jan82-385
Boorstin, D.J. L'esprit d'exploration.
   P-Y. Petillon, 98:Dec81-1255
Booth, M., ed. Decadal.
   T. Eagleton, 565:Vol122No2-73
Booth, M.R. Victorian Spectacular Theatre
   1850-1910.*
   J.R. Taylor, 157:Winter81-51
Booth, P. Before Sleep.*
   J.F. Cotter, 249(HudR):Summer81-287
   S. Lea, 472:Fall/Winter81-131
   639(VQR):Summer81-95
Booth, S. - see Shakespeare, W.
Booth, W.C. Critical Understanding.*
   W. Bache, 395(MFS):Summer80-372
   T. Heller, 50(ArQ):Spring81-85
   D. O'Hara, 659(ConL):Winter82-105
   D.H. Richter, 349:Summer81-232
   S. Trombley, 541(RES):Aug81-365
   B.A. Wilson, 529(QQ):Spring81-179
de Booy, J.T. - see Diderot, D.
Borchmeyer, D. Die Weimarer Klassik.
   H.R. Vaget, 221(GQ):Nov81-507
von Borcke, A. and G. Simon. Neue Wege
   der Sowjetunion-Forschung.
   R.E. Kanet, 550(RusR):Oct81-466

39

Bothwell, R., I. Drummond and J. English.
Canada Since 1945.*
    D. Smiley, 99:Nov81-33
Bots, H. and P. Leroy, with J. Wijnhoven -
see Rivet, A. and C. Sarrau
Botsch, R.E. We Shall Not Overcome.
    W.W. Braden, 583:Fall81-88
Böttcher, K., with H. Greiner-Mai, eds.
Schriftsteller der DDR.
    D. Herberg, 682(ZPSK):Band32Heft2-220
Bottomore, T.B. Karl Marx.
    J-M. Gabaude, 542:Oct-Dec81-478
Bottoms, D. Shooting Rats at the Bibb
County Dump.
    D.M. Cicotello, 502(PrS):Spring-
    Summer81-311
Botwinick, A. Ethics, Politics and Episte-
mology.
    A.C.B., 185:Jul82-775
Botz, G. Wien vom Anschluss zum Krieg.
    E. Wangermann, 575(SEER):Apr81-310
Bouacha, A.A. - see under Ali Bouacha, A.
Bouboulidis, P. and G. Bibliographia
Neoellēnikēs Philologias tōn Etōn 1974-
1976.
    J.E. Rexine, 399(MLJ):Autumn81-335
Boucé, P-G. - see Smollett, T.
du Bouchet, A. Rapides.
    M. Bishop, 207(FR):May82-923
Boudjedra, R. Les 1001 Années de la nos-
talgie.
    M. Mortimer, 207(FR):Mar81-617
Boudoin, E.M. and others. Reader's Choice.
    E. Hamp-Lyons, 608:Jun82-253
Boudon, R. The Crisis in Sociology.
    K.E. Soltan, 185:Jul82-765
Boudon, R. The Unintended Consequences of
Social Action.
    A. Giddens, 617(TLS):27Aug82-927
Boudot, P. La jouissance de Dieu ou le
roman courtois de Thérèse d'Avila.
    A. Reix, 542:Jul-Sep81-343
Boudot-Lamotte, A. Aḥmad Šawqī.
    F. Malti-Douglas, 318(JAOS):Apr/Jun80-
    149
Boué, A. William Carleton.
    R. Tracy, 445(NCF):Sep81-214
Bouffard, E.N. Studying Spanish and Spain
in Spain.
    J.R. Stamm, 238:May81-325
Bouillier, H. Portraits et Miroirs.
    J. Seznec, 208(FS):Jan81-108
Bouissac, P. La mesure des gestes.
    G.F. Meier, 682(ZPSK):Band32Heft2-223
Boulby, M. Karl Philipp Moritz.*
    A.W. Riley, 627(UTQ):Summer81-150
Boulez, P. and others. Alban Berg, Lulu.
    J. Le Rider, 98:Oct80-962
Boullata, I.J., ed and trans. Modern Arab
Poets.
    C. Wilcockson, 294:Vol 11-115
Boulter, C.G. and K.T. Luckner. Corpus
Vasorum Antiquorum, USA 17: The Toledo
Museum of Art, I.
    H.A.G. Brijder, 394:Vol34fasc1/2-199
Boulton, A. Reverón.
    Á. Hurtado, 37:Nov-Dec81-21
Boulton, J.T. - see Lawrence, D.H.
Boumelha, P. Thomas Hardy and Women.
    A. Leighton, 617(TLS):16Jul82-760
Bouquiaux, L. and others. Dictionnaire
Sango-Français.
    W.J. Samarin, 69:Vol50No2-233

Bourassa, A. Surréalisme et littérature
québécoise.
    C. Bayard, 102(CanL):Winter80-141
Bourcelot, H. Atlas linguistique et ethno-
graphique de la Champagne et de la Brie.
(Vol 3)
    J. Chaurand, 209(FM):Jul81-277
Bourdache, C. Les Années cinquante.
    A. Douglas, 207(FR):Oct81-172
Bourderon, R. and others. Le PCF.
    D. Johnson, 617(TLS):2Jul82-707
Bourdieu, P. La Distinction.*
    P. Vogt, 207(FR):Feb81-486
Bourel, D. - see Mendelssohn, M.
Bourgeade, P. Le Camp.
    P.L. Horn, 207(FR):Feb81-500
Bourgeade, P. Le Football, c'est la
guerre poursuivie par d'autres moyens.
    P-L. Rey, 450(NRF):Jun81-126
Bourget, J-L. Les humbles choses.
    A. Masson, 98:Aug-Sep81-875
Bourlier, K. Marcel Proust et l'architec-
ture.
    J. McClelland, 627(UTQ):Summer81-145
Bourne, K. Palmerston: The Early Years
1784-1841.
    N. Gash, 617(TLS):22Oct82-1152
    J. Grigg, 362:23Sep82-21
Bourniquel, C. Le Soleil sur la rade.
    P.A. Mankin, 207(FR):Dec80-360
Bournonville, A. My Theatre Life.
    F.J. Marker, 612(ThS):Nov81-245
Bousoño, C. Superrealismo poético y
simbolización.
    M. Durán, 240(HR):Summer81-370
Bousquet, F. Camus le Méditerranéen,
Camus l'Ancien.*
    J.F. Rigaud, 207(FR):Oct80-175
Bousquet, J. La Connaissance du Soir.
    G. Gouérou, 450(NRF):Oct81-131
Boussard, I. Vichy et la corporation pay-
sanne.
    C.W. Obuchowski, 207(FR):Feb81-488
Boutang, P. Apocalypse du désir.
    P. Legendre, 98:Jan80-63
Boutang, P. La Fontaine politique.
    G. Sartoris, 450(NRF):Dec81-123
Boutet, D. and A. Strubel. Littérature,
politique et société dans la France du
Moyen Age.
    G.J. Brault, 207(FR):Dec80-337
    C.T. Wood, 589:Oct81-854
Bouton, C. La Linguistique Appliquée.
    F. Gomes de Matos, 257(IRAL):May81-157
Bouttes, J-L. Le destructeur d'intensité.
    P. Bonitzer, 98:Aug-Sep81-870
Bové, P.A. Destructive Poetics.*
    C. Molesworth, 141:Winter81-98
Boveland, K., C.P. Burger and R. Steffen.
Der Antichrist und die Fünfzehn Zeichen
vor dem Jüngsten Gericht.
    R.K. Emmerson, 589:Jan81-91
Bovenschen, S. Die imaginierte Weiblich-
keit.
    J. Le Rider, 98:Oct80-962
Bovesse, J. Une visite au Musée des
Archives de l'Etat à Namur.
    P. Christopher, 14:Winter80-87
Bovio Marconi, J. La Grotta del Vecchi-
uzzo.
    R. Adam, 555:Vol54fasc2-389

Bozzolo, C. and E. Ornato. Pour une
Histoire du Livre Manuscrit au Moyen Age.
78(BC):Spring81-17
Bracco, V. Volcei.
M.H. Crawford, 313:Vol71-153
Brachin, P. La langue néerlandaise.*
R.E. Wood, 660(Word):Aug80-225
C. Zinsser, 72:Band217Heftl-95
Brackenbury, A. Dreams of Power.*
D. Davis, 362:7Jan82-22
Brackenbury, R. The Woman in the Tower.
L. Taylor, 617(TLS):15Oct82-1122
Bradbrook, M.C. Collected Papers. (Vol 1)
C. Martindale, 617(TLS):22Oct82-1158
Bradbrook, M.C. Collected Papers. (Vol 2)
V. Glendinning, 362:16Dec82-22
Bradbrook, M.C. Shakespeare.*
V.M. Carr, 179(ES):Oct81-484
Bradbrook, M.C. John Webster.*
C.R. Forker, 401(MLQ):Sep81-294
S.G. Putt, 175:Autumn81-291
L. Tennenhouse, 141:Spring81-181
J.C. Trewin, 157:1stQtr81-50
Bradbury, M. Saul Bellow.
P. Kemp, 362:22Jul82-20
C. Rawson, 617(TLS):3Sep82-941
Bradbury, M. and D. Palmer, eds. The Con-
temporary English Novel.*
M. Allott, 541(RES):May81-211
J.J. Riley, 395(MFS):Winter80/81-698
Bradbury, M. and H. Temperley, eds.
Introduction to American Studies.
Z. Leader, 617(TLS):19Feb82-178
Bradbury, N. Henry James: The Later
Novels.*
K. Flint, 175:Autumn81-302
P. Horne, 184(EIC):Apr81-149
A. Hynes, 148:Summer81-89
W. Veeder, 405(MP):Aug81-104
295(JML):Vol18No3/4-529
Bradby, D., L. James and B. Sharratt, eds.
Performance and Politics in Popular
Drama.*
C. Barker, 610:Spring81-154
M.R. Booth, 611(TN):Vol135No1-45
Braden, G. The Classics and English Ren-
aissance Poetry.*
D. Attridge, 402(MLR):Apr81-437
D. Crane, 161(DUJ):Dec80-109
K. Duncan-Jones, 447(N&Q):Oct80-427
M-M. Martinet, 189(EA):Jul-Sep81-336
Braden, S. Artists and People.
C. Crouch, 437:Spring81-189
Bradford, A.S. A Prosopography of Lacedae-
monians from the Death of Alexander the
Great, 323 B.C., to the Sack of Sparta
by Alaric, A.D. 396.*
R.S. Stroud, 122:Jul81-237
Bradford, C.B. - see Yeats, W.B.
Bradford, E. Hannibal.
B.H. Warmington, 617(TLS):29Jan82-117
Bradford, E. The Story of the Mary Rose.
D. Thomas, 362:14Oct82-29
Bradford, R. The Last Ditch.
P. Craig, 617(TLS):5Feb82-131
Brading, D.A., ed. Caudillo and Peasant
in the Mexican Revolution.
M.P. Costeloe, 86(BHS):Apr81-157
Bradley, A., ed. Contemporary Irish
Poetry.
F. ffolliott, 305(JIL):Jan81-95
J.W. Foster, 134(CP):Fal181-116
[continued]

[continuing]
R. Pybus, 565:Vol22No3-72
639(VQR):Summer81-95
Bradley, A. William Butler Yeats.*
R. Bonaccorso, 174(Éire):Winter81-131
N.C. Schmitt, 397(MD):Mar81-107
Bradley, B.L. Zu Rilkes "Malte Laurids
Brigge."
R. Hauptman, 395(MFS):Winter80/81-739
L.S. Pickle, 301(JEGP):Oct81-611
Bradley, D. Proto-Loloish.
G. Thurgood, 350:Dec82-951
Bradley, I. The English Middle Classes
Are Alive and Kicking.
V. Glendinning, 617(TLS):16Apr82-431
R. Hoggart, 362:11Feb82-20
Bradley, K.R. Suetonius' Life of Nero.*
P. Jal, 555:Vol54fasc1-197
G.V. Sumner, 487:Winter81-378
Bradley, R. and N. Swartz. Possible
Worlds.
T. Karmo, 63:Jun81-239
Bradley, S. and others - see Whitman, W.
Bradshaw, G. Kingdom of Summer.
S.D. Lavine, 385(MQR):Winter82-189
Bradshaw, P. 18th Century English Porce-
lain Figures 1745-1795.
B. Wedgwood, 617(TLS):7May82-512
Bradt, H. and G. Backpacking in Mexico
and Central America. Backpacking in
Venezuela, Colombia and Ecuador. Back-
packing and Trekking in Peru and Bolivia.
(3rd ed)
G. de Reparaz, 37:Mar81-46
Bradt, H. and J. Pilkington. Backpacking
in Chile and Argentina Plus the Falkland
Islands.
37:Mar81-47
Brady, F. and W.K. Wimsatt - see Johnson,
S.
Brady, J. The Unmaking of a Dancer.
J. Dunning, 441:1Aug82-9
Brady, K. The Short Stories of Thomas
Hardy.
J. Adlard, 617(TLS):22Oct82-1173
J. Bayley, 453(NYRB):7Oct82-9
Brady, P. Le bouc émissaire chez Emile
Zola.
B.L. Knapp, 446(NCFS):Spring-Summer82-
364
Brady, P. Marcel Proust.*
W.L. Hodson, 402(MLR):Jan81-199
Braegger, C. Das Visuelle und das Plas-
tische.
H.R. Klieneberger, 402(MLR):Jan81-249
R.E. Lorbe, 301(JEGP):Oct81-609
Braestrup, P. Big Story. (rev)
D.P. Chandler, 293(JASt):Nov80-77
Braga, G. Per una teoria della comunica-
zione verbale.
M. Danesi, 355(LSoc):Apr81-82
Bragg, M. Autumn Manoeuvres. Kingdom
Come.
P. Lewis, 565:Vol22No3-55
Brague, R. Le Restant.*
P. Louis, 555:Vol54fasc2-355
Braham, A. The Architecture of the French
Enlightenment.*
E.G. Grossman, 505:Jul81-143
D. Wiebenson, 54:Sep81-518
Braham, R.L. The Politics of Genocide.*
I. Deak, 453(NYRB):4Feb82-24

Brainerd, B. and others. Linguistique
expérimentale et appliquée au Canada/
Experimental and Applied Linguistics
in Canada.* (P.R. Léon, ed)
  G. Bourcier, 189(EA):Jan-Mar81-87
  A.W. Grundstrom, 207(FR):Feb81-481
  C. Sabourin, 209(FM):Apr81-183
Brambila, D. Diccionario rarámuri-castel-
lano.
  W. Bright, 350:Dec81-975
Bramly, S. Un Piège à lumière.
  D.M. Church, 207(FR):Oct80-188
Brams, S.J. Biblical Games.*
  N.R.M., 185:Jan82-397
Brams, S.J. The Presidential Election
Game.
  E.M.U., 185:Jan81-350
Branca, D.D. - see under Delcorno Branca,
D.
Branca, P. Silent Sisterhood.
  F. Ducrocq, 98:Feb-Mar81-138
Brancaforte, B. Guzmán de Alfarache.
  F.L. Trice, 238:Dec81-635
Brancaforte, B. and C.L., eds. La primera
traducción italiana del "Lazarillo de
Tormes" por Giulio Strozzi.*
  C. Stern, 545(RPh):Feb81-303
Branch, E.M. and R.H. Hirst, with H.E.
Smith - see Twain, M.
Branch, T. and E.M. Propper. Labyrinth.
  P. Taubman, 441:21Mar82-8
  442(NY):19Apr82-178
Brand, G. - see Wittgenstein, L.
Brand, M. Peace March.
  J. Schley, 434:Winter81-334
Branden, V. Mrs. Job.
  P. Klovan, 102(CanL):Autumn81-147
Brander, M. The Emigrant Scots.
  J. Hunter, 617(TLS):10Dec82-1373
Brandon, P., ed. The South Saxons.
  D.A. White, 589:Jul81-589
Brandt, G.W., ed. British Television
Drama.*
  N. Berry, 364:Jun81-83
Brandt, H. and N. Kakabadse, eds. Erzähl-
te Welt. (2nd ed)
  H-J. Sander, 654(WB):6/1981-181
Brandt, W. and others. The Comprehensive
Study of Music.
  J. Straus, 308:Fall81-334
Branfman, F. The Village of the Deep
Pond. (J.A. Hafner and J.M. Halpern,
eds) The Old Man. (J.M. Halpern and
J.A. Hafner, eds)
  C.J. Compton, 293(JASt):May81-645
Branford, J. A Dictionary of South
African English.*
  M. Görlach, 38:Band99Heft1/2-196
Branford, K.A. A Study of Jean-Jacques
Bernard's "Théâtre de l'inexprimé."
  D. Knowles, 208(FS):Jul81-360
Branigan, K. and M. Vickers. Hellas.
  P. MacKendrick, 124:Sep-Oct81-56
Brantôme. Les Dames galantes. (P. Pia,
ed)
  J.G. Beaudry, 207(FR):Apr82-672
"Brassaï: The Artists of My Life." (R.
Miller, trans)
  P-L. Adams, 61:Dec82-107
  A. Grundberg, 441:5Dec82-58
Braude, B. and B. Coste. Engagements.
  H. Peyre, 207(FR):Oct81-173

Braudel, F. On History.
  W.H.D., 185:Apr82-584
  639(VQR):Spring81-49
Braudel, F. The Structures of Everyday
Life.* (Vol 1)
  R. Holmes, 231:May82-66
  P. Robinson, 441:16May82-9
Braudy, S. Who Killed Sal Mineo?
  N. Johnson, 441:30May82-9
Brault, G.J. - see "The Song of Roland"
Braun, A. Romanian Foreign Policy since
1965.
  H. Hanak, 575(SEER):Jul81-470
Braun, E. The Theatre of Meyerhold.*
  A.V. Knowles, 402(MLR):Jul81-766
  F. Williams, 575(SEER):Jan81-97
Braun, E. and H. Radermacher, eds. Wissen-
schaftstheoretisches Lexikon.
  U. Charpa, 679:Band11Heft1-196
Braun, J. and G. Conviva Ludibundus.
  W. Förster, 654(WB):12/1981-151
Braun, L. Histoire de l'histoire de la
philosophie.
  K. Bärthlein, 53(AGP):Band63Heft2-180
Braun, L., ed and trans. Scenae Suppositi-
ciae oder Der falsche Plautus.
  H.D. Jocelyn, 123:Vol31No2-196
Braun, R. and J. Richer, eds. L'empereur
Julien.* (Vol 1)
  J. Bompaire, 555:Vol54fasc2-331
Braun, S.D. and S. Lainoff. Transatlantic
Mirrors.*
  H.U. York, 446(NCFS):Spring-Summer81-
  287
Braun, T. Disraeli the Novelist.*
  445(NCF):Dec81-381
Brauner, S. Lehrbuch des Bambara.
  G.F. Meier, 682(ZPSK):Band32Heft2-223
Braunfels, W. Die Kunst im Heiligen Römis-
chen Reich Deutscher Nation. (Vol 1)
  H. Boockmann, 683:Band43Heft2-219
Braunfels, W. Die Kunst im Heiligen Römis-
chen Reich Deutscher Nation. (Vol 2)
  H. Boockmann, 683:Band43Heft4-414
Brautigan, R. The Hawkline Monster.
  L.L. Willis, 145(Crit):Vol23No2-37
Brautigan, R. So the Wind Won't Blow It
All Away.
  E. Ottenberg, 441:7Nov82-13
  442(NY):13Sep82-172
Bray, A. Homosexuality in Renaissance
England.
  I. Salusinszky, 617(TLS):29Oct82-1187
de Bray, R.G.A. Guide to the Slavonic
Languages. (3rd ed) (Vols 1 and 2)
  R.D. Fulk, 350:Dec81-971
de Bray, R.G.A. Guide to the Slavonic
Languages. (3rd ed) (Vol 3)
  R.D. Fulk, 350:Dec81-971
  P.J. Mayo, 575(SEER):Oct81-589
Braynard, F.O. The Big Ship. (R.H. Bur-
gess, ed)
  R. Goold-Adams, 324:Jun82-439
Brearley, M. Phoenix from the Ashes.
  J.R. Pole, 362:22Jul82-23
  T.D. Smith, 617(TLS):27Aug82-929
Breatnach, P.A. Die Regensburger Schotten-
legende.
  D.A. Binchy, 112:Vol 14-155
Breazeale, D. - see Nietzsche, F.
Brecher, C. and R.D. Horton, eds. Setting
Municipal Priorities, 1982.
  N. Glazer, 441:31Jan82-7

43

Brecht, B. Briefe. (G. Glaeser, ed)
    J. Willett, 617(TLS):19Feb82-189
Brecht, B. The Life of Galileo. (H. Brenton, trans)
    D. Devlin, 157:Oct80-72
Brecht, B. Poems 1913-1956.* (J. Willett and R. Manheim, with E. Fried, eds)
    C. Davies, 148:Winter81-85
Breckenridge, M. Lap Quilting.
    M. Cowan, 614:Fall81-17
Brednich, R.W. Mennonite Folklife and Folklore.
    R. Wehse, 196:Band21Heft3/4-296
Bredsdorff, E. Kjeld Abells billedkunst.
    H.G. Carlson, 563(SS):Winter81-107
    F.J. Marker, 562(Scan):May81-106
Brée, G. Narcissus Absconditus.
    G. Idt, 535(RHL):May-Jun81-483
    205(FMLS):Jan80-81
Breen, T.H. Puritans and Adventurers.*
    J. Butler, 432(NEQ):Jun81-272
    C.M. Jedrey, 165(EAL):Winter81/82-287
Breen, T.H. and S. Innes. "Myne Owne Ground."*
    L.S. Walsh, 656(WMQ):Apr81-315
de Breffny, B. and B. O'Riordain. Castles of Ireland.
    D. Guinness, 576:May81-154
Bregenhøj, C. Helligtrekongersløb på Agersø.
    H.R.E. Davidson, 203:Vol92No1-119
Breitinger, E., ed. Black Literature.*
    M.F., 189(EA):Jul-Sep81-365
Brejon de Lavergnée, A., comp. Dijon, musée Magnin: Catalogue des tableaux et dessins italiens (XVe — XIXe siècles).
    J.T. Spike, 90:Jun81-365
Brekle, H.E. and D. Kastovsky, eds. Perspektiven der Wortbildungsforschung.
    H. Schendl, 38:Band99Heft3/4-435
von Bremen, T. Lord Byron als Erfolgsautor.
    R.P. Lessenich, 72:Band217Heft2-427
Brenan, G. Thoughts in a Dry Season.
    205(FMLS):Jan80-81
Brend, R.M. and E. Lansing, eds. Studies in Tone and Intonation.*
    G.F. Meier, 682(ZPSK):Band33Heft5-627
Brendel, O.J. Prolegomena to the Study of Roman Art.*
    M.A.R. Colledge, 123:Vol31No1-99
Brendon, P. Eminent Edwardians.
    R. Binion, 651(WHR):Spring81-70
    J.D. Cushman, 569(SR):Spring81-xlvi
    H.L. Malchow, 637(VS):Spring81-373
Brendon, P. The Life and Death of the Press Barons.
    A. Watkins, 362:25Nov82-24
Brenman-Gibson, M. Clifford Odets.*
    R. Brustein, 453(NYRB):4Feb82-10
Brennan, R. The Sea of Fire.
    T. Eagleton, 565:Vol22No2-73
Brenner, T., with B. Nagler. Only the Ring Was Square.
    P. Andrews, 441:10Jan82-6
Brent, J. A Few Days in Weasel Creek.
    A. Horton, 435:Winter81-110
Brent, P. Charles Darwin.
    R.W. Clark, 441:7Feb82-28

Brentano, C. Sämtliche Werke und Briefe.* (Vols 6-8 and Vol 9, Pts 1-3) (H. Rölleke, ed)
    J.F. Fetzer, 221(GQ):Mar81-224
    H. Henel, 406:Winter81-465
Brentano, F. The Theory of Categories.
    A. Reix, 542:Oct-Dec81-480
Brentjes, B. Mittelasien — Kunst des Islam.
    J.W. Allan, 463:Winter81/82-432
Brenton, H. Magnificence. Plays for the Poor Theatre.
    D. Devlin, 157:1stQtr81-54
Brenton, H. The Romans in Britain.
    D. Devlin, 157:2ndQtr81-55
    R.J., 214:Vol 10No37-128
    M. Martin, 148:Winter81-49
Brereton, G. French Comic Drama from the Sixteenth to the Eighteenth Century.*
    M. Gutwirth, 612(ThS):May81-107
Breslin, J. Forsaking All Others.
    E. Hunter, 441:20Jun82-10
Bresson, R. Notes sur le cinématographe.
    D. Knowles, 208(FS):Oct81-494
Breton, A. What is Surrealism?* (F. Rosemont, ed and trans)
    R. Cardinal, 529(QQ):Spring81-19
Bretone, M. Diritto e pensiero giuridico romano.
    P. Stein, 313:Vol71-226
Brett, H. and B. Promises to Keep.
    N. Callendar, 441:10Jan82-29
Brett, R.L., ed. Andrew Marvell.*
    G.D. Lord, 677(YES):Vol 11-258
    M-M. Martinet, 189(EA):Oct-Dec81-468
    J.L. Selzer, 568(SCN):Winter81-88
Brett, S. Murder Unprompted.
    T.J. Binyon, 617(TLS):12Mar82-276
    N. Callendar, 441:12Dec82-37
Brett, S. Situation Tragedy.*
    N. Callendar, 441:24Jan82-34
Brettell, R. and C. Lloyd. A Catalogue of the Drawings by Camille Pissarro in the Ashmolean Museum, Oxford.*
    K. Adler, 208(FS):Jul81-351
    R. Hobbs, 59:Mar81-121
    D. Thistlewood, 89(BJA):Autumn81-378
Bretz, M.L. Concha Espina.
    L.B. Barr, 345(KRQ):Vol28No4-427
Bretz, M.L. La evolución novelística de Pío Baroja.
    P.A. Bly, 268(IFR):Winter82-69
Breuilly, J. Nationalism and the State.
    S.J. Woolf, 617(TLS):19Nov82-1281
Breunig, L.C. and others. Forme et Fond. (2nd ed)
    J-M. Salien, 207(FR):Apr81-772
Brewer, A. Marxist Theories of Imperialism.
    L.E.L., 185:Jul82-790
Brewer, A.M., ed. Abbreviations, Acronyms, Ciphers and Signs.
    K.B. Harder, 424:Dec81-314
Brewer, A.M., ed. Dictionaries, Encyclopedias, and Other Word-Related Books. (2nd ed)
    K.B. Harder, 424:Mar80-94
Brewer, D., ed. Chaucer: The Critical Heritage.* (Vols 1 and 2)
    D. Pearsall, 402(MLR):Jan81-158
Brewer, D. Symbolic Stories.*
    W.R.J.B., 148:Spring82-92

[continued]

[continuing]
P.V. Neuss, 155:Summer81-108
E. Robertson, 175:Summer81-170
Brewer, J. and J. Styles, eds. An Ungovernable People.
H.T. Dickinson, 566:Autumn81-50
M. Rediker, 656(WMQ):Jan81-132
Brewster, E. It's Easy to Fall on the Ice.
J.R. Struthers, 296(JCF):No31/32-244
Brice, W.C., ed. An Historical Atlas of Islam.
R. Irwin, 617(TLS):10Sep82-960
Bricke, J. Hume's Philosophy of Mind.
A. Baier, 185:Jan82-346
N.C., 543:Mar81-599
Briçonnet, G. and M. d'Angoulême. Correspondance (1521-1524), II. (C. Martineau and M. Veissière, with H. Heller, eds)
J-C. Margolin, 535(RHL):Jul-Oct81-748
Bridge, F.R. and R. Bullen. The Great Powers and the European States System, 1815-1914.*
D. Kirby, 575(SEER):Jul81-451
Bridgman, J.M. The Revolt of the Hereros.
S. Uys, 617(TLS):5Mar82-261
Bridgwater, P. Gissing and Germany.
P. Keating, 617(TLS):31Dec82-1447
Bridgwater, P. Kafka and Nietzsche.
B. Goldstein, 406:Spring81-67
Brierley, D. Big Bear, Little Bear.*
H. Saal, 441.24Jan82-12
Briggs, A. The Power of Steam.
J. Morgan, 617(TLS):21May82-560
Briggs, A.D.P. Vladimir Mayakovsky.*
E.J. Brown, 104(CASS):Winter81 565
J. Graffy, 575(SEER):Jan81-86
Briggs, C.L. The Wood Carvers of Cordova, New Mexico.
G.F. Giffords, 50(ArQ):Autumn81-280
L. Milazzo, 584(SWR):Spring81-v
Briggs, D. The Partners.
D.J. Enright, 617(TLS):2Jul82-725
J. Mellors, 362:5Aug82-22
Briggs, J. Night Visitors.
G.R. Thompson, 395(MFS):Winter80/81-714
Briggs, K. Abbey Lubbers, Banshees and Boggarts.
J. Simpson, 203:Vol91No1-123
Briggs, K.M. Nine Lives.
A.C. Percival, 203:Vol92No2-251
Briggs, W.W., Jr. Narrative and Simile from the "Georgics" in the "Aeneid."
J. Griffin, 123:Vol31No1-23
Brigham, J.A. - see Durrell, L.
Bright, D.F. "Haec mihi fingebam."*
G.K. Galinsky, 122:Jan81-72
Bright-Holmes, J. - see Muggeridge, M.
Brillant, J. Le Soleil, se cherche tout l'été.
R. Hodgson, 102(CanL):Spring81-96
Brink, A. A Chain of Voices.
J. Kramer, 453(NYRB):2Dec82-8
J. Moynahan, 441:13Jun82-1
R. Owen, 617(TLS):14May82-536
J. Simpson, 362:13May82-26
442(NY):19Jul82-99
Brinkhaus, H. Die Altindischen Mischkastensysteme.
S. Pollock, 318(JAOS):Jul/Sep80-322
Brinkley, A. Voices of Protest.
R. Sherrill, 441:11Jul82-13
C.V. Woodward, 453(NYRB):23Sep82-3

Brinkmann, R., ed. Romantik in Deutschland.
M. Adams, 67:Nov81-266
W. Heise, 654(WB):7/1981-165
Brinkschulte, B. Formen und Funktionen wirtschaftlicher Kooperation in traditionalen Gesellschaften Westafrikas.
A. Wirz, 69:Vol50No2-228
Brinnin, J.M. Sextet.*
R. Fuller, 362:11Feb82-21
A. Hollinghurst, 617(TLS):9Apr82-415
385(MQR):Winter82-219
Briscoe, J. A Commentary on Livy. (Bks 34-37)
P. Green, 617(TLS):26Feb82-206
Brisebarre, J. Li Restor du paon. (E. Donkin, ed)
P.S. Noble, 382(MAE):1981/1-194
205(FMLS):Oct80-372
Brisman, L. Romantic Origins.*
C. Bond, 529(QQ):Winter81-777
S. Peterfreund, 494:Autumn80-218
S.M. Tave, 677(YES):Vol 11-290
Brissenden, A. Shakespeare and the Dance.
J. Kavanagh, 617(TLS):23Apr82-469
Brissenden, R.F. The Whale in Darkness.*
F. Adcock, 617(TLS):29Jan82-114
Britain, I. Fabianism and Culture.
K.O. Morgan, 617(TLS):23Jul82-783
"British Music Yearbook 1981." (M. Barton, ed)
N. Goodwin, 415:Mar81-178
Brittain, V. Account Rendered. Born 1925.
P. Craig, 617(TLS):12Nov82-1243
Brittan, A. The Privatised World.
J. Posner, 488:Mar81-117
Brittan, G.G., Jr. Kant's Theory of Science.*
D. Knight, 161(DUJ):Dec80-131
Britton, J. and J. Gilmour. The Weakest Link.
I.D. Chapman, 298:Summer81-119
Brize, P. Die Geryoneis des Stesichoros und die frühe griechische Kunst.
D.C. Kurtz, 123:Vol131No2-260
Brizio, A.M., M.V. Brugnoli and A. Chastel. Leonardo the Artist.
M. Kemp, 617(TLS):16Apr82-443
Broad, C.D. Kant.* (C. Lewy, ed)
A.L. Loades, 161(DUJ):Jun81-272
H. Robinson, 342:Band71Heft2-270
M-B. Zeldin, 319:Apr81-260
Broadbent, G., R. Bunt and C. Jencks. Signs, Symbols and Architecture.
G. Necipoğlu, 576:Oct81-259
Broccia, G. "Enchiridion."
J. Schneider, 555:Vol54fasc2-365
Broccia, G. La questione omerica.
F.M. Combellack, 122:Jul81-228
F. Vian, 555:Vol54fasc1-153
Broch, H. La mort de Virgile.
A. Serre, 450(NRF):Jan81-154
Brochu, A. and G. Marcotte. La Littérature et le reste (livre de lettres).
J. Michon, 627(UTQ):Summer81-174
Brock, M. and E. - see Asquith, H.H.
Brock, R. Ceux du canal.
R.A. Champagne, 207(FR):Apr81-761
Brock, W.R. Scotus Americanus.
G. Donaldson, 617(TLS):23Jul82-806

Brockhaus, H.A. and K. Niemann, eds.
Musikgeschichte der Deutschen Demokra-
tischen Republik 1945-1976.
    A. Cross, 415:Jul81-480
"Brockhaus Wahrig Deutsches Wörterbuch."
(Vol 3) (G. Wahrig, H. Krämer and H.
Zimmermann, eds)
    G.P. Butler, 617(TLS):3Sep82-952
Brockmeier, P., R. Desné and J. Voss, eds.
Voltaire und Deutschland.*
    P.H. Meyer, 173(ECS):Winter80/81-213
Brockmeyer, N. Antike Sklaverei.
    B.D. Shaw, 487:Fall81-272
Brod, P. Die Antizionismus — und Israel-
politik der UdSSR.
    A. Krammer, 550(RusR):Jul81-346
Brod, R.I., ed. Language Study for the
1980's.
    R.V. Teschner, 238:May81-322
Brode, H. Günter Grass.
    I.M. Goessl, 221(GQ):May81-377
Broder, D.S. Changing of the Guard.
    L. Sabato, 639(VQR):Winter81-147
Broderick, J. The Trial of Father
Dillingham.
    M.G. McCulloch, 617(TLS):19Feb82-198
Brodeur, P. The Stunt Man.
    A.M. Saltzman, 145(Crit):Vol22No1-32
Brodsky, J. A Part of Speech.*
    J. Bayley, 472:Spring/Summer81-83
    J. Saunders, 565:Vol22No3-61
    639(VQR):Winter81-27
Brodsly, D. L.A. Freeway.
    R. Banham, 617(TLS):23Apr82-465
    J.Q. Wilson, 441:18Apr82-11
Brody, B.A. Identity and Essence.*
    J.B., 543:Jun81-782
    G. Forbes, 479(PhQ):Oct81-368
Brody, B.A. and H.T. Engelhardt, Jr., eds.
Mental Illness.
    J.C. Moskop, 185:Jan82-381
Brody, H. Maps and Dreams.
    M. Abley, 617(TLS):19Mar82-308
    P-L. Adams, 61:Apr82-110
    J.E. Chamberlin, 99:Dec81/Jan82-33
Brody, H. Placebos and the Philosophy of
Medicine.
    J.C.M., 185:Apr82-594
Brody, J. Du style à la pensé.
    E.C. Knox, 207(FR):May82-905
Broe, M.L. Protean Poetic.
    J.B. Rollins, 27(AL):Nov81-553
    A. Thwaite, 651(WHR):Autumn81-283
Broehl, W.G., Jr. The Village Entrepre-
neur.
    R.J. Herring, 293(JASt):Feb81-403
Brogyanyi, B., ed. Studies in Diachronic,
Synchronic, and Typological Linguistics.
    P. Baldi, 215(GL):Spring81-47
    C. Justus, 350:Sep82-681
Broide, E. Chekhov — myslitel'-khudozhnik.
    R. Cockrell, 402(MLR):Oct81-1005
    S. Karlinsky, 550(RusR):Oct81-473
Brommer, F. The Sculptures of the Parthe-
non.* (German title: Die Parthenon-
Skulpturen.)
    D. Williams, 303(JoHS):Vol 101-212
Brøndsted, M. Bibliografisk vejledning
til studiet af nordisk litteratur og
sprog.
    T. Geddes, 562(Scan):Nov81-240
Broneer, O. Terracotta Lamps.
    J.J.V.M. Derksen, 394:Vol34fasc1/2-205

Bronne, C. Beloeil et la Maison de Ligne.
    E. de la Rochefoucauld, 161(DUJ):Dec80-
    84
Brontë, A. The Poems of Anne Brontë.*
(E. Chitham, ed)
    J. Dusinberre, 447(N&Q):Aug80-379
Brontë, C. Shirley. (H. Rosengarten and
M. Smith, eds)
    C. Alexander, 67:Nov81-249
    S. Monod, 445(NCF):Sep80-200
    P. Thomson, 541(RES):Nov81-470
Brontë, C. Two Tales by Charlotte Brontë.
(W. Holtz, ed)
    P. Thomson, 541(RES):Aug81-344
Brontë, C. Villette. (M. Lilly, ed)
    P. Thomson, 541(RES):Nov81-470
Brook-Shepherd, G. November 1918.
    442(NY):17May82-141
Brooke, J. The Orchid Trilogy.*
    A. Seymour, 364:Dec81/Jan82-116
Brooke, J. and M. Sorensen - see Gladstone,
W.E.
Brooke, N. Horrid Laughter in Jacobean
Tragedy.*
    S.G. Putt, 175:Autumn81-291
Brookner, A. Jacques-Louis David.*
    W. Allan, 324:Jan82-108
    F. Haskell, 90:Dec81-749
    M. Jordan, 135:Sep81-8
Brookner, A. Providence.
    J. Mellors, 362:3Jun82-22
    G. Strawson, 617(TLS):28May82-579
Brookner, A. A Start in Life.*
    C. Hawtree, 364:Oct81-99
Brooks, C. William Faulkner.*
    R. Gray, 677(YES):Vol 11-358
    E. McKinsey, 587(SAF):Spring81-123
Brooks, H.F. - see Shakespeare, W.
Brooks, J. Jacob Hamblin.
    C.S. Peterson, 649(WAL):Spring81-59
Brooks, L. Faith Never Lost.
    D. Crane, 617(TLS):5Nov82-1227
Brooks, L. Lulu in Hollywood.
    J. Lahr, 441:30May82-7
    S. Laschever, 453(NYRB):21Oct82-27
    J. Updike, 442(NY):16Aug82-84
Brooks, L. Portrait d'une anti-star.
    J. Le Rider, 98:Oct80-962
Brooks, M. and C. Knight. A Complete
Guide to British Butterflies.
    J. Mellanby, 617(TLS):2Jul82-727
Brooks, P. Speaking for Nature.*
    R.W. Bradford, 27(AL):Nov81-560
    J. Elder, 434:Autumn81-152
Brooks, P. and J. Halpern, eds. Genet: A
Collection of Critical Essays.*
    R. Sandarg, 207(FR):Mar81-606
Brooks-Davies, D. Spenser's "Faerie
Queene."*
    T.P. Roche, 402(MLR):Jul81-660
Broome, P. Henri Michaux.*
    M. Bowie, 402(MLR):Apr81-480
Broome, P. - see Michaux, H.
Brossard, N. Le Centre Blanc.
    G.V. Downes, 102(CanL):Winter80-105
Brosseau, M. Gothic Revival in Canadian
Architecture.
    H. Kalman, 576:Oct81-253
Brostrøm, T. and M. Winge, eds. Danske
digtere i det 20. århundrede. (Vol 1)
    F. Hugus, 563(SS):Autumn81-486
Broszat, M. The Hitler State.
    N. Stone, 453(NYRB):13May82-24

Broughton, G. and others. Teaching English as a Foreign Language.
F.W. Gester, 38:Band99Heft1/2-214
Broughton, G. and others. Teaching English as a Foreign Language.* (2nd ed)
J.D. Bowen, 399(MLJ):Winter81-421
Broughton, P.R., ed. The Art of Walker Percy.*
W.J. Stuckey, 395(MFS):Winter80/81-662
J.P. Telotte, 577(SHR):Spring81-174
Broughton, T.A. Far From Home.
S.M. Gilbert, 491:Oct81-35
Brouillet, G. La passion de l'égalité.
L. Marcil-Lacoste, 154:Mar81-145
Broussard, J.H. The Southern Federalists, 1800-1816.*
R.E. Ellis, 656(WMQ):Apr81-322
Brouwer, D. and others. Vrouwentaal en mannepraat.
J. Williams, 355(LSoc):Apr81-122
Broven, J. Rhythm and Blues in New Orleans.
S.J. Bronner, 292(JAF):Jan-Mar81-115
Brow, J. Vedda Villages of Anuradhapura.
E.R. Leach, 293(JASt):May81-622
Brower, K. Micronesia.
P-L. Adams, 61:Sep82-95
Brown, A. By Green Mountain.
T. Whalen, 628(UWR):Spring-Summer82-96
Brown, A. Bartolomeo Scala, 1430-1497.*
A. Molho, 551(RenQ):Autumn80-420
Brown, A. and others, eds. The Cambridge Encyclopedia of Russia and the Soviet Union.
P. Frank, 617(TLS):9Jul82-747
Brown, A.C. Ancient Italy Before the Romans.
M.H. Crawford, 313:Vol71-153
Brown, A.C. and C.B. Macdonald - see under Cave Brown, A. and C.B. Macdonald
Brown, A.P. - see d'Ordonez, C.
Brown, B. Mountain in the Clouds.
F. Randall, 441:10Oct82-16
Brown, B. Victims and Traders.
C. Dunsford, 368:Sep81-364
Brown, B.W. and J.M. Rose. Black Roots in Southeastern Connecticut, 1650-1900.
K.B. Harder, 424:Sep80-218
K.B. Harder, 424:Mar81-93
Brown, C. Carel Fabritius.*
J. Ferguson, 324:May82-366
Brown, C. A Promising Career.
F. Tuohy, 617(TLS):13Aug82-888
Brown, C. and L. Cunliffe. The Book of Royal Lists.
B. Masters, 617(TLS):24Dec82-1429
Brown, C.B. Arthur Mervyn.* (S.J. Krause and others, eds)
H. Parker, 445(NCF):Sep81-196
Brown, D. Creek Mary's Blood.
P. Pavich, 649(WAL):Spring81-72
Brown, D. Walter Scott and the Historical Imagination.*
R. Fadem, 478:Fall81-241
R.C. Gordon, 445(NCF):Jun80-103
F.R. Hart, 191(ELN):Dec80-146
L. Hartveit, 571(ScLJ):Summer80-99
H.L. Hennedy, 594:Winter81-459
D.A. Low, 541(RES):May81-231
P.H. Sosnoski, 125:Winter81-228
G.A.M. Wood, 447(N&Q):Oct80-455

Brown, D. Soviet Russian Literature Since Stalin.*
M. Friedberg, 131(CL):Winter81-111
Brown, D. Tchaikovsky. (Vol 2: The Crisis Years, 1874-1878.)
J. Warrack, 617(TLS):24Dec82-1412
Brown, D.S. A World of Books.
G. Guntermann, 608:Mar82-95
Brown, E.K. and J.E. Miller. Syntax.
A. Hochster, 350:Dec81-966
Brown, F. Theater and Revolution.*
A.J. Bingham, 577(SHR):Summer81-271
L. Brown, 612(ThS):May81-113
Brown, F.E. Cosa.*
M.H. Crawford, 313:Vol71-153
Brown, F.M. The Diary of Ford Madox Brown.* (V. Surtees, ed)
R. Jefferies, 324:Jun82-437
Brown, G. Sensational Silk.
P. Bach, 614:Fall82-20
Brown, G., K.L. Currie and J. Kenworthy. Questions of Intonation.
D.R. Ladd, 350:Mar82-204
Brown, G. and K. Dillon. Sew a Beautiful Wedding.
P. Bach, 614:Summer82-18
Brown, G.M. - see under Mackay Brown, G.
Brown, H. Hamish's Groats End Walk.
J. Hunter, 617(TLS):8Jan82-36
Brown, H.D. Principles of Language Learning and Teaching.*
A.S. Horning, 399(MLJ):Winter81-417
T.D. Terrell, 350:Sep81-781
Brown, J. Feminist Drama.
R. Curb, 397(MD):Mar81-102
Brown, J. Gardens of a Golden Afternoon.
J. Buxton, 617(TLS):26Nov82-1321
Brown, J. and J.H. Elliott. A Palace for a King.*
J. Connors, 576:Oct81-244
A. Delaforce, 59:Jun81-234
H.G. Koenigsberger, 39:Oct81-273
P. Reuterswärd, 341:Vol50No3-153
Brown, J.C. In the Shadow of Florence.
J.K. Hyde, 617(TLS):26Nov82-1319
Brown, J.M. Dickens: Novelist in the Market-Place.
S. Weintraub, 617(TLS):9Jul82-746
Brown, J.P. Jane Austen's Novels.*
J. McMaster, 191(ELN):Jun81-304
Brown, J.R. Discovering Shakespeare.
J. Hankey, 617(TLS):8Jan82-33
Brown, J.W. Heriberto Frías.
P.R. Beardsell, 86(BHS):Apr81-162
Brown, L. A Catalogue of British Historical Medals 1760-1960.* (Vol 1)
J.K.D. Cooper, 135:Jun81-88
Brown, L. English Dramatic Form, 1660-1760.
E. Burns, 617(TLS):15Jan82-57
R.D. Hume, 401(MLQ):Sep81-297
Brown, M. The Shape of German Romanticism.*
N. Fruman, 599:Winter81-35
E. Glass, 221(GQ):Jan81-97
P.M. Lützeler, 301(JEGP):Jan81-94
W.G. Regier, 400(MLN):Apr81-676
Brown, M. and N. Madge. Despite the Welfare State.
R. Klein, 617(TLS):17Dec82-1401
Brown, M.E. Double Lyric.*
M. Kirkham, 569(SR):Summer81-474

Bruegmann, R., S. Chappell and J. Zukowsky. The Plan of Chicago: 1909-1979.
  A.L. Van Zanten, 576:Oct81-255
Brugger, B., ed. China Since the "Gang of Four."*
  H.S. Klein, 293(JASt):Aug81-751
Brugière, B. L'univers imaginaire de Robert Browning.
  N. Fruman, 189(EA):Jul-Sep81-350
  J-J. Mayoux, 98:Feb-Mar81-199
Brugnoli, G. and R. Scarcia - see Dante Alighieri
Brühl, C. Urkunden und Kanzlei König Rogers II. von Sizilien.
  J.M. Powell, 589:Apr81-358
Bruhns, H. Caesar und die römische Oberschicht in den Jahren 49-44 v. Chr.*
  D.C.A. Shotter, 313:Vol71-189
Brumbaugh, J. and J. Mowat. His and Her Tailoring.
  P. Bach, 614:Spring81-19
Bruneau, J. - see Flaubert, G.
Brunel-Roche, A. La haine entre les dents.
  M. Recurt, 102(CanL):Spring80-115
Brunet, É. Index-Concordance d'"Émile ou de l'Éducation."
  C. Muller, 209(FM):Jul81-268
Brunetti, G. Nine Symphonies. (N. Jenkins, ed)
  P. Weiss, 414(MusQ):Apr81-282
Brunhölzl, F. Geschichte der lateinischen Literatur des Mittelalters.
  W. Berschin, 684(ZDA):Band109Heft4-139
Brunkhorst, M. Tradition und Transformation.
  M. Mueller, 678(YCGL):No29-52
Brunner, A. Kant und die Wirklichkeit des Geistigen.
  N. Fischer, 342:Band71Heft2-272
Brunner, H. and J. Rettelbach, eds. Die Töne der Meistersinger.
  G.F. Jones, 221(GQ):May81-339
  E. Schumann, 684(ZDA):Band110Heft4-164
Brunner-Lachaux, H. Somaśambhupaddhati. (Pts 1-3)
  J.W. de Jong, 259(IIJ):Apr81-159
Brunner-Traut, E., comp. Altägyptische Märchen. (4th ed)
  H-J. Uther, 196:Band21Heft1/2-102
Brunot, F. Histoire de la langue français des origines à nos jours. (Vol 11, Pt 2)
  G. Von Proschwitz, 209(FM):Apr81-161
Brunskill, R.W. Traditional Farm Buildings of Britain.
  J.M. Robinson, 617(TLS):10Dec82-1379
Brunvand, J.H., ed. Readings in American Folklore.*
  R.L. Baker, 650(WF):Jul81-270
Brunvand, J.H. The Vanishing Hitchhiker.
  M. Abley, 617(TLS):13Aug82-873
Bruschi, A. Bramante.
  M.N. Rosenfeld, 551(RenQ):Winter80-763
Bruss, E. Autobiographical Acts.
  G.W. Allen, 219(GaR):Summer81-411
Bruss, P. Conrad's Early Sea Fiction.
  K. Cushman, 573(SSF):Fall81-469
  R. Davis, 395(MFS):Summer80-299
  H. Hawkins, 136:Vol 13No2-151
  S. Raval, 594:Winter81-439
  295(JML):Vol8No3/4-470
Brustein, R. Making Scenes.*
  G. Houston, 108:Fall81-117

Bruun, P. and others. Studies in the Romanisation of Etruria.
  M.H. Crawford, 313:Vol71-153
  W.V. Harris, 122:Jan81-67
van den Bruwaene, M. - see Cicero
Bruyere, C. Walls.
  J. Wasserman, 102(CanL):Autumn80-88
de Bruyn, L. Woman and The Devil in Sixteenth-Century Literature.*
  G. Bourquin, 189(EA):Apr-Jun81-214
  J. Couchman, 539:Aug82-210
Bryan, C.D.B. The National Air and Space Museum.
  E.C. Ezell, 658:Spring81-123
Bryant, A. Spirit of England.
  J. Ridley, 617(TLS):31Dec82-1436
Bryant, E. Pennell's New York Etchings.
  J.V. Turano, 16:Summer81-86
Bryant, K.E. Poems to the Child-God.
  J.S. Hawley, 318(JAOS):Apr/Jun80-160
  F.W. Pritchett, 314:Summer-Fall81-234
Bryant, M. Recall the Poppies.
  R.L. Barth, 598(SoR):Spring82-458
Bryant, N. - see "The High Book of the Grail"
Bryer, B.J. - see Trollope, A.
Bryer, J.R., ed. F. Scott Fitzgerald: The Critical Reception.
  J. Ellis, 577(SHR):Spring81-173
Brym, R.J. Intellectuals and Politics.
  A.L., 185:Jan82-393
Brynner, R. The Ballad of Habit and Accident.
  639(VQR):Summer81-100
Bryusov, V. The Diary of Valery Bryusov, 1893-1905. (J.D. Grossman, ed and trans)
  M. Ehre, 405(MP):Feb82-331
  J.M. King, 574(SEEJ):Fall81-116
Bubner, R. Modern German Philosophy.
  E. Förster, 617(TLS):19Mar82-326
Buchan, J. The Best Short Stories of John Buchan. (Vol 2) (D. Daniell, ed)
  J. Grigg, 362:3Jun82-21
  M. Trend, 617(TLS):9Jul82-751
Buchan, J. The Dancing Floor. The Courts of the Morning.
  T.J.B., 617(TLS):29Oct82-1197
Buchan, W. John Buchan.
  D. Daniell, 617(TLS):9Jul82-751
  J. Grigg, 362:3Jun82-21
Buchanan, G. Possible Being.*
  J. Cotton, 493:Sep81-74
Buchanan, K., C.P. Fitz Gerald and C.A. Ronan. China.
  J. Spence, 453(NYRB):1Apr82-45
Büchel, W. Die Macht des Fortschritts.
  H-J. Braun, 679:Band12Heft2-401
Bucher, F. Architector. (Vol 1)
  C.F. Barnes, Jr., 589:Jul81-595
  E. Fernie, 90:Jan81-47
  P. Kidson, 576:Dec81-329
Buchholz, P. Vorzeitkunde.*
  T.M. Andersson, 301(JEGP):Apr81-291
  P.M. Sørensen, 196:Band22Heft3/4-325
Buchloh, B.H.D. - see Andre, C. and H. Frampton
Büchner, K., ed. Latein und Europa.
  E. Kessler, 52:Band15Heft1-69
Büchner, K. Studien zur römischen Literatur. (Vol 9)
  G.M. Paul, 487:Summer81-176

Buchthal, H. and H. Belting. Patronage in Thirteenth-Century Constantinople.
A. Cutler, 589:Jan81-100
G. Vikan, 54:Jun81-325
Buchwald, A. Laid Back in Washington.
C.D. May, 441:3Jan82-10
Buck, A. and M. Pfister. Studien zu den "volgarizzamenti" römischer Autoren in der italienischen Literatur des 13. und 14. Jahrhunderts.
G. Costa, 545(RPh):Feb81(supp)-364
Buck, G. The History of King Richard the Third (1619).* (A.N. Kincaid, ed)
J.D. Cox, 405(MP):Nov81-200
Buck, J.J. The Only Place to Be.
R. Billington, 441:18Jul82-12
Buck, L.A. Autonomy Psychotherapy.
K. Baier, 185:Apr81-499
Buck, R.J. A History of Boeotia.*
P. Roesch, 487:Fall81-267
"Samuel Buck's Yorkshire Sketchbook."
R. Hyde, 325:Oct81-508
Buckland, G. Fox Talbot and the Invention of Photography.*
R. Whelan, 55:Jan81-33
Buckle, R. Buckle at the Ballet.*
P. Migel, 151:Nov81-89
Buckle, R. In the Wake of Diaghilev.
G. Annan, 617(TLS):3Dec82-1335
Buckle, R., ed. U and Non-U Revisited.
M. Dilkes, 35(AS):Summer81-139
Buckler, W.E. The Victorian Imagination.*
W.D. Shaw, 401(MLQ):Jun81-199
Buckley, C. Steaming to Bamboola.
P-L. Adams, 61:May82-106
W. Goodman, 441:31Oct82-18
A. Ross, 617(TLS):20Aug82-898
Buckley, V. Late Winter Child.* The Pattern.*
G. Bitcon, 581:Dec81-469
Buckley, W.F., Jr. Atlantic High.
M. Hunt, 441:5Sep82-6
Buckley, W.F., Jr. Marco Polo, If You Can.
E. Hunter, 441:24Jan82-12
Budde, A. Zur Syntax geschriebener und gesprochener Sprache von Grundschülern.*
G. Starke, 682(ZPSK):Band32Heft2-241
Budden, J. The Operas of Verdi.* (Vols 1 and 2)
G. Tomlinson, 451:Fall81-170
Budden, J. The Operas of Verdi.* (Vol 3)
J. Kerman, 453(NYRB):4Mar82-18
R. Osborne, 617(TLS):5Mar82-263
Budge, D.M. - see Gibbon, L.G.
Buechner, F. The Sacred Journey.
R. Price, 441:11Apr82-12
Buescu, M.L.C. - see under Carvalhão Buescu, M.L.
Buetin, W. and others. Deutsche Literaturgeschichte.
J. Hermand, 406:Fall81-338
Buffet-Challie, L. Art Nouveau Style.
R.L. Shep, 614:Fall82-13
Bugialli, G. Classic Techniques of Italian Cooking.
M. Sheraton, 441:5Dec82-12
Bugliani, A. La presenza di D'Annunzio in Valle-Inclán.*
H. Hatzfeld, 552(REH):Jan81-136
Bühler, W., with E.M. Voigt, eds. Lexikon des frühgriechischen Epos. (Pt 9)
W.J. Verdenius, 394:Vol34fasc1/2-144

Buijtenhuijs, R. Le FROLINAT et les révoltes populaires du Tchad, 1965-1976.
E. Conte, 69:Vol150No4-438
Buin, Y. Maël.
R.H. Simon, 207(FR):May81-891
Bukdahl, E.M. Diderot, Critique d'Art. (Vol 1)
J. Chouillet, 208(FS):Jul81-340
B. Scott, 39:Aug81-135
Bukowcowa, Z. and M. Kucała. Bibliografia podręczna gramatyki historycznej i historii języka polskiego, cz. I: Gramatyka.
H. Leeming, 575(SEER):Jan81-78
Bukowski, C. Dangling in the Tournefortia.
W. Logan, 617(TLS):12Nov82-1251
P. Schjeldahl, 441:17Jan82-13
Bukowski, C. Ham on Rye.
D. Montrose, 617(TLS):3Dec82-1344
Bulciolu, M.T. L'Ecole saint-simonienne et la femme.
L.S. Herrmann, 446(NCFS):Spring-Summer82-372
H.C. Staples, 207(FR):Apr82-697
Bull, G. Inside the Vatican.
C.C. O'Brien, 362:27May82-20
M. Walsh, 617(TLS):28May82-574
"Bulletin de l'Institut de Phonétique de Grenoble." (Vol 3)
G.F. Meier, 682(ZPSK):Band33Heft6-738
Bulliet, R.W. Conversion to Islam in the Medieval Period.
J. Waltz, 589:Apr81-360
Bullivant, K. and H. Ridley, eds. Industrie und deutsche Literatur.
W.B. Fischer, 221(GQ):Jan81-116
Bullock, A-M. Lace and Lace Making.
P. Bach, 614:Spring82-14
Bullock, M.B. An American Transplant.
C.W. Hayford, 293(JASt):Aug81-753
Bullock-Davies, C. Menestrellorum multitudo.*
U. Peters, 684(ZDA):Band109Heft4-158
Bullowa, M., ed. Before Speech.
S. Foster, 350:Jun81-518
Bülow, E. and P. Schmitter, eds. Integrale Linguistik.
H. Penzl, 350:Mar81-231
Bumke, J. Mäzene im Mittelalter.
M. Curschmann, 301(JEGP):Apr81-296
Bumke, J. and others, eds. Literatur — Publikum — historischer Kontext.*
V. Mertens, 684(ZDA):Band109Heft2-55
Bunbury, E.H. A History of Ancient Geography Among the Greeks and Romans from the Earliest Ages till the Fall of the Roman Empire. (Vols 1 and 2)
L. Casson, 124:Sep-Oct81-60
Bungarten, T. Präsentische Partizipialkonstruktionen in der deutschen Gegenwartssprache.
E. Beneš, 685(ZDL):1/1981-104
G. Starke, 682(ZPSK):Band33Heft5-584
Bunge, M. The Mind-Body Problem.
R. Puccetti, 84:Sep81-282
Bunge, M. Treatise on Basic Philosophy. (Vols 1 and 2)
B. Linsky, 154:Jun81-384
Bunge, M. A World of Systems.
G. Vollmer, 679:Band12Heft1-178
Bungert, H., ed. Die amerikanische Literatur der Gegenwart.*
K. Müller, 38:Band99Heft3/4-544
[continued]

[continuing]
W. Zacharasiewicz, 224(GRM):Band30
Heft3-371
Bunkle, P. and B. Hughes, eds. Women in
New Zealand Society.
P. Smart, 368:Jun81-170
Bunting, B. Briggflatts.
A. Cluysenaar, 565:Vol22No2-62
Bunyan, J. Grace Abounding [and] The Life
and Death of Mr. Badman. (G.B. Harrison,
ed)
E.B., 189(EA):Apr-Jun81-238
Bunyan, J. The Holy War. (R. Sharrock
and J.F. Forrest, eds)
J. Barnard, 617(TLS):23Apr82-470
E.F. Daniels, 568(SCN):Winter81-89
Bunyan, J. The Miscellaneous Works of
John Bunyan.* (Vol 2)(R.L. Greaves, ed)
J.B.H. Alblas, 179(ES):Feb81-65
Bunyan, J. The Miscellaneous Works of
John Bunyan.* (Vol 8)(R.L. Greaves, ed)
J.B.H. Alblas, 179(ES):Feb81-65
E. Bourcier, 189(EA):Jan-Mar81-91
N.H. Keeble, 447(N&Q):Aug80-369
Burbank, J. and P. Steiner - see Mukařov-
ský, J.
Burbidge, P. and R. Sutton, eds. The Wag-
ner Companion.*
J. Deathridge, 451:Summer81-81
R.L.J., 412:May80-146
H.R. Vaget, 221(GQ):Mar81-202
Burch, P.H. Elites in American History:
The Federalist Years to the Civil War.
E. Wright, 617(TLS):4Jun82-603
Burchardt-Dose, H. Das Junge Deutschland
und die Familie.
G. Friesen, 400(MLN):Apr81-679
Burchfield, R.W. - see "A Supplement to
the Oxford English Dictionary"
Burckhardt, J. Reflections on History.
H. McDonald, 396(ModA):Spring81-209
Burckhardt, J. Über das Studium der
Geschichte. (P. Ganz, ed)
H. Trevor-Roper, 617(TLS):8Oct82-1087
Burd, V.A. Ruskin, Lady Mount-Temple and
the Spiritualists.
T. Hilton, 617(TLS):22Oct82-1153
Burd, V.A. - see La Touche, R.
Bürgel, P. Die Briefe des frühen Gutzkow
1830-1848.
G. Friesen, 400(MLN):Apr81-678
Burger, R. Plato's "Phaedrus."
M.F. Burnyeat, 123:Vol31No2-299
D.S. Kaufer, 583:Spring81-305
S. Rosen, 480(P&R):Spring81-112
Burgess, A. Earthly Powers.*
42(AR):Summer81-393
639(VQR):Spring81-59
Burgess, A. The End of the World News.
E. Korn, 617(TLS):5Nov82-1211
M. Poole, 362:25Nov82-27
Burgess, A. On Going to Bed.
P-L. Adams, 61:Jul82-94
C. Brown, 617(TLS):8Oct82-1104
E.S. Turner, 362:19Aug82-22
Burgess, A. This Man and Music.
C. Wintle, 617(TLS):24Dec82-1412
Burgess, G.S., ed. Court and Poet.
H.F. Williams, 304(JHP):Winter82-159
Burgess, G.S., comp. Marie de France.*
K. Brightenback, 545(RPh):Feb81(supp)-
349
Burgess, R.H. - see Braynard, F.O.

Burghardt, W. and K. Hölker, eds. Text
Processing.
B. Lindemann, 307:Apr81-52
Bürgin, H. and H-O. Mayer, eds. Die
Briefe Thomas Manns, Regesten und Regis-
ter.* (Vol 1) (Y. Schmidlin, comp)
K.W. Jonas, 221(GQ):May81-373
H. Lehnert, 462(OL):Vol35No2-185
Bürgin, H. and H-O. Mayer, eds. Die
Briefe Thomas Manns, Regesten und Regis-
ter. (Vol 2) (Y. Schmidlin, comp)
K.W. Jonas, 221(GQ):May81-373
Burgis, N. - see Dickens, C.
Burgos, J. Lecture plurielle du texte
poétique.*
R.A. York, 208(FS):Jan81-111
Burk, K., ed. War and the State.
K.O. Morgan, 617(TLS):29Oct82-1186
Burke, D.B. American Paintings in the
Metropolitan Museum of Art. (Vol 3)
J.V. Turano, 16:Winter81-92
Burke, E. The Writings and Speeches of
Edmund Burke. (Vol 5) (P.J. Marshall,
ed)
K. Ballhatchet, 617(TLS):5Feb82-142
Burke, P. Popular Culture in Early Modern
Europe.*
K. Roth, 196:Band21Heft3/4-297
Burkert, W. Structure and History in
Greek Mythology and Ritual.*
B.C. Dietrich, 487:Summer81-156
N.J. Richardson, 123:Vol31No1-63
Burkhard, M. and G. Labroisse, eds. Zur
Literatur der deutschsprachigen Schweiz.
A. Arnold, 133:Band14Heft4-378
Burkhardt, F.H. and I.K. Skrupskelis - see
James, W.
Burkholder, M.A. Politics of a Colonial
Career.
S.E. Ramírez-Horton, 263(RIB):Vol31No4
546
Burks, D.M., ed. Rhetoric, Philosophy,
and Literature.*
J.S.M., 543:Jun81-783
Burl, A. Prehistoric Avebury.
R. Fonseca, 576:Dec81-326
S. Piggott, 447(N&Q):Apr80-183
Burley, W.J. The House of Care.
N. Callendar, 441:12Sep82-38
Burley, W.J. Wycliffe's Wild-Goose Chase.
T.J. Binyon, 617(TLS):12Mar82-276
Burman, S. Chiefdom Politics and Alien
Law.
A. Atmore, 617(TLS):7May82-516
Burman, S. Fit Work for Women.
F. Ducrocq, 98:Feb-Mar81-138
Burnam, T. More Misinformation.
639(VQR):Winter81-28
Burne-Jones, E.C. Burne-Jones Talking,
His Conversations 1895-1898. (M. Lago,
ed)
M. Lutyens, 617(TLS):11Jun82-645
R.L. Smith, 362:27May82-23
Burnett, J. Destiny Obscure.
N. Roberts, 617(TLS):12Nov82-1240
Burnett, T.A.J. The Rise and Fall of a
Regency Dandy.*
F. Taliaferro, 441:21Mar82-6
Burney, F. The Journals and Letters of
Fanny Burney (Madame d'Arblay). (Vol 8)
(P. Hughes, with others, eds)
P.B. Steese, 446(NCFS):Spring-Summer82-
376

Burney, F. The Journals and Letters of
Fanny Burney. (Vols 9 and 10) (W. Derry,
ed)
P. Rogers, 617(TLS):18Jun82-660
Burnham, D.K. The Comfortable Arts.
S.W. Keene, 99:Mar82-34
R.L. Shep, 614:Winter82-16
Burnham, D.K. Warp and Weft.
F.H. Pettit, 37:May81-26
Burnham, L.F. Bob and Bob: The First Five
Years, 1975-1980.
62:Apr81-62
Burnham, W.D. and M. Weinberg, eds.
American Politics and Public Policy.
J. Alexander, 106:Spring81-89
Burnier, M.A. and P. Rambaud. Le Roland-
Barthes sans peine.
C. Rigolot, 207(FR):Oct80-179
Burnley, J. Unrepentant Women.
J. Astor, 362:18Mar82-24
L. Hughes-Hallett, 617(TLS):19Mar82-
306
Burnley, J.D. Chaucer's Language and the
Philosophers' Tradition.
J.H. Fisher, 589:Apr81-448
B. Quinn, 599:Fall81-499
A.V.C. Schmidt, 382(MAE):1981/2-344
Burns, A. The Day Daddy Died.*
J. Mellors, 362:14Jan82-24
Burns, A. Nature and Culture in D.H.
Lawrence.*
J. King-Farlow, 478:Fall81-234
Burns, A. and C. Sugnet. The Imagination
on Trial.
L. Mackinnon, 617(TLS):25Jun82-701
Burns, C.A., ed. Literature and Society.
A.E. Pilkington, 208(FS):Oct81-488
Burns, D.M. Language, Thought, and Logi-
cal Paradoxes.
D.D. Daye, 485(PE&W):Jul81-382
Burns, E.B. The Poverty of Progress.
J.A. Rayfield, 263(RIB):Vol31No2-274
Burns, J.M. The Vineyard of Liberty.
N. Bliven, 442(NY):17May82-135
P. Maier, 441:21Feb82-9
G.S. Wood, 453(NYRB):18Feb82-3
Burns, M.U. - see Woollcott, A.
Burns, T.S. The Ostrogoths.
C. Morton, 589:Oct81-924
Burnshaw, S. The Refusers.
R. Alter, 441:4Apr82-18
J.M. Cameron, 453(NYRB):1Apr82-33
Burr, B. Up North.
N. Johnson, 441:28Mar82-14
Burrell, D.B. Aquinas.*
E. Stump, 482(PhR):Jan81-162
Burrell, D.B. - see Lonergan, B.J.
Burrell, P. The Isle, the Sea and the
Crown.
D. Devlin, 157:Autumn81-51
Burridge, K. Someone, No One.
R.W. Lovin, 185:Oct81-176
Burroughs, J.M. On the Trail.
W. Gard, 584(SWR):Winter81-vii
P.A. Owens, 649(WAL):Fall81-252
Burroughs, P. Thomas Hart Benton.
A. Berman, 55:Nov81-38
J.V. Turano, 16:Summer81-87
Burroughs, W.S. Cities of the Red Night.*
639(VQR):Summer81-102
Burrow, J.A. Medieval Writers and Their
Work.
H. O'Donoghue, 617(TLS):24Dec82-1425

Burrow, J.W. A Liberal Descent.*
J. Clive, 453(NYRB):24Jun82-41
Burrow, T. The Problem of shwa in
Sanskrit.
L. Dubois, 555:Vol54fasc2-339
J.S. Klein, 350:Jun81-446
A. Lubotsky, 361:Sep81-75
Burrow, T. The Sanskrit Language.
B. Barschel, 682(ZPSK):Band33Heft6-739
Burroway, J. Material Goods.
W. Scammell, 617(TLS):28May82-592
Burrs, M. Children on the Edge of Space.
A.R. Shucard, 102(CanL):Winter80-110
Bursch, H. Die lateinisch-romanische
Wortfamilie von *Interpedare und seine
Parallelbildungen.*
M. Pfister, 72:Band217Heft2-461
Bursen, H.A. Dismantling the Memory
Machine.*
J. Heil, 518:Jan81-52
C. Mortensen, 63:Mar81-130
S. Munsat, 482(PhR):Jan81-120
Bursill-Hall, G.L. - see Hunt, R.W.
Burt, E.C. An Annotated Bibliography of
the Visual Arts of East Africa.
M. Posnansky, 2(AfrA):Aug81-22
Burt, J.R. From Phonology to Philology.
T.A. Lathrop, 304(JHP):Spring81-227
Burton, A. The Changing River.
A. Wheeler, 617(TLS):12Mar82-287
Burton, I. A Book of Poems.
L. Sail, 565:Vol22No1-66
Burton, I.J. All Along the Skyline.
L. Duguid, 617(TLS):20Aug82-910
Burton, T.G. Some Ballad Folks.
R.D. Morse, 650(WF):Jul81-278
Bury, J.P.T. Gambetta's Final Years.
M. Larkin, 617(TLS):11Jun82-646
Burzyński, T. and Z. Osiński. Grotowski's
Laboratory.
H. Filipowicz, 574(SEEJ):Fall81-134
Busby, K. Gauvain in Old French Litera-
ture.
W.W. Kibler, 207(FR):Mar82-541
P. Nykrog, 589:Jul81-667
D.J. Shirt, 402(MLR):Oct81-956
205(FMLS):Oct81-375
Busch, F. Take This Man.*
E. Milton, 676(YR):Winter82-254
Busch, W. Die Entstehung der kritischen
Rechtsphilosophie Kants 1762-1780.
L. Guillermit, 542:Jul-Sep81-376
R.B.P., 543:Dec80-373
Busch, W. The Genius of Wilhelm Busch.
(W. Arndt, ed and trans)
G. Annan, 453(NYRB):1Apr82-6
Buschhausen, H. Die süditalienische Bau-
plastik im Königreich Jerusalem von
König Wilhelm II. bis Kaiser Fried-
rich II.*
M. Burgoyne and J. Folda, 54:Jun81-321
Buschor, E. On the Meaning of Greek
Statues.
R. Higgins, 39:Jun81-414
G.B. Waywell, 123:Vol31No2-318
R. Woodfield, 89(BJA):Spring81-175
Bush, A. In My Eighth Decade and Other
Essays.
R. Evans, 607:Jun81-46
P. Griffiths, 415:Jun81-380

Buyssens, E. Epistémologie de la phoné-
matique.
   P. Swiggers, 603:Vol5No2-287
Buzaljko, G. - see Kroeber, A.L. and E.W.
Gifford
Byers, J.R., Jr. and J.J. Owen. A Concor-
dance to the Five Novels of Nathaniel
Hawthorne.
   E.A. Dryden, 445(NCF):Jun81-107
Byers, R.B. and R.W. Reford, eds. Canada
Challenged.
   V. Lyon, 298:Summer81-122
Bylinsky, G. Life in Darwin's Universe.
   T. Ferris, 441:4Apr82-17
Bynum, C.W. "Docere verbo et exemplo."
   R.M. Thomson, 589:Jul81-598
Bynum, D.E. The Daemon in the Wood.*
   H.R.E. Davidson, 203:Vol91No1-120
Bynum, D.E. - see Parry, M., A.B. Lord and
D.E. Bynum
Bynum, W.F., E.J. Browne and R. Porter,
eds. Dictionary of the History of
Science.
   J.M. Ziman, 617(TLS):4Jun82-606
Byrd, D. Charles Olson's "Maximus."*
   J. Mazzaro, 27(AL):Nov81-530
Byrd, M. London Transformed.*
   J.T. Boulton, 161(DUJ):Dec80-114
Byrne, M.S., ed. The Lisle Letters.*
   R. Holmes, 231:Jan82-65
   W.T. MacCaffrey, 405(MP):May82-414
Lord Byron. The Complete Poetical Works.*
   (Vol 1) (J.J. McGann, ed)
   A. Levine, 661(WC):Summer81-178
   W.R., 148:Spring81-92
Lord Byron. The Complete Poetical Works.
   (Vol 2) (J.J. McGann, ed)
   A. Levine, 661(WC):Summer81-178
Lord Byron. Byron's Letters and Journals.
   (Vols 1-7) (L.A. Marchand, ed)
   W.H. Pritchard, 249(HudR):Winter81/82-
   569
Lord Byron. Byron's Letters and Journals.*
   (Vol 8) (L.A. Marchand, ed)
   W.H. Pritchard, 249(HudR):Winter81/82-
   569
   A. Rutherford, 161(DUJ):Dec80-117
Lord Byron. Byron's Letters and Journals.*
   (Vol 9) (L.A. Marchand, ed)
   W.H. Pritchard, 249(HudR):Winter81/82-
   569
   F.W. Shilstone, 577(SHR):Winter81-79
Lord Byron. Byron's Letters and Journals.
   (Vol 10) (L.A. Marchand, ed)
   J.A. Davies, 506(PSt):May81-101
   W.H. Pritchard, 249(HudR):Winter81/82-
   569
   C.E. Robinson, 661(WC):Summer81-176
Lord Byron. Byron's Letters and Journals.*
   (Vol 11) (L.A. Marchand, ed)
   W.H. Pritchard, 249(HudR):Winter81/82-
   569
   639(VQR):Autumn81-124
Lord Byron. Selected Letters and Journals.
   (L.A. Marchand, ed)
   D.J.R. Bruckner, 441:7Nov82-9
   H.R., 231:Oct82-75
Byron, W. Cervantes.*
   A. Close, 402(MLR):Jul81-722

Caballero Calderón, E. Manuel Pacho. (M.
Lichtblau, ed)
   L.E. Ben-Ur, 238:Dec81-646
Cabanis, J. Lacordaire et quelques autres.
   J. McManners, 617(TLS):3Dec82-1342
Cabanis, J. Petit entracte à la guerre.
   P. Bourgeade, 450(NRF):Jun81-113
Cable, M. Avery's Knot.
   V. Miner, 441:17Jan82-12
Cable, M. Lost New Orleans.
   J.J. Poesch, 576:Oct81-255
Cabot, T.D. Beggar on Horseback.
   H. Lee, 432(NEQ):Mar81-149
Cabourdin, G. and G. Viard. Lexique his-
torique de la France d'Ancien Régime.
   W. Leiner, 475:No14Pt1-161
Cabrera, V. and H. Boyer. Critical Views
on Vicente Aleixandre's Poetry.
   I.R.M. Galbis, 238:May81-316
Cachero, J.M.M. - see under Martínez
Cachero, J.M.
de Cadalso, J. Escritos autobiográficos y
Epistolario. (N. Glendinning and N.
Harrison, eds)
   J. Dowling, 402(MLR):Jul81-726
   I.L. McClelland, 86(BHS):Jul81-268
   J.H.R. Polt, 405(MP):May82-413
Cadogan, G. Palaces of Minoan Crete.
   J.W. Shaw, 124:Jul-Aug82-378
Cady, E.H. The Big Game.
   W.E. Akin, 106:Winter81-351
Cady, E.H. Stephen Crane. (rev)
   J.B. Colvert, 26(ALR):Autumn81-303
Cady, J.F. The History of Post-war
Southeast Asia.
   D.K. Emmerson, 293(JASt):Nov80-43
Caerwyn Williams, J.E. The Poets of the
Welsh Princes.
   L. Breatnach, 112:Vol 14-169
Caesar, J. The Battle for Gaul.* (A. and
P. Wiseman, trans)
   J.D. Leach, 123:Vol31No2-312
Caesar, S., with B. Davidson. Where Have
I Been?
   F. Rich, 441:24Oct82-7
Cagnon, M., ed. Ethique et esthétique
dans la littérature française du XXe
siècle.
   A-M. Boyer, 207(FR):Dec80-348
"Cahier de poésie 3."
   D. Pobel, 450(NRF):Sep81-118
"Cahiers du communisme: 24e Congrès du
parti communiste français, Février 1982."
   D. Johnson, 617(TLS):2Jul82-707
"Cahiers Saint-John Perse 2."
   M. Autrand, 535(RHL):Mar-Apr81-334
"Cahiers Paul Valéry 3."* (J. Levaillant,
ed)
   P. Gifford, 402(MLR):Apr81-476
Cahill, J. Parting at the Shore.
   R. Barnhart, 54:Jun81-344
   E.J. Laing, 318(JAOS):Apr/Jun80-202
Cahlander, A., with E. Zorn and A.P. Rowe.
Sling Braiding of the Andes.
   P. Bach, 614:Winter81-18
Cahn, V.L. Beyond Absurdity.*
   M. Silverstein, 397(MD):Jun81-240
Cahn, W. Masterpieces.
   B. Wind, 568(SCN):Winter81-92
   B.M. Stafford, 446(NCFS):Fall-Win-
   ter80/81-149

Cahn, W. and L. Seidel. Romanesque Sculp-
ture in American Collections. (Vol 1)
  P. Fergusson, 589:Jan81-214
Caie, G.D. The Judgment Day Theme in Old
English Poetry.
  T.D. Hill, 38:Band99Heft3/4-490
Cain, J.M. The Baby in the Icebox and
Other Short Fiction.* (R. Hoopes, ed)
  T.J. Binyon, 617(TLS):31Dec82-1448
Cain, T.G.S., ed. Jacobean and Caroline
Poetry.
  J. Roe, 617(TLS):19Mar82-324
Cain, T.H. Praise in "The Faerie Queene."*
  J. Carscallen, 178:Spring81-107
  F.P., 604:Spring-Summer81-29
Caird, G.B. The Language and Imagery of
the Bible.
  506(PSt):May81-115
Cairns, F. Tibullus.
  J.A. Barsby, 67:Nov81-234
  R. Maltby, 123:Vol31No1-37
Calabresi, G. A Common Law for the Age of
Statutes.
  J.R. Pole, 617(TLS):24Sep82-1029
Caldarola, C. Christianity: The Japanese
Way.
  W. Davis, 293(JASt):Feb81-379
Calder, D.G., ed. Old English Poetry.
  J.F. Vickrey, 589:Apr81-366
Calder, J. Robert Louis Stevenson: A Life
Study.*
  E.M. Eigner, 445(NCF):Mar82-492
Calder, J.H. Jacques Offenbach.
  H. MacDonald, 415:Jul81-479
Calderón, E.C. - see under Caballero Cal-
derón, E.
Calderón de la Barca, P. Celos aun del
aire matan. (M.D. Stroud, ed and trans)
  G.H. Sumner, 304(JHP):Spring81-240
Calderón de la Barca, P. Four Comedies.
(A.L. Mackenzie, ed)
  R. ter Horst, 405(MP):May82-435
Calderón de la Barca, P. Mística y real
Babilonia. (K. Uppendahl, ed)
  D.W. Cruickshank, 86(BHS):Jan81-84
Calderón de la Barca, P. El postrer duelo
de España.* (G. Rossetti, ed)
  G. Edwards, 402(MLR):Jan81-221
Calderón de la Barca, P. La vida es sueño.
(E.W. Hesse, ed)
  R.W. Listerman, 238:Mar81-154
Calderwood, J.L. Metadrama in Shake-
speare's Henriad.*
  M. Coyle, 447(N&Q):Oct80-434
  M. Grivelet, 189(EA):Jan-Mar81-90
  T. Hawkes, 541(RES):Aug81-320
  C.M. Shaw, 551(RenQ):Autumn80-476
Caldini, R.M. Horos e Properzio, ovvero
l'ispirazione necessaria.
  J.A. Richmond, 123:Vol31No2-292
Caldwell, D.H. Scottish Weapons and Forti-
fications 1100-1800.
  G.M. Wilson, 617(TLS):7May82-504
Caldwell, G. The Screaming Frog that
Ralph Ate.
  G. Bitcon, 581:Dec81-469
Calhoun, J.C. The Papers of John C. Cal-
houn, 1829-1832. (C.N. Wilson, ed)
  G. Anastaplo, 396(ModA):Winter81-106
Calhoun, T.O. Henry Vaughan.
  G.B. Christopher, 401(MLQ):Dec81-391
Califano, J.A., Jr. Governing America.*
  639(VQR):Autumn81-133

"California Slavic Studies." (Vol 11)
(N.V. Riasanovsky, G. Struve and T.
Eekman, eds)
  M. Banerjee, 574(SEEJ):Fall81-109
Calin, W. A Poet at the Fountain.
  R. Deschaux, 545(RPh):Aug80-113
Calinescu, M. Faces of Modernity.*
  R. Langbaum, 473(PR):1/1981-151
  A. Rodway, 447(N&Q):Jun80-285
  M. Spariosu, 131(CL):Winter81-79
Calisher, H., with S. Ravenel, eds. The
Best American Short Stories 1981.
  B. Allen, 434:Spring82-478
Calkins, R.G. Distribution of Labor.*
  K. Gould, 589:Jul81-601
Calkins, R.G. Monuments of Medieval Art.
  D. Buckton, 39:Mar81-202
Callaghan, B. The Hogg Poems and Drawings.
  D. Headon, 102(CanL):Autumn80-115
Callaghan, M. No Man's Meat and "The
Enchanted Pimp."
  R. Miles, 102(CanL):Spring80-120
Callaghan, M.M. - see de Lasphrise, M.P.
Callahan, D. and S. Bok, eds. Ethics
Teaching in Higher Education.
  J.M. Giarelli, 185:Apr82-549
Callen, A. Women Artists of the Arts and
Crafts Movement 1870-1914.
  E. Boris, 637(VS):Spring81-382
Calleo, D.P. The Imperious Economy.
  R.J. Barnet, 441:18Jul82-1
  J. Epstein, 453(NYRB):23Sep82-17
Callimachus. Hymn to Zeus. (G.R. McLen-
nan, ed)
  A. Griffiths, 303(JoHS):Vol 101-159
Callot, E. La philosophie de la science
et de la nature.
  J-M. Gabaude, 542:Jan-Mar81-138
Callow, P. Cave Light.
  W. Scammell, 617(TLS):2Apr82-393
Calloway, S. English Prints for the
Collector.
  D. Alexander, 135:Aug81-250
Callwood, J. Portrait of Canada.
  E.Z. Friedenberg, 453(NYRB):4Nov82-37
Calvet, L-J. Les Sigles.
  J. Duvignaud, 450(NRF):Feb81-128
Calvino, I. If on a winter's night a
traveler.*
  H.O. Brown, 141:Fall81-335
  T. Le Clair, 659(ConL):Winter82-83
  J.D. O'Hara, 434:Summer82-603
  G. Perez, 249(HudR):Winter81/82-606
Calvino, I., ed. Italian Folktales.*
  N. Philip, 203:Vol192No2-253
Calvino, I., ed. L'Uccel Belverde.
  R. Davies, 617(TLS):26Mar82-348
da Câmara Cascudo, L. Contes tradition-
nels du Brésil.*
  M-L. Tenèze, 196:Band21Heft1/2-108
de Cambrai, J. - see under Jacques de
Cambrai
Cameron, A. Circus Factions.
  A.B. Breebaart, 394:Vol34fasc1/2-194
Cameron, A. and others. Christianisme et
formes littéraires de l'antiquité tar-
dive en occident.
  E.D. Hunt, 313:Vol71-193
Cameron, C. and J. Wright. Second Empire
Style in Canadian Architecture.
  H. Kalman, 576:Oct81-253
Cameron, E. Hugh MacLennan.*
  T.D. MacLulich, 102(CanL):Autumn81-126

55

Cameron, I. To the Farthest Ends of the Earth.
639(VQR):Spring81-52
Cameron, I.A. Crime and Repression in the Auvergne and the Guyenne 1720-1790.
G. Rudé, 617(TLS):30Jul82-833
Cameron, K. Henri III — A Maligned or Malignant King?
M.M. McGowan, 208(FS):Jul81-326
205(FMLS):Jan80-81
Cameron, K. - see Meigret, L.
Cameron, S. Lyric Time.*
D.V. Fuller, 50(ArQ):Spring81-83
M.D. Uroff, 301(JEGP):Jul81-461
A. Woodlief, 577(SHR):Summer81-268
Cameron, S.D. Dragon Lady.*
P. Barclay, 102(CanL):Summer81-133
Camfield, W.A. Francis Picabia.*
C. Green, 90:Nov81-683
Camon, F. Apothéose.
J-N. Schifano, 450(NRF):Nov81-146
Campa, A.L. Hispanic Culture in the Southwest.*
J.O. West, 292(JAF):Apr-Jun81-263
Campagna, A. and P. Grundleher. Points de vue.
N.D. Savage, 207(FR):May82-917
Campanile, E. and C. Letta. Studi sulle magistrature indigine e municipali in area italica.
M.H. Crawford, 313:Vol71-153
Campbell, I., ed. Nineteenth-Century Scottish Fiction.
R.C. Gordon, 445(NCF):Jun80-103
L. Hartveit, 179(ES):Oct81-485
K. Sutherland, 571(ScLJ):Winter81-119
Campbell, I.R. "Kudrun."*
E.S. Dick, 301(JEGP):Apr81-293
Campbell, J. Grammatical Man.
442(NY):9Aug82-95
Campbell, J., P. Wormald and E. John. The Anglo-Saxons.
S. Keynes, 617(TLS):5Nov82-1229
Campbell, J.L., ed and trans. Hebridean Folksongs II.*
V. Blankenhorn, 112:Vol 14-164
Campbell, J.L., ed and trans. Hebridean Folksongs III.
D. Sealy, 617(TLS):12Feb82-171
Campbell, K. Skungpoomery.
O. Wymark, 157:Oct80-73
Campbell, L. Van der Weyden.
639(VQR):Winter81-12
Campbell, L. and M. Mithun, eds. The Languages of Native America.*
H. Berman, 269(IJAL):Jul81-248
A.R. Taylor, 350:Jun82-440
Campbell, M. The Great Violinists.
R. Anderson, 415:Jun81-383
Campbell, M. The Way Back.
E. Crayford, 368:Dec81-489
Campbell, P.J. Refuge from Fear.
A. Brett-James, 617(TLS):29Oct82-1202
Campbell, R. Self-Love and Self-Respect.
D.P.L., 185:Oct81-190
Campbell, R.H. and A.S. Skinner, eds. The Origins and Nature of the Scottish Enlightenment.
N. Phillipson, 617(TLS):17Sep82-1015
Campbell, R.H. and A.S. Skinner. Adam Smith.
N. Phillipson, 617(TLS):17Sep82-1015

Campbell, S.C. Only Begotten Sonnets.
J. Fuzier, 189(EA):Apr-Jun81-215
Campbell, S.C. - see Shakespeare, W.
Campe, J. Der programmatische Roman von Wielands "Agathon" zu Jean Pauls "Hesperus."*
G. Müller, 684(ZDA):Band109Heft1-43
W.D. Wilson, 133:Band14Heft1-73
Campion, E.J. - see Quinault, P.
Campos, E. Die Kantkritik Brentanos.
W. Steinbeck, 342:Band72Heft1-120
Camps, W.A. An Introduction to Homer.*
J.B. Hainsworth, 123:Vol31No2-284
Campus, E. The Little Entente and the Balkan Alliance.
P.S. Wandycz, 575(SEER):Jan81-128
Camurati, M. Enfoques.
T.B. Kalivoda, 399(MLJ):Spring81-103
Camurati, M. La fábula en Hispanoamérica.
B. Miller, 238:Mar81-159
Camurati, M. Poesía y poética de Vicente Huidobro.
E. Rivero, 263(RIB):Vol31No1-79
Camus, A. The Outsider.
A. Ryan, 362:29Apr82-25
Camus, A. and J. Grenier. Correspondance 1932-1960.* (M. Dobrenn, ed)
G. Barrière, 450(NRF):Jun81-110
Camus, J-P. Trente nouvelles.* (R. Favret, ed)
J. Serroy, 535(RHL):Jul-Oct81-762
Canaday, J. What Is Art?
D.M. Ebitz, 289:Jul81-122
M.S. Young, 39:Sep81-206
"Canadian Archives."
T. Walch, 14:Spring81-158
Candaux, J-D. and others - see de Charrière, I.
Candelaria, F. Foraging.
L. Ricou, 102(CanL):Spring81-142
Candida, B. Altari e cippi nel museo nazionale romano.
A. Hus, 555:Vol54fasc2-393
Canetti, E. Histoire d'une jeunesse.*
S. Koster, 98:Oct80-1012
Canetti, E. Kafka's Other Trial.
V.S. Pritchett, 453(NYRB):4Feb82-6
Canetti, E. The Torch in My Ear.
A. Kazin, 441:19Sep82-11
S.S. Prawer, 453(NYRB):4Nov82-41
G. Steiner, 442(NY):22Nov82-186
Canning, V. Memory Boy.
H. Saal, 441:24Jan82-12
Cannon, J. Italo Calvino.
D.S. Watson, 617(TLS):12Feb82-167
Cannon, J., ed. The Historian at Work.
J.H. Brumfitt, 83:Autumn81-229
Cannon, J. Stranger to Sereno.*
D. Durrant, 364:Nov81-85
Cannon, J., ed. The Whig Ascendancy.
J.C.D. Clark, 83:Autumn81-232
Cannon, L. Reagan.
C. Wilkie, 441:3Oct82-1
Canovan, M. G.K. Chesterton.
L. Hunter, 506(PSt):Dec81-353
Cantarella, E. Norma e sanzione in Omero.
D.M. MacDowell, 123:Vol31No1-66
Cantarino, V. Entre monjes y musulmanes.
D.E. Carpenter, 545(RPh):Feb81(supp)-373
J.F. Powers, 589:Apr81-368
Cantone, G. La Città di marmo.
M. Licht, 576:Mar81-65

Cantor, M., ed. American Workingclass Culture.
  E.T. May, 658:Spring81-103
Cantor, M.G. Prime-Time Television.
  B. Sweeney, 583:Fall81-94
Capecci, A. Struttura e fine.*
  R.W. Sharples, 123:Vol31No2-223
Capin, J. L'Effet télévision.
  D.T. Stephens, 207(FR):Mar81-633
Caplan, A.L., ed. The Sociobiology Debate.
  J. Beatty, 529(QQ):Winter81-607
  R.L. Simon, 185:Jan82-327
Caplan, D., ed. Biological Studies of Mental Processes.
  E.H. Matthei, 350:Jun81-517
Caplan, G., with R. Caplan. Arab and Jew in Jerusalem.
  P.S. Appelbaum, 287:May81-21
Caplow, T. and others. Middletown Families.
  J. Herbers, 441:18Apr82-11
Capote, T. Music for Chameleons.*
  S. Brown, 569(SR):Summer81-431
  A.H. Carter 3d, 573(SSF):Winter81-111
  G. Johnson, 461:Spring-Summer81-92
  A. Ross, 364:Apr/May81-6
  M.R. Winchell, 649(WAL):Summer81-168
Capozza, M., ed. Schiavitù, manomissione e classi dipendenti nel mondo antico.
  B.D. Shaw, 487:Fall81-272
Capp, B. Astrology and the Popular Press.
  L. James, 541(RES):May81-208
  G. Williams, 354:Sep81-253
Capp, B. English Almanacs, 1500-1800.
  A.L. Birney, 568(SCN):Spring81-25
  H. Leventhal, 173(ECS):Winter80/81-194
Cappeller, C. Kleine Schriften. (S. Lienhard, ed)
  L. Sternbach, 318(JAOS):Jul/Sep80-313
Capponi, F. Ornithologia Latina.
  W.G. Arnott, 123:Vol31No2-269
Caprioglio, S. - see Gramsci, A.
Caputo, J.D. The Mystical Element in Heidegger's Thought.
  S.L. Bartky, 484(PPR):Sep81-140
Caputo-Mayr, M.L., ed. Franz Kafka.
  C. Koelb, 406:Summer81-239
Caradec, F. and A. Weill. Le Café-Concert.
  E. Brody, 446(NCFS):Fall-Winter81/82-176
Carandini, A. and others. Ostia: Le terme del nuotatore.
  G.E. Rickman, 313:Vol71-215
Caras, R. A Celebration of Dogs.
  R.R. Harris, 441:19Dec82-15
Caraway, C. Appliqué Quilts to Color. Pieced Quilts to Color.
  R.L. Shep, 614:Winter82-14
Caraway, C. The Mola Design Coloring Book.
  P. Bach, 614:Spring82-15
Cardenal, E. Zero Hour. (D.D. Walsh, ed)
  J.F. Cotter, 249(HudR):Summer81-280
Cardinal, R. Figures of Reality.
  M. Bowie, 617(TLS):25Jun82-696
  C. Clausen, 569(SR):Summer81-lxxvi
Cardona, G. Pāṇini.
  R. Rocher, 318(JAOS):Jan/Mar80-59
Carduner, S. and M.P. Hagiwara. D'accord.
  A. Malinowski, 207(FR):Feb81-510
Cardus, N. The Roses Matches, 1919-1939.
  H. Wilson, 362:11Nov82-22
Cardwell, R.A. Juan R. Jiménez.*
  H.F. Grant, 86(BHS):Jan81-87

Caré, J-M. Paris.
  J. Laroche, 207(FR):May81-909
Careless, J.M.S., ed. The Pre-Confederation Premiers: Ontario Government Leaders, 1841-1867.*
  G.W., 102(CanL):Autumn80-156
Carens, J.F. Surpassing Wit.*
  H. Pyle, 541(RES):Aug81-356
Carey, G. All the Stars in Heaven.*
  R. Combs, 617(TLS):23Apr82-465
Carey, J. The Black Rabbit and the Mantra.*
  J. Cotton, 493:Sep81-74
Carey, J. John Donne.*
  F. Manley, 569(SR):Fall81-635
  A. Phillips, 364:Aug-Sep81-137
  W.H. Pritchard, 249(HudR):Autumn81-413
  639(VQR):Summer81-84
Carey, J., ed. English Renaissance Studies Presented to Dame Helen Gardner in honour of her Seventieth Birthday.
  G.M. Ridden, 366:Autumn81-250
Carey, J. Thackeray.*
  S.M., 189(EA):Oct-Dec81-498
Carey, J.A. Judicial Reform in France before the Revolution of 1789.
  J.M.J. Rogister, 617(TLS):30Jul82-833
Carey, P. Bliss.*
  D. Durrant, 364:Feb82-97
  442(NY):23Aug82-92
Cargher, J. - see Melba, N.
Cargile, J. Paradoxes.*
  T. Baldwin, 518:Jan81-29
  P.F. Strawson, 393(Mind):Apr81-306
  R.C.S. Walker, 479(PhQ):Jan81-79
Cargill, J. The Second Athenian League.*
  N. Jones, 124:Jul-Aug82-375
Carin, M. Five Hundred Keys.
  P. Morley, 102(CanL):Summer81-139
Carkesse, J. Lucinda Intervalla (1679).*
  P.R. Backscheider, 568(SCN):Winter81-89
Carl, R-P. Franz Xaver Kroetz.*
  H. Kreuzer, 133:Band14Heft3-261
Carleton, W. Valentine M'Clutchy, the Irish Agent.
  R. Tracy, 445(NCF):Sep81-214
Carline, R. Stanley Spencer at War.
  M. Chamot, 39:Jul81-68
Carline, R. and A. Causey. Stanley Spencer R.A.
  J. Beckett, 59:Dec81-461
Carlsen, G.R. Books and the Teenage Reader.
  T.W. Hipple and B. Bartholomew, 128(CE):Nov81-724
Carlsnaes, W. The Concept of Ideology and Political Analysis.
  S.B.S., 185:Jul82-798
Carlson, E.A. Genes, Radiation, and Society.
  S. Rose, 617(TLS):19Nov82-1274
Carlson, I., ed. The Pastoral Care. (Pt 2)
  P.E. Szarmach, 589:Apr81-449
Carlson, M. Goethe and the Weimar Theatre.*
  M.K. Flavell, 402(MLR):Jan81-242
Carlson, P.A. Hawthorne's Functional Settings.
  M.J. Colacurcio, 183(ESQ):Vol127No2-108

Carlson, R., ed. Contemporary Northwest Writing.
M. Lewis, 649(WAL):Winter81-297
Carlson, R. Truants.*
T.O. Treadwell, 617(TLS):26Mar82-361
Carlton, D. Anthony Eden.*
A.J.P. Taylor, 453(NYRB):15Apr82-17
Carlut, C., ed. Essais sur Flaubert.*
D. Aynesworth, 446(NCFS):Spring-Summer81-275
B.F. Bart, 399(MLJ):Spring81-95
J. Bem, 535(RHL):Jul-Oct81-810
M. Bertrand, 210(FrF):May81-178
R.T. Denommé, 207(FR):Feb81-472
Carlut, C., P.H. Dubé and J.R. Dugan, eds. A Concordance to Flaubert's "La Tentation de Saint Antoine."* A Concordance to Flaubert's "Trois Contes."*
B.F. Bart, 446(NCFS):Fall-Winter80/81-146
M. Issacharoff, 207(FR):May81-872
Carlut, C., P. Dubé and J.R. Dugan, eds. A Concordance to Flaubert's "L'Education sentimentale."*
B.F. Bart, 210(FrF):Jan81-93
E.F. Gray, 446(NCFS):Fall-Winter80/81-144
N. Schor, 207(FR):Oct80-167
Carlut, C., P.H. Dubé and J.R. Dugan, eds. A Concordance to Flaubert's "Madame Bovary."*
B.F. Bart, 207(FR):Dec80-345
Carlut, C., P.H. Dubé and J.R. Dugan, eds. A Concordance to Flaubert's "Salammbô."* A Concordance to Flaubert's "Bouvard et Pécuchet."
B.F. Bart, 446(NCFS):Fall-Winter80/81-146
Carlyle, T. and J.W. The Collected Letters of Thomas and Jane Welsh Carlyle. (Vols 8 and 9) (C.R. Sanders and K.J. Fielding, eds)
A.J.S., 148:Winter81-94
Carlyle, T. and J. Ruskin. The Correspondence of Thomas Carlyle and John Ruskin. (G.A. Cate, ed)
T. Hilton, 617(TLS):22Oct82-1153
Carmi, T., ed and trans. The Penguin Book of Hebrew Verse.
H. Bloom, 453(NYRB):23Sep82-12
M.L. Rosenthal, 617(TLS):11Jun82-633
Carnall, G. - see Butt, J.
Carner, M. Alban Berg.
J. Le Rider, 98:Oct80-962
Carner, M. Major and Minor.
W. Dean, 415:Aug81-537
Carnero, G. Los orígenes del romanticismo reaccionario en España.
D.T. Gies, 240(HR):Autumn81-427
Caro, R.A. The Path to Power.
D.H. Donald, 441:21Nov82-1
Caron, A. Le père Emile Legault et le théâtre au Québec.
M. Moore, 108:Spring81-122
Caron, J-B., M. Fortin and G. Maloney, eds. Mélanges d'études anciennes offerts à Maurice Lebel.
J. de Romilly, 487:Winter81-389
Caron, L. Le Bonhomme Sept-heures.*
V. Raoul, 102(CanL):Spring81-106

Carotenuto, A. A Secret Symmetry.
P-L. Adams, 61:Jun82-100
R. Dinnage, 617(TLS):10Dec82-1351
A. Storr, 441:16May82-1
D.M. Thomas, 453(NYRB):13May82-3
Carozzi, C. - see Adalbero of Laon
Carpenter, D.B. - see Emerson, E.T.
Carpenter, H. W.H. Auden.*
J.D. McClatchy, 676(YR):Winter82-293
W. Scammell, 364:Jul81-80
Carpenter, H. The Inklings.
C.E. Lloyd, 569(SR):Spring81-281
C.W. Pollard, 295(JML):Vol8No3/4-376
Carpenter, H. J.R.R. Tolkien.
M. Verch, 196:Band21Heft3/4-299
Carpentier, A. L'aigle volera à travers le soleil.
C. Rubinger, 102(CanL):Spring80-118
Carpio, L.D. - see under de Vega Carpio, L.
Carr, I. Miles Davis.
B. Zavatsky, 441:12Sep82-11
Carr, M.H. The Surface of Mars.
B. Lovell, 453(NYRB):10Jun82-32
Carr, R. and J.P. Fusi Aizpurua. Spain.
R.P. Clark, 529(QQ):Spring81-177
Carr, R.A. Pierre Boaistuau's "Histoires tragiques."
P. Chilton, 402(MLR):Oct81-960
R. Reynolds, 207(FR):May81-865
Carras, M.C. Indira Gandhi in the Crucible of Leadership.
P. Oldenburg, 293(JASt):Nov80-155
Carrascou, M. and C. Tieck - see Fondane, B.
Carré, R-M. Cyrano de Bergerac, voyages imaginaires à la recherche de la vérité humaine.
J. Prévot, 535(RHL):Mar-Apr81-286
Carreño, A. El romancero lírico de Lope de Vega.*
A.S. Trueblood, 240(HR):Autumn81-501
Carrera Andrade, J. Selected Poems of Jorge Carrera Andrade. (H.R. Hayes, ed)
M. Agosin, 552(REH):Jan81-134
Carrère d'Encausse, H. Le Pouvoir confisqué.*
H. Cronel, 450(NRF):Apr81-135
Carrier, J-G. A Cage of Bone.
K. Mezei, 102(CanL):Autumn80-119
Carrier, J-G. Family.
J. Doyle, 296(JCF):No31/32-241
Carrier, R. The Garden of Delights.
K. Garebian, 102(CanL):Spring81-98
Carriere, D. and F. Day. Solar Houses for a Cold Climate.
D. Michaelis, 46:Mar81-192
Carrière, J. Le Choeur secondaire dans le drame grec.
A.M. van Erp Taalman Kip, 394:Vol134 fasc3/4-417
Carrington, S.M. - see Jamyn, A.
Carrión, B. - see Montalvo, J.
Carroll, B.J. Testing Communicative Performance.
P.L. Carrell, 399(MLJ):Summer81-206
Carroll, D. - see Simpson, R.
Carroll, J. Family Trade.
A. Cheuse, 441:11Jul82-14
442(NY):16Aug82-94
Carroll, J. Fault Lines.
D. Flower, 249(HudR):Spring81-108
Carroll, J. Sceptical Sociology.
K.S., 185:Jul81-697

Castagnoli, P.G., A. Conti and M. Ferretti.
Pittura Bolognese del '300 — scritti di
Francesco Arcangeli.
   R. Gibbs, 90:Feb81-101
Castañeda, S.G. - see under García
Castañeda, S.
Castel, R., F. Castel and A. Lovell. The
Psychiatric Society.
   G.M. Carstairs, 617(TLS):18Jun82-671
Castellani, G. - see Saba, U.
Castellani Pollidori, O. Niccolò Machia-
velli e il "Dialogo intorno alla nostra
lingua," con una edizione critica del
testo.
   A.L. Lepschy, 545(RPh):Feb81(supp)-367
de Castells, M.O. Mundo hispano.
   M.E. Beeson, 399(MLJ):Winter81-451
Castells, M.O. and H.E. Lionetti. La
lengua española. (2nd ed)
   S.C. Griswold, 238:May81-326
Casterline, G.F. Archives and Manuscripts:
Exhibits.
   M.H. Kabakoff, 14:Winter81-56
Castle, T. Clarissa's Ciphers.
   S. French, 617(TLS):24Dec82-1416
Castleman, C. Getting Up.
   R.R. Harris, 441:19Dec82-14
Castoriadis, C. Devant la guerre.
(Vol 1)
   V. Descombes, 98:Aug-Sep81-723
   C. Ost and G. Lourmel, 98:Aug-Sep81-
   744
Castro, R. Arrivals.
   H.B. Norland, 502(PrS):Spring-Summer81-
   318
Castro Díaz, A. Los "Coloquios" de Pedro
Mexía.*
   M.A. Van Antwerp, 545(RPh):Aug80-135
Catach, N., ed. La ponctuation. (Pts 1
and 2)
   H. Bonnard, 209(FM):Apr81-175
Catalán, D., ed. Gran crónica de Alfonso
XI.*
   C. Smith, 402(MLR):Jan81-216
Catalán, D., K. Lamb and E. Phipps, eds.
La dama y el pastor.
   J.G. Cummins, 86(BHS):Apr81-136
   S.H. Petersen, 238:May81-311
Catalano, G. The Years of Hope.
   I. Jeffrey, 364:Mar82-92
   C. Wallace-Crabbe, 617(TLS):14May82-
   542
"The Catalogue of the West India Reference
Library."
   T.L. Welch, 263(RIB):Vol31No1-90
"Catalogue sommaire illustré des peintures
du musée du Louvre." (Vol 2)
   90:Dec81-778
Catan, J.R. - see Owens, J.
Catanoy, N. The Fiddlehead Republic.*
   D.S. West, 102(CanL):Winter80-112
Catanoy, N., ed. Modern Rumanian Poetry.
   A. Cluysenaar, 565:Vol22No2-62
Cate, G.A. - see Carlyle, T. and J. Ruskin
Cátedra, P.M., J.M. Tatjer and C. Yarza -
see Petrarch
Cater, W.F. - see Fountaine, M.
Cates, G.T. and J.K. Swaffar. Reading a
Second Language.
   T.D. Terrell, 399(MLJ):Autumn81-327
Cather, W. My Mortal Enemy.
   P. Craig, 617(TLS):13Aug82-888
   P. Craig, 617(TLS):22Oct82-1175

St. Catherine of Siena. I, Catherine. (K.
Foster and M.J. Ronayne, eds and trans)
   M. Davie, 402(MLR):Jul81-714
Catteau, J., ed. Bakounine.
   M. Confino, 104(CASS):Winter81-584
Catteau, J. La Création littéraire chez
Dostoïevski.*
   R.L. Busch, 104(CASS):Winter81-561
Cattin, G. Storia della Musica: Il
Medioevo I.
   G. Capovilla, 228(GSLI):Vol 157fasc499-
   470
Catudal, H.M. Kennedy and the Berlin Wall
Crisis.
   A.L. George, 550(RusR):Oct81-467
Catullus. The Poems of Catullus. (P.
Whigham, trans)
   G.M. Erickson, 399(MLJ):Summer81-230
"Catullus, A Critical Edition."* (D.F.S.
Thomson, ed)
   A. Sheppard, 161(DUJ):Dec80-88
Catz, R. A sátira social de Fernão Mendes
Pinto.
   O.T. Almeida, 238:Mar81-158
   N.J. Lamb, 86(BHS):Apr81-152
Causey, A. Paul Nash.*
   R. Calvocoressi, 90:Nov81-684
   D. Farr, 324:Sep82-680
   C. Harrison, 59:Mar81-123
   D. Thistlewood, 89(BJA):Spring81-185
Causey, R.L. Unity of Science.*
   P. Achinstein, 449:Mar81-67
   W. Demopoulos, 482(PhR):Jan81-150
Caute, D. Les compagnons de route 1917-
1968.
   J-P. Morel, 98:Dec80-1124
Cavaglion, A. Nella notte straniera.
   J. Gatt-Rutter, 617(TLS):30Apr82-489
Cavajoni, G.A. Supplementum adnotationum
super Lucanum I, libri I-V.
   R. Mayer, 123:Vol31No1-117
Cavalieri, L.F. The Double-edged Helix.*
   K.S., 185:Jul82-799
Cavaliero, G. A Reading of E.M. Forster.*
   S. Arkin, 395(MFS):Summer80-285
   J. Colmer, 677(YES):Vol 11-349
   K.M. Hewitt, 541(RES):Aug81-360
Cavallini, G. La decima giornata del
"Decameron."
   M. Marti, 228(GSLI):Vol 158fasc504-600
Cavallo, A.S. Needlework.
   P. Bach, 614:Spring81-21
Cave, M. Computers and Economic Planning.
   P. Jonas, 550(RusR):Oct81-454
Cave, R.A. A Study of the Novels of
George Moore.*
   N. Grene, 447(N&Q):Dec80-562
Cave, T.C. The Cornucopian Text.*
   J. Birkett, 366:Autumn81-248
   B.C. Bowen, 551(RenQ):Autumn80-458
   E.C. Forsyth, 67:Nov81-254
   R. Griffin, 210(FrF):May81-173
   S.F.R., 131(CL):Winter81-95
   F. Rigolot, 188(ECr):Winter81-110
   R. Zuber, 535(RHL):Mar-Apr81-280
   205(FMLS):Apr80-186
Cave Brown, A. and C.B. Macdonald. On a
Field of Red.
   W. Kendall, 617(TLS):23Jul82-784
   639(VQR):Autumn81-135

Cavell, S. The Claim of Reason.*
 C. Bernstein, 81:Winter81-295
 D. Ducker, 258:Mar81-109
 D.W. Hamlyn, 518:Jul81-186
 V. Hope, 262:Dec81-470
 H.O. Mounce, 479(PhQ):Jul81-280
 R. Rorty, 543:Jun81-759
 W.L.S., 543:Mar81-601
 M. Weitz, 311(JP):Jan81-50
Cavell, S. Pursuits of Happiness.
 S.S. Prawer, 617(TLS):26Feb82-203
 M. Wood, 453(NYRB):21Jan82-29
Cavell, S. The Senses of Walden.
 G. Burns, 584(SWR):Autumn81-422
Caviness, M.H. The Early Stained Glass of
 Canterbury Cathedral, circa 1174-1220.
 V.C. Raguin, 54:Mar81-148
Caws, M.A. La Main de Pierre Reverdy.
 A. Rizzuto, 207(FR):Dec81-281
Caws, M.A. The Presence of René Char.*
 C.A. Hackett, 208(FS):Jul81-362
Caws, M.A. and J. Griffin - see Char, R.
Caws, P. Sartre.*
 W.L. McBride, 185:Apr82-561
 P.K. McInerney, 482(PhR):Oct81-610
 C. Mohanty, 207(FR):Oct81-146
 P.S. Morris, 518:Jul81-147
 R.E. Santoni, 258:Sep81-343
Caws, P., ed. Two Centuries of Philosophy
 in America.
 D.L., 185:Jul82-700
"H.W. Caylor, Frontier Artist."
 L. Milazzo, 584(SWR):Summer81-v
Cayrol, J. Il Était Une Fois Jean Cayrol.
 A. Whitmarsh, 617(TLS):23Apr82 471
Cayrol, J. L'Homme dans le rétroviseur.
 F. de Martinoir, 450(NRF):Apr81-125
 M. Naudin, 207(FR):Dec81-301
Cazelles, B. La Faiblesse chez Gautier de
 Coinci.*
 P.F. Dembowski, 545(RPh):Feb81-361
 M.A. Freeman, 207(FR):Dec80-337
 E.J. Mickel, 210(FrF):Jan81-84
Ceaser, J.W. Presidential Selection.*
 J. Alexander, 106:Spring81-89
Cèbe, J-P. - see Varro
Cebik, L.B. Concepts, Events and History.
 W.H. Dray, 125:Fall80-102
Cecil, D. A Portrait of Jane Austen.*
 R. Folkenflik, 445(NCF):Jun81-95
Cedeño, R.A.N. - see under Núñez Cedeño,
 R.A.
Celan, P. Poems.* (M. Hamburger, ed and
 trans)
 J. Saunders, 565:Vol22No3-61
 K. Washburn and M. Guillemin, 472:
 Spring/Summer81-33
Celan, P. Speech-Grille and Selected
 Poems.
 K. Washburn and M. Guillemin, 472:
 Spring/Summer81-33
Celeyrette-Pietri, N. Valéry et le Moi.*
 U. Franklin, 207(FR):Mar81-602
 P. Gifford, 402(MLR):Jul81-709
Cellard, J. and M. Sommant. 500 mots nou-
 veaux définis et expliqués.
 J-C. Boulanger, 209(FM):Oct81-379
Censorinus. Le jour natal. (G. Rocca-
 Serra, trans)
 M. Winterbottom, 123:Vol31No2-296
Centore, F.F. Persons.
 G. Englebretsen, 154:Jun81-407
 P.S., 185:Oct81-193

Ceplair, L. and S. Englund. The Inquisi-
 tion in Hollywood.*
 R.L. Davis, 584(SWR):Summer81-333
 S. Pinsker, 560:Fall81-155
 G. Weales, 219(GaR):Spring81-166
 639(VQR):Spring81-64
Ceravolo, J. Transmigration Solo.
 P. Schjeldahl, 472:Spring/Summer81-284
Cercignani, F. Shakespeare's Works and
 Elizabethan Pronunciation.
 V. Salmon, 617(TLS):1Jan82-10
Cerf, M. Amérindiennes.
 M.G. Hydak, 207(FR):Oct80-189
Cerf, M. Les Seigneurs du Ponant.
 P. Astier, 207(FR):Feb81-501
Cerf, W. and H.S. Harris - see Hegel,
 G.W.F.
Černov, G.V. Teorija i praktika sinxron-
 nogo perevoda.
 H. Salevsky, 75:3/1980-176
Cernuda, L. Cartas a Eugénio de Andrade.
 (Á. Crespo, ed)
 D. Harris, 240(HR):Summer81-372
Cernuda, L. Selected Poems of Luis Cer-
 nuda. (R. Gibbons, ed and trans)
 J.M. Labanyi, 447(N&Q):Dec80-574
 G. Rabassa, 472:Spring/Summer81-140
Černyšev, V.A. Dynamika jazykovoj situa-
 cii v severnoj Indii (chindijazyčnyj
 areal posle 1947 g.).
 M. Gatzlaff, 602(ZPSK):Band33Heft6-741
Cerri, G. Legislazione orale e tragedia
 greca.
 J. Diggle, 123:Vol31No1-107
 C. Bonnet, 555:Vol54fasc2 348
de Certeau, M. La Fable Mystique: XVIe-
 XVIIe Siècle.
 A. Levi, 617(TLS):24Dec82-1427
de Cervantes Saavedra, M. Don Quijote de
 la Mancha. (J.B. Avalle-Arce, ed)
 L.A. Murillo, 240(HR):Autumn81-499
Cervera Vera, L. Documentos biográficos
 de Juan de Herrera. (Vol 1)
 D. Angulo Íñiguez, 48:Jan-Mar81-107
Cervigni, D.S. The "Vita" of Benvenuto
 Cellini.
 G. Guarino, 551(RenQ):Winter80-755
Cesbron, G. Leur pesant d'écume. Passé
 un certain âge.
 D. O'Connell, 207(FR):Dec81-302
Cevasco, G.A. J-K. Huysmans.
 E. Gilcher, 177(ELT):Vol24No1-52
Chabanis, C. Dieu existe? Oui.
 D.T. Stephens, 207(FR):Feb82-456
Chabot, D. L'Eldorado des glaces.
 C. Rubinger, 102(CanL):Spring80-118
Chace, J. Solvency.*
 639(VQR):Autumn81-132
Chace, W.M. Lionel Trilling.*
 R.G. Cox, 569(SR):Winter81-118
 E. Goodheart, 473(PR):3/1981-469
 W. Sutton, 27(AL):Mar81-156
 639(VQR):Spring81-56
Chadbourne, R.M. Charles-Augustin Sainte-
 Beuve.*
 F. Rigolot, 207(FR):Mar82-552
 L.M. Schwartz, 446(NCFS):Spring-Sum-
 mer81-265
Chadwick, C. Rimbaud.*
 M. Davies, 402(MLR):Jan81-198
 A. Guyaux, 535(RHL):May-Jun81-474
 205(FMLS):Apr80-82

61

Chadwick, H. Boethius.
  R.A. Markus, 617(TLS):8Jan82-29
Chafe, W.H. Civilities and Civil Rights.*
  C.N. Stone, 185:Jan82-378
Chafe, W.L. The Caddoan, Iroquoian, and
Siouan Languages.
  R.L. Rankin, 269(IJAL):Apr81-172
Chafe, W.L., ed. The Pear Stories.
  D. Schiffrin, 350:Dec81-959
  K.A. Watson-Gegeo, 355(LSoc):Dec81-451
Chaffin, A. and F. L'Art Kota.
  L. Siroto, 2(AfrA):Aug81-80
Chailley, J. La musique grecque antique.
  M.L. West, 303(JoHS):Vol 101-188
Chaillou, M. La Petite Vertu.
  P. Reumaux, 450(NRF):Feb81-101
Chakrabarti, K.K. The Logic of Gotama.*
  D.D. Daye, 293(JASt):May81-624
Chakravorty, D.K. India in English Fic-
tion.
  R.J. Lewis, 314:Summer-Fall181-228
Chalfant, F.C. Ben Jonson's London.
  M.C. Bradbrook, 570(SQ):Spring81-118
  J.A. Riddell, 551(RenQ):Summer80-295
Chalfen, I. Paul Celan.
  J. Glenn, 221(GQ):Jan81-110
  K. Weissenberger, 133:Band14Heft3-276
Lord Chalfont, ed. Waterloo.
  639(VQR):Winter81-8
Challe, R. Journal d'un voyage fait aux
Indes Orientales (1690-1691) par Robert
Challe, écrivain du Roi.* (F. Deloffre
and M. Menemencioglu, eds)
  O.A. Haac, 546(RR):May81-357
  P. Hourcade, 475:No14Pt1-178
  E. Joliat, 627(UTQ):Spring81-337
Chaloemtiarana, T. - see under Thak Chal-
oemtiarana
Chamberlain, L. The Food and Cooking of
Russia.
  A. Davidson, 617(TLS):22Oct82-1165
Chamberland, P. Terre souveraine.
  R. Sutherland, 102(CanL):Spring81-92
Chambers, C. Other Spaces.*
  R. James, 214:Vol 10No37-125
  J. Roose-Evans, 157:1stQtr81-51
Chambers, J.K. and P. Trudgill. Dialectol-
ogy.
  C. Feagin, 350:Sep82-690
Chambers, J.W. 2d. The Tyranny of Change.
  G. Adams, Jr., 106:Fall181-245
Chambers, R. Meaning and Meaningfulness.*
  J.M. Cocking, 208(FS):Apr81-239
  L. Frappier-Mazur, 210(FrF):May81-185
  P. Murphy, 402(MLR):Oct81-904
  M. Spencer, 67:May81-103
  205(FMLS):Oct80-372
Champion, J.J. The Periphrastic Futures
Formed by the Romance Reflexes of "Vado
(ad)" Plus Infinitive.*
  S. Fleischman, 545(RPh):Feb81(supp)-
  144
Champion, L.S. Perspective in Shake-
speare's English Histories.
  E.I. Berry, 301(JEGP):Jul81-405
  W.M. Jones, 130:Fall81-277
Champion, L.S. Tragic Patterns in
Jacobean and Caroline Drama.*
  A.R. Dutton, 179(ES):Feb81-59
  P. Edwards, 402(MLR):Jul81-669
Champlin, E. Fronto and Antonine Rome.
  K.R. Bradley, 121(CJ):Apr/May82-369

Chan, A. The Glory and Fall of the Ming
Dynasty.
  R.L. Shep, 614:Summer82-16
Chan, F.G., ed. China at the Crossroads.
  L.E. Eastman, 293(JASt):May81-576
Chan Kam-po. Chinese Art and Archaeology.
  A. Juliano, 318(JAOS):Jan/Mar80-98
Chan, M. Music in the Theatre of Ben
Jonson.*
  T. McCavera, 184(EIC):Oct81-356
Chand, M. Last Quadrant.*
  E. Milton, 441:9May82-12
  442(NY):26Apr82-142
de Chandieu, A. Octonaires sur la vanité
et inconstance du monde. (F. Bonali-
Fiquet, ed)
  T.C. Cave, 208(FS):Apr81-190
  J. Pineaux, 535(RHL):Jul-Oct81-755
Chandler, R. Selected Letters of Raymond
Chandler.* (F. MacShane, ed)
  B. Andrews, 364:Nov81-77
  W. Balliett, 442(NY):8Mar82-138
Chandra, J. Bibliography of Indian Art,
History and Archaeology.
  R. Morris, 463:Autumn81-323
Chandra, S. Identity and Thought Experi-
ment.
  H.A.D., 543:Mar81-602
Chandrasekhar, S. - see Knowlton, C. and A.
Besant
Chaney, D. Fictions and Ceremonies.
  G. Scharnhorst, 395(MFS):Winter80/81-
  724
Chaney, L. and M. Cieply. The Hearsts.
  639(VQR):Summer81-96
Chang, A. Painting in the People's
Republic of China.
  E.J. Laing, 293(JASt):Aug81-755
Chang, G.C.C., ed and trans. The Hundred
Thousand Songs of Milarepa.
  T.V. Wylie, 293(JASt):Feb81-370
Chang, K.S. The Evolution of Chinese
"Tz'u" Poetry.
  J.J.Y. Liu, 244(HJAS):Dec81-672
Chang, P.H. Power and Policy in China.
(2nd ed)
  D.C. Sanford, 293(JASt):Aug81-757
Chanock, M. Unconsummated Union.
  S. Marks, 69:Vol150No1-98
"La Chanson de Roland." (P. Jonin, ed)
  P.H. Stäblein, 207(FR):Apr81-731
Chantraine, P. and others. Dictionnaire
étymologique de la langue grecque.
(Vol 4, Pt 2)
  M. Casevitz, 555:Vol54fasc2-334
  D.M. Jones, 123:Vol31No2-306
  J.H.W. Penney, 303(JoHS):Vol 101-176
  J.W. Poultney, 24:Summer81-239
Chantreau, A., ed. Stendhal et Balzac,
II.*
  F.W. Saunders, 208(FS):Jul81-347
Chapin, H. The Haunt of Time.
  H. Williams, 617(TLS):5Feb82-141
Chapman, G., B. Jonson and J. Marston.
Eastward Ho.* (R.W. Van Fossen, ed)
  J. Creaser, 541(RES):May81-209
  C. Spencer, 130:Spring81-87
Chapman, R., I. Kinnes and K. Randsborg,
eds. The Archaeology of Death.
  D. Ridgway, 617(TLS):27Aug82-926

Chappell, F. Earthsleep. Wind Mountain. River. Bloodfire.
K. Cherry, 472:Fall/Winter81-115
R. Morgan, 29:Jul/Aug82-45
Chappell, F. Moments of Light.
M. Kreyling, 573(SSF):Fall81-462
Chappell, W. A Short History of the Printed Word.
F.C. Robinson, 569(SR):Summer81-423
Chapple, J.A.V., with J.G. Sharps. Elizabeth Gaskell.*
C.J. Worth, 155:Autumn81-178
Chapple, R.L. Soviet Satire of the Twenties.
E. Draitser, 574(SEEJ):Winter81-94
M. Friedberg, 651(WHR):Winter81-374
Chaput, H. Donatien Frémont.
S. Knutson, 102(CanL):Autumn81-164
Char, R. Fenêtres dormantes et porte sur le toit.
M. Bishop, 207(FR):Feb81-502
Char, R. Poems of René Char. (M.A. Caws and J. Griffin, eds and trans) Le Nu perdu et autres poèmes 1964-1975.
C.A. Hackett, 208(FS):Jul81-362
Chardin, P. Un roman du clair-obscur, l'"Idiot" de Dostoïevski.
M. Watthee-Delmotte, 356(LR):Nov81-367
Chardri. La Vie des Set Dormanz.* (B.S. Merrilees, ed)
P.F. Dembowski, 545(RPh):Feb81(supp)-350
Chariton. Le roman de Chairéas et Callirhoé. (G. Molinié, ed and trans)
G. Anderson, 303(JoHS):Vol 101-163
F. Vian, 555:Vol54fasc1-168
Charitonova, I.J. Theoretische Grammatik der deutschen Sprache.
K-E. Sommerfeldt, 682(ZPSK):Band33 Heft5-587
Charle, C. La Crise littéraire à l'epoque du naturalisme.
J. Dubois, 535(RHL):May-Jun81-477
Charles, M. Rhétorique de la lecture.
R. Amossy, 546(RR):Mar81-226
L.D. Kritzman, 494:Autumn79-410
Charleston, R.J. Masterpieces of Glass.
A. Polak, 135:Jul81-166
G. Wills, 39:Oct81-275
Charlton, D.G., ed. France.* (2nd ed)
T.H. Geno, 399(MLJ):Spring81-87
205(FMLS):Apr80-188
Charlton, M. and A. Moncrieff. Many Reasons Why.
D.P. Chandler, 293(JAst):Nov80-77
Charney, M. Comedy High and Low.*
G. Bas, 189(EA):Jan-Mar81-84
205(FMLS):Apr80-82
Charpentier, G. Trente années d'amité. (C. Becker, ed)
J. Newton, 188(ECr):Winter81-114
Charpin, F. L'idée de phrase grammaticale et son expression en latin.
H. Pinkster, 394:Vol34fasc3/4-425
Charpin, F. - see Lucilius, G.
de Charrière, I. Oeuvres complètes.* (Vol 1) (J-D. Candaux and others, eds.)
G. Van de Louw, 535(RHL):Nov-Dec81-1012
Charron, D. - see Rotrou, J.
Charron, G. Freud et le problème de la culpabilité.
C. Brodeur, 154:Mar81-149

Charters, A. Kerouac.
D. Stanley, 649(WAL):Summer81-138
Charters, A. and S. I Love.*
J. Graffy, 575(SEER):Jan81-86
Charters, S. The Roots of the Blues.*
W. Collins, 187:Sep82-469
T. Russell, 617(TLS):15Jan82-50
Charvet, J. A Critique of Freedom and Equality.
J. Waldron, 617(TLS):12Mar82-285
Charvet, J. Feminism.
K. Lennon, 617(TLS):3Dec82-1333
Charyn, J. Panna Maria.
R.P. Brickner, 441:27Jun82-12
Chase, W.M. Lionel Trilling.
J.P. McWilliams, Jr., 587(SAF):Autumn81-282
Chasins, A. Leopold Stokowski.
N. Goodwin, 415:Nov81-751
Chastain, K. Spanish Grammar in Review.
E.M. Dial, 238:Mar81-167
Chastain, K. Toward a Philosophy of Second-Language Learning and Teaching.
E. Hocking, 207(FR):Oct81-174
Chastel, A. Fables, formes figures.
J. Wirth, 98:Apr80-382
Château, J., ed. La psychologie de l'enfant en langue française.
J-M. Gabaude, 542:Jan-Mar81-127
de Chateaubriand, F.R. Correspondance générale.* (Vol 1) (B. d'Andlau, P. Christophorov and P. Riberette, eds)
F. Bassan, 446(NCFS):Fall-Winter80/81-130
de Chateaubriand, F.R. Correspondance générale. (Vol 2) (P. Riberette, ed)
F. Bassan, 446(NCFS):Fall-Winter80/81-130
R. Lebègue, 535(RHL):Jan-Feb81-145
de Chateaubriand, F.R. Correspondance générale. (Vol 3) (P. Riberette, ed)
G.D. Painter, 617(TLS):16Jul82-762
Chatham, J.R. and C.C. McClendon, with others. Dissertations in Hispanic Languages and Literatures. (Vol 2)
D. Eisenberg, 304(JHP):Autumn81-73
Chatman, S. Story and Discourse.*
H.F. Mosher, 494:Spring80-171
R. Scholes, 494:Spring80-190
P. Tammi, 439(NM):1980/1-88
Chatwin, B. On The Black Hill.
A. Duchêne, 617(TLS):10Oct82-1063
Chaudenson, R. Les créoles français.*
A. Bollée, 72:Band217Heft1-206
Chaudhuri, P. The Indian Economy.
J.S. Uppal, 293(JAst):Feb81-404
Chaudhury, N.C. Hinduism.*
A. Sharma, 314:Summer-Fall81-221
Chaussinand-Nogaret, G. Mirabeau.
P. Higonnet, 617(TLS):10Oct82-1071
Chavane, M-J. and M. Yon. Salamine de Chypre.* (Vol 10, Pts 1-3)
R.W., 555:Vol54fasc1-158
Chavrukov, G. Bulgarian Monasteries.
M. Chamot, 39:Feb81-131
Chawaf, C. Crépusculaires.
R. Linkhorn, 207(FR):May82-921
Chawaf, C. Landes.
C. Reeder, 207(FR):Oct81-153
Chazaud, J. La souffrance de l'idéal.
J-M. Gabaude, 542:Jan-Mar81-127
Cheape, C. Moving the Masses.
P.L. Clay, 432(NEQ):Sep81-449

Checchini, A.D., ed. Il Vergier de cunsol-
lacion e altri scritti (manoscritto GE
209).*
　E. Hirsch, 685(ZDL):1/1981-113
Chedid, A. Les Marches de sable.
　R. Linkhorn, 207(FR):May82-922
Cheever, J. Oh What a Paradise It Seems.
　R.M. Adams, 453(NYRB):29Apr82-8
　J. Leonard, 441:7Mar82-1
　A. Mars-Jones, 617(TLS):30Jul82-815
　R. Ottaway, 362:12Aug82-24
　J. Updike, 442(NY):5Apr82-193
Cheever, J. The Stories of John Cheever.*
　S. Pinsker, 573(SSF):Winter81-87
Cheever, J. The Cage.
　S. Ballantyne, 441:3Oct82-9
Chefdor, M. Blaise Cendrars.
　S. Taylor-Horrex, 208(FS):Jul81-359
Chekhov, A. The Early Stories 1883-88.
　(P. Miles and H. Pitcher, eds and trans)
　K. Fitz Lyon, 617(TLS):24Sep82-1044
Chekhov, A. The Oxford Chekhov.* (Vol 4)
　(R. Hingley, ed and trans)
　M. Ehre, 574(SEEJ):Summer81-92
Chekki, D.A. The Sociology of Contempo-
rary India.
　G.R. Gupta, 293(JASt):Feb81-405
Chellas, B.F. Modal Logic.
　D. Makinson, 316:Sep81-670
Ch'en, J. China and the West.
　P.A. Cohen, 293(JASt):Feb81-339
　D.E. Waterfall, 529(QQ):Summer81-279
Ch'en, J. The Military-Gentry Coalition.
　P. Suleski, 293(JASt):Nov80-98
Mme. Chen Jo-shi. Le Préfet Yin.
　Y. Kempf, 450(NRF):Apr81-144
Ch'en Ku-Ying. Lao Tzu.
　H. Welch, 293(JASt):Feb81-359
Chen, P.S.J. and J.T. Fawcett, eds. Pub-
lic Policy and Population Change in
Singapore.
　J.T. Johnson, 293(JASt):May81-647
Chenery, H. Structural Change and Develop-
ment Policy.
　J.G. Gurley, 293(JASt):Feb81-329
Cheng, F. L'Espace du Rêve.
　Y. Kempf, 450(NRF):Apr81-144
Chénier, A. Elegies and Camille.
　M.J. O'Regan, 402(MLR):Jan81-189
Cheong, W.E. Mandarins and Merchants.
　R. Murphey, 293(JASt):Nov80-101
　A.J. Youngson, 302:Vol 18-166
Cherkovski, N. Ferlinghetti.
　D. Street, 584(SWR):Spring81-228
　648(WCR):Vol 15No3-72
Cherlin, A.J. Marriage Divorce Remarriage.
　A. Hacker, 453(NYRB):18Mar82-37
Chernaik, J. The Daughter.*
　J. Mellors, 364:Jun81-93
Cherniss, H. Selected Papers. (L. Tarán,
ed)
　R.K. Sprague, 122:Apr81-151
Chernoff, J.M. African Rhythm and African
Sensibility.
　R.A. Dendinger, 2(AfrA):Nov80-80
Cherry, C. Nature and Religious Imagina-
tion From Edwards to Bushnell.
　W. Breitenbach, 656(WMQ):Jul81-525
Chertok, L. Le non-savoir des psy.
　J-M. Cabaude, 542:Jan-Mar81-132
　F. Roustang, 98:Dec80-1192
Cherubim, D., ed. Fehllinguistik.
　T.A. Lovik, 350:Sep81-779

Cherubim, D. Grammatische Kategorien.*
　K.R. Jankowsky, 685(ZDL):1/1981-68
Chervel, A. "...et il fallut apprendre à
écrire à tous les petits Français."*
　K. Connors, 545(RPh):Feb81(supp)-189
Chesnut, G.F. The First Christian His-
tories.
　J. Helgeland, 125:Winter81-236
Chesnut, M. Mary Chesnut's Civil War.*
　(C.V. Woodward, ed)
　N.F. Cott, 676(YR):Autumn81-121
　M. O'Brien, 385(MQR):Summer82-515
Chesnutt, M. and others, eds. Essays Pre-
sented to Knud Schibsbye.
　P. Steller, 179(ES):Feb81-88
Chessick, R.D. Freud Teaches Psycho-
therapy.
　D. Duncalfe, 529(QQ):Winter81-800
Chester, L. My Pleasure.
　P. Schjeldahl, 472:Spring/Summer81-284
"The Chester Mystery Cycle: A Reduced Fac-
simile of Huntington Library MS 2."
　L.M. Clopper, 130:Winter81/82-384
Chesterton, G.K. Le Poète et les Luna-
tiques.
　H. Cronel, 450(NRF):Jun81-132
Chetrit, J. L'influence du français dans
les langues judéo-arabes d'Afrique du
Nord.
　H. Wise, 208(FS):Oct81-503
Cheung, D. Feng Chih.
　R. Vohra, 293(JASt):May81-578
Cheuse, A. The Bohemians.
　P. Andrews, 441:28Mar82-14
Chevalley, S. La Comédie-Française hier
et aujourd'hui.
　F. Bassan, 446(NCFS):Fall-Winter81/82-
165
　A. Blanc, 475:No13Pt1-140
Chevalley, S. and P. Dux. La Comédie
Française.
　F. Bassan, 446(NCFS):Fall-Winter81/82-
165
Cheyfitz, E. The Trans-Parent.
　C. Daly, 400(MLN):Dec81-1227
　385(MQR):Spring82-378
Chia, C.S. Turned Clay.
　P. Monk, 150(DR):Winter81/82-763
Chiarenza, C. Aaron Siskind.
　A. Grundberg, 441:5Dec82-58
Chiarini, G. La Recita.
　H.D. Jocelyn, 123:Vol31No2-194
Chiavacci Leonardi, A.M. La guerra de la
pietate.
　M. Marti, 228(GSLI):Vol 158fasc503-441
　M.U. Sowell, 589:Jul81-632
Chiavacci Leonardi, A.M. Il "Secolo di
Dante" nella critica del Foscolo.
　M. Marti, 228(GSLI):Vol 158fasc503-441
Chibnall, M. - see Orderic Vitalis
Chicoteau, C. Chère Rose.
　R.B. Leal, 67:Nov81-258
Ch'ien Chung-shu. Fortress Besieged.
　A.J. Palandri, 293(JASt):Nov80-102
Chierici, S. Romanische Lombardei.
　W. Haas, 43:Band11Heft1-87
Chiesa, G. - see under Sena Chiesa, G.
Chikafusa, K. A Chronicle of Gods and
Sovereigns. (H.P. Varley, trans)
　J.S. Brownlee, 407(MN):Summer81-206
　J.P. Mass, 293(JASt):May81-612

Christine de Pisan. The Middle English Translation of Christine de Pisan's "Livre du Corps de Policie." (D. Bornstein, ed)
D. Pearsall, 72:Band217Heft1-190

Christine de Pisan and others. Le Débat sur le "Roman de la Rose."* (E. Hicks, ed)
P.H. Stäblein, 545(RPh):May81-562

Christison, M.A. and S. Bassano. Look Who's Talking!
K.D. Pechilis, 608:Dec82-551

Christoff, P.K. K.S. Aksakov.
L. Schapiro, 617(TLS):220ct82-1165

Christophilopoulos, A.P. Nomika epigraphika.
A.G. Woodhead, 303(JoHS):Vol 101-224

Christy, J. Rough Road to the North.
G.W., 102(CanL):Autumn80-156

Chu, G.C. and F.L.K. Hsu, eds. Moving a Mountain.
R. Crozier, 293(JASt):Feb81-341

Chubb, J.N. Assertion and Fact.
T.S. Champlin, 518:Jan81-31

Chung, S. Case Marking and Grammatical Relations in Polynesian.
R. Clark, 350:Mar81-198

Chung-shu, C. - see under Ch'ien Chung-shu

Churba, J. Retreat from Freedom.
R. Saidel, 390:Feb81-56

Church, E.F. and T. George, eds. Continuity and Discontinuity in Church History.
G. Strauss, 551(RenQ):Summer80-246

"Churches in Greece, 1453-1850."
T.E. Gregory, 576:Dec81-328

Churchland, P.M. Scientific Realism and the Plasticity of Mind.*
J.M. Hinton, 518:Jul81-163
S.P.S., 185:Oct81-197

Cianci, G., ed. Wyndham Lewis: Letteratura/Pittura.
A. Mars-Jones, 617(TLS):3Dec82-1334

Ciardi, J. A Browser's Dictionary and Native's Guide to the Unknown American Language.
G. Core, 249(HudR):Autumn81-475
N. Miller, 42(AR):Winter81-123
639(VQR):Winter81-30

Ciccone, A.A. The Comedy of Language.
G. Montbertrand, 210(FrF):Sep81-277

Cicero. Cicéron, "De Natura Deorum." (Bk 2) (M. van den Bruwaene, ed and trans)
M. Winterbottom, 123:Vol31No2-295

Cicero. Epistulae ad Familiares.* (D.R. Shackleton Bailey, ed)
J.M. Hunt, 122:Jul81-215

Cicero. Epistulae ad Quintum fratrem et M. Brutum. (D.R. Shackleton Bailey, ed)
E. Rawson, 123:Vol31No2-211

Cicero. Select Letters. (D.R. Shackleton Bailey, ed)
E. Rawson, 123:Vol31No1-119

Cicourel, A.V. Sprache in der sozialen Interaktion.
R. Hopfer, 682(ZPSK):Band33Heft5-588

Cieszkowski, A. Selected Writings of August Cieszkowski. (A. Liebich, ed and trans)
D. McLellan, 575(SEER):Apr81-304
N. Naimark, 104(CASS):Winter81-625

"Cinquante ans de théâtre: André Barsacq."
D. Knowles, 208(FS):Jan81-100

Cioran, E.M. Ecartèlement.*
A. Compagnon, 98:May80-457

Cirerol, M. Etats d'âme.
D.E. Rivas, 207(FR):May82-923

Citti, V. Tragedia e lotta di classe in Grecia.
R.G.A. Buxton, 303(JoHS):Vol 101-172
F. Jouan, 555:Vol54fasc2-345
C.W. MacLeod, 123:Vol31No1-107

Ciucci, G. and others. The American City: From the Civil War to the New Deal.*
P.R. Baker, 658:Winter81-351

Clabburn, P. Shawls.
R.L. Shep, 614:Spring82-16

Clack, D.H., ed. The Making of a Code.
N.B. Parker, 14:Spring81-159

Clader, L.L. Helen.
J. Bremmer, 394:Vol34fasc1/2-148

Claesges, U. Geschichte des Selbstbewusstseins.
E. Fuchs, 53(AGP):Band62Heft1-99

Claiborne, C. A Feast Made for Laughter.
B.H. Fussell, 441:10Oct82-12

Claiborne, C., with P. Franey. The New New York Times Cookbook.
W. and C. Cowen, 639(VQR):Spring81-71

Clairmont, R.E. A Commentary on Seneca's Apocolocyntosis Divi Claudii.
P.T. Eden, 123:Vol31No2-328

Clanchy, M.T. From Memory to Written Record.*
J.H. Mundy, 589:Jan81-109

Clancy, J. Christmas Cookbook.
M. Sheraton, 441:5Dec82-12

Clapham, J. Dvořák.*
J.H., 412:Feb80-68

Clardy, J.V. and B.S. The Superfluous Man in Russian Letters.
M. Friedberg, 651(WHR):Winter81-374
T. Pachmuss, 550(RusR):Jan81-81
S. Rabinowitz, 574(SEEJ):Spring81-111

Clare, G. Last Waltz in Vienna.
E. de Mauny, 617(TLS):26Mar82-356
F. Morton, 441:28Mar82-9
442(NY):17May82-140

Claremon, N. Easy Favors.
P. Varner, 649(WAL):Spring81-71

Clarence-Smith, W.G. Slaves, Peasants and Capitalists in Southern Angola 1840-1926.*
C. Henfrey, 69:Vol50No3-321

Clarfield, G.H. Timothy Pickering and the American Republic.
W.B. Fowler, 432(NEQ):Dec81-595
W. Stinchcombe, 656(WMQ):Apr81-331

Clark, A. Christopher Brennan.
D. Green, 381:Apr81-93

Clark, A. Lewis Carroll, A Biography.*
K. Blake, 637(VS):Autumn80-128

Clark, A. Psychological Models and Neural Mechanisms.
R. Puccetti, 518:Jul81-166

Clark, A. The Real Alice.*
442(NY):20Sep82-152

Clark, A.M. Anthony Morris Clark — Studies in Roman Eighteenth-Century Painting. (E.P. Bowron, ed)
A. Blunt, 617(TLS):19Mar82-319

Clark, A.M. Murder Under Trust or the Topical Macbeth.
J. Briggs, 617(TLS):29Oct82-1187

Clark, C. Thomas Moran.
W.G. Bell, 649(WAL):Summer81-156
J. Lunsford, 584(SWR):Spring81-220
Clark, C. The Web of Metaphor.*
W.H. Bowen, 551(RenQ):Spring80-114
S.J. Holyoake, 402(MLR):Apr81-465
205(FMLS):Apr80-82
Clark, D. Between Pulpit and Pew.
D. Martin, 617(TLS):15Oct82-1138
Clark, D. Doone Walk.
T.J. Binyon, 617(TLS):31Dec82-1448
Clark, D. Roast Eggs.
N. Callendar, 441:10Jan82-29
Clark, D. Shelf Life.
T.J.B., 617(TLS):16Jul82-775
Clark, E.C. Francis Warrington Dawson and
the Politics of Restoration.
E.M. Lander, Jr., 9(AlaR):Jul81-233
W.M. Strickland, 583:Summer82-455
Clark, E.E. and M. Edmonds. Sacagawea of
the Lewis and Clark Expedition.
R.E. Robinson, 649(WAL):Summer81-152
Clark, J. and others, eds. Culture and
Crisis in Britain in the 30s.
M. Green, 366:Autumn81-267
Clark, J.D., ed. The Cambridge History of
Africa. (Vol 1)
C.T. Shaw, 617(TLS):18Jun82-673
Clark, K. An Introduction to Rembrandt.
B. Wind, 568(SCN):Summer-Fall81-57
Clark, K. The Soviet Novel.
G. Hosking, 617(TLS):2Apr82-367
V.D. Mihailovich, 268(IFR):Summer82-
152
Clark, K. and D. Finn. The Florence
Baptistery Doors.*
P. Cannon-Brookes, 39:Jul81-68
Clark, L.D. Is This Naomi? And Other
Stories.
M.R. Bennett, 649(WAL):Spring81-68
Clark, L.D. The Minoan Distance.
C. Boebel, 50(ArQ):Winter81-373
G.H. Ford, 651(WHR):Autumn81-280
D.C. Haberman, 177(ELT):Vol24No4-214
295(JML):Vol8No3/4-547
Clark, L.M.G. and L. Lange, eds. The Sex-
ism of Social and Political Theory.
N. Holmstrom, 185:Jan82-368
Clark, M. and M. Mowlam, eds. Debate on
Disarmament.
C.M. Woodhouse, 617(TLS):24Sep82-1030
Clark, M.H. A Cry in the Night.
E. Jakab, 441:14Nov82-15
Clark, M.J., ed. Politics and the Media.
H.P. Raleigh, 289:Apr81-111
Clark, P., A.G.R. Smith and N. Tyacke, eds.
The English Commonwealth, 1547-1640.*
A.J. Slavin, 551(RenQ):Autumn80-440
Clark, R. Bertrand Russell and his World.
483:Jul81-437
Clark, R.J. Catabasis.
D.E. Hill, 487:Spring81-98
N. Horsfall, 313:Vol71-220
C. Segal, 24:Summer81-237
Clark, R.L., ed. Afro-American History:
Sources for Research.
L.J. Henry, 14:Fall81-363
Clark, R.P. The Basques.
R.L. Trask, 86(BHS):Jul81-272
Clark, R.W. Freud.*
D. Duncalfe, 529(QQ):Spring81-158
Clark, R.W. The Greatest Power on Earth.
639(VQR):Autumn81-134

Clark, S. Social Origins of the Irish
Land War.
D.H. Akenson, 529(QQ):Autumn81-490
A. O'Day, 637(VS):Spring81-384
Clark, S.R.L. The Moral Status of Animals.
D. Jamieson, 449:May81-230
Clark, S.R.L. The Nature of the Beast.
B. Brophy, 617(TLS):15Oct82-1124
Clark, T. and L.E. Bannon. Handbook of
Audubon Prints.
E. Hardy, 39:Aug81-138
Clark, T.A. Madder Lake.
C. Inez, 472:Fall/Winter81-231
Clarke, A. Growing Up Stupid Under The
Union Jack.
C. Dabydeen, 150(DR):Spring81-156
K. Garebian, 102(CanL):Autumn81-136
D. Pinckney, 453(NYRB):27May82-46
Clarke, A.C. 2010: Odyssey Two.
442(NY):20Dec82-138
Clarke, B., ed. Architectural Stained
Glass.
G. Russell, 324:Jan82-106
Clarke, B.K. and H. Ferrar. The Dublin
Drama League 1919-1941.
G. Phillips, 174(Éire):Winter81-133
Clarke, D. Louison.
J.Z. Brown, 174(Éire):Winter81-157
Clarke, E.H. Demand Revelation and the
Provision of Public Goods.
N.R.M., 185:Jan82-396
Clarke, G.W. Street Names of Kahului and
Wailuki.
K.B. Harder, 424:Jun81-174
Clarke, H.D.B. and M. Hamamura. Collo-
quial Japanese.
T.M. Critchfield, 399(MLJ):Winter81-
435
Clarke, J.M. The Life and Adventures of
John Muir.
W.F. Kimes, 649(WAL):Spring81-63
Clarke, J.R. Roman Black-and-White
Figural Mosaics.
E. Waywell, 123:Vol31No1-140
Clarke, J.W. American Assassins.
J.B., 231:Sep82-76
M. Kammen, 441:29Aug82-9
Clarke, M. The Tempting Prospect.
D. Thomas, 324:May82-367
Clarke, M.L. The Noblest Roman.*
E. Rawson, 123:Vol31No2-327
Clarke, M.W. The Slaughter Ranches and
Their Makers.
W. Gard, 584(SWR):Winter81-vi
Clarke, R. Anglo-American Economic Col-
laboration in War and Peace 1942-1949.
M. Beloff, 617(TLS):4Jun82-620
Clarke, S. The Foundations of Structural-
ism.*
V.V., 185:Jul82-803
Clarke, S. and others. One-Dimensional
Marxism.
T. Eagleton, 208(FS):Jul81-369
Clarke, T.E.B. Murder at Buckingham
Palace.
P-L. Adams, 61:Mar82-89
Clarkson, A. and G.B. Cross, eds. World
Folktales.
J.R. Reaver, 650(WF):Jul81-281
Clarkson, E. The Many-Forked Branch.
A. Schimpf, 649(WAL):Fall81-249
Claro Valdés, S. Oyendo a Chile.
E. Garmendia, 263(RIB):Vol31No1-80

Claude, D. Geschichte des Erzbistums
Magdeburg bis in das 12. Jahrhundert.
(Vol 2)
  B.H. Hill, Jr., 589:Jan81-215
Claudel, C.A. Fools and Rascals.
  E.C. Lynskey, 577(SHR):Fall81-370
  R. Wehse, 196:Band22Heft1/2-117
Claudel, P. and F. Mauriac. Chroniques du
"Journal de Clichy" [together with]
Claudel, P. and D. Fontaine. Corres-
pondance. (F. Morlot and J. Touzot, eds)
  A. Blanc, 535(RHL):Mar-Apr81-321
Clausen, C. The Place of Poetry.
  D. Donoghue, 441:24Jan82-10
  C. Martin, 472:Spring/Summer82-254
Clavel, M. La suite appartient à d'autres.
  P. Legendre, 98:Jan80-63
Clavet, A. Guide to Canadian Photographic
Archives/Guide des archives photogra-
phiques canadienne.
  W. Rundell, Jr., 14:Winter80-81
Clayman, D.L. Callimachus' Iambi.
  F. Cairns, 123:Vol31No2-287
Clayton, T., ed. Cavalier Poets.*
  J. Creaser, 447(N&Q):Oct80-442
Cleary, T., ed. Timeless Spring.
  A. Bloom, 407(MN):Spring81-109
Cleaver, H. Reading "Capital" Politically.
  A.L., 185:Jan82-391
Clegg, J.S. The Structure of Plato's
Philosophy.
  N.D. Smith, 319:Jan81-105
Clegg, S. The Theory of Power and
Organization.
  T. Ball, 185:Apr81-532
Clemen, W. Originalität und Tradition in
der englischen Dichtungsgeschichte.
  W. Bies, 604:Fall81-65
Clemens, P.G.E. The Atlantic Economy and
Colonial Maryland's Eastern Shore.
  R.E. Gallman, 656(WMQ):Jul81-521
Clemenson, H.A. English Country Houses
and Landed Estates.
  A. Saint, 617(TLS):26Nov82-1295
Clément, F. Le Canton des nuages.
  G.R. Besser, 207(FR):Oct80-190
Clements, B.E. Bolshevik Feminist.*
  R.C. Williams, 104(CASS):Winter81-603
Clements, G.N., ed. Harvard Studies in
Phonology. (Vol 2)
  E. Kaisse, 350:Jun82-479
Clements, P. and J. Grindle, eds. The
Poetry of Thomas Hardy.*
  I. Goody, 627(UTQ):Summer81-126
Clements, R.J. and J. Gibaldi. Anatomy of
the Novella.
  V. Ugalde, 552(REH):May81-301
Clements, R.J. and L. Levant, eds. Renais-
sance Letters.
  K.R. Bartlett, 539:Feb82-66
Clendennen, G.W., with I.C. Cunningham,
comps. David Livingstone.
  R. Seton, 325:Apr81-438
Cleomedes. Cléomède: "Theorie Elémen-
taire." (R. Goulet, ed and trans)
  R. Beck, 487:Fall81-287
  I. Bulmer-Thomas, 123:Vol31No2-277
Clerc, F., ed. Le Monde paysan.
  A. Duhamel-Ketchum, 207(FR):Dec80-374
Clift, D. and S. Arnopoulos. Le Fait
anglais au Québec.
  R. Sutherland, 102(CanL):Spring81-92

Clifton-Everest, J.M. The Tragedy of
Knighthood.*
  K. Smits, 67:Nov81-264
  H.B. Willson, 402(MLR):Jan81-235
Clifton-Taylor, A. Six English Towns.
  J. Rykwert, 576:May81-172
Clitandre, P. Cathédrale du mois d'août.
  J. Kirkup, 617(TLS):9Jul82-750
Cloonan, W. Racine's Theatre.
  C.G.S. Williams, 207(FR):Mar81-592
Clopper, L.M., ed. Records of Early
English Drama: Chester.*
  P. Neuss, 611(TN):Vol35No1-33
Close, A. The Romantic Approach to "Don
Quixote."*
  I. Azar, 400(MLN):Mar81-440
Closs, A. - see Priebsch, R. and E. von
Steinmeyer
Clothey, F.W. The Many Faces of Murukaṇ.
  J.B. Long, 293(JASt):May81-625
Clothier, C. Death Mask.
  S. Ellis, 617(TLS):22Jan82-90
Clough, S.D.P. Homage to the Haiku
Masters.
  W. Cope, 617(TLS):29Jan82-114
Cloutier, C. Chaleuils.
  G.V. Downes, 102(CanL):Winter80-105
Cloutier, D., ed and trans. Spirit,
Spirit, Shaman Songs.
  M. Heller, 472:Spring/Summer81-269
Cloutier, G. Cette Profondeur Parfois.
  D. Festa-McCormick, 207(FR):Apr82-701
Clover, H. and M. Gibson - see Lanfranc
Clowney, P. and T. Exploring Churches.
  P. Goldberger, 441:26Dec82-3
Clubbe, J. - see Froude, J.A.
Clube, V. and B. Napier. The Cosmic Ser-
pent.
  J. North, 617(TLS):24Dec82-1407
Clucas, H. Gods and Mortals.
  G. Szirtes, 617(TLS):15Oct82-1139
Clutton-Brock, J. Domesticated Animals
from Early Times.
  D.R. Harris, 617(TLS):9Apr82-420
Clüver, C. Thornton Wilder und André
Obey.
  F.H. Link, 52:Band15Heft2-223
Clyne, R. djarp.
  G. Bitcon, 581:Dec81-469
Coale, A.J., B. Anderson and E. Harm.
Human Fertility in Russia Since the
Nineteenth Century.
  R.A. French, 575(SEER):Jan81-109
  104(CASS):Winter81-597
Coates, W.H., A.S. Young and V.F. Snow,
eds. The Private Journals of the Long
Parliament: 3 January to 5 March 1642.
  D. Pennington, 617(TLS):18Jun82-670
Cobb, B.E., Jr. The Sacred Harp.*
  G.W. Boswell, 650(WF):Jul81-276
Cobb, G. English Cathedrals.
  A. Clifton-Taylor, 135:Feb81-164
Cobb, R. Promenades.*
  J. Cruickshank, 208(FS):Apr81-246
Cobb, R. The Streets of Paris.
  J. Rykwert, 437:Winter80/81-136
Cobo, M.A. - see under Agulló y Cobo, M.
Coburn, A. Company Secrets.
  T.J. Binyon, 617(TLS):2Jul82-725
Coburn, K. Experience into Thought.*
  A.J. Harding, 178:Dec81-488
  L.S. Lockridge, 661(WC):Summer81-148
  J.R. Watson, 83:Autumn81-202

Coburn, K. - see Coleridge, S.T.
Cocco, M. La tradizione cortese ed il petrarchismo nella poesia di Clément Marot.*
  J.T. Nothnagle, 551(RenQ):Spring80-111
Cochrane, E. Historians and Historiography in the Italian Renaissance.
  D. Hay, 617(TLS):12Feb82-153
Cockburn, J.S., ed. Calendar of Assize Records: Kent Indictments, Elizabeth I.*
  C. Cross, 325:Apr81-433
Cockburn, J.S., ed. Calendar of Assize Records: Kent Indictments, James I.
  C. Cross, 325:Oct81-507
Cockfield, J.H., ed. Dollars and Diplomacy.
  C.F. Smith, 550(RusR):Oct81-452
Cocking, J.M. Proust.
  R. Shattuck, 617(TLS):5Nov82-1222
Cocks, A.S. The Victoria and Albert Museum.
  90:Mar81-192
Cocks, P.M. Science Policy: U.S.A./USSR. (Vol 2)
  R.W. Campbell, 550(RusR):Oct81-455
Cockshut, A.O.J. Anthony Trollope.
  J. Roubaud, 98:Feb-Mar81-166
Cockshut, A.O.J. - see Thackeray, W.M.
Cody, J., H. Hughes and D. Wall, eds. Policies for Industrial Progress in Developing Countries.
  B. Ward, 293(JASt):Feb81-335
Cody, L. Bad Company.
  T.J. Binyon, 617(TLS):31Dec82-1448
Cody, L. Dupe.*
  N. Callendar, 441:7Feb82-20
van Coetsem, F. and H.L. Kufner, eds. Toward a Grammar of Proto-Germanic.
  J.B. Voyles, 361:Oct/Nov81-249
van Coetsem, F. and L.R. Waugh, eds. Contributions to Historical Linguistics.
  J. Klausenburger, 350:Jun82-480
Coetzee, J.M. Waiting for the Barbarians.*
  P-L. Adams, 61:Jun82-101
  C. Hope, 364:Apr/May81-136
  I. Howe, 441:18Apr82-1
  J. Kramer, 453(NYRB):2Dec82-8
  G. Steiner, 442(NY):12Jul82-102
Coffin, D.R. The Villa in the Life of Renaissance Rome.*
  D. Cast, 43:Band11Heft2-190
  A. Laing, 161(DUJ):Dec80-83
  L. Partridge, 54:Jun81-336
Coffin, L. Human Trappings.
  H. Thomas, 385(MQR):Winter82-200
Coffman, R.J. Solomon Stoddard.*
  K. Keller, 568(SCN):Spring81-22
Cogan, M. The Human Thing.
  A.W.H.A., 185:Jul82-773
Cogny, P. and others. Nouvelles Recherches sur "Bouvard et Pécuchet" de Flaubert.
  C.A. Levinson, 446(NCFS):Spring-Summer82-362
Cohen, A.D. Testing Language Ability in the Classroom.
  A.C. Omaggio, 399(MLJ):Autumn81-328
  A. Pousada, 350:Dec81-978
Cohen, C.E. The Drawings of Giovanni Antonio da Pordenone.
  K. Andrews, 90:Feb81-103

Cohen, G.A. Karl Marx's Theory of History.*
  W.L. McBride, 185:Jan82-316
  R.W. Miller, 482(PhR):Jan81-91
  J. Rée, 98:Aug-Sep80-802
Cohen, H. Equal Rights for Children.
  P.H.J., 185:Apr82-589
Cohen, H. Werke. (Vol 4: Kommentar zu Immanuel Kants Kritik der reinen Vernunft.)(H. Holzhey, ed)
  W. Marx, 53(AGP):Band63Heft1-96
Cohen, H. Werke. (Vol 6, Pt 1: Logik der reinen Erkenntnis.) (H. Holzhey, ed)
  W. Marx, 53(AGP):Band63Heft2-204
Cohen, H.S. Elusive Reform.
  B. Petit, 207(FR):Oct80-206
Cohen, J. The Friars and the Jews.
  G. Leff, 617(TLS):5Nov82-1208
Cohen, J. Le haut langage.
  J-L. Chrétien, 98:Feb80-135
Cohen, J.R. Charles Dickens and His Original Illustrators.*
  R.L. Patten, 445(NCF):Sep81-226
  A. Powell, 39:Feb81-125
  A. Sanders, 155:Spring81-41
Cohen, K. Film and Fiction.*
  G. Mast, 405(MP):May82-458
  P. Nordon, 189(EA):Jan-Mar81-87
Cohen, L.J. The Probable and the Provable.*
  S. Stoljar, 482(PhR):Jul81-457
Cohen, L.J. and M. Hesse, eds. Applications of Inductive Logic.
  J. Largeault, 542:Oct-Dec81-501
Cohen, M. Flowers of Darkness.
  G. Woodcock, 102(CanL):Summer81-137
Cohen, M. The Inconvenience of Living.
  R.J. Stout, 435:Winter81-100
Cohen, M. Miroirs.
  N.Q. Maurer, 450(NRF):Mar81-126
Cohen, M. The Sweet Second Summer of Kitty Malone.*
  M. Northey, 102(CanL):Autumn80-122
Cohen, M.E. Balag-Compositions.
  S.D. Sperling, 318(JAOS):Jul/Sep80-371
Cohen, M.N., with R.L. Green - see Carroll, L.
Cohen, R. Domestic Tranquility.*
  S.D. Lavine, 385(MQR):Winter82-189
Cohen, R. - see Nzula, A.T., I.I. Potekhin and A.Z. Zusmanovich
Cohen, R., P.K. Feyerabend and M.W. Wartofsky, eds. Essays in Memory of Imre Lakatos.
  J.F. Fox, 63:Mar81-92
Cohen, S. Norman Mailer's Novels.
  P. Bufithis, 395(MFS):Winter80/81-680
Cohen, S. The Man in the Crowd.*
  R. Blount, Jr., 441:10Jan82-6
Cohen, S.B., ed. Comic Relief.*
  H. Hill, 395(MFS):Summer80-320
Cohen, S.F., ed. An End to Silence.
  A. Austin, 441:7Feb82-11
  J.B. Dunlop, 617(TLS):29Oct82-1195
  442(NY):8Feb82-130
Cohen, S.F., A. Rabinowitch and R. Sharlet, eds. The Soviet Union Since Stalin.
  A. Dallin, 550(RusR):Jan81-67
Cohen, S.J.D. Josephus in Galilee and Rome.
  M.D. Goodman, 313:Vol71-222
  T. Rajak, 123:Vol31No2-250

Cohen, S.P. and C.V. Raghavulu. The
Andhra Cyclone of 1977.
  P. Greenough, 293(JASt):Aug81-815
Cohen, W.B. The French Encounter with
Africans.
  J.J. Lafontant, 446(NCFS):Fall-Win-
  ter81/82-182
Cohen, W.S. Roll Call.*
  639(VQR):Summer81-93
Cohen-Tanugi, P. and C. Morrisson. Sal-
aires, intérêts, profits dans l'indus-
trie française.
  J-M. Guieu, 207(FR):Dec81-286
Cohler, D.K. Freemartin.
  N. Callendar, 441:31Jan82-22
Cohn, D. Transparent Minds.*
  J.M. Ellis, 301(JEGP):Apr81-308
  H. Foltinek, 402(MLR):Jul81-643
  S. Jackiw, 221(GQ):Jan81-118
  B. McHale, 494:Winter81-183
  S. Soupel, 189(EA):Jul-Sep81-328
  W. Wittkowski, 406:Summer81-225
Cohn, J. Improbable Fiction.
  E. Ammons, 587(SAF):Spring81-132
Cohn, J. The Palace or the Poorhouse.
  M. Filler, 576:Oct81-254
Cohn, R. Just Play.*
  J. Acheson, 67:May81-120
  J. Acheson, 295(JML):Vol8No3/4-449
  D.G., 214:Vol 10No37-111
  D. Ketterer, 529(QQ):Spring81-188
  J.G. Miller, 397(MD):Dec81-561
Cohn, R. New American Dramatists 1960-
1980.
  N. de Jongh, 617(TLS):3Dec82-1347
Cohn, R.G. Mallarmé: "Igitur."
  M. Bishop, 150(DR):Winter81/82-692
  G.D. Martin, 617(TLS):2Apr82-386
Cohn, S.K., Jr. The Laboring Classes in
Renaissance Florence.
  F. Gilbert, 453(NYRB):21Jan82-62
  J. Larner, 617(TLS):15Jan82-61
Coja, M. and P. Dupont. Histria. (Vol 5)
  R.M. Cook, 303(JoHS):Vol 101-214
Colace, P.R. - see Choerilus of Samos
Colby, R.A. Thackeray's Canvass of Human-
ity.*
  D. Hawes, 541(RES):Nov81-462
  C. MacKay, 445(NCF):Jun80-109
  S. Monod, 189(EA):Apr-Jun81-228
  R. ap Roberts, 579(SAQ):Spring81-237
Cole, B. Agnolo Gaddi.
  J. White, 551(RenQ):Winter80-758
Cole, B. Masaccio and the Art of Early
Renaissance Florence.
  C. Eisler, 39:Sep81-205
  R. Linnenkamp, 471:Jul/Aug/Sep81-293
  T. Tolley, 59:Mar81-124
Cole, B. Sienese Painting.*
  E. Fahy, 39:Aug81-130
  F. Russell, 324:Jan82-107
Cole, B., ed. Television Today.
  R. Sklar, 18:Jun81-60
Cole, D. The Work of Sir Gilbert Scott.*
  J. Summerson, 90:Feb81-108
Cole, H.C. The "All's Well" Story from
Boccaccio to Shakespeare.
  B. Vickers, 617(TLS):18Jun82-678
Cole, J.M. Exile in the Wilderness.*
  C.W., 102(CanL):Summer80 180
Cole, L. Dream Team.
  R. Blount, Jr., 441:10Jan82-6

Cole, P., ed. Syntax and Semantics.
(Vol 9)
  E.A. Moravcsik, 215(GL):Spring81-62
Colecchia, F. García Lorca.
  G. Roberts, 238:May81-315
Colegate, I. The Shooting Party.*
  639(VQR):Autumn81-136
Coleiro, E. An Introduction to Vergil's
"Bucolics" with a Critical Edition of
the Text.
  W.W. Briggs, Jr., 121(CJ):Apr/May82-
  359
Coleman, A. Eça de Queirós and European
Realism.
  A. Freeland, 86(BHS):Oct81-353
  A.J. MacAdam, 345(KRQ):Vol28No3-324
  E.W. White, 395(MFS):Winter80/81-745
Coleman, C. Sergeant Back Again.
  G. Kearns, 249(HudR):Summer81-302
Coleman, D.G. The Chaste Muse.
  L.V.R., 568(SCN):Spring81-31
Coleman, D.G. The Gallo-Roman Muse.*
  T.C. Cave, 402(MLR):Apr81-461
  D. Stone, Jr., 207(FR):Oct81-134
  205(FMLS):Apr80-187
Coleman, D.G. Rabelais.
  A.R. Mackay, 539:Nov82-291
Coleman, J.S., T. Hoffer and S. Kilgore.
High School Achievement.
  M.J. Bane, 441:28Nov82-11
Coleman, K. Colonial Georgia.
  J. Sainsbury, 106:Spring81-57
Coleman, N.G. A Moonbeam's Metamorphosis.
  G. Bitcon, 581:Dec81-469
Coleman, T. Thanksgiving.
  W. Logan, 617(TLS):28May82-594
Coleridge, S.T. The Collected Works of
Samuel Taylor Coleridge. (Marginalia, 1)
(G. Whalley, ed)
  J. Curtis, 648(WCR):Vol 15No3-80
  W.J.B. Owen, 402(UTQ):Summer81-119
  S.V. Pradhan, 150(DR):Spring81-143
Coleridge, S.T. Inquiring Spirit. (rev)
(K. Coburn, ed)
  J.R. Watson, 83:Autumn81-202
Coleridge-Taylor, A. The Heritage of
Samuel Coleridge-Taylor.
  S. Banfield, 415:Jan81-31
Coles, D. Anniversaries.*
  P. Stevens, 529(QQ):Autumn81-504
  A. Suknaski, 102(CanL):Autumn80-130
Coles, R. Flannery O'Connor's South.*
  J. Conarroe, 27(AL):Mar81-138
  M.J. Friedman, 578:Fal182-120
  M. Orvell, 295(JML):Vol8No3/4-578
Coles, R.A. and others. The Oxyrhynchus
Papyri. (Vol 47)
  W. Luppe, 123:Vol131No2-267
Colette. Le Blé en herbe. (B. Stimpson,
ed)
  J.H. Stewart, 207(FR):Feb82-417
Colette. Letters from Colette.* (R.
Phillips, ed and trans)
  639(VQR):Autumn81-126
Colignon, J-P. and P.V. Berthier. Pièges
du langage.
  R.J. Melpignano, 399(MLJ):Summer81-218
Colin, R-P. Schopenhauer en France.
  J.T. Baer, 207(FR):May82-907
  R. Ripoll, 535(RHL):Jul-Oct81-820
Collard, D. Altruism and Economy.
  B.B., 185:Jan81-344

Collard, E. Decade of Change.
R.L. Shep, 614:Spring82-12
Collard, E. Women's Dress in the 1920's.
R.L. Shep, 614:Winter82-21
Collart, J. Varron, grammaire antique et
stylistique latine.
C. Moussy, 555:Vol54fasc1-184
Collcutt, M. Five Mountains.
H.P. Varley, 407(MN):Winter81-463
Colledge, E. and J. Walsh, eds. A Book of
Showings to the Anchoress Julian of Nor-
wich.*
M. Glasscoe, 382(MAE):1981/1-170
"College and University Archives: Selected
Readings."
C. Densmore, 14:Spring80-214
Collet, G.P. - see Gide, A. and J-É.
Blanche
Collett, P. Elgar Lived Here. Elgar
Country.
R. Anderson, 415:Dec81-822
Colley, I. Dos Passos and the Fiction of
Despair.*
R. Belflower, 541(RES):Nov81-476
L. Hughson, 594:Fall81-334
D. Seed, 677(YES):Vol 11-357
R.P. Weeks, 395(MFS):Autumn80-520
Colley, L. In Defiance of Oligarchy.
E. Cruickshanks, 617(TLS):28May82-581
Colli, G. La sapienza greca. (Vol 3)
J. Barnes, 123:Vol131No1-126
Colli, G. and M. Montinari - see Nietzsche,
F.
Collie, M. The Alien Art.*
J. Korg, 637(VS):Autumn00-130
J. Powers, 445(NCF):Jun80-115
Collie, M. George Borrow, Eccentric.
M. Mason, 617(TLS):10Dec82-1353
Collier, B. Hidden Weapons.
D. Hunt, 617(TLS):28May82-586
Colligan, J.P., ed. The Image of Chris-
tianity in Japan.
W. Davis, 293(JASt):Feb81-379
Collin, P. and others - see "Harrap's
Shorter French and English Dictionary"
Collinder, B. Sprache und Sprachen.
E. Alanne, 439(NM):1981/1-95
G.F. Meier, 682(ZPSK):Band33Heft5-592
Collini, S. Liberalism and Sociology.*
R.H.H., 185:Oct81-194
Collins, D. Sartre as Biographer.
G.H. Bauer, 207(FR):May81-879
W. Fowlie, 569(SR):Spring81-xlix
Collins, G.R., ed. Visionary Drawings of
Architecture and Planning.
T. Walton, 576:Oct81-256
Collins, L. and D. Lapierre. Mountbatten
and the Partition of India: March 22 -
August 15, 1947.
B.N. Pandey, 617(TLS):6Aug82-849
Collins, R.K.L., ed. Constitutional Gov-
ernment in America.
G.E.T., 543:Dec80-374
Collins, S. Selfless Persons.
G. Strawson, 617(TLS):31Dec82-1445
Collins, W. The Works of William Collins.
(R. Wendorf and C. Ryskamp, eds)
O.F. Sigworth, 405(MP):Aug81-86
"Collins Dictionary of the English Lan-
guage." (P. Hanks and others, eds)
J. De Clercq-D'hondt, 179(ES):Dec81-
548

"Collins Robert French-English, English-
French Dictionary." (By B.T. Atkins and
others) "Collins Gem French-English,
English-French Dictionary." (By P-H.
Cousin with others) "Collins Gem Fran-
çais-Espagnol, Español-Francés." (By
C. Giordano and S. Yurkievich)
E. Woods, 208(FS):Jan81-113
"Colloque Eugène Fromentin."
P. Berthier, 535(RHL):Mar-Apr81-315
Collot, A. Ventres pleins, ventres creux.
M.F. Meurice, 450(NRF):Mar81-139
Collot, M. Horizon de Reverdy.
P. Bady, 98:Aug-Sep81-872
Colmer, J. Coleridge to "Catch-22."
W. Bache, 395(MFS):Summer80-372
Colodny, R.G., ed. Logic, Laws and Life.
N. Roll-Hansen, 84:Mar81-104
Colombel, J. Sartre ou le parti de vivre.
L.S. Roudiez, 546(RR):Nov81-504
Colombi, J-P. Leçons de ténèbres.
D. Pobel, 450(NRF):Mar81-120
Colombo, J.R., ed. Other Canadas.
T.M. Green, 526:Autumn81-174
Colonna, A. - see Sophocles
Colonna, F. Hypnerotomachia Poliphili.
D.J. McKitterick, 617(TLS):29Jan82-119
Colquhoun, K. Filthy Rich.
J.K.L. Walker, 617(TLS):30Jul82-839
Colquhoun, K. Goebbels and Gladys.*
C. Hawtree, 364:Oct81-99
P. Lewis, 565:Vol122No4-69
Colson, T. The Beauty of It.*
M. Hurley, 102(CanL):Summer81-166
Cult, C.F., with A. Miall. The Early
Piano.
C. Ehrlich, 415:Sep81-606
Coltheart, M., K. Patterson and J.C.
Marshall, eds. Deep Dyslexia.
P.G. Patel, 350:Jun82-490
Colton, J.P. The "Parnase François."*
C. Goldstein, 54:Jun81-342
B. Scott, 39:Jan81-61
Colton, T.J. Big Daddy.
G.W., 102(CanL):Summer81-87
Colucci, M. and A. Danti - see Zatočnik, D.
Colum, P. The Poet's Circuits.
R. Garfitt, 617(TLS):2Apr82-392
Colwin, L. Family Happiness.
T.G., 231:Sep82-76
C. See, 441:19Sep82-13
442(NY):4Oct82-146
Comaroff, J.L. and S. Roberts. Rules and
Processes.
L. Mair, 617(TLS):7May82-516
Combet, L. Cervantès ou les incertitudes
du désir.
J.B. Avalle-Acre, 304(JHP):Winter82-
167
Combs, R. Vision of the Voyage.
P.R. Yannella, 295(JML):Vol8No3/4-473
"Comecon Data, 1979."
A.H. Smith, 575(SEER):Jul81-478
Comino, M. Gimson and the Barnsleys.
P. Davey, 46:Oct81-258
Comito, T. The Idea of the Garden in the
Renaissance.*
M.A. Di Cesare, 125:Winter81-232
Common, J. Kiddar's Luck [and] the Amper-
sand.
P. Lewis, 565:Vol22No3-55
"Common Security."
M. Mandelbaum, 441:18Jul82-10

de Commynes, P. Mémoires sur Louis XI
(1464-1483). (J. Dufournet, ed)
G.T. Diller, 207(FR):Oct81-132
A.H. Diverres, 208(FS):Oct81-427
Comoth, K. Die "Verwiklichung der Philos-
ophie."
H. Faes, 542:Jul-Sep81-382
Compagnon, A. Le seconde main ou le tra-
vail de la citation.
L. Marin, 98:Apr80-355
"Comparative Criticism." (Vol 1) (E.
Shaffer, ed)
K. Petherick, 562(Scan):May81-112
205(FMLS):Oct80-372
"Comparative Criticism." (Vol 2) (E.
Shaffer, ed)
M. Bowie, 208(FS):Oct81-490
"Comparisons."
639(VQR):Spring81-68
Compton, C. The Diary of Charles Compton
(1828-1884).* (E.H. Turner, ed)
A.S., 155:Summer81-111
Compton, L.F. Andalusian Lyrical Poetry
and Old Spanish Love Songs.*
D. Wulstan, 318(JAOS):Jul/Sep80-340
Comrie, B. and G. Stone. The Russian Lan-
guage Since the Revolution.*
V.M. Živov, 559:Dec80-181
Comstock, G. Television in America.
B. Sweeney, 583:Fall81-94
"La comunicación en los monasterios
medievales."
I. Mateo Gómez, 48:Oct-Dec81-461
Comyn, J. Irish at Law.
C. Davidson, 617(TLS):9Apr82-416
J. Vaizey, 362:7Jan82-25
Conacher, D.J. Aeschylus' "Prometheus
Bound."
G.M. Kirkwood, 99:Dec81/Jan82-38
Conarroe, J. John Berryman.
S. Fender, 677(YES):Vol 11-365
da Conceição, M., with N. Grubb. Wearable
Art.
F.H. Pettit, 37:May81-26
"The Concise Oxford Dictionary of Current
English." (7th ed) (J.B. Sykes, ed)
R.R.K. Hartmann, 617(TLS):3Sep82-953
"The Concise Oxford French Dictionary."*
(2nd ed) (H. Ferrar, J.A. Hutchinson and
J-D. Biard, eds)
M. Harris, 206(FS):Jul81-374
205(FMLS):Oct81-375
Conde, F.J.F. - see under Fernández Conde,
F.J.
de Condillac, E.B. Essai sur l'origine
des connaissances humaines.
Z. Kouřím, 542:Jul-Sep81-367
de Condillac, E.B. Les Monades. (L.L.
Bongie, ed)
D. Leduc-Fayette, 542:Jul-Sep81-366
R. McRae, 627(UTQ):Summer81-143
Condit, C.W. The Port of New York.
[... from the Grand Central Electrifica-
tion to the Present]
E. Jones, 617(TLS):18Jun82-663
Condon, R. Prizzi's Honour.
R. Asahina, 441:18Apr82-12
A. Bold, 617(TLS):11Jun82-642
442(NY):3May82-165
Cone, E.T. - see Sessions, R.
Cone, M. and R.F. Gombrich. The Perfect
Generosity of Prince Vessantara.
B.G. Gokhale, 318(JAOS):Jul/Sep80-320

Conisbee, P. Painting in Eighteenth-
Century France.
N. Bryson, 617(TLS):19Mar82-319
Conklin, W.E. In Defence of Fundamental
Rights.
M.K., 185:Jan82-390
Connell, E.S. Saint Augustine's Pigeon.
(G. Blaisdell, ed)
J. Gerlach, 573(SSF):Fall81-481
F.M. Link, 502(PrS):Fall81-99
Connellan, L. Massachusetts Poems.
D.W. Faulkner, 434:Winter81-340
Conner, M.W., ed. New Frontiers in For-
eign Language Education.
S.L. Shinall, 399(MLJ):Spring81-107
Conner, P. Savage Ruskin.*
P.M. Ball, 677(YES):Vol 11-326
M. Steveni, 289:Jul81-370
F.G. Townsend, 637(VS):Winter81-248
Connolly, J. Jerome K. Jerome.
H. Carpenter, 617(TLS):10Sep82-968
Connolly, S.J. Priests and People in Pre-
Famine Ireland 1760-1845.
P. Hebblethwaite, 617(TLS):18Jun82-652
Connolly, W.E. Appearance and Reality in
Politics.
G. Ionescu, 617(TLS):26Mar82-359
C.N.S., 185:Jul82-801
Connoly, G. Linguistique descriptive.
A. Valdman, 207(FR):Dec80-384
Connor, J. Ann Miller.
D. McClelland, 200:May81-309
Connors, J.J. Borromini and the Roman
Oratory.*
T.G. Smith, 505:May81-188
Conover, R.L. - see Loy, M.
Conquest, R. Present Danger.*
G.H. Bolsover, 575(SEER):Jan81-139
Conrad, G. Johann Nepomuk Nestroy 1801-
1862.
W.E. Yates, 402(MLR):Oct81-996
Conrad, J. Au coeur des ténèbres, Amy
Foster, Le Compagnon secret. (J-J.
Mayoux, trans)
C. Jordis, 450(NRF):Mar81-149
Conrad, J. Joseph Conrad.*
L.M. Whitehead, 150(DR):Winter81/82-
743
Conrad, J.P. Justice and Consequences.
T.M.R., 185:Apr82-598
Conrad, P. Imagining America.*
R.H. Fogle, 27(AL):Mar81-134
C. Mulvey, 366:Autumn81-245
Conrad, P. Shandyism.*
M. New, 173(ECS):Spring81-361
Conrad, P. Television.
P. Lennon, 362:19Aug82-20
M. Mason, 617(TLS):25Jun82-691
Conrad, R. Studien zur Syntax und Seman-
tik von Frage und Antwort.
R. Schmidt, 682(ZPSK):Band33Heft6-776
Conradi, P. John Fowles.
P. Kemp, 362:22Jul182-20
C. Rawson, 617(TLS):3Sep82-941
Conran, S. Lace.
E.R. Lipson, 441:30Oct82-27
F. Taliaferro, 231:Oct82-71
Conron, J. and C.A. Denne - see Cooper,
J.F.
Conroy, M. 300 Years of Canada's Quilts.
P. Bach, 614:Winter82-21

Cordry, D. Mexican Masks.*
  J.B. Esser, 2(AfrA):May81-86
  B.L. Fontana, 50(ArQ):Spring81-81
Coren, A., ed. Pick of Punch.
  V. Glendinning, 617(TLS):24Dec82-1431
Corfield, P.J. The Impact of English
  Towns: 1700-1800.
  P. Slack, 617(TLS):30Jul82-829
Corinth, T. Lovis Corinth.
  H. Keller, 471:Apr/May/Jun81-186
Cormier, R. and J.L. Pallister. Waiting
  for Death.
  J. Acheson, 49:Oct81-103
  D. Jones, 207(FR):Mar81-604
  K. Morrison, 397(MD):Mar81-121
Corn, A. The Various Light.*
  639(VQR):Winter81-25
Corneille, P. Oeuvres complètes. (Vol 1)
  (G. Couton, ed)
  C.J. Gossip, 208(FS):Jul81-328
  W.L., 475:No14Pt1-167
  G. Steiner, 617(TLS):19Nov82-1259
Corneille, T. Camma.* (D.A. Watts, ed)
  P. Hourcade, 475:No14Pt1-191
Cornell, T. and J. Matthews. Atlas of the
  Roman World.
  J.J. Wilkes, 617(TLS):4Jun82-616
Cornet, J. Pictographies Woyo.
  W. MacGaffey, 2(AfrA):Aug81-24
Cornwell, J. Earth to Earth.
  P. Boer, 362:28Oct82-26
  W. Trevor, 617(TLS):5Nov82-1210
"Corpus des notes marginales de Voltaire."
  (Vol 1)
  M. Laurent-Hubert, 535(RHL):Nov-Dec81-
  996
  H. Mason, 402(MLR):Jan81-188
Corraze, J., ed. Image spéculaire du
  corps.
  J-M. Gabaude 542:Jan-Mar81-127
Corrêa Barbosa, E.C. O ciclo do ouro.
  G.H. Béhague, 263(RIB):Vol31No3-406
Correia-Afonso, J., ed. Indo-Portuguese
  History.
  C.R. Boxer, 617(TLS):6Aug82-859
Corrigan, J.T., ed. Archives: The Light
  of Faith.
  D.M. Dougherty, 14:Summer81-250
Corrigan, R.W., ed. Comedy, Meaning and
  Form. (2nd ed)
  R.K. Simon, 594:Fall81-322
Corrington, J.W. The Actes and Monuments.
  P. Lewis, 565:Vol22No1-60
Corrington, J.W. The Southern Reporter.*
  B. Allen, 434:Spring82-478
  J.D. O'Hara, 434:Summer82-603
Corriveau, H.G. Gilles Hénault.*
  J. Viswanathan, 102(CanL):Spring81-108
Corry, J.A. Memoirs of J.A. Corry.
  D. Smiley, 99:Mar82-30
Corson, J.C., ed. Notes and Index to Sir
  Herbert Grierson's Edition of the Let-
  ters of Sir Walter Scott.*
  L. Hartveit, 179(ES):Aug81-389
  D. Hewitt, 571(ScLJ):Winter81-109
  D.A. Low, 541(RES):Aug81-338
  J. Mitchie, 506(PSt):Sep81-209
  G.A.M. Wood, 447(N&Q):Oct80-456
Cort, L.A. Shigaraki, Potters' Valley.*
  D. Rhodes, 293(JASt):May81-599
  U. Roberts, 60:Jan-Feb81-133
Cortazzi, H. - see Fraser, M.C.

Cortey, T. Le Rêve dans les contes de
  Charles Nodier.
  S.F. Daniel, 207(FR):Oct80-165
  D.P. Haase, 546(RR):May81-361
Corti, M. Dante a un nuovo crocevia.
  Z.G. Barański, 617(TLS):22Jan82-88
Corti, M. An Introduction to Literary
  Semiotics.*
  T. de Lauretis, 125:Fall80-93
  R.N. St. Clair, 599:Winter81-89
Corti, M. - see Fenoglio, B.
Corum, R.T., Jr. Other Worlds and Other
  Seas.
  F.L. Lawrence, 210(FrF):Jan81-86
  B. Nicholas, 402(MLR):Oct81-962
  B. Norman, 207(FR):Dec81-263
  M.J. O'Regan, 208(FS):Apr81-192
  C. Rolfe, 535(RHL):Nov-Dec81-983
  205(FMLS):Apr80-187
Cosgrave, P. R.A. Butler.*
  A. Dickins, 364:Aug-Sep81-142
Cosgrove, R.A. The Rule of Law.*
  A. Brundage, 50(ArQ):Summer81-190
Cosman, M.P. and B. Chandler, eds.
  Machaut's World.
  R.S. Sturges, 546(RR):Nov81-496
de Cossart, M. The Food of Love.
  C. Zimra, 207(FR):Dec81-288
Costa, G. Le antichità germaniche nella
  cultura italiana da Machiavelli a Vico.*
  M. Moss, 319:Jan81-112
Costa, M.O. - see under Ortega Costa, M.
Costa, R.H. Edmund Wilson.*
  G. Burns, 584(SWR):Autumn81-422
  295(JML):Vol8No3/4-641
Costello, B. Marianne Moore.
  A. Brownjohn, 617(TLS):28May82-577
Costello, C., with R. Strait. Lou's on
  First.
  D. McClelland, 200:Nov81-572
Costelloe, M.J. - see Schurhammer, G.
Costich, J.F. Antonin Artaud.
  C. Campos, 402(MLR):Apr81-479
  I.A. Kuhn, 207(FR):Dec80-352
Costich, J.F. The Poetry of Change.
  E.R. Jackson, 207(FR):Feb82-418
Cotera, M. and L. Hufford, eds. Bridging
  Two Cultures.
  D. Ballesteros, 238:Dec81-651
Cotnam, J., A. Oliver and C.D.E. Tolton,
  eds. Perspectives contemporaines.
  D. Moutote, 535(RHL):Jul-Oct81-831
Cott, J. and C. Doudna, eds. The Ballad
  of John and Yoko.
  R. Asahina, 441:28Nov82-16
Cotten, J-P. La pensée de Louis Althusser.
  J-M. Gabaude, 542:Oct-Dec81-478
Cottino-Jones, M. and E.F. Tuttle, eds.
  Boccaccio: Secoli di vita.*
  G. Costa, 545(RPh):May81-525
Cotton, M.A. The Late Republican Villa at
  Posto, Francolise.
  T.W. Potter, 313:Vol71-233
Coughlin, E.V., F.R. Jiménez and B.L.
  Jiménez - see de la Cruz, R.
Coulet du Gard, R. Le Prisonnier. Les
  fruits verts.
  A. Thiher, 207(FR):Dec80-361
Coulet du Gard, R. and D.C. Western. The
  Handbook of American Counties, Parishes,
  and Independent Cities.
  W.F.H. Nicolaisen, 424:Mar81-89

75

Coulson, J. Religion and Imagination.
I. Ker, 617(TLS):12Feb82-154
Coulter, J. François Bigot.
J. Ripley, 102(CanL):Summer80-113
Coulter, J. The Social Construction of
Mind.
R.T. Craig, 480(P&R):Spring81-119
J.D., 185:Apr82-584
Coulter, J.A. The Literary Microcosm.*
E.B., 604:Spring-Summer81-35
Coulthard, R.M. An Introduction to Dis-
course Analysis.*
R. de Beaugrande, 599:Winter81-83
Coulton, J.J. The Architectural Develop-
ment of the Greek Stoa.
J.S. Boersma, 394:Vol34fasc1/2-201
"Country Champions."
T.D. Smith, 617(TLS):27Aug82-929
Couper-Kuhlen, E. The Prepositional Pas-
sive in English.*
H. Ulherr, 38:Band99Heft3/4-451
Courage, J. Such Separate Creatures.
C. Hankin, 368:Dec73-351
Couratier, M., ed. Étienne Gilson et nous.
J-P. Guinle, 450(NRF):Jul-Aug81-195
de Courcel, M. L'Impossible Coïncidence.
J. Blot, 450(NRF):Jun81-114
Courrier, J. - see Sand, G.
Court, F.E. Pater and his Early Critics.
G. Monsman, 177(ELT):Vol24No4-213
"Courtauld Institute Illustration
Archives." (Archive 1, Pts 1-9; Archive
3, Pts 1-9)
N. Coldstream, 90:Mar81-173
Courtenay, W.J. Adam Wodeham.
S.F. Brown, 551(RenQ):Winter80-737
Courtine, J-F. and E. Martineau - see
Schelling, F.W.J.
Courtney, C.P. A Preliminary Bibliography
of Isabelle de Charrière (Belle de Zuy-
len).
M.B. Lacy, 207(FR):Dec81-272
D. Wood, 208(FS):Oct81-452
Courtney, E. A Commentary on the Satires
of Juvenal.*
T.G. Palaima, 124:Jan-Feb82-190
Courtney, W.F. Young Charles Lamb 1775-
1802.
J. Keates, 617(TLS):26Nov82-1315
Courtwright, D.T. Dark Paradise.
A. Hayter, 617(TLS):5Nov82-1209
Couser, G.T. American Autobiography.*
G.W. Allen, 219(GaR):Summer81-411
M.M. Mangini, 77:Fall81-354
J. Mazzaro, 560:Spring-Summer81-188
Cousin, J. - see Quintilian
Cousin, P-H. with others - see under
"Collins Robert French English, English-
French Dictionary"
Cousins, E.H. Bonaventure and the Coinci-
dence of Opposites.
T.M. Tomasic, 589:Jan81-111
Coustillas, P. George Gissing and Ivan
Turgenev.
P. Keating, 617(TLS):31Dec82-1447
Coustillas, P. - see Gissing, G.
Coustillas, P., J-P. Petit and J. Raimond.
Le Roman anglais au XIXe siècle.
T.J. Winnifrith, 677(YES):Vol 11-312
Couton, G. - see Corneille, P.
Couzyn, J. House of Changes.
D. Livesay, 102(CanL):Winter80-122

Covington, J. Confessions of a Single
Father.
G. Wolff, 441:21Nov82-15
Cowan, E.J., ed. The People's Past.
M.E. Brown, 571(ScLJ):Winter81-101
Cowan, P. An Orphan in History.
C.E. Silberman, 441:10Oct82-13
Cowan, W., ed. Papers of the Tenth
Algonquian Conference.*
P.V. Kroskrity, 350:Jun81-509
Cowan, W., ed. Papers of the Eleventh
Algonquian Conference.
D.H. Pentland, 320(CJL):Fall81-239
Coward, E.W., Jr., ed. Irrigation and
Agricultural Development in Asia.
B. Ward, 293(JASt):Feb81-335
Coward, N. The Noël Coward Diaries. (G.
Payn and S. Morley, eds)
P-L. Adams, 61:Nov82-170
D. Hare, 617(TLS):10Oct82-1062
J. Lahr, 231:Oct82-64
J. Osborne, 441:3Oct82-7
K. Waterhouse, 362:2Sep82-20
442(NY):25Oct82-174
Cowart, D. Thomas Pynchon.
S. Brivic, 295(JML):Vol18No3/4-599
J.J. Waldmeir, 395(MFS):Winter80/81-
675
Cowasjee, S. Nude Therapy.
L. Rogers, 102(CanL):Autumn81-156
Cowasjee, S. So Many Freedoms.*
M. Fisher, 314:Summer-Fall81-230
Cowasjee, S., ed. Stories from the Raj.
P. Mason, 617(TLS):6Aug82-863
J. Mellors, 362:15Apr82-23
Cowasjee, S. - see Anand, M.R.
Cowen, R.C. Hauptmann Kommentar zum
dramatischen Werk.
J. Glenn, 221(GQ):May81-369
Cowie, P. Ingmar Bergman.
S. Peck, 441:19Dec82-7
Cowley, M. The Dream of the Golden Moun-
tains.*
M. Brown, 639(VQR):Winter81-168
G. Bullert, 396(ModA):Spring81-204
J. Lydenberg, 432(NEQ):Jun81-292
D. Pizer, 27(AL):Mar81-155
Cowley, M. The View from 80.
639(VQR):Winter81-14
Cowper, W. The Letters and Prose Writings
of William Cowper.* (Vol 1) (J. King
and C. Ryskamp, eds)
F. Kermode, 453(NYRB):21Oct82-39
Cowper, W. The Letters and Prose Writings
of William Cowper.* (Vol 2) (J. King
and C. Ryskamp, eds)
W.H., 148:Winter81-90
F. Kermode, 453(NYRB):21Oct82-39
Cowper, W. The Poems of William Cowper.*
(Vol 1) (J.D. Baird and C. Ryskamp, eds)
F. Kermode, 453(NYRB):21Oct82-39
Cox, A. The Cox Report on the American
Corporation.
P. Lewis, 441:26Dec82-9
Cox, A. Freedom of Expression.
G. Marshall, 617(TLS):22Oct82-1169
Cox, C.B. Every Common Sight.*
A.E. Dyson, 148:Summer81-3
C. Hope, 364:Apr/May81-119
R. Phillips, 249(HudR):Autumn81-430
Cox, G.S.A. Folk Music in a Newfoundland
Outport.
B. Nettl, 650(WF):Oct81-344

Cox, R. Figures of Transformation.
  M. Jacobs, 402(MLR):Jul81-754
  205(FMLS):Oct80-373
Cox, R. The KGB Directive.
  H. Saal, 441:24Jan82-12
Cox, R.M. Eighteenth-Century Spanish
  Literature.
  P. Deacon, 86(BHS):Apr81-144
  S. García Castañeda, 173(ECS):Spring81-
    359
  I.L. McClelland, 402(MLR):Jan81-222
Cozens, A. A New Method of Assisting the
  Invention in Drawing Original Composi-
  tions of Landscape (1785). (P. Lavez-
  zari, ed)
  E.H. Ramsden, 39:Sep81-206
Crabbe, J. Hector Berlioz.*
  J. Rushton, 415:May81-313
Craddock, P. Young Edward Gibbon.
  W.B. Carnochan, 617(TLS):6Aug82-857
Craemer-Ruegenberg, I. Die Naturphilos-
  ophie des Aristoteles.
  D.C.L., 543:Jun81-784
Craft, R. - see Stravinsky, I.
Crafton, D. Before Mickey.
  T. Hunter, 441:26Sep82-12
Cragg, K. Islam and the Muslim.
  S. Vahiduddin, 273(IC):Oct80-243
Craig, D. and M. Egan. Extreme Situations.
  J. Klinkowitz, 395(MFS):Winter80/81-
    719
Craig, G.A. The Germans.
  F. Stern, 441:14Mar82-10
  442(NY):8Feb82-129
Craig, L. and others. The Federal Pres-
  ence.*
  D.A. Grimsted, 658:Summer/Autumn81-229
  B. Lowry, 576:May81-146
Craig, P. and M. Cadogan. The Lady
  Investigates.*
  G. Ewart, 364:Apr/May81-141
Craig, S., ed. Dreams and Deconstruc-
  tions.*
  J. Roose-Evans, 157:1stQtr81-51
Craig, W.L. The Kalām Cosmological Argu-
  ment.*
  J.A. Sadowsky, 258:Jun81-222
Craige, B.J. Lorca's Poet in New York.
  R. Johnson, 552(REH):May81-310
Craighead, F.C., Jr. Track of the Grizzly.
  C. Beyers, 649(WAL):Winter81-302
Craik, E.M. The Dorian Aegean.
  A.R. Burn, 303(JoHS):Vol 101-198
  S. Hood, 123:Vol31No2-315
Cramer, C. and S. Harris. Hostage.
  A. Holden, 617(TLS):30Jul82-837
Cramer, T. Die kleineren Liederdichter
  des 14. und 15. Jahrhunderts. (Vol 1)
  D. Merzbacher, 680(ZDP):Band99Heft1-
    116
Cramer, T., ed. Die kleineren Liederdich-
  ter des 14. und 15. Jahrhunderts. (Vol
  2)
  C. Petzsch, 72:Band217Heft1-180
  H-G. Richert, 221(GQ):Jan81-85
Cramer, T., ed. Maeren-Dichtung.
  D. Blamires, 402(MLR):Oct81-984
Cramer, T., ed. Till Eulenspiegel in
  Geschichte und Gegenwart.
  G. Bollenbeck, 196:Band21Heft3/4-301
Crampton, C.G. The Zunis of Cibola.
  K.I. Periman, 292(JAF):Jan-Mar81-121

Crampton, E.P.T. Christianity in Northern
  Nigeria.
  M. Bray, 69:Vol50No3-322
Crandall, J.A. Adult Vocational ESL.
  T.D. Terrell, 399(MLJ):Autumn81-327
Crane, D., ed. Beyond the Monetarists.
  M. Ignatieff, 99:Nov81-32
Crane, H. Playbill.
  M. Toms, 611(TN):Vol35No2-94
Crane, H. and Y. Winters. Hart Crane and
  Yvor Winters: Their Literary Correspon-
  dence. (T. Parkinson, ed)
  P. Makin, 402(MLR):Oct81-948
  N. Shrimpton, 447(N&Q):Jun80-274
Crane, L.B., E. Yeager and R.L. Whitman.
  An Introduction to Linguistics.
  A. Pousada, 350:Mar82-238
Crane, P. Gays and the Law.
  D. Pannick, 362:11Nov82-25
Crankshaw, E. Bismarck.*
  F.L. Carsten, 617(TLS):26Mar82-362
  G.L. Mosse, 441:17Jan82-9
Cranz, F.E. and P.O. Kristeller, eds.
  Catalogus Translationum et Commentario-
  rum. (Vol 4)
  J.G. Plante, 124:May-Jun82-310
Crase, D. The Revisionist.*
  R. von Hallberg, 659(ConL):Fall182-550
  H. McNeil, 617(TLS):29Jan82-113
  V. Shetley, 453(NYRB):29Apr82-43
Craven, P. "An Impartial Umpire."
  D. McCalla, 298:Fall-Winter81-212
Cravens, G. Love and Work.
  C. Duchen, 617(TLS):10Sep82-982
  R. Miner, 441:28Mar82-11
  442(NY):10May82-168
Crawford, A. Thunder on the Right.
  639(VQR):Winter81-24
Crawford, D. Kafka.
  B. Goldstein, 406:Spring81-67
Crawford, J.M. The Mobilian Trade Lan-
  guage.
  B.K. Dumas, 269(IJAL):Jul81-262
Crawley, A. The Shadow of God.
  S. Altinel, 617(TLS):20Aug82-910
de Crébillon, C.P.J. Electre. (J. Dunk-
  ley, ed)
  R. Niklaus, 83:Autumn81-225
Cree, E.H. The Cree Journals. (M. Levien,
  ed)
  R. O'Hanlon, 617(TLS):24Dec82-1428
Creed, D. Travellers in an Antique Land.
  S. Brook, 617(TLS):20Aug82-910
Creeley, R. Later.*
  D.K. Boyer, 649(WAL):Winter82-317
  D. Graham, 565:Vol22No1-73
  C. Lambert, 472:Fall/Winter81-255
Creeley, R. Was That a Real Poem and
  Other Essays. (D. Allen, ed) Later
  (1-10).*
  C. Lambert, 472:Fall/Winter81-255
Creighton, D. The Passionate Observer.*
  G.W., 102(CanL):Spring81-172
Creighton, J.V. Joyce Carol Oates.*
  L.W. Wagner, 573(SSF):Winter81-107
Crépeau, P. and S. Bizimana. Proverbes du
  Rwanda.
  W. Mieder, 196:Band22Heft1/2-117
  W. Mieder, 292(JAF):Apr-Jun81-240
Crespo, Á. - see Cernuda, L.
Crespo, E. Elementos antiguos y modernos
  en la prosodia Homérica.*
  A. Heubeck, 260(IF):Band85-342

Cressey, W.W. Spanish Phonology and
Morphology.*
   M.T. Ward, 240(HR):Summer81-349
Cressy, D. Literacy and the Social Order.*
   M.A. Kishlansky, 656(WMQ):Oct81-738
   F.C. Robinson, 569(SR):Summer81-423
Crevel, R. Êtes-vous fous?
   F. Trémolières, 450(NRF):Oct81-141
Crichton Smith, I. A Field Full of Folk.
   S.J. Newman, 617(TLS):21May82-566
   442(NY):16Aug82-89
Crichton Smith, I. On the Island.
   D. MacAulay, 571(ScLJ):Summer80-136
Crichton Smith, I. Selected Poems 1955-
1980.
   D. Dunn, 617(TLS):13Aug82-876
Crick, B. George Orwell.*
   J.A. Glusman, 363(LitR):Spring82-431
   W. Scammell, 364:Apr/May81-121
   G. Woodcock, 529(QQ):Summer81-250
Crick, M. Explorations in Language and
Meaning.
   D. Dutton, 488:Jun80-229
Crickillon, J. Nuit la Neige.
   J. Decock, 207(FR):Apr82-701
Crisp, N.J. The Brink.
   A. Cheuse, 441:11Jul82-14
Crist, T.J., with others - see Wing, D.
Cristiani, M. Dall'Unanimitas all'Univer-
sitas de Alcuino a Giovanni Eriugena.
   T.F.X. Noble, 589:Apr81-372
Cristofani, M. Etruschi.
   P. Swiggers, 350:Dec81-968
"Critique et Création littéraires en
France au XVIIe siècle."
   H.T. Barnwell, 208(FS):Apr81-204
Croce, A. Going to the Dance.
   R. Craft, 453(NYRB):12Aug82-28
   E. Denby, 441:1Aug82-9
Crocker, L. Positive Liberty.
   J.A. Gould, 63:Jun81-254
Croll, E. Feminism and Socialism in China.
   V.L. Hsu, 293(JASt):May81-579
Cronin, J. The Anglo-Irish Novel: The
Nineteenth Century.
   L.V. Harrod, 174(Éire):Winter81-152
   R. Tracy, 445(NCF):Sep81-214
Cronin, J. Gerald Griffin, 1803-1840.*
   C.W. Barrow, 174(Éire):Winter81-154
   G. O'Brien, 677(YES):Vol 11-317
Cronin, S. Irish Nationalism.*
   C.C. O'Brien, 453(NYRB):29Apr82-30
Cronin, S. Frank Ryan.
   G. Freyer, 174(Éire):Summer81-155
Cronin, T.E., T.Z. Cronin and M.E. Milako-
vich. U.S. v. Crime in the Streets.
   W. Goodman, 441:7Feb82-18
Cronin, V., ed. Essays by Divers Hands.
   L.L. Lee, 599:Fall81-473
Cronin, V. The View from Planet Earth.*
   442(NY):25Jan82-106
Crook, I. and D. Ten Mile Inn.
   G. Bennett, 293(JASt):Nov80-107
Crook, J.M. William Burges and the High
Victorian Dream.*
   J.S. Curl, 324:May82-368
   135:Oct81-92
de Croome, D.E. - see under Empaytaz de
Croome, D.
Cropsey, J. Political Philosophy and the
Issues of Politics.*
   H.T. Wilson, 488:Jun80-215

Cros, E. Ideología y genética textual.
   J. Iffland, 304(JHP):Winter82-171
Cros, E. Proposition pour une socio-
critique.
   H.G. Hall, 208(FS):Apr81-202
Crosby, B. Durham Cathedral Choristers
and their Masters.
   W. Shaw, 415:Feb81-110
Crosby, J.O. Guía bibliográfica para el
estudio crítico de Quevedo.
   H. Sieber, 240(HR):Winter81-126
Crosland, S. Tony Crosland.
   R. Hattersley, 362:3Jun82-20
Crosman, I.K. Metaphoric Narration.*
   G. Brée, 207(FR):Apr81-742
   P. Newman-Gordon, 399(MLJ):Summer81-
214
Crosman, R. Reading "Paradise Lost."
   W.E. Cain, 400(MLN):Dec81-1121
   J. Mason, 184(EIC):Oct81-362
Cross, A. Death in a Tenured Position.*
   J.D. O'Hara, 434:Summer82-603
Cross, A.G. "By the Banks of the Thames."*
   W. Harrison, 83:Autumn81-243
   C.A. Johnson, 402(MLR):Oct81-1003
   I. de Madariaga, 575(SEER):Jul81-446
Cross, A.G., ed. Great Britain and Russia
in the Eighteenth Century.
   I-H.L. Ryu, 104(CASS):Winter81-578
Cross, A.G., ed. Russian Literature in
the Age of Catherine the Great.*
   C.L. Drage, 575(SEER):Jan81-155
Cross, R.K. Malcolm Lowry.*
   R.H. Costa, 405(MP):Aug81-109
   W.N., 102(CanL):Autumn80-inside back
   cover
   J.J. Riley, 395(MFS):Winter80/81-698
   R.I. Smyer, 50(ArQ):Autumn81-279
"Cross Stitch: 300 Motifs."
   P. Bach, 614:Summer82-14
Crothers, E.J. Paragraph Structure Infer-
ence.*
   Z. Szabó, 353:Vol 18No5/6-572
Crotty, K. Song and Action.
   M. Lefkowitz, 617(TLS):29Oct82-1183
Crouzet, F. The Victorian Economy.
   R. Floud, 617(TLS):27Aug82-930
Crouzet, M. Stendhal et le langage.
   P. Bayard, 450(NRF):Jul-Aug81-200
Crovetto, P.L., ed. Gabriel García
Márquez.
   J. Higgins, 86(BHS):Apr81-165
Crow, C.L. Janet Lewis.
   A. Frietzsche, 649(WAL):Fall81-231
Crow, C.M. Paul Valéry and the Poetry of
Voice.
   G.W. Ireland, 617(TLS):3Sep82-938
Crow, J.A., ed. An Anthology of Spanish
Poetry.*
   A. Otten, 42(AR):Fall81-513
   T.J. Rogers, 238:Dec81-632
Crow, J.A. and G.D. Panorama de las Améri-
cas. (5th ed)
   D.R. McKay, 399(MLJ):Autumn81-337
Crowe, S. Garden Design.
   G.S. Thomas, 324:Nov82-828
Crowell, J. and S.J. Searl, Jr. - see
Miller, P.
Crowley, E.T., ed. Acronyms, Initialisms,
and Abbreviations Dictionary. (7th ed)
(Vol 1)
   K.B. Harder, 424:Dec80-293

Crowley, E.T., ed. New Acronyms, Initial-
isms, Abbreviations 1979. Trade Names
Dictionary. (2nd ed)
K.B. Harder, 424:Mar80-94
Crowley, J. Little, Big.
A. Bold, 617(TLS):28May82-593
Crowley, T.E. The Beam Engine.
D. Bowen, 324:Oct82-757
Crowson, L. The Esthetic of Jean Cocteau.
L.C. Breunig, 546(RR):Mar81-247
P.A. Mankin, 207(FR):Oct80-174
Crozier, M. Le mal américain.
F. Ewald, 98:Aug-Sep81-797
J. Paulhan, 207(FR):Feb82-452
Crozier, M. On ne change pas la société
par décret.
F. Ewald, 98:Aug-Sep81-797
Crozier, M. and E. Friedberg. L'acteur et
le système.
F. Ewald, 98:Aug-Sep81-797
Crubellier, M. L'Enfance et la jeunesse
dans la société française, 1800-1950.
J-F. Brière, 207(FR):Feb81-485
Cruickshank, J. Variations on Catastrophe.
M. Tilby, 617(TLS):3Dec82-1342
Cruikshank, M. Thomas Babington Macaulay.
S. Shatto, 677(YES):Vol 11-316
Crump, G.B. The Novels of Wright Morris.*
K. Carabine, 447(N&Q):Jun80-275
Crump, J.I. Chinese Theater in the Days
of Kublai Khan.
W. Dolby, 610:Spring81-146
G.A. Hayden, 244(HJAS):Dec81-663
W.J. Meserve, 612(ThS):Nov81-241
Crutch, D. - see Williams, S.H. and F.F.
Madan
Crutchley, B. To Be A Printer.
M. Oliver, 324:Dec81-63
de la Cruz, R. Tres obras inéditas de don
Ramón de la Cruz. (E.V. Coughlin, F.R.
Jiménez and D.L. Jiménez, eds)
R.M. Cox, 240(HR):Autumn81-505
de Cruz-Sáenz, M.S. - see under Schiavone
de Cruz-Sáenz, M.
Crystal, D. A First Dictionary of Linguis-
tics and Phonetics.*
D.H., 355(LSoc):Aug81-310
Crystal, D. - see Partridge, E.
Csáth, G. The Magician's Garden and Other
Stories.* (M.D. Birnbaum, ed)
A.H. Carter 3d, 573(SSF):Winter81-91
Csonka, F. - see Schesaeus, C.
Cuadra, P.A. Songs of Cifar and the Sweet
Sea.* (G. Schulman and A.M. de Zavala,
eds and trans)
D. Oliphant, 436(NewL):Winter81/82-105
G. Rabassa, 472:Spring/Summer81-140
Cuartero Sancho, M.P. Fuentes clásicas de
la literatura paremiológica española del
siglo XVI.
J.J. Reynolds, 304(JHP):Winter82-162
Cude, W. A Due Sense of Differences.
W.J. Keith, 99:Mar82-33
Cuenca, J.R.A. - see under Araluce Cuenca,
J.R.
Cuénin, M. Roman et société sous Louis
XIV.
M. Bertaud, 535(RHL):Jul-Oct81-768
M-O. Sweetser, 207(FR):Mar81-594
M-O. Sweetser, 475:No14Pt1-168
Cuénin, M. - see Madame de Lafayette

Cuisenier, J., ed. Récits et contes
populaires.
G. Calame-Griaule, 98:Mar80-278
R. Schenda, 196:Band22Heft1/2-151
Cule, J. Wales and Medicine.
P. Davison, 354:Mar81-77
Culhane, T. Russian.
D. Phillips, 558(RLJ):Spring-Fall81-
275
Cullen, M. The Curried Chicken Apocalypse.
D. Barbour, 648(WCR):Jun80-77
Cullen, P. and T.P. Roche - see "Spenser
Studies"
Cullen, S. In Praise of Panic.
J. Simpson, 362:4Feb82-24
Culler, J. The Pursuit of Signs.
J. Bayley, 617(TLS):1Jan82-3
M. Brown, 401(MLQ):Jun81-208
N. Cotton, 435:Fall81-304
P. Dickinson, 364:Nov81-75
J. van Luxemburg, 204(FdL):Dec81-350
M. Zavarzadeh, 290(JAAC):Spring82-329
Culler, J. Ferdinand de Saussure.*
E. Buyssens, 567:Vol33No1/2-151
A. van der Hoven, 494:Winter80/81-203
R.G. Schuh, 350:Sep82-725
Cullinan, E. A Change of Scene.
442(NY):17May82-138
Cullingford, E. Yeats, Ireland and Fas-
cism.*
G. Davenport, 569(SR):Summer81-469
Culme, J. Nineteenth Century Silver.
C. Oman, 39:Apr81-273
Culot, P. - see Grétry, A-E-M.
Culshaw, J. Putting the Record Straight.
D. Hamilton, 453(NYRB):13May82-37
R. Osborne, 617(TLS):26Feb82-208
"La cultura italica: Atti del convegno
della società italiana di glottologia,
Pisa, dicembre 1977."
M.H. Crawford, 313:Vol71-153
"Cultura/letteratura popolare/dotta del
Seicento francese."
J.B. Atkinson, 207(FR):Oct81-136
C. Rizza, 535(RHL):Jul-Oct81-764
"Les cultures ibériques en devenir."
A. Reix, 542:Jan-Mar81-139
Cumings, B. The Origins of the Korean War.
J.C. Perry, 441:11Apr82-8
Cumming, R.D. Starting Point.
D.I., 543:Mar81-604
D. Leland, 185:Jan81-331
M. Murray, 482(PhR):Oct81-608
Cummings, A.L., ed. Architecture in Colo-
nial Massachusetts.
D.J. Coolidge, 432(NEQ):Mar81-153
Cummings, A.L. The Framed Houses of
Massachusetts Bay, 1625-1725.*
R. Harris, 46:Apr81-256
Cummings, E.E. Complete Poems 1910-1962.
J. Bayley, 617(TLS):5Mar82-235
Cummings, E.E. The Enormous Room. (G.J.
Firmage, ed)
R. Belflower, 541(RES):Nov81-476
Cummings, W.K. Education and Equality in
Japan.
Nishijima Takeo, 285(JapQ):Apr-Jun81-
285
J. Singleton, 407(MN):Winter81-479
Cummins, J.G., ed. The Spanish Tradi-
tional Lyric.*
P. Gallagher, 86(BHS):Jan81-77

Cummins, M.W. The Tache-Yokuts.
R. Keeling, 187:Sep82-465
Cuneo, A. Une cuillerée de bleu.
J. Devaud, 207(FR):Dec80-362
Cuniberti, J. The Birth of a Nation.
A. Slide, 200:May81-306
Cunliffe, L., C. Brown and J. Connell, eds.
The Dirty Bits.
G. Ewart, 617(TLS):22Jan82-91
Cunliffe, M. Chattel Slavery and Wage
Slavery.
D.L. Lightner, 106:Fall81-225
B. Wyatt-Brown, 9(AlaR):Apr81-132
Cunningham, C. Victorian and Edwardian
Town Halls.*
135:Oct81-92
Cunningham, G. The New Woman and the Vic-
torian Novel.*
J.P. Brown, 445(NCF):Mar81-559
J. Dusinberre, 447(N&Q):Jun80-255
A. Easson, 366:Autumn81-263
R. Miles, 677(YES):Vol 11-328
Cunningham, H. Leisure in the Industrial
Revolution.
P. Bailey, 637(VS):Spring81-366
Cunningham, J.I. and W.D. Wilson. A Con-
cordance to André Gide's "La Symphonie
pastorale."
A. Spacagna, 207(FR):Apr81-744
D.H. Walker, 208(FS):Jul81-356
Cunningham, J.S. - see Marlowe, C.
Cunningham, K. and M. Ballard. Conversa-
tions with a Dancer.*
R. Philp, 151:Sep81-98
Cunningham, N.E., Jr. The Image of Thomas
Jefferson in the Public Eye.
J.V. Turano, 16:Summer81-88
Cunningham, R.L., ed. Liberty and the
Rule of Law.
T.D. Campbell, 393(Mind):Jul81-446
Cunningham, S. Largesse.
G. Bitcon, 581:Dec81-469
Cunningham, W.J. Agony at Galloway.
E.N. Akin, 392:Spring81-135
Cunninghame Graham, R.B. The Scottish
Sketches of R.B. Cunninghame Graham.
(J. Walker, ed) Selected Writings of
Cunninghame Graham. (C. Watts, ed)
B. Urquhart, 617(TLS):10Dec82-1373
Cunninghame Graham, R.B. The South Ameri-
can Sketches of R.B. Cunninghame Graham.*
(J. Walker, ed)
J. Herdman, 571(ScLJ):Summer80-113
Cupitt, D. The World to Come.
G. Priestland, 362:26Aug82-22
S.R. Sutherland, 617(TLS):28May82-574
Čurčić, S. Gračanica.
B. Cox, 575(SEER):Jul81-429
A.W. Epstein, 589:Apr81-374
J. Morganstern, 576:Dec81-328
T.T. Rice, 46:Feb81-128
Curcuru, M. Childhood and Adolescence in
the Novels of L.P. Hartley.
H.D. Spear, 454:Fall81-94
Curl, J.S. Moneymore and Draperstown.
The History, Architecture and Planning
of the Estates of the Fishmongers'
Company in Ulster.
A. Whittick, 324:Oct82-756
Curley, E.M. Descartes Against the Skep-
tics.*
G. Brykman, 542:Jul-Sep81-350

Curnow, A. An Incorrigible Music.*
D. Graham, 565:Vol22No4-62
Curnow, W., ed. Essays on New Zealand Lit-
erature.
A.R. Wells, 368:Sep73-250
Curreli, M. and A. Martino, eds. Critical
Dimensions.
W. Ross, 52:Band15Heft1-61
A.J. Smith, 541(RES):May81-248
Curri, C.B. Vetulonia.* (Vol 1)
M.H. Crawford, 313:Vol71-153
Currie, J.T. Enclave.
E.N. Akin, 392:Spring81-135
Currie, R. Industrial Politics.
J. Lovell, 161(DUJ):Jun81-272
Currie, R. Yarrow.
G.A. Boire, 102(CanL):Summer81-168
Curry, L.P. The Free Black in Urban
America, 1800-1850.
J.H. Silverman, 676(YR):Spring82-458
Curteis, I. Churchill and the Generals.
Suez 1956.
T.A. Dunn, 610:Spring81-156
Curti, M. Human Nature in American
Thought.
A.N., 185:Jul82-793
L. Ratner, 125:Spring81-351
Curtin, M. The Replay.*
D. Quammen, 441:1Aug82-12
442(NY):8Mar82-141
Curtis, J. Eagles Over Big Sur.
D.W. Madden, 649(WAL):Fall81-247
Curtis, J.M. Culture as Polyphony.
J. Radway, 658:Summer/Autumn81-249
Curtis, L.A. - see Defoe, D.
Curtis, T. Preparations.*
D. Graham, 565:Vol22No4-62
Curtiss, J.S. Russia's Crimean War.*
M.J.D. Holman, 575(SEER):Jan81-108
Curtius, E.R. European Literature and the
Latin Middle Ages.
A. Crépin, 189(EA):Jul-Sep81-335
Curval, P. Brave Old World.
B. Shaw, 617(TLS):19Feb82-198
Cushing, F.H. Zuñi. (J. Green, ed)
W.M. Clements, 292(JAF):Apr-Jun81-248
Cushion, J.P., with W.B. Honey. Handbook
of Pottery and Porcelain Marks.
G. Wills, 39:Mar81-201
Cushman, K. D.H. Lawrence at Work.*
H.T. Moore, 402(MLR):Oct81-941
Cushner, N.P. Lords of the Land.
E.J. Burrus, 377:Jul81-121
F. Pease, 263(RIB):Vol31No1-82
Custance, R., ed. Winchester College.
W. Oakeshott, 617(TLS):20Aug82-907
Cuthbertson, B.C. - see Payzant, J.
Cutler, H. The Cutler Files.
T. Judge, 362:11Mar82-24
Cutul, A-M. Twentieth-Century European
Painting.
J. Masheck, 62:Feb81-72
Cyr, G. Sol Inapparent.
G.V. Downes, 102(CanL):Winter80-105
de Cyrano de Bergerac, S. Oeuvres com-
plètes. (J. Prévot, ed)
M. Gaume, 535(RHL):Mar-Apr81-285

Dabney, V. The Jefferson Scandals.*
639(VQR):Autumn81-119
Dabydeen, C. Heart's Frame.
D. Precosky, 102(CanL):Winter80-142

Dabydeen, C. This Planet Earth.
   M. Hurley, 102(CanL):Summer81-166
Dacey, P. The Boy Under the Bed.
   R. Phillips, 249(HudR):Autumn81-426
   V. Young, 472:Fall/Winter81-155
   639(VQR):Autumn81-130
Dacos, N. Le Logge di Raffaello.
   N.W. Canedy, 54:Mar81-154
Dadié, B. Mhoi-Ceul.
   T.N. Hammond, 95(CLAJ):Jun81-529
Daemmrich, H.S. and I. Wiederholte
Spiegelungen.
   M. Beller, 52:Band15Heft2-186
   E. Frenzel, 196:Band21Heft3/4-303
   M.S. Fries, 395(MFS):Summer80-362
   U. Weisstein, 301(JEGP):Jan81-104
Dagerman, S. Automne allemand.
   J-M. le Sidaner, 450(NRF):Apr81-154
Dagron, G., ed and trans. Vie et miracles
de sainte Thècle.
   H.D. Watson, 303(JoHS):Vol 101-230
Dahl, H. Word Frequencies of Spoken
American English.
   K.B. Harder, 424:Mar81-93
   H. Käsmann, 38:Band99Heft3/4-471
Dahl, S. Relativität und Absolutheit.
   P.M. Lützeler, 680(ZDP):Band100Heft4-
   626
Dahlhaus, C. Richard Wagner's Music
Dramas.*
   R.L.J., 412:May80-145
   H.R. Vaget, 221(GQ):Mar81-202
Dahmen-Dallapiccola, A.L. Rāgamālā-
Miniaturen von 1475 bis 1700.
   H. Powers, 318(JAOS):Oct/Dec80-473
Dahrendorf, M. Das Mädchenbuch und seine
Leserin. (3rd ed)
   H. Euler, 196:Band21Heft1/2-110
Dahrendorf, R. Life Chances.
   N.F., 185:Oct81-183
Daiber, H. Aetius Arabus.
   C.S.F. Burnett, 123:Vol31No2-304
Lady Daibu. The Poetic Memoirs of Lady
Daibu. (P.T. Harries, trans)
   H. McCullough, 293(JASt):May81-601
   K.L. Richard, 407(MN):Autumn81-341
Daiches, D. Literature and Gentility in
Scotland.
   J. Campbell, 617(TLS):9Jul82-751
Daix, P. Cubists and Cubism.
   J. Russell, 441:5Dec82-66
Daix, P. and J. Rosselet. Picasso: The
Cubist Years, 1907-1916.*
   E.F. Fry, 127:Spring81-91
Dalbor, J.B. Spanish Pronunciation. (2nd
ed)
   R.M. Barasch, 399(MLJ):Autumn81-338
Dalbor, J.B. and H.T. Sturcken. Spanish
in Review.
   F. Viña, 238:Mar81-168
Dalby, D. Language Map of Africa and the
Adjacent Islands.
   S. Brauner, 682(ZPSK):Band33Heft2-273
Dale, A. The Theatre Royal Brighton.
   S. Rosenfeld, 611(TN):Vol35No1-39
Dale, P.A. The Victorian Critic and the
Idea of History.
   P. Morgan, 179(ES):Apr81-183
Daleski, H.M. Joseph Conrad.
   E.K. Hay, 405(MP):Nov81-177
Dalfen, J. - see Marcus Aurelius
Dalisi, R. Gaudi: Furniture and Objects.
   J. Glancey, 46:Dec81-369

Dallapiccola, L. Parole e musica.
   C. Shaw, 607:Sep81-45
d'Alleva, J. and A. Bee. Incontri cultur-
ali.*
   G.L. Ervin, 399(MLJ):Spring81-118
Dalley, S., C.B.F. Walker and J.D. Hawkins.
The Old Babylonian Tablets from Tell al
Rimah.
   J.M. Sasson, 318(JAOS):Oct/Dec80-453
Dalton, E. Unconscious Structure in "The
Idiot."*
   G.S. Morson, 574(SEEJ):Winter81-62
D'Alton, M. Fatal Finish.
   N. Callendar, 441:12Dec82-37
Daly, P.M., ed. The European Emblem.
   V.W. Callahan, 570(SQ):Spring81-121
Daly, P.M. Literature in the Light of the
Emblem.*
   V.W. Callahan, 570(SQ):Spring81-121
   S. Gottlieb, 568(SCN):Summer-Fall81-63
   W.J. Ong, 377:Jul81-120
   H. Stegemeier, 301(JEGP):Jan81-86
d'Amboise, F. Oeuvres Complètes. (Vol 2)
(R.T. de Rosa, ed)
   G. Cesbron, 356(LR):Feb-May81-159
   M. Gaume, 535(RHL):Jul-Oct81-757
Damiani, B.M. Francisco López de Ubeda.
   R.V. Piluso, 552(REH):Jan81-142
Damico, A.J. Individuality and Community.
   J.D. Greenstone, 185:Oct81-152
D'Amico, J. Knowledge and Power in the
Renaissance.
   L.G. Black, 541(RES):May81-205
D'Amico, J. - see Petrarch
Damiens, S. La vie affective.
   J-M. Gabaude, 542:Jan-Mar81-132
Dammann, G., K.L. Schneider and J. Schö-
berl. Georg Heyms Gedicht "Der Krieg."
   H. Scher, 406:Summer81-238
Damrosch, L., Jr. Symbol and Truth in
Blake's Myth.*
   S. Curran, 401(MLQ):Sep81-303
Damsteegt, T. Epigraphical Hybrid San-
skrit.*
   J.S. Klein, 318(JAOS):Apr/Jun80-150
Dana, R. In a Fugitive Season.
   S. Corey, 639(VQR):Autumn81-732
   P. Mariani, 472:Spring/Summer82-265
Dance, D.C. Shuckin' and Jivin'.
   P.B. Mullen, 292(JAF):Jan-Mar81-119
d'Andlau, B., P. Christophorov and P.
Riberette - see de Chateaubriand, F.R.
Danell, K.J. Remarques sur la construc-
tion dite causative.
   M. Currie, 209(FM):Apr81-180
Daneman, M. The Groundling.
   J. Astor, 362:15Jul82-23
   L. Taylor, 617(TLS):11Jun82-643
Danesi, M. La lingua dei "Sermoni Subal-
pini."
   E. Hirsch, 685(ZDL):1/1981-88
Danforth, K.C. and M.B. Dickinson, eds.
Journey Into China.
   D.J.R. Bruckner, 441:12Dec82-13
Daniel, G. A Short History of Archaeology.
   D.W. Harding, 617(TLS):9Apr82-420
Daniel, G., ed. Towards a History of
Archaeology.
   D.W. Harding, 617(TLS):9Apr82-420
Daniel, L. Towards a New Compass.
   R. Willmot, 102(CanL):Autumn80-138
Daniel, O. Stokowski.
   R. Dyer, 441:19Dec82-3

Daniel, W. The Life of Ailred of Rievaulx.
(M. Powicke, ed and trans)
    A.G. Dyson, 325:Apr81-429
Daniell, D. "Coriolanus" in Europe.*
    M. Esslin, 157:2ndQtr81-52
    R.J., 214:Vol 10No37-126
    G. Taylor, 570(SQ):Summer81-286
Daniell, D. - see Buchan, J.
Daniels, B.C. The Connecticut Town.*
    D. Hoerder, 656(WMQ):Jan81-134
Daniels, C.B. The Evaluation of Ethical
Theories.*
    D.P.L., 185:Oct81-189
Daniels, P. and K. Weingarten. Sooner or
Later.
    C. Tavris, 441:4Apr82-14
Daniels, R.L. Laurence Olivier.
    D. McClelland, 200:Mar81-178
Danielsson, B. - see Smith, T.
Danielsson, B. - see Twiti, W.
d'Anjou, R. - see under René d'Anjou
Dann, J.C., ed. The Revolution Remembered.
    G.B. Kirsch, 432(NEQ):Sep81-435
    H.F. Rankin, 656(WMQ):Jan81-140
    W.C. Wright, 14:Fall80-492
Dannheimer, H. Torhalle auf Frauen-
chiemsee.
    W. Haas, 43:Band11Heft1-86
Danon, S. and S.N. Rosenberg - see "Ami
and Amile"
Dansel, M. Dictionnaire des inconnus aux
noms communs.
    J-Y. Dugas, 209(FM):Apr81-184
Danson, L. The Harmonies of "The Merchant
of Venice."*
    A.R. Dutton, 179(ES):Feb81-59
    G. Salgādo, 402(MLR):Jul81-665
Danson, L., ed. On "King Lear."
    B. Vickers, 617(TLS):20Aug82-911
Dante Alighieri. Dante's "Rime."* (P.S.
Diehl, trans)
    D.M. Di Orio, 577(SHR):Fall81-359
    A. Scaglione, 545(RPh):Feb81(supp)-32
Dante Alighieri. La Divina Commedia.*
(U. Bosco and G. Reggio, eds)
    T. Barolini, 276:Autumn81-214
Dante Alighieri. Inferno.* (A. Mandel-
baum, trans)
    J.R.B., 148:Spring81-19
    A.R.C. Duncan, 529(QQ):Winter81-758
Dante Alighieri. Opere minori. (Vol 2)
(P.V. Mengaldo and others, eds) Le
Ecloghe. (G. Brugnoli and R. Scarcia,
eds and trans)
    M. Marti, 228(GSLI):Vol 158fasc501-146
Dante Alighieri. La Vita nuova. (D. De
Robertis, ed)
    M. Marti, 228(GSLI):Vol 158fasc502-286
Danto, A.C. The Transfiguration of the
Commonplace.
    M.M. Eaton, 290(JAAC):Winter81-206
Dany, M. and J-R. Laloy. Le Français de
l'hôtellerie et du tourisme.
    B. Braude, 207(FR):Oct81-174
Daphinoff, D. - see Echlin, E.
Daphnopates, T. Correspondance. (J.
Darrouzès and L.G. Westerink, eds and
trans)
    R. Browning, 303(JoHS):Vol 101-231
Dardano, M. G.I. Ascoli e la questione
della lingua.
    F. Bruni, 545(RPh):Aug80-127

Dārdano, M. (S)parliamo italiano?
    R.A. Hall, Jr., 350:Jun81-495
D'Ardenne, S.T.R.O. The Katherine Group,
edited from MS. Bodley 34.
    B. Diensberg, 38:Band99Heft1/2-226
    A. Rynell, 597(SN):Vol53No2-385
Dardón, C.H.M. - see under Monsanto Dardón,
C.H.
D'Argence, R-Y.L. and D. Turner, eds.
5,000 Years of Korean Art.
    J.W. Best, 293(JASt):May81-559
d'Argenteuil, R. The ME Prose Translation
of Roger d'Argenteuil's "Bible en Fran-
çois."* (P. Moe, ed)
    D. Pearsall, 72:Band217Heft1-190
Darian, S.G. The Ganges in Myth and His-
tory.
    C.R. King, 314:Summer-Fall81-229
Darley, G. The National Trust Book of the
Farm.
    J.N. White, 324:Oct82-755
Darlington, B. - see Wordsworth, W.
Darlington, B. - see Wordsworth, W. and M.
D'Arms, J.H. Commerce and Social Standing
in Ancient Rome.
    R.P. Duncan-Jones, 617(TLS):19Mar82-
321
D'Arms, J.H. and E.C. Kopff, eds. The Sea-
borne Commerce of Ancient Rome.
    N. Purcell, 313:Vol71-197
Darmstaedter, R. Reclams Künstlerlexikon.
    J. Kronjäger, 471:Jan/Feb/Mar81-94
Darnton, R. The Business of Enlighten-
ment.*
    G.E.G., 543:Jun81-785
Darnton, R. The Literary Underground of
the Old Regime.
    N. Hampson, 453(NYRB):7Oct82-43
    M. Peters, 441:21Nov82-16
Darracott, J. The World of Charles Rick-
etts.*
    A. Ross, 364:Jun81-9
d'Arras, J. Le Roman de Mélusine ou
l'Histoire des Lusignan.
    M. Hugues, 535(RHL):May-Jun81-453
Darrouzès, J. and L.G. Westerink - see
Daphnopates, T.
Dars, J. - see Shi Nai-an and Luo Guan-
zhong
Dart, A.K. ESL Grammar Handbook for Inter-
mediate to Advanced Students of English
as a Second Language.
    R.F. Van Trieste, 608:Sep82-399
Darton, F.J.H., ed. Children's Books in
England. (3rd ed rev by B. Alderson)
    J. Briggs, 617(TLS):26Mar82-341
Darwin, C. Metaphysics, Materialism, and
the Evolution of Mind. (P.H. Barrett
and H.E. Gruber, eds)
    M. Ruse, 529(QQ):Summer81-373
Darwin, E. The Letters of Erasmus Darwin.
(D. King-Hele, ed)
    R. O'Hanlon, 617(TLS):19Mar82-299
Dary, D. Cowboy Culture.
    L. Milazzo, 584(SWR):Autumn81-413
Dary, D. True Tales of the Old-Time
Plains.
    K.I. Periman, 650(WF):Oct81-351
Das, A.K. Mughal Painting During Jahan-
gir's Time.
    M.C. Beach, 57:Vol42No1-119

Das, G.K. and J. Beer, eds. E.M. Forster.*
    S. Arkin, 395(MFS):Summer80-285
    K.M. Hewitt, 541(RES):Aug81-360
Das, K. The Old Playhouse and Other Poems.
    A.R.K. Zide, 314:Winter-Spring81-233
Das, R.J. Joseph Conrad.
    R. Roussel, 445(NCF):Sep81-249
Das, V. Structure and Cognition.
    H.P. Alper, 318(JAOS):Jan/Mar80-55
Daschkewitsch, V. Japanische Tuschmaler-
eien.
    J. Meech-Pekarik, 57:Vol42No2/3-235
Das Gupta, A. Indian Merchants and the
    Decline of Surat: c. 1700-1750.*
    F.F. Conlon, 293(JASt):Aug81-816
Dash, I.G. Wooing, Wedding, and Power.
    L. Lerner, 617(TLS):4Jun82-619
Da Silva, E.R. - see under Rosa Da Silva,
E.
Da Silva, Z.S. Spanish. (2nd ed)
    M.S. Yates, 399(MLJ):Winter81-447
"Dat narren schyp, Lübeck 1497." (T.
Sodmann, ed)
    H. Tervooren, 680(ZDP):Band100Heft3-
    450
Dathorne, O.R. Dark Ancestor.
    E. O'Callaghan, 617(TLS):2Apr82-391
Dauber, K. Rediscovering Hawthorne.*
    M.J. Colacurcio, 183(ESQ):Vol127No2-108
Dauer, A. and F. Kerschbaumer - see "Jazz
    Forschung 10"
Daugherty, S.B. - see James, H.
Daumal, R. Le Mont Analogue.
    F. Trémolières, 450(NRF):Jul-Aug81-191
d'Aurevilly, J-A.B. - see under Barbey
    d'Aurevilly, J-A.
Daval, J-L. Modern Art 1884-1914.
    S. Preston, 39:Jan81-63
Davenport, B.L. Textures and Patterns for
    the Rigid Heddle Loom.
    P. Bach, 614:Spring82-13
Davenport, G., ed and trans. Archilochos,
    Sappho, Alkman.*
    C.R. Beye, 472:Spring/Summer81-199
Davenport, G. Da Vinci's Bicycle.*
    E. Inness-Brown, 585(SoQ):Winter81-86
Davenport, G. Eclogues.*
    C.R. Beye, 472:Spring/Summer82-75
    J. Ditsky, 628(UWR):Spring-Summer82-
    105
Davenport, G. The Geography of the Imagin-
    ation.*
    C.R. Beye, 472:Spring/Summer82-75
    D. Hamilton, 271:Winter81-157
Davenport, W.A. The Art of the Gawain-
    Poet.
    M. Andrew, 179(ES):Oct81-471
    P.M. Kean, 677(YES):Vol 11-227
    M. Markus, 72:Band217Heft2-418
    D. Mehl, 38:Band99Heft1/2-223
    A.C. Spearing, 161(DUJ):Dec80-108
Davern, J. and others. Architecture 1970-
    1980.
    F. Gutheim, 45:Jan81-51
Davey, F. The Arches.
    D. McCarthy, 628(UWR):Fall-Winter81-
    104
Davey, F. Louis Dudek and Raymond Souster.
    B. Whiteman, 105:Spring/Summer81-98
Davey, J. Murder in Paradise.
    N. Callendar, 441:10Oct82-22

Davey, P. Arts and Crafts Architecture.*
    J.B. Smith, 39:Sep81-207
    135:Oct81-92
Daviau, D.G. - see Schnitzler, A.
David, A.R. The Ancient Egyptians.
    B.J. Kemp, 617(TLS):17Dec82-1400
David, C., ed. Franz Kafka.
    J.M. Grandin, 406:Spring81-97
David, C. - see Kafka, F.
David, D. Fictions of Resolution in
    Three Victorian Novels.*
    M. Irwin, 445(NCF):Dec81-366
    F.S. Schwarzbach, 155:Autumn81-177
David, J. Brave New Wave.
    G. Clever, 102(CanL):Winter80-130
David, R. Shakespeare in the Theatre.
    W.A. Armstrong, 611(TN):Vol35No1-36
    P. Thomson, 677(YES):Vol 11-238
    H.S. Weil, Jr., 570(SQ):Summer81-278
Davids, R.C. and D. Guravich. Lords of
    the Arctic.
    P-L. Adams, 61:Nov82-170
Davidsen, E. Henrik Ibsen og Det konge-
    lige teater.
    R. Rudler, 172(Edda):1981/2-125
Davidsen-Nielsen, N. Neutralization and
    Archiphoneme.
    M.S. Flier, 350:Mar81-225
    D.L. Goyvaerts, 361:Jan81-61
    G. Lepschy, 297(JL):Mar81-175
Davidson, A.A. Early American Modernist
    Painting, 1910-1935.*
    D. Anfam, 617(TLS):19Mar82-316
Davidson, C. A Woman's Work is Never Done.
    R. Delmar, 617(TLS):3Dec82-1343
Davidson, C. and D.E. O'Connor. York Art.*
    M.H. Caviness, 589:Jan81-114
Davidson, D. Essays on Actions and
    Events.*
    P. Engel, 98:Jun-Jul81-578
    A.R. White, 518:Jul81-158
Davidson, D. and G. Harman, eds. Seman-
    tics of Natural Language.
    G.F. Meier, 682(ZPSK):Band33Heft6-763
Davidson, H.E. - see Saxo Grammaticus
Davidson, H.M. The Origins of Certainty.*
    E.J. Campion, 583:Winter81-188
    J. De Jean, 188(ECr):Spring81-107
    C.G.S. Williams, 131(CL):Fall81-386
Davidson, H.M. and P.H. Dubé. A Concor-
    dance to Pascal's "Les Provinciales."
    E. Morot-Sir, 207(FR):Oct81-137
Davidson, H.R.E. and W.M.S. Russell, eds.
    The Folklore of Ghosts.
    G. Hough, 617(TLS):29Jan82-97
    E.S. Turner, 362:15Jul82-21
Davidson, J.P. David Teniers the Younger.
    C. Brown, 39:Dec81-429
Davidson, J.W. and M.H. Lytle. After the
    Fact.
    C.V. Woodward, 453(NYRB):27May82-42
    442(NY):19Apr82-177
Davidson, M.B. The Bantam Illustrated
    Guide to Early American Furniture.
    J.V. Turano, 16:Winter81-92
Davidson, P. International Money and The
    Real World.
    E. Roll, 617(TLS):4Jun82-620
Davidson, P. and J. Norman. Russian
    Phrase Book. (2nd ed)
    D. Matual, 399(MLJ):Winter81-441

Davie, D. Dissentient Voice.
    V. Cunningham, 362:26Aug82-21
    C. Rawson, 617(TLS):8Oct82-1097
Davie, D. A Gathered Church.*
    J. Seed, 580(SCR):Fall80-93
Davie, D., ed. The New Oxford Book of
    Christian Verse.*
    F. Kermode, 453(NYRB):21Oct82-39
    P. Ramsey, 472:Spring/Summer82-172
    J. Updike, 441:11Apr82-1
Davie, D. These the Companions.
    C. Rawson, 617(TLS):8Oct82-1097
    L. Simpson, 441:21Nov82-9
Davie, D. Three for Water-Music.
    G. Szirtes, 617(TLS):8Jan82-38
Davie, D. Trying to Explain.*
    P. Hobsbaum, 560:Fall81-121
    M. Kirkham, 569(SR):Summer81-474
Davies, A. - see Ormond, R. and M. Rogers
Davies, C. Latin Writers of the Renais-
    sance.
    H. Lloyd-Jones, 617(TLS):8Jan82-29
Davies, C.W. Theatre for the People.*
    D. Longhurst, 366:Autumn81-269
Davies, E.C. On the Semantics of Syntax.*
    R. Huddleston, 297(JL):Mar81-121
Davies, H. The Grades.
    M. Church, 617(TLS):26Feb82-204
Davies, H. William Wordsworth.*
    J. Hunter, 249(HudR):Spring81-135
    639(VQR):Spring81-48
Davies, J., ed. Esenin.
    J. Graffy, 617(TLS):29Oct82-1195
Davies, J. The Realism of Luigi Capuana.
    205(FMLS):Oct80-373
Davies, J.K. Democracy in Classical
    Greece.*
    A.L. Boegehold, 122:Jan81-62
Davies, K.G., ed. Documents of the Ameri-
    can Revolution 1770-83. (Colonial
    Office series)
    E. Wright, 617(TLS):12Feb82-152
Davies, M. Apologia pro Marcel Lefebvre.
    (Pt 1)
    M.M. Brennan, 396(ModA):Fall81-438
Davies, N. The Ancient Kingdom of Mexico.
    C. Tickell, 617(TLS):17Dec82-1400
Davies, N. God's Playground.
    L. Kolakowski, 441:15Aug82-6
    H. Seton-Watson, 617(TLS):19Mar82-297
Davies, P. The Edge of Infinity.
    J. Bernstein, 441:25Apr82-10
Davies, P. Roots.
    R.G. Schuh, 350:Sep82-726
Davies, P.C.W. The Forces of Nature.
    R.N. Bracewell, 529(QQ):Summer81-336
Davies, R. The Best of Rhys Davies.*
    A.R. Jones, 573(SSF):Spring81-197
Davies, R. The Enthusiasms of Robertson
    Davies. (J.S. Grant, ed)
    H. Hoy, 627(UTQ):Summer81-166
Davies, R. The Rebel Angels.
    P. Kemp, 617(TLS):26Mar82-339
    P. Monk, 150(DR):Autumn81-578
    K.C. O'Brien, 362:25Mar82-27
    S. Solecki, 99:Dec81/Jan82-30
    F. Taliaferro, 231:Feb82-66
    442(NY):15Feb82-138
Davies, R. The Well-Tempered Critic.
    S. Solecki, 99:Dec81/Jan82-30
Davies, R. - see Leacock, S.

Davies, R.T. and B.G. Beatty, eds. Litera-
    ture of the Romantic Period 1750-1850.*
    J.R. Strugnell, 677(YES):Vol 11-285
Davies, R.W. The Industrialisation of
    Soviet Russia.
    639(VQR):Winter81-7
Davies, S., ed. Renaissance Views of Man.
    H. Woudhuysen, 447(N&Q):Oct80-426
Davies, W. The Llandaff Charters.
    S.S. Walker, 589:Jan81-216
Davies, W. - see Hopkins, G.M.
Davies, W.H. Young Emma.*
    D. Severn, 364:Apr/May81-126
Davin, D., ed. Short Stories from the
    Second World War.
    I. Hamilton, 617(TLS):12Nov82-1243
Davis, A.R., ed. Modern Japanese Poetry.*
    D. Graham, 565:Vol22No1-73
Davis, A.Y. Women, Race and Class.
    A. Jones, 441:10Jan82-8
Davis, B.H. and R.K. O'Cain, eds. First
    Person Singular.
    R.A. Hall, Jr., 350:Sep81-701
Davis, B.J. The Storytellers in Margue-
    rite de Navarre's "Heptaméron."*
    205(FMLS):Jan80-83
Davis, D. Seeing the World.*
    D. Graham, 565:Vol22No4-62
Davis, F. A Fearful Innocence.*
    C. Schine, 441:10Jan82-12
Davis, G. Marriage.
    C. See, 441:14Feb82-14
Davis, G. and G. Watson. Black Life in
    Corporate America.
    A. Young, 441:24Oct82-12
Davis, G.V. Arnold Zweig in der DDR.
    J. Steakley, 406:Summer81-243
Davis, J.C. Utopia and the Ideal Society.
    Q. Skinner, 617(TLS):29Jan82-96
Davis, J.G. Fear No Evil.
    D. Profumo, 617(TLS):30Jul82-839
Davis, J.H., Jr. Fénelon.
    J. Cruickshank, 402(MLR):Apr81-467
    L. Mathieu-Kerns, 207(FR):Dec81-271
    205(FMLS):Oct80-373
Davis, J.L. and J.F. Cherry, eds. Papers
    in Cycladic Prehistory.
    J.B. Hennessy, 303(JoHS):Vol 101-205
Davis, J.M. Farce.*
    W.D. Howarth, 208(FS):Jan81-107
    205(FMLS):Apr80-187
Davis, L.H. Theory of Action.*
    I. Thalberg, 185:Jan82-343
Davis, M. Interpreters for Nigeria.
    P.F. Wilmot, 69:Vol50No2-234
Davis, M.E. Voces del Purgatorio.
    D.A. Olsen, 187:Sep82-466
Davis, M.T. - see under Thomson Davis, M.
Davis, N. Non-Cycle Plays and the Winches-
    ter Dialogues.
    W. Tydeman, 382(MAE):1981/2-350
Davis, N. and others, comps. A Chaucer
    Glossary.*
    J.J. Anderson, 148:Summer81-82
    M. Gretsch, 38:Band99Heft3/4-500
    R.A. Waldron, 447(N&Q):Aug80-357
Davis, P. Hometown.
    T.R. Edwards, 453(NYRB):15Jul82-28
    S.A. Toth, 441:4Apr82-9
Davis, P. Three Days.
    639(VQR):Winter81-8

Davis, P.J. and R. Hersh. The Mathemati-
cal Experience.*
  R.E.L., 185:Jul82-787
  R. Penrose, 617(TLS):14May82-523
Davis, R.B. A Colonial Southern Book-
shelf.*
  C. Dolmetsch, 392:Winter80/81-68
  J.L. Idol, Jr., 580(SCR):Fall80-102
  D.E. Stanford, 9(AlaR):Jul81-223
Davis, R.B. Intellectual Life in the
Colonial South, 1585-1763.*
  K. Silverman, 173(ECS):Spring81-344
Davis, R.B. George William Russell
('AE').
  G. O'Brien, 402(MLR):Oct81-939
Davis, R.C., ed. The Fictional Father.
  L. Mackinnon, 617(TLS):19Feb82-178
  R. Schleifer, 400(MLN):Dec81-1185
Davis, R.G. and L.A. Miller, eds. Guide
to the Catalogued Collections in the
Manuscript Department of the William F.
Perkins Library, Duke University.
  M.G. Martin, Jr., 14:Winter81-54
Davis, R.M. Evelyn Waugh, Writer.
  R.L. Montgomery, 617(TLS):9Jul82-746
Davis, S., ed. The Form of Housing.
  G. Anselevicius, 576:May81-166
Davis, S. Views of Medieval Bhutan. (M.
Aris, ed)
  A. Motion, 617(TLS):6Aug82-860
Davis, S.A., ed. 1982/83 National Direc-
tory of Shops/Galleries, Shows/Fairs.
  P. Bach, 614:Summer82-17
Davis, S.T.W. Intellectual Change and
Political Development in Early Modern
Japan.
  T.R.H. Havens, 407(MN):Summer81-210
Davis, T. Vision Quest.
  W. Bloodworth, 649(WAL):Winter81-314
Davis, W. Dojo.
  H.B. Earhart, 407(MN):Autumn81-329
Davis, W. The Rich.
  J. Stokes, 617(TLS):19Nov82-1263
Davis, W.A. The Act of Interpretation.*
  T. Heller, 50(ArQ):Spring81-85
  D. Richter, 599:Winter81-98
Davis, W.C., ed. The Image of War, 1861-
65. (Vol 2)
  442(NY):22Mar82-165
Davis, W.C., ed. The Image of War, 1861-
65. (Vol 3)
  442(NY):27Sep82-147
Davis-Gardner, A. Felice.
  P-L. Adams, 61:Aug82-96
  M. Gordon, 441:6Jun82-12
  442(NY):26Jul82-95
Davison, J.D. The Squeeze.
  A. Kemp, 396(ModA):Winter81-78
Davison, M. The Glory of Greece and the
World of Alexander.
  R. Higgins, 39:Jul81-69
Davison, P. - see Mowat, F.
Davison, P. - see Sissman, L.E.
Daw, S. The Music of Johann Sebastian
Bach: The Choral Works.
  W. Mellers, 617(TLS):29Oct82-1201
Dawe, G., ed. The Younger Irish Poets.
  P. Craig, 617(TLS):17Dec82-1399
Dawe, R.D. Studies on the Text of
Sophocles.* (Vol 3)
  J.C. Kamerbeek, 394:Vol34fasc1/2-154
  H. Lloyd-Jones, 123:Vol131No2-167
Dawe, R.D. - see Sophocles

Dawe, R.D., J. Diggle and P.E. Easterling,
eds. Dionysiaca.*
  G.L. Koniaris, 24:Spring81-94
Dawidoff, R. The Education of John Ran-
dolph.*
  N.R. McMillen, 585(SoQ):Winter81-84
  L.P. Simpson, 639(VQR):Winter81-158
Dawidowicz, L.S. The Holocaust and the
Historians.*
  T. Taylor, 441:24Jan82-8
"The Dawn of Modern Banking."*
  R. Ashton, 551(RenQ):Summer80-240
Daws, G. A Dream of Islands.
  S. Firth, 381:Apr81-124
Dawson, A.B. Indirections.*
  R. Huebert, 178:Fall81-353
Dawson, C. Victorian Noon.*
  J.P. Farrell, 637(VS):Autumn80-134
  N. McEwan, 447(N&Q):Aug80-379
  S. Monod, 189(EA):Jan-Mar81-99
  T. Peltason, 580(SCR):Fall80-97
  P. Turner, 541(RES):Aug81-349
Dawson, F.W. Reminiscences of Confeder-
ate Service, 1861-1865.
  639(VQR):Spring81-49
Dawson, P.M.S. The Unacknowledged Legis-
lator.*
  W. Galperin, 301(JEGP):Jul81-423
  D. Hughes, 591(SIR):Summer81-262
  G. McNiece, 661(WC):Summer81-181
  J. Raimond, 189(EA):Oct-Dec81-473
  P.S., 148:Spring81-93
Daxelmüller, C. Disputationes curiosae.
  R. Schenda, 196:Band21Heft1/2-110
Day, A.G. Modern Australian Prose, 1901-
1975.
  354:Jun81-180
"The Day Before Yesterday."
  J. Myerscough, 637(VS):Winter81-249
Day-Lewis, C. Poems of C. Day-Lewis 1925-
1972. (I. Parsons, ed) Posthumous
Poems.
  J. Whitehead, 184(EIC):Apr81-162
Day-Lewis, S. C. Day-Lewis.
  J. Whitehead, 184(EIC):Apr81-162
Daymond, D. and L. Monkman, eds. Stories
of Quebec.*
  S. Beckmann, 102(CanL):Summer81-152
Dayus, K. Her People.
  D.J. Enright, 617(TLS):12Nov82-1240
D'Costa, J. Roger Mais.
  K. Williamson, 541(RES):May81-245
De, B., ed. Perspectives in Social
Sciences I.
  D.L. Curley, 293(JASt):Nov80-158
Deák, I. The Lawful Revolution.*
  A. Sked, 575(SEER):Jan81-106
  G.F.G. Stanley, 529(QQ):Summer81-380
Deal, S.S. No Moving Parts.
  K.W. Cohen, 649(WAL):Winter82-318
Deal, T.E. and A.A. Kennedy. Corporate
Cultures.
  R. Krulwich, 441:4Jul82-6
Dean, J.F. Tom Stoppard.
  C.W.E. Bigsby, 617(TLS):8Jan82-33
Dean, S.F.X. By Frequent Anguish.
  T.J. Binyon, 617(TLS):29Oct82-1196
De Andrea, W. Killed in the Act.
  N. Callendar, 441:25Apr82-21
Deane, P. The First Industrial Revolution.
(2nd ed)
  D.B. Welbourn, 111:27Feb81-141

Dearlove, J.E. Accommodating the Chaos.
  P.J. Schwartz, 268(IFR):Summer82-149
Debesse, M. and G. Mialaret. Traité des
  sciences pédagogiques. (Vol 5)
  E. Diet, 542:Jul-Sep81-319
Debray, R. Teachers, Writers, Celebri-
  ties.*
  E. Le Roy Ladurie, 453(NYRB):21Jan82-
  59
Debray-Genette, R., ed. Flaubert à
  l'oeuvre.*
  J. Bem, 535(RHL):Jul-Oct81-812
  M. Lukacher, 400(MLN):May81-944
  N. Schor, 446(NCFS):Fall-Winter81/82-
  151
Debreuille, J-Y. Éluard ou le Pouvoir du
  Mot.
  F.R. Smith, 208(FS):Apr81-227
De Bruyne, J. Spaanse Spraakkunst.
  N. Delbecque, 277(ITL):No48-107
Debus, A.G. Man and Nature in the Renais-
  sance.*
  W.B. Ashworth, Jr., 551(RenQ):Autumn80-
  431
"Claude Debussy: Esquisses de 'Pelléas et
  Mélisande' (1893-1895)."
  R.H., 412:Nov80-320
Décarie, V., with R. Houde-Sauvé - see
  Aristotle
De Carlo, A. Uccelli da gabbia e da
  voliera.
  D. Robey, 617(TLS):3Dec82-1345
Décaudin, M. - see Toulet, P-J.
Deckart, G. - see Ertl, A.W.
De Coster, C. Pedro Antonio de Alarcón.
  R. Kirsner, 238:Sep81-477
Decottignies, J. L'Ecriture de la fiction.
  J. Alter, 188(ECr):Fall81-98
  J.M. Cocking, 208(FS):Apr81-240
  G. May, 207(FR):May81-862
  P. Somville, 542:Jan-Mar81-118
Dedijer, V. Novi prilozi za biografiju
  Josipa Broza Tita.
  S. Clissold, 617(TLS):16Jul82-763
Dedmond, F.B. Sylvester Judd.
  L. Neufeldt, 432(NEQ):Sep81-444
Dees, A., with P.T. van Reenan and J.A. de
  ·Vries. Atlas des formes et des construc-
  tions des chartes françaises du 13e
  siècle.
  A. McIntosh, 382(MAE):1981/1-136
Defaux, G. Molière, ou les métamorphoses
  du comique.
  R. Albanese, Jr., 207(FR):Dec81-270
  C. Garaud, 546(RR):Nov81-498
  F.L. Lawrence, 400(MLN):May81-918
  M-O. Sweetser, 475:No14Pt1-173
  R.W. Tobin, 188(ECr):Winter81-112
  205(FMLS):Oct80-373
Defoe, D. Atalantis Major.
  P-G.B., 189(EA):Jul-Sep81-364
Defoe, D. The Versatile Defoe.* (L.A.
  Curtis, ed)
  I. McGowan, 506(PSt):Dec81-344
  J. Wilkinson, 566:Autumn80-45
De George, R.T. The Philosopher's Guide
  to Sources, Research Tools, Profes-
  sional Life, and Related Fields.
  B.L., 185:Jul82-788
Deger-Jalkotzy, S. E-QE-TA.*
  H. Mühlestein, 260(IF):Band85-338

Dégh, L., ed. Studies in East European
  Folk Narrative.*
  G.K. Beynen, 574(SEEJ):Fall81-138
  D. Simonides, 196:Band22Heft1/2-119
Degler, C.N. At Odds.
  W.H. Chafe, 676(YR):Spring82-426
  N. Sahli, 432(NEQ):Jun81-290
Deguy, M. Donnant donnant.
  M. Chaillou, 98:Aug-Sep81-827
  D. Leuwers, 450(NRF):Sep81-115
Deguy, M. and J. Roubaud, eds. Vingt
  poètes américains.
  J. Stéfan, 450(NRF):Mar81-153
Dehejia, V. Early Stone Temples of
  Orissa.*
  M.W. Meister, 318(JAOS):Apr/Jun80-155
De Heusch, L. Why Marry Her?
  P. Rivière, 617(TLS):19Feb82-195
Deighton, L. Goodbye, Mickey Mouse.
  P-L. Adams, 61:Dec82-107
  P. Andrews, 441:14Nov82-15
  H.R., 231:Nov82-76
Deiritz, K. Geschichtsbewusstsein, Satire,
  Zensur.*
  J. Biener, 654(WB):7/1981-155
Deist, W. The Wehrmacht and German Rearma-
  ment.
  N. Stone, 453(NYRB):13May82-24
"Dejiny francouzské literatury 19. a 20.
  stoleti, 3: od 30 let do soucasnosti."
  M. Girard, 535(RHL):Jul-Oct81-852
De Jong, F. Names, Religious Denomination
  and Ethnicity of Settlements in Western
  Thrace.
  J.G. Nandris, 575(SEER):Oct81-634
Dekeyser, X. Number and Case Relations in
  19th Century British English.
  L. Lipka, 38:Band99Heft3/4-432
Dekker, R. and L. Van de Pol. Daat was
  Laatst een meisje loos.
  C.R. Boxer, 617(TLS):19Feb82-199
Dekker, T. The Shoemaker's Holiday.
  (R.L. Smallwood and S. Wells, eds)
  C. Spencer, 130:Spring81-87
  R.K. Turner, Jr., 568(SCN):Summer-
  Fall81-41
Delacampagne, C. and R. Maggiori, eds.
  Philosopher.
  J-C. Michéa, 98:Oct80-975
Delacroix, E. The Journal of Eugène Dela-
  croix. (H. Wellington, ed)
  E.J. Talbot, 207(FR):May81-905
Delahaye, M. The Sale of Lot 236.*
  T.J. Binyon, 617(TLS):1Jan82-12
Delaney, C.F., ed. Rationality and Reli-
  gious Belief.
  R. Hepburn, 393(Mind):Oct81-631
Delaney, J.J. Dictionary of Saints.
  G. Irvine, 617(TLS):5Nov82-1223
Delany, P. D.H. Lawrence's Nightmare.*
  J.A.V. Chapple, 366:Autumn81-232
  R.P. Wheeler, 301(JEGP):Jan81-149
  295(JML):Vol18No3/4-547
Delany, V. - see Cary, P.
Delas, D. Poetique/Pratique.
  W. Beauchamp, 599:Fall81-498
Delay, F. L'insuccès de la fête.*
  S. Koster, 98:Apr80-431
Delay, F. and J. Roubaud. Joseph d'Ari-
  mathie [et] Merlin l'Enchanteur.
  F. Trémolières, 450(NRF):Jun81-116
Delay, J. Avant Mémoire. (Vol 3)
  R. Buss, 617(TLS):24Dec82-1427

Delbanco, A. William Ellery Channing.*
639(VQR):Autumn81-126
Delbanco, N. Group Portrait.
P-L. Adams, 61:May82-106
E. Eichman, 231:Apr82-108
V. Glendinning, 362:28Oct82-20
H. Moss, 441:30May82-4
F. Tuohy, 617(TLS):22Oct82-1148
442(NY):21Jun82-122
Delbono, F. - see Oswald von Wolkenstein
Delclos, J-C. Le témoignage de Georges
Chastellain, Historiographie de Philippe
le Bon et de Charles le Téméraire.
D.R. Kelley, 589:Oct81-925
Delcorno Branca, D. Sulla tradizione
delle "Rime" del Poliziano.
P. Viti, 228(GSLI):Vol 158fasc503-451
Delebecque, É. - see Xénophon
Deleule, D. Hume et la naissance du
libéralisme économique.
F. Guery, 98:Nov80-1061
Deleuze, G. Francis Bacon, logique de la
sensation.
C. Gordon, 617(TLS):14May82-542
Deleuze, G. and F. Guattari. Mille pla-
teaux.*
P. Dulac, 450(NRF):Feb81-122
Deleuze, G. and F. Guattari. Politique et
Psychanalyse.
J. Forrester, 208(FS):Apr81-170
Delevoy, R.L., C. de Croës and G. Ollinger-
Zinque. Fernand Khnopff — Catalogue de
l'oeuvre.
H. Dorra, 90:Apr81-241
De Lillo, D. The Names.
J. Rubins, 453(NYRB):16Dec82-46
F. Taliaferro, 231:Dec82-70
M. Wood, 441:10Oct82-1
Delisle, J. L'Analyse du discours comme
méthode de traduction.
M-T. Caron, 628(UWR):Spring-Summer82-
110
Dell, F. Generative Phonology.
A. Carstairs, 353:Vol 18No9/10-943
Dell, F. Generative Phonology and French
Phonology.
B. Tranel, 350:Dec82-907
Dell, F. La langue bai.
G. Thurgood, 350:Sep82-732
Della Volpe, G. Rousseau and Marx.
S.G.S., 543:Dec80-375
Del Mar, N. Anatomy of the Orchestra.
H. Cole, 362:4Feb82-25
Del Mar, N. Mahler's Sixth Symphony.*
M. Carner, 415:Sep81-604
Deloffre, F. and M. Menemencioglu - see
Challe, R.
Delorko, O. Zanemareno blago.
M. Bošković-Stulli, 196:Band21Heft3/4-
Delorme, R.L., comp. Latin America.
M.H. Sable, 263(RIB):Vol31No4-549
Delouche, D. Peintres de la Bretagne.
N. McWilliam, 59:Dec81-466
Del Sesto, S.L. Science, Politics, and
Controversy.
R.E.G., 185:Oct80-172
Del Tredici, R. The People of Three Mile
Island.
J.S. Walker, 14:Fall81-365
Delumeau, J. La Peur en Occident (XIVe-
XVIIIe siècles).
S. Bayne, 475:No13Pt1-141

Delvalle, A.G. - see under González
Delvalle, A.
Del Vecchio, J.M. The 13th Valley.
J. Klein, 441:15Aug82-1
Dem, T. Masseni.
C.R. Larson, 441:4Jul82-8
Demaitre, L.E. Doctor Bernard de Gordon.
Y.V. O'Neill, 589:Oct81-857
Demandt, A. Metaphern für Geschichte.
D. Peil, 224(GRM):Band31Heft2-245
Demaray, J.G. Milton's Theatrical Epic.*
W.B. Hunter, Jr., 301(JEGP):Apr81-250
H. MacCallum, 627(UTQ):Spring81-314
L.E. Orange, 568(SCN):Summer-Fall81-37
J. Wittreich, 401(MLQ):Jun81-184
Demaris, O. The Last Mafioso.*
639(VQR):Spring81-65
De Martino, F. Storia economica di Roma
antica.
J. Briscoe, 123:Vol31No2-253
Dembowski, P.F., ed. "La Vie de sainte
Marie l'Égyptienne."
D. Robertson, 545(RPh):Nov80-258
Demerson, G. - see Dorat, J.
Demetz, P. - see Fontane, T.
De Molen, R.L., ed. Essays on the Works
of Erasmus.
M.O. Boyle, 551(RenQ):Summer80-265
A.H.T. Levi, 402(MLR):Jan81-150
Demos, J.P. Entertaining Satan.
P-L. Adams, 61:Oct82-105
E.S. Morgan, 453(NYRB):4Nov82-39
J.N. Rakove, 441:19Sep82-14
Demouzon, A. Quidam.
M.G. Hydak, 207(FR):May81-893
Dempster, N. Princess Margaret.^
C. Curtis, 441:4Apr82-11
d'Encausse, H.C. - see under Carrère
d'Encausse, H.
Dendle, B.J. Galdós: The Mature Thought.
639(VQR):Spring81-58
Dendurent, H.O. John Clare.
J. Barrell, 541(RES):Feb81-114
M. Storey, 447(N&Q):Aug80-378
Dendurent, H.O. Thomas De Quincey.
S.M. Tave, 677(YES):Vol 11-305
De Negri, E. Ottocento e rinnovamento
urbano.
F. Sborgi, 576:Mar81-60
Denham, R.D. - see Frye, N.
Denholm, A. Lord Ripon 1827-1909.
H.C.G. Matthew, 617(TLS):22Oct82-1155
Denholm, D. - see Cooper, C.E.
De Nicola, F. - see Edo, P.
Denis, A. Charles VIII et les Italiens.
D. Hay, 551(RenQ):Autumn80-438
Denis, C.P. The Films of Shirley MacLaine.
D. McClelland, 200:Apr81-241
Denis, E. La Lokapaññatti et les Idées
cosmologiques du Bouddhisme ancien.
J.P. McDermott, 318(JAOS):Jan/Mar80-56
Denis, H. L'"Economie" de Marx.
M. Lagueux, 154:Dec81-804
Denis, P. Carnet d'un aveuglement.
M. Bishop, 207(FR):May81-893
Denison, C., H.B. Mules and J. Shoaf.
European Drawings 1375-1825.
J.B. Shaw, 39:Dec81-429
Denisov, P.N. and V.V. Morkovkin. Učebnyj
slovar' sočetaemosti slov russkogo
jazyka.
G.F. Holliday, 574(SEEJ):Spring81-132

Denker, E. and B. The Rocking Chair Book.
P. Talbott, 658:Winter81-339
Denman, P. Sour Grapes.
R. Pybus, 565:Vol22No3-72
Dennett, D.C. Brainstorms.*
K. Sterelny, 63:Dec81-442
M. Thornton, 154:Sep81-610
Lord Denning. What Next in the Law.
N. MacCormick, 617(TLS):1Oct82-1076
D. Pannick, 362:12Aug82-21
Dennis, A., P. Foote and R. Perkins. Laws
of Early Iceland: Grágás I.
J.M. Jochens, 563(SS):Spring81-217
Dennis, C. Signs and Wonders.*
D. Graham, 565:Vol22No1-73
R.T. Smith, 577(SHR):Spring81-176
Dennis, J. The Plays of John Dennis.
(J.W. Johnson, ed)
C.D. Lein, 566:Autumn80-41
Dennison, S. Sidehill Gouger; or, What's
So Deadly about Caterpillars?
B. Rasporich, 296(JCF):No31/32-252
Dennys, R. Heraldry and the Heralds.
P.L. Dickinson, 617(TLS):3Sep82-949
Dent, R.W. Shakespeare's Proverbial Lan-
guage: An Index.
S. Wells, 617(TLS):16Apr82-435
Denyer, N. Time, Action and Necessity.
G. Strawson, 617(TLS):21May82-565
Deonanan, V.E. and C.E. Teaching Spanish
in the Secondary School in Trinidad,
West Indies.
F.H. Nuessel, Jr., 238:Sep81-488
Depestre, R. Le Mât de Cocagne.
J. Decock, 207(FR):Feb81-502
Depland, D. Le Fossoyeur.
J. Carleton, 207(FR):Feb81-504
De Poorter, N. - see under de Poorter, N.
De Porte, A.W. Europe Between the Super-
powers.
639(VQR):Summer81-94
Depreux, J-C. and T. Ici, il n'y a point
de chemin.
J-M. Gabaude, 542:Jan-Mar81-132
Deprun, J. La philosophie de l'inquiétude
en France au XVIIIe siècle.*
D. Leduc-Fayette, 542:Jul-Sep81-371
R. Mortier, 535(RHL):Nov-Dec81-1006
Derbolav, J. Platons Sprachphilosophie im
Kratylos und in den späteren Schriften.
G.B. Kerferd, 303(JoHS):Vol 101-155
Derbyshire, D.C. Hixkaryana.
P.K. Andersen, 215(GL):Winter81-292
De Robertis, D. - see Dante Alighieri
De Rocher, F. and G. Options.
A.S. Caprio, 207(FR):Mar81-609
Derolez, A. The Library of Raphael de
Marcatellis, Abbot of St. Bavon's, Ghent,
1437-1508.
J.J.G. Alexander, 382(MAE):1981/2-324
A.G. Watson, 447(N&Q):Aug80-359
Derré, J-R. - see de Rémusat, C.
Derrett, J.D.M. The Anastasis.
A.E. Harvey, 617(TLS):5Nov82-1226
Derrida, J. La Carte Postale.
G.L. Ulmer, 153:Fall81-39
Derrida, J. Positions. (A. Bass, ed and
trans)
N.M. Flax, 478:Fall81-237
C. Norris, 89(BJA):Autumn81-372
A. Parker, 114(ChiR):Spring81-135
A. Parker, 153:Fall81-57
[continued]

[continuing]
S.S., 148:Autumn81-92
J.H. Smith, 400(MLN):Dec81-1160
G. Strickland, 111:1Jun81-229
Derrida, J. Spurs.* (French title:
Éperons.)
B. Draine, 81:Spring-Fall81-425
D.G. Marshall, 473(PR):2/1981-294
T.B. Strong, 185:Jan81-324
C.S. Taylor, 518:Oct81-208
Derry, W. - see Burney, F.
Dershowitz, A.M. The Best Defense.
T. Goldstein, 441:13Jun82-13
G. Hughes, 453(NYRB):24Jun82-27
Derwing, B.L. and T.M.S. Priestly. Read-
ing Rules for Russian.*
J.G. Sowerby, 575(SEER):Oct81-593
C.E. Townsend, 399(MLJ):Winter81-440
Desai, A. Clear Light of Day.*
G. Kearns, 249(HudR):Summer81-311
De Salvo, L.A. Virginia Woolf's First
Voyage.
J. Haule, 659(ConL):Winter82-100
De Salvo, L.A. - see Woolf, V.
Desanti, D. Daniel ou le visage secret
d'une comtesse romantique, Marie
d'Agoult.
M.A. Garnett, 446(NCFS):Fall-Win-
ter81/82-187
C. Zimra, 207(FR):Dec81-288
Desbarats, P. Canada Lost/Canada Found.
V. Lyon, 298:Summer81-122
Deschamps, N., R. Héroux and N. Villeneuve.
Le Mythe de Maria Chapdelaine.
B-Z. Shek, 627(UTQ):Summer81-184
Descharnes, R. and C. Prévost. Gaudí.
P. Goldberger, 441:12Dec82-12
Deschner, G. Reinhard Heydrich.
J. Grigg, 362:25Mar82-22
N. Stone, 453(NYRB):13May82-24
Descoeudres, J-P. and others. Eretria:
Fouilles et recherches. (Vol 6)
O.T.P.K. Dickinson, 303(JoHS):Vol 101-
207
Descotes, D. La Première critique des
"Pensées."
P. Sellier, 475:No15Pt1-160
Desheriev, J.D. Social'naja lingvistika.
J.F. Levin, 355(LSoc):Apr81-85
Deshpande, M.M. Evolution of Syntactic
Theory in Sanskrit Grammar.
D. Disterheft, 350:Jun81-492
Deshpande, M.M. Sociolinguistic Attitudes
in India.
F.C. Southworth, 350:Dec81-932
Deshpande, M.M. and P.E. Hook, eds. Aryan
and Non-Aryan in India.
M.B. Emeneau, 350:Jun81-468
Deshusses, J. The Eighth Night of Crea-
tion.
M. Berman, 441:7Mar82-10
Désiré, A. Le Contrepoison des Cinquante-
deux Chansons de Clément Marot. (J.
Pineaux, ed)
C.A. Mayer, 208(FS):Oct81-432
Desmarests de Saint-Sorlin, J. Clovis, ou
la France chrestienne.* (F.R. Freud-
mann, ed)
A. Niderst, 535(RHL):Jan-Feb81-129
205(FMLS):Jan80-83

De Smedt, R. La Collaboration de Franz
Hellens aux périodiques de 1899 à 1972.*
[shown in prev under de Smedt, R.]
J. Decreus, 208(FS):Apr81-228
Desmond, R. The India Museum, 1801-1879.
A.C. Davies, 324:Jul82-505
De Souza, T.R. Medieval Goa.
D. Alden, 293(JASt):Nov80-160
Desowitz, R.S. New Guinea Tapeworms and
Jewish Grandmothers.*
J.F. Watkins, 617(TLS):24Sep82-1027
Despalatatović, E.M. Ljudevit Gaj and the
Illyrian Movement.
T. Eekman, 279:Vol24-190
Des Périers, B. Nouvelles Récréations et
joyeux devis I-XC. (K. Kasprzyk, ed)
J.S. Dugan, 207(FR):May82-900
G-A. Pérouse, 535(RHL):Nov-Dec81-979
Desportes, P. Reims et les Rémois aux
XIIIe et XIVe siècles.
K.L. Reyerson, 589:Jan81-116
Desrosiers, T. Les relations d'Haïti.
G. Breathett, 263(RIB):Vol31No4-550
Dessaint, A.Y. Minorities of Southwest
China.
D.J. Solinger, 293(JASt):May81-581
Dessaix, R. and M. Ulman - see Svirski, G.
Dessau, J. Lord of the Ladies.
617(TLS):8Jan82-35
d'Étaples, J.L. - see under Lefèvre
d'Étaples, J.
Dethier, F. and J. Wathelet-Willem, eds.
Six littératures romanes.
C. Di Girolamo, 545(RPh):Aug80-104
Detienne, M. and J-P. Vernant. La cuisine
du sacrifice en pays grec.*
R.G.A. Buxton, 123:Vol31No1-131
J. Pollard, 303(JoHS):Vol 101-184
Detrez, C. Le Dragueur de Dieu.*
M. Naudin, 207(FR):Dec81-303
Detweiler, R. and G. Meeter, eds. Faith
and Fiction.
O.B. Emerson, 573(SSF):Fall81-474
Deufert, W. Narr, Moral und Gesellschaft.
H. Heinen, 680(ZDP):Band99Heft3-457
Deutrich, M.E. and V.C. Purdy, eds. Clio
Was a Woman.
M.I. Crawford, 14:Fall80-493
Deutsch, E. On Truth.
L.E. Johnson, 63:Mar81-129
"Deutsche Märchen." (illustrations by F.
Hechelmann)
R. Wehse, 196:Band22Heft1/2-128
"Deuxième Rapport sur les revenus des Fran-
çais."
J-M. Guieu, 207(FR):Dec81-286
Devaulx, N. Le Manuscrit inachevé.
F. de Martinoir, 450(NRF):Jul-Aug81-
193
Devaulx, N. La Plume et la racine.*
D.B. Brautman, 207(FR):May81-894
Develin, R. Patterns in Office-Holding,
366-49 B.C.
J. Briscoe, 313:Vol71-230
P. Jal, 555:Vol54fasc2-383
Deverell, R. Boiler Room Suite.*
J. Wasserman, 102(CanL):Autumn80-88
Devine, P.E. The Ethics of Homicide.*
B. Cohen, 393(Mind):Jan81-142
G.W. Trianosky-Stillwell, 482(PhR):
Oct81-633

De Vitoria, F. Leçon sur le pouvoir
politique. (M. Barbier, ed and trans)
A. Reix, 542:Jul-Sep81-346
Devkota, L. Nepali Visions, Nepali Dreams.
(D. Rubin, trans)
L. Nathan, 293(JASt):Aug81-838
Devlin, D. A Speaking Part.
S. Wall, 617(TLS):24Dec82-1417
Devlin, D.D. Jane Austen and Education.
J.F. Burrows, 402(MLR):Oct81-936
Devlin, K.J. Fundamentals of Contemporary
Set Theory.
R. Chuaqui, 316:Jun81-419
The Duchess of Devonshire. The House.
J. Lees-Milne, 617(TLS):30Jul82-823
Devos, R. and others. La Pratique des
Documents Anciens.
C. Dolan, 14:Summer80-381
De Vries, P. Sauce for the Goose.*
G. Craig, 617(TLS):22Jan82-76
J. Mellors, 362:14Jan82-24
Dewdney, C. Alter Sublime.
P. Smith, 150(DR):Winter81/82-760
Dewdney, S. The Hungry Time.
K. Kealy, 102(CanL):Summer81-149
Dewhurst, C.K., B. MacDowell and M.
MacDowell. Artists in Aprons.
J.A. Chinn, 650(WF):Apr81-188
Dewhurst, E. Whoever I Am.
M. Laski, 362:29Apr82-27
Dewhurst, K. The Captain of the Sands.
J.K.L. Walker, 617(TLS):2Apr82-395
Dewhurst, K. Lark Rise/Candleford.
D. Devlin, 157:1stQtr81-54
Dewhurst, K. and N. Reeves. Friedrich
Schiller.*
M. Bragg, 406:Winter81 458
E. Slater, 447(N&Q):Oct80-449
Deyermond, A.D. "Lazarillo de Tormes": A
Critical Guide.
C. Stern, 545(RPh):Feb81-303
Deyermond, A.D., ed. Medieval Hispanic
Studies, presented to Rita Hamilton.*
F. Marquez Villanueva, 545(RPh):
Feb81(supp)-371
Deyon, P. Le mercantilisme.
J-P. Lefebvre, 98:Dec81-1278
Diaconoff, S. Eros and Power in "Les
Liaisons dangereuses."*
P. Clancy, 67:Nov81-256
S.K. Jackson, 399(MLJ):Winter81-427
R.C. Rosbottom, 535(RHL):Jul-Oct81-790
J. Undank, 210(FrF):May81-177
Diallo, N. A Dakar Childhood.
J. Kirkup, 617(TLS):29Oct82-1202
Diamond, C. and J. Teichman, eds. Inten-
tions and Intentionality.
S. Candlish, 479(PhQ):Apr81-170
M.J. Harney, 63:Sep81-365
I. Thalberg, 482(PhR):Oct81-624
Diamond, E. Good News, Bad News.
J. Alexander, 106:Spring81-89
Diamond, E. Sign Off.
J. Powers, 231:Dec82-61
Diamonstein, B. American Architecture
Now.*
H. Senie, 55:Summer81-28
Diamonstein, B., ed. Collaboration.
H. Senie, 55:Summer81-30
Díaz, A.C. - see under Castro Díaz, A.
Díaz, A.E. - see under Espinós Díaz, A.
Díaz Migoyo, G. Estructura de la novela.
C.B. Johnson, 240(HR):Summer81-357

Díaz y Díaz, M.C. Libros y librerías en
la Rioja altomedieval.
J.N. Hillgarth, 589:Jan81-119
Di Battista, M. Virginia Woolf's Major
Novels.*
M. Magalaner, 395(MFS):Winter80/81-684
D. Watt, 301(JEGP):Jul81-449
295(JML):Vol18No3/4-643
Dibble, J.A. The Pythia's Drunken Song.*
G.B. Tennyson, 599:Winter81-37
Di Camillo, O. El humanismo castellano
del siglo XV.*
C. Stern, 545(RPh):May81-544
Di Cesare, M.A. and E. Fogel. A Concor-
dance to the Poems of Ben Jonson.*
H.S. Donow, 365:Fall81-165
"1922-1943: vent'anni di moda italiana."
R.L. Shep, 614:Summer82-20
Di Cicco, P.G. Dancing in the House of
Cards.
R. Willmot, 102(CanL):Autumn80-138
Di Cicco, P.G., ed. Roman Candles.*
L. Ricou, 102(CanL):Autumn80-128
Di Cicco, P.G. The Tough Romance.*
E. Nicol, 102(CanL):Winter80-108
Dick, J. Violence and Oppression.
G. Ostergaard, 185:Oct81-140
Dickens, A.G., ed. The Courts of Europe,
Politics, Patronage and Royalty, 1400-
1800.
T.D. Kaufmann, 576:Mar81-70
Dickens, C. David Copperfield.* (N.
Burgis, ed)
J.H. Buckley, 155:Autumn81-172
A. Welsh, 676(YR):Autumn81-149
Dickens, C. Dickens on America and the
Americans.* (M. Slater, ed)
S. Monod, 189(EA):Oct-Dec81-477
Dickens, C. Dickens on England and the
English.* (M. Andrews, ed) [shown in
prev under ed]
S. Monod, 189(EA):Oct-Dec81-477
445(NCF):Dec81-378
Dickens, C. The Letters of Charles Dick-
ens.* (Vol 4) (K. Tillotson, with N.
Burgis, eds)
T. Blount, 447(N&Q):Jun80-253
T.J. Cribb, 541(RES):Nov81-465
A. Easson, 366:Autumn81-265
Dickens, C. The Letters of Charles
Dickens.* (Vol 5) (G. Storey and
K.J. Fielding, eds)
A. Sanders, 155:Autumn81-170
A. Welsh, 676(YR):Autumn81-149
Dickens, C. Little Dorrit.* (H.P. Suck-
smith, ed)
T. Davis, 301(JEGP):Oct81-585
K.J. Fielding, 677(YES):Vol 11-321
J. Gattégno, 189(EA):Jul-Sep81-349
S. Gill, 541(RES):Nov81-468
J. Stillinger, 445(NCF):Mar81-543
Dickens, C. La Maison d'Âpre-Vent.* (S.
Monod, ed and trans)
G.H. Ford, 189(EA):Oct-Dec81-475
Dickens, C. and L. Garfield. The Mystery
of Edwin Drood.*
K.M. Longley, 155:Summer81-102
"Dickens Studies Annual." (Vol 8) (M.
Timko, F. Kaplan and E. Guiliano, eds)
R. Ashton, 155:Autumn81-175
"Dickens Studies Annual." (Vol 9) (M.
Timko, F. Kaplan and E. Guiliano, eds)
J. Batchelor, 617(TLS):28May82-591

Dicker, G. Perceptual Knowledge.
P. Snowdon, 617(TLS):19Feb82-194
Dickey, D.W. The Kennedy Corridos.
P. Sonnichsen, 650(WF):Jul81-274
Dickey, J. The Strength of Fields.*
C. Molesworth, 473(PR):2/1981-315
Dickey, J.S. Canada and the American
Presence.
G.A. Rawlyk, 106:Winter81-405
Dickinson, E. The Manuscript Books of
Emily Dickinson: A Facsimile Edition.
(R.W. Franklin, ed)
M.L. Rosenthal, 617(TLS):26Mar82-357
Dickinson, H.T. Liberty and Property.*
A.N. Newman, 366:Autumn81-254
Dickinson, J.C. The Later Middle Ages.
R.W. Pfaff, 589:Apr81-376
Dickinson, P. The Last House Party.
P-L. Adams, 61:Nov82-171
P. Craig, 617(TLS):4Jun82-622
Dickson, J. Victoria Hotel.
R.T. Smith, 577(SHR):Spring81-177
Dickson, K.A. Towards Utopia.*
S. Mews, 301(JEGP):Jan81-107
205(FMLS):Jan80-84
Dickson, M.B. and S.C. Welch - see "The
Houghton 'Shahnameh'"
Dickstein, M. Gates of Eden.
W. Marling, 50(ArQ):Spring81-94
S. O'Connell, 418(MR):Spring81-185
Di Clerico, R.E. The American President.
J. Alexander, 106:Spring81-89
"Dicţionarul literaturii române de la
origini pînă la 1900."
D.J. Deletant, 575(SEER):Jul81-414
"Dictionary of Canadian Biography." (Vol
4) (F.G. Halpenny, general ed)
C.F. Klinck, 178:Dec81-496
Diderot, D. Ecrits inconnus de jeunesse,
1745.* (J.T. de Booy, ed)
J. Lough, 535(RHL):May-Jun81-463
G. May, 546(RR):Jan81-111
"Diderot Studies XIX." (O. Fellows and
D.G. Carr, eds)
P.D. Jimack, 208(FS):Jul81-338
R. Niklaus, 535(RHL):Jan-Feb81-134
Diebner, S. "Aesernia-Venafrum."
M.H. Crawford, 313:Vol71-153
A. Hus, 555:Vol54fasc2-390
Diehl, J.F. Dickinson and the Romantic
Imagination.
R. Christiansen, 617(TLS):6Aug82-867
Diehl, W. Chameleon.
E. Jakab, 441:7Feb82-13
Dierauer, U. Tier und Mensch im Denken
der Antike.*
W.J. Verdenius, 394:Vol134fasc1/2-185
Dierse, U. Enzyklopädie.*
R.A. Müller, 489(PJGG):Band88Heft2-425
Dietiker, S.R. Franc-Parler. (2nd ed)
P.J. Edwards, 207(FR):Oct81-175
J.W. Zdenek, 399(MLJ):Summer81-215
Dietz, H.A. Poverty and Problem-Solving
Under Military Rule.
C.A. Astiz, 263(RIB):Vol31No1-83
Dietz, K. Senatus contra principem.
T.D. Barnes, 487:Winter81-386
Dietz, J. Frequenzwörterbuch zur Synodal-
handschrift der Ersten Novgoroder
Chronik.
G.F. Meier, 682(ZPSK):Band33Heft5-631
Dietzsch, S. - see Kant, I.
Dietzsch, S. and B. - see Kant, I.

Díez Borque, J.M., ed. Historia de la
  literatura española. (Vol 1)
    A. Deyermond, 86(BHS):Apr81-135
Di Gaetani, J.L., ed. Penetrating Wag-
  ner's Ring.
    J. Deathridge, 451:Summer81-81
Diggett, C. and W.C. Mulligan. Hypnocop.
    M. Peters, 441:21Nov82-16
van Dijk, T.A., ed. Pragmatics of Lan-
  guage and Literature.
    N.E. Enkvist, 599:Winter81-90
Dik, S.C. Functional Grammar.*
    G.D. Prideaux, 350:Sep81-717
Dik, S.C. Stepwise Lexical Decomposition.
    G.B., 189(EA):Apr-Jun81-237
Dik, S.C. Studies in Fuctional Grammar.
    E.A. Edwards, 350:Sep82-727
Dil, A.S. - see Emeneau, M.B.
Dil, A.S. - see Friedrich, P.
Dil, A.S. - see Haugen, E.
Dil, A.S. - see McDavid, R.I., Jr.
Dil, A.S. - see Nida, E.A.
Dillard, A. Living by Fiction.
    V. Bourjaily, 441:9May82-10
    442(NY):17May82-140
Dillard, A. Teaching a Stone to Talk.
    H. Bevington, 441:28Nov82-13
Dillard, J.L. - see Marckwardt, A.H.
Dillenberger, J. Benjamin West.
    A. Staley, 90:May81-307
Diller, H-J. Metrik und Verslehre.
    E. Standop, 38:Band99Heft3/4-478
Diller, H-J. and J. Kornelius. Linguis-
  tische Probleme der Übersetzung.*
    D. Stein, 38:Band99Heft1/2-204
Diller, K.C. The Language Teaching Contro-
  versy.
    I. Andrews, 257(IRAL):Feb81-77
Dillon, G.L. Constructing Texts.
    A.D. and A.M. Zwicky, 350:Sep82-740
Dillon, G.L. Language Processing and the
  Reading of Literature.*
    E.C. Traugott, 599:Winter81-77
Dillon, J. The Middle Platonists.*
    K. Bärthlein, 53(AGP):Band62Heft2-204
Dillon, K.J. Scholars' Guide to Washing-
  ton, D.C.: Central and East European
  Studies.
    A. South, 14:Spring81-161
Dillon, N. Mother's Gone Fishing.* (D.
  Cooley, ed)
    D. Barbour, 648(WCR):Jun80-75
Dilman, I. Morality and the Inner Life.
    G.E.T., 543:Dec80-377
Dilthey, W. Selected Writings. (H.P.
  Rickman, ed) Descriptive Psychology and
  Historical Understanding.
    T.E. Huff, 488:Dec81-461
Di Marco, V. and L. Perelman, eds. The
  Middle English "Letter of Alexander to
  Aristotle."*
    A. Hudson, 447(N&Q):Jun80-249
Dimić, M.V. and E. Kushner, eds. Pro-
  ceedings of the 7th Congress of the
  International Comparative Literature
  Association.
    D.W. Fokkema, 204(FdL):Jun81-216
Dimmitt, C. and J.A.B. van Buitenen, eds
  and trans. Classical Hindu Mythology.
    D. Dell, 485(PE&W):Apr81-240
Dinesen, I. Letters from Africa, 1914-
  1931.* (F. Lasson, ed)
    V. Young, 249(HudR):Winter81/82-625

Dingle, A.E. The Campaign for Prohibition
  in Victorian England.
    D.M. Fahey, 637(VS):Summer81-524
Dinneen, F.P. Linguistics.
    G.F. Meier, 682(ZPSK):Band32Heft2-224
Dinnsen, D.A., ed. Current Approaches to
  Phonological Theory.
    E. Gussmann, 297(JL):Sep81-371
    A. Liberman, 353:Vol 18No11/12-1105
    P. Tiersma, 361:Jun/Jul81-227
    A.M. Zwicky, 350:Dec82-873
Dinsmoor, W.B., Jr. The Propylaia to the
  Athenian Akropolis. (Vol 1)
    J.J. Coulton, 123:Vol31No2-319
    S.G. Miller, 576:May81-151
Dintenfass, M. Old World, New World.
    D. Merkin, 441:28Feb82-9
D'Introno, F. Sintaxis transformacional
  del español.
    C. Silva-Corvalán, 350:Jun81-496
Diodorus Siculus. Diodore de Sicile, "Bib-
  liothèque historique." (Vol 13, Bk 18)
  (P. Goukowsky, ed and trans)
    M. Casevitz, 555:Vol54fasc2-361
Dion, M. and others. La Classe ouvrière
  française et la politique.
    J-P. Ponchie, 207(FR):Oct81-168
Dion, P-E. La langue de Ya'udi.
    P. Swiggers, 350:Jun81-505
Dionysius of Halicarnassus. Denys d'Hali-
  carnasse, "Opuscules rhétoriques."*
  (Vol 1) (G. Aujac, ed and trans)
    D.C. Innes, 123:Vol31No1-111
Diószegi, V. and M. Hoppál, eds. Shaman-
  ism in Siberia.
    R. Grambo, 196:Band21Heft1/2-113
Di Pietro, R.J. The Semiotics of Musical
  Theatre.
    M. Danesi, 399(MLJ):Summer81-227
Dippie, B.W., ed. Nomad.
    W. Price, 649(WAL):Fall81-235
Dipple, E. Iris Murdoch.
    P. Kemp, 362:21Jan82-24
    S. Newman, 617(TLS):12Feb82-167
Disch, T. Burn This.
    D. Lehman, 617(TLS):27Aug82-919
"Discourse in Action."
    E. Hamp-Lyons, 608:Jun82-253
Dismukes, B. and J.M. McConnell, eds.
  Soviet Naval Diplomacy.*
    J.N. Westwood, 575(SEER):Apr81-313
"La dispersión del Manierismo."
    F. Marías, 48:Apr-Jun81-224
Disraeli, B. Benjamin Disraeli: Letters.
  (Vols 1 and 2) (J.A.W. Gunn and others,
  eds)
    J.W. Burrow, 617(TLS):22Oct82-1155
    N. St. John-Stevas, 362:9Sep82-20
Disraeli, B. The Works of Benjamin
  Disraeli. Sybil.
    F. Coblence, 98:Feb-Mar81-276
d'Istria, H. and J-J. Breton, with P. Gavi.
  Les Relations Parents-Enfants.
    A. Duhamel-Ketchum, 207(FR):Oct80-205
Dittert, A.E., Jr. and F. Plog. Genera-
  tions in Clay.
    L. Milazzo, 584(SWR):Autumn81-414
Dittmann, J., ed. Arbeiten zur Konversa-
  tionsanalyse.
    U.M. Quasthoff, 350:Sep81-755
Dittmar, K. Assimilation und Dissimila-
  tion.
    T. Hergt, 52:Band15Heft2-217

Dix, C. D.H. Lawrence and Women.
  N. Clausson, 395(MFS):Winter80/81-687
"Le Dix-Septième siècle."
  J. Stéfan, 450(NRF):Apr81-117
Dixon, D. After Man.
  T. Ferris, 441:4Apr82-17
Dixon, R.M.W. The Languages of Australia.
  D. Laycock, 350:Sep82-701
  G.N. O'Grady, 67:Nov81-273
Dixon, R.M.W. and B.J. Blake, eds. Hand-
  book of Australian Languages.* (Vol 1)
  B. Rigsby, 350:Sep82-704
Dixon, S. 14 Stories.*
  L. Abbott, 580(SCR):Fall81-133
  W. Cummins, 363(LitR):Spring82-462
  W. Koon, 573(SSF):Summer81-337
Dixon, S. Quite Contrary.*
  L. Abbott, 580(SCR):Fall81-133
  R. Orodenker, 573(SSF):Fall81-478
Dixon, S. Too Late.
  L. Abbott, 580(SCR):Fall81-133
Dixon, V. - see de Vega Carpio, L.
al-Djawbarî, 'A.R. Le Voile arraché.
  J-L. Gautier, 450(NRF):May81-148
Djébar, A. Femmes d'Alger dans leur
  appartement.
  M. Mortimer, 207(FR):Mar82-564
Djordjevic, D. and S. Fischer-Galati. The
  Balkan Revolutionary Tradition.
  639(VQR):Summer81-93
Djurić, M. Mythos, Wissenschaft, Ideolo-
  gie.*
  E. Blondel, 542:Oct-Dec81-497
Dmytryshyn, B. and E.A.P. Crownhart-
  Vaughan - see Golovin, P.N.
Doane, A.N., ed. Genesis A.* (new ed)
  U. Schwab, 179(ES):Oct81-474
  T.A. Shippey, 402(MLR):Apr81-430
Dobbs, C.M. The Unwanted Symbol.
  W. Goodman, 441:17Jan82-14
Dobie, J.F. Wild and Wily.
  L. Milazzo, 584(SWR):Autumn81-413
Dobkowski, M.N. The Tarnished Dream.
  M. Friedman, 390:Oct81-58
Dobrenn, M. - see Camus, A. and J. Grenier
Dobroszycki, L. and B. Kirshenblatt-
  Gimblett. Image Before My Eyes.
  H. Niedzielski, 497(PolR):Vol26No3-111
Dobson, E.J. The Origins of "Ancrene
  Wisse."
  G. Kristensson, 597(SN):Vol53No2-371
Dobson, E.J. and F.L. Harrison, eds.
  Medieval English Songs.
  N.C. Carpenter, 301(JEGP):Oct81-571
  L. Clopper and H. Tischler, 589:Oct81-
  859
  T.G. Duncan, 382(MAE):1981/2-338
  A.A. MacDonald, 179(ES):Oct81-479
  D. Stevens, 414(MusQ):Jul81-437
Dobson, R., ed. Sisters Poets 1.
  C. Pollnitz, 581:Jun81-221
Dobson, R. and D. Campbell - see "Seven
  Russian Poets"
Doctorow, E.L. Drinks before Dinner.*
  D.L. Zins, 584(SWR):Winter81-96
Doctorow, E.L. Loon Lake.*
  D. Flower, 249(HudR):Spring81-105
  R.H. King, 639(VQR):Spring81-341
  N. Schmitz, 473(PR):4/1981-629
Dodd, P. - see Pater, W.
Doderer, K., ed. Lexikon der Kinder- und
  Jugendliteratur.
  R. Schenda, 196:Band22Heft1/2-121

Dodge, E. Morning Was Starlight.
  P-L. Adams, 61:May82-106
Dodge, G.H. Benjamin Constant's Philoso-
  phy of Liberalism.
  D.J., 185:Jul82-786
Dodgshon, R.A. Land and Society in Early
  Scotland.
  T.C. Smout, 617(TLS):2Apr82-389
Doehaerd, R. The Early Middle Ages in the
  West.
  B.S. Bachrach, 589:Apr81-452
D'Oench, E.G. The Conversation Piece.
  R. Wark, 54:Sep81-520
Doerner, K. Madmen and the Bourgeoisie.
  R. Brown, 617(TLS):8Jan82-23
Dōgen. Record of Things Heard from the
  Treasury of the Eye of the True Teaching.
  (as recorded by Ejō, trans by T. Cleary)
  T.J. Kodera, 407(MN):Autumn81-353
Doggett, F. Wallace Stevens.*
  M.J. Bates, 295(JML):Vol8No3/4-620
  W. Harmon, 27(AL):May81-316
Doggett, F. and R. Buttel, eds. Wallace
  Stevens.*
  W. Harmon, 27(AL):May81-316
Doglio, M.L. - see Giovio, P.
Doig, A. The Architectural Drawings
  Collection of King's College, Cambridge.*
  P. Willis, 83:Autumn81-255
Doig, I. The Sea Runners.
  M.L. Settle, 441:3Oct82-9
Doig, I. Winter Brothers.*
  H.P. Simonson, 649(WAL):Summer81-169
Dolan, C. Entre tours et clochers.
  C.E. Campbell, 207(FR):Feb82-457
  D. Hickey, 539:Nov82-306
Dolci, D. Sicilian Lives.*
  L. Barzini, 453(NYRB):10Jun82-26
  T. Morgan, 441:7Feb82-11
Dolet, É. Préfaces françaises. (C. Lon-
  geon, ed)
  R. Cholakian, 207(FR):Dec81-262
  G. Gueudet, 535(RHL):Jul-Oct81-750
Dolgopolova, L.K. - see Bely, A.
Dolgopolova, Z., ed. Russia Dies Laughing.
  K. Fitz Lyon, 617(TLS):11Jun82-641
Dolle, J-M. De Freud à Piaget.
  J-M. Gabaude, 542:Jan-Mar81-132
Dölling, I. Naturwesen — Individuum —
  Persönlichkeit.
  H.M. Nickel, 654(WB):12/1981-187
Dolphin, C. Méthodes de la statistique
  linguistique et vocabulaire fantastique
  de "Malpertuis."
  A. Schneider, 209(FM):Jul81-273
Dölz Blackburn, I. Antología crítica de
  la poesía tradicional chilena.
  S.G. Armistead, 240(HR):Summer81-375
  A.M. Pasero, 399(MLJ):Summer81-219
Domandl, S. Jugendbewegung aus dem Geiste
  Kants und Goethes.
  R. Malter, 342:Band71Heft2-275
Domes, J. Socialism in the Chinese Coun-
  tryside.
  D.E. Waterfall, 529(QQ):Summer81-279
Domínguez, F., ed. Cancionero de obras de
  burlas provocantes a risa.
  C. Stern, 552(REH):May81-318
Domínguez, F.A. The Medieval Argonautica.
  R.G. Keightley, 382(MAE):1981/2-336
  F.P. Norris, 589:Oct81-862

Domínguez Moltó, A. El Abate D. Juan
Andrés Morell (Un erudito del siglo
XVIII).
G.E. Mazzeo, 240(HR):Spring81-244
Dominian, J. Marriage, Faith and Love.
R. Haughton, 617(TLS):30Jul82-836
Dominicis, M.C. and J.A. Cussen. Casos y
cosas.
E. Spinelli, 399(MLJ):Winter81-448
Dömötör, T. János Honti.*
J. Gulya, 196:Band21Heftl/2-114
Donadio, S. Nietzsche, Henry James, and
the Artistic Will.*
J. Arac, 81:Spring-Fall81-437
Donaghue, M.R. and J.F. Kunkle. Second
Language in Primary Education.
R.W. Newman, 207(FR):Mar81-610
Donahue, T.J. The Theater of Fernando
Arrabal.
B.L. Knapp, 397(MD):Mar81-104
N. Lane, 207(FR):Mar81-606
C. Marowitz, 157:Oct80-48
Donakowski, C.L. A Muse for the Masses.*
H.B.R., 412:Feb80-63
Donaldson, F. P.G. Wodehouse.
P-L. Adams, 61:Jun82-100
B. Brophy, 362:30Sep82-17
A. Cockburn, 453(NYRB):23Sep82-22
P. De Vries, 442(NY):23Aug82-87
H. Spurling, 617(TLS):12Nov82-1239
Donaldson, I. The Rapes of Lucretia.
L. Sage, 617(TLS):24Dec82-1410
Donaldson, M. Children's Minds.
S. and F. Plank, 257(IRAL):May81-167
Donaldson, S. By Force of Will.
D. Hewitt, 447(N&Q):Jun80-272
Donat, A. The Death Camp, Treblinka.
M.W. Kiel, 287:Apr81-26
Doncaster, S. Some Notes on Bewick's
Trade Blocks.
354:Jun81-177
Dondaine, H-F. - see Aquinas, T.
Donehoo, G.P. Indian Villages and Place
Names in Pennsylvania.
K.B. Harder, 424:Mar80-93
Donelson, K.L. and A.P. Nilsen. Litera-
ture for Today's Young Adults.
T.W. Hipple and B. Bartholomew,
128(CE):Nov81-724
Dönhoff, M. Foe into Friend.
M. Balfour, 617(TLS):12Nov82-1238
Donington, R. The Rise of Opera.
H. Cole, 362:4Feb82-25
J. Glover, 617(TLS):12Feb82-156
Donkin, E. - see Brisebarre, J.
Donne, J. The Divine Poems.* (2nd ed) (H.
Gardner, ed)
R. Ellrodt, 189(EA):Apr-Jun81-218
A.F. Marotti, 551(RenQ):Autumn80-479
G. Pursglove, 161(DUJ):Jun81-253
M. Roberts, 447(N&Q):Aug80-364
Donne, J. The Epithalamions, Anniversar-
ies and Epicedes of John Donne.* (W.
Milgate, ed)
D.F. Bratchell, 447(N&Q):Oct80-436
A.F. Marotti, 551(RenQ):Autumn80-479
Donne, J. Paradoxes and Problems. (H.
Peters, ed)
G.M. Ridden, 366:Autumn81-250
639(VQR):Spring81-56
Donne, M. and C. Fowler. Per Ardua Ad
Astra.
B. Bond, 617(TLS):13Aug82-886

Donnell, D. Dangerous Crossings.
G.A. Boire, 102(CanL):Summer81-168
Donner, F. Shabono.
C. Turnbull, 441:27Jun82-10
Donner, F.M. The Early Islamic Conquests.
H. Kennedy, 617(TLS):10Sep82-980
Donno, E.S. - see Madox, R.
Donoghue, D. Ferocious Alphabets.*
S. Helmling, 249(HudR):Winter81/82-631
P. Rogers, 617(TLS):5Feb82-132
Donoghue, M.R. and J.F. Kunkle. Second
Languages in Primary Education.
T. Andersson, 399(MLJ):Summer81-204
S.L. Fischer, 238:Sep81-477
Donovan, J. Sarah Orne Jewett.
T.R. Hovet, 26(ALR):Spring81-152
Donovan, R.J. Tumultuous Years.
M. Miller, 441:30Oct82-1
Donson, T.B. Prints and the Print Market.
T. Crombie, 39:Jun81-415
Doob, L.W. - see Pound, E.
Dooley, D.J. Moral Vision in the Canadian
Novel.*
R. Lecker, 102(CanL):Autumn80-104
Dooley, R. From Scarface to Scarlett.
R. Haver, 18:Jun81-63
M. McCreadie, 200:Oct81-506
Doolittle, H. - see under H.D.
Doolittle, J. and Z. Barnieh. A Mirror of
Our Dreams.
P. Moss, 108:Winter81-135
P. Nodelman, 102(CanL):Summer80-109
Doppelfeld, O. and W. Weyres. Die Ausgra-
bungen im Dom zu Köln. (H. Hellenkemper,
ed)
W. Haas, 43:Band11Hcft2-185
Doran, M. Shakespeare's Dramatic Lan-
guage.*
J. Schäfer, 402(MLR):Jul81-663
Dorat, J. Les Odes latines. (G. Demerson,
ed and trans)
G. de Rocher, 345(KRQ):Vol28No4-428
d'Ordonez, C. Seven Symphonies. (A.P.
Brown, ed)
P. Weiss, 414(MusQ):Apr81-282
Doret, M. Cinq Dialogues.
A. Moorhead, 207(FR):Feb82-434
Doret, M. Isolement.
D.E. Rivas, 207(FR):Apr81-761
Dorge, C. Le Roitelet.
L. Filteau, 108:Spring81-123
Doria, C., ed. The Tenth Muse.
J. Herington, 472:Fall/Winter81-217
Dorian, N.C. Language Death.
W.U. Dressler, 350:Jun82-432
Dorigo, S.M. - see Einaudi, L.
Dorin, F. Les Lits à une place.
N. Aronson, 207(FR):Apr81-758
Döring, J.R., ed. Zur Analyse dreier
Erzählungen von Vl. I. Dal'.
J.T. Baer, 688(ZSP):Band41Heft2-440
Döring, K. Exemplum Socratis.
A.A. Long, 123:Vol31No2-298
Doring, P.F. Colloquial German. (4th ed)
(I. Hubmann-Uhlich, ed)
C.E. Putnam, 399(MLJ):Autumn81-355
Dorival, B., ed. Album Pascal.
P. Sellier, 535(RHL):Nov-Dec81-985
Dormeier, H. Montecassino und die Laien
im 11. und 12. Jahrhundert.
G. Constable, 589:Jan81-121
d'Ormesson, J. Dieu, sa vie, son oeuvre.
A. Clerval, 450(NRF):Apr81-128

d'Ormesson, J. Mon dernier rêve sera pour vous.
  P.L. Bowles, 617(TLS):5Nov82-1222
Dorn, E. Interviews. Views. (D. Allen, ed of both)
  D.K. Boyer, 649(WAL):Winter82-317
Dorn, E. Yellow Lola, Formerly Titled Japanese Neon.
  R. von Hallberg, 659(ConL):Spring82-225
Dorn, R. Mittelalterliche Kirchen in Braunschweig.
  J. Cramer, 43:Band10Heft2-185
Dornberg, J. Munich 1923.
  W. Goodman, 441:19Sep82-16
Dörner, F.K. and M-B. von Stritzky, eds. Tituli Bithyniae. (Vol 1)
  A.G. Woodhead, 303(JoHS):Vol 101-224
Dorner-Bachmann, H. Erzählstruktur und Texttheorie.
  J.H. Petersen, 680(ZDP):Band99Heft4-597
Dörrie, H. Platonica minora.
  R.T. Wallis, 123:Vol131No1-129
Dorson, R.M., ed. Folklore in the Modern World.*
  T.A. Green, 650(WF):Jul81-267
  U. Kutter, 196:Band21Heft3/4-305
Dorward, D. Scotland's Place-Names.
  W.F.H. Nicolaisen, 424:Mar80-88
Dossin, G., with A. Finet, eds and trans. Archives royales de Mari. (Vol 10)
  W.L. Moran, 318(JAOS):Apr/Jun80-186
Dostál, A. and H. Rothe, eds. Der altrussische Kondakar'.
  A.E. Pennington, 575(SEER):Jul81-415
"Dostoïevski et les Lettres françaises."
  O. Scherer, 549(RLC):Jul-Dec81-489
Dothan, T. The Philistines and their Material Culture.
  K. Kitchen, 617(TLS):17Dec82-1400
Doty, C. A Day Late.*
  T. Helbert, 649(WAL):Spring81-62
Doubrovsky, S. Parcours critique.
  P. Bayard, 450(NRF):Jan81-142
Douglas, C. Swans of Other Worlds.
  V.D. Barooshian, 550(RusR):Apr81-227
Douglas, E. A Lifetime Burning.
  S. Isaacs, 441:31Oct82-11
Douglas, K. The Complete Poems of Keith Douglas. Alamein to Zem Zem. (D. Graham, ed of both)
  R. Gibbons, 472:Spring/Summer81-315
Douglas, M. In the Active Voice.
  S. Sutherland, 617(TLS):13Aug82-889
Douglas, M. and A. Wildavsky. Risk and Culture.
  I. Hacking, 453(NYRB):23Sep82-30
  L. Winner, 441:8Aug82-8
Douglas, R. New Alliances 1940-41.
  K. Jeffery, 617(TLS):31Dec82-1450
Douglas, W.O. The Court Years, 1939-1975.*
  385(MQR):Spring82-376
Douglass, F. The Frederick Douglass Papers.* (Ser 1, Vol 1) (J.W. Blassingame, with others, eds)
  G.B. Mills, 9(AlaR):Apr81-133
  J.C. Williams, 583:Winter81-189
Doumas, C., ed. Thera and the Aegean World.* (Vol 1)
  E. Schofield, 123:Vol131No1-96
Dourado, A. The Voices of the Dead.*
  K. Pollitt, 441:24Jan82-13

Dove, R. The Yellow House on the Corner.
  D. Smith, 29:Jan/Feb82-36
Dover, K. - see Plato
Dover, K.J., ed. Ancient Greek Literature.
  L.M. Styler, 123:Vol131No2-214
Dover, K.J. Greek Homosexuality.*
  T.M. Robinson, 487:Summer81-160
Dower, J.W. Empire and Aftermath.
  Hosoya Chihiro, 285(JapQ):Jan-Mar81-103
Dowling, W.C. The Boswellian Hero.*
  G.M. Buresch, 447(N&Q):Oct80-447
  D. Crane, 179(ES):Aug81-387
  C. Fox, 77:Summer81-268
  A.F.T. Lurcock, 541(RES):Aug81-334
  A. Pailler, 189(EA):Apr-Jun81-222
  P.M. Spacks, 173(ECS):Summer81-470
  A. Varney, 506(PSt):May81-97
Downes, D.A. Ruskin's Landscape of Beatitude.
  F.G. Townsend, 637(VS):Winter81-248
Downes, K. The Architecture of Wren.
  A. Hollinghurst, 617(TLS):24Dec82-1413
Downes, K. Rubens.*
  A. Hughes, 90:Feb81-106
Downes, K. Vanbrugh.*
  D. Cast, 43:Band10Heft1-92
Downes, R. - see Porter, F.
Downie, F. Plainsong.
  H. Lomas, 364:Nov81-68
Downie, J.A. Robert Harley and the Press.
  J. Barnard, 148:Autumn81-85
  J. Feather, 517(PBSA):Jan-Mar81-112
  L.S. Horsley, 506(PSt):Dec81-341
  M. Treadwell, 354:Sep81-254
Downie, M.A. and M. Hamilton. "And Some brought Flowers."
  W.N., 102(CanL):Spring81-174
  529(QQ):Spring81-194
Downs, B. Sacred Places.
  E.D. Layman, 576:Dec81-341
Dowrick, F.E., ed. Human Rights.
  R.P.C., 185:Oct80-171
Dowty, D.R. Word Meaning and Montague Grammar.
  T.J. Taylor, 307:Oct81-127
Doxey, M.P. Economic Sanctions and International Enforcement.
  O.R.Y., 185:Oct81-197
Doyle, A.C. Uncollected Stories. Essays on Photography. (J.M. Gibson and R.L. Green, eds of both)
  P. Craig, 617(TLS):24Dec82-1414
  H. Greene, 362:23and30Dec82-45
Doyle, C. R.A.K. Mason.
  A. Paterson, 368:Dec73-361
Doyle, C., ed. William Carlos Williams: The Critical Heritage.
  E. Domville, 627(UTQ):Summer81-140
Doyle, E.M. and V.H. Floyd, eds. Studies in Interpretation.* (Vol 2)
  K.T. Loesch, 290(JAAC):Fall81-105
Doyle, R. Journal, 1840.
  A.S., 155:Summer81-110
Doyle, W. Origins of the French Revolution.*
  R. Tombs, 208(FS):Oct81-456
Drabble, M. The Middle Ground.*
  J. Deckenbach, 114(ChiR):Spring81-131
  D. Flower, 249(HudR):Spring81-115
  E.C. Rose, 145(Crit):Vol123No3-69
  L.V. Sadler, 145(Crit):Vol123No3-83

Drachenberg, E., K-J. Maercker and C. Schmidt. Die mittelalterliche Glasmalerei in den Ordenskirchen und im Angermuseum zu Erfurt.
G. Fritzsche, 683:Band43Heft4-423

Drage, C.L. Russian Literature in the Eighteenth Century.*
W.G. Jones, 402(MLR):Apr81-510
G.S. Smith, 575(SEER):Apr81-287

Dragonetti, R. La Vie de la lettre au Moyen Age (Le Conte du Graal).*
D. Hult, 400(MLN):May81-951
L. Marin, 98:Jan81-40

Drake, D.B. Cervantes' "Novelas ejemplares." (2nd ed)
H.C. Woodbridge, 304(JHP):Spring81-235

Drake, D.B. "Don Quijote" (1894-1970). (Vols 1 and 2)
W.F. King, 238:Mar81-153

Drake, D.B. "Don Quijote" (1894-1970).* (Vol 3)
E.H. Friedman, 238:Dec81-636

Drake, G.C. and C.A. Forbes - see Vida, M.G.

Drake, G.F. The Role of Prescriptivism in American Linguistics, 1820-1970.
J.L. Subbiondo, 350:Jun82-485

Drake, R. The Home Place.
T. Hubert, 396(ModA):Fall81-410

Drake, S. Galileo at Work.*
G.A.J. Rogers, 518:Apr81-84

Drake, W. Sara Teasdale.
A. Kolodny, 27(AL):May81-320

Draper, R.P., ed. George Eliot: "The Mill on the Floss" and "Silas Marner."
P. Preston, 447(N&Q):Dec80-558

Draper, R.P., ed. D.H. Lawrence: The Critical Heritage.
J.A.V. Chapple, 366:Autumn81-232

Dray, W. Perspectives on History.*
A.D., 185:Jul81-693
A.P. Fell, 529(QQ):Autumn81-580

Drea, E.J. The 1942 Japanese General Election.
G.M. Berger, 407(MN):Summer81-214

Dreessen, W-O. and H-J. Müller, eds. Daniel: Das altjiddische Danielbuch.
P. Trost, 680(ZDP):Band100Heft1-143

Dreiser, T. Theodore Dreiser: American Diaries 1902-26. (T.P. Riggio, J.L.W. West 3d and N.M. Westlake, eds)
P.K. Bell, 617(TLS):24Sep82-1023
A. Kazin, 441:22Aug82-9
442(NY):28Jun82-119

Dreiser, T. Sister Carrie.* (J.L.W. West 3d and others, eds)
R.H. Brodhead, 676(YR):Summer82-597
P.L. Gerber, 26(ALR):Autumn81-299
D. Pizer, 27(AL):Jan82-731

Dresden, S. and others - see Erasmus

Dresser, C. The Art of Decorative Design.
C.M. Porter, 658:Spring81-106

Dressler, W.U. Grundfragen der Morphonologie.*
A. Carstairs, 353:Vol 18No11/12-1153
W.U. Wurzel, 682(ZPSK):Band32Heft2-248

Dressler, W.U. and others, eds. Proceedings of the Twelfth International Congress of Linguists.
W. Euler 260(IF):Band85-298

Dretske, F.I. Knowledge and the Flow of Information.
A. Margalit, 617(TLS):22Oct82-1170

Drew, E. Portrait of an Election.*
T.J. Farer, 453(NYRB):21Jan82-40
E. Wright, 617(TLS):30Apr82-482

Drew, P. The Architecture of Arata Isozaki.
P. Goldberger, 441:8Aug82-9

Drew, P. The Meaning of Freedom.
A.D. Nuttall, 617(TLS):9Jul82-746

Drewes, G.W.J. Directions for Travellers on the Mystic Path.
R. Jones, 293(JASt):Feb81-418

Drexler, R. Bad Guy.
S. Isaacs, 441:8Aug82-13

Dreyfus, J. A History of the Nonesuch Press.
R. McLean, 617(TLS):2Apr82-372
H. Schmoller, 324:Nov82-824

Dreyfus, K. Music by Percy Aldridge Grainger.
J.H., 412:Feb80-69

Dreyfuss, J. and C. Lawrence 3d. The Bakke Case.
I. Thalberg, 185:Oct80-138

Drieu la Rochelle, P. The Man on Horseback.
J. Cruickshank, 208(FS):Jan81-93

Drinnon, R. Facing West.
S.M. Bennett, 651(WHR):Winter81-387

Driscoll, P. Heritage.
S. Ellin, 441:3Oct82-12

Driver, C.E. - see Moore, M.

Droixhe, D. La linguistique et l'appel de l'histoire (1600-1800).*
G. Price, 208(FS):Jul81-373
R. Rocher, 318(JAOS):Jan/Mar80-60

Drooker, P.B. Hammock Making Techniques.
P. Bach, 614:Fall82-17

von Droste-Hülshoff, A. Historisch-kritische Ausgabe. (Vol 3, Pt 1 ed by L. Jordan; Vol 5, Pt 1 ed by W. Huge)
E. Care, 402(MLR):Jul81-750

Drozdowski, M.M. Ignacy Jan Paderewski.
P.S. Wandycz, 497(PolR):Vol26No1-127

Drucker, H.M. - see Mackintosh, J.P.

Drucker, P.F. The Last of All Possible Worlds.
J. Mellors, 362:26Aug82-24

Drüe, H. Psychologie aus dem Begriff.*
R. Aschenberg, 53(AGP):Band62Heft2-225

Drummond, D. New and Selected Poems 1938-1978.
M. Bucco, 649(WAL):Winter82-309

Drummond, P. The German Concerto.
G.R. Seaman, 83:Autumn81-246

Drummond de Andrade, C. The Minus Sign.
H.J.F. de Aguilar, 472:Spring/Summer82-23

Drury, A. The Hill of Summer.*
M. Haltrecht, 617(TLS):30Apr82-493

Druzhinin, N.M. Russkaia derevnia na perelome, 1861-1880 gg.
D. Field, 550(RusR):Apr81-189

Dryden, D.M. Fabric Painting and Dyeing for the Theatre.
R.L. Shep, 614:Summer82-15

Dryden, E.A. Nathaniel Hawthorne.*
M.J. Colacurcio, 183(ESQ):Vol127No2-108

Dryden, J. The Works of John Dryden. (Vol 19) (A. Roper and V.A. Dearing, eds)
J.V. Guerinot, 568(SCN):Spring81-15
A. Poyet, 189(EA):Jan-Mar81-92

Drysdale, R. Miniature Crocheting and
Knitting for Dollhouses.
  M.Z. Cowan, 614:Fall82-19
Du Bartas, S. The Divine Weeks and Works
of Guillaume de Saluste, Sieur du Bartas.
(S. Snyder, ed)
  A.L. Prescott, 551(RenQ):Autumn80-460
Du Bartas, S. La Sepmaine (Texte de 1581).
(Y. Bellenger, ed)
  G. Echard, 539:Nov82-300
Dubé, M. Octobre.
  D.M. Hayne, 102(CanL):Summer80-129
Dubie, N. The Everlastings.*
  F. Garber, 29:May/Jun82-44
  V. Shetley, 453(NYRB):29Apr82-43
Dubois, A-J. L'Oeil de la mouche.
  R. Linkhorn, 207(FR):Mar82-565
Dubois, C. - see "Petit Larousse en
couleurs 1980"
Dubois, C-G. Le Maniérisme.
  M. Simonin, 535(RHL):Mar-Apr81-337
Dubois, J., ed. Dictionnaire du français
langue étrangère, Niveau 1.*
  R.J. Steiner, 399(MLJ):Summer81-217
Dubois, J. L'Institution de la littéra-
ture.*
  M. Grimaud, 494:Autumn80-202
Dubois, J. Les martyrologes du moyen âge
latin.
  J.M. McCulloh, 589:Jan81-122
Du Bruck, E. - see Rivière, P.
Duby, G. Le chevalier, la femme et le
prêtre.
  R. Chartier, 98:Aug-Sep81-822
Duby, G. The Three Orders.* (French
title: Les trois ordres ou l'imaginaire
du féodalisme.)
  E. Benson, 207(FR):Oct80-203
Duca, I.G. Amintiri politice. (G. Duca,
ed)
  V. Nemoianu, 617(TLS):6Aug82-845
Ducatillon, J. Polémiques dans la Collec-
tion hippocratique.
  M-P. Duminil, 555:Vol54fasc2-350
Duchac, J. The Poems of Emily Dickinson.
  B.L. St. Armand, 365:Fall81-174
Ducháček, O. L'évolution de l'articula-
tion linguistique du domaine esthétique
du latin au français contemporain.*
  J. Chaurand, 209(FM):Apr81-168
Duchet, C., ed. Balzac et "La Peau de
chagrin."
  D. Adamson, 208(FS):Apr81-214
  D. Bellos, 402(MLR):Jan81-196
Duchet, C., with B. Merigot and A.P. van
Teslaar, eds. Sociocritique.
  M. Hays, 210(FrF):May81-189
Ducout, F. Séductrices du cinéma français,
1936-1956.
  M.G. Hydak, 207(FR):Oct81-149
Ducrocq, J., S. Halimi and M. Lévy. Roman
et société en Angleterre au XVIIIe
siècle.*
  J.C. Dales, 677(YES):Vol 11-270
Ducrot, O. and others. Les mots du dis-
cours.
  J.M. Julien, 350:Mar81-238
  D. Nebig, 361:Jun/Jul81-269
Ducrot, O. and T. Todorov. Encyclopedic
Dictionary of the Sciences of Language.*
  T. Eaton, 599:Fall81-506
  D.H., 355(LSoc):Aug81-311

Dudek, L. Selected Essays and Criticism.
  T. Goldie, 178:Spring81-120
Dudek, L. Technology and Culture.*
  M. Ross, 102(CanL):Autumn80-105
"DUDEN - Das grosse Wörterbuch der deut-
schen Sprache in sechs Bänden." (Vols
1-5)
  B. Brogyanyi, 215(GL):Fall81-205
Dudley Edwards, O. The Quest for Sherlock
Holmes.
  P. Craig, 617(TLS):24Dec82-1414
Dudley Edwards, R. Corridors of Death.
  N. Callendar, 441:12Sep82-38
  K. Jeffery, 617(TLS):11Jun82-642
  M. Laski, 362:29Apr82-27
Duerr, H.P. Traumzeit.
  J. Agassi, 262:Dec81-455
Duff, S.G. - see under Grant Duff, S.
Duffey, B. Poetry in America.
  R. Asselineau, 189(EA):Apr-Jun81-234
  S. Fender, 677(YES):Vol 11-365
  A. Hook, 447(N&Q):Jun80-268
Duffy, C. Russia's Military Way to the
West.
  I. Vinogradoff, 617(TLS):23Jul82-802
Duffy, C. Siege Warfare.
  N. Adams, 576:Dec81-331
Duffy, E., ed. Challoner and His Church.
  P. Hebblethwaite, 617(TLS):21May82-554
Duffy, E. Rousseau in England.*
  J. Clubbe, 340(KSJ):Vol30-196
  C.H. Ketcham, 191(ELN):Mar81-219
Duffy, M. The Erotic World of Faery.
  G. Macdonald, 435:Summer81-208
Dufournet, J. Nouvelles recherches sur
Villon.
  J-C. Aubailly, 535(RHL):Nov-Dec81-976
Dufournet, J. - see de Commynes, P.
Dufrenne, M. L'Inventaire des a-priori,
Recherche de l'originaire.
  T. Cordellier, 450(NRF):Nov81-138
Dufrenne, M., ed. Main Trends in Aes-
thetics and the Sciences of Art.
  E.F. Kaelin, 127:Summer81-183
Dufrenne, S. Tableaux synoptiques de 15
Psautiers medievaux. Les Illustrations
du Psautier d'Utrecht.
  H.L. Kessler, 54:Mar81-142
Dugast, D. La statistique lexicale.
  J. Breuillard, 209(FM):Jul81-271
Duggan, J.J. A Guide to Studies on the
"Chanson de Roland."*
  G.S. Burgess, 545(RPh):Aug80-136
Duggan, M. Collected Stories. (C.K.
Stead, ed)
  V. Cunningham, 617(TLS):9Apr82-404
Duggan, M.M. and R. Layman - see "Fitz-
gerald/Hemingway Annual, 1977"
Dugger, R. The Politician.
  A. Latham, 441:9May82-1
Duignan, P. and A. Rabushka, eds. The
United States in the 1890s.*
  D.J. Senese, 396(ModA):Spring81-199
Duiker, W.J. Cultures in Collision.
  J.W. Esherick, 293(JASt):Nov80-108
Duisit, L. Satire, Parodie, Calembour.
  C. Abastado, 535(RHL):May-Jun81-493
  J.A. Flieger, 207(FR):Oct80-157
Dujardin, É. Les Lauriers sont coupés.
  P-L. Rey, 450(NRF):Nov81-124
Duke, M. Flashpoint.
  M. Laski, 362:29Jul82-27

Duke, M.S. Lu You.*
  J.T. Wixted, 293(JASt):Aug81-758
Dukelskaya, L., comp. The Hermitage:
  English Art.
  A.G. Cross, 575(SEER):Apr81-299
  G. Wills, 39:May81-338
Dukes, P., ed and trans. Russia under
  Catherine the Great.* (Vol 1)
  R.E.F. Smith, 575(SEER):Oct81-637
Dukore, B.F. Money and Politics in Ibsen,
  Shaw, and Brecht.*
  J. Coakley, 130:Fall81-281
  C.G. Rand, 572:Vol 1-251
Dukore, B.F. Harold Pinter.
  N. de Jongh, 617(TLS):3Dec82-1347
Dukore, B.F. - see Shaw, G.B.
Dulière, C. "Lupa Romana."
  A. Hus, 555:Vol154fasc2-391
Dull, J.L. - see Hsu, C-Y.
Dulong, G. and G. Bergeron. Le Parler
  populaire du Québec et de ses régions
  voisines.
  N. Beauchemin, 320(CJL):Fall81-230
Dumas, A. Nommer Dieu.
  E. Blondel, 542:Oct-Dec81-497
Dumitriu, A. History of Logic.* (Vols
  1-4)
  P.V. Spade, 449:May81-239
Dumitriu, P. Au Dieu inconnu.
  J. Kirkup, 617(TLS):15Jan82-62
Dummett, M. Frege: Philosophy of Langu-
  age. What is a Theory of Meaning.
  J. Bouveresse, 98:Aug-Sep80-881
Dummett, M. The Interpretation of Frege's
  Philosophy. Frege: Philosophy of Lan-
  guage. (2nd ed)
  G. Harman, 617(TLS):16Apr82-433
Dummett, M. Truth and Other Enigmas.*
  J. Bouveresse, 98:Aug-Sep80-881
  J.E. Llewelyn, 262:Oct81-374
  M. Schirn, 84:Dec81-419
  C. Wright, 479(PhQ):Jan81-47
Dumont, L. From Mandeville to Marx.*
  P.D. Shaw, 488:Jun80-232
Dumoulin, H. Zen Enlightenment.
  J.M. Kitagawa, 407(MN):Spring81-107
Dunbabin, K.M.D. The Mosaics of Roman
  North Africa.*
  S.D. Campbell, 487:Summer81-188
  R.J.A. Wilson, 313:Vol71-173
Dunbar, A.P. Against the Grain.
  W. Goodman, 441:17Jan82-14
Dunbar, P. William Blake's Illustrations
  to the Poetry of Milton.*
  M. Pointon, 90:May81-313
  P. Quennell, 39:Aug81-136
Dunbar, W. The Poems of William Dunbar.
  (J. Kinsley, ed)
  P. Bawcutt, 382(MAE):1981/1-88
  A. Hudson, 541(RES):Nov81-440
  R.J. Lyall, 571(ScLJ):Winter81-105
  P. Morère, 189(EA):Jan-Mar81-89
Duncan, A. Tiffany Windows.
  I. Anscombe, 135:Jan81-84
  L. Ormond, 39:May81-340
Duncan, D. Ben Jonson and the Lucianic
  Tradition.*
  I. Donaldson, 541(RES):Aug81-323
  G.R. Hibbard, 178:Fall81-357
  D. Riggs, 405(MP):Nov81-192
Duncan, W.R. The Queen's Messenger.
  M. Laski, 362:29Jul82-27

Dundes, A. Interpreting Folklore.*
  205(FMLS):Apr81-198
Dundes, A., ed. Varia folklorica.
  T.A. Green, 650(WF):Jul81-267
  U. Kutter, 196:Band21Heft3/4-307
Dunham, V. and M. Hayward - see Voznesen-
  sky, A.
Dunkley, J. - see de Crébillon, C.P.J.
Dunleavy, P. The Politics of Mass Housing
  in Britain, 1945-1975.
  J.N. Tarn, 617(TLS):15Oct82-1143
Dunlop, I. The Cathedrals' Crusade.
  J. Sumption, 617(TLS):26Mar82-336
Dunmore, T. The Stalinist Command Economy.
  H. Hunter, 550(RusR):Oct81-453
  M. McCauley, 575(SEER):Oct81-621
Dunn, A. and P. Porter. Sock Bunnies.
  P. Bach, 614:Fall81-21
Dunn, C.W. and E.T. Byrnes, eds. Middle
  English Literature.
  J. Kleinstück, 38:Band99Heft1/2-225
Dunn, D. St. Kilda's Parliament.*
  D. Davis, 362:7Jan82-22
  H. Lomas, 364:Dec81/Jan82-97
Dunn, J. Political Obligation in its His-
  torical Context.*
  C.R.B., 185:Jan82-386
  K. Ingham, 437:Summer81-384
Dunn, J.A. A Practical Dictionary of the
  Coast Tsimshian Language.
  C.M. Eastman, 350:Sep82-733
Dunn, L.A. Controlling the Bomb.
  G.T. Seaborg, 441:25Apr82-10
  C.M. Woodhouse, 617(TLS):24Sep82-1030
Dunn, R.E. Resistance in the Desert.
  P. Bonte, 69:Vol50No1-99
Dunne, D. The Winners.
  N. Johnson, 441:30May82-9
Dunne, J.G. Dutch Shea, Jr.
  R.M. Adams, 453(NYRB):10Jun82-31
  A. Mars-Jones, 617(TLS):17Sep82-992
  G. Stade, 441:28Mar82-1
  442(NY):24May82-134
Dunne, P. Take Two.
  A. Sarris, 18:Oct80-82
Dunnett, D. King Hereafter.
  J. Zorn, 441:25Jul82-11
Dunning, S.N. The Tongues of Men.
  R.F. Brown, 258:Mar81-99
Dupâquier, J. La Population française aux
  XVIIe et XVIIIe siècles.
  T.H. Goetz, 207(FR):Mar81-629
Du Perron, E. Le Pays d'Origine.
  L. Kovacs, 450(NRF):Jan81-161
Duplat, A. - see de la Vigne, A.
Dupon, J-F. Contraintes Insulaires et
  Fait Colonial aux Mascareignes et aux
  Seychelles.
  G. Shepherd, 69:Vol50No2-221
Dupont-Roc, R. and J. Lallot - see Aris-
  totle
Dupré, G. Le Grand Coucher.
  A. Clerval, 450(NRF):Dec81-114
  D. Gascoyne, 617(TLS):7May82-502
Dupré, L. A Dubious Heritage.
  B.M.B., 543:Jun81-787
Dupriez, B. L'Étude des styles.
  J-J. Thomas, 207(FR):May81-912
Dupuy, T.N. Elusive Victory.*
  B. Morris, 390:Oct81-60

Durán, G.B.   The Archetypes of Carlos
Fuentes.
  M. Coddou, 238:Dec81-647
  L.B. Hall, 584(SWR):Winter81-101
Durán, M.   Quevedo.*
  G. Díaz-Migoyo, 240(HR):Autumn81-503
Durán, M. - see Marqués de Santillana
Durán, M. and R. González Echevarría.
Calderón y la crítica.
  D.H. Darst, 552(REH):May81-308
Durán, R.   Catálogo de los dibujos de los
siglos XVI y XVII en la colección del
Museo de la Casa de la Moneda.
  M. Mena, 48:Jul-Sep81-375
Durand, R., ed.   Le Discours de la vio-
lence dans la culture américaine.
  R.A. Day, 189(EA):Jul-Sep81-362
Durant, A.   Ezra Pound.*
  P. Smith, 150(DR):Summer81-356
Duranton, H., ed.   Correspondance littér-
aire du Président Bouhier.
  P. Rétat, 535(RHL):Nov-Dec81-990
Duranty, L.E.   Le Malheur d'Henriette Gér-
ard.
  P-J. Founau, 450(NRF):Jul-Aug81-187
Duras, M.   Agatha.
  B.L. Knapp, 207(FR):Apr82-702
Duras, M.   L'Homme assis dans le couloir.
  B.L. Knapp, 207(FR):Apr81-762
Duras, M.   Outside.
  P. Dulac, 450(NRF):May81-118
Durbach, E., ed.   Ibsen and the Theatre.*
[shown in prev under Durback, E.]
  J. Lyons, 214:Vol 10No37-120
  O. Reinert, 130:Fall81-272
Durbin, P.T., ed.   A Guide to the Culture
of Science, Technology, and Medicine.
  S.P., 185:Jul82-794
Durchslag, A. and J. Litman-Demeestère -
see Lasker-Schüler, E.
Dürer, A.   L'Oeuvre graphique.
  L. Finas, 450(NRF):May81-153
Lady Durham.   Letters and Diaries of Lady
Durham.*   (P. Godsell, ed)
  V. Strong-Boag, 298:Fall-Winter81-217
Durham, M.   Flambard's Confession.
  P-L. Adams, 61:Oct82-105
  M. Simpson, 441:19Dec82-13
Durling, R.M. - see Petrarch
Dürmüller, U. and H. Utz.   Altenglisch.*
  F. Wenisch, 38:Band99Heft1/2-162
Durova, N.   Zapiski kavaperist-devicy.
  J.J. Gebhard, 574(SEEJ):Spring81-96
Dürr, V. and G. von Molnár, eds.   Versuche
zu Goethe.*
  P. Boerner, 173(ECS):Spring81-329
Durrell, G.   The Mockery Bird.
  442(NY):19Apr82-176
Durrell, L.   Collected Poems, 1931-1974.*
  (J.A. Brigham, ed)
  V. Young, 249(HudR):Spring81-144
Durrell, L.   Constance.
  V. Cunningham, 617(TLS):15Oct82-1122
  P. Kemp, 362:14Oct82-31
  442(NY):29Nov82-174
Durrell, L.   Livia: Or Buried Alive.*
  (French title: Livia ou Enterrée vive.)
  C. Jordis, 450(NRF):May81-144
Dürrenmatt, F.   Stoffe.   (Vols 1-3)
  M. Butler, 617(TLS):29Oct82-1202
Durso, J.   Madison Square Garden.
  639(VQR):Winter81-30

Dürst, R.   Heinrich von Kleist.*   (2nd ed)
  M.M. Tatar, 406:Winter81-461
Durzak, M.   Das expressionistische Drama.*
  K. Kändler, 654(WB):1/1981-168
  F.R. Love, 406:Fall81-361
Düsberg, K.J.   Zur Messung von Raum und
Zeit.
  A. Kamlah, 679:Band12Heft1-182
Dusinberre, W.   Henry Adams.*
  E.N. Harbert, 432(NEQ):Jun81-267
  R.F. Sommer, 577(SHR):Fall81-366
  R.E. Spiller, 27(AL):Mar81-131
Düsing, K.   Das Problem der Subjektivität
in Hegels Logik.*
  K. Hartmann, 53(AGP):Band63Heft2-206
Dussault, L.   Moman, [précédé de] Itiné-
aire pour une moman.
  C.F. Coates, 207(FR):Apr82-703
Duteil, F.P. - see under Pouradier Duteil,
F.
Duthie, E.L.   The Themes of Elizabeth
Gaskell.*
  I. Ferris, 445(NCF):Jun81-110
Dutka, J.   Music in the English Mystery
Plays.
  B. Boyd, 130:Spring81-80
  R. Rastall, 627(UTQ):Summer81-105
Dutra, F.A.   A Guide to the History of
Brazil, 1500-1822.
  M.H. Sable, 263(RIB):Vol31No3-407
Dutton, H.I. and J.E. King.   Ten Per Cent
and No Surrender.*
  P.S. Bagwell, 324:Apr82-293
Dutu, A.   La culture roumaine dans la
civilisation européenne moderne.
  J. Amsler, 549(RLC):Jan-Mar81-129
Duţu, A.   Modele, imagini, privelisti.
  V. Nemoianu, 678(YCGL):No29-53
Duval, E-F.   Anthologie thématique du thé-
âtre Québécois au XIXe siècle.
  D.M. Hayne, 102(CanL):Summer80-118
Duval, F.Y. and I.B. Rigby.   Early Ameri-
can Gravestone Art in Photographs.
  G.L. Pocius, 292(JAF):Jul-Sep81-381
Duval, P.   La pensée alchimique et le
Conte du Graal.
  E.R. Sienaert, 356(LR):Feb-May81-155
Duval, P-M.   Les Dieux de la Gaule.
  B. Ó Cuív, 112:Vol 14-171
Düwell, H.   Fremdsprachenunterricht im
Schülerurteil.
  F.J. Hausmann, 257(IRAL):Aug81-259
  M. Spoelders, 277(ITL):No47-77
Dvořák, K.   Soupis staročeských exempel.
  H-J. Uther, 196:Band22Heft3/4-327
Dworkin, A.   Pornography.*
  J.G. Weightman, 617(TLS):1Jan82-5
Dwyer, J.   The Portraits and Landscapes of
Alfred J. Wiggin, 1823-1883.
  M.B. Péladeau, 658:Winter81-349
Dybek, S.   Brass Knuckles.*
  S.P. Estess, 577(SHR):Winter81-91
  S.M. Gilbert, 491:Oct81-35
Dyck, J.   Athen und Jerusalem.
  F.M. Eybl, 224(GRM):Band31Heft1-111
  R. von Tiedemann, 52:Band15Heft1-85
Dye, J.M.   Ways to Shiva.
  U. Roberts, 60:Nov-Dec81-157
Dyer, C.   Lords and Peasants in a Changing
Society.*
  R.B. Patterson, 589:Oct81-926
Dyer, G.   Advertising as Communication.
  G. Ewart, 617(TLS):10Dec82-1352

Dyke, C. Philosophy of Economics.
  J.H.A., 185:Apr82-579
Dyserinck, H. Komparatistik.*
  H.S. Daemmrich, 222(GR):Spring81-80
Dyson, F. Disturbing the Universe.*
  M. Green, 128(CE):Oct81-569
  T.C. Holyoke, 42(AR):Winter81-125
Dyson, K.K. A Various Universe.*
  P.S. Guptara, 541(RES):Aug81-335

Eager, A.R. A Guide to Irish Bibliographi-
  cal Material. (2nd ed)
  R.G. Yeed, 305(JIL):May81-130
Eagleton, M. and D. Pierce. Attitudes to
  Class in the English Novel.*
  P. Lewis, 565:Vol122No3-55
Eagleton, T. The Rape of "Clarissa."
  M. Butler, 617(TLS):12Nov82-1241
Earle, J. A Trial of Strength.*
  V. Young, 249(HudR):Spring81-143
Earle, P. The Sack of Panama.*
  P-L. Adams, 61:Apr82-108
Earle, W. Mystical Reason.
  H.M. Curtler, 396(ModA):Summer81-316
Earley, T. Rebel's Progress.
  L. Sail, 565:Vol122No1-66
Easlea, B. Witch Hunting, Magic and the
  New Philosophy.
  G.S. Rousseau, 566:Spring82-127
Easson, A. Elizabeth Gaskell.*
  I. Ferris, 445(NCF):Jun81-110
  T.J. Winnifrith, 677(YES):Vol 11-318
Eastlake, W. Go in Beauty.
  W. Gard, 584(SWR):Winter81-vii
Easton, B. Pragmatism and Progress.
  C.N.S., 185:Jul82-802
Eaton, C.E. Colophon of the Rover.*
  M.L. Hester, 577(SHR):Fall81-374
  P.B. Newman, 601:Fall81-75
Eaton, R.M. Sufis of Bijapur, 1300-1700.*
  G. Böwering, 318(JAOS):Jan/Mar80-39
Eatwell, J. Whatever Happened to Britain?
  H. Land, 617(TLS):27Aug82-930
Ebbatson, R. Lawrence and the Nature Tra-
  dition.*
  W.J. Keith, 150(DR):Summer81-386
  J. Meyers, 594:Winter81-449
Ebel, C. Transalpine Gaul.
  A. Dirkzwager, 394:Vol134fasc3/4-455
Ebeling, H. Selbsterhaltung und Selbst-
  bewusstsein. Der Tod in der Moderne.
  H-L. Ollig, 342:Band72Heft4-495
Ebeling, K. Rāgamālā Painting.
  H. Powers, 318(JAOS):Oct/Dec80-473
Ebeling, W. The Fruited Plain.
  G.C. Fite, 658:Winter81-340
Eberhart, M. Next of Kin.
  N. Callendar, 441:24Oct82-28
Eberhart, R. Of Poetry and Poets.*
  B. Duffey, 27(AL):May81-324
Eberhart, R. Ways of Light.*
  J.F. Cotter, 249(HudR):Summer81-281
  R. Hornsey, 461:Fall-Winter81/82-101
  639(VQR):Spring81-65
Ebersole, A.V., ed. Perspectivas de la
  novela.
  E. Rodgers, 86(BHS):Jan81-85
Ebersole, F.B. Meaning and Saying.* Lan-
  guage and Perception.*
  D. Evans, 393(Mind):Jul81-459

Ebied, R.Y. and M.J.L. Young, eds and
  trans. Some Arabic Legal Documents of
  the Ottoman Period.
  A-K. Rafeq, 318(JAOS):Jan/Mar80-36
Ebner, P. Der Erfolgreiche.
  J. Neves, 617(TLS):9Jul82-750
von Ebner-Eschenbach, M. Kritische Texte
  und Deutungen.* (Vol 1) (B. Bittrich,
  ed)
  H. Böschenstein, 133:Band14Heft4-375
von Ebner-Eschenbach, M. Kritische Texte
  und Deutungen. (Vol 2) (K. Binneberg,
  ed)
  H. Böschenstein, 133:Band14Heft4-375
  F. Martini, 680(ZDP):Band100Heft2-307
Ebrey, P.B., ed. Chinese Civilization
  and Society.
  J. Spence, 453(NYRB):1Apr82-45
Eça de Queiroz. A Tragédia da Rua das
  Flores. (J. Medina and A. Campos Matos,
  eds)
  A. Freeland, 86(BHS):Apr81-153
Eccles, R. - see Shakespeare, W.
Echeruo, M.J.C. Joyce Cary and the Dimen-
  sions of Order.
  F. McCombie, 447(N&Q):Jun80-261
  P. Murphy, 541(RES):Feb81-106
  B.J. Murray, 395(MFS):Summer80-307
Echlin, E. An Alternative Ending to Rich-
  ardson's "Clarissa." (D. Daphinoff, ed)
  M. Butler, 617(TLS):12Nov82-1241
Eck, W. Die staatliche Organisation
  Italiens in der hohen Kaiserzeit.
  N. Purcell, 123:Vol31No1-137
Eckert, H. Lexical Field Analysis and
  Interpersonal Terms in German.
  W. Kühlwein, 277(ITL):No48-94
Eckhardt, A. Dictionnaire hongrois-
  français. (2nd ed)
  G. Radó, 75:1/1980-50
Eckstein, A. China's Economic Revolution.
  S.M. Jones, 293(JASt):May81-539
Eckstein, F., ed. Antike Plastik. (Pt 18)
  M. Robertson, 90:Oct81-624
"Eclair: A Multi-Media Course in French,
  Year 1."
  P. Siegel, 207(FR):Oct80-213
Eco, U. The Role of the Reader.*
  E. Block, Jr., 659(ConL):Winter82-97
  L. Doležel, 494:Summer80-181
  W.O. Hendricks, 567:Vol35No3/4-361
  E.R. Kintgen, 599:Fall81-479
  T. de Lauretis, 125:Fall80-93
  J.J. White, 402(MLR):Jan81-142
  205(FMLS):Jul81-288
École de Tartu. Travaux sur les systèmes
  de signes.
  H. Cronel, 450(NRF):Mar81-143
"Economic Report of the President Transmit-
  ted to the Congress, February 1982."
  E. Rothschild, 453(NYRB):15Apr82-19
Economou, G. - see Blackburn, P.
Eddy, B.D. Abbeys, Ghosts, and Castles.
  W.D. Keel, 399(MLJ):Spring81-116
Eddy, D.D. Samuel Johnson: Book Reviewer
  in the "Literary Magazine: or, Universal
  Review," 1756-1758.*
  T.M. Curley, 405(MP):Nov81-203
Edel, A. Science, Ideology, and Value.
  (Vol 2)
  D.G.T., 185:Jan82-402

99

Edel, L. Bloomsbury.*
 E.C. Bufkin, 219(GaR):Spring81-190
 J.B. Bullen, 541(RES):Nov81-478
 D.J. Cahill, 395(MFS):Summer80-287
 295(JML):Vol8No3/4-346
Edel, L. Stuff of Sleep and Dreams.
 P-L. Adams, 61:Apr82-108
 D. Trotter, 617(TLS):19Nov82-1267
 442(NY):14Jun82-134
Edel, L. - see James, H.
Edel, L. - see Wilson, E.
Edel, L. and others. Telling Lives.* (M.
 Pachter, ed)
 D.J. Cahill, 395(MFS):Summer80-287
Edelberg, C. Robert Creeley's Poetry.
 C. Lambert, 472:Fall/Winter81-255
Edelberg, L. and S. Jones. Nuristan.
 K.L. Michaelson, 293(JASt):Aug81-818
Edelen, G. - see Hooker, R.
Edelhertz, H. and C. Rogovin, eds. A
 National Strategy for Containing White-
 Collar Crime.
 C.S., 185:Apr82-602
Edelman, J.C. Sämtliche Schriften in
 Einzelausgaben. (Vol 12) (W. Grossmann,
 ed)
 T.P. Saine, 680(ZDP):Band100Heft2-292
Edelman, R. Gentry Politics on the Eve of
 the Russian Revolution.
 D.C.B. Lieven, 575(SEER):Oct81-614
 G. Yaney, 550(RusR):Apr81-194
Eden, E. The Semi-Attached Couple and the
 Semi-Detached House.
 P. Rose, 441:25Apr82-9
Eder, M. Geschichte der japanischen
 Religion.
 A. Schwade, 407(MN):Spring81-105
The Duke of Edinburgh. A Question of Bal-
 ance.
 D.R. Harris, 324:Oct82-751
Edinger, E.F. Melville's "Moby-Dick."*
 E.A. Dryden, 50(ArQ):Winter81-371
Edler, E. Die Anfänge des sozialen Romans
 und der sozialen Novelle in Deutschland.
 G. Müller, 684(ZDA):Band109Heft2-77
Edmonson, M.S. The Ancient Future of the
 Itza.
 G. Brotherston, 617(TLS):3Dec82-1341
Edo, P. Il rimedio amoroso. (F. De
 Nicola, ed)
 M. Marti, 228(GSLI):Vol 157fasc497-143
Edsman, B.M. Lawyers in Gold Coast
 Politics, c. 1900-1945.
 R. Rathbone, 69:Vol150No2-239
Edwards, A. Sonya.*
 L. Kelly, 617(TLS):26Feb82-222
 639(VQR):Autumn81-122
Edwards, A.D. Language in Culture and
 Class.
 D. Eder, 355(LSoc):Aug81-283
Edwards, A.S.G., ed. Skelton: The Criti-
 cal Heritage.
 V. Adams, 617(TLS):1Jan82-14
Edwards, B. Drawing on the Right Side of
 the Brain.
 N.M. Bailey, 289:Apr81-114
Edwards, C.H. Hallie Farmer.
 L. Griffith, 9(AlaR):Apr81-127
Edwards, D.L. Christian England.
 B.M. Bolton, 617(TLS):5Feb82-146
Edwards, G. Lorca.*
 J. Alberich, 402(MLR):Jul81-729
 H. Hobson, 157:2ndQtr81-51

Edwards, G. The Second Century of the
 English Parliament.
 B. Lyon, 589:Jan81-125
Edwards, G.B. The Book of Ebenezer Le
 Page.*
 R. Buffington, 569(SR):Summer81-lxxiv
 D. Kubal, 249(HudR):Autumn81-456
 E. Milton, 676(YR):Winter82-254
 639(VQR):Summer81-100
Edwards, J.D. The Afro-American Trickster
 Tale.
 J.W. Roberts, 292(JAF):Jul-Sep81-392
Edwards, M., ed. Prospice 10.
 M. Smith, 607:Mar81-35
Edwards, M., ed. Raymond Queneau.
 C. Shorley, 208(FS):Jan81-97
Edwards, O.D. - see under Dudley Edwards,
 O.
Edwards, P. Threshold of a Nation.*
 B. Benstock, 301(JEGP):Jul81-447
 R. Fréchet, 189(EA):Oct-Dec81-460
Edwards, P., I-S. Ewbank and G.K. Hunter,
 eds. Shakespeare's Styles.*
 R. Jacobs, 175:Summer81-177
Edwards, P.D. Anthony Trollope.*
 J. Carlisle, 639(VQR):Winter81-176
 A. Easson, 366:Autumn81-263
 V. Shaw, 677(YES):Vol 11-322
Edwards, R. The Montecassino Passion and
 the Poetics of Medieval Drama.
 S.J. Kahrl, 589:Jan81-126
Edwards, R. and P. Steptoe. A Matter of
 Life.
 K.G. Millar, 529(QQ):Autumn81-590
Edwards, R.B. Kadmos the Phoenician.
 R.F. Willetts, 123:Vol31No2-236
Edwards, R.B. Pleasures and Pains.
 J. Gosling, 393(Mind):Oct81-619
 J.M. Howarth, 518:Oct81-250
 D. Mitchell, 63:Sep81-354
 S.C. Patten, 154:Dec81-799
 H.R. West, 185:Jan81-314
Edwards, R.D. - see under Dudley Edwards,
 R.
Edwards, S.A. French Structures in Review.
 (3rd ed)
 P.J. Edwards, 399(MLJ):Summer81-216
Eekman, T. Thirty Years of Yugoslav Lit-
 erature (1945-1975).
 V.D. Mihailovich, 577(SHR):Spring81-
 187
Eells, G. and S. Musgrove. Mae West.
 J. Haskins, 441:13Jun82-16
 442(NY):12Apr82-156
Eengels, J. Vivaldi in Early Fall.
 W. Scammell, 617(TLS):28May82-592
Effe, B. Dichtung und Lehre.
 M. von Albrecht, 52:Band15Heft1-67
Egan, D.R. and M.A. Leo Tolstoy.*
 L.S. Herrmann, 365:Spring-Summer82-117
 M.J.D. Holman, 575(SEER):Jan81-84
 205(FMLS):Oct80-374
Egan, J. The Inward Teacher.
 J.G. Rechtien, 599:Fall81-476
Egejuru, P.A. Towards African Literary
 Independence.
 D.F. Dorsey, 95(CLAJ):Dec80-230
Egerton, J. British Sporting and Animal
 Paintings 1665-1867 [together with]
 Egerton, J. and D. Snelgrove. British
 Sporting and Animal Drawings 1500-1850.*
 S. Gore, 39:Oct81-272

100

Eggleston, W. Literary Friends.
 A. Bailey, 105:Spring/Summer81-95
 W.J. Keith, 627(UTQ):Summer81-157
Ehle, J. The Winter People.
 I. Gold, 441:9May82-13
Ehrard, J., ed. Études sur le XVIIIe
 siècle.
 M. Gilot, 535(RHL):Mar-Apr81-301
Ehre, M. - see Gogol, N.
Ehrenburg, I. and V. Grossman, eds. Chor-
 naya Kniga (The Black Book).
 W. Goodman, 441:14Mar82-16
 S.L. Shneiderman, 390:Dec81-49
Ehrenfeld, D. The Arrogance of Humanism.*
 D.D. Todd, 154:Sep81-620
Ehrenpreis, I. Acts of Implication.*
 H.D. Weinbrot, 566:Autumn81-38
Ehret, C. The Historical Reconstruction
 of Southern Cushitic Phonology and Vocab-
 ulary.
 D. Biber, 350:Dec82-949
Ehrhardt, H. Der Stabreim in altnordis-
 chen Rechtstexten.
 H. Fix, 680(ZDP):Band100Heft1-119
Ehrhart, W.D. Matters of the Heart.
 639(VQR):Autumn81-130
Ehrlich, E. and others - see "Oxford
 American Dictionary"
Ehrlich, G. To Touch the Water.
 A.G. Hart, 649(WAL):Winter81-337
Ehrlich, M. Shaitan.
 P. Andrews, 441:28Feb82-14
Ehrlich, R. Norman Mailer.
 P. Bufithis, 395(MFS):Winter80/81-680
Ehrlichman, J. Witness to Power.
 N. von Hoffman, 453(NYRB):18Mar82-18
 R. Sherrill, 441:24Jan82-1
 442(NY):1Mar82-128
Ehrmann, G. Georg von Ehingen, Reisen
 nach der Ritterschaft.
 V. Honemann, 684(ZDA):Band110Heft1-44
Eich, G. Träume.
 L. Volke, 654(WB):7/1981-134
Eicher, J.B. Nigerian Handicrafted Tex-
 tiles.
 J. Picton, 69:Vol50No1-107
Eickelpasch, R. Mythos und Sozialstruktur.
 N.O., 52:Band15Heft1-112
Eigeldinger, M., ed. Études sur les
 "Poésies" de Rimbaud.*
 E.R. Peschel, 207(FR):Oct81-142
Eigeldinger, M. - see Hugo, V.
"The Eighteenth Century: A Current Bibliog-
 raphy."* (Vol 2) (R.R. Allen, ed)
 P-G. Boucé, 189(EA):Jul-Sep81-341
Eigner, E.M. The Metaphysical Novel in
 England and America.
 R. Belflower, 541(RES):Aug81-342
 E.J. Sundquist, 580(SCR):Fall80-104
 R.E. Wiehe, 179(ES):Dec81-572
Eikhenbaum, B. Tolstoi in the Sixties.
 Tolstoi in the Seventies.
 H. McLean, 441:18Apr82-14
"Eilhart von Oberge's 'Tristrant.'"* (J.W.
 Thomas, trans)
 R.H. Firestone, 406:Winter81-446
 P.S. Noble, 208(FS):Jan81-64
Eimer, H. Bodhipathapradīpa.
 P. Harrison, 259(IIJ):Oct81-314
Einarsson, B., ed. Hallfređar Saga.*
 H. Beck, 684(ZDA):Band110Heft1-6
Einarsson, J. Talad och skriven Svenska.
 C.B. Paulston, 355(LSoc):Dec81-459

Einaudi, L. Interventi e Ralazioni parla-
 mentari. (Vols 1 and 2) (S.M. Dorigo,
 ed)
 J. Rosselli, 617(TLS):17Dec82-1397
von Einem, H. Deutsche Malerei des
 Klassizismus und der Romantik, 1760
 bis 1840.*
 T. Pelzel, 54:Dec81-688
Einhorn, E. Old French.
 W.D. Paden, Jr., 545(RPh):Feb81-335
Einhorn, L.J., P.H. Bradley and J.E. Baird,
 Jr. Effective Employment Interviewing.
 P.E. King, 583:Summer82-459
Eis, G. Kleine Schriften zur altdeutschen
 weltlichen Dichtung.
 F.G. Gentry, 406:Fall81-343
Eisenberg, D. Castilian Romances of
 Chivalry in the Sixteenth Century.
 R.E. Barbera, 238:Dec81-634
 F. Pierce, 86(BHS):Jan81-80
 H.L. Sharrer, 304(JHP):Winter82-163
Eisenberg, D. - see Lorca, F.G.
Eisenberg, P. Oberflächenstruktur und
 logische Struktur.
 W. Motsch, 682(ZPSK):Band33Heft5-593
Eisenhower, J.S.D. Allies.
 N. Johnston, 441:24Oct82-18
Eisenstein, E.L. The Printing Press as an
 Agent of Change.*
 F.X. Blouin, Jr., 14:Spring81-157
 O. Gingerich, 517(PBSA):Apr-Jun81-228
 D.R. Kelley, 125:Winter81-213
 F.C. Robinson, 569(SR):Summer81-423
 D. Shaw, 354:Sep81-261
Eisler, C. The Master of the Unicorn.*
 H. Zerner, 54:Jun81-332
Eisner, E.W. The Educational Imagination.
 M.C. Beardsley, 289:Jan81-115
 E.R. House and R.S. Mayer, 289:Jan81-
 117
 E. Steiner, 289:Jan81-107
Eisner, S. - see Nicholas of Lynn
Eitel, W. Balzac in Deutschland.
 K. Wingård, 597(SN):Vol53No2-411
Eiximenis, F. Lo libre de les dones. (F.
 Naccarato, ed; rev by C. Wittlin)
 E.J. Neugaard, 304(JHP):Winter82-161
Ejō - see Dōgen
Ekelöf, G. Guide to the Underworld. (R.
 Lesser, trans)
 J. Lutz, 563(SS):Spring81-241
Ekert-Rotholz, A. Rice in Silver Bowls.
 442(NY):16Aug82-89
Ekman, B. The End of a Legend.*
 M.F., 189(EA):Apr-Jun81-240
Elam, K. The Semiotics of Theatre and
 Drama.*
 J. Alter, 494:Spring81-264
 J.G. Barry, 290(JAAC):Summer82-439
Elam, Y. The Social and Sexual Roles of
 Hima Women.
 E.E. Hopkins, 69:Vol50No4-426
Elcock, H. and M. Wheaton. Local Govern-
 ment.
 I. McLean, 617(TLS):15Oct82-1143
Elder, A.A. The "Hindered Hand."*
 H. Jarrett, 27(AL):Mar81-142
Elert, C-C., ed. Internordisk språkför-
 ståelse.
 J.T. Jensen, 350:Jun82-486

101

Elert, K. Portraits of Women in Selected
Novels by Virginia Woolf and E.M. For-
ster.
A.L. McLaughlin, 395(MFS):Summer80-282
Eley, G. Reshaping the German Right.
639(VQR):Winter81-7
Elgin, S.H. The Gentle Art of Verbal Self
Defense.
H.L. Goodall, Jr., 583:Spring82-348
A.D. Grimshaw, 350:Sep82-743
Eliach, Y. Hasidic Tales of the Holocaust.
P-L. Adams, 61:Nov82-171
Eliade, M. Autobiography.* (Vol 1)
V. Nemoianu, 617(TLS):2Apr82-375
Eliade, M. A History of Religious Ideas.
(Vol 1)
E. Webb, 648(WCR):Jun80-65
Eliade, M. The Old Man and the Bureau-
crats.
W. Buchanan, 573(SSF):Spring81-196
W.A. Strauss, 651(WHR):Autumn81-276
Elias, A.C. Swift at Moor Park.
M. Hodgart, 617(TLS):15Oct82-1135
Elias, N. Power and Civility.
G. Barraclough, 453(NYRB):21Oct82-36
Elias, N. State Formation and Civiliza-
tion.
R.M. Adams, 617(TLS):10Sep82-983
P.N. Furbank, 362:5Aug82-21
Eliav-Feldon, M. Realistic Utopias.
P. Burke, 617(TLS):26Nov82-1319
Elie, R. Oeuvres.
A.B. Chartier, 207(FR):Oct81-154
Eliot, G. The George Eliot Letters.*
(Vols 8 and 9) (G.S. Haight, ed)
F. Bolton, 189(EA):Jan-Mar81-99
Eliot, G. George Eliot's "Middlemarch"
Notebooks.* (J.C. Pratt and V.A. Neu-
feldt, eds)
J. Wiesenfarth, 445(NCF):Jun81-113
G.J. Worth, 405(MP):Nov81-213
Eliot, G. The Mill on the Floss.* (G.S.
Haight, ed)
S. Gill, 541(RES):Nov81-468
P. Shillingsburg, 301(JEGP):Oct81-590
G.J. Worth, 405(MP):Nov81-213
Eliot, G. Some George Eliot Notebooks.
(Vol 3) (W. Baker, ed)
354:Jun81-178
"George Eliot." [exhibition catalog]
B. Hardy, 175:Spring81-87
Eliot, T.S. Old Possum's Book of Practi-
cal Cats. (Illustrated by E. Gorey)
P-L. Adams, 61:Oct82-105
Elkhadem, S. The York Companion to Themes
and Motifs of World Literature.
A. Bloch, 268(IFR):Winter82-73
Elkin, J.L. Jews of the Latin American
Republics.
B.D. Ansel, 263(RIB):Vol31No1-85
G. Böhm, 37:Sep81-27
Elkin, S. Stanley Elkin's Greatest Hits.
639(VQR):Summer81-103
Elkin, S. George Mills.
L. Epstein, 441:31Oct82-11
J. Rubins, 453(NYRB):16Dec82-46
F. Taliaferro, 231:Nov82-74
Elkin, S., with S. Ravenel, eds. The Best
American Short Stories 1980.
B. Allen, 434:Spring82-478
J. Mcnew, 639(VQR):Autumn81-744
639(VQR):Spring81-59

Elkind, D. The Hurried Child.
C. May, 441:7Mar82-22
Elkins, D.J. and R. Simeon. Small Worlds.
R. Gibbins, 529(QQ):Winter81-797
Ellegård, A. The Syntactic Structure of
English Texts.*
N. Davis, 541(RES):May81-198
S. Greenbaum, 597(SN):Vol53No2-389
Elleinstein, J. Une certaine idée du
communisme.
V. Descombes, 98:Jan80-5
Ellen, R.F. Nuaulu Settlement and Ecology.
P.M. Taylor, 293(JASt):Feb81-420
Ellenberger, B. The Latin Element in the
Vocabulary of the Earlier Makars Henry-
son and Dunbar.*
M. Görlach, 72:Band217Heft2-410
Elliot, A. Talking Back.
D. Davis, 362:16Dec82-23
Elliot, A. - see Vergil
Elliott, D., ed. Rodchenko.
M.B. Betz, 127:Fall/Winter80-417
Elliott, E., ed. Puritan Influences in
American Literature.*
L. Buell, 432(NEQ):Mar81-136
R.B. Davis, 579(SAQ):Winter81-108
E. Emerson, 301(JEGP):Jul81-459
D. Weber, 445(NCF):Jun81-83
Elliott, E. Revolutionary Writers.
C.N. Davidson, 165(EAL):Fall82-182
Elliott, J. The Country of Her Dreams.
S. Altinel, 617(TLS):19Mar82-306
J. Astor, 362:18Mar82-24
Elliott, J. Secret Places.*
G. Ewart, 364:Jul81-88
442(NY):8Feb82-127
Elliott, J.R., Jr. and G.A. Runnalls, eds
and trans. The Baptism and Temptation
of Christ.*
A.C. Cawley, 541(RES):Feb81-75
A. Foulet, 545(RPh):Nov80-273
C. Gauvin, 189(EA):Apr-Jun81-213
A. Hindley, 402(MLR):Jan81-182
Elliott, S.L. Water Under the Bridge.
C. Hanna, 581:Sep80-360
Ellis, A.T. The Birds of the Air.*
W. Boyd, 364:Apr/May81-129
Ellis, A.T. The 27th Kingdom.
K.C. O'Brien, 362:22Jul82-24
L. Taylor, 617(TLS):2Jul82-710
Ellis, B. Rational Belief Systems.*
J. Cargile, 482(PhR):Jul81-454
B. Carr, 393(Mind):Jul81-457
R. Kennedy, 316:Sep81-668
Ellis, G. Napoleon's Continental Blockade.
J. Rogister, 617(TLS):2Apr82-394
Ellis, J.J. After the Revolution.*
Q. Anderson, 165(EAL):Spring82-87
Ellis, M.D. Agriculture and the State in
Ancient Mesopotamia.
R.F.G. Sweet, 318(JAOS):Jan/Mar80-77
Ellis, P.B. H. Rider Haggard.*
B.J. Murray, 395(MFS):Summer80-308
Ellis, P.B. The Liberty Tree.
D. Nokes, 617(TLS):26Mar82-339
Ellis, R. Dolphins and Porpoises.
S.D. Smith, 441:5Dec82-64
Ellis, S.H. New Mexico Colcha Embroidery.
P. Bach, 614:Winter82-18
Ellison, H. Shatterday.
C. Greenland, 617(TLS):9Jul82-739
Ellmann, R. James Joyce. (new ed)
H. Kenner, 617(TLS):17Dec82-1383

Ellmann, R. - see Joyce, J.
Ellsworth, E.W. Liberators of the Female
Mind.
  J.S. Pedersen, 637(VS):Autumn80-126
Elphick, R. and H. Giliomee, eds. The
Shaping of South African Society, 1652-
1820.
  G.M. Fredrickson, 453(NYRB):18Mar82-51
  A.J. Greenberger, 637(VS):Spring81-351
Elrod, J.W. Kierkegaard and Christendom.
  J.Z., 185:Apr82-607
van Els, T.J.M. The Kassel Manuscript of
Bede's "Historia Ecclesiastica Gentis
Anglorum" and its Old English Material.*
  L-G. Hallander, 179(ES):Dec81-556
Elshtain, J.B. Public Man, Private Woman.
  S.M. Clark, 150(DR):Autumn81-594
Elsom, J., ed. Post-War British Theatre
Criticism.*
  A.P.H., 148:Winter81-92
  J. Lahr, 157:Winter81-48
Elson, R.E. The Cultivation System and
"Agricultural Involution."
  R. Van Niel, 293(JASt):Nov80-210
Elster, J. Ulysses and the Sirens.*
  R. Phillips, 63:Dec81-454
Elton, J. Bridges, Docks and Harbours:
Catalogue 45.
  S. Gardiner, 362:15Apr82-20
Eluard, P. Last Love Poems.
  639(VQR):Winter81-27
Éluard, P. Le Poète et son Ombre. (R.D.
Valette, ed)
  D. Gascoyne, 208(FS):Oct81-475
Elwert, W.T. Die romanischen Sprachen und
Literaturen.
  A.L. Mackenzie, 86(BHS):Jan81-73
Elyot, T. The Letters of Sir Thomas Elyot.
(K.J. Wilson, ed)
  M.J. Tucker, 551(RenQ):Autumn80-462
Elytis, O. The Axion Esti.* (E. Keeley
and G. Savidis, eds and trans)
  J. Saunders, 565:Vol22No3-62
Elytis, O. Odysseus Elytis. (E. Keeley
and P. Sherrard, eds) Maria Nephele.
  R. Hadas, 441:7Feb82-29
Embree, L. - see Gurwitsch, A.
Emecheta, B. Destination Biafra.
  Chinweizu, 617(TLS):26Feb82-228
  A. Huth, 362:21Jan82-25
Emeneau, M.B. Language and Linguistic
Area. (A.S. Dil, ed)
  H.F. Schiffman, 350:Mar82-185
  F.C. Southworth, 355(LSoc):Apr81-125
"The Emergence of Man."
  J.S. Weiner, 617(TLS):29Jan82-102
Emerson, E.T. The Life of Lidian Jackson
Emerson. (D.B. Carpenter, ed)
  J. Porte, 27(AL):Jan82-750
Emerson, R.W. Emerson in His Journals.
(J. Porte, ed)
  R. Poirier, 441:20Jun82-14
  L. Ziff, 617(TLS):27Aug82-915
  442(NY):24May82-134
Emery, N. Alexander Hamilton.
  P-L. Adams, 61:Oct82-105
Emlyn-Jones, C.J. The Ionians and Hellen-
ism.*
  P. Walcot, 123:Vol31No2-310
Emmanuelli, F-X. Pouvoir royal et Vie
régionale en Provence au Déclin de la
Monarchie. La Crise marseillaise de

1774 et la Chute des Courtiers.
  N. Hampson, 208(FS):Apr81-211
Emmerson, J.S., ed. Catalogue of the
Pybus Collection of Medical Books, Let-
ters and Engravings, 15th-20th Centuries,
held in the University Library, Newcas-
tle upon Tyne.
  D. McKitterick, 617(TLS):7May82-519
Emmert, R. and M. Yuki, eds. Musical
Voices of Asia.
  K. Benitez, 187:Jan82-171
Emmet, A. and others. Cambridge, Massachu-
setts.
  C. Zaitzevsky, 576:Mar81-73
Emmet, D. The Moral Prism.*
  F. Sparshott, 185:Apr81-510
Emmison, F.G., ed. Elizabethan Life.
  M.A. Havinden, 325:Apr81-433
Emmison, F.G. Introduction to Archives.*
  P. Christopher, 14:Winter80-87
Emons, R. Valenzgrammatik für das
Englische.*
  H.U. Boas, 38:Band99Heft3/4-438
Empaytaz de Croome, D. Albor.
  205(FMLS):Oct81-376
Empedocles. The Extant Fragments.* (M.R.
Wright, ed)
  J.P. Hershbell, 124:May-Jun82-316
Emrich, W. Poetische Wirklichkeit.
  I.M. Goessl, 221(GQ):May81-388
En-lai, C. - see under Chou En-lai
Enayat, H. Modern Islamic Political
Thought.
  E. Mortimer, 617(TLS):10Sep82-963
del Encina, J. Poesía lírica y "Cancion-
ero musical." (R.O. Jones and C.R. Lee,
eds)
  R. Gimeno, 545(RPh):Feb81(supp)-251
Ende, S.A. Keats and the Sublime.*
  A. Clayborough, 179(ES):Feb81-79
Enderton, H.B. Elements of Set Theory.
  K. Kunen, 316:Mar81-164
Endicott, K. Batek Negrito Religion.
  R.K. Dentan, 293(JASt):Feb81-421
Endicott, S. James G. Endicott.
  G.W., 102(CanL):Spring81-175
  D.E. Waterfall, 529(QQ):Summer81-279
Endo, S. The Samurai.
  L. Allen, 617(TLS):21May82-567
  I. Howe, 453(NYRB):4Nov82-31
  J. Moynahan, 441:26Dec82-7
Endo, S. The Sea and Poison.
  G. Kearns, 249(HudR):Summer81-310
  639(VQR):Spring81-61
Endres, C. Johannes Secundus.*
  D. Brearley, 539:Nov82-303
  L.V.R., 568(SCN):Summer-Fall81-80
Engel, M. Lunatic Villas.
  H. Kirkwood, 99:Feb82-43
Engel, U. Syntax der deutschen Gegenwarts-
sprache.
  G. Van der Elst, 685(ZDL):1/1981-70
Engelen, B. Untersuchungen zu Satzbauplan
und Wortfeld in der geschriebenen deuts-
chen Sprache der Gegenwart.
  G. Van der Elst, 685(ZDL):1/1981-74
Engelhardt, H.T., Jr. and S.F. Spicker,
eds. Explanation and Evaluation in the
Biomedical Sciences. Mental Health.
  J.C. Moskop, 185:Jan82-381
Engelhardt, H.T., Jr., S.F. Spicker and B.
Towers, eds. Clinical Judgment.
  J.C. Moskop, 185:Jan82-381

103

Engelhardt, K. and V. Roloff. Daten der
französischen Literatur.
  F.S., 52:Band15Heft1-111
Engelhardt, P. Danerne fra fødsel til dåb.
  J.M. Jochens, 563(SS):Autumn81-471
Engell, J. The Creative Imagination.
  W.J. Bate, 453(NYRB):18Nov82-71
  C.B. Hausman, 290(JAAC):Summer82-437
  J.D. O'Hara, 434:Summer82-603
  J.P. Russo, 617(TLS):5Feb82-143
Engels, J. Vivaldi in Early Fall.
  J. Schley, 434:Summer82-621
Engen, R. Kate Greenaway.*
  A. Lurie, 453(NYRB):18Mar82-15
Engen, R.K. Dictionary of Victorian
Engravers, Print Publishers and their
Works.
  D. Alexander, 135:Aug81-251
Enggass, C. and R. - see Pio, N.
Engineer, A. The Bohras.
  T.P. Wright, Jr., 293(JASt):Aug81-819
England, A.B. Energy and Order in the
Poetry of Swift.*
  N.C. Jaffe, 566:Spring81-112
England, J., ed. Hispanic Studies in
Honour of Frank Pierce.
  R. Arias, 238:Dec81-633
  C. Smith, 402(MLR):Jul81-715
English, B. The Lords of Holderness,
1086-1260.*
  P. Niles, 589:Oct81-865
English, J., ed. Sex Equality.
  K. Hanson, 449:Mar81-95
"English National Opera Guides." (No. 1-4)
  T. Coombs, 214:Vol 10No37-127
Engman, M. and J.A. Erikson. Mannen i
kolboxen.
  D. Kirby, 575(SEER):Jan81-116
Engster, H. Der Januskopf des Bürgers.
  E. Eide, 562(Scan):Nov81-222
Ennius. Quinto Ennio. (P. Magno, ed and
trans)
  H.D. Joycelyn, 123:Vol31No1-114
Enns, V. Jimmy Bang Poems.
  D. Barbour, 648(WCR):Jun80-76
  J. Giltrow, 102(CanL):Spring81-145
Enright, D.J. Collected Poems.*
  P. Bland, 364:Oct81-79
Enstice, A. Thomas Hardy.
  L. Elsbree, 637(VS):Autumn80-139
  J. Halperin, 395(MFS):Summer80-302
  S. Hunter, 677(YES):Vol 11-331
  M. Millgate, 445(NCF):Sep80-216
  B. Richards, 541(RES):Nov81-472
  M. Williams, 447(N&Q):Jun80-257
  295(JML):Vol18No3/4-514
Enteen, G.M. The Soviet Scholar-Bureau-
crat.*
  J. Barber, 575(SEER):Oct81-619
de Entrambasaguas, J. - see Ruiz de
Alarcón, J.
Entrekin, D. Make Your Own Silk Flowers.
  P. Bach, 614:Fall81-18
Enyeart, J., ed. Heinecken.
  H. Fischer, 62:Sep81-73
Enyedi, G. and J. Mészaros, eds. Develop-
ment of Settlement Systems.
  L.A. Kosiński, 104(CASS):Winter81-618
Enzensberger, H.M. The Sinking of the
Titanic.*
  J. Monroe, 448:Vol 19No3-188
  P. West, 472:Spring/Summer81-91

Epictetus. Epiktet, "Vom Kynismus."* (M.
Billerbeck, ed and trans)
  J. Dillon, 122:Jul81-247
  A.A. Long, 303(JoHS):Vol 101-163
Epps, B. Pilgarlic the Death.
  S.E. Grace, 102(CanL):Summer81-155
Epstein, B.L. The Politics of Domestic-
ity.*
  K.J. Blair, 432(NEQ):Sep81-456
Epstein, D. Beyond Orpheus.
  A. Whittall, 308:Fall81-319
Epstein, E.J. The Rise and Fall of Dia-
monds.
  P. Erdman, 441:20Jun82-7
Epstein, E.L. Language and Style.*
  G.B., 189(EA):Apr-Jun81-241
  R. Hasan, 494:Autumn80-207
Epstein, J. The Lion of Freedom.
  D. Jones, 617(TLS):25Jun82-686
Epstein, L. Regina.
  G. Stade, 441:21Nov82-12
Eran, O. Mezhdunarodniki.*
  A. Dallin, 550(RusR):Jan81-73
Erasmus. Collected Works of Erasmus.*
(Vols 23 and 24) (C.R. Thompson, ed)
  J.W. Blench, 551(RenQ):Summer80-262
Erasmus. La Correspondance d'Erasme.
(Vol 8) (J. Chomarat and others, eds)
  B. Beaulieu, 539:Feb82-46
Erasmus. The Correspondence of Erasmus.
(Vol 5) (P.G. Bietenholz, ed; R.A.B.
Mynors and D.F.S. Thomson, trans)
  J.H. Bentley, 539:Feb82-67
  R.L. De Molen, 551(RenQ):Winter80-752
  L.V.R., 568(SCN):Spring81-33
Erasmus. Opera omnia, recognita et
adnotatione critica instructa notisque
illustrata. (Pt 5, Vol 1) (S. Dresden
and others, eds)
  H.A. Oberman, 551(RenQ):Spring80-88
Erasmus. The Praise of Folly. (C.H.
Miller, ed and trans)
  J. Mezciems, 402(MLR):Apr81-421
  J.T. Rhodes, 161(DUJ):Jun81-249
de Ercilla, A. La Araucana. (M.A. Mor-
ínigo and I. Lerner, eds)
  H. Betancourt, 240(HR):Summer81-351
  G.A. Davies, 86(BHS):Jul81-262
  F. Pierce, 402(MLR):Apr81-486
Erdelyi, H.T., ed. Literatur und Litera-
turgeschichte in Österreich.
  D.G. Daviau, 678(YCGL):No29-42
Erdman, D.V. and others - see Blake, W.
Erdt, W. Christentum und heidnisch-antike
Bildung bei Paulin von Nola mit Kommen-
tar und Übersetzung des 16. Briefes.
  E.D. Hunt, 313:Vol71-193
Ereira, A. The Invergordon Mutiny.*
  B. Ranft, 617(TLS):5Feb82-145
Ereira, A. The People's England.*
  N. Miller, 42(AR):Summer81-389
Erickson, J.D. Nommo.*
  D.S. Blair, 402(MLR):Jan81-209
  A.A. Renaud, 210(FrF):Jan81-93
  H.A. Waters, 207(FR):Feb81-460
Erickson, J.D. and I. Pagès, eds. Proust
et le texte producteur.
  G. Brée, 188(ECr):Summer81-101
  P. Perron, 627(UTQ):Summer81-190
  L.B. Price, 207(FR):Apr81-743
Ericson, E.E., Jr. Solzhenitsyn.
  D. Pospielovsky, 550(RusR):Oct81-479

Ericson, L. and D.E. Frode. Design it
Yourself. Print it Yourself. Sewing it
Yourself.
P. Bach, 614:Fall82-15
Eriksson, E. L'emploi des modes dans la
subordonnée relative en français
moderne.*
J. Chaurand, 209(FM):Apr81-185
K. Hunnius, 72:Band217Heft2-465
Erkkila, B. Walt Whitman Among the
French.*
D. Burdick, 646(WWR):Mar81-42
A. Golden, 27(AL):May81-326
J.P. Houston, 207(FR):May82-906
Erkkila, B.H. Hammers on Stone.
J.E. Garland, 432(NEQ):Dec81-604
Ermolaev, H. Mikhail Sholokhov and His
Art.
J. Grayson, 617(TLS):30Jul82-819
Ernaux, A. La Femme gelée.
F. de Martinoir, 450(NRF):Jun81-123
Ernst, G. Der Wortschatz der franzö-
sischen Übersetzungen von Plutarchs
"Vies parallèles" (1559-1694).*
H. and R. Kahane, 545(RPh):Feb81(supp)-
24
Erofeev, B. Moscow Circles.
G. Hosking, 617(TLS):15Jan82-63
Erofeev, V. Moscow to the End of the
Line.*
639(VQR):Winter81-20
Erskine-Hill, H. and A. Smith, eds. The
Art of Alexander Pope.*
G.S. Rousseau, 173(ECS):Winter80/81-
181
Ertl, A.W. Grösste Denkwürdigkeiten
Bayerns. (G. Deckart, ed)
H. Gerndt, 196:Band21Heft1/2-115
Ertz, K. Jan Brueghel de Altere: die
Gemalde.
C. Brown, 39:Dec81-429
J.K., 471:Jan/Feb/Mar81-91
Ervin, S.J., Jr. The Whole Truth.*
639(VQR):Summer81-92
Erwin, E. Behavior Therapy.*
K. Baier, 185:Apr81-499
M.E. Grenander, 84:Mar81-85
Erzgräber, W., ed. Neues Handbuch der Lit-
eraturwissenschaft.* (Vol 8)
W.T.H. Jackson, 589:Jan81-128
Esau, H., ed. Language and Communication.
D.R. Ladd, 350:Dec82-890
Esberey, J.E. Knight of the Holy Spirit.*
G.W., 102(CanL):Summer81-87
Escarpit, R., ed. Dictionnaire Interna-
tional des terms littéraires. (fasc 1
and 2)
L. Orr, 599:Fall81-501
Eschbach, A. Pragmasemiotik und Theater.
E.W.B. Hess-Lüttich, 680(ZDP):Band99
Heft3-473
Eschbach, A. and W. Rader, eds. Literatur-
semiotik I-II.
A. Schwarz, 196:Band22Heft3/4-332
Esche, A. Wörterbuch Burmesisch-Deutsch.
K. Kaden, 682(ZPSK):Band33Heft2-243
Eschebach, H. Die stabianer Thermen in
Pompeji.
R. Ling, 313:Vol71-212
von Eschenbach, W. - see under Wolfram von
Eschenbach

Eschwege, H. Die Synagoge in der deutsch-
en Geschichte.
C.H. Krinsky, 576:Oct81-246
Escobar, A. Variaciones sociolingüísticas
del castellano en el Perú.
B. Schuchard, 72:Band217Heft1-211
Esher, L. A Broken Wave.
S. Cantacuzino, 324:Aug82-596
S. Gardiner, 364:Feb82-76
Eshleman, C. The Gospel of Celine Arnauld.
T. Olson, 436(NewL):Winter81/82-108
Esmeijer, A.C. Divina Quaternitas.*
A. van Run, 600:Vol 12No1-70
Espener, M.I.W. - see under Watson Espener,
M.I.
Espey, J. The Empty Box Haiku.
T. Cassity, 472:Fall/Winter81-184
Espiau de la Maëstre, A. Humanisme clas-
sique et syncrétisme mythique chez Paul
Claudel (1880-1892).*
M. Wood, 208(FS):Jul81-354
Espinós Díaz, A. Museo de Bellas Artes de
Valencia: Catálogo de Dibujos I.
A.E.P.S., 48:Jan-Mar81-102
Espinosa, M.T. - see under Torreblanca
Espinosa, M.
Esser, J. Intonationszeichen im Englis-
chen.*
M. Schubiger, 685(ZDL):1/1981-97
Essich, R.N. and M.D. Paley - see Blair, R.
Essick, R.N. William Blake, Printmaker.*
D. Alexander, 90:May81-311
L. Damrosch, Jr., 591(SIR):Winter81-
544
J. Gage, 59:Dec81-470
R.E. Johnson, 435:Summer81-204
P. Quennell, 39:Aug81-136
42(AR):Winter81-131
Esslin, M. Mediations.*
S. Gooch, 214:Vol 10No37-128
H. Hobson, 157:Autumn81-49
G. Woodcock, 569(SR):Fall81-611
Estergreen, M.M. Kit Carson.
W.T. Jackson, 651(WHR):Summer81-179
Estermann, A. Die deutschen Literatur-
Zeitschriften 1815-1850.
P.U. Hohendahl, 406:Summer81-230
G. Sautermeister, 680(ZDP):Band100
Heft2-303
H. Steinecke, 221(GQ):Mar81-222
Estermann, P.C. Ethnographie du Sud-Ouest
de l'Angola.
D. Birmingham, 69:Vol50No1-111
Estes, J.W. Hall Jackson and the Purple
Foxglove.
H.A. Leventhal, 656(WMQ):Oct81-744
Estève, M. - see under Jurt, J.
Estienne, H. Deux dialogues du nouveau
langage françois. (P.M. Smith, ed)
D.G. Coleman, 208(FS):Apr81-189
P. Rickard, 402(MLR):Jul81-696
Estleman, L. The Midnight Man.
N. Callendar, 441:22Aug82-26
Estrada, A. Maria Sabina.
F. Randall, 441:28Feb82-18
Estrada, F.L. - see under López Estrada, F.
Estragon, V. Waiting for Dessert.
J. Leonard, 441:4Jul82-2
"Estudios sefardíes." (Vol 1) (I.M.
Hassán, ed)
R. Haboucha, 240(HR):Autumn81-493

Etcheverry, J-P. Elvire ou la guerre
perdue.
  C.W. Obuchowski, 207(FR):Oct80-191
Ethe, J. Easy-to-Make Felt Bean Bag Toys.
  P. Bach, 614:Winter82-17
Ethier-Blais, J. Autour de Borduas.
  L. Shouldice, 102(CanL):Summer81-162
Ethier-Blais, J. Petits poèmes presque en
prose.
  G.V. Downes, 102(CanL):Winter80-105
Étiemble. Comment lire un roman japonais?
  D. Aury, 450(NRF):Jul-Aug81-180
Etiemble. Quelques essais de littérature
universelle.
  J. Weightman, 617(TLS):10Dec82-1369
"Étoffes imprimées françaises."
  R.L. Shep, 614:Summer82-15
Ettinger, E. - see Luxemburg, R.
Ettinger, S. Form und Funktion in der
Wortbildung. (2nd ed)
  W.B. Lockwood, 297(JL):Sep81-385
"Études Celtiques." (Vols 16 and 17)
  B. Ó Cuív, 112:Vol 14-183
"Études de statistique linguistique."
  J. Schmidely, 209(FM):Apr81-189
"Études Finno-Ougriennes." (Vol 12)
  G.F. Meier, 682(ZPSK):Band33Heft5-597
"Études Gobiniennes, 1976-78."
  M.D. Biddiss, 208(FS):Jan81-85
"Etudes rabelaisiennes."* (Vol 14)
  W.H. Bowen, 551(RenQ):Spring80-114
"Études Romanes de Brno." (Vol 8)
  G.F. Meier, 682(ZPSK):Band33Heft5-598
"Études sur le XVIIIe siècle."
  P. Larthomas, 209(FM):Apr81-177
Etulain, R.W. - see London, J.
Euripides. Andromacha. (A. Garzya, ed)
  J. Diggle, 123:Vol31No1-4
Euripides. The Bakkhai. (R. Bagg, trans)
  J. Herington, 472:Fall/Winter81-217
Euripides. The Phoenician Women. (P.
  Burian and B. Swann, trans) Helen. (J.
  Michie and C. Leach, trans) The Chil-
  dren of Herakles. (H. Taylor and R.A.
  Brooks, trans)
  D. Bain, 617(TLS):30Apr82-491
"Euskera." (Vol 18)
  G.F. Meier, 682(ZPSK):Band33Heft4-497
Evans, B. Shakespeare's Tragic Practice.*
  H.C. Cole, 301(JEGP):Apr81-244
  B. McElroy, 405(MP):Aug81-73
Evans, D. Big Road Blues.
  B. Luckin, 617(TLS):24Sep82-1047
Evans, D. Faith, Authenticity, and Moral-
ity.
  L. Angel, 627(UTQ):Summer81-211
Evans, E. Eudora Welty.
  P.W. Prenshaw, 578:Spring82-69
Evans, F. - see Marx, J., L. and E.
Evans, F.B., comp. The History of
Archives Administration.
  M. Cook, 325:Oct81-512
  D.H. Winfrey, 14:Summer80-379
Evans, G. and J. McDowell, eds. Truth and
Meaning.*
  P. Engel, 98:Jun-Jul81-578
Evans, G.R. Anselm and a New Generation.
  W.J. Courtenay, 589:Jul81-607
Evans, G.R. Anselm and Talking About
God.*
  P.A. Clarke, 518:Apr81-82
  R.A. Herrera, 319:Apr81-248

Evans, G.R. Old Arts and New Theology.
  C. Reel, 382(MAE):1981/2-314
Evans, H. Intrusions.
  P-L. Adams, 61:Mar82-89
Evans, H. O Time In Your Flight.
  P. Barclay, 102(CanL):Summer81-133
Evans, J.D., B. Cunliffe and C. Renfrew,
  eds. Antiquity and Man.
  D.W. Harding, 617(TLS):9Apr82-420
Evans, J.D.G. Aristotle's Concept of
Dialectic.
  E. Stump, 319:Jan81-108
Evans, J.G., comp. Llyfr Hwiangerddi y
Dref Wen.
  J. Davies, 617(TLS):26Mar82-352
Evans, M. Lucien Goldmann.
  C. Norris, 617(TLS):5Feb82-144
Evans, P. The Music of Benjamin Britten.*
  J.B., 412:May80-151
Evans, R.J. and W.R. Lee, eds. The German
Family.*
  G.P. Butler, 220(GL&L):Apr82-275
Evans, R.J.W. The Making of the Habsburg
Monarchy 1500-1700.
  T.D. Kaufmann, 576:Mar81-70
  E. Wangermann, 575(SEER):Oct81-605
Evans, S. Temporary Hearths.
  P. Lewis, 617(TLS):25Jun82-702
  J. Mellors, 362:3Jun82-22
Evans, T. and C.L. Green. English
Cottages.
  P. Goldberger, 441:12Dec82-22
Evans, T.F., ed. Shaw: The Critical Heri-
tage.
  W.R. Evans, 174(Éire):Winter81-136
Evans, T.S. Formen der Ironie in Conrad
Ferdinand Meyers Novellen.
  K. Fehr, 133:Band14Heft4-380
Evans, W.R. - see "Robert Frost and Sidney
Cox"
"Walker Evans at Work."
  A. Grundberg, 441:5Dec82-11
Evens, M.W. and others. Lexical-Semantic
Relations.
  J. Gallant, 350:Mar82-242
Evenson, N. Paris: A Century of Change,
1878-1978.*
  M.G. Hydak, 207(FR):May82-931
  42(AR):Fall81-516
Everest, K. Coleridge's Secret Ministry.
  W.J.B. Owen, 541(RES):May81-233
Evers, L., ed. The South Corner of Time.*
  P.G. Beidler, 50(ArQ):Summer81-184
  J.L. Davis, 649(WAL):Summer81-146
Eversmann, S. Poetik und Erzählstruktur
in den Romanen Italo Calvinos.
  J. Woodhouse, 402(MLR):Oct81-979
Everson, W. The Masks of Drought.
  M. Beilke, 649(WAL):Spring81-67
"Evolution of Fashion 1835-1895."
  R.L. Shep, 614:Winter81-19
Ewans, M. Wagner and Aeschylus.
  H. Lloyd-Jones, 617(TLS):10ct82-1073
Ewart, G. The Collected Ewart, 1933-1980.
  T. Eagleton, 565:Vol22No4-74
Ewart, G. The New Ewart.
  D. Davis, 362:6May82-26
  W. Scammell, 617(TLS):30Jul82-830
Ewers, H-H. Kinder- und Jugendliteratur
der Aufklärung.
  D.C.G. Lorenz, 221(GQ):Nov81-505
  R. Schenda, 196:Band22Heft3/4-334

Ewing, E. Fur in Dress.
R.L. Shep, 614:Spring82-13
"Expressionism — A German Intuition 1905-20."
J. Lloyd, 59:Jun81-220
Eyben, E. De jonge Romein volgens de literaire bronnen der periode ca. 200 v. Chr. tot ca. 500 n. Chr.
J.N. Bremmer, 394:Vol134fasc3/4-453
G. Thomas, 67:Nov81-236
Eyck, F. G.P. Gooch.
K. Robbins, 617(TLS):30Jul82-820
Eylat, O. Le Psy-chat.
P.L. Bowles, 617(TLS):23Apr82-471
Eyler, J.M. Victorian Social Medicine.
W.F. Bynum, 637(VS):Autumn80-141
Eyles, D. The Doulton Burslem Wares.
K. Baker, 135:Feb81-164
Eyo, E. and F. Willett. Treasures of Ancient Nigeria.
D. Fraser, 2(AfrA):Nov80-15
Eysell, M. Wohlfart und Etatismus.
S. Oakley, 562(Scan):Nov81-224
Eysenck, H.J. and D.K.B. Nias. Astrology.
J.B. Brackenridge, 617(TLS):9Jul82-731
Ezrahi, S.D. By Words Alone.
S. Cohen, 577(SHR):Fall81-350
J. Klinkowitz, 395(MFS):Winter80/81-719

Faas, E. Ted Hughes.*
C. Bradshaw, 97(CQ):Vol 10No2-172
von Faber, H., ed. Kreativität im Fremdsprachenunterricht.
M.P. Alter, 399(MLJ):Spring81-113
"Fabliaux" - see under Rouger, G.
Fabre, J. Idées sur le roman: De Madame de Lafayette au Marquis de Sade.
R.C. Rosbottom, 207(FR):Mar82-550
Fabre, J. Maigret: Enquête sur un enquêteur.
D. Johnson, 617(TLS):10ct82-1058
de Fabry, A.S. - see under Srabian de Fabry, A.
"Faces of Findhorn."
W. Tulecke, 42(AR):Fall81-512
"Facétie et littérature facétieuse à l'époque de la Renaissance."
K.M. Hall, 208(FS):Jul81-321
Facione, P.A. and D. Scherer. Logic and Logical Thinking.
R. Rogers, 316:Sep81-672
Fadda, A.M.L. - see under Luiselli Fadda, A.M.
Faderman, L. Surpassing the Love of Men.*
N. Baym, 587(SAF):Autumn81-278
Fagerholm, K-A. Talmannens röst.
H.P. Krosby, 563(SS):Spring81-228
Fagg, W. Masques d'Afrique dans les collections du Musée Barbier-Müller.
M-T. Brincard, 2(AfrA):Aug81-19
Fagg, W. Yoruba Beadwork. (B. Holcombe, ed)
J.B. Donne, 617(TLS):30Jul82-818
E.L.R. Meyerowitz, 39:Aug81-134
Fagg, W. and J. Pemberton 3d. Yoruba: Sculpture of West Africa. (B. Holcombe, ed)
J.B. Donne, 617(TLS):30Jul82-818
Fagiolo, M., D. Fonti and P. Vivarelli. Alberto Savinio.
S. Fauchereau, 98:Dec80-1164

Faïk-Njuzi, C. Devinettes tonales: Tusumwinu.
P.A. Noss, 69:Vol50No1-107
Fainlight, R. Sibyls and Others.*
D. Graham, 565:Vol22No4-62
Fair, J.D. British Interparty Conferences.
J.L. Godfrey, 579(SAQ):Summer81-374
Fairbairn, D. Down and Out in Cambridge.
442(NY):8Mar82-143
Fairbank, J.K. Chinabound.
H.R. Isaacs, 441:28Feb82-11
D.S. Nivison, 453(NYRB):13May82-33
Fairbank, J.K., ed. The Missionary Enterprise in China and America.
C.W. Hayford, 318(.JAOS):Apr/Jun80-207
Fairbank, J.K. and K-C. Liu, eds. The Cambridge History of China. (Vol 11)
M.B. Rankin, 293(JASt):Aug81-760
Fairchild, B.H. Such Holy Song.
M.W. England, 591(SIR):Winter81-545
S. Peterfreund, 661(WC):Summer81-167
Faiss, K. Verdunkelte Compounds im Englischen.*
W. Hüllen, 72:Band217Heft2-402
Faith, N. Safety in Numbers.
J.K. Galbraith, 61:Nov82-163
J. Steinberg, 617(TLS):6Aug82-853
Fáj, A. Le thème de Jonas dans la littérature mondiale (A Jónástema a világirodalomban).
A. Karátson, 549(RLC):Apr-Jun81-255
Falcione, R.L. and H.H. Greenbaum. Organizational Communication.
P. Hobor, 583:Summer81-434
Faldella, C. Zibaldone. (C. Marazzini, ed)
G. Tesio, 228(GSLI):Vol 158fasc501-150
Falk, D.V. Lillian Hellman.
M.W. Estrin, 397(MD):Sep81-379
Falk, E.H. The Poetics of Roman Ingarden.
J. Flzer, 478:Fall81 245
G.D. Pollick, 290(JAAC):Spring82-345
Falk, H. Quellen des Pañcatantra.
L. Sternbach, 318(JAOS):Jan/Mar80-49
Falk, J. "Ser y estar" con atributos adjetivales.
C. Silva-Corvalán, 350:Mar82-245
Falk, S. Tennessee Williams. (2nd ed)
A.E. Kalson, 585(SoQ):Winter81-81
Falk, T. and M. Archer. Indian Miniatures in the India Office Library.
A. Topsfield, 617(TLS):6Aug82-860
Fall, A.S. La Grève des bàttu ou les déchets humains.
T.N. Hammond, 207(FR):Dec80-363
Fall, A.S. Le Revenant.
T.N. Hammond, 207(FR):Mar81-618
de Falla, M. On Music and Musicians. (F. Sopena, ed)
R. Crichton, 415:Feb81-107
Fallani, G. - see Saba, U.
Fallico, A. G.B. Casti e l'utopia di una intellettualità non subalterna.
F. Žaboklicki, 228(GSLI):Vol 157fasc 497-150
Fallis, R. The Irish Renaissance.*
H. Kosok, 38:Band99Heft3/4-528
Fallon, D. The German University.
C.V. Miller, 399(MLJ):Winter81-434
Fallon, P. and S. Golden, eds. Soft Day.*
T. Kelly, 174(Éire):Spring81-149
K. Skinner, 134(CP):Fall81-121

Fallowell, D. and A. Ashley. April Ash-
ley's Odyssey.
A. Motion, 617(TLS):14May82-525
H. Wackett, 362:29Apr82-18
Fane, J. Gentleman's Gentleman.*
J. Betjeman, 364:Dec81/Jan82-142
Fanelli, M. Aujourd'hui. (2nd ed)
D.C. Spinelli, 207(FR):May81-882
Fanger, D. The Creation of Nikolai Gogol.*
K. Klotz, 219(GaR):Fall81-681
Fanning, C. Finley Peter Dunne and Mr.
Dooley: The Chicago Years.
S. Poger, 174(Éire):Spring81-140
Fantazzi, C. - see Vives, J.L.
Fanthorpe, U.A. Side Effects.*
B. Ruddick, 148:Winter81-71
Fantoni, B. Stickman.
R. Davies, 617(TLS):22Oct82-1156
Fantosme, J. Jordan Fantosme's Chronicle.*
(R.C. Johnston, ed and trans)
205(FMLS):Oct81-377
Far, I. De Chirico.
M. Zarader, 98:Feb80-155
Farber, M. "Somebody is Lying."
E.J. Bloustein, 441:22Aug82-6
Farber, T. Hazards to the Human Heart.
M. McQuade, 114(ChiR):Autumn80-117
Farer, T.J. The Future of the Inter-
American System.
R. Perina, 263(RIB):Vol31No1-70
Fargher, D.C. Fargher's English-Manx
Dictionary.
B. Ó Cuív, 112:Vol 14-175
de Faria, N. Structures et unité dans
"Les Rougon-Macquart" (La Poétique du
cycle).*
C. Bertrand-Jennings, 446(NCFS):Fall-
Winter80/81-141
C.B. Jennings, 627(UTQ):Spring81-323
Farington, J. The Diary of Joseph Faring-
ton.* (Vols 1 and 2) (K. Garlick and A.
Macintyre, eds)
E. Waterhouse, 447(N&Q):Oct80-451
Faris, A. Jacques Offenbach.*
J.B., 412:Nov80-314
H. MacDonald, 415:Jul81-479
Farkas, E. and others. The Véhicule Poets.
D. Barbour, 648(WCR):Jun80-73
J. Giltrow, 102(CanL):Spring81-145
Farkas, J., ed. Räterepublik und Kultur
Ungarn 1919.
R. Begemann, 654(WB):4/1981-175
Farley-Hills, D. Rochester's Poetry.*
J.H. O'Neill, 173(ECS):Summer81-483
566:Spring81-121
Farmer, D.H. The Oxford Dictionary of
Saints.*
J.M. McCulloh, 589:Oct81-867
Farmer, K.C. Ukrainian Nationalism in the
Post-Stalin Era.
F.E. Sysyn, 575(SEER):Oct81-624
Farmer, P. Music in the Comprehensive
School.
P. Standford, 415:Apr81-244
Farnsworth, B. Aleksandra Kollontai.*
R. Glickman, 550(RusR):Jul81-343
R.C. Williams, 104(CASS):Winter81-603
Farnsworth, R.M. - see Tolson, M.B.
Farooqi, A.H.Z. Allama Ibn-Taymiyyah and
his Contemporary Ulama.
S.A. Akbarabadi, 273(IC):Apr80-132
Farooqi, N.A. - see Imdadullah, H.

Farquhar, G. The Beaux' Stratagem. (C.N.
Fifer, ed)
W. Myers, 541(RES):Aug81-332
Farr, D. Gilbert Cannan.
295(JML):Vol18No3/4-463
Farr, D.M. John Ford and the Caroline
Theatre.*
G. Bas, 189(EA):Oct-Dec81-465
Farrand, J., Jr., ed. The Audubon Society
Encyclopedia of Animal Life.
S.D. Smith, 441:5Dec82-12
Farrell, J.P. Revolution as Tragedy.*
R.B. Henkle, 637(VS):Spring81-389
J. Millgate, 301(JEGP):Oct81-583
Farrington, J. Wyndham Lewis.
J. Beckett, 59:Dec81-461
Farris, J. Catacombs.
T.J. Binyon, 617(TLS):12Feb82-170
Farris, J. Me and Gallagher.
442(NY):27Sep82-145
Farrow, A. George Moore.
M. Harmon, 541(RES):Nov81-503
Farson, D. Henry.
J. Symons, 617(TLS):24Sep82-1033
Faruqi, N.A. Early Muslim Historiography
(612-750 A.D.).
M.A. Nayeem, 273(IC):Oct80-246
Faruqui, Z.H. and M. ul-Haque, eds.
Fikr-e Islami Ki Tashkil-e Jadid.
S.A. Khundmiri, 273(IC):Jan81-67
Farwell, B. For Queen and Country.
N. Best, 617(TLS):29Jan82-118
Farwell, B. Mr. Kipling's Army.*
M. Green, 676(YR):Autumn81-145
Fasholé-Luke, E. and others, eds. Chris-
tianity in Independent Africa.
A. Redmayne, 69:Vol50No2-210
Fassler, D. and N.D. Lay. Encounter with
a New World.
B. Kroll, 399(MLJ):Summer81-233
Fassnidge, V. Something Else.
M. Furness, 617(TLS):12Feb82-170
Fast, H. Max.
S. Ellin, 441:3Oct82-12
Faugère, A. Les Origines Orientales du
Graal chez Wolfram von Eschenbach.
M.E. Gibbs, 406:Fall81-344
Faulhaber, U.K. and P.B. Goff. German
Literature.
S. Lehmann, 221(GQ):May81-396
Faulkner, P. Robert Bage.
A. Rodway, 447(N&Q):Oct80-453
Faulkner, P. Angus Wilson.
I. Malin, 639(VQR):Summer81-566
Faulkner, R.F.J. and O.R. Impey. Shino
and Oribe Kiln Sites.
U. Roberts, 60:Nov-Dec81-156
Faulkner, W. Mayday.*
A.F. Kinney, 395(MFS):Summer80-336
Faulkner, W. Mississippi Poems.
P.D. Morrow, 577(SHR):Spring81-174
Faulkner, W. Uncollected Stories of
William Faulkner.* (J. Blotner, ed)
T.A. Gullason, 573(SSF):Spring81-189
T.L. Heller, 50(ArQ):Summer81-173
L.P. Simpson, 385(MQR):Spring82-365
Faulstich, W., ed. Kritische Stichwörter
zur Medienwissenschaft.
H-F. Foltin, 196:Band22Heft1/2-123
Faust, C. Metamorphosed from the Adjacent
Cold.
G. Catalano, 381:Apr81-114

Faust, N. Lecciones para el Aprendizaje del Idioma Shipibo-Conibo.
K.M. Kensinger, 269(IJAL):Jan81-68
Favier, J. Philippe le Bel.
J.B. Henneman, 589:Jan81-131
Favre, R. La Mort dans la littérature et la pensée françaises au siècle des Lumières.*
H. Cohen, 207(FR):Mar81-630
Favre, Y-A. Giono et l'art du récit.*
M. Scott, 208(FS):Oct81-476
Favre, Y-A. La Recherche de la grandeur dans l'oeuvre de Suarès.*
H. Godin, 208(FS):Oct81-472
Favre, Y-A. - see de Boschère, J.
Favre, Y-A. - see Suarès, A.
Favret, R. - see Camus, J-P.
Favretti, R.J. and J.P. Landscapes and Gardens for Historic Buildings.
C. Zaitzevsky, 576:Mar81-73
Fawcett, E. and T. Thomas. The American Condition.
N. Lemann, 441:19Dec82-9
Fawcett, T. Music in Eighteenth-Century Norwich and Suffolk.*
C.N. Smith, 83:Autumn81-249
Fawkes, R. Dion Boucicault.*
R. Jackson, 611(TN):Vol35No2-90
Fay, S. Beyond Greed.
J.K. Galbraith, 61:May82-100
W. Goodman, 441:18Apr82-26
442(NY):31May82-108
Fay, S. The Great Silver Bubble.
R. Lambert, 617(TLS):6Aug82-853
Feagin, C. Variation and Change in Alabama English.*
R.R. Butters, 350:Sep81-735
M.I. Miller, 35(AS):Winter81-288
H.B. Woods, 320(CJL):Fall81-250
Feaver, V. Close Relatives.*
P. Bland, 364:Jul81-72
Fedeli, P. - see Propertius
Feder, L. Madness in Literature.
E. Butscher, 219(GaR):Fall81-675
W. Fowlie, 569(SR):Winter81-xv
Federman, R. The Twofold Vibration.
B. Morton, 617(TLS):3Dec82-1344
M. Rose, 441:7Nov82-12
Federman, R. La Voix dans le cabinet de débarras/The Voice in the Closet.
M. Cagnon, 207(FR):Dec80-364
P. Quartermain, 114(ChiR):Autumn80-65
Fedorowicz, J.K. England's Baltic Trade in the Early Seventeenth Century.
D. Kirby, 575(SEER):Jul81-443
Fedorowicz, J.K., ed and trans. A Republic of Nobles.
J. Ciechanowski, 617(TLS):10Dec82-1375
Feenberg, A. Lukács, Marx and the Sources of Critical Theory.
J-J. Goux, 400(MLN):Dec81-1171
Fehling, D. Amor und Psyche.*
C.C. Schlam, 122:Apr81-164
Fehrman, C. Poetic Creation.
A. Berleant, 478:Spring81-117
G. Della Piana, 599:Fall81-474
D. Callen, 290(JAAC):Spring82-342
R.D. Spector, 563(SS):Winter81-103
Fei, J.C.H. and others. Growth with Equity.
A.J. Gregor, 293(JASt):Feb81-355
Feick, H. - see Heidegger, M.

Feifer, M. Everyman's France.
I. Bell, 617(TLS):22Oct82-1172
"Feiffer." (S. Heller, ed)
N. Perrin, 441:19Dec82-8
Feige, P. Die Anfänge des portugiesischen Königtums und seiner Landeskirche.
P. Freedman, 589:Apr81-378
Feigs, W. Deskriptive Edition auf Allograph-, Wort- und Satzniveau, demonstriert an handschriftlich überlieferten, deutschsprachigen Briefen von H. Steffens. (Pt 1)
R. Schröder, 462(OL):Vol36No3-265
Feinberg, J. Rights, Justice and the Bounds of Liberty.
R.L.S., 185:Jul82-798
Feingold, R. Nature and Society.*
P.M. Spacks, 402(MLR):Jan81-166
Feinstein, E. The Survivors.
P. Lewis, 617(TLS):26Feb82-224
J. Mellors, 362:11Mar82-23
Feirstein, F. Manhattan Carnival.
P. Mariani, 472:Spring/Summer82-265
Fekete, É. and É. Karádi, eds. György Lukács.
G. Steiner, 617(TLS):22Jan82-67
Fekete, J. The Critical Twilight.
T.H. Adamowski, 529(QQ):Autumn81-442
Feldbrugge, F.J.M., ed. The Constitutions of the USSR and The Union Republics.
W.E. Butler, 575(SEER):Jan81-143
Feldbuch, M., ed. Der Brief Alexanders an Aristoteles über die Wunder Indiens.
C. Minis, 684(ZDA):Band10Heft3-113
Feldman, A. and E. O'Doherty, eds. The Northern Fiddler.
L. Herrmann, 187:Sep82-464
L.E. McCullough, 174(Éire):Fall81-154
Feldman, E.J. and N. Nevitte, eds. The Future of North America.
G.A. Rawlyk, 106:Winter81-405
Feldman, I. New and Selected Poems.*
R. Asselineau, 189(EA):Oct-Dec81-494
Feldman, J. La Sexualité du Petit Larousse ou le jeu du dictionnaire.
W. Woodhull, 207(FR):Mar82-583
Felix, S.W. Linguistische Untersuchungen zum natürlichen Zweitsprachenerwerb.
H.W. Dechert, 257(IRAL):May81-171
H. Ulherr, 38:Band99Heft3/4-477
Fell, J.P. Heidegger and Sartre.*
J.D. Rabb, 518:Jul81-146
J.W., 543:Sep80-129
Fell, M. Womens Speaking Justified (1667) [and] Epistle from the Womens Yearly Meeting at York 1688 (1688) [together with] Waite, M. A Warning to All Friends (1688).*
E.B., 189(EA):Apr-Jun81-238
Fellows, J. Ruskin's Maze.
R. Trickett, 617(TLS):12Mar82-273
Fellows, O. and D.G. Carr - see "Diderot Studies XIX"
Felman, S. La Folie et la chose littéraire.*
R.C. Carroll, 400(MLN):May81-897
G.D. Chaitin, 131(CL):Fall81-389
A. Demaitre, 207(FR):Mar82-539
C. Prendergast, 208(FS):Jan81-103
S. Tinter, 546(RR):May81-363
Felman, S., ed. Literature and Psychoanalysis.
J. Forrester, 208(FS):Apr81-170

109

Felman, S. Le Scandale du corps parlant.
 R.C. Carroll, 400(MLN):May81-897
 C.P. James, 207(FR):Dec81-268
 H.C. Knutson, 402(MLR):Oct81-963
 R. Lloyd, 208(FS):Jan81-105
 M. Schneider, 153:Fall81-27
 205(FMLS):Oct80-375
Fels, L. Living Together.
 M. Fox, 529(QQ):Winter81-817
Felsenstein, F. - see Smollett, T.
Felten, H. María de Zayas y Sotomayor.
 W. Krömer, 602:Vol 12No2-402
 H.W. Sullivan, 240(HR):Spring81-236
Femia, J.V. Gramsci's Political Thought.
 J. Joll, 617(TLS):12Feb82-159
Femmel, G., ed. Die Gemmen aus Goethes
 Sammlung.
 G. Seidmann, 90:Jun81-370
Fen, E. Tomorrow We Die.
 J. Uglow, 617(TLS):30Jul82-839
Fender, S. Plotting the Golden West.
 R. Christiansen, 617(TLS):8Oct82-1112
Fenlon, I. Music and Patronage in
 Sixteenth-Century Mantua.*
 D. Stevens, 414(MusQ):Oct81-592
Fenn, R.K. Liturgies and Trials.
 D. Crane, 617(TLS):30Jul82-836
Fennario, D. Balconville.
 T. Beaupre, 108:Fall81-113
Fennario, D. Nothing to Lose.
 J. Ripley, 102(CanL):Summer80-113
Fennis, J. La "Stolonomie" et son vocab-
 ulaire maritime marseillais.
 A.G. Gordon, 551(RenQ):Autumn80-442
 C. Schmitt, 72:Band217Heft1-215
Fenoglio, B. Opere. (M. Corti, ed)
 E. Bonora, 228(GSLI):Vol 157fasc498-
 305
 M.G. Di Paolo, 276:Winter81-330
Fensch, T. Steinbeck and Covici.*
 R. De Mott, 295(JML):Vol8No3/4-617
Fenton, J. Dead Soldiers.
 J. Mole, 617(TLS):2Apr82-392
Fenton, J. A German Requiem.*
 D. Davis, 362:7Jan82-22
Fenton, J. The Memory of War.
 J. Bayley, 617(TLS):27Aug82-919
 G. Grigson, 362:25Nov82-25
Fenton, W.N. and E.L. Moore - see Lafitau,
 J.
de Ferdinandy, M. Philipp II.
 E. Spivakovsky, 551(RenQ):Summer80-253
Ferebee, A. A History of Design from the
 Victorian Era to the Present.
 T. Benton, 59:Sep81-348
Ferencz, B.B. Less Than Slaves.
 D. Stone, 287:Apr81-27
Ferenczi, L. Voltaire-problémák.
 É. Martonyi, 535(RHL):May-Jun81-462
Ferguson, A.B. Clio Unbound.*
 C.S.L. Davies, 541(RES):Aug81-318
 L.C. Knights, 402(MLR):Jul81-656
Ferguson, J. and others. Greece 478-336
 B.C.
 H.D. Westlake, 303(JoHS):Vol 101-193
Ferguson, M. The Aquarian Conspiracy.
 P. Morgan, 529(QQ):Spring81-169
Ferguson, N. The Gordian Knot.
 M.J. Buscaglia, 399(MLJ):Autumn81-329
Ferguson, T. Desperate Siege.
 W.N., 102(CanL):Summer81-171

Ferguson, T. and J. Rogers, eds. The Hid-
 den Election.
 T.J. Farer, 453(NYRB):21Jan82-40
Ferguson, W. La versificación imitativa
 en Fernando de Herrera.
 A. Bianchini, 304(JHP):Autumn81-79
Ferlinghetti, L. Landscapes of Living and
 Dying.
 D. Street, 584(SWR):Autumn81-419
 648(WCR):Vol 15No3-72
Fermigier, A. - see Renard, J.
Fernández, A.L. - see under Labandeira
 Fernández, A.
Fernández-Armesto, F. The Canary Islands
 After the Conquest.
 G. Scammell, 617(TLS):2Jul82-723
Fernández Conde, F.J. Gutierre de Toledo,
 obispo de Oviedo (1377-1389).
 J. Edwards, 86(BHS):Jul81-257
Fernández de Moratín, L. Teatro completo.
 (M. Fernández Nieto, ed)
 S.M. Scales, 552(REH):May81-316
Fernández-Galiano, E. Léxico de los
 himnos de Calímaco.
 A. Griffiths, 123:Vol31No1-9
Fernández Jiménez, J. Suma de cosmo-
 graphia.
 C. Iranzo, 241:Sep81-95
Fernández Moreno, C., J. Ortega and I.A.
 Shulman, eds. Latin America in Its
 Literature.*
 R.A. Paredes, 651(WHR):Winter81-372
Fernández Nieto, M. - see Fernández de
 Moratín, L.
Fernández Santos, J. Cuentos completos.
 J. Ferrán, 552(REH):Jan81-146
Fernández-Sevilla, J. Problemas de lexico-
 grafía actual.
 P.M. Lloyd, 545(RPh):May81-471
Fernando, E.M.G., ed. Lanka Flags.
 N.D. Wijesekera, 60:Sep-Oct81-146
Fernier, R. La vie et l'oeuvre de Gustave
 Courbet.
 K. Herding, 471:Jul/Aug/Sep81-282
Ferns, C.S. Aldous Huxley: Novelist.
 W.M. Lebans, 49:Oct81-99
Ferrar, H., J.A. Hutchinson and J-D. Biard
 - see "The Concise Oxford French Diction-
 ary"
de Ferraresi, A.C. De amor y poesía en la
 España medieval.
 C.B. Faulhaber, 545(RPh):Feb81(supp)-
 240
Ferrars, E. Skeleton in Search of a Cup-
 board.
 T.J. Binyon, 617(TLS):29Oct82-1196
Ferrars, E. Thinner Than Water.
 T.J. Binyon, 617(TLS):1Jan82-12
Ferraté, J. Lectura de "La Terra Gastada"
 de T.S. Eliot.
 A. Terry, 107(CRCL):Winter81-151
Ferrater Mora, J. Diccionario de Filoso-
 fía. (6th ed)
 J. Bernhardt, 542:Apr-Jun81-239
Ferrater Mora, J. De la materia a la
 razón.
 A. Reix, 542:Jan-Mar81-141
Ferrell, R.H. - see Truman, H.S.
Ferreres, R. - see March, A.
Ferreri, R. Innovazione e tradizione nel
 Boccaccio.
 M. Marti, 228(GSLI):Vol 158fasc504-600

Ferrier, R.W. The History of The British Petroleum Company. (Vol 1)
    E. Penrose, 617(TLS):31Dec82-1451
Ferrini, V. Know Fish.
    A. Golding, 114(ChiR):Autumn80-51
Ferris, P. Richard Burton.*
    J.C. Trewin, 617(TLS):1Jan82-18
Ferris, W. Blues from the Delta.*
    S.J. Bronner, 292(JAF):Apr-Jun81-243
Festa-McCormick, D. Honoré de Balzac.
    G.R. Besser, 446(NCFS):Fall-Winter80/81-135
    M. Kanes, 399(MLJ):Winter81-429
    R. Merker, 207(FR):Apr81-738
Festa-McCormick, D. The City as Catalyst.*
    F.S. Heck, 207(FR):Feb81-461
    H. Wirth-Nesher, 395(MFS):Summer80-385
Fetherling, D. Gold Diggers of 1929.
    G.W., 102(CanL):Summer80-180
Fetterley, J. The Resisting Reader.*
    C. Zwarg, 454:Fall81-76
Feuer, J. The Hollywood Musical.
    G. Kaufman, 362:23and30Dec82-42
Feyerabend, P. Science in a Free Society.*
    J.R. Brown, 154:Mar81-169
Feyerabend, P.K. Philosophical Papers.
    D. Papineau, 617(TLS):29Oct82-1198
Fiamengo, M. North of the Cold Star.
    D. Headon, 102(CanL):Autumn80-115
"The Fiberarts Design Book."
    P. Bach, 614:Spring81-19
Fichte, J.G. Lo Stato commerciale chiuso. (H. Hirsch, ed)
    C.C., 227(GCFI):May-Aug81-267
Fichte, J.O. Chaucer's "Art Poetical."
    A.T. Gaylord, 589:Jul81-608
Fichtner, E.G. English and German Syntax.
    M.M. Bryant, 660(Word):Aug80-230
Fickelson, M. La Vie Intérieure.
    M.G. McCulloch, 617(TLS):9Jul82-750
Fickert, K.J. Kafka's Doubles.
    M.L. Caputo-Mayr, 221(GQ):May81-371
    M. Swales, 402(MLR):Jul81-760
Fickert, K.J. Signs and Portents.
    G.B. Mathieu, 221(GQ):Nov81-529
Fiddian, R. Ignacio Aldecoa.*
    R. Landeira, 238:Mar81-157
Fidjestøl, B. Sólarjóð.
    R. Perkins, 562(Scan):Nov81-219
Fido, F. Guida a Goldoni.
    G. Nuvoli, 228(GSLI):Vol 156fasc495-471
Fido, F. - see Baretti, G.
Fiedler, C. On Judging Works of Visual Art.
    R.L. Wilson, 289:Apr81-110
Fiedler, L. What Was Literature?
    442(NY):29Nov82-174
Fiedler, L.A. and H.A. Baker, Jr., eds. English Literature.
    J. Briggs, 617(TLS):15Oct82-1140
Fiedler, W. Analogiemodelle bei Aristoteles.*
    P. Louis, 555:Vol54fasc2-356
Field, G.L. and J. Higly. Elitism.
    B.S.S., 185:Jan82-400
Field, H.H. Science Without Numbers.*
    R. Farrell, 63:Jun81-235
    M. Friedman, 486:Sep81-505
    J. Largeault, 542:Oct-Dec81-502
Field, J. Place-Names of Breat Britain and Ireland.
    E.C. Smith, 424:Dec80-303

Field, J. Place-Names of Greater London.
    E.C. Smith, 424:Sep80-223
Fiennes, C. The Illustrated Journeys of Celia Fiennes 1685 - c. 1712. (C. Morris, ed)
    P. Earle, 617(TLS):13Aug82-874
Fiest, C.F. Native Arts of North America.
    62:Feb81-71
Fifer, C.N. - see Farquhar, G.
Figes, E. Waking.*
    A. Alvarez, 453(NYRB):13May82-22
    D.M. Thomas, 441:28Feb82-9
de Figueroa y Melgar, A. Estudio histórico sobre algunas familias españolas. (Vol 5)
    S. Stoudemire, 424:Mar81-91
Fika, A.M. The Kano Civil War and British Over-Rule 1881-1940.
    M. Bray, 69:Vol50No3-322
Filby, W.P. and M.K. Meyer, eds. Passenger and Immigration Lists Index. (preliminary vol)
    K.B. Harder, 424:Dec80-293
Filin, F.P. - see "Russkij jazyk"
Filion, J-P. Cap Tourmente.
    D.F. Rogers, 102(CanL):Summer81-148
Filip, J. Celtic Civilization and its Heritage.* (2nd ed)
    B. Ó Cuív, 112:Vol 14-171
Fill, A. Wortdurchsichtigkeit im Englischen.
    J. Vachek, 361:Jun/Jul81-273
Filliozat, J., ed and trans. Yogaśataka.
    K.G. Zysk, 259(IIJ):Oct81-309
Filliozat, P-S. Le Mahābhāṣya de Patañjali avec le Pradīpa de Kaiyaṭa et l'Uddyota de Nāgeśa.
    Yutaka Ojihara, 259(IIJ):Jan81-45
Fillmore, C.J., D. Kempler and W.S-Y. Wang, eds. Individual Differences in Language Ability and Language Behavior.
    J.C. Marshall, 353:Vol 18No3/4-357
"Film Cataloging."
    J.T. Guénette, 14:Spring80-215
Filstrup, C. and J. Beadazzled.
    R.L. Shep, 614:Summer82-12
Finch, M.H.J. A Political Economy of Uruguay Since 1870.
    A. Angell, 617(TLS):26Feb82-225
Finch, R. and E. Joliat - see de Saint-Évremond, C.
Findlay, J.N. Kant and the Transcendental Object.
    S. Körner, 617(TLS):8Jan82-37
Findlay, L.M. - see Swinburne, A.C.
Findley, T. Can You See Me Yet?
    J. Wasserman, 102(CanL):Summer80-104
Findley, T. Famous Last Words.
    P-L. Adams, 61:Aug82-94
    I. Gold, 441:15Aug82-10
    R. Schieder, 99:Feb82-36
    442(NY):9Aug82-94
"Fine Crochet Lace."
    P. Bach, 614:Summer82-12
Fineberg, L. Five Plays by Larry Fineberg.
    K. Garebian, 102(CanL):Summer80-122
Finegold, L. Linguadex: Key-Word Index to Spoken Russian.
    A. Rugaleva, 558(RLJ):Spring-Fall81-266
Fingar, T. and P. Blencoe, eds. China's Quest for Independence.
    P.G. Maddox, 293(JASt):Feb81-343

111

Fingarette, H. and A.F. Hasse. Mental Dis-
abilities and Criminal Responsibility.
R.A. Duff, 518:Jan81-1
Finger, H. Untersuchungen zum "Muspilli."*
C. Minis, 684(ZDA):Band109Heft2-50
J. Splett, 680(ZDP):Band100Heft3-419
Fingleton, J. Batting from Memory.
G. Moorhouse, 364:Nov81-95
Fink, E. Hegel: Phaenomenologische Inter-
pretationen der "Phaenomenologie des
Geistes." (J. Holl, ed)
W. Bonsiepen, 125:Summer81-429
Fink, G. I Testimoni dell'Immaginario.*
R. Asselineau, 189(EA):Apr-Jun81-233
Fink, K.J. and J.W. Marchand, eds. The
Quest for the New Science.
H. Reiss, 133:Band14Heft2-177
Finkel, D. What Manner of Beast.
R. von Hallberg, 659(ConL):Fall82-550
J. Parini, 617(TLS):2Jul82-720
Finkelman, P. An Imperfect Union.
639(VQR):Autumn81-120
Finkielkraut, A. Le Juif imaginaire.
S. Koster, 98:Dec80-1191
Finlay, I. Columba.
W.H.C. Frend, 571(ScLJ):Summer80-80
Finlay, J.L. and D.N. Sprague. The Struc-
ture of Canadian History.
G.W., 102(CanL):Spring80-149
Finlay, R. Population and Metropolis.
V. Pearl, 617(TLS):22Jan82-72
Finley, G. Landscapes of Memory.*
L. Errington, 59:Jun81-232
E. Joll, 90:Apr81-244
G. Reynolds, 39:Jul81-68
A. Welsh, 445(NCF):Dec81-358
Finley, J.H., Jr. Homer's "Odyssey."*
F.M. Combellack, 131(CL):Winter81-87
Finley, M.I. Ancient Sicily.* (2nd ed)
R.J.A. Talbert, 303(JoHS):Vol 101-199
Finley, M.I. Ancient Slavery and Modern
Ideology.*
K.R. Bradley, 487:Winter81-367
P.A. Brunt, 123:Vol31No1-70
J.H. D'Arms, 121(CJ):Apr/May82-366
Finley, M.I. Economy and Society in
Ancient Greece. (B.D. Shaw and R.P.
Saller, eds)
S.C. Humphreys, 617(TLS):2Jul82-721
D.A.N. Jones, 362:7Jan82-24
Finley, M.I., ed. The Legacy of Greece.
J. Appleton, 453(NYRB):4Feb82-38
D.A.N. Jones, 362:7Jan82-24
O. Taplin, 617(TLS):30Apr82-491
Finley, M.I. Le monde d'Ulysse. (new ed)
L. Kahn, 98:Feb80-116
Finnane, M. Insanity and the Insane in
Post-Famine Ireland.
V. Skultans, 617(TLS):12Feb82-171
Finnegan, R., ed. A World Treasury of
Oral Poetry.
J.P. Leary, 292(JAF):Jan-Mar81-92
Finney, B. Christopher Isherwood.*
L. Blanchard, 395(MFS):Summer80-295
J. Hamard, 189(EA):Jan-Mar81-106
Finnigan, J. This Series Has Been Discon-
tinued.
G. Coggins, 628(UWR):Spring-Summer82-
112
Finnis, J.M. Natural Law and Natural
Rights.
J. Langan, 258:Jun81-217
[continued]

[continuing]
S.L. Paulson, 518:Oct81-215
R. Tuck, 479(PhQ):Jul81-282·
Finocchiaro, M.A. History of Science as
Explanation.
C.E. Perrin, 488:Mar81-119
Fiore, F.P. Città e macchine del'400 nei
disegni di Francesco di Giorgio Martini.
R. Betts, 576:Mar81-64
Fiorentino, F. I Gendarmi e la Macchia.
D. Ferri and P. Jeoffroy-Faggianelli,
535(RHL):Mar-Apr81-314
Firbank, R. Five Novels.
J.D. O'Hara, 434:Summer82-603
Firchow, P.E. and E.S., eds and trans.
East German Short Stories.*
P. Herminghouse, 400(MLN):Apr81-680
D.C. Stern, 399(MLJ):Spring81-114
Firmage, G.J. - see Cummings, E.E.
Firmani, A. Il lessico degli Annali di
Quinto Ennio (vv. 1-226) attraverso le
edizioni dal 1564.
H.D. Jocelyn, 123:Vol31No1-115
Firpo, M. Antitrinitari nell'Europa
orientale del '500.
A.J. Schutte, 551(RenQ):Summer80-242
First, R. and A. Scott. Olive Schreiner.*
C.E. Bastian, 637(VS):Summer81-526
U. Edmands, 69:Vol50No4-428
Firth, K.R. The Apocalyptic Tradition in
Reformation Britain, 1530-1645.
D.R. Kelley, 551(RenQ):Summer80-272
J. Wittreich, 568(SCN):Spring81-1
Fischer, B., ed. Novae concordantiae Bib-
lorum Sacrorum iuxta vulgatam versionem.*
P. Meyvaert and S. Lusignan, 589:Jul81-
611
Fischer, F.W. Der Maler Max Beckmann.
P. Selz, 54:Mar81-170
Fischer, G.N. La Formation, quelle utopie!
M.R. Morris, 207(FR):Mar81-634
Fischer, H. Erzählgut der Gegenwart.
R. Schenda, 196:Band21Heft1/2-116
Fischer, J.I. On Swift's Poetry.*
M.E. Lawlis, 301(JEGP):Jan81-138
Fischer, K. Erotik und Askese in Kult und
Kunst der Inder.
G. Gropp, 259(IIJ):Jan81-72
Fischer, M., comp. Kunstbibliothek Berlin:
Katalog der Architektur- und Ornament-
stichsammlung.* (Pt 1)
E. Forssman, 683:Band43Heft1-109
Fischer, M.M.J. Iran.*
W.L. Cleveland, 529(QQ):Summer81-273
Fischer, N. Die Transzendenz in der Trans-
zendentalphilosophie.
W. Steinbeck, 342:Band72Heft1-114
Fischer, S.R. The Dream in the Middle
High German Epic.
J.M. Clifton-Everest, 67:May81-122
Fischer-Galati, S., ed. Eastern Europe in
the 1980s.
A. Pravda, 617(TLS):28May82-578
Fischer-Lichte, E. Bedeutung.*
K.E. Kuhn-Osius, 222(GR):Fall81-165
P. Somville, 542:Jan-Mar81-119
Fischhoff, B. and others. Acceptable Risk.
I. Hacking, 453(NYRB):23Sep82-30
Fish, R.L. Rough Diamond.
G. Wheatcroft, 617(TLS):6Aug82-853
Fish, S. Is There a Text in This Class?*
R.L. Bogue, 141:Spring81-177
[continued]

Flanagan, T. Louis "David" Riel.
  G. Woodcock, 102(CanL):Spring80-116
Flanary, D.A. Champfleury.
  H.O. Borowitz, 446(NCFS):Fall-Winter81/82-172
Flannery, J.W. W.B. Yeats and the Idea of a Theatre.*
  E. Mackenzie, 447(N&Q):Oct80-471
Flannery, M.C. Yeats and Magic.
  P.L. Marcus, 677(YES):Vol 11-344
Flannery, P. and M. Ford. The Adventures of Awful Knawful.
  O. Wymark, 157:Oct80-73
Flasche, H. Geschichte der spanischen Literatur.* (Vol 1)
  H-J. Lope, 224(GRM):Band31Heft3-380
Flasche, H., K-H. Körner and H. Mattauch, eds. Hacia Calderón.
  S. Neumeister, 72:Band217Heft2-473
Flashar, H., ed. Le Classicisme à Rome aux lers siècles avant et après J.-C.
  R. Mayer, 123:Vol31No2-222
Flaubert, G. Bouvard et Pécuchet.*
  (C. Gothot-Mersch, ed)
  C. Mouchard, 98:Feb80-181
Flaubert, G. Correspondance II (1851-1858).* (J. Bruneau, ed)
  B.F. Bart, 446(NCFS):Fall-Winter81/82-146
  R. Bismut, 356(LR):Nov81-362
  R. Bismut, 535(RHL):Jul-Oct81-814
  S. Haig, 207(FR):Feb82-413
Flaubert, G. L'Éducation sentimentale.*
  (A. Raitt, ed)
  P.M. Wetherill, 535(RHL):Jul-Oct81-809
Flaubert, G. The Letters of Gustave Flaubert 1830-1857.* (F. Steegmuller, ed and trans)
  M. Mudrick, 249(HudR):Spring81-126
Flaubert, G. The Letters of Gustave Flaubert 1857-1880. (F. Steegmuller, ed and trans)
  J. Atlas, 441:17Oct82-3
  S. Hampshire, 453(NYRB):16Dec82-26
  V.S. Pritchett, 61:Nov82-167
  442(NY):22Nov82-196
Flaubert, G. Plans, notes et scénarios d'"Un Coeur Simple." (F. Fleury, ed)
  B.F. Bart, 207(FR):Oct80-168
  R. Debray-Genette, 535(RHL):Jul-Oct81-804
Fleck, R.F. Clearing of the Mist.
  B. Baines, 649(WAL):Fall81-250
Fleetwood, H. The Beast.
  G.W. Jarecke, 577(SHR):Spring81-176
Fleetwood, H. A Young Fair God.
  D. Montrose, 617(TLS):12Feb82-169
Flegg, J., ed. A Notebook of Birds 1907-1980.
  R. O'Hanlon, 617(TLS):20Aug82-905
Fleischman, S. Cultural and Linguistic Factors in Word Formation.*
  C. Blaylock, 545(RPh):Aug80-100
Fleishman, A. Fiction and the Ways of Knowing.*
  G. Good, 131(CL):Spring81-204
  D.G. Marshall, 445(NCF):Mar81-563
Fleissner, R.F. Resolved to Love.
  E.W. Taylor, 95(CLAJ):Dec80-233
Flemming, L.A. Another Lonely Voice.
  C. Coppola, 314:Winter-Spring81-219
  M.U. Memon, 293(JASt):May81-627

Flemmons, J. and D. Muench. Texas.
  L. Milazzo, 584(SWR):Spring81-v
Flershem, R.G. and Y.N. Kaga.
  H.J. Jones, 407(MN):Winter81-475
Fletcher, A. The Outbreak of the English Civil War.
  V. Pearl, 617(TLS):18Jun82-670
  K. Sharpe, 453(NYRB):2Dec82-43
Fletcher, B. Don't Blame the Stork.
  K.B. Harder, 424:Jun81-166
Fletcher, P. and M. Garman, eds. Language Acquisition.
  R.A. Berman, 361:Jun/Jul81-256
  N.V. Smith, 350:Jun82-470
Fleuriot, L. Les Origines de la Bretagne.
  J.E. Doan, 589:Oct81-868
  A.G. Suozzo, Jr., 207(FR):Dec81-290
Fleury, F. - see Flaubert, G.
Fleutiaux, P. La Forteresse.
  H. Le Mansec, 207(FR):Feb81-505
Flew, A., ed. A Dictionary of Philosophy.
  A.C. Purton, 518:Jan81-25
  D.D. Todd, 154:Sep81-625
Flew, A. The Politics of Procrustes.
  J.P.S., 185:Jul82-801
Flexner, J.T. America's Old Masters. (rev)
  J.V. Turano, 16:Winter81-92
Fliegelman, J. Prodigals and Pilgrims.
  R.A. Ferguson, 617(TLS):22Oct82-1169
Flint, A., ed. Insights.
  E. Hamp-Lyons, 608:Jun82-253
  A. Silverman, 399(MLJ):Winter81-422
Flint, J.E., ed. The Cambridge History of Africa. (Vol 5)
  D.D. Cordell, 69:Vol150No1-96
Flippo, C. Your Cheatin' Heart.
  M. Colyer, 362:19Aug82-22
Floeck, W. Die Literarästhetik des französischen Barock.*
  A. Buck, 490:Band12Heft2-264
  M. Israel, 535(RHL):Jul-Oct81-759
  P.J. Yarrow, 402(MLR):Oct81-961
Florenne, Y., ed. Lettres de la Religieuse portugaise.
  W. Leiner, 475:No3Pt1-146
Florenne, Y. Ouvertures.
  P-L. Rey, 450(NRF):Jun81-128
Flores, A., ed. Orígenes del cuento hispanoamericano.
  D. Rhoades, 238:May81-322
Flores, E. Latinità arcaica e produzione linguistica.
  P. Flobert, 555:Vol154fasc1-177
Flory, S. A Winter's Journey.
  P. Schjeldahl, 472:Spring/Summer81-284
Flory, W.S. Ezra Pound and "The Cantos."*
  C. Emery, 468:Fall81-445
  C. Sanders, 301(JEGP):Apr81-280
  P. Smith, 150(DR):Summer81-356
  S. West, 49:Apr81-95
Flower, D. - see de Voltaire, F.M.A.
Floyd, V. - see O'Neill, E.
Flynn, J.R. Race, IQ, and Jensen.*
  J.L.H., 185:Apr82-587
Flynn, T. A Strange Routine.*
  J. Cassidy, 493:Sep81-81
  C. Hope, 364:Apr/May81-120
Flynt, J.W. Dixie's Forgotten People.
  J.M. Richardson, 9(AlaR):Apr81-146
Fo, D. and F. Rame. Female Parts.
  D. Devlin, 157:Winter81-51

Foa, S.M. Feminismo y forma narrativa.
H.D. Smith, 86(BHS):Apr81-143
Fodor, J.A. Representations.
C. McGinn, 617(TLS)29Jan82-115
Foerst, G. Die Gravierungen der pränestinischen Cisten.
R. Adam, 555:Vol54fasc1-200
Fog, D. Dansk Musikfortegnelse, I. Kompositionen von C.E.F. Weyse.
J.H., 412:May80-156
Fogarty, R.S. Dictionary of American Communal and Utopian History.
K.M. Roemer, 26(ALR):Spring81-122
Fogarty, R.S. The Righteous Remnant.
M. Bayles, 441:31Jan82-12
B. Wilson, 617(TLS):5Nov82-1223
Fogel, D.M. Henry James and the Structure of the Romantic Imagination.
S. Weintraub, 617(TLS):18Jun82-678
Fokkelman, J. Oog in oog met Jakob.
M. Bal, 204(FdL):Jun81-225
Fokkema, D.W. and E. Kunne-Ibsch. Theories of Literature in the Twentieth Century.
H. Jechova, 549(RLC):Apr-Jun81-258
Foladare, J. Boswell's Paoli.*
D. Crane, 179(ES):Aug81-387
Folb, E.A. Runnin' Down Some Lines.
J. Baugh, 350:Jun81-475
J. Baugh, 355(LSoc):Dec81-461
Folda, J. Crusader Manuscript Illumination at Saint-Jean d'Acre — 1275-1291.
H. Stahl, 683:Band43Heft4-416
Folejewski, Z. Futurism and Its Place in the Development of Modern Poetry.
A.M. Lawton, 574(SEEJ):Fall81-124
Foley, J.A. Theoretical Morphology of the French Verb.*
D.C. Walker, 361:Feb-Mar81-291
Foley, M. The Go Situation.
W. Scammell, 617(TLS):30Jul82-830
Foley, M. The Story of "Story" Magazine. (J. Neugeboren, ed)
T.A. Gullason, 573(SSF):Winter81-97
B. Targan, 569(SR):Winter81-xxv
L. Wertenbaker, 219(GaR):Spring81-200
W.E. Wilson, 27(AL):Mar81-151
Foley, M.M. The American House.
M. Filler, 576:Oct81-254
Folkenflik, R. Samuel Johnson, Biographer.*
W.C. Dowling, 677(YES):Vol 11-283
Folkenflik, R. - see Swift, J.
Follet, L. Lionel Follet lit Aragon.
S. Ravis-Françon, 535(RHL):Jul-Oct81-843
Follet, S. Athènes au IIe et au IIIe siècle.
J.S. Traill, 487:Spring81-85
Follett, K. The Man from St. Petersburg.
T.J. Binyon, 617(TLS):4Jun82-622
S. Ellin, 441:9May82-12
442(NY):16Aug82-93
Fónagy, I. La métaphore en phonétique.
H. Birnbaum, 350:Dec82-899
Fónagy, I. and P.R. Léon, eds. L'accent en français contemporain.
G.B., 189(EA):Oct-Dec81-497
Fonda, C. Svevo e Freud.*
B. Weiss, 276:Winter81-327

Fondane, B. Rimbaud le voyou.* Faux traité d'esthétique.* La conscience malheureuse.* Le mal des fantômes. (M. Carrascou and C. Tieck, eds of all)
S. Koster, 98:Aug-Sep81-869
Fone, B.R.S., ed. Hidden Heritage.
K.J. Dover, 123:Vol31No2-326
Foner, E. Politics and Ideology in the Age of the Civil War.
W.R. Brock, 617(TLS):14May82-537
P.D. Escott, 579(SAQ):Autumn81-492
Fong, W., ed. The Great Bronze Age of China.*
R. Kerr, 463:Autumn81-324
A.C. Soper, 57:Vol142No2/3-223
Fontaine, J. - see Ammianus Marcellinus
Fontane, T. Theodor Fontane: Short Novels and other Writings. (P. Demetz, ed)
G. Annan, 453(NYRB):7Oct82-26
Fontane, T. Le Stechlin.
J-M. le Sidaner, 450(NRF):Dec81-129
de Fontenay, E. Diderot.
442(NY):8Nov82-171
de Fontenay, É. Diderot ou le matérialisme enchanté.
A. Clerval, 450(NRF):Oct81-149
Fontenilles, A. and M. Heimerdinger. La Vie des affaires.
J.S. Dugan, 207(FR):Feb82-446
Fontenrose, J. The Delphic Oracle.*
J. Pollard, 303(JoHS):Vol 101-182
Fontes, M.D. Romanceiro Português do Canadá.
J.G. Cummins, 86(BHS):Apr81-136
J.B. Purcell, 650(WF):Apr81-192
C. Slater, 240(HR):Autumn81-519
Foon, D. Heracles. The Windigo. Raft Baby.
P. Nodelman, 102(CanL):Summer80-109
Foot, M.M. A Collection of Bookbindings: The Henry Davis Gift.* (Vol 1)
R. Nikirk, 517(PBSA):Oct-Dec81-498
Foot, P. Red Shelley.*
P.M.S. Dawson, 148:Winter81-77
Forbes, B. That Despicable Race.
M. Norgate, 157:2ndQtr81-54
Forbes, J. Stalin's Holiday.
F. Adcock, 617(TLS):29Jan82-114
Forbes, P. The Aerial Noctiluca.
R. Garfitt, 617(TLS):2Apr82-392
Forcadel, É. Oeuvres poétiques. (F. Joukovsky, ed)
L. Terreaux, 535(RHL):Jan-Feb81-124
Forché, C. The Country Between Us.
J. Gleason, 472:Spring/Summer82-9
J.C. Oates, 441:4Apr82-13
Ford, C. Histoire du cinéma français contemporain, 1945-1977.
A. Thiher, 207(FR):Apr82-698
Ford, C. Tall Trees.
R. Willmot, 102(CanL):Autumn80-138
Ford, D. The Cult of the Atom.
E. Zuckerman, 441:31Oct82-9
Ford, D.F. Three Mile Island.
F. Randall, 441:11Apr82-14
Ford, E. The Playhouse.
G. Johnson, 461:Spring-Summer81-92
Ford, F.M. The Rash Act.
R. Green, 362:12Aug82-23
Ford, G.H., ed. Victorian Fiction: A Second Guide to Research.*
M. Harris, 72:Band217Heft2-432
S. Monod, 677(YES):Vol 11-310

Ford, J. The Broken Heart.
    J.C. Trewin, 157:2ndQtr81-53
Ford, J. and J. Images of Brighton.
    C. Fox, 617(TLS):19Mar82-302
Ford, R. The Ultimate Good Luck.*
    G. Perez, 249(HudR):Winter81/82-620
Ford, R.A.D. Holes In Space.*
    P. Stevens, 102(CanL):Spring81-155
Fordyce, C.J. - see Vergil
"Foreign Versions of English Names, and
    Foreign Equivalents of United States
    Military and Civilian Titles."
    K.B. Harder, 424:Dec80-293
Forell, G.W. History of Christian Ethics.
    (Vol 1)
    J. Stout, 185:Jan81-328
Foreman, L., ed. The Percy Grainger Com-
    panion.
    P. O'Connor, 617(TLS):9Apr82-418
Foreman, W.C., Jr. The Music of the
    Close.*
    N. Cotton, 551(RenQ):Spring80-134
    G. Taylor, 541(RES):Feb81-76
Förg, A., ed. Schiess-Scheiben.
    W. Harms, 196:Band22Heft1/2-124
Forge, A. Traditional Balinese Paintings.
    J.S. Lansing, 293(JASt):Aug81-849
Forgue, G.J. Les Mots américains.*
    R.A. Hall, Jr., 35(AS):Spring-Summer77-
    150
Forgue, G.J., with R.I. McDavid, Jr. La
    Langue des Américains.
    R.A. Hall, Jr., 35(AS):Spring-Summer77-
    150
Forkner, B., ed. Modern Irish Short
    Stories, 1980.*
    P. Drewniany, 305(JIL):May81-133
    J.A. Glusman, 174(Éire):Winter81-147
"Forms of Prayer: Daily, Sabbath and
    Occasional Prayers." (7th ed)
    A.H. Podet, 390:Oct81-62
Forrest, A. The Pandora Secret.
    S. Altinel, 617(TLS):17Dec82-1398
Forrester, J. Language and the Origins of
    Psychoanalysis.*
    S.M. Albert, 114(ChiR):Spring81-75
Forschner, M. Rousseau.
    M. Neumann, 319:Apr81-258
Forsdale, L. Perspectives on Communica-
    tion.
    J.R. Edwards, 583:Fall81-96
Forssman, E. The Palazzo da Porto Festa
    in Vicenza.
    D. Howard, 90:Feb81-108
Forssman, E. and others. Palladio: la sua
    eredità nel mondo.
    C. Elam, 59:Sep81-350
Förster, E. Romanstruktur und Weltanschau-
    ung im Werk L-F. Célines.*
    L. Davis, 208(FS):Jan81-96
Forster, E.M. Alexandria.
    A. Hollinghurst, 617(TLS):16Apr82-429
Forster, E.M. Arctic Summer and Other
    Fiction.* (E. Heine and O. Stallybrass,
    eds)
    A. Dickins, 364:Jul81-94
Forster, E.M. The Manuscripts of "A Pas-
    sage to India."* (O. Stallybrass, ed)
    S. Arkin, 395(MFS):Summer80-285
    J. Colmer, 402(MLR):Apr81-452
    D. Kramer, 301(JEGP):Oct81-597

Forster, E.M. A Passage to India.* (O.
    Stallybrass, ed)
    J. Colmer, 402(MLR):Apr81-452
    D. Kramer, 301(JEGP):Oct81-597
Forster, K. A Pronouncing Dictionary of
    English Place-Names.*
    K.B. Harder, 424:Dec80-297
Forster, L. The Icy Fire.
    A. Scaglione, 545(RPh):Feb81-352
Forster, L. Kleine Schriften zur deut-
    schen Literatur im 17. Jahrhundert.*
    D. Gutzen, 52:Band15Heft1-80
Forsyte, C. The Decoding of Edwin Drood.*
    K.M. Longley, 155:Summer81-102
Forsyth, F. No Comebacks.
    M. Watkins, 441:9May82-14
Forsyth, P.Y. Atlantis.
    J.E. Rexine, 124:Sep-Oct81-55
Fort, B. Le Langage de l'ambiguïté dans
    l'oeuvre de Crébillon fils.*
    M.B. Lacy, 207(FR):Mar81-595
    G.E. Rodmell, 208(FS):Oct81-449
Fortescue, M.D. A Discourse Production
    Model for "Twenty Questions."
    J.H. McDowell, 355(LSoc):Dec81-453
    J. Mey, 350:Dec82-930
Fortier, A. Le Texte et la scène.
    J.M. Weiss, 102(CanL):Spring81-119
Fortin, E.L. Dissidence et philosophie au
    Moyen Age.
    A. Reix, 542:Jul-Sep81-341
Fortoul, H. Journal d'Hippolyte Fortoul.
    (Vol 1) (G. Massa-Gille, ed)
    W.V. Gugli, 446(NCFS):Fall-Winter81/82-
    185
Fortuna, J.L., Jr. "The Unsearchable Wis-
    dom of God."
    P. Sabor, 566:Autumn81-47
Foscolo, U. Lèttera apologetica. (G.
    Nicoletti, ed)
    M. Chiesa, 228(GSLI):Vol 158fasc502-
    301
Foscolo, U. Scritti vari di critica
    storica e letteraria (1817-1827).* (U.
    Limentani, with J.M. Lindon, eds)
    G. Barbarisi, 228(GSLI):Vol 158fasc501-
    125
Foscolo, U. Studi su Dante. (Pt 1) (G.
    da Pozzo, ed)
    M. Chiesa, 228(GSLI):Vol 158fasc503-
    454
Foscue, V.O. The Place Names of Sumter
    County, Alabama.*
    P. Munro, 350:Jun81-510
Foss, D.C. The Value Controversy in Soci-
    ology.
    E.S. Lyon, 488:Dec81-521
Foss, D.J. and D.T. Hakes. Psycholinguis-
    tics.*
    A. Chandrasekhar, 261:Sep79-206
Fossaert, R. La Société. (Vols 1-4)
    C. Gruson, 98:Apr81-397
Foster, D.W. Studies in the Contemporary
    Spanish-American Short Story.*
    M.E. Beeson, 552(REH):Oct81-474
Foster, F. Witnessing Slavery.
    J. Mazzaro, 560:Spring-Summer81-188
Foster, J. The Case for Idealism.
    D.M. Armstrong, 617(TLS):22Oct82-1170
Foster, J.B. Heirs to Dionysus.
    D. Trotter, 617(TLS):18Jun82-672

Foster, K. and P. Boyde, eds. Cambridge
Readings in Dante's Comedy.
  D. Robey, 617(TLS):30Apr82-489
Foster, K. and M.J. Ronayne - see St. Cath-
erine of Siena
Foster, K.P. Aegean Faience of the Bronze
Age.
  S. Hood, 123:Vol31No2-258
Foster, M.K. From the Earth to Beyond the
Sky.
  K.T. Loesch, 269(IJAL):Apr81-178
Foster, P. The Blue-Eyed Sheiks.
  N. Ward, 529(QQ):Autumn81-551
Foster, P.E. A Study of Lorenzo de'
Medici's Villa at Poggio a Caiano.*
  E.B. MacDougall, 551(RenQ):Summer80-
  260
Foster, R. Across the White Lawn.
  D. Barbour, 648(WCR):Jun80-76
  J. Giltrow, 102(CanL):Spring81-145
Foster, S.C. and R.E. Kuenzli, eds. Dada
Spectrum.*
  J. Koppensteiner, 221(GQ):May81-383
  G. Mead, 207(FR):Feb81-475
  M. Perloff, 402(MLR):Jan81-152
Foster, V. Bags and Purses.
  R.L. Shep, 614:Summer82-14
Foster, V.R. Baltasar Gracián.
  S.A. Stoudemire, 241:Jan81-74
Fothergill-Payne, L. La alegoría en los
autos y farsas anteriores a Calderón.
  C. Stern, 545(RPh):Nov80-273
Fougeyrollas, P. Savoirs et idéologie
dans les sciences sociales.
  J-M. Gabaude, 542:Oct-Dec81-478
Foulet, A. and M.B. Speer. On Editing Old
French Texts.*
  M.W. Epro, 207(FR):Dec81-261
Foulkes, D. A Grammar of Dreams.
  F. Peraldi, 567:Vol34No3/4-343
Fountaine, M. Love among the Butterflies.*
  (W.F. Cater, ed)
  E. Claridge, 364:Jul81-60
Fournier, M-A. 35000 Prénoms d'hier et
d'aujourd'hui.
  D.C. Cooper, 424:Mar80-84
Fourrier, A. - see Froissart, J.
Fowler, A. From the Domain of Arnheim.
  I. Crichton Smith, 617(TLS):19Nov82-
  1282
Fowler, C. A Knot in the Thread.
  L-F. Hoffmann, 535(RHL):Jul-Oct81-850
Fowler, J.W. Stages of Faith.
  M.G.H., 185:Jul82-785
Fowles, J. The Magus: A Revised Version.
  M. Boccia, 295(JML):Vol18No2-235
  R.L. Nadeau, 295(JML):Vol18No2-261
Fowles, J. Mantissa.
  P-L. Adams, 61:Nov82-170
  B. De Mott, 441:29Aug82-3
  P. Kemp, 617(TLS):8Oct82-1091
  M. Richler, 453(NYRB):18Nov82-28
  442(NY):13Sep82-171
Fowles, J. and R. Legg - see Aubrey, J.
Fox, B. Hidden in the Household.
  A. Miles, 99:Nov81-36
Fox, F. Great Ships.
  D.C., 90:Jun81-386
Fox, G. In Search of Living Things.
  G.A. Boire, 102(CanL):Summer81-168
  P. Stevens, 529(QQ):Autumn81-504

Fox, J. White Mischief.
  D. Pryce-Jones, 617(TLS):19Nov82-1261
  E.S. Turner, 362:9Dec82-22
Fox, J.P. Germany and the Far Eastern
Crisis 1931-1938.
  P. Kennedy, 617(TLS):5Nov82-1212
Fox, M.J. and K.A. McDonough. Wisconsin
Municipal Records Manual.
  J.L. Mims, 14:Summer81-243
Fox, N. Pueblo Weaving and Textile Arts.
  P. Bach, 614:Spring81-21
Fox, R. and G. Weisz, eds. The Organiza-
tion of Science and Technology in France
1808-1914.
  W.R. Paulson, 446(NCFS):Spring-Sum-
  mer82-387
Fox, R.L. - see under Lane Fox, R.
Fox-Lockert, L. Women Novelists in Spain
and Spanish America.*
  C.M. Tatum, 238:May81-318
"Foxfire 6." (E. Wigginton, ed)
  C. Oblinger, 14:Summer81-245
"Fra barn til kvinne."
  M. Winge, 172(Edda):1981/2-123
van Fraassen, B.C. The Scientific Image.*
  Y. Gauthier, 154:Sep81-579
  S.W., 185:Apr82-606
Fraisse, G. Femmes toutes mains.
  A. Corbin, 98:Jun-Jul80-595
Fraisse, J-C. L'oeuvre de Spinoza.
  J-L. Poirier, 542:Jul-Sep81-357
Fraisse, S. Péguy.
  F. Gerbod, 535(RHL):Mar-Apr81-319
Fraisse, S. Péguy et le Moyen Age.*
  R. Burac, 535(RHL):Jan-Feb81-154
  N. Wilson, 208(FS):Jan81-92
Fraisse, S. Renan au pied de l'Acropole.
  L. Rétat, 535(RHL):May-Jun81-475
Frame, D. The Myth of Return in Early
Greek Epic.*
  F.M. Combellack, 122:Jul81-225
Frame, J. To the Is-land.
  H. Bevington, 441:21Nov82-14
Frame, R. English Lordship in Ireland
1318-1361.
  J.R. Maddicott, 617(TLS):25Jun82-698
Frampton, K. Modern Architecture.
  R.L. Castro, 529(QQ):Autumn81-547
  W. Curtis, 576:May81-168
  D. Dunster, 505:Jun81-65
France, A. Croquis féminins; Mendès, C.
  Figurines des poètes; Racot, A. Por-
  traits-cartes. (M. Pakenham, ed)
  C. Becker, 535(RHL):Nov-Dec81-1018
"France."
  S. Smith, 207(FR):Feb82-454
"Le France et les Français; Vus par Piem
et F. Tomiche."
  J-F. Brière, 207(FR):Oct80-210
Franchini, A. Il Rendenglese.
  R.A. Hall, Jr., 350:Dec82-946
Francis, A. Picaresca, decandencia,
historia.*
  C. Stern, 545(RPh):Feb81-303
Francis, C. and F. Gontier. Les Écrits de
Simone de Beauvoir.*
  É. Marks, 535(RHL):Jul-Oct81-841
  T. Pagès, 188(ECr):Winter81-115
  S. Reynolds, 402(MLR):Jan81-206
Francis, D. Banker.
  T.J. Binyon, 617(TLS):10Dec82-1378

Francis, D. Twice Shy.*
    P-L. Adams, 61:Jul82-96
    T.J. Binyon, 617(TLS):1Jan82-12
    S. Ellin, 441:25Apr82-13
    442(NY):17May82-141
Francis, H.E. Naming Things.*
    C. Stetler, 573(SSF):Fall81-475
Francis, M. Forme et signification de
    l'attente dans l'oeuvre romanesque de
    Julien Gracq.
    J. Roach, 208(FS):Jan81-99
Francisco, R.A., B.A. Laird and R.D. Laird,
    eds. The Political Economy of Collectiv-
    ized Agriculture.
    A. Brzeski, 550(RusR):Jan81-79
    G. Kolankiewicz, 575(SEER):Jan81-147
Franck, F. - see Blyth, R.H.
de Franclieu, F. - see "Le Corbusier
    Sketchbooks"
François, C. Raison et déraison dans le
    théâtre de Pierre Corneille.
    H.B. McDermott, 207(FR):Feb81-465
Francos, A. Il était des femmes dans la
    Résistance.
    I. de Courtivron, 207(FR):Mar81-631
Francovich, G. Los mitos profundos de
    Bolivia.
    H.E. Davis, 263(RIB):Vol31No2-275
von Frank, A.A. Family Policy in the USSR
    Since 1944.
    B. Madison, 550(RusR):Apr81-214
Frank, B. Solde.
    A. Clerval, 450(NRF):Mar81-124
Frank, E.E. Literary Architecture.*
    E. Block, Jr., 651(WHR):Spring81-72
    A. Whittick, 89(BJA):Spring81-176
Frank, M., F.A. Kittler and S. Weber - see
    "Fugen: Deutsch-Französisches Jahrbuch
    für Text-Analytik"
Frank, R.M. Beings and Their Attributes.
    D. Gimaret, 318(JAOS):Apr/Jun80-131
Frank, V., comp. Bibliographie des
    oeuvres de Simon Frank.
    L.B. Schapiro, 575(SEER):Jul81-422
Franke, H-P. Der Pest-"Brief an die Frau
    von Plauen."
    B.D. Haage, 680(ZDP):Band100Heft3-441
Frankel, E.R. Novy Mir.
    G. Hosking, 617(TLS):2Apr82-367
Frankel, J. Prophecy and Politics.
    I. Howe, 453(NYRB):15Jul82-31
    B. Wasserstein, 617(TLS):21May82-550
Frankenthaler, M. José Revueltas.*
    S.L. Slick, 238:Sep81-485
Franklin, B. The Autobiography of Benja-
    min Franklin, a Genetic Text. (J.A.L.
    Lemay and P.M. Zall, eds)
    M.H. Buxbaum, 165(EAL):Spring82-75
Franklin, J. The Gentleman's Country
    House and its Plan 1835-1914.*
    J. Brandon-Jones, 324:Feb82-166
    P. Davey, 46:Mar81-191
    N. Powell, 39:Apr81-267
Franklin, J.C. Mystical Transformations.
    H. Popper, 406:Spring81-108
Franklin, J.H. John Locke and the Theory
    of Sovereignty.
    G. Parry, 185:Jan82-358
Franklin, P.R. - see Bauer-Lechner, N.
Franklin, R.W. - see Dickinson, E.

Franklin, U. The Rhetoric of Valéry's
    Prose "Aubades."*
    R. Geen, 399(MLJ):Spring81-89
    P. Gifford, 402(MLR):Jul81-709
    L. Vines, 207(FR):Mar81-601
    205(FMLS):Apr80-188
Franklin, W. Discoverers, Explorers,
    Settlers.*
    R.C. Davis, 106:Winter81-301
    J.R. Leo, 141:Winter81-93
    L.C. Mitchell, 301(JEGP):Apr81-267
    W.N., 102(CanL):Spring81-174
    C.L. Sanford, 656(WMQ):Jul81-509
Franko, I. The Master's Jests (Pans'ki
    žarty).
    D.B. Chopyk, 574(SEEJ):Spring81-121
Franks, A. Boychester's Bugle.
    J. Mellors, 362:8Jul82-23
    J.K.L. Walker, 617(TLS):18Jun82-677
Franks, K.A., P.F. Lambert and C.N. Tyson.
    Early Oklahoma Oil.
    L. Milazzo, 584(SWR):Summer81-v
Franolić, B. A Short History of Literary
    Coratian.
    C. Spalatin, 350:Jun81-504
Franzke, A. Dubuffet.*
    J. Russell, 441:28Mar82-12
Frappier, J. and R.R. Grimm, eds. Grund-
    riss der romanischen Literaturen des
    Mittelalters. (Vol 4, Pt 1)
    N.J. Lacy, 589:Jan81-132
Fraser, A. Cool Repentance.
    T.J. Binyon, 617(TLS):2Jul82-725
Fraser, A. Royal Charles.* (British
    title: King Charles II.)
    M. Brownley, 77:Winter81-90
Fraser, D. Alanbrooke.
    M. Carver, 617(TLS):7May82-504
    R. Trevelyan, 362:22Apr82-20
Fraser, G.M. Flashman and the Redskins.
    P-L. Adams, 61:Sep82-96
    E.S. Turner, 617(TLS):16Jul82-775
    442(NY):13Sep82-172
Fraser, G.S. Alexander Pope.
    W.B. Carnochan, 677(YES):Vol 11-275
    D.E. Richardson, 569(SR):Fall81-638
Fraser, J. The Chinese.* (French title:
    Les nouveaux Chinois.)
    V. Alleton, 98:Aug-Sep81-762
    D.E. Waterfall, 529(QQ):Summer81-279
Fraser, J.F. Round the World on a Wheel.
    D. Murphy, 617(TLS):21May82-560
Fraser, K. The Fashionable Mind.*
    A. Hollander, 453(NYRB):15Apr82-38
Fraser, M.C. A Diplomat's Wife in Japan.
    (H. Cortazzi, ed)
    H. Cooke, 441:30Oct82-14
    442(NY):25Oct82-172
Fraser, O. The Pure Account. (H.M. Shire,
    ed)
    A. Bold, 617(TLS):7May82-515
Fraser, P.M. Rhodian Funerary Monuments.
    E.M. Craik, 303(JoHS):Vol 101-227
    E.G. Pemberton, 54:Mar81-139
Fraser, R. A Mingled Yarn.*
    D. Donoghue, 617(TLS):22Oct82-1147
    442(NY):18Jan82-129
Fraser, R. The Novels of Ayi Kwei Armah.
    P. Sabor, 49:Jul81-113
Fraser, S. A Casual Affair.
    L. Gottlieb, 296(JCF):No31/32-261

Frassica, P. and A. Carrara. Per modo di
dire.
   J. Siracusa, 399(MLJ):Winter81-438
Frayling, C. Spaghetti Westerns.*
   18:May81-75
Frayne, J.P. and C. Johnson - see Yeats,
W.B.
Frede, H.J., ed. Vetus Latina. (Pt 7)
   P. Courcelle, 555:Vol54fasc2-380
Fredrickson, N.J. and S. Gibb. The Cove-
nant Chain.
   K.E. Kidd, 298:Fall-Winter81-222
   J. Murray, 529(QQ):Summer81-353
Fredrickson, R.S. Hjalmar Hjorth Boyesen.
   C.A. Glasrud, 26(ALR):Spring81-149
Free, L.R., ed. Laclos — Critical Ap-
proaches to "Les Liaisons dangereuses."*
   S. Harvey, 208(FS):Jul81-343
Freed, A.F. The Semantics of English
Aspectual Complementation.
   K. Allan, 350:Jun81-497
Freed, L. T.S. Eliot.*
   295(JML):Vol8No3/4-486
Freedberg, D. Dutch Landscape Prints.
   D. Alexander, 135:Feb81-168
   K. Andrews, 39:Jun81-416
Freedland, M. Maurice Chevalier.
   G. Kaufman, 362:25Mar82-24
Freedle, R.O., ed. New Directions in
Discourse Processing.*
   T.A. van Dijk, 297(JL):Mar81-140
Freedman, D.G. Human Sociobiology.
   R.L. Simon, 185:Jan82-327
Freedman, L. The Evolution of Nuclear
Strategy.
   M. Howard, 617(TLS):16Apr82-427
Freedman, M. The Study of Chinese Soci-
ety. (G.W. Skinner, ed)
   B. Gallin, 293(JASt):Feb81-345
Freedman, R. Hermann Hesse.
   E. Webb, 648(WCR):Jun80-60
Freedman, R., ed. Virginia Woolf.*
   M. Magalaner, 395(MFS):Winter80/81-684
   D. Watt, 301(JEGP):Jul81-449
Freedman, W. Laurence Sterne and the
Origins of the Musical Novel.*
   N.C. Carpenter, 107(CRCL):Winter81-127
   R. Folkenflik, 301(JEGP):Jan81-142
   S. Soupel, 189(EA):Jul-Sep81-345
Freehling, W.W. - see Rose, W.L.
Freeling, N. Castang's City.
   639(VQR):Winter81-20
Freeling, N. Wolfnight.
   M. Laski, 362:29Jul82-27
Freeman, A. Elizabeth's Misfits.
   D.C. Kay, 447(N&Q):Oct80-428
Freeman, J.A. Milton and the Martial
Muse.*
   W.E. Cain, 400(MLN):Dec81-1121
   G.M. Crump, 569(SR):Fall81-628
   S.P. Revard, 141:Fall81-359
Freeman, L.J. Nuclear Witnesses.
   J.N. Wilford, 441:31Jan82-6
Freeman, M. Edmund Burke and the Critique
of Political Radicalism.
   P.J. Stanlis, 396(ModA):Summer81-301
Freeman, M.A. The Poetics of "translatio
studii" and "conjointure."*
   T. Hunt, 402(MLR):Jan81-181
   205(FMLS):Apr80-188
Freeman, M.J. - see de Larivey, P.

Freeman, R.B. British Natural History
Books, 1495-1900.*
   354:Dec81-361
Freer, C. The Poetics of Jacobean Drama.
   A. Mackie, 617(TLS):17Dec82-1402
Freese, P., H. Groene and L. Hermes, eds.
Die Short Story im Englischunterricht
der Sekundarstufe II.
   S.L. Tiefenthaler, 602:Vol 12No1-288
Freeze, R.A., ed. A Fragment of an Early
K'ekchi' Vocabulary with Comments on
the Cultural Content.
   S.O. Stewart, 269(IJAL):Oct81-358
Frege, G. On the Foundations of Geometry
and Formal Theories of Arithmetic.
(E-H.W. Kluge, ed and trans)
   H. Jackson, 316:Mar81-175
Frege, G. Philosophical and Mathematical
Correspondence. (H. Kaal, trans)
   D. Bell, 518:Apr81-117
Frege, G. Posthumous Writings. (H.
Hermes, K. Kambartel and F. Kaulbach,
eds)
   D. Bell, 518:Apr81-117
   G. Currie, 84:Jun81-197
   S. Rosen, 480(P&R):Summer81-196
   R.H. Stoothoff, 63:Jun81-217
Frege, G. Translations from the Philosoph-
ical Writings of Gottlob Frege. (3rd ed)
(P. Geach and M. Black, eds)
   C. Parsons, 316:Dec81-870
Frei, N. Theodor Fontane.
   A.F. Bance, 402(MLR):Oct81-998
Freijeiro, A.B. - see under Blanco Frei-
jeiro, A.
von Freimar, H. - see under Heinrich von
Freimar
Freire, P. Pedagogy in Process.
   C.S. Taylor, 142:Summer80-217
Fremlin, C. The Parasite Person.
   M. Laski, 362:29Jul82-27
Frémont, D. Les Français dans l'Ouest
Canadien.
   S. Knutson, 102(CanL):Autumn81-164
Frénaud, A. Notre inhabileté fatale.*
   C.A. Hackett, 208(FS):Apr81-231
French, D. British Economic and Strategic
Planning 1905-1915.
   K. Jeffery, 617(TLS):9Apr82-402
French, M. The Book as World.
   U. Schneider, 38:Band99Heft3/4-529
French, M. Shakespeare's Division of
Experience.*
   L. Lerner, 617(TLS):4Jun82-619
French, P., ed. Three Honest Men.
   R.G. Cox, 569(SR):Winter81-118
   J. Oakley, 506(PSt):Sep81-227
French, P.A. The Scope of Morality.
   K. Lennon, 393(Mind):Oct81-622
French, P.A. and others, eds. Midwest
Studies in Philosophy. (Vol 4)
   M. Dentscher, 63:Jun81-222
French, P.A., T.E. Uehling, Jr. and H.K.
Wettstein, eds. Contemporary Perspec-
tives in the Philosophy of Language.
   M. Devitt, 63:Jun81-211
French, R.K. The History and Virtues of
Cyder.
   P.J. Kavanagh, 617(TLS):12Mar82-287
French, S.G., ed. Philosophers Look at
Canadian Confederation.*
   A.W.J. Harper, 488:Mar81-97

119

Frenkin, M. Russkaia armiia i revoliut-
siia, 1917-1918.
P. Kenez, 550(RusR):Apr81-195
Frenzel, E. Motive der Weltliteratur.
H. Lixfeld, 196:Band21Heft1/2-118
Freud, A. Psychoanalytic Psychology of
Normal Development.
D. Ingleby, 617(TLS):9Apr82-401
Freudenstein, R., ed. Teaching Foreign
Languages to the Very Young.
R. Masciantonio, 399(MLJ):Summer81-204
Freudmann, F.R. - see Desmarests de Saint-
Sorlin, J.
Freund, J. La fin de la Renaissance.
A. Reix, 542:Apr-Jun81-240
Freundlieb, D. Zur Wissenschaftstheorie
der Literaturwissenschaft.
D. Firmenich, 679:Band11Heft2-385
Frey, D.L. The First Tetralogy.*
H-J. Müllenbrock, 38:Band99Heft3/4-514
Frey, H.H. Therobiblia. (H. Reinitzer,
ed)
C. Gerhardt, 224(GRM):Band30Heft2-227
P.W. Tax, 589:Jan81-134
Frey, H-J. and O. Lorenz. Kritik des
Freien Verses.
B. Bjorklund, 221(GQ):May81-391
Frey, J.A. The Aesthetics of the Rougon-
Macquart.
F.E. Humphreys 3d, 207(FR):Feb81-473
L. Kamm, 395(MFS):Summer80-357
Frey, R.G. Interests and Rights.
M. Midgley, 479(PhQ):Oct81-379
B. Steinbock, 518:Oct81-217
C.W., 185:Jul81-692
Frey, W. and others. Einführung in die
deutsche Literatur des 12. bis 16.
Jahrhunderts. (Vol 1)
W. Breuer, 680(ZDP):Band100Heft3-434
S.M. Johnson, 301(JEGP):Jan81-85
Freyer, G. W.B. Yeats and the Anti-
Democratic Tradition.
B. Martin, 617(TLS):6Aug82-867
Fricke, H. Die Sprache der Literaturwis-
senschaft.*
D. Firmenich, 679:Band11Heft2-385
Frickx, R. and J. Muno, eds. Littérature
française de Belgique.
M-C. Bancquart, 535(RHL):Mar-Apr81-338
Fridh, Ä. L'emploi causal de la conjonc-
tion "ut" en latin tardif.
P. Flobert, 555:Vol54fasc1-174
Fried, C. Contract as Promise.
R.H., 185:Apr82-586
Fried, C. Right and Wrong.*
E. Regis, Jr., 449:Sep81-414
A.J. Simmons, 482(PhR):Jan81-125
Fried, E. One Hundred Poems Without a
Country.
L. Rosenwald, 114(ChiR):Spring81-125
G. Stern, 133:Band14Heft3-286
Fried, M. Absorption and Theatricality.*
D. Rosand, 55:Nov81-37
B. Scott, 39:Aug81-135
B.M. Stafford, 400(MLN):Dec81-1212
Fried, Y. and J. Agassi. Paranoia.
J.O. Wisdom, 488:Dec80-459
Friedan, B. The Second Stage.*
M. Warnock, 617(TLS):30Jul82-822
Friedemann, J. Alexandre Weill écrivain
contestataire et historien engagé, 1811-
[continued]

[continuing]
1899.
B.L. Knapp, 446(NCFS):Spring-Summer82-
380
Friedenberg, E.Z. Deference to Authority.
P.J. Wood, 529(QQ):Spring81-163
Friedenreich, H.P. The Jews of Yugoslavia.
M. Stanislawski, 104(CASS):Winter81-
637
Friedenreich, K., ed. Tercentenary Essays
in Honor of Andrew Marvell.
G.D. Lord, 677(YES):Vol 11-258
Friederich, W. Die Interpunktion im
Englischen.
G. Graustein, 682(ZPSK):Band33Heft6-
748
H. Ulherr, 38:Band99Heft1/2-190
Friedgut, T.H. Political Participation in
the USSR.*
R.C. Gripp, 104(CASS):Winter81-606
Friedhof, G. Kasusgrammatik und lokaler
Ausdruck im Russischen.
G. Corbett, 297(JL):Mar81-178
Friedländer, M. Lehrbuch des Susu.
G.F. Meier, 682(ZPSK):Band33Heft4-498
Friedländer, S. When Memory Comes.*
P. Lewis, 565:Vol22No4-69
Friedman, A. - see Wycherley, W.
Friedman, A.W. Multivalence.*
J.L. Sutherland, 481(PQ):Summer80-386
Friedman, E.G. Joyce Carol Oates.
M. Fuchs, 628(UWR):Fall-Winter81-102
Friedman, L.M. The Legal System.
R. Kevelson, 567:Vol135No1/2-183
Friedman, M. and R. Free to Choose.
W.H. Peterson, 396(ModA):Spring81-202
Friedman, M.H. The Making of a Tory Human-
ist.*
W.H. Galperin, 301(JEGP):Apr81-257
W. Heath, 591(SIR):Spring81-117
W.J.B. Owen, 677(YES):Vol 11-300
Friedman, R. Hermann Hesse.
M. Boulby, 220(GL&L):Apr82-272
Friedmann, J. The Good Society.
J. Mechling, 658:Spring81-130
Friedrich, J. and A. Kammenhuber. Hethit-
isches Wörterbuch. (Pt 2) (2nd ed)
J. Puhvel, 318(JAOS):Apr/Jun80-167
Friedrich, J. and A. Kammenhuber. Hethit-
isches Wörterbuch. (Pt 3) (2nd ed)
J. Puhvel, 318(JAOS):Apr/Jun80-168
Friedrich, O. The End of the World.
N. Johnston, 441:24Oct82-16
Friedrich, P. Language, Context and the
Imagination. (A.S. Dil, ed)
J. Sherzer, 350:Sep81-765
Friedrichs von Sonnenburg. Die Sprüche
Friedrichs von Sonnenburg. (A. Masser,
ed)
E. Kiepe-Willms, 684(ZDA):Band109Heft3-
106
O. Sayce, 402(MLR):Jul81-739
Friel, B. Translations.
D. Devlin, 157:Autumn81-51
Friendly, F.W. Minnesota Rag.*
S. Donaldson, 569(SR):Fall81-604
Frier, B.W. Libri annales pontificum maxi-
morum.
J. Briscoe, 123:Vol31No2-311
R.M. Ogilvie, 313:Vol71-199
Frier, W. and G. Labroisse, eds. Grundfra-
gen der Textwissenschaft.
W.U. Dressler, 602:Vol 12No1-286

Frier-Wantiez, M. Sémiotique du fantas-
tique.
  P. Imbert, 567:Vol33No3/4-377
Fries, M.S. The Changing Consciousness of
Reality.
  F. Betz, 221(GQ):May81-365
Fries, S.D. The Urban Idea in Colonial
America.
  J. Archer, 173(ECS):Winter80/81-198
Friese, W., ed. Strindberg und die
deutschsprachigen Länder.*
  G.P. Knapp, 406:Winter81-471
  C. Westling, 562(Scan):May81-103
Friess, H.L. Felix Adler and Ethical Cul-
ture.
  J.M.G., 185:Jul82-779
Frimmer, S. Dead Matter.
  N. Callendar, 441:16May82-27
Frindall, B. The Wisden Book of Cricket
Records.
  T.D. Smith, 617(TLS):1Jan82-19
Frings, M.S. - see Heidegger, M.
Frings, T. and E. Linke, eds. Morant und
Galie.
  H. Beckers, 684(ZDA):Band109Heft2-62
Frisbie, C.J. and D.P. McAllester - see
Mitchell, F.
Frisch, M. Blaubart.
  M. Butler, 617(TLS):4Jun82-622
Frisch, M. Don Juan oder Die Liebe zur
Geometrie. (D.G. and S.M. Matthews, eds)
  205(FMLS):Oct80-375
Frisch, M. I'm Not Stiller.
  S.S. Prawer, 617(TLS):30Jul82-814
Frisch, M. Montauk.
  T. Shipe, 145(CritI):Vol22No3-55
Frisch, M. Triptych.* (French title:
Triptyque.)
  J-L. Gautier, 450(NRF):Jan81-158
Frisch, O. What Little I Remember.
  Alceste, 111:7Nov80-31
Frisé, A. - see Musil, R.
Frith, J.R., ed. Measuring Spoken Lan-
guage Proficiency.
  A. Pousada, 350:Mar82-254
Frith, N. The Legend of Krishna.
  N.E. Falk, 314:Winter-Spring81-223
Frith, S. Sound Effects.
  L. Winner, 441:7Feb82-14
von Fritz, K. Schriften zur griechischen
Logik.* (Vols 1 and 2)
  I. Mueller, 53(AGP):Band63Heft1-41
Fritz, P. and R. Morton, eds. Women in
the 18th Century and Other Essays.
  S. Staves, 402(MLR):Oct81-933
Fröhlich, H. Studien zur langobardischen
Thronfolge von den Anfängen bis zur
Eroberung des italienischen Reiches
durch Karl den Grossen (774).
  T.F.X. Noble, 589:Jul81-613
Froissart, J. Le Joli Buisson de Jonece.
(A. Fourrier, ed)
  M.A. Freeman, 545(RPh):Feb81-366
Frolic, B.M. Mao's People.*
  K. Lieberthal, 293(JASt):May81-583
  D.E. Waterfall, 529(QQ):Summer81-279
Fromkin, V.A., ed. Errors in Linguistic
Performance.
  A.M. Peters, 350:Dec82-926
Fromkin, V.A., ed. Speech Errors as
Linguistic Evidence.
  A.S. Kaye, 35(AS):Summer81-131

Fromm, E. The Greatness and Limitations
of Freud's Thought.
  T. Murphy, 258:Mar81-111
Fromm, E. and R.E. Shor, eds. Hypnosis.
(2nd ed)
  E.A. Barnett, 529(QQ):Summer81-383
Fromson, B.D. Running and Fighting.
  S.J. Ungar, 441:7Feb82-14
Frontinus, S.J. Frontin, "Kriegslisten."
(2nd ed) (G. Bendz, ed and trans)
  J. André, 555:Vol54fasc1-179
Fröschle, H. and W. Scheffler - see Uhland,
L.
Frost, C. Liar's Dice.
  P. Thompson, 502(PrS):Fall81-100
Frost, D. and M. Deakin. I Could Have
Kicked Myself.
  E.S. Turner, 362:27May82-21
Frost, D.L. - see Middleton, T.
Frost, F.J. Plutarch's "Themistocles."
  F.E. Romer, 24:Summer81-226
  G.S. Shrimpton, 487:Winter81-375
Frost, R. Robert Frost: Farm-Poultryman.*
(E.C. Lathem and L. Thompson, eds)
  A. Motion, 617(TLS):26Mar82-333
"Robert Frost and Sidney Cox."* (W.R.
Evans, ed)
  R. Buffington, 569(SR):Fall81-c
  A. Motion, 617(TLS):26Mar82-333
Froude, J.A. Froude's Life of Carlyle.*
(ed and abridged by J. Clubbe)
  I.B. Nadel, 77:Spring81-187
Frumkin, V., ed. Bulat Okudzhava.
  S.F. Starr, 550(RusR):Jan81-88
Fry, J., ed. Twenty-five African Sculp-
tures.
  E.L.R. Meyerowitz, 39:Mar81-202
Fry, J.L., ed. Limits of the Welfare
State.
  R.F. Tomasson, 563(SS):Spring81-232
Fry, P.H. The Poet's Calling in the Eng-
lish Ode.
  J. Baxter, 150(DR):Summer81-382
  M. Brown, 591(SIR):Summer81-249
  D. Bush, 301(JEGP):Jan81-133
  J. Haney-Peritz, 405(MP):Nov81-226
  A. Rodway, 89(BJA):Spring81-178
  H. Vendler, 401(MLQ):Mar81-87
  C. Woodring, 340(KSJ):Vol30-191
Fry, P.S. and F.S. - see under Somerset
Fry, P. and F.
Fryde, N. The Tyranny and Fall of Edward
II, 1321-1326.
  R.M. Haines, 589:Jan81-135
Frye, N. Creation and Recreation.
  M. Ross, 627(UTQ):Summer81-95
Frye, N. Northrop Frye on Culture and
Literature.* (R.D. Denham, ed)
  R. Bates, 296(JCF):No31/32-227
  L. Lane, Jr., 178:Spring81-123
Frye, N. The Great Code.
  N. Bliven, 442(NY):31May82-104
  J.M. Cameron, 453(NYRB):15Apr82-28
  H. Kenner, 441:11Apr82-10
  S. Medcalf, 362:23Sep82-23
  R. Trickett, 617(TLS):2Jul82-712
Frye, N. The Secular Scripture.
  K.L. Pfeiffer, 38:Band99Heft1/2-241
Frye, R.M. Milton's Imagery and the
Visual Arts.*
  W.E. Cain, 400(MLN):Dec81-1121
  M. Hollington, 161(DUJ):Dec80-111
                                [continued]

Frye, R.M. Milton's Imagery and the
Visual Arts. [continuing]
    M. Praz, 179(ES):Dec81-566
    J.M. Steadman, 131(CL):Winter81-100
    J. Sturrock, 648(WCR):Jun80-63
Frye, R.N., ed. The Cambridge History of
Iran. (Vol 4)
    H. Algar, 318(JAOS):Apr/Jun80-143
Frykenberg, R.E., ed. Land Tenure and
Peasant in South Asia.
    C. Dewey, 293(JASt):May81-629
Fu, C.W-H. and W-T. Chan. Guide to Chi-
nese Philosophy.*
    D. Bodde, 318(JAOS):Jan/Mar80-88
Fu, J.S. Mythic and Comic Aspects of the
Quest.
    A.E. Kunst, 678(YCGL):No29-50
Fu, S.C.Y., with others. Traces of the
Brush.
    S. Goldberg, 318(JAOS):Jan/Mar80-98
Fubini, R. - see de' Medici, L.
Fuchs, E., with R. Lauth and W. Schieche,
eds. J.G. Fichte im Gespräch. (Vol 1)
    J. Widmann, 489(PJGG):Band88Heft1-203
de Fuentes, Á.G. - see under Galmés de
Fuentes, Á.
Fuentes, C. Distant Relations.
    G. Davenport, 441:21Mar82-3
    A. Mars-Jones, 617(TLS):9Jul82-739
    J. Mellors, 362:5Aug82-22
Fuentes, C. Una Familia Lejana.
    P. Sáenz, 37:Jan81-47
Fugard, A. A Lesson from Aloes.
    D. Walder, 617(TLS):23Apr82-468
Fugard, A. Tsotsi.*
    G. Kearns, 249(HudR):Summer81-309
"Fugen: Deutsch-Französisches Jahrbuch für
Text-Analytik."* (Vol 1) (M. Frank, F.A.
Kittler and S. Weber, eds)
    G. von Graevenitz, 680(ZDP):Band100
    Heft4-629
Füger, W., ed. Concordance to James
Joyce's "Dubliners."
    H.W. Gabler, 329(JJQ):Winter81-217
Fuhrmann, F. - see Plutarch
Fukui, K. and D. Turton, eds. Warfare
among East African Herders.
    P. Spencer, 69:Vol50No4-443
Fukutake Tadashi. Rural Society in Japan.
    Ishikawa Takeo, 285(JapQ):Apr-Jun81-
    288
    E. Norbeck, 407(MN):Summer81-225
Fuld, W. Walter Benjamin.*
    P. Missac, 98:Apr80-370
Fulford, R. - see Queen Victoria
Fulford, R.W. Powerland Minds.
    R. Sward, 102(CanL):Summer81-143
Fullenwider, H.F. Rilke and his Reviewers.
    K. Phillips, 406:Spring81-114
Fuller, J. The Illusionists.*
    C. Hope, 364:Apr/May81-120
Fuller, J. Waiting for the Music.
    D. Davis, 362:16Dec82-23
    L. Mackinnon, 617(TLS):17Dec82-1399
Fuller, P. Beyond the Crisis in Art.
    I. Jeffrey, 364:Apr/May81-106
Fuller, P. Seeing Berger.
    H. Foster, 62:Summer81-88
Fuller, R. Fellow Mortals.
    A. Motion, 617(TLS):8Jan82-27

Fuller, R. The Individual and His Times.
(V.J. Lee, ed)
    R. Blythe, 362:12Aug82-20
    A. Brownjohn, 617(TLS):17Sep82-998
Fuller, R. The Reign of Sparrows.*
    B. Ruddick, 148:Winter81-71
    L. Sail, 565:Vol122No1-66
Fuller, R. Vamp Till Ready.
    R. Blythe, 362:12Aug82-20
    D.A.N. Jones, 617(TLS):30Jul82-812
Fullinwider, R.K. The Reverse Discrimina-
tion Controversy.
    J.L.H., 185:Oct81-186
Fumaroli, M., ed. Critique et création
littéraires en France au XVIIe siècle.
    J. Barchilon, 207(FR):Oct80-160
Fumaroli, M. L'Age de l'Eloquence.*
    M-O. Sweetser, 207(FR):Dec81-265
    M-O. Sweetser, 475:No15Pt1-162
Funke, G. Von der Aktualität Kants.
    R. Lüthe, 342:Band72Heft2-196
von Fürer-Haimendorf, C., with E. von
Fürer-Haimendorf. The Gonds of Andhra
Pradesh.
    E.J. Jay, 293(JASt):Aug81-847
Furlong, M. Merton.*
    295(JML):Vol8No3/4-568
Furman, L. The Glass House.
    42(AR):Spring81-266
Furnas, J.C. Fanny Kemble.
    442(NY):1Feb82-132
Furness, R. Wagner and Literature.
    L. Beckett, 617(TLS):1Oct82-1073
Fürnkäs, J. Der Ursprung des psycholo-
gischen Romans.*
    M. Boulby, 221(GQ):Jan81-92
Furst, L.R. The Contours of European
Romanticism.
    E. Boa, 89(BJA):Winter81-85
    G. Hoffmeister, 406:Winter81-459
Furst, L.R., ed. European Romanticism.
    R.T. Denommé, 207(FR):Feb82-411
    E. Kern, 402(MLR):Oct81-918
Furst, P.T. and J.L. North American
Indian Art.
    P-L. Adams, 61:Dec82-107
Fussell, B.H. Mabel.
    J. Lahr, 441:30May82-7
    442(NY):2Aug82-88
Fussell, P. Abroad.*
    D.L. Eder, 639(VQR):Summer81-543
    J. Halperin, 579(SAQ):Summer81-366
    A. Zwerdling, 141:Summer81-279
Fussell, P. The Boy Scout Handbook and
Other Observations.
    N. Perrin, 441:29Aug82-6
    442(NY):4Oct82-151
Futrell, A.W. and C.B. Wordell - see
Maurer, D.W.
Fyfield, J.A. Re-educating Chinese Anti-
Communists.
    D. Duncanson, 617(TLS):21May82-553
Fyle, C.M. Almamy Suluku of Sierra Leone,
c. 1820-1906.
    J.A. Karimu, 69:Vol50No4-440
Fyler, J.M. Chaucer and Ovid.*
    H. Cooper, 447(N&Q):Feb80-89
    C. Gauvin, 189(EA):Oct-Dec81-462
    P. Hardman, 541(RES):May81-204
    R.L. Hoffman, 301(JEGP):Apr81-231
Fyvel, T.R. George Orwell.
    M. Bayles, 441:7Nov82-15
                                    [continued]

[continuing]
S. Jacobson, 362:9Sep82-22
R. Mayne, 617(TLS):26Nov82-1292

Gaál, L. and P. Gunszt. Animal Husbandry
in Hungary in the 19th and 20th Cen-
turies.
I. Volgyes, 104(CASS):Winter81-614
von Gabain, A. Einführung in die Zentral-
asienkunde.
J.W. de Jong, 259(IIJ):Jul81-236
Gabba, E. Republican Rome, the Army and
the Allies.
M.H. Crawford, 313:Vol71-153
Gabba, E. and G. Vallet, eds. La Sicilia
Antica.
D. Ridgway, 617(TLS):12Mar82-286
Gabinskij, M.A. Grammatičeskoe var'iro-
vanie v moldavskom jazyke.
Y. Malkiel, 350:Mar81-239
Gablik, S. Magritte.
R. Cardinal, 529(QQ):Spring81-19
Gaborit-Chopin, D. Invoires du Moyen Age.
L.Z. Gross, 589:Jan81-137
Gadamer, H-G. Dialogue and Dialectic.*
R. Bernasconi, 323:Oct81-290
S. Rosen, 480(P&R):Spring81-112
Gadamer, H-G. Reason in the Age of
Science.
M. Rosen, 617(TLS):19Nov82-1283
Gadd, B. Childsong and Other Verses.
N. Monin, 368:Sep81-368
Gaddis, J.L. Strategies of Containment.
W. Laqueur, 617(TLS):5Mar82-243
J.S. Nye, 441:17Jan82-8
Gaede, F. Poetik und Logik.*
M. Beetz, 680(ZDP):Band99Heft4-616
H. Entner, 654(WB):7/1981-178
J. Mahr, 52:Band15Heft2-201
Gaeng, P.A. A Study of Nominal Inflection
in Latin Inscriptions.
S.N. Dworkin, 545(RPh):May81-458
Gage, J. - see von Goethe, J.W.
Gage, J. - see Turner, J.M.W.
Gage, J.T. In the Arresting Eye.*
R. Kern, 659(ConL):Summer82-368
Gagliardo, J.G. Reich and Nation.
T.P. Saine, 221(GQ):Mar81-221
des Gagniers, J. and V. Karageorghis.
Vases et figurines de l'âge du bronze à
chypre: Céramique rouge et noire polie.
P. Åström, 487:Summer81-193
J.B. Hennessy, 303(JoHS):Vol 101-213
Gagnon, J. Les Vaches sont de braves
types.
M.A. Fitzpatrick, 207(FR):Mar82-566
Gaide, F. - see Avianus
Gaillard, D. Dorothy L. Sayers.
D. Brown, 435:Fall81-305
Gaines, C. Dangler.*
C. Hawtree, 364:Oct81-99
Gaines, E.J. In My Father's House.
J. McCluskey, Jr., 459:Spring-Summer80-
239
Gair, W.R. - see Marston, J.
Gaiser, K. Das Philosophenmosaik in
Neapel.
R.J. Ling, 123:Vol31No2-322
Gaite, C.M. - see under Martín Gaite, C.

Gajecky, G. The Cossack Administration of
the Hetmanate.*
G.E. Orchard, 104(CASS):Winter81-574
J.E.O. Screen, 575(SEER):Jan81-156
Gajek, B., ed. Johann Georg Hamman: Acta
des internationalen Hamann-Colloqiums in
Lüneburg 1976.*
S-A. Jørgensen, 462(OL):Vol36No3-260
Gak, V.G. Teoretitcheskaïa grammatika
frantsuzskovo yazyka.
C. Hyart, 209(FM):Jan81-79
Gal, H. Schumann Orchestral Music.
J.B., 412:Aug80-238.*
Gal, S. Language Shift.*
R. Coates, 297(JL):Mar81-131
Galante, P. Operation Valkyrie.
N. Stone, 453(NYRB):13May82-24
Galarneau, C. Les Collèges classiques au
Canada français (1620-1970).
P. Savard, 193(ELit):Dec81-559
Galassi, J. - see Montale, E.
Galbraith, J.K. Théorie de la pauvreté de
masse.
H. Cronel, 450(NRF):Jan81-148
Galdon, J.A., ed. Essays on the Philip-
pine Novel in English.
N. Rosca, 293(JASt):Aug81-859
Galdós, B.P. Benito Pérez Galdós: Etapas
preliminares de "Gloria." (W.T. Patti-
son, ed)
G. Cullón, 240(HR):Summer81-368
E. Rodgers, 86(BHS):Jan81-86
G. Smith, 238:May81-313
Gale, R.L. Luke Short.
J.D. Nesbitt, 649(WAL):Fall81-230
Galenson, D.W. White Servitude in Colo-
nial America.
E. Wright, 617(TLS):24Sep82-1040
Galenson, W., ed. Economic Growth and
Structural Change in Taiwan.
A.Y.C. Koo, 293(JASt):Nov80-109
Galera Andreu, P.A. Arquitectura de los
siglos XVII y XVIII en Jaén.
V. Tovar Martín, 48:Oct-Dec81-461
Galileo. Galileo Galilei, "Operations of
the Geometric and Military Compass"
(1606). (S. Drake, trans)
R. Palter, 551(RenQ):Autumn80-433
Galinsky, H. Das Amerikanische Englisch.
B. Carstensen, 38:Band99Heft3/4-469
Galisson, R. Lexicologie et enseignement
des langues.*
M.M. Heiser, 399(MLJ):Summer81-215
Gallagher, C.T. Brass Images.
M. Zachary, 70:Nov/Dec80-66
Gallagher, E.J., J.A. Mistichelli and J.A.
Van Eerde. Jules Verne.
M.G. Rose, 446(NCFS):Fall-Winter81/82-
193
Gallais-Hamonno, J. The Language of Basic
Economics: Manuel d'anglais économique.
J.L., 189(EA):Oct-Dec81-499
Gallant, J. Russian Verbal Prefixation
and Semantic Features.
F.Y. Gladney, 574(SEEJ):Spring81-130
Gallant, M. From the Fifteenth District.*
G. Merler, 648(WCR):Jun80-34
W.H. New, 102(CanL):Summer80-153
Gallant, M. Home Truths.
M. Thorpe, 99:Feb82-40
Gallardo, E.G. - see under Godoy Gallardo,
E.

Gallez, P. Das Geheimnis des Drachen-
schwanzes.
  R. Etchepareborda, 263(RIB):Vol31No1-
  86
Gallico, C. Storia della Musica: L'età
dell'Umanesimo e del Rinascimento.
  G. Capovilla, 228(GSLI):Vol 157fasc499-
  470
Gallie, W.B. Philosophers of Peace and
War.*
  L. Thiry, 154:Mar81-174
Gallix, F. - see White, T.H. and L.J.
.Potts
Gallo, F.A. Storia della Musica: Il
Medioevo II.
  G. Capovilla, 228(GSLI):Vol 157fasc499-
  470
Gallo, I. Un papiro della "Vita del filo-
sofo Secondo" e la tradizione medioevale
del "bios."
  S. West, 123:Vol31No1-113
Gallo, P.L. and F. Sedwick. French for
Careers.
  B. Braude, 207(FR):Mar82-562
Gallup, D. - see O'Neill, E.
Gallup, G., Jr., with W. Proctor. Adven-
tures in Immortality.
  F.R. Schumer, 441:5Sep82-14
Galmés de Fuentes, Á., ed. "El Libro de
las batallas."
  J. Aguadé, 545(RPh):Nov80-266
Galsterer, H. Herrschaft und Verwaltung
im republikanischen Italien.
  M.H. Crawford, 313:Vol71-153
Galt, J. John Galt: Selected Short Sto-
ries.* (I.A. Gordon, ed)
  R.C. Gordon, 445(NCF):Jun80-103
  D.S. Mack, 447(N&Q):Oct80-458
Galton, H. Freedom — From Illusions.
  H.A. Stammler, 396(ModA):Fall81-435
Galvin, B. Atlantic Flyway.
  G.E. Murray, 249(HudR):Spring81-159
  T. Reiter, 134(CP):Spring81-86
Galvin, J. Imaginary Timber.
  R. Hornsey, 461:Fall-Winter81/82-101
Gamerschlag, K. Sir Walter Scott und die
Waverley Novels.
  K. Wittig, 588(SSL):Vol 16-301
Gammond, P. Offenbach.
  H. MacDonald, 415:Jul81-479
Gammond, P. and R. Horricks, eds. The
Music Goes Round and Round.
  M. Harrison, 415:May81-316
Gandhi, R. Presuppositions of Human Commu-
nication.
  T.S. Champlin, 518:Jan81-34
Gangemi, K. Lydia/Corroborée.
  C. Minière, 98:May80-523
Gann, L.H. and P. Duignan. The Rulers of
German Africa, 1884-1914. The Rulers
of British Africa, 1870-1914. The
Rulers of Belgian Africa, 1884-1914.
  A.H.M. Kirk-Greene, 69:Vol50No4-433
Gannon, T. Newport Mansions.
  P-L. Adams, 61:Oct82-106
Gans-Ruedin, E. Chinese Carpets.
  P. Bach, 614:Fall82-14
Gant, P. Islands.
  R.A. Copland, 368:Sep73-257
Gant, R. - see Thomas, E.
Ganz, P. - see Burckhardt, J.
Ganz, P. - see Gottfried von Strassburg

Garaudy, R. Appel aux vivants.
  V. Descombes, 98:Jan80-5
Garaudy, R. Il est encore temps de vivre.
  A. Jacob, 542:Jan-Mar81-142
Garavini, F. La Casa dei giochi.
  R.G. Pellegrini, 535(RHL):Jul-Oct81-
  760
Garber, E.K. Metaphysical Tales.
  W. Cummins, 363(LitR):Spring82-462
Garber, F. Thoreau's Redemptive Imagina-
tion.*
  H.D. Peck, 131(CL):Winter81-106
  R.J. Schneider, 183(ESQ):Vol27No1-57
  M.F. Schulz, 678(YCGL):No29-55
Garber, K., ed. Europäische Bukolik und
Georgik.*
  E. Zillekens, 447(N&Q):Oct80-422
Garber, K. Der locus amoenus und der
locus terribilis.
  E. Mazingue, 549(RLC):Jan-Mar81-126
Garber, M. Coming of Age in Shakespeare.
  J. Stachniewski, 617(TLS):29Jan82-100
García, C. La oposición y conjunción de
los dos grandes Luminares de la tierra o
la antipatía de Franceses y Españoles.*
(M. Bareau, ed)
  R. Arbour, 539:Feb82-58
  F.A. de Armas, 678(YCGL):No29-38
García, F.M. - see under Martínez García,
F.
García Antón, I. La arquitectura de prin-
cipios de siglo en Alicante y provincia.
  E. Casado, 48:Oct-Dec81-463
García-Baquero González, A. Cádiz y el
Atlántico (1717-1778).
  M.T. Hamerly, 37:Jan81-45
García Castañeda, S. Miguel de los Santos
Álvarez (1818-1892).
  J. Alberich, 86(BHS):Apr81-146
  D.T. Gies, 240(HR):Summer81-364
García Castañeda, S. Don Telesforo de
Trueba y Cosío (1799-1835).
  A.H. Clarke, 86(BHS):Jul81-269
  J. Dowling, 240(HR):Winter81-128
  P.B. Goldman, 405(MP):Nov81-205
García Hernandez, B. El campo semantico
de "ver" en la lengua latina.*
  P. Flobert, 555:Vol54fasc1-175
García Hortelano, J. Cuentos completos.
  J.F. Spencer, 552(REH):Oct81-476
García Márquez, G. Chronicle of a Death
Foretold.
  J. Archer, 362:9Sep82-21
  B. Buford, 617(TLS):10Sep82-965
García Mateo, R. Dialektik als Polemik.
  F. Niedermayer, 72:Band217Heft2-479
Garcilaso de la Vega. Obra completa.
(A.I. Sotelo Salas, ed)
  J. Lihani, 552(REH):Jan81-139
du Gard, R.C. - see under Coulet du Gard,
R.
du Gard, R.C. and D.C. Western - see under
Coulet du Gard, R. and D.C. Western
du Gard, R.M. - see under Martin du Gard,
R.
Gardair, J-M. - see Renard, J.
Garde, P. Histoire de l'accentuation
slave.
  M. Halle and P. Kiparsky, 350:Mar81-
  150
Gardet, L. Les Hommes de l'Islam.
  J.M. Pessagno, 318(JAOS):Jan/Mar80-27

126

Gbadamosi, T.G.O. The Growth of Islam among the Yoruba, 1841-1980.
  R. Law, 69:Vol50No4-441
Geach, P. and M. Black - see Frege, G.
Geach, P.T. Truth, Love and Immortality.*
  A. MacIntyre, 185:Jul81-667
  T.L.S. Sprigge, 518:Apr81-126
Geanakoplos, D.J. Medieval Western Civilization and the Byzantine and Islamic Worlds.
  P. Charanis, 551(RenQ):Spring80-63
Geary, P. Living in Ether.
  F. Levine, 441:22Aug82-11
Geary, P.J. Furta Sacra.*
  W. Rothwell, 208(FS):Jan81-67
Gebauer, H.D. Bücherauktionen in Deutschland im 17. Jahrhundert.
  D.L. Paisey, 354:Dec81-355
Gebauer, P. Art of Cameroon.
  M.B. Joseph, 2(AfrA):Feb81-15
Gebhardt, C. - see de Spinoza, B.
Gebhardt, P., ed. Literaturkritik und literarische Wertung.
  K. Kändler, 654(WB):8/1981-179
Cecadze, I.O. Očerki po sintaksisu abchaskogo jazyka.
  G.F. Meier, 682(ZPSK):Band33Heft4-499
Geddes, G. Conrad's Later Novels.*
  M. Kreiswirth, 627(UTQ):Summer81-131
  L.M. Whitehead, 150(DR):Winter81/82-743
Geddes, G., ed. Divided We Stand.
  G.A. Boire, 102(CanL):Spring80-95
Gedo, M.M. Picasso.
  90.Nov01-712
Gee, M. Dying, in Other Words.*
  J. Mellors, 364:Nov81-88
Gee, M. Meg.*
  D. Durrant, 364:Feb82-97
Geertz, C. Negara.*
  S.F. Moore, 676(YR):Winter82-280
Geggus, D. Slavery, War, and Revolution.
  P. Mackesy, 617(TLS):24Sep82-1040
Gehlen, A. Arnold Gehlen Gesamtausgabe. (Vols 1, 2 and 7) (L. Samson and K-S. Rehberg, eds)
  H. Ottmann, 489(PJGG):Band88Heft2-423
Geier, M., M. Kohrt and C. Küper. Sprache als Struktur.
  H. Singer, 685(ZDL):1/1981-76
Geier, S. - see Belyj, A.
Geiger, W.E. Phytonymic Derivational Systems in the Romance Languages.*
  M.R. Harris, 545(RPh):Feb81(supp)-135
Geijer, A. A History of Textile Art.*
  L. von Wilckens, 471:Jan/Feb/Mar81-92
Geil, G. Gottfried von Strassburg und Wolfram von Eschenbach als literarische Antipoden.
  M.G. Scholz, 680(ZDP):Band99Heft1-126
Geiogamah, H. New Native American Drama.
  N.C. Greenberg, 130:Summer81-187
  T. King, 649(WAL):Summer81-158
Geith, K-E. Carolus Magnus.*
  R. Schnell, 680(ZDP):Band99Heft3-433
  W. Schröder, 684(ZDA):Band110Heft1-11
Gekoski, R.A. Conrad.*
  J. Batchelor, 447(N&Q):Jun80-259
  D. Hewitt, 541(RES):Aug81-353
  C. Watts, 677(YES):Vol 11-341
Gelb, L.H., with R.K. Betts. The Irony of Vietnam.
  D.P. Chandler, 293(JASt):Nov80-77

Gelber, H.G. Technology, Defense, and External Relations in China, 1975-1978.
  T. Fingar, 293(JASt):Feb81-347
Gellius, A. Aulu-Gelle, "Les Nuits Attiques." (Vol 2) (R. Marache, ed and trans)
  M. Baratin, 555:Vol54fasc2-372
Gellner, E. Muslim Society.*
  C. Geertz, 453(NYRB):27May82-25
Gellner, E. Spectacles and Predicaments.
  B. Fay, 185:Apr82-569
Gelsinger, B.E. Icelandic Enterprise.
  H. Davidson, 617(TLS):15Jan82-61
Gelwick, R. The Way of Discovery.
  H.A.D., 543:Mar81-606
Gemar, R.S-L. - see under Sánchez-Lafuente Gemar, R.
van Gemert, G. Die Werke des Aegidius Albertinus (1560-1620).
  F.M. Eybl, 602:Vol 12No2-392
"Genesis profeta, nordiska studier i gammaltestamentlig ikonografi."
  R. Zeitler, 341:Vol50No2-101
Genette, G. Figures III.
  K. Schomer, 545(RPh):Nov80-245
Genette, G. Introduction à l'architexte.*
  J. Pier, 567:Vol35No3/4-381
  G. Prince, 454:Autumn80-189
Genette, G. Mimologiques.*
  S. Merrim, 153:Spring81-44
Genette, G. and T. Todorov, eds. Recherche de Proust.
  C. Lang, 400(MLN):May81-906
Gennari, G. La Neuvième Vague.
  R. Linkhorn, 207(FR):Oct81-157
Genno, C.N. and H. Wetzel, eds. The First World War in German Narrative Prose.
  D. Barnouw, 133:Band14Heft4-381
Geno, T.H., ed. Our Profession.
  R.G. Royer, 399(MLJ):Summer81-207
Genot, G. Grammatica trasformazionale dell'italiano.
  G. Lepschy, 545(RPh):Aug80-128
"Gens et paroles d'Afrique."
  J-C. Monteil, 98:Jun-Jul81-652
Gensler, K. Without Roof.
  639(VQR):Autumn81-131
Gentikow, B. Skandinavien als präkapitalistische Idylle.*
  B. Henningsen, 462(OL):Vol35No1-92
Gentili, B. and C. Prato, eds. Poetarum elegiacorum testimonia et fragmenta. (Pt 1)
  M. Davies, 303(JoHS):Vol 101-167
  M.L. West, 123:Vol31No1-1
Genuist, P. La Faillite du Canada anglais.
  C.F. Coates, 207(FR):Mar82-582
"Geography of Japan."
  D.H. Kornhauser, 407(MN):Summer81-229
Georgacas, D.J. Ichthyological Terms for the Sturgeon and Etymology of the International Terms Botargo, Caviar and Congeners.*
  A. Heubeck, 260(IF):Band85-346
  G.M. Messing, 122:Oct81-344
  L. Zgusta, 660(Word):Aug80-235
George, D. The Real Duke Ellington.
  C. Fox, 617(TLS):25Jun82-691
George, D.H. Blake and Freud.*
  A. Ostriker, 661(WC):Summer81-161
  639(VQR):Winter81-16
George, E. Kate's Death.
  H. Thomas, 385(MQR):Winter82-200

George, E., ed. Was sieht die Ringeltaube.
  T. Di Napoli, 221(GQ):May81-398
George, E. - see Radnóti, M.
George, F.H. Problem Solving.
  W.H.P., 185:Jul81-697
George, S. Frog Salad.*
  E. Friedman, 461:Fall-Winter81/82-93
George, T.J.S. Revolt in Mindanao.
  G.C. Bentley, 293(JASt):May81-649
George, W. Darwin.
  R. O'Hanlon, 617(TLS):18Jun82-653
Lord George-Brown. The Voices of History.
  639(VQR):Spring81-50
Georgiev, N. Bǎlgarskata narodna pesen.
  A. Zander, 688(ZSP):Band42Heft1-179
Georgiev, V.A. and others. Vostochnyi
  vopros vo vneshnei politike Rossii
  (konets XVII — nachalo XX v.).
  W.S. Vucinich, 550(RusR):Jan81-60
Georgiev, V.T. La lingua e l'origine
  degli Etruschi.
  B.A. Rudes, 350:Dec81-967
Geppert, H.V. Achim von Arnims Romanfrag-
  ment "Die Kronenwächter."*
  R. Hoermann, 221(GQ):Jan81-97
Geraëts, T.F., ed. Rationality To-day/La
  rationalité aujourd'hui.
  R.H., 185:Apr82-586
  J.N. Kaufmann, 154:Mar81-114
Gérard, J. Juvénal et la réalité contem-
  poraine.
  M.S. Smith, 313:Vol71-225
Gérard, J. L'exclamation en français.
  J. Chaurand, 209(FM):Oct81-375
Gerber, A. Le Faubourg des Coups-de-
  Trique.
  J. Laroche, 207(FR):Apr81-753
Gerber, A. and D. Bryen. Language and
  Learning Disabilities.
  J.F. Schmitt, 583:Winter82-231
Gerdts, W.H. and T.E. Stebbins, Jr. "A
  Man of Genius."*
  B.J. Wolf, 219(GaR):Spring81-195
Gere, J.A. and J. Sparrow - see Madan, G.
Gerhard, P. A Guide to the Historical
  Geography of New Spain.
  J.L. Arbena, 37:Feb81-47
Gerhard, P. The Southeast Frontier of New
  Spain.
  J.L. Arbena, 37:Feb81-47
  J.S. Bromley, 161(DUJ):Dec80-94
Gerhard, U. and others, eds. "Dem Reich
  der Freiheit werb' ich Bürgerinnen."
  R-E.B. Joeres, 221(GQ):Nov81-534
Gerhardie, W. God's Fifth Column.* (M.
  Holroyd and R. Skidelsky, eds)
  M. Muggeridge, 453(NYRB):1Apr82-26
  J. Turner, 364:Jul81-90
Gerhardt, V. and F. Kaulbach. Kant.
  W. Steinbeck, 342:Band72Heft4-510
Gérin, W. Anne Thackeray Ritchie.*
  A.J.S., 148:Autumn81-87
Gerlach, K. Heinrich von Kleist.* (Pt 3)
  M.M. Tatar, 406:Winter81-461
Gerlach-Nielsen, M., H. Hertel and M. Nøj-
  gaard, eds. Romanteori og romananalyse.
  E. Lunding, 52:Band15Heft3-309
Gerli, M. - see Martínez de Toledo, A.
Germain-Thomas, O. La Tentation des Indes.
  J. Blot, 450(NRF):Sep81-133
German, T.J. Hamann on Language and
  Religion.
  P. Gardiner, 617(TLS):6Aug82-864

"Germanistische Studientexte: Wort — Satz —
  Text."
  D. Herberg, 682(ZPSK):Band33Heft2-275
Gernet, J. A History of Chinese Civiliza-
  tion.
  J. Spence, 453(NYRB):1Apr82-45
Gernet, L. The Anthropology of Ancient
  Greece.
  J. Griffin, 617(TLS):12Nov82-1235
Gersh, S. From Iamblichus to Eriugena.*
  J. Pépin, 589:Apr81-380
Gervais, C.H. The Believable Body.
  D. Barbour, 648(WCR):Vol 15No3-43
Gervais, C.H. Up Country Lines.
  D. Barbour, 648(WCR):Vol 15No3-43
  K.P. Stich, 628(UWR):Fall-Winter81-126
Gervais, D. Flaubert and Henry James.*
  R.K. Cross, 445(NCF):Jun80-96
  K. Cushman, 594:Fall81-337
Gerver, D. and H.W. Sinaiko, eds. Lan-
  guage Interpretation and Communication.
  M.M. Bryant, 660(Word):Dec80-321
"Geschichte der deutschen Literatur."
  (Vol 6)
  P. Weber, 654(WB):2/1981-154
"Gesta Hungarorum." (D. Pais, trans)
  B. Brogyanyi, 688(ZSP):Band42Heft1-210
Getlein, F. Mary Cassatt.
  J.V. Turano, 16:Spring81-92
Gettleman, M.E. and others, eds. El
  Salvador.
  R. Bonner, 441:17Oct82-7
Geuss, R. The Idea of a Critical Theory.
  M. Rosen, 617(TLS):6Aug82-864
  Q. Skinner, 453(NYRB):7Oct82-35
Gewirth, A. Reason and Morality.*
  E. Regis, Jr., 311(JP):Dec81-786
  D.M. Taylor, 483:Apr81-266
Ghai, Y., ed. Law in the Political
  Economy of Public Enterprises.
  J. Vanderlinden, 69:Vol50No1-104
Ghanānand. Love Poems of Ghanānand.*
  (K.P. Bahadur, trans)
  C.R. King, 314:Summer-Fall81-247
Gharghoury, M. L'Erotique méditerranéenne
  dans le roman français contemporain
  (1920-1965).
  A. Nuccitelli, 207(FR):Apr81-747
  J. Onimus, 535(RHL):Mar-Apr81-334
Ghatage, A.M., general ed. An Encyclopae-
  dic Dictionary of Sanskrit on Historical
  Principles. (Vol 1, Pt 1)
  W. Morgenroth, 682(ZPSK):Band33Heft6-
  734
Ghatage, A.M., general ed. An Encyclopae-
  dic Dictionary of Sanskrit on Historical
  Principles. (Vol 1, Pt 2)
  G. Cardona, 261:Sep79-198
  O. von Hinüber, 259(IIJ):Jan81-41
  W. Morgenroth, 682(ZPSK):Band33Heft6-
  734
Ghatage, A.M., general ed. An Encyclopae-
  dic Dictionary of Sanskrit on Historical
  Principles. (Vol 1, Pt 3)
  O. von Hinüber, 259(IIJ):Jan81-41
Ghil, R. "Traité du Verbe."* (T. Goruppi,
  ed)
  V.J. Daniel, 208(FS):Oct81-462
Ghirshman, R. Terasses Sacrées de Bard-è
  Néchandeh et Masjid-i Solaiman.
  R.N. Frye, 318(JAOS):Jan/Mar80-82
Ghiselin, B. Windrose.*
  V. Young, 249(HudR):Spring81-146

Ghose, Z. Hamlet, Prufrock and Language.
  C. Richards, 447(N&Q):Oct80-476
Ghose, Z. A New History of Torments.
  A. Bold, 617(TLS):10Sep82-981
Giani Rotelli, G. Du studi sul simbol-
  ismo.
  A. Guyaux, 535(RHL):May-Jun81-475
Giaquinto, A. Dragão de mofo.
  W.A. Luchting, 399(MLJ):Summer81-209
Gibault, H. John Galt romancier écossais.
  E. Frykman, 571(ScLJ):Summer80-102
Gibbon, L.G. Smeddum. (D.M. Budge, ed)
  D. Young, 571(ScLJ):Winter81-131
Gibbon, M. The Pupil.
  V. Mercier, 617(TLS):2Apr82-369
Gibbons, R., ed. The Poet's Work.*
  M.K. Spears, 579(SAQ):Winter81-116
Gibbons, R. The Ruined Motel.
  J.R. Reed, 385(MQR):Fall82-680
Gibbons, R. - see Cernuda, L.
Gibbs, R. I've Always Felt Sorry for
  Decimals.
  A. Schroeder, 102(CanL):Summer80-144
Gibellini, P., ed. Folengo e dintorni.
  M. Chiesa, 228(GSLI):Vol 158fasc504-
  608
Gibson, A. Biblical Semantic Logic.
  P. Ellingworth, 617(TLS):15Jan82-62
Gibson, A.M. - see Kipling, R.
Gibson, C. - see Massinger, P.
Gibson, E. The "Christians for Chris-
  tians" Inscriptions of Phrygia.*
  É. Des Places, 555:Vol54fasc1-172
Gibson, E.K. C.S. Lewis, Spinner of Tales.
  C.E. Lloyd, 569(SR):Spring81-281
Gibson, G., with C. Renison. Bull of the
  Woods.
  G.W., 102(CanL):Autumn81-193
Gibson, I. La noche en que mataron a
  Calvo Sotelo.
  H. Southworth, 617(TLS):8Oct82-1107
Gibson, J. - see Hardy, T.
Gibson, J.C.L. Textbook of Syrian Semitic
  Inscriptions. (Vols 1 and 2)
  D.R. Hillers, 318(JAOS):Apr/Jun80-177
Gibson, J.J. The Ecological Approach to
  Visual Perception.*
  K. James, 576:Mar81-86
Gibson, J.M. and R.L. Green - see Doyle,
  A.C.
Gibson, M., ed. Boethius.
  R.A. Markus, 617(TLS):8Jan82-29
Gibson, R., ed. Modern French Poets on
  Poetry.
  205(FMLS):Apr80-191
Gibson, T. A Soldier of India.
  S. Altinel, 617(TLS):20Aug82-910
Gibson, W.M. Theodore Roosevelt Among the
  Humorists.*
  R.B. Hauck, 395(MFS):Winter80/81-652
  J.S. Tuckey, 27(AL):Nov81-558
Giddens, A. A Contemporary Critique of
  Historical Materialism. (Vol 1)
  T.B. Bottomore, 617(TLS):12Mar82-271
Gide, A. and J-É. Blanche. Correspondance
  André Gide - Jacques Émile Blanche 1892-
  1939. (G-P. Collet, ed)
  D. Moutote, 535(RHL):Jul-Oct81-834
Gide, A. and D. Bussy. Correspondance
  André Gide-Dorothy Bussy. (Vol 3)
  (J. Lambert and R. Tedeschi, eds)
  P. Pollard, 617(TLS):10ct82-1072

Gidel, H. Le Théâtre de Feydeau.*
  B.T. Cooper, 446(NCFS):Fall-Win-
  ter80/81-143
  M. Corvin, 535(RHL):Jul-Oct81-828
  A.G. Tunks, 207(FR):Feb81-474
Gielgud, K.T. A Victorian Playgoer.*
  B.A. Young, 157:2ndQtr81-50
Gier, H. Die Entstehung des deutschen
  Expressionismus und die antisymbolis-
  tische Reaktion in Frankreich.*
  W.D. Elfe, 406:Summer81-237
Giergelewicz, M., with L. Krzyżanowski,
  eds. Polish Civilization.
  J.T. Baer, 497(PolR):Vol26No1-118
Gies, D.T. Nicolás Fernández de Moratín.
  P. Deacon, 402(MLR):Jul81-724
  J. Dowling, 240(HR):Summer81-359
  R.B. Klein, 238:Sep81-477
  I.L. McClelland, 86(BHS):Jul81-267
Gies, F. and J. Women in the Middle Ages.
  G. Macdonald, 435:Winter81-113
Gifford, B. and L. Lee. Jack's Book.*
  D. Stanley, 649(WAL):Summer81-138
Gifford, H. Tolstoy.
  A. Ryan, 362:18Mar82-21
Gigante, M. Civiltà delle forme letter-
  arie nell'antico Pompei.
  M.S. Smith, 123:Vol31No1-52
Gigante, M., ed. Poeti bizantini di terra
  d'Otranto nel secolo XIII. (2nd ed)
  A.R. Littlewood, 589:Jul81-615
Gigante, M. and W. Schmid - see Usener, H.
Gignac, F.T. A Grammar of the Greek Pap-
  yri of the Roman and Byzantine Periods.
  (Vol 1)
  H. Schmoll, 260(IF):Band85-351
Gigon, O., ed. Entretiens sur l'antiquité
  classique.* (Vol 24: Lucrèce.)
  D.P. Fowler, 313:Vol71-218
  J. Perret, 555:Vol54fasc1-184
Giguère, D. Wings in the Wind.*
  C. Gerson, 102(CanL):Spring81-124
Giguère, R. Forêt vierge folle.
  E-M. Kroller, 102(CanL):Winter80-132
Gilbert, A. Marx's Politics.
  D. McLellan, 617(TLS):5Feb82-140
Gilbert, A.J. Literary Language from
  Chaucer to Johnson.
  M. Cooley, 350:Jun81-501
  R.J. Corthell, 506(PSt):Dec81-337
  S. Peterfreund, 566:Autumn80-43
Gilbert, A.T. Ann Taylor Gilbert's Album.*
  (C.D. Stewart, ed)
  P.H. Muir, 78(BC):Winter81-558
Gilbert, C. Nerval's Double.
  O. Avni, 546(RR):May81-362
  M-F.E. Baer, 207(FR):Feb81-471
  H. Cassou-Yager, 446(NCFS):Spring-Sum-
  mer81-269
Gilbert, C.B. A Bibliography of the Works
  of Dorothy L. Sayers.*
  L. Madden, 447(N&Q):Jun80-262
Gilbert, C.E. Italian Art 1400-1500.*
  (H.W. Janson, ed)
  90:Oct81-642
Gilbert, G.G. - see Schuchardt, H.
Gilbert, G.G. and J. Ornstein, eds. Prob-
  lems in Applied Educational Sociolinguis-
  tics.
  A. Pousada, 350:Sep82-740
  205(FMLS):Apr80-191

Gilbert, J. Monolithos.
    M. Kinzie, 29:Sep/Oct82-37
    R. Tillinghast, 441:12Sep82-42
    H. Vendler, 453(NYRB):23Sep82-41
Gilbert, J.G. Edmund Waller.
    J.L. Selzer, 568(SCN):Spring81-11
Gilbert, M. Winston S. Churchill. (Companion Vol 5, Pt 3)
    J. Grigg, 362:18Nov82-26
Gilbert, M. End-Game.
    C.G. Heilbrun, 441:12Sep82-9
    442(NY):30Aug82-92
Gilbert, M. Mr. Calder and Mr. Behrens.
    T.J. Binyon, 617(TLS):25Jun82-702
    C.G. Heilbrun, 441:12Sep82-9
    M. Laski, 362:29Jul82-27
Gilbert, S.M. and S. Gubar. The Madwoman in the Attic.*
    B.T. Bennett, 340(KSJ):Vol30-207
    J.P. Brown, 591(SIR):Spring81-132
    A. Coombes, 366:Autumn81-261
    K. Frank, 481(PQ):Summer80-381
    A. Lebowitz, 648(WCR):Vol 15No3-58
    M. Miller, 639(VQR):Spring81-358
    H. Moglen, 445(NCF):Sep80-225
    E. Simmons, 184(EIC):Jul81-249
    J. Wilt, 81:Spring80-285
Gilbert, S.M. and S. Gubar, eds. Shakespeare's Sisters.*
    L.T. Hanley, 81:Spring80-301
Gilbert, W.S. The Lost Stories of W.S. Gilbert. (P. Haining, ed)
    P. Kemp, 362:11Nov82-26
Gilbert, W.S. Plays by W.S. Gilbert. (G. Rowell, ed)
    J. Hankey, 617(TLS):20Aug82-901
Gilboa, A. The Light of Lost Suns.
    A. Cluysenaar, 565:Vol22No2-62
    D.R. Mesher, 390:May81-61
Gilchrist, E. In the Land of Dreamy Dreams.
    B. Allen, 434:Spring82-478
    J. Crace, 617(TLS):15Oct82-1142
    J. Thompson, 435:Fall81-306
Gilder, G. Wealth and Poverty.*
    R. Klein, 617(TLS):10Sep82-967
    E.C. Pasour, Jr., 396(ModA):Fall81-388
    W.H. Peterson, 396(ModA):Summer81-306
    D. Usher, 529(QQ):Winter81-651
Gildner, G. Letters from Vicksburg.
    W. Slesinger, 448:Vol 19No1/2-246
Gildon, C. The Plays of Charles Gildon.
    566:Spring82-130
Giles, H. and R. St. Clair, eds. Language and Social Psychology.*
    J. Fishman, 350:Mar81-220
Giles, M.E. and K. Hohlwein, eds. Enter the Heart of the Fire.
    P. Ramsey, 472:Spring/Summer82-172
Giles, P., with D. Mallinder. The Counter Tenor.
    A. Burgess, 617(TLS):2Apr82-378
Gill, A. The Early Mallarmé.* (Vol 1)
    M.L. Assad, 446(NCFS):Fall-Winter81/82-160
    U. Franklin, 207(FR):Dec81-276
    A.J. Steele, 402(MLR):Oct81-974
    205(FMLS):Oct80-375
Gill, B., with D. Moore. The Dream Come True.*
    M.S. Young, 39:Jun81-415
    505:Jan81-208

Gill, D. Quest.*
    639(VQR):Spring81-47
Gill, P.E. Moral Judgments of Violence among Irish and Swedish Adolescents.
    M.G.H., 185:Jul82-784
Gille, K.F., ed. Goethes "Wilhelm Meister."
    E. Boa, 402(MLR):Apr81-504
    H.M.K. Riley, 406:Fall81-349
Gillel'son, M.I. and I.B. Musina. Povest' A.S. Puškina "Kapitanskaja Dočka."
    P. Debreczeny, 558(RLJ):Winter81-221
Gillespie, N.C. Charles Darwin and the Problem of Creation.*
    F.B. Churchill, 637(VS):Winter81-255
Gillet, J. Le "Paradis perdu" dans la littérature française de Voltaire à Chateaubriand.
    T. Logé, 356(LR):Feb-May81-161
Gilliard, F. L'expérience juridique, Esquisse d'une dialectique.
    G.A. Legault, 154:Mar81-152
Gilliatt, P. Quotations From Other Lives.
    R. Dinnage, 441:11Apr82-6
    V. Glendinning, 617(TLS):20Aug82-910
Gilligan, C. In a Different Voice.
    C. Tavris, 441:2May82-14
Gillis, E.A. South By West.
    P. Varner, 649(WAL):Fall81-242
Gillon, A. Conrad and Shakespeare.
    J. Batchelor, 447(N&Q):Dec80-561
    D. Hewitt, 541(RES):Aug81-353
Gillon, W. Collecting African Art.*
    A. Rubin, 2(AfrA):Nov80-79
Gilman, E.B. The Curious Perspective.*
    J. Harvey, 184(EIC):Oct80-346
    F.J. Warnke, 301(JEGP):Jan81-128
Gilman, S. Galdós and the Art of the European Novel: 1867-1887.
    P.A. Bly, 268(IFR):Summer82-154
    A. Terry, 617(TLS):4Jun82-601
Gilmore, M. Letters of Mary Gilmore. (W.H. Wilde and T.I. Moore, eds)
    F.H. Mares, 71(ALS):May81-139
Gilpin, R. War and Change in World Politics.
    J. Keegan, 453(NYRB):23Sep82-27
Gilsenan, M. Recognising Islam.
    P. Mansfield, 362:21Oct82-23
Gilson, D. A Bibliography of Jane Austen.
    P. Rogers, 617(TLS):12Nov82-1242
Gimson, A.C. - see Jones, D.
Gindin, J. The English Climate.
    D.E. Van Tassel, 395(MFS):Summer80-310
Gingrich, F.W. and F.W. Danker - see Bauer, W.
Ginsberg, A. Plutonian Ode.
    W. Logan, 617(TLS):12Nov82-1251
Ginsberg, A. and P. Orlofsky. Straight Hearts' Delight. (W. Leyland, ed)
    D. Pinckney, 472:Spring/Summer82-99
Ginsburgs, G. and C.F. Pinkele. The Sino-Soviet Territorial Dispute, 1949-1964.
    J. Harris, 550(RusR):Apr81-206
Ginzburg, C. Les batailles nocturnes. Le fromage et les vers.
    R. Chartier, 98:Jan81-72
Ginzburg, C. The Cheese and the Worms.
    J.L. Pearl, 539:May82-142
Ginzburg, C. Indagini su Piero.
    J. White, 617(TLS):1Oct82-1077

Giono, J. Angélique.
  M.I. Madden, 207(FR):Oct81-158
  F. de Martinoir, 450(NRF):Feb81-105
Giono, J. Blue Boy. The Song of the
  World. Joy of Man's Desiring. The
  Horseman on the Roof.
  L. Davis, 441:4Jul82-4
Giono, J. Coeurs, passions, caractères.
  W.D. Redfern, 617(TLS):8Oct82-1113
Giordano, C. and S. Yurkievich - see under
  "Collins Robert French-English, English-
  French Dictionary"
Giorello, G. and S. Morini - see Thom, R.
Giovanoli, S. Form und Funktion des
  Schuldramas im 16. Jahrhundert.
  T.W. Best, 221(GQ):Nov81-502
Giovio, P. Dialogo dell'imprese militari
  e amorose. (M.L. Doglio, ed)
  T.C.P. Zimmermann, 551(RenQ):Winter80-
  780
Gipper, H. and P. Schmitter. Sprachwissen-
  schaft und Sprachphilosophie im Zeit-
  alter der Romantik.
  H. Birnbaum, 350:Mar81-226
  W. Oesterreicher, 224(GRM):Band31Heft1-
  106
Gipper, H. and H. Schwarz, eds. Biblio-
  graphisches Handbuch zur Sprachinhalts-
  forschung. (Vol 1)
  P. Swiggers, 350:Jun81-489
Girard, R. "To double business bound."
  A. Demaitre, 207(FR):Dec81-258
Girard, R. Violence and the Sacred.*
  (French title: La violence et le sacré.)
  T. Molnar, 396(ModA):Summer81-329
Girard, R., with J.M. Oughourlian and G.
  Lefort. Des choses cachées depuis la
  fondation du monde.*
  B. Bassoff, 577(SHR):Summer81-262
de Girardin, R-L. De la composition des
  paysages.
  J-R. Mantion, 98:Dec81-1301
Girbal de Blacha, N.M. Los centros agrí-
  colas en la Provincia de Buenos Aires.
  P.S. Bollo Cabrios, 263(RIB):Vol31No3-
  408
Girgus, S.B. The Law of the Heart.*
  L. Cederstrom, 106:Fall81-235
Girgus, S.N., ed. The American Self.
  27(AL):Nov81-574
  639(VQR):Summer81-92
Girling, J.L.S. America and the Third
  World.
  M. Selden, 293(JASt):May81-568
de la Giroday, V. Die Übersetzertätigkeit
  des Münchner Dichterkreises.
  J.K. Fugate, 406:Summer81-232
Girouard, M. Life in the English Country
  House.*
  K. Garlick, 447(N&Q):Oct80-424
Girouard, M. The Return to Camelot.*
  G. Mortimer, 364:Feb82-89
Girouard, M. The Victorian Country House.*
  J.D. Hunt, 43:Band10Heft2-190
Girouard, M. Alfred Waterhouse and The
  Natural History Museum.*
  G. Stamp, 324:Feb82-167
Giroux, R. The Book Known as Q.
  P-L. Adams, 61:Jun82-101
  F. Taliaferro, 441:29Aug82-13
  442(NY):7Jun82-144
Giroux, R. Voici. S. L'arbre de temps.
  D. Cahen, 98:Jun-Jul80-666

Gissing, G. Born in Exile. (P. Coustil-
  las, ed)
  R. Barrow, 541(RES):Nov81-475
  S. Monod, 189(EA):Jan-Mar81-100
Gissing, G. Denzil Quarrier. (J. Hal-
  perin, ed)
  R. Barrow, 541(RES):Nov81-475
Gissing, G. London and the Life of Litera-
  ture in Late Victorian England.* (P.
  Coustillas, ed)
  J. Halperin, 677(YES):Vol 11-339
  J. Korg, 637(VS):Autumn80-130
  M. Squires, 395(MFS):Summer80-314
Gissing, G. Will Warburton. (C. Part-
  ridge, ed) The Town Traveller. (P.
  Coustillas, ed)
  P. Keating, 617(TLS):31Dec82-1447
Gittings, R. and J. Manton. The Second
  Mrs. Hardy.*
  P.J. Casagrande, 445(NCF):Sep80-219
  J. Halperin, 395(MFS):Summer80-302
  C. Lock, 184(EIC):Oct80-367
  295(JML):Vol18No3/4-514
Gittins, D. Fair Sex.
  P. Willmott, 617(TLS):15Oct82-1143
Giudici, E. Louise Labé.
  S. Petrey, 207(FR):May82-902
"Ciuffrè, Una Apertura Hacia lo Real."
  L.J. Penay, 37:Nov-Dec81-22
Giuliani, O. Allegoria retorica e poetica
  nel "Secretum" del Petrarca.*
  G. Costa, 545(RPh):Feb81 354
Giustiniani, V.R. Neulateinische Dichtung
  in Italien 1850-1950.
  E. Loos, 72:Band217Heft2-391
Givner, J. Katherine Anne Porter.
  P-L. Adams, 61:Dec82-105
  E. Hardwick, 441:7Nov82-3
Givón, T. Discourse and Syntax.
  G.M. Green, 350:Sep82-672
  W.A. Smalley, 361:Feb-Mar81-275
Givón, T. On Understanding Grammar.*
  R.W. Langacker, 350:Jun81-436
  R.D. Van Valin, Jr., 361:May81-47
Givón, T., ed. Syntax and Semantics.
  (Vol 12)
  M.L. Owen, 353:Vol 18No7/8-721
Gladstone, W.E. The Gladstone Diaries.
  (Vols 7 and 8) (H.C.G. Matthew, ed)
  S. Koss, 617(TLS):22Oct82-1151
Gladstone, W.E. The Prime Ministers'
  Papers Series, W.E. Gladstone. (Vol 4)
  (J. Brooke and M. Sorensen, eds)
  R. Foster, 617(TLS):16Apr82-430
Glaesemer, J. Paul Klee.
  R. Hohl, 471:Jan/Feb/Mar81-93
Glaeser, G. - see Brecht, B.
Glaister, G.A. Glaister's Glossary of the
  Book.* (2nd ed)
  P.S. Koda, 517(PBSA):Apr-Jun81-219
Glang-Süberkrüb, A. Der Liebesgarten.
  R. Verdi, 90:Feb81-106
Glaser, E. Peripheral Vision.*
  M. Kinzie, 29:Mar/Apr82-13
Glass, M. Bone Love.
  S.T. Ryan, 436(NewL):Winter81/82-118
Glassey, L.K.J. Politics and the Appoint-
  ment of Justices of the Peace, 1675-
  1720.*
  H.T. Dickinson, 566:Spring82-128
Glassie, H. Irish Folk History.
  P. Craig, 617(TLS):5Nov82-1214
  E. Larkin, 441:25Jul82-9

131

Glassie, H. Passing the Time in Ballymen-
one.
P. Craig, 617(TLS):5Nov82-1214
E. Larkin, 441:25Jul82-9
442(NY):16Aug82-92
Glasson, S. - see Marguerite de Navarre
Glatz, F., ed. Ostmitteleuropa im zweiten
Weltkrieg.*
G.R. Kleinfeld, 104(CASS):Winter81-619
Glatzer, N.N. - see Kafka, F.
Glauche, G. and H. Knaus - see Bischoff, B.
Glauert, B., ed. Carl Zuckmayer: Das Büh-
nenwerk im Spiegel der Kritik.
H. Glade, 400(MLN):Apr81-684
Glauser, A. Le faux Rabelais ou De
l'inauthenticité du Cinquième Livre.
S. Bisarello, 356(LR):Aug81-249
Glauser, A. La Poétique de Hugo.*
S. Nash, 210(FrF):Jan81-91
P.A. Ward, 207(FR):Oct80-168
Glavin, A. One for Sorrow.
A. Douglas, 305(JIL):Sep81-111
Glazer, M., ed. Burning Air and a Clear
Mind.
385(MQR):Spring82-374
Glazier, S.D. Perspectives on Pentecostal-
ism.
C.L. Dow, 37:Jun-Jul81-23
Gleason, A. Young Russia.*
R.K. Debo, 529(QQ):Spring81-115
Gleeck, L.E., Jr. The Manila Americans
(1901-1964).
D.R. Sturtevant, 293(JASt):Feb81-423
Glen, D. Realities Poems.
C. Craig, 571(ScLJ):Winter81-140
Glenday, A. Follow, Follow.
L. Wilson, 368:Dec73-353
Glendinning, N. and N. Harrison - see de
Cadalso, J.
Glendinning, V. Edith Sitwell.*
A. Ross, 364:Nov81-92
Glennon, J. Understanding Music.
G. Poole, 415:Aug81-536
Gless, D.J. "Measure for Measure," the
Law, and the Convent.*
R. Battenhouse, 125:Spring81-323
W. Blissett, 539:May82-154
G.M. Ridden, 366:Autumn81-250
R.P. Wheeler, 405(MP):Nov81-193
Glickman, N.J. The Growth and Management
of the Japanese Urban System.
G.D. Allinson, 293(JASt):Feb81-381
Glickman, R.J. - see del Casal, J.
Glissant, É. La Case du Commandeur.
L. Kovacs, 450(NRF):Oct81-147
J. Silenieks, 207(FR):Apr82-704
Gloag, J. Sleeping Dogs Lie.*
W. Boyd, 364:Apr/May81-129
Glofcheskie, J.M. Folk Music of Canada's
Oldest Polish Community.
B. Nettl, 650(WF):Oct81-344
Glover, D. The Lost Village.
F. Tuohy, 617(TLS):26Nov82-1318
Glover, M. A Very Slippery Fellow.
A.J. Hessom, 161(DUJ):Dec80-86
Gloversmith, F., ed. Class, Culture and
Social Change.*
P. Lewis, 565:Vol22No3-55
Gloy, K. Die Kantische Theorie der Natur-
wissenschaft.
H. Hoppe, 342:Band71Heft3-373

Gluck, B.R. Beckett and Joyce.*
C.C. Andonian, 188(ECr):Fall81-100
M. Beja, 395(MFS):Summer80-276
Glück, L. Descending Figure.*
C. Bedient, 472:Spring/Summer81-168
J.F. Cotter, 249(HudR):Summer81-285
T. Diggory, 560:Fall81-146
R. von Hallberg, 659(ConL):Spring82-
225
M. Kinzie, 29:Sep/Oct82-37
D. Smith, 29:Jan/Feb82-36
P. Stitt, 219(GaR):Spring81-182
S. Yenser, 676(YR):Autumn81-97
639(VQR):Spring81-66
Glucker, J. Antiochus and the Late
Academy.
J. Barnes, 313:Vol71-205
J. Dillon, 123:Vol31No1-60
Glymour, C. Theory and Evidence.*
F.J. Clendinnen, 63:Mar81-104
M.A.F., 543:Sep80-135
A. Morton, 486:Sep81-498
R. Swinburne, 84:Sep81-314
Glynn, P. Skin to Skin.
P-L. Adams, 61:Dec82-107
Gmelin, H.G. Wilhelm Busch als Maler.
E. Ruhmer, 471:Apr/May/Jun81-187
Gmelin, O.F. Böses aus Kinderbüchern und
ein roter Elefant. (2nd ed)
K.F. Geiger, 196:Band21Heft3/4-310
Gnoli, G. and J-P. Vernant, eds. La mort,
les morts dans les sociétés anciennes.
J. Griffin, 617(TLS):12Nov82-1235
Gobert, I. La vie publique et privée dans
l'Inde ancienne. (fasc 2)
F. Wilhelm, 318(JAOS):Apr/Jun80-162
Gobin, P. Le Fou et ses doubles.*
A.B. Chartier, 207(FR):Dec80-335
D.W. Russell, 102(CanL):Summer80-130
Gochet, P. Outline of a Nominalist Theory
of Propositions.
S. Leblanc, 154:Sep81-592
Gochet, P. Quine en perspective.*
C. Imbert, 98:Apr80-393
Gockel, H. Max Frisch: "Gantenbein."*
(2nd ed)
H.F. Pfanner, 406:Fall81-366
Godard, H. Album Giono.
R. Ricatte, 535(RHL):Jul-Oct81-839
Godard, H., ed. Cahiers Giono 2.
W.D. Redfern, 617(TLS):8Oct82-1113
Godbout, J. Dragon Isle.
K. Mezei, 102(CanL):Autumn80-119
Godbout, J. Les têtes à Papineau.
P. France, 617(TLS):15Jan82-63
Goddard, V. Skies to Dunkirk.
B. Bond, 617(TLS):13Aug82-886
Godden, M. - see Aelfric
Godden, R. The Dark Horse.*
P-L. Adams, 61:Feb82-87
442(NY):8Feb82-128
Goder-Stark, P. Das Kurt-Tucholsky-Archiv.
H. Mörchen, 680(ZDP):Band99Heft2-298
Godfrey, R.T. Printmaking in Britain.*
D. Alexander, 135:Aug81-250
Godin, J-C. and L. Mailhot. Théâtre québé-
cois II.
L.E. Doucette, 627(UTQ):Summer81-177
J.M. Weiss, 102(CanL):Spring81-119
Godiveau, R. 1000 difficultés courantes
du français parlé.
R.J. Melpignano, 399(MLJ):Summer81-218

Godoy Gallardo, E. La infancia en la
narrativa española de posguerra, 1939-
1978.
    L. Hickey, 86(BHS):Jan81-90
Godsell, P. - see Lady Durham
Godwin, G. A Mother and Two Daughters.*
    J. Hendin, 441:10Jan82-3
    J. Uglow, 617(TLS):5Mar82-246
    442(NY):18Jan82-129
Godwin, J. Mystery Religions in the
Ancient World.
    M. Beard, 617(TLS):15Jan82-60
Goebel, J. The Struggle for the Falkland
Islands.
    H.S. Ferns, 617(TLS):2Jul82-709
Goedert, G. Nietzsche.
    J. Salaquarda, 53(AGP):Band63Heft1-97
Goedicke, H. The Protocol of Neferty (The
Prophecy of Neferti).
    D.B. Redford, 318(JAOS):Jul/Sep80-369
Goertz, H-J., ed. Radikale Reformatoren.
    W. Wegstein, 684(ZDA):Band11OHeft2-81
von Goethe, J.W. Goethe on Art.* (J.
Gage, ed and trans)
    P. Fingesten, 290(JAAC):Winter81-229
von Goethe, J.W. Goethe's Plays.* (C.E.
Passage, trans)
    D. Devlin, 157:Oct80-72
    L. Dieckmann, 130:Spring81-95
Goetsch, P. Bauformen des modernen englis-
chen und amerikanischen Dramas.*
    A. Klein, 38:Band99Heft3/4-541
Goetz, H. Rajput Art and Architecture.
(J. Jain and J. Jain-Neubauer, eds)
    M.C. Beach, 293(JASt):May81-631
Goetz-Stankiewicz, M. The Silenced Thea-
tre.
    H. Eagle, 627(UTQ):Summer81-152
    R.B. Pynsent, 575(SEER):Jan81-93
    P.I. Trensky, 574(SEEJ):Spring81-124
    G.W., 102(CanL):Summer80-179
le Goff, J. La Naissance du Purgatoire.
    R.W. Southern, 617(TLS):18Jun82-651
le Goff, J. and J.C. Schmitt, eds. Le
Charivari.
    B. Stock, 617(TLS):25Jun82-698
Goff, T.W. Marx and Mead.
    G.F., 543:Jun81-788
Goffman, E. Forms of Talk.*
    H.L. Goodall, Jr., 583:Winter82-235
    P.M. Spacks, 676(YR):Winter82-274
Gogarty, O.S. Tumbling in the Hay.
    R. Brown, 617(TLS):12Mar82-289
Gogol, N. The Theater of Nikolay Gogol.*
(M. Ehre, ed)
    E.J. Czerwinski, 130:Spring81-90
    M. Green, 574(SEEJ):Spring81-100
Gohin, Y. - see Hugo, V.
Goins, C.R. and J.W. Morris. Oklahoma
Homes Past and Present.
    L. Milazzo, 584(SWR):Spring81-v
Goitein, S.D. A Mediterranean Society.*
(Vol 3)
    M.A. Friedman, 318(JAOS):Apr/Jun80-128
Gokhale, B.G. Surat in the Seventeenth
Century.
    M.N. Pearson, 293(JASt):Aug81-821
Golan, G. Yom Kippur and After.
    H. Hanak, 575(SEER):Apr81-317
Golan, M. Shimon Peres.
    C.C. O'Brien, 362:30Sep82-18
Gold, A. Some of the Cat Poems.
    J. Giltrow, 102(CanL):Spring81-145

Gold, A. and R. Fizdale. Misia.*
    M. Wagner, 207(FR):Feb81-490
Gold, B.K., ed. Literary and Artistic
Patronage in Ancient Rome.
    N.M. Horsfall, 617(TLS):13Aug82-877
Gold, H. True Love.
    P. Andrews, 441:12Dec82-14
Goldbarth, A. Different Fleshes.
    W. Harmon, 577(SHR):Spring81-182
Goldberg, G.J. Heart Payments.
    P-L. Adams, 61:Mar82-88
Goldberg, M. Namesake.
    P. Fussell, 441:5Sep82-3
    S. Jacobson, 362:14Oct82-28
Goldberg, S.M. The Making of Menander's
Comedy.
    P. Arnott, 130:Fall81-278
    D. Thompson, 157:1stQtr81-54
Goldberg, V., ed. Photography in Print.*
    42(AR):Summer81-392
Goldberger, P. The Skyscraper.* The City
Observed: New York.
    S. Gardiner, 362:4Mar82-24
    S. Gardiner, 617(TLS):26Mar82-338
Goldblat, J. Agreements for Arms Control.
    C.M. Woodhouse, 617(TLS):24Sep82-1030
"The Golden Age: Cincinnati Painters of
the Nineteenth Century Represented in
the Cincinnati Art Museum."
    H.W. Morgan, 658:Summer/Autumn81-232
Coldfarb, R.L. Migrant Farmworkers.
    M. Bayles, 441:2May82-18
Goldin, F. - see "The Song of Roland"
Golding, W. Darkness Visible.*
    J. Mills, 648(WCR):Vol 15No3-70
Golding, W. A Moving Target.
    G. Josipovici, 617(TLS):23Jul82-785
    J. Morris, 441:11Jul82-9
    C. Sigal, 362:24Jun82-22
Golding, W. Rites of Passage.*
    D. Flower, 249(HudR):Spring81-111
    R. Gray, 97(CQ):Vol 10No3-242
    P. Lewis, 565:Vol22No3-55
    S. Monod, 189(EA):Oct-Dec81-489
    E. Owen, 175:Summer81-195
Goldman, A. Elvis.*
    B. Morrison, 617(TLS):29Jan82-111
    442(NY):4Jan82-90
Goldman, A.H. Justice and Reverse Discrim-
ination.*
    I. Thalberg, 185:Oct80-138
Goldman, A.H. The Moral Foundations of
Professional Ethics.
    R. Goodin, 185:Oct81-137
Goldman, A.I. and J. Kim, eds. Values and
Morals.*
    N.J.H. Dent, 393(Mind):Jan81-144
    G. Wallace, 479(PhQ):Jan81-81
Goldman, B. - see Hopkins, C.
Goldman, L. Sounding the Territory.
    E. Eichman, 231:Apr82-107
    J.C. Oates, 441:21Feb82-1
    G. Strawson, 617(TLS):17Sep82-992
Goldman, M. China's Intellectuals.*
    R. Garside, 441:3Jan82-7
Goldman, R. and J. Children's Sexual
Thinking.
    A. Clare, 362:29Apr82-22
Goldman, R.F. Selected Essays and Reviews
1948-1968. (D. Klotzman, ed)
    P. Dickinson, 415:Sep81-606

Goldman, R.P. Gods, Priests, and War-
riors.*
    N.E. Falk, 314:Winter-Spring81-223
Goldman, W. Control.
    E. Hunter, 441:25Apr82-13
Goldmann, L. Towards a Sociology of the
Novel.
    205(FMLS):Apr80-188
Goldring, M. and Y. Quilès. Sous le mar-
teau, la plume.
    D. Johnson, 617(TLS):2Jul82-707
Goldschmidt, H., ed. Zu Beethoven.
    W. Drabkin, 415:Oct81-671
Goldschmidt, L. and W. Naef. The Truthful
Lens.
    R.W., 55:Nov81-44
Goldschmidt, W. Culture and Behaviour of
the Sebei.
    A. Bourgeot, 69:Vol50No1-108
Goldsmith, M.E. The Figure of Piers Plow-
man.
    P. Neuss, 617(TLS):23Apr82-470
Goldsmith, U.K., with T. Schneider and
S.S. Coleman, eds. Rainer Maria Rilke:
A Verse Concordance to His Complete
Lyrical Poetry.
    B.L. Bradley, 301(JEGP):Oct81-612
Goldstein, J.K. The Modern American Vice-
Presidency.
    H.G. Nicholas, 617(TLS):8Oct82-1092
Goldstein, K. and N.V. Rosenberg, with
others, eds. Folklore Studies in
Honour of Herbert Halpert.
    U. Kutter, 196:Band22Heft3/4-342
Goldstein, L. Ruins and Empire.*
    B.S. Hammond, 179(ES):Apr81-178
Goldstein, L.F. The Constitutional Rights
of Women.
    N.O.K., 185:Oct80-175
Goldstein, M., ed. Tibetan-English Dic-
tionary of Modern Tibetan.
    T.V. Wylie, 293(JASt):Nov80-123
Goldsworthy, M. Clothes for Disabled
People.
    P. Bach, 614:Summer82-13
Goldthrope, J.H., with C. Llewellyn and C.
Payne. Social Mobility and Class Struc-
ture in Modern Britain.
    T.C. Miller, 185:Jul82-766
Goldthwaite, R.A. The Building of Renais-
sance Florence.*
    F. Gilbert, 453(NYRB):21Jan82-62
    I. Hyman, 576:Dec81-332
Goldziher, I. Introduction to Islamic
Theology and Law.
    F.W. Zimmermann, 617(TLS):5Feb82-146
Goldziher, I. Tagebuch. (A. Scheiber, ed)
    G.M. Wickens, 318(JAOS):Jan/Mar80-34
Göller, K.H. - see Gutch, D.
Gollin, R.K. Nathaniel Hawthorne and the
Truth of Dreams.*
    M.J. Colacurcio, 183(ESQ):Vol27No2-108
Golovin, P.N. The End of Russian America.
(B. Dmytryshyn and E.A.P. Crownhart-
Vaughan, eds and trans)
    L.T. Black, 550(RusR):Apr81-188
    R.A. Pierce, 104(CASS):Winter81-592
Golt, R. Eternal Saudi Arabia.
    P-L. Adams, 61:Feb82-88
Gom, L. Land of the Peace.
    B.K. Filson, 526:Spring81-72
Gombrich, E.H. Art and Illusion.*
    A. Woods, 97(CQ):Vol 10No2-130

Gombrich, E.H. The Image and the Eye.
    R. Arnheim, 617(TLS):29Oct82-1179
    M. Vaizey, 441:26Sep82-9
Gombrich, E.H. The Sense of Order.*
    F. Sparshott, 289:Jan81-126
Gomes de Matos, F. and S.S. Biazioli, eds.
Instituto de Idiomas Yázigi: Portugês do
Brasil para Estrangeiros.
    J.B. Jensen, 399(MLJ):Spring81-85
Gómez, I.M. - see under Mateo Gómez, I.
Gomez, J. Entwicklung und Perspektiven
der Literaturwissenschaft in der DDR.*
    W. Brettschneider, 52:Band15Heft1-107
Gómez, R.J. Las Teorías Científicas.
(Vol 1)
    R. Torretti, 449:May81-244
Gomme, A.H., ed. D.H. Lawrence.*
    H.T. Moore, 402(MLR):Oct81-943
Gomme, A.W., A. Andrewes and K.J. Dover.
A Historical Commentary on Thucydides.*
(Vol 5)
    J.T. Roberts, 24:Winter81-448
    D.L. Stockton, 123:Vol31No2-180
Gompertz, G.S.G.M. Chinese Celadon Wares.*
    M. Kim, 60:Jul-Aug81-140
Gonda, J. Vedic Literature (Saṃhitās and
Brāhmaṇas). The Ritual Sūtras.
    L. Rocher, 318(JAOS):Jan/Mar80-41
Gonda, J. - see Nijenhuis, E.T.
Gondebeaud, L. Le Roman "picaresque"
anglais 1650-1730.
    P. Rogers, 189(EA):Oct-Dec81-470
"Göngu-Hrolfs Saga." (H. Pálsson and P.
Edwards, trans)
    O.D. MacRae-Gibson, 571(ScLJ):Winter81-
    103
Gonon, M., ed. Documents Linguistiques de
la France (série francoprovençale).
    M.S. La Du, 545(RPh):Feb81(supp)-325
González, A.G-B. - see under García-
Baquero González, A.
González, A.N. - see under Navarro Gon-
zález, A.
González-Cruz, L.F. Neruda.
    L. Guerra-Cunningham, 238:Mar81-161
    D.L. Shaw, 86(BHS):Apr81-159
González Delvalle, A. Función Patronal.
    F.E. Feito, 37:Oct81-26
González-del-Valle, L. and B.A. Shaw.
Luis Romero.
    D.K. Benson, 399(MLJ):Spring81-97
    M. Bieder, 238:Mar81-164
González-del-Valle, L.T. El teatro de
Federico García Lorca y otros ensayos
sobre literatura española e hispano-
americana.
    J. Lyon, 86(BHS):Oct81-349
González Ollé, F. - see de Horozco, S.
González Real, O. Anticipación y Reflex-
ión.
    F.E. Feito, 37:Oct81-26
Gooch, A. and Á. García de Paredes - see
"Cassell's Spanish-English English-
Spanish Dictionary"
Good, E.M. Giraffes, Black Dragons, and
Other Pianos.
    C. Ehrlich, 617(TLS):10Dec82-1374
"The Good Pub Guide 1983."
    R. Gilbert, 362:23and30Dec82-42
Goode, J. George Gissing.*
    J. Powers, 445(NCF):Jun80-115
Goode, J.M. Capital Losses.
    E. Verheyen, 576:May81-149

Goodenough, W.H. and H. Sugita. Trukese-
English Dictionary.
   D. Sherwood, 350:Dec81-975
Goodfield, J. An Imagined World.*
   639(VQR):Summer81-104
Goodheart, E. The Failure of Criticism.*
   M. Baumgarten, 125:Fall80-115
   H. Feldmann, 396(ModA):Fall81-430
   S. O'Connell, 418(MR):Spring81-185
Goodin, R.E. Manipulatory Politics.
   S.P. Gwin, 583:Spring81-310
Goodman, A.E. The Lost Peace.
   D.P. Chandler, 293(JASt):Nov80-77
Goodman, G.K. - see de Asis, L.
Goodman, J. American Genesis.*
   P. Riesman, 649(WAL):Winter81-335
Goodman, J. The Mond Legacy.
   S. Koss, 617(TLS):16Apr82-430
Goodman, J. National Health Care in Great
Britain.
   A. Bobak, 651(WHR):Spring81-69
Goodpaster, K.E. and K.M. Sayre, eds.
Ethics and Problems of the 21st Century.*
   R.E. Goodin, 185:Oct80-154
   O. O'Neill, 393(Mind):Oct81-624
Goodwin, A. The Friends of Liberty.*
   M. Fitzpatrick, 83:Spring81-101
Goodwin, C. The Oak Park Strategy.
   N.B. Bross, 185:Jan81-339
Goody, E.N. Parenthood and Social Repro-
duction.
   E. Gillies, 617(TLS):26Feb82-210
Goody, J. La raison graphique. (J. Bazin
and A. Bensa, eds and trans)
   R. Bautier, 209(FM):Oct81-373
Goodyear, F.R.D. - see Tacitus
Gopal, S. Jawaharlal Nehru. (Vol 2)
   R.L. Park, 293(JASt):Aug81-821
Göpel, E. and B., comps. Max Beckmann,
Katalog der Gemälde.*
   P. Selz, 54:Mar81-170
Goquingco, L.O. The Dances of the Emerald
Isles.
   U. Roberts, 60:Nov-Dec81-154
Gorceix, B., ed and trans. Alchimie.
   G. Auclair, 450(NRF):May81-132
Gordimer, N. Burger's Daughter.*
   B. King, 569(SR):Summer81-461
Gordimer, N. July's People.*
   E. Milton, 676(YR):Winter82-254
   J.D. O'Hara, 434:Summer82-603
   G. Perez, 249(HudR):Winter81/82-617
   639(VQR):Autumn81-136
Gordimer, N. Selected Stories.
   E.W. Githii, 145(Crit):Vol22No3-45
Gordimer, N. A Soldier's Embrace.*
   G. Johnson, 461(Spring-Summer81-92
   B. King, 569(SR):Summer81-461
   B. Lyons, 573(SSF):Summer81-335
   639(VQR):Spring81-60
Gordon, A. An American Dreamer.
   P. Bufithis, 659(ConL):Summer82-400
Gordon, A.D.D. Businessmen and Politics.
   B.R. Tomlinson, 293(JASt):May81-633
Gordon, B. Domestic American Textiles.
   P. Bach, 614:Winter82-17
Gordon, B. Shaker Textile Arts.
   P. Bach, 614:Winter81-19
Gordon, B.M. Collaborationism in France
during the Second World War.*
   H. Peyre, 207(FR):Apr82-690
   639(VQR):Winter81-9

Gordon, C. The Collected Stories of
Caroline Gordon.*
   H. Baker, 598(SoR):Spring82-427
   R.H. Brinkmeyer, Jr., 578:Spring82-62
   D. Kubal, 249(HudR):Autumn81-457
   J. Mellors, 362:15Apr82-23
Gordon, C. Aleck Maury, Sportsman.*
   R.H. Brinkmeyer, Jr., 578:Spring82-62
Gordon, G., ed. Shakespeare Stories.
   D. Nokes, 617(TLS):12Nov82-1243
Gordon, H. The Minister's Wife.
   J.A.S. Miller, 571(ScLJ):Summer80-115
Gordon, I.A. - see Galt, J.
Gordon, J. James Joyce's Metamorphoses.
   E. Neill, 617(TLS):22Oct82-1173
Gordon, M. The Company of Women.*
   P. Craig, 617(TLS):26Nov82-1318
Gordon, P. and J. White. Philosophers as
Educational Reformers.
   S.S., 543:Mar81-607
Gordon, R. Shady Lady.
   442(NY):31May82-106
Gordon, S. A Modest Harmony.
   R. Blythe, 441:25Jul82-8
Gordon, S. Welfare, Justice, and Freedom.
   W.J. Samuels, 185:Jul82-754
Gordon, W.T. Semantics: A Bibliography,
1965-1978.
   K. Allan, 350:Mar81-254
Gorges, J-G. Les villas hispano-romaines.
   J.C. Edmondson, 313:Vol71-217
Gorgoniev, J.A. Khmersko-Russkij Slovar'.
   R. Gaudes, 682(ZPSK):Band33Heft4-500
Gorham, G.L. and J.M. Warth. Charted
Designs for Holidays and Special Occa-
sions.
   M.Z. Cowan, 614:Fall82-14
Gori, F. and C. Questa, eds. La fortuna
di Tacito dal sec. XV ad oggi.
   D. Leduc-Fayette, 542:Jul-Sep81-333
Görlach, M. Einführung ins Frühneu-
englische.
   P.A. Jorgensen, 35(AS):Summer81-133
   H. Sauer, 38:Band99Heft3/4-424
   M. Scheler, 72:Band217Heft1-189
Cörland, I. Die Konkrete Freiheit des
Individuums bei Hegel und Sartre.
   A.D. Schrift, 125:Summer81-427
Görland, I. - see Heidegger, M.
Gormley, J. Battered Cherub.
   J. Grant, 362:8Apr82-22
   K.O. Morgan, 617(TLS):30Apr82-477
Görner, H. Redensarten.
   R. Eckert, 682(ZPSK):Band33Heft5-631
de Gorog, R. and L.S. Concordancias del
"Arcipreste de Talavera."*
   J. González Muela, 240(HR):Spring81-
   232
Görög, V. and A. Diarra, eds and trans.
Contes Bambara du Mali.*
   J. Simpson, 203:Vol192No1-127
Görög-Karady, V. Noirs et blancs.*
   W.J. Samarin, 69:Vol50No1-106
Goruppi, T. - see Ghil, R.
Gose, E.B., Jr. The Transformation
Process in Joyce's "Ulysses."*
   M.J. Sidnell, 627(UTQ):Summer81-133
   42(AR):Winter81-133
   295(JML):Vol8No3/4-536
Gosselin, M. L'Écriture du Surnaturel
dans l'oeuvre romanesque de Bernanos.
   G. Antoine, 209(FM):Jan81-56

135

Goswamy, B.N. Painters at the Sikh Court.
  S.L. Huntington, 318(JAOS):Apr/Jun80-
  158
Gothot-Mersch, C. - see Flaubert, G.
Gotlieb, P. The Works.
  R. Miles, 102(CanL):Summer80-140
Gotoff, H.C. Cicero's Elegant Style.*
  C.E. Murgia, 122:Oct81-301
Gotshalk, D.W. Art and the Social Order.
  (2nd ed)
  B. Lang, 290(JAAC):Fall81-85
Gottfried von Strassburg. Tristan. (P.
  Ganz, ed)
  K. Ruh, 684(ZDA):Band110Heft4-149
Gottfried, R.S. Bury St. Edmunds and the
  Urban Crisis: 1290-1539.
  R.B. Dobson, 617(TLS):22Oct82-1171
Gottlieb, C. The Window in Art.
  D.R., 55:Nov81-38
Gottlieb, D. Ontological Economy.
  J. Largeault, 542:Oct-Dec81-503
Gottlieb, G. Ost und West in der christ-
  lichen Kirche des 4. und 5. Jahrhunderts.
  E.D. Hunt, 123:Vol131No2-313
Gottlieb, L.C. Rachel Crothers.
  M.W. Estrin, 397(MD):Sep81-379
Gottlieb, V. Chekhov and the Vaudeville.
  V.L. Smith, 617(TLS):31Dec82-1446
Göttner, H. Logik der Interpretation.
  H. Göttner, 494:Winter80/81-171
Göttner, H. and J. Jacobs. Der Logische
  Bau von Literaturtheorien.
  E. Nierlich, 494:Autumn80-213
Goudsblom, J. Nihilism and Culture.
  A. Stevenson, 437:Summer81-378
Gough, B.M. Distant Dominion.
  P. Roy, 298:Fall-Winter81-205
Gouhier, H. Cartésianisme et augustinisme
  au XVIIe siècle.
  M. Adam, 542:Jul-Sep81-351
Gouhier, H. Fénelon philosophe.*
  P. Riley, 482(PhR):Apr81-285
Goukowsky, P. Essai sur les origines du
  mythe d'Alexandre (336-270 av. J-C.).*
  (Vol 1)
  C.R. Rubincam, 487:Summer81-168
Goukowsky, P. - see Diodorus Siculus
Gould, A., ed. Masters of Caricature.*
  R.E. Shikes, 441:10Jan82-19
Gould, C. Bernini in France.
  J. Rykwert, 617(TLS):19Mar82-317
Gould, C.C. Marx's Social Ontology.*
  W.L. Adamson, 488:Mar81-108
  H. Gamberg, 150(DR):Autumn81-590
Gould, H. Glitterburn.
  N. Callendar, 441:17Jan82-29
Gould, K. The Psalter and Hours of
  Yolande of Soissons.*
  J. Backhouse, 90:Mar81-173
Gould, K.L. Claude Simon's Mythic Muse.*
  A. Finch, 208(FS):Oct81-479
  A.C. Pugh, 402(MLR):Jan81-208
Gould, L. La Presidenta.*
  E. Friedman, 461:Fall-Winter81/82-93
Gould, S.J. The Mismeasure of Man.*
  P-L. Adams, 61:Jan82-87
  J. Bernstein, 442(NY):12Apr82-144
Goulden, J.C. Korea.
  J.C. Perry, 441:11Apr82-8
Goulden, J.C. Jerry Wurf.
  W. Serrin, 441:12Sep82-14

Goulet, A.S-M. L'Univers théâtral de
  Corneille.*
  H. Verhoeff, 535(RHL):Mar-Apr81-288
  A.G. Wood, 399(MLJ):Summer81-213
Goulet, P. Les Lois de la Pesanteur.
  J. Ripley, 102(CanL):Summer80-113
Goulet, R. - see Cleomedes
Gourlay, K.A. Sound-Producing Instruments
  in Traditional Society.
  D. Niles, 187:May82-330
Gouy, P. Pérégrinations des "Barcelon-
  nettes" au Mexique.
  G.E. Saunders, 207(FR):Dec81-291
Gowar, N. An Invitation to Mathematics.
  C. Small, 529(QQ):Autumn81-586
Gowland, D.A. Methodist Secessions.
  W.L. Arnstein, 637(VS):Winter81-230
Goyet, T. and J-P. Collinet, eds. Jour-
  nées Bossuet.
  A. Reix, 542:Jul-Sep81-349
Grabar, A. Les voies de la création en
  iconographie chrétienne.
  A. Reix, 542:Jul-Sep81-331
Grabar, O. La formación del Arte Islámico.
  M. Lillo, 48:Jul-Sep81-376
Grabar, O. and S. Blair. Epic Images and
  Contemporary History.
  B. Gray, 39:Nov81-349
Grabo, N.S. The Coincidental Art of
  Charles Brockden Brown.
  R.S. Levine, 165(EAL):Spring82-92
Graburn, N.H.H., ed. Ethnic and Tourist
  Arts.
  S.J. Bronner, 292(JAF):Jul-Sep81-383
Grace, G. The Man With the Styrofoam Head.
  D. Barbour, 648(WCR):Jun80-77
Grace, P. The Dream Sleepers, and Other
  Stories.
  D. Norton, 368:Sep81-330
Grace, S. Violent Duality.
  T. Goldie, 102(CanL):Spring81-133
  D.G. Jones, 105:Fall/Winter81-106
Gracia, J.J.E., ed. El hombre y su
  conducta/Man and his Conduct.
  W.J. Kilgore, 263(RIB):Vol31No1-87
Gracq, J. En lisant, en écrivant.
  J-C. Gateau, 98:Dec81-1329
  J. Pfeiffer, 450(NRF):Oct81-135
  J-Y. Tadié, 208(FS):Oct81-478
Grade, C. Rabbis and Wives.
  R.R. Wisse, 441:14Nov82-3
  442(NY):27Dec82-77
Gradenwitz, P. Musik zwischen Orient und
  Okzident.
  K.P. Etzkorn, 187:Sep82-461
Gradidge, R. Dream Houses.*
  A. Saint, 576:Oct81-248
  135:Oct81-93
Gradman, B. Metamorphosis in Keats.*
  639(VQR):Spring81-56
Gradon, P. - see Michel, D.
Grady, W., ed. The Penguin Book of Cana-
  dian Short Stories.*
  D.O. Spettigue, 529(QQ):Autumn81-558
Graebner, W. A History of Retirement.*
  639(VQR):Summer81-86
Graefe, R. Vela erunt.
  L. Casson, 576:Mar81-56
  R. Ling, 313:Vol71-231
Graf, A. Il diavolo. (C. Perrone, ed)
  G. de Liguori, 227(GCFI):Sep-Dec81-373

Graf, R. Der Konjunktiv in gesprochener
  Sprache.
    J. Schmidt, 682(ZPSK):Band33Heft2-251
Graff, G. Literature Against Itself.*
    C. Caramello, 125:Winter81-223
    G. Levine, 128(CE):Feb81-146
    S. Raval, 50(ArQ):Spring81-90
    D.H. Richter, 349:Summer81-232
    J. Sherwood, 648(WCR):Vol 15No3-55
Graff, G. Poetic Statement and Critical
  Dogma.
    S. Raval, 50(ArQ):Spring81-90
Grafton, S. "A" is for Alibi.
    N. Callendar, 441:23May82-41
Gragg, L.D. Migration in Early America.
    B. Levy, 656(WMQ):Apr81-318
Graham, A.C. Later Mohist Logic, Ethics
  and Science.
    C. Hansen, 485(PE&W):Apr81-241
Graham, D. The Fiction of Frank Norris.
    R. Belflower, 541(RES):Nov81-476
    J. Bochner, 106:Winter81-345
Graham, D. - see Douglas, K.
Graham, G.S. The China Station.*
    T.L. Kennedy, 293(JASt):Feb81-349
Graham, J. Hybrids of Plants and of
  Ghosts.*
    S.H. Madoff, 434:Summer82-617
    D. Smith, 29:Jan/Feb82-36
Graham, L.R. Between Science and Values.
    J.M. Ziman, 617(TLS):21May82-561
Graham, R.B.C. - see under Cunninghame
  Graham, R.B.
Graham, V.E. and W.M. Johnson. The Royal
  Tour of France by Charles IX and Cather-
  ine de' Medici: Festivals and Entries
  1564-1566.*
    E. Limbrick, 627(UTQ):Summer81-141
    R.J. van Pelt, 402(MLR):Apr81-463
    J.H.M. Salmon, 551(RenQ):Winter80-778
    D.F. Yates, 576:Mar81-68
Graham, W.S. Selected Poems.
    J. Wainwright, 472:Spring/Summer81-242
    639(VQR):Winter81-26
Graham-Campbell, D. Scotland's Story in
  Her Monuments.
    D. Walker, 617(TLS):10Dec82-1373
Graham-Campbell, J. Viking Artefacts.
    H. Chickering, 589:Apr81-383
Graham-Campbell, J. The Viking World.
    H. Chickering, 589:Apr81-383
    M. Cormack, 563(SS):Spring81-211
Graham-Campbell, J. and D. Kidd. The Vik-
  ings.
    H. Chickering, 589:Apr81-383
Graham-Yooll, A. The Forgotten Colony.*
  Portrait of an Exile.
    D. Tipton, 364:Dec81/Jan82-126
Graivoronskii, V.V. Ot kochevogo obraza
  zhizni k osedlosti (na opyte MNR).
    G. Ginsburgs, 293(JASt):Nov80-124
Grammaticus, S. - see under Saxo Gram-
  maticus
Gramsci, A. Cronache Torinesi 1913-1917.
  La Città Futura 1917-1918. (S. Capriog-
  lio, ed of both)
    M. Clark, 617(TLS):8Oct82-1107
Granatstein, J.L. A Man of Influence.*
    A. Andrew, 150(DR):Summer81-366
de Granda, G. Estudios lingüísticos his-
  pánicos, afro-hispánicos y criollos.
    M.B. Fontanella de Weinberg, 545(RPh):
      Feb81(supp)-158   [continued]

[continuing]
    G.L. Guitarte, 240(HR):Spring81-227
    W.W. Megenney, 350:Dec81-928
Grand'maison, J. Une Foi ensouchée dans
  ce pays.
    R. Sutherland, 102(CanL):Spring81-92
Granger, B. American Essay Serials from
  Franklin to Irving.
    R.V. Sparks, 432(NEQ):Mar81-139
Granger, B. Schism.
    M. Laski, 362:2Dec82-23
Granoff, P.E. Philosophy and Argument in
  Late Vedānta.
    L. Davis, 293(JASt):Nov80-161
    J.W. de Jong, 259(IIJ):Jan81-63
Grant, C. Canyon de Chelly.
    M.J. Young, 292(JAF):Apr-Jun81-254
Grant, D. Tobias Smollett.*
    P. Danchin, 179(ES):Feb81-76
Grant, J.S. Their Children Will See and
  Other Stories.
    D. MacAulay, 571(ScLJ):Summer80-136
Grant, J.S. - see Davies, R.
Grant, M. The Etruscans.*
    R.M. Ogilvie, 123:Vol31No2-243
Grant, M.K. The Tragic Vision of Joyce
  Carol Oates.*
    M.F. Schulz, 402(MLR):Oct81-951
Grant, P. Images and Ideas in Literature
  of the English Renaissance.*
    R.M. Frye, 677(YES):Vol 11-232
    J. Wittreich, 301(JEGP):Apr81-237
Grant, P. Six Modern Authors and Problems
  of Belief.*
    J.J. Riley, 395(MFS):Winter80/81-698
Grant, R.J.S. Cambridge, Corpus Christi
  College 41: The Loricas and the Missal.*
    L.E. Voigts, 589:Oct81-927
Grant Duff, S. The Parting of Ways.
    B. Bergonzi, 617(TLS):12Mar82-274
Grantham, D.W. The Regional Imagination.
    W.D. Barnard, 9(AlaR):Jul81-237
Grass, G. Headbirths, or The Germans are
  Dying Out.
    P-L. Adams, 61:Apr82-110
    D.J. Enright, 453(NYRB):18Mar82-46
    G. Josipovici, 617(TLS):23Apr82-455
    J. Leonard, 441:14Mar82-11
    C. Lock, 362:22Apr82-24
    J. Updike, 442(NY):14Jun82-129
Grass, G. The Meeting at Telgte.*
    G. Perez, 249(HudR):Winter81/82-615
Grass, G. Une Rencontre en Westphalie.
    L. Kovacs, 450(NRF):Sep81-145
    J-P. Lefebvre, 98:Dec81-1278
Grass, R. and W.R. Risley, eds. Waiting
  for Pegasus.
    P. Ilie, 238:Sep81-474
Grassegger, H. Merkmalsredundanz und
  Sprachverständlichkeit.
    K. Kohler, 260(IF):Band85-312
Grassi, E. Rhetoric as Philosophy.*
    R.D. Harrison, 583:Winter81-191
    L. Pennachetti, 539:Aug82-211
Grassian, V. Moral Reasoning.
    D.G.T., 185:Jan82-403
Grattan-Guinness, I. Dear Russell — Dear
  Jourdain.
    M. Hallett, 84:Dec81-381
Graumann, G. "La Guerre de Troie" aura
  lieu.
    M.M. Celler, 207(FR):Dec81-279

Graur, A. Mic tratat de ortografie.
    G.F. Meier, 682(ZPSK):Band32Heft2-226
Graus, F. Lebendige Vergangenheit.
    O. Ehrismann, 680(ZDP):Band99Heft1-142
Gravagnuolo, B. Adolf Loos.
    P. Goldberger, 441:8Aug82-9
Graver, L. and R. Federman, eds. Samuel
  Beckett: The Critical Heritage.*
    L.S. Butler, 447(N&Q):Dec80-572
    D. Sherzer, 395(MFS):Summer80-355
Graversen, P. The Fagin.
    N. Callendar, 441:16May82-26
Graves, J. From a Limestone Ledge.
    S. Brown, 569(SR):Summer81-431
    S. Kremp, 649(WAL):Fall81-248
    L. Milazzo, 584(SWR):Winter81-v
Graves, M.A.R. The House of Lords in the
  Parliaments of Edward VI and Mary I.
    C.S.L. Davies, 617(TLS):22Jan82-72
Graves, R. In Broken Images. (P. O'Prey,
  ed)
    A. Burgess, 617(TLS):21May82-547
    P. Kemp, 362:20May82-23
Graves, R.P. A.E. Housman.*
    J. Diggle, 123:Vol31No1-148
    E.S. Fisher, 295(JML):Vol18No3/4-524
    A.A. Imholtz, Jr., 639(VQR):Autumn81-
      755
    B.J. Leggett, 651(WHR):Autumn81-287
    P.G. Naiditch, 121(CJ):Apr/May82-361
    42(AR):Spring81-264
Gray, A. Lanark.*
    A.M., 148:Autumn81-86
Gray, C., with J. Boswell and P. Brown.
  Blueprints.
    P. Goldberger, 441:12Dec82-12
Gray, D. Robert Henryson.*
    P. Bawcutt, 382(MAE):1981/2-352
    G. Clark, 529(QQ):Winter81-772
Gray, D., ed. A Selection of Religious
  Lyrics.
    C.G., 189(EA):Oct-Dec81-498
Gray, F. La Poétique de Du Bellay.*
    D.G. Coleman, 208(FS):Jul81-319
Gray, F., ed. Poétiques.
    R.L. Mitchell, 207(FR):Dec80-332
Gray, F. and M. Tetel, eds. Textes et
  intertextes.
    T.C. Cave, 402(MLR):Jul81-694
    R.D. Cottrell, 207(FR):Mar81-589
    E.M. Duval, 210(FrF):May81-172
Gray, F.D. World Without End.*
    G. Perez, 249(HudR):Winter81/82-619
Gray, J.M. Fun Tomorrow.
    G.L. Parker, 102(CanL):Spring80-93
Gray, J.M. Thro' the Vision of the Night.
    W.D. Shaw, 627(UTQ):Summer81-125
    636(VP):Summer81-201
Gray, N. Nineteenth Century Ornamented
  Typefaces. (2nd ed)
    M. Twyman, 39:Apr81-269
Gray, P. T.S. Eliot's Intellectual and
  Poetic Development 1909-1922.
    J. Casey, 617(TLS):10Sep82-975
Gray, R. Ibsen — A Dissenting View.
    R.B. Vowles, 562(Scan):May81-101
Gray, S. Close of Play.
    D. Devlin, 157:1stQtr81-54
Gray, S. Quartermaine's Terms.
    D. Devlin, 157:Winter81-51
Gray, V.B. "Invisible Man"'s Literary
  Heritage.*
    205(FMLS):Jan80-85

Grayson, A.K. Assyrian and Babylonian
  Chronicles.
    A.R. Millard, 318(JAOS):Jul/Sep80-364
Grayson, A.K. Assyrian Royal Inscriptions.
  (Pt 2)
    A.R. Millard, 318(JAOS):Jul/Sep80-368
Grayson, C., ed. The World of Dante.
    639(VQR):Summer81-83
Grayson, G.W. The Politics of Mexican Oil.
    E.J. Williams, 263(RIB):Vol31No4-551
Grayson, J.P., ed. Class, State, Ideology
  and Change.
    D. Swartz, 529(QQ):Summer81-394
Grayson, R. The Monterant Affair.
    639(VQR):Spring81-62
Grayson, R. The Montmartre Murders.
    T.J. Binyon, 617(TLS):28May82-594
    N. Callendar, 441:24Oct82-28
    M. Laski, 362:29Apr82-27
de Grazia, V. The Culture of Consent.
    M. Clark, 617(TLS):26Mar82-356
Graziosi, M.T. - see Guidiccioni, G.
Greaves, R.L. - see Bunyan, J.
Greaves, R.L. and R. Zaller, eds. Bio-
  graphical Dictionary of British Radicals
  in the Seventeenth Century. (Vol 1)
    C. Hill, 617(TLS):6Aug82-848
Greber, J.M. Abraham und David Roentgen:
  Möbel für Europa.
    P. Thornton, 39:Jan81-60
Greeley, A.M. Thy Brother's Wife.
    W. Schott, 441:11Apr82-7
Green, A. Flaubert and the Historical
  Novel.
    F.W.J. Hemmings, 617(TLS):29Jan82-98
Green, A. The Tragic Effect.*
    D.W. Harding, 402(MLR):Jan81-146
    W.D. Howarth, 208(FS):Apr81-235
    205(FMLS):Apr81-199
Green, A.K. The Leavenworth Case.
    P. Craig, 617(TLS):13Aug82-888
    P. Craig, 617(TLS):22Oct82-1175
Green, C.L. Edward Albee.
    T.P. Adler, 130:Summer81-180
Green, D.H. Irony in the Medieval
  Romance.*
    P. Gradon, 541(RES):Nov81-502
    T. Hunt, 220(GL&L):Oct81-98
    W. Schröder, 684(ZDA):Band110Heft1-25
    205(FMLS):Apr80-188
Green, D.H. and L.P. Johnson. Approaches
  to Wolfram von Eschenbach.*
    A. Groos, 406:Fall81-344
Green, E.P. - see Piñero Green, E.
Green, J. La Terre est si belle ... 1976-
  1978.
    D. Gascoyne, 617(TLS):10Oct82-1072
Green, J. - see Cushing, F.H.
Green, J.A. - see Schwob, M.
Green, J.R. Grass-Roots Socialism.
    G. Adams, Jr., 106:Fall81-245
Green, J.R. Corpus Vasorum Antiquorum.
  (New Zealand, fasc 1)
    D.J.R. Williams, 123:Vol31No2-320
Green, J.R. The World of the Workers.
    639(VQR):Spring81-64
Green, M. Dreams of Adventure, Deeds of
  Empire.*
    J.A. Downie, 566:Spring82-125
    A.A. Noble, 571(ScLJ):Winter81-91
    W.L. Reed, 445(NCF):Sep80-236
    S. Soupel, 189(EA):Oct-Dec81-458

Green, M.J.M. Louis Guilloux.
  F.J. Greene, 207(FR):Apr82-689
  W.D. Redfern, 402(MLR):Jul81-712
Green, P. The Pursuit of Inequality.*
  J. Sumption, 617(TLS):19Feb82-181
  639(VQR):Autumn81-133
Green, R. Ford Madox Ford.*
  P.S., 148:Winter81-91
Green, R., ed. The Train.
  P. Parker, 617(TLS):18Jun82-663
Green, R. and others. Herrad of Hohen-
  bourg, "Hortus Deliciarum."
  C.M. Kauffmann, 90:Mar81-172
Green, R.F. Poets and Princepleasers.*
  D. Bornstein, 589:Oct81-874
  L. Eldredge, 539:May82-147
Green, R.H., K. Kiljunen and M-L. Kiljunen,
  eds. Namibia.
  R. Rathbone, 617(TLS):5Mar82-261
Green, R.L. - see Williams, S.H. and F.F.
  Madan
Green, R.W. Six French Poets of Our Time.
  V.A. La Charité, 210(FrF):May81-183
Green, S. Encyclopaedia of the Musical
  Film.*
  A. Croce, 442(NY):18Jan82-128
Greenbaum, S., ed. Acceptability in
  Language.
  P.C. Collins, 215(GL):Spring81-22
Greenbaum, S., G. Leech and J. Svartvik,
  eds. Studies in English Linguistics for
  Randolph Quirk.*
  D. Young, 349:Summer81-246
Greenberg, A. The Discovery of America
  and Other Tales of Terror and Self-
  Exploration.*
  P. Lewis, 565:Vol22No1-60
Greenberg, J.H., C.A. Ferguson and E.A.
  Moravcsik, eds. Universals of Human
  Language.* (Vols 1-4)
  C.P. Masica, 215(GL):Summer81-126
Greenblatt, S. Renaissance Self-Fashion-
  ing.*
  M.W. Ferguson, 676(YR):Spring82-414
  J. Goldberg, 400(MLN):Dec81-1201
  L.A. Montrose, 141:Fall81-349
Greenburg, D. What Do Women Want?
  C. Schine, 441:16May82-18
Greene, D.J. - see Johnson, S.
Greene, E.J.H. Menander to Marivaux.*
  M. Leisner-Jensen, 462(OL):Vol36No4-
  349
  C. Miething, 224(GRM):Band30Heft3-356
Greene, G. Doctor Fischer of Geneva, or,
  the Bomb Party.*
  L.T. Lemon, 502(PrS):Spring-Summer81-
  318
  S. Monod, 189(EA):Oct-Dec81-487
Greene, G. Doctor Love.
  N. Johnson, 441:11Jul82-14
Greene, G. J'Accuse.
  J. Raban, 453(NYRB):4Nov82-18
Greene, G. Monsignor Quixote.
  R. Davies, 362:16Sep82-25
  M. Muggeridge, 61:Nov82-165
  J. Raban, 453(NYRB):4Nov82-18
  J. Symons, 617(TLS):8Oct82-1089
  R. Towers, 441:19Sep82-1
  442(NY):18Oct82-179
Greene, G. Ways of Escape.*
  D.L. Eder, 639(VQR):Summer81-543
Greene, H. Inference of Guilt.
  T.J. Binyon, 617(TLS):31Dec82-1448

Greene, J.C. Science, Ideology, and
  World View.
  D.M. Knight, 617(TLS):12Mar82-279
Greene, R.W. Six French Poets of Our
  Time.*
  M. Sheringham, 402(MLR):Jan81-207
Greenewalt, C.H. Ritual Dinners in Early
  Historic Sardis.
  J. Pollard, 303(JoHS):Vol 101-184
Greenfeld, H. Puccini.*
  A. Fitz Lyon, 617(TLS):9Apr82-418
Greenfield, J. China and the Law of the
  Sea, Air and Environment.
  R. O'Brien, 302:Vol 18-154
Greenfield, J. The Real Campaign.
  L. Sabato, 441:20Jun82-9
Greenfield, J. Yale University Library
  Preservation Pamphlets.
  G. Trinkaus-Randall, 14:Summer81-249
Greenhalgh, M. and V. Megaw, eds. Art in
  Society.
  E.L.R. Meyerowitz, 39:Mar81-202
Greenhalgh, P. Pompey.* (Vols 1 and 2)
  D.L. Stockton, 123:Vol31No2-248
Greenhowe, J. Making Mascot Dolls.
  P. Bach, 614:Fall81-18
Greenleaf, S. State's Evidence.
  442(NY):6Sep82-110
Greenough, S. and J. Hamilton - see
  "Alfred Stieglitz: Photographs and Writ-
  ings"
Greenstein, F.I. The Hidden-Hand Presi-
  dency.
  442(NY):20Dec82-139
Greenwood, F.M., ed and trans. Land of a
  Thousand Sorrows.
  W.N., 102(CanL):Winter80-160
Greer, G. The Obstacle Race.*
  N.F. Broude, 127:Summer81-180
Greet, A.H. Apollinaire et le livre de
  peintre.*
  W. Bohn, 131(CL):Summer81-296
Greger, D. Movable Islands.*
  D. Smith, 29:Jan/Feb82-36
Gregerson, K.J. and D. Thomas, eds. Mon-
  Khmer Studies V.*
  G.F. Meier, 682(ZPSK):Band33Heft4-506
Gregg, E. Queen Anne.*
  L.K.J. Glassey, 566:Spring81-114
Gregg, J.Y. Communication and Culture.
  E. Hamp-Lyons, 608:Jun82-253
Gregg, L. Too Bright to See.
  D. Smith, 29:Jan/Feb82-36
  S. Yenser, 676(YR):Autumn81-97
Gregor, I., ed. Reading the Victorian
  Novel.
  A.M. Duckworth, 445(NCF):Jun81-89
  S. Monod, 189(EA):Oct-Dec81-481
  M. Moseley, 569(SR):Winter81-xxi
  C. Richards, 175:Spring81-79
Gregor-Dellin, M. and D. Mack - see Wagner,
  C.
Lady Gregory. Lady Gregory's Journals.*
  (Vol 1) (D.J. Murphy, ed)
  R. Fréchet, 189(EA):Apr-Jun81-231
  P.L. Marcus, 677(YES):Vol 11-345
Saint Gregory of Nazianzus. Grégoire de
  Nazianze, "Discours 1-3." (J. Bernardi,
  ed and trans)
  P. Nautin, 555:Vol54fasc1-170
Gregory, A. Me & Nu.
  R. Fréchet, 189(EA):Apr-Jun81-233

Gregory, R.L. Mind in Science.*
  D. Joravsky, 453(NYRB):21Oct82-44
Greider, W. The Education of David Stock-
  man and Other Americans.
  L.C. Thurow, 453(NYRB):7Oct82-6
Greifenstein, E. Der Hiob-Traktat des
  Marquard von Lindau.
  K. Kunze, 680(ZDP):Band100Heft3-445
Greiff, C.M. John Notman, Architect:
  1810-1865.
  G.A. Danzer, 658:Summer/Autumn81-242
Greimas, A.J. Sémiotique et sciences
  sociales.
  T.G. Pavel, 154:Mar81-162
Greimas, A.J. and E. Landowski, eds.
  Introduction à l'analyse du discours en
  sciences sociales.
  J-J. Thomas, 207(FR):Mar81-637
Greiner, J. The Red Snow.
  J.C. George, 649(WAL):Fall81-240
Greiner, N. "Idealism" und "realism" im
  Frühwerk Shaws.
  W. Kluge, 179(ES):Aug81-395
Greiner, U. Der Tod des Nachsommers.
  E. Schwarz, 221(GQ):Jan81-120
Gren-Eklund, G. A Study of Nominal Sen-
  tences in the Oldest Upaniṣads.
  J-M. Verpoorten, 259(IIJ):Jan81-44
Grenzmann, R.R. Studien zur bildhaften
  Sprache in der "Goldenen Schmiede"
  Konrads von Würzburg.
  F.L. Decker, 406:Winter81-449
Grese, W.C. Corpus Hermeticum XIII and
  Early Christian Literature.
  É. Des Places, 555:Vol54fasc1-171
Grétry, A-E-M. Le Jugement de Midas. (P.
  Culot, ed)
  K.P., 412:Nov80-318
Greve, T. Haakon VII.
  T.I. Leiren, 563(SS):Summer81-350
Grewendorf, G. Argumentation and Interpre-
  tation.
  H. Göttner, 494:Winter80/81-171
Grewendorf, G., ed. Sprechakttheorie und
  Semantik.
  N. Fries and J. Meibauer, 603:Vol5No1-
  148
Grey, I. Stalin.
  H.J. Ellison, 550(RusR):Apr81-200
Gribben, A. Mark Twain's Library.*
  L.J. Budd, 365:Spring-Summer82-129
Gribbin, J. Genesis — The Origins of Man
  and the Universe.
  639(VQR):Autumn81-137
Gribbin, J. and J. Cherfas. The Monkey
  Puzzle.
  P-L. Adams, 61:Nov82-170
  A. Manning, 362:20May82-24
Gribbon, M.J. Walter J. Phillips.
  W.H.N., 102(CanL):Spring80-152
Grieder, J.B. Intellectuals and the State
  in Modern China.
  R. Garside, 441:3Jan82-7
Griego y Maestas, J. Cuentos.
  R.G. Lint, 649(WAL):Fall81-251
Grier, P.T. Marxist Ethical Theory in the
  Soviet Union.*
  K.M.J., 543:Sep80-137
  D. McLellan, 575(SEER):Jan81-119
Grierson, J. Grierson on the Movies. (F.
  Hardy, ed)
  E. Anstey, 324:Jan82-104

Griesbach, H. Deutsch x 3.
  K.E.H. Liedtke, 399(MLJ):Spring81-116
Grieve, A. Victor Pasmore.
  D. Thistlewood, 59:Mar81-123
Griffin, A. Sikyon.
  R.A. Tomlinson, 617(TLS):14May82-538
Griffin, D.H. Alexander Pope.*
  H. Erskine-Hill, 541(RES):Nov81-451
  D.E. Richardson, 569(SR):Fall81-638
  P. Rogers, 677(YES):Vol 11-278
  G.S. Rousseau, 173(ECS):Winter80/81-
  181
Griffin, D.R. The Question of Animal
  Awareness.* (rev)
  D. Joravsky, 453(NYRB):21Oct82-44
Griffin, D.R. and D.W. Sherburne - see
  Whitehead, A.N.
Griffin, E.M. Old Brick.*
  P.F. Gura, 656(WMQ):Jan81-137
Griffin, J. Homer on Life and Death.*
  Homer.*
  A.M. Bowie, 123:Vol31No2-157
  F. Rosslyn, 97(CQ):Vol 10No2-169
Griffin, M.T. Seneca.
  B.L. Hijmans, Jr., 394:Vol34fasc3/4-
  438
Griffin, N. Relative Identity.*
  R.H. Feldman, 154:Jun81-365
Griffin, P.E. The Chinese Communist Treat-
  ment of Counterrevolutionaries, 1924-
  1949.
  R.R. Edwards, 318(JAOS):Apr/Jun80-204
Griffin, S. Pornography and Silence.*
  J.G. Weightman, 617(TLS):1Jan82-5
Griffith, B. Time for Frankie Coolin.
  S. Ellin, 441:9May82-12
Griffiths, A. Prints and Printmaking.
  J. Glynne, 59:Mar81-122
  A. Wilton, 324:Mar82-232
Griffiths, F.T. Theocritus at Court.
  F. Williams, 303(JoHS):Vol 101-158
Griffiths, J. Three Tomorrows.*
  295(JML):Vol8No3/4-409
Griffiths, L., with P. Thompson. Maggie
  and Pierre.
  T. Beaupre, 108:Fall81-113
Griffiths, P. Peter Maxwell Davies.
  H. Cole, 362:22Jul82-22
  P. Driver, 617(TLS):4Jun82-609
Griffiths, T. Occupations.
  D. Devlin, 157:2ndQtr81-55
  M. Martin, 148:Winter81-49
Grigson, G., ed. Faber Book of Nonsense
  Verse.
  J.G., 189(EA):Apr-Jun81-237
Grigson, G. Freedom of the Parish.
  C. Causley, 617(TLS):28May82-576
Grigson, G., ed. The Oxford Book of
  Satirical Verse.*
  W. Harmon, 569(SR):Spring81-278
  566:Autumn81-52
Grigson, G. The Private Art. Blessings,
  Kicks and Curses. Collected Poems 1963-
  1980.
  P. Kemp, 362:9Dec82-24
Grigson, J. Food with the Famous.
  W. and C. Cowen, 639(VQR):Autumn81-138
Grillone, A. - see Pseudo Hyginus
Grimal, P. Le Lyrisme à Rome.*
  J-M. André, 555:Vol54fasc1-187
Grimal, P. Le théâtre antique.
  R.W., 555:Vol54fasc1-159

von der Grün, M. Späte Liebe.
    J. Neves, 617(TLS):1Oct82-1083
Grundlehner, P. The Lyrical Bridge.*
    N. Ritter, 221(GQ):Mar81-253
Grundtvig, N.F.S. Dag- og Udtogsbøger.*
    (G. Albeck, ed)
    S.E. Larsen, 562(Scan):Nov81-225
Grundy, J. Hardy and the Sister Arts.*
    L. Elsbree, 637(VS):Autumn80-139
    S. Hunter, 677(YES):Vol 11-331
    M. Millgate, 445(NCF):Sep80-216
    M. Williams, 447(N&Q):Jun80-257
Grünewald, B. Der Phänomenologische
    Ursprung des Logischen.
    J.N. Mohanty, 53(AGP):Band63Heft1-100
Grunfeld, F.V. Prophets Without Honour.*
    M. Swales, 529(QQ):Autumn81-545
de Grunne, B. Terres cuites anciennes de
    l'ouest africain.
    P.C. Coronel, 2(AfrA):Feb81-82
Gruša, J. The Questionnaire.
    P-L. Adams, 61:Aug82-94
    N. Ascherson, 453(NYRB):23Sep82-48
    C. Sinclair, 617(TLS):1Oct82-1064
    442(NY):30Aug82-90
Gruyer, F. Les Ruines du soleil.*
    L.S. Crist, 207(FR):Mar82-568
Gruzinov, V.P. The USSR's Management of
    Foreign Trade.* (E.A. Hewett, ed)
    J. Salter, 575(SEER):Jul81-472
Grylls, D. Guardians and Angels.*
    L.A. Schoch, 637(VS):Winter81-240
Gryphius, A. Catharina von Georgien.
    (J.E. Oyler and A.H. Schulze, eds)
    J.R. Mehl, 406:Fall81-347
Gschwind, U., ed. Le Roman de "Flamenca."
    S. Fleischman, 545(RPh):May81-513
Gualdo Rosa, L. - see Luiso, F.P.
Gualís, G.B. and M. García Guatas - see
    under Borrás y Gualís, G. and M. García
    Guatas
Gualís, G.M.B. - see under Borrás Gualís,
    G.M.
Guarnieri, P. La "Rivista filosofica"
    (1899-1908).
    G.O., 227(GCFI):May-Aug81-269
Gude, M.L. "Le Page Disgracié."
    205(FMLS):Apr80-189
Guenther, H.V. Tibetan Buddhism in West-
    ern Perspective.*
    T.V. Wylie, 293(JASt):Nov80-126
Guenthner, F. and C. Rohrer, eds. Studies
    in Formal Semantics.
    L.M. Faltz, 350:Jun82-455
Guenthner, F. and S.J. Schmidt, eds. For-
    mal Semantics and Pragmatics for Natural
    Languages.
    E.S. Wheeler, 320(CJL):Fall81-247
Guerard, A.J. The Triumph of the Novel.*
    M. Christadler, 38:Band99Heft1/2-256
    D. Hewitt, 447(N&Q):Jun80-277
Gueret, M., A. Robinet and P. Tombeur.
    Spinoza, "Ethica."*
    E.G. Boscherini, 53(AGP):Band62Heft3-
    333
Guerlac, H. Newton on the Continent.
    R. Fox, 617(TLS):22Oct82-1159
Guerlac, R. - see Vives, J.L.
Guerman, M., comp. Art of the October
    Revolution.*
    M.B. Betz, 127:Fall/Winter80-417

Guest, J. Second Heaven.
    N. Rosen, 441:30Oct82-12
    F. Taliaferro, 231:Oct82-71
    442(NY):22Nov82-196
Guetti, J. Word-Music.
    C. Holte, 395(MFS):Winter80/81-694
    D.G. Marshall, 445(NCF):Mar81-563
Gueunier, N., É. Genouvrier and A. Khomsi.
    Les Français devant la norme.*
    D. Godard, 355(LSoc):Aug81-299
    F.J. Hausmann, 257(IRAL):Feb81-88
de Guevera, L.V. - see under Vélez de
    Guevera, L.
Gugler, J. and W.G. Flanagan. Urbaniza-
    tion and Social Change in West Africa.
    V. Pons, 69:Vol50No2-228
Guglielmetti, A. Feu et lumière dans la
    "Peau de Chagrin" de Balzac.
    D. Bellos, 402(MLR):Jan81-196
    P. Mustière, 535(RHL):Mar-Apr81-306
Guha, A.S. An Evolutionary View of
    Economic Growth.
    P. Seabright, 617(TLS):9Apr82-402
"Guida Generale degli Archivi di Stato
    Italiani." (Vol 1)
    S.J. Woolf, 617(TLS):17Dec82-1397
"Guide documentaire à l'intention des prof-
    esseurs de français à l'étranger."
    M.G. Hydak, 207(FR):Feb81-491
"Guide to Literary Manuscripts in the
    Huntington Library."
    R.A., 189(EA):Apr-Jun81-241
Guidiccioni, G. Le lettere. (M.T.
    Graziosi, ed)
    M.L. Doglio, 228(GSLI):Vol 158fasc504-
    612
Guidoni, E. Primitive Architecture.
    T.K. Seligman, 2(AfrA):May81-23
Guidoni, E. and A. Marino. Storia dell'-
    urbanistica: Il Seicento.
    A.M. Matteucci, 576:May81-171
Guiles, F.L. Stan.*
    E. Wagenknecht, 200:Oct81-506
Guiliano, E., ed. Lewis Carroll: A Cele-
    bration.
    442(NY):15Feb82-139
Guiliano, E. Lewis Carroll: An Annotated
    International Bibliography 1960-77.
    E. Wakeling, 283:Winter80/81-24
Guillain, R. I Saw Tokyo Burning.
    639(VQR):Summer81-99
Guillemin, H. Charles Péguy.*
    J. Bastaire, 450(NRF):Sep81-124
Guillén, J. Guillén on Guillén.*
    H.J.F. de Aguilar, 472:Spring/Summer81-
    253
    A. Cluysenaar, 565:Vol22No2-62
Guillén, J. Mientras el aire es nuestro.
    (P.W. Silver, ed)
    J. Ruiz-de-Conde, 238:May81-315
Guillevic. Autres, poèmes 1969-79.*
    S. Lawall, 207(FR):Oct81-159
Guillevic, E. Etier, poèmes 1965-1975.
    S.N. Lawall, 207(FR):Oct80-193
Guilloux, L. Souvenirs sur Georges
    Palante.*
    W.D. Redfern, 402(MLR):Jul81-712
Guinness, B. Potpourri from the Thirties.
    A. Forbes, 617(TLS):24Dec82-1411
Guiral, P. and G. Thuillier. La vie
    quotidienne des domestiques en France
    au XIXe siècle.
    A. Corbin, 98:Jun-Jul80-595

142

Guise, H. Great Victorian Engravings.
D. Alexander, 135:Aug81-251
R. Mander, 39:Apr81-269
Guisti-Lanham, H. and A. Dodi. The Cuisine of Venice.
W. and C. Cowen, 639(VQR):Spring81-71
Gülich, E. and W. Raible. Linguistische Textmodelle.
E.U. Grosse, 224(GRM):Band30Heft1-108
Gulick, S.L. A Chesterfield Bibliography to 1800.* (2nd ed)
354:Dec81-367
Gullans, C. Imperfect Correspondences. Many Houses.
T. Cassity, 472:Fall/Winter81-184
Gullberg, H. Gentleman, Single, Refined and Selected Poems, 1937-1959.*
K. Petherick, 563(SS):Winter81-118
Gullón, R., ed. El modernismo visto por los modernistas.
I.M. Zuleta, 263(RIB):Vol31No4-552
Gullón, R. Psicologías del autor y lógicas del personaje.
D. Villanueva, 240(HR):Summer81-366
Gumbert, H.L. - see Lichtenberg, G.C.
Gumbrecht, H-U., K. Stierle and R. Warning, eds. Honoré de Balzac.
D. Bellos, 402(MLR):Oct81-971
Gumilev, N. On Russian Poetry. (D. Lapeza, ed and trans)
E.D. Sampson, 574(SEEJ):Fall81-118
Cunawardana, R.A.L.H. Robe and Plough.
H.L. Seneviratne, 293(JASt):Nov80-163
Gundert, H. Pindar und sein Dichterberuf.
F.J. Nisetich, 122:Jan81-57
Güngerich, R. Kommentar zum Dialogus des Tacitus. (H. Heubner, ed)
M. Winterbottom, 123:Vol31No1-44
Gunn, Mrs. A. We of the Never-Never.
A. Chisholm, 617(TLS):30Jul82-832
Gunn, D.W. Tennessee Williams.
T.P. Adler, 365:Spring-Summer82-127
Gunn, E.M., Jr. Unwelcome Muse.
H. Goldblatt, 293(JASt):May81-584
B.S. McDougall, 244(IIJAS):Jun81-278
Gunn, J.A.W. and others - see Disraeli, B.
Gunn, T. The Passages of Joy. The Occasions of Poetry.
I. Hamilton, 617(TLS):23Jul82-782
P. Kemp, 362:12Aug82-21
Gunnars, K. Settlement Poems 1. One-Eyed Moon Maps.
R. Brown, 99:Feb82-37
Gunnemann, J.P. The Moral Meaning of Revolution.
J. Nagel, 185:Jan81-330
S. Sherwin, 150(DR):Summer81-374
Gunnlaugsdóttir, Á. Tristán en el Norte.*
A. Deyermond, 203:Vol191No1-121
P. Schach, 589:Jul81-616
Gunny, A. Voltaire and English Literature.*
O.R. Taylor, 402(MLR):Jan81-186
Guntern, J., ed. Volkserzählungen aus dem Oberwallis.
L.G. Meister, 196:Band21Heft3/4-312
Güntert, G., M-R. Jung and K. Ringger, eds. Orbis Mediaevalis.*
A.H. Diverres, 402(MLR):Jan81-148
W. Rothwell, 208(FS):Jul81-315

Günther, G., A.A. Volgina and S. Seifert, eds. Herder-Bibliographie.*
E. Loeb, 221(GQ):May81-347
Günther, H. - see Moritz, K.P.
Guo Tingyi. Zhonghua minguo shishi rizhi. (Vol 1)
A.J. Nathan, 293(JASt):Feb81-350
Gupta, S., D.J. Hoens and T. Goudriaan. Hindu Tantrism.*
H. Brunner, 259(IIJ):Apr81-139
Gura, V. Kak sozdavalsja "Tixij Don."
H. Ermolaev, 574(SEEJ):Fall81-123
Gurney, I. Collected Poems. (P.J. Kavanagh, ed)
A. Motion, 617(TLS):15Oct82-1121
Gurney, J. Wheal Zion.*
D. Graham, 565:Vol22No4-62
Gürsel, N. Un long été à Istanbul.
L. Kovacs, 450(NRF):Jun81-141
Gürttler, K.R. "Künec Artûs der guote."*
P.K. Stein, 680(ZDP):Band100Heft1-134
Gurwitsch, A. Human Encounters in the Social World. (A. Métraux, ed)
E.K., 543:Mar81-609
L. Langsdorf, 323:May81-179
Gurwitsch, A. Leibniz.
F. Kersten, 323:May81-189
Gurwitsch, A. Marginal Consciousness. (L. Embree, ed)
P. Richer, 323:May81-184
Gurwitsch, A. Phenomenology and the Theory of Science. (L. Embree, ed)
G. Null, 323:May81-187
Gusdorf, G. La conscience révolutionnaire.
D. Leduc-Fayette, 542:Jul-Sep81-372
Gusdorf, G. Fondements du Savoir Romantique.
A. Thorlby, 617(TLS):8Oct82-1108
Güse, E-G. Das Frühwerk Max Beckmanns.
P. Selz, 54:Mar81-170
Gusfield, J. The Culture of Public Problems.
K.S., 185:Jan82-401
Gusler, W.B. Furniture of Williamsburg and Eastern Virginia, 1710-1790.
D.M. Sokol, 658:Spring81-94
Gustafson, D.F. and B.L. Tapscott, eds. Body, Mind, and Method.*
M.B. Mahowald, 484(PPR):Dec81-300
Gustafson, P. Salish Weaving.
P. Bach, 614:Summer81-21
K.E. Kidd, 298:Fall-Winter81-222
W.N., 102(CanL):Autumn81-193
Gustafson, R. Landscape with Rain.*
D. Barbour, 648(WCR):Vol 15No3-47
A.J. Harding, 102(CanL):Spring81-138
P. Stevens, 529(QQ):Autumn81-504
Gustafson, R. Soviet Poems.
P.K. Smith, 102(CanL):Summer80-136
Gustafsson, L. The Death of a Beekeeper.
J. Updike, 442(NY):11Jan82-92
Gustafsson, L. Nominalpräpositionen untersucht besonders an Hand deutscher und niederländischer Urkunden 1250-1550.
D. Rosenthal, 597(SN):Vol53No1-190
Gustafsson, M. Binomial Expressions in Present-Day English.
B. Sundby, 597(SN):Vol53No1-188
Gutch, D. Einführung in die anglistische Sprachwissenschaft. (Vol 2) (K.H. Göller, ed)
B. Hansen, 682(ZPSK):Band33Heft2-253

"Gutenberg–Jahrbuch 1980." (H–J. Koppitz, ed)
    J.L. Flood, 617(TLS):29Jan82–119
"Gutenberg–Jahrbuch 1981." (H–J. Koppitz, ed)
    D.L. Paisey, 617(TLS):2Jul82–726
Guth, P. Lettre ouverte aux futurs illettrés.
    J. Berkowitz, 207(FR):Oct81–169
Guthrie, W.K.C. A History of Greek Philosophy. (Vol 4)
    J.M. Rist, 487:Summer81–163
    W.J. Verdenius, 394:Vol34fasc3/4–415
Guthrie, W.K.C. A History of Greek Philosophy.* (Vol 5)
    M.F. Burnyeat, 482(PhR):Jan81–157
    J.M. Rist, 487:Summer81–163
    R.K. Sprague, 122:Jul81–230
    W.J. Verdenius, 394:Vol34fasc3/4–415
    R.W., 555:Vol54fasc1–164
Gutierrez, D. Lapsing Out.
    D.C. Haberman, 177(ELT):Vol24No4–214
    J. Meyers, 594:Winter81–449
Gutiérrez, G. A Theology of Liberation.
    (C. Inda and J. Eagleson, eds and trans)
    D. Sturm, 185:Jul82–733
Gutkin, H. Journey Into Our Heritage.
    W.N., 102(CanL):Winter80–inside back cover
Gutknecht, C., ed. Contemporary English.
    A.B. Kulkarni, 682(ZPSK):Band33Heft5–632
Gutknecht, C. Kontrastive Linguistik.*
    E. Burgschmidt, 38:Band99Heft1/2–207
Gutman, J.M. Through Indian Eyes.
    A. Grundberg, 441:5Sep82–10
Gutman, R.J.S. and E. Kaufman, with D. Slovic. American Diner.*
    F.T. Kihlstedt, 576:Dec81–339
Gutting, G., ed. Paradigms and Revolutions.
    M.A. Kaplan, 185:Jan82–355
Guttmann, A. From Ritual to Record.
    C. Messenger, 658:Summer/Autumn81–246
Gutwirth, M. Michel de Montaigne ou le Pari d'exemplarité.*
    D.G. Coleman, 208(FS):Oct81–434
Gutwirth, M. Madame de Staël, Novelist.*
    N. King, 402(MLR):Jan81–190
Guy, J. The Destruction of the Zulu Kingdom.
    A.J. Greenberger, 637(VS):Spring81–351
Guy, J. Oriental Trade Ceramics in Southeast Asia, 10th to 16th Century.
    B. Harrisson, 463:Summer81–205
Guyer, P. Kant and the Claims of Taste.*
    P. Kivy, 185:Jan81–317
Guzzetti, A. Two or Three Things I Know About Her.*
    P. Brunette, 18:Mar81–71
Guzzoni, U., B. Rang and L. Siep, eds. Der Idealismus und seine Gegenwart.
    K. Albert, 53(AGP):Band63Heft1–108
Gvozdanović, J. Tone and Accent in Standard Serbo-Croatian.
    R. Alexander, 350:Mar82–250
Gwaltney, J.L. Drylongso.*
    639(VQR):Winter81–12
Gwyn, R. The Northern Magus.
    R. Paine, 99:Dec81/Jan82–32
    G.W., 102(CanL):Spring81–172
Győry, J. A Francia dráma kialakulása.
    É. Martonyi, 535(RHL):May–Jun81–457

H.D. End to Torment.* (N.H. Pearson and M. King, ed)
    B. Duffey, 27(AL):May81–324
    J. Kerblat-Blanchenay, 189(EA):Jul–Sep81–359
H.D. The Gift.
    442(NY):27Dec82–78
H.D. HERmione.
    P-L. Adams, 61:Jan82–86
    C. Camper, 659(ConL):Summer82–377
Ha, K.C. – see under Kim Chi Ha
Haack, S. Philosophy of Logics.*
    M. Black, 483:Jul81–435
    N. Tennant, 84:Sep81–287
Haakonsen, D., ed. Ibsenårbok 1977.
    M. Ritzu, 462(OL):Vol35No3–283
Haakonssen, K. The Science of a Legislator.
    D.D. Raphael, 617(TLS):5Feb82–140
de Haan, G.J. Conditions on Rules.
    T. van den Hoek, 204(FdL):Dec81–339
Haarmann, H. Elemente einer Soziologie der kleinen Sprachen Europas. (Vol 2)
    B. Comrie, 350:Sep81–780
Haarmann, H. Grundzüge der Sprachtypologie.
    H. and R. Kahane, 545(RPh):Feb81(supp)–10
Haarmann, H. Quantitative Aspekte des Multilingualismus.
    B. Comrie, 350:Jun81–511
Haarmann, H. Spracherhaltung und Sprachwechsel als Probleme der interlingualen Soziolinguistik.
    B. Comrie, 350:Mar81–242
Haarmann, H., ed. Wissenschaftsgeschichtliche Beiträge zur Erforschung indogermanischer, finnisch-ugrischer und kaukasischer Sprachen bei Pallas.
    B. Comrie, 350:Jun81–487
Haarmann, H. and A-L.V., eds. Sprachen und Staaten: Festschrift Heinz Kloss.*
    J. Pool, 355(LSoc):Aug81–285
Haas, A.M. Sermo mysticus.
    W. Blank, 680(ZDP):Band100Heft3–438
Haas, D.F. Interaction in the Thai Bureaucracy.
    W.J. Siffin, 293(JASt):May81–650
Habel, C. and S. Kanngiesser, eds. Sprachdynamik und Sprachstruktur.
    H. Harnisch, 682(ZPSK):Band33Heft6–765
Haberman, D. The Furtive Wall.
    C. Inez, 472:Fall/Winter81–231
Haberman, J. Maimondies and Aquinas.*
    J. Jolivet, 542:Jul–Sep81–337
Habermas, J. Communication and the Evolution of Society.* Knowledge and Human Interests. Theory and Practice. Legitimation Crisis.
    R.S. Gottlieb, 185:Jan81–280
    Q. Skinner, 453(NYRB):7Oct82–35
Habermas, J. Raison et Légitimité.
    A. Compagnon, 98:Oct80–925
Habermas, J. Toward a Rational Society.
    Q. Skinner, 453(NYRB):7Oct82–35
Habermas, J. and N. Luhmann. Theorie der Gesellschaft oder Sozialtechnologie.
    Q. Skinner, 453(NYRB):7Oct82–35
Habersetzer, K-H. Bibliographie der deutschen Barockliteratur.
    B. Becker-Cantarino, 221(GQ):Jan81–88

Halberstam, D. The Breaks of the Game.*
  R. Blount, Jr., 441:10Jan82-6
Hald, M. Ancient Danish Textiles from
  Bogs and Burials.
  614:Winter82-13
Hale, J.R., ed. A Concise Encyclopedia of
  the Italian Renaissance.
  H. Honour, 453(NYRB):12Aug82-23
Hale, L. Turn South at the Second Bridge.
  W. Gard, 584(SWR):Winter81-vii
Hale, T.A. Les Ecrits d'Aimé Césaire.
  F.I. Case, 627(UTQ):Winter80/81-251
  F.R. Smith, 208(FS):Oct81-480
Hale, W. The Political and Economic
  Development of Modern Turkey.
  C.H. Dodd, 617(TLS):8Jan82-28
Halévy, D. Péguy et les Cahiers de la
  Quinzaine.
  205(FMLS):Jan80-85
Haley, A. Wurzeln.
  H. Ihde, 654(WB):1/1981-138
Haley, J.L. Apaches.
  L. Milazzo, 584(SWR):Summer81-v
Halfmann, H. Die Senatoren aus dem öst-
  lichen Teil des Imperium Romanum bis zum
  Ende des 2. Jh. n. Chr.
  S. Mitchell, 313:Vol71-191
Halford, M-B. Illustration and Text in
  Lutwin's "Eva und Adam."
  J.A. Davidson, 221(GQ):Nov81-495
Halkett, A. and A. Fanshawe. The Memoirs
  of Anne, Lady Halkett and Ann, Lady Fan-
  shawe.* (J. Loftis, ed)
  P.M. Spacks, 301(JEGP):Jul81-415
Hall, A.R. Philosophers at War.
  T.M. Lennon, 486:Sep81-502
Hall, C.V. Soft Sculpture.
  P. Bach, 614:Summer82-19
Hall, D. To Keep Moving.
  639(VQR):Autumn81-128
Hall, H. Selected Poems. (B. Bentley, ed)
  V.L. Nielsen, 649(WAL):Summer81-159
Hall, J. Another World and Yet the Same.
  (J.M. Wands, ed and trans)
  C. Hill, 617(TLS):16Apr82-432
Hall, J. The Sociology of Literature.*
  D. Watson, 366:Spring81-127
Hall, J. The Transforming Image.*
  639(VQR):Summer81-85
Hall, J.W., Nagahara Keiji and Kozo Yama-
  mura, eds. Japan Before Tokugawa.
  C. Totman, 407(MN):Autumn81-344
Hall, M.B. Renovation and Counter-
  Reformation.*
  F. Ames-Lewis, 161(DUJ):Jun81-227
  D.D. Bohlin, 551(RenQ):Summer80-257
  W.C. Kirwin, 54:Dec81-687
Hall, N. The Moon and the Virgin.
  B. Kohn, 42(AR):Summer81-390
Hall, N.J. Trollope and his Illustrators.*
  A. Wright, 445(NCF):Dec81-368
Hall, N.J., ed. The Trollope Critics.
  A. Wright, 617(TLS):19Mar82-322
Hall, O. Lullaby.
  R. Rhodes, 441:28Mar82-15
Hall, R. Lovers on the Nile.*
  G. and A. Macdonald, 435:Summer81-206
Hall, R. The Well of Loneliness.
  P. Craig, 617(TLS):13Aug82-888
Hall, R.A., Jr. External History of the
  Romance Languages.*
  G.F. Meier, 682(ZPSK):Band32Heft2-227

Hall, R.A., Jr. Language, Literature and
  Life.*
  M. Danesi, 320(CJL):Fall81-233
Hall, R.A., Jr. Proto-Romance Phonology.*
  G.F. Meier, 682(ZPSK):Band33Heft4-501
  T.J. Walsh, 545(RPh):Aug80-64
Hall, S. The Godmothers.
  T. Warr, 617(TLS):5Nov82-1231
Hall, S. and others, eds. Culture, Media,
  Language.
  B. Robbins, 366:Autumn81-239
Hall, T. Charles and Diana.
  V. Glendinning, 617(TLS):25Jun82-689
Hall, W. Raising Caine.
  T.J. Binyon, 617(TLS):15Jan82-51
Hallam, A.H. The Letters of Arthur Henry
  Hallam. (J. Kolb, ed)
  R.B. Martin, 617(TLS):14May82-527
  442(NY):15Mar82-144
von Hallberg, R. Charles Olson.*
  P. Yannella, 295(JML):Vol8No3/4-580
Halle, M., J. Bresnan and G.A. Miller, eds.
  Linguistic Theory and Psychological
  Reality.*
  R. Coates, 603:Vol5No1-111
  D.H., 355(LSoc):Apr81-145
  T. Roeper, 350:Jun82-467
Hallett, C.A. and E.S. The Revenger's Mad-
  ness.
  W. Blissett, 539:Nov82-289
Halley, A. The Bearded Mother.
  L. Sondern, 436(NewL):Fall81-121
Halley Mora, M. Los Hombres de Celina.
  F.E. Feito, 37:Oct81-28
Halliday, F.E. Shakespeare and His World.*
  N.A. Brittin, 577(SHR):Winter81-77
Halliday, M.A.K. Language as a Social
  Semiotic.*
  J. Ard, 351(LL):Jun81-257
Halliday, M.A.K. and R. Hasan. Cohesion
  in English.*
  N.E. Enkvist, 597(SN):Vol53No2-391
  G. Rauh, 260(IF):Band85-378
Halliday, M.A.K. and R. Hasan. Text and
  Context.
  N.E. Enkvist, 597(SN):Vol53No2-391
Hallie, P.P. Lest Innocent Blood Be Shed.
  C.W. Obuchowski, 207(FR):Dec80-378
Halligan, T.A., ed. The Booke of Gostlye
  Grace of Mechtild of Hackeborn.
  N.F. Blake, 589:Apr81-386
Hallmark, R. The Genesis of Schumann's
  Dichterliebe.
  E. Sams, 415:Jun81-382
Halls, G. Talking to Strangers.
  R. Belben, 617(TLS):6Aug82-865
  J. Mellors, 362:5Aug82-22
Halls, W.D. The Youth of Vichy France.*
  B. Braude, 207(FR):Apr82-692
Halm, W. Spanisch für Sie — Grammatik.
  G.F. Meier, 682(ZPSK):Band33Heft5-633
Halmos, I. The Music of the Nambicuara
  Indians.
  A. Seeger, 187:Jan82-165
Halpenny, F.G. - see "Dictionary of Cana-
  dian Biography"
Halperin, J., ed. Jane Austen.
  J.F. Burrows, 402(MLR):Oct81-936
Halperin, J. Gissing.
  P. Keating, 617(TLS):31Dec82-1447
Halperin, J. Trollope and Politics.*
  J. Carlisle, 639(VQR):Winter81-176
Halperin, J. - see Gissing, G.

Hampe, R. and E. Simon. The Birth of
Greek Art.
   B.F. Cook, 617(TLS):14May82-538
Hampl, F. Geschichte als kritische Wissen-
schaft. (Vol 3) (I. Weiler, ed)
   J-C. Richard, 555:Vol54fasc2-384
Hampshire, S. Two Theories of Morality.
   J.D. Wallace, 449:Mar81-76
Hampson, N. Danton.
   J.F. Traer, 173(ECS):Summer81-490
Hanagan, E. A Knock at the Door.
   J. Mellors, 362:26Aug82-24
   D. Montrose, 617(TLS):23Jul82-781
Hanan, P. The Chinese Vernacular Story.*
   J.C. Miller, 573(SSF):Fall81-479
   D. Roy, 293(JASt):Aug81-764
Hanawalt, B.A. Crime and Conflict in
English Communities, 1300-1348.
   J. Given, 589:Jan81-139
Hancock, G., ed. Magic Realism.
   S. Beckmann, 102(CanL):Summer81-152
Hancock, I.F. and others, eds. Readings
in Creole Studies.
   G. Aub-Buscher, 297(JL):Sep81-382
   P. Mohan, 350:Dec81-904
Handke, P. La Leçon de la Sainte-Victoire.
   B. Bayen, 450(NRF):Jul-Aug81-212
Handke, P. Le poids du monde.
   A. Ferry, 98:Oct80-948
Handlin, D.P. The American Home.
   M. Filler, 576:Oct81-254
   D. Schuyler, 658:Winter81-350
Handlin, O. Truth in History.*
   H.A. Tulloch, 366:Spring81-133
Handlin, O. and L. A Restless People.
   P-L. Adams, 61:Apr82-110
   W. Goodman, 441:14Mar82-16
Hane, M. Peasants, Rebels and Outcastes.
   J. Halliday, 617(TLS):17Dec82-1390
   E.J. Hobsbawm, 453(NYRB):15Apr82-15
Hanefeld, E. Philosophische Haupttexte
der älteren Upaniṣaden.
   L. Rocher, 318(JAOS):Jul/Sep80-319
Hanf, T., H. Weiland and G. Vierdag.
South Africa.
   G. Wheatcroft, 617(TLS):26Feb82-229
Hanfling, O., ed. Essential Readings in
Logical Positivism.
   N. Tennant, 617(TLS):19Mar82-326
Hanfling, O. Logical Positivism.
   N. Tennant, 617(TLS):19Mar82-326
Hanfling, O. The Uses and Abuses of Argu-
ment.
   E.J. Borowski, 479(PhQ):Apr81-184
Hanford, R.T. The Complete Book of Pup-
pets and Puppeteering.
   R.L. Shep, 614:Summer82-13
Hani, J. La religion égyptienne dans la
pensée de Plutarque.
   P.W. van der Horst, 394:Vol34fasc1/2-
165
Hanisch, G.S. Love Elegies of the Renais-
sance.
   R.E. Hallowell, 210(FrF):Sep81-275
Hanke, L. Guía de las fuentes en Hispano-
américa para el estudio de la administra-
ción virreinal española en México y en
el Perú, 1535-1700.
   W.L. Sherman, 263(RIB):Vol31No2-276
Hankins, J.E. Backgrounds of Shake-
speare's Thought.*
   V.M. Carr, 179(ES):Dec81-565

Hankinson, A. Man of Wars.
   H. Brogan, 617(TLS):31Dec82-1439
Hanks, P. and others - see "Collins Dic-
tionary of the English Language"
Hanley, J. Against the Stream.
   F. Tuohy, 617(TLS):21May82-549
   A. Tyler, 441:17Jan82-7
   442(NY):11Jan82-95
Hann, C.M. Tázlár.
   P. Bogdanowicz, 575(SEER):Jul81-468
Hannappel, H. and H. Melenk. Alltags-
sprache.
   R. Kloepfer, 490:Band12Heft3/4-509
Hannay, A. Kierkegaard.
   M. Warnock, 617(TLS):24Dec82-1423
Hannay, A. Love and Other Natural Disas-
ters.
   442(NY):14Jun82-134
Hannemann, J. and L. Zschuckelt. Schrift-
steller in der Diskussion.
   K. Rauschek, 654(WB):8/1981-189
Hannibal, E. A Trace of Red.
   S. Ellin, 441:28Feb82-14
Hannick, C., ed. Fundamental Problems of
Early Slavic Music and Poetry.*
   H. Keipert, 688(ZSP):Band42Heft2-417
Hanning, R. and J. Ferrante - see Marie de
France
Hanrahan, B. and R. Fox. I Counted Them
All Out and I Counted Them All Back.
   A. Ryan, 362:9Sep82-22
Hans, J.S. The Play of the World.
   L. Rosenstein, 290(JAAC):Spring82-344
   K.S., 185:Jul82-799
Hansel, C.E.M. ESP and Parapsychology.
   D.J. Murray, 529(QQ):Winter81-764
   639(VQR):Spring81-68
Hansen, B. Mexican Cookery.
   A.B.E., 37:Mar81-48
Hansen, J. Gravedigger.
   N. Callendar, 441:30May82-15
Hansen, K.C. and L.E. The Core of Pintupi
Grammar.
   R.M.W. Dixon, 350:Mar81-245
Hansen, M.A. Against the Wind.* The Book.
   F. Ingwersen, 563(SS):Winter81-109
Hansen, P.A. - see Plutarch
Hansen-Löve, A.A. Der russische Formalis-
mus.*
   J-U. Peters, 688(ZSP):Band42Heft1-172
   W-D. Stempel, 490:Band12Heft3/4-537
Hanslik, R. - see Propertius
Hanson, A. Burgundy.
   J. Robinson, 617(TLS):27Aug82-929
   A. Watkins, 362:10Jun82-27
Hanson, A.T. and R.P.C. Reasonable
Belief.
   D. Cupitt, 617(TLS):12Feb82-154
Hanson, D. The New Alchemists.
   442(NY):25Oct82-174
Hanson, J.A. The Voyageur's Sketchbook.
   R.L. Shep, 614:Fall81-22
Hanson, R.P.C., with C. Blanc - see Saint
Patrick
Häny, A. Die Dichter und ihre Heimat.*
   S. Steffensen, 301(JEGP):Jan81-113
Happ, H. Grundfragen einer Dependenz-
Grammatik des Lateinischen.
   E. Vester, 394:Vol34fasc1/2-169
Harari, J.V., ed. Textual Strategies.
   J. Alter, 494:Winter80/81-213
   J. Arac, 81:Spring80-241
[continued]

[continuing]
W.E. Cain, 210(FrF):May81-186
D. O'Hara, 290(JAAC):Fall81-101
Harari, J.V. and D.F. Bell - see Serres, M.
Harari, M. Il "Gruppo Clusium" della
ceramografia etrusca.
A.D. Trendall, 303(JoHS):Vol 101-216
Harbison, P., H. Potterton and J. Sheehy.
Irish Art and Architecture from Prehis-
tory to the Present.
D. Guinness, 576:May81-154
Harbsmeier, C. Wilhelm von Humboldts
Brief an Abel-Rémusat und die philoso-
phische Grammatik des Altchinesischen.
R.C.S. Walker, 307:Apr81-46
Harden, E.F. The Emergence of Thackeray's
Serial Fiction.*
S. Monod, 189(EA):Apr-Jun81-227
R. Sheets, 637(VS):Winter81-238
J. Sutherland, 445(NCF):Sep80-206
Harden, E.J. The Murder of Griboedov —
New Materials.
D. Rayfield, 575(SEER):Apr81-289
Hardin, G. Promethean Ethics.*
I.M., 185:Oct81-193
Hardin, R., ed. Survivals of Pastoral.
J. Quinlan, 579(SAQ):Winter81-115
Harding, D.W. Words into Rhythm.
W. Bernhart, 224(GRM):Band30Heft1-119
D.G. Marshall, 402(MLR):Oct81-920
Harding, G. and A. Hollo, eds. Modern
Swedish Poetry in Translation.
R. Jarvi, 563(SS):Spring81-239
Harding, J. Folies de Paris.
R. Shattuck, 207(FR):Dec81-289
Harding, J. Jacques Offenbach.
J.B., 412:Nov80-314
Harding, R.R. Anatomy of a Power Elite.*
M. Greengrass, 161(DUJ):Jun81-241
Harding, W. and M. Meyer. The New Thoreau
Handbook.
J.C. Broderick, 365:Fall81-162
R.J. Schneider, 183(ESQ):Vol127No1-57
M.F. Schulz, 678(YCGL):No29-55
Hardinge, G., ed. Winter's Crimes 13.
R.D. Edwards, 617(TLS):1Jan82-12
Hardjono, J.M. Transmigration in Indo-
nesia.
L. Manderson, 293(JASt):Nov80-201
Hardtwig, B., comp. Bestandskatalog der
Bayerischen Staatsgemäldesammlungen.
(Vol 3)
S. Röttgen, 471:Jan/Feb/Mar81-90
Hardwick, M. Bergerac.
N. Callendar, 441:19Dec82-30
Hardwick, M. Prisoner of the Devil.
639(VQR):Winter81-18
Hardy, A. Coriolan.* (T. Allott, ed)
C. Nutton, 208(FS):Jul81-327
Hardy, B. Particularities.
J. Bayley, 617(TLS):23Jul82-779
Hardy, F. Who Shot George Kirkland?
P. Pierce, 381:Apr81-106
Hardy, F. - see Grierson, J.
Hardy, H. - see Berlin, I.
Hardy, H. and A. Kelly - see Berlin, I.
Hardy, J.C. A Catalogue of English Prose
Fiction Mainly of the Eighteenth Century
from a Private Library.
D.J.M., 617(TLS):17Dec82-1403
Hardy, R. and others. The Weather Book.
O.M. Ashford, 617(TLS):4Jun82-616

Hardy, R.W. China's Oil Future.
C.T. Hu, 293(JASt):Aug81-765
Hardy, T. The Collected Letters of Thomas
Hardy.* (Vol 1) (R.L. Purdy and M. Mill-
gate, eds)
P. Coustillas, 189(EA):Oct-Dec81-483
Hardy, T. The Collected Letters of Thomas
Hardy.* (Vol 2) (R.L. Purdy and M. Mill-
gate, eds)
R.G.C., 148:Autumn81-91
P. Coustillas, 189(EA):Oct-Dec81-483
P. Zietlow, 445(NCF):Mar82-489
Hardy, T. The Collected Letters of Thomas
Hardy. (Vol 3) (R.L. Purdy and M. Mill-
gate, eds)
J. Bayley, 453(NYRB):7Oct82-9
C. Lock, 362:2Dec82-22
J.I.M. Stewart, 617(TLS):10Sep82-968
Hardy, T. The Complete Poems of Thomas
Hardy. (J. Gibson, ed)
C. Lock, 184(EIC):Oct80-367
Hardy, T. Far from the Madding Crowd. (R.
Blythe, ed) Jude the Obscure. (C.H.
Sisson, ed) The Mayor of Casterbridge.
(M. Seymour-Smith, ed) The Return of
the Native. (G. Woodcock, ed) Tess of
the d'Urbervilles. (D. Skilton, ed)
Under the Greenwood Tree. (D. Wright,
ed)
I. Ousby, 161(DUJ):Jun81-261
Hardy, T. The Personal Notebooks of
Thomas Hardy.* (R.H. Taylor, ed)
L.A. Björk, 445(NCF):Sep80-213
J.L. Bradley, 677(YES):Vol 11-330
C. Lock, 184(EIC):Oct80-367
M. Williams, 447(N&Q):Jun80-257
Hardy, W.G. Language, Thought, and Experi-
ence.
B. Bjorklund, 494:Autumn80-226
Hare, A. George Frederick Cooke.*
J.C. Trewin, 157:Autumn81-51
Hare, G.E. Alphonse Daudet.
M. Sachs, 207(FR):Mar81-600
Hare, J.E. and C.B. Joynt. Ethics and
International Affairs.
B. Barry, 617(TLS):13Aug82-878
Hare, R.M. Moral Thinking.
R.B. Brandt, 617(TLS):2Jul82-713
M. Warnock, 362:18Feb82-22
Hare, W. Open-Mindedness and Education.
O. Reboul, 154:Sep81-602
Haren, M.J., ed. Calendar of Entries in
the Papal Registers Relating to Great
Britain and Ireland. (Papal Letters,
Vol 15)
J.E. Sayers, 325:Oct81-505
Hares, R.J. Teaching French.
205(FMLS):Apr80-189
Hargrove, N.D. Landscape as Symbol in the
Poetry of T.S. Eliot.*
W. Harmon, 577(SHR):Summer81-276
Haring, N.M. - see Alan of Lille
Harivaṃś, Ś.H. The "Caurāsī Pad" of Śrī
Hit Harivaṃś.* (C.S.J. White, ed and
trans)
F.W. Pritchett, 314:Summer-Fall81-234
Harjan, G. Leonid Leonov.
P. Petro, 104(CASS):Winter81-566
Harker, M.E. The Linked Ring.*
T. Powell, 39:Apr81-275

Harkins, W.E. and P.I. Trensky, eds.
Czech Literature Since 1956.
  M. Heim, 574(SEEJ):Spring81-127
  R.B. Pynsent, 575(SEER):Oct81-601
Harlfinger, D. and M. Sicherl, with others.
Griechische Handschriften und Aldinen.*
  N.G. Wilson, 122:Apr81-169
Harlow, M. Nothing But Switzerland and
Lemonade.
  W. Slinn, 368:Dec81-495
Harlow, R. Making Arrangements.*
  M. Benazon, 102(CanL):Winter80-134
  J. Harris, 296(JCF):No31/32-248
Härmä, J. Recherches sur les construc-
tions imbriquées relatives et interroga-
tives en français.
  J.M. Julien, 350:Mar81-237
  L. Lindgren, 439(NM):1981/2-220
Harman, C. - see Warner, S.T.
Harman, M., comp. Incunabula in the Uni-
versity of Illinois Library at Urbana-
Champaign.
  F.R. Goff, 517(PBSA):Jan-Mar81-111
Harman, P.M. Energy, Force, and Matter.
  D.M. Knight, 617(TLS):6Aug82-864
Harmer, L.C. Uncertainties in French Gram-
mar.* (P. Rickard and T.G.S. Combe, eds)
  S.N. Rosenberg, 207(FR):Feb81-482
  J. Walz, 399(MLJ):Autumn81-358
Harmon, M., ed. Irish Poetry After Yeats.*
  J.W. Foster, 134(CP):Fall81-116
Harmon, M., ed. Richard Murphy.
  C.W. Barrow, 174(Éire):Winter81-144
Harmon, W., ed. The Oxford Book of Ameri-
can Light Verse.*
  R. Asselineau, 189(EA):Jul-Sep81-356
Harmon, W. Time in Ezra Pound's Work.
  P. Stevens, 106:Winter81-355
Harms, R.W. River of Wealth, River of
Sorrow.
  R. Oliver, 617(TLS):26Feb82-211
Harner, J.L. Samuel Daniel and Michael
Drayton.
  P.J. Klemp, 365:Spring-Summer82-116
Harner, J.L. English Renaissance Prose
Fiction 1500-1660.*
  J. Belfield, 354:Mar81-73
  R. Yeager, 594:Fall81-340
Harpas, E. - see Constant, B.
Harper, D.A. Good Company.
  M. Abley, 617(TLS):13Aug82-873
Harper, F.M.H. - see Lincoln, M.
Harper, G.M., ed. Yeats and the Occult.
  E. Mackenzie, 447(N&Q):Oct80-471
Harper, G.M. W.B. Yeats and W.T. Horton.*
  M. Sidnell, 150(DR):Winter81/82-752
Harper, M.S. - see Brown, S.A.
Harper, M.S. and R.B. Stepto, eds. Chant
of Saints.
  M. Fabre, 189(EA):Jan-Mar81-111
  J.O. Perry, 219(GaR):Spring81-170
Harper, N.L. Human Communication Theory.
  D.E. Williams, 583:Fall80-86
Harprath, R. Papst Paul III. als Alex-
ander der Grosse.*
  C. Hope, 90:Feb81-104
"Harrap's New Standard French and English
Dictionary." (Vols 3 and 4) (by J.E.
Mansion; rev by D.M. and R.P.L. Ledésert)
  G. Price, 208(FS):Jan81-114
"Harrap's Shorter French and English Dic-
tionary." (P. Collin and others, eds)
  J. Weightman, 617(TLS):3Sep82-952

Harré, R. Social Being.
  D.A. Lloyd Thomas, 483:Jan81-133
Harrigan, S. Aransas.
  W. Bloodworth, 649(WAL):Winter81-307
Harrington, E. and A.J. Abadie, eds.
Faulkner, Modernism, and Film.*
  A.F. Kinney, 395(MFS):Summer80-337
Harrington, M. Decade of Decision.*
  G. McKenna, 396(ModA):Summer81-312
Harrington, R.E. Proud Man.
  A. Bold, 617(TLS):26Mar82-361
Harrington, W. The English Lady.
  S. Ellin, 441:30May82-19
Harriot, T. The Last Proud Rider.*
  C. Hope, 364:Dec81/Jan82-136
Harris, B. - see Sackville, C.
Harris, C. Mystery at the Edge of Two
Worlds.
  J.K. Kealy, 102(CanL):Spring80-113
Harris, C. The Trouble with Princesses.
  K. Kealy, 102(CanL):Summer81-149
Harris, D. Dreams Die Hard.
  J. Klein, 441:13Jun82-3
Harris, E.P. and R.E. Schade, eds. Less-
ing in heutiger Sicht.*
  S. Suesse-Fiedler, 133:Band14Heft2-179
Harris, E.T. Handel and the Pastoral
Tradition.
  L. Lindgren, 317:Summer81-352
Harris, G.G. Casting Out Anger.
  A. Redmayne, 69:Vol150No2-216
Harris, H.S. and T.M. Knox - see Hegel,
G.W.F.
Harris, J. The Artist and the Country
House.*
  D. Irwin, 83:Spring81-113
Harris, J. Violence and Responsibility.*
  B. Barry, 185:Apr82-555
  D.M. Evans, 483:Apr81-273
  H. Kuhse, 63:Jun81-252
Harris, J. Without Trace.
  R. O'Hanlon, 617(TLS):23Jul82-805
Harris, J.G. - see Mandelstam, O.
Harris, J.W. Law and Legal Science.
  T.M. Benditt, 518:Oct81-213
  G. Marshall, 393(Mind):Jul81-443
  S.E. Marshall, 479(PhQ):Jan81-89
Harris, K. Attlee.
  K.O. Morgan, 617(TLS):24Sep82-1026
  H. Wilson, 362:23Sep82-20
Harris, K.E. and S.D. Tilley, comps.
Index: Journals of the Continental Con-
gress, 1774-1789.
  C.H. Lesser, 14:Summer80-373
Harris, K.G., ed. Robert Frost: Studies
of the Poetry.
  T. Lieber, 651(WHR):Spring81-92
Harris, K.M. Carlyle and Emerson.*
  B. Kuklick, 319:Oct81-515
  J.S. Martin, 106:Fall81-209
Harris, M. America Now.
  A. Hacker, 453(NYRB):18Mar82-37
  R. Lekachman, 441:31Jan82-7
Harris, M. Saul Bellow: Drumlin Wood-
chuck.*
  S. Pinsker, 219(GaR):Spring81-178
  B. Stonehill, 114(ChiR):Spring81-119
Harris, M. Herma.*
  J. Moody, 617(TLS):12Feb82-169
Harris, M. Screenplay.
  C. See, 441:31Oct82-14
Harris, R. Honor Bound.
  J. Casey, 441:22Aug82-10

Harris, R. The Language-Maker.*
  C-J.N. Bailey, 307:Oct81-116
  M.L. Pratt, 350:Sep81-698
Harris, R.D. Necker.
  J.C. Riley, 173(ECS):Fall80-97
Harris, T. Red Dragon.*
  442(NY):18Jan82-130
Harris, W. The Angel at the Gate.
  J.P. Durix, 617(TLS):15Oct82-1141
Harris, W.C. The Day of the Carpetbagger.*
  E.N. Akin, 392:Spring81-135
Harris, W.V. British Short Fiction in the
  Nineteenth Century.*
  R.A. Colby, 637(VS):Winter81-254
  J. Harkey, 573(SSF):Fall81-472
  D.D. Stone, 445(NCF):Sep80-234
Harrison, B. An Introduction to the Phi-
  losophy of Language.
  M. McGinn, 479(PhQ):Apr81-163
  J.E. Tiles, 518:Jul81-182
Harrison, B. Separate Spheres.*
  V. Cromwell, 161(DUJ):Dec80-102
Harrison, B. and P. Hollis, eds. Robert
  Lowery.
  J. Epstein, 637(VS):Spring81-380
Harrison, C. English Art and Modernism
  1900-1939.*
  J. Beckett, 59:Dec81-461
  R. Morphet, 90:Nov81-679
  G.P. Weisberg, 55:Nov81-48
Harrison, D. The White Tribe of Africa.
  G. Wheatcroft, 617(TLS):26Feb82-229
Harrison, F. Strange Land.
  P. Beer, 362:4Mar82-22
  K. Mellanby, 617(TLS):12Mar82-287
Harrison, G.B. - see Bunyan, J.
Harrison, J. Hume's Theory of Justice.*
  R.H., 185:Apr82-587
Harrison, J. Selected and New Poems.
  R. Tillinghast, 441:12Dec82-14
Harrison, J. Warlock.*
  T.O. Treadwell, 617(TLS):15Jan82-48
Harrison, J.F.C. The Second Coming.
  W.L. Arnstein, 637(VS):Winter81-230
Harrison, J.P. The Endless War.
  G. Smith, 441:2May82-3
Harrison, M. Victorian Stained Glass.*
  R. Hubbuck, 46:Feb81-128
  R. Mander, 39:Apr81-269
Harrison, M.J. In Viriconium.
  C. Greenland, 617(TLS):29Oct82-1203
Harrison, R., ed. Independent Collier.
  I. Prothero, 637(VS):Winter81-245
Harrison, R., ed. Rational Action.*
  G. Marshall, 63:Mar81-106
Harrison, S.M. The Pilgrimage of Grace in
  the Lake Counties, 1536-7.
  C. Cross, 617(TLS):21May82-554
Harrison, S.P. and S. Albert. Mokilese-
  English Dictionary.*
  G.F. Meier, 682(ZPSK):Band33Heft5-634
Harrison, S.P. and S.Y. Albert. Mokilese
  Reference Grammar.*
  G.F. Meier, 682(ZPSK):Band33Heft5-600
Harrison, T. Continuous.
  D. Davis, 362:6May82-26
  C. Reid, 617(TLS):15Jan82-49
  A. Ross, 364:Mar82-5
  S. Spender, 453(NYRB):15Jul82-26
Harrison, T. U.S. Martial. A Kumquat for
  John Keats.
  C. Reid, 617(TLS):15Jan82-49

Harrison, W. Burton and Speke.
  J.S., 231:Oct82-76
Harrison, W. and A. Pyman, eds. To Honor
  Nikolay Andreyev.
  J. Dingley, 575(SEER):Jul81-430
Harrop, D.A. A History of the Gregynog
  Press.
  P. Morgan, 78(BC):Summer81-260
  G. Walters, 354:Sep81-263
Harrop, L. The Hum of the Old Suit.*
  C. Pollnitz, 581:Jun81-221
Hart, A.A. Historic Boise.
  J.M. Neil, 576:Dec81-343
't Hart, A.C. Recht en Staat in het den-
  ken van Giambattista Vico.*
  R. Crease, 480(P&R):Spring81-133
Hart, F.R. and J.B. Pick. Neil M. Gunn.*
  E. Morgan, 617(TLS):19Feb82-192
Hart, G.L. 3d. Poets of the Tamil Antholo-
  gies.
  D. Shulman, 293(JASt):Nov80-165
Hart, J. Hiking the Great Basin.
  T.J. Lyon, 649(WAL):Fall81-236
Hart, J. When the Going Was Good!
  R.M.K., 231:Sep82-74
  H. Schwartz, 441:14Nov82-16
Hart, K. The Lines of the Hand.
  C. Wallace-Crabbe, 617(TLS):19Nov82-
  1282
Hart, M. Rats.
  P. Highsmith, 617(TLS):24Sep82-1027
Hart, P. Conductors.
  N. Goodwin, 415:Jun81-385
Hart, P. - see Merton, T.
Hart, P.R. G.R. Derzhavin.*
  I.K. Lilly, 575(SEER):Apr81-288
  I. Sherman, 550(RusR):Apr81-216
Hart, T. Cradle Song.
  L. Marcus, 617(TLS):16Jul82-775
Hart-Davis, D. Level Five.
  M. Trend, 617(TLS):12Feb82-169
Hart-Davis, R. - see Lyttelton, G. and R.
  Hart-Davis
Hart-Davis, R. - see Sassoon, S.
Harter, C. The Seven.
  D. Devlin, 157:Oct80-72
Harter, E. Bosom of the Family.
  J.P. Gemill, 314:Summer-Fall81-239
Hartford, R., ed. Bayreuth: The Early
  Years.*
  R. Anderson, 415:May81-310
Harth, E. Windows on the Mind.
  D.M. MacKay, 617(TLS):26Mar82-360
  R.M. Restak, 441:7Mar82-6
  442(NY):4Jan82-90
Hartig, M. and R. Binnick. Grammatik und
  Sprachgebrauch.
  E. Bense, 353:Vol 18No7/8-745
Hartigan, K. The Poets and the Cities.*
  G. Lawall, 122:Oct81-319
Hartley, L. Laurence Sterne.
  C.J. Rawson, 677:Vol 11-268
Hartley, R.A., ed. Keats, Shelley, Byron,
  Hunt and their Circles.*
  J.D. Bone, 677(YES):Vol 11-304
Härtling, P. Die dreifache Maria.
  M. McHaffie, 617(TLS):1Oct82-1083
Härtling, P. Hölderlin.
  G. Quinsat, 450(NRF):Apr81-121
  A. Reix, 542:Oct-Dec81-481
Hartman, C.O. Free Verse.*
  A. Helms, 569(SR):Fall81-cxvii
  A. Welsh, 141:Fall81-367

151

Hartman, E. Substance, Body, and Soul.*
  H.S. Lang, 319:Oct81-500
Hartman, G.H. Criticism in the Wilderness.*
  T.H. Adamowski, 529(QQ):Autumn81-442
  J.M. Flora, 573(SSF):Fall81-463
  S. Handelman, 661(WC):Summer81-202
  D. Hughes, 400(MLN):Dec81-1134
  K. Johnston, 128(CE):Sep81-471
  R. Levin, 405(MP):Feb82-340
  J. Mall, 290(JAAC):Winter81-227
  D.G. Marshall, 676(YR):Autumn81-129
  R. Moynihan, 50(ArQ):Summer81-187
  P.C. Ray, 651(WHR):Winter81-367
  D.H. Richter, 349:Summer81-232
  M. Sprinker, 81:Fall80-217
  H. Vendler, 442(NY):3May82-158
  H. White, 473(PR):4/1981-646
Hartman, G.H., ed. Psychoanalysis and the
  Question of the Text.
  D. Gordon, 107(CRCL):Winter81-112
  A.D. Nuttall, 541(RES):Feb81-113
Hartman, G.H. Saving the Text.
  D. Hughes, 400(MLN):Dec81-1134
  J. Mall, 290(JAAC):Winter81-227
  D.G. Marshall, 676(YR):Autumn81-129
  D. O'Hara, 659(ConL):Summer82-381
  639(VQR):Autumn81-126
Hartmann von Aue. Iwein.* (J.W. Thomas,
  trans)
  205(FMLS):Apr80-189
Hartmann, J.B. Antike Motive bei Thorvaldsen.
  N. Penny, 90:Jan81-41
Hartmann, K., ed. Die ontologische Option.
  M. Baum, 53(AGP):Band63Heft2-213
Hartmann, K-H. Wiederholungen im Erzählen.
  J.H. Petersen, 680(ZDP):Band99Heft4-597
Hartog, F. Le Miroir d'Hérodote.
  J-P. Guinle, 450(NRF):Mar81-136
Hartung, A.E., ed. A Manual of the Writings in Middle English: 1050-1500. (Vol 6)
  R.L. Hoffman, 365:Winter82-30
Hartung, W., ed. Normen in der sprachlichen Kommunikation.
  U. Teleman, 353:Vol 18No3/4-335
Harvey, A.E., ed. God Incarnate.
  J.L. Houlden, 617(TLS):28May82-589
Harvey, A.E. Jesus and the Constraints of History.
  A.N. Sherwin-White, 617(TLS):9Apr82-408
Harvey, G. The Art of Anthony Trollope.
  J. McMaster, 445(NCF):Sep81-234
  42(AR):Fall81-518
Harvey, J. Mediaeval Gardens.
  G. Jellicoe, 324:Aug82-597
Harvey, N. The Guide to Successful Tapestry Weaving.
  P. Bach, 614:Winter82-21
Harvey, S. and others, eds. Reappraisals of Rousseau.*
  R. Grimsley, 208(FS):Jul81-336
  T. Scanlan, 207(FR):Dec81-273
Harvey, V. Color and Design in Macramé.
  R.L. Shep, 614:Summer81-16
Harvey, V.I. - see Bateman, W.G.
Harvey, W. Disputations touching the Generation of Animals.
  M. Pollock, 617(TLS):11Jun82-629

Harvey, Y.K. Six Korean Women.
  T. Pak, 77:Winter81-85
Harwood, G. The Lion's Bride.
  C. Wallace-Crabbe, 617(TLS):19Nov82-1282
Harwood, L. and J. Walker. All the wrong notes.
  S. Ellis, 617(TLS):2Apr82-393
Hasan, M. - see Ansari, M.A.
Hasegawa, T. The February Revolution.
  H. Shukman, 617(TLS):19Feb82-184
Haseloff, C.H. Ride South!
  J.D. Nesbitt, 649(WAL):Spring81-84
Haseman, J.B. The Thai Resistance Movement During the Second World War.
  C.A. Trocki, 293(JASt):Nov80-191
Hashmi, A. The Oath and Amen.
  J.P. Gemmill, 314:Winter-Spring81-244
Haskell, F. and N. Penny. Taste and the Antique.*
  A. Potts, 90:Oct81-618
  135:Dec81-250
Haslam, G. The Wages of Sin.
  B. Baines, 649(WAL):Fall81-228
  L. Clayton, 95(CLAJ):Jun81-533
Hass, R. Praise.*
  W. Scammell, 617(TLS):28May82-592
Hass, U. Theodor Fontane.*
  R.L. Jamison, 406:Fall81-360
Hassall, A.J. Henry Fielding's "Tom Jones."
  E. Moon, 67:May81-110
Hassan, I. The Right Promethean Fire.*
  S.B. Girgus, 560:Spring-Summer81-208
  J. Klinkowitz, 395(MFS):Winter80/81-719
  A. Otten, 42(AR):Summer81-391
Hassán, I.M. - see "Estudios sefardíes"
Hassel, R.C., Jr. Renaissance Drama and the English Church Year.
  D. Mills, 541(RES):Aug81-315
  N.C. Strout, 568(SCN):Summer-Fall81-53
  G.W. Williams, 551(RenQ):Autumn80-468
Hasselbeck, O. Illusion und Fiktion.
  G. Kurscheidt, 680(ZDP):Band100Heft4-592
  E. Rentschler, 400(MLN):Apr81-685
Hassenstein a Lobkowicz, B. Bohvslai Hassensteinii a Lobkowicz Epistvlae. (Vol 2) (J. Martínek and B. Martínková, eds)
  L.V.R., 568(SCN):Winter81-106
Hassine, J. Essai sur Proust et Baudelaire.
  M-H. Thomas, 535(RHL):Nov-Dec81-1019
Hastings, A. A History of African Christianity 1950-1975.
  J.D.Y. Peel, 69:Vol150No3-323
Hastings, M. Sir Richard Burton.
  R. Pankhurst, 69:Vol150No2-213
Hastings, M. Gloo Joo, Full Frontal, For the West (Uganda).
  D. Devlin, 157:1stQtr81-54
Hastings, M. Das Reich.*
  W. Goodman, 441:1Aug82-23
Hasubek, P. - see Immermann, K.L.
Hatch, R.M. Thrust for Canada.
  M.H. Gorn, 432(NEQ):Mar81-125
Hatfield, H. From the Magic Mountain.*
  F.D. Horvay, 395(MFS):Winter80/81-735
  K. Schröter, 222(GR):Winter81-38
Hatfield, M. Spy Fever.
  K. Jeffery, 617(TLS):11Jun82-642

Hatlen, B., ed. George Oppen.
  N. Wheale, 617(TLS):30Jul82-838
Hatt, J. The Tropical Traveller.
  D. Murphy, 617(TLS):30Apr82-490
Hattaway, M. Elizabethan Popular Theatre.
  S. Wells, 617(TLS):17Dec82-1402
Hattersley, R. Politics Apart.
  A. Chancellor, 362:15Jul82-20
Hatto, A.T., ed. The Memorial Feast for
  Kökötöy-Khan (Kökötöydun Aši).
  J.J. Duggan, 131(CL):Winter81-86
Hatzfeld, H. Estudios de estilística.
  C. Stern, 545(RPh):Feb81-332
Hatzfeld, H., ed. Romanistische Stilfor-
  schung.
  E.J. Richards, 545(RPh):Feb81(supp)-
  212
Haubrichs, W., ed. Erzählforschung 2.
  R. Kloepfer, 196:Band21Heft3/4-314
Haubrichs, W., ed. Erzählforschung 3.
  J.H. Petersen, 680(ZDP):Band99Heft4-
  597
  D. Ward, 196:Band22Heft1/2-129
Haubtmann, P. La philosophie sociale de
  P-J. Proudhon.
  A. Reix, 542:Oct-Dec81-482
Haudressy, D. Thèmes russes extraits du
  journal Le Monde. (Vol 1)
  N.J. Brown, 575(SEER):Jan81-155
Haufe, H. Funktion und Wandel christ-
  licher Themen in der mexikanischen
  Malerei des 20. Jahrhunderts.
  H. Prignitz, 683:Band44Heft1-101
Häufle, H. Aufklärung und Ökonomie.
  F. Schalk, 72:Band217Heft1-223
Haug, W. "Das Land, von welchem niemand
  wiederkehrt."*
  C. Cormeau, 684(ZDA):Band109Heft1-23
Haugan, J. Henrik Ibsens metode.
  M. Ritzu, 462(OL):Vol35No3-206
Hauge, R., ed. Drinking and Driving in
  Scandinavia.
  D. Orrick, 563(SS):Winter81-94
Haugen, E. The Ecology of Language. (A.S.
  Dil, ed)
  L. Pederson, 35(AS):Summer81-118
Haugen, E. Ibsen's Drama.*
  S.G. McLellan, 130:Spring81-85
  A. van Marken, 562(Scan):May81-100
Haugen, E. The Vocabulary of Bjørnson's
  Literary Works.
  H. Noreng, 562(Scan):Nov81-229
Haugen, E., with others, eds. A Bibliog-
  raphy of Scandinavian Languages and Lin-
  guistics, 1900-1970.
  L. Pederson, 35(AS):Summer81-125
Haumont, T. Les Petits Prophètes du nord.
  R. Robe, 207(FR):Feb82-435
Hauner, M. India in Axis Strategy.
  M.E. Yapp, 617(TLS):6Aug82-851
Haupt, J. Heinrich Mann.
  U. Weisstein, 221(GQ):Nov81-522
Hauri, H.W. Kontrahiertes und sigma-
  tisches Futur.*
  A. Heubeck, 260(IF):Band85-332
Haus, A. Moholy-Nagy: Photographs and
  Photograms.
  J. Masheck, 62:Jan81-64
Hauser, A. The Sociology of Art.
  T. Eagleton, 617(TLS):22Oct82-1168
Hauser, E.O. Italy.
  H. Honour, 453(NYRB):12Aug82-23

Hauser, G. The Ordinary Invisbile Woman.
  D. Cooper-Clark, 102(CanL):Autumn80-
  108
Häusler, F. Das Problem Phonetik und
  Phonologie bei Baudouin de Courtenay
  und in seiner Nachfolge. (2nd ed)
  L.R. Zinder, 682(ZPSK):Band33Heft5-602
Hausman, J.J., with J. Wright, eds. Arts
  and the Schools.
  S.G. Weiner, 127:Summer81-189
Hausmann, F.J. Einführung in die Benut-
  zung der neufranzösischen Wörterbücher.*
  H. and R. Kahane, 545(RPh):Feb81(supp)-
  6
Hausmann, F.J. Louis Meigret humaniste et
  linguiste.
  P. Rickard, 208(FS):Jul81-325
Hausmann, F.J. - see Meigret, L.
Havel, V. Audience; Vernissage; Pétition.
  J-L. Gautier, 450(NRF):Mar81-154
Havelock, E.A. The Greek Concept of
  Justice.*
  J.A.S. Evans, 529(QQ):Spring81-87
Haver, R. David O. Selznick's Hollywood.*
  D. Bodeen, 200:Mar81-179
  A. Sarris, 18:Jan-Feb81-60
Haverkamp, A. Typik und Politik im
  Annolied.
  D.H. Green, 402(MLR):Oct81-982
Haverkate, H. Impositive Sentences in
  Spanish.*
  J.M. Guitart, 238:Sep81-492
Haverstock, M.S. An American Bestiary.
  R.M. Peck, 658:Summer/Autumn81-236
Hawke, D.F. Those Tremendous Mountains.
  L.J. Cappon, 656(WMQ):Oct81-751
Hawkes, C. Britain and Julius Caesar.
  R. Goodburn, 123:Vol31No1-135
Hawkes, J. Adventures in Archaeology.
  P-L. Adams, 61:Aug82-97
Hawkes, J. Virginie.
  A. Friedman, 441:27Jun82-3
  J. Wolcott, 453(NYRB):10Jun82-14
Hawkes, J. Mortimer Wheeler.
  S. Piggott, 617(TLS):23Apr82-467
Hawkes, S.C., D. Brown and J. Campbell,
  eds. Anglo-Saxon Studies in Archaeology
  and History. (Vol 1)
  H. Chickering, 589:Apr81-389
Hawkins, J.A. Definiteness and Indefinite-
  ness.*
  N. Burton-Roberts, 350:Mar81-191
  F. Corblin, 209(FM):Jan81-84
  E. Klein, 353:Vol 18No1/2-147
Hawkins, J.D., ed. Trade in the Ancient
  Near East.
  J.D. Muhly, 318(JAOS):Apr/Jun80-173
Hawkins, J.M. - see "The Oxford Senior Dic-
  tionary"
Hawley, D. L'Oeuvre insolite de Georges
  Bataille, une hiérophanie moderne.*
  V. Conley, 207(FR):Feb82-420
Haworth, L. Decadence and Objectivity.
  D.G. Sloan, 488:Mar81-114
Hawthorn, J. Joseph Conrad.*
  J. Batchelor, 447(N&Q):Jun80-259
  T.K. Bender, 577(SHR):Winter81-85
  R. Davis, 395(MFS):Summer80-299
  E.K. Hay, 405(MP):Nov81-177
  D. Hewitt, 541(RES):Aug81-353
  B. Johnson, 637(VS):Winter81-257
  S. Raval, 594:Winter81-439
  M.W. Stewart, 136:Vol 13No2-155

Heath, J. Ngandi Grammar, Texts, and
Dictionary.* Linguistic Diffusion in
Arnhem Land.
   I. Smith, 350:Jun82-435
Heath, R.A.K. Genetha.
   H. Eley, 617(TLS):1Jan82-8
   J. Mellors, 362:14Jan82-24
Heath, R.A.K. Kwaku.
   A. Bold, 617(TLS):12Nov82-1243
   K.C. O'Brien, 362:11Nov82-27
Heath, R.A.K. One Generation.*
   A. Ross, 364:Jun81-12
Heath, T. Interstices of Night.*
   E. Popham, 102(CanL):Autumn81-157
Heath-Stubbs, J. Naming the Beasts.
   D. Davis, 362:6May82-26
   G. Szirtes, 617(TLS):11Jun82-633
Hebblethwaite, B. The Problems of
Theology.*
   483:Jan81-139
Hebblethwaite, P. Introducing John Paul
II.
   D. Crane, 617(TLS):5Nov82-1227
Hebden, M. Pel is Puzzled.
   N. Callendar, 441:10Jan82-29
Hébert, A. Héloise.
   P.G. Lewis, 207(FR):Apr81-763
Hebert, E. A Little More Than Kin.
   P-L. Adams, 61:Sep82-96
   N. Delbanco, 441:12Sep82-12
Hébert, F. Triptyque de la mort.*
   R.S. Thornberry, 107(CRCL):Winter81-
148
Hechelmann, F. - see "Deutsche Märchen"
Hecht, A. The Venetian Vespers.*
   D. Graham, 565:Vol22No1-73
   B. Howard, 502(PrS):Winter81/82-84
Hecht, J. - see Süssmilch, J.P.
Hecht, J.J. The Domestic Servant in
Eighteenth-Century England.
   D. Watson, 83:Autumn81-241
Hecht, M.B. Odd Destiny.
   G.C. Ward, 441:1Aug82-11
   442(NY):21Jun82-123
Heckscher, A., with P. Robinson. Open
Spaces.
   C. Zaitzevsky, 576:Mar81-73
Hector, L.C., ed. Curia Regis Rolls of
the Reign of Henry III. (Vol 16)
   R.B. Pugh, 325:Apr81-431
Hector, L.C. and B. Harvey, eds. The West-
minster Chronicle 1381-1394.
   J. Catto, 617(TLS):5Nov82-1229
Hedayetullah, M. Kabir.*
   H.A. Ali, 273(IC):Jul80-194
Hederer, O. Leo von Klenze.
   R. Elvin, 46:Aug81-129
Hedges, E. - see Le Sueur, M.
Hedin, M. Fly Away Home.
   W. Cummins, 363(LitR):Spring82-462
   G. Johnson, 461:Spring-Summer81-92
Hedvall, Y.O. Harry Järv.
   L. Thompson, 562(Scan):Nov81-237
Heenan, D.A. The Re-United States of
America.
   P. Lewis, 441:26Dec82-9
Heer, F. Der Kampf um die österreichische
Identität.
   D. Johnson, 617(TLS):9Jul82-748
Heertje, A., ed. Schumpeter's Vision.
   T.W. Hutchison, 617(TLS):5Feb82-130

Heesakkers, C.L. Praecidanea Dousana:
Materials for a Biography of Janus
Dousa Pater (1545-1604), His Youth.
   P.R. Sellin, 551(RenQ):Spring80-108
Heess, M. Blaise Pascal.*
   R. Behrens, 224(GRM):Band31Heft1-117
Hefner, L.L., comp. The WPA Historical
Records Survey.
   E. Barrese, 14:Spring81-161
Hefner, R.J., ed. East Hampton's Heritage.
   P. Goldberger, 441:12Dec82-22
Hegel, G.W.F. The Christian Religion.
(P.C. Hodgson, ed and trans)
   R.F. Brown, 258:Mar81-99
Hegel, G.W.F. Faith and Knowledge.* (W.
Cerf and H.S. Harris, eds and trans)
   A.W.J. Harper, 154:Jun81-396
Hegel, G.W.F. Gesammelte Werke. (Vol 11)
(F. Hogemann and W. Jaeschke, eds)
   T.M. Seebohm, 125:Summer81-440
Hegel, G.W.F. Hegel's Introduction to
Aesthetics. (T.W. Knox, trans)
   J. Kaminsky, 482(PhR):Jul81-439
   G. Shapiro, 290(JAAC):Winter81-231
Hegel, G.W.F. Natural Law. (T.M. Knox,
trans)
   A.W.J. Harper, 154:Mar81-160
Hegel, G.W.F. System of Ethical Life
(1802/3) [and] First Philosophy of
Spirit.* (H.S. Harris and T.M. Knox,
eds and trans)
   B.C. Sax, 185:Oct80-164
Heger, H. - see Wolfram von Eschenbach
Heger, K. Monem, Wort, Satz und Text.
(2nd ed)
   G. Ineichen, 260(IF):Band85-311
Heggelund, K., S. Skjønsberg and H. Vold,
eds. Forfatternes litteraturhistorie.
   H.S. Naess, 563(SS):Autumn81-491
Heidegger, M. The Basic Problems of Phe-
nomenology. (A. Hofstadter, trans)
   H.L. Dreyfus, 617(TLS):17Sep82-1011
Heidegger, M. Die Grundprobleme der Phän-
omenologie. (F-W. von Herrmann, ed)
   C. Strube, 53(AGP):Band63Heft1-104
Heidegger, M. Hegel's Phänomenologie des
Geistes. (I. Görland, ed)
   M.E. Zimmerman, 323:Jan81-89
Heidegger, M. Heraklit. (M.S. Frings, ed)
   M.E. Zimmerman, 323:Oct81-282
Heidegger, M. Nietzsche.* (Vol 1)
   B.C. Sax, 185:Jul82-761
Heidegger, M. Phänomenologische Interpre-
tation von Kants Kritik der reinen Ver-
nunft.
   J. Kopper, 342:Band72Heft2-204
Heidegger, M. Prolegomena zur Geschichte
des Zeitbegriffs. (P. Jaeger, ed)
   M.E. Zimmerman, 323:Jan81-87
Heidegger, M. Schelling: Le traité de
1809 sur l'essence de la liberté humaine.
(H. Feick, ed)
   J-M. Monnoyer, 450(NRF):Feb81-110
Heidegger, M. Sein und Zeit.* (14th ed)
   S. Rosen, 480(P&R):Winter81-57
Heideking, J. Areopag der Diplomaten.
   F.L. Carsten, 575(SEER):Jan81-123
Heidler, K., H. Hermes and F-K. Mahn.
Rekursive Funktionen.
   A.S. Ferebee, 316:Mar81-165

Heidtmann, F., E. Fertig and P.S. Ulrich.
Wie finde ich Literatur zur deutschen
Literatur?
   L. Newman, 402(MLR):Jan81-227
Heikal, M. Iran.
   S. Bakhash, 453(NYRB):18Nov82-19
Heikal, M. The Return of the Ayatollah.
   H. Enayat, 617(TLS):21May82-553
Heilbron, J.L. Electricity in the 17th
and 18th Centuries.
   L.P. Williams, 84:Dec81-426
Heilbroner, R.L. and L.C. Thurow. Five
Economic Challenges.
   H.L. Robinson, 99:Dec81/Jan82-39
Heim, M.H. The Russian Journey of Karel
Havlíček Borovský.*
   A-M. Kiessl, 688(ZSP):Band42Heft1-198
Heims, S.J. John von Neumann and Norbert
Wiener.*
   J. Coleman, 529(QQ):Winter81-806
   R.E.L., 185:Apr82-590
   R. Peierls, 453(NYRB):18Feb82-16
Heindl, W., ed. Die Protokolle des öster-
reichischen Ministerrates, 1848-1867.
(Section 3, Vol 2)
   T.V. Thomas, 575(SEER):Apr81-306
Heindrichs, W., F-W. Gester and H.P. Kelz.
Sprachlehrforschung.
   R.W. Dunbar, 399(MLJ):Winter81-415
Heine, B. Pidgin-Sprachen im Bantubereich.
   S. Brauner, 682(ZPSK):Band33Heft6-750
Heine, E. and O. Stallybrass - see Forster,
E.M.
Heine, H. The Complete Poems of Heinrich
Heine. (H. Draper, trans)
   R. Lesser, 441:8Aug82-11
   S.S. Prawer, 617(TLS):9Jul82-738
Heine, H. The Lazarus Poems.* (A. Elliot,
trans)
   D.J. Constantine, 161(DUJ):Jun81-256
Heineman, H. Mrs. Trollope.*
   A. Wright, 445(NCF):Dec81-368
Heinemann, M. Puritanism and Theatre.
   R. Clare, 111:7Nov80-25
   A.D. Cousins, 67:Nov81-244
   P.J. Finkelpearl, 141:Summer81-265
   C. Hill, 366:Autumn81-252
   D.L. Russell, 568(SCN):Summer-Fall81-
46
Heinemann, R.K. Der Weg des Übens im
ostasiatischen Mahāyāna.
   J.W. de Jong, 259(IIJ):Jul81-240
Heinesen, W. Arctis.
   J. Saunders, 565:Vol22No3-62
Heinl, R.D. and N.G. Written in Blood.
   A. Gouraige, 207(FR):May82-933
Heinlein, R.A. Friday.
   H.B. Franklin, 441:4Jul82-8
Heinlein, R.A. The Number of the Beast.
   D. Sherwin, 283:Spring81-50
Heinrich von Freimar. Der Traktat Hein-
richs von Freimar über die Unterschei-
dung der Geister. (R.G. Warnock and A.
Zumkeller, eds)
   F.L. Borchardt, 221(GQ):Jan81-86
   T. Hohmann, 684(ZDA):Band109Heft1-39
Heinrichs, H-J. - see Bachofen, J.K.
Heinzelman, K. The Economics of the
Imagination.*
   J.H. Kavanagh, 301(JEGP):Apr81-228
Heinzelmann, M. Translationsberichte und
andere Quellen des Reliquienkultes.
   P.J. Geary, 589:Oct81-929

Heinzle, J. Mittelhochdeutsche Dietrich-
epik.*
   M. Curschmann, 684(ZDA):Band109Heft1-
32
   R.H. Firestone, 406:Winter81-450
   W. Haug, 196:Band21Heft1/2-119
   E.R. Haymes, 221(GQ):Jan81-84
Heissig, W. Mongolische Epen VIII.
   E. Rosner, 196:Band22Heft3/4-345
Heissig, W., ed. Die mongolischen Epen.
   E. Rosner, 196:Band22Heft3/4-344
Heissig, W. The Religions of Mongolia.
   G.W. Houston, 485(PE&W):Oct81-556
Heitman, S. The Soviet Germans in the
USSR Today.
   D.M. Crowe, Jr., 550(RusR):Oct81-464
Heitmann, K. Der französische Realismus
von Stendhal bis Flaubert.
   F.W.J. Hemmings, 402(MLR):Apr81-470
Heizer, R.F. - see Merriam, C.H.
Hélal, G. La Philosophie comme pan-
physique.
   M. Gagnon, 154:Sep81-596
   A.H. Johnson, 627(UTQ):Summer81-210
Helbig, G. and J. Buscha. Deutsche Übungs-
grammatik.
   U. Schröter, 682(ZPSK):Band33Heft4-502
Helbling, R. and others. Arts and Letters.
(2nd ed) Current Issues. (2nd ed)
   B.S. Jurasek, 399(MLJ):Autumn81-352
Helbo, A., ed. Le Champ sémiologique.
   J-M. Klinkenberg, 209(FM):Jan81-60
Helbo, A. L'Enjeu du discours, lecture de
Sartre.
   G. Idt, 535(RHL):Nov-Dec81-1031
Helck, W. Die Lehre für König Merikare.
   E.S. Meltzer, 318(JAOS):Jan/Mar80-70
Held, J.S. The Oil Sketches of Peter Paul
Rubens.*
   D. Freedberg, 59:Dec81-484
   P. Cannon-Brookes, 161(DUJ):Jun81-228
   A-M. Logan, 54:Sep81-512
   D. Rosand, 55:Apr81-38
Held, J.S. Rubens and His Circle. (A.W.
Lowenthal, D. Rosand and J. Walsh, eds)
   C. Brown, 617(TLS):15Oct82-1127
Held, V. Property, Profits, and Economic
Justice.
   B.B., 185:Jan81-342
Heldal, A. and A. Linneberg, eds. Struk-
turalisme i litteraturvitenskapen.
   L. Saetre, 172(Edda):1981/1-65
Helen, T. Organization of Roman Brick
Production in the First and Second
Centuries A.D.
   N. Purcell, 313:Vol71-214
Heleniak, K.M. William Mulready.*
   D. Cherry, 59:Sep81-335
   J. Murdoch, 90:Apr81-244
   L. Ormond, 39:Apr81-272
Helgesen, S. Wildcatters.
   L. Milazzo, 584(SWR):Summer81-v
Helleman-Elgersma, W. Soul-Sisters.
   A. Reix, 542:Jul-Sep81-330
Hellenkemper, H. - see Doppelfeld, O. and
W. Weyres
Heller, A. On Instincts.
   P. Thomas, 482(PhR):Jul81-441
Heller, A. Renaissance Man.
   G.H.R. Parkinson, 518:Apr81-109
Heller, A. The Theory of Feeling.
   P.S., 185:Oct81-194
   P. Thomas, 482(PhR):Jul81-441

Heller, G. Un Allemand à Paris, 1940-
1944.*
  L. Vines, 207(FR):Apr82-691
Heller, J. Good as Gold.*
  C. Berryman, 114(ChiR):Spring81-108
Heller, M. Knowledge.
  T. Olson, 436(NewL):Winter81/82-108
  A. Williamson, 472:Fall/Winter81-247
Heller, M. and A. Nekrich. L'Utopie au
pouvoir.
  A. Nove, 617(TLS):28May82-578
Heller, P. Probleme der Zivilisation.
  W. Hoffmeister, 221(GQ):Mar81-251
Heller, S. - see "Feiffer"
Heller, U. Village Portraits.
  E. Amer, 99:Feb82-43
Hellerstein, E.O., L.P. Hume and K.M.
Offen, eds. Victorian Women.
  K.J. Crecelius, 446(NCFS):Fall-Win-
  ter81/82-181
Hellman, J. Emmanuel Mounier and the New
Catholic Left, 1930-1950.
  P. McCarthy, 617(TLS):12Feb82-159
Hellman, P. The Auschwitz Album.*
  T. Taylor, 441:24Jan82-8
Hellmann, J. Fables of Fact.
  P.K. Bell, 617(TLS):15Jan82-47
  27(AL):Nov81-571
Hellmann, M-C. and P. Fraisse. Delos.
(Fasc 32)
  R.A. Tomlinson, 303(JoHS):Vol 101-209
Hellyer, P. Exit Inflation.
  H.L. Robinson, 99:Dec81/Jan82-39
Helms, C. An Ambassador's Wife in Iran.*
  639(VQR):Summer81-98
Helms, R. Tolkien and the Silmarils.
  P.W., 148:Winter81-92
Helprin, M. Ellis Island and Other
Stories.*
  W. Cummins, 363(LitR):Spring82-462
  G. Locklin, 573(SSF):Summer81-339
  J.D. O'Hara, 434:Summer82-603
Helsinger, E.K. Ruskin and the Art of the
Beholder.
  T. Hilton, 617(TLS):22Oct82-1153
  442(NY):6Sep82-109
Helwig, D. A Book Of The Hours.*
  P. Stevens, 102(CanL):Spring81-155
Helwig, D., ed. The Human Elements.
  G. Clever, 102(CanL):Winter80-130
Helwig, D. The King's Evil.
  E.L. Bobak, 150(DR):Autumn81-585
  H. Kirkwood, 99:Feb82-44
Helwig, D., ed. Love and Money.
  E.L. Bobak, 150(DR):Autumn81-585
  D. Duffy, 627(UTQ):Summer81-160
  G. Woodcock, 529(QQ):Winter81-672
van Hemeldonck, W. Antieke en bijbelse
metaforiek in de moderne Nederlandse
letteren (1880-ca. 1914).*
  P. Brachin, 549(RLC):Apr-Jun81-249
Hemenway, R.E. Zora Neale Hurston.*
  R.L. Brittin, 577(SHR):Fall81-369
Hemingway, A. Pzyche.
  D. Montrose, 617(TLS):18Jun82-677
Hemingway, E. Selected Letters, 1917-
1961.* (C. Baker, ed)
  S. Baker, 385(MQR):Summer82-505
  R.W. Lewis, 234:Fall81-59
  M. Mudrick, 249(HudR):Autumn81-441
  D.E. Schoonover, 676(YR):Autumn81-x
Hemingway, J. Conflict and Democracy.
  J. Lovell, 161(DUJ):Jun81-272

Hemming, D. Guldhornenes tale.
  J.M. Jochens, 563(SS):Autumn81-471
Hemming, J. Monuments of the Incas.
  D.J.R. Bruckner, 441:12Dec82-24
Hemmings, F.W.J. Baudelaire the Damned.
  V. Brombert, 441:21Nov82-39
  M. Wood, 453(NYRB):2Dec82-16
  442(NY):18Oct82-180
Hémon, L. Maria Chapdelaine. (illus-
trated by C. Gagnon)
  B-Z. Shek, 627(UTQ):Summer81-185
Hémon, L. Maria Chapdelaine, Récit du
Canada français. (G. Legendre, ed)
  B-Z. Shek, 627(UTQ):Summer81-184
Hemon, R. La Marie-Morgane.
  J-M. le Sidaner, 450(NRF):Nov81-130
Hemperley, M.R., comp. Cities, Towns and
Communities of Georgia between 1847-1962.
  K.B. Harder, 424:Jun81-170
Henderson, D. The Low East.
  C. Inez, 472:Fall/Winter81-231
Henderson, P.V.N. Félix Díaz, the Por-
firians, and the Mexican Revolution.
  S.R. Ross, 263(RIB):Vol31No3-409
Henderson, R. Into the Wind.
  B. Allen, 434:Spring82-478
Hendin, H. Suicide in America.
  M. Bayles, 441:20Jun82-16
Hendin, J. Vulnerable People.*
  S. O'Connell, 418(MR):Spring81-185
Hendrick, G. - see Hosmer, H.
Hendricks, J.E. Charles Thomson and the
Making of a New Nation, 1729-1824.
  R.F. Jones, 656(WMQ):Apr81-330
Hendrickson, D. Quiet Presence.
  R. Le Page, 207(FR):Apr81-756
Hendrickson, R. The Literary Life and
Other Curiosities.*
  442(NY):1Feb82-133
Henege, T. A Cargo of Tin.
  T.J. Binyon, 617(TLS):30Apr82-493
Heng-yü, K. - see under Kuo Heng-yü
Hengel, M. The Charismatic Leader and
His Followers.
  J.L. Houlden, 617(TLS):8Oct82-1099
Heninger, S.K., Jr. The Cosmographical
Glass.*
  A.M.L., 125:Fall80-116
  A.G. Petti, 178:Spring81-112
Henisz-Dostert, B., R.R. Macdonald and M.
Zarechnak. Machine Translation.
  S.M. Embleton, 320(CJL):Fall81-234
  G. Radó, 75:2/1980-122
  205(FMLS):Apr81-199
Henkel, A. - see Hamann, J.G.
Henkel, H. Beiträge zum historischen
Cembalobau.
  H. Schott, 415:Jan81-32
Henkels, R.M., Jr. Robert Pinget.
  B.L. Knapp, 399(MLJ):Autumn81-359
  J-C. Liéber, 98:Apr81-418
  J.O. Lowrie, 207(FR):Feb82-419
  A. Thiher, 395(MFS):Summer80-352
Henkle, R.B. Comedy and Culture, England
1820-1900.
  P. Brantlinger, 454:Winter82-185
  S. Hudson, 577(SHR):Summer81-267
  L. James, 191(ELN):Mar81-223
  H. Levin, 445(NCF):Mar81-551
  S. Pickering, 569(SR):Spring81-lii
  J.R. Reed, 141:Winter81-87
  S. Rothblatt, 637(VS):Spring81-362
                              [continued]

Henkle, R.B. Comedy and Culture, England
   1820-1900.   [continuing]
   R.K. Simon, 594:Fall181-322
   S.M. Tave, 405(MP):Nov81-208
Henne, H. and H. Rehbock. Einführung in
   die Gesprächsanalyse.*
   205(FMLS):Oct81-376
Hennequin, J. Henri IV dans ses oraisons
   funèbres ou la naissance d'une légende.*
   P.J. Bayley, 208(FS):Apr81-191
   J.D. Lyons, 207(FR):Dec80-339
Hennessy, M. The Bright Blue Sky.
   M. Trend, 617(TLS):22Oct82-1174
Hennig, J. and L. Huth. Kommunikation als
   Problem der Linguistik.
   H. Bussmann, 685(ZDL):1/1981-100
   W. Hartung, 682(ZPSK):Band33Heft4-503
Henning, P. Der Buchstabe und der Geist.
   R. Nägele, 400(MLN):Dec81-1241
Henrich, D., ed. Stuttgarter Hegel-
   Kongress 1975.
   G. Di Giovanni, 154:Mar81-178
Henriksen, C. Dansk rigssprog.
   K. Nilsson, 563(SS):Winter81-85
Henry, A. - see Perse, S-J.
Henry, B-M. L'Anjou dans les textes
   anciens.
   J-C. Richard, 555:Vol54fasc1-199
Henry, E. Chinese Amusement.
   N.K. Mao, 130:Winter81/82-389
Henry, E. Disraeli, Derby, and the Con-
   servative Party. (J. Vincent, ed)
   A.J. Heesom, 161(DUJ):Dec80-99
Henry, M. The Intoxication of Power.*
   G.E.T., 543:Sep80-138
Henry, M. Marx. (Vols 1 and 2)
   W.L. McBride, 185:Jan82-316
Henry, P. and H-R. Schwyzer - see Plotinus
Hentoff, N. Blues for Charlie Darwin.
   R. Freedman, 441:24Oct82-42
   442(NY):27Sep82-147
Henze, H.W. Music and Politics.
   H. Cole, 362:11Nov82-25
   P. Driver, 617(TLS):19Nov82-1266
   E. Rothstein, 441:26Dec82-5
Hepburn, J. - see Bennett, A.
Hepp, N. and J. Hennequin, eds. Les val-
   eurs chez les Mémorialistes français du
   XVIIe siècle avant la Fronde.
   S. Romanowski, 475:No14Pt1-188
   M-O. Sweetser, 207(FR):Dec80-340
Heppell, M. The Ecclesiastical Career of
   Gregory Camblak.
   D.M. Nicol, 575(SEER):Jan81-100
Hepworth, B. Robert Lowth.*
   F.M. Keener, 677(YES):Vol 11-286
Hepworth, M. and B.S. Turner. Confession.
   B. Goodwin, 617(TLS):17Dec82-1387
Heraclitus. Héraclite. (2nd ed) (A. Jean-
   nière, ed)
   J-L. Poirier, 542:Apr-Jun81-259
Herbart, P. Inédits.
   J.S., 450(NRF):Oct81-171
Herbert, F. The White Plague.
   G. Jonas, 441:26Sep82-15
Herbert, I. - see "Who's Who in the
   Theatre"
Herbert, M.C. and B. McNeil, eds. Bio-
   graphical Dictionaries Master Index:
   First Supplement.
   K.B. Harder, 424:Mar80-94
   K.B. Harder, 424:Sep80-218

Herbert, M.C. and B. McNeil, eds. Biogra-
   phy and Genealogy Master Index. (2nd ed)
   K.B. Harder, 424:Dec80-293
Herbert, R.T. Paradox and Identity in
   Theology.
   J. Newman, 185:Jan81-327
   P.L. Quinn, 482(PhR):Jan81-164
Herbert, T.W. Oberon's Mazéd World.
   L.G. Black, 541(RES):May81-205
Herbert, T.W., Jr. Marquesan Encounters.*
   A. Krupat, 27(AL):Nov81-541
   D. Leverenz, 445(NCF):Sep81-238
Herbert, Z. Selected Poems.
   J. Aaron, 472:Spring/Summer81-110
Herdeck, D.E., ed. Caribbean Writers.*
   L-F. Hoffmann, 535(RHL):Jul-Oct81-850
Herdman, J. Pagan's Pilgrimage.
   I. Murray, 571(ScLJ):Summer80-134
de Heredia, J-M. Les Trophées. (W.N.
   Ince, ed)
   J. Lowin, 446(NCFS):Fall-Winter81/82-
   158
   R.A. York, 402(MLR):Jul81-707
   205(FMLS):Oct80-376
van Herk, A. Judith.
   M. Waddington, 102(CanL):Spring80-101
Herlin, L. Couleur de temps.
   D.L., 450(NRF):Oct81-169
Hermann, A., K.V. Meyenn and V.F. Weiss-
   kopf - see Pauli, W.
Hermann, E.R. and E.H. Spitz, eds. German
   Women Writers of the Twentieth Century.
   A-C. Andersen, 172(Edda):1981/3-197
Hermansen, G. Ostia.
   R. Meiggs, 617(TLS):19Nov82-1276
Hermerén, L. On Modality in English.*
   H. Wekker, 297(JL):Sep81-359
   P. Westney, 257(IRAL):Feb81-81
Hermes, H., K. Kambartel and F. Kaulbach -
   see Frege, G.
Hernadi, P., ed. What is Criticism?
   L. Mackinnon, 617(TLS):5Feb82-144
Hernadi, P., ed. What Is Literature?*
   R.G. Cox, 447(N&Q):Jun80-282
   K. Steiner, 323:Jan81-97
Hernadez, B.G. - see under García
   Hernandez, B.
Hernández, J. Martín Fierro. (L. Sáinz
   de Medrano, ed)
   P.R. Beardsell, 86(BHS):Apr81-162
Hernández, J.L.A. - see under Alonso
   Hernández, J.L.
Hernández, M. Poemas sociales, de guerra
   y de muerte. (L. de Luis, ed)
   C.W. Cobb, 552(REH):Jan81-154
Herndon, M. Native American Music.
   B. Nettl, 187:Jan82-161
Hernekamp, K. Der argentinisch-chilen-
   ische Greinzstreit am Beagle-Kanal.
   A.E. Gropp, 263(RIB):Vol31No1-89
Hernton, C. Medicine Man.
   T. Dent, 459:Spring-Summer80-244
Herrera Zapién, T. - see Ovid
Herring, G.C. America's Longest War.
   D.P. Chandler, 293(JASt):Nov80-77
Herring, H., ed. Immanuel Kant: Proceed-
   ings of the Seminars at Calcutta and
   Madras in September and December 1974.
   R. Malter, 342:Band72Heft3-375
Herrmann, F. Sotheby's.*
   M. Secrest, 55:Nov81-42

von Herrmann, F-W. Heideggers Philosophie der Kunst.
M.E.Z., 543:Mar81-621
von Herrmann, F-W. - see Heidegger, M.
Herrnstein-Smith, B. On the Margins of Discourse.
R. Carter, 307:Apr81-63
Hershinow, S.J. Bernard Malamud.
J.J. Waldmeir, 395(MFS):Winter80/81-675
Hershon, R. The Public Hug.
S.M. Gilbert, 491:Oct81-35
Herskowitz, L. and M.M. Klein, eds. Courts and Law in Early New York.
J.E. Crowley, 106:Spring81-67
Hertel, H. and S.M. Kristensen, eds. The Activist Critic.
R. Wellek, 462(OL):Vol36No4-354
Herttrich, E. - see Kobylańska, K.
Hervey, S.G.J. Axiomatic Semantics.
G. Sampson, 307:Apr81-49
205(FMLS):Apr80-189
von Herwarth, J. Against Two Evils.
E. de Mauny, 617(TLS):14May82-531
Herz, J.S. and R.K. Martin, eds. E.M. Forster.
D.J. Enright, 362:20May82-28
B. Martin, 617(TLS):30Jul82-838
Herzberg, J. - see Salomon, C.
Herzog, C. The Arab-Israeli Wars.
E. Luttwak, 617(TLS):19Nov82-1262
J.R. Moskin, 441:28Nov82-10
C.C. O'Brien, 362:24Jun82-20
442(NY):29Nov82-176
Herzog, U. Deutsche Barocklyrik.*
J.F. Hyde, Jr., 406:Winter81-452
J. Leighton, 402(MLR):Jul81-743
S. Rusterholz, 684(ZDA):Band109Heft3-131
Heschong, L. Thermal Delight in Architecture.*
D. Kelbaugh, 505:Apr81-99
Hesiod. Hesiodo, "Teogonía."* (P. Vianello de Córdova, ed)
P. Monteil, 555:Vol54fasc1-155
Hesiod. Works and Days.* (M.L. West, ed)
W. McLeod, 487:Winter81-364
Hesketh, P. The Eighth Day.*
B. Ruddick, 148:Winter81-71
Heskett, J. Industrial Design.
T. Benton, 59:Sep81-348
Hess, H-J. Die obersten Grundsätze Kantischer Ethik und ihre Konkretisierbarkeit.
W. Teichner, 53(AGP):Band62Heft1-94
Hesse, E.W. - see Calderón de la Barca, P.
Hesse, H. Hours in the Garden.
J. Saunders, 565:Vol22No3-62
Hesse, H. Pictor's Metamorphoses and other Fantasies. (R. Lesser, trans)
I. Parry, 617(TLS):10Sep82-965
Hesse, H. and R. Rolland. Correspondence, Diary Entries and Reflections, 1915-1940.
M.S. Fries, 395(MFS):Summer80-362
Hesse, M. Revolutions and Reconstructions in the Philosophy of Science.*
M.A.K., 185:Oct81-188
A.B. Stewart, 42(AR):Summer81-387
R. Trigg, 483:Jul81-430
R.S. Woolhouse, 518:Jan81-64
Hessing, S., ed. Speculum Spinozanum, 1677-1977.
E. Alexander, 485(PE&W):Jan81-101

Hessling, D.C. On the Origin and Formation of Creoles.
E. Woolford, 355(LSoc):Apr81-128
Hetata, S. - see El Saadawi, N.
Hetmann, F., ed. Irischer Zaubergarten.
K.H. Schmidt, 196:Band21Heft3/4-315
Heubeck, A. Schrift.
J. Chadwick, 303(JoHS):Vol 101-222
Heubner, H. - see Güngerich, R.
Heussler, R. British Rule in Malaya.
P. Mason, 617(TLS):19Feb82-199
Hewett, C.A. Church Carpentry.
G. Cavaliero, 324:Oct82-753
Hewett, C.A. English Historic Carpentry.
J.S. Curl, 324:Jan82-109
Hewett, D. Greenhouse.
C. Pollnitz, 581:Jun81-221
Hewett, E.A. - see Gruzinov, V.P.
Hewison, R. In Anger.*
639(VQR):Summer81-93
Hewison, R., ed. New Approaches to Ruskin.
R. Trickett, 617(TLS):12Mar82-273
Hewitt, G.R. Scotland under Morton 1572-80.
G. Donaldson, 617(TLS):17Sep82-1015
Hewitt, J. The Selected John Hewitt. (A. Warner, ed) Mosaic.
N. Corcoran, 617(TLS):14May82-540
Hewitt, N. - see Troyat, H.
Hexham, I. The Irony of Apartheid.
K. Ingham, 617(TLS):23Apr82-468
Heyd, D. Supererogation.
J. Griffin, 617(TLS):24Dec82-1423
Heydenreich, L.H., B. Dibner and L. Reti. Leonardo the Inventor.
M. Kemp, 617(TLS):16Apr82-443
Heyder, W. and A. Mallwitz. Das Kabirenheiligtum bei Theben.* (Vol 2)
H.W. Parke, 303(JoHS):Vol 101-208
Heyen, W. Long Island Light.* The Swastika Poems.* Lord Dragonfly. The Bees. The City Parables.
M. McFee, 472:Spring/Summer82-153
Heymann, C.D. American Aristocracy.
M. Goldstein, 569(SR):Spring81-287
M. Holton, 295(JML):Vol8No3/4-377
T. Wortham, 27(AL):Nov81-546
Heytesbury, W. William Heytesbury on "Insoluble" Sentences. (P.V. Spade, ed and trans)
P.A. Clarke, 479(PhQ):Jan81-70
P.T. Geach, 382(MAE):1981/1-125
M.M. Tweedale, 482(PhR):Oct81-605
Hiatt, M.P. The Way Women Write.*
M.R. Key, 599:Fall81-456
Hibbard, D. Weiser.
K. Harrington, 658:Spring81-112
Hibbard, G. - see Jonson, B.
Hibbard, G.R., ed. The Elizabethan Theatre VI.*
P. Finkelpearl, 677(YES):Vol 11-235
Hibbert, C. Africa Explored.
R. Oliver, 617(TLS):19Nov82-1261
Hibbert, C. The Great Mutiny.*
J.R. McLane, 637(VS):Winter81-237
Hickey, G.C. Sons of the Mountains.
D.J. Duncanson, 617(TLS):13Aug82-885
Hickman, L. Modern Theories of Higher Level Predicates.
H.B. Veatch, 258:Mar81-114
Hickman, W.C. - see Babinger, F.

Hicks, E. - see Christine de Pisan and others
Hicks, J. Causality in Economics.
    M. Hollis, 479(PhQ):Apr81-189
Hicks, J. In the Singer's Temple.
    J.D. O'Hara, 434:Summer82-603
Hicks, J.V. Now Is a Far Country.
    D. Barbour, 648(WCR):Jun80-79
    A.R. Shucard, 102(CanL):Winter80-110
Hiddleston, J.A. Essais sur Laforgue et "Les Derniers Vers" suivi de Laforgue et Baudelaire.
    B.L. Knapp, 446(NCFS):Spring-Summer82-365
Hideomi, T. - see under Tsuge Hideomi
Hieatt, A.K. and M. Lorch - see Valla, L.
"Hier pour Demain: Arts, Traditions et Patrimoine."
    N. McWilliam, 59:Dec81-466
Higgins, D.S. Rider Haggard.*
    B. Andrews, 364:Dec81/Jan82-129
Higgins, G.V. The Patriot Game.
    P-L. Adams, 61:May82-106
    S. Ellin, 441:25Apr82-13
    442(NY):7Jun82-144
Higgins, I. Francis Ponge.*
    B. Beugnot, 535(RHL):Mar-Apr81-332
    F. Caro, 67:May81-116
    M.R. Sorrell, 402(MLR):Apr81-481
    205(FMLS):Oct80-376
Higgins, I. - see Ponge, F.
Higgins, J. Touch the Devil.
    E. Hunter, 441:5Sep82-8
Higgins, W.E. Xenophon the Athenian.*
    W. den Boer, 394:Vol34fasc1/2-161
Higginson, S. Coward's Country.
    T. Irwin, 368:Mar81-117
"The High Book of the Grail."* (N. Bryant, trans)
    R.H. Ivy, Jr., 161(DUJ):Dec80-106
Higham, J. and P.K. Conkin, eds. New Directions in American Intellectual History.*
    F. Matthews, 529(QQ):Summer81-377
Highfield, A.R. The French Dialect of St. Thomas, U.S. Virgin Islands.
    P. Stevens, 207(FR):Mar82-589
Highfill, P.H., Jr., K.A. Burnim and E.A. Langhans. A Biographical Dictionary of Actors, Actresses, Musicians, Dancers, Managers, and other Stage Personnel in London, 1660-1800.* (Vols 5 and 6)
    F. Blessington, 566:Autumn80-40
    R.D. Hume, 173(ECS):Fall80-78
Highsaw, R.B. Edward Douglass White.
    639(VQR):Autumn81-124
Higman, F.M. Censorship and the Sorbonne.*
    M-M. de La Garanderie, 535(RHL):Jul-Oct81-747
    P. Sharratt, 402(MLR):Apr81-460
Higonnet, P. Class, Ideology, and the Rights of Nobles during the French Revolution.
    C. Lucas, 617(TLS):17Dec82-1388
Hijmans, B.J., Jr. and others. Apuleius Madaurensis, "Metamorphoses." (Bk 4, Pts 1-27)
    H.J. Mason, 487:Summer81-184
Hilberry, C. Man in the Attic.
    M. Kinzie, 29:Mar/Apr82-13
Hildebrand, R.C. Power and the People.
    T. Moore, 583:Spring82-344

Hildebrandt, D. Lessing.
    R.R. Heitner, 221(GQ):Jan81-93
Hildesheimer, W. Mozart.
    E. Rothstein, 441:31Oct82-7
    A. Tyson, 453(NYRB):18Nov82-3
Hiley, J. Theatre at Work.*
    A.P.H., 148:Winter81-93
Hilfer, A.C. The Ethics of Intensity in American Fiction.
    R. Christiansen, 617(TLS):3Dec82-1330
Hill, C. Milton and the English Revolution.*
    R. Lejosne, 189(EA):Apr-Jun81-220
Hill, D. - see Spenser, E.
Hill, D.L. - see Pater, W.
Hill, D.R. The Impact of Migration on the Metropolitan and Folk Society of Carriacou, Grenada.
    J.C. Beck, 292(JAF):Jul-Sep81-395
Hill, I., ed. The Ethical Basis of Economic Freedom. (2nd ed)
    M.S.M., 185:Apr82-591
Hill, I. - see de la Sale, A.
Hill, J.S., ed. Imagination in Coleridge.*
    G. Dekker, 677(YES):Vol 11-302
    L. Tyler, 580(SCR):Spring82-116
Hill, K.C., ed. The Genesis of Language.
    P. Mühlhäusler, 350:Mar82-221
    H. Tinelli, 207(FR):Mar81-639
Hill, M.A. Charlotte Perkins Gilman.
    D. Arzt, 77:Spring81-180
    S.A. Zagarell, 432(NEQ):Jun81-288
Hill, P. Fire Opal.
    J.A.S. Miller, 571(ScLJ):Winter81-146
Hill, R. Who Guards a Prince.
    T.J. Binyon, 617(TLS):2Jul82-725
    M. Laski, 362:29Jul82-27
Hill, R.C. and T.G. Bergin. Anthology of the Provençal Troubadours. (rev by T.G. Bergin, with others)
    F.M. Chambers, 545(RPh):Aug80-130
Hill, R.D. Rice in Malaya.
    J.A. Hafner, 293(JASt):Nov80-194
Hill, R.J. Soviet Politics, Political Science and Reform.
    R. Amann, 575(SEER):Jan81-135
Hill, S. and I. Quigly, eds. New Stories 5.
    P. Lewis, 565:Vol22No1-60
Hill, W.S. - see Hooker, R.
Hill-Tout, C. The Salish People.* (R. Maud, ed)
    G.W., 102(CanL):Spring80-149
Hillebrand, B., ed. Zur Struktur des Romans.
    H. Kurzke, 684(ZDA):Band109Heft3-136
Hiller, J. and P. Neary, eds. Newfoundland in the Nineteenth and Twentieth Centuries.
    R. MacLean, 529(QQ):Winter81-783
    G.W., 102(CanL):Spring81-174
Hillerman, T. The Dark Wind.
    P-L. Adams, 61:Jun82-102
    N. Callendar, 441:17Oct82-41
Hillerman, T. People of Darkness.*
    T.J. Binyon, 617(TLS):29Oct82-1196
Hillier, J. The Art of Hokusai in Book Illustration.*
    K. Gardner, 407(MN):Summer81-216
Hillman, H. The Art of Winning Corporate Grants.
    639(VQR):Winter81-29

Hirschberg, J., G. Szépe and E. Vass-
Kovács, eds. Papers in Interdisciplin-
ary Speech Research.
    G.F. Meier, 682(ZPSK):Band33Heft5-609
Hirschen, J. - see Auboyer, J. and others
Hirschhorn, C. The Hollywood Musical.*
    A. Croce, 442(NY):18Jan82-128
Hirschman, A.O. Essays in Trespassing.
    K. Griffin, 617(TLS):19Feb82-191
    R.L. Heilbroner, 453(NYRB):24Jun82-44
Hirschman, A.O. Shifting Involvements.
    P.L. Berger, 441:18Apr82-9
    R.L. Heilbroner, 453(NYRB):24Jun82-44
Hirsh, J.E. The Structure of Shakespear-
ean Scenes.
    J. Stachniewski, 617(TLS):20Aug82-911
Hirshorn, P. and S. Izenour. White Towers.
    F.T. Kihlstedt, 576:Dec81-339
    T.J. Schlereth, 658:Spring81-121
Hirst, D. and I. Beeson. Sadat.*
    M.E. Yapp, 617(TLS):8Jan82-28
Hirst, D.L. Comedy of Manners.*
    G. Bas, 189(EA):Jan-Mar81-85
Hirst, M. Sebastiano del Piombo.
    M. Kemp, 617(TLS):19Mar82-305
Hirst, M. and J. Shearman - see Wilde, J.
Hirszowicz, M. The Bureaucratic Leviathan.
    M. McAuley, 575(SEER):Oct81-628
Hitchcock, B. Richard Malcolm Johnston.*
    K. King, 392:Winter80/81-83
Hitchcock, D.R. The Appeal of Adam to
Lazarus in Hell.*
    W.F. Ryan, 575(SEER):Apr81-277
Hitchcock, H-R. German Renaissance
Architecture.
    A. Blunt, 617(TLS):17Sep82-1017
Hitchcock, H-R. Netherlandish Scrolled
Gables of the 16th and Early 17th Cen-
turies.*
    E.R.M. Taverne, 43:Band11Heft2-192
Hitching, F. The Neck of the Giraffe.
    442(NY):21Jun82-123
Hitchman, S. The World as Theatre in the
Works of Franz Grillparzer.
    U. Fülleborn, 67:Nov81-267
Hitkari, S.S. Ganesha-Sthapana.
    R.L. Shep, 614:Fall82-17
Hitkari, S.S. Phulkari.
    R.L. Shep, 614:Summer81-20
Hittle, J.M. The Service City.*
    J.M. Hartley, 575(SEER):Apr81-301
Hixon, R. and M. The Place Names of the
White Mountains.
    K.B. Harder, 424:Sep81-249
Ho, W-K. and others. Eight Dynasties of
Chinese Painting.
    B. Gray, 39:Aug81-131
Ho Wing Meng. Straits Chinese Silver.
    E.H. Moore, 60:Sep-Oct81-145
Hoagland, E. The Tugman's Passage.
    G. Stokes, 441:21Mar82-7
    442(NY):26Apr82-143
Hobbes, T. Les Éléments du Droit Naturel
et Politique.* (L. Roux, ed and trans)
    T.W. Hayes, 568(SCN):Summer-Fall81-65
Hobbs, R. Robert Smithson: Sculpture.
    F. Spalding, 617(TLS):13Aug82-873
Hobbs, W. Stage Combat.
    D. Robb, 157:Oct80-70
Hoben, W. Terminologische Studien zu den
Sklavenerhebungen der römischen Repub-
lik.*
    B.D. Shaw, 487:Fall81-272

Hoberman, G. The Art of Coins and Their
Photography.
    D.J.R.B., 441:4Apr82-15
    A. Burnett, 617(TLS):28May82-575
Hobhouse, J. Nellie Without Hugo.
    J. Astor, 362:18Mar82-24
    P. Kemp, 617(TLS):12Mar82-289
    K. Pollitt, 441:18Apr82-13
Hobsbaum, P. A Reader's Guide to D.H.
Lawrence.
    J. Meyers, 594:Winter81-449
Hobsbaum, P. Tradition and Experiment in
English Poetry.*
    P. Levi, 541(RES):Aug81-362
Hobson, A. The Art and Life of J.W. Water-
house, R.A., 1849-1917.*
    A. Goodchild, 135:Mar81-243
    R. Mander, 39:Apr81-269
    M. Warner, 324:Oct82-754
Hobson, C. and R. Rutland - see Madison, J.
Hobson, D. Crossroads.
    C. Brown, 617(TLS):24Sep82-1047
Hobson, G., ed. The Remembered Earth.
    27(AL):Nov81-564
Hobson, L.Z. Untold Millions.
    N. Johnson, 441:28Mar82-14
Hobson, M. Poor Tom.
    P. Craig, 617(TLS):2Apr82-395
Hocevar, T. The Economic History of
Slovenia, 1828-1918.
    J.A. Wrench, 575(SEER):Apr81-318
Hočevar, T. Slovenski družbeni razvoj.
    S. Slak, 104(CASS):Winter81-635
Hochberg, H. Thought, Fact and Reference.*
    A. Fisher, 393(Mind):Oct81-633
    N. Griffin, 482(PhR):Apr81-292
Hochegger, H. Sculptures nouvelles de
Bandundu.
    D.J. Crowley, 2(AfrA):Aug81-23
Hochstedler, C. - see "The Tale of Nezame"
Hochwälder, F. The Public Prosecutor and
Other Plays.
    W.L. Nahrgang, 399(MLJ):Winter81-431
Höck, C. Zur syntaktischen und kommunika-
tiven Struktur slavischer Partizipial-
und Gerundialkonstruktionen.
    V.M. Du Feu, 575(SEER):Oct81-591
Hockett, C.F. The View from Language.*
    C.T. Hodge, 350:Sep82-686
Hockey, S. A Guide to Computer Applica-
tions in the Humanities.*
    L.T. Milic, 405(MP):Nov81-233
    M.J. Preston, 191(ELN):Dec80-153
Hocquard, E. Album d'images de la villa
Harris.*
    D.E. Rivas, 207(FR):Dec80-365
Hocquard, E. Une Journée dans le détroit.*
    M. Bishop, 207(FR):May81-896
Hocutt, M. The Elements of Logical Analy-
sis and Inference.
    M. Partridge, 479(PhQ):Jan81-90
Hodcroft, F.W. and others, eds. Mediaeval
and Renaissance Studies on Spain and Por-
tugal in Honour of P.E. Russell.
    D. Eisenberg, 304(JHP):Spring81-229
Hodgart, M. James Joyce.*
    D. Davin, 541(RES):Nov81-479
    K. Williamson, 447(N&Q):Dec80-566
Hodge, R.I.V. Foreshortened Time.*
    R.M. Cummings, 402(MLR):Jul81-669
    J.H. Summers, 125:Fall80-112

Hodges, C.W., S. Schoenbaum and L. Leone,
eds. The Third Globe.
J. Hankey, 617(TLS):23Apr82-469
Hodgins, J. The Ressurection of Joseph
Bourne.*
D.L. Jeffrey, 102(CanL):Spring80-74
J. Mills, 648(WCR):Jun80-38
Hodgson, G. All Things to All Men.
639(VQR):Spring81-62
Hodgson, J.A. Wordsworth's Philosophical
Poetry, 1797-1814.*
P.J. Manning, 661(WC):Summer81-151
639(VQR):Winter81-16
Hodgson, P.C. - see Hegel, G.W.F.
Hodnett, E. Image and Text.
W. Feaver, 617(TLS):2Jul82-722
Hodnett, G. Leadership in the Soviet Na-
tional Republics.
R.J. Hill, 575(SEER):Jan81-141
Høedt, J. and R. Turner, eds. The World
of LSP. New Bearings in LSP.
J. Yalden, 350:Sep82-739
Hoeges, D. Literatur und Evolution.
A. Gier, 224(GRM):Band31Heft4-476
Hoekstra, T. and H. van der Hulst, eds.
Morfologie in Nederland.
F. Plank, 361:Feb-Mar81-279
Hoenigswald, H.M., ed. The European Back-
ground of American Linguistics.
B.H. Davis, 350:Jun81-454
Hoensch, J.K. Sowjetische Osteuropa-
Politik, 1945-1975.
M. McCauley, 575(SEER):Jan81-131
Hoerder, D. Crowd Action in Revolutionary
Massachusetts, 1765-1780.*
I. Mugridge, 106:Fall81-199
Hoevels, F.E. Märchen und Magie in den
"Metamorphosen" des Apuleius von Mad-
aura.*
C.C. Schlam, 122:Jul81-244
Hofacker, E.P. Christian Morgenstern.
H. Gumtau, 406:Winter81-475
vom Hofe, G. and P. Pfaff. Das Elend des
Polyphem.
K. Wagner, 602:Vol 12No2-398
Höfer, A. The Caste Hierarchy and the
State in Nepal.
D.A. Messerschmidt, 293(JASt):Aug81-
824
Hofer, H., ed. Louis-Sébastien Mercier
précurseur et sa fortune.*
P-E. Knabe, 72:Band21Heft1-228
Hoffman, A. Square Dancing in the Ice Age.
F. Randall, 441:15Aug82-12
Hoffman, A. White Horses.
A. Tyler, 441:28Mar82-11
442(NY):3May82-165
Hoffman, D. Brotherly Love.*
J.F. Cotter, 249(HudR):Autumn81-435
J. Hollander, 617(TLS):12Feb82-166
P. Mariani, 472:Spring/Summer82-265
Hoffman, D., ed. Harvard Guide to Contem-
porary American Literature.*
R. Asselineau, 189(EA):Jul-Sep81-358
D. Davie, 569(SR):Winter81-110
Hoffman, E. and J. McCoy. Concrete Mama.
R.M. Kaus, 441:25Apr82-14
Hoffman, H.W. Sagas of Old Western Travel
and Transport.
L. Milazzo, 584(SWR):Spring81-v
Hoffman, M.A. Egypt Before the Pharaohs.
D.B. Redford, 529(QQ):Summer81-398

Hoffman, N.J. Spenser's Pastorals.*
M. Evans, 402(MLR):Apr81-438
H.R. Woudhuysen, 447(N&Q):Aug80-363
Hoffman, P. Lions of the Eighties.
F.R. Schumer, 441:5Sep82-11
Hoffman, W. The Land That Drank the Rain.
T.O. Treadwell, 617(TLS):13Aug82-888
Hoffman, W. Virginia Reels.
P. Lewis, 565:Vol122No1-60
Hoffmann, C. Max Frischs Roman "Homo
Faber."
I.M. Goessl, 221(GQ):Jan81-112
Hoffmann, F. and J. Berlinger. Die Neue
Deutsche Mundartdichtung.
C. Wickham, 406:Spring81-118
Hoffmann, G. Raum, Situation, erzählte
Wirklichkeit.
K.L. Pfeiffer, 490:Band12Heft2-249
Hoffmann, G. and H. Rölleke - see Grimm,
F.P.
Hoffmann, L., ed. Fachwortschatz Mathe-
matik, Häufigkeitswörterbuch.
J. Kunze, 682(ZPSK):Band33Heft2-275
Hoffmann, L-F. Le nègre romantique, per-
sonnage littéraire et obsession collec-
tive.
T. Logé, 356(LR):Aug81-253
Hoffmann, P. La Femme dans la pensée des
Lumières.*
D. Williams, 83:Spring81-97
Hoffmann, S. Duties Beyond Borders.
R. Falk, 676(YR):Winter82-267
Hoffmann, W. Kafkas Aphorismen.
B. Goldstein, 406:Spring81-67
Hoffmann, W. Mittelhochdeutsche Helden-
dichtung.
W. Dinkelacker, 680(ZDP):Band99Heft1-
132
Hoffmeister, G. Deutsche und europäische
Romantik.*
205(FMLS):Jan80-86
Hofheins, R., Jr. and K.E. Calder. The
Eastasia Edge.
R.B. Reich, 453(NYRB):24Jun82-37
Höfler, M. Zur Integration der neulatein-
ischen Kompositionsweise im Franzö-
sischen.
H. and R. Kahane, 545(RPh):Feb81(supp)-
22
Höfler, O. Über somatische, psychische
und kulturelle Homologie.
U. Kutter, 196:Band22Heft1/2-132
Hofmann, A. LSD.
B. Kohn, 42(AR):Summer81-389
Hofmann, P. Rome.
M. Bayles, 441:20Jun82-16
Hofstadter, D. - see Sand, G.
Hofstadter, D.R. Gödel, Escher, Bach.*
M. Green, 128(CE):Oct81-569
S.W. Smoliar, 513:Fall-Winter80/Spring-
Summer81-501
Hofstadter, D.R. and D.C. Dennett, eds.
The Mind's I.*
J. and A. Laski, 362:22Apr82-22
J.R. Searle, 453(NYRB):29Apr82-3
Hogan, H.M., ed. My Poem is a Bubble.
P. Godsiff, 368:Dec73-358
Hogan, J.C. A Guide to the "Iliad."*
F.M. Combellack, 122:Apr81-143
Hogarth, P., with V. Clery. Dragons.
J. Simpson, 203:Vol91No1-122
Hoge, J.O. - see "Lady Tennyson's Journal"

Hoge, J.O. and J.L.W. West 3d – see "Review"

Hogemann, F. and W. Jaeschke – see Hegel, G.W.F.

Höger, A. Frank Wedekind.
    J.L. Hibberd, 402(MLR):Jan81-250
    H-J. Irmer, 654(WB):7/1981-162

Hogg, R. Of Light.
    D. Barbour, 648(WCR):Vol 15No3-46

Hoggart, R. An English Temper.
    P. Lennon, 362:19Aug82-20
    G. Watson, 617(TLS):26Mar82-334
    442(NY):14Jun82-135

Hoggart, S. Back on the House.
    C. Moore, 617(TLS):24Dec82-1431

B.-Hogue, M. C'était dimanche.
    V. Raoul, 102(CanL):Spring81-106

Hogwood, C. Music at Court.
    F.R.C. Clarke, 529(QQ):Summer81-396

Hohendahl-Zoetelief, I.M. Manners in the Homeric Epic.
    J.E. Rexine, 124:Jul-Aug82-376

Hohl, L. Une Ascension.
    L. Kovacs, 450(NRF):Feb81-143

Höhle, T.N. Lexikalistische Syntax.
    J. Lenerz, 603:Vol5No3-407
    T.F. Shannon, 350:Sep81-774

Hohmann, T. Heinrichs von Langenstein "Unterscheidung der Geister" lateinisch und deutsch.
    F.V. Spechtler, 680(ZDP):Band100Heft3-449

Hohti, P. The Interrelation of Speech and Action in the Histories of Herodotus.
    A. Mantel, 394:Vol34fasc1/2-159

Holan, V. A Night with Hamlet.
    J. Saunders, 565:Vol22No3-62

Hölbl, G. Zeugnisse Ägyptischer Religions-vorstellungen für Ephesus.
    F. Solmsen, 318(JAOS):Jan/Mar80-76

Holbrook, D. English for Meaning.
    A.C. Capey, 437:Winter80/81-139
    F. Whitehead, 148:Summer81-90

Holbrook, D. Selected Poems 1961-1978.*
    C.B.C., 148:Spring81-94

Holcombe, B. – see Fagg, W.

Holcombe, B. – see Fagg, W. and J. Pemberton 3d

Holdcroft, D. Words and Deeds.*
    J.A. Mason, 307:Oct81-129

Holden, D. and R. Johns. The House of Saud.*
    J. Hoagland, 453(NYRB):1Apr82-23
    D. Pipes, 441:14Mar82-3

Holden, E. The Edwardian Lady. (I. Taylor, comp)
    639(VQR):Spring81-48

Holden, J. The Rhetoric of the Contemporary Lyric.*
    R. Kern, 659(ConL):Summer82-368
    S. Lea, 434:Autumn81-165

Holden, U. Penny Links.*
    J. Mellors, 364:Jun81-93

Holden, U. Sing About It.
    L. Taylor, 617(TLS):19Feb82-179

Holder, P.A. The Roman Army in Britain.
    D.J. Breeze, 617(TLS):25Jun82-703

Holderness, G. D.H. Lawrence.
    M. Tanner, 617(TLS):26Nov82-1316

Holdsworth, R.V., ed. Jonson: "Every Man is his Humour" and "The Alchemist."
    D.C. Kay, 447(N&Q):Apr80-192

Holenstein, E. Roman Jakobson's Approach to Language.
    R.B. Sangster, 350:Dec82-897

Holl, J. – see Fink, E.

Holland, C. The Sea Beggars.
    S. Altinel, 617(TLS):17Dec82-1398

Holland, L.A. Lucretius and the Trans-padanes.
    A.M. Devine, 122:Oct81-333
    H.M. Hoenigswald, 355(LSoc):Aug81-313
    R. Maltby, 123:Vol31No1-21

Holland, N.N. Laughing.
    D.J. Enright, 617(TLS):24Dec82-1430

Holland, P. The Ornament of Action.*
    B. Corman, 405(MP):Aug81-81
    K. Muir, 677(YES):Vol 11-274

Holland, R.F. Against Empiricism.
    J.B., 543:Jun81-790
    R.G. Frey, 518:Oct81-254

Holland, R.F. Britain and the Commonwealth Alliance.
    C. Thorne, 617(TLS):5Feb82-145

Hollander, A. Seeing Through Clothes.*
    E. Fox-Genovese, 473(PR):4/1981-633

Hollander, J. Blue Wine and Other Poems.
    C. Molesworth, 473(PR):2/1981-315
    L. Sail, 565:Vol22No1-66

Hollander, J. The Figure of Echo.
    J. Bayley, 617(TLS):7May82-499

Hollander, P. Political Pilgrims.*
    H. Thomas, 362:18Feb82-21

Hollen, N. Pattern Making by the Flat-Pattern Method. (5th ed)
    T. Cowan, 614:Fall81-20

Hollerman, L., ed. Japan and the United States.
    K. Sato, 293(JASt):Feb81-383

Holliday, J.S. The World Rushed In.
    E. Connell, 441:17Jan82-11

Hollien, H. and P., eds. Current Issues in the Phonetic Sciences.
    I. Maddieson, 350:Jun81-488

Hollier, D., ed. Le Collège de Sociologie (1937-1939).*
    V. Descombes, 98:May80-441

Hollier, D., with D. Lemann – see Bataille, G.

Hollingdale, R.J. – see Nietzsche, F.

Hollinghurst, A. Confidential Chats with Boys.
    D. Davis, 362:16Dec82-23
    L. Mackinnon, 617(TLS):17Dec82-1399

Hollingsworth, S. The Complete Book of Traditional Aran Knitting.
    R.L. Shep, 614:Fall82-15

Hollingsworth, S. Knitting and Crochet for the Physically Handicapped and Elderly.
    C.J. Mouton, 614:Fall82-18

Hollis, M. Models of Man.*
    G.W. Trompf, 488:Sep80-336

Holloway, J. Narrative and Structure.*
    T. Eagleton, 541(RES):Nov81-498
    M. Maclean, 67:May81-102
    D.G. Marshall, 445(NCF):Mar81-563
    E.S. Rabkin, 131(CL):Fall81-375
    205(FMLS):Apr80-190

Holloway, J. and S. Picciotto, eds. State and Capital.
    J.J. Flynn, 185:Jul81-668

Holloway, R. Debussy and Wagner.*
    R. Nichols, 415:May81-311

Holloway, T.H. Immigrants on the Land.
   A.M. Pescatello, 263(RIB):Vol31No4-554
Hollowell, J. Fact and Fiction.
   R. Vanderauwera, 494:Spring80-187
Holm, B. and G.I. Quimby. Edward S.
   Curtis in the Land of the War Canoes.
   W.N., 102(CanL):Winter80-159
   T. Sobchack, 649(WAL):Fall81-248
   639(VQR):Winter81-29
Holman, C.H. Windows on the World.*
   L.J. Budd, 395(MFS):Summer80-345
   J. Fletcher, 125:Fall80-104
   M. Orvell, 295(JML):Vol8No3/4-410
   H.D. Piper, 191(ELN):Dec80-152
Holme, B., ed. A Present of Laughter.
   P-L. Adams, 61:Sep82-96
Holmer, P.L. The Grammar of Faith.
   H.A.D., 543:Mar81-611
Holmes, E. The Diary of Miss Emma Holmes.
   (J.F. Marszalek, ed)
   A.F. Scott, 579(SAQ):Winter81-116
Holmes, H.B., B.B. Hoskins and M. Gross,
   eds. The Custom-made Child?
   T.M.R., 185:Apr82-599
Holmes, P. Vilhelm Moberg.
   G. Eidevall, 562(Scan):Nov81-233
   R. Wright, 563(SS):Autumn81-504
Holmes, P. Resistance and Compromise.
   J.J. Scarisbrick, 617(TLS):5Nov82-1228
Holmes, R. Coleridge.
   A. Ryan, 362:18Mar82-21
Holmes, R. Communities in Transition.
   L. Auwers, 656(WMQ):Oct81-740
Holmström, R., K. Segerberg and C. Zillia-
   cus, eds. Pegas och snöbollskrig.
   L. Thompson, 562(Scan):May81-108
Holroyd, M. and P. Levy - see Strachey, L.
Holroyd, M. and R. Skidelsky - see Ger-
   hardie, W.
Holt, C.E. and D.A. Pacyga. Chicago.
   R.M. McReynolds, 14:Fall80-496
Holt, J.C. Robin Hood.
   R. Hardy, 362:10Jun82-21
   R.H. Hilton, 617(TLS):11Jun82-631
Höltgen, K.J. Francis Quarles, 1592-1644.*
   T.A.B., 179(ES):Apr81-194
   P. Daly, 72:Band217Heft1-195
   H. Stegemeier, 301(JEGP):Jan81-122
Holton, G. and Y. Elkana, eds. Albert
   Einstein.
   T. Ferris, 441:26Sep82-18
   442(NY):16Aug82-91
Holton, G. and R.S. Morrison, eds. Limits
   of Scientific Inquiry.
   S.A. Lakoff, 185:Oct80-100
Holton, M. and P. Vangelisti, eds. The
   New Polish Poetry.*
   J. Aaron, 472:Spring/Summer81-110
Holtz, W. - see Brontë, C.
Holtzmann, S.H. and C.M. Leich, eds.
   Wittgenstein: to Follow a Rule.
   B. Stroud, 617(TLS):8Jan82-37
Holtzman, W. Judy Holliday.
   N. Johnston, 441:28Mar82-18
Holwerda, D. Scholia in Aristophanum.*
   (Pt 1, fasc 3, section 1)
   K.J. Dover, 123:Vol31No1-6
Holz, A. Deutsches Dichterjubiläum.
   R.H. Lawson, 133:Band14Heft1-95
Holz, H. Die Idee der Philosophie bei
   Schelling.
   J. Jantzen, 53(AGP):Band63Heft1-91

Holz, H. Mensch und Menschheit.
   W.G. Jacobs, 489(PJGG):Band88Heft2-421
Holz, H. Thomas von Aquin und die Phil-
   osophie.
   A. Zimmermann, 53(AGP):Band63Heft2-191
Holz, L. Developing Your Doll Collection.
   R.L. Shep, 614:Fall82-15
Holzapfel, O. Det balladeske.
   W.E. Richmond, 563(SS):Summer81-342
Holzapfel, O. "Catholisch Gesangbuechlein"
   Munchen 1613.
   J. Dittmar, 196:Band22Heft1/2-133
Holzapfel, O., with J. McGrew and I. Piø,
   eds. The European Medieval Ballad.*
   R. Wehse, 196:Band22Heft1/2-134
Holzhey, H. - see Cohen, H.
Holzman, M. Avec les Chinois.
   V. Alleton, 98:Aug-Sep81-762
Homan, S., ed. Shakespeare's "More Than
   Words Can Witness."
   D.M. Bergeron, 130:Fall81-283
Homand, J-P. - see Mme. de Villedieu
Homans, M. Women Writers and Poetic Iden-
   tity.*
   S. Gubar, 676(YR):Spring82-446
"Homenaje a Tirso."
   D.H. Darst, 304(JHP):Autumn81-81
Homer, W.I. Seurat and the Science of
   Painting.
   J.A. Richardson, 289:Apr81-119
Homeyer, H., ed and trans. Dichterinnen
   des Altertums und des frühen Mittel-
   alters. (2nd ed)
   H.R., 52:Band15Heft3-340
Hommel, H. Bocksbeutel und Aryballos.
   Y. Calvet, 555:Vol54fasc1-158
Honan, P. Matthew Arnold.*
   A. Phillips, 364:Nov81-73
Honderich, T. Violence for Equality.*
   P. Singer, 479(PhQ):Jul81-284
   L.W. Sumner, 529(QQ):Autumn81-593
Hone, J. Gone Tomorrow.
   E. de Mauny, 617(TLS):12Mar82-284
   C. Sigal, 362:7Jan82-23
Hone, J., ed. Irish Ghost Stories.
   J.R. Moore, 573(SSF):Winter81-91
Hone, J.A. For the Cause of Truth.
   W. Thomas, 617(TLS):4Jun82-602
Honegger, J.B. Das Phänomen der Angst bei
   Franz Kafka.
   B. Goldstein, 406:Spring81-67
Honemann, V. Die "Epistula ad fratres de
   Monte Dei" des Wilhelm von Saint-
   Thierry.*
   H. Gindele, 684(ZDA):Band109Heft3-111
Honemann, V. and others, eds. Poesie und
   Gebrauchsliteratur im deutschen Mittel-
   alter.
   W.C. Crossgrove, 589:Jan81-140
Honeycombe, G. The Edge of Heaven.
   M.G. McCulloch, 617(TLS):1Jan82-12
Hong, H.V. and E. - see Kierkegaard, S.
Honig, E. Selected Poems.
   B.L. Estrin, 560:Spring-Summer81-217
Honigmann, E.A.J. Shakespeare's Impact on
   his Contemporaries.
   G. Bradshaw, 617(TLS):8Oct82-1110
Honoré, T. Emperors and Lawyers.
   A.R. Birley, 617(TLS):19Mar82-321
Honour, H. Romanticism.*
   L. Eitner, 90:Jun81-368
   K. Kroeber, 591(SIR):Summer81-268

Honsza, N., Z. Światłowski and B. Wen-
gierek. Profile współczesności.
  A. Sąpoliński, 654(WB):4/1981-163
Hood, A.B.E., ed and trans. St. Patrick:
His Writings and Muirchu's Life.
  J.F. Kelly, 589:Jul81-669
Hood, H. A New Athens.
  M. Northey, 296(JCF):No30-165
Hood, H. Reservoir Ravine.*
  D. Brydon, 102(CanL):Winter80-139
Hood, M. The Evolution of Javanese Game-
lan. (Bk 1)
  M.J. Kartomi, 187:May82-328
Hood, W. Mole.
  P. Taubman, 441:23May82-14
Hoogeveen, J. Funktionalistische Rezep-
tionstheorie.
  F. Betz, 406:Fall81-340
Hook, P.E. Hindi Structures. (Inter-
mediate Level)
  M.C. Shapiro, 293(JASt):Aug81-825
Hook, S. Philosophy and Public Policy.*
  J.B. Colburn, 396(ModA):Summer81-308
  A.G.N. Flew, 518:Oct81-232
Hooker, C.A., J.J. Leach and E.F. McClen-
nen, eds. Foundations and Applications
of Decision Theory.*
  M.A.F., 543:Sep80-141
Hooker, J. Englishman's Road.*
  P. Mills, 493:Jun81-63
Hooker, J. The Poetry of Place.
  D.A.N. Jones, 362:9Dec82-25
  A. Stevenson, 617(TLS):15Oct82-1139
Hooker, J. Jown Cowper Powys and David
Jones.
  W.J. Keith, 627(UTQ):Spring81-330
Hooker, J. A View from the Source.
  A. Stevenson, 617(TLS):15Oct82-1139
Hooker, J.T. Linear B.
  J-C. Billigmeier, 24:Fall81-347
Hooker, M., ed. Descartes.*
  D.M. Clarke, 518:Jan81-12
Hooker, M.D. and S.G. Wilson, eds. Paul
and Paulinism.
  J.L. Houlden, 617(TLS):5Nov82-1226
Hooker, R. Of the Laws of Ecclesiastical
Polity. (A.S. McGrade and B. Vickers,
eds)
  D. Bevington, 539:Aug82-219
Hooker, R. Of the Laws of Ecclesiastical
Polity.* (Vol 1: Bks 1-4 ed by G. Edel-
en; Vol 2: Bk 5 ed by W.S. Hill)
  D. Bevington, 539:Aug82-219
  L.G. Black, 447(N&Q):Oct80-429
Hooker, R. Of the Laws of Ecclesiastical
Polity. (Vol 3, Bks 6-8) (P.G. Stanwood,
ed)
  D. Bevington, 539:Aug82-219
Hookway, C. and P. Pettit, eds. Action
and Interpretation.*
  C.D. Peters, 488:Dec81-513
Hooper, W. - see Lewis, C.S.
Hoopes, J. Oral History.
  E.C. Clark, 9(AlaR):Jan81-73
Hoopes, J. - see Miller, P.
Hoopes, R. Cain.
  N. Johnson, 441:28Nov82-13
Hoopes, R. - see Cain, J.M.
Hoover, T. Zen Culture.
  F.H. Cook, 318(JAOS):Apr/Jun80-208
Hooykaas, R. Religion and the Rise of
Modern Science.
  D. Steinberg, 186(ETC.):Winter81-423

Hopcraft, A. Mid-Century Men.
  K.C. O'Brien, 362:25Mar82-27
  J.K.L. Walker, 617(TLS):16Apr82-446
Hope, A.D. The New Cratylus.*
  C.R. Beye, 472:Spring/Summer82-75
Hope, C. In the Country of the Black Pig.
  P. Bland, 364:Oct81-79
  D. Dunn, 617(TLS):8Jan82-38
Hope, C. Private Parts and Other Tales.
  A. Delius, 617(TLS):5Nov82-1231
Hope, C. A Separate Development.*
  P-L. Adams, 61:Feb82-86
  A. Delius, 617(TLS):5Nov82-1231
  D. Durrant, 364:Feb82-97
Hope, C. Titian.
  C. McCorquodale, 135:Sep81-9
  T. Pignatti, 39:May81-336
  J. Steer, 59:Sep81-351
Hope, E.R. The Deep Syntax of Lisu Sen-
tences.
  J.A. Matisoff, 318(JAOS):Jul/Sep80-386
Hopes, D.B. The Glacier's Daughters.
  H. Chatfield, 236:Fall-Winter82-57
Hopkins, A. Beating Time.
  H. Cole, 362:22Jul82-22
Hopkins, A. Understanding Music.
  J.H., 412:Nov80-316
Hopkins, C. The Discovery of Dura-Europos.
  (B. Goldman, ed)
  J.A.S. Evans, 529(QQ):Winter81-686
Hopkins, E. and R. Grotjahn, eds. Studies
in Language Teaching and Language Acqui-
sition.
  J. Yalden, 350:Sep82-739
Hopkins, G.M. Gerard Manley Hopkins: The
Major Poems. (W. Davies, ed)
  R.K.R. Thornton, 541(RES):Nov81-474
Hopkins, J. Nicholas of Cusa's Debate
with John Wenck. Nicholas of Cusa on
Learned Ignorance.
  D.F. Duclow, 589:Oct81-930
Hopkins, J.K. A Woman to Deliver Her
People.
  D. Martin, 617(TLS):26Nov82-1287
Hopkins, K. Conquerors and Slaves.*
  K.R. Bradley, 122:Jan81-82
Hopkinson, C. A Bibliography of the Musi-
cal and Literary Works of Hector Berlioz
1803-1869. (2nd ed)
  R. Jacoby, 354:Jun81-166
  D.W. Krummel, 415:Sep81-605
Hopkinson, T. Of This Our Time.
  S. Jacobson, 362:20May82-25
  C. Madge, 617(TLS):30Apr82-478
Hopkirk, P. Foreign Devils on the Silk
Road.
  N. Malcolm, 111:5Dec80-60
  639(VQR):Summer81-86
Hopkirk, P. Trespassers on the Roof of
the World.
  C. von Fürer-Haimendorf, 617(TLS):
  30Jul82-813
Horálek, K. - see Barnetová, V. and others
Horan, D.J. and D. Mall, eds. Death,
Dying, and Euthanasia.
  T.M.R., 185:Apr82-598
Horan, J.D. The Peking Agent.
  N. Callendar, 441:12Sep82-38
Horbury, W. and B. McNeil, eds. Suffering
and Martyrdom in the New Testament.
  J.L. Houlden, 617(TLS):14May82-543
Horgan, E.R. The Shaker Holy Land.
  J. Demos, 441:15Aug82-12

Horgan, J., ed. The Golden Years of
Ginger Meggs 1921-1952.
B. Andrews, 71(ALS):May81-133
Horgan, P. Mexico Bay.
J. Kaplan, 441:28Mar82-15
Hormann, H. Psycholinguistics. (2nd ed)
R. Goodwin, 353:Vol 18No11/12-1164
Horn, A. Das Literarische — Formalis-
tische Versuche zu seiner Bestimmung.
A. Corbineau-Hoffmann, 490:Band12
Heft3/4-524
B. Sorg, 52:Band15Heft2-182
Horn, N., ed. Rights and Responsibilities.
R.L.S., 185:Jul82-797
Horn, W. and E. Born. The Plan of St.
Gall.*
F. Bucher, 576:Mar81-58
S. Kostof, 54:Jun81-317
Horn-Oncken, A. Ausflug in elysische Ge-
filde.
H. Sichtermann, 52:Band15Heft2-199
Hornblower, J. Hieronymus of Cardia.
J. Briscoe, 617(TLS):6Aug82-847
Hornblower, S. Mausolus.
P. Cartledge, 617(TLS):23Apr82-459
Hornbostel-Hüttner, G. Studien zur römis-
chen Nischenarchitektur.
R. Ling, 313:Vol71-232
N. Neuerburg, 576:May81-153
Hornby, A.S., with A.P. Cowie. Oxford
Advanced Learner's Dictionary of
Current English. (3rd ed)
H. Ulherr, 38:Band99Heft3/4-466
Hornby, A.S. and E.C. Parnwell. The
Oxford English Reader's Dictionary.
(new ed)
H. Ulherr, 38:Band99Heft3/4-467
Hornby, R. Danske Personnavne.
G.B. Droege, 424:Mar80-90
Horner, I.B., ed and trans. The Minor
Anthologies of the Pali Canon. (Pt 4)
C.S. Prebish, 318(JAOS):Jan/Mar80-56
Hornsby, J. Actions.
D.W.D. Owen, 479(PhQ):Jul81-271
C.S. Ripley, 518:Jul81-161
B.F. Scarlett, 63:Mar81-136
I. Thalberg, 185:Jan82-343
Horoszowski, P. Economic Special-Opportun-
ity Conduct and Crime.
C.S., 185:Apr82-601
de Horozco, S. Representaciones. (F.
González Ollé, ed)
P.N. Dunn, 86(BHS):Apr81-143
N. Griffin, 402(MLR):Jul81-721
Horrall, S.M., ed. The Southern Version
of "Cursor Mundi."* (Vol 1)
O.S. Pickering, 38:Band99Heft3/4-498
Horrent, J. Les Versions françaises et
étrangères des Enfances de Charlemagne.
G. West, 86(BHS):Jul81-255
Horrocks, J. My Dear Parents. (A.S.
Lewis, ed)
S. Fender, 617(TLS):10Dec82-1377
Horrox, R. The Changing Plan of Hull,
1290-1650.
D. Keene, 325:Oct81-506
Horrox, R. and P.W. Hammond, eds. British
Library Harleian Manuscript 433. (Vol 1)
R.W. Kaeuper, 589:Apr81-453
Horsman, R. Race and Manifest Destiny.
K.S. Lynn, 617(TLS):12Mar82-272
J.H. Silverman, 676(YR):Spring82-458

Horster, M. Andrea del Castagno.*
F. Ames-Lewis, 59:Sep81-339
K. Christiansen, 39:Jul81-66
Hortelano, J.G. - see under García Horte-
lano, J.
Horton, A.S. and J. Magretta, eds. Modern
European Filmmakers and the Art of
Adaptation.
R. Greenspun, 18:May81-73
A.G. Robson, 399(MLJ):Winter81-424
H. Weinberg, 200:Aug-Sep81-445
Horton, J.O. and L.E. Black Bostonians.
H.L. Armour, 14:Fall81-366
Horton, R.A. The Unity of "The Faerie
Queene."*
J.S. Dees, 580(SCR):Fall80-95
Horton, S.R. Interpreting Interpreting.*
S. Mailloux, 131(CL):Summer81-289
D. Overton, 637(VS):Winter81-229
Horvat, B. The Political Economy of
Socialism.
R.L. Heilbroner, 453(NYRB):10Jun82-41
Horwath, P. Der Kampf gegen die religiöse
Tradition.*
B. Bittrich, 52:Band15Heft2-211
Horwitz, R. Buber's Way to "I and Thou."
M.L.M., 543:Mar81-612
Horwitz, S.L. The Find of a Lifetime.*
639(VQR):Summer81-98
Horwood, H. Bartlett.
T.D. MacLulich, 102(CanL):Spring80-90
Horwood, W. Adolphe Sax, 1814-1894.
P. Bate, 415:May81-313
Hosking, G. Beyond Socialist Realism.*
J.M. Curtis, 574(SEEJ):Spring81-112
D. Milivojević, 558(RLJ):Spring-Fall81-
313
J.A. Schillinger, 395(MFS):Winter80/81-
742
D. Skillen, 575(SEER):Jan81-92
Hoskins, J.W. Casimir Pulaski 1747-1779.
The USSR and East Central and Southeast-
ern Europe: Periodicals in Western Lan-
guages. (4th ed)
W. Zalewski, 497(PolR):Vol26No3-108
Hoskins, K.B. Anderson County.
D.W. Bowen, 9(AlaR):Apr81-150
Hoskins, W.G. Fieldwork in Local History.
(2nd ed)
K.E. Jermy, 324:Sep82-677
Hoskyns, E.C. and F.N. Davey. Crucifixion
— Resurrection. (G.S. Wakefield, ed)
B. Lindars, 617(TLS):9Apr82-406
Hösle, J. Molières Komödie Dom Juan.
W.D. Howarth, 208(FS):Oct81-495
Hosmer, H. Remembrances of Concord and
the Thoreaus. (G. Hendrick, ed)
A. Hook, 447(N&Q):Oct80-469
R.J. Schneider, 183(ESQ):Vol127No1-57
Hotchkiss, B. The Medicine Calf.
R.E. Morsberger, 649(WAL):Winter82-327
Hotchner, A.E. The Man Who Lived at the
Ritz.
A. Cheuse, 441:28Feb82-15
M. Haltrecht, 617(TLS):9Apr82-422
Hou, C-M. and T-S. Yu, eds. Modern Chi-
nese Economic History.
S.M. Jones, 293(JASt):Nov80-111
Houben, H. St. Blasianer Handschriften
des 11. und 12. Jahrhunderts unter
besonderer Berücksichtigung der Ochsen-
hauser Klosterbibliothek.
C.E. Ineichen-Eder, 589:Oct81-876

Houck, C. The Fashion Encyclopedia.
   P. Bach, 614:Fall82-16
Houfe, S. Sir Albert Richardson: The
Professor.*
   J.M. Robinson, 135:Mar81-242
Hough, J.F. Soviet Leadership in Transi-
tion.
   G.W. Breslauer, 550(RusR):Apr81-210
Hough, S.J. The Italians and the Creation
of America.
   J. Tedeschi, 517(PBSA):Jul-Sep81-360
Houghton, W.E., with E.R. Houghton, eds.
The Wellesley Index to Victorian Periodi-
cals 1824-1900.* (Vol 3)
   I. Jack, 541(RES):Aug81-346
   J.M. Robson, 637(VS):Winter81-243
"The Houghton 'Shahnameh.'" (M.B. Dickson
and S.C. Welch, eds)
   M. Levey, 453(NYRB):7Oct82-13
Houlbrooke, R. Church Courts and the
People during the English Reformation,
1520-1570.
   R.M. Kingdon, 551(RenQ):Winter80-792
   D. Loades, 161(DUJ):Jun81-240
Houlgate, L.D. The Child and the State.
   F.G.M., 185:Jan82-396
Hourcade, P. Temas de Literatura Portu-
guesa.*
   205(FMLS):Jan80-86
Hourmouziadis, G. To neolithiko Dimēni.
   P. Halstead, 303(JoHS):Vol 101-206
House, A., comp. Black South African
Women Writers in English.
   D. Dorsey, 95(CLAJ):Mar81-416
House, J. A Model for Translation Quality
Assessment.
   K. Faiss, 257(IRAL):Feb81-79
House, J. and M. Stevens, eds. Post-
Impressionism.
   R.R. Brettell, 127:Fall/Winter80-409
Household, G. Summon the Bright Water.*
   N. Callendar, 441:10Jan82-29
"Household and Family Characteristics."
   A. Hacker, 453(NYRB):18Mar82-37
Housley, N. The Italian Crusades.
   D.P. Waley, 617(TLS):25Jun82-698
Houston, C.J. and W.J. Smyth. The Sash
Canada Wore.
   D.H. Akenson, 529(QQ):Autumn81-490
Houston, J. Eskimo Prints.
   W.N., 102(CanL):Spring81-176
Houston, J. Spirit Wrestler.
   P. Barclay, 102(CanL):Summer81-133
   P. Klovan, 102(CanL):Autumn81-147
Houston, J.P. French Symbolism and the
Modernist Movement.*
   B.L. Knapp, 446(NCFS):Spring-Summer81-
284
   205(FMLS):Oct81-376
Houston, J.P. and M. Tobin, eds and trans.
French Symbolist Poetry.
   U. Franklin, 446(NCFS):Spring-Summer82-
367
Houston, L. At the Mercy.*
   J. Cotton, 493:Sep81-74
Hovanec, E.A. Henry James and Germany.*
   A.W. Bellringer, 677(YES):Vol 11-336
Hovenkamp, H. Science and Religion in
America, 1800-1860.
   W.R. Ward, 161(DUJ):Dec80-96

Hover, C.F. "Aucassin et Nicolette."
   (L.H. Silverstein, ed)
   P.F. Dembowski, 545(RPh):Aug80-137
   N. Mann, 447(N&Q):Feb80-87
Hovi, K. Cordon sanitaire or barrière de
l'est?
   D. Kirby, 575(SEER):Apr81-272
Hovi, O. The Baltic Area in British Pol-
icy, 1918-1921. (Vol 1)
   D. Kirby, 575(SEER):Apr81-272
Hoving, T. King of the Confessors.*
   P-L. Adams, 61:Jan82-88
   J. Richardson, 453(NYRB):21Jan82-16
Howard, C. Coleridge's Idealism.
   K. Oedingen, 342:Band71Heft1-126
Howard, D. The Architectural History of
Venice.*
   J.G. Links, 39:May81-339
   J. Onians, 324:Feb82-164
Howard, D. and J. Ayers. Masterpieces of
Chinese Export Porcelain from the Mot-
tahedeh Collection in the Virginia
Museum.
   W.B.R. Neave-Hill, 135:May81-75
Howard, D.R. Writers and Pilgrims.*
   A.S.G. Edwards, 405(MP):May82-421
   P. Strohm, 141:Spring81-180
Howard, E.J. Getting it Right.
   A. Duchêne, 617(TLS):14May82-536
   J. Mellors, 362:3Jun82-22
   442(NY):15Nov82-203
Howard, J. Darwin.
   R. O'Hanlon, 617(TLS):18Jun82-653
   A. Ryan, 362:18Mar82-21
Howard, L. Trivial Fond Records. (R.
Howard, ed)
   H. Hobson, 617(TLS):1Oct82-1062
Howard, M. Eppie.
   F.R. Schumer, 441:5Sep82-11
Howard, M. Facts of Life.
   M. Ellmann, 569(SR):Summer81-454
Howard, M. Grace Abounding.
   A. Long, 453(NYRB):2Dec82-46
   N. Perrin, 441:26Sep82-7
   442(NY):18Oct82-179
Howard, P., ed. C.W. von Gluck "Orfeo."
   M. Tanner, 617(TLS):8Jan82-25
Howard, P. Words Fail Me.*
   G. Core, 249(HudR):Autumn81-475
Howard, R. Contemporary Chinese Theatre.
   C. Mackerras, 293(JASt):Nov80-114
Howard-Hill, T.H. Index to British Liter-
ary Bibliography. (Vols 4 and 5)
   J.D. Fleeman, 447(N&Q):Oct80-424
Howard-Hill, T.H. Literary Concordances.
   H.S. Donow, 365:Winter82-46
   M.J. Preston, 191(ELN):Jun81-321
Howarth, S. The Knights Templar.
   J. Riley-Smith, 617(TLS):12Feb82-155
Howarth, W. The Book of Concord.
   M. Bayles, 441:12Sep82-11
Howarth, W.D., ed. Comic Drama.
   205(FMLS):Apr80-82
Howarth, W.D. Molière.
   J.H. Mason, 617(TLS):17Sep82-1018
Howe, C. China's Economy.
   S.M. Jones, 293(JASt):May81-539
Howe, D.W. The Political Culture of the
American Whigs.
   T.H. O'Connor, 432(NEQ):Sep81-440
Howe, F. Holy Smoke.
   S. Scott-Fleming, 436(NewL):Fall81-124

Howe, I. A Margin of Hope.
   J. Atlas, 441:31Oct82-1
Howe, I. and I.W., eds. Short Shorts.
   442(NY):19Jul82-98
Howe, J.R. Marlowe, Tamburlaine and Magic.
   G.D. Aggeler, 179(ES):Apr81-173
Howe, P. Origins.
   D. Dunn, 617(TLS):8Jan82-38
Howe, T. Myself in the Rain.*
   P. Stevens, 529(QQ):Autumn81-504
Howell, B. A Mere Formality.
   L. Taylor, 617(TLS):13Aug82-888
Howell, C. Though Silence.
   C. Inez, 472:Fall/Winter81-231
Howell, S.C. Designing for Aging.
   T.O. Byerts, 505:Aug81-114
Howells, C. Sartre's Theory of Litera-
   ture.*
   G. Idt, 535(RHL):Nov-Dec81-1030
   T. Keefe, 208(FS):Jan81-97
   A. Young, 323:Jan81-95
   205(FMLS):Oct81-377
Howells, C.A. Love, Mystery, and Misery.*
   R. Jackson, 677(YES):Vol 11-293
   C. Lamont, 161(DUJ):Jun81-255
Howells, W.D. Selected Letters.* (Vol 1)
   (G. Arms and others, eds)
   J. Katz, 579(SAQ):Autumn81-491
   K.S. Lynn, 445(NCF):Jun80-92
Howells, W.D. Selected Letters.* (Vol 2)
   (G. Arms, C. Lohmann and J. Herron, eds)
   J. Katz, 579(SAQ):Autumn81-491
Howells, W.D. Selected Letters. (Vol 3)
   (R.C. Leitz 3d, R.H. Ballinger and C.
   Lohmann, eds)
   J. Katz, 579(SAQ):Autumn81-491
Hower, A. and R.A. Preto-Rodas, eds. Crôn-
   icas brasileiras.
   M. Harvey, 238:May81-329
Howlett, C.F. Troubled Philosopher.
   J.D. Moreno, 319:Jan81-129
Howse, D. Greenwich Time and the Dis-
   covery of the Longitude.
   B. Castel, 529(QQ):Spring81-173
Howson, C., ed. Method and Appraisal in
   the Physical Sciences.*
   A.F. Chalmers, 167:Mar81-167
Hoy, C. Introductions, Notes, and Commen-
   taries to Texts in "The Dramatic Works
   of Thomas Dekker."
   R. Berry, 529(QQ):Summer81-392
   J.C. Trewin, 157:2ndQtr81-53
Hoy, D.C. The Critical Circle.*
   L. Orr, 599:Fall81-508
Hoyle, F. and N.C. Wickramasinghe.
   Diseases from Space.
   R. Bieri, 42(AR):Spring81-261
Hoyt, E.P. Guerilla.
   D.J.R. Bruckner, 441:24Jan82-16
Hoyt, R. Trotsky's Run.
   N. Callendar, 441:22Aug82-26
Hraste, M. and P. Šimunović. Čakavisch-
   deutsches Lexikon. (Pt 1) (R. Olesch,
   ed)
   P. Herrity, 575(SEER):Jan81-73
   W. Potthoff, 688(ZSP):Band42Heft2-435
Hsia, A., ed. Hermann Hesse heute.
   E.A. Metzger, 133:Band14Heft3-282
Hsia, R. and L. Chau. Industrialization,
   Employment and Income Distribution.
   S. Richards, 302:Vol 18-168

Hsiao Kung-ch'üan. A History of Chinese
   Political Thought. (Vol 1)
   L.S. Chang and Y-O. Kim, 485(PE&W):
   Jul81-355
Hsieh, S-Y. The Life and Thought of Li
   Kou, 1009-1059.
   C. Schirokauer and J.T.C. Liu,
   244(HJAS):Dec81-692
Hsu, C-Y. Han Agriculture. (J.L. Dull,
   ed)
   R.M. Myers, 302:Vol 18-149
Hsü Chin-hsiung. Ming Yi-shih shou-ts'ang
   chia-ku shih-wen pien. (Vol 2)
   D.N. Keightley, 318(JAOS):Jan/Mar80-96
Hsu, K-Y. and T. Wang, eds. Literature in
   the People's Republic of China.
   M. Egan, 293(JASt):May81-586
Hsu, R.S.W. The Style of Lu Hsun.
   C.L. McClenon, 350:Jun82-488
Hsueh, F.S. Phonology of Old Mandarin.
   P-H. Ting, 318(JAOS):Jan/Mar80-94
Hu, K-Z. Der Gebrauch des Artikels in der
   deutschen Gegenwartssprache.
   205(FMLS):Oct81-377
Hu, S-C. The Development of the Chinese
   Collection in the Library of Congress.
   A. Marr, 293(JASt):Feb81-352
Huang San, A. Pino and L. Epstein, eds.
   Un bol de nids d'hirondelles ne fait pas
   le printemps de Pékin.
   V. Alleton, 98:Aug-Sep81-762
Hubbard, W. Complicity and Conviction.
   L. Wright, 46:Aug81-128
Hubbs, G.W. - see Barr, J.G.
Huber, H.D. Historische Romane in der
   ersten Hälfte des 19. Jahrhunderts.
   N.A. Kaiser, 221(GQ):Mar81-232
Huber, R. and R. Reith. Festungen.
   N. Adams, 576:Dec81-331
Hubert, C. Dreamspeaker and Tem Eyos Ki
   and the Land Claims Question.
   M. Whitaker, 102(CanL):Autumn80-134
Hubig, C. and W. von Rahden, eds. Konse-
   quenzen kritischer Wissenschaftstheorie.
   C. Lendhardt, 488:Dec81-509
Hubmann-Uhlich, I. - see Doring, P.F.
Hübner, K. Kritik der wissenschaftlichen
   Vernunft.
   H. Reinhardt, 489(PJGG):Band88Heft2-
   402
Hübner, K. and others, eds. Die politis-
   che Herausforderung der Wissenschaft.
   C. Lenhardt, 488:Dec81-509
Hübscher, A. - see Schopenhauer, A.
Hucke, K-H. Utopie und Ideologie in der
   expressionistischen Lyrik.
   G.P. Knapp, 133:Band14Heft3-284
Huddle, D. Paper Boy.
   S.P. Estess, 577(SHR):Winter81-91
Huddleston, E.L. and D.A. Noverr, eds.
   The Relationship of Painting and Litera-
   ture.
   R. Stewart, 658:Summer/Autumn81-238
Hudelson, S., ed. Learning to Read in
   Different Languages.
   A. Pousada, 350:Mar82-253
Huder, W. and T. Koebner, eds. Alfred
   Kerr.
   R. Grimm, 406:Winter81-478
Hudson, C. Insider Out.
   K. Jeffery, 617(TLS):26Nov82-1318
   J. Mellors, 362:21Oct82-23

Hudson, C.M., ed. Black Drink.
  J. Duffy, 9(AlaR):Jan81-64
  L.J. Sass, 292(JAF):Apr-Jun81-260
Hudson, K. Pawnbroking.
  P. Keating, 617(TLS):30Apr82-490
Hudson, R.A. Sociolinguistics.
  R.R. Day, 608:Mar82-91
  P. Eckert, 355(LSoc):Aug81-259
  J.T. Platt, 361:Feb-Mar81-288
Hudson, W.D. A Century of Moral Philoso-
  phy.
  T.M.R., 185:Jan82-399
Hudson, W.H., with M. Beaven. Birds of a
  Feather. (D. Shrubsall, ed)
  R. O'Hanlon, 617(TLS):17Sep82-996
Hue, B. Littératures et arts de l'Orient
  dans l'oeuvre de Claudel.*
  G. Gadoffre, 208(FS):Oct81-470
  G. Gadoffre, 535(RHL):Mar-Apr81-323
Huebel, H.R. Jack Kerouac.
  D. Stanley, 649(WAL):Summer81-138
Huebener, T. Opportunities in Foreign
  Language Careers.
  B. Braude, 207(FR):Oct81-176
  R.I. Brod, 399(MLJ):Winter81-413
Huebert, R. John Ford.*
  G. Bas, 189(EA):Oct-Dec81-465
Huemer, F. Corpus Rubenianum Ludwig
  Burchard. (Pt 19, Vol 1)
  J.D. Stewart, 90:Jun81-365
Huettich, H.G. Theater in the Planned
  Society.*
  D. Sevin, 406:Summer81-250
Huffman, J.L. Politics of the Meiji
  Press.*
  W.R. Braisted, 293(JASt):Nov80-131
Huge, W. - see von Droste-Hülshoff, A.
Hügel, H-O. Untersuchungsrichter, Diebes-
  fänger, Detektive.*
  P. Bekes, 224(GRM):Band30Heft3-362
Hughes, A. Henry Irving, Shakespearean.*
  R. Harwood, 157:2ndQtr81-49
Hughes, A. and P. Trudgill. English
  Accents and Dialects.
  R.R. Butters, 35(AS):Fall81-234
  M.R. Key, 350:Mar82-243
  S. Rixon, 277(ITL):No48-93
  B.M.H. Strang, 447(N&Q):Feb80-85
  J. Vachek, 682(ZPSK):Band33Heft6-751
  205(FMLS):Jan80-87
Hughes, C., ed. American Theatre Annual
  1978-79.
  L. Senelick, 610:Autumn81-233
Hughes, D. Dryden's Heroic Plays.*
  A.B. Gardiner, 566:Spring82-119
  J. Loftis, 130:Winter81/82-387
Hughes, G. Where I Used to Play on the
  Green.
  V. Cunningham, 617(TLS):29Jan82-104
  J. Mellors, 362:11Mar82-23
Hughes, G. - see Laycock, S.
Hughes, G.T. Romantic German Literature.*
  D.G. Little, 402(MLR):Apr81-508
Hughes, K.J. The Life and Art of Jackson
  Beardy.
  K.E. Kidd, 298:Fall-Winter81-222
  W.N., 102(CanL):Spring81-174
Hughes, M. The Ghost Dance Caper.
  J.K. Kealy, 102(CanL):Spring80-113
Hughes, P., with others - see Burney, F.

Hughes, R. The Shock of the New.*
  D. Cooper, 39:Dec81-425
  N. Foote, 62:Summer81-89
  C. Harrison, 59:Sep81-328
  B. Wolmer, 55:Summer81-27
Hughes, R. Unholy Communion.
  N. Callendar, 441:23May82-41
Hughes, S.S. Surveyors and Statesmen.
  J.R. Stilgoe, 656(WMQ):Jan81-136
Hughes, T. Moortown.*
  G. Burns, 584(SWR):Spring81-230
  S. McPherson, 29:Jan/Feb82-18
  R. Murphy, 453(NYRB):10Jun82-38
Hughes, T. New Selected Poems.
  D. Donoghue, 441:14Mar82-12
  R. Murphy, 453(NYRB):10Jun82-38
Hughes, T. Remains of Elmet.* Under the
  North Star.* Cave Birds.*
  R. Murphy, 453(NYRB):10Jun82-38
Hughes, T. Selected Poems 1957-1981.
  A. Thwaite, 617(TLS):25Jun82-696
Hughes, T. - see Plath, S.
Hughes, T. and F. McCullough - see Plath,
  S.
Hughes, W. The Maniac in the Cellar.*
  P. Brantlinger, 141:Summer81-270
  C. Crosby, 454:Winter81-91
  P.D. Edwards, 445(NCF):Sep81-221
"Hugo von Montfort." (Vols 1 and 2) (E.
  Thurnher and others, eds)
  B. Wachinger, 684(ZDA):Band110Heft4-
  160
Hugo, R. The Hitler Diaries.
  K. Jeffery, 617(TLS):6Aug82-865
Hugo, R. The Right Madness on Skye.
  M. Allen, 649(WAL):Winter81-312
  R. Hornsey, 461:Fall-Winter81/82-101
  P. Serchuk, 569(SR):Spring81-271
  P. Stitt, 219(GaR):Spring81-182
Hugo, R. Selected Poems.*
  M. Allen, 649(WAL):Winter81-308
Hugo, R. White Center.*
  M. Allen, 649(WAL):Winter81-312
  P. Serchuk, 569(SR):Spring81-271
  P. Stitt, 219(GaR):Spring81-182
Hugo, V. Quatrevingt-treize. (Y. Gohin,
  ed)
  W.J.S. Kirton, 208(FS):Oct81-459
Hugo, V. Les Travailleurs de la mer. (M.
  Eigeldinger, ed) Les Travailleurs de la
  mer. (Y. Gohin, ed)
  W. Greenberg, 207(FR):Apr82-683
Hugo, V. and P-J. Hetzel. Correspondance.
  (Vol 1) (S. Gaudon, ed)
  P.L. Horn, 446(NCFS):Fall-Winter80/81-
  131
Huguet, L. L'oeuvre d'Alfred Döblin ou la
  dialectique de l'exode, 1878-1918.
  K. Weissenberger, 133:Band14Heft2-190
Huhm, H.P. Kut.
  A.C. Heyman, 187:Jan82-173
Huish, I. Horváth.
  K. Winston, 221(GQ):Nov81-520
Hull, R.E. Nathaniel Hawthorne.*
  J. Franzosa, 141:Summer81-278
Hull, S.W. Chaste, Silent and Obedient.
  J. Briggs, 617(TLS):19Nov82-1264
Hulse, C. Metamorphic Verse.
  K. Duncan-Jones, 617(TLS):11Jun82-647
Hulse, M. Knowing and Forgetting.*
  H. Lomas, 364:Nov81-72

Hulsewé, A.F.P. China in Central Asia;
The Early Stage: 125 B.C. - A.D. 23.
J.W. de Jong, 259(IIJ):Jul81-242
Hulsker, J. The Complete van Gogh.*
G. Pollock, 59:Sep81-349
N. Powell, 39:Jul81-69
Hult, G. and D. McCaslin. Hala Sultan
Tekke.* (Vol 4)
Y. Calvet, 555:Vol54fasc2-338
"Humanitas."
F. Niedermayer, 72:Band217Heft1-172
"Humanitas Religiosa: Festschrift für
Haralds Biezais dargebracht von
Freunden und Kollegen."
E. Ettlinger, 203:Vol92No1-125
"The Humanities in American Life."*
K. Johnston, 128(CE):Sep81-471
B. Lang, 651(WHR):Winter81-349
Humber, J.M. and R.F. Almeder, eds. Bio-
medical Ethics and the Law. (2nd ed)
J.C.M., 185:Jan82-397
Humbert, A. and D. Danctis. La Jeunesse
et l'espace urbain.
J. Laroche, 207(FR):Dec81-287
Humbert, M. Municipium et Civitas sine
suffragio.
M.H. Crawford, 313:Vol171-153
Humbert, M-T. A l'autre bout de moi.
M. Le Clézio, 207(FR):Mar82-568
Hume, I.N. Martin's Hundred.
P-L. Adams, 61:Jun82-102
442(NY):12Jul82-104
Hume, L.J. Bentham and Bureaucracy.
A. Ryan, 617(TLS):29Jan82-96
Hume, R.D., ed. The London Theatre World,
1660-1800.*
J.D. Durant, 566:Autumn81-52
Humes, J.N. Two Against Time.*
A. Barnes, 535(RHL):Mar-Apr81-320
Humfrey, B., ed. Recollections of the
Powys Brothers.
J.L. Mitchell, 77:Spring81-183
Humpherys, A. Travels into the Poor Man's
Country.*
T.C. Barker, 366:Autumn81-264
S. Pickering, 569(SR):Spring81-306
Humphreys, A.R. - see Shakespeare, W.
Humphreys, R.A. Latin America and the
Second World War. (Vol 1)
L. Whitehead, 617(TLS):18Jun82-656
Humphreys, R.A. Latin America and the
Second World War. (Vol 2)
L. Whitehead, 617(TLS):17Dec82-1391
Humphreys, R.S. From Saladin to the
Mongols.
B. Lewis, 589:Apr81-393
Humphreys, S.C. Anthropology and the
Greeks.*
V. Hunter, 487:Summer81-145
V. Valeri, 122:Jan81-63
Hundley, D.R. Social Relations in Our
Southern States. (W.J. Cooper, Jr., ed)
R. Mathis, 9(AlaR):Jan81-71
Hunger, H. Die hochsprachliche profane
Literatur der Byzantiner.* (Vols 1
and 2)
G. Huxley, 303(JoHS):Vol 101-229
Huning, A. Das Schaffen des Ingenieurs.
(2nd ed)
W. Strombach, 489(PJGG):Band88Heft1-
194

Hunnisett, B. A Dictionary of British
Steel Engravers.
T. Russell-Cobb, 324:Dec81-64
Hunnisett, B. Steel-Engraved Book Illus-
trations in England.*
J. Glynne, 59:Mar81-122
Hunt, A. The Language of Television.*
N. Berry, 364:Jun81-82
P. Lennon, 362:19Aug82-20
Hunt, C. "Lycidas" and the Italian
Critics.
A. Burnett, 447(N&Q):Feb80-92
M. Evans, 541(RES):Aug81-329
R.H. Peake, 551(RenQ):Summer80-303
Hunt, E.D. Holy Land Pilgrimage in the
Later Roman Empire AD 312-460.
G. Fowden, 617(TLS):1Oct82-1082
Hunt, G.D. Communication Skills in the
Organization.
L. Moore, 583:Winter82-229
Hunt, H. The Abbey.*
S. Carney, 476:Vol 11-129
A. Parkin, 397(MD):Jun81-243
K. Reardon, 579(SAQ):Winter81-109
Hunt, J.D. Andrew Marvell.*
G.D. Lord, 677(YES):Vol 11-258
Hunt, J.D. The Wider Sea.
D. Donoghue, 441:22Aug82-8
R. Trickett, 617(TLS):12Mar82-273
442(NY):6Sep82-109
Hunt, J.D. and F.M. Holland, eds. The Rus-
kin Polygon.
R. Trickett, 617(TLS):12Mar82-273
Hunt, M. The Universe Within.
D. Joravsky, 453(NYRB):21Oct82-44
R.M. Restak, 441:7Mar82-6
Hunt, R.W. The History of Grammar in the
Middle Ages. (G.L. Bursill-Hall, ed)
B. Löfstedt, 350:Jun81-487
Hunt, S. Collected Poems 1963-1980.
W.S. Broughton, 368:Sep81-282
Hunter, A. Fields of Heather.
T.J. Binyon, 617(TLS):5Feb82-147
Hunter, A. Gently Between Tides.
T.J. Binyon, 617(TLS):31Dec82-1448
Hunter, F. Community Power Succession.
639(VQR):Spring81-64
Hunter, G.K. Dramatic Identities and
Cultural Tradition.*
M.C. Bradbrook, 402(MLR):Jan81-162
R.W. Dent, 551(RenQ):Summer80-290
Hunter, G.K. "Paradise Lost."
W.E. Cain, 400(MLN):Dec81-1121
G.M. Crump, 569(SR):Fall81-628
M.A. Radzinowicz, 402(MLR):Oct81-930
Hunter, G.K. and C.J. Rawson - see "The
Yearbook of English Studies"
Hunter, J. Edwardian Fiction.
R. Brown, 617(TLS):26Nov82-1316
442(NY):10May82-169
Hunter, J., ed. Modern Poets Five.
D. Gioia, 249(HudR):Winter81/82-585
Hunter, J.F.M. Thinking about Sex and
Love.
S.L.B., 185:Apr82-581
B. Hendley, 529(QQ):Winter81-809
Hunter, L. G.K. Chesterton.
D.E. Van Tassel, 395(MFS):Summer80-310
Huntingford, G.W.B. The Periplus of the
Erythraean Sea.
E.W. Gray, 123:Vol131No2-275

Huntley, F.L. Bishop Joseph Hall, 1574-
1656.*
A. Fotheringham, 447(N&Q):Oct80-441
P. Horden, 568(SCN):Winter81-87
D. Loades, 161(DUJ):Jun81-233
Hurd, M. The Orchestra.
P. Standford, 415:Nov81-750
Hurd, M. The Oxford Junior Companion to
Music.
P. Standford, 415:Apr81-244
Hurewitz, J.C., ed. The Middle East and
North Africa in World Politics. (Vol 2)
(2nd ed)
R. Bidwell, 69:Vol50No3-326
Hurst, A.E. and J.H. Goodier. Painting
and Decorating. (9th ed)
I. Bristow, 324:May82-369
Hursthouse, R. Introduction to Philosophy.
E.J. Borowski, 479(PhQ):Apr81-184
Hurston, Z.N. Their Eyes Were Watching
God.*
R.L. Brittin, 577(SHR):Fall81-369
Hurt, L.J. A History of Writing-on-Stone
N.W.M.P. Post.
R.D. Francis, 298:Summer81-129
Hurt, L.J. The Victoria Settlement 1862-
1922.
R.D. Francis, 298:Summer81-129
Husain, T. A Passage to France.
T. Le Gassick, 318(JAOS):Jan/Mar80-30
Husar Struk, D. Ukrainian for Undergrad-
uates.
M. Jenkala, 575(SEER):Jul81-417
Huseboe, A.R., ed. Big Sioux Pioneers.
K.E.R. Johnson, 649(WAL):Summer81-169
Hüskens-Hasselbeck, K. Stil und Kritik.
H.H.F. Henning, 406:Spring81-111
Husserl, E. Aufsätze und Rezensionen
(1890-1910). (B. Rang, ed)
D. Willard, 323:Oct81-275
Husserl, E. Phantasie, Bildbewusstsein,
Erinnerung. (E. Marbach, ed)
R. Lüthe, 323:Oct81-277
Huston, N. Les Variations Goldberg.
A. Clerval, 450(NRF):Nov81-128
Hutchins, E. Culture and Inference.
C.O. Frake, 350:Jun82-474
Hutchins, F.G. Young Krishna.
A. Topsfield, 39:Mar81-202
Hutchinson, P. Literary Presentations of
Divided Germany.*
J. Steakley, 406:Summer81-252
Hutchison, R. The Politics of the Arts
Council.
M. Laski, 617(TLS):13Aug82-877
Hutchison, T.W. The Politics and Philos-
ophy of Economics.
D. Pearce, 617(TLS):26Mar82-359
Hütsch, V. Der Münchner Glaspalast 1854-
1931.
D. Nehring, 43:Band11Heft1-88
Hutson, J.H. John Adams and the Diplomacy
of the American Revolution.*
G.H. Clarfield, 656(WMQ):Jul81-536
Hütt, W. Grafik in der DDR.
H. Möbius, 654(WB):3/1981-182
Hüttner, J. and O.G. Schindler - see
Schwarz, H.
Hutton, M. Address Unknown.
N. Callendar, 441:7Feb82-20
Hutton, P.H. The Cult of the Revolution-
ary Tradition.
S. Englund, 617(TLS):11Jun82-646

Hutton, R. The Royalist War Effort 1642-
1646.
V. Pearl, 617(TLS):15Oct82-1128
K. Sharpe, 453(NYRB):2Dec82-43
Huxley, A. The Penguin Encyclopedia of
Gardening.
R.I. Ross, 617(TLS):12Mar82-288
Huxley, E. The Prince Buys the Manor.
M. Furness, 617(TLS):29Oct82-1203
J. Mellors, 362:18Nov82-28
Huxley, F. The Dragon.
J. Simpson, 203:Vol91No1-122
Huzar, E.G. Mark Antony.*
P. Jal, 555:Vol54fascl-199
A.J. Marshall, 487:Fall81-281
Hyde, H.M. The Atom Bomb Spies.*
639(VQR):Spring81-63
Hyde, H.M. Secret Intelligence Agent.
D. Hunt, 617(TLS):3Sep82-948
Hyde, M. - see Shaw, G.B. and A. Douglas
Hyman, A. Charles Babbage.
H.C. Longuet-Higgins, 617(TLS):26Nov82-
1290
R. O'Hanlon, 441:14Nov82-26
442(NY):23Aug82-93
Hyman, I. Fifteenth Century Florentine
Studies.
P. Morselli, 576:Oct81-240
Hyman, L.M., ed. Studies in Stress and
Accent.
B. de Chene, 350:Jun81-463
Hyman, P. From Dreyfus to Vichy.
F. Busi, 390:Jun/Jul81-60
Hyman, S. Edward Lear's Birds.
H. Crawley, 39:Apr81-274
Hynes, W.G. The Economics of Empire.
A.J. Greenberger, 637(VS):Spring81-351
Hyppolite, M.P. Phonétique historique
haïtienne.
A. Hull, 207(FR):Oct80-200
Hyslop, L.B. Baudelaire.
R. Galand, 207(FR):Apr82-684
J.T. Harskamp, 89(BJA):Summer81-280
J.C. McLaren, 446(NCFS):Spring-Sum-
mer81-273
D. Schier, 569(SR):Winter81-140

I-ch'ing, L. - see under Liu I-ch'ing
"Iberiul-k'avk'asiuri enatmecnierebis
c'elic'deuli II."
G.F. Meier, 682(ZPSK):Band32Heft2-230
Ibrahim, S. The Smell of It and other
Stories.
G. Bowder, 294:Vol 11-120
Ibsen, H. Peer Gynt. (R. Fjelde, trans)
D. Devlin, 157:Winter81-51
C. Leland, 397(MD):Dec81-564
Ide, R.S. Possessed with Greatness.*
L.S. Champion, 579(SAQ):Summer81-373
E. Pechter, 401(MLQ):Mar81-85
Idiens, D. and K.G. Ponting, eds.
Textiles of Africa.
E.L.R. Meyerowitz, 39:Aug81-134
Ignatow, D. Whisper to the Earth.
P. Stitt, 441:14Feb82-15
Ihde, D. Technics and Praxis.
H.A.D., 543:Dec80-380
K. Dorter, 154:Sep81-606
Ihimaera, W. Tangi.
H.W. Rhodes, 368:Dec73-348

Israeli, R. Muslims in China.
    M. Hasan, 273(IC):Jul81-209
Israelowitz, O. Synagogues of New York
City.
    P. Goldberger, 441:26Dec82-3
Issawi, C. An Economic History of the
Middle East and North Africa.
    P.K. O'Brien, 617(TLS):31Dec82-1451
Issenhuth, J-P. Entretien d'un autre
temps.
    A. Moorhead, 207(FR):Mar82-569
Isserman, M. Which Side Were You On?
    H. Klehr, 453(NYRB):18Nov82-55
    J. Klein, 441:14Feb82-12
"Issues in Stylistics."
    J.R. Bennett, 599:Fall81-483
Ito, M. John Gower, the Medieval Poet.
    R.F. Yeager, 402(MLR):Jul81-654
Itoh, H. and L.W. Beer, eds. The Constitu-
tional Case Law of Japan.
    J.M. Maki, 293(JASt):Feb81-384
Itzin, C. Stages in the Revolution.*
    M.B., 214:Vol 10No37-131
    J. Roose-Evans, 157:1stQtr81-51
Ivanov, S.N. Kurs tureckoj grammatiki.
    A. Achundov, 682(ZPSK):Band33Heft4-504
Ives, E.D., ed. Argyle Boom.
    D. Tebbetts, 292(JAF):Jul-Sep81-387
Ives, E.D. Joe Scott.*
    J. and U. Rempel, 106:Winter81-331
    R.D. Renwick, 292(JAF):Jan-Mar81-113
Ives, E.D. The Tape-Recorded Interview.
    C.T. Morrissey, 14:Fall80-491
Iwamura, S.G. The Verbal Games of Pre-
School Children.
    L. Löfstedt, 350:Sep81-754
Izmajlov, N.V. - see Puškin, A.S.
Izzo, H.J., ed. Italic and Romance.
    B. Löfstedt, 350:Mar82-216

"The JACT Greek Course."
    H.J.K. Usher, 123:Vol31No1-68
Jaakko, L. Die Logik im XVII. Jahrhundert
in Finnland.
    H. Burkhardt, 53(AGP):Band63Heft2-200
al-Jabartī, 'A.R. Al-Jabartī's Chronicle
of the First Seven Months of the French
Occupation of Egypt, Muḥarram-Rajab 1213,
15 June-December 1798. (S. Moreh, ed
and trans)
    W.M. Brinner, 318(JAOS):Apr/Jun80-136
Jachnow, H. and others. Zur Erklärung und
Modellierung diachroner Wortbildungspro-
zesse (anhand russischer substantiv-
ischer Neologismen).
    G. Stone, 575(SEER):Oct81-636
Jack, R.D.S., ed. A Choice of Scottish
Verse 1560-1660.
    D.S. Hewitt, 402(MLR):Oct81-928
    F. Ridley, 588(SSL):Vol 16-272
Jackowska, N. Dr. Marbles and Marianne.
    J. Mellors, 362:16Dec82-24
    L. Taylor, 617(TLS):26Nov82-1318
Jackson, A. The Papers of Andrew Jackson.
(Vol 1) (S.B. Smith and H.C. Owsley,
eds)
    R.W. Coakley, 14:Winter81-55
    M.J. McDaniel, 9(AlaR):Jul81-227
Jackson, A.M. Illustration and the Novels
of Thomas Hardy.
    J. Keates, 617(TLS):5Mar82-248

Jackson, C. Color Me Beautiful.
    P. Bach, 614:Fall82-15
Jackson, D. The Story of Writing.
    J.D. O'Hara, 434:Summer82-603
Jackson, D.A. and S.P. Stich, eds. The
Recombinant DNA Debate.
    S.A. Lakoff, 185:Oct80-100
Jackson, D.D. Gold Dust.*
    W.F. Kimes, 649(WAL):Spring81-79
Jackson, E.R. Worlds Apart.
    F.R. Smith, 208(FS):Jan81-91
Jackson, H.F. From the Congo to Soweto.
    J.S. Whitaker, 441:27Jun82-7
Jackson, I.V., comp. Afro-American Reli-
gious Music.*
    B. Feintuch, 292(JAF):Apr-Jun81-242
Jackson, J.E. La Question du Moi.*
    H-P. Bayerdörfer, 52:Band15Heft1-101
    H. Godin, 402(MLR):Jan81-151
    205(FMLS):Jan80-88
Jackson, J.R.D. Poetry of the Romantic
Period.*
    G. Dekker, 661(WC):Summer81-186
    R. Hoffpauir, 627(UTQ):Summer81-114
    J.E. Jordan, 191(ELN):Jun81-307
    D.H. Reiman, 591(SIR):Summer81-254
    J. Stillinger, 301(JEGP):Oct81-581
Jackson, L. (Riding) The Poems of Laura
Riding.*
    B. Adams, 398(MPS):Vol 11Noland2-189
    R. Fraser, 175:Spring81-84
    H. Lomas, 364:Aug-Sep81-132
Jackson, L.E.B. Elli, Coming of Age in
the Holocaust.
    D. Stern, 390:Apr81-57
Jackson, M. The Kuranko.
    E. Tonkin, 69:Vol50No1-111
Jackson, M. Wall.
    R. Jackaman, 368:Jun81-220
Jackson, R. Fantasy.*
    T. Siebers, 385(MQR):Summer82-520
Jackson, R. - see Wilde, O.
Jackson, R.L. The Afro-Spanish American
Author.
    J. Hebert, 263(RIB):Vol31No2-277
    C.C. Rabassa, 238:Sep81-480
Jackson, R.L. The Art of Dostoevsky.
    M.V. Jones, 617(TLS):4Jun82-621
Jackson, R.L. Black Writers in Latin
America.
    M.K. Cobb, 238:May81-318
    L. King, 86(BHS):Apr81-156
Jackson, T., ed. Learning through Theatre.
    M.B., 214:Vol 10No37-122
Jackson, W. The Probable and the Marvel-
ous.*
    S.M. Tave, 677(YES):Vol 11-290
Jacob, F. The Possible and the Actual.
    P-L. Adams, 61:Apr82-110
    T. Ferris, 441:4Apr82-16
    M.F. Perutz, 617(TLS):24Sep82-1028
    J.M. Smith, 453(NYRB):13May82-41
Jacob, J.R. Robert Boyle and the English
Revolution.
    A.M.L., 125:Fall80-117
Jacob, M. The Dice Cup. (M. Brownstein,
ed)
    J. Saunders, 565:Vol22No3-62
    W.M. Spackman, 472:Spring/Summer81-233
Jacob, M. Lettres à Marcel Jouhandeau.
(A.S. Kimball, ed)
    D. Steel, 402(MLR):Apr81-478

Jacob, M.C. The Radical Enlightenment.
   M. Goldie, 566:Spring82-129
Jacob, S. Italienische Zeichnungen der
   Kunstbibliothek Berlin: Architektur und
   Dekoration 16. bis 18. Jahrhundert.
   H. Hager, 576:Mar81-69
Jacobi, K. Die Modalbegriffe in den logis-
   chen Schriften des Wilhelm von Shyres-
   wood und in anderen Kompendien des 12.
   und 13. Jahrhundert.
   P.V. Spade, 589:Oct81-878
Jacobs, C. The Dissimulating Harmony.
   D.B. Allison, 131(CL):Winter81-76
   B. Draine, 81:Spring-Fall81-425
Jacobs, D. The Magic of Woody Allen.
   G. Kaufman, 362:23and30Dec82-42
Jacobs, D.N. Borodin.*
   639(VQR):Autumn81-122
Jacobs, E. and others, eds. Woman and
   Society in Eighteenth-Century France.*
   P. Hoffmann, 535(RHL):Jul-Oct81-773
   R. Veasey, 402(MLR):Jul81-700
Jacobs, J. The Question of Separatism.*
   639(VQR):Spring81-63
Jacobsen, J. The Chinese Insomniacs.
   J.C. Oates, 441:4Apr82-13
Jacobson, D. The Story of the Stories.
   H. Bloom, 441:17Oct82-25
   D.J. Enright, 362:2Sep82-21
   D. Lodge, 617(TLS):5Nov82-1207
Jacobson, N. Pride and Solace.
   L.D. Spence, 480(P&R):Spring81-124
Jacobson, R., with others - see Trubetzkoy,
   N.S.
Jacobson, S. On the Use, Meaning and
   Syntax of English Preverbal Adverbs.*
   Factors Influencing the Placement of
   English Adverbs in Relation to Auxilia-
   ries.
   B.M.H. Strang, 597(SN):Vol53No1-184
Jacobus, M., ed. Women Writing and
   Writing About Women.
   A. Kolodny, 301(JEGP):Jul81-442
   E. Simmons, 184(EIC):Jul81-249
Jacques de Cambrai. Les Poésies du
   trouvère Jacques de Cambrai.* (J-C.
   Rivière, ed)
   T.H. Newcombe, 402(MLR):Jan81-180
   N. Wilkins, 208(FS):Jul81-313
Jaeger, C.S. Medieval Humanism in Gott-
   fried von Strassburg's "Tristan und
   Isolde."
   W. McConnell, 400(MLN):Apr81-689
Jaeger, P. - see Heidegger, M.
Jaffa, H.C. Modern Australian Poetry,
   1920-1970.*
   M. Duwell, 71(ALS):May81-135
Jaffa, H.V. How to Think About the
   American Revolution.
   J.S. Rubin, 106:Spring81-79
Jaffe, I.B. The Sculpture of Leonard
   Baskin.
   A. Berman, 55:Apr81-40
Jaffe, N.C. The Poet Swift.*
   M.E. Lawlis, 301(JEGP):Jan81-138
Jaffee, A.W. Adult Education.*
   J. Astor, 362:18Mar82-24
   E. Friedman, 461:Fall-Winter81/82-93
   C. Rumens, 617(TLS):5Mar82-246
Jaffke, F. Making Soft Toys.
   M. Cowan, 614:Fall81-18

Jäger, B. "Durch reimen gute lere geben"
   — Untersuchung zu Überlieferung und
   Rezeption Freidanks im Spätmittelalter.
   N.A. Perrin, 221(GQ):May81-338
"Jahrbuch des Wiener Goethe-Vereins."
   (Vols 81-83) (W. Martens and H. Zeman,
   eds)
   J. Müller, 680(ZDP):Band100Heft4-598
Jain, J. and J. Jain-Neubauer - see Goetz,
   H.
Jain, R.K. Soviet-South Asian Relations,
   1947-1978.* (Vols 1 and 2)
   C.H. Heimsath, 293(JASt):Feb81-407
Jakes, J. North and South.
   S. Altinel, 617(TLS):20Aug82-910
   M. Watkins, 441:7Mar82-24
Jakobson, R. Selected Writings. (Vol 5)
   (S. Rudy and M. Taylor, eds)
   R.D.B. Thomson, 575(SEER):Apr81-292
   205(FMLS):Oct80-377
Jakobson, R. and S. Rudy. Yeats's "Sorrow
   of Love" Through the Years.
   M.W. Bloomfield, 494:Autumn79-409
Jakobson, R. and L.R. Waugh. The Sound
   Shape of Language.*
   I. Fónagy and G. Kassai, 361:Oct/Nov81-
   221
   J. Graham, 153:Spring81-29
   D.H., 355(LSoc):Aug81-314
   G. Rappaport, 574(SEEJ):Fall81-94
   J. Vachek, 567:Vol33No3/4-301
James, A. The Death and Letters of Alice
   James.* (R.B. Yeazell, ed)
   L.Y. Gossett, 569(SR):Fall81-641
   J.V. Gunn, 27(AL):Jan82-750
   R.E. Long, 26(ALR):Spring81-139
   A. Niemtzow, 284:Fall81-65
James, B. Manuel de Falla and the Spanish
   Musical Renaissance.
   R. Crichton, 415:Feb81-107
James, B. The Bill James Baseball
   Abstract 1982.
   R. Yglesias, 441:23May82-3
James, C. The Crystal Bucket.*
   N. Berry, 364:Jun81-80
James, C. First Reactions.*
   W.H. Pritchard, 249(HudR):Spring81-117
   G. Woodcock, 569(SR):Fall81-611
James, C. From the Land of Shadows.
   T.J. Binyon, 617(TLS):7May81-506
James, D.E. Written Within and Without.*
   S. Pritchard, 447(N&Q):Dec80-551
James, D.W. St. David's and Dewisland.
   P. Stead, 617(TLS):29Jan82-116
James, E. Swans Reflecting Elephants.
   (G. Melly, ed)
   A. Forbes, 617(TLS):24Dec82-1411
   D.A.N. Jones, 362:22Jul82-21
James, E., ed. Visigothic Spain.*
   D.W. Lomax, 86(BHS):Jan81-76
James, G., C.G. Whitley and S. Bode. Lis-
   tening In and Speaking Out. (Interme-
   diate)
   D.D. Matthews, 608:Sep82-395
James, H. Henry James: Letters. (Vol 1)
   (L. Edel, ed)
   B. Richards, 184(EIC):Jan81-61
James, H. Henry James: Letters. (Vol 2)
   (L. Edel, ed)
   B. Richards, 184(EIC):Jan81-61
   D. Seed, 189(EA):Jan-Mar81-110

James, H. Henry James: Letters.* (Vol 3)
(L. Edel, ed)
    R.D. Bamberg, 284:Spring82-200
    J. Katz, 27(AL):Jan82-729
    D. Kirby, 573(SSF):Summer81-329
    R.E. Long, 26(ALR):Spring81-137
    639(VQR):Summer81-96
James, H. The Literary Criticism of Henry
James. (S.B. Daugherty, ed)
    R.E. Long, 26(ALR):Autumn81-300
James, H. Selected Literary Criticism.
(M. Shapira, ed)
    G. Hough, 208(FS):Oct81-466
James, H. The Tales of Henry James. (Vol
1) (M. Aziz, ed)
    A. Massa, 447(N&Q):Jun80-270
James, H. The Tales of Henry James. (Vol
2) (M. Aziz, ed)
    A.W. Bellringer, 677(YES):Vol 11-336
    A. Massa, 447(N&Q):Jun80-270
James, J.J. The Contractors of Chartres.
(Vol 1)(French title: Chartres, les
constructeurs.)
    S. Murray, 54:Mar81-149
    L.R. Shelby, 589:Apr81-395
James, N.D.G. A History of English For-
estry.
    S. Leathart, 617(TLS):8Jan82-36
James, P.D. The Skull Beneath the Skin.
    T. Sutcliffe, 617(TLS):29Oct82-1197
    J. Symons, 441:12Sep82-9
    442(NY):8Nov82-173
James, S.V. Colonial Rhode Island.
    J. Sainsbury, 106:Spring81-57
James, W. Essays in Philosophy. (F.H.
Burkhardt and I.K. Skrupskelis, eds)
    J.B., 543:Dec80-384
Jameson, F. Fables of Aggression.*
    D. Donoghue, 453(NYRB):29Apr82-28
    B. Hatlen, 295(JML):Vol8No3/4-555
    B. Lafourcade, 189(EA):Jan-Mar81-101
    B.J. Murray, 395(MFS):Summer80-307
    H.N. Schneidau, 405(MP):Nov81-220
Jameson, F. The Political Unconscious.*
    J. Alter, 188(ECr):Fall81-79
    W.E. Cain, 569(SR):Fall81-cxii
    R.W. Dasenbrock, 435:Fall81-307
    D. O'Hara, 659(ConL):Summer82-381
    M. Poster, 445(NCF):Sep81-252
    D. Punter, 141:Fall81-362
Jameson, S. Women Against Men. Company
Parade.
    N. Mitchison, 617(TLS):22Oct82-1175
Jamyn, A. Les Oeuvres poétiques: Livres
II, III et IV (1575).* (S.M. Carrington,
ed)
    M. Simonin, 535(RHL):Mar-Apr81-282
Janáček, L. Janáček: Leaves from His Life.
(V. and M. Tausky, eds and trans)
    442(NY):25Oct82-174
Janicaud, D. Hegel et le destin de la
Grèce.
    P. Garniron, 53(AGP):Band62Heft1-107
Janke, J. - see Szymborska, W.
Janke, W. Historische Dialektik.
    W. Steinbeck, 342:Band72Heft1-117
Jankélévitch, V. Le Je-ne-sais quoi et le
Presque-rien.
    M. Le Doeuff, 98:May80-474
Janni, P. Etnografia e mito.
    J. Desanges, 555:Vol54fasc2-387

Janning, J., H. Gehrts and H. Ossowski.
Vom Menschenbild im Märchen.
    E-D. Güting, 196:Band22Heft3/4-347
Janota, J., ed. Eine Wissenschaft etabl-
iert sich.
    U. Wyss, 684(ZDA):Band110Heft3-143
Jansen, M.B. Japan and Its World.*
    A. Iriye, 407(MN):Autumn81-347
    Uete Michiari, 285(JapQ):Jul-Sep81-428
Janson, H.W. - see Gilbert, C.E.
Janson, T. Mechanisms of Language Change
in Latin.
    P. Baldi, 215(GL):Summer81-120
    N. De Wandel, 350:Jun81-493
    B. Löfstedt, 439(NM):1980/3-347
Janssens de Bishoven, A., with M. Baes-
Dondeyne and D. De Vos. De Vlaamse
Primitieven, I. (3rd ed) (Vol 1)
    L. Campbell, 39:Nov81-352
Jantz, H. The Form of Faust.
    J.R. Williams, 402(MLR):Apr81-506
Janzen, R. Albrecht Altdorfer.
    M. Baxandall, 59:Dec81-484
"Japan's Dirty Old Man." (H.S. Levy and M.
Kawatani, trans)
    J.W. Schiffeler, 292(JAF):Apr-Jun81-
    234
Jara, R. and others. Diccionario de
términos e "ismos" literarios.
    R. de Gorog, 545(RPh):Feb81-345
Jarczyk, G. Système et liberté dans la
logique de Hegel.
    H. Faës, 542:Oct-Dec81-483
Jardin, P. La Bête à bon dieu.
    T. Greene, 207(FR):Dec81-304
Jarman, D. The Music of Alban Berg.*
    P.J.P., 412:Feb80-71
Jarman, M.R., G.N. Bailey and H.N. Jarman,
eds. Early European Agriculture.
    G.W. Dimbleby, 617(TLS):17Dec82-1400
Jarmatz, K., S. Barck and P. Diezel. Exil
in der UdSSR.
    G. Wenzel, 654(WB):7/1981-148
Jarnow, J.A., B. Judelle and M. Guerreiro.
Inside the Fashion Business. (3rd ed)
    P. Bach, 614:Spring82-14
Jarrell, R. Kipling, Auden & Co.*
    W. Pratt, 392:Fall81-477
    639(VQR):Winter81-16
Jarrell, R.A. and N.R. Ball, eds. Science,
Technology and Canadian History.
    I.D. Chapman, 298:Summer81-119
Jarry, A. Selected Works of Alfred Jarry.
(R. Shattuck and S.W. Taylor, eds)
    M. Heath, 214:Vol 10No37-124
Jarry, A. Ubu. (N. Arnaud and H. Bordil-
lon, eds)
    K.S. Beaumont, 208(FS):Jan81-93
Jarvis, A.C., R. Lebredo and F. Mena.
Basic Spanish Grammar.
    R.W. Hatton, 238:Sep81-490
    C. Stansfield, 399(MLJ):Summer81-222
Jarvis, C.E. Visions of Kerouac.
    D. Stanley, 649(WAL):Summer81-138
Jarvis, G.A. and others. Connaître et se
connaître. (2nd ed)
    R. Danner, 207(FR):Apr81-774
Jarvis, G.A. and others. Vivent les
Différences. (2nd ed)
    A.S. Caprio, 207(FR):Dec81-283
Jarvis, G.A. and S.J. Adams. Evaluating a
Second Language Program.
    T.D. Terrell, 399(MLJ):Autumn81-327

Jasen, D.A.   P.G. Wodehouse.
   B. Brophy, 362:30Sep82-17
Jasen, D.A. - see Jerome, J.K.
Jasen, D.A. - see McCutcheon, G.B.
Jasen, D.A. - see Wodehouse, P.G.
Jasen, D₂A. and J. Tichenor.   Rags and Rag-
   time.
   R. Riddle, 187:Sep82-471
Jasinski, B.W. - see Madame de Staël
Jasmin, C.   La Sablière.
   E-M. Kroller, 102(CanL):Spring81-93
Jaspers, G.J.   Stephan von Landskron.
   N.F. Palmer, 447(N&Q):Oct80-480
Jaspers, K.   Philosophische Autobiographie.
   H.A.D., 543:Dec80-386
Jastrow, R.   The Enchanted Loom.*
   S.J. Gould, 453(NYRB):15Apr82-26
   R.M. Restak, 441:7Mar82-6
Jaulin, R.   Mon Thibaud ou le jeu de vivre.
   J. Duvignaud, 450(NRF):Jan81-152
Jauss, H.R.   Aesthetische Erfahrung und
   literarische Hermeneutik.   (Vol 1)
   D. Barnouw, 494:Summer80-213
Jauss, H.R.   Alterität und Modernität der
   mittelalterlichen Literatur.*
   H. Kolb, 72:Band217Heft1-158
Javitch, D.   Poetry and Courtliness in
   Renaissance England.*
   S.J. Greenblatt, 677(YES):Vol 11-229
Jávor, K., I. Küllös and Z. Tátrai, eds.
   Kis magyar néprajz a Rádióban.
   A. Scheiber, 196:Band21Heft1/2-124
Jay, E.   The Religion of the Heart.*
   H.R. Harrington, 637(VS):Winter81-232
   S. Nash, 301(JEGP):Apr81-262
   G.B. Tennyson, 445(NCF):Jun80-117
Jayadevá.   Love Song of the Dark Lord:
   Jayadeva's "Gītagovinda."*   (B.S. Miller,
   ed and trans)
   N.E. Falk, 314:Winter-Spring81-223
Jaynes, J.   The Origin of Consciousness in
   the Breakdown of the Bicameral Mind.
   P.A. Pilkonis, 480(P&R):Spring81-127
Jayyusi, S.K.   Trends and Movements in
   Modern Arabic Poetry.
   T.M. Johnstone, 318(JAOS):Apr/Jun80-
   142
Jazayery, M.A., E.C. Polomé and W. Winter,
   eds.   Linguistic and Literary Studies in
   Honor of Archibald A. Hill.   (Vols 1-3)
   205(FMLS):Jan80-90
Jazayery, M.A., E.C. Polomé and W. Winter,
   eds.   Linguistic and Literary Studies in
   Honor of Archibald A. Hill.*   (Vol 4)
   R. Dirven, 277(ITL):No47-81
   205(FMLS):Jan80-90
"Jazz Forschung 10."   (A. Dauer and F.
   Kerschbaumer, eds)
   M. Harrison, 415:Jun81-387
Jean, M. - see Arp, J.
Jean-Richard, P.   L'Oeuvre Gravé de
   François Boucher dans le collection
   Edmond de Rothschild.*
   B. Scott, 39:Jan81-61
Jeanne, M.   La Chasse au racoon.
   M.G. Paulson, 207(FR):Apr82-705
Jeanneret, M.   La Lettre perdue.*
   A. Fairlie, 402(MLR):Apr81-472
Jeannière, A. - see Heraclitus
Jeanson, F.   Sartre and the Problem of
   Morality.
   R.E. Santoni, 258:Sep81-333

Jeauneau, E.   Quatre thèmes érigéniens.
   T.M. Tomasic, 589:Jan81-142
Jech, J. - see Němcová, B.
Jech, T.   Set Theory.
   K.J. Devlin, 316:Dec81-876
Jechova, H. and M-F. Vieuille, eds and
   trans.   Anthologie de la poésie baroque
   tchèque.
   G. Mathieu-Castellani, 549(RLC):Jul-
   Dec81-487
Jedrey, C.M.   The World of John Cleave-
   land.*
   P. Drummey, 432(NEQ):Mar81-129
Jeffares, A.N., ed.   W.B. Yeats: The Criti-
   cal Heritage.
   J. Kelly, 447(N&Q):Dec80-564
Jeffares, A.N.   Yeats, Sligo and Ireland.
   R. Burnham, 305(JIL):Sep81-112
Jeffares, A.N. and A.S. Knowland.   A Com-
   mentary on the Collected Plays of W.B.
   Yeats.
   A.V.C. Schmidt, 447(N&Q):Aug80-380
Jeffares, B.   The Artist in Nineteenth Cen-
   tury English Fiction.
   N. Auerbach, 445(NCF):Mar81-555
Jefferies, A.   Among the Living.
   G. Bitcon, 581:Dec81-469
Jeffers, R.   What Odd Expedients and Other
   Poems.   (R.I. Scott, ed)
   L.C. Powell, 50(ArQ):Winter81-377
Jeffers, R.J. and I. Lehiste.   Principles
   and Methods for Historical Linguistics.*
   J. Aitchison, 353:Vol 18No5/6-560
Jefferson, A.   The Nouveau Roman and the
   Poetics of Fiction.*
   C. Krance, 405(MP):May82-454
   V. Minogue, 208(FS):Oct81-487
   B.T. Rahv, 207(FR):Mar82-558
   B. Stoltzfus, 188(ECr):Winter81-115
Jefferson, A. and D. Robey, eds.   Modern
   Literary Theory.
   C. Norris, 617(TLS):11Jun82-628
Jefferson, G.   Edward Garnett.
   R. Blythe, 362:29Apr82-19
   H. Lee, 617(TLS):4Jun82-604
Jeffrey, R.   Chess in the Mirror.
   M.B., 214:Vol 10No37-119
Jeffrey, R., ed.   People, Princes and
   Paramount Power.
   D.A. Washbrook, 293(JASt):May81-634
Jeffreys-Jones, R.   Violence and Reform in
   American History.
   G. Adams, Jr., 106:Fall81-245
Jeffri, J.   The Emerging Art.
   P.E. Aarons, 476:Vol 11-132
Jeffries, R.   Class, Power and Ideology in
   Ghana.
   J. Silver, 69:Vol50No2-230
Jehasse, L.   Salamine de Chypre.   (Vol 8)
   B.A. Sparkes, 303(JoHS):Vol 101-214
Jehmlich, R.   Science Fiction.
   M. Nagl, 196:Band22Heft3/4-350
Jelinek, E.C., ed.   Women's Autobiogra-
   phy.*
   T.R. Smith, 249(HudR):Summer81-293
   M.D. Uroff, 301(JEGP):Jul81-440
Jelinek, H.   Madame le Président de la
   République française.
   N. Aronson, 207(FR):Apr82-706
Jenaczek, F. - see Weinheber, J.
Jencks, C.   Late Modern Architecture.
   R. Banham, 46:Jan81-64

179

Jodogne, P., ed. Antonio Alamanni, "Commedia della conversione di Santa Maria Maddalena."
F. Bruni, 545(RPh):Aug80-132
Joes, A.J. Mussolini.
M. Kempton, 453(NYRB):7Oct82-19
Johannessen, K.S. and T. Nordenstam, eds. Wittgenstein: Aesthetics and Transcendental Philosophy.
B.R. Tilghman, 290(JAAC):Summer82-444
Johannesson, H-E. Studier i Lars Gyllenstens estetik.*
B. Lide, 563(SS):Summer81-363
Johannesson, K. Saxo Grammaticus.
J. Martínez-Pizarro, 589:Apr81-398
Johannesson, N-L. The English Modal Auxiliaries.*
P. Westney, 257(IRAL):Feb81-81
Johansen, H.B. Stendhal et le roman.
P. Berthier, 535(RHL):May-Jun81-470
Johansen, R.C. The National Interest and the Human Interest.
R. Ranger, 529(QQ):Winter81-812
Johanson, D.C. and M.A. Edey. Lucy.*
J.S. Weiner, 617(TLS):29Jan82-102
Johansson, S. Some Aspects of the Vocabulary of Learned and Scientific English.
G.B., 189(EA):Apr-Jun81-238
N. Davis, 541(RES):May81-198
Johansson, S. Studies of Error Gravity.*
A. Chesterman, 439(NM):1980/1-90
John of Salisbury. The Letters of John of Salisbury. (Vol 2) (W.J. Millor and C.N.L. Brooke, eds)
M. Chibnall, 382(MAE):1981/1-123
R.E. Pepin, 589:Apr81-415
J.E. Sayers, 325:Apr81-429
John, N., ed. English National Opera Guides.* (Vols 1-4)
P. Howard, 415:Mar81-177
Johnsen, A.O. and P. King, eds. The Tax Book of the Cistercian Order.
D.S. Buczek, 589:Apr81-454
Johnson, A.L. Sign and Structure in the Poetry of T.S. Eliot.
G. Chesters, 494:Autumn79-405
Johnson, B. The Critical Difference.
D. Bleich, 188(ECr):Fall81-97
L. Mackinnon, 617(TLS):8Jan82-34
R.E. Palmer, 478:Fall81-244
P.T. Starr, 400(MLN):Dec81-1163
639(VQR):Summer81-84
Johnson, B. Défigurations du langage poétique.
W.T. Bandy, 207(FR):Mar82-555
E.K. Kaplan, 210(FrF):Sep81-284
C. Lang, 131(CL):Fall81-394
M. Whitford, 208(FS):Jan81-85
Johnson, B.L.C. Pakistan.
W.E. Gustafson, 293(JASt):Nov80-168
Johnson, C. MITI and the Japanese Miracle.
R.B. Reich, 453(NYRB):24Jun82-37
Johnson, C. Oxherding Tale.
442(NY):20Dec82-138
Johnson, C. - see under "The Life and Adventures of Capt. John Avery (1709?)"
Johnson, D. The Incognito Lounge and Other Poems.
A. Williamson, 441:10Oct82-30
Johnson, D. Lying Low.*
B. Rosecrance, 473(PR):4/1981-639
Johnson, D. Terrorists and Novelists.
B. De Mott, 441:31Oct82-12

Johnson, D.B. - see Lotman, Y.
Johnson, D.C. American Art Nouveau.
G.W.R. Ward, 658:Spring81-115
62:Feb81-72
Johnson, D.G. The Medieval Chinese Oligarchy.
B.E. Wallacker, 318(JAOS):Jan/Mar80-93
Johnson, D.L. and G. Landow. Fantastic Illustration and Design in Great Britain, 1850-1930.*
C. Cannon-Brookes, 39:Apr81-273
S.H. Goodacre, 283:Spring81-48
Johnson, D.R. Policing the Urban Underworld.
M. Fellman, 106:Winter81-323
Johnson, E. Charles Dickens.
M. Andrews, 161(DUJ):Jun81-257
Johnson, E.C. Oscar W. Underwood.
B. Brandon, 9(AlaR):Jul81-218
Johnson, F. Out of Order.
A. Howard, 362:28Oct82-26
C. Moore, 617(TLS):24Dec82-1431
Johnson, F. - see "Rockwell Kent: An Anthology of His Work"
Johnson, H.J., J.J. Leach and R.G. Muehlmann, eds. Revolutions, Systems, and Theories.
D.R., 185:Jan81-350
Johnson, J. Maroni de Chypre.
M. Popham, 123:Vol31No1-139
Johnson, J.T. Just War Tradition and the Restraint of War.
G. Best, 617(TLS):19Feb82-175
Johnson, J.W. - see Dennis, J.
Johnson, L. The Cultural Critics.*
R.H. Hagman, 185:Jan81-307
G. Merle, 189(EA):Apr-Jun81-205
S. Trombley, 541(RES):Aug81-365
Johnson, L. Onion.
A. Baysting, 368:Dec73-355
Johnson, L. The Paintings of Eugène Delacroix.
J. Whiteley, 90:Dec81-750
Johnson, L.A. Mary Hallock Foote.
S. Armitage, 26(ALR):Spring81-146
J.H. Maguire, 649(WAL):Spring81-83
Johnson, M. The Borgias.
442(NY):8Feb82-130
Johnson, M.K. and D.K. Hilton. Japanese Prints Today.
R.G. Robertson, 407(MN):Autumn81-361
Johnson, N. You Can Go Home Again.
A. Adams, 441:7Nov82-14
Johnson, N.R. Louis XIV and the Age of the Enlightenment.*
J.H. Brumfitt, 208(FS):Jan81-73
Johnson, O.A. Skepticism and Cognitivism.*
R.W. Newell, 393(Mind):Jan81-137
D. Odegard, 154:Mar81-171
Johnson, P. Pope John Paul II and the Catholic Restoration.
C.C. O'Brien, 362:25Feb82-20
Johnson, P. and B. Cazelles. Le vain siècle guerpir.
K.A. Knutsen, 207(FR):Apr81-730
K.D. Uitti, 402(MLR):Apr81-458
R. Vermette, 589:Jan81-144
Johnson, P.D. Prayer, Patronage and Power.
C.N.L. Brooke, 617(TLS):16Apr82-445
Johnson, R. Ark: The Foundations.
W. Harmon, 472:Spring/Summer81-217

Johnson, R.E. Peasant and Proletariat.
R.H. Rowland, 104(CASS):Winter81-596
A. Wildman, 550(RusR):Jan81-63
Johnson, R.H. and J.A. Blair. Logical
Self-Defense.
A.S. Carson, 154:Jun81-403
Johnson, R.R. Adjustment to Empire.
J.R. Pole, 617(TLS):14May82-537
Johnson, S. Samuel Johnson: Selected
Poetry and Prose.* (F. Brady and W.K.
Wimsatt, eds)
F.M. Keener, 402(MLR):Jan81-165
Johnson, S. Johnson's Dictionary: A
Modern Selection. (E.L. McAdam and G.
Milne, eds)
P. Rogers, 617(TLS):3Sep82-936
Johnson, S. Later Roman Britain.
P. Bartholomew, 123:Vol31No1-94
Johnson, S. The Marburg Virus.
S. Brook, 617(TLS):16Apr82-446
Johnson, S. Walk a Winter Beach.
N. Callendar, 441:7Nov82-39
Johnson, S. The Works of Samuel Johnson.*
(Vol 10: Political Writings.) (D.J.
Greene, ed)
D. Crane, 179(ES):Aug81-387
Johnson, S. The Works of Samuel Johnson.*
(Vol 14: Sermons.) (J.H. Hagstrum and J.
Gray, eds)
M.C. Battestin, 677(YES):Vol 11-281
J.T. Boulton, 541(RES):Feb81-86
D. Crane, 179(ES):Aug81-387
Johnson, T.W. and J. Crime Fiction Criti-
cism.
354:Dec81-368
Johnson, U.E. American Prints and Print-
makers.
R. Broner, 62:Jan81-63
Johnson, W.C. Milton Criticism.*
R. Lejosne, 189(EA):Apr Jun81-221
Johnson-Davies, D., ed and trans. Egyp-
tian Short Stories.
F.X. Paz, 294:Vol 11-117
Johnston, A.F. and M. Rogerson, eds.
Records of Early English Drama: York.*
B.B. Adams, 551(RenQ):Summer80-278
B. Dobson, 539:Feb82-47
C. Gauvin, 189(EA):Apr-Jun81-210
Johnston, A.W. Trademarks on Greek Vases.
J. Boardman, 123:Vol31No1-139
R.M. Cook, 303(JoHS):Vol 101-224
Johnston, B. To the Third Empire.
C. Leland, 397(MD):Dec81-564
J. Templeton, 563(SS):Autumn81-494
T.F. Van Laan, 130:Spring81-72
Johnston, C. Talk About the Last Poet.*
G. Annan, 362:8Apr82-20
Johnston, G., ed and trans. Rocky Shores.*
H. Brønner, 563(SS):Autumn81-479
Johnston, M.P. and G. Kaufman. Designs on
Fabrics. (2nd ed)
P. Bach, 614:Summer81-18
Johnston, P.A. Vergil's Agricultural
Golden Age.
J. Griffin, 123:Vol31No1-23
Johnston, R.C. - see Fantosme, J.
Johnston, W. The Mirror Mind.
G. Jantzen, 617(TLS):18Jun82-679
Johnstone, H.W., Jr. Validity and Rheto-
ric in Philosophical Argument.*
M.A.F., 543:Sep80-143
Johnstone, R. The Will to Believe.
J. Newman, 617(TLS):22Oct82-1173

Johnstone, T.M. Ḥarsūsi Lexicon and
English-Ḥarsūsi Word-List.
P. Swiggers, 353:Vol 18No9/10-939
de Joia, A. and A. Stenton, comps. Terms
in Systemic Linguistics.
A.D. Grimshaw, 350:Sep81-769
Joly, A., ed. Grammaire générative trans-
formationnelle et psychomécanique du
langage.
N. Stenson, 353:Vol 18No3/4-347
Joly, A. and W. Hirtle, eds. Langage et
psychomécanique du langage.
L.G. Kelly, 350:Dec82-945
Joly, A. and J. Stéfanini, eds. La Gram-
maire générale des modistes aux idéo-
logues.*
K.D. Uitti, 545(RPh):Nov80-222
Jonas, H. Das Prinzip Verantwortung.
O.P. Obermeier, 489(PJGG):Band88Heft2-
426
Jonas, I.B. Thomas Mann and Italy.*
K.J. Fickert, 395(MFS):Summer80-359
Jonas, K.W. and others, comps. Die Thomas-
Mann-Literatur.* (Vol 2)
H. Lehnert, 221(GQ):Jan81-102
J.H. Petersen, 680(ZDP):Band99Heft2-
296
Jones, A.G. Tomorrow is Another Day.
H. McNeil, 617(TLS):6Aug82-867
Jones, A.J. Game Theory.
D.S., 185:Oct81-196
Jones, B. The Island Normal.*
P. Mills, 493:Jun81-63
L. Sail, 565:Vol22No1-66
Jones, B. and M.V. Dixon. The Macmillan
Dictionary of Biography.
W. Haley, 617(TLS):4Jun82-606
Jones, B.W. Domitian and the Senatorial
Order.
B.M. Levick, 123:Vol31No1-93
Jones, C.W. Saint Nicholas of Myra, Bari,
and Manhattan.^
F.J. Coppa, 77:Fall81-365
Jones, D. The Dying Gaul and Other Writ-
ings.* (H. Grisewood, ed) Dai Great-
coat. (R. Hague, ed)
W.J. Keith, 627(UTQ):Spring81-330
Jones, D. Everyman's English Pronouncing
Dictionary.* (14th ed rev by A.C. Gim-
son)
K. Hansen, 682(ZPSK):Band33Heft2-247
W. Sauer, 38:Band99Heft1/2-189
F. Zaic, 224(GRM):Band30Heft2-243
Jones, D. Introducing David Jones.* (J.
Matthias, ed)
W. Blissett, 651(WHR):Spring81-79
T. Dilworth, 219(GaR):Summer81-437
W.J. Keith, 627(UTQ):Spring81-330
Jones, D. Letters to William Hayward.*
(C. Wilcockson, ed)
N. Jacobs, 541(RES):May81-241
W.J. Keith, 627(UTQ):Spring81-330
Jones, D. The Roman Quarry.* (H. Grise-
wood and R. Hague, eds)
G. Davenport, 441:17Oct82-9
Jones, D.C. The Barefoot Brigade.
M.L. Settle, 441:3Oct82-9
Jones, D.C. Elkhorn Tavern.
639(VQR):Spring81-61
Jones, D.F. Jean de Campistron.*
A. Blanc, 535(RHL):Jul-Oct81-770
C.J. Gossip, 402(MLR):Jan81-185

Jones, D.G. Under the Thunder the Flowers Light Up the Earth.*
  E.D. Blodgett, 102(CanL):Spring80-99
Jones, D.R., ed. Soviet Armed Forces Review Annual. (Vol 3)
  P.H. Vigor, 575(SEER):Jan81-150
Jones, G. Times Like These.
  P. Lewis, 565:Vol22No3-55
Jones, G.D. and R.R. Kautz, eds. The Transition to Statehood in the New World.
  N. Hammond, 617(TLS):26Nov82-1323
Jones, H.G., comp. Hispanic Manuscripts and Printed Books in the Barberini Collection.
  C.B. Faulhaber, 545(RPh):Feb81(supp)-369
Jones, H.G. Local Government Records.
  N. Olsberg, 14:Summer80-376
Jones, H.J. Live Machines.
  D. Roden, 293(JASt):May81-604
Jones, I.G. Explorations and Explanations.
  K.O. Morgan, 617(TLS):19Feb82-196
Jones, J. Soldiers of Light and Love.
  R.N. Current, 9(AlaR):Jul81-231
  639(VQR):Spring81-52
Jones, J. and E. The Book of Bread.
  M. Sheraton, 441:5Dec82-66
Jones, J.F., Jr. "La Nouvelle Héloïse."*
  J.S. Spink, 208(FS):Oct81-450
Jones, J.G. Tales and Teachings of the Buddha.
  J.P. McDermott, 293(JASt):Nov80-169
Jones, J.L. Adam's Dream.
  R. Bonaccorso, 174(Éire):Spring81-152
Jones, J.P. Thomas More.
  S. Gresham, 577(SHR):Winter81-75
  J.B. Trapp, 677(YES):Vol 11-230
Jones, L. Cwmardy. We Live.
  P. Lewis, 565:Vol22No3-55
Jones, L.E. The "Cort d'Amor."*
  L.M. Paterson, 208(FS):Oct81-425
Jones, M. Season of a Strangler.
  C. Rose, 598(SoR):Summer82-678
Jones, M. Two Women and Their Man.
  J. Mellors, 362:11Mar82-23
Jones, O. Chinese Design and Pattern.
  P. Bach, 614:Fall82-14
Jones, P. D'un espace renoué.
  F.C. St. Aubyn, 207(FR):Mar82-570
Jones, P. and M. Schmidt, eds. British Poetry Since 1970.*
  V. Young, 249(HudR):Spring81-141
Jones, R. Camus: "L'Étranger" and "La Chute."
  J. Cruickshank, 208(FS):Oct81-483
Jones, R.O. and C.R. Lee - see del Encina, J.
Jones, S. Alfonsina Storni.*
  C. Freixas, 238:Mar81-159
Jones, T.B. In the Twilight of Antiquity.*
  E.D. Hunt, 123:Vol31No2-313
Jones, W.M., ed. The Present State of Scholarship in Sixteenth-Century Literature.*
  W.J. Beck, 207(FR):Mar82-544
de Jonge, A. Fire and Water.*
  M. Raeff, 550(RusR):Jan81-58
de Jonge, A. The Life and Times of Grigorii Rasputin.
  E. Crankshaw, 453(NYRB):27May82-12
  R. Massie, 441:18Apr82-32
  N. Mosley, 362:10Jun82-22

de Jonge, P. Philological and Historical Commentary on Ammianus Marcellinus XVIII.
  R. Browning, 123:Vol31No2-296
Jonin, P. - see "La Chanson de Roland"
Jönsjö, J. Studies on Middle English Nicknames. (Vol 1)
  E.C. Smith, 424:Mar80-89
Jonson, B. Bartholmew Fair.* (G. Hibbard, ed)
  J.E. Neufeld, 627(UTQ):Summer81-107
Jonson, B. Ben Jonson's Plays and Masques. (R.M. Adams, ed)
  J. Kelly, 568(SCN):Summer-Fall181-43
Jonson, B. Three by Ben Jonson. (J. Price, ed)
  D.L. Russell, 568(SCN):Summer-Fall181-43
Jonsson, B.R., S. Solheim and E. Danielson, eds. The Types of the Scandinavian Medieval Ballad.*
  P.J. Frankis, 447(N&Q):Jun80-286
  D.K. Wilgus, 187:May82-323
Jónsson, J.H. Das Partizip Perfekt der schwachen "ja"-Verben.
  J.E. Cathey, 563(SS):Winter81-83
de Joode, T. and A. Stolk. The Backyard Bestiary.
  S.D. Smith, 441:5Dec82-64
Joós, E., ed. Scolastique.
  J.A. Trentman, 627(UTQ):Summer81-208
Joost-Gaugier, C.L., ed. Jacopo Bellini — Selected Drawings.
  J.B. Shaw, 39:Sep81-203
Jordan, B. The Athenian Navy in the Classical Period.
  F.D. Harvey, 123:Vol31No1-83
Jordan, H. Crisis.
  J. Fallows, 453(NYRB):16Dec82-3
  R. Sherrill, 441:3Oct82-1
  442(NY):25Oct82-171
Jordan, L. - see von Droste-Hülshoff, A.
Jordan, M.V. De ta soeur, Sara Riel.
  D. Morton, 627(UTQ):Summer81-204
Jordan, N. The Past.*
  W. Boyd, 364:Apr/May81-129
  P. Craig, 617(TLS):13Aug82-888
Jordan, S.D. Ludwig Ferdinand Huber (1764-1804).
  S.L. Cocalis, 406:Fall81-349
Jordan, T.G. Trails to Texas.
  L. Milazzo, 584(SWR):Autumn81-413
Jordan, W.C. Louis IX and the Challenge of the Crusade.*
  J.A. Brundage, 377:Mar81-54
  N. Housley, 382(MAE):1981/1-186
  G.M. Spiegel, 589:Jan81-147
Jordens, A-M. The Stenhouse Circle.*
  R. Wilson, 67:May81-113
Jorstad, E. The Politics of Moralism.
  R.B., 185:Apr82-582
José. Finding the Sky.
  P. Varner, 649(WAL):Fall81-241
Joseph, K. and J. Sumption. Equality.
  R.J. Delahunty, 161(DUJ):Jun81-268
Josephus. Josèphe, Guerre des Juifs. (Bk 1) (A. Pelletier, ed and trans)
  M.A. Beek, 394:Vol34fasc1/2-164
Joshi, A. The Last Labyrinth.
  H.R.F. Keating, 617(TLS):6Aug82-863
Josipovici, G. - see Blanchot, M.
Josselson, M. and D. The Commander.*
  C. Duffy, 575(SEER):Jan81-104
  A. McConnell, 550(RusR):Apr81-187

Kadhani, M. and M. Zimunya, eds. And Now
the Poets Speak.
  C. Style, 362:18Mar82-23
Kadish, D.Y. Practices of the New Novel
in Claude Simon's "L'Herbe" and "La
Route des Flandres."
  S.J. Fajardo, 207(FR):May81-881
  A. Thiher, 395(MFS):Summer80-352
Kael, P. 5001 Nights at the Movies.
  S. Farber, 441:14Nov82-9
Kaempf-Dimitriadou, S. Die Liebe der Göt-
ter in der attischen Kunst des 5. Jahr-
hunderts v. Chr.*
  S. Woodford, 303(JoHS):Vol 101-221
Kaes, A., ed. Kino-Debatte.*
  H. Kreuzer, 133:Band14Heft1-92
Kafitz, D. Figurenkonstellation als
Mittel der Wirklichkeitserfassung.
  L.A. Lensing, 221(GQ):May81-363
Kafka, F. Letters to Ottla and the
Family. (N.N. Glatzer, ed)
  J. Atlas, 441:17Jan82-1
  V.S. Pritchett, 453(NYRB):4Feb82-6
  442(NY):1Feb82-132
Kafka, F. Oeuvres complètes. (Vol 2) (C.
David, ed)
  J. Borel, 450(NRF):Apr81-150
Kagan, D. The Peace of Nicias and the
Sicilian Expedition.
  R. Seager, 617(TLS):25Jun82-703
Kagan, J., R.B. Kearsley and P.R. Zelazo.
Infancy.
  G.R. Lowe, 529(QQ):Spring81-13
Kagan, M.S., ed. Vorlesungen zur Geschich-
te der Ästhetik.
  K. Schimmelpfennig, 654(WB):6/1981-175
Kagan, R.L. Lawsuits and Litigants in
Castile 1500-1700.
  H.G. Koenigsberger, 617(TLS):1Jan82-17
Kaganoff, N.M. and M.I. Urofsky, eds.
"Turn to the South."
  B. Gitenstein, 392:Winter80/81-69
Kagle, S.E. American Diary Literature:
1620-1799.*
  R.C. Davis, 106:Winter81-301
Kähler, H., ed. Handbuch der Oriental-
istic. (Section 3, Vol 2, Pt 1)
  A.J.W. Huisman, 318(JAOS):Jul/Sep80-
  353
Kahn, C.H., ed and trans. The Art and
Thought of Heraclitus.
  M.F. Burnyeat, 453(NYRB):13May82-45
  A.R. Lacey, 518:Apr81-80
  E. des Places, 555:Vol54fasc2-342
  M.R. Wright, 123:Vol131No1-53
Kahn, H. The Coming Boom.
  J. Epstein, 453(NYRB):23Sep82-17
  P. Passell, 441:12Sep82-15
  442(NY):13Sep82-174
Kahn, R. The Seventh Game.
  D. Okrent, 441:25Jul82-10
Kahr, M.M. Dutch Painting in the Seven-
teenth Century.
  Å. Bengtsson, 341:Vol150No3-151
Kahrl, W.L., ed. The California Water
Atlas.
  J.G. Dunne, 453(NYRB):21Oct82-6
Kahrl, W.L. Water and Power.
  J.G. Dunne, 453(NYRB):21Oct82-6
  B. Stein, 441:11Jul82-12
Kaikō, T. Into a Black Sun.*
  Tokumoto Mitsumasa, 285(JapQ):
  Apr-Jun81-290

Kaimio, J. The Romans and the Greek Lan-
guage.
  A.M. Devine and L.D. Stephens, 350:
  Mar82-211
Kainz, H.P. Ethica Dialectica.
  J.P. Dobel, 185:Jan81-313
Kaiser, G. and F.A. Kittler. Dichtung als
Sozialisationsspiel.
  J. Link, 490:Band12Heft2-268
Kaiser, G.R. Einführung in die Vergleich-
ende Literaturwissenschaft.
  W. Schröder, 654(WB):11/1981-171
Kaiser, R.G. and H.J. Russia from the
Inside.
  J.W. Strong, 529(QQ):Winter81-805
Kaivola-Bregenhøj, A. The Nominativus
Absolutus Formula.*
  S.F. Sanderson, 203:Vol91No2-245
Kajima, M. The Diplomacy of Japan, 1894-
1922. (Vol 3)
  H. Conroy, 407(MN):Spring81-101
Kalb, M.G. The Congo Cables.
  J.S. Whitaker, 441:27Jun82-7
Kaldor, M. The Baroque Arsenal.*
  M. Howard, 617(TLS):16Apr82-427
Kaldor, M. and D. Smith, eds. Disarming
Europe.
  C.M. Woodhouse, 617(TLS):24Sep82-1030
Kallen, L. C.B. Greenfield: No Lady in
the House.
  T.J. Binyon, 617(TLS):29Oct82-1196
  N. Callendar, 441:18Apr82-20
Kalman, R., ed. A Collection of Canadian
Plays. (Vol 5)
  A. Messenger, 102(CanL):Summer80-111
  J. Noonan, 529(QQ):Spring81-190
Kalman, R. and others, eds. A Collection
of Canadian Plays. (Vols 1-4)
  A. Messenger, 102(CanL):Summer80-111
Kalsi, M-L.S. - see Meinong, A.
Kalstone, D. Five Temperaments.*
  R. Langbaum, 473(PR):1/1981-151
Kaluza, I. The Functioning of Sentence
Structure in the Stream-of-Consciousness
Technique of William Faulkner's "The
Sound and the Fury."
  T.L. McHaney, 395(MFS):Winter80/81-654
Kalverkämper, H. Textlinguistik der
Eigennamen.*
  H. and R. Kahane, 545(RPh):Feb81(supp)-
  19
  R. Wimmer, 353:Vol 18No7/8-749
Kalwies, H.H. Hugues Salel.
  F. Rigolot, 207(FR):Mar81-590
Kam-po, C. - see under Chan Kam-po
Kamenka, E. and A.E-S. Tay, eds. Justice.
  D. Browne, 63:Mar81-126
  M.H. Lessnoff, 518:Oct81-234
Kamerbeek, J.C. The Plays of Sophocles:
Commentaries.* (Pt 3: The Antigone.)
  D.A. Hester, 394:Vol34fasc1/2-157
  H. Lloyd-Jones, 123:Vol131No2-173
Kamerbeek, J.C. The Plays of Sophocles:
Commentaries. (Pt 6: The Philoctetes.)
  H. Lloyd-Jones, 123:Vol131No2-173
Kaminsky, S. Never Cross A Vampire.
  639(VQR):Winter81-22
Kamm, L. The Object in Zola's "Rougon-
Macquart."*
  C.B. Jennings, 627(UTQ):Spring81-323
  C. Smethurst, 208(FS):Jan81-86
Kammen, M. Colonial New York.
  J. Sainsbury, 106:Spring81-57

Kammen, M., ed. The Past Before Us.
639(VQR):Winter81-8
Kammen, M. A Season of Youth.*
H. Green, 658:Winter81-343
Kanafani, G. Men in the Sun and other
Palestinian Stories.
G. Bowder, 294:Vol 11-120
Kanazawa, H. Japanese Ink Painting: Early
Zen Masterpieces.
M. Hickman, 407(MN):Spring81-103
Kandinsky, V. Kandinsky: Die Gesammelten
Schriften. (Vol 1) (H.K. Roethel and J.
Hahl-Koch, eds)
S. Selwood, 90:Nov81-685
P. Vergo, 135:Jul81-166
Kandinsky, W. Sounds.*
T. Phillips, 148:Winter81-79
Kanellos, N. and J.A. Huerta, eds. Nuevos
Pasos.
S.D. Elizondo, 238:Mar81-165
Kanin, G. Cordelia?
P-L. Adams, 61:Aug82-94
J. Coleman, 441:22Aug82-10
Kant, I. Anthropologie in pragmatischer
Absicht. (K. Vorländer, ed)
W. Steinbeck, 342:Band72Heft3-380
Kant, I. Briefwechsel. (O. Schöndörffer,
ed)
R. Cadenbach, 53(AGP):Band62Heft1-96
Kant, I. Crítica de la Razón Práctica.
(4th ed) (J. Rovira Armengol, trans;
A. Klein, ed)
M. Caimi, 342:Band72Heft2-206
Kant, I. Crítica de la Razón Pura. (new
ed) (Vol 1 trans by J. del Perojo, Vol
2 trans by J. Rovira Armengol; both ed
by A. Klein)
M. Caimi, 342:Band72Heft2-204
Kant, I. Critica della ragion pura. (V.
Mathieu, ed)
F. Pfurtscheller, 342:Band71Heft4 509
Kant, I. Fondements de la Métaphysique
des moeurs. (V. Delbos, trans; A.
Philonenko, ed)
L. Guillermit, 542:Jul-Sep81-374
J. Kopper, 342:Band72Heft2-205
Kant, I. Grundlegung zur Metaphysik der
Sitten. (T. Valentiner, ed) Kritik der
praktischen Vernunft. (J. Kopper, ed)
R. Malter, 342:Band71Heft3-379
Kant, I. Kant's Gesammelte Schriften.
[Akademie der Wissenschaften der DDR]
(Vol 27)
J. Kopper, 342:Band71Heft1-127
Kant, I. Kritik der praktischen Vernunft.
(M. Thom, ed)
R. Malter, 342:Band72Heft4-515
Kant, I. Lectures on Philosophical Theol-
ogy.* (A.W. Wood, ed)
K. Ward, 518:Apr81-100
Kant, I. Prolegomena zu einer jeden künf-
tigen Metaphysik, die als Wissenschaft
wird auftreten können. (S. Dietzsch, ed)
R. Malter, 342:Band72Heft1-112
Kant, I. Über die Wiederherstellung der
ursprünglichen Anlage zum Guten in ihre
Kraft.
R. Malter, 342:Band72Heft1-114
Kant, I. Von den Träumen der Vernunft.
(S. and B. Dietzsch, eds)
R. Malter, 342:Band72Heft4-516

Kanta, A. The Late Minoan III Period in
Crete.
M. Popham, 123:Vol31No1-137
Kanzog, K. Edition und Engagement.
M. Gelus, 221(GQ):May81-350
W. Schröder, 684(ZDA):Band110Heft3-138
W. Wittkowski, 133:Band14Heft1-85
Kao Ming. The Lute. (J. Mulligan, trans)
R.E. Strassberg, 244(HJAS):Dec81-695
Kapelle, W.E. The Norman Conquest of the
North.*
R.L. Fleming and C.W. Hollister, 589:
Apr81-401
Kaplan, F.M. and J.M. Sobin. Encyclopedia
of China Today. (3rd ed)
D. Rimmington, 617(TLS):4Jun82-618
Kaplan, J. Walt Whitman.*
G.W. Allen, 646(WWR):Mar81-40
J.D. McClatchy, 249(HudR):Summer81-315
C.C. Nash, 50(ArQ):Spring81-75
J. Porte, 27(AL):Jan82-744
Kaplan, J. - see Whitman, W.
Kaplan, M.A., ed. The Many Faces of Com-
munism.
R. Wesson, 550(RusR):Jan81-76
Kaplan, R.B., ed. On the Scope of Applied
Linguistics.
M.M. Azevedo, 350:Jun81-521
Kaplan, R.B., R.L. Jones and G.R. Tucker -
see "Annual Review of Applied Linguis-
tics"
Kapp, D.B. Das Verbum paraba in seiner
Funktion als Simplex und Explikativum in
Jāyasī Padumāvatī.
G.H. Schokker, 259(IIJ):Apr81-133
Kapp, E. Grundlinien einer Philosophie
der Technik. (H-M. Sass, ed)
W. Strombach, 489(PJGG):Band88Heft1-
194
Kappeler, S. Writing and Reading in Henry
James.*
K. Flint, 175:Autumn81-302
J.C. Rowe, 284:Fall81-67
Kappler, C. Le Monstre.
S.S. Prawer, 208(FS):Jul81-370
Kappler, C. Monstres, démons et merveil-
les à la fin du Moyen Age.
G.R. Mermier, 207(FR):Mar81-628
205(FMLS):Oct80-378
Karadžić, V.S., ed. Serbische Volkslieder.
F. Hahn, 654(WB):11/1981-163
Karageorghis, J. La grande déesse de
Chypre et son culte, à travers l'icono-
graphie, de l'epoque néolithique au
VIème siècle a.C.
A. Peatfield, 303(JoHS):Vol 101-185
Karcher, C. Shadow Over the Promised Land.
G.T. Hull, 27(AL):Mar81-144
D. Leverenz, 445(NCF):Sep81-238
A. Nadel, 219(GaR):Spring81-203
H. Welsh, 651(WHR):Spring81-81
Karginov, G. Rodchenko.
M.B. Betz, 127:Fall/Winter80-417
Kargon, R.H. The Rise of Robert Millikan.
R. Peierls, 453(NYRB):29Apr82-34
Karim, A. The Bauls of Bangladesh.
C. Salomon, 293(JASt):May81-637
Karim, W-J. Ma' Betisék Concepts of Liv-
ing Things.
R.H. Barnes, 617(TLS):19Mar82-327

Kaufmann, M.S. The Love of Elspeth Baker.
   A. Gottlieb, 441:5Sep82-9
Kaufmann, S. Before My Eyes.
   O. Owomoyela, 502(PrS):Spring-Summer81-316
Kaufmann, W. Discovering the Mind. (Vol 1)
   D.L.L., 543:Dec80-389
Kaufmann, W. Discovering the Mind. (Vol 2)
   S.J. Antosik, 222(GR):Winter81-37
Kaufmann, W. Musical References in the Chinese Classics.
   J.M. Boltz, 318(JAOS):Jan/Mar80-95
Kaukonen, V. Lönnrot ja Kalevala.
   J.I. Kolehmainen, 563(SS):Winter81-127
Kauuttila, S. Akseli Gallen-Kallelan Väinämöiset.
   J.I. Kolehmainen, 563(SS):Winter81-127
Kavanagh, J.F. and J.E. Cutting, eds. The Role of Speech in Language.*
   A.S. Kaye, 35(AS):Summer81-128
Kavanagh, P.J. Selected Poems.
   D. Davis, 362:6May82-26
   E. Longley, 617(TLS):16Jul82-770
Kavanagh, P.J. - see Gurney, I.
Kavanagh, R.M., ed. South African People's Plays.
   D. Walder, 617(TLS):23Apr82-468
Kawabata, Y. Tristesse et Beauté.
   L. Arénilla, 450(NRF):Sep81-143
Kawin, B.F. Mindscreen.*
   W. Beard, 107(CRCL):Winter81-164
Kay, C.M. and H.E. Jacobs, eds. Shakespeare's Romances Reconsidered.*
   D. Lindley, 447(N&Q):Oct80-433
Kay, J.H. Lost Boston.
   J.F. O'Gorman, 576:May81-147
   R. Urquhart, 432(NEQ):Sep81-447
Kay, R. Dante's Swift and Strong.*
   A. Scaglione, 545(RPh):Feb81(supp)-32
Kay-Robinson, D. The First Mrs. Thomas Hardy.*
   P.J. Casagrande, 445(NCF):Sep80-219
   J. Halporin, 395(MFS):Summer80-302
   J. Marcus, 637(VS):Spring81-378
   B. Richards, 541(RES):Aug81-350
   295(JML):Vol8No3/4-515
Kaye, M.M. The Far Pavilions.*
   F. Weinbaum, 314:Winter-Spring81-247
Kaye, M.M., ed. The Golden Calm.*
   B. Llewellyn, 135:Jun81-89
Kayser, W. 500 Jahre wissenschaftliche Bibliothek in Hamburg, 1479-1979.*
   J.L. Flood, 354:Jun81-159
Kazan, E. The Anatolian.
   E. Wagner, 441:15Aug82-10
Kazantzakis, N. Serpent and Lily.* The Suffering God.
   K. Oderman, 584(SWR):Autumn81-425
Kealey, E.J. Medieval Medicus.
   J. Sumption, 617(TLS):5Mar82-262
Kealey, G.S. Toronto Workers Respond to Industrial Capitalism, 1867-1892.*
   M. Dubofsky, 529(QQ):Autumn81-552
Keane, M. Good Behaviour.*
   J. Mellors, 364:Feb82-93
Kearney, L. Kingdom Come.*
   K. Fontenot, 435:Winter81-115
Kearns, E.J. Ideas in Seventeenth-Century France.*
   J. Cruickshank, 402(MLR):Apr81-467
                     [continued]

[continuing]
   C. Greenberg, 568(SCN):Winter81-92
   J.P. Wright, 518:Apr81-90
   205(FMLS):Apr80-190
Kearns, G. Guide to Ezra Pound's "Selected Cantos."*
   W.H. Pritchard, 249(HudR):Autumn81-419
   C. Seelye, 27(AL):Nov81-531
   W. Sutton, 468:Winter81-641
Kearns, L. Practicing Up to Be Human.*
   D. Barbour, 648(WCR):Vol 15No3-46
Keating, H.R.F. The Lucky Alphonse.
   A. Hislop, 617(TLS):29Oct82-1203
Keating, P.J. The Working Classes in Victorian Fiction.
   P.C., 189(EA):Apr-Jun81-239
Keaton, D. Reservations.
   P. Hodges, 62:Jan81-65
Keay, J. Eccentric Travellers.
   G. Moorhouse, 617(TLS):29Oct82-1202
Kebric, R.B. In the Shadow of Macedon: Duris of Samos.
   G.J.D. Aalders H. Wzn., 394:Vol34 fasc3/4-451
Kech, H. Hagiographie als christliche Unterhaltungsliteratur.
   K. Kunze, 680(ZDP):Band99Heft3-451
Keddie, N.R., with Y. Richard. Roots of Revolution.*
   H. Enayat, 617(TLS):21May82-553
Kedourie, E. Islam in the Modern World and Other Studies.*
   C. Geertz, 453(NYRB):27May82-25
Kee, A. Constantine versus Christ.
   H. Chadwick, 617(TLS):28May82-573
Kee, R. A Crowd Is Not Company.
   D.J. Enright, 362:10Jun82-25
Kee, R. Ireland.*
   P-L. Adams, 61:May82-106
Keeble, J. Yellowfish.
   R.B. Olafson, 649(WAL):Summer81-166
Keeble, N.H. Richard Baxter.
   C.H. Sisson, 617(TLS):6Aug82-848
Keefe, R. Charlotte Brontë's World of Death.*
   C. Proudfit, 191(ELN):Jun81-313
Keefer, S.L. The Old English Metrical Psalter.
   P.E. Szarmach, 589:Jul81-618
Keeffe, B. A Mad World, My Masters.
   D. Devlin, 157:1stQtr81-54
   M. Martin, 148:Winter81-49
Keegan, J. Six Armies in Normandy.
   J. Beatty, 61:Aug82-93
   D. Middleton, 441:15Aug82-7
   A.J.P. Taylor, 453(NYRB):12Aug82-25
   J. Terraine, 617(TLS):25Jun82-684
Keeler, M.F., ed. Sir Francis Drake's West Indian Voyage 1585-86.
   A.N. Ryan, 617(TLS):29Jan82-103
Keeley, E. and G. Savidis - see Elytis, O.
Keeley, E. and P. Sherrard - see Elytis, O.
Keene, D. Yokomitsu Riichi: Modernist.*
   V.H. Viglielmo, 407(MN):Summer81-202
Keene, D. Surviving.
   D. Graham, 565:Vol122No4-62
Keep, J.L.H., ed and trans. The Debate on Soviet Power.*
   M. McCauley, 575(SEER):Jan81-114
Keeran, R. The Communist Party and the Auto Workers Unions.*
   P. Le Blanc, 385(MQR):Summer82-486

Kegg, M. Gabekanaansing/At the End of the
Trail. (J. Nichols, ed)
G.F. Aubin, 269(IJAL):Jan81-87
Keightley, D.N. Sources of Shang History.*
K.C. Chang, 244(HJAS):Dec81-633
J.A. Lefeuvre, 293(JASt):May81-588
Keil, C. Tiv Song.*
J.T. Irvine, 355(LSoc):Apr81-139
Keil, F.C. Semantic and Conceptual Devel-
opment.*
C.E. Caton, 350:Jun82-457
Keillor, G. Happy to be Here.
R. Blount, Jr., 441:28Feb82-12
Keisler, H.J. Elementary Calculus. Foun-
dations of Infinitesimal Calculus.
P.A. Loeb, 316:Sep81-673
Keith, W.J. Epic Fiction.
T. Marshall, 99:Mar82-30
Keith, W.J. The Poetry of Nature.*
T. Brownlow, 627(UTQ):Summer81-123
M.K. Sutton, 661(WC):Summer81-187
G.W., 102(CanL):Spring81-172
Keith, W.J. - see Wiebe, R. and others
Keith, W.J. and B-Z. Shek, eds. The Arts
in Canada.*
G. Woodcock, 529(QQ):Winter81-672
Kekes, J. The Nature of Philosophy.
E.A. Hacker, 484(PPR):Sep81-139
B.L., 185:Jul82-789
R.W. Newell, 483:Jan81-126
Kelder, D. The Great Book of French
Impressionism.*
62:Jan81-66
Kelen, C. punks travels.
G. Bitcon, 581:Dec81-469
Kelen, S.K. Zen Maniacs.
G. Catalano, 381:Apr81-114
Kellas, J.G. Modern Scotland.
P. Davidson, 111:7Nov80-30
Keller, J. Die russisch-kirchenslavische
Fassung des Weihnachtskontakions und
seiner Prosomoia.
E. Trapp, 688(ZSP):Band42Heft2-421
Keller, G.D. and F. Jiménez, eds. His-
panics in the United States.
E.N. Eger, 238:Dec81-643
S.A. Williams, 399(MLJ):Autumn81-339
Keller, H. Adelsherrschaft und städtische
Gesellschaft in Oberitalien, 9. bis 12.
Jahrhundert.
R. Schumann, 589:Jul81-619
Keller, H. The Art of the Impressionists.
R. Pickvance, 39:Jan81-63
Keller, H. The Great Book of French
Impressionism.*
42(AR):Summer81-394
62:Jan81-66
Keller, H. and M. Cosman. Stravinsky Seen
and Heard.
H. Cole, 362:22Jul82-22
Keller, H.H. New Perspectives on Teaching
Vocabulary.
M. Celce-Murcia, 350:Dec81-979
Keller, J.E. and R.W. Linker, eds. Bar-
laam e Josafat.
L.A. Sharpe, 345(KRQ):Vol28No2-211
Keller, K. The Only Kangaroo Among the
Beauty.*
D.V. Fuller, 50(ArQ):Autumn81-286
F. Lentricchia, 579(SAQ):Winter81-107
Keller, L. - see Proust, M.
Keller, P. States of Belonging.
J. McDermott, 106:Spring81-101

Keller, W. Strukturen der Unterentwick-
lung, Indien 1757-1914.
D.H.A. Kolff, 293(JASt):Feb81-408
Kelley, D.R., ed. Soviet Politics in the
Brezhnev Era.
A. Dallin, 550(RusR):Jan81-67
Kelley, G. The English Jacobin Novel 1780-
1805.
G. Lottes, 38:Band99Heft1/2-248
Kelley, M.R. Flamboyant Drama.*
D. Staines, 130:Spring81-82
Kelling, G.W. Blind Mazes.
J. Jordan, 42(AR):Fall81-514
Kellman, S.G. The Self-Begetting Novel.
M. Danahy, 651(WHR):Spring81-76
M.J. Friedman, 454:Winter82-175
R. Hauptman, 395(MFS):Winter80/81-739
E. Kern, 402(MLR):Oct81-916
H. Nitzberg, 207(FR):Feb81-462
Kellner, S. "Le Docteur Pascal" de Zola.
R. Stanley, 446(NCFS):Fall-Winter81/82-
153
Kelly, A.A. Mary Lavin.*
R.F. Peterson, 174(Éire):Fall81-150
Kelly, D. Medieval Imagination.*
R.T. Davies, 402(MLR):Jan81-149
B. Davis, 599:Winter81-39
B.N. Sargent-Baur, 545(RPh):
Feb81(supp)-219
J. Stevens, 131(CL):Winter81-90
205(FMLS):Jan80-88
Kelly, G.A. Hegel's Retreat from Eleusis.
E.S. Dalrymple, 482(PhR):Jan81-135
Kelly, H.A. Love and Marriage in the Age
of Chaucer.
E. Brown, Jr. and S. Fleischman,
545(RPh):May81-496
Kelly, L. The Kemble Era.*
639(VQR):Winter81-12
Kelly, L.G. The True Interpreter.
H. Birnbaum, 350:Mar81-247
M.G. Rose, 599:Fall81-482
W. Wilss, 603:Vol5No3-412
Kelly, M.T. The More Loving One.*
L. Rogers, 102(CanL):Autumn81-156
Kelly, T.E. Le Haut Livre du Graal:
Perlesvaus.
G.A. Savage, 545(RPh):Aug80-108
Kelso, R. Doctrine for the Lady of the
Renaissance.
L.G. Black, 541(RES):May81-205
K. Duncan-Jones, 447(N&Q):Apr80-189
Kelton, E. The Wolf and the Buffalo.
D. Grover, 649(WAL):Summer81-166
Kemal, Y. Meurtre au marché des forgerons.
H. Cronel, 450(NRF):Dec81-130
Kemball, R. - see Tsvetaeva, M.
Kemp, B. English Church Monuments.
J.S. Curl, 324:Jul82-504
Kemp, E.C. Manuscript Solicitation for
Libraries, Special Collections, Museums,
and Archives.
A. Bell, 325:Apr81-440
Kemp, J.A. - see Lepsius, R.
Kemp, J.C. Robert Frost and New England.*
L. Perrine, 191(ELN):Sep80-72
Kemp, M. Leonardo da Vinci.
J. Beck, 441:10Jan82-11
E.H. Gombrich, 617(TLS):15Jan82-43
Kemp, P. Changing Place.
D. Barbour, 648(WCR):Vol 15No3-45

Kemp, P. H.G. Wells and the Culminating
Ape.
  D.J. Enright, 362:9Dec82-22
Kempe-Oettinger, C. Rudolf Kempe.
  P.J.P., 412:Feb80-73
Kempinski, T. Duet for One.
  D. Devlin, 157:Autumn81-51
Kempner, B.M. Nonnen unter dem Hakenkreuz.
  F.L. Carsten, 575(SEER):Jul81-477
Kempowski, W. Days of Greatness.*
  K.C. O'Brien, 362:28Jan82-24
  I. Parry, 617(TLS):22Jan82-76
Kempton, R. French Literature.
  S. Haig, 207(FR):Oct81-176
Kendal, G. Facts.
  R.P.A., 185:Apr82-578
Kendall, E. The End of an Era.
  T.G. Christensen, 69:Vol50No4-449
Kendle, J. John Bracken.
  G.W., 102(CanL):Winter80-150
Kendler, H.H. Psychology.
  J.D., 185:Jul82-778
Kendon, A. Studies on the Behavior of
Social Interaction.
  M. Mathiot, 567:Vol36No3/4-329
Kendrick, W.M. The Novel-Machine.*
  J. Carlisle, 639(VQR):Winter81-176
  J. McMaster, 445(NCF):Sep81-234
Keneally, T. Confederates.*
  B. King, 569(SR):Summer81-461
  639(VQR):Winter81-22
Keneally, T. Schindler's List. (British
title: Schindler's Ark.)
  D.J. Enright, 617(TLS):29Oct82-1189
  P. Kemp, 362:14Oct82-31
  P. Zweig, 441:24Oct82-1
  442(NY):13Dec82-184
Kenedi, J. Do It Yourself.
  G. Mikes, 617(TLS):5Feb82-129
Kengen, J.H.L., ed. Memoriale Credencium.
  H. Forshaw, 179(ES):Aug81-381
  P. Gradon, 382(MAE):1981/2-346
  R. Hanna 3d, 589:Jan81-151
  S. Wenzel, 38:Band99Heft3/4-511
Kenkel, K. Medea-Dramen.
  G. Chancellor, 221(GQ):Jan81-123
Kennan, G.F. The Decline of Bismarck's
European Order.*
  H. Seton-Watson, 575(SEER):Jul81-453
Kennan, G.F. The Nuclear Delusion.
  S. Hoffmann, 61:Dec82-96
  M.J. Sherwin, 441:7Nov82-7
  S. Zuckerman, 453(NYRB):16Dec82-19
  442(NY):1Nov82-156
Kennard, J.E. Victims of Convention.
  T.J. Winnifrith, 677(YES):Vol 11-315
Kennaway, J. and S. The Kennaway Papers.*
  A. Ross, 364:Apr/May81-5
Kennedy, A. Meaning and Signs in Fiction.*
  R.L. Caserio, 445(NCF):Sep80-229
  H. Foltinek, 402(MLR):Jul81-643
  A. Jefferson, 447(N&Q):Jun80-281
Kennedy, E., ed. Lancelot do Lac.*
  W.W. Kibler, 207(FR):May82-898
Kennedy, E. A Philosophe in the Age of
Revolution.*
  A. Vartanian, 319:Oct81-512
Kennedy, G.A. Classical Rhetoric and its
Christian and Secular Tradition from
Ancient to Modern Times.
  M.W. Bloomfield, 589:Jan81-218
  K. Jamieson, 377:Jul81-119

[continued]

[continuing]
  W.J. Kennedy, 131(CL):Summer81-282
  J.J. Murphy, 480(P&R):Winter81-51
  D.E. Williams, 583:Fall80-86
  M. Winterbottom, 123:Vol31No1-125
Kennedy, J.G. Herbert Spencer.
  C.B. Jones, 506(PSt):Sep81-216
  A.J.M. Milne, 161(DUJ):Jun81-270
Kennedy, L., comp. A Book of Sea Journeys.
  N. Shakespeare, 617(TLS):19Mar82-308
Kennedy, M. Britten.*
  A. Whittall, 415:Jun81-379
  C. Wintle, 607:Sep81-43
Kennedy, M., ed. Oxford Concise Dictio-
nary of Music.* (3rd ed)
  A. Jacobs, 415:Apr81-243
Kennedy, M. The Works of Ralph Vaughan
Williams. (2nd ed)
  P.J. Pirie, 415:Feb81-108
Kennedy, M.L. The Jacobin Clubs in the
French Revolution: The First Years.
  W. Scott, 617(TLS):2Jul82-723
Kennedy, R.G. American Churches.
  P. Goldberger, 441:26Dec82-3
Kennedy, R.S. Dreams in the Mirror.*
  J. Bayley, 617(TLS):5Mar82-235
  T. Ludington, 639(VQR):Spring81-362
Kennedy, T. Die a Little.
  K. Jeffery, 617(TLS):6Aug82-865
Kennedy, T. Durango.
  R.J. Stout, 584(SWR):Winter81-110
Kennedy, W.L. Rhetorical Norms in Renais-
sance Literature.*
  C. Chiappelli, 678(YCGL):No29-40
  H.A. Marshall, 447(N&Q):Apr80-190
Kennedy, X.J., ed. Tygers of Wrath.
  V. Young, 472:Spring/Summer82-241
Kenner, H. Joyce's Voices.*
  D. Davin, 541(RES):Nov81-479
  B.K. Scott, 305(JIL):May81-128
Kenner, H. "Ulysses."*
  A. Goldman, 402(MLR):Jul81-687
  L.V. Harrod, 174(Éire):Summer81-158
  M. Sabin, 454:Spring82-271
  B.K. Scott, 305(JIL):May81-128
  H.B. Staples, 329(JJQ):Spring81-360
  295(JML):Vol8No3/4-537
Kennett, L. The French Forces in America,
1780-1783.*
  J. Lough, 208(FS):Apr81-212
Kenney, E.J. and W.V. Clausen, eds. The
Cambridge History of Classical Litera-
ture. (Vol 2)
  J.P. Sullivan, 617(TLS):10Sep82-966
Kenny, A. The Aristotelian Ethics.*
  J.M. Cooper, 449:Sep81-381
  J-L. Poirier, 542:Apr-Jun81-266
  N. Sherman and M. Presser, 319:Jul81-
  380
Kenny, A. Aristotle's Theory of the Will.*
  S.R.L. Clark, 393(Mind):Apr81-302
  C.A. Freeland, 482(PhR):Jan81-159
  W.F.R. Hardie, 483:Jan81-120
  C.L., 543:Sep80-144
Kenny, A. The Computation of Style.
  A.Q. Morton, 617(TLS):26Nov82-1290
Kenny, A. The God of the Philosophers.*
  W. Hasker, 482(PhR):Oct81-621
  H. Palmer, 518:Jan81-50
  S.R. Sutherland, 393(Mind):Apr81-312

189

Ketchum, W.C., Jr. The Catalog of American Collectibles.
  R.A. Fischer, 658:Winter81-337
Ketner, K.L. and J.E. Cook - see Peirce, C.S.
Ketner, K.L. and J.M. Ransdell - see "Peirce Studies"
Ketteler, V. Soziale Erfahrung und Erzählen.
  J.H. Petersen, 680(ZDP):Band99Heft4-597
Ketterer, D. The Rationale of Deception in Poe.
  J.W. Gargano, 573(SSF):Winter81-100
  D. Hill, 178:Fall81-364
  P.F. Quinn, 445(NCF):Jun80-88
  J.A. Robbins, 27(AL):Mar81-130
  205(FMLS):Oct80-378
Kettering, S. Judicial Politics and Urban Revolt in Seventeenth-Century France.
  J. Lough, 208(FS):Jul81-331
Kettle, M. The Allies and the Russian Collapse.* (Vol 1)
  639(VQR):Summer81-90
Keuls, E.C. Plato and Greek Painting.*
  A.W.H. Adkins, 487:Fall81-289
Key, M.R. Catherine the Great's Linguistic Contribution.
  B. Comrie, 350:Mar82-240
Key, M.R. Nonverbal Communication.
  A.S. Kaye, 35(AS):Winter81-305
  A.S. Kaye, 361.:Jun/Jul81-253
Keynes, G. - see Blake, W.
Keynes, J.M. Activities 1922-9. (D. Moggridge, ed)
  A. Cairncross, 617(TLS):19Feb82-191
Keypour, N.D. André Gide.
  R. Le Huenen, 627(UTQ):Summer81-146
Keys, I. Mozart.*
  N. Zaslaw, 415:Jun81-381
Kezich, T. Il campeggio di Duttogliano.
  J. Gatt-Rutter, 617(TLS):15Jan82-63
Al-Khalesi, Y.M. The Court of the Psalms.
  A. Finet, 318(JAOS):Apr/Jun80-190
Khatibi, A. Le Livre du sang.
  J.D. Erickson, 207(FR):Apr81-765
Khera, A. Hermann Hesses Romane der Krisenzeit in der Sicht seiner Kritiker.*
  A. Otten, 406:Spring81-116
Khleif, B.D. Language, Ethnicity, and Education in Wales.
  N.C. Dorian, 355(LSoc):Dec81-463
Iman Khomeini. Islam and Revolution. (H. Algar, ed and trans)
  C. Geertz, 453(NYRB):27May82-25
Khosla, G.D. Never the Twain.
  H.R.F. Keating, 617(TLS):6Aug82-863
Khwaja, J. Quest for Islam.
  S.K. Miri, 273(IC):Jan81-64
Kibler, W.W., J-L.G. Picherit, and T.S. Fenster, eds. Lion de Bourges.
  G.J. Brault, 589:Oct81-879
Kicklighter, C.E. and R.J. Baird. Crafts.
  P. Bach, 614:Spring82-12
Kidd, B. Who's A Soccer Player?
  K. Kealy, 102(CanL):Summer81-149
Kidder, T. The Soul of a New Machine.*
  J. Naughton, 362:11Mar82-21
"Kids Plays: Six Canadian Plays for Children."
  J. Doolittle, 108:Fall81-112

Kiefer, K.H. Wiedergeburt und Neues Leben.*
  A. Corbineau-Hoffmann, 224(GRM): Band31Heft2-249
  C. Michel, 52:Band15Heft2-205
Kiely, B. The State of Ireland.*
  D. Flower, 249(HudR):Spring81-113
  639(VQR):Spring81-60
Kiely, R. Beyond Egotism.*
  J.M. Kertzer, 49:Oct81-93
  J. Meyers, 594:Winter81-449
  J. Rivkin, 659(ConL):Summer82-390
Kienast, D. Cato der Zensor.
  R. Goujard, 555:Vol54fasc2-374
Kienitz, F-K. Völker im Schatten.
  P.L. MacKendrick, 124:Jul-Aug82-380
Kienzle, W.X. Assault with Intent.
  N. Callendar, 441:23May82-41
Kierkegaard, S. Letters and Documents.* (H. Rosenmeier, ed and trans)
  P. Bové, 81:Fall80-233
  A.L. Jakobsen, 462(OL):Vol36No4-351
Kierkegaard, S. Two Ages.* (H.V. and E. Hong, eds and trans)
  P. Bové, 81:Fall80-233
Kiernan, D. Existentiale Themen bei Max Frisch.
  H.F. Pfanner, 406:Fall81-366
Kiernan, T. The Intricate Music.
  R. De Mott, 295(JML):Vol8No3/4-617
  P. Lisca, 395(MFS):Winter80/81-669
Kiernan, V.G. From Conquest to Collapse. (British title: European Empires from Conquest to Collapse, 1815-1960.)
  J. Keegan, 453(NYRB):23Sep82-27
  P.J. Marshall, 617(TLS):16Jul82-758
Kierpatrich, S. Larra.
  J. Sánchez-Boudy, 552(REH):Jan81-145
Kiesling, S. The Shell Game.
  R. Blount, Jr., 441:30May82-6
Kiger, R., ed. Kate Greenaway.
  J. Baker, 503:Winter81-176
Kilby, C.S. Images of Salvation in the Fiction of C.S. Lewis.
  T.T. Howard, 396(ModA):Winter81-98
  C.E. Lloyd, 569(SR):Spring81-281
Kilby, C.S. and M.L. Mead - see Lewis, W.H.
Kilby, D.A. Deep and Superficial Cases in Russian.
  G. Corbett, 297(JL):Mar81-178
Kilmurray, E. - see Ormond, R. and M. Rogers
Kim, C.L., ed. Political Participation in Korea.
  J.K.C. Oh, 293(JASt):Aug81-799
Kim, C-W., ed. Papers in Korean Linguistics.*
  C.C. Kubler, 350:Mar81-244
Kim Chi Ha. The Middle Hour.
  Ko Won, 293(JASt):May81-614
Kim, H-C., ed. The Korean Diaspora.
  D.N. Clark, 293(JASt):Nov80-146
Kim, J-H. Prehistory of Korea. (K. and R. Pearson, eds and trans)
  E.B. McCune, 293(JASt):Aug81-801
Kim, K-H. The Last Phase of the East Asian World Order.
  C.K. Quinones, 293(JASt):Feb81-386
Kim, K.K., ed. Islam di Malaysia. Lembaran Akhbar Melayu. Malaysia.
  W.R. Roff, 293(JASt):Feb81-425
Kimball, A.S. - see Jacob, M.

Kippur, S.A.   Jules Michelet.
  O.A. Haac, 446(NCFS):Fall-Winter81/82-
  188
  E.K. Kaplan, 207(FR):Feb82-414
Király, B.K. and G.E. Rothenburg, eds.
  War and Society in East Central Europe.
  (Vol 1)
  L.E. Hill, 104(CASS):Winter81-609
  N. Stone, 575(SEER):Jan81-157
Kirby, D.   America's Hive of Honey, or,
  Foreign Influences on American Fiction
  through Henry James.
  354:Dec81-369
Kirby, D.   Grace King.
  E.T. Arnold, 26(ALR):Spring81-145
  R.S. Moore, 578:Spring82-72
Kirby, D.G.   Finland in the Twentieth Cen-
  tury.*
  A.F. Upton, 575(SEER):Jan81-111
Kircher, H., ed.   Deutsche Sonette.
  W.E. Yates, 402(MLR):Jan81-237
Kirchert, K.   Der Windberger Psalter.
  H. Eggers, 684(ZDA):Band110Heft2-67
Kirchherr, E.C.   Abyssinia to Zimbabwe.
  H.A. Raup, 424:Mar80-92
"Ernst Ludwig Kirchner 1880-1938."
  J. Lloyd, 59:Jun81-220
Kirk, J. and D. Schmidt - see Agustín, J.
Kirk, M. and A. Strathern.   Man as Art.*
  R. Kushner, 62:Mar82-64
Kirk, R.   Lord of the Hollow Dark.   The
  Princess of All Lands.
  E. Wagenknecht, 396(ModA):Fall81-415
Kirk, R., ed.   The Portable Conservative
  Reader.
  T. Paulin, 617(TLS):8Oct82-1094
Kirkegaard, P.   Knut Hamsun som modernist.
  T. Schiff, 563(SS):Summer81-360
Kirkland, S.   The Journal of Samuel Kirk-
  land.   (W. Pilkington, ed)
  J.H. Smylie, 656(WMQ):Oct81-742
Kirkness, A.   Zur Sprachreinigung im Deuts-
  chen 1789-1871.
  N.R. Wolf, 685(ZDL):1/1981-77
Kirkpatrick, B.J.   A Bibliography of
  Edmund Blunden.
  N. Rogers, 78(BC):Autumn81-418
Kirkpatrick, J.J.   Dictatorships and
  Double Standards.
  T. Draper, 441:25Jul82-1
  442(NY):2Aug82-88
Kirkup, J.   Dengonban Messages.
  W. Cope, 617(TLS):29Jan82-114
Kirsch, A.   Shakespeare and the Experience
  of Love.
  S. Wintle, 617(TLS):5Feb82-124
Kirsch, D.   La Bruyère ou le Style cruel.
  A.R. Curtis, 627(UTQ):Winter80/81-248
  L. van Delft, 535(RHL):Mar-Apr81-293
Kirschbaum, E-G. and M. Wolter.   Enzyklo-
  pädie-Reisesprachführer Deutsch-Russisch.
  (2nd ed)
  H. Zikmund, 682(ZPSK):Band33Heft2-276
Kirsner, D.   The Schizoid World of Jean-
  Paul Sartre and R.D. Laing.
  M. Harney, 63:Mar81-133
Kirsner, R.S.   The Problem of Presentative
  Sentences in Modern Dutch.
  W.Z. Shetter, 350:Jun82-429
Kirst, H.H.   Party Games.
  A. Otten, 42(AR):Spring81-258
Kisch, G.   Immanuel Kant im Medaillenbild.
  R.M., 342:Band71Heft1-128

Kiseleva, L.I.   Katalog rukopiseĭ i frag-
  mentov latinskogo alfavita, khranyasbchi-
  ksya v Matenadarane.   (A.D. Lyublinskaya,
  ed)
  354:Mar81-85
Kissinger, H.   Years of Upheaval.
  M. Frankel, 441:4Apr82-1
  S. Hoffmann, 453(NYRB):29Apr82-14
  K. Kyle, 362:1Apr82-21
  E.N. Luttwak, 617(TLS):15Oct82-1125
  W. Pfaff, 442(NY):13Sep82-156
Kitchen, P.   Gerard Manley Hopkins.
  295(JML):Vol8No3/4-523
Kitcher, P.   Abusing Science.
  P-L. Adams, 61:Oct82-105
Kittler, F.A.   Der Traum und die Rede.
  W. Kudszus, 221(GQ):Mar81-230
Kittrie, N.N. and J. Susman, eds.   Legal-
  ity, Morality, and Ethics in Criminal
  Justice.
  D.A.J. Richards, 185:Apr82-563
Kivy, P.   The Corded Shell.*
  639(VQR):Spring81-67
Kiyota, M., with E.W. Jones, eds.   Mahā-
  yāna Buddhist Meditation.
  R.K. Payne, 485(PE&W):Jul81-378
Kizer, C., ed.   Woman Poet.
  V.L. Nielsen, 649(WAL):Summer81-159
Kizer, C. - see Peterson, R.
Kjellén, A.   Bakom den officiella fasaden.
  W. Johnson, 563(SS):Winter81-115
Klaas, R.M., ed.   Piano-Jahrbuch.
  C. Ehrlich, 415:Mar81-180
Klaassen, W.   Michael Gaismair.
  J.A. Strouss, 551(RenQ):Autumn80-430
Klappenbach, R.   Studien zur modernen
  deutschen Lexikographie.   (W. Abraham,
  with J.F. Brand, eds)
  J. Eichhoff, 603:Vol5No3-416
Klar, K., M. Langdon and S. Silver, eds.
  American Indian and Indoeuropean Studies.
  W. Bright, 350:Jun81-508
  D.H., 355(LSoc):Dec81-491
Klassen, I., ed.   D'Sonoqua.
  D. Barbour, 648(WCR):Jun80-73
  P. Brennan, 102(CanL):Winter80-125
Klaus, G.   Philosophiehistorische Abhand-
  lungen.
  R.M., 342:Band71Heft1-129
Klausenburger, J.   Historische franzö-
  sische Phonologie aus generativer Sicht.
  J. Klare, 682(ZPSK):Band33Heft6-751
Klausner, C.   The Seljuk Vezirate.
  S.C. Fairbanks, 318(JAOS):Jan/Mar80-28
Klegraf, J. and others, eds.   Beowulf und
  die kleineren Denkmäler der altenglis-
  chen Heldensage Waldere und Finnsburg.
  R.P.M. Lehmann, 589:Jan81-157
Kleiber, G.   Le Mot "IRE" en ancien fran-
  çais (XIe-XIIIe siècles).*
  N.L. Corbett, 545(RPh):Feb81(supp)-194
Kleiber, W., ed.   Otfrid von Weissenburg.*
  G. Vollmann-Profe, 684(ZDA):Band110
  Heft1-8
Klein, A. - see Kant, I.
Klein, C.   Aline.*
  L. Field, 395(MFS):Winter80/81-668
Klein, E., K.J. Mattheier and H. Mivkartz.
  Rheinisch.
  H. Fischer, 680(ZDP):Band99Heft3-467
Klein, H.G.   Making It Perfectly Clear.*
  R. de Toledano, 396(ModA):Fall81-419
  639(VQR):Winter81-23

Kluger, P. and R. Good Goods.
    N. Johnson, 441:14Nov82-14
Kluger, R. Un-American Activities.
    M. Simpson, 441:25Jul82-10
    442(NY):16Aug82-90
Knabe, P-E. Die Rezeption der französis-
    chen Aufklärung in den "Göttingischen
    Gelehrten Anzeigen" (1739-1779).*
    R. Mortier, 52:Band15Heft2-203
Knapp, B.L. Maurice Maeterlinck.
    D. Knowles, 208(FS):Apr81-218
Knapp, B.L. Gérard de Nerval.*
    R. Chambers, 446(NCFS):Spring-Summer81-
    268
    S. Dunn, 207(FR):Apr81-739
    M. Tison-Braun, 188(ECr):Summer81-98
Knapp, B.L. Anaïs Nin.*
    E.B. Tenenbaum, 395(MFS):Summer80-290
Knapp, B.L. Theatre and Alchemy.
    G.R. Besser, 446(NCFS):Spring-Summer82-
    369
    D. Gerould, 397(MD):Dec81-572
Knapp, B.L. Emile Zola.
    L. Kamm, 207(FR):Oct81-144
    N.D. Savage, 446(NCFS):Fall-Win-
    ter81/82-192
Knapp, F.P. Das lateinische Tierepos.
    F. Wagner, 196:Band21Heft3/4-318
Knapp, F.P. Der Selbstmord in der abend-
    ländischen Epik des Hochmittelalters.
    D.H. Green, 402(MLR):Jan81-232
Knapp, G.P., ed. Max Frisch: Aspekte des
    Bühnenwerks.
    I.M. Goessl, 221(GQ):Jan81-114
Knapp, G.P., ed. Max Frisch: Aspekte des
    Prosawerks.*
    I.M. Goessl, 221(GQ):Jan81-112
    Y. Perczuk, 67:Nov81-272
    H.F. Pfanner, 406:Fall81-366
Knapp, C.P. Die Literatur des deutschen
    Expressionismus.
    G.C. Avery, 400(MLN):Apr81-693
    E. Glass, 222(GR):Winter81-39
    J.H. Petersen, 680(ZDP):Band100Heft2-
    309
    T. Rietzschel, 654(WB):12/1981-181
    J.M. Ritchie, 402(MLR):Jul81-758
Knapp, H-W. Die französische Arbeiter-
    dichtung in der Epoche der Julimonarchie.
    H. Stenzel, 224(GRM):Band30Heft4-468
Knapp, R.C. Aspects of the Roman Experi-
    ence in Iberia, 206-100 B.C.
    N. Mackie, 313:Vol71-187
Knaus, W.A. Inside Russian Medicine.
    639(VQR):Autumn81-133
Knebel, F. Crossing in Berlin.*
    D. Profumo, 617(TLS):26Mar82-339
Knecht, E. Le Mythe du juif errant.
    M-M. Münch, 549(RLC):Jan-Mar81-127
Knecht, R.J. Francis I.
    P.S. Lewis, 617(TLS):7May82-514
Kneepkens, C.H. and H.F. Reijnders - see
    Magister Siguinus
Knell, H. Grundzüge der griechischen
    Architektur.
    R.A. Tomlinson, 123:Vol31No2-321
Knepler, G. Geschichte als Weg zum Musik-
    verständnis.
    R.L.J., 412:Aug80-244
    K. Mehner, 654(WB):11/1981-156
Kneževič, B. History, the Anatomy of Time.
    H.J. Birx, 484(PPR):Sep81-137

Knies, E. Streets After Rain.
    G.E. Murray, 249(HudR):Spring81-158
Knieter, G.L. and J. Stallings, eds. The
    Teaching Process and Arts and Aesthetics.
    P. Meeson, 89(BJA):Spring81-180
    M.J. Parsons, 290(JAAC):Winter81-234
"Kniga: Issledovaniya i Materialy." (Vols
    34-38, 40 and 41)
    J.S.G. Simmons, 78(BC):Winter81-557
Knight, B. Rug Weaving.
    P. Bach, 614:Summer81-21
Knight, E. Born of a Woman.
    D. Pinckney, 472:Spring/Summer81-306
    639(VQR):Winter81-27
Knight, G.N. Indexing, The Art of.
    H. Ostroff, 14:Summer80-375
    R. Phillips, 354:Jun81-174
Knight, G.W. Shakespeare's Dramatic
    Challenge.*
    A.R. Dutton, 179(ES):Feb81-59
Knight, G.W. Symbol of Man.
    P. Redgrove, 617(TLS):30Jul82-828
Knight, R.C. - see Racine, J.
Knight, S. and M. Wilding, eds. The Radi-
    cal Reader.*
    G. Jenkins, 366:Spring81-128
Knights, L.C. "Hamlet" and other Shake-
    spearean Essays.*
    M. Grivelet, 189(EA):Apr-Jun81-218
"Knigopečatanie i knižnye sobranija v
    Rossii do serediny XIX v."
    R.H. Burger, 574(SEEJ):Spring81-119
Knipe, H. Die Doppelfunktion des Irra-
    tionalen in Hermann Brochs "Die Schuld-
    losen."
    P.M. Lützeler, 406:Winter81-479
"Knizhnye sokrovishcha Gosudarstvennoĭ
    biblioteki SSSR im. V. I. Lenina."
    (Vols 1-3)
    354:Mar81-85
Knobloch, H. Herr Moses in Berlin.
    G. Hartung, 654(WB):9/1981-165
Knoepfli, A. and others. Der Altar des 18.
    Jahrhunderts.
    F. Brauen, 90:Dec81-754
Knoll, A.J. Togo under Imperial Germany
    1884-1914.
    R. Cornevin, 69:Vol50No2-226
Knoop, U. Das mittelhochdeutsche Tage-
    lied.*
    R. Schnell, 680(ZDP):Band99Heft1-111
Knopf, J. Brecht-Handbuch: Theater.
    J. Milfull, 67:Nov81-267
Knopp, K. Französischer Schülerargot.
    M.P. Hagiwara, 207(FR):Dec81-294
Knops, P. Les Anciens Senufo 1923-1935.
    D. Richter, 2(AfrA):May81-30
Knorringa, R. Fonction phatique et tradi-
    tion orale.
    D. Deletant, 575(SEER):Jan81-154
Knott, J.R., Jr. The Sword of the Spirit.*
    I. Bell, 401(MLQ):Mar81-90
    B. Berry, 141:Summer81-267
Knowles, A.V., ed. Tolstoy: The Critical
    Heritage.*
    J. Bayley, 541(RES):Feb81-91
Knowles, C. Typings (1974-1977).
    42(AR):Winter81-132
Knowles, R. - see Shakespeare, W.
Knowlson, J. and J. Pilling. Frescoes of
    the Skull.*
    S.E. Gontarski, 397(MD):Dec81-559

Knowlton, C. and A. Besant. "A Dirty,
Filthy Book." (S. Chandrasekhar, ed)
   B. Harrison, 617(TLS):12Nov82-1252
Knox, B. - see Sophocles
Knox, D. Death March.
   D.J.R. Bruckner, 441:24Jan82-14
Knox, E.C. and C.D. Rifelj. C'est-à-dire.
   A.S. Caprio, 207(FR):Oct80-215
Knox, M. Mussolini Unleashed, 1939-1941.
   M. Kempton, 453(NYRB):7Oct82-19
   C. Seton-Watson, 617(TLS):30Jul82-831
Knox, O. From Rose to San Marino.
   P. Johnson, 362:29Jul82-26
   J. Ridley, 617(TLS):30Jul82-831
Knust, H. - see Grosz, G.
Kobayashi, H. The Human Comedy of Heian
Japan.
   W.M. Kelsey, 293(JASt):Nov80-132
Koblas, J.J. F. Scott Fitzgerald in Minne-
sota.
   S. Donaldson, 395(MFS):Summer80-332
Koblischke, H. Grosses Abkürzungsbuch.
   D. Herberg, 682(ZPSK):Band33Heft5-635
Kobylańska, K. Frédéric Chopin: Thema-
tisch-bibliographisches Werkverzeichnis.
(E. Herttrich, ed)
   J. Kallberg, 317:Summer81-357
   N. Temperley, 415:Mar81-177
Koch, F. The New Corporate Philanthropy.
   T. Russell-Cobb, 324:Apr82-294
Koch, L., J.H. Meter and T. Paroli, eds.
Studi per Mario Gabrieli.
   W.G. Jones, 562(Scan):Nov81-236
Koder, J. and T. Weber. Liutprand von
Cremona in Konstantinopel.
   M. Arbagi, 589:Oct81-932
Kodera, T.J. Dōgen's Formative Years in
China.
   C. Bielefeldt, 293(JASt):Feb81-387
   T.P. Kasulis, 485(PE&W):Oct81-552
Kodjak, A. Pushkin's I.P. Belkin.*
   P. Austin, 104(CASS):Winter81-556
Kodjak, A., M.J. Connolly and K. Pomorska,
eds. The Structural Analysis of Narra-
tive Texts.
   J. Graffy, 575(SEER):Oct81-594
   N. Perlina, 558(RLJ):Spring-Fall81-309
Kodjak, A., K. Pomorska and K. Taranovsky,
eds. Alexander Puškin: Symposium II.
   E.D. Sampson, 558(RLJ):Spring-Fall81-
285
Koefoed, O. Le verbe comme objet d'étude.
   A. Klum, 597(SN):Vol53No2-394
Koehler, J.W. and J.I. Sisco. Public Com-
munication in Business and the Profes-
sions.
   D.C. Corr, 583:Spring82-350
Koehler, L. N.F. Fedorov.
   L.K.D. Kristof, 550(RusR):Oct81-449
   J.P. Scanlan, 574(SEEJ):Spring81-115
   M-B. Zeldin, 104(CASS):Winter81-594
Koehler, L. A Search for Power.
   H.M. Pycior, 432(NEQ):Dec81-592
Koenig, M. and G. Speirs. Making Rugs for
Pleasure and Profit.
   P. Bach, 614:Fall81-18
Koenigsberger, D. Renaissance Man and
Creative Thinking.
   S.K. Heninger, Jr., 125:Winter81-216
   M.L. Kuntz, 551(RenQ):Autumn80-424
Koepke, W. Erfolglosigkeit.
   R-R. Wuthenow, 133:Band14Heft2-181

Koerner, E.F.K., ed. Progress in Linguis-
tic Historiography.
   P. Swiggers, 350:Mar82-194
Koerner, E.F.K. Toward a Historiography
of Linguistics.*
   P. Swiggers, 353:Vol 18No7/8-703
Koerner, E.F.K. Western Histories of Lin-
guistic Thought.
   E. Finegan, 350:Mar82-239
   P. Swiggers, 353:Vol 18No7/8-703
Koerner, E.F.K., H-J. Niederehe and R.H.
Robins, eds. Studies in Medieval Lin-
guistic Thought.
   M.A. Covington, 350:Mar82-239
Koesters, P-H. Deutschland, deine Denker.
(2nd ed) (H. Nannen, ed)
   R. Malter, 342:Band72Heft2-203
Kogan, D. and M. The Battle for the La-
bour Party.
   D.A.N. Jones, 362:21Jan82-22
Kogawa, J. Obasan.
   S. Kelman, 99:Feb82-39
   E. Milton, 441:5Sep82-8
   442(NY):14Jun82-134
Kohák, E. Idea and Experience.*
   D. Blinder, 393(Mind):Jul81-465
Kohl, B.G. and R.G. Witt, with E.B. Welles,
eds. The Earthly Republic.*
   A.J. Hunt, 402(MLR):Apr81-485
Kohl-Larsen, L., ed. Die Leute im Baum.
   E. Dammann, 196:Band21Heft1/2-125
Kohlberg, L. The Philosophy of Moral
Development.*
   T.M.R., 185:Jul82-794
Köhler, E., ed. Der altfranzösische
höfische Roman.
   D. Evans, 447(N&Q):Apr80-186
Köhler, H. Welfare and Planning.
   C.W. Anderson, 185:Jul81-675
Köhler, I. Baudelaire et Hoffmann.*
   R. Beilharz, 597(SN):Vol53No2-418
Kohler, K.J. Einführung in die Phonetik
des Deutschen.
   W.A. Benware, 350:Mar81-234
Kohlschmidt, W., ed. Bürgerlichkeit und
Unbürgerlichkeit in der Literatur der
Deutschen Schweiz.*
   R. Kieser, 406:Winter81-445
Kohlwes, K. Christliche Dichtung und
stilistische Form bei Paulinus von Nola.
   P.G. Walsh, 123:Vol31No1-119
Kohn, H. Who Killed Karen Silkwood?*
   J.M. Crewdson, 453(NYRB):21Jan82-31
Kohonen, J. Studien zu Dependenz, Valenz
und Satzmodell. (Pts 1 and 2)
   G. Kolde, 260(IF):Band85-317
Kohs, E.B. Musical Composition.
   P. Standford, 415:Dec81-824
Kohut, H. The Restoration of the Self.
   R. Harper, 529(QQ):Summer81-256
Kojève, A. Introduction à la lecture de
Hegel. (R. Queneau, ed)
   J-M. Gabaude, 542:Oct-Dec81-488
Kokott, H. Literatur und Herrschaftsbewus-
stein.*
   W. Röcke, 680(ZDP):Band100Heft3-431
Kolakowski, L. Main Currents of Marxism.*
   J. Daly, 518:Apr81-105
   J. Elster, 185:Jul81-634
   A. Levine, 185:Jul81-645

Kolakowski, L. Religion: If there is no God ...
  J.M. Cameron, 453(NYRB):23Sep82-55
  A. Ryan, 362:25Feb82-22
Kolander, C. A Silk Worker's Notebook.
  R.L. Shep, 614:Winter82-20
Kolatch, A.J. Dictionary of First Names. The Name Dictionary.
  E.C. Smith, 424:Jun81-169
Kolatkar, A. Jejuri.
  J.P. Gemmill, 314:Summer-Fall81-207
Kolb, E., with others. Atlas of English Sounds.*
  N. Davis, 541(RES):Aug81-309
  R.I. McDavid, Jr., 300:Mar81-45
Kolb, H. and H. Lauffer, eds. Sprachliche Interferenz.
  G. Bellmann, 685(ZDL):1/1981-116
Kolb, J. - see Hallam, A.H.
Kolb, P. - see Proust, M.
Kolenda, K. - see Ryle, G.
Kolers, P.A., M.E. Wrolstad and H. Bouma, eds. Processing of Visible Language. (Vol 1)
  G. Corbett, 307:Oct81-135
  G. Mounin, 567:Vol33No3/4-383
Koljevic, S. The Epic in the Making.
  E.D. Goy, 575(SEER):Jul81-417
  205(FMLS):Oct81-377
Kolker, R.P. A Cinema of Loneliness.
  A. Aleiss, 400(MLN):Dec81-1257
Kollontai, A. A Great Love.*
  H. Robinson, 441:25Apr82-9
Kölving, U. - see Grimm, F.M.
Komar, A. Music and Human Experience.
  G. Poole, 415:Aug81-536
Komarov, B. The Destruction of Nature in the Soviet Union.
  L.K.D. Kristof, 550(RusR):Oct81-458
Komjathy, A. and R. Stockwell. German Minorities and the Third Reich.
  J. Hiden, 575(SEER):Oct81-620
"Kommunikative Sozialforschung."
  E.W.B. Hess-Lüttich, 680(ZDP):Band100 Heft3-468
Konig, D.T. Law and Society in Puritan Massachusetts: Essex County, 1629-1692.*
  H.A. Johnson, 656(WMQ):Oct81-730
  I.K. Steele, 106:Winter81-313
Konig, D.T., ed. Plymouth Court Records, 1686-1859. (Vols 1-3)
  H.A. Johnson, 656(WMQ):Oct81-730
König, E. Form und Funktion.*
  W. Bublitz, 277(ITL):No47-74
  U. Oomen, 38:Band99Heft1/2-169
König, T., ed. Sartres Flaubert lesen.
  R. Neudeck, 489(PJGG):Band88Heft1-225
Konopacki, S.A. The Descent into Words.
  F.L. Borchardt, 221(GQ):Jan81-87
  E.A. Ebbinghaus, 568(SCN):Summer-Fall81-66
Konopnicki, G. Balades dans la culture.
  M. Kovacovic, 207(FR):Oct80-209
Konrád, G. The Loser.
  R. Sennett, 441:26Sep82-1
  442(NY):25Oct82-171
Konrád, G. and I. Szelényi. The Intellectuals on the Road to Class Power.*
  D.W. Treadgold, 396(ModA):Spring81-192
Konski, B. Poems.
  A. Cluysenaar, 565:Vol22No2-62

Kontos, A., ed. Powers, Possessions, and Freedom.*
  J.A.W. Gunn, 529(QQ):Winter81-794
Kontra, M. A nyelvek közötti kölcsönzés néhány kérdéséről.
  M.D. Birnbaum, 350:Jun82-486
Konwicki, T. The Polish Complex.* (Polish title: Kompleks polski.)
  J. Anders, 453(NYRB):4Mar82-16
  D.J. Enright, 617(TLS):10ct82-1063
  E. Hoffman, 441:10Jan82-3
van der Kooi, J., ed. Volksverhalen uit Friesland.
  H.L. Cox, 196:Band22Heft1/2-136
Kook, A.I. Abraham Isaac Kook. (B.Z. Bosker, ed and trans)
  L. Fine, 390:Jan81-61
Koon, H. and R. Switzer. Eugène Scribe.
  F. Bassan, 446(NCFS):Spring-Summer81-278
Koopmann, H., ed. Mythos und Mythologie in der Literatur des 19. Jahrhunderts.
  J. Müller, 680(ZDP):Band100Heft2-299
Kooser, T. Sure Signs.*
  M. Kinzie, 29:Sep/Oct82-37
  F.M. Link, 502(PrS):Spring-Summer81-307
Kooser, T., ed. The Windflower Home Almanac of Poetry.
  F.M. Link, 502(PrS):Spring-Summer81-307
Köpke, W. Erfolglosigkeit.
  C. Müller, 680(ZDP):Band99Heft2-306
Koppe, F. Sprache und Bedürfnis.*
  E. Albrecht, 682(ZPSK):Band33Heft2-256
  R. Welter, 679:Band11Heft2-387
Köppen, U. Die "Dialoghi d'amore" des Leone Ebreo in ihren französischen Übersetzungen.
  R. Schwaderer, 52:Band15Heft3-327
Kopper, E.A., Jr. John Millington Synge.*
  C.A. Carpenter, 397(MD):Mar81-119
  M. Kelsall, 610:Spring81-154
  D. Kiberd, 541(RES):Feb81-97
Kopper, J. - see Kant, I.
Koppitz, H-J. Studien zur Tradierung der weltlichen mittelhochdeutschen Epik im 15. und beginnenden 16. Jahrhundert.
  G. Lohse, 684(ZDA):Band110Heft4-172
  M.W. Wierschin, 133:Band14Heft4-361
Koppitz, H-J. - see "Gutenberg-Jahrbuch"
Köppl, S. Die Rezeption George Herberts im 17. und 18. Jahrhundert.*
  I. Leimberg, 72:Band217Heft2-420
Korda, M. Worldly Goods.
  J. Symons, 441:30May82-8
Korg, J. Language in Modern Literature.*
  G.L. Bruns, 401(MLQ):Jun81-204
  R. Fowler, 301(JEGP):Jul81-457
  W. French, 191(ELN):Jun81-319
Korhonen, J. Studien zu Dependenz, Valenz und Satzmodell. (Pt 1)
  T. Kotschi, 353:Vol 18No11/12-1157
Kornemann, E. Geschichte der Spätantike.
  J-P. Callu, 555:Vol154fasc2-387
Körner, G. Wendisches oder slavonisch-deutsches ausführliches und vollständiges Wörterbuch: eine Handschrift des 18. Jahrhunderts. (Pt 1, Vols 1-3)
  G. Stone, 575(SEER):Jan81-72
Körner, G. Wendisches oder slavonisch-deutsches ausführliches und vollständiges Wörterbuch: eine Handschrift des

18. Jahrhunderts. (Pt 2, Vols 1 and 2)
 G. Stone, 575(SEER):Oct81-588
Kors, A.C. D'Holbach's Coterie.*
 M.H. Waddicor, 208(FS):Apr81-207
Korte, H., ed. Film und Realität in der
 Weimarer Republik.
 D. Wöhrle, 602:Vol 12No1-282
Kortländer, B. Annette von Droste-
 Hülshoff und die deutsche Literatur.
 L.D. Wells, 221(GQ):Mar81-228
Kos, M.Š. Inscriptiones latinae in
 Graecia repertae.
 A.J.S. Spawforth, 313:Vol71-231
Kosáry, D. Művelődés a XVIII. századi
 Magyarországon.
 R.J.W. Evans, 575(SEER):Jul81-443
Koselleck, R. Le règne de la critique.
 M-P. Edmond, 98:Jun-Jul80-614
Koshal, S. Ladakhi Grammar. (B.G. Misra,
 ed)
 S. De Lancey, 350:Dec81-972
Kosík, K. Dialectics of the Concrete.*
 R. Albritton, 488:Jun80-233
Kosinski, J. Pinball.
 B. De Mott, 441:7Mar82-8
 A. Mars-Jones, 617(TLS):28May82-579
Koskinen, K.E. Nilal.
 A. Fox, 350:Sep82-726
Kosok, H. and H. Priessnitz, eds. Litera-
 turen in englischer Sprache.*
 K.G. Knight, 447(N&Q):Jun80-267
 W. Zacharasiewicz, 224(GRM):Band30
 Heft4-475
Kostelanetz, R., ed. The Avant-Garde Tra-
 dition in Literature.
 442(NY):30Aug82-91
Kostelanetz, R. - see Stein, G.
Koster, J. Locality Principles in Syntax.*
 P.W. Culicover, 350:Sep81-711
Koster, R.M. The Dissertation.
 T.J. Lewis, 37:Jun-Jul81-24
Koster, W.J.W. Scholia in Aristophanum.*
 (Pt 2, fasc 1)
 K.J. Dover, 123:Vol31No1-6
Kostis, N. The Exorcism of Sex and Death
 in Julien Green's Novels.
 A. Davin, 356(LR):Feb-May81-168
Kostiuk, H. Okaianni roky.
 R. Szporluk, 550(RusR):Apr81-203
Kōtarō, T. - see under Takamura Kōtarō
Kotin, A.A. The Narrative Imagination.*
 A. Iker-Gittleman, 545(RPh):
 Feb81(supp)-357
Kotošixin, G. O Rossii v carstvovanie
 Alekseja Mixajloviča. (A.E. Pennington,
 ed)
 C.E. Gribble, 574(SEEJ):Summer81-91
 W.E. Harkins, 550(RusR):Jan81-57
Kotschi, T. Probleme der Beschreibung
 lexikalischer Strukturen.
 G.F. Meier, 682(ZPSK):Band33Heft6-753
Köttelwesch, C., ed. Bibliographisches
 Handbuch der deutschen Literaturwissen-
 schaft 1945-1969. (Vol 2)
 S. Seifert, 654(WB):4:1981-169
Kotzwinkle, W. Christmas at Fontaine's.
 E. Ottenberg, 441:7Nov82-13
Kotzwinkle, W. E.T.
 G. Jonas, 441:29Aug82-10
Kouidis, V.M. Mina Loy.
 R.E. Mielke, 27(AL):Nov81-533
 E. Williams, 405(MP):Feb82-338

Kovačević, R., D.E. Stefanović and D. Bog-
 danović, eds. Matičin Apostol (XIII
 vek).
 A.E. Pennington, 575(SEER):Oct81-587
Köves-Zulauf, T. Reden und Schweigen.
 D.W.L. van Son, 394:Vol34fasc3/4-439
Kowalke, K.H. Kurt Weill in Europe.*
 D. Puffett, 415:Jan81-30
Koyano, M. Japanese Scroll Paintings.
 R. Lewis, 60:Jan-Feb81-136
Koyré, A. Galileo Studies.
 G.A.J. Rogers, 518:Apr81-84
Kozicki, H. Tennyson and Clio.*
 G.L. Bruns, 191(ELN):Dec80-150
 G. Joseph, 637(VS):Winter81-235
Koziełek, G., ed. Mittelalterrezeption.
 O. Ehrismann, 680(ZDP):Band100Heft1-
 144
 U. Meves, 224(GRM):Band30Heft2-233
Kozloff, M. Photography and Fascination.*
 P. Roussin, 98:Nov80-1065
Kraditor, A.S. The Radical Persuasion,
 1890-1917.
 P. Gottfried, 396(ModA):Fall81-413
von Kraemer, E., ed. "Le Jeu d'amour."
 D.A. Fein, 545(RPh):Feb81-369
Kraft, K-F.O. Iweins Triuwe.
 B. Nagel, 221(GQ):May81-336
 B. Nagel, 680(ZDP):Band100Heft3-425
Kraft, S. No Castles on Main Street.
 J.M. Mudge, 658:Spring81-105
Krailsheimer, A. Pascal.
 E. Moles, 208(FS):Apr81-198
Kramarae, C. Women and Men Speaking.
 S.H. Elgin, 350:Dec82-940
Kramer, A. Carousel Parkway and Other
 Poems.
 J. Schley, 434:Winter81-334
Kramer, D., ed. Critical Approaches to
 the Fiction of Thomas Hardy.*
 R.K. Anderson, 395(MFS):Winter80/81-
 704
 S. Curtis, 148:Summer81-87
 B. Harkness, 405(MP):Feb82-333
 S. Hunter, 677(YES):Vol 11-331
 M. Millgate, 445(NCF):Sep80-216
Kramer, J. Unsettling Europe.*
 S. Brown, 569(SR):Summer81-431
 P. Karmel, 219(GaR):Summer81-433
Kramer, L., ed. The Oxford History of
 Australian Literature.
 J.F. Burrows, 581:Sep81-358
Kramer, R. and D. White - see Pellaprat,
 H.P.
Kramer, T. Der Mensch zwischen Individuum
 und Kollektiv.
 K. Weissenberger, 133:Band14Heft1-94
Krannich, R.L. Mayors and Managers in
 Thailand.
 W.J. Siffin, 293(JASt):May81-650
Kranz, G. Lexikon der christlichen Welt-
 literatur.
 D. Gutzen, 52:Band15Heft1-64
Kranzberg, M., ed. Ethics in an Age of
 Pervasive Technology.
 T.M.R., 185:Jan82-399
Krapf, L. Germanenmythus und Reichs-
 ideologie.
 F.L. Borchardt, 133:Band14Heft4-363
 G. Hoffmeister, 406:Winter81-451
 U-K. Ketelsen, 221(GQ):May81-339
Krapf, L. and C. Wagenknecht - see Weckher-
 lin, G.R.

Krapf, M. Die Baumeister Gumpp.
    A. Laing, 576:Oct81-247
    N. Powell, 90:Mar81-176
Krashen, S.D. Second Language Acquisition
and Second Language Learning.
    P. Munsell and T.H. Carr, 351(LL):
    Dec81-493
Krasnov, V. Solzhenitsyn and Dostoevsky.*
    J.A. Schillinger, 395(MFS):Winter80/81-
    742
"Kratkaja literaturnaja Enciklopedija."
(A.A. Surkov, general ed)
    J. Glad, 574(SEEJ):Summer81-80
Kratzmann, G. Anglo-Scottish Literary
Relations, 1430-1550.*
    L. Ebin, 589:Oct81-881
Kraulis, J.A., ed. The Art of Canadian
Nature Photography.
    W.N., 102(CanL):Spring81-173
Kraus, E.M. The Metaphysics of Experi-
ence.*
    T.E. Burke, 518:Apr81-123
Kraus, H. Gold was the Mortar.*
    S. Murray, 54:Mar81-152
Kraus, J.W. Messrs. Copeland & Day.
    N. Barker, 78(BC):Autumn81-418
Krause, D. and R.G. Lowery, eds. Sean
O'Casey Centenary Essays.
    B. Dolan, 305(JIL):May81-132
Krause, H. Feder kontra Degen.*
    J. Hardin, 221(GQ):Mar81-214
Krause, S.J. and others - see Brown, C.B.
Krauss, H., ed. Altfranzösische Epik.
    T.D. Hemming, 208(FS):Oct81-423
    U. Mölk, 196:Band21Heft1/2-126
Krauss, J. Le "Dom Juan" de Molière.
    H.C. Hall, 475:No14Pt1-182
Krautheimer, R. Rome: Profile of a City,
312-1308.*
    R. Brentano, 589:Jul81-622
    A. Chastel, 576:Mar81-57
    P. Partner, 46:Jul81-63
Krawschack, R., with R. Mahlker. Mary
Lavin.
    R.F. Peterson, 174(Éire):Fall81-150
    M. Rohrberger, 395(MFS):Winter80/81-
    692
Krebs, H. Reminiscences and Reflections.
    J.F. Watkins, 617(TLS):21May82-561
Krebs, I. Paul Natorps Ästhetik.
    W. de Schmidt, 53(AGP):Band62Heft2-235
Kreisel, H. The Almost Meeting, and Other
Stories.
    W.J. Keith, 150(DR):Winter81/82-758
Krentz, P. The Thirty at Athens.
    P.J. Rhodes, 617(TLS):19Nov82-1276
Krepp, E. The Estonian War of Indepen-
dence, 1918-1920.
    D. Kirby, 575(SEER):Apr81-272
Kresh, P. Isaac Bashevis Singer.
    L. Field, 395(MFS):Winter80/81-653
Kress, G. and R. Hodge. Language as Ideol-
ogy.*
    A.D. Grimshaw, 350:Sep81-759
    H. Ormsby-Lennon, 402(MLR):Jan81-139
Krestan, L., comp. Vorarbeiten zu einem
Lexicon Ambrosianum.
    P. Courcelle, 555:Vol54fasc2-381
Kretzenbacher, L. Legendenbilder aus dem
Feuerjenseits.
    L. Intorp, 196:Band22Heft3/4-353

Kretzmann, N., ed. Infinity and Contin-
uity in Ancient and Medieval Thought.
    J. Barnes, 617(TLS):27Aug82-931
Kretzschmar, W.A., Jr. - see McDavid, R.I.,
Jr.
Kreutzer, H.J. Überlieferung und Edition.*
    W. Schröder, 684(ZDA):Band110Heft3-138
Kreutzer, L. Mein Gott Goethe.
    J. Jacobs, 680(ZDP):Band100Heft2-297
Kreyling, M. Eudora Welty's Achievement
of Order.*
    J.A. Allen, 573(SSF):Spring81-188
    M.J. Bolsterli, 295(JML):Vol8No3/4-635
    J. Givner, 268(IFR):Winter82-61
    R.E. McGowan, 435:Summer81-204
    W.J. Stuckey, 395(MFS):Winter80/81-662
Krich, J. A Totally Free Man.
    L. Marcus, 617(TLS):28May82-594
Krieger, E. A Marxist Study of Shake-
speare's Comedies.
    W.L. Godshalk, 130:Spring81-91
    C. Hill, 570(SQ):Autumn81-408
Krieger, L. Ranke.*
    P.H. Reill, 319:Jan81-125
Krieger, M. Arts on the Level.
    K. Harries, 290(JAAC):Spring82-333
Krieger, M. Poetic Presence and Illusion.*
    G. Webster, 599:Fall81-495
Kring, W.D. Henry Whitney Bellows.
    L. Neufeldt, 432(NEQ):Mar81-141
Kripke, S.A. Naming and Necessity.*
    J.E.J. Altham, 518:Jan81-36
    T.L.S. Sprigge, 483:Jul81-431
Krippner, S. Human Possibilities
    D.J. Murray, 529(QQ):Winter81-765
Kris, E. Die ästhetische Illusion.
    C. Pietzcker, 224(GRM):Band30Heft3-355
Krishna, D. Political Development.
    J.J. Sylvan, 185:Oct81-165
Krishnamoorthy, K. - see Kuntaka
Krisman, S. Ducks and Drakes.*
    C. Hawtree, 364:Oct81-99
Krissdottir, M. John Cowper Powys and the
Magical Quest.
    M. Moran, 627(UTQ):Summer81-136
Kristensen, S.M. Georg Brandes.
    E. Sprinchorn, 563(SS):Autumn81-485
Kristeva, J. Desire in Language. (L.S.
Roudiez, ed)
    E. Baer, 141:Summer81-261
    C.J. Jannone, 435:Fall81-309
    J. Mall, 290(JAAC):Fall81-93
Kristeva, J. Pouvoirs de l'horreur.*
    C. Norris, 208(FS):Oct81-492
Kristjánsson, J., ed. Gripla I-III.
    H. Beck, 684(ZDA):Band110Heft1-1
"Kristusfremstillinger, Foredrag holdt ved
det 5. nordiske symposium for ikonogra-
fiske studier på Fuglsang 29. aug. — 3.
sept. 1976."
    R. Zeitler, 341:Vol50No2-101
Kritzman, L.D. Destruction/Découverte.
    R.D. Cottrell, 207(FR):Apr82-673
Kroeber, A.L. and E.W. Gifford. Karok
Myths. (G. Buzaljko, ed)
    J.L. Davis, 649(WAL):Winter82-320
Kroeber, K., ed. Traditional Literatures
of the American Indian.
    J.L. Davis, 649(WAL):Winter82-320
Kroeber, K. and W. Walling, eds. Images
of Romanticism.*
    K. Garlick, 447(N&Q):Oct80-452
    S.M. Tave, 677(YES):Vol 11-290

Kroetsch, R. The Crow Journals.*
  J. Kertzer, 627(UTQ):Summer81-170
Kröger, W. Das Publikum als Richter.*
  E.M. Batley, 402(MLR):Apr81-501
Krohn, R., B. Thum and P. Wapnewski, eds.
  Stauferzeit.
  D.H. Green, 402(MLR):Jan81-230
Król, M. Style politycznego myślenia.
  A.J. Matejko, 497(PolR):Vol26No3-94
Kröll, F. Gruppe 47.*
  D.C.G. Lorenz, 221(GQ):Jan81-110
Kronenberg, A. and W., eds and trans.
  Nubische Märchen.
  E. Brunner-Traut, 196:Band21Heft1/2-
  127
Krönig, W. - see di Stefano, G.
Krotkov, Y. The Nobel Prize.*
  T.C. Holyoke, 42(AR):Winter81-127
Krotkov, Y. The Red Monarch. (C.H. Smith,
  ed)
  H.J. Ellison, 550(RusR):Apr81-200
Kruck, W.E. Looking for Dr. Condom.
  P. Rogers, 617(TLS):19Feb82-185
Krueger, J.R. - see Pozdneyev, A.M.
Kruft, H-W. Antonello Gagini und seine
  Söhne.*
  J.D. Draper, 90:Jan81-42
Krummacher, H-H., ed. Briefe deutscher
  Barockautoren.
  B. Becker-Cantarino, 221(GQ):Jan81-88
Krusche, D. Kafka und Kafka-Deutung.
  B. Goldstein, 406:Spring81-67
Krusche, D. Kommunikation im Erzähltext.
  J.H. Petersen, 680(ZDP):Band99Heft4-
  597
  M. Pfister, 490:Band12Heft1-140
Kruse, J. Red Omega.*
  T.J. Binyon, 617(TLS):9Apr82-422
Krustev, V. Bulgarian Music.
  I. Markoff, 187:May82-324
Kryger, E. La Notion de liberté chez
  Rousseau et ses répercussions sur Kant.
  J.F. Jones, Jr., 207(FR):May81-870
Krysin, L.P. and D.N. Shmelev, eds.
  Social'no-lingvisticheskie issledovanija.
  J.F. Levin, 355(LSoc):Apr81-85
Kšicová, D. Ruská poezie v interpretaci
  Františka Táborského.
  D. Short, 575(SEER):Jul81-476
Ku-Ying, C. - see under Ch'en Ku-Ying
Kubach, H.E. and A. Verbeek. Romanische
  Baukunst an Rhein und Maas.
  W.E. Kleinbauer, 54:Sep81-508
Kubik, G. The Kachamba Brothers' Band.
  J.E. Kaemmer, 187:Sep82-474
Kubler, G. Building the Escorial.
  V. Fraser, 617(TLS):17Sep82-1017
Kugler, R.C. William Allen Wall.
  M.B. Péladeau, 658:Winter81-349
Kühebacher, E., ed. Deutsche Heldenepik
  in Tirol.
  U. Hennig, 684(ZDA):Band109Heft4-148
Kühlewind, G. Présence du logos selon les
  données de Jean l'évangéliste.
  A. Reix, 542:Jul-Sep81-339
Kuhn, H. Entwürfe zu einer Literatur-
  systematik des Spätmittelalters.
  H. Kratz, 133:Band14Heft4-357
Kühn, P. Deutsche Wörterbücher.*
  D. Herberg, 682(ZPSK):Band33Heft5-635
  J. Splett, 680(ZDP):Band100Heft3-472
Kühn, P. Der Grundwortschatz.*
  A. Kirkness, 680(ZDP):Band100Heft1-149

Kuhn, T.S. Black-Body Theory and the
  Quantum Discontinuity, 1894-1912.*
  P. Galison, 84:Mar81-71
Kuhn, T.S. The Essential Tension.*
  D. Zaret, 482(PhR):Jan81-146
Kühnel, J., H-D. Mück and U. Müller, eds.
  Mittelalter-Rezeption.
  G.F. Jones, 221(GQ):Nov81-506
Kuiper, F.B.J. Varuṇa and Vidūṣaka.
  M. Biardeau, 259(IIJ):Oct81-293
Kuipers, T.A.F. Studies in Inductive Prob-
  ability and Rational Expectation.
  R.J. Ackermann, 518:Jan81-44
Kuizenga, D. Narrative Strategies in "La
  Princesse de Clèves."
  205(FMLS):Apr80-190
Kulcsár, P. - see Ransanus, P.
Kulenkampff, J. Kants Logik des ästheti-
  schen Urteils.
  P. Guyer, 290(JAAC):Winter81-212
Kulsdom, G. Die Strophenschlüsse im
  "Nibelungenlied."
  E.R. Haymes, 406:Winter81-447
  D.R. McLintock, 447(N&Q):Jun80-287
Kulshrestha, C. Saul Bellow.
  J.J. Waldmeir, 395(MFS):Winter80/81-
  675
Kulshrestha, J.P. Graham Greene.
  U. Böker, 224(GRM):Band31Heft4-482
  R.H. Costa, 395(MFS):Summer80-293
  K. Williamson, 447(N&Q):Jun80-264
"Kul'tura razvitogo socializma."
  H. Schlemm, 654(WB):2/1981-186
"Kul'turnoe nasledie drevnej Rusi."
  G.A. Levinton, 559:Aug81-329
Kumin, M. Our Ground Time Here Will Be
  Brief. Why Can't We Live Together Like
  Civilized Human Beings?
  A. Ostriker, 441:8Aug82-10
Kummer, I.E. Blaise Pascal.
  A.v.S., 543:Sep80-147
Kuna, F. Franz Kafka.
  B. Goldstein, 406:Spring81-67
Kundera, M. The Book of Laughter and For-
  getting.* (French title: Le Livre du
  rire et de l'oubli.)
  A. Bold, 617(TLS):5Feb82-131
  G. Kearns, 249(HudR):Summer81-307
  J. Mellors, 362:11Feb82-24
  N. Miller, 42(AR):Spring81-260
Kundera, M. The Joke.
  I. Howe, 441:24Oct82-3
Kuné, J.H. Die Auferstehung Christi im
  deutschen religiösen Drama des Mittel-
  alters.*
  B. Thoran, 680(ZDP):Band100Heft3-443
Kunene, M. Anthem of the Decades.
  A. Delius, 617(TLS):14May82-541
Küng, H. Does God Exist?*
  R. Harper, 400(MLN):Dec81-1195
Kung-ch'üan, H. - see under Hsiao Kung-
  ch'üan
Kuniczak, W.S. The March.
  A.C. Lupack, 497(PolR):Vol26No3-100
Kuniholm, B.R. The Origins of the Cold
  War in the Near East.*
  W.T. Wooley, 106:Winter81-387
Kunnás, T. Nietzsche ou l'esprit de con-
  tradiction.
  E. Blondel, 542:Oct-Dec81-497
"Die Künste in der DDR."
  H. Möbius, 654(WB):3/1981-182

"Künstlerinnen der russischen Avantgarde/
Women-Artists of the Russian Avantgarde,
1910-1930."
  M.B. Betz, 127:Fall/Winter80-417
Kunstmann, P., ed. Jean le Marchant,
"Miracles de Notre-Dame de Chartres."
  P. Ménard, 545(RPh):Feb81(supp)-264
Kuntaka. The Vakrokti-jīvita of Kuntaka.
(K. Krishnamoorthy, ed and trans)
  R.W. Lariviere, 318(JAOS):Jul/Sep80-
  324
Kuntz, J.M. and N.C. Martinez. Poetry
Explication.
  27(AL):Nov81-577
Kunz, J. Die deutsche Novelle im 19. Jahr-
hundert. Die deutsche Novelle im 20.
Jahrhundert.
  J. Müller, 680(ZDP):Band99Heft2-314
Kunzang, R.R.J. - see under Rechung Rin-
poche Jampal Kunzang
Kunze, M. Die Funktion der bukolischen
Klischees in der englischen Literatur
von Spenser bis Pope und Philips.
  R. Borgmeier, 52:Band15Heft2-196
Kunze, M., ed. Johann Joachim Winckelmann
und Adam Friedrich Oeser.
  G. Schwarz, 52:Band15Heft1-90
Kunzle, D. Fashion and Fetishism.
  A. Hollander, 453(NYRB):4Mar82-21
Kuo Heng-yü. Die Komintern und die Chine-
sische Revolution.
  W. Kirby, 293(JASt):Feb81-353
Kuper, A. Wives for Cattle.
  E. Gillies, 617(TLS):2Jul82-724
Kuper, H. Sobhuza II, Ngwenyama and King
of Swaziland.
  R.P. Werbner, 69:Vol50No4-431
Kuper, L. Genocide.
  M. Banton, 617(TLS):2Jul82-715
  T. Taylor, 441:28Mar82-9
Kuper, L. International Action Against
Genocide.
  M. Banton, 617(TLS):2Jul82-715
Kupper, H.J. Robert Burns im deutschen
Sprachraum unter besonderer Berücksichti-
gung der schweizerdeutschen Übersetzun-
gen von August Corrodi.
  A.M. Stewart, 571(ScLJ):Summer80-96
  C.J. Wickham, 406:Fall81-357
  W. Witte, 402(MLR):Jul81-748
Kupperman, K.O. Settling with the Indians.
  H.C. Rountree, 656(WMQ):Apr81-308
  W.S. Simmons, 432(NEQ):Jun81-269
Küppers, J. Die Fabeln Avians.
  P. Flobert, 555:Vol54fasc2-379
Kurczaba, A. Gombrowicz and Frisch.
  R. Grol-Prokopczyk, 497(PolR):Vol26No3-
  82
Kurelek, W. Someone With Me.
  K. Garebian, 102(CanL):Autumn81-136
Kuretsky, S.D. The Paintings of Jacob
Ochtervelt.*
  B. Wind, 568(SCN):Winter81-97
Kuriyama, C.B. Hammer or Anvil.
  T.B. Stroup, 130:Summer81-178
  639(VQR):Spring81-56
Kuroda, S-Y. Aux quatre coins de la lin-
guistique.
  A. Zribi-Hertz, 209(FM):Oct81-382
Kurosawa, A. Something Like An Autobiogra-
phy.
  P-L. Adams, 61:Jul82-94
[continued]

[continuing]
  F. Gibney, 441:27Jun82-8
  442(NY):12Jul82-106
Kuroyanagi, T. Totto-chan.
  S. Chira, 441:21Nov82-15
Kurtz, L.S. Historical Dictionary of
Tanzania.
  A. Redmayne, 69:Vol50No1-101
Kurtz, M.L. Crime of the Century.
  J. Sparrow, 617(TLS):8Oct82-1092
Kuryłowicz, J. Problèmes de linguistique
indo-européenne.*
  R. Ködderitzsch, 260(IF):Band85-322
Kurz, G. Traum-Schrecken.
  T. Elm, 680(ZDP):Band100Heft4-619
  J.M. Grandin, 406:Spring81-97
Kurzweil, E. The Age of Structuralism.
  M. Green, 363(LitR):Spring82-448
  C.J. Jannone, 435:Fall81-311
Kušakov, A.V. Puškin i Pol'ša.
  V. Perelešin, 558(RLJ):Winter81-229
Kushner, E. and R. Struc, eds. Litera-
tures of America.
  E. Caracciolo-Trejo, 678(YCGL):No29-39
Kushner, H.S. When Bad Things Happen to
Good People.
  C.D. May, 441:3Jan82-10
Kuśniewicz, A. La Leçon de langue morte.
  L. Kovacs, 450(NRF):Nov81-149
Kuśniewicz, A. L'état d'apesanteur.* Le
roi des Deux-Siciles.
  R. Micha, 98:Dec80-1148
Kussmaul, A. Servants in Husbandry in
Early Modern England.
  J. Thirsk, 617(TLS):15Oct82-1128
Kuzma, G., ed. A Book of Rereadings.
  P.B. Newman, 601:Spring81-75
Kuzminsky, K.K. and G.L. Kovalev, eds.
The Blue Lagoon Anthology of Modern
Russian Poetry. (Vol 1)
  C. Janecek, 574(SEEJ):Fall81-130
Kuznetsov, Y. and I. Linnik. Dutch Paint-
ing in Soviet Museums.
  J. Russell, 441:5Dec82-13
Kvam, W.E. Hemingway in Germany.
  J. Utz, 72:Band21Heft1-170
Kvideland, R. Lita-Frid-Kirsti.
  O. Holzapfel, 196:Band22Heft1/2-111
Kvist, H-O. Zum Verhältnis von Wissen und
Glauben in der kritischen Philosophie
Immanuel Kants.
  A.v.S., 543:Sep80-145
  W. Steinbeck, 342:Band71Heft3-372
Kwanten, L. Imperial Nomads.
  Chin-Fu Hung, 244(HJAS):Dec81-597
Kwock, C.H. and V. McHugh, eds and trans.
Old Friend From Far Away.
  639(VQR):Autumn81-132
Kwong, J. Chinese Education in Transition.
  J. Glassman, 293(JASt):Feb81-362
Kyria, P. L'Heure froide.
  C.J. Murphy, 207(FR):Apr82-707

Laage, K.E. Theodor Storm.
  W.N.B. Mullan, 402(MLR):Jan81-247
Laage, K-E. and V. Hand - see "Schriften
der Theodor-Storm Gesellschaft"
Labandeira Fernández, A. - see Rodríguez
de Lena, P.
Labaree, B.W. Colonial Massachusetts.
  R. Zemsky, 656(WMQ):Jul81-519

Laforgue, J. Moralités légendaires.* (D. Grojnowski, ed)
P.G. Lewis, 207(FR):Oct81-143
Lafourcade, B. - see Lewis, W.
Lagarde, F. - see Mason, J.
Lagerberg, K. West Irian and Jakarta Imperialism.
J.M. van der Kroef, 293(JASt):Feb81-426
Lagerlöf, K.E., ed. Modern Swedish Prose in Translation.
R. Jarvi, 563(SS):Spring81-239
Lago, M. - see Burne-Jones, E.C.
Lahougue, J. Comptine des Height.*
C.V. Jacquemont, 207(FR):Mar82-570
Lahr, J. Coward the Playwright.
N. Shrimpton, 617(TLS):1Oct82-1061
Lahr, J. Prick Up Your Ears.*
D.R. Noble, 577(SHR):Summer81-272
Lai, T.C. Understanding Chinese Painting.
P. Mole, 135:May81-74
Lainé, P. L'Eau du miroir.*
L. de Vitry-Maubrey, 207(FR):May81-896
Laing, R.D. The Voice of Experience.
D. Ingleby, 617(TLS):3Sep82-939
Lakatos, I. The Methodology of Scientific Research Programmes. Mathematics, Science and Epistemology. (J. Worrall and G. Currie, eds of both)
J.F. Fox, 63:Mar81-92
Lakatos, I. Proofs and Refutations.* (J. Worrall and E. Zahar, eds)
P. Marchi, 488:Dec80-445
Lake, P. Moderate Puritans and the Elizabethan Church.
C. Cross, 617(TLS):3Sep82-954
Lakebrink, B. Kommentar zu Hegels "Logik" in seiner "Enzyklopädie" von 1830. (Vol 1)
M.G., 543:Dec80-390
Lakier, A.B. A Russian Looks at America!* (A. Schrier and J. Story, eds and trans)
J.I. Gow, 104(CASS):Winter81-591
Lakoff, G. and M. Johnson. Metaphors We Live By.*
M. Black, 290(JAAC):Winter81-208
R. Greene, 400(MLN):Dec81-1173
Lakshin, V. Solzhenitsyn, Tvardovsky, and "Novy Mir."
E.R. Frankel, 550(RusR):Oct81-477
Lalande, J. Journal d'un voyage en Angleterre, 1763. (H. Monod-Cassidy, ed)
S. Diaconoff, 207(FR):Dec81-272
J. Renwick, 402(MLR):Oct81-968
Lalanne-Berdouticq, P. Appel aus Francophones pour le français, langue de l'Europe.
J-F. Brière, 207(FR):Feb82-451
Lalonde, M. Défense et illustration de la langue québécoise suivie de prose et poèmes.
A.B. Chartier, 207(FR):Mar82-571
P. Merivale, 102(CanL):Spring81-127
Lalonde, M. Dernier recours de Baptiste à Catherine.
D.M. Hayne, 102(CanL):Summer80-129
Lam, B. Beethoven String Quartets.
J.B., 412:Aug80-238
Lamar, H. and L. Thompson, eds. The Frontier in History.
G.M. Fredrickson, 453(NYRB):18Mar82-51

Lamb, C. and M.A. The Letters of Charles and Mary Lamb. (Vol 1) (E.W. Marrs, Jr., ed)
H-J. Schild, 38:Band99Heft1/2-250
Lamb, C. and M.A. The Letters of Charles and Mary Anne Lamb.* (Vol 3) (E.W. Marrs, Jr., ed)
P. Morgan, 179(ES):Feb81-83
Lamb, C. and M.A. Tales from Shakespeare.
42(AR):Winter81-133
Lamb, M. "Antony and Cleopatra" on the English Stage.
C.H. Shattuck, 570(SQ):Summer81-281
Lamb, V. and A. Au Cameroun: Weaving — Tissage.
J.B. Donne, 617(TLS):17Sep82-994
Lambek, M. Human Spirits.
I.M. Lewis, 617(TLS):2Jul82-724
Lambersy, W. Maîtres et maisons de thé.
S. Lawall, 207(FR):Apr82-708
Lambert, B. Bring Down the Sun.
639(VQR):Winter81-20
Lambert, B. Clouds of Glory.
A. Ravel, 102(CanL):Summer81-158
Lambert, D. The Red Dove.
T.J. Binyon, 617(TLS):29Oct82-1196
Lambert, E.Z. Placing Sorrow.*
F. Mouret, 549(RLC):Jul-Dec81-501
Lambert, G. Running Time.
J. Astor, 362:28Oct82-28
Lambert, J. and R. Tedeschi - see Gide, A. and D. Bussy
Lambert, M. Dickens and the Suspended Quotation.*
M. Wheeler, 155:Autumn81-176
Lamberz, E. and E.K. Litsas. Katalogos cheirographōn tēs Batopedinēs skētēs Hagiou Dēmētriou.
N.G. Wilson, 303(JoHS):Vol 101-227
Lambourne, L. Utopian Craftsmen.
G. Darley, 135:Oct81-93
J.E. Nuttgens, 46:Jan81-64
Lambourne, L. and J. Hamilton, comps. British Watercolours in the Victoria and Albert Museum.
J.E., 90:Jul81-449
Lambton, A.K.S. State and Government in Medieval Islam.
C.J. Wickham, 617(TLS):30Apr82-495
Lämmert, E. and H. Eggert, with others, eds. Romantheorie.
M. Wegner, 654(WB):9/1981-185
Lamonde, Y. La Philosophie et son enseignement au Québec (1665-1920).
L. Marcil-Lacoste, 154:Sep81-600
J.T. Stevenson, 627(UTQ):Summer81-206
Lamont, C. - see Scott, W.
Lamont, C. and L. - see Masefield, J.
Lamott, A. Hard Laughter.
639(VQR):Spring81-60
L'Amour, L. Bendigo Shafter. Comstock Lode.
J.D. Nesbitt, 649(WAL):Winter82-315
Lamp, F. African Art of the West Atlantic Coast.
W.L. d'Azevedo, 2(AfrA):Nov80-81
Lamparter, H. Prüfet die Geister. (6th ed)
R.M., 342:Band71Heft4-511

Langbaum, R. The Mysteries of Identity.*
  M. McKie, 184(EIC):Jul81-263
  P. Stevick, 473(PR):2/1981-323
Lange, W-D., ed. Französische Literatur
  des 19. Jahrhunderts.
  D.P. Haase, 446(NCFS):Spring-Summer82-
  360
Lange-Seidl, A. Approaches to Theories
  for Nonverbal Signs.
  I. Rauch, 567:Vol34No1/2-167
Langer, G. Das Märchen in der tschechis-
  chen Literatur von 1790 bis 1860.
  J. Jech, 196:Band22Heft1/2-137
  R.B. Pynsent, 575(SEER):Apr81-290
Langford, G. The Adventures of Dreaded
  Ned.
  C. Ackerley, 368:Sep81-371
Langguth, A.J. Saki.*
  C. Hawtree, 364:Feb82-103
Langham, I. The Building of British
  Social Anthropology.
  R. Needham, 617(TLS):12Feb82-164
Langholf, V. Syntaktische Untersuchungen
  zu Hippokrates-Texten.
  F. Kudlien, 260(IF):Band85-344
Langland, J. Any Body's Song.*
  R. Tillinghast, 569(SR):Spring81-265
Langland, W. Piers Plowman.* (D. Pear-
  sall, ed)
  S.A. Barney, 589:Jan81-161
  D.C. Fowler, 677(YES):Vol 11-224
  C. Gauvin, 189(EA):Apr-Jun81-211
Langland, W. The Vision of Piers Plowman.
  (A.V.C. Schmidt, ed)
  S.A. Barney, 589:Jan81-161
  D.C. Fowler, 677(YES):Vol 11-224
  C. Gauvin, 189(EA):Apr-Jun81-211
  B. Raw, 447(N&Q):Feb80-85
  C. Wilcockson, 382(MAE):1981/1-166
Langley, L.D. The United States and the
  Caribbean, 1900-1970.
  W.T. Wooley, 106:Winter81-387
Langlois, W.G., ed. André Malraux, 4.
  A. Vandegans, 535(RHL):May-Jun81-483
Langton, J. Natural Enemy.
  N. Callendar, 441:16May82-26
Langton, S. Selected Sermons of Stephen
  Langton. (P.B. Roberts, ed)
  G.R. Evans, 382(MAE):1981/1-125
"Language Files."
  D.R. Ladd, 350:Dec82-890
Langvik-Johannessen, K. Litteraturen i
  Nederlandene gjennom 800 år.
  J.W. Dietrichson, 172(Edda):1981/5-335
Lanham, L.W. and C.A. Macdonald. The Stan-
  dard in South African English and its
  Social History.
  D. Blair, 67:May81-134
  U. Dürmüller, 350:Jun81-498
  H. Ulherr, 38:Band99Heft3/4-476
Lanham, L.W. and K.P. Prinsloo, eds.
  Language and Communication Studies in
  South Africa.
  M. Görlach, 72:Band217Heft2-407
Lanham, R.A. The Motives of Eloquence.
  L.S. Lerner, 545(RPh):May81-503
Lanher, J., ed. Documents linguistiques
  de la France, série française. (Vol 2)
  M.S. La Du, 545(RPh):Feb81-336
Lankheit, K. Friedrich Weinbrenner und
  der Denkmalskult um 1800.
  R. Dorn, 43:Band11Heft1-83

Lanly, A. Morphologie historique des
  verbes français.*
  M.W. Epro, 545(RPh):Nov80-241
"L'Année balzacienne 1980."
  O. Heathcote, 446(NCFS):Fall-Win-
  ter81/82-139
Lansbury, C. The Reasonable Man.
  R.D. McMaster, 445(NCF):Mar82-487
  A. Wright, 617(TLS):19Mar82-322
Lansdown, A. Homecoming.
  C. Pollnitz, 581:Jun81-221
Lansing, R.H. From Image to Idea.
  G. Costa, 545(RPh):May81-521
Lant, J.L. Insubstantial Pageant.
  F. Hardie, 637(VS):Spring81-357
Lantolf, J.P. and others, eds. Colloquium
  on Spanish and Luso-Brazilian Linguis-
  tics.
  T.D. Terrell, 350:Mar81-235
Lantz, K.A. Nikolay Leskov.*
  F.C.M. Kitch, 575(SEER):Oct81-597
  J.J. Rinkus, 104(CASS):Winter81-559
Lao She. Rikschakuli. (L. Frender, trans)
  I. Fessen-Henjes, 654(WB):4/1981-133
Lao Tzu. A Translation of Lao Tzu's "Tao
  Te Ching" and Wang Pi's Commentary.
  (P.J. Lin, trans)
  W.G. Boltz, 318(JAOS):Jan/Mar80-84
  H. Welch, 293(JASt):Feb81-359
Lapesa, R. Historia de la lengua española.
  (8th ed)
  R. Wright, 86(BHS):Jan81-74
Lapesa, R. Poetas y prosistas de ayer y
  de hoy.
  J. Snow, 545(RPh):May81-575
Lapeza, D. - see Gumilev, N.
Lapierre, R. Les Masques du récit.
  F. Iqbal, 102(CanL):Spring81-105
La Plantz, S. Plaited Basketry.
  P. Bach, 614:Fall82-19
Lapointe, G. Arbre-Radar.
  M. Cagnon, 207(FR):Dec81-305
Laporte, H. - see de Nerval, G.
Lappé, M. Genetic Politics.
  G.R. Fraser, 529(QQ):Autumn81-575
Laqueur, W. The Terrible Secret.*
  K. Kellen, 390:Aug/Sep81-58
  L.D. Stokes, 150(DR):Summer81-372
Laqueur, W. and B. Rubin, eds. The Human
  Rights Reader.
  R.P.C., 185:Oct80-171
Lara, L.F. En concepto de forma en lin-
  güística.
  R. Posner, 545(RPh):Aug80-95
Larbaud, V. and M. Ray. Correspondance.*
  (Vol 3)
  P. Bayard, 450(NRF):Mar81-120
"Valery Larbaud et la littérature de son
  temps."*
  R. Gay-Crosier, 207(FR):Dec80-350
Largeault, J. Enigmes et controverses.
  J-L. Gardies, 542:Oct-Dec81-505
  Y. Gauthier, 154:Dec81-820
Largeault, J. Hasards, probabilités,
  inductions.
  J-L. Gardies, 542:Oct-Dec81-503
Largeault, J. Quine, Questions de mots,
  Questions de faits.
  J-L. Gardies, 542:Oct-Dec81-508
de Larivey, P. Les Esprits.* (D. Stone,
  Jr., ed) Les Esprits. (M.J. Freeman,
  ed)
  J. Beck, 545(RPh):Feb81(supp)-311

Larkin, E. The Making of the Roman Catholic Church in Ireland, 1850-1860.
 D. Bowen, 529(QQ):Summer81-381
 A. O'Day, 637(VS):Spring81-384
Larmat, J. Le Moyen âge dans le Gargantua de Rabelais.
 J.S. Kittay, 546(RR):Jan81-105
Laroch, P. Petits-maîtres et roués.
 M. Therrien, 535(RHL):Nov-Dec81-989
de La Rochefoucauld, E. Courts métrages II.
 J.M.J. Rogister, 161(DUJ):Jun81-237
de La Rochefoucauld, J.D., C. Wolikow and G. Ikni. Le duc de La Rochefoucauld Liancourt, 1747-1827.
 J.M.J. Rogister, 161(DUJ):Jun81-237
Larochette, J. Le langage et la réalité.
 S. Norwood, 545(RPh):Feb81(supp)-321
Larocque, G. Le Refuge.
 M. Cagnon, 207(FR):Apr82-709
Larsen, E., with J.P. Davidson. Calvanistic Economy and 17th Century Dutch Art.
 C. Brown, 39:Dec81-429
Larsen, S.U., B. Hagvet and J.P. Myklebust, eds. Who Were the Fascists?
 A. Beichman, 617(TLS):19Feb82-180
Larson, C.F.W., comp. American Regional Theatre History to 1900.
 T.F. Marshall, 610:Autumn81-226
Larson, D.R. The Honor Plays of Lope de Vega.*
 J.A. Parr, 240(HR):Summer81-354
"L'Arte del Settecento Emiliano."
 M. Jacobs, 90:Aug81-494
Larteguy, J. Les Naufragés du soleil 3.
 D.B. Brautman, 207(FR):Apr82-710
Larthomas, P. Le Langage dramatique, sa nature, ses procédés. (new ed)
 G. Montbertrand, 207(FR):May82-895
Larthomas, P. Le Théâtre en France au XVIIIe siècle.
 G. Antoine, 209(FM):Jan81-59
La Rue, J. Guidelines for Style Analysis.
 E. Sams, 415:Apr81-243
Larue, M. La Cohorte fictive.
 D. Brautman, 207(FR):Feb81-506
Laruelle, F. Le principe de minorité.
 A. Reix, 542:Apr-Jun81-241
Lascault, G. Escrits timides sur le visible.
 G. Raillard, 98:Nov80-1107
Lascaut, G. Boucles et noeuds. La Destinée de Jean Simon Castor.
 O. Juilliard, 450(NRF):Jul-Aug81-184
Lascelles, M. The Story-Teller Retrieves the Past.
 A.S. Byatt, 617(TLS):28May82-591
 E.M. Eigner, 445(NCF):Mar82-492
Lasch, C. The Culture of Narcissism.*
 P. Nachbar, 186(ETC.):Summer81-205
Lasdun, S. The Victorians at Home.*
 A. Stumpf, 46:Dec81-370
Lash, J.P. Love, Eleanor.
 N. Bliven, 442(NY):9Aug82-89
 G.C. Ward, 441:13Jun82-11
Lasher, P. and B. Bentley. Texas Women.
 J.M. Johnson, 584(SWR):Autumn81-437
Lasker-Schüler, E. Hebrew Ballads and Other Poems.* (A. Durchslag and J. Litman-Demeestère, eds and trans)
 L. Elkin, 287:Aug-Sep81-45

Laskowski, R. Studia nad morfonologią współczesnego języka polskiego.
 R.D. Steele, 279:Vol24-183
Laslett, P. and J. Fishkin, eds. Philosophy, Politics and Society.
 R. Abrams, 185:Oct80-156
Lasnier, R. Matin d'Oiseaux. Paliers de Paroles.
 G.V. Downes, 102(CanL):Winter80-105
Lasocki, D. and B.B. Mather. The Classical Woodwind Cadenza.
 N. O'Loughlin, 415:Jun81-383
de Lasphrise, M.P. "Les Amours de Théophile" et "L'Amour passionnée de Noémie." (M.M. Callaghan, ed)
 J.C. Nash, 207(FR):Mar82-546
Lass, N.J., ed. Speech and Language.
 H.W. Buckingham, 215(GL):Winter81-272
 M.R. Smith, 350:Dec81-964
Lass, R. On Explaining Language Change.*
 F. D'Agostino, 63:Dec81-457
 E. Itkonen, 350:Sep81-688
 G. Sampson, 84:Mar81-98
 J. Vachek, 361:Jun/Jul81-249
Lassner, J. The Shaping of 'Abbāsid Rule.
 R.W. Bulliet, 589:Jul81-629
Lasson, F. - see Dinesen, I.
Latacz, J., ed. Homer: Tradition und Neuerung.
 F. Vian, 555:Vol54fasc2-340
"Lateinisches Hexameter-Lexikon." (Pt 1) (O. Schumann and B. Bischoff, comps)
 P. Godman, 382(MAE):1981/2-311
 L. Wenger, 589:Jan81-222
Lathem, E.C. and L. Thompson - see Frost, R.
Lathen, E. Green Grow the Dollars.
 T.J. Binyon, 617(TLS):28May82-594
 N. Callendar, 441:4Apr82-29
 M. Laski, 362:29Apr82-27
Lathrop, T.A. The Evolution of Spanish.
 R.M. Barasch, 399(MLJ):Winter81-446
Latortue, R. and G.R.W. Adams. "Les Cenelles."
 L-F. Hoffmann, 535(RHL):May-Jun81-495
La Touche, R. John Ruskin and Rose La Touche.* (V.A. Burd, ed)
 F.G. Townsend, 637(VS):Winter81-248
Latsis, S., ed. Method and Appraisal in Economics.
 A. Rosenberg, 449:May81-225
Latta, F.F. Joaquin Murrieta and His Horse Gangs.
 G. Haslam, 649(WAL):Fall81-237
"L'Attentat de Damiens: Discours sur l'événement au XVIIIe siècle."
 H.T. Mason, 400(MLN):May81-942
de Lattre, A. La Doctrine de la réalité chez Proust.
 J.N. Megay, 207(FR):May81-874
Lauben, P. A Surfeit of Alibis.
 T.J. Binyon, 617(TLS):31Dec82-1448
Laubin, R. and G. American Indian Archery.
 L.D. Olsen, 649(WAL):Fall81-233
Laudan, L. Progress and its Problems.*
 G. Doppelt, 262:Jun81-253
 P.K. Feyerabend, 84:Mar81-57
Lauer, Q. Essays in Hegelian Dialectic.
 C. Butler, 319:Apr81-264
 W.E. Steinkraus, 125:Summer81-444
Lauerbach, G. Form und Funktion englischer Konditionalsätze mit "if."
 G. Deimer, 38:Band99Heft3/4-453

Lauf, D-I. Verborgene Botschaft tibetis-
cher Thangkas.
  J.C. Huntington, 318(JAOS):Jul/Sep80-
  326
Laufhütte, H. Die deutsche Kunstballade.
  W. Ruttkowski, 221(GQ):Nov81-491
Launey, M. Introduction à la langue et à
la littérature aztèques.
  W. Bright, 350:Jun81-511
Laur, W. Die Ortsnamen im Kreise Pinne-
berg.
  G.B. Droege, 424:Dec80-301
Laurance, A. and I. Asimov, eds. Who Done
It?
  T.C. Holyoke, 42(AR):Summer81-390
Laurence, D.H. - see Shaw, G.B.
Laurence, M. The Christmas Birthday Story.
  W.N., 102(CanL):Summer81-171
Laurens, A. Le Métier politique.
  H.L. Butler, 207(FR):Apr81-753
Laurenti, H. - see "Paul Valéry 2"
Laurie, B. Working People of Philadelphia,
1800-1850.
  H.B. Rock, 658:Winter81-347
Laurie, P. Electronics Explained.
  L.E. Peppard, 529(QQ):Winter81-763
Lauriol, C. La Beaumelle.*
  D.A. Bonneville, 207(FR):Oct80-161
  J. Lough, 208(FS):Jul81-332
Lausberg, H. Der Hymnus "Veni Creator
Spiritus."
  P. Courcelle, 555:Vol54fasc2-382
Lauterer, J. Wouldn't Take Nothin' for My
Journey Now.
  42(AR):Spring81-265
Lauth, R. Die Entstehung von Schellings
Identitätsphilosophie in der Auseinander-
setzung mit Fichtes Wissenschaftslehre,
1795-1801.
  H. Holz, 53(AGP):Band62Heft1-103
Lauth, R. Theorie des philosophische
Arguments.
  H-J. Schild, 480(P&R):Spring81-122
"L'autobiographie dans le monde hispan-
ique."
  R. Ricard, 356(LR):Feb-May81-152
Lavagne, H. Recueil général des mosaïques
de la Guale III: Province de Narbon-
naise I.
  J. André, 555:Vol54fasc2-392
  R.J.A. Wilson, 313:Vol71-173
Lavater, J.K. Unveränderte Fragmente aus
dem Tagebuche eines Beobachters seiner
Selbst. (C. Siegrist, ed)
  K.J. Fink, 133:Band14Heft1-72
Lavender, D. The Southwest.
  E.W. Gaston, 649(WAL):Winter81-301
de Lavergnée, A.B. - see under Brejon de
Lavergnée, A.
Lavers, A. Roland Barthes.
  S. Heath, 617(TLS):10Dec82-1372
Lavezzari, P. - see Cozens, A.
Lavin, I. Bernini and the Unity of the
Visual Arts.*
  J. Coolidge, 576:Oct81-242
  C. Gould, 324:Apr82-295
  T.A. Marder, 46:Jul81-65
  O. Raggio, 39:Sep81-200
Lavin, I. Drawings by Gianlorenzo Bernini
from the Museum der Bildenden Künste,
Leipzig.
  M. Jaffé, 617(TLS):15Oct82-1127

Lavin, I. and J. Plummer, eds. Studies in
Late Medieval and Renaissance Painting
in Honor of Millard Meiss.
  D. Rosand, 551(RenQ):Autumn80-446
Lavin, M. Selected Short Stories.
  A. Douglas, 305(JIL):Sep81-109
Lavin, M.A. Piero della Francesca's Bap-
tism of Christ.
  J. White, 617(TLS):1Oct82-1077
Lavoie, C-A. A Deux contre la nuit.
  J. Viswanathan, 102(CanL):Spring81-122
Law, T.S. and T. Berwick - see MacDiarmid,
H.
Lawhorne, C.O. The Supreme Court and
Libel.
  G. Phifer, 583:Winter82-227
Lawler, J.G. Celestial Pantomime.
  J. Hollander, 473(PR):3/1981-478
  B. Michelson, 301(JEGP):Apr81-226
Lawler, J.R. René Char.*
  P. Aspel, 207(FR):May81-880
  C.A. Hackett, 208(FS):Jul81-362
  205(FMLS):Jan80-89
Lawler, T. The One and the Many in the
"Canterbury Tales."*
  R.B. Burlin, 589:Jul81-630
Lawn, B., ed. The Prose Salernitan Ques-
tions.
  C.S.F. Burnett, 203:Vol91No2-249
  L. Demaitre, 589:Jan81-166
Lawrance, J.N.H., ed. Un tratado de
Alonso de Cartagena sobre la educación y
los estudios literarios.
  A. Deyermond, 400(MLN):Mar81-445
  N.G. Round, 402(MLR):Jul81-719
Lawrence, A.W. Greek Aims in Fortifica-
tion.
  R.A. Tomlinson, 303(JoHS):Vol 101-211
Lawrence, B.B. Notes from a Distant Flute.
  S.S. Alvi, 293(JASt):Nov80-170
Lawrence, D.H. The Letters of D.H. Law-
rence.+ (Vol 1) (J.T. Boulton, ed)
  J.A.V. Chapple, 366:Autumn81-232
  K.M. Hewitt, 541(RES):Feb81-102
  S. Hynes, 569(SR):Winter81-125
  J. Lucas, 617(TLS):17Sep82-995
  M. Mudrick, 249(HudR):Spring81-125
Lawrence, D.H. The Letters of D.H. Law-
rence. (Vol 2) (G.J. Zytaruk and J.T.
Boulton, eds)
  J. Lucas, 617(TLS):17Sep82-995
  S. Spender, 362:10Jun82-24
Lawrence, D.H. The Lost Girl. (J. Worth-
en, ed)
  S. Gill, 617(TLS):19Mar82-313
Lawrence, E. and others, eds. Haida
Dictionary.
  R.D. Levine, 269(IJAL):Oct81-354
Lawrence, K. The Odyssey of Style in
"Ulysses."
  R. Brown, 617(TLS):20Aug82-909
  M. Sabin, 454:Spring82-271
Lawrence, R.D. Secret Go the Wolves.
  G.H. Tweney, 649(WAL):Winter81-313
Lawrence, R.G. and S.L. Macey, eds.
Studies in Robertson Davies' Deptford
Trilogy.
  J.S. Grant, 627(UTQ):Summer81-168
  S. Solecki, 99:Dec81/Jan82-30
Lawson, B.S. Joaquin Miller.
  A. Frietzsche, 649(WAL):Fall81-231

Lawvere, F.W., C. Maurer and G.C. Wraith,
eds. Model Theory and Topoi.
M.E. Szabo, 316:Mar81-158
Laxer, J. Canada's Economic Strategy.
P. Phillips, 99:Nov81-31
A.M. Sinclair, 150(DR):Autumn81-588
Laxness, H. The Atom Station.
P-L. Adams, 61:Aug82-97
442(NY):12Jul82-103
Laycock, D.C. The Complete Enochian
Dictionary.
W.J. Samarin, 350:Jun81-523
Laycock, S. Selected Poems. (G. Hughes,
ed)
R. Garfitt, 617(TLS):2Apr82-392
Layton, I. Droppings from Heaven.*
D. Barbour, 648(WCR):Jun80-74
L. Daniel, 102(CanL):Winter80-128
Layton, I. For My Neighbours In Hell.
P.K. Smith, 102(CanL):Spring81-153
Layton, I. The Love Poems of Irving Lay-
ton.*
D. Barbour, 648(WCR):Jun80-74
P.K. Smith, 102(CanL):Spring81-153
Layton, I. Taking Sides. (H. Aster, ed)
J. Robinson, 102(CanL):Spring80-127
Layton, I. The Tightrope Dancer.
M.J. Edwards, 102(CanL):Autumn80-113
Layton, M., P.A. Walker and M. Williams.
The I'd-Rather-Be-Quilting Cookbook.
R.L. Shep, 614:Fall82-17
Layton, R. The Anthropology of Art.
R. Firth, 617(TLS):15Jan82-58
Lazard, M. Rabelais et la Renaissance.*
J. Larmat, 535(RHL):Jul-Oct81-749
Lazard, M. Le Théâtre en France au XVIe
siècle.
R. Griffiths, 208(FS):Jul81-323
R.J. Melpignano, 207(FR):May82-901
Lazaridès, A. Valéry.*
V.J. Daniel, 208(FS):Jan81-90
Lazcano, J.M. - see under Marchant Lazcano,
J.
Lazzarini, J. and R. Pavlova.*
P. Migel, 151:Nov81-86
Lazzarino, G. and others. Prego!
M. Danesi, 399(MLJ):Autumn81-345
G.P. Orwen, 276:Autumn81-221
Lea, C.A. Emancipation, Assimilation and
Stereotype.*
R.C. Reimer, 406:Fall81-358
Lea, J.F. Kazantzakis.*
A.O. Aldridge, 125:Spring81-338
M. Koutsoudaki, 395(MFS):Summer80-370
Lea, S. Searching the Drowned Man.*
J. Bullis, 502(PrS):Winter81/82-89
G.E. Murray, 249(HudR):Spring81-156
T. Swiss, 569(SR):Spring81-lvi
Leab, D.J. and K.K. The Auction Companion.
G. Naylor, 617(TLS):1Jan82-7
Leach, C. A Killing Frost.
T.O. Treadwell, 617(TLS):18Jun82-677
Leach, C. Scars and Other Ceremonies.
P. Lewis, 565:Vol22No1-60
Leach, E. L'Unité de l'Homme.
H. Cronel, 450(NRF):Oct81-154
Leach, E. Social Anthropology.
M. Bloch, 617(TLS):16Apr82-444
A. Ryan, 362:25Feb82-22
Leach, J. Pompey the Great.*
A.J. Marshall, 487:Fall81-281

Leach, W. True Love and Perfect Union.
W.H. Chafe, 676(YR):Spring82-426
639(VQR):Summer81-103
Leacock, S. The Penguin Stephen Leacock.
(R. Davies, ed)
G. Ewart, 364:Mar82-87
Leader, Z. Reading Blake's Songs.*
S. Matthews, 175:Autumn81-296
Leakey, R. The Making of Mankind.*
J.S. Weiner, 617(TLS):29Jan82-102
Leaming, B. Polanski.
M. Wood, 453(NYRB):10Jun82-34
Leapman, M. Yankee Doodles.
J. Lahr, 617(TLS):30Jul82-837
C. Sigal, 362:15Apr82-21
Lear, E. Bosh and Nonsense.
R. Fuller, 362:16Sep82-26
Lear, J. Aristotle and Logical Theory.
D. Charles, 123:Vol131No2-301
A.R. Lacey, 303(JoHS):Vol 101-157
R.L. Purtill, 124:Jan-Feb82-194
R.L. Purtill, 258:Dec81-468
S.R., 543:Sep80-148
Lears, T.J.J. No Place of Grace.*
J.F. Kasson, 676(YR):Summer82-601
K.S. Lynn, 441:10Jan82-8
Leary, H.F.M. and M.R. Stirewalt, eds.
North Carolina Research: Genealogy and
Local History.
P.M. Vanorny, 14:Fall81-362
Leary, L. Ralph Waldo Emerson.
A.M. Woodlief, 577(SHR):Fall81-364
Lease, B. Anglo-American Encounters.
B. Nevius, 617(TLS):17Sep82-1013
Leavis, F.R. The Critic as Anti-Philoso-
pher. (G. Singh, ed)
C. Rawson, 617(TLS):10Dec82-1371
Leavis, F.R. Reading Out Poetry [and]
Eugenio Montale — A Tribute.
D.K.M. MacKenzie, 506(PSt):Sep81-229
Leavitt, C. Meeting Rozzy Halfway.*
C. Rumens, 617(TLS):5Mar82-246
Leavy, S.A. The Psychoanalytic Dialogue.
R. Ambrester, 583:Summer81-431
Lebeaux, R. Young Man Thoreau.
R.J. Schneider, 183(ESQ):Vol127No1-57
Lebègue, R. Aspects de Chateaubriand.
P. Riberette, 535(RHL):Nov-Dec81-1013
R. Switzer, 446(NCFS):Spring-Summer81-
260
P.J. Whyte, 402(MLR):Oct81-969
Lebègue, R. Etudes sur le Théâtre fran-
çais.
M-O. Sweetser, 475:No14Pt1-184
Lebensztejn, J-C., with A. Parronchi - see
da Pontormo, J.
Leblanc, A. La Vie comme je te pousse.
D.B. Brautman, 207(FR):May81-897
Leblanc, B. Y sont fous le grand monde!
R. Hodgson, 102(CanL):Spring81-96
Leblanc, B.B. Joseph-Philémon Sanschagrin,
ministre.
D.M. Hayne, 102(CanL):Summer80-129
Leblanc, B.B. Les Trottoirs de bois.
G. Marcotte, 102(CanL):Autumn80-93
Le Blanc, C. and D. Borei - see Bodde, D.
Le Blon, J-C. Coloritto, or the Harmony
of Colouring in Painting.
J. Gage, 59:Dec81-470
Le Bon, G. Gustave Le Bon: The Man and
His Works. (A. Widener, ed and trans)
S.I. Gurney, 396(ModA):Summer81-314

208

Lebowitz, F. Social Studies.*
    J.D. O'Hara, 434:Summer82-603
Le Bris, M. Romantics and Romanticism.*
    J.D. O'Hara, 434:Summer82-603
Le Brun, C. A Method to Learn to Design
    the Passions. (J. Williams, trans)
    J. Freehafer, 566:Autumn81-49
Lecherbonnier, B., ed. Textes français et
    histoire littéraire: XXe siècle.
    R.T. Denommé, 207(FR):Dec81-284
Lecker, R. and J. David, eds. The Anno-
    tated Bibliography of Canada's Major
    Authors. (Vol 1)
    D. Jackel, 102(CanL):Spring81-147
    W.J. Keith, 627(UTQ):Summer81-155
    D.G. Lochhead, 105:Fall/Winter81-100
Lecker, R. and J. David, eds. The Anno-
    tated Bibliography of Canada's Major
    Authors. (Vol 2)
    D.G. Lochhead, 105:Fall/Winter81-100
Leckey, R.G. Some Aspects of Balladesque
    Art and Their Relevance for the Novels
    of Theodor Fontane.
    A. Bance, 402(MLR):Jul81-754
Leclanche, J-L. - see "Le Conte de Floire
    et Blancheflor"
Leclercq, J. Monks and Love in Twelfth-
    Century France.*
    D.W. Robertson, 161(DUJ):Jun81-239
Leclercq, P-R. Introduction à "Monsieur
    Ouine," de Bernanos.
    J. Onimus, 535(RHL):Mar-Apr81-329
Le Clézio, J.M.G. Désert.* Trois Villes
    saintes.
    S. Smith, 207(FR):May81-898
Le Clézio, J.M.G. La Ronde et autres
    faits divers.
    J. Pilling, 617(TLS):8Oct82-1113
Le Comte, E. A Dictionary of Puns in Mil-
    ton's English Poetry.*
    G.M. Crump, 569(SR):Fall81-628
Le Comte, E. The Professor and the Coed.*
    G.W. Oldham, 42(AR):Fall81-513
"Le Corbusier Sketchbooks."* (Vol 1) (F.
    de Franclieu, ed)
    M. McLeod, 127:Fall81-275
"Le Corbusier Sketchbooks." (Vols 3 and 4)
    (notes by F. de Franclieu)
    P. Goldberger, 441:12Dec82-12
Le Corsu, F. Isis.
    F. Solmsen, 318(JAOS):Jan/Mar80-76
Lecourt, D. L'ordre et les jeux.
    J. Largeault, 542:Oct-Dec81-511
Ledbetter, S. and P. Myers - see Marenzio,
    L.
Ledeen, M. and W. Lewis. Debacle.*
    639(VQR):Autumn81-134
Lederer, K. Lillian Hellman.
    J.H. Adler, 392:Fall81-463
    M.W. Estrin, 397(MD):Sep81-379
Ledésert, D.M. and R.P.L. - see "Harrap's
    New Standard French and English Diction-
    ary"
Le Dressay, A. This Body That I Live In.*
    (D. Cooley, ed)
    D. Barbour, 648(WCR):Jun80-75
    D. Precosky, 102(CanL):Winter80-142
Lee, A. Russian Journal.*
    A. Brown, 617(TLS):13Aug82-891
Lee, A.R., ed. Black Fiction.*
    S.L. Blake, 395(MFS):Winter80/81-673
Lee, A.R., ed. Nathaniel Hawthorne.
    R. Christiansen, 617(TLS):12Nov82-1249

Lee, B. The Novels of Henry James.*
    R.K. Cross, 445(NCF):Jun80-96
Lee, B. Theory and Personality.*
    E. Larrisy, 506(PSt):May81-108
    295(JML):Vol8No3/4-486
Lee, D. The Gods.*
    D. Barbour, 648(WCR):Vol 15No3-47
Lee, D. - see King, J. and D. Lee
Lee, D.N. and H.C. Woodhouse. Art on the
    Rocks of Southern Africa.
    D. Brokensha, 2(AfrA):Feb81-78
Lee, H. Elizabeth Bowen.*
    P.S., 148:Winter81-91
Lee, J.M. and M. Petter. The Colonial
    Office, War and Development Policy.
    I. Duffield, 617(TLS):17Sep82-988
Lee, M. Studies in Goethe's Lyric Cycles.*
    K.J. Fink, 133:Band14Heft1-80
Lee, M.O. Fathers and Sons in Virgil's
    "Aeneid:" Tum Genitor Natum.*
    C.E. Finch, 377:Mar81-54
    W.R. Johnson, 487:Spring81-97
Lee, M.P. Your Name — All About It.
    E.C. Smith, 424:Sep80-224
Lee, P.H. Celebration of Continuity.
    J. Chaves, 293(JASt):Aug81-749
Lee Poh Ping. Chinese Society in Nine-
    teenth Century Singapore.*
    C.M. Turnbull, 302:Vol 18-172
Lee, R.B. The !Kung San.
    A. Barnard, 69:Vol50No3-328
Lee, V.J. - see Fuller, R.
Leech, G.N. Explorations in Semantics and
    Pragmatics.
    A. Davison, 350:Mar82-242
Leedy, W.C., Jr. Fan Vaulting.
    P. Crossly, 576:May81-155
    R. Mainstone, 46:Sep81-196
    F. Woodman, 59:Mar81-124
Leemhuis, F. The D and H Stems in Koranic
    Arabic.
    J.H. Rodgers, 318(JAOS):Apr/Jun80-127
Lees, L.H. Exiles of Erin.*
    A. Sutcliffe, 637(VS):Autumn80-124
Lees-Milne, J. William Beckford.*
    F. Fergusson, 576:Mar81-61
Lees-Milne, J. Harold Nicolson.* (Vol 1)
    J. Sparrow, 364:Jun81-89
Lees-Milne, J. and D. Ford. Images of
    Bath.
    P. Rogers, 617(TLS):13Aug82-871
Leete-Hodge, L. Diana: Princess of Wales.
    V. Glendinning, 617(TLS):25Jun82-689
Lefay-Toury, M-N. La Tentation du suicide
    dans le roman français du XIIe siècle.
    R. Jones, 402(MLR):Apr81-457
Lefebvre, H. La présence et l'absence.
    M. Adam, 542:Apr-Jun81-241
Lefebvre, J-P. - see Marx, K.
Lefèvre, E., ed. Der Einfluss Senecas auf
    das europäische Drama.
    C.W. Thomsen, 490:Band12Heft2-257
Lefèvre, E. Der "Phormio" des Terenz und
    der "Epidikazomenos" des Apollodor von
    Karystos.*
    J.N. Grant, 487:Summer81-178
Lefèvre d'Étaples, J. Quincuplex Psalter-
    ium [together with] Bedouelle, G. Le
    "Quincuplex Psalterium" de Lefèvre
    d'Étaples.
    J. Pineaux, 535(RHL):Jan-Feb81-121

Leiter, J.C., Jr. and J. Stanley. Dis-
cover Dressmaking as a Professional
Career.
P. Bach, 614:Fall82-16
Leiter, S.L., ed and trans. The Art of
Kabuki.
F.T. Motofuji, 293(JASt):Feb81-389
Leiter, S.L. Kabuki Encyclopedia.
L.C. Pronko, 293(JASt):Nov80-134
R. Rann, 187:May82-327
A.T. Tsubaki, 407(MN):Autumn81-355
Leith, J.A., ed. Images of the Commune/
Images de la Commune.
J. Flower, 208(FS):Oct81-468
Leithauser, B. Hundreds of Fireflies.
B. Bennett, 441:14Mar82-12
H. Vendler, 453(NYRB):23Sep82-41
Leitz, R.C. 3d, R.H. Ballinger and C.
Lohmann - see Howells, W.D.
Leiva Vivas, R. Vigencia del sabio Valle.
F. Parker, 263(RIB):Vol31No4-555
Leivant, D.M.R. Absoluteness of Intuition-
istic Logic.
G.E. Minc, 316:Dec81-873
Lejeune, M. Ateste à l'heure de la romani-
sation.
M.H. Crawford, 313:Vol71-153
P. Flobert, 555:Vol54fasc1-172
Lejeune, M. L'anthroponymie Osque.
M.H. Crawford, 313:Vol71-153
Lejeune, P. Je est un autre.*
P. Bayard, 450(NRF):Feb81-126
J-M. Klinkenberg, 209(FM):Jan81-60
Lekachman, R. Greed is Not Enough.
A. Wildavsky, 441:14Mar82-9
442(NY):22Mar82-166
Lem, S. Memoirs of a Space Traveler.
A. Mars-Jones, 617(TLS):19Mar82-306
M. Rose, 441:19Sep82-13
Lem, S. More Tales of Pirx the Pilot.
M. Rose, 441:19Sep82-13
442(NY):1Nov82-156
Lem, S. Tales of Pirx the Pilot.*
T.H. Hoisington, 497(PolR):Vol26No3-
103
Lemaire, A. Inscriptions hébraïques.
(Vol 1)
P.E. Dion, 318(JAOS):Jul/Sep80-362
Lemaire, J-P. Les Marges du jour.
P. Jaccottet, 450(NRF):Dec81-107
Lemaître, J-L. Répertoire des documents
nécrologiques français.
G. Constable, 589:Oct81-884
Le Master, J.R. Jesse Stuart.*
B.T. Spencer, 27(AL):Mar81-150
Le May, G.H.L. The Victorian Constitution.
J.B. Conacher, 637(VS):Spring81-376
Lemay, J.A.L., ed. Essays in Early Vir-
ginia Literature Honoring Richard Beale
Davis.*
J. Rambeau, 568(SCN):Spring81-20
Lemay, J.A.L. and G.S. Rousseau. The
Renaissance Man in the Eighteenth Cen-
tury.
P. Rogers, 541(RES):Aug81-368
Lemay, J.A.L. and P.M. Zall - see Franklin,
B.
Le Mée, K.W. A Metrical Study of Five
"Lais" of Marie de France.*
K. Brightenback, 545(RPh):Feb81(supp)-
347
J. Fox, 208(FS):Jul81-308

Lemelin, R. Les Voies de l'espérance.
L. Mailhot, 102(CanL):Spring81-110
Lemerle, P. and others, eds. Actes de
Lavra. (Pt 3)
D.M. Nicol, 303(JoHS):Vol 101-232
Lemhagen, G. La concurrence entre
l'infinitif et la subordonnée complé-
tive.* (Vol 1)
A. Boone, 209(FM):Jan81-82
Lemire, M., ed. Dictionnaire des oeuvres
littéraires du Québec.* (Vol 1)
B-Z. Shek, 627(UTQ):Summer81-171
Lemire, M. and others. Dictionnaire des
oeuvres littéraires du Québec. (Vol 2)
A.B. Chartier, 207(FR):Feb82-400
B-Z. Shek, 627(UTQ):Summer81-171
Lemmon, E.J. Beginning Logic. (G.W.D.
Berry, ed)
S. Stebbins, 316:Jun81-421
Lempp, O. Das Problem der Theodizee in
der Philosophie und Literatur des 18.
Jahrhunderts bis auf Kant und Schiller.
R. Malter, 342:Band72Heft3-380
de Lena, P.R. - see under Rodríguez de
Lena, P.
Lenard, Y. Elan.
N.A. Poulin, 207(FR):Apr81-776
Lenčo, J. Das letzte Kollegium.
L. Richter, 654(WB):11/1981-139
Lengauer, W. Greek Commanders in the 5th
and 4th Centuries B.C. — Politics and
Ideology.
H.D. Westlake, 303(JoHS):Vol 101-196
Lenger, M-T. Corpus des Ordonnances des
Ptolémées (C. Ord. Ptol.).
R.S. Bagnall, 24:Fall81-349
Lengyel, A. and C.T.B. Radan, eds. The
Archaeology of Roman Pannonia.
J.J. Wilkes, 617(TLS):15Jan82-60
Lenihan, J.H. Showdown.
E. Brater, 651(WHR):Summer81-190
P.A. Hutton, 649(WAL):Fall81-228
Lennon, C. Richard Stanihurst the Dub-
liner, 1547-1618.
J. Bossy, 617(TLS):15Oct82-1128
Lenoir, M. - see Pseudo Hyginus
Lensi-Orlandi, G. Il Palazzo Vecchio di
Firenze.
J. Paul, 576:Oct81-238
Lent, J.A., ed. Broadcasting in Asia and
the Pacific.
J. Lyle, 293(JASt):Feb81-334
Lentricchia, F. After the New Criticism.*
T.H. Adamowski, 529(QQ):Autumn81-442
M. Black, 175:Summer81-207
W.F. Cain, 651(WHR):Summer81-192
A. Durant, 506(PSt):Sep81-186
G. Levine, 128(CE):Feb81-146
T. Martin, 295(JML):Vol8No3/4-399
W. Martin, 131(CL):Summer81-271
C. Molesworth, 560:Winter82-242
D. O'Hara, 659(ConL):Winter82-105
A. Parker, 153:Fall81-57
Lenz, C.R.S., G. Greene and C.T. Neely,
eds. The Woman's Part.
C.W. Cary, 130:Fall81-280
M.W. Ferguson, 676(YR):Spring82-414
M. Taylor, 49:Oct81-97
Lenz, S. Der Verlust.
G.P. Butler, 617(TLS):15Jan82-63
Lenzer, R. and P. Palijewski, eds. Kon-
text.
H-J. Lehnert, 654(WB):10/1981-177

Léon, A. Introduction à l'histoire des faits éducatifs.
J-M. Gabaude, 542:Jan-Mar81-127
de León, L. The Unknown Light. (W. Barnstone, trans)
F. Pierce, 86(BHS):Jul81-263
Leon, N.H. Character Indexes of Modern Chinese.
C.L. McClenon, 350:Jun82-488
Léon, P. and M. Rossi, eds. Problèmes de Prosodie. (Vol 1)
N.A. Poulin, 207(FR):Mar82-588
Léon, P.R. - see Brainerd, B. and others
Léon, P.R. and H. Mitterand. L'analyse du discours.
D. Bouverot, 209(FM):Jul81-284
Leonard, E. Cat Chaser.
N. Callendar, 441:5Sep82-20
442(NY):12Jul82-107
Leonard, E. Split Images.
N. Callendar, 441:18Apr82-20
Leonard, H. Da/A Life/Time Was.*
D. Devlin, 157:Winter81-51
Leonard, H. A Life.
D. Devlin, 157:Autumn81-51
Leonard, J. Private Lives in the Imperial City.
R.B. Shwartz, 569(SR):Winter81-ii
Leonardi, A.M.C. - see under Chiavacci Leonardi, A.M.
Leonardsson, S. Den franska grammatikens historia i Sverige I. Histoire de la grammaire française en Suède II.
L-G. Sundell, 597(SN):Vol53No2-409
Leone, D. The Sampler Quilt. (Bk 2)
M. Cowan, 614:Winter82-19
Leonhard, K. Der menschliche Ausdruck in Mimik, Gestik und Phonik.
I. Gorelov and A. Šachnarovič, 682(ZPSK):Band32Heft2-219
Leonhard, W. Eurocommunism.*
D.W. Treadgold, 396(ModA):Spring81-192
Leopardi, G. A Leopardi Reader. (O.M. Casale, ed and trans) Pensieri. (W.S. Di Piero, trans)
R.W. Flint, 472:Spring/Summer82-42
Leopold, C. The Night Fishers of Antibes.*
N. Callendar, 441:30May82-15
442(NY):15Mar82-145
Leopold, J. Culture in Comparative and Evolutionary Perspective.
R. Ackerman, 637(VS):Summer81-518
Leospo, E. La Mensa Isiaca di Torino.
F. Solmsen, 318(JAOS):Jan/Mar80-76
Lepage, Y.G., ed. Les Rédactions en Vers du Couronnement de Louis.*
D.G. Hoggan, 208(FS):Oct81-424
S. Kay, 545(RPh):Feb81(supp)-274
Le Pan, D. Bright Glass of Memory.*
R.L. McDougall, 102(CanL):Winter80-120
Lepecki, M.L. José Cardoso Pires.
M. Guterres, 86(BHS):Apr81-155
Lepschy, A.L. and G. The Italian Language Today.
T. Barrett, 545(RPh):Feb81(supp)-167
Y. Malkiel, 545(RPh):Feb81(supp)-170
Lepsius, R. Standard Alphabet for Reducing Unwritten Languages and Foreign Graphic Systems to a Uniform Orthography in European Letters. (2nd ed) (J.A. Kemp, ed)
C.M. Eastman, 350:Sep82-724

Le Quesne, A.L. Carlyle.
R. Ashton, 617(TLS):24Sep82-1046
A. Ryan, 362:18Mar82-21
Leray, Y., A. Pradeilles and N. Vigouroux-Frey. This Quiet Revolution.
J.H., 189(EA):Oct-Dec81-499
Lerhis-Puškaitis, A. Džūkstes Pasakas.
V. Voigt, 196:Band22Heft3/4-355
Le Rider, P. Le Chevalier dans "Le Conte du Graal" de Chrétien de Troyes.
D.J. Shirt, 208(FS):Jul81-308
Lerner, G. The Majority Finds its Past.
W.H. Chafe, 676(YR):Spring82-426
Lerner, L. Love and Marriage.
J.P. Brown, 445(NCF):Mar81-559
Lerner, L. The Man I Killed.*
T. Eagleton, 565:Vol122No4-74
Lerner, L., ed. The Victorians.*
F.W. Bradbrook, 447(N&Q):Dec80-555
A. Easson, 366:Autumn81-263
Lerond, A. Dictionnaire de la prononciation.
M. Grimaud, 207(FR):Dec81-293
Leroux, P. Corso di Frenologia. (A. Prontera and F. Fiorentino, eds and trans)
J. Viard, 535(RHL):Nov-Dec81-1016
Leroux, P. La Grève de Samarez, Poème Philosophique. (J-P. Lacassagne, ed)
J. Gaulmier, 535(RHL):Jul-Oct81-823
N.D. Savage, 446(NCFS):Spring-Summer81-266
Leroy, M. Les grands courants de la linguistique moderne.
P. Swiggers, 361:Sep81-63
Le Roy Ladurie, E. Love, Death and Money in the Pays d'oc.* (French title: L'Argent, l'amour et la mort en pays d'oc.)
E. Benson, 207(FR):May82-929
P. Robinson, 441:12Dec82-7
Le Roy Ladurie, E. Montaillou.
V.S. Pritchett, 442(NY):1Feb82-128
Le Roy Ladurie, E. Paris-Montpellier.
D. Johnson, 617(TLS):2Jul82-707
Le Roy Ladurie, E. and J. Goy. Tithe and Agrarian History from the Fourteenth to the Nineteenth Centuries.
G.E. Mingay, 617(TLS):28May82-590
Lervik, Å.H., ed. Gjennom kvinneøyne.
S.A. Aarnes, 172(Edda):1981/4-257
E.L. Haugen, 563(SS):Autumn81-497
Lerzundi, P. - see Lihn, E.
Lesberg, S. The Master Chefs Cookbook.
W. and C. Cowen, 639(VQR):Spring81-72
Lescoe, F.J. God as First Principle in Ulrich of Strasbourg.
M.D.J., 543:Sep80-151
Lescourret, M-A. - see Wittgenstein, L.
Lescure, M. Psychologie de la première enfance, de la conception à trois ans.
J-M. Gabaude, 542:Jan-Mar81-130
Lescure, P. Voilier.
F.J. Greene, 207(FR):Feb82-437
Leslie, B.R. Ronsard's Successful Epic Venture.*
Y. Bellenger, 535(RHL):Nov-Dec81-983
M. Dassonville, 210(FrF):Jan81-85
205(FMLS):Apr80-190
Leslie, C., ed. Asian Medical Systems.
B.J. Good, 318(JAOS):Jul/Sep80-383
Leslie, J. Value and Existence.*
W.J. Wainwright, 482(PhR):Apr81-318

Leslie, R.F., ed. The History of Poland
since 1863.*
P.S. Wandycz, 575(SEER):Jul81-452
639(VQR):Spring81-50
Lessa, B. Rodeio dos Ventos.
C.E. Cortés, 399(MLJ):Spring81-84
Lessenich, R.P. Lord Byron and the Nature
of Man.*
G. Hoffmeister, 72:Band217Heft2-428
I. Scott-Kilvert, 677(YES):Vol 11-306
Lessing, D. The Making of the Representa-
tive for Planet 8.
J. Leonard, 441:7Feb82-1
G. Mortimer, 364:Mar82-82
L. Taylor, 617(TLS):2Apr82-370
Lessing, D. The Sirian Experiments.*
E. Milton, 676(YR):Winter82-254
Lessing, G.E. Meine liebste Madam.
(G. and U. Schulz, eds)
R.R. Heitner, 221(CQ):Mar81-218
"Lessing Yearbook 10."* (R.E. Schade and
J. Glenn, eds)
G. Flaherty, 173(ECS):Winter80/81-208
Lessmann, J. Italienische Majolika.
R. Joppien, 471:Oct/Nov/Dec81-378
Le Sueur, M. Ripening. (E. Hedges, ed)
B. Gelfant, 441:4Apr82-7
Lesueur, R. L'Enéide de Virgile.
P.F. Hovingh, 394:Vol34fasc3/4-434
Le Sueur, W.D. A Critical Spirit.* (A.B.
McKillop, ed)
G.W., 102(CanL):Winter80-inside back
cover
Le Sueur, W.D. William Lyon Mackenzie.
(A.B. McKillop, ed)
C.G. Holland, 99:Nov81-35
G.W., 102(CanL):Winter80-inside back
cover
Lesure, F., ed. Igor Stravinsky: "Le
sacre du printemps:" dossier de presse.
P. Griffiths, 415:Mar81-180
Lesy, M. Time Frames.
62:Apr81-62
Lethaby, W.R. Philip Webb and his Work.
(G. Rubens, ed)
P. Davey, 46:Oct81-258
P. Faulkner, 506(PSt):Sep81-221
Le Touzé, P. Le Mystère du Réel dans les
romans de Bernanos.
G. Antoine, 209(FM):Jan81-56
G. Cesbron, 535(RHL):Jul-Oct81-835
Letta, C. and S. D'Amato. Epigrafia della
regione dei marsi.
M.H. Crawford, 313:Vol71-153
"Letter to a Russian Friend."
A. McMillin, 575(SEER):Jan81-151
Letwin, S.R. The Gentleman in Trollope.
R. Foster, 617(TLS):25Jun82-700
P. Kemp, 362:22Apr82-22
Leube, E. and L. Schrader, eds. Interpre-
tation und Vergleich.
C. Stern, 545(RPh):May81-488
Leuschner, J. Germany in the Late Middle
Ages.
B.M. Kaczynski, 589:Apr81-404
Levaillant, J. - see "Cahiers Paul Valéry
3"
Levcik, F. and J. Stankovsky. Industrial
Cooperation between East and West.*
C.W. Lawson, 575(SEER):Jul81-473
Levelt, W.J.M. Formal Grammars in Linguis-
tics and Psycholinguistics. (Vols 1-3)
G.F. Meier, 682(ZPSK):Band33Heft6-755

Levelt, W.J.M. and G.B. Flores d'Arcais,
eds. Studies in the Perception of Lan-
guage.
D.G. MacKay and M.C. MacDonald, 350:
Sep82-735
Leven, J. Satan.
P. Andrews, 441:1Aug82-12
442(NY):9Aug82-94
Levenberg, D. Out of the Desert.*
J. Rosenberg, 390:Nov81-59
Leverenz, D. The Language of Puritan Feel-
ing.*
T. Toulouse, 432(NEQ):Mar81-133
Lévesque, G. Louis Hémon, aventurier ou
philosophe?
B-Z. Shek, 627(UTQ):Summer81-185
Lévesque, J. The USSR and the Cuban Revol-
ution.* (French title: L'URSS et la
Révolution Cubaine.)
H. Hanak, 575(SEER):Jan81-149
Lévesque, R. My Québec.
G.W., 102(CanL):Spring80-150
Levet, H.J-M. Poèmes.
G. Gouérou, 450(NRF):Jun81-107
Levey, M. The Case of Walter Pater.*
E. Block, 481(PQ):Summer80-384
P. Mauriès, 98:Apr81-376
Levey, M. Tempting Fate.
S. Altinel, 617(TLS):3Sep82-940
J. Astor, 362:23Sep82-23
Levey, S.H. The Messiah.
B. Grossfeld, 318(JAOS):Jan/Mar80-63
Levi, H. Honour Your Partner.
P. Barclay, 102(CanL):Summer81-133
Levi, P. Private Ground.
T. Dooley, 617(TLS):2Apr82-393
Levi, P. 3e non ora, quando?
A.L. Lepschy, 617(TLS):3Dec82-1345
Levi, R. L'homme et le temps.
M. Adam, 542:Jan-Mar81-144
Lévi-Strauss, C. The Naked Man.
M. Green, 363(LitR):Spring82-448
Levien, M. - see Cree, E.H.
Levin, B. Conducted Tour.
H. Cole, 362:4Feb82-25
C. Osborne, 364:Dec81/Jan82-139
Levin, D. Cotton Mather.*
R. Morton, 106:Fall81-191
Levin, G. Edward Hopper: The Art and the
Artist.
D. Anfam, 59:Dec81-457
Levin, G. Edward Hopper: The Complete
Prints. Edward Hopper as Illustrator.
D. Anfam, 59:Dec81-457
S. Ball, 658:Winter81-358
Levin, G. Richardson the Novelist.*
J.C. Dales, 677(YES):Vol 11-279
Levin, H. Memories of the Moderns.*
639(VQR):Spring81-56
Levin, I., ed. Märchen aus dem Kaukasus.*
H-J. Uther, 196:Band21Heft1/2-102
Levin, J. Water Dancer.
B. Caplan, 441:28Nov82-12
Levin, J.F. The Slavic Element in the Old
Prussian Elbing Vocabulary.
V.N. Toporov, 279:Vol124-174
Levin, J.F. and P.D. Haikalis, with A.A.
Forostenko. Reading Modern Russian.*
N.J. Brown, 575(SEER):Jan81-75
Levin, M. The Architect.*
D. Fuchs, 441:3Jan82-9

213

Levin, M.E. Metaphysics and the Mind-Body
Problem.*
   A.G.N. Flew, 518:Jul81-168
   G. Harman, 185:Oct81-174
Levin, M.I. Russian Declension and Conju-
gation.
   C.E. Townsend, 558(RLJ):Spring-Fall81-
259
Levin, R. New Readings vs. Old Plays.*
   M. Charney, 551(RenQ):Winter80-808
   R.K. Turner, Jr., 568(SCN):Summer-
Fall81-39
   D. Young, 191(ELN):Jun81-298
Levin, S.R. The Semantics of Metaphor.*
   C.R. Hausman, 480(P&R):Fall81-249
   T.J. Taylor, 307:Apr81-54
Levinas, E. Existence and Existents.
   E.W., 543:Mar81-613
Levine, B.B. Benjy Lopez.
   G. Guinness, 37:Apr81-27
Levine, G. The Realistic Imagination.*
   A.M. Duckworth, 445(NCF):Mar82-475
   A. Fleishman, 401(MLQ):Dec81-400
   J.R. Kincaid, 441:24Jan82-10
   639(VQR):Autumn81-130
Levin, G. and U.C. Knoepflmacher, eds.
The Endurance of "Frankenstein."*
   B.T. Bennett, 340(KSJ):Vol30-207
   M.G. Cooke, 445(NCF):Jun80-99
   C.A. Howells, 175:Summer81-185
Levine, L.W. Black Culture and Black
Consciousness.*
   J. Mason, 392:Fall81-472
Levine, P. Don't Ask.*
   M. Perloff, 472:Spring/Summer82-209
Levine, P. One for the Rose.*
   J. Parini, 617(TLS):2Jul82-720
   M. Perloff, 472:Spring/Summer82-209
   R. Tillinghast, 441:12Sep82-42
Levine, R.M. Historical Dictionary of
Brazil.*
   E.C. Rehder, 238:Mar81-160
Levine, R.M. Race and Ethnic Relations in
Latin America and the Caribbean.
   H.D. Sims, 263(RIB):Vol31No3-410
Levine, S. Mothers and Wives.
   P. Caplan, 69:Vol50No2-219
Levine, S.B. and H. Kawada. Human
Resources in Japanese Industrial
Development.
   W.M. Fruin, 293(JASt):Aug81-787
   Kobayashi Ken'ichi, 285(JapQ):
Oct-Dec81-561
Levinson, P., ed. In Pursuit of Truth.
   J. Lieberson, 453(NYRB):2Dec82-51
Levinson, R. and W. Link. Stay Tuned.
   H. Alpert, 18:Jul-Aug81-66
Levis, L. The Dollmaker's Ghost.*
   W. Scammell, 617(TLS):28May82-592
   P. Stitt, 219(GaR):Fall81-647
Levitan, S.R. and R.S. Belous. What's
Happening to the American Family?
   A. Hacker, 453(NYRB):18Mar82-37
   R. Mitchison, 617(TLS):2Jul82-714
Levitine, G. The Dawn of Bohemianism.*
   F.H. Dowley, 173(ECS):Spring81-351
Levitsky, S.L. Copyright, Defamation, and
Privacy in Soviet Civil Law.*
   I. Lapenna, 575(SEER):Apr81-314
Levitt, H., J.M. Pickett and R.A. Houde,
eds. Sensory Aids for the Hearing
Impaired.
   P. Howell, 353:Vol 18No9/10-951

Levitt, I. and C. Smout. The State of the
Scottish Working-Class in 1843.
   W. Donaldson, 571(ScLJ):Winter81-116
   J. Epstein, 637(VS):Spring81-380
Levitt, M.P. The Cretan Glance.
   M. Koutsoudaki, 395(MFS):Winter80/81-
748
Levitz, K. and H. Logic and Boolean
Algebra.
   D. Resek, 316:Jun81-420
Levno, A. Rencontres Culturelles.
   G.L. Ervin, 399(MLJ):Spring81-118
Levowitz-Treu, M. L'Amour et la mort chez
Stendhal.*
   M. Sachs, 207(FR):Oct80-166
Levtzion, N. and J.F.P. Hopkins, eds.
Corpus of Early Arabic Sources for
West African History.
   R. Oliver, 617(TLS):12Feb82-155
Levy, A. Basic Set Theory.
   H.T. Hodes, 492(PhR):Apr81-298
   W. Mitchell, 316:Jun81-417
Levy, A. Etudes sur le conte et le roman
chinois.
   V. Alleton, 98:Mar80-217
Levy, A. Inventaire analytique et cri-
tique du conte chinois en langue vul-
gaire.* (Vols 1 and 2)
   V. Alleton, 98:Mar80-217
Lévy, B-H. L'Idéologie française.*
   P. Bourgeade, 450(NRF):Apr81-146
Lévy, B-H. The Testament of God. (French
title: Le testament de Dieu.)
   B. Anderson, 560:Fall81-132
   P. Legendre, 98:Jan80-63
Levy, B.J., ed. Selected Fabliaux.
   A. Foulet, 545(RPh):May81-577
Levy, D.C. University and Government in
Mexico.
   J.P. Harrison, 263(RIB):Vol31No4-556
Levy, D.G., H.B. Applewhite and M.D. John-
son. Women in Revolutionary Paris, 1789-
1795.
   B.E. Todd, 207(FR):Feb81-484
Lévy, E. Athènes devant la défaite de 404.
   N.R.E. Fisher, 123:Vol31No1-81
Levy, E. The Habima.*
   S. Carney, 476:Vol 11-129
Levy, E.P. Beckett and the Voice of
Species.*
   A. Otten, 42(AR):Fall81-514
Levy, F. "Le Mariage de Figaro."*
   H.G. Hall, 402(MLR):Apr81-469
   W.D. Howarth, 208(FS):Jul81-342
Levy, H.S. and M. Kawatani - see "Japan's
Dirty Old Man"
Levy, I.H. - see "The Ten Thousand Leaves"
Levy, K.L. Tomás Carrasquilla.
   G. Pontiero, 86(BHS):Jul81-274
Levy, P. Moore.*
   M.S. Quinn, 584(SWR):Summer81-318
   D.D. Todd, 154:Dec81-822
Lewalski, B.K. Protestant Poetics and the
Seventeenth-Century Religious Lyric.*
   W. Halewood, 568(SCN):Winter81-86
   D. Haskin, 613:Jun81-226
   A. Raspa, 539:Feb82-71
   H.M. Richmond, 551(RenQ):Summer80-298
Lewcock, R. Traditional Architecture in
Kuwait and the Northern Gulf.
   K. Fischer, 43:Band10Heft1-95

Lewin, M.Z. Missing Woman.
T.J. Binyon, 617(TLS):2Jul82-725
Lewin, R. The Other Ultra.
D. Hunt, 362:6May82-25
Lewis, A.S. - see Horrocks, J.
Lewis, B. The Muslim Discovery of Europe.
R.W. Southern, 453(NYRB):4Nov82-23
Lewis, B.R. HRH The Princess of Wales.
V. Glendinning, 617(TLS):25Jun82-689
Lewis, C.S. Of This and Other Worlds.
(W. Hooper, ed)
G. Watson, 617(TLS):24Sep82-1024
Lewis, C.S. They Stand Together. (W. Hooper, ed)
C.E. Lloyd, 569(SR):Spring81-281
Lewis, D. The Drawings of Andrea Palladio.
B. Boucher, 39:Dec81-430
Lewis, D. The Maori.
617(TLS):3Sep82-955
Lewis, D.L. When Harlem Was in Vogue.*
R.G. O'Meally, 617(TLS):31Dec82-1441
Lewis, D.M. Sparta and Persia.*
P.A. Stadter, 318(JAOS):Jul/Sep80-374
Lewis, H.D. The Elusive Self.
K. Lennon, 617(TLS):15Oct82-1136
Lewis, J. The Birthday of the Infanta.
T. Cassity, 472:Fall/Winter81-184
D. Gioia, 249(HudR):Winter81/82-593
Lewis, J. Poems Old and New, 1918-1978.*
The Indians in the Woods.
D. Gioia, 249(HudR):Winter81/82-592
H.P. Trimpi, 598(SoR):Spring82-251
Lewis, J.D. and R.L. Smith. American Sociology and Pragmatism.
D.N.L., 185:Apr82-590
Lewis, M., ed. Concerning Western Poetry.
C. Larson, 649(WAL):Winter81-334
Lewis, M., with M. Silver. Great Balls of Fire.
R. Asahina, 441:28Nov82-17
Lewis, N. Cuban Passage.
J. Mellors, 362:8Jul82-23
N. Shakespeare, 617(TLS):14May82-536
442(NY):2Aug82-87
Lewis, N. A Dragon Apparent.
A. Davidson, 617(TLS):13Aug82-885
Lewis, O., R.M. Lewis and S. Rigdon.
Trois femmes dans la Révolution cubaine.
H. Cronel, 450(NRF):Jul-Aug81-203
Lewis, P. George Orwell.
P. Martin, 364:Dec81/Jan82-138
Lewis, P.H. Paraguay under Stroessner.
M.J. Kryzanek, 263(RIB):Vol31No3-411
Lewis, R. A Gathering of Ghosts.
T.J. Binyon, 617(TLS):31Dec82-1448
Lewis, R. Science and Industrialization in the USSR.
R. Hutchings, 575(SEER):Jan81-122
R.H. Randolph, 550(RusR):Jul81-351
Lewis, R.E. - see dei Segni, L.
Lewis, R.H. The Manuscript Murders.
N. Callendar, 441:24Oct82-28
Lewis, R.J. E.M. Forster's Passages to India.*
S. Arkin, 395(MFS):Summer80-285
J. Colmer, 677(YES):Vol 11-349
Lewis, S. Art: African American.
J. Hotton, 69:Vol150No2-208
Lewis, W. Collected Poems and Plays. (A. Munton, ed)
B. Lafourcade, 189(EA):Jan-Mar81-103
Lewis, W. The Complete Wild Body. (B. Lafourcade, ed) Tarr.
A. Mars-Jones, 617(TLS):3Dec82-1334
Lewis, W. Mrs. Dukes' Million.
A. Kerrigan, 396(ModA):Spring81-220
Lewis, W.A. The Evolution of the International Economic Order.
N. Gemmell, 161(DUJ):Dec80-101
Lewis, W.D. and W.P. Newton. Delta.
K.C. Carter 3d, 9(AlaR):Apr81-142
Lewis, W.H. Brothers and Friends. (C.S. Kilby and M.L. Mead, eds)
D.J.R. Bruckner, 441:22Aug82-12
Lewis, W.S. Rescuing Horace Walpole.*
H. Forster, 447(N&Q):Oct80-448
R. Lonsdale, 677(YES):Vol 11-287
Le Witt, S. Autobiography.
B.W., 55:Nov81-50
Lewsen, P. John X. Merriman.
K. Ingham, 617(TLS):29Oct82-1184
J. Lewin, 362:15Jul82-23
Lewy, C. - see Broad, C.D.
Lewy, G. America in Vietnam.
D.P. Chandler, 293(JASt):Nov80-77
"Lexikon: Archivwesen der DDR."
J. Mendelsohn, 14:Winter80-88
"Lexikon des Mittelalters."* (Vol 1, fasc 1 and 6-10)
F.C. Gentry, 406:Summer81-226
"Lexikon des Mittelalters."* (Vol 1, fasc 2-5)
F.G. Gentry, 406:Summer81-226
J. Vezin, 555:Vol54fasc2-393
Ley, R. Brecht as Thinker.
S.L. Gilman, 221(GQ):Jan81-109
H.T. Tewarson, 222(GR):Winter81-36
Leyland, W. - see Ginsberg, A. and P. Orlofsky
Leymarie, J. Balthus.*
G. Raillard, 98:Jun-Jul81-631
Leys, S. Broken Images.
T.B. Gold, 293(JASt):Aug81-769
Leyser, K.J. Rule and Conflict in an Early Medieval Society: Ottonian Saxony.
L.G. Duggan, 589:Jan81-168
L'Hermitte, R. La phrase nominale en russe.*
H. Birnbaum, 559:Jun80-99
D.S. Worth, 550(RusR):Jan81-89
Lhundup Sopa, G. and J. Hopkins, eds and trans. Practice and Theory of Tibetan Buddhism.
J.W. de Jong, 259(IIJ):Jan81-79
Li, C.N., ed. Subject and Topic.
A.S. Kaye, 35(AS):Fall81-238
Li Ch'ing-chao. Complete Poems.* (K. Rexroth and Ling Chung, eds and trans)
T. Enslin, 472:Spring/Summer81-301
S. Watson, 435:Winter81-98
Li, F.K. A Handbook of Comparative Tai.
R.B. Jones, 318(JAOS):Apr/Jun80-212
Li, L.M. China's Silk Trade.
J. Spence, 453(NYRB):1Apr82-45
Li Shu-Huan. Tao-chia ta tz'u-tien.
T-C. Yao, 293(JASt):Nov80-115
Li, V.H., ed. The Future of Taiwan.
A.J. Gregor, 293(JASt):Feb81-355
Libanius. Discours. (Vol 1) (J. Martin, ed)
J.H.W.G. Liebeschuetz, 303(JoHS): Vol 101-165

Lichem, K. and H.J. Simon, eds. Hugo
Schuchardt, *Gotha 1842 — †Graz 1927.
  T.L. Markey, 350:Sep82-683
Lichem, K. and H.J. Simon, eds. Studien
zu Dante and zu anderen Themen der roman-
ischen Literaturen.
  A. Scaglione, 545(RPh):Feb81(supp)-32
Lichtblau, M. - see Caballero Calderón, E.
Lichtenberg, G.C. Lichtenberg in England.*
(Vols 1 and 2) (H.L. Grumbert, ed)
  H. Reiss, 133:Band14Heft1-69
Lichtman, A.J. and V. French. Historians
and the Living Past.
  J.W. Zophy, 125:Spring81-349
Lida de Malkiel, M.R. Estudios sobre la
literatura española del siglo XV.
  C.B. Faulhaber, 545(RPh):Aug80-123
  O. Tudorica-Impey, 402(MLR):Jan81-217
Lida de Malkiel, M.R. Juan Ruiz: Selec-
ción del "Libro de buen amor" y estudios
críticos.
  D. Seidenspinner-Núñez, 545(RPh):
    Feb81(supp)-231
Lieberman, F. Chinese Music. (2nd ed)
  Han Kuo-huang, 187:Sep82-484
Lieberman, H. Night Call From a Distant
Time Zone.
  I. Hislop, 617(TLS):30Apr82-493
Lieberman, L. God's Measurements.*
  P. Serchuk, 569(SR):Spring81-271
  H. Thomas, 385(MQR):Winter82-200
Lieberthal, K.G. Revolution and Tradition
in Tientsin, 1949-52.
  W.T. Rowe, 293(JASt):Feb81-358
Liebeschuetz, J.H.W.G. Continuity and
Change in Roman Religion.*
  M. Beard, 313:Vol71-203
  D.P. Harmon, 121(CJ):Oct/Nov81-74
  C.B. Pascal, 122:Jul81-249
Liebich, A. Between Ideology and Utopia.
  D. McLellan, 575(SEER):Apr81-304
  N. Naimark, 104(CASS):Winter81-625
  L.S. Stepelevich, 125:Summer81-437
Liebich, A. - see Cieszkowski, A.
Lieblich, A. Kibbutz Makom.
  A.E. Shapiro, 441:4Apr82-14
Liebling, A.J. Liebling at Home.
  W. Goodman, 441:1Aug82-23
Liem, N.D., ed. South-East Asian Linguis-
tic Studies. (Vol 4)
  S. De Lancey, 350:Dec81-974
Liénard, E. Répertoires prosodiques et
métriques.*
  E.J. Kenney, 123:Vol31No1-115
Lienhard, J.T. Paulinus of Nola and Early
Western Monasticism.
  E.D. Hunt, 313:Vol71-193
Lienhard, S. - see Cappeller, C.
van Lieshout, R.G.A. Greeks on Dreams.
  R.J. White, 124:May-Jun82-318
Lietz, R. At Park and East Division.
  C. Inez, 472:Fall/Winter81-231
"Le Lieu et la Formule: Hommage à Marc
Eigeldinger."*
  J.M. Cocking, 208(FS):Apr82-237
  205(FMLS):Jan80-89
Lievsay, J.L., ed. The Seventeenth-
Century Resolve.
  J. Robertson, 161(DUJ):Jun81-254
Life, P.W. Sir Thomas Malory and the
Morte Darthur.
  P. Brown, 354:Sep81-246
  D. Staines, 589:Apr81-456

"The Life and Adventures of Capt. John
Avery (1709?)" [and] Johnson, C. The
Successful Pyrate (1713).
  P.J. De Gategno, 566:Spring82-129
Ligeti, L., ed. Proceedings of the Csoma
de Körös Memorial Symposium.
  J.W. de Jong, 259(IIJ):Jan81-75
Lightbown, R. Sandro Botticelli.
  D.G. Wilkins, 551(RenQ):Spring80-100
Lightbown, R. and A. Caiger-Smith - see
Piccolpasso, C.
Lightbown, R.W. Donatello and Michelozzo.*
  F. Ames-Lewis, 59:Sep81-339
  V. Herzner, 683:Band44Heft3-300
Lightfoot, D.W. Principles of Diachronic
Syntax.*
  J. Aitchison, 353:Vol 18No1/2-137
  O.C.M. Fischer and F.C. van der Leek,
    361:Dec81-301
  205(FMLS):Jan80-89
Lightstone, A.H. and A. Robinson. Nonarch-
imedean Fields and Asymptotic Expansions.
  C.W. Henson, 316:Mar81-163
Lihani, J. Bartolomé de Torres Naharro.
  E.M. Malinak, 238:Mar81-152
  J.E. Varey, 86(BHS):Jul81-262
Lihn, E. The Dark Room and Other Poems.
(P. Lerzundi, ed)
  G. Rabassa, 472:Spring/Summer81-140
Likhachov, D.S., ed. Perepiska Ivana
Groznogo s Andreyem Kurbskim.
  N. Andreyev, 575(SEER):Apr81-278
Lilienthal, D. Atomic Energy.
  T.C. Holyoke, 42(AR):Winter81-129
Lillo, G. The Plays of George Lillo.
  F.M. Link, 566:Autumn80-47
Lilly, M. - see Brontë, C.
Lillyman, W.J. Reality's Dark Dream.*
  E. Behler, 680(ZDP):Band100Heft4-608
  J. Trainer, 402(MLR):Oct81-991
Limentani, A. - see Iordan, I. and M.M.
Manea
Limentani, A. - see Rutebeuf
Limentani, U., with J.M. Lindon - see
Foscolo, U.
Limonov, È. Èto ja — Edička.
  D.M. Fiene, 399(MLJ):Winter81-443
Lin, S-F. The Transformation of the Chi-
nese Lyrical Tradition.*
  W. Schlepp, 318(JAOS):Jan/Mar80-87
Lincoln, A.T. Paradise Now and Not Yet.
  J.L. Houlden, 617(TLS):15Jan82-62
Lincoln, B. Emerging from the Chrysalis.
  P. Rivière, 617(TLS):16Apr82-444
Lincoln, M. Début at the Gewandhaus and
After. (F.M.H. Harper, ed)
  E. Forbes, 415:Jun81-385
Lincoln, W.B. Nicholas I.*
  M. Beresford, 161(DUJ):Dec80-98
Lincoln, W.B. The Romanovs.
  K. Fitz Lyon, 617(TLS):19Mar82-298
Lincoln, W.B. Petr Petrovich Semenov-Tian-
Shanskii.
  R.A. French, 575(SEER):Oct81-612
  R.E. McGrew, 550(RusR):Apr81-191
Lind, J. Travels to the Enu.
  F. Tuohy, 617(TLS):12Mar82-289
  P. Zweig, 441:20Jun82-10
  442(NY):17May82-139
Lind, T. and G.A. Mackay. Norwegian Oil
Policies.
  P.K. Kresl, 563(SS):Spring81-230

Lindahl, J. Decorating with Fabric. (rev ed)
P. Bach, 614:Summer82-15
Lindahl, J. The Shade Book. (rev ed)
P. Bach, 614:Summer82-19
Lindberg, C. The Middle English Bible: Prefatory Epistles of St. Jerome.*
H. Hargreaves, 541(RES):May81-201
Lindberg, D.C., ed. Science in the Middle Ages.
R.C. Dales, 589:Oct81-932
Lindberg-Seyersted, B. - see Pound, E. and F.M. Ford
Lindblom, C.E. Politics and Markets.
S.L. Elkin, 185:Jul82-720
Lindblom, C.E. and D.K. Cohen. Usable Knowledge.
W.H. Panning, 185:Oct81-162
Linden, E. City of Razors.*
J. Cotton, 493:Sep81-74
Linden, R.H. Bear and Foxes.
S. Kirschbaum, 104(CASS):Winter81-634
Linder, C., ed. Oral Communication Testing.
E. Hocking, 207(FR):Oct80-216
Linder, C.A. Romantic Imagery in the Novels of Charlotte Brontë.*
J. Dusinberre, 447(N&Q):Aug80-379
R. Miles, 677(YES):Vol 11-313
P. Thomson, 541(RES):Aug81-344
Lindey, C. Superrealist Painting and Sculpture.
90:Jun81-386
Lindfors, B. Black African Literature in English.
M. Banham, 610:Autumn81-232
M.F., 189(EA):Jul-Sep81-365
Lindfors, J.W. Children's Language and Learning.
M.W. Salus, 350:Sep82-738
Lindgren, A. Das Utrechter Arzneibuch.
B.D. Haage, 680(ZDP):Band99Heft3-459
Lindholm, C. Generosity and Jealousy.
C. von Fürer-Haimendorf, 617(TLS): 17Dec82-1390
Lindkvist, K-G. AT versus ON, IN, BY.
J.L. Mackenzie, 38:Band99Heft1/2-182
205(FMLS):Jan80-89
Lindkvist, K-G. A Comprehensive Study of Conceptions of Locality in which English Prepositions Occur.
J. Monaghan, 38:Band99Heft1/2-181
Lindkvist, T. Landborna i Norden under äldre medeltid.
B.E. Gelsinger, 589:Jan81-170
Lindman, S. - see Wiik, K.H.
Lindop, G. The Opium Eater.*
A. Phillips, 364:Mar82-77
Lindow, J., ed and trans. Swedish Legends and Folktales.*
G. Petschel, 196:Band21Heft1/2-130
Lindqvist, K. Individ grupp gemenskap.
I.M. Gabrieli, 562(Scan):Nov81-231
Lindsay, M. Collected Poems.
C. Rush, 571(ScLJ):Summer80-125
Lindsay, M. Lowland Scottish Villages.
J.A.S. Miller, 571(ScLJ):Winter81-147
Lindsay, M. Francis George Scott and the Scottish Renaissance.
C.T. Davie, 571(ScLJ):Winter81-132
Lindsey, K. Friends as Family.
A. Hacker, 453(NYRB):18Mar82-37

Lindskog-Wallenburg, G. Bezeichnungen für Frauenkleidungsstücke und Kleiderschmuck im Mittelniederdeutschen.*
D. Rosenthal, 680(ZDP):Band99Heft1-150
Lindström, O. Aspects of English Intonation.
N. Davis, 541(RES):May81-198
Lindstrom, T.S. A Concise History of Russian Literature.* (Vol 2)
R. Sheldon, 550(RusR):Jul81-352
Lindung, Y., ed. Kiosklitteraturen.
R.J. Jensen, 563(SS):Winter81-124
Linell, P. Psychological Reality in Phonology.
G. Drachman, 350:Sep81-728
J. Fought, 355(LSoc):Dec81-466
J.T. Jensen, 320(CJL):Fall81-236
I.R. Smith, 67:Nov81-277
"Linen-Making in New England 1640-1860 (All Sorts of Good Sufficient Cloth)."
P. Bach, 614:Spring81-20
Ling, T. Buddhism, Imperialism and War.
C.F. Keyes, 293(JASt):Nov80-196
"Lingua e contesto."
R. Posner, 545(RPh):Aug80-95
Linhart, R. Le sucre et la faim.
N. Michel, 98:Jan81-54
Link, A.S. - see Wilson, W.
Link, F. Geschichte der amerikanischen Erzählkunst im 19. Jahrhundert.*
C. Wegelin, 27(AL):Nov81-519
Linker, R.W. A Bibliography of Old French Lyrics.
F.M. Chambers, 545(RPh):Feb81(supp)-296
D.A. Fein, 207(FR):Oct81-131
N.B. Smith, 589:Jan81-171
Linklater, E. Orkney and Shetland. (rev)
J.B. Caird, 571(ScLJ):Winter81-148
Linklater, M. Massacre.
J. Hunter, 617(TLS):2Apr82-387
Links, J.G. Canaletto.
J. Russell, 441:5Dec82-13
J. Steer, 617(TLS):31Dec82-1440
Linn, N. A Book of Songs.
R. Minor, 441:28Nov82-27
Linz, J.J. and A. Stepan, eds. The Break-down of Democratic Regimes.
J. Dunn, 185:Jul81-685
Lipgens, W. A History of European Integration. (Vol 1)
R. Mayne, 617(TLS):15Oct82-1126
Lipinsky, A. Oro, argento, gemme e smalti.
W. Krönig, 471:Jul/Aug/Sep81-291
Lipking, L., ed. High Romantic Argument.
C. Salvesen, 617(TLS):26Feb82-231
Lipking, L. The Life of the Poet.
C. Martindale, 617(TLS):20Aug82-897
Lipman, J. and T. Armstrong, eds. American Folk Painters of Three Centuries.
C.K. Dewhurst and M. MacDowell, 658: Winter81-341
Lipman, S. Music After Modernism.
A. Berger, 473(PR):4/1981-624
D. Pond, 396(ModA):Spring81-211
Lipp, S. Leopoldo Zea.*
I.A. Leonard, 37:Mar81-45
J.W. Robb, 238:Dec81-647
de Lippe, A. Indian Mediaeval Sculpture.*
C.R. Bolon, 318(JAOS):Apr/Jun80-157
Lippi, M. Value and Naturalism in Marx.
A.L., 185:Oct81-192

Lippit, N.M. Reality and Fiction in Modern Japanese Literature.
  A.R. Davis, 302:Vol 18-161
Lippman, C. Lyrical Positivism.
  205(FMLS):Jan80-90
Lipscomb, J. and R.W. David, eds. John Raven.
  M. Grant, 617(TLS):19Feb82-176
Lipsey, R. Coomaraswamy 3.*
  M.W. Meister, 318(JAOS):Apr/Jun80-151
Lipsey, R. - see Coomaraswamy, A.K.
Lipsius, J. and P. Cunaeus. Two Neo-Latin Menippean Satires. (C. Matheeussen and C.L. Heesakkers, eds)
  L.V.R., 568(SCN):Spring81-32
Liria Montañés, P. - see Mandeville, J.
Lisca, P. John Steinbeck.
  R. Astro, 395(MFS):Summer80-325
Liscombe, R.W. William Wilkins 1778-1839.*
  H. Colvin, 46:Mar81-192
  P.F. Norton, 576:Dec81-335
  D. Watkin, 90:May81-316
Liska, G. Russia and World Order.
  A.C. Janos, 550(RusR):Jan81-74
Lisle, L. Portrait of an Artist.
  A. Oktenberg, 436(NewL):Winter81/82-113
  J.R. Williams, 658:Winter81-361
List, S. Forgiving.
  N. Johnson, 441:14Nov82-14
Littell, K.M. Jeremias Gotthelf's "Die Käserei in der Vehfreude."*
  H.M. Waidson, 133:Band14Heft4-379
Littell, R. The Amateur.*
  T.J. Binyon, 617(TLS):29Jan82-104
  T.J. Binyon, 617(TLS):5Feb82-147
"Litteraturtolkninger 1979."
  A. Jørgensen, 172(Edda):1981/4-261
Little, B. Abbeys and Priories in England and Wales.
  P. Draper, 576:May81-157
Little, D.P., ed. Essays on Islamic Civilization Presented to Niyazi Berkes.
  W.C. Hickman, 318(JAOS):Apr/Jun80-148
Little, J.P. Simone Weil. (supp 1)
  P.J. Kingston, 208(FS):Jul81-365
Little, N.F. Neat and Tidy.
  42(AR):Winter81-131
Littlewood, W. Communicative Language Teaching.
  T. Light, 350:Dec82-952
Litwack, L.F. Been in the Storm So Long.*
  R.F. Durden, 579(SAQ):Winter81-117
  G.S. Hasson, 9(AlaR):Jul81-232
Liu I-ch'ing. Shih-shuo Hsin-yü. (R.B. Mather, ed and trans)
  D.E. Gjertson, 318(JAOS):Jul/Sep80-380
Liu Wu-chi and others, eds. K'uei Hsing.
  D.R. Knechtges, 318(JAOS):Jul/Sep80-381
Lively, P. Next to Nature, Art.
  A. Brownjohn, 617(TLS):23Apr82-455
  K.C. O'Brien, 362:22Jul82-24
Liver, R. Die Nachwirkung der antiken Sakralsprache im christlichen Gebet des lateinischen und italienischen Mittelalters.
  G. Wieland, 589:Jan81-174
Livingston, J. A Piece of the Silence.
  N. Callendar, 441:26Sep82-41
Livingston, J.C. Fair Game?
  I. Thalberg, 185:Oct80-138

Livingston, P. Ingmar Bergman and the Rituals of Art.
  I-S. Ewbank, 617(TLS):3Dec82-1347
Livingstone, M. David Hockney.*
  M. Glazebrook, 364:Oct81-85
Livni, A. La Recherche du Dieu chez Paul Valéry.*
  P. Gifford, 208(FS):Jan81-89
"Livres et auteurs québécois 1978."
  A.B. Chartier, 207(FR):Feb81-463
Lizé, E. Voltaire, Grimm et la "Correspondance Littéraire."
  J. Pappas, 207(FR):Oct81-139
  J. Schlobach, 535(RHL):Nov-Dec81-994
  D. Williams, 402(MLR):Jul81-703
Ljung, M. Reflections on the English Progressive.
  A. Davison, 350:Sep82-729
Llamzon, T.A. Handbook of Philippine Language Groups.
  J.U. Wolff, 293(JASt):Feb81-427
Llorach, E.A. - see under Alarcos Llorach, E.
Llorens, V. El romanticismo español.
  D.L. Shaw, 402(MLR):Jul81-727
Llosa, M.V. - see under Vargas Llosa, M.
Lloyd, A.L. Anatomy of the Verb.
  P.J. Hopper, 350:Dec81-926
  R.H. Lawson, 301(JEGP):Apr81-288
Lloyd, A.L., ed. Come All Ye Bold Miners. (rev)
  L. Fish, 292(JAF):Jan-Mar81-125
  P. Lewis, 565:Vol22No3-55
Lloyd, G.E.R. Magic, Reason and Experience.*
  J. Barnes, 483:Jul81-433
Lloyd, R. Baudelaire et Hoffmann.*
  D.P. Haase, 446(NCFS):Spring-Summer81-285
  E. Hartman, 207(FR):Mar81-599
  F.S. Heck, 188(ECr):Spring81-110
  I. Köhler, 597(SN):Vol153No1-205
  J.M. McGlathery, 221(GQ):May81-354
  S.S. Prawer, 402(MLR):Jan81-248
  205(FMLS):Apr80-191
Lloyd, R. Baudelaire's Literary Criticism.*
  M. Wood, 453(NYRB):2Dec82-16
Lloyd, S.M. - see "Roget's Thesaurus of English Words and Phrases"
Lloyd, T.H. Alien Merchants in England in the High Middle Ages.
  E. Miller, 617(TLS):22Oct82-1171
Lloyd-Jones, H. Blood for the Ghosts. Classical Survivals.
  B. Knox, 617(TLS):6Aug82-847
Lloyd-Jones, H. - see von Wilamowitz-Moellendorff, U.
Loades, D.M. The Reign of Mary Tudor.
  S.E. Lehmberg, 551(RenQ):Winter80-790
Loar, B. Mind and Meaning.
  P.F. Strawson, 617(TLS):2Jul82-713
Lobban, R. Historical Dictionary of the Republics of Guinea-Bissau and Cape Verde.
  C. Fyfe, 69:Vol50No3-329
Lobbenberg, S. Using Urban Wasteland.
  T. Cantell, 324:Aug82-598
Lobkowicz, B.H. - see under Hassenstein a Lobkowicz, B.
Lobsien, E. Der Alltag des "Ulysses."*
  U. Schneider, 38:Band99Heft3/4-529

Lo Cascio, F. Sulla autenticità delle
epistole di Apollonio Tianeo.
 G.W. Bowersock, 123:Vol31No2-289
Locher, G.W. Die Zwinglische Reformation
im Rahmen der europaischen Kirchenge-
schichte.
 J.M. Estes, 539:Aug82-206
Locher, J.L., general ed. Escher.
 A.L. Loeb, 617(TLS):17Sep82-997
Lochhead, D. High Marsh Road.*
 M. Darling, 102(CanL):Summer81-135
 A. Munton, 150(DR):Autumn81-569
Lochhead, M. Renaissance of Wonder.
 C.E. Lloyd, 569(SR):Spring81-281
Lock, A., ed. Action, Gesture and Sym-
bol.*
 I. Vine, 567:Vol35No1/2-157
Lock, F. and A. Lawson, comps. Australian
Literature.* (2nd ed)
 J.F. Burrows, 402(MLR):Oct81-952
Lock, F.P. Susanna Centlivre.*
 B. Yearling, 610:Winter80/81-75
Lock, F.P. The Politics of "Gulliver's
Travels."
 J.B., 148:Autumn81-87
 C. Fabricant, 301(JEGP):Jul81-419
 B.A. Goldgar, 566:Autumn80-35
 R. Quintana, 402(MLR):Jul81-671
Lock, M.M. East Asian Medicine in Urban
Japan.*
 A. Kleinman, 407(MN):Winter81-485
 W.E. Steslicke, 293(JASt):May81-606
Locke, D. A Fantasy of Reason.*
 B.B., 185:Jan81-343
 B.R. Pollin, 340(KSJ):Vol30-213
 M.S. Quinn, 584(SWR):Autumn81-433
 K.E. Smith, 83:Autumn81-216
 D.O. Thomas, 518:Apr81-102
Locke, E. Student at the Gates.
 P. Smart, 368:Dec81-475
Locke, J. The Correspondence of John
Locke.* (Vol 6) (E.S. de Beer, ed)
 J. Dunn, 362:17Jun82-22
Locke, J. The Correspondence of John
Locke. (Vol 7) (E.S. de Beer, ed)
 J. Dunn, 362:17Jun82-22
 K.H.D. Haley, 617(TLS):14May82-524
Locker, D., ed. Symptoms and Illness.
 P. Sedgwick, 617(TLS):8Jan82-24
Lockridge, L.S. Coleridge the Moralist.*
 P. Lim, Jr., 179(ES):Aug81-390
Lockspeiser, E. Debussy.
 R. Nichols, 415:Sep81-604
Lockwood, M. and A.V. Bhat - see King
Mahendra
Lockwood, T. Post-Augustan Satire.*
 J.J. Gold, 301(JEGP):Apr81-255
 C.N. Manlove, 447(N&Q):Aug80-374
 C.J. Rawson, 541(RES):Nov81-457
Lockyer, R. Buckingham.
 P. Collinson, 617(TLS):29Oct82-1187
Loder, J.E. The Transforming Moment.
 R.B., 185:Apr82-583
Lodge, D. Souls and Bodies.* (British
title: How Far Can You Go?)
 E. Eichman, 231:Apr82-107
 P. Theroux, 441:31Jan82-3
 442(NY):25Jan82-103
Lodge, D. Working with Structuralism.*
 P. Dickinson, 364:Nov81-75
Lods, J. La Morte-saison.
 M.B. Kline, 207(FR):Feb82-438
 L. Kovacs, 450(NRF):Mar81-129

Loeb, E.H. Die Geburt der Götter in der
griechischen Kunst der klassischen Zeit.
 J. Boardman, 123:Vol31No1-140
 S. Woodford, 303(JoHS):Vol 101-221
Loeb, J., ed. Feminist Collage.*
 N.F. Broude, 127:Summer81-180
Loeb, P. Nuclear Culture.
 R. Sale, 453(NYRB):29Apr82-12
Loeber, R. A Biographical Dictionary of
Architects in Ireland 1600-1720.
 N. Sheaff, 324:Jul82-502
Loehr, M. The Great Painters of China.
 H. Crawley, 39:Feb81-127
 M. Tregear, 324:Jun82-436
Loehr, M., with L.G.F. Huber. Ancient
Chinese Jades from the Grenville L.
Winthrop Collection in the Fogg Art
Museum, Harvard University.
 J.M. Hartman, 318(JAOS):Jul/Sep80-377
Loeser, K. A Thousand Pardons.
 H. Bevington, 441:3Oct82-14
Loewenstein, J.I. Marx against Marxism.
 A.L., 185:Jul81-694
Loewy, E., ed. Exil.
 A. Stephan, 406:Winter81-481
Loewy, R. Industrial Design.*
 T. Benton, 59:Sep81-408
Löffler, A. and J-C. Rojahn, eds. Eng-
lische Lyrik.
 J. Kleinstück, 38:Band99Heft1/2-240
Löffler, H. and W. Besch. Alemannisch.
 H. Fischer, 680(ZDP):Band99Heft3-467
Löffler, H., K. Pestalozzi and M. Stern,
eds. Standard und Dialekt.
 M. Durrell, 402(MLR):Apr81-493
 K-H. Jäger, 406:Winter81-443
Löfstedt, L., ed. "Li abregemenz noble
honme Vegesce Flave René des establis-
semenz apartenanz a chevalerie," traduc-
tion par Jean de Meun de "Flavii Vegeti
Renati Viri Illustris Epitoma Instituto-
rum Rei Militaris."
 G.S. Burgess, 545(RPh):Feb81(supp)-355
Loftis, J. - see Halkett, A. and A. Fan-
shawe
Logan, J. Only the Dreamer Can Change the
Dream.* The Bridge of Change.*
 R.W. Flint, 472:Fall/Winter81-45
 J. Mazzaro, 219(GaR):Winter81-892
Logue, C. Ode to the Dodo.* War Music.
 L. Durrell, 364:Jul81-74
Lohmeier, D., ed. Jürgen Andersen und
Volquard Iversen.
 V. Meid, 406:Winter81-454
Lohmeier, D. and B. Olsson, eds. Welt-
liches und Geistliches Lied des Barock.
 A.J. Harper, 402(MLR):Jul81-745
Loi, V. Origini e caratteristiche della
latinità cristiana.
 L.A. Holford-Strevens, 123:Vol31No2-
230
Loizos, P. The Heart Grown Bitter.
 J.K. Campbell, 617(TLS):26Nov82-1291
Lomas, H. Public Footpath.*
 P. Bland, 364:Jul81-72
 R. Phillips, 249(HudR):Autumn81-431
 B. Ruddick, 148:Winter81-71
Lomas, H., ed and trans. Territorial
Song.*
 P. Elstob, 364:Mar82-94
Lombard, C.M. Xavier de Maistre.
 P.J. Whyte, 208(FS):Oct81-453

Lombard, J.   Courtilz de Sandras et la
crise du roman à la fin du grand siècle.
   D. Kuizenga, 207(FR):Mar82-549
Lombardi, L.   Conversazioni con Petrassi.
   C. Bennett, 607:Dec81-47
Lomnäs, E., ed.   Franz Berwald.
   J. Horton, 415:Jun81-381
London, J.   Jack London on the Road. (R.W.
Etulain, ed)
   H. Lachtman, 573(SSF):Spring81-200
   H. Lachtman, 649(WAL):Spring81-58
London, J.   Thirteen Tales of Terror by
Jack London. (J. Perry, ed)
   H. Lachtman, 649(WAL):Winter82-322
Londré, F.H.   Tom Stoppard.
   C.W.E. Bigsby, 617(TLS):8Jan82-33
Londré, F.H.   Tennessee Williams.
   A.E. Kalson, 585(SoQ):Winter81-81
   M. Yacowar, 397(MD):Mar81-112
Lonergan, B.J.   Verbum — Word and Idea in
Aquinas. (D.B. Burrell, ed)
   J. Burbidge, 154:Mar81-155
Long, D.G.   Bentham on Liberty.*
   H.W. Schneider, 319:Jan81-123
Long, J.L.   Introduced Birds of the World.
   C. Lever, 617(TLS):12Mar82-291
Long, M.H. and others.   Reading English
For Academic Study.
   E. Hamp-Lyons, 608:Jun82-253
Long, R-C.W.   Kandinsky.
   S. Selwood, 90:Nov81-685
   R. Woodfield, 89(BJA):Autumn81-380
Long, R.E.   The Achieving of "The Great
Gatsby."
   S. Donaldson, 395(MFS):Summer80-332
Long, R.E.   The Great Succession.*
   P.J. Eakin, 27(AL):Mar81-153
   P. McCarthy, 284:Fall81-70
   E. Nettels, 445(NCF):Jun81-123
   D.J. Schneider, 395(MFS):Winter80/81-
646
   M.R. Winchell, 577(SHR):Fall81-367
Long, R.J. - see Bartholomaeus Anglicus
Longeon, C. - see Dolet, É.
Lord Longford.   Diary of a Year.
   V. Glendinning, 617(TLS):3Sep82-949
   J. Vaizey, 362:5Aug82-20
Lord Longford.   Pope John Paul II.
   D. Crane, 617(TLS):5Nov82-1227
   C.C. O'Brien, 362:27May82-20
Lord Longford and A. McHardy.   Ulster.
   K. Jeffery, 617(TLS):5Mar82-238
Longford, E.   Images of Chelsea.*
   G. Walters, 354:Dec81-357
Longford, E.   A Pilgrimage of Passion.
   M. Goldstein, 569(SR):Spring81-287
Longford, E. - see Antrim, L.
Longley, M.   The Echo Gate.*
   L. Sail, 565:Vol22No1-66
Longley, M.   Selected Poems 1963-1980.*
   M. De Shazer, 134(CP):Fall81-125
   V. Young, 472:Fall/Winter81-155
Longrigg, R.   Bad Bet.
   R. Mortimer, 617(TLS):21May82-566
Longtin, R.C.   Three Writers of the Far
West.
   J.H. Maguire, 26(ALR):Spring81-134
Longville, T. - see Riley, J.
Lonigan, P.R.   The "Gormont et Isembart."
   A. Iker-Gittleman, 545(RPh):Feb81-356
Lonis, R.   Guerre et religion en Grèce à
l'époque classique.
   N.J. Richardson, 303(JoHS):Vol 101-185

Lønning, P.   Cet effrayant pari.
   M. Adam, 542:Jul-Sep81-354
Lönnroth, L.   Den dubbla scenen.*
   H. Kuhn, 563(SS):Autumn81-475
Loos, E.E., ed.   Estudios Panos I.
Estudios Panos II.
   K.M. Kensinger, 269(IJAL):Jan81-68
Loos, E.E.   Estudios Panos V.
   K.M. Kensinger, 269(IJAL):Jan81-68
Loose, G.   Der junge Heinrich Mann.
   H.R. Vaget, 221(GQ):May81-372
Lope, H-J., ed.   Aufsätze zum 18. Jahr-
hundert in Frankreich.
   J. Rustin, 535(RHL):Jul-Oct81-788
Lopes, J.L. and M. Paty, eds.   Quantum
Mechanics, a Half Century Later.
   R.T.W. Arthur, 486:Mar81-156
Lopez, B.H.   Winter Count.*
   639(VQR):Autumn81-137
Lopez, E.H.   Conversations with Katherine
Anne Porter.*
   A. Phillips, 617(TLS):25Jun82-701
López Estrada, F., ed.   El Abencerraje.
   E.R. Rogers, 238:Dec81-674
López Estrada, F.   Tomás Moro y España.
   S. Cro, 304(JHP):Autumn81-78
López-Heredia, J.   Matéria e forma narra-
tiva d'O Ateneu.
   M-O.L. McBride, 238:Sep81-487
López Morales, H.   Historia de la litera-
tura medieval española. (Vol 1)
   P.O. Gericke, 545(RPh):May81-530
López Portillo, J., D. Sodi and F. Díaz
Infante.   Quetzalcoatl.
   D.J.R. Bruckner, 441:12Dec82-24
Loraine, P.   Sea-Change.
   M. Laski, 362:2Dec82-23
Lorber, F.   Inschriften auf korinthischen
Vasen.
   A. Johnston, 303(JoHS):Vol 101-223
Lorca, F.G.   Bodas de sangre. (H. Ramsden,
ed)
   205(FMLS):Oct80-375
Lorca, F.G.   The Cricket Sings.
   H.J.F. de Aguilar, 472:Spring/Summer81-
253
Lorca, F.G.   Deep Song and Other Prose.*
(C. Maurer, ed and trans)
   H.J.F. de Aguilar, 472:Spring/Summer81-
253
Lorca, F.G.   Songs. (P. Cummings, trans;
D. Eisenberg, ed)
   J.W. Zdenek, 552(REH):Jan81-138
Lord, S.   Golden Hill.
   M. Mewshaw, 441:24Oct82-43
Lorde, A.   Zami: A New Spelling of My
Name. Chosen Poems Old and New.
   R. Daniell, 441:19Dec82-12
Loreau, M.   Michel Deguy, la poursuite de
la poésie tout entière.
   M. de Diéguez, 98:Oct80-1011
Loreck, J.   Wie man früher Sozialdemokrat
wurde.
   H. Groschopp, 654(WB):4/1981-183
Lorentz, O.   Norsk setningsform.
   T.L. Markey, 562(Scan):Nov81-213
Lorenzatos, Z.   The Lost Center and other
Essays in Greek Poetry.
   P. Bien, 651(WHR):Winter81-369
Lorenzi, J-H., O. Pastre and J. Toledano.
La crise du XXe siècle.
   J. Piel, 98:Oct80-980

de Lorenzo, P. Episodios de la era del tiburón.
C.D. Ley, 617(TLS):12Nov82-1254
Lorenzo-Rivero, L. Larra.
P.L. Ullman, 399(MLJ):Spring81-99
Lőrincz, L. Mongol mesetípusok.
V. Voigt, 196:Band21Heft1/2-131
Lőrincz, L. Mongolische Märchentypen.
H-J. Uther, 196:Band22Heft3/4-359
Lortat-Jacob, B. Musique et fêtes au Haut-Atlas.
B. Yarmolinsky, 187:Jan82-170
Losemann, V. Nationalsozialismus und Antike.
W.M. Calder 3d, 122:Apr81-166
T.E.J. Wiedemann, 313:Vol71-229
Losse, D.N. Rhetoric at Play.
G. de Rocher, 207(FR):Dec81-262
Lossky, B. and N., eds. Bibliographie des oeuvres de Nicolas Lossky.
M. Everitt, 575(SEER):Jan81-89
Losty, J.P. The Art of the Book in India.
T. Falk, 617(TLS):17Sep82-1019
Lőte, L., ed. Transylvania and the Theory of Daco — Roman — Rumanian Continuity.
D. Deletant, 575(SEER):Jul81-431
Lotman, Y. Analysis of the Poetic Text. (D.B. Johnson, ed and trans)
R. Reeder, 567:Vol135No3/4-317
Lottman, H.R. The Left Bank.
N. Bliven, 442(NY):5Jul82-98
N. Fraser, 362:2/May82-22
M. Gallant, 441:4Apr82-3
P. Thody, 617(TLS):1Oct82-1057
Loucks, J.F. - see Browning, R.
Loudon, J.H. James Scott and William Scott, Bookbinders.*
D.A. Harrop, 354:Mar81-74
Lougee, C.C. Le Paradis des Femmes.
S. Bayne, 475:No14Pt1-146
Lough, J. The Philosophes and Post-Revolutionary France.
L.A. Siedentop, 617(TLS):8Oct82-1108
Lough, J. Seventeenth-Century French Drama: The Background.*
H.T. Barnwell, 610:Spring81-147
J. Berkowitz, 612(ThS):May81-109
E.M. Tilton, 568(SCN):Summer-Fall81-56
Lough, J. Writer and Public in France.*
P.P. Clark, 131(CL):Winter81-92
R. Pouilliart, 356(LR):Aug81-254
Loughran, D.K. Federico García Lorca.*
A. Josephs, 238:Mar81-155
Louis, C. - see Reynes, R.
Loulis, J.C. The Greek Communist Party 1940-1944.
C.M. Woodhouse, 617(TLS):20Aug82-908
Lounela, P. Hella Wuolijoki, legenda jo eläessään.
M.N. Deschner, 563(SS):Summer81-372
Lourie, M.A. - see Morris, W.
Love, J.L. São Paulo in the Brazilian Federation, 1889-1937.
J.A. Ellis, 263(RIB):Vol31No2-278
Love, J.O. Virginia Woolf.*
V. Shaw, 677(YES):Vol 11-353
Lovelace, R.F. The American Pietism of Cotton Mather.
D.D. Hall, 165(EAL):Spring82-89
C.E. Hambrick-Stowe, 656(WMQ):Apr81-309

Lovell, M. The Spy with His Head in the Clouds.
N. Callendar, 441:18Apr82-20
Lovelock, Y., ed. The Colour of the Weather.
J. Saunders, 565:Vol122No3-62
Lovesey, P. The False Inspector Dew.
T.J. Binyon, 617(TLS):25Jun82-702
N. Callendar, 441:3Oct82-16
M. Laski, 362:29Apr82-27
Lovoll, O.S., ed. Makers of an American Immigrant Legacy.
H. Naess, 562(Scan):Nov81-238
Low, A. Love's Architecture.
M. Elsky, 551(RenQ):Spring80-138
K. Lynch, 568(SCN):Spring81-7
A. Rudrum, 677(YES):Vol 11-251
Low, A.D. Jews in the Eyes of the Germans.*
E. Glass, 221(GQ):Jan81-124
Low, D.A. That Sunny Dome.*
A. Noble, 571(ScLJ):Summer80-105
Low, D.A. Thieves' Kitchen.
J. Adlard, 617(TLS):9Apr82-417
Low, J.T. Doctors, Devils, Saints and Sinners.
D. Hutchison, 571(ScLJ):Winter81-128
Löw, R. Philosophie des Lebendigen.
M.G., 543:Jun81-790
Lowance, M.I., Jr. The Language of Canaan.*
M.J. Crawford, 432(NEQ):Sep81-432
P.F. Gura, 27(AL):Nov81-508
K. Keller, 141:Summer81-275
Lowden, D. Sunspot.*
N. Callendar, 441:21Feb82-42
Lowe, D.K. Benjamin Constant.
B. Fink, 207(FR):Mar81-599
Lowe, R. Delius Collection of the Grainger Museum.
R. Anderson, 415:Aug81-537
Lowe, S. Touched.
M. Martin, 148:Winter81-49
Lowenthal, A.W., D. Rosand and J. Walsh - see Held, J.S.
Lower, J.A. Ocean of Destiny.*
P. Roy, 298:Fall-Winter81-205
Lowman, A. Printing Arts in Texas.
L. Milazzo, 584(SWR):Autumn81-414
Lownes, V. The Autobiography of Victor Lownes: Playboy Extraordinary.
M. Furness, 617(TLS):1Oct82-1056
Lowry, B. Daddy's Girl.*
442(NY):4Jan82-89
Lowry, J.M.P. The Logical Principles of Proclus' "Stoicheiōsis Theologikē" as Systematic Ground of the Cosmos.
A. Sheppard, 123:Vol31No2-303
Lowry, M. Le Garde-fantôme.
J-M. le Sidaner, 450(NRF):Mar81-151
Lowry, M. The World of Aldus Manutius.*
L.V.R., 568(SCN):Summer-Fall81-78
Lowry, T.P. and T.S. The Clitoris.
D.W. Maurer, 35(AS):Spring-Summer77-157
Loy, M. The Last Lunar Baedeker. (R.L. Conover, ed)
H. Kenner, 441:16May82-7
Loyn, H.R. The Vikings in Britain.
E.S. Firchow, 563(SS):Winter81-78
Lozerec'h, B. L'Intérimaire.
P.L. Bowles, 617(TLS):12Nov82-1254

Luard, E. A History of the United Nations.
(Vol 1)
    S. Hazzard, 617(TLS):17Sep82-987
Lubin, G. - see Sand, G.
Lucas, G.A. The Diary of George A. Lucas.*
(L.M.C. Randall, ed and trans)
    F. Haskell, 90:Apr81-243
    H.W. Morgan, 658:Summer/Autumn81-233
Lucas, J. The Literature of Change.*
    P. Coustillas, 189(EA):Apr-Jun81-226
Lucas, J., ed. The 1930s.*
    M. Green, 366:Autumn81-267
    J. Newman, 161(DUJ):Jun81-263
    295(JML):Vol8No3/4-348
Lucas, J. War in the Desert.
    S. Bidwell, 617(TLS):31Dec82-1450
Lucas, J. War on the Eastern Front, 1941-
1945.
    639(VQR):Summer81-86
Lucas, J.R. On Justice.
    T.D. Campbell, 518:Oct81-236
Lucas, L.W. Grammar of Ros Goill Irish,
Co. Donegal.
    B. Ó Cuív, 112:Vol 14-172
    T. Thomas-Flinders, 350:Jun81-503
Luce, S. A Glossary of Celine's Fiction.
    R. Hauptman, 395(MFS):Winter80/81-739
Lucid, D.P., ed and trans. Soviet Semiot-
ics.*
    M. Corti, 599:Winter81-52
Lucie-Smith, E. Art in the Seventies.
    90:Jun81-386
Lucie-Smith, E. The Art of Caricature.
    R.E. Shikes, 441:10Jan82-30
Lucie-Smith, E., S. Hunter and A.M. Vogt.
Kunst der Gegenwart (Propyläen Kunst-
geschichte, Supplementband II).
    S. Muthesius, 576:May81-159
Lucier, A. and D. Simon. Chambers.
    P. Griffiths, 415:Jun81-382
Lucilius, G. Satires. (Vol 2) (F. Char-
pin, ed and trans)
    J. André, 555:Vol54fasc2-367
Luckert, K.W., with J.C. Cooke. Coyoteway.
    D.P. McAllester, 292(JAF):Apr-Jun81-
247
Ludendorff, M. Ein Wort der Kritik an
Kant und Schopenhauer.
    R. Malter, 342:Band72Heft1-117
Lüders, D., ed. Clemens Brentano.
    E.W. Herd, 67:Nov81-271
    H.M.K. Riley, 133:Band14Heft2-187
Ludington, T. John Dos Passos.*
    A. Chapman, 37:Jun-Jul81-22
    R.S. Kennedy, 295(JML):Vol8No3/4-481
    T.K. Meier, 659(ConL):Spring82-263
    D. Pizer, 639(VQR):Summer81-537
    W.B. Rideout, 27(AL):Jan82-739
Ludlum, R. The Parsifal Mosaic.
    E. Hunter, 441:21Mar82-11
Ludz, P.C., ed. Geheime Gesellschaften.
    K.F. Otto, Jr., 406:Winter81-455
Luecke, J-M. Measuring Old English
Rhythm.*
    W. Obst, 38:Band99Heft3/4-482
Luft, D.S. Robert Musil and the Crisis of
European Culture 1880-1942.*
    A. Janik, 478:Fall81-240
    P.W. Nutting, 221(GQ):Nov81-527
de Luis, L. - see Hernández, M.

Luiselli Fadda, A.M., ed. Nuove Omelie
Anglosassoni della Rinascenza Benedet-
tina.*
    M.R. Godden, 402(MLR):Apr81-431
    H. Sauer, 38:Band99Heft1/2-216
Luiso, F.P. Studi su l'Epistolario di
Leonardo Bruni. (L. Gualdo Rosa, ed)
    H. Baron, 589:Oct81-831
Lukács, G. Eine Autobiographie im Dialog.
    G. Steiner, 617(TLS):22Jan82-67
Lukacs, J. 1945: Year Zero.
    H.M. Adams, 396(ModA):Fall81-417
Lukatsky, D. and S.B. Toback. The Jewish
American Princess Handbook.
    M. Lefkowitz, 617(TLS):24Dec82-1429
Luke, D. - see Grimm, J. and W.
Luker, N., ed and trans. An Anthology of
Russian Neo-Realism.
    G. Donchin, 617(TLS):31Dec82-1446
Luker, N.J.L. Aleksandr Grin.
    B.P. Scherr, 550(RusR):Apr81-222
Lukes, S. Émile Durkheim.
    R. Griffiths, 208(FS):Oct81-469
Lumsden, C.J. and E.O. Wilson. Genes,
Mind and Culture.*
    R.J.P., 185:Jul82-793
Lund, H.P. La Critique du siècle chez
Nodier.
    D.P. Haase, 546(RR):May81-361
    A-M. Roux, 535(RHL):Jan-Feb81-148
Lund, R.D. Restoration and Early Eigh-
teenth-Century English Literature 1660-
1740.*
    566:Autumn81-51
Lundkvist, A. Agadir.*
    J.F. Cotter, 249(HudR):Summer81-280
Lundquist, J. J.D. Salinger.*
    G.F. Waller, 106:Winter81-413
Lundqvist, Å. Masslitteraturen.
    R.J. Jensen, 563(SS):Winter81-124
Lundström, S. Ovids Metamorphosen und die
Politik des Kaisers.
    J.C. McKeown, 123:Vol31No2-292
Luplow, C. Isaac Babel's Red Cavalry.
    J. Grayson, 617(TLS):31Dec82-1446
Lurati, O. Dialetto e italiano regionale
nella Svizzera italiana.
    R. Stefanini, 545(RPh):Feb81(supp)-174
Lurie, A. The Language of Clothes.*
    P. Bach, 614:Winter82-18
    S. Gardiner, 362:6May82-24
    W. Goodman, 441:17Jan82-16
    A. Hollander, 453(NYRB):15Apr82-38
    L. Sage, 617(TLS):14May82-525
Lurker, M., ed. Wörterbuch der Symbolik.
    C. Burckhardt-Seebass, 196:Band22
Heft1/2-139
Lustick, I. Arabs in the Jewish State.*
    639(VQR):Winter81-23
Lustig, I.S. and F.A. Pottle - see Boswell,
J.
Lüthi, M. Märchen. (7th ed) Once Upon a
Time.
    E. Tucker, 292(JAF):Jul-Sep81-390
Lütkehaus, L. Hebbel.*
    E. McInnes, 402(MLR):Jan81-245
Lütterfelds, W. Kants Dialektik der
Erfahrung.
    W. Steinbeck, 342:Band71Heft3-367
Lutz, C.E. The Oldest Library Motto and
Other Library Essays.
    C. Smith, 377:Mar81-59

Lutz, D.S. Popular Consent and Popular Control.
  J.H. Kettner, 656(WMQ):Oct81-749
  639(VQR):Winter81-7
Lutz, K.B. and F.P. Leffler. Nos Amis French 1.
  P. Siegel, 207(FR):Apr82-716
Luwel, M. H.H. Johnston et H.M. Stanley sur le Congo.
  P. van Leynseele, 69:Vol50No4-440
van Luxemburg, J., M. Bal and W.G. Weststeijn. Inleiding in de literatuurwetenschap.
  J. Goedegebuure, 204(FdL):Sep81-286
Luxemburg, R. Comrade and Lover.* (E. Ettinger, ed and trans)
  D. Barnouw, 221(GQ):Jan81-105
  L. Lawner, 473(PR):3/1981-485
Luxton, M. More Than a Labour of Love.
  V. Strong-Boag, 298:Fall-Winter81-217
Lyall, G. The Conduct of Major Maxim.
  T.J. Binyon, 617(TLS):31Dec82-1448
Lyday, L.F. and G.W. Woodyard, eds. Dramatists in Revolt.
  D. Zalacaín, 241:Jan81-79
Lyman, C.M. The Vanishing Race and Other Illusions.
  A. Grundberg, 441:5Sep82-10
Lynch, D. Yeats.*
  D. O'Hara, 295(JML):Vol8No3/4-647
  H. Pyle, 541(RES):Aug81-356
Lynch, J. Argentine Dictator.
  M. Deas, 617(TLS):23Apr82-453
Lynch, L.W. Eighteenth-Century French Novelists and the Novel.
  M.B. Lacy, 207(FR):May81-867
  V. Mylne, 208(FS):Oct81-455
Lynch, M. Edinburgh and the Reformation.
  E. Playfair, 617(TLS):21May82-554
Lyndon, D. The City Observed: Boston.
  M. Bayles, 441:12Sep82-15
Lyne, R.O.A.M. The Latin Love Poets from Catullus to Horace.*
  N. Rudd, 123:Vol131No2-216
Lynn, H. - see Lampman, A. and E.W. Thomson
Lynton, N. The Story of Modern Art.
  D. Cooper, 39:Dec81-425
  D. Hall, 90:Nov81-680
  C. Harrison, 59:Sep81-328
  K. Morand, 529(QQ):Winter81-748
  42(AR):Fall81-515
Lyon, J.K. Bertolt Brecht in America.*
  J.M. Ritchie, 220(GL&L):Jan82-182
Lyons, F.S.L. Culture and Anarchy in Ireland 1890-1939.
  A. O'Day, 637(VS):Spring81-384
Lyons, J. Language and Linguistics.*
  P.A. Lee, 350:Jun82-478
Lyons, J. Semantics.* (Vol 1)
  G.L. Milsark, 215(GL):Summer81-141
Lyons, J. Semantics.* (Vol 2)
  R.M. Kempson, 603:Vol5No1-123
  G.L. Milsark, 215(GL):Summer81-141
Lyons, J.B. Oliver St. John Gogarty.* Brief Lives of Irish Doctors, 1600-1965.
  R.H., 305(JIL):Sep81-113
Lyons, J.O. The Invention of the Self.
  S. Soupel, 189(EA):Jul-Sep81-342
Lyons, M.C. and D.E.P. Jackson. Saladin.
  J. Hackett, 617(TLS):10Sep82-959
Lyons, N. and I. Sold!
  M. Simpson, 441:25Apr82-12

Lyotard, J-F. La Condition postmoderne.
  P. Coleman, 207(FR):Apr81-754
Lypp, M., ed. Literatur für Kinder.*
  O.F. Gmelin and K. Hammarberg, 196:Band21Heft1/2-134
Lyttelton, G. and R. Hart-Davis. The Lyttelton Hart-Davis Letters.* (Vol 3) (R. Hart-Davis, ed)
  P. Dickinson, 364:Jul81-96
Lyttelton, G. and R. Hart-Davis. The Lyttelton Hart-Davis Letters. (Vol 4) (R. Hart-Davis, ed)
  G. Annan, 362:29Apr82-21
  A. Bell, 617(TLS):24Sep82-1033
Lyublinskaya, A.D. - see Kiseleva, L.I.
Lyytinen, E. Finland in British Politics in the First World War.
  A.F. Upton, 575(SEER):Jul81-460

"MLA Directory of Periodicals."* (E.M. Mackesy, K. Mateyak and N.B. Hoover, eds)
  M.C. Patterson, 365:Spring-Summer82-121
McAdam, E.L. and G. Milne - see Johnson, S.
MacAfee, N., with L. Martinengo - see Pasolini, P.P.
McAfee, T. Whatever Isn't Glory.*
  H. Levine, 573(SSF):Fall81-480
McAleer, E.C. The Brownings of Casa Guidi.*
  C.C. Murrah, 628(UWR):Fall-Winter81-109
McAlester, D.P. Hogans.
  F.E. Hoxie, 42(AR):Spring81-258
McAlexander, H.H. The Prodigal Daughter.
  A. Rowe, 578:Fall82-130
McAlpine, M.E. The Genre of "Troilus and Criseyde."*
  T.A. Kirby, 179(ES):Dec81-560
MacAndrew, E. The Gothic Tradition in Fiction.*
  C.A. Howells, 175:Summer81-185
  W. Jackson, 579(SAQ):Spring81-239
  M.E. Novak, 445(NCF):Mar82-471
  G.R. Thompson, 395(MFS):Winter80/81-714
McAndrew, J. Venetian Architecture of the Early Renaissance.*
  D. Howard, 90:Aug81-493
  J.G. Links, 39:May81-339
MacAndrews, C. Mobility and Modernisation.
  M-H. Lim, 293(JASt):Nov80-197
McArdle, A.D. and D.B. Carpenter Gothic.*
  K. Harrington, 658:Spring81-112
McAulay, S. Chance.
  A. Cheuse, 441:27Jun82-12
McBain, E. Beauty and the Beast.
  T.J. Binyon, 617(TLS):25Jun82-702
McBain, E. Heat.
  M. Laski, 362:29Apr82-27
McBain, E. The McBain Brief.
  T.J. Binyon, 617(TLS):10Dec82-1378
McBarnet, D.J. Conviction.
  J.C. Alderson, 617(TLS):17May82-526
MacBeth, G. A Kind of Treason.
  K. Jeffery, 617(TLS):19Feb82-179
  M. Laski, 362:29Apr82-27
MacBeth, G. Poems from Oby.
  E. Morgan, 617(TLS):19Nov82-1282
MacBeth, G. Poems of Love and Death.*
  T. Eagleton, 565:Vol22No4-74

McConnell, F. Storytelling and Mythmak-
ing.*
    G. Mast, 405(MP):May82-458
McConnell, F.D. Four Postwar American
Novelists.*
    R. Langbaum, 473(PR):1/1981-151
    S. O'Connell, 418(MR):Spring81-185
McConnor, V. The Paris Puzzle.
    N. Callendar, 441:16May82-26
McConville, M. and J. Baldwin. Courts,
Prosecution, and Conviction.
    A.W.B. Simpson, 617(TLS):9Apr82-417
McCormack, G. Chang Tso-lin in Northeast
China, 1911-1928.
    Yuen Kwok Keung, 302:Vol 18-141
MacCormack, S.G. Art and Ceremony in Late
Antiquity.
    J. Trilling, 617(TLS):13Aug82-884
McCormack, W.C. and S.E. Wurm, eds.
Approaches to Language.
    205(FMLS):Apr80-186
McCormack, W.J. Sheridan Le Fanu and
Victorian Ireland.
    M. Harmon, 637(VS):Summer81-515
    K. Sullivan, 445(NCF):Sep81-244
    R. Tracy, 174(Éire):Winter81-128
McCormick, C. Résumé for Murder.
    N. Callendar, 441:12Sep82-36
McCormick, E.H. Omai, Pacific Envoy.
    J. Mangan, 318(JAOS):Apr/Jun80-211
McCormick, E.H. Portrait of Frances Hodg-
kins.
    K. Flint, 617(TLS):19Mar82-320
    A. Ross, 364:Dec81/Jan82-138
McCormick, R.P. The Presidential Game.
    H.G. Nicholas, 617(TLS):80ct82-1092
McCormmach, R. Night Thoughts of a Clas-
sical Physicist.
    D.J. Kevles, 441:7Feb82-12
    R. Peierls, 453(NYRB):29Apr82-34
    S.S. Prawer, 617(TLS):220ct82-1159
McCorquodale, C. Bronzino.
    C.H. Smyth, 453(NYRB):23Sep82-50
McCoy, D.R. The Elusive Republic.
    P. Conkin, 656(WMQ):Apr81-301
    R. Ketcham, 639(VQR):Autumn81-723
McCoy, R.C. Sir Philip Sidney.*
    N. Lindheim, 568(SCN):Spring81-5
    J. Robertson, 551(RenQ):Spring80-127
McCracken, J. The Overlord of the Little
Prairie.
    R.D. Francis, 298:Summer81-129
McCrank, L.J. Education for Rare Book
Librarianship.
    M.U. Russell, 14:Winter81-57
McCrary, W.C. and J.A. Madrigal, eds.
Studies in Honor of Everett W. Hesse.
    A.E. Foley, 304(JHP):Winter82-169
McCrea, B. Henry Fielding and the Poli-
tics of Mid-Eighteenth-Century England.*
    J.B. Kern, 405(MP):Feb82-326
    W.A. Speck, 566:Spring82-117
McCrum, R. A Loss of Heart.
    J. Mellors, 362:11Mar82-23
    A. Motion, 617(TLS):26Feb82-214
McCullough, H.C. - see "Ōkagami, the Great
Mirror"
McCullough, W.H. and H.C., eds and trans.
A Tale of Flowering Fortunes.*
    E. Seidensticker, 407(MN):Summer81-195
    Tsunoda Bun'ei, 285(JapQ):Jan-Mar81-
113
    H.P. Varley, 293(JASt):May81-608

McCurdy, J.D. Visionary Appropriation.
    H.H. Rudnick, 480(P&R):Winter81-62
McCutcheon, G.B. Brewster's Millions.
(D.A. Jasen, ed)
    S. Pickering, 219(GaR):Fall81-678
McDavid, R.I., Jr. Dialects in Culture.
(W.A. Kretzschmar, Jr., ed)
    H.B. Allen, 355(LSoc):Dec81-472
    R.R. Butters, 579(SAQ):Winter81-113
    A.R. Duckert, 300:Mar81-33
    K.B. Harder, 424:Sep80-217
    J.L. Idol, Jr., 580(SCR):Fall81-133
McDavid, R.I., Jr. Varieties of American
English. (A.S. Dil, ed)
    A.R. Duckert, 300:Mar81-33
    U. Dürmüller, 350:Jun81-499
    J.L. Idol, Jr., 580(SCR):Fall81-133
    R.W. Shuy, 355(LSoc):Dec81-470
McDavid, R.I., Jr. and R.K. O'Cain, eds.
Linguistic Atlas of the Middle and South
Atlantic States. (Vol 1, fasc 1 and 2)
    H.B. Allen, 300:Mar81-30
    E. Finegan, 350:Mar82-244
    J.R. Gaskin, 569(SR):Spring81-298
    K.B. Harder, 424:Sep81-251
McDermott, A. A Bigamist's Daughter.
    A. Tyler, 441:21Feb82-1
McDermott, A.C.S. - see Boethius
McDermott, M.Y. and M.M. Ahsan. The
Muslim Guide.
    K. Kemal, 273(IC):Oct81-295
MacDiarmid, H. The Socialist Poems of
Hugh MacDiarmid. (T.S. Law and T. Ber-
wick, eds)
    R. Watson, 571(ScLJ):Summer80-122
MacDonald, A.W. and A.V. Stahl. Newar Art.
    R.M. Bernier, 293(JASt):Nov80-172
McDonald, F. Alexander Hamilton.
    W.P. Murchison, 396(ModA):Winter81-90
Mcdonald, G. The Buck Passes Flynn.
Fletch and the Widow Bradley.
    N. Callendar, 441:31Jan82-22
Mcdonald, G. Fletch's Moxie.
    N. Callendar, 441:19Dec82-30
MacDonald, G. Phantastes.
    P. Craig, 617(TLS):22Oct82-1175
Macdonald, G. and P. Pettit. Semantics
and Social Science.
    A. Morton, 617(TLS):29Jan82-115
MacDonald, G.F., ed. Perception and Iden-
tity.
    M. Smithurst, 518:Jul81-184
    A. White, 479(PhQ):Jan81-74
Macdonald, H. Berlioz.
    M. Tanner, 617(TLS):15Oct82-1129
MacDonald, J.D. Cinnamon Skin.
    T.J. Binyon, 617(TLS):29Oct82-1196
    J. Casey, 441:22Aug82-10
    442(NY):19Jul82-100
MacDonald, J.D. Free Fall in Crimson.*
    639(VQR):Autumn81-135
MacDonald, M. Mystical Bedlam.
    R. Robbins, 617(TLS):30Jul82-816
    L. Stone, 453(NYRB):16Dec82-28
McDonald, M. A Semilemmatized Concordance
to Euripides' "Alcestis," "Cyclops,"
"Andromache," and "Medea."*
    P. Elbert, 122:Jan81-61
McDonald, M. and S.A. Wurm. Basic Materi-
als in Wankumara (Galali).
    P. Austin, 350:Sep82-732

Macdonald, R. Self-Portrait. (R. Sipper, ed)
    J. Symons, 617(TLS):2Apr82-369
"The Macdonald Encyclopedia of Shells."
    J. Mellanby, 617(TLS):12Mar82-291
"The Macdonald Encyclopedia of Trees."
    J. Mellanby, 617(TLS):20Aug82-905
McDonough, J.L. Shiloh — In Hell Before Night.
    S.E. Ambrose, 9(AlaR):Jan81-72
McDonough, P. and A. De Souza. The Politics of Population in Brazil.
    R.T. Daland, 263(RIB):Vol31No3-412
MacDougall, E., ed. Fons Sapientiae, Renaissance Garden Fountains.
    A.A. Tait, 90:Jan81-43
    P.F. Watson, 551(RenQ):Winter80-783
Macdougall, N. James III.
    G.W.S. Barrow, 617(TLS):5Nov82-1228
McDougall, W.A. France's Rhineland Diplomacy, 1914-1924.
    A. Orde, 161(DUJ):Dec80-103
Macdowall, D.W. The Western Coinage of Nero.
    C.M. Kraay, 313:Vol71-206
    D. Sinos, 24:Winter81-472
MacDowell, D.M. The Law in Classical Athens.* (H.H. Scullard, ed)
    J.A.S. Evans, 529(QQ):Spring81-87
McDowell, E. To Keep Our Honor Clean.
    639(VQR):Winter81-22
McDowell, R.B. and D.A. Webb. Trinity College Dublin 1592-1952.
    R. Foster, 617(TLS):9Jul82-735
Macé, G. Leçon de chinois.
    R. Blin, 450(NRF):Sep81-134
McEwan, I. The Comfort of Strangers.*
    J. Mellors, 364:Oct81-93
MacEwen, G. Mermaids and Ikons.
    L. Rogers, 102(CanL):Spring80-122
MacEwen, G. The Trojan Women.
    A. Ravel, 102(CanL):Summer81-158
Macey, S.L. Clocks and the Cosmos.
    W. Harmon, 173(ECS):Winter80/81-196
    J.M. Hill, 566:Autumn80-45
McFadden, D. On The Road Again.
    J. Ferns, 102(CanL):Spring80-126
McFadden, R. A Watching Brief.
    T. Eagleton, 565:Vol22No2-73
McFadzean, R. The Life and Work of Alexander Thomson.*
    J. Bassin, 637(VS):Winter81-239
McFarland, T. Romanticism and the Forms of Ruin.*
    R. Ginsberg, 290(JAAC):Winter81-219
    A.K. Mellor, 401(MLQ):Jun81-194
    V. Nemoianu, 400(MLN):Dec81-1216
    L. Tyler, 580(SCR):Spring82-116
Macfarlane, A. The Origins of English Individualism.
    B. Donagan, 185:Oct80-168
McFarlane, I.D., ed. Renaissance Latin Poetry.
    J.R.C. Martyn, 67:Nov81-238
    L.V.R., 568(SCN):Spring81-31
    J.E. Ziolkowski, 124:Sep-Oct81-58
    205(FMLS):Oct80-379
Macfarlane, K.N. Isidore of Seville on the Pagan Gods.
    P. Godman, 123:Vol31No2-297
    P.K. Marshall, 589:Apr81-456

McFate, P. The Writings of James Stephens.*
    R.A. Cave, 677(YES):Vol 11-351
    P. Diskin, 447(N&Q):Dec80-567
McFeely, W.S. Grant.*
    P.J. Parish, 617(TLS):12Feb82-151
    639(VQR):Autumn81-124
McGaha, M.D. The Theatre in Madrid during the Second Republic.
    M.T. Halsey, 238:Dec81-641
McGahern, J. Getting Through.
    W.P. Keen, 573(SSF):Summer81-336
    639(VQR):Spring81-61
McGann, J.J. - see Lord Byron
McGarry, J. Place Names in the Writings of William Butler Yeats.
    K.B. Harder, 424:Sep80-216
McGhee, R.D. Marriage, Duty, and Desire in Victorian Poetry and Drama.
    M. Doane, 85(SBHC):Spring81-99
McGilchrist, I. Against Criticism.
    J. Bayley, 362:28Oct82-22
    C.J. Rawson, 617(TLS):11Jun82-627
McGinley, P. Goosefoot.
    R. Freedman, 441:24Oct82-42
    442(NY):22Nov82-196
McGinn, B. Visions of the End.
    H. Kaminsky, 589:Apr81-412
McGinnis, B. Sweet Cane.
    A. Cheuse, 441:28Feb82-15
McGivern, W.P. Summitt.
    S. Trachtenberg, 441:24Oct82-43
McGough, J.P., ed and trans. Fei Hsiao-tsung.
    R.D. Arkush, 293(JASt):Aug81-771
McGough, R. Unlucky for Some.
    S. Ellis, 617(TLS):22Jan82-90
McGowan, B. Economic Life in Ottoman Europe.
    C.J. Heywood, 617(TLS):10Sep82-980
McGrade, A.S. and B. Vickers - see Hooker, R.
McGrath, D.F. - see "Bookman's Price Index"
McGrath, J. A Good Night Out.
    H. Hobson, 617(TLS):1Jan82-18
McGrath, J. Joe's Drum.
    D. Devlin, 157:2ndQtr81-55
McGrath, P. and M.E. Williams, eds. Bristol Inns and Alehouses in the Mid-Eighteenth Century.
    W.E. Minchinton, 325:Apr81-435
MacGregor, R. Shore Lines.
    P. Barclay, 102(CanL):Summer81-133
McGregor, S. The Complete Book of Traditional Fair Isle Knitting.
    R.L. Shep, 614:Summer82-13
McGuane, T. Nobody's Angel.
    V. Bourjaily, 441:7Mar82-9
    442(NY):22Mar82-165
McGuane, T. An Outside Chance.*
    S. Brown, 569(SR):Summer81-431
    639(VQR):Spring81-67
McGuckian, M. The Flower Master.
    D. Davis, 362:16Dec82-23
    T. Dooley, 617(TLS):29Oct82-1200
McGuckian, M. Portrait of Joanna.*
    R. Pybus, 565:Vol22No3-72
McGuinness, B. - see Waismann, F.
McGuire, W. Bollingen.
    T. Bender, 441:14Nov82-24
    A. Storr, 617(TLS):17Dec82-1387

Mach, E. Great Pianists Speak for Themselves.
  C. Ehrlich, 415:Mar81-180
  E. Ronsheim, 42(AR):Winter81-129
Machado, A. Selected Poems.* (B.J. Craige, trans)
  G.R. Barrow, 86(BHS):Apr81-161
McHale, T. Dear Friends.
  I. Gold, 441:14Feb82-14
  S. Lardner, 442(NY):8Feb82-125
Maché, U. and V. Meid, eds. Gedichte des Barock.
  D.G., 52:Band15Heft3-341
Machery, P. A Theory of Literary Production.*
  D.G. Marshall, 473(PR):2/1981-294
Machlup, F. Methodology of Economics and Other Social Sciences.
  J. Bien, 484(PPR):Sep81-135
Machtey, M. and P. Young. An Introduction to the General Theory of Algorithms.
  N. Lynch, 316:Dec81-877
McHugh, P. Prostitution and Victorian Social Reform.
  J.A. Banks, 637(VS):Summer81-513
McHugh, R. Annotations to "Finnegans Wake."*
  B. Benstock, 329(JJQ):Fall80-103
  L.O. Mink, 329(JJQ):Fall80-97
McInerny, R. Thicker Than Water.
  N. Callendar, 441:31Jan82-22
McInnes, E. German Social Drama 1840-1900.
  T. Meyer, 680(ZDP):Band99Heft2-310
MacInnes, H. Cloak of Darkness.
  M. Slung, 441:26Sep82-15
McIntosh, P. Fair Play.
  T.R.M., 185:Apr81-534
MacIntyre, A. After Virtue.*
  N.S. Struever, 400(MLN):Dec81-1193
  M. Warnock, 362:18Feb82-22
Mack, J.E. A Prince of Our Disorder.
  S. Lug, 318(JAOS):Jan/Mar80-29
Mack, M. and J.A. Winn, eds. Pope: Recent Essays by Several Hands.*
  C.R. Kropf, 566:Autumn80-39
Mack, S. Patterns of Time in Vergil.*
  A. Crabbe, 123:Vol31No2-290
Mack Smith, D. Mussolini.
  H.S. Hughes, 441:16May82-11
  D. Hunt, 362:25Feb82-21
  M. Kempton, 453(NYRB):7Oct82-19
  A. Lyttelton, 617(TLS):9Apr82-399
  G. Steiner, 442(NY):30Aug82-86
Mackay, A. Death on the Eno.
  N. Callendar, 441:7Feb82-20
MacKay, A. Money, Prices and Politics in Fifteenth-Century Castile.
  J. Edwards, 617(TLS):30Jul82-833
MacKay, A.F. Arrow's Theorem.
  P. Urbach, 84:Dec81-425
McKay, G. The Pat Lowther Poem.
  D. Barbour, 648(WCR):Vol 15No3-44
MacKay, I.R.A. Introducing Practical Phonetics.
  T.C. Frazer, 35(AS):Summer81-135
McKay, J.C. A Guide to Romance Reference Grammars.
  S. Fleischman, 350:Sep81-771
Mackay, M. The Indomitable Servant.
  A.H.M. Kirk-Greene, 69:Vol50No4-439
Mackay, R., B. Barkman and R.R. Jordan, eds. Reading in a Second Language.
  R.A. Schulz, 399(MLJ):Spring81-106

Mackay, R. and J.D. Palmer, eds. Languages for Specific Purposes.
  J.J. Hafernik, 608:Mar82-93
Mackay Brown, G. Under Brinkie's Brae.
  J.B. Caird, 571(ScLJ):Winter81-148
McKee, A. How We Found the Mary Rose.
  D. Thomas, 362:14Oct82-29
McKee, J.O. and J.A. Schlenker. The Choctaws.
  J.L. Loos, 9(AlaR):Jul81-220
Mackenzie, A.L. - see Calderón de la Barca, P.
Mackenzie, B.D. Behaviourism and the Limits of Scientific Method.
  E.S. Reed, 488:Dec81-477
Mackenzie, C.C. Sarah Barnwell Elliott.
  R.S. Moore, 578:Spring82-72
MacKenzie, D. Raven's Revenge.
  T.J. Binyon, 617(TLS):28May82-594
  N. Callendar, 441:3Oct82-16
Mackenzie, D. - see Rodríguez de Almela, D.
MacKenzie, G.C. The Politics of Presidential Appointments.
  A. Beichman, 617(TLS):12Mar82-290
Mackenzie, J., comp. Cycling.*
  C. Hawtree, 364:Dec81/Jan82-140
MacKenzie, J. A Victorian Courtship.
  J. Marcus, 637(VS):Spring81-378
Mackenzie, M.M. Plato on Punishment.
  A.W. Price, 617(TLS):21May82-565
MacKenzie, N. The Escape from Elba.
  W. Goodman, 441:30May82-10
  442(NY):7Jun82-146
MacKenzie, N. and J. Dickens.*
  M. Andrews, 161(DUJ):Jun81-257
MacKenzie, N. and J. - see Webb, B.
McKenzie, R.B. The Political Economy of the Educational Process.
  W.L. Boyd, 185:Oct81-172
Mackenzie-Grieve, A. Clara Novello (1818-1908).
  E.T. Harris, 414(MusQ):Apr81-290
McKerrow, M. The Faeds.
  P. Keating, 617(TLS):2Apr82-387
Mackesy, E.M., K. Mateyak and N.B. Hoover - see "MLA Directory of Periodicals"
MacKethan, L.H. The Dream of Arcady.
  L. Brown, 585(SoQ):Winter81-90
  J.H. Justus, 639(VQR):Spring81-373
  M. Kreyling, 392:Spring81-146
  T.D. Young, 569(SR):Summer81-480
Mackie, J.L. Ethics.
  J.M., 543:Sep80-152
  N. Rotenstreich, 321:Vol 15No3-253
Mackie, J.L. Hume's Moral Theory.
  I.M. Fowlie, 518:Apr81-95
  R.G.H., 185:Jul82-781
Mackie, J.L. Truth Probability and Paradox.
  J.T. Kearns, 316:Mar81-174
McKillop, A.B. A Disciplined Intelligence.*
  B. Hunter and J. King-Farlow, 518:Oct81-211
McKillop, A.B. - see Le Sueur, W.D.
McKillop, A.B. - see Morton, W.L.
MacKinnon, S. Mazinaw.*
  T. Goldie, 526:Spring81-69
  G. McWhirter, 102(CanL):Autumn81-160
Mackintosh, J.P. On Parliament and Social Democracy. (D. Marquand, ed) On Scotland. (H.M. Drucker, ed)
  P. Whitehead, 362:30Sep82-20

227

McKitterick, D. - see Morison, S.
McKitterick, D. - see Morison, S. and D.B. Updike
McKnight, R. Moberg's Emigrant Novels and the Journals of Andrew Peterson.
　　P. Holmes, 563(SS):Autumn81-503
MacLachlan, C.M. and J.E. Rodríguez O. The Forging of the Cosmic Race.*
　　E. Couturier, 263(RIB):Vol31No3-413
Maclachlan, M. All the Roses Falling.
　　J.A.S. Miller, 571(ScLJ):Winter81-146
McLaren, D. - see Marsden, S.
McLaurin, M.A. and M.V. Thomason. The Image of Progress.
　　W. Flynt, 9(AlaR):Jul81-217
MacLaverty, B. Secrets and Other Stories.
　　T. Kelly, 174(Éire):Spring81-155
MacLaverty, B. A Time to Dance.
　　A. Mars-Jones, 617(TLS):14May82-536
　　442(NY):20Sep82-151
MacLean, A. Cuentos Based on the Folk Tales of the Spanish Californians.
　　H.H. Lee, 650(WF):Jul81-279
Maclean, I. The Renaissance Notion of Woman.
　　J. Cadden, 377:Mar81-57
　　J. Couchman, 539:Aug82-210
　　S.M. Okin, 185:Apr82-567
MacLean, S. Spring Tide and Neap Tide/ Reothairt is Contraigh.
　　R. Hugo, 588(SSL):Vol 16-282
　　A. MacNeacail, 588(SSL):Vol 16-298
McLean, S. - see Snyder, G.
MacLeish, A. Six Plays.
　　D. Devlin, 157:Oct80-72
McLeish, K. The Theatre of Aristophanes.
　　D.M. MacDowell, 303(JoHS):Vol 101-152
　　N.G. Wilson, 123:Vol31No1-109
McLennan, G.R. - see Callimachus
MacLeod, C. Devil in the Wind.
　　D. MacAulay, 571(ScLJ):Summer80-136
Macleod, C.W., ed. Homer: "Iliad," Book 24.
　　S. West, 617(TLS):23Jul82-803
MacLeod, D. Down-to-Earth Women.
　　T. McLean, 617(TLS):30Jul82-823
McLeod, E. Living Twice.
　　I. Bell, 617(TLS):26Nov82-1313
McLeod, N. and M. Herndon, eds. The Ethnography of Musical Performance.
　　M.I. Asch, 187:May82-317
McLeod, R. and P. Collins, eds. The Parliament of Science.
　　J. Taylor, 324:Jun82-434
MacLeod, S. The Art of Starvation.*
　　M. Scarf, 441:8Aug82-7
McLeod, S.H. Dramatic Imagery in the Plays of John Webster.
　　R.P. Merrix, 568(SCN):Summer-Fall81-47
McLeod, W.R. and V.B., eds. Anglo-Scottish Tracts, 1701-1714.
　　F.M. Link, 566:Autumn80-47
　　G.M. Straka, 173(ECS):Fall80-105
McLeod, W.T. and P. Hanks, eds. The New Collins Concise Dictionary of the English Language.
　　R.R.K. Hartmann, 617(TLS):3Sep82-953
MacLure, M., ed. Marlowe: The Critical Heritage, 1588-1896.*
　　H. Cooper, 447(N&Q):Aug80-362
　　A. Leggatt, 529(QQ):Spring81-93
McMahan, J. British Nuclear Weapons.
　　M. Howard, 617(TLS):16Apr82-427

McManners, J. Death and the Enlightenment.
　　O. Chadwick, 617(TLS):14May82-539
　　R. Darnton, 453(NYRB):13May82-8
McMaster, G. Scott and Society.
　　R. Ashton, 617(TLS):13Aug82-890
McMaster, J. Jane Austen on Love.*
　　S.O. Taylor, 173(ECS):Summer81-492
McMaster, J. Trollope's Palliser Novels.*
　　J. Carlisle, 639(VQR):Winter81-176
　　J. Dusinberre, 447(N&Q):Aug80-382
　　J.R. Kincaid, 445(NCF):Sep80-210
　　R.M. Polhemus, 301(JEGP):Apr81-264
　　V. Shaw, 677(YES):Vol 11-322
McMaster, R.K., with S.L. Horst and R.F. Ulle. Conscience in Crisis.
　　J.A.H., 185:Jan81-348
McMichael, J. Four Good Things.*
　　R. von Hallberg, 659(ConL):Spring82-225
MacMillan, D.J., ed. The Stoic Strain in American Literature.
　　T.T. Barker, 594:Winter81-463
McMullen, E.W., ed. Pubs, Place-Names, and Patronymics.
　　K.B. Harder, 424:Mar81-85
McMullen, L. Sinclair Ross.*
　　P. Stevens, 649(WAL):Spring81-75
McMullen, M. The Other Shoe.
　　M. Laski, 362:2Dec82-23
MacMullen, R. Paganism in the Roman Empire.
　　H. Chadwick, 617(TLS):9Apr82-407
　　R.J. Penella, 124:May-Jun82-313
McMullin, E. Newton on Matter and Activity.*
　　M.A. Finocchiaro, 319:Oct81-507
McMurray, G.R. José Donoso.
　　D. Castiel, 238:Mar81-162
McMurrin, S.M., ed. The Tanner Lectures of Human Values.* (Vol 1)
　　R.L.S., 185:Apr82-603
McMurtry, J. Victorian Life and Victorian Fiction.*
　　R. Miles, 677(YES):Vol 11-313
McMurtry, J.R. The Structure of Marx's World View.*
　　W.L. McBride, 185:Jan82-316
　　J. Urry, 488:Mar81-69
McMurtry, L. Cadillac Jack.
　　E.R. Lipson, 441:21Nov82-13
　　442(NY):13Dec82-184
McNab, T. Flanagan's Run.
　　M. Simpson, 441:25Jul82-10
　　R. Twisk, 362:29Apr82-24
McNairn, A. The Young Van Dyck.
　　G. Martin, 39:Feb81-131
McNally, D. Desolate Angel.*
　　S. Pinsker, 27(AL):Nov81-524
　　D. Stanley, 649(WAL):Summer81-138
McNeil, F. A Balancing Act.*
　　D. Barbour, 648(WCR):Vol 15No3-44
　　R. Hornsey, 461:Fall-Winter81/82-101
　　P. Stevens, 529(QQ):Autumn81-504
MacNeil, R. The Right Place at the Right Time.
　　442(NY):6Sep82-109
McNeill, W.H. The Pursuit of Power.
　　S. Hoffmann, 441:28Nov82-7
McNickle, D. Wind from an Enemy Sky.
　　J.W. Schneider, 649(WAL):Spring81-87

Magagnato, L. and P. Marini – see Palladio, A.

Magaziner, I.C. and R.B. Reich. Minding America's Business.
L.C. Thurow, 453(NYRB):1Apr82-3

Magdalen, I.I. The Search for Anderson.
T.J. Binyon, 617(TLS):29Oct82-1196
M. Laski, 362:2Dec82-23

Magee, B., ed. Men of Ideas.
O. Hanfling, 518:Jan81-23

Magee, W. A Dark Age.
G. Lindop, 617(TLS):24Sep82-1041

Maggs, T., ed. Major Rock Paintings of Southern Africa.
D. Brokensha, 2(AfrA):Feb81-78

Magno, P. – see Ennius

Magnus, B. Nietzsche's Existential Imperative.*
C.S. Taylor, 518:Oct81-208
J.T. Wilcox, 319:Oct81-516

de Magny, O. Les Souspirs.* (D. Wilkin, ed)
G. Castor, 208(FS):Apr81-188

Magocsi, P.R., ed. The Ukrainian Experience in the United States.
G.A. Rawlyk, 104(CASS):Winter81-638

Magrì, M.A. – see under Arco Magrì, M.

Maguire, D.C. The Moral Choice.
M. Vertin, 154:Jun81-405

Maguire, H. Art and Eloquence in Byzantium.
R. Cormack, 617(TLS):19Nov82-1278

Maguire, R.A. and J.E. Malmstad – see Bely, A.

Mahadevan, T.M.P. and G.E. Cairns, eds. Contemporary Indian Philosophers of History.
R.W. Lariviere, 318(JAOS):Jul/Sep80-324

Mahapatra, J. A Rain of Rites. Waiting.
F. Allen, 472:Spring/Summer81-332

Maharg, J. A Call to Authenticity.
M.S. Stabb, 552(REH):May81-305

Mahé, J-P. – see Tertullian

King Mahendra. Bhagavadajjuka Prahasana. (M. Lockwood and A.V. Bhat, eds and trans)
F.W. Blackwell, 314:Winter-Spring81-250

King Mahendra. The Farce of the Drunk Monk. (P. Lal, trans)
F.W. Blackwell, 314:Winter-Spring81-249

Maher, J.P. Papers on Language Theory and History.* (Vol 1)
H. and R. Kahane, 350:Dec81-919

Maheux-Forcier, L. En toutes lettres.
M. Cagnon, 207(FR):Dec81-306

Mahfouz, N. Miramar.
F.X. Paz, 294:Vol 11-117

Mahieu le Poirier. "Le Court d'Amours" de Mahieu le Poirier et la "Suite Anonyme de la 'Court d'Amours.'" (T. Scully, ed)
S. Kay, 545(RPh):Feb81-364

Mahler, G. Gustav Mahler und Holland. (E. Reeser, ed)
M. Carner, 415:Jul81-480

Mahn-Lot, M. Bartolomé de las Casas et le droit des Indiens.
A. Pagden, 617(TLS):1Oct82-1081

Mahon, D. Poems, 1962-1978.*
A.E. McGuinness, 174(Éire):Spring81-135
L. Sail, 565:Vol22No1-66
J. Sisson, 174(Éire):Winter81-143
639(VQR):Winter81-28

Mahony, R., ed. Different Styles of Poetry.
P.F. Hammond, 83:Spring81-96

Maiastra. Renaissance de l'Occident.
Y. Michaud, 98:Jan80-31

Maiden, J. The Border Loss.*
C. Pollnitz, 581:Jun81-221

Mailer, N. The Essential Mailer.
P.K. Bell, 617(TLS):10Dec82-1378

Mailer, N. The Executioner's Song.*
J. Mills, 529(QQ):Spring81-145

Mailer, N. Pieces and Pontifications.
E. Hoagland, 441:6Jun82-3

Maillard, K. Alex Driving South.
C. Blaise, 102(CanL):Summer81-131

Maillet, A. Cent Ans dans les bois.
H.R. Runte, 150(DR):Autumn81-583

Maillet, A. Pélagie.* (French and British title: Pélagie-la-charrette.)
M. Abley, 617(TLS):3Dec82-1344
P-L. Adams, 61:Apr82-108
D. Plante, 441:7Mar82-8

Maillet, A. La Veuve enragée.
D.M. Hayne, 102(CanL):Summer80-129

Maillet, A., M. G. Le Blanc and B. Emont, eds. Anthologie de textes littéraires acadiens.
A.B. Chartier, 207(FR):Apr81-766

Mails, T.E. Sundancing at Rosebud and Pine Ridge.
W.K. Powers, 187:Jan82-163

Maïmonide, M. Le guide des égarés; Traité des huit chapitres. (C. Mopsik, ed)
A. Reix, 542:Jul-Sep81-340

Mainer, J.C. – see "Revista Nueva: 1899"

Maingueneau, D. Les Livres d'école de la République: 1870-1914.
R.H. Simon, 207(FR):Oct80-204

Mair, P.B. Shared Enthusiasm.
H. Wilson, 362:9Dec82-20

Maisani-Leonard, M. André Gide ou l'ironie de l'écriture.
P. Somville, 102(CanL):Spring81-114

de Maistre, J. Considérations sur la France (1796). (J. Tulard, ed)
A. Reix, 542:Oct-Dec81-487

Maital, S. Minds, Markets, and Money.
P. Passell, 441:15Aug82-8

Maixner, P., ed. Robert Louis Stevenson: The Critical Heritage.*
E.M. Eigner, 445(NCF):Mar82-492

Majid bin Zainuddin, A. The Wandering Thoughts of a Dying Man.* (W.R. Roff, ed)
C.S. Kessler, 318(JAOS):Jan/Mar80-40

Major, A. The Scarecrows of Saint-Emmanuel.
M.A. Peterman, 102(CanL):Spring81-100

Major, C. Emergency Exit.
P. Quartermain, 114(ChiR):Autumn80-65

Major, H. Comment vivent les Québécois.
J. Laroche, 207(FR):May81-909

Major, R. Parti Pris.*
A.B. Chartier, 207(FR):Oct80-208
L. Hutcheon, 102(CanL):Winter80-145

Maki, J.M., ed and trans. Japan's Commission on the Constitution: The Final Report.
  Kobayashi Naoki, 285(JapQ):Oct-Dec81-557
  T. McNelly, 407(MN):Autumn81-351
Makin, P. Provence and Pound.*
  H.M. Dennis, 402(MLR):Oct81-945
  J.H. Marshall, 208(FS):Oct81-421
  L.M. Paterson, 131(CL):Summer81-284
  M.C. Ward, 382(MAE):1981/1-190
  J.J. Wilhelm, 107(CRCL):Winter81-144
Makouta-Mboukou, J-P. Jacques Roumain.
  L-F. Hoffmann, 535(RHL):Jul-Oct81-850
Makowsky, V.A. - see Blackmur, R.P.
Makuck, P. Breaking and Entering.
  B. Allen, 434:Spring82-478
Malamud, B. God's Grace.
  A. Lelchuk, 441:29Aug82-1
  R. Ottaway, 362:4Nov82-23
  M. Richler, 453(NYRB):18Nov82-28
  C. Sinclair, 617(TLS):29Oct82-1188
  J. Updike, 442(NY):8Nov82-167
Malarewicz, J-A. Itinéraire d'une absence.
  J-M. Gabaude, 542:Jan-Mar81-131
Malchow, H.L. Population Pressures.
  A. Brundage, 637(VS):Spring81-364
Malcolm, J. Diana and Nikon.*
  P. Wollheim, 648(WCR):Jun80-57
Malcolm, N. Memory and Mind.
  R. Amundson, 449:Mar81-101
Male, R.R. Enter, Mysterious Stranger.*
  J.S. Martin, 49:Apr81-102
  W.B. Stone, 573(SSF):Winter81-103
Male, R.R., ed. Money Talks.*
  B.C., 284:Spring82-208
Malebranche, N. Oeuvres I. (G. Rodis-Lewis, with G. Malbreil, eds)
  J. Bernhardt, 542:Jul-Sep81-356
  H. Wagner, 53(AGP):Band63Heft1-88
El Malch, E.A. Parcours immobile.
  B.L. Knapp, 207(FR):Oct81-155
Małek, E. Historia o Meluzynie.
  W. Baumann, 196:Band22Heft3/4-361
de Malesherbes, C.G.D. Mémoires sur la librairie et sur la liberté de la presse. (G.E. Rodmell, ed)
  G. Barber, 83:Autumn81-220
Malévitch, K.S. Ecrits. (A.B. Nakov, ed)
  A. Reix, 542:Jan-Mar81-121
Maley, A. and A. Duff. Drama Techniques in Language Learning.*
  J. Penfield, 608:Mar82-96
Maley, C.A. Dans le vent.
  M.M. Celler, 207(FR):Feb82-448
Malin, E. A World of Faces.
  G.S. Nickerson, 292(JAF):Jan-Mar81-103
Malins, E. and P. Bowe. Irish Gardens and Demesnes from 1830.
  K. Woodbridge, 39:Apr81-271
Malinvaud, E. Réexamen de la théorie du chômage.
  F. Bourcier, 98:Jan81-90
Malke, L. Italienische Zeichnungen des 15. und 16. Jahrhunderts.
  K. Andrews, 90:Feb81-105
de Malkiel, M.R.L. - see under Lida de Malkiel, M.R.
Malkin, C. The Journeys of David Toback.
  E. King, 287:Nov81-21
Mall, R.A. Naturalism and Criticism.
  J. Kopper, 342:Band72Heft2-195

de Mallac, G. Boris Pasternak.
  442(NY):25Jan82-106
El Mallakh, D.H. The Slovak Autonomy Movement, 1935-1939.
  O.V. Johnson, 104(CASS):Winter81-630
Mallarmé, S. Un coup de Dés jamais n'abolira le Hasard.
  J-C. Lebenstejn, 98:Jun-Jul80-633
Mallarmé, S. Stéphane Mallarmé: Correspondance.* (Vol 5) (H. Mondor and L.J. Austin, eds)
  E. Souffrin-Le Breton, 208(FS):Oct81-461
Mallarmé, S. Stéphane Mallarmé: Correspondance. (Vols 6 and 7) (H. Mondor and L.J. Austin, eds)
  J.M. Cocking, 617(TLS):11Jun82-628
Mallea, J.R., ed. Quebec's Language Policies.*
  L-J. Dorais, 355(LSoc):Aug81-301
Mallebrera, R.N. - see under Navarro Mallebrera, R.
Mallette, R. Spenser, Milton, and Renaissance Pastoral.
  604:Fall81-57
Mallos, T. The Complete Middle East Cookbook.
  W. and C. Cowen, 639(VQR):Autumn81-139
Malmström, S. and M. Poulsen, eds. The Experience of Literature.
  L.P. Rømhild, 462(OL):Vol36No4-357
Malone, B.C. Southern Music/American Music.*
  N. Cohen, 650(WF):Oct81-348
  J. and U. Rempel, 106:Winter81-331
  639(VQR):Winter81-29
Malone, M. Heroes of Eros.
  H. Ashmore, 436(NewL):Winter81/82-123
Malouf, D. Child's Play.
  P. Kemp, 617(TLS):21May82-549
Malouf, D. First Things Last.
  F. Adcock, 617(TLS):29Jan82-114
  G. Catalano, 381:Apr81-114
  J. Tulip, 581:Dec81-392
Malouf, D. Fly Away Peter.
  A. Brownjohn, 617(TLS):15Oct82-1141
Malthus, T.R. Essai sur le principe de population. (E. Vilquin, trans)
  A. Reix, 542:Jul-Sep81-376
Maltin, L. Of Mice and Magic.
  J.F. Weldon, 529(QQ):Autumn81-568
Maltin, L., ed. TV Movies 1981-1982. (rev)
  R. Edelman, 200:Feb81-118
Mamalakis, M.J. Historical Statistics of Chile.
  L. Roberts Luis, 263(RIB):Vol31No2-279
Mambrino, J. L'Oiseau-coeur.
  T. Greene, 207(FR):Feb82-439
de Man, P. Allegories of Reading.*
  J. Arac, 81:Spring-Fall81-437
  J.D. Black, 494:Summer80-189
  G.L. Bruns, 599:Winter81-75
  D. Carrier, 478:Spring81-124
  R. Gaschè, 153:Winter81-36
  J. McLelland, 400(MLN):May81-888
  J. Rolleston, 301(JEGP):Jan81-102
  R.C. Rosbottom, 173(ECS):Spring81-317
  M. Sabin, 131(CL):Winter81-69
  W.A. Strauss, 651(WHR):Spring81-89
  H. White, 473(PR):2/1981-311
Manacorda, D. Un' officina lapidaria sulla Via Appia.
  M. Beard, 313:Vol71-231

Manceaux, M. Grand Reportage.
  N. Aronson, 207(FR):Apr81-758
Manceron, C. Their Gracious Pleasure.*
  639(VQR):Summer81-90
Mandel, E. Dreaming Backwards.
  J. Kertzer, 99:Dec81/Jan82-41
Mandel, O. Collected Lyrics and Epigrams.
  V. Young, 472:Spring/Summer82-241
Mandelbaum, M. The Anatomy of Historical
  Knowledge.*
  L.J. Goldstein, 488:Sep80-341
Mandelkow, K.R., ed. Goethe im Urteil
  seiner Kritiker. (Pt 3)
  W.H. Bruford, 402(MLR):Jul81-748
  C.E. Schweitzer, 301(JEGP):Apr81-300
Mandell, M. Nazi Hunter.
  N. Callendar, 441:17Oct82-41
Mandelstam, N. Hope Abandoned.
  J. Griffith, 436(NewL):Winter81/82-108
Mandelstam, N. Hope Against Hope.
  S. Birkerts, 271:Fall81-182
  J. Griffith, 436(NewL):Winter81/82-115
Mandelstam, O. Journey to Armenia.*
  J.G. Harris, 574(SEEJ):Fall81-120
  R. Silbajoris, 550(RusR):Jan81-85
Mandelstam, O. Mandelstam: The Complete
  Critical Prose and Letters. (J.G.
  Harris, ed) The Prose of Osip Mandel-
  stam. (C. Brown, trans)
  S. Birkerts, 271:Fall81-182
Mander, R. Mrs. Browning.
  636(VP):Summer81-200
Mandeville, J. "Libro de las maravillas
  del mundo" de Juan de Mandevilla. (P.
  Liria Montañés, ed)
  G.A. Davies, 86(BHS):Jan81-78
Mandrou, R. From Humanism to Science,
  1480-1700.*
  W.E. Cain, 125:Winter81-239
  P. Sharratt, 208(FS):Oct81-443
Manet, J. Journal (1893-1899).
  R. Pickvance, 90:Apr81-242
Manfred, F. American Roads.
  R. Gish, 649(WAL):Spring81-66
Manfred, F. Sons of Adam.
  B.K. Morton, 649(WAL):Summer81-148
Manganelli, G. Discorso dell'ombra e
  dello stemma.
  U. Varnai, 617(TLS):3Dec82-1345
Manganiello, D. Joyce's Politics.*
  N. Miller, 42(AR):Summer81-388
  M.T. Reynolds, 676(YR):Winter82-xiii
Mango, C. Byzantium.*
  M. Angold, 123:Vol31No2-278
  639(VQR):Summer81-88
Manheimer, R.J. Kierkegaard as Educator.
  G.J. Stack, 319:Jul81-398
Manherz, K. Sprachgeographie und Sprach-
  soziologie der deutschen Mundarten in
  Westungarn.*
  G. Lerchner, 682(ZPSK):Band33Heft5-608
  R. Muhr, 680(ZDP):Band100Heft3-461
Manhire, B. Good Looks.
  F. Adcock, 617(TLS):17Dec82-1399
Maniates, M.R. Mannerism in Italian Music
  and Culture, 1530-1630.
  I. Fenlon, 415:Apr81-243
  J. Haar, 551(RenQ):Winter80-766
  J.E. Kreider, 539:Nov82-284
  J.G. Kurtzman, 414(MusQ):Jan81-125
  D.S., 412:Nov80-309
  G. Tomlinson, 317:Fall81-552

Mank, G.W. It's Alive!
  D. McClelland, 200:Nov81-573
Mankowitz, W. Mazeppa.
  J. Stokes, 617(TLS):20Aug82-901
Manley, L. Convention: 1500-1750.*
  M. McCanles, 141:Winter81-82
Manlove, C.N. The Gap in Shakespeare.
  P. Taylor, 617(TLS):23Apr82-469
Mann, C. Modigliani.
  90:Apr81-270
Mann, P.H. From Author to Reader.
  N. Cross, 617(TLS):31Dec82-1447
  D.J. Enright, 362:28Oct82-24
Mann, R., ed and trans. The Song of
  Prince Igor.
  A.E. Alexander, 292(JAF):Jan-Mar81-
  124
Mann, T. Les maîtres.
  E. Blondel, 542:Oct-Dec81-497
Mann, T. Thomas Mann Diaries 1918-1939.
  (H. Kesten, ed)
  G.A. Craig, 453(NYRB):2Dec82-32
  E. Pawel, 441:14Nov82-13
Mann, T. Tagebücher 1918-1921.* (P. de
  Mendelssohn, ed)
  H. Lehnert, 462(OL):Vol36No4-343
  K. Schröter, 406:Fall81-364
Mann, T. Tagebücher 1935-1936.* (P. de
  Mendelssohn, ed)
  H. Lehnert, 462(OL):Vol35No2-185
  F. Rau, 224(GRM):Band31Heft2-253
  K. Schröter, 406:Fall81-364
"Thomas Mann 1875-1975: Homenaje en su
  centenario."
  E. Lunding, 680(ZDP):Band99Heft2-288
Manni, T.R. - see under Rogledi Manni, T.
Manniche, L. Musical Instruments from the
  Tomb of Tut'ankhamûn.
  R.D.A., 412:Aug80-234
Manninen, O. Suur-Suomen ääriviivat.
  T. Vihavainen, 550(RusR):Jul81-345
Manning, D.J., ed. The Form of Ideology.*
  R.A., 185:Oct81-180
Manning, E. Marble and Bronze.
  F. Pearson, 617(TLS):31Dec82-1440
Manning, P.J. Byron and his Fictions.*
  F.W. Shilstone, 134(CP):Spring81-75
  L. Waldoff, 301(JEGP):Jan81-144
Manningham, J. The Diary of John Manning-
  ham of the Middle Temple, 1602-3. (R.P.
  Sorlien, ed)
  M.C. Bradbrook, 570(SQ):Spring81-118
Mannison, D., M. McRobbie and R. Routley,
  eds. Environmental Philosophy.
  J.L. Thompson, 63:Dec81-461
Mannoni, M. La Théorie comme fiction.
  C. Gordon, 208(FS):Jul81-367
Mannoni, O. Fictions freudiennes.
  C. Gordon, 208(FS):Jul81-367
Manns, P. Martin Luther.
  R.M. Brown, 441:26Dec82-1
Mano, D.K. Take Five.
  R.M. Adams, 453(NYRB):10Jun82-31
  I. Gold, 441:23May82-13
Manoliu, M. El estructuralismo lingüís-
  tico.
  O.T. Myers, 545(RPh):Feb81(supp)-116
Manrique, J. Coplas de amor y de muerte.
  (J.M. Aguirre, ed)
  D.S. Severin, 402(MLR):Oct81-980
Mansergh, N. and others, eds. The Trans-
  fer of Power 1942-47. (Vol 10)
  B.N. Pandey, 617(TLS):6Aug82-849

Mansergh, N. and P. Moon, eds. The Transfer of Power 1942-47. (Vol 8)
M. Cook, 325:Apr81-438
Mansfield, B.E. Phoenix of His Age.*
G.A. Hoar, 377:Mar81-60
Mansfield, P., ed. The Middle East. (5th ed)
A.J. Rawick, 287:Nov81-26
Mansfield, P. The New Arabians.
D. Pipes, 441:14Mar82-3
Mansion, J.E. - see "Harrap's New Standard French and English Dictionary"
Mansour, J. Birds of Prey (Rapaces).
E.R. Peschel, 207(FR):Mar81-622
Mansvelt, W.M.F. and P. Creutzberg. Rice Prices.
R. Van Niel, 293(JASt):Nov80-210
Manteiga, R.C. The Poetry of Rafael Alberti.*
C.G. Bellver, 238:Mar81-155
G. Connell, 86(BHS):Jan81-88
Mantell, L. Murder and Chips.*
N. Callendar, 441:12Sep82-38
Manuel, F.E. and F.P. Utopian Thought in the Western World.*
M.E. Blanchard, 131(CL):Fall81-358
K.M. Roemer, 26(ALR):Spring81-122
W. Stafford, 366:Autumn81-257
L.B. Zimmer, 173(ECS):Spring81-338
Manuel, J. Juan Manuel: A Selection. (I. Macpherson, ed)
H.T. Sturcken, 304(JHP):Spring81-230
Manuel, J. 2d and J. Manuel. The Manueline Succession. (I. Macpherson, ed)
R. Boase, 86(BHS):Jul81-259
D.S. Severin, 402(MLR):Jul81-720
205(FMLS):Oct80-379
Manuwald, B. Cassius Dio und Augustus.
T.E.J. Wiedemann, 313:Vol71-201
Manwaring, R. The Swifts of Maggiore.
R. Garfitt, 617(TLS):2Apr82-392
Manzalaoui, M.A., ed. Secretum Secretorum. (Vol 1)
R.W. Hanning, 551(RenQ):Spring80-65
Mar, J.M. and J. Mejía Mejía - see under Matos Mar, J. and J. Mejía Mejía
Mara, T. The Thames and Hudson Manual of Screen Printing.
P. Bach, 614:Spring81-22
Marache, R. - see Gellius, A.
Maragall, J.A. Història de la Sala Parés.
E. Casado, 48:Jan-Mar81-104
Maravall, J.A. Poder, honor y élites en el siglo XVII.
R.A. Stradling, 86(BHS):Jan81-82
Marazzini, C. - see Faldella, G.
Marbach, E. - see Husserl, E.
March, A. Obra poètica completa. (R. Ferreres, ed)
R.L.A. Archer, 86(BHS):Oct81-354
Marchand, B. After the Fact.
A. Brooks, 526:Autumn81-160
Marchand, B. Évaluation des élèves et conseil de classe.
M.R. Morris, 207(FR):Mar81-634
Marchand, L.A., ed. Byron's Letters and Journals. (Vol 12: Index.)
P. Johnson, 362:20May82-27
Marchand, L.A. - see Lord Byron
Marchant Lazcano, J. Así escriben los chilenos.
M. Agosin, 552(REH):Jan81-150

Marchello-Nizia, C. Histoire de la langue française aux XIVe et XVe siècles.*
R. de Gorog, 589:Jan81-176
M. Léonard, 209(FM):Apr81-165
B. Tranel, 350:Dec81-968
Marchescou, M. El concepto de literariedad.
E. Bejel, 240(HR):Autumn81-515
Marchione, M. Clemente Rebora.
C. Klopp, 276:Winter81-335
Marckwardt, A.H. American English.* (2nd ed rev by J.L. Dillard)
J.R. Gaskin, 569(SR):Spring81-298
K.B. Harder, 424:Sep81-253
Marckwardt, A.H. The Place of Literature in the Teaching of English as a Second or Foreign Language.
H.B. Allen, 351(LL):Jun81-243
Marconi, J.B. - see under Bovio Marconi, J.
Marcos Marín, F. Estudios sobre el pronombre.*
S.N. Dworkin, 240(HR):Spring81-225
Marcus, J. - see West, R.
Marcus, L.S. Childhood and Cultural Despair.*
J. Carey, 541(RES):May81-217
W.L. Godshalk, 551(RenQ):Spring80-140
M. McCanles, 301(JEGP):Jul81-409
D.L. Russell, 568(SCN):Spring81-9
Marcus, M.J. An Allegory of Form.
A. Iovino, 545(RPh):Feb81(supp)-259
K. Pennington, 589:Oct81-090
Marcus, M.P. A Theory of Syntactic Recognition for Natural Language.
M.B. Kac, 350:Jun82-447
Marcus Aurelius. Marcus Aurelius, ad se ipsum libri xii. (J. Dalfen, ed)
F.H. Sandbach, 123:Vol31No2-188
Marcuse, H. The Aesthetic Dimension. (rev by H. Marcuse and E. Sherover)
E.F. Kaelin, 127:Summer81-183
Mardersteig, G. The Officina Bodoni.* (H. Schmoller, ed and trans)
78(BC):Autumn81-303
de Maré, E. The Victorian Woodblock Illustrators.*
G. Reynolds, 39:Jan81-63
A.S., 155:Summer81-109
M. Steig, 637(VS):Summer81-517
van Marwar, J.W. Marquard von Lindau, Die zehe gebot (Strassburg 1516 und 1520).
K. Kunze, 680(ZDP):Band100Heft3-445
Marenzio, L. Madrigali a quattro, cinque e sei voci, libro primo (1588). (Vol 7) (S. Ledbetter and P. Myers, eds)
H.W. Kaufmann, 551(RenQ):Spring80-90
Maresca, T.E. Three English Epics.
M.E. McAlpine, 589:Apr81-457
J.M. Steadman, 301(JEGP):Apr81-234
Marfurt, B. Textsorte Witz.
R. Wehse, 196:Band21Heft3/4-323
Margalit, A., ed. Meaning and Use.
B. Harrison, 393(Mind):Oct81-614
C. Hookway, 479(PhQ):Apr81-173
Margenau, H. Physics and Philosophy.*
D. Hockney, 518:Jan81-46
H. Krips, 63:Mar81-135
Marghieri, C. Trilogia.
A.F. Price, 617(TLS):8Oct82-1109
Margitić, M. Essai sur la mythologie du "Cid."*
D. Judovitz, 546(RR):Jan81-108

Margittai, T. and P. Kovi. The Four Seasons.
  W. and C. Cowen, 639(VQR):Spring81-71
Margolies, E. and D. Bakish, eds. Afro-American Fiction, 1853-1976.
  M.F., 189(EA):Jul-Sep81-365
Margolies, J. The End of the Road.
  F.T. Kihlstedt, 576:Dec81-339
Margolin, P.M. The Last Innocent Man.*
  M. Laski, 362:2Dec82-23
Margolis, H. Selfishness, Altruism and Rationality.
  P. Seabright, 617(TLS):10Dec82-1354
Margolis, J. Art and Philosophy.*
  K. Walton, 617(TLS):4Jun82-600
Margolis, J. Persons and Minds.*
  D.M. Armstrong, 488:Jun80-227
Margolis, J.D. Joseph Wood Krutch.
  A.J. Angyal, 27(AL):Nov81-527
Marguerite de Navarre. Les Prisons.* (S. Glasson, ed)
  H.G. Collins, 207(FR):Dec81-264
  K.M. Hall, 208(FS):Oct81-430
Marianella, C.H. "Dueñas" and "Doncellas."
  F. Pierce, 402(MLR):Jul81-723
Mariani, P. William Carlos Williams.*
  J. Wilson, 271:Fall81-201
Marías, F. and A. Bustamante. Les ideas artísticas de El Greco.
  D. Angulo Íñiguez, 48:Apr-Jun81-224
Marie de France. Les "Lais" of Marie de France."* (R. Hanning and J. Ferrante, eds and trans)
  P.F. Dembowski, 545(RPh):Feb81(supp)-279
Mariën, M. L'Activité surréaliste en Belgique.
  J.H. Matthews, 593:Summer80-180
Mariengof, A. Roman bez vran'ya. (2nd ed)
  J. Graffy, 575(SEER):Oct81-600
Marill, A.H. Movies Made for Television.
  D. McClelland, 200:Mar81-180
Marín, D. Poesía paisajística española (1940-1970).
  205(FMLS):Jan80-91
Marín, F.M. - see under Marcos Marín, F.
Marín, J.L.M. - see under Morales y Marín, J.L.
Marinetti, F.T. Le Futurisme. Le futurisme dans les collections du MOMA.
  M. Dachy, 98:Jan81-85
Marini, P., ed. Palladio e Verona.
  C. Elam, 59:Sep81-350
Marini, S.A. Radical Sects of Revolutionary New England.
  J. Demos, 441:15Aug82-12
Marino, A. La Critique des idées littéraires.* (German title: Kritik der literarischen Begriff.)
  G. Cesbron, 356(LR):Nov81-374
Marino, A. Etiemble ou le comparatisme militant.
  J. Weightman, 617(TLS):10Dec82-1369
Marino, A. L'Herméneutique de Mircea Eliade.
  P. Bayard, 450(NRF):Sep81-138
Marino, L. The Decameron "Cornice."
  B.J. Layman, 589:Apr81-405
  J.J. Wilhelm, 551(RenQ):Autumn80-443
Marion, J.F. The Fine Old House.
  K.M. Kovacs, 14:Spring81-162
"Marital Status and Living Arrangements."
  A. Hacker, 453(NYRB):18Mar82-37

"Maritime History."
  78(BC):Winter81-447
Mark, M.E. Falkland Road.*
  M. Kozloff, 62:Nov81-76
Markandaya, K. The Nowhere Man.
  A.L. Weir, 314:Winter-Spring81-230
Markandaya, K. Pleasure City.
  J. Astor, 362:23Sep82-23
  A. Motion, 617(TLS):17Sep82-993
Markel, J.D. and A.H. Gray, Jr. Linear Prediction of Speech.
  H.K. Kubzdela, 682(ZPSK):Band33Heft2-258
Marken, J.W. and H.T. Hoover. Bibliography of the Sioux.
  C.A. Milner 2d, 649(WAL):Fall81-234
Marker, L-L. and F.J. Ingmar Bergman.
  I-S. Ewbank, 617(TLS):3Dec82-1347
Markey, T.L. - see Schuchardt, H.
Markham, E.A. Love, Politics and Food.
  T. Dooley, 617(TLS):24Sep82-1041
Markkanen, R. Tense and Aspect in English and Finnish.
  M. Gustafsson, 439(NM):1980/4-443
Markov, V. Russian Imagism, 1919-1924.
  R.D.B. Thomson, 575(SEER):Jul81-426
Markowski, G. Der schlaue Peter.
  D. Witschew, 654(WB):12/1981-159
Marks, E. and I. de Courtivron, eds. New French Feminisms.
  B. Braude, 207(FR):Dec81-292
Marks, E.R. Coleridge on the Language of Verse.
  L. Tyler, 580(SCR):Spring82-116
  639(VQR):Autumn81-129
Marks, R.B. The Medieval Manuscript Library of the Charterhouse of St. Barbara in Cologne.
  A.I. Doyle, 382(MAE):1981/1-109
Marks, S. and A. Atmore, eds. Economy and Society in Pre-Industrial South Africa.
  G.M. Fredrickson, 453(NYRB):18Mar82-51
Markson, D. Malcolm Lowry's Volcano.
  S.E. Grace, 102(CanL):Spring80-110
Márkus, G. Marxism and Anthropology.
  J.N. Gray, 518:Apr81-111
Marlatt, D. What Matters.
  C. Hall, 628(UWR):Spring-Summer82-119
Marling, K.A. Wall-to-Wall America.
  M. Kammen, 441:14Nov82-9
Marlowe, C. The Complete Works of Christopher Marlowe. (2nd ed) (F. Bowers, ed)
  354:Dec81-366
Marlowe, C. The Jew of Malta.* (N.W. Bawcutt, ed)
  T.W. Craik, 677(YES):Vol 11-243
  A. Leggatt, 529(QQ):Spring81-93
Marlowe, C. Tamburlaine the Great. (J.S. Cunningham, ed)
  S. Wells, 617(TLS):8Jan82-33
Marmontel, J-F. Correspondance. (J. Renwick, ed)
  J. Grieder, 207(FR):Oct80-162
Marnham, P. The "Private Eye" Story.
  R. Maxwell, 362:18Nov82-24
Marot, C. Oeuvres complètes. (Vol 6) (C.A. Mayer, ed)
  H.W. Lawton, 208(FS):Oct81-431
  B.L.O. Richter, 207(FR):Feb82-404
Marquand, D. - see Mackintosh, J.P.

234

Martin, F.D. Sculpture and Enlivened
Space.
    R. Arnheim, 290(JAAC):Summer82-435
    M. Yorke, 324:Nov82-828
Martin, G. A Companion to Twentieth Cen-
tury Opera.
    A. Jacobs, 415:Jan81-30
Martin, G.D. The Architecture of Experi-
ence.
    G. Strickland, 617(TLS):8Jan82-34
Martin, G.D. - see Renard, J-C.
Martin, H.B. The Polynesian Journal of
Captain Henry Byam Martin, R.N.
    P-L. Adams, 61:Feb82-86
Martin, J. Always Merry and Bright.*
    J. Nelson, 587(SAF):Spring81-133
    D.R. Noble, 577(SHR):Summer81-272
Martin, J. Gilbert.
    P-L. Adams, 61:Dec82-107
    442(NY):13Dec82-184
Martin, J. Miss Manners' Guide to
Excruciatingly Correct Behavior.
    P-L. Adams, 61:Sep82-94
    D. Ephron, 441:6Jun82-9
    442(NY):2Aug82-89
Martin, J. - see Libanius
Martin, J.R. and G. Feigenbaum. Van Dyck
as Religious Artist.*
    C.D. Cuttler, 551(RenQ):Spring80-106
    B. Wind, 568(SCN):Summer-Fall81-60
Martin, L. The Two-Edged Sword.
    M. Howard, 617(TLS):16Apr82-427
Martin, M. The Decline and Fall of the
Roman Church.
    C.C. O'Brien, 362:27May82-20
Martin, P. "Piers Plowman."
    J.J. Anderson, 148:Summer81-82
    P.M. Kean, 541(RES):May81-202
    D. Pearsall, 402(MLR):Apr81-435
Martin, P.W. Byron.
    K. Walker, 617(TLS):5Nov82-1213
Martin, R. La Notion de recevabilité en
linguistique.*
    K.E.M. George, 208(FS):Oct81-499
Martin, R. Tacitus.
    M. Grant, 617(TLS):29Jan82-117
Martin, R.B. Tennyson.*
    J.H. Buckley, 637(VS):Summer81-511
    J. Hunter, 249(HudR):Spring81-138
    G. Joseph, 636(VP):Summer81-196
    H. Kozicki, 651(WHR):Autumn81-273
    J.D. O'Hara, 434:Summer82-603
    C.D. Ryals, 579(SAQ):Autumn81-485
Martin, R.H. - see Terence
Martin, R.M. Semiotics and Linguistic
Structure.
    F.B. Fitch, 484(PPR):Mar82-453
    R. Nolan, 316:Mar81-167
Martin, S. Wagner to "The Waste Land."
    L. Beckett, 617(TLS):1Oct82-1073
Martin, S.E. A Reference Grammar of
Japanese.
    C. Kitagawa, 318(JAOS):Jan/Mar80-18
Martin, V. Alexandra.
    J.M. Davis, Jr., 435:Winter81-109
Martín, V.T. - see under Tovar Martín, V.
Martin du Gard, R. Correspondance géné-
rale.* (Vols 1 and 2) (M. Rieuneau, ed)
    G.J. Barberet, 207(FR):Apr81-743
Martin-Fugier, A. La place des bonnes.
    A. Corbin, 98:Jun-Jul80-595

Martín Gaite, C. Cuentos completos.
    G. Crescioni Neggers, 552(REH):Oct81-
    473
Martín Zorraquino, M.A. Las construc-
ciones pronominales en español.
    C.J. Pountain, 86(BHS):Jul81-251
Martindale, A. The Triumphs of Caesar by
Andrea Mantegna in the Collection of Her
Majesty the Queen at Hampton Court.*
    J. Anderson, 313:Vol71-227
    J.M. Massing, 90:Jun81-360
Martindale, J.R. The Prosopography of the
Later Roman Empire. (Vol 2)
    R.S. Bagnall, 121(CJ):Dec81/Jan82-183
    J.H.W.G. Liebeschuetz, 123:Vol31No2-
    256
Martine, J.J., ed. Critical Essays on
Arthur Miller.
    L. Moss, 397(MD):Mar81-110
Martineau, C. and M. Veissière, with H.
Heller - see Briçonnet, G. and M.
d'Angoulème
Martineau-Génieys, C. Le Thème de la mort
dans la poésie française de 1450 à 1550.*
    T. Sankovitch, 545(RPh):May81-569
    C.M. Scollen-Jimack, 208(FS):Apr81-187
Martínek, J. and D. Martínková - see
Hassenstein a Lobkowicz, B.
Martines, L. Power and Imagination.*
    R.A. Goldthwaite, 551(RenQ):Winter80-
    750
    D. Hay, 589:Apr81-408
    C.J. Nederman, 539:May82-149
Martinet, A. and others. Grammaire fonc-
tionnelle du français.
    D. Birdsong, 207(FR):May81-910
Martinet, M-M., ed. Art et Nature en
Grande-Bretagne au XVIIIe siècle.
    J-R. Mantion, 98:Dec81-1301
    H. Osborne, 89(BJA):Winter81-89
    C.J. Rawson, 189(EA):Oct-Dec81-472
    P. Somville, 542:Jan-Mar81-122
Martínez-Bonati, F. Fictive Discourse and
the Structures of Literature.
    639(VQR):Autumn81-129
Martínez Cachero, J.M. Historia de la
novela española entre 1936 y 1975.*
    J.J. Macklin, 86(BHS):Apr81-162
Martínez de Toledo, A. Arcipreste de Tala-
vera o Corbacho. (M. Gerli, ed)
    D.L. Heiple, 238:Mar81-151
Martínez García, F. César Vallejo.
    J. Higgins, 86(BHS):Oct81-355
Martínková, D. - see Proxenus a Sudetis, S.
Martino, A. Daniel Casper von Lohenstein.*
(Vol 1)
    B.L. Spahr, 133:Band14Heft3-265
Martino, N.F. - see de Baena, J.A.
de Martinoir, F. Née Rostopchine.
    M.E. Birkett, 207(FR):Feb82-439
Martinson, S.D. On Imitation, Imagination
and Beauty.*
    O.F. Best, 406:Fall81-348
Martland, T.R. Religion as Art.
    D. Burke, 290(JAAC):Winter81-217
Martz, L.L. Poet of Exile.
    H. MacCallum, 627(UTQ):Spring81-314
    W. Myers, 569(SR):Fall81-622
    A.M. Patterson, 141:Spring81-183
    B. Rajan, 405(MP):May82-433
    D.E. Ray, 49:Oct81-101
    J. Wittreich, 401(MLQ):Jun81-184
    639(VQR):Winter81-14

Marvan, J. Prehistoric Slavic Contraction.
    H. Leeming, 575(SEER):Jul81-413
Marwick, A. British Society since 1945.
    P. Clarke, 617(TLS):23Jul82-783
    P. Whitehead, 362:17Jun82-24
Marx, B. Bartolomeo Pagello.
    M.L. King, 551(RenQ):Winter80-739
Marx, J., L. and E. The Daughters of Karl
    Marx. (F. Evans, ed and trans)
    H. Wackett, 362:26Aug82-20
    442(NY):3May82-167
Marx, K. Manuscrits de 1861-1863. (J-P.
    Lefebvre, ed)
    J-M. Gabaude, 542:Oct-Dec81-488
Marx, K. and F. Engels. Correspondance.*
    (Vol 7) (G. Badia and J. Mortier, eds)
    J-M. Gabaude, 542:Oct-Dec81-488
Marx, K. and F. Engels. Selected Letters.
    (F.J. Raddatz, ed)
    A. Oakley, 441:2May82-15
    442(NY):22Mar82-165
Marx, W. Schelling.*
    H. Holz, 319:Apr81-262
Marzio, P.C. The Democratic Art.*
    D. Glanz, 658:Spring81-96
Masao, T., Akai Tatsurō and Fujii Manabu -
    see under Takatori Masao, Akai Tatsurō
    and Fujii Manabu
Masefield, J. Letters of John Masefield
    to Florence Lamont. (C. and L. Lamont,
    eds)
    F.W. Mellown, 579(SAQ):Spring81-241
Maser, S. - see de Baïf, J-A.
Masini, F. Dialettica dall'avanguardia.
    R.A. Cavell, 107(CRCL):Winter81-137
Mason, B. Betty's Basic Boxes.
    T. Cowan, 614:Fall81-15
Mason, B. Betty's Basic Dolls.
    P. Bach, 614:Spring81-16
Mason, B. Michel Butor.
    D. Rice, 207(FR):Apr82-690
Mason, B.A. Shiloh and Other Stories.
    D. Quammen, 441:21Nov82-7
    R. Towers, 453(NYRB):16Dec82-38
Mason, E.B. and L.M. Starr, eds. The
    Oral History Collection of Columbia
    University.
    J.E. Fogerty, 14:Spring80-216
Mason, H., ed. Studies on Voltaire and
    the Eighteenth Century.* (Vol 174)
    M.H. Waddicor, 208(FS):Jan81-75
Mason, H., ed. Studies on Voltaire and
    the Eighteenth Century. (Vol 176)
    J. Geffriaud-Rosso, 535(RHL):Nov-Dec81-
    1000
    M.H. Waddicor, 208(FS):Oct81-447
Mason, H., ed. Studies on Voltaire and
    the Eighteenth Century. (Vol 182)
    M. Delon, 535(RHL):Jul-Oct81-783
Mason, H., ed. Studies on Voltaire and
    the Eighteenth Century. (Vol 183)
    D. Fletcher, 402(MLR):Oct81-966
    P. Testud, 535(RHL):Nov-Dec81-1002
Mason, H., ed. Studies on Voltaire and
    the Eighteenth Century. (Vol 185)
    D. Fletcher, 402(MLR):Oct81-966
Mason, H. Voltaire.*
    M. Mudrick, 249(HudR):Winter81/82-531
    R. Runte, 150(DR):Spring81-158
    D. Schier, 569(SR):Summer81-xc
Mason, J. The Turk. (F. Lagarde, ed)
    N. Strout, 568(SCN):Summer-Fall81-48

Mason, J.H. The Irresistible Diderot.
    P. Jimack, 617(TLS):5Nov82-1222
Mason, P. The English Gentleman.
    J. Rae, 362:30Sep82-25
Mass, J.P. The Development of Kamakura
    Rule, 1180-1250.
    W.H. McCullough, 244(HJAS):Jun81-263
"Mass Communication Review Yearbook."
    (Vol 1) (G.C. Wilhoit and H. de Bock,
    eds)
    R.K. Tiemens, 583:Summer81-429
Massa-Gille, G. - see Fortoul, H.
Massa-Pairault, F-H. and J.M. Pailler. La
    Maison aux Salles Souterraines (Bolsena
    V).
    R.M. Ogilvie, 123:Vol31No2-323
Masser, A. - see Friedrichs von Sonnenburg
Massicotte, M. Le Parler rural de l'Île-
    aux-grues (Québec).*
    G. Price, 208(FS):Apr81-243
Massie, A. The Death of Men.*
    J. Mellors, 364:Oct81-93
    442(NY):19Apr82-176
Massie, R.K. Peter the Great.*
    M. Raeff, 550(RusR):Jan81-58
Massinger, P. The Selected Plays of
    Philip Massinger.* (C. Gibson, ed)
    P. Hollindale, 677(YES):Vol 11-245
Massip, R. Belle à jamais ...
    R.J. Scaly, 207(FR):Dec80-366
Maoooli, M. - see "Frey Íñigo de Mendoza,
    'Coplas de Vita Christi'"
Mast, G. The Comic Mind. (2nd ed)
    M. Wreen, 290(JAAC):Winter81-226
Mast, G. Howard Hawks, Storyteller.
    S. Peck, 441:19Dec82-7
Mastandrea, P. Un neoplatonico latino,
    Cornelio Labeone.
    G. Fowden, 313:Vol71-178
    R.M. Ogilvie, 123:Vol31No1-128
Masters, B. Great Hostesses.
    M. Amory, 617(TLS):19Nov82-1263
    P. Johnson, 362:25Nov82-21
Masters, H. Last Stands.
    P-L. Adams, 61:Dec82-106
    D. Hall, 441:19Dec82-11
    442(NY):13Dec82-184
Masthay, C. Mahican-Language Hymns, Bib-
    lical Prose, and Vocabularies from Mora-
    vian Sources.
    I. Goddard, 350:Sep81-776
Mastny, V. Russia's Road to the Cold War.*
    A.M. Cienciala, 497(PolR):Vol26No2-76
Mastrocinque, A. La Caria e la Ionia
    meridionale in epoca ellenistica
    (323-188 a.C.).
    N.S.R. Hornblower, 303(JoHS):Vol 101-
    202
Mastromarco, G. Il pubblico di Eronda.
    I.C. Cunningham, 303(JoHS):Vol 101-161
    P. Monteil, 555:Vol54fasc1-166
    P.J. Parsons, 123:Vol31No1-110
Masur, H.Q. The Broker.
    N. Callendar, 441:7Feb82-20
Masur, H.Q. The Mourning After.
    T.J. Binyon, 617(TLS):31Dec82-1448
Matarasso, P. The Redemption of Chivalry.
    N.J. Lacy, 207(FR):Mar81-588
    C.C. Morse, 589:Apr81-410
    C.E. Pickford, 382(MAE):1981/1-143
Matas, J. La cuestión del género litera-
    rio.
    D. Harris, 86(BHS):Apr81-135

Matejka, L. and I.R. Titunik, eds. Semi-
otics of Art.
   W. Holmes, 567:Vol33No1/2-155
Mateo, I. La sillería del coro de la
Catedral.
   D. Angulo Íñiguez, 48:Apr-Jun81-227
Mateo, R.G. - see under García Mateo, R.
Mateo Gómez, I. Temas profanos en la
escultura gotica española: Las sillerias
de coro.
   J. Gardner, 90:Jan81-47
   E. Young, 39:Oct81-274
Materer, T. Vortex.*
   C.C. Clark, 396(ModA):Fall81-428
   D. Messerli, 295(JML):Vol8No3/4-357
   H.N. Schneidau, 405(MP):Nov81-220
Mates, B. Skeptical Essays.
   M.T., 185:Apr82-606
Mateus, M.H.M. Aspectos da fonologia
portuguesa.
   J. Tláskal, 682(ZPSK):Band33Heft6-756
Matheeussen, C. and C.L. Heesakkers - see
Lipsius, J. and P. Cunaeus
Mather, R.B. - see Liu I-ch'ing
Matheson, D.K. Ideology, Political Action
and the Finnish Working Class.
   M. Rintala, 563(SS):Summer81-354
Matheson, P. The Third Reich and the
Christian Churches.
   N. Stone, 453(NYRB):13May82-24
Mathews, H. Le Naufrage du stade Odradek.
   C. Jordis, 450(NRF):Jul-Aug81-221
Mathews, T.F. The Byzantine Churches of
Istanbul.
   G. Stričević, 54:Mar81-145
Mathieu, V. - see Kant, I.
Mathieu-Castellani, G., ed. Eros baroque.*
   Y. Bellenger, 535(RHL):May-Jun81-454
   W. Leiner, 475:No13Pt1-148
Mathieu-Castellani, G. Mythes de l'éros
baroque.
   T. Cave, 617(TLS):26Feb82-226
Mathiot, M., ed. Ethnolinguistics.*
   J. Manes, 355(LSoc):Aug81-261
   205(FMLS):Apr80-187
Mathis, C. Aerial View of Louisiana.*
   K. Chamberlain, 134(CP):Spring81-95
Mathis, R. John Horry Dent.
   B.H. Wall, 9(AlaR):Apr81-125
Mathis, U. Wirklichkeitssicht und Stil in
"Le Rouge et le Noir."*
   H. Charney, 207(FR):Dec80-345
   R. Rie, 446(NCFS):Fall-Winter80/81-132
   F.W. Saunders, 208(FS):Oct81-457
Matisoff, J.A. Variational Semantics in
Tibeto-Burman.*
   G. Thurgood, 261:Jun80-116
de Matos, F.G. and S.S. Biazioli - see
under Gomes de Matos, F. and S.S.
Biazioli
Matos Mar, J. and J. Mejía Mejía. Reforma
agraria.
   O. Bedini, 263(RIB):Vol31No1-92
Matson, K. Short Lives.
   W.N., 102(CanL):Spring81-176
Mattessich, R. Instrumental Reasoning and
Systems Methodology.*
   P. Diesing, 488:Dec81-516
Matthaei, J.A. An Economic History of
Women in America.
   F. Randall, 441:12Dec82-16
Matthew, C. and B. Green - see Jerome, J.K.
Matthew, H.C.G. - see Gladstone, W.E.

Matthews, D. Arturo Toscanini.
   N. Del Mar, 617(TLS):19Nov82-1266
Matthews, D.G. and S.M. - see Frisch, M.
Matthews, J. Dubious Persuasions.
   L.K. Abbott, Jr., 580(SCR):Spring82-
133
   T. O'Brien, 441:7Feb82-12
Matthews, J.H. The Imagery of Surrealism.
   R. Cardinal, 529(QQ):Spring81-19
Matthews, J.H. The Inner Dream.*
   D. O'Connell, 207(FR):Oct80-172
Matthews, J.V. Rufus Choate.
   D.W. Howe, 432(NEQ):Jun81-282
Matthews, M.R. The Marxist Theory of
Schooling.
   A.L., 185:Jan82-394
Matthews, P.H. Generative Grammar and
Linguistic Competence.*
   D.E. Gulstad, 399(MLJ):Spring81-108
Matthews, P.H. Morphology.
   P. Swiggers, 350:Dec81-965
Matthews, R.T. and P. Mellini. In "Vanity
Fair."
   C. Fox, 617(TLS):19Nov82-1263
   E. Sorel, 441:26Sep82-12
Matthiae, P. Ebla.*
   P-L. Adams, 61:Feb82-88
Matthias, J. Crossing.*
   L. Sail, 565:Vol22No1-66
Matthias, J. - see Jones, D.
Matthias, J. and G. Printz-Påhlson - see
"Contemporary Swedish Poetry"
Matthiessen, P. Sand Rivers.*
   S. Pickering, Jr., 219(GaR):Winter81-
883
   V. Young, 249(HudR):Winter81/82-625
Mattielli, S., ed. Virtues in Conflict.
   G. Dix, 293(JASt):May81-616
Matto, J.B.R. - see under Rivarola Matto,
J.B.
Matura, M. Nice, Rum an' Coca Cola,
Welcome Home Jacko.
   D. Devlin, 157:1stQtr81-54
Maud, R. - see Hill-Tout, C.
de Maupassant, G. Bel-Ami. (M-C. Banc-
quart, ed)
   P. Cogny, 535(RHL):Jul-Oct81-819
Mauquoy-Hendrickx, M. Les Estampes des
Wierix, I and II.
   C. Brown, 39:Dec81-429
von Maur, K. Oskar Schlemmer.
   W. Herzogenrath, 471:Apr/May/Jun81-184
Sister Maura. What We Women Know.
   P. Ramsey, 472:Spring/Summer82-172
Maurer, C. - see Lorca, F.G.
Maurer, D.W. Language of the Underworld.
   (A.W. Futrell and C.B. Wordell, eds)
   A. Burgess, 617(TLS):22Jan82-74
   G. Nunberg, 441:2May82-9
Maurer, H. Der Herzog von Schwaben.
   J.M. Bak, 589:Jan81-179
du Maurier, D. L'escalier en colimaçon.
Golden Lads. The Winding Stairs.
   P. Mauriès, 98:Feb80-149
Mauser, W. Hugo von Hofmannsthal.*
   S.P. Sondrup, 133:Band14Heft3-264
Maxwell, M.F. Handbook for AACR2.
   N.B. Parker, 14:Spring81-159
Maxwell, S. The Princess of Wales.
   V. Glendinning, 617(TLS):25Jun82-689
Maxwell, W. - see Warner, S.T.

Medvedev, P.N. and M.M. Bakhtin. The For-
mal Method in Literary Scholarship.*
  C. Norris, 402(MLR):Jan81-143
  E. Thompson, 599:Winter81-71
Medvedev, R.A. The October Revolution.*
  R.A. Wade, 104(CASS):Winter81-599
Medvedev, R.A. On Stalin and Stalinism.*
  A. Dallin, 550(RusR):Jan81-66
Medvedev, R.A., with P. Ostellino. Roy
  Medvedev: On Soviet Dissent.
  639(VQR):Winter81-23
Medvedev, Z.A. Nuclear Disaster in the
  Urals.
  E. Teller, 550(RusR):Jan81-69
Medwall, H. The Plays of Henry Medwall.
  (A.H. Nelson, ed)
  D. Bevington, 130:Summer81-176
Mee, C.L., Jr. The End of Order.*
  639(VQR):Spring81-50
Mee, C.L., Jr. The Ohio Gang.
  F. Russell, 453(NYRB):24Jun82-30
Meehan, E. Reasoned Argument in Social
  Science.
  K.S., 185:Jul82-800
Meek, C. Lucca 1369-1400.*
  M.B. Becker, 551(RenQ):Spring80-62
Meek, M. Learning to Read.
  B. Rotman, 617(TLS):26Mar82-351
Meeker, M.E. Literature and Violence in
  Northern Arabia.
  R. Bidwell, 294:Vol 12-160
van der Meer, N.C.V. Sawah Cultivation in
  Ancient Java.
  R.D. Hill, 302:Vol 18-178
Meerman, J. Public Expenditure in Malay-
  sia.
  L.Y.C. Lim, 293(JASt):Nov80-199
Meersseman, G.G., with G.P. Pacini. Ordo
  Fraternitas.
  A. Vitale-Brovarone, 228(GSLI):
  Vol 157fasc500-607
Megenney, W.W. A Bahian Heritage.
  Q.A. Pizzini, 238:May81-324
Megenney, W.W., ed. Five Essays on Martín
  Luis Guzmán.
  P. Turton, 86(BHS):Apr81-163
Meggle, G. and M. Beetz. Interpretations-
  theorie und Interpretationspraxis.
  H. Göttner, 494:Winter80/81-171
Meghani, J. Earthen Lamps.
  G.V. Gopalan, 314:Summer-Fall81-243
Mehan, H. Learning Lessons.
  J.L. Heap, 355(LSoc):Aug81-279
  D. Tannen, 355(LSoc):Aug81-274
von der Mehden, F.R. South-East Asia
  1930-1970.
  D.K. Emmerson, 293(JASt):Nov80-43
Mehendale, M.A. Nirukta Notes. (Ser 2)
  R.L. Turner, 261:Sep79-212
Mehlman, J. Cataract.
  H. Cohen, 207(FR):Mar81-596
  D. Krauss, 345(KRQ):Vol28No4-429
Mehnert, H. Melancholie und Inspiration.
  A. Corbineau-Hoffmann, 490:Band12Heft1-
  119
  H. Stenzel, 224(GRM):Band30Heft3-364
Mehra, P. Tibetan Polity, 1904-1937.
  E. Sperling, 318(JAOS):Jul/Sep80-395
Mehrotra, A.K. Nine Enclosures.
  J.P. Gemmill, 314:Summer-Fall81-207
Mehta, P.C. The Yesterdays of My Life.
  A.L. Weir, 314:Summer-Fall81-226

Mehta, V. A Family Affair.
  C. Blaise, 441:17Oct82-12
Mehta, V. Vedi.
  C. Blaise, 441:17Oct82-12
  J. Malcolm, 453(NYRB):7Oct82-3
Meier, M. -íó-, Zur Geschichte eines
  griechischen Nominalsuffixes.
  A. Sideras, 260(IF):Band85-335
Meier, O., with F. Evans, eds and trans.
  The Daughters of Karl Marx.
  A. Oakley, 441:2May82-15
  A. Ryan, 617(TLS):13Aug82-872
Meier-Lenz, D.P. Heinrich Heine — Wolf
  Biermann: Deutschland.*
  V. Hansen, 133:Band14Heft1-86
Meigret, L. Le Traité de la Grammaire
  française (1550). (F.J. Hausmann, ed)
  K. Cameron, 208(FS):Jul81-324
Meigret, L. Traité touchant le commun
  usage de l'escriture françoise. (K.
  Cameron, ed)
  C-G. Dubois, 535(RHL):Jul-Oct81-751
Meikle, J.L. Twentieth Century Limited.*
  W. Belasco, 658:Spring81-120
Meilaender, G. The Taste for the Other.*
  B. Reynolds, 677(YES):Vol 11-359
Meillier, C. Callimaque et son temps.
  F. Cairns, 123:Vol31No1-110
Meinong, A. On Objects of Higher Order
  and Husserl's Phenomenology.* (M-L.S.
  Kalsi, ed and trans)
  Q. Smith, 484(PPR):Mar82-451
Meisel, J.M. and M.D. Pam, eds. Linear
  Order and Generative Theory.
  M.A. Covington, 350:Sep81-770
Meisel, L.K. Photo-Realism.
  W. Zimmer, 55:Nov81-46
  62:Feb81-71
Meisel, P. The Absent Father.*
  J. Gindin, 301(JEGP):Jan81-151
  M. Magalaner, 395(MFS):Winter80/81-684
  J. Marcus, 637(VS):Spring81-378
  I. Milligan, 506(PSt):Dec81-355
Meiselas, S. Nicaragua: June 1978-July
  1979.* (C. Rosenberg, ed)
  M. Kozloff, 62:Nov81-76
Meiss, M. French Painting in the Time of
  Jean de Berry.
  C. Eisler, 54:Jun81-328
Meiss, M. and E.H. Beatson, eds. "La Vie
  de Nostre Benoit Sauveur Ihesuscrist" et
  "La Saincte Vie de Nostre Dame."*
  J.L. Grigsby, 545(RPh):Feb81(supp)-64
Meissner, F-J. Wortgeschichte Untersuchun-
  gen im Umkreis von französisch Enthousi-
  asme und Genie.
  O. Ducháček, 209(FM):Apr81-171
Meissner, W. Learning to Breathe Under-
  water.
  T. Swiss, 436(NewL):Fall81-119
Meister, B. Nineteenth-Century French
  Song.
  J. Fulcher, 446(NCFS):Fall-Winter81/82-
  174
  N. Suckling, 208(FS):Oct81-467
Mekhitarian, A. Egyptian Painting.
  T.G.H. James, 39:Oct81-270
"Melanges de langue et de littérature du
  Moyen Age offerts à Teruo Sato, profes-
  seur honoraire à l'Université Waseda,
  par ses amis et ses collègues." (Pt 1)
  W.D. Paden, Jr., 545(RPh):May81-493

"Mélanges de langue et littérature françaises du Moyen Age et de la Renaissance, offerts à Monsieur Charles Foulon." (Vol 1)
    N.J. Lacy, 207(FR):Mar82-543
"Mélanges de linguistique et de littérature offerts à Lein Geschiere par ses amis, collègues et élèves."
    C. Stern, 545(RPh):May81-480
Melba, N. Melodies and Memories.* (J. Cargher, ed)
    E. Forbes, 415:Jun81-385
Melchinger, S. Die Welt als Tragödie.
    P.G. Mason, 303(JoHS):Vol 101-170
Melchiori, G., ed. Le Forme del Teatro.
    K. Richards, 611(TN):Vol35No3-133
Meléndez Valdés, J. Poesías. (E. Palacios, ed)
    J.H.R. Polt, 240(HR):Summer81-361
Melgar, A.D. - see under de Figueroa y Melgar, A.
"Meliadus de Leonnoys, 1532." (C.E. Pickford, ed)
    D.J. Shaw, 617(TLS):17Sep82-1019
Melillo, G. Economia e giurisprudenza a Roma.
    P. Stein, 313:Vol71-226
Melis, G. Jean de Sponde, Poésies.
    J. Pineaux, 535(RHL):Jan-Feb81-125
Melitz, J. and D. Winch - see Viner, J.
Mellard, J.M. The Exploded Form.*
    P. Butithis, 659(ConL):Summer82-400
    P. Buitenhuis, 150(DR):Summer81-380
    I. Malin, 27(AL):Jan82-742
Mellen, J. Privilege.
    S. Jacoby, 441:10Oct82-12
Mellen, J. The Waves at Genji's Door.
    P. McCarthy, 293(JASt):Nov80-136
Melli, E. - see Buvalelli, R.
Mellor, A.K. English Romantic Irony.*
    P.A. Cantor, 141:Spring81-187
    L.J. Swingle, 401(MLQ):Mar81-99
    S. Wolfson, 661(WC):Summer81-192
Mellor, D.H., ed. Science, Belief and Behaviour.
    R.G. Swinburne, 393(Mind):Jul81-468
Mellow, J.R. Nathaniel Hawthorne in His Times.*
    N. Baym, 445(NCF):Jun81-102
    M.J. Colacurcio, 183(ESQ):Vol127No2-108
    R. Conway, 432(NEQ):Sep81-442
    J.H. Justus, 651(WHR):Autumn81-285
    J.D. McClatchy, 249(HudR):Summer81-315
    T. Martin, 27(AL):Jan82-726
    42(AR):Spring81-264
Mellown, E.W. Edwin Muir.
    P. Butter, 571(ScLJ):Summer80-118
Melly, G. A Tribe of One.
    A. Ross, 364:Mar82-8
Melly, G. - see James, E.
Melnikas, A. The Corpus of the Miniatures in the Manuscripts of the Decretum Gratiani.
    C. Nordenfalk, 683:Band43Heft3-318
Melosi, M.V. Garbage in the Cities.
    F. Randall, 441:11Apr82-14
Melville, A. and C. Johnson. Cured to Death.
    D. Gould, 617(TLS):17Dec82-1401
Melville, H. Typee; Omoo; Mardi. (G.T. Tanselle, ed)
    M. Cowley, 441:25Apr82-3

Melville, J. The Ninth Netsuke.
    T.J. Binyon, 617(TLS):28May82-594
    M. Laski, 362:29Jul82-27
Melville-Ross, A. Trigger.
    M. Laski, 362:29Apr82-27
Mena, J.L. Du mythe à l'ontologie.
    R.S., 543:Mar81-615
Ménager, D. Ronsard.
    M. Glatigny, 535(RHL):Nov-Dec81-981
    M.M. McGowan, 402(MLR):Jan81-184
Ménard, C. La formation d'une rationalité économique.
    M. Lagueux, 154:Mar81-102
Ménard, G. Fragments.
    G.V. Downes, 102(CanL):Winter80-105
Ménard, J-É., ed and trans. L'authentikos logos.
    O. Wintermute, 318(JAOS):Apr/Jun80-172
Ménard, P., ed. Fabliaux français du Moyen Age.* (Vol 1)
    W. Rothwell, 208(FS):Oct81-426
Ménard, P. Les Lais de Marie de France.*
    P.F. Dembowski, 545(RPh):Feb81(supp)-279
    D. Grokenberger, 196:Band22Heft1/2-140
    T.D. Hemming, 208(FS):Apr81-184
Mendel, A.P. Michael Bakunin.
    J.H. Billington, 441:9May82-9
Mendelson, D. Metaphor in Babel's Short Stories.
    J. Grayson, 617(TLS):31Dec82-1446
Mendelson, E. Early Auden.*
    J.D. McClatchy, 676(YR):Winter82-293
    J.D. O'Hara, 434:Summer82-603
    W.H. Pritchard, 491:Feb82-292
Mendelson, E., ed. Pynchon.
    D. Tallack, 541(RES):Feb81-109
Mendelson, E. - see Auden, W.H.
Mendelssohn, M. Morgenstunden oder Vorlesungen über das Dasein Gottes. (D. Bourel, ed)
    R. Malter, 342:Band71Heft3-379
Mendelssohn, M. Rezensionsartikel in der Bibliothek der schönen Wissenschaften und der freyen Künste (1756-1759).
    W. Koepke, 221(GQ):Jan81-76
de Mendelssohn, P. - see Mann, T.
Mendès, C. - see France, A.
Méndez, M.D.P. - see under Pallares Méndez, M.D.
Menegazzi, L., ed. Tomaso da Modena.
    R. Gibbs, 90:Feb81-101
Meneghetti, M.L., ed. I Fatti di Bretagna.
    R. Morris, 382(MAE):1981/1-131
Meneghini, G.B., with R. Allegri. My Wife Maria Callas.
    P.G. Davis, 441:21Nov82-14
de Menezes, P. Crafts from the Countryside.
    P. Bach, 614:Spring82-12
Meng, H.W. - see under Ho Wing Meng
Mengaldo, P.V. Linguistica e retorica di Dante.
    N. Vincent, 402(MLR):Apr81-483
Mengaldo, P.V. and others - see Dante Alighieri
Menger, K. Selected Papers in Logic and Foundations, Didactics, Economics.
    D. Gillies, 84:Jun81-183
    M. Hallett, 479(PhQ):Jan81-92
Menhennet, A. The Romantic Movement.*
    H.S. Daemmrich, 221(GQ):Nov81-494

Menninger, K.   Number Words and Number
Symbols.*
M. Jackson, 545(RPh):Nov80-217
Menocal, N.G.   Architecture as Nature.
J.V. Turano, 16:Autumn81-88
Menocal, N.G.   Keck and Keck, Architects.
B. Pickens, 576:May81-150
Mensching, E.   Caesar und die Germanen
im 20. Jahrhundert.
T.E.J. Wiedemann, 313:Vol71-229
Menton, S., ed.   The Spanish American
Short Story.*
L.E. Ben-Ur, 238:Dec81-645
E. Echevarria, 573(SSF):Spring81-194
639(VQR):Winter81-22
Mentrup, W., ed.   Materialien zur historis-
chen entwicklung der gross- und klein-
schreibungsregeln.
H. Penzl, 350:Mar81-230
G. Schmidt-Wilpert, 680(ZDP):Band100
Heft3-465
Menuhin, Y. and C.W. Davis.   The Music of
Man.
G. Poole, 415:Aug81-536
Menyuk, P.   Language and Maturation.
A. Elliot, 297(JL):Mar81-125
Mephan, J. and D-H. Ruben.   Issues in
Marxist Philosophy.
J. Rée, 98:Aug-Sep80-802
Mercer, D.   Collected TV Plays.
C. Hampton, 157:Winter81-47
Mercer, R.G.G.   The Teaching of Gasparino
Barzizza.*
A.J. Hunt, 402(MLR):Apr81-484
Merchant, W.M.   R.S. Thomas.
J. Hamard, 189(EA):Oct-Dec81-490
Mercier, C. - see Philo of Alexandria
Mercier, V.   Beckett/Beckett.*
T. Fischer-Seidel, 38:Band99Heft1/2-
260
Mercier-Josa, S.   Pour lier Hegel et Marx.
J-M. Gabaude, 542:Oct-Dec81-488
Mercken-Spaas, G.   Alienation in Con-
stant's "Adolphe."*
I.W. Alexander, 402(MLR):Jan81-195
Meredith, G.   The Poems of George Mere-
dith.*   (P.B. Bartlett, ed)
C. Cook, 447(N&Q):Oct80-465
Meredith, W.   The Cheer.*
B. Costello, 472:Fall/Winter81-169
R.B. Shaw, 491:Dec81-171
P. Stitt, 219(GaR):Winter81-874
V. Young, 249(HudR):Spring81-149
639(VQR):Summer81-94
Meriwether, J.B. and M. Millgate, eds.
Lion in the Garden.
P.G. Hogan, Jr., 573(SSF):Fall81-464
Merlan, P.   Kleine philosophische
Schriften.   (F. Merlan, ed)
K. Bärthlein, 53(AGP):Band62Heft1-91
Merle, R.   Culture occitane per avançar.
M.G. Hydak, 207(FR):Dec80-373
Merle, R.   Fortune de France.   En nos
vertes années.
R.D. Frye, 207(FR):May81-901
Meron, E.   Les idées morales des interlocu-
teurs de Socrate dans les dialogues pla-
toniciens de jeunesse.
J-L. Poirier, 542:Apr-Jun81-263
Merquior, J.G.   The Veil and the Mask.
J. Burnheim, 63:Mar81-125
S. Smith, 185:Oct80-159

Merrett, R.J.   Daniel Defoe's Moral and
Rhetorical Ideas.
J. Black, 150(DR):Autumn81-596
D. Blewett, 627(UTQ):Summer81-110
P. Sabor, 566:Spring81-123
Merriam, C.H.   Indian Names for Plants and
Animals Among Californian and Other Wes-
tern North American Tribes.   (R.F. Hei-
zer, ed)
B. Berlin, 350:Mar81-245
Merrilees, B.S. - see Chardri
Merrill, J.   Mirabell: Books of Number.*
Scripts for the Pageant.*   Divine Come-
dies.
W.G. Regier, 502(PrS):Spring-Summer81-
303
D. Yeaton, 434:Winter81-330
Merrill, W.M. - see Garrison, W.L.
Merriman, J.M.   The Agony of the Republic.
D.H. Barry, 161(DUJ):Jun81-244
Merryman, J.H. and A.E. Elsen.   Law,
Ethics and the Visual Arts.
R. Brilliant, 127:Fall/Winter80-427
Mertens, J., ed.   Ordona.   (Vol 6)
A. Hus, 555:Vol154fasc2-389
Mertens, V.   Gregorius Eremita.*
C. Cormeau, 684(ZDA):Band109Heft3-99
R. Schmidt, 680(ZDP):Band100Heft3-422
Merton, A.H.   Enemies of Choice.
F. Randall, 441:28Feb82-16
Merton, T.   The Literary Essays of Thomas
Merton.   (P. Hart, ed)
D.J.R. Bruckner, 441:23May82-15
Merwin, W.S.   Unframed Originals.
J.C. Oates, 441:1Aug82-7
Merwin, W.S. and J.M. Masson - see "San-
skrit Love Poetry"
de Mesa, D.P. - see under Pérez de Mesa, D.
Meschery, J.   In a High Place.*
V. Miner, 441:17Jan82-12
R. Scruton, 617(TLS):2Apr82-395
Meschonnic, H.   Légendaire chaque jour.*
M. Bishop, 207(FR):Feb81-506
Mesqui, J.   Provins.
J. Beeler, 589:Apr81-413
Messagier, M.   Poèmes (1967-1971).
E.R. Jackson, 207(FR):Oct80-196
Messer, R.L.   The End of an Alliance.
J.L. Gaddis, 441:21Mar82-9
Messner, D.   Chronologische und etymolo-
gische Studien zu den iberoromanischen
Sprachen und zum Französischen.
P.M. Lloyd, 545(RPh):May81-471
Messner, D.   Einführung in die Geschichte
des französischen Wortschatzes.*
R. De Gorog, 545(RPh):Feb81(supp)-184
Mestas, J-P.   Pays nuptial.   Cette Idée
qui ne vivra pas.
T. Greene, 207(FR):Feb82-440
Mészáros, I.   The Work of Sartre.   (Vol 1)
P. Caws, 482(PhR):Oct81-613
W.L. McBride, 185:Apr82-561
P.S. Morris, 518:Jul81-147
Metcalf, A.A.   Chicano English.
T.D. Terrell, 399(MLJ):Autumn81-327
Metcalf, J.   General Ludd.*
D.R. Bartlett, 628(UWR):Fall-Winter81-
116
P. Monk, 150(DR):Spring81-161
L. Rogers, 102(CanL):Autumn81-156
Metcalf, J.   Girl in Gingham.*
R.W. Harvey, 102(CanL):Spring80-129

Metcalf, J. and C. Blaise, eds. 78: Best
Canadian Stories.*
   A.J. Harding, 102(CanL):Summer80-149
Metcalf, J.C. Taxidermy.
   R. O'Hanlon, 617(TLS):1Jan82-19
Metcalf, P. James Knowles.
   J.H. Wiener, 637(VS):Spring81-359
Metellus, J. Jacmel au crépuscule.
   J. Kirkup, 617(TLS):12Mar82-276
Meter, H. Apollinaire und der Futurismus.
   H. Felten, 602:Vol 12No1-281
   R. Lloyd, 208(FS):Apr81-226
   J. Schultz, 535(RHL):May-Jun81-480
Metford, D.A. and J.S. Kaléidoscope.
   W. Staaks, 207(FR):Dec80-354
"Méthodes chez Pascal."*
   J.H. Broome, 208(FS):Apr81-196
Methuen-Campbell, J. Chopin Playing.*
   N. Temperley, 415:Sep81-604
Metken, G. Herbert List: Photographs
1930-1970.*
   A. Ross, 364:Jun81-5
Metlitzki, D. The Matter of Araby in
Medieval England.*
   N. Daniel, 318(JAOS):Jul/Sep80-343
   M.A. Manzalaoui, 382(MAE):1981/1-180
   R.H. Robbins, 72:Band217Heft2-414
Métraux, A. - see Gurwitsch, A.
"Metropol'."*
   D. Milivojević, 558(RLJ):Spring-Fall181-
303
Metz, J.B. Faith in History and Society.
Theology of the World.
   D. Sturm, 185:Jul82-733
Metzeltin, M. Altspanisches Ememantar-
buch. (Vol 1)
   T.J. Walsh, 350:Jun81-495
Meuli, K. and others - see Bachofen, J.K.
Meunier, P. Anecdotes Asquinoises.
   M.G. Hydak, 207(FR):Dec80-373
Meves, H. Studien zu König Rother, Herzog
Ernst und Grauer Rock (Orendel).*
   P.K. Stein, 680(ZDP):Band99Heft3-441
Mey, J.L., ed. Pragmalinguistics.*
   E. Burgschmidt, 38:Band99Heft3/4-414
205(FMLS):Jan80-93
Meyer, C. Facing Reality.
   639(VQR):Spring81-64
Meyer, L. Israel Now.
   S. Stern, 441:18Jul82-10
Meyer, M. Several More Lives to Live.
   R.J. Schneider, 183(ESQ):Vol27No1-57
Meyer, M., ed. Summer Days.
   J. Lucas, 617(TLS):22Jan82-91
Meyer, N. Confessions of a Homing Pigeon.*
   P. Taylor, 617(TLS):26Mar82-361
Meyer, P. The Yale Murder.
   R. Coles, 442(NY):26Jul82-89
   V.S. Navasky, 441:6Jun82-7
Meyer, P.A. and C. MacAndrews. Transmi-
gration in Indonesia.
   L. Manderson, 293(JASt):Nov80-201
Meyer, P.G. Satzverknüpfungsrelationen.
   W. Wildgen, 685(ZDL):1/1981-79
Meyer-Hermann, D., ed. Sprechen — Handeln —
Interaktion.
   H. Harnisch, 682(ZPSK):Band33Heft5-625
Meyerhold, V. Ecrits sur le Théâtre.
(Vol 3) (B. Picon-Vallin, ed and trans)
   C. Amiard-Chevrel, 549(RLC):Jul-Dec81-
491
Meyerowitz, J. St. Louis and the Arch.
   P. Hodges, 62:Jan81-66

Meyers, J. The Enemy.*
   J. Beckett, 59:Dec81-461
   D. Donoghue, 453(NYRB):29Apr82-28
   442(NY):3May82-166
Meyers, J., ed. Wyndham Lewis.*
   J. Beckett, 59:Dec81-461
   G. Woodcock, 102(CanL):Spring81-150
Meyers, J. Katherine Mansfield.*
   D.B. Kesterson, 573(SSF):Summer81-327
Meyers, J. Married to Genius.
   C. MacCulloch, 526:Winter81-89
Meyers, W.E. Aliens and Linguists.*
   S. Gresham, 577(SHR):Spring81-188
   D. Ketterer, 106:Winter81-361
Meyfart, J.M. Tuba novissima Das ist Von
den vier letzten Dingen des Menschen
1626. (E. Trunz, ed)
   H-H. Krummacher, 224(GRM):Band31Heft3-
378
Meyrick, B. Cockles is Convenient.
   J.K.L. Walker, 617(TLS):12Feb82-170
Micha, A. - see "Lancelot, roman en prose
du XIIIe siècle"
Michael, J. Deceptions.
   C. Schine, 441:16May82-18
Michaels, L. The Men's Club.*
   D. Kubal, 249(HudR):Autumn81-460
   W. Scammell, 364:Oct81-96
Michaels, L. and C. Ricks, eds. The State
of the Language.*
   J.R. Gaskin, 569(SR):Spring81-298
   529(QQ):Spring81-195
Michaud, G. and E. Marc. Vers une science
des civilisations?
   W. Greenberg, 207(FR):Feb82-450
Michaux, H. Au pays de la Magie.* (P.
Broome, ed)
   M. Bowie, 402(MLR):Apr81-480
Michaux, H. Poteaux d'angle.*
   D. Leuwers, 450(NRF):May81-112
Michaux, H. Une Voie pour l'insubordina-
tion.
   P-J. Founau, 98:Jun-Jul81-709
   D. Leuwers, 450(NRF):Jan81-116
Michaux, J-P., ed. George Gissing.
   R.S.P., 148:Autumn81-90
   445(NCF):Dec81-380
Michel, D. Ayenbite of Inwyt. (Vol 2)
(P. Gradon, ed)
   T. Heffernan, 589:Jul81-673
Michel, H. Paris Allemand.
   M.R.D. Foot, 617(TLS):12Feb82-158
Michel, H. Paris résistant.
   M.R.D. Foot, 617(TLS):31Dec82-1450
Michel, N. Le repos de Penthésilée.
   A. Badiou, 98:Jun-Jul81-680
   R.A. Champagne, 207(FR):Oct81-161
Michel, P. Mirage.
   K. Mezei, 102(CanL):Autumn80-119
   A. Pokorny, 296(JCF):No31/32-238
di Michele, M. Bread and Chocolate
[together with] Wallace, B. Marrying
into the Family.
   R. Brown, 99:Feb82-37
di Michele, M. Mimosa and Other Poems.
   G. Coggins, 628(UWR):Spring-Summer82-
112
   P. Smith, 150(DR):Winter81/82-760
Michelet, C. Les Palombes ne passeront
plus.
   A. Thiher, 207(FR):Dec81-307

Michell, G. An Architectural Description
and Analysis of the Early Western Caluk-
yan Temples.*
    M. Meister, 318(JAOS):Apr/Jun80-154
Michels, V. Mittelhochdeutsche Grammatik.
(5th ed) (H. Stopp, ed)
    M.L. Wentzler, 215(GL):Winter81-290
Michelsen, P. Der Bruch mit der Vater-
Welt.
    J.L. Sammons, 221(GQ):May81-349
Michelson, W. and others. The Child in
the City. (Vol 2)
    G.R. Lowe, 529(QQ):Spring81-13
Michelson, W., S.V. Levine and E. Michel-
son, eds. The Child in the City. (Vol
1)
    G.R. Lowe, 529(QQ):Spring81-13
Michener, J.A. Space.
    J.N. Wilford, 441:19Sep82-3
Michielsen, G. The Preparation of the
Future.
    C. Hill, 400(MLN):Apr81-697
Michon, J. Mallarmé et "Les Mots
anglais."*
    D.M. Betz, 207(FR):Mar81-600
    M. Lemaire, 107(CRCL):Winter81-131
Mickelsen, W.C. Hugo Riemann's Theory of
Harmony [together with] Riemann, H.
History of Music Theory. (Bk 3) (W.C.
Mickelsen, ed and trans)
    P.J.P., 412:Aug80-246
Mickelsson, U. Bibliografier och uppslags-
verk.
    T. Geddes, 562(Scan):Nov81-240
Micros, M. Upstairs Over the Ice Cream.
    L. Mathews, 628(UWR):Fall-Winter81-119
Midbøe, H. Peer Gynt — teatret og tiden
Hans Jacob Nilsen og den "antiromantiske"
revolt.
    M. Ritzu, 462(OL):Vol36No1-92
Middell, E. and others. Exil in den USA.
    T. Rietzschel, 654(WB):4/1981-149
Middlebrook, D. Sweet My Love.
    J. Wilson, 617(TLS):26Feb82-220
Middlekauff, R. The Glorious Cause.
    H. Brogan, 362:2Sep82-23
    P. Marshall, 617(TLS):12Nov82-1249
    G.S. Wood, 453(NYRB):12Aug82-4
    442(NY):26Jul82-96
Middleton, C. Carminalenia.*
    T. Eagleton, 565:Vol22No2-73
    C. Lambert, 97(CQ):Vol 10No1-84
Middleton, C.F. The Dance in the Village.
    A. Bold, 617(TLS):7May82-515
Middleton, S. Blind Understanding.
    J. Mellors, 362:13May82-27
Middleton, T. The Second Maiden's Trag-
edy.* (A. Lancashire, ed)
    R. Gill, 541(RES):Aug81-324
    J.E. Neufeld, 627(UTQ):Summer81-107
    M.L. Wine, 677(YES):Vol 11-247
Middleton, T. The Selected Plays of
Thomas Middleton.* (D.L. Frost, ed)
    P. Hollindale, 677(YES):Vol 11-245
    G.B. Shand, 539:Feb82-60
Midgley, M. Beast and Man.*
    J. Beatty, 529(QQ):Winter81-607
    D.L. Hull, 482(PhR):Apr81-307
Midgley, M. Heart and Mind.
    D. Locke, 617(TLS):15Jan82-46
Mieses, M. Die Entstehungsursache der
jüdischen Dialekte.
    P. Wexler, 355(LSoc):Aug81-294

Mieth, G. Friedrich Hölderlin.
    C.F. Köpp, 654(WB):2/1981-182
Miething, C. Marivaux.
    S. Jüttner, 72:Band217Heft2-476
Mignucci, M. L'Argomentazione Dimostra-
tiva in Aristotele.
    T. Ebert, 53(AGP):Band62Heft1-85
Migoyo, G.D. - see under Díaz Migoyo, G.
Míguez Bonino, J. Christians and Marxists.
Doing Theology in a Revolutionary Situa-
tion.
    D. Sturm, 185:Jul82-733
Mihura, M. Tres sombreros de copa. (J.
Rodríguez Padrón, ed)
    J.E. Dial, 238:Mar81-156
Mijuskovic, B.L. Loneliness in Philosophy,
Psychology, and Literature.
    P.S., 185:Oct81-195
    W.E. Steinkraus, 484(PPR):Dec81-298
Mikes, G. How to be Seventy.
    K. Fitz Lyon, 617(TLS):5Mar82-247
    F. Watson, 362:18Mar82-23
Mikhail, E.H. The Art of Brendan Behan.
    A. Boué, 189(EA):Oct-Dec81-492
    W.T. O'Malley, 70:Oct80-35
Mikhail, E.H. Brendan Behan, An Annotated
Bibliography of Criticism.
    R.H., 305(JIL):Jan81-94
    M. Levin, 174(Éire):Winter81-155
Mikhail, E.H., ed. Lady Gregory, Inter-
views and Recollections.*
    C. Abbott, 174(Éire):Spring81-146
    A. Clune, 447(N&Q):Oct80-470
Mikhail, E.H. Oscar Wilde: An Annotated
Bibliography of Criticism.*
    M. Levin, 174(Éire):Winter81-155
Milanesi, V. Logica della valutazione et
etica naturalistica in Dewey.
    H.W. Schneider, 319:Apr81-273
Milbury-Steen, S.L. European and African
Stereotypes in Twentieth-Century Fic-
tion.*
    E. Palmer, 268(IFR):Winter82-47
Mileck, J. Hermann Hesse: Biography and
Bibliography.*
    G. Kleine, 680(ZDP):Band99Heft4-623
Mileck, J. Hermann Hesse: Life and Art.
    D. Bathrick, 406:Summer81-240
Miles, B. and J.C. Trewin. Curtain Calls.
    H. Hobson, 617(TLS):22Jan82-86
Miles, G.B. Virgil's "Georgics."
    J. Griffin, 123:Vol31No1-23
    D.M. Halperin, 121(CJ):Oct/Nov81-70
Miles, J. Coming To Terms.
    S.M. Gilbert, 491:Oct81-35
Miles, M.W. The Odyssey of the American
Right.
    J. Rieder, 676(YR):Winter82-xvii
Miles, P. and H. Pitcher - see Chekhov, A.
Mileur, J-P. Vision and Revision.
    J. Beer, 617(TLS):17Dec82-1389
Milgate, W. - see Donne, J.
Milhous, J. Thomas Betterton and the
Management of Lincoln's Inn Fields,
1695-1708.*
    566:Spring81-120
Milik, J.T., ed. The Books of Enoch.
    J. Vander Kam, 318(JAOS):Jul/Sep80-360
Miliukov, P.N. The Russian Revolution.*
(Vol 1) (R. Stites, ed)
    J. Keep, 575(SEER):Apr81-309

Mill, J.S. The Collected Works of John
Stuart Mill.* (Vol 1: Autobiography and
Literary Essays.) (J.M. Robson and J.
Stillinger, eds)
B.B., 185:Jan82-404
S. Collini, 617(TLS):26Mar82-331
J.B. Schneewind, 400(MLN):Dec81-1231
Mill, J.S. The Collected Works of John
Stuart Mill. (Vol 9: An Examination
of Sir William Hamilton's Philosophy
and of the Principal Philosophical
Questions Discussed in his Writings.)
(J.M. Robson, ed)
K. Britton, 483:Apr81-264
F. Sparshott, 178:Summer81-239
Millar, F. The Emperor in the Roman
World (31 B.C. — A.D. 337).*
A. Chastagnol, 555:Vol54fasc1-196
Millar, M. Mermaid.
N. Callendar, 441:14Feb82-22
442(NY):18Jan82-130
de Mille, A. America Dances.*
P. Migel, 151:Nov81-87
de Mille, R. The Don Juan Papers.
T.J. Lyon, 649(WAL):Summer81-149
Miller, A. Arthur Miller's Collected
Plays. (Vol 2)
385(MQR):Winter82-218
Miller, B.S. - see Jayadeva
Miller, C. A Childhood in Scotland.
T. Fitton, 617(TLS):19Feb82-192
Miller, C. and K. Swift. The Handbook of
Nonsexist Writing.
M. Shear, 35(AS):Winter81-301
Miller, C.H. - see Erasmus
Miller, D. Philosophy and Ideology in
Hume's Political Thought.
D. Forbes, 617(TLS):19Feb82-183
Miller, D.A. Narrative and Its Discon-
tents.*
D.P. Deneau, 268(IFR):Winter82-66
Miller, G. History and Human Existence.
J.N. Gray, 518:Apr81-111
Miller, G.A. Language and Speech.
S. Sutherland, 617(TLS):1Jan82-16
A.M. Zwicky, 350:Sep82-735
Miller, G.A. and E. Lenneberg, eds. Psy-
chology and Biology of Language and
Thought.
D. Bekerian, 297(JL):Mar81-134
Miller, H. Joey. Book of Friends. (Vol
1)
R. Jones, 649(WAL):Winter81-304
Miller, H. Hugh Miller, Outrage and Order.
(G. Rosie, ed)
O.D. Edwards, 617(TLS):2Apr82-387
Miller, H. The World of Lawrence.* (E.J.
Hinz and J.J. Teunissen, eds)
D. Gutierrez, 649(WAL):Summer81-147
J. Meyers, 594:Winter81-449
Miller, H. and W. Fowlie. Letters of
Henry Miller and Wallace Fowlie (1943-
1972).
R. Jones, 649(WAL):Winter81-304
Miller, J. History and Human Existence
from Marx to Merleau-Ponty.
B. Rigby, 208(FS):Apr81-245
Miller, J. Many Junipers, Heartbeats.
P. Schjeldahl, 472:Spring/Summer81-284
T. Swiss, 436(NewL):Fall81-119
Miller, J. and B. Van Loon. Darwin for
Beginners.
442(NY):8Nov82-172

Miller, J.C., ed. The African Past Speaks.
D. Ben-Amos, 2(AfrA):May81-28
Miller, J.C., ed. Poe's Helen Remembers.
R.D. Jacobs, 495(PoeS):Jun81-11
J. Porte, 27(AL):Mar81-124
Miller, J.D., J. Drayton and T. Lyon. USA-
Hispanic South America Culture Capsules.
M.E. Beeson, 399(MLJ):Summer81-224
Miller, J.E., Jr. The American Quest for
a Supreme Fiction.*
L. Cederstrom, 106:Fall81-235
D.W. Hiscoe, 301(JEGP):Apr81-269
M. Johnson, 295(JML):Vol8No3/4-429
C.C. Walcutt, 50(ArQ):Spring81-77
Miller, J.F., with others. Assessing Com-
municative Behavior. (Vol 1)
P.P. Phillips, 583:Summer82-457
Miller, J.H. Fiction and Repetition.
R. Brown, 617(TLS):10Sep82-975
R. Langbaum, 441:4Apr82-15
Miller, J.W. The Definition of the Thing.
S.B., 185:Oct81-181
Miller, L.B., ed. The Collected Papers of
Charles Willson Peale and His Family.
L.B. Miller, 165(EAL):Winter81/82-288
Miller, M. The Logic of Language Develop-
ment in Early Childhood.
S. Foster, 350:Jun81-520
Miller, M.H. The Philosopher in Plato's
"Statesman."
S. Rosen, 480(P&R):Spring81-112
S.U., 543:Jun81-796
Miller, N.K. The Heroine's Text.
M. Butler, 184(EIC):Jul81-246
C. Crosby, 454:Winter82-171
N. Le Coat, 400(MLN):May81-937
J.C. O'Neal, 188(ECr):Winter81-113
E. Showalter, 546(RR):Jan81-112
J.H. Stewart, 207(FR):Apr81-737
Miller, P. The Responsibility of Mind in
a Civilization of Machines.* (J. Crow-
ell and S.J. Searl, Jr., eds)
J. Rambeau, 568(SCN):Summer-Fall81-68
J. Rosenmeier, 165(EAL):Winter81/82-
282
Miller, P. Sources for "The New England
Mind." (J. Hoopes, ed)
E. Elliott, 165(EAL):Fall82-180
Miller, P.B. - see von Kleist, H.
Miller, R. - see "Brassaï: The Artists of
My Life"
Miller, R., C.T. Smith and J. Fisher, eds.
Social and Economic Change in Modern
Peru.
R.B. St. John, 37:Apr81-26
Miller, R.A. Origins of the Japanese Lan-
guage.
Ozawa Shigeo, 285(JapQ):Oct-Dec81-566
J. Patrie, 350:Sep82-699
G. Wenck, 407(MN):Autumn81-335
Miller, R.F. Dostoevsky and "The Idiot."
M.V. Jones, 617(TLS):4Jun82-621
G. Rosenshield, 268(IFR):Summer82-142
Miller, R.H. Graham Greene.*
A.R. Redway, 78(BC):Spring81-106
Miller, R.J. Japan's First Bureaucracy.
A.R. Lewis, 318(JAOS):Apr/Jun80-209
Miller, R.M., ed. "Dear Master."
C.B. Dew, 9(AlaR):Jan81-65
Miller, S.C. "Benevolent Assimilation."
R.E. Welch, Jr., 441:21Nov82-11

Miller, W.D. Dorothy Day.
M. Harrington, 441:13Jun82-3
442(NY):30Aug82-91
Millett, K. Going to Iran.
C.D. May, 441:16May82-14
Millgate, J., ed. Editing Nineteenth-
Century Fiction.*
J. Gold, 178:Spring81-114
Millgate, M. Thomas Hardy.
J. Bayley, 453(NYRB):7Oct82-9
M. Jacobus, 617(TLS):16Jul82-759
F. Kermode, 61:Jun82-93
G. Levine, 441:9May82-11
C. Lock, 362:10Jun82-26
Milligan, D. Reasoning and the Explana-
tion of Actions.*
A.R. White, 518:Jul81-162
Milligan, S. Indefinite Articles and
Scunthorpe.
V. Cunningham, 617(TLS):15Jan82-51
Millor, W.J. and C.N.L. Brooke - see John
of Salisbury
Mills, A.D. The Place-Names of Dorset.
(Pt 2)
K.B. Harder, 424:Mar81-90
M.F. Wakelin, 382(MAE):1981/2-353
Mills, F.V., Sr. Bishop By Ballot.
J.B. Bell, 656(WMQ):Oct81-747
Mills, H. Mailer.
M. Harris, 441:19Dec82-10
Mills, J. Skevington's Daughter.
R.W. Harvey, 102(CanL):Spring80-129
Mills, R.F. - see Wojowasito, S.
Milne, C. The Hollow on the Hill.
B. Sibley, 362:19Aug82-23
Milne, J. Tyro.
J. Melmoth, 617(TLS):17Dec82-1398
Milne, P. John David.
S.J. Newman, 617(TLS):25Jun82-702
Milner, A. John Milton and the English
Revolution.*
C. Hill, 366:Autumn81-228
Milner, J-C. De la syntaxe à l'interpréta-
tion.
K.E.M. George, 208(FS):Apr81-242
Milner, M. - see Bertrand, A.
Miłosz, C. Bells in Winter.*
A. Cluysenaar, 565:Vol22No2-62
A. Young, 148:Winter81-81
Miłosz, C. The Issa Valley.*
G. Perez, 249(HudR):Winter81/82-614
Miłosz, C. Native Realm.* Selected Poems.
S. Baranczak, 472:Fall/Winter81-62
Miłosz, C. Visions from San Francisco Bay.
L. Edel, 441:17Oct82-24
J. Symons, 617(TLS):24Dec82-1426
442(NY):20Sep82-155
Miłosz, C. - see Wat, A.
Milrad, A. and E. Agnew. The Art World.
K. Kritzwiser, 73:Sep/Oct80-57
Milroy, J. Regional Accents of English:
Belfast.
P. Craig, 617(TLS):19Feb82-192
Milroy, L. Language and Social Networks.
J.B. Pride, 350:Mar82-231
Milton, J. Complete Prose Works of John
Milton. (Vol 7) (R.W. Ayers, ed)
G.M. Crump, 569(SR):Fall81-628
C. Hill, 366:Autumn81-228
639(VQR):Autumn81-129

Milton, J.R. The Novel of the American
West.
S. Atherton, 268(IFR):Summer82-152
W. Bloodworth, 584(SWR):Summer81-321
J.H. Maguire, 27(AL):May81-336
M. Westbrook, 649(WAL):Spring81-61
"Milton Studies."* (Vol 12) (J.D.
Simmonds, ed)
J. Egan, 568(SCN):Summer-Fall81-37
D. Haskin, 613:Jun81-226
"Milton Studies."* (Vol 13) (J.D. Sim-
monds, ed)
D.L. Russell, 568(SCN):Winter81-83
B. Sherry, 67:Nov81-247
"Milton Studies." (Vol 14) (J.D. Simmonds,
ed)
G.M. Crump, 569(SR):Fall81-628
Milward, P. Religious Controversies of
the Elizabethan Age.* Religious Contro-
versies of the Jacobean Age.*
T.N. Corns, 506(PSt):May81-96
Minai, N. Women in Islam.*
A. Soueif, 617(TLS):10Sep82-977
Minčeva, A. Starob"lgarski kirilski
otk"sleci.
A. Martini, 688(ZSP):Band42Heft1-208
Minenko, N.A. Russkaia krest'ianskaia
sem'ia v zapadnoi Sibiri, XVIII-pervoi
XIX v.
P. Czap, Jr., 550(RusR):Oct81-447
Miner, E. Japanese Linked Poetry.*
E. Ramirez-Christensen, 244(HJAS):
Dec81-555
Miner, E., ed. Literary Uses of Typology
from the Late Middle Ages to the Pres-
ent.*
G. Reedy, 173(ECS):Spring81-324
Miner, V. Blood Sisters.*
A. Gottlieb, 441:22Aug82-11
Miner, V. Murder in the English Depart-
ment.
T. Warr, 617(TLS):5Nov82-1231
Ming, K. - see under Kao Ming
Mingay, G. Mrs. Hurst Dancing.
V. Glendinning, 617(TLS):22Jan82-91
Mingay, G.E., ed. The Victorian Country-
side.*
135:Oct81-92
Mingtao, Z. and others - see under Zhang
Mingtao and others
Minguet, P. Esthétique du rococo.
P. Somville, 542:Jan-Mar81-122
Minicucci, M.J. Una biblioteca all'-
incanto.
O. Ragusa, 276:Spring81-67
Mink, L.O. A "Finnegans Wake" Gazetteer.*
M. Beja, 395(MFS):Summer80-276
R. Boyle, 577(SHR):Winter81-86
Minninger, M. Von Clermont zum Wormser
Konkordat.
H.E.J. Cowdrey, 382(MAE):1981/1-188
Mino, Y., comp. Boîtes à encens japon-
aises redécouvertes.
M. Hickman, 318(JAOS):Apr/Jun80-210
Minogue, V. Nathalie Sarraute and the War
of the Words.*
L.S. Roudiez, 268(IFR):Summer82-136
Minor, R.N. Sri Aurobindo.
P. Mundschenk, 293(JASt):Nov80-174
Minta, S. Love Poetry in Sixteenth-
Century France.*
B.L.O. Richter, 551(RenQ):Spring80-112

Minta, S. Petrarch and Petrarchism.*
  J.G. Beaudry, 207(FR):Feb81-465
  N. Mann, 402(MLR):Apr81-423
  205(FMLS):Apr81-199
Minter, D. William Faulkner.*
  J. Bassett, 141:Summer81-281
  L. Paddock, 150(DR):Summer81-379
  N. Polk, 573(SSF):Fall81-466
  639(VQR):Autumn81-128
Minton, W.W. Concordance to the Hesiodic
  Corpus.
  A. Hoekstra, 394:Vol34fasc1/2-149
Mintz, J.R. The Anarchists of Casas
  Viejas.
  R. Carr, 453(NYRB):23Sep82-54
Minz, A. George Eliot and the Novel of
  Vocation.
  W. Myers, 677(YES):Vol 11-324
Miron, G. The Agonized Life.
  E. Dansereau, 526:Winter81-79
Mirow, K.R. and H. Maurer. Webs of Power.
  442(NY):22Mar82-165
Misenheimer, H.E. Rousseau on the Educa-
  tion of Women.
  M. Raaphorst-Rousseau, 207(FR):Apr82-
  679
von Mises, L. Economic Policy.
  M.N. Rothbard, 396(ModA):Summer81-304
Mishima, Y. La Mer de la Fertilité. (Vol
  3) [entry in prev was of Vols 1 and 2]
  L. Kovacs, 450(NRF):May81-138
Mishra, J.B. John Dryden.
  J. Freehafer, 566:Spring81-120
Mishra, V., ed. Rama's Banishment.
  U. Parameswaran, 314:Summer-Fall81-244
Misra, B.G. - see Koshal, S.
Misra, K.P., ed. Janata's Foreign Policy.
  N.D. Palmer, 293(JASt):Aug81-835
Misra, K.S. Terms of Address and Second
  Person Pronominal Usage in Hindi.
  O.N. Koul, 261:Dec79-315
Misrahi, R. Construction d'un château.
  T. Cordellier, 450(NRF):Oct81-138
Missfeldt, A. Die Abschnittsgliederung
  und ihre Funktion in mittelhochdeutscher
  Epik.*
  B. Schirok, 680(ZDP):Band100Heft1-129
"La Mission française de Pékin aux XVIIe
  et XVIIIe siècles."
  J.D. Spence, 318(JAOS):Jul/Sep80-378
Mitcalfe, B. Country Road. Uncle and
  Others. Harvestman.
  C. Dunsford, 368:Jun81-223
Mitcalfe, B. Pighunter.
  N. Simms, 292(JAF):Jan-Mar81-126
Mitcham, A. Inuit Summer.
  D. Barbour, 648(WCR):Jun80-74
Mitchell, A. For Beauty Douglas.
  C. Rumens, 617(TLS):29Oct82-1200
Mitchell, A. Westminster Man.
  P. Whitehead, 362:18Nov82-25
Mitchell, B. Morality.*
  R.L., 185:Apr82-591
  D.Z. Phillips, 479(PhQ):Apr81-179
Mitchell, D. Britten and Auden in the
  Thirties: The Year 1936.*
  M. Kennedy, 415:Jun81-379
  J.D. O'Hara, 434:Summer82-603
  M. Smith, 607:Jun81-42
Mitchell, D. "I'm a Man That Works."
  (R.E. Mitchell, ed)
  D. Tebbetts, 292(JAF):Jul-Sep81-387

Mitchell, D. and H. Keller, eds. Music
  Survey. (New series 1949-1952)
  M. Kennedy, 617(TLS):30Apr82-488
Mitchell, F. Navajo Blessingway Singer.
  (C.J. Frisbie and D.P. McAllester, eds)
  R. Zumwalt, 292(JAF):Jul-Sep81-385
Mitchell, G. Death of a Burrowing Mole.
  T.J. Binyon, 617(TLS):29Oct82-1196
Mitchell, H. The Essential Earthman.
  N. Johnston, 441:28Mar82-16
Mitchell, H.L. Mean Things Happening in
  This Land.
  V.F. Durr, 9(AlaR):Apr81-128
Mitchell, J.G. The Hunt.*
  R.G. Benson, 569(SR):Spring81-lxx
  J.P. Kilgo, 219(GaR):Fall81-673
Mitchell, J.T. A Thematic Analysis of Mme.
  d'Aulnoy's "contes de fées."*
  C.G.S. Williams, 399(MLJ):Spring81-92
Mitchell, L.C. Witnesses to a Vanishing
  America.
  H.D. Peck, 445(NCF):Mar82-482
Mitchell, P.M. Halldór Hermannsson.
  E.S. Firchow, 563(SS):Winter81-80
Mitchell, P.M. Henrik Pontoppidan.
  W.G. Jones, 563(SS):Winter81-106
Mitchell, R.L. Tristan Corbière.*
  A. Guyaux, 535(RHL):Jul-Oct81-825
  R. Killick, 402(MLR):Apr81-473
  E.R. Peschel, 207(FR):Oct80-169
Mitchell, R.L. The Poetic Voice of
  Charles Cros.
  L.C. Breunig, 546(RR):Jan81-114
Mitchell, T.N. Cicero: The Ascending
  Years.
  J. Linderski, 121(CJ):Feb/Mar82-275
Mitchell, W.J.T. Blake's Composite Art.*
  J. Beer, 402(MLR):Jul81-676
  J.M.Q. Davies, 161(DUJ):Dec80-116
  V.A. De Luca, 627(UTQ):Winter80/81-238
Mitchiner, J.E. Studies in the Indus
  Valley Inscriptions.
  R.J. Cohen, 293(JASt):May81-638
Mitnick, B.M. The Political Economy of
  Regulation.
  J.R.H., 185:Jul82-785
Mitrofanova, V.V. Russkie narodnye
  zagadki.
  J.L. Conrad, 574(SEEJ):Summer81-101
Mittelstrass, J., ed. Enzyklopädie Philos-
  ophie und Wissenschaftstheorie. (Vol 1)
  J. Bernhardt, 542:Apr-Jun81-242
Mitterand, H. Le Discours du roman.
  B. Picard, 207(FR):Dec81-258
Mitterrand, F. The Wheat and the Chaff.
  D.P. Calleo, 441:22Aug82-1
  S. Hoffmann, 453(NYRB):12Aug82-37
  F. Kersaudy, 362:21Oct82-21
  P. McCarthy, 617(TLS):19Nov82-1260
  442(NY):20Sep82-156
Mittner, L. Storia della letteratura
  tedesca.
  F. Delbono, 684(ZDA):Band109Heft1-4
Mitton, R. Master and Son.
  P. Morley, 102(CanL):Summer81-139
Miyajima, S. The Theatre of Man.*
  G.H.V. Bunt, 179(ES):Dec81-561
  C. Gauvin, 189(EA):Apr-Jun81-212
Mizuno, H. Folk Kilns I.
  W. Bates, 139:Dec81/Jan82-42
Mlikotin, A.M., ed. Western Philosophical
  Systems in Russian Literature.* (Vol 3)
  V. Setchkarev, 550(RusR):Jul81-357

Mlynář, Z. Nightfrost in Prague.*
  P.E. Zinner, 550(RusR):Apr81-214
Mo, T. Sour Sweet.
  P. Lewis, 617(TLS):7May82-502
  J. Mellors, 362:3Jun82-22
"La Mode et les poupées."
  R.L. Shep, 614:Fall82-19
"Modern Patchwork."
  P. Bach, 614:Summer82-17
Moe, P. - see d'Argenteuil, R.
Moe, T.M. The Organization of Interests.
  R.H., 185:Jan81-345
Moehlmann, J.F. A Concordance to the
  Complete Poems of John Wilmot, Earl
  of Rochester.
  566:Autumn81-49
Moelleken, W.W., G. Agler-Beck and R.E.
  Lewis, eds. Die Kleindichtung des
  Strickers. (Vols 4 and 5)
  E. Stutz, 684(ZDA):Band110Heft1-36
Moeller, J. and H. Liedloff. Deutsch
  heute, Grundstufe. (2nd ed)
  R.J. Rundell, 399(MLJ):Autumn81-354
Moffat, G. The Buckskin Girl.
  L. Duguid, 617(TLS):12Feb82-169
Moggach, D. Hot Water Man.
  J. Astor, 362:6May82-27
  L. Duguid, 617(TLS):30Apr82-481
Moggridge, D. - see Keynes, J.M.
Mohanty, B.C. Appliqué Craft of Orissa.
  R.L. Shep, 614:Spring82-11
Mohanty, B.C. Patachitras of Orissa.
  R.L. Shep, 614:Spring82-15
Mohr, W. Gottfried von Strassburg: Tris-
  tan und Isold.
  D.H. Green, 402(MLR):Jul81-737
Mohr, W. and W. Haug. Zweimal "Muspilli."
  C. Minis, 684(ZDA):Band109Heft2-50
Moinot, P. Le Guetteur d'ombre.
  P.A. Mankin, 207(FR):Apr81-767
Moisan, C. Poésie des frontières.*
  L. Hutcheon, 102(CanL):Winter80-145
Mojtabai, A.G. Autumn.
  B. De Mott, 441:8Aug82-1
  442(NY):6Sep82-106
Mok, Q.I.M. Manuel pratique de morpholo-
  gie d'ancien occitan.*
  M.S. Breslin, 545(RPh):Feb81-340
Molas, P.R. - see under Ramírez Molas, P.
Mole, J. Feeding the Lake.
  S. Ellis, 617(TLS):22Jan82-90
Molesworth, C. The Fierce Embrace.*
  L. Gallo, 134(CP):Spring81-78
Molho, M. Cervantes: "Raices folkloricas."
  J. Fribourg, 98:Mar80-312
Molin, S.E. and R. Goodefellowe. Dion
  Boucicault, The Shaughgran. (Pt 1)
  M. Levin, 174(Éire):Winter81-155
de Molina, T. - see under Tirso de Molina
Molinié, G. - see Chariton
Moll, K. Der junge Leibniz I.*
  J. Moreau, 542:Jul-Sep81-361
  G.H.R. Parkinson, 53(AGP):Band63Heft1-
  89
Mollenhauer, P. Friedrich Nicolais
  Satiren.
  R. Terras, 406:Winter81-457
Moller, M.E. Thoreau in the Human Commu-
  nity.
  D.G. Rohman, 27(AL):Nov81-544
  R.J. Schneider, 183(ESQ):Vol27No1-57
  639(VQR):Spring81-58

Molloy, T. The Green Line.
  A. Cheuse, 441:19Sep82-31
Molnar, T. Christian Humanism.
  D.J. Levy, 396(ModA):Winter81-87
Molnar, T. Theists and Atheists.
  A. Reix, 542:Apr-Jun81-243
Molony, C., H. Zobl and W. Stölting, eds.
  Deutsch im kontakt mit anderen Sprachen/
  German in Contact with Other Languages.*
  A.D. Foolen, 355(LSoc):Aug81-290
Moltmann, J. The Church in the Power of
  the Spirit. The Crucified God. Theol-
  ogy of Hope.
  D. Sturm, 185:Jul82-733
Moltó, A.D. - see under Domínguez Moltó, A.
Molyneux, W. The Case of Ireland Stated.*
  G. Midgley, 447(N&Q):Feb80-95
Mombello, G. Les avatars de "TALENTUM."
  L.S. Lerner, 545(RPh):May81-463
Momigliano, A. Essays in Ancient and
  Modern Historiography.
  R. Drews, 122:Jan81-56
Monaghan, D. Jane Austen.*
  A. Duckworth, 405(MP):Aug81-96
  D. Kaplan, 454:Spring82-267
  T. Lockwood, 445(NCF):Jun81-99
Monaghan, D., ed. Jane Austen in Social
  Context.
  D. Kaplan, 454:Spring82-267
Monaghan, J. The Neo-Firthian Tradition
  and its Contribution to General Linguis-
  tics.*
  C.S. Butler, 38:Band99Heft3/4-408
Monaghan, P. Women in Myth and Legend.
  L. Lerner, 617(TLS):4Jun82-619
Monahan, B.J. The Art of Singing.
  H.B.R., 412:Nov80-315
Monahan, J. Zsuzsi Roboz.
  J.P. Hodin, 89(BJA):Autumn81-381
Moncreiffe of that Ilk, I. Royal Highness.
  S. Runciman, 617(TLS):3Sep82-949
Mondjannagni, A.C. Campagnes et villes au
  sud de la Republique Populaire du Bénin.
  R. Clignet, 69:Vol150No2-232
Mondor, H. and L.J. Austin - see Mallarmé,
  S.
Monegal, E.R. - see under Rodríguez
  Monegal, E.
Monegal, E.R. and A. Reid - see under
  Rodríguez Monegal, E. and A. Reid
Monesi, I. La Voie lactée.
  N.Q. Maurer, 450(NRF):Apr81-133
"Money Income and Poverty Status of Fami-
  lies and Persons."
  A. Hacker, 453(NYRB):18Mar82-37
Mongrédien, J. Jean-François Le Sueur.
  Catalogue thématique de l'oeuvre com-
  plète du compositeur Jean-François Le
  Sueur (1760-1837).
  D.K. Holoman, 317:Fall81-566
Monière, D. Ideologies in Quebec.
  J. Hutcheson, 99:Feb82-41
Moñino, A.R.R. - see under Rodríguez
  Moñino, A.R.
Monkman, L. A Native Heritage.
  V.P. and R.H. Miller, 150(DR):Winter81/
  82-771
Monnier, A. Un Publiciste Frondeur sous
  Catherine II: Nicolas Novikov.
  I. de Madariaga, 617(TLS):23Jul82-802
Monnier, G. and B. Rose. History of an
  Art: Drawing.*
  C. Eisler, 127:Summer81-183

Moore, J.H. Growth with Self-Management.
  D. McGlue, 575(SEER):Oct81-622
Moore, M. The Complete Poems of Marianne
  Moore.* (C.E. Driver, ed)
  D. Bromwich, 491:Mar82-340
  B.F. Engel, 659(ConL):Winter82-114
  G. Schulman, 29:Jul/Aug82-35
Moore, M.J., ed. Quincentennial Essays on
  St. Thomas More.
  J.N. King, 541(RES):Feb81-73
  J.B. Trapp, 677(YES):Vol 11-230
Moore, R. The Social Impact of Oil.
  J. Hunter, 617(TLS):10Sep82-967
Moore, S. Marx and the Choice between
  Socialism and Communism.
  S. Hook, 550(RusR):Jan81-55
  M.W. Howard, 142:Summer80-187
Moore, S. My Old Sweetheart.
  A. Tyler, 441:17Oct82-14
  442(NY):8Nov82-171
Moorey, P.R.S. Kish Excavations 1923-1933.
  N. Yoffee, 318(JAOS):Apr/Jun80-198
Moorman, M. George Macaulay Trevelyan.*
  R.H. Evans, 366:Spring81-135
Mopsik, C. - see Maïmonide, M.
Mora, J.F. - see under Ferrater Mora, J.
Mora, M.H. - see under Halley Mora, M.
Morales, A.I. El ayuntamiento de Sevilla.
  I. Mateo Gómez, 48:Jul-Sep81-377
Morales, H.L. - see under López Morales, H.
Morales y Marín, J.L. Vicente López.
  J.E. Arias Anglés, 48:Apr-Jun81-228
Morales Oliver, L. Sinopsis de "Don
  Quijote."*
  J.J. Allen, 552(REH):Jan81-151
de Moratín, L.F. - see under Fernández de
  Moratín, L.
Moraux, P. Le commentaire d'Alexandre
  d'Aphrodise aux "Seconds Analytiques"
  d'Aristote.
  E. Berti, 53(AGP):Band63Heft1-84
  É. des Places, 555:Vol54fasc2-363
Moravcsik, E.A. and J.R. Wirth, eds. Cur-
  rent Approaches to Syntax.
  R.W. Langacker, 350:Jun82-399
Moravia, A. and G. Prezzolini. Lettere.
  S. Vinall, 617(TLS):3Dec82-1345
Morawetz, T. The Philosophy of Law.
  D.T. Ozar, 185:Apr82-572
Morawetz, T. Wittgenstein and Knowledge.*
  H.P. Gallacher, 518:Jan81-20
Mordden, E. The Hollywood Musical.*
  A. Croce, 442(NY):18Jan82-128
  G. Kaufman, 362:20May82-26
More, T. The Complete Works of St. Thomas
  More.* (Vol 9: The Apology.) (J.B.
  Trapp, ed)
  J. Mezciems, 447(N&Q):Aug80-361
More, T. Écrits de prison. (P. Leyris,
  trans)
  M.F. Meurice, 450(NRF):Apr81-147
More, T. L'"Utopie" de Thomas More.* (A.
  Prévost, ed and trans)
  A. Reix, 542:Jul-Sep81-344
"Thomas More 1477-1977."
  J-C. Margolin, 535(RHL):Mar-Apr81-279
Moreau, C. Freud et l'occultisme.
  J-M. Gabaude, 542:Jan-Mar81-132
Moreau, J. Stoïcisme.
  M. Adam, 542:Apr-Jun81-270
Moreau, M-L. "C'est."*
  N.L. Corbett, 545(RPh):Feb81(supp)-203
Moreau, P.F. - see Spinoza, B.

Moreh, S. - see al-Jabartī, 'A.R.
Morel, J. and A. Viala - see Racine, J.
Moreland, F.L., ed. Strategies in Teach-
  ing Greek and Latin.
  G.W. Lawall, 124:Jul-Aug82-381
Morello, J. Jean Rotrou.
  J. Moravcevich, 207(FR):Mar82-547
Morency, P. Torrentiel.
  E-M. Kroller, 102(CanL):Winter80-132
Morency, P. Tournebire et le Malin Frigo
  [and] Les Écoles de Bon Bazou.
  J. Ripley, 102(CanL):Summer80-113
Moreno, C.F., J. Ortega and I.A. Shulman -
  see under Fernández Moreno, C., J.
  Ortega and I.A. Shulman
Moreno Baéz, E. - see de Montemayor, J.
Morère, P. L'Oeuvre de James Beattie.
  I. Ross, 571(ScLJ):Winter81-108
Moretti, L., ed. Inscriptiones Graecae
  urbis Romae. (Vol 3)
  A.G. Woodhead, 303(JoHS):Vol 101-224
Morf, G. The Polish Shades and Ghosts of
  Joseph Conrad.
  J. Batchelor, 447(N&Q):Aug80-383
  D. Hewitt, 541(RES):Aug81-353
Morgan, C. Heirlooms.
  C. Grill, 287:May81-25
Morgan, D.H. Harvesters and Harvesting
  1840-1900.
  P. Horn, 617(TLS):28May82-590
Morgan, E. Poems of Thirty Years.
  D. Davis, 362:16Dec82-23
  C. Rumens, 617(TLS):10Dec82-1376
Morgan, E.G. Provenance and Problematics
  of "Sublime and Alarming Images" in
  Poetry.
  G. Carnall, 571(ScLJ):Summer80-91
Morgan, F. Northbook.
  J. Parini, 617(TLS):2Jul82-720
Morgan, H.W. New Muses.
  J. Bochner, 106:Winter81-345
Morgan, K.O. Rebirth of a Nation.*
  G. Hughes, 453(NYRB):18Nov82-69
Morgan, M.J. Molyneux's Question.*
  C.A.J. Coady, 63:Mar81-118
  S. Shute, 319:Apr81-255
Morgan, P. Oxford Libraries outside the
  Bodleian.* (2nd ed)
  354:Mar81-81
Morgan, R. Depth Perception.
  J. Parini, 617(TLS):12Nov82-1251
Morgan, R. Groundwork.* Zirconia Poems.
  Red Owl. Land Diving. Trunk and
  Thicket. Bronze Age.
  W. Harmon, 472:Fall/Winter81-5
Morgan, S. In the Meantime.*
  A. Duckworth, 405(MP):Aug81-96
  R. Folkenflik, 445(NCF):Jun81-95
  J. McMaster, 191(ELN):Jun81-304
  G.W. Ruoff, 661(WC):Summer81-169
Morgan, T. Churchill.
  P. Stansky, 441:13Jun82-12
  A.J.P. Taylor, 453(NYRB):15Jul82-33
  442(NY):12Jul82-104
Morgan, T. Maugham.*
  D.L. Higdon, 395(MFS):Winter80/81-708
Morgan, V. Babes in the Wood.
  O. Wymark, 157:Oct80-73
Morgan, W. Louisville, Architecture and
  the Urban Environment.
  M.R. Corbett, 576:May81-148

Morgan, W.N. Prehistoric Architecture in the Eastern United States.
B. Lewis, 576:Dec81-327
Morgenthaler, W. Bedrängte Positivität.
R.L. Jamison, 406:Fall81-359
Mōri, H. Japanese Portrait Sculpture.*
V. Harris, 39:Feb81-129
Mori, T. The Chauvinist and Other Stories.
C.L. Chua, 573(SSF):Fall81-470
Moriconi, V. Black Annis.
H. Eley, 617(TLS):10ct82-1075
Morin, E. Essai de stylistique comparée.
J. Morehen, 415:May81-316
Morin, E. La Vie de la vie.
J. Duvignaud, 450(NRF):Apr81-142
Morin, M. Les Annales de l'Hôtel-Dieu de Montréal 1659-1725. (G. Legendre, ed)
M. Lebel, 102(CanL):Autumn81-133
C. Poirier, 320(CJL):Fall81-241
Morin, M. and C. Bertrand. Le territoire imaginaire de la culture.
P. Coleman, 207(FR):Apr81-754
L. Hutcheon, 102(CanL):Winter80-145
Morínigo, M.A. and I. Lerner - see de Ercilla, A.
Morishima, M. Why has Japan "Succeeded"?
J. Hardie, 617(TLS):9Jul82-745
Morison, S. Selected Essays on the History of Letter-Forms in Manuscript and Print. (D. McKitterick, ed)
S.N. Antupit, 441:28Mar82-13
A. Bell, 617(TLS):2Apr82-372
H. Schmoller, 324:Apr82-292
Morison, S. and D.B. Updike. Selected Correspondence. (D. McKitterick, ed)
N. Barker, 78(BC):Summer81-259
Morisseau, R. Chanson de Roland.
A. Moorhead, 207(FR):May81-900
Morita, J.R. Kaneko Mitsuharu.
J. O'Brien, 407(MN):Spring81-97
Moritz, K.P. Karl Philipp Moritz: Werke. (H. Günther, ed)
T.J. Reed, 617(TLS):1Oct82-1083
Morley, F. Literary Britain.
529(QQ):Summer81-401
639(VQR):Spring81-58
Morley, J.W., ed. The Fateful Choice.
J. Lebra, 407(MN):Summer81-212
Morley, P. Morley Callaghan.
J. Orange, 296(JCF):No31/32-223
Morley, S., ed. Punch at the Theatre.
D.G., 214:Vol 10No37-118
Morlot, F. and J. Touzot - see Claudel, P. and F. Mauriac
Morón Arroyo, C. Nuevas meditaciones del "Quijote."
D.J. Viera, 552(REH):May81-300
Morón Arroyo, C. Sentido y forma de "La Celestina."
D.S. Severin, 545(RPh):Feb81-376
Morrall, J.B. Aristotle.*
D. Keyt, 479(PhQ):Jan81-68
Morrell, D. Blood Oath.
N. Callendar, 441:12Dec82-37
Morrice, K. For All I Know.
A. Bold, 617(TLS):7May82-515
Morris, B. - see Shakespeare, W.
Morris, C. - see Fiennes, C.
Morris, E. Corregidor.
C. Thorne, 617(TLS):20Aug82-906
Morris, F.O. British Birds. (T. Soper, ed)
R. O'Hanlon, 617(TLS):4Jun82-615

Morris, J. Londinium. (rev by S. Macready)
B. Cunliffe, 617(TLS):24Sep82-1039
Morris, J. Oxford. (rev)
S. Pickering, 569(SR):Winter81-xxiii
Morris, J., ed. The Oxford Book of Oxford.
S. Pickering, 569(SR):Winter81-xxiii
Morris, J. A Venetian Bestiary.
S.D. Smith, 441:5Dec82-65
442(NY):20Dec82-140
Morris, J. - see Ruskin, J.
Morris, M.F. Le Chevalier de Jaucourt.
A.W. Fairbairn, 402(MLR):Apr81-468
G. Vidan, 535(RHL):Jul-Oct81-782
Morris, N. and M. Tonry, eds. Crime and Justice. (Vol 2)
R.P.A., 185:Apr82-579
Morris, R. The Fate of the Universe.
T. Ferris, 441:4Apr82-16
Morris, R. Haig.
K. Kyle, 362:2Dec82-21
N. Lemann, 441:15Aug82-9
Morris, R.J. Cholera 1832.
S.E.D. Shortt, 529(QQ):Spring81-130
Morris, W. The Defence of Guenevere and other Poems. (M.A. Lourie, ed)
L. Goldstein, 385(MQR):Summer82-528
Morris, W. Earthly Delights, Unearthly Adornments.
J.J. Wydeven, 395(MFS):Summer80-348
Morris, W. Friday's Footprint.*
J.A. Boon, 454:Spring82-260
F. Merrell, 395(MFS):Winter80/81-726
Morris, W. James Jones.
D.R. Noble, 577(SHR):Summer81-272
Morris, W. Plains Song.*
J. Hafer, 649(WAL):Winter81-306
Morris, W. and M. Harper Dictionary of Contemporary Usage.*
T.J. Creswell, 35(AS):Spring-Summer77-145
"Wright Morris: Photographs and Words." (J. Alinder, ed)
A. Grundberg, 441:5Dec82-11
Morris-Jones, W.H. Politics Mainly Indian.
D.C. Potter, 293(JASt):May81-640
Morrison, B. Seamus Heaney.
P. Kemp, 362:22Jul82-20
C. Rawson, 617(TLS):3Sep82-941
Morrison, B. The Movement.*
M. Kirkham, 569(SR):Summer81-474
G. Ward, 97(CQ):Vol 10No1-67
639(VQR):Winter81-16
Morrison, B. and A. Motion, eds. The Penguin Book of Contemporary British Poetry.
G. Grigson, 362:25Nov82-25
Morrison, J. and C.F. Zabusky. American Mosaic.
639(VQR):Summer81-90
Morrison, K. The Mimetic Tradition of Reform in the West.
B. Stock, 617(TLS):5Nov82-1229
Morrison, P. Spiders' Games.
P. Bach, 614:Spring82-16
Morrison, T. Tar Baby.*
D. Kubal, 249(HudR):Autumn81-463
E. Milton, 676(YR):Winter82-254
V.A. Smith, 569(SR):Fall81-cxv
639(VQR):Autumn81-135
Morrissette, B. Intertextual Assemblage in Robbe-Grillet From "Topology" to "The Golden Triangle."
A. Thiher, 395(MFS):Summer80-352

Motsch, W., ed. Kontexte der Grammatik-
theorie.
G. Starke, 682(ZPSK):Band33Heft5-604
Mottahedeh, R.P. Loyalty and Leadership
in an Early Islamic Society.
M.W. Dols, 589:Oct81-891
C. Geertz, 453(NYRB):27May82-25
Motyl, A.J. The Turn to the Right.
R. Szporluk, 550(RusR):Apr81-202
Motz, R. Time as Joyce Tells It.
M. Beja, 395(MFS):Summer80-276
Mouchard, C. Perdre.
P. Pachet, 98:May80-481
Mouffe, C., ed. Gramsci and Marxist The-
ory.
F.H. Adler, 185:Jan82-365
Moule, C.F.D. Essays in New Testament
Interpretation.
J.L. Houlden, 617(TLS):5Nov82-1226
Moulton, E. Fatal Demonstrations.
639(VQR):Winter81-20
Moulton, J. and G.M. Robinson. The Organi-
zation of Language.
D.G. MacKay and J. Meister, 350:Sep82-
715
Mounier, J. La Fortune des écrits de J.-J.
Rousseau dans les pays de langue alle-
mande de 1782 à 1813.
L.R. Furst, 131(CL):Fall81-387
Mount, F. The Subversive Family.
R. Dinnage, 617(TLS):27Aug82-927
V. Glendinning, 362:8Jul82-21
Mouré, E. Empire, York Street.*
E. Nicol, 102(CanL):Winter80-108
Moure, N.D.W. William Louis Sonntag.
J.V. Turano, 16:Spring81-92
Moureau, F. Dufresny, auteur dramatique
(1657-1724).
J. Dickson, 207(FR):Apr82-678
R. Cuichemerre, 535(RHL):May-Jun81-459
P. Hourcade, 475:No15Pt1-174
Mourelatos, A.P.D., ed. The Pre-Socratics.
D. Pralon, 542:Apr-Jun81-255
Mouret, F.J-L. Les Traducteurs Anglais de
Pétrarque, 1754-1798.*
W. von Koppenfels, 72:Band217Heft1-162
Mourey, L. Grimm et Perrault, histoire,
structure, mise en texte des contes.
J. Prévot, 535(RHL):Mar-Apr81-294
de Mourgues, O. Two French Moralists.*
A.R. Curtis, 627(UTQ):Winter80/81-248
Moutsopoulos, E. Conformisme et déforma-
tion.
J-M. Cabaude, 542:Jan-Mar81-123
Moutsopoulos, E. La philosophie de la
musique dans la dramaturgie antique.
Le problème de l'imaginaire chez
Plotin.
J-M. Gabaude, 542:Jul-Sep81-333
Mowat, F. And No Birds Sang.
J.F. McLean, 102(CanL):Summer81-146
Mowat, F. The World of Farley Mowat. (P.
Davison, ed)
E. Thompson, 102(CanL):Autumn81-163
Mowrer, O.H., ed. Psychology of Language
and Learning.
P.H. Salus, 350:Dec81-976
Moxey, K.P.G. Pieter Aertsen, Joachim
Beuckelaer, and the Rise of Secular
Painting in the Context of the Reforma-
tion.
J. Spicer, 539:Feb82-63

Moyle, R.M. Songs of the Pintupi.
T.A. Jones, 187:Sep82-489
Moynihan, E.B. Paradise as a Garden in
Persia and Mughal India.
A. Topsfield, 90:Jul81-428
Muchembled, R. La Sorcière au Village —
XVe/XVIIIe siècle.
H. Cronel, 450(NRF):Feb81-132
Mück, H-D. Untersuchungen zur Überliefe-
rung und Rezeption spätmittelalterlicher
Lieder und Spruchgedichte im 15. und 16.
Jahrhundert.
G.F. Jones, 221(GQ):Nov81-498
Mück, H-D. and U. Müller, eds. Gesammelte
Vorträge der 600-Jahrfeier Oswalds von
Wolkenstein, Seis am Schlern 1977.
O. Sayce, 402(MLR):Apr81-498
Mudford, P. The Art of Celebration.
J-P. Vernier, 189(EA):Oct-Dec81-486
Mudrick, M. Nobody Here But Us Chickens.*
M. Bayles, 441:31Jan82-12
J. Wolcott, 453(NYRB):21Jan82-51
Mueller, D.C. Public Choice.
N. Frohlich, 185:Apr82-560
Mueller, L. The Need to Hold Still.*
S. Corey, 639(VQR):Autumn81-732
T. Hansen, 460(OhR):No28-124
Mueller, M. Children of Oedipus and Other
Essays on the Imitation of Greek Tragedy
1550-1800.
R.Y. Hathorn, 678(YCGL):No29-46
Mueller, R.K. Buzzwords.
W.W. Evans, 35(AS):Spring-Summer77-134
Mueller, R.K. Festival and Fiction in
Heinrich Wittenwiler's "Ring."*
H-J. Behr, 680(ZDP):Band99Heft1-139
Mugdan, J. Flexionsmorphologie und
Psycholinguistik.
K. Maroldt, 257(IRAL):Feb81-86
Muggeridge, M. Chronicles of Wasted Time.
(Vols 1 and 2)
N. Annan, 453(NYRB):10Jun82-18
Muggeridge, M. Like It Was.* (J. Bright-
Holmes, ed)
N. Annan, 453(NYRB):10Jun82-18
D. Lodge, 441:21Feb82-3
Muhlenfeld, E. Mary Boykin Chesnut.*
N.F. Cott, 676(YR):Autumn81-121
Mühlhäusler, P. Growth and Structure of
the Lexicon of New Guinea Pidgin.
E. Woolford, 350:Mar82-225
Muir, E. Civic Ritual in Renaissance
Venice.
R. Mackenney, 617(TLS):2Apr82-394
Muir, E. Poor Tom.
A. Bold, 617(TLS):2Apr82-388
Muir, E. Uncollected Scottish Criticism.
(A. Noble, ed)
J. Campbell, 617(TLS):2Apr82-388
Muir, F. A Book at Bathtime.
V. Glendinning, 617(TLS):24Dec82-1431
Muir, K., ed. Shakespeare Survey. (Vol
31)
T. Hawkes, 541(RES):Nov81-446
D.G. Watson, 551(RenQ):Summer80-282
Muir, K., ed. Shakespeare Survey.* (Vol
32)
M. Grivelet, 189(EA):Apr-Jun81-217
H. Jenkins, 611(TN):Vol35No3-140
Muir, K., ed. Shakespeare Survey.*
(Vol 33)
J.C. Trewin, 157:2ndQtr81-53

Muir, K. Shakespeare's Comic Sequence.*
  M. Campbell, 67:May81-107
  T.W. Craik, 161(DUJ):Jun81-251
Muir, K. Shakespeare's Sonnets.*
  J. Fuzier, 189(EA):Apr-Jun81-215
  R.L. Smallwood, 402(MLR):Jul81-667
Muir, K. Shakespeare's Tragic Sequence.*
  T.W. Craik, 161(DUJ):Jun81-251
Muir, K. The Singularity of Shakespeare
  and Other Essays.*
  M-M. Martinet, 189(EA):Jul-Sep81-338
Muir, K. The Sources of Shakespeare's
  Plays.* (rev)
  C. Hoy, 301(JEGP):Apr81-243
Muir, M. Charlotte Barton.
  E. Webby, 581:Sep81-363
Mujica, B. Aquí y ahora.*
  B.M. Class, 399(MLJ):Summer81-223
  A.E. Singer, 238:Mar81-168
Mujū, I. Collection de Sable et de
  pierres (Shasekishū).* (H.O. Rotermund,
  ed and trans)
  R.E. Morrell, 407(MN):Summer81-201
Mukarovsky, H. A Study of Western Nigri-
  tic.
  S. Brauner, 682(ZPSK):Band33Heft2-277
Mukařovský, J. Structure, Sign, and Func-
  tion.* (J. Burbank and P. Steiner, eds
  and trans) The Word and Verbal Art.
  L. Doležel, 599:Winter81-64
Mukherjee, M., ed. Considerations.
  U. Parameswaran, 314:Winter-Spring81-
  227
Mukherjee, M. The Twice Born Fiction.
  F.W. Blackwell, 314:Winter-Spring81-
  252
Mulder, J.W.F. and S.G.J. Hervey. The
  Strategy of Linguistics.
  H. Pilch, 660(Word):Aug80-239
  205(FMLS):Oct80-380
Muldoon, J. Popes, Lawyers, and Infidels.*
  J.A. Brundage, 377:Jul81-118
Muldoon, P. Why Brownlee Left.*
  M. De Shazer, 134(CP):Fall81-125
  H. Lomas, 364:Jun81-75
  S. O'Brien, 493:Jun81-60
  R. Pybus, 565:Vol22No3-72
Mulgan, R.G. Aristotle's Political
  Theory.*
  D. Keyt, 479(PhQ):Jan81-68
Mulhern, F. The Moment of "Scrutiny."*
  A. Wald, 42(AR):Winter81-130
  R. Wellek, 402(MLR):Jan81-175
Mullen, D.J. and J.F. Garganigo. El
  cuento hispánico.
  E. Echevarria, 399(MLJ):Winter81-450
Mullen, M. Kelly.
  T.O. Treadwell, 617(TLS):1Jan82-8
Müllenbrock, H-J. Popes Gesellschafts-
  lehre in "An Essay on Man."*
  U. Böker, 224(GRM):Band30Heft3-370
Müllenbrock, H-J. Whigs Kontra Tories.*
  A. Löffler, 224(GRM):Band30Heft4-472
von Müllenheim-Rechberg, B. Battleship
  Bismarck.
  J. Russell, 396(ModA):Summer81-331
Muller, C. Langue française et linguis-
  tique quantitative.
  R. Jolivet, 209(FM):Jul81-263
Muller, C. Le Vocabulaire du théâtre de
  Pierre Corneille.
  M.R. Margitić, 475:No15Pt1-186

Müller, C.W. Die Kurzdialoge der Appendix
  Platonica.
  H-J. Horn, 53(AGP):Band63Heft2-194
Müller, E.E. Grossvater, Enkel, Schwieger-
  sohn.
  J. Erben, 684(ZDA):Band110Heft4-175
von Müller, I. Handbuch der Altertumswis-
  senschaft. (Vol 10)
  J.A.C. Thomas, 303(JoHS):Vol 101-205
Muller, M. Ask the Cards.
  N. Callendar, 441:7Nov82-39
Müller, M. Philosophische Anthropologie.
  (W. Vossenkuhl, ed) Erfahrung und
  Geschichte. Sinn-Deutungen der
  Geschichte. Der Kompromiss oder Vom
  Unsinn und Sinn menschlichen Lebens.
  S. Müller, 489(PJGG):Band88Heft2-378
Muller, M. Préfiguration et structure
  romanesque dans "A la recherche du temps
  perdu."
  J. Murray, 207(FR):May81-875
  M-H. Thomas, 535(RHL):Nov-Dec81-1020
Müller, M. Sein und Geist. (2nd ed)
  W. Vossenkuhl, 489(PJGG):Band88Heft2-
  393
Müller, P. Löwen und Mischwesen in der
  archaischen griechischen Kunst.
  J.M. Cook, 303(JoHS):Vol 101-220
Müller, R., ed. Kulturgeschichte der
  Antike. (Vol 1) (2nd ed)
  A.H.M. Kessels, 394:Vol134fasc3/4-444
Muller, R. Virginities.
  J.K.L. Walker, 617(TLS):10Sep82-982
Müller, S. Vernunft und Technik.
  R. Maurer, 489(PJGG):Band88Heft1-190
Müller, U., ed. Oswald von Wolkenstein.
  F. Delbono, 684(ZDA):Band110Heft4-155
Müller, W.G. Die politische Rede bei
  Shakespeare.
  H.F. Plett, 490:Band12Heft3/4-526
Müller-Mertens, E. Die Reichsstruktur im
  Spiegel der Herrschaftspraxis Ottos des
  Grossen.
  T.F.X. Noble, 589:Jul81-634
Mullet, M. and R. Scott, eds. Byzantium
  and the Classical Tradition.
  A. Kazhdan, 617(TLS):2Apr82-394
Mullett, G.M. Spider Woman Stories.
  S.F. Sanderson, 203:Vol91No2-246
Mullin, C. A Very British Coup.
  T.J. Binyon, 617(TLS):29Oct82-1196
Mullin, M., with K.M. Muriello, eds.
  Theatre at Stratford-upon-Avon.
  R. Berry, 108:Summer81-146
  J.L. Styan, 130:Summer81-190
Muma, J.R. Language Handbook.
  L. Wilder, 583:Summer81-427
Mumford, L. My Works and Days.*
  M. Birnbaum, 396(ModA):Winter81-99
  B. Singer, 77:Summer81-278
Mumford, L. Sketches from Life: The Early
  Years.
  P. Goldberger, 441:16May82-13
  442(NY):10May82-168
Munby, J. Communicative Syllabus Design.*
  205(FMLS):Apr80-191
Munch-Petersen, E. Kilder til litteratur-
  søgning. (2nd ed)
  T. Geddes, 562(Scan):Nov81-240
Mundt, M., ed. Hákonar saga Hákonarsonar
  etter Sth. 8 fol., AM 325 VIII, 4° og AM
  304, 4°.
  J.E. Knirk, 563(SS):Spring81-218

Mundy, S. Elgar.
R. Anderson, 415:Feb81-108
Mungello, D.E. Leibniz and Confucianism.*
J.C. Creutz, 318(JAOS):Jan/Mar80-90
Y-T. Lai, 293(JASt):Aug81-767
Mungoshi, C. Some Kinds of Wounds.
C. Style, 362:18Nov82-27
Munitz, M.K. Contemporary Analytic Philosophy.
R.S.N., 185:Jul82-791
Muñoz, G.P. - see under Porras Muñoz, G.
Munro, D. Alexandre Dumas père.*
F.W.J. Hemmings, 208(FS):Jan81-79
Munro, E. Originals.*
N.F. Broude, 127:Summer81-180
Munsche, P.B. Gentlemen and Poachers.
E. Hobsbawm, 617(TLS):16Jul82-772
Muntéano, B. Corespondente. (E. Muntéano, ed)
T.J. Barbulesco, 549(RLC):Jul-Dec81-497
Munton, A. - see Lewis, W.
Munz, P. The Shapes of Time.
A.P. Fell, 125:Fall80-106
Münz-Koenen, I. and others. Literarisches Leben in der DDR 1945 bis 1960.
E. Röhner, 654(WB):10/1981-182
Murakami, S. Sānkuya Tetsugaku Kenkyū.
Masaaki Hattori, 259(IIJ):Oct81-302
Murakami Shigeyoshi. Japanese Religion in the Modern Century.
Morioka Kiyomi, 285(JapQ):Jan-Mar81-106
Murata, K., ed. An Industrial Geography of Japan.
D.H. Kornhauser, 293(JASt):Aug81-792
Muratorio, R. A Feast of Color.
R.L. Shep, 614:Winter82-17
Murdoch, A. "The People Above."
I.R. Christie, 83:Autumn81-240
Murdoch, B.O. and M. Read. Siegfried Lenz.*
205(FMLS):Jan80-91
Murdoch, I. The Fire and the Sun.*
J.P. Anton, 319:Apr81-239
J. Sprute, 53(AGP):Band63Heft2-183
Murdoch, I. Nuns and Soldiers.*
P.J. Conradi, 148:Autumn81-63
639(VQR):Autumn81-135
Murdoch, J. and others. The English Miniature.
M. Edmond, 617(TLS):19Mar82-304
Murin, C. Nietzsche-Problème.
H. Weinmann, 154:Dec81-812
Muro, A.J. The Collected Stories of Amado Muro.*
L. McMurtry, 441:30May82-8
Murphy, B. The Enigma Variations.
N. Callendar, 441:7Feb82-20
P. Kemp, 617(TLS):19Feb82-198
Murphy, B.A. The Brandeis/Frankfurter Connection.
A. Schlesinger, Jr., 441:21Mar82-5
442(NY):5Apr82-198
Murphy, D.J. - see Lady Gregory
Murphy, F.X. The Papacy Today.
P. Hebblethwaite, 617(TLS):12Feb82-154
Murphy, J.A. Ireland in the Twentieth Century.
A. Mitchell, 174(Éire):Summer81-157

Murphy, J.G. Retribution, Justice, and Therapy.
A.L. Allen, 482(PhR):Jul81-484
J.G. Cottingham, 518:Oct81-241
J. Kleinig, 63:Sep81-352
Murphy, R.T. Hume and Husserl.
V. Cobb-Stevens, 258:Jun81-223
B.J. Jones, 323:Oct81-280
Murrah, D.J. C.C. Slaughter.
L. Milazzo, 584(SWR):Autumn81-413
Murray, C. Hamewith.
D. Buchan, 571(ScLJ):Winter81-122
Murray, G.E. Repairs.
D. Oliphant, 436(NewL):Winter81/82-105
Murray, I. - see Wilde, O.
Murray, J., ed. Cultural Atlas of Africa.
H. Fisher, 617(TLS):26Feb82-230
Murray, J. The Proustian Comedy.
D. Festa-McCormick, 207(FR):Mar81-603
Murray, J.H. Strong-Minded Women.
P. Maier, 441:16May82-10
442(NY):7Jun82-145
Murray, J.K. A Decade of Discovery.
S.C. Chuang, 302:Vol 18-135
Murray, J.L., ed. Canadian Cultural Nationalism.
G.A. Rawlyk, 106:Winter81-405
Murray, L.A. The Vernacular Republic.
F. Adcock, 617(TLS):30Jul82-830
Murray, M., ed. Heidegger and Modern Philosophy.
J.J. Kockelmans, 480(P&R):Winter81-58
Murray, P.J. The Life of John Banim.
R. Tracy, 445(NCF):Sep80-193
Murray, R. Journey.
G. Coggins, 628(UWR):Spring-Summer82-112
Murray Parkes, C. and J. Stevenson-Hinde, eds. The Place of Attachment in Human Behaviour.
A. Storr, 617(TLS):30Jul82-822
Murrell, J. Waiting for the Parade.
T. Beaupre, 108:Fall81-113
Murrin, M. The Allegorical Epic.*
K.W. Gransden, 123:Vol31No1-146
W.H. Herendeen, 539:Aug82-224
F.P., 604:Winter81-3
J. Ziolkowski, 121(CJ):Apr/May82-364
Murtaugh, D.M. "Piers Plowman" and the Image of God.*
A.J. Colaianne, 481(PQ):Winter80-115
J.S. Wittig, 589:Apr81-417
Muschg, A. Gottfried Keller.
D. Goltschnigg, 224(GRM):Band31Heft4-471
Musgrave, S. A Man to Marry, A Man to Bury.*
E. Nicol, 102(CanL):Winter80-108
Musil, J. Urbanization in Socialist Countries.
L.A. Kosiński, 104(CASS):Winter81-618
Musil, R. Briefe 1901-1942. (A. Frisé, ed)
S.S. Prawer, 617(TLS):1Oct81-1051
Musil, R. Gesammelte Werke in neun Banden. (A. Frisé, ed)
J. Strelka, 680(ZDP):Band99Heft4-619
Musin, L., M. Joannes and G. Bogaert. Le Ciel est pour demain.
J. Decock, 207(FR):May82-925
Muthesius, H. The English House.* (D. Sharp, ed)
R.G. Wilson, 505:Nov81-168

Muthesius, S. The English Terraced House.
  S. Gardiner, 362:25Nov82-21
Muyskens, J.L. The Sufficiency of Hope.*
  J.M.G., 185:Apr82-585
Muzzioli, M.P. Cures sabini.
  M.H. Crawford, 313:Vol71-153
Myant, M.R. Socialism and Democracy in
  Czechoslovakia.
  A. Pravda, 617(TLS):12Mar82-290
Myers, J. Katherine Mansfield.
  42(AR):Fall81-518
Myers, R. and M. Harris, eds. Development
  of the English Book Trade, 1700-1899.
  P. Rogers, 617(TLS):2Apr82-373
Myers, R.H. The Chinese Economy.
  S.M. Jones, 293(JASt):May81-539
Myers, T., ed. The Development of Conver-
  sation and Discourse.
  S. Foster, 350:Jun81-517
  R.C. Mehrotra, 261:Sep/Dec80-208
Myerson, J., ed. Antebellum Writers in
  New York and the South.
  T.L. McHaney, 392:Fall81-496
  B.R. Pollin, 495(PoeS):Jun81-18
Myerson, J., ed. Critical Essays on Marga-
  ret Fuller.
  V.M. Kouidis, 577(SHR):Summer81-269
Myerson, J. The New England Transcenden-
  talists and the Dial.*
  L. Buell, 27(AL):Nov81-513
Myrer, A. A Green Desire.
  N. Johnson, 441:28Mar82-14
  442(NY):15Mar82-143
Myron, M-R. and J. Smetana. Perspectives.
  (2nd ed)
  W. Staaks, 207(FR):Feb82-449

Naaman, A., comp. Répertoire des thèses
  littéraires canadiennes de 1921 à 1976.
  A.L. Amprimoz, 102(CanL):Spring80-97
Nabb, M. Death of a Dutchman.
  T.J. Binyon, 617(TLS):29Oct82-1196
  M. Laski, 362:2Dec82-23
Nabb, M. Death of an Englishman.
  T.J. Binyon, 617(TLS):1Jan82-12
Nablow, R.A. A Study of Voltaire's Light-
  er Verse.
  P. Henry, 546(RR):May81-360
Nabokov, V. Feu pâle.
  P. Dulac, 450(NRF):Jun81-134
Nabokov, V. Lectures on Literature.*
  (F. Bowers, ed)
  J. Agee, 231:Jan82-70
  J.D. O'Hara, 434:Summer82-603
  P. Pachet, 98:Jun-Jul81-693
  B. Stonehill, 114(ChiR):Autumn80-115
  G. Woodcock, 569(SR):Fall81-611
  639(VQR):Summer81-83
Nabokov, V. Lectures on Russian Litera-
  ture.* (F. Bowers, ed)
  J. Agee, 231:Jan82-70
  J.D. O'Hara, 434:Summer82-603
Nabokov, V. and E. Wilson. The Nabokov-
  Wilson Letters: 1940-1971.* (S. Karlin-
  sky, ed)
  R. Hingley, 575(SEER):Jan81-90
  P. Pachet, 98:Jun-Jul81-693
  G.S. Smith, 402(MLR):Jan81-254
Nabrings, K. and P. Schmitter. Spracher-
  werbsforschung.
  K. Meng, 682(ZPSK):Band33Heft6-777
Naccarato, F. - see Eiximenis, F.

Nadel, I.B. and F.S. Schwarzbach, eds.
  Victorian Artists and the City.
  A. Sanders, 155:Spring81-41
Nader, H. The Mendoza Family in the
  Spanish Renaissance, 1350-1550.
  G.M. Addy, 551(RenQ):Summer80-250
Nadler, J. Die Hamannausgabe.
  E.J. Krzywon, 489(PJGG):Band88Heft1-
  204
Nadvi, S.A.H.A. Muhammad Rasulullah.
  R. Kemal, 273(IC):Oct80-251
Naef, W.J., ed. Era of Exploration.*
  S. Armitage, 649(WAL):Spring81-78
Naff, T. and R. Owen, eds. Studies in
  Eighteenth Century Islamic History.
  L.C. Rose, 318(JAOS):Jan/Mar80-40
Nagata, J.A. Malaysian Mosaic.
  M.L. Lyon, 293(JASt):May81-652
Nagel, B. Franz Kafka.
  D. Naumann, 224(GRM):Band30Heft4-466
Nagel, E. Teleology Revisited.
  C.B. Wright, 518:Jul81-177
Nagel, J. Stephen Crane and Literary
  Impressionism.
  J.B. Colvert, 587(SAF):Autumn81-281
  M. Foster, 268(IFR):Summer82-160
  J.W. Gargano, 573(SSF):Summer81-330
  T.A. Gullason, 26(ALR):Autumn81-302
  C.K. Lohmann, 27(AL):Jan82-737
  E. Solomon, 445(NCF):Sep81-246
  A. Young, 617(TLS):12Feb82-152
Nagel, T. Mortal Questions.*
  J. Glover, 393(Mind):Apr81-292
  V. Haksar, 262:Mar81-105
Nägele, R. Literatur und Utopie.*
  M. Gelus, 406:Fall81-354
  R.B. Harrison, 402(MLR):Jul81-747
  S. McLean, 400(MLN):Apr81-699
Nagorni, D. Die Kirche Sv. Petar in
  Bijelo Polje (Montenegro).
  S. Čurčić, 589:Jul81-637
Nagy, Á.N. Selected Poems.
  J. Saunders, 565:Vol22No3-62
Nagy, G. The Best of the Achaeans.*
  W.B. Ingalls, 487:Fall81-276
  F. Solmsen, 24:Spring81-81
Nagy, P. Vous et Nous.
  L.K., 450(NRF):Oct81-172
Nagy, S., ed. Pedagógiai Lexikon. (Vols
  1-4)
  J. Kölzow, 682(ZPSK):Band33Heft6-779
Nahal, C. My True Faces.
  J.P. Gemill, 314:Summer-Fall81-239
Nahrebecky, R. Wackenroder, Tieck, E.T.A.
  Hoffmann, Bettina von Arnim.
  C.V. Miller, 406:Winter81-469
Nai-an, S. and Luo Guan-zhong - see under
  Shi Nai-an and Luo Guan-zhong
Naik, J.A., ed. Russia in Asia and Africa.
  S.K. Gupta, 550(RusR):Apr81-207
Naimark, N.M. The History of the "Prole-
  tariat."
  S.A. Blejwas, 104(CASS):Winter81-627
Naipaul, V.S. Among the Believers.*
  V.S. Pritchett, 442(NY):4Jan82-86
Naipaul, V.S. Guérilleros.
  C. Jordis, 450(NRF):Nov81-152
Naipaul, V.S. Three Novels.
  J.S., 231:Dec82-71
Nair, S.B. - see Sternbach, L.
Naisbitt, J. Megatrends.
  K.E. Meyer, 441:26Dec82-8

Nakagawa, S. Kutani Ware.
    O. Impey, 463:Spring81-92
Nakano, T.U., with L. Nakano. Within the
    Barbed Wire Fence.
    W.N., 102(CanL):Spring81-173
Nakhimovsky, A.D. and R.L. Leed. Advanced
    Russian.*
    N.J. Brown, 575(SEER):Jan81-76
    J.S. Levine, 574(SEEJ):Spring81-128
    D. Phillips, 399(MJL):Spring81-83
Nakov, A.B. - see Malévitch, K.S.
Nalivkin, D.V. Geology of the USSR. (N.
    Rast and T.S. Westoll, eds)
    M. Churkin, Jr., 550(RusR):Apr81-229
Namer, E. Le beau roman de la physique
    cartésienne et la science exacte de
    Galilée.
    A. Nardi, 227(GCFI):Jan-Apr81-129
Namer, E. La Vie et l'Oeuvre de J-C.
    Vanini.
    J. Bernhardt, 542:Jul-Sep81-343
Namer, G. Rousseau sociologue de la con-
    naissance.
    M.R. Raaphorst, 207(FR):Dec80-342
Nancy, J-L. Ego sum.*
    D. Judovitz, 400(MLN):May81-916
Nandakumari, P. Poems of Subramania
    Bharati.
    R. Kennedy, 314:Summer-Fall81-249
Nannen, H. - see Koesters, P-H.
Napley, D. Not Without Prejudice.
    D. Pannick, 362:2Dec82-20
Napoleon I. Napoléon: Lettres d'amour à
    Joséphine. (C. de Tourtier-Bonazzi, ed)
    J.E. Howard, 617(TLS):16Jul82-762
Napoli, D.J. and E.N. Rando, eds. Linguis-
    tic Muse.
    L. Hinton, 350:Dec81-979
Napoli, D.J. and E.N. Rando, eds. Syntac-
    tic Argumentation.
    G.M. Green, 350:Sep81-703
Naravane, V.S. Premchand.
    R.K. Narayan, 617(TLS):6Aug82-863
Narayan, J. Towards Total Revolution.
    R.N. Iyer, 293(JASt):Aug81-831
Narayan, R.K. Malgudi Days.
    P-L. Adams, 61:Apr82-108
    A. Desai, 441:7Mar82-1
    R. Towers, 453(NYRB):1Apr82-21
    J. Updike, 442(NY):2Aug82-84
Narboni, J., ed. Alfred Hitchcock.
    P. French, 617(TLS):8Oct82-1103
Nardi, P. Studi sul banchiere nel pen-
    siero dei Glossatori.
    R.S. Lopez, 589:Apr81-458
Nardo, A.K. Milton's Sonnets and the
    Ideal Community.
    W. Myers, 569(SR):Fall81-622
Narducci, E. La provvidenza crudele,
    Lucano e la distruzione dei miti
    augustei.
    F. Delarue, 555:Vol54fasc2-377
    R. Mayer, 123:Vol31No1-118
Narmour, E. Beyond Schenkerism.*
    D.C., 412:May80-154
Narváez, L. Ambientes hispánicos I.
    E.D. Allen, 399(MLJ):Summer81-221
    A. Schrade, 238:Sep81-489
Narváez, L. Ambientes hispánicos 2.
    B.P. Flam, 238:Dec81-649
    R. Largmann, 399(MLJ):Autumn81-336
Nash, G.B. The Urban Crucible.*
    I. Mugridge, 106:Fall81-199

Nash, J.R. The Dark Fountain.
    N. Callendar, 441:10Oct82-22
Nash, R. and D. Belaval, eds. Readings in
    Spanish-English Contrastive Linguistics.*
    (Vol 2)
    J.J. Bergen, 238:Dec81-651
    J.D. Bowen, 355(LSoc):Dec81-492
Nash, R.H. Freedom, Justice, and the
    State.
    J.L.H., 185:Oct81-187
Nason, R: A Modern Dunciad.
    P. Mariani, 472:Spring/Summer82-265
Nasr, S.H. Islamic Life and Thought.
    S. Nuseibeh, 617(TLS):5Mar82-267
Nathan, L. Dear Blood.*
    J.T. Gage, 448:Vol 19No3-180
Nathan, L. The Likeness.
    A.R.K. Zide, 314:Winter-Spring81-233
Nathan, N.M.L. Evidence and Assurance.
    R. Kirk, 393(Mind):Oct81-612
    D. McQueen, 483:Jan81-129
"National Film Archive Catalogue." (Vol 1)
    W.T. Murphy, 14:Fall81-361
Natwar-Singh, K. Maharaja Suraj Mal 1707-
    1763.
    H. Tinker, 617(TLS):5Feb82-142
Naubert, Y. Tales of Solitude.*
    P. Merivale, 102(CanL):Spring81-127
Naumann, G. Probleme des griechischen
    Weihreliefs.
    B.S. Ridgway, 54:Dec81-674
Naumann, H. Der Fall Stiller.
    K. Haberkamm, 400(MLN):Apr81-666
Naumann, M.T. Blue Evenings in Berlin.*
    J. Grayson, 575(SEER):Apr81-297
Naumann, U. Adalbert Stifter.
    L.D. Wells, 221(GQ):Mar81-227
Navarane, V.S. An Introduction to Rabin-
    dranath Tagore.
    S.M. Asnani, 314:Summer-Fall81-215
de Navarre, M. - see under Marguerite de
    Navarre
Navarre, Y. Le Jardin d'acclimatation.
    H. Le Mansec, 207(FR):Oct81-162
Navarro, J.M. and others, eds. Homenaje
    al Profesor Hans Karl Schneider.
    C. Stern, 545(RPh):May81-485
Navarro González, A. - see de Alarcón, P.A.
Navarro Mallebrera, R. Los arquitectos
    del templo de Santa María de Elche.
    V. Tovar Martín, 48:Oct-Dec81-460
Navascués, M., ed. Lecturas modernas de
    Hispanoamérica.
    M.E. Beeson, 238:May81-328
Navasky, V.S. Naming Names.*
    S. Pinsker, 560:Fall81-155
    R. Sklar, 18:Jan-Feb81-64
Navia, L.E. and E. Kelly, eds. Ethics and
    The Search for Values.
    D.G.T., 185:Jan82-403
Nawata, T. Shughni.
    B. Comrie, 350:Mar81-243
Naylor, G. The Arts and Crafts Movement.
    62:Jan81-64
Naylor, G. The Women of Brewster Place.
    A. Gottlieb, 441:22Aug82-11
Naylor, J.A. and J. Lockyer. Auf ins
    Rheinland.
    S.P. Jebe, 399(MLJ):Spring81-115
Naylor, P.B., ed. Austronesian Studies.
    A.B. Hudson, 293(JASt):Aug81-849

Ndayishinguje, P. L'Intronisation d'un Mwami [together with] Chrétien, J-P. La Royauté Capture les Rois.
R.G. Abrahams, 69:Vol50No2-240

Nectoux, J-M. Phonographies: Gabriel Fauré 1900-1977.
R. Nichols, 415:Feb81-108

Needham, J. Science in Traditional China.*
J. Spence, 441:18Apr82-7

Needham, J., with Ho Ping-yü and Lu Gwei-djen. Science and Civilization in China. (Vol 5, Pt 3)
N. Sivin, 244(HJAS):Jun81-219

Needham, P. Twelve Centuries of Book-binding: 400-1600.*
M.M. Foot, 78(BC):Summer81-268

Neesen, L. Untersuchungen zu den direkten Staatsabgaben der römischen Kaiserzeit (27 v. Chr. — 284 n. Chr.).
P.A. Brunt, 313:Vol71-161

Neff, N.A. The Big Cats.
S.D. Smith, 441:5Dec82-12

Negley, G. Utopian Literature.*
C. Spivack, 365:Winter82-48

Negri, A. L'anomalia selvaggia, saggio su potere e potenza in Baruch Spinoza.
E. Alliez, 98:Aug-Sep81-812

Negro, O. Conversational Italian.
205(FMLS):Oct80-380

Nehls, D. Semantik und Syntax des englischen Verbs. (Pt 1)
F.W. Gester, 38:Band99Heft3/4-444
A.R.T., 189(EA):Jul-Sep81-364

Nehls, D., ed. Studies in Contrastive Linguistics and Error Analysis.* (Vol 1)
Y. Kachru, 399(MLJ):Summer81-232

Nehls, D., ed. Studies in Descriptive English Grammar.*
Y. Kachru, 399(MLJ):Summer81-232
N.N. Kharma, 257(IRAL):May81-160

Nehls, D., ed. Studies in Language Acquisition.
I. Andrews, 257(IRAL):Aug81-256

Neider, C. - see under Twain, M.

Neighbour, O. The Consort and Keyboard Music of William Byrd.*
M. Lefkowitz, 551(RenQ):Winter80-776

Neighbour, O., ed. Music and Bibliography.*
H. Cobbe, 78(BC):Winter81-561
S. Sadie, 415:Feb81-110

Neijt, A. Gapping.
G. Mallinson, 603:Vol5No3-418
N. van der Zee, 204(FdL):Sep81-280

Neill, W.T. Archeology and a Science of Man.
G. Gibbon, 84:Mar81-106

Neilsen, P. The Art of Lying.*
C. Pollnitz, 581:Jun81-221

Nelson, A.H. - see Medwall, H.

Nelson, D.A. - see de Berceo, G.

Nelson, K. Cold Wind River.*
J.K. Folsom, 649(WAL):Winter81-339

Nelson, R.F. The Almanac of American Letters.
27(AL):Jan82-759

Nelson, R.J. Pascal.
R. Parish, 617(TLS):30Jul82-834

Nelson, R.S. Hemingway.*
S. Donaldson, 395(MFS):Summer80-332
295(JML):Vol18No3/4-520

Nelson, S., J.R. Barrett and R. Ruck. Steve Nelson, American Radical.
H. Klehr, 453(NYRB):18Nov82-55
P. Le Blanc, 385(MQR):Summer82-486

Nelson, T.A. Kubrick.
N. Roddick, 617(TLS):24Sep82-1047

Němcová, B. Učeň nad Mistra. (J. Jech, ed)
S. Schenda, 196:Band21Heft3/4-327

Nemerov, H. Sentences.*
B. Costello, 472:Fall/Winter81-169
J.F. Cotter, 249(HudR):Summer81-278
639(VQR):Summer81-95

Nemes, D. and others, eds. Études historiques hongroises 1980.
P. Longworth, 575(SEER):Oct81-603

Nemo, J. Patrick Kavanagh.*
E. Wagner, 134(CP):Fall81-137

Nemoianu, A.M. The Boat's Gonna Leave.
J. Mey, 350:Dec82-930

Nepveu, P. Les mots à l'écoute.*
R. Giguere, 102(CanL):Autumn80-106

Nerlich, G. The Shape of Space.
C.A. Hooker, 154:Dec81-783

Neruda, P. Isla Negra.
R. Bly, 441:23May82-9
R. Blythe, 362:25Nov82-28

de Nerval, G. Paris et alentours. (M. Laporte, ed)
P-L. Rey, 450(NRF):Jan81-123

Nestosa, J.R. - see under Ruiz Nestosa, J.

Nestroy, J. Johann Nestroy: Stücke I. (F. Walla, ed) Johann Nestroy Briefe. (W. Obermaier, ed)
A. Obermayer, 67:Nov81-269

Netter, L. Heine et la peinture de la civilisation parisienne 1840-1848.
R.C. Holub, 221(GQ):May81-351

Neu, J. Emotion, Thought, and Therapy.*
H.R. Bernstein, 319:Jan81-114

Neubauer, J. Novalis.
D.P. Haase, 221(GQ):Nov81-516

Neubauer, J. Symbolismus und symbolische Logik.
S.L. Gilman, 400(MLN):Apr81-702
G. von Molnár, 173(ECS):Winter80/81-207

Neubecker, O. Heraldik. (French title: Le grand livre de l'héraldique.)
P. Missac, 98:Jun-Jul80-660

Neubert, W. Skrupel, Reue und Chancen des Kritikers.
C. Molle, 654(WB):5/1981-181

Neugebauer, O. A History of Ancient Mathematical Astronomy.
J. Bernhardt, 542:Apr-Jun81-244

Neugeboren, J. - see Foley, M.

Neuhaus, V. Günter Grass.
I.M. Goessl, 221(GQ):May81-376

Neuhaus, V. Der zeitgeschichtliche Sensationsroman in Deutschland 1855-1878.
H. Steinecke, 680(ZDP):Band100Heft4-611

Neuman, S.C. Gertrude Stein.*
S. Dick, 178:Fall81-367

Neumann, F. Ornamentation in Baroque and Post-Baroque Music, with Special Emphasis on J.S. Bach.*
C.M.B., 412:Feb80-60

Neumeister, S. Der Dichter als Dandy.
B. Goldstein, 406:Spring81-67

Neumeister, S. Mythos und Repräsentation.*
C. Rodiek, 52:Band15Heft1-82

Neumeyer, P. Homage to John Clare.*
   L.J. Swingle, 651(WHR):Autumn81-293
Neuner, G., H. Wilms and M. Zirkel.
   Deutsch aktiv.
   K.E.H. Liedtke, 399(MLJ):Spring81-119
Neuschäfer, H-J. Der Naturalismus in der
   Romania.
   C. Bevernis, 535(RHL):Nov-Dec81-1018
Neusner, J. Judaism.
   H. Maccoby, 617(TLS):13Aug82-887
Neuss, P. - see Skelton, J.
Nevett, T.R. Advertising in Britain.
   J. Vaizey, 362:25Feb82-23
Neville, G. Incidents in the Life of
   Joseph Grimaldi.
   M. Norgate, 157:1stQtr81-53
Neville, G.H. A Memoir of D.H. Lawrence,
   (C. Baron, ed)
   P. Craig, 617(TLS):19Mar82-313
Nevins, A. and M.H. Thomas - see Strong,
   G.T.
Nevins, A.J. A Saint for Your Name;
   Saints for Boys. A Saint for Your Name;
   Saints for Girls.
   E.C. Smith, 424:Sep80-224
Nevins, D. and R.A.M. Stern. The Archi-
   tect's Eye — American Architectural Draw-
   ings from 1799-1978.
   L.I. Mitnick, 576:Mar81-78
New, W., ed. Margaret Laurence.*
   A. Pasold, 296(JCF):No31/32-257
New, W.H., ed. A Political Art.*
   H. Kreisel, 102(CanL):Spring80-82
"The New American Quilt."
   M.Z. Cowan, 614:Spring82-15
"The New Sunday Missal."
   D. Crane, 617(TLS):5Nov82-1227
Newall, V.J., ed. Folklore Studies in
   the Twentieth Century.
   J. Simpson, 203:Vol192No2-249
Newby, E. A Short Walk in the Hindu Kush.
   J.D. O'Hara, 434:Summer82-603
Newby, E. A Traveller's Life.
   J. Hone, 617(TLS):20Aug82-898
   R. Trevelyan, 362:1Jul82-26
Newby, P.H. Feelings Have Changed.*
   D. Durrant, 364:Feb82-97
Newcomb, A. The Madrigal at Ferrara, 1579-
   1597.*
   I. Fenlon, 415:Jun81-381
Newcombe, T.H. - see Thibaut de Blaison
Newell, P.E. Zapata of Mexico.
   M.P. Costeloe, 86(BHS):Jul81-278
Newey, V., ed. "The Pilgrim's Progress" —
   Critical and Historical Views.
   J. Barnard, 617(TLS):23Apr82-470
   D.L. Russell, 568(SCN):Winter81-90
Newhall, B. The History of Photography.
   A. Grundberg, 441:5Dec82-59
Newhall, B., ed. Photography: Essays and
   Images.*
   C. Hagen, 62:Apr81-61
Newhouse, J. The Sporty Game.
   R. Witkin, 441:11Jul82-12
Newlin, D. Bruckner — Mahler — Schoen-
   berg.* (rev)
   E.S., 412:May80-148
Newlin, D. Schoenberg Remembered.
   P.P. Nash, 607:Jun81-44
Newman, A. Artists.
   C. Nadelman, 55:Mar81-38
Newman, E. Strictly Speaking.
   W.W. Evans, 35(AS):Spring-Summer77-134

Newman, G.F. The Men with the Guns.
   D. Profumo, 617(TLS):2Jul82-725
Newman, J.H. The Letters and Diaries of
   John Henry Newman.* (Vol 1) (I. Ker and
   T. Gornall, eds)
   D.J. De Laura, 402(MLR):Jan81-169
Newman, J.H. The Letters and Diaries of
   John Henry Newman. (Vols 2 and 3) (I.
   Ker and T. Gornall, eds)
   D.J. De Laura, 402(MLR):Jul81-682
   A.G. Hill, 541(RES):Feb81-87
Newman, J.H. The Letters and Diaries of
   John Henry Newman. (Vol 4) (I. Ker and
   T. Gornall, eds)
   E.D. Mackerness, 506(PSt):May81-103
Newman, J.H. Mélange pour le Centenaire
   du Cardinalat. (M.K. Strolz, ed)
   J.G., 189(EA):Apr-Jun81-239
Newman, L.W. - see Barsov, A.A.
Newman, P. and R.M., eds. Modern Hausa-
   English Dictionary. (2nd ed)
   P. Jaggar, 350:Jun81-505
Newman, P.C. Bronfman Dynasty.
   G.W., 102(CanL):Spring80-150
Newman, P.R. Marston Moor, 2 July 1644.
   I. Roy, 325:Apr81-434
Newman, S.J. Dickens at Play.*
   T. Braun, 155:Summer81-105
Newmeyer, F.J. Linguistic Theory in
   America.
   J.D. McCawley, 353:Vol 18No9/10-911
   C. Mallinson, 361:Apr81-371
   D.J. Napoli, 350:Jun81-456
Newmyer, S.T. The "Silvae" of Statius.*
   M. Morford, 122:Oct81-331
Newsome, D. On the Edge of Paradise.
   R. Hyam, 111:5Dec80-56
Newton, N. On the Broken Mountain.^
   K.P. Stich, 628(UWR):Fall-Winter81-126
Newton, P.A., with J. Kerr. The County of
   Oxford: A Catalogue of Medieval Stained
   Glass.
   M.P. Lillich, 589:Apr81-460
Newton, R.P. Leaves of Quest.
   205(FMLS):Oct80-380
   295(JML):Vol8No3/4-487
Newton, S.M. Fashion in the Age of the
   Black Prince.
   J. Gardner, 39:Jul81-65
Newton-Smith, W.H. The Rationality of
   Science.
   B. Barnes, 617(TLS):19Feb82-194
Newton-Smith, W.H. The Structure of Time.
   C.W. Kilmister, 84:Jun81-206
Ngapo Ngawang Jigmei and others. Tibet.
   J.H. Crook, 617(TLS):19Feb82-199
Ngugi wa Thiong'o. Devil on the Cross.
   J. Mellors, 362:26Aug82-24
   D. Sweetman, 617(TLS):18Jun82-676
Ngumu, P-C. Les Mendzan des chanteurs de
   Yaoundé.
   K.A. Gourlay, 187:Sep82-475
Niatum, D. Songs for the Harvester of
   Dreams.
   W. Scammell, 617(TLS):28May82-592
Nichiren. Nichiren: Selected Writings.
   (L.R. Rodd, ed)
   D.W. Chappell, 407(MN):Winter81-482
Nichol, bp. Journal.* Craft Dinner.*
   E.E. Greengrass, 102(CanL):Summer80-
   142

259

Nicholas of Cusa. Nicolo Cusano, "Scritti filosofici." (G. Santinello, ed) On Learned Ignorance. (J. Hopkins, trans)
M. de Gandillac, 542:Jul-Sep81-341
Nicholas of Lynn. The Kalendarium of Nicholas of Lynn.* (S. Eisner, ed; G. MacEoin and S. Eisner, trans)
P. Brown, 354:Sep81-246
Nicholas, H.G., ed. Washington Despatches 1941-1945.*
M. Gilbert, 617(TLS):30Apr82-482
Nicholas, J.M., ed. Images, Perceptions, and Knowledge.
G. Thrane, 488:Mar80-116
Nicholas, W.R. The Folk Poets.
L. Breatnach, 112:Vol 14-169
Nicholls, J.C. - see Riccoboni, M-J.
Nichols, B. Ideology and the Image.
T. Cripps, 18:Jul-Aug81-64
Nichols, F.D. and R.E. Griswold. Thomas Jefferson, Landscape Architect.
C. Zaitzevsky, 576:Mar81-73
Nichols, F.J., ed and trans. An Anthology of Neo-Latin Poetry.*
J.W. Binns, 551(RenQ):Autumn80-454
M. Pope, 123:Vol31No1-100
J.E. Ziolkowski, 124:Sep-Oct81-58
Nichols, G.C. Miguel Hernández.*
J. Cano-Ballesta, 400(MLN):Mar81-459
Nichols, J. - see Kegg, M.
Nichols, P. The Pope's Divisions.*
D.J. Dooley, 99:Mar82-35
Nichols, R.L. and T.G. Stavrou, eds. Russian Orthodoxy under the Old Regime.
S. Hackel, 575(SEER):Apr81-303
A.J. Rieber, 104(CASS):Winter81-593
Nicholson, N. Sea to the West.*
H. Lomas, 364:Dec81/Jan82-97
Nicholson, N. Selected Poems 1940-1982.
A. Motion, 617(TLS):10Dec82-1376
Nickel, G. Einführung in die Linguistik.*
W. Kühlwein, 277(ITL):No48-97
Nickel, G., ed. Proceedings of the Fourth International Congress of Applied Linguistics.
G.F. Meier, 682(ZPSK):Band33Heft5-613
Nickel, G. - see "'Beowulf' und die kleineren Denkmäler der altenglischen Heldensage Waldere und Finnsburg"
Nickles, T., ed. Scientific Discovery, Logic, and Rationality.
R. McLaughlin, 63:Jun81-248
R.S.N., 185:Jul82-791
Nicol, D.M. The End of the Byzantine Empire.
M.E. Martin, 303(JoHS):Vol 101-234
Nicolai, R.R. Ende ohne Anfang.
J.M. Grandin, 406:Spring81-97
Nicolet, C. Rome et la conquête du monde méditerranéen 264-27 avant J-C. (Vol 1)
M.H. Crawford, 313:Vol71-153
Nicoletti, G. Il "metodo" dell'"Ortis" e altri studi foscoliani.
M. Chiesa, 228(GSLI):Vol 158fasc502-301
Nicoletti, G. - see Foscolo, U.
Nicoll, A. The Garrick Stage.* (S. Rosenfeld, ed)
J. Milhous, 130:Fall81-275
Nicolle, J. Madame de Pompadour et la société de son temps.
H. Cohen, 207(FR):May81-904

Nicolson, B. The International Caravaggesque Movement.*
L.J. Slatkes, 600:Vol 12No2/3-167
Nicolson, N. and J. Trautmann - see Woolf, V.
Nida, E.A. Language Structure and Translation. (A.S. Dil, ed)
M. Okrand, 545(RPh):Nov80-229
Niderst, A. Racine et la tragédie classique.*
E.J. Campion, 475:No13Pt1-150
G. Jondorf, 208(FS):Apr81-200
Niebaum, H. Westfälisch.
H. Fischer, 680(ZDP):Band99Heft3-467
Nieh, H., ed. Literature of the Hundred Flowers.
R.E. Hegel, 268(IFR):Summer82-133
Nienhauser, W.H., Jr., ed. Critical Essays on Chinese Literature.
D.R. Knechtges, 318(JAOS):Jan/Mar80-92
Nies, F., with J. Rehbein, eds. Genres mineurs.*
D. Beyerle, 72:Band217Heft1-221
L. van Delft, 210(FrF):Jan81-87
Nieto, J.C. Mystic, Rebel, Saint.
E.A. Maio, 238:May81-312
C.P. Thompson, 86(BHS):Jul81-265
Nieto, M.F. - see under Fernández Nieto, M.
Nietzsche, F. Daybreak. (R.J. Hollingdale, trans)
A.C. Danto, 617(TLS):1Oct82-1074
D.J. Enright, 362:29Jul82-25
Nietzsche, F. A Nietzsche Reader. (R.J. Hollingdale, ed and trans) Ecce Homo.
T. Martin, 81:Spring-Fall81-417
Nietzsche, F. Philosophy and Truth. (D. Breazeale, ed and trans)
C.S. Taylor, 518:Apr81-114
Nietzsche, F. Werke. (Vol 3) (G. Colli and M. Montinari, eds)
W.J.D., 543:Dec80-392
Nieuwenhuys, R., ed. Memory and Agony.
P.D. Westbrook, 573(SSF):Winter81-94
Niewyk, D.L. The Jews in Weimar Germany.*
639(VQR):Summer81-50
Nijenhuis, E.T. Musicological Literature. (Vol 6, Pt 3) (J. Gonda, ed)
M.J. Curtiss, 318(JAOS):Apr/Jun80-159
Nijinska, B. Early Memoirs.* (I. Nijinska and J. Rawlinson, eds and trans)
J. Kavanagh, 617(TLS):9Jul82-744
442(NY):15Feb82-140
Niklewski, G. Versuch über Symbol und Allegorie.
N. Oellers, 52:Band15Heft3-334
Nikolaev, P.A., ed. Vozniknovenie russkoj nauki o literature. Akademičeskie školy v russkom literaturovedenii.
M. Lotman, 559:Aug81-337
Nilsen, D.L.F. and A.P. Language Play.*
M.M. Bryant, 660(Word):Aug80-243
L.A. Hughes, 355(LSoc):Aug81-314
Nilsson, N.Å., ed. Art, Society, Revolution.
P. Carden, 574(SEEJ):Fall81-128
J. Graffy, 575(SEER):Jul81-422
J.L. Laychuk, 104(CASS):Winter81-602
D.J. Youngblood, 550(RusR):Apr81-196
Nilsson, N.Å., ed. Russian Romanticism.
L. Burnett, 558(RLJ):Winter81-217
B.H. Scherr, 574(SEEJ):Fall81-126
Nilstun, T. Moral Reasoning.
T. Thorson, 185:Jan81-320

Norris, C. and S.D. Washington. The Last of the Scottsboro Boys.
D.E. Alsobrook, 9(AlaR):Apr81-130
Norris, C.C. William Empson and the Philosophy of Literary Criticism.*
R. Gill, 447(N&Q):Jun80-265
M. Megaw, 184(EIC):Jan81-73
Norris, K. The Book of Fall.
J. Giltrow, 102(CanL):Spring81-145
Norris, L. Walking the White Fields.
J.F. Cotter, 249(HudR):Summer81-285
Norris, L. Water Voices.*
D. Graham, 565:Vol22No4-62
Norrman, R. Techniques of Ambiguity in the Fiction of Henry James.*
J.F. Blackall, 494:Autumn79-417
J.W. Tuttleton, 402(MLR):Oct81-938
Norstedt, J.A. Thomas MacDonagh.*
T.C. Ware, 174(Éire):Winter81-139
North, D.C. Structure and Change in Economic History.
D.C. Coleman, 617(TLS):15Jan82-61
North, E. Ancient Enemies.
J. Mellors, 362:18Nov82-28
L. Taylor, 617(TLS):5Nov82-1231
North, E. Dames.*
G. Ewart, 364:Jul81-88
North, H.F. From Myth to Icon.*
M. Volpe, 480(P&R):Fall81-258
North, H.F., ed. Interpretations of Plato.*
H.G. Ingenkamp, 53(AGP):Band62Heft2-191
North, M. A Vision of Eden.*
E. Claridge, 364:Apr/May81-138
Norton, D.F., N. Capaldi and W.L. Robison, eds. McGill Hume Studies.
A. Baier, 185:Jan82-346
Norton, F.J. A Descriptive Catalogue of Printing in Spain and Portugal, 1501-1520.*
R. Mortimer, 551(RenQ):Spring80-82
"Norwegian-American Studies." (Vol 28) (K.O. Bjork, ed)
T.I. Leiren, 563(SS):Summer81-352
Norwich, J.J. A History of Venice.
L. Barzini, 441:30May82-3
P. Partner, 453(NYRB):27May82-22
442(NY):10May82-169
Norwich, J.J. Venice: The Greatness and the Fall.
N. Davidson, 617(TLS):11Jun82-632
Noske, F. The Signifier and the Signified.*
M. Baroni, 187:May82-319
H. Busch, 414(MusQ):Jul81-440
Nossack, H.E. Wait for November.
J. Agee, 441:18Jul82-9
442(NY):21Jun82-121
"La notion de personne en Afrique noire."
J. Beattie, 69:Vol50No3-313
Notker der Deutsche. Martianus Capella. (J.C. King, ed)
J. Dishington, 589:Apr81-461
R.H. Lawson, 301(JEGP):Jan81-81
A.L. Lloyd, 400(MLN):Apr81-691
Notley, A. How Spring Comes. Waltzing Matilda.
P. Schjeldahl, 441:17Jan82-13
Nouaros, A.M. Une fable grecque moderne.
M. Meraklis, 196:Band22Heft1/2-143
J. Simpson, 203:Vol191No2-251
Nougué, A. - see Tirso de Molina

Noussan-Lettry, L. Spekulatives Denken in Platons Frühschriften.
J. Dillon, 122:Apr81-150
El Nouty, H. Théâtre et pré-cinéma.
A.B. Smith, 207(FR):Oct81-141
S.M. Taylor, 446(NCFS):Spring-Summer81-276
Nova, C. The Good Son.
J. Irving, 441:3Oct82-3
Novak, B. Nature and Culture.*
E. Johns, 127:Spring81-85
M.S. Young, 39:Feb81-129
Novak, B. and others. Next to Nature.
639(VQR):Summer81-103
Novak, M. The Spirit of Democratic Capitalism.
R.M.K., 231:Aug82-76
Novarina, V. La lutte des morts.
A. Clavel, 98:Feb80-184
Novarr, D. The Disinterred Muse.*
R. Bozanich, 651(WHR):Autumn81-289
F. Manley, 569(SR):Fall81-635
Noveck, M. The Mark of Ancient Man.
P. Amiet, 318(JAOS):Apr/Jun80-185
Novikov, N.N. and others. Birmansko-russkij slovař.
K. Kaden, 682(ZPSK):Band33Heft2-245
Novo Villaverde, Y. Vicente Aleixandre, poeta surrealista.
D. Harris, 402(MLR):Oct81-982
Nowak, C. Wart nicht auf einen Orden.
R. Bernhardt, 654(WB):11/1981-130
Nowak, J. Courier from Warsaw.* (Polish title: Kurier z Warszawy.)
J. Kott, 441:31Oct82-3
H. Seton-Watson, 617(TLS):10Dec82-1375
442(NY):15Nov82-203
Noyes, R.W. The Sun, Our Star.
442(NY):27Dec82-78
Nozick, R. Anarchy, State, and Utopia.*
G. Kortian, 98:Jan81-3
Nozick, R. Philosophical Explanations.*
B. Blanshard, 676(YR):Spring82-404
M.F. Burnyeat, 617(TLS):15Oct82-1136
B. Williams, 453(NYRB):18Feb82-32
de la Nuez, S. - see Iriarte, T.
Nuiten, H. Les Variantes des "Fleurs du mal" et des "Épaves" de Charles Baudelaire.
H. Cassou-Yager, 207(FR):Apr81-739
G. Chesters, 402(MLR):Jul81-706
205(FMLS):Oct80-380
Núñez, B. Dictionary of Afro-Latin American Civilization.
S. Miranda, 263(RIB):Vol31No3-414
Núñez Cedeño, R.A. La fonología moderna y el español de Santo Domingo.
J.R. Gutiérrez, 350:Dec81-971
Nuss, A.M.F. Export Marketing French.
J.S. Dugan, 207(FR):Feb81-511
Nussbaum, M.C. - see Aristotle
Nusser, P. Der Kriminalroman.
S.S. Prawer, 221(GQ):Nov81-488
Nwezeh, E.C. Africa in French and German Fiction, 1911-1933.
J. Mounier, 549(RLC):Apr-Jun81-250
"Nya namnregler."
J. Leighly, 424:Jun80-152
Nyberg, M. The Crazy Horse Suite.
D. Barbour, 648(WCR):Jun80-79
Nye, N.S. Different Ways to Pray.
D. Oliphant, 436(NewL):Winter81/82-105

Nye, R. The Voyage of the Destiny.
V. Cunningham, 617(TLS):30Apr82-481
J. Mellors, 362:13May82-27
Nylander, J.C. Fabrics for Historic
Buildings. (2nd ed)
P. Bach, 614:Spring81-18
Nylen, E. and J.P. Lamm. Bildstenar.
H.R.E. Davidson, 203:Vol92No1-119
Nzula, A.T., I.I. Potekhin and A.Z. Zusman-
ovich. Forced Labour in Colonial Africa.
(R. Cohen, ed)
P. O'Keefe, 69:Vol50No4-435

Oakes, J. The Ruling Race.
E. Foner, 441:23May82-11
Oakes, P. Dwellers All in Time and Space.
P. Beer, 362:8Apr82-21
J. Mellors, 364:Mar82-91
V. Scannell, 617(TLS):7May82-517
Oakeshott, W. The Two Winchester Bibles.
J.J.G. Alexander, 617(TLS):21May82-563
78(BC):Summer81-151
Oakley, F. The Western Church in the
Later Middle Ages.*
R.M. Fraher, 589:Oct81-893
J. Riley-Smith, 382(MAE):1981/1-195
Oakman, R.L. Computer Methods for Liter-
ary Research.*
M.L. Flowers, 399(MLJ):Spring81-111
L.T. Milic, 405(MP):Nov81-233
Oates, J.C. Angel of Light.*
H.S. Arnow, 385(MQR):Fall82-674
P. Kemp, 617(TLS):29Jan82-105
J. Mellors, 362:11Feb82-24
Oates, J.C. Bellefleur.*
D. Durrant, 364:Jul81-86
639(VQR):Winter81-18
Oates, J.C. A Bloodsmoor Romance.
D. Donoghue, 453(NYRB):21Oct82-12
D. Johnson, 441:5Sep82-1
J. Wolcott, 231:Sep82-67
442(NY):27Sep82-145
Oates, J.C. Contraries.
D. Kirby, 150(DR):Summer81-384
Oates, J.C. The Lamb of Abyssalia.
S. Pinsker, 573(SSF):Winter81-111
Oates, J.C. A Sentimental Education.*
J. Mellors, 364:Aug-Sep81-139
Oates, J.C., with S. Ravenel, eds. The
Best American Short Stories 1979.*
T.A. Gullason, 573(SSF):Winter81-89
Oates, S.B. Let the Trumpet Sound.
E. Foner, 441:12Sep82-14
O'Ballance, E. No Victor, No Vanquished.
B. Morris, 390:Oct81-60
Obbo, C. African Women.
C. Brantley, 69:Vol50No4-425
Obenauer, H-G. Études de syntaxe inter-
rogative du français.
N.L. Corbett, 545(RPh):Feb81-338
Ober, W.B. Boswell's Clap and Other
Essays.
J.H. O'Neill, 173(ECS):Spring81-366
T. Ziolkowski, 569(SR):Fall81-652
Ober, W.U., ed. The Story of the Three
Bears.
T. Shippey, 617(TLS):26Mar82-347
Oberg, A. Anna's Song.
S.I. Bellman, 649(WAL):Spring81-82
K. MacLean, 134(CP):Spring81-61

Oberhammer, G. Strukturen Yogischer Medi-
tation.*
P. Olivelle, 318(JAOS):Jan/Mar80-48
Obermaier, W. - see Nestroy, J. •
Oberman, H.A. Werden und Wertung der
Reformation.
H.J. Hillerbrand, 551(RenQ):Spring80-
84
Oberman, H.A., with T. Brady, Jr., eds.
Itinerarium Italicum.
F. Caspari, 551(RenQ):Summer80-231
Obermayer, A., ed. Festschrift for E.W.
Herd.
H. Kreuzer, 67:Nov81-260
Obholzer, K. The Wolf-Man. (French title:
Entretiens avec l'Homme aux loups.)
R. Dinnage, 617(TLS):10Dec82-1351
J. le Hardi, 450(NRF):Nov81-135
O'Brien, E. Returning.
V. Glendinning, 617(TLS):23Apr82-456
J. Mellors, 362:13May82-27
O'Brien, E. Virginia.
D. Devlin, 157:2ndQtr81-55
O'Brien, G. Hardboiled America.*
N. Callendar, 441:7Feb82-20
R. Flood, 62:Feb82-81
O'Brien, M. The Idea of the American
South: 1920-1941.*
M. Kreyling, 392:Winter80/81-60
T.D. Young, 569(SR):Summer81-480
O'Brien, M.L. and M. Foulds, with H.A.
Link. The Art of Shibata Zeshin.
U. Roberts, 60:Nov-Dec81-156
O'Brien, P. The Promise of Punishment.
M. Ignatieff, 617(TLS):16Jul82-762
O'Brien, T. Going After Cacciato.*
A.M. Saltzman, 145(Crit):Vol22No1-32
O'Brien, V. Techniques of Stained Glass.
G. Russell, 324:Jan82-106
O'Buachalla, S. - see Pearse, P.H.
Obuchowski, C.W. Mars on Trial.
J. Cruickshank, 208(FS):Oct81-481
A.D. Hytier, 207(FR):Dec80-349
A. Thiher, 395(MFS):Summer80-351
B. Thompson, 399(MLJ):Winter81-428
Ocampo, V. Against the Wind and Tide.
N. Lindstrom, 399(MLJ):Summer81-220
Ochs, E. and B. Schieffelin, eds. Develop-
mental Pragmatics.
A.D. Pellegrini, 351(LL):Jun81-249
M. Shatz, 350:Jun81-479
Ockham, William of. Guillaume d'Occam,
"Commentaire sur le Livre des Pré-
dicables de Porphyry."* (L. Valcke, ed;
R. Galbois, trans)
C. Panaccio, 154:Jun81-318
O'Collins, G. Fundamental Theology.
J. Coventry, 617(TLS):15Jan82-62
O'Connell, M. Mirror and Veil.*
A.K. Hieatt, 191(ELN):Mar81-212
O'Connor, D. and J. Jiminez. The Images
of Jesus.
J.S. Ackerman, 599:Fall81-503
O'Connor, F. The Habit of Being.* (S.
Fitzgerald, ed)
E. Bartlett, 435:Summer81-211
J.V. Gunn, 27(AL):Nov81-522
W. Leamon, 651(WHR):Summer81-177
O'Connor, G. Ralph Richardson.
J. Mortimer, 441:19Dec82-7
S. Wall, 617(TLS):24Dec82-1417

O'Connor, J.E. and M.A. Johnson, eds.
American History/American Film.
J.M. Skinner, 106:Spring81-123
O'Connor, P.W. and A.M. Pasquariello, eds.
Contemporary Spanish Theater.
A. Dias, 399(MLJ):Summer81-221
R.B. Klein, 238:Sep81-489
O'Connor, U. Three Noh Plays.
D. Devlin, 157:Oct80-72
OCork, S. End of the Line.
N. Callendar, 441:14Feb82-22
Ó Cróinín, S. and D. Seanachas Amhlaoibh
í Luínse.
B. Ó Cuív, 112:Vol 14-181
O'Day, A., ed. The Edwardian Age.
H.L. Malchow, 637(VS):Spring81-373
Odelain, O. and R. Séguineau. Dictionary
of Proper Names and Places in the Bible.
E.C. Smith, 424:Dec81-313
O'Dell, F.A. Socialisation through Chil-
dren's Literature.*
J.J. Tomiak, 575(SEER):Jul81-463
Odenkirchen, C.J., ed. The Life of St.
Alexius in the Old French Version of the
Hildesheim Manuscript.*
M.D. Legge, 382(MAE):1981/1-133
O'Donnell, J.J. Cassiodorus.*
G. Bonner, 589:Jan81-184
A. Cameron, 313:Vol71-183
M. McCormick, 24:Fall81-344
O'Donnell, M. The Devil's Prison.
T.J. Binyon, 617(TLS):6Aug82-865
O'Donnell, P. The Night of Morningstar.
T.J. Binyon, 617(TLS):31Dec82-1448
O'Donnell, W.R. and L. Todd. Variety in
Contemporary English.
J.T. Jensen, 350:Jun82-485
O'Donohue, B. From the Edge of the World.
C. Pollnitz, 581:Jun81-221
Oehler, D. Pariser Bilder I (1830-1848).*
H. Nuiten, 535(RHL):Jul-Oct81-803
Oehlschlaeger, F. and G. Hendrick, eds.
Toward the Making of Thoreau's Modern
Reputation.*
D. Fussell, 506(PSt):Sep81-213
R.J. Schneider, 183(ESQ):Vol27No1-57
T. Woodson, 651(WHR):Spring81-94
Oelmuller, W. Die unbefriedigte Aufklä-
rung.
W. Steinbeck, 342:Band71Heft1-127
Oeser, E. and R. Schubert-Soldern. Die
Evolutionstheorie.
H.W. Ingensiep, 53(AGP):Band62Heft1-
121
O'Faolain, J. The Obedient Wife.
P. Craig, 617(TLS):23Jul82-807
J. Mellors, 362:3Jun82-22
O'Faolain, S. Collected Stories. (Vol 3)
P. Craig, 617(TLS):3Dec82-1344
O'Flaherty, J.C. Johann Georg Hamann.
S-A. Jørgensen, 462(OL):Vol36No3-260
O'Flaherty, L. The Black Soul. Shame the
Devil.
F. Tuohy, 617(TLS):1Jan82-8
O'Flaherty, P. The Rock Observed.*
F. Cogswell, 529(QQ):Winter81-786
R.G. Moyles, 102(CanL):Winter80-138
Ogden, S.M. The Point of Christology.
J.L. Houlden, 617(TLS):24Sep82-1045
Ogilvie, R.M. The Library of Lactantius.*
E.D. Hunt, 313:Vol71-193

Oh, C-K. and D.A. Dinneen, eds. Syntax
and Semantics. (Vol 11: Presupposition.)
T. Burge, 316:Jun81-412
D.T. Langendoen, 350:Mar81-214
O'Hara, D.T. Tragic Knowledge.*
H. Adams, 290(JAAC):Summer82-434
W. Martin, 659(ConL):Spring82-239
O'Hara, J. An Artist Is His Own Fault.
Selected Letters of John O'Hara. (M.J.
Bruccoli, ed of both)
M. Light, 395(MFS):Winter80/81-658
O'Hara, J. Two by O'Hara.
T.K. Meier, 50(ArQ):Summer81-183
O'Hara, K. Nightmares' Nest.
T.J. Binyon, 617(TLS):31Dec82-1448
Ohashi, K., ed. The Traditional and the
Anti-Traditional.
D.L. Cook, 27(AL):Jan82-753
O'Hear, A. Education, Society, and Human
Nature.
P.H., 185:Jul82-779
O'Hear, A. Karl Popper.
J. Lieberson, 453(NYRB):18Nov82-67 and
cont in 2Dec82-51
Ó hEithir, B. Lead Us Not Into Tempta-
tion.*
C.W. Barrow, 174(Éire):Fall81-152
Ohkawa, K. and H. Rosovsky. Japanese
Economic Growth.
L. Hollerman, 293(JASt):Aug81-735
Ohkawa, K. and M. Shinohara, with L.
Meissner, eds. Patterns of Japanese
Economic Development.
L. Hollerman, 293(JASt):Aug81-735
Ohlsson, R. The Moral Import of Evil.*
D.P.L., 185:Oct81-190
A. Montefiore, 482(PhR):Jul81-492
Ohlsson, S.O. Skånes språkliga försvensk-
ning.
N. Hasselmo, 563(SS):Spring81-221
Ohrn, K.B. Dorothea Lange and the Documen-
tary Tradition.
639(VQR):Winter81-28
Oikonomidès, N. Actes de Kastamonitou.*
J. Chrysostomides, 303(JoHS):Vol 101-
231
Oinas, F.J., ed. Folklore, Nationalism,
and Politics.*
F. Hemmersam, 196:Band21Heft1/2-136
Oinas, F.J., ed. Heroic Epic and Saga.*
W. Haug, 196:Band21Heft3/4-329
J. Ruud, 125:Spring81-350
Oinas, F.J. Kalevipoeg kütkeis ja muid
esseid rahvaluulest, mütoloogiast ja
kirjandusest/Kalevipoeg in Fetters and
Other Essays on Folklore, Mythology and
Literature.
V. Terras, 292(JAF):Apr-Jun81-259
Ojigbo, O. Shehu Shagari.
A.H.M. Kirk-Greene, 617(TLS):3Dec82-
1346
Ojo, J.O. Yoruba Customs from Ondo.
J. Clarke, 69:Vol150No1-110
D.B. Welch, 187:Jan82-167
"Ōkagami, the Great Mirror." (H.C.
McCullough, trans)
S. Matisoff, 407(MN):Winter81-469
D.E. Mills, 244(HJAS):Jun81-280
Tsunoda Bun'ei, 285(JapQ):Jan-Mar81-
113
M. Ury, 293(JASt):Aug81-790
O'Keefe, D. The Cheese Buyer's Handbook.
W. and C. Cowen, 639(VQR):Spring81-73

O'Keefe, P. and B. Wisner, eds. Landuse and Development.
C. Frantz, 69:Vol50No2-236
O'Kelly, H.W. Melancholie und die melancholische Landschaft.
A. Corbineau-Hoffmann, 490:Band12Heft1-119
Okenfuss, M.J. The Discovery of Childhood in Russia.
H.A. Bennett, 550(RusR):Apr81-183
J.J. Tomiak, 575(SEER):Jul81-438
Okpewho, I. The Epic in Africa.
R. Knight, 187:Sep82-477
Olafson, F.A. The Dialectic of Action.*
R.F. Atkinson, 185:Jan82-354
M.D., 543:Sep80-153
Olbrich, H., with others, eds. Sozialistische deutsche Karikatur 1848-1978.
H.W. Rohls, 654(WB):4/1981-188
Olcott, A. Murder at the Red October.*
S. Altinel, 617(TLS):28May82-593
M. Laski, 362:2Dec82-23
"Old and New Architecture: Design Relationship."
R. Wagner, 576:May81-148
Oldenbourg, Z. La Joie-Souffrance.
C. Faraggi, 450(NRF):Oct81-142
Oldenbourg, Z. Le procès du rêve.
R. Buss, 617(TLS):23Apr82-471
Olds, P. Lady Moss Revived.
A. Baysting, 368:Dec73-355
Olds, S. Satan Says.*
G.E. Murray, 249(HudR):Spring81-158
Oldsey, B. Hemingway's Hidden Craft.*
S. Donaldson, 395(MFS):Summer80-332
O'Leary, G. The Shaping of Chinese Foreign Policy.*
T.S. An, 293(JASt):Aug81-773
Olender, M., ed. Pour Léon Poliakov.
S. Koster, 98:Dec81-1332
Oles, C. The Loneliness Factor.*
S.M. Gilbert, 491:Oct81-35
Olesch, R. - see Hrastě, M. and P. Šimunović
de Oliveira, F. A gramática da linguagem portuguesa. (M.L. Carvalhão Buescu, ed)
R. Nagel, 72:Band217Heft1-214
Olivella, J.M., C. Rey i Grangé and A. Porqueras-Mayo - see under Martí i Olivella, J., C. Rey i Grangé and A. Porqueras-Mayo
Olivelle, P. Vāsudevāśrama Yatidharmaprakāśa.
S. Pollock, 318(JAOS):Jan/Mar80-48
Oliver, A. Michel, Job, Pierre, Paul.
A. Goulet, 535(RHL):Jul-Oct81-834
Oliver, A. and J.B. Peabody, eds. The Records of Trinity Church, Boston, 1728-1830.
B.A. Norton, 432(NEQ):Dec81-590
Oliver, H. Flaubert and an English Governess.
B.F. Bart, 446(NCFS):Spring-Summer82-383
205(FMLS):Oct80-380
639(VQR):Winter81-12
Oliver, L.M. - see under Morales Oliver, L.
Oliver, R. and M. Crowder, general eds. The Cambridge Encyclopedia of Africa.
H. Fisher, 617(TLS):26Feb82-230
Oliver, W.H. Out of Season.
C. Doyle, 368:Mar81-114

Oliver, W.H. and B.R. Williams, eds. The Oxford History of New Zealand.
C. Newbury, 617(TLS):30Jul82-832
Olivier, L. Confessions of an Actor.
D.A.N. Jones, 362:21Oct82-22
J. Mortimer, 441:19Dec82-7
S. Wall, 617(TLS):24Dec82-1417
Olivier-Martin, Y. Histoire du roman populaire en France de 1840 à 1980.
D. Coste, 207(FR):Apr81-729
Ollard, R. An English Education.
J.H.C. Leach, 617(TLS):12Nov82-1244
Ollé, F.G. - see under González Ollé, F.
Ollier, C. Marrakch Médine.*
R.A. Champagne, 207(FR):Dec80-368
A. Meddeb, 98:Jun-Jul80-661
del Olmo, J.M.P. - see under Parrado del Olmo, J.M.
Olmsted, F.L. Civilizing American Cities. (S.B. Sutton, ed)
C. Zaitzevsky, 576:Mar81-73
Olney, J. The Rhizome and the Flower.*
G. Davenport, 569(SR):Summer81-469
G.M. Harper, 579(SAQ):Spring81-233
H.J. Levine, 639(VQR):Summer81-554
C. McDowell, 67:May81-111
M. Sprinker, 478:Fall81-243
Olney, J.B., ed. Autobiography.*
G.W. Allen, 219(GaR):Summer81-411
D. Barnouw, 221(GQ):May81-392
J. Clubbe, 301(JEGP):Jul81-435
M. Ellmann, 569(SR):Summer81-454
R. Gray, 560:Spring-Summer81-175
E. Kern, 402(MLR):Oct81-918
J. Mazzaro, 560:Spring-Summer81-188
J.N. Morris, 405(MP):Aug81-114
R.J. Porter, 191(ELN):Mar81-233
T.R. Smith, 249(HudR):Summer81-295
S.J. Whitfield, 579(SAQ):Spring81-234
Olsen, D. The State Elite.*
G.W., 102(CanL):Winter80-160
Olsen, O.H., ed. Reconstruction and Redemption in the South.
J.M. Wiener, 9(AlaR):Apr81-139
639(VQR):Winter81-7
Olsen, S.H. The Structure of Literary Understanding.*
M. Warner, 478:Spring81-118
Olshen, B.N. John Fowles.*
L. Hutcheon, 178:Spring81-116
Olson, C. and R. Creeley. The Complete Correspondence. (Vols 1 and 2) (G.F. Butterick, ed)
G. Burns, 584(SWR):Summer81-339
S. Paul, 472:Fall/Winter81-269
Olson, E. Teoría de la comedia [together with] Wardropper, B.W. La comedia española del Siglo de Oro.*
E.H. Friedman, 400(MLN):Mar81-451
205(FMLS):Jan80-92
Olson, M. The Rise and Decline of Nations.
M. Lilla, 231:Oct82-68
P. Passell, 441:21Nov82-11
Olson, R.J.M. Italian Drawings 1780-1890.
J. Masheck, 62:Feb81-71
Olsson, M. Intelligibility.
A. Chesterman, 439(NM):1980/1-90
Olwell, C. and J.L. Waldhorn. A Gift to the Street. (rev)
K. Harrington, 658:Spring81-112
Omacini, L. - see Madame de Staël

Omaggio, A.C. Games and Simulations in the Foreign Language Classroom.
  M.P. Leamon and F.L. Jenks, 399(MLJ):Autumn81-326
O'Malley, J.W. Praise and Blame in Renaissance Rome.*
  R.P. Sonkowsky, 589:Jan81-186
Omar, S. Das Archiv des Soterichos (P. Soterichos).
  J.D. Thomas, 123:Vol31No1-144
O'Meally, R.G. The Craft of Ralph Ellison.*
  N. Harris, 459:Winter80-106
  639(VQR):Summer81-84
Omesco, I. La Métamorphose de la tragédie.
  W.D. Howarth, 208(FS):Jan81-106
Omu, F.I.A. Press and Politics in Nigeria, 1880-1937.
  A.H.M. Kirk-Greene, 69:Vol50No2-229
Ondaatje, M. Elimination Dance.*
  R. Willmot, 102(CanL):Autumn80-138
Ondaatje, M., ed. The Long Poem Anthology.*
  D. Brydon, 102(CanL):Autumn80-99
Ondaatje, M. Rat Jelly and Other Poems 1963-78.
  L. Sail, 565:Vol22No1-66
Ondaatje, M. Running in the Family.
  P-L. Adams, 61:Dec82-107
  W. Balliett, 442(NY):27Dec82-76
Ondaatje, M. There's a Trick with a Knife I'm Learning to Do.*
  D. Barbour, 648(WCR):Vol 15No3-48
  E. Prato, 102(CanL):Winter80-103
Ondráčková, J. The Physiological Activity of the Speech Organs.
  G.F. Meier, 682(ZPSK):Band33Heft6-778
"One of a Kind."
  N. Rosenblum, 658:Summer/Autumn81-251
O'Neill, E. Eugene O'Neill at Work. (V. Floyd, ed)
  R. Coppenger, 609:Summer/Fall82-65
O'Neill, E. Eugene O'Neill: Poems, 1912-1944.* (D. Gallup, ed)
  R. Merritt, 150(DR):Summer81-376
  C. Molesworth, 580(SCR):Spring81-111
O'Neill, J. Essaying Montaigne.
  C. Clark, 617(TLS):30Jul82-834
O'Neill, J. On Critical Theory.
  F.R. Dallmayr, 488:Mar80-93
  L.J. Ray, 488:Mar81-99
O'Neill, J. Musée des Beaux-Arts d'Orléans: Les Peintures de l'école française des XVIIe et XVIIIe siècles.
  A.F.B., 90:Dec81-778
O'Neill, O. and W. Ruddick, eds. Having Children.
  P.J., 185:Jul81-695
O'Neill, T.R. The Individuated Hobbit.*
  C.E. Lloyd, 569(SR):Spring81-281
Onerva, L. Eino Leino Runoilija ja ihminen.
  R. Virtanen, 563(SS):Summer81-369
Onians, J. Art and Thought in the Hellenistic Age.*
  J.J. Gahan, 487:Winter81-370
  O. Murray, 90:Jan81-41
  R.R.R. Smith, 303(JoHS):Vol 101-222
Onnau, H.E. Das Schrifttum der Görresgesellschaft zur Pflege der Wissenschaft 1876-1976.
  R.A. Müller, 489(PJGG):Band88Heft2-425

Onwuejeogwu, M.A. An Igbo Civilization.
  G.I. Jones, 617(TLS):7May82-516
Onyeberechi, S. Africa.
  P.L. Thompson, 95(CLAJ):Sep80-116
Opitz, M. Gesammelte Werke.* (Vol 2, Pt 2) (G. Schulz-Behrend, ed)
  K.F. Otto, Jr., 221(GQ):Jan81-90
  P. Skrine, 402(MLR):Jul81-746
Oppenheim, F.E. Political Concepts.
  T.A., 185:Apr82-580
Oppenheim, L. Intentionality and Intersubjectivity.
  M. Lydon, 207(FR):May82-911
  D. McWilliams, 210(FrF):Sep81-285
Opperby, P. Leopold Stokowski.
  P. O'Connor, 617(TLS):24Sep82-1038
O'Prey, P. - see Graves, R.
Oqueli, R. - see del Valle, J.C.
Orbach, W.W. The American Movement to Aid Soviet Jews.*
  P.S. Appelbaum, 390:May81-59
Orban, O. - see Pedron, F.
Orderic Vitalis. The Ecclesiastical History of Orderic Vitalis. (Vol 1) (M. Chibnall, ed)
  B.M. Bolton, 617(TLS):21May82-564
Orderic Vitalis. The Ecclesiastical History of Orderic Vitalis.* (Vol 6) (M. Chibnall, ed and trans)
  R.B. Patterson, 589:Jul81-674
O'Regan, M.J. The Mannerist Aesthetic.
  M.B. Nelson, 207(FR):Apr82-676
Orenstein, A. Willard Van Orman Quine.*
  M.C. Bradley, 63:Mar81-109
Organ, D.M. Tennyson's Drama.
  T. Otten, 637(VS):Autumn80-136
Orgel, S. The Jonsonian Masque.
  B. Worden, 617(TLS):5Feb82-123
Orjuela, H.H. Literatura hispanoamericana.
  P. Barreda, 263(RIB):Vol31No4-557
Orjuela, H.H. - see Silva, J.A.
Orlando, F. Toward a Freudian Theory of Literature.*
  G. Craig, 402(MLR):Oct81-909
  R. Sussman, 207(FR):Mar81-593
Orlev, U. The Lead Soldiers.
  H. Newman, 390:Mar81-52
Orlov, V. Hamayun.
  S. Karlinsky, 441:9May82-8
Orlovsky, D.T. The Limits of Reform.
  N.V. Riasanovsky, 550(RusR):Oct81-448
Ormond, R., with J. Rishel and R. Hamlyn. Sir Edwin Landseer.*
  M. Warner, 324:Jul82-501
Ormond, R. and M. Rogers, eds. Dictionary of British Portraiture. (Vol 3 comp by E. Kilmurray, Vol 4 comp by A. Davies)
  T. Russell-Cobb, 324:Sep82-678
Ormsby, F., ed. Poets from the North of Ireland.*
  J.W. Foster, 134(CP):Fall81-116
Orozco Acuaviva, A. La gaditana Frasquita Larrea, primera romántica española.
  D.T. Gies, 240(HR):Autumn81-427
Orr, G. The Red House.*
  H. Lazer, 271:Winter81-148
  G.E. Murray, 249(HudR):Spring81-159
Orr, J. Tragic Drama and Modern Society.
  B. Rotman, 617(TLS):11Jun82-644
Orr, J. Tragic Realism and Modern Society.*
  J. Batchelor, 447(N&Q):Dec80-575

Orr, L. Existentialism and Phenomenology.*
  A.C.R.G. Montefiore, 447(N&Q):Jun80-
  280
Orrego Vicuña, F. Los estudios inter-
  nacionales en América Latina.
  A.F. Lowenthal, 263(RIB):Vol31No4-559
Orringer, N.R. Ortega y sus fuentes ger-
  mánicas.
  T. Mermall, 593:Winter81/82-372
Orsenna, É. Une comédie française.*
  J. le Hardi, 98:Apr81-438
Orso, E.G. Modern Greek Humor.
  H.R. Bernard, 292(JAF):Apr-Jun81-256
  G. Morgan, 203:Vol92No1-124
Ortega, J. La cultura peruana.
  N. Lindstrom, 399(MLJ):Winter81-447
Ortega Costa, M. Proceso de la Inquisi-
  ción contra María de Cazalla.
  A.G. Kinder, 86(BHS):Apr81-142
Ortiz, A., ed. Handbook of North American
  Indians. (Vol 9)
  W. Gard, 584(SWR):Winter81-vi
Ortner, S.B. Sherpas Through Their Ritu-
  als.
  M.C. Goldstein, 318(JAOS):Apr/Jun80-
  216
  F.A. Hanson, 567:Vol33No1/2-169
  D. Martin, 302:Vol 18-184
Orton, D. Made of Gold.
  B. Kanner, 637(VS):Summer81-520
  S. Monod, 189(EA):Oct-Dec81-478
Orton, H., S. Sanderson and J. Widdowson,
  eds. The Linguistic Atlas of England.*
  R.I. McDavid, Jr., 35(AS):Fall81-219
  B. Southard, 300:Mar81-53
Ortony, A., ed. Metaphor and Thought.*
  C.R. Hausman, 480(P&R):Summer81-188
  D.H. Hirsch, 569(SR):Winter81-95
  C. Norris, 393(Mind):Jul81-448
  G. Sampson, 361:Jun/Jul81-211
  M. Warner, 402(MLR):Apr81-426
Osborn, E. The Beginning of Christian Phi-
  losophy.
  H. Chadwick, 617(TLS):14May82-543
Osborn, F.J. and A. Whittick. New Towns.
  J. Rykwert, 576:May81-172
Osborn, K. Real Lush.
  C. Phillpot, 62:May82-77
Osborne, C. W.H. Auden.*
  R.V. Arana, 77:Spring81-169
  T. Mallon, 134(CP):Spring81-82
Osborne, C. The Life and Crimes of Agatha
  Christie.
  N. Andrew, 362:9Sep82-24
  T.J. Binyon, 617(TLS):24Sep82-1033
Osborne, H. Abstraction and Artifice in
  Twentieth-Century Art.*
  W.L. King, 289:Apr81-107
Osborne, H., ed. The Oxford Companion to
  20th-Century Art.
  S. Bayley, 362:14Jan82-23
Osborne, J. A Better Class of Person.*
  P. Bland, 364:Dec81/Jan82-124
  V.S. Pritchett, 442(NY):15Mar82-136
Osborne, M. Southeast Asia.
  D.K. Emmerson, 293(JASt):Nov80-43
Osgood, C.E. Lectures on Language Perform-
  ance.
  J.M. Carroll, 350:Sep82-711
Oshima. Écrits 1956-1978.
  H. Cronel, 450(NRF):Nov81-140
Osiński, Z. Grotowski i jego Laboratorium.
  H. Filipowicz, 574(SEEJ):Fall81-134

Osley, A.S., ed and trans. Scribes and
  Sources.
  639(VQR):Winter81-9
de Osma, G. Mariano Fortuny.
  J. Rutherford, 135:May81-75
  R.L. Shep, 614:Summer81-19
Osmund, A. and D. Hurd. War Without
  Frontiers.
  T.J. Binyon, 617(TLS):31Dec82-1448
Osofsky, S. Peter Kropotkin.
  M.A. Miller, 550(RusR):Jan81-62
Ossar, M. Anarchism in the Dramas of
  Ernst Toller.*
  E. Lachman-Kalitzki, 397(MD):Dec81-570
Ostberg, K. The Old High German Isidor in
  its Relationship to the Extant Manu-
  scripts (Eighth to Twelfth Century) of
  Isidorus De Fide Catholica.
  H.U. Schmid, 684(ZDA):Band110Heft2-59
von der Osten Sacken, C. San Lorenzo el
  Real de El Escorial.
  J.B. Bury, 90:Jun81-366
Oster, E. - see Schenker, H.
Oster, K. Islam Reconsidered.
  S. Vahiduddin, 273(IC):Oct80-249
Oster Soussouev, P. Pratique de l'éloge.*
  Requêtes.* Les dieux.* Cérémonial de
  la réalité.
  B. Saint-Sernin, 98:Aug-Sep81-845
von Osterhausen, F. Georg Christoph Sturm.
  R. Dorn, 683:Band44Heft1-99
  H. Heckmann, 43:Band11Heft2-194
Osterkamp, E. Lucifer.*
  T. Ziolkowski, 52:Band15Heft3-324
Osterwalder, H. T.S. Eliot.
  M. Lojkine-Morelec, 189(EA):Jul-Sep81-
  353
Ostle, R.C. Studies in Modern Arabic
  Literature.
  C.F. Audebert, 318(JAOS):Jul/Sep80-341
Ostriker, A. A Dream of Springtime.
  R.J. Stout, 584(SWR):Winter81-110
Ostriker, A.S. The Mother/Child Papers.*
  J. McGowan, 236:Fall-Winter82-55
Ostry, B. The Cultural Connection.
  G. Woodcock, 102(CanL):Spring80-78
Oswald von Wolkenstein. Handschrift A.
  (F. Delbono, ed)
  U. Müller, 680(ZDP):Band100Heft1-138
Otero, C-P. Evolución y revolución en
  romance.
  E. Torrego, 240(HR):Winter81-119
Otis, R. Little Valley.
  W. Gard, 584(SWR):Winter81-vii
Ott, I., ed. Kalevala.
  A. Nenola-Kallio, 196:Band21Heft1/2-
  139
Ott, S. The Circle of Mountains.
  J. Davis, 617(TLS):1Jan82-17
Otto, W.F. Les Dieux de la Grèce.
  J-P. Guinle, 450(NRF):Oct81-157
Ó Tuama, S., ed. An Duanaire.
  P. Craig, 453(NYRB):13May82-48
Ouellet, F. Lower Canada: 1791-1840.
  G.W., 102(CanL):Winter80-159
Ouellette, F. Ecrire en notre temps
  Essais.
  M. Lebel, 102(CanL):Winter80-124
Ouellette-Michalska, M. Le Plat de len-
  tilles.
  E.R. Babby, 207(FR):Feb81-507
Oukada, L. Louisiana French.
  R. Le Page, 207(FR):Dec81-296

Outerbridge, P. [title unknown; a selection of photos 1921-1939]
  A. Ross, 364:Apr/May81-10
Outhwaite, R.B., ed. Marriage and Society.
  R. Mitchison, 617(TLS):2Jul82-714
Ovendon, G. and P. Mendes. Victorian Erotic Photography.
  S. Heath, 98:Feb-Mar81-152
Overholt, W.H., ed. The Future of Brazil.
  T.E. Skidmore, 399(MLJ):Spring81-86
Ovid. Publio Ovidio Nasón, "Heróidas."
  (T. Herrera Zapién, ed)
  E.J. Kenney, 123:Vol31No2-293
Owen, G. and M.C. Williams, eds. Contemporary Southern Poetry.*
  D. Graham, 565:Vol22No1-73
  R.T. Smith, 577(SHR):Summer81-270
Owen, L. and M. Wolfe, eds. The Best Modern Canadian Short Stories.
  A.J. Harding, 102(CanL):Summer80-149
Owen, S. Indonesian Food and Cookery.
  W. and C. Cowen, 639(VQR):Spring81-73
Owens, J. Aristotle. (J.R. Catan, ed)
  R.S. Brumbaugh, 124:Jul-Aug82-377
"Oxford American Dictionary."* (E. Ehrlich and others, eds)
  G. Core, 249(HudR):Autumn81-475
  J.R. Gaskin, 569(SR):Spring81-298
"The Oxford Dictionary of Quotations." (3rd ed)
  G. Core, 249(HudR):Autumn81-475
  S. Monod, 189(EA):Jan-Mar81-83
"The Oxford-Duden Pictorial German-English Dictionary."
  G.P. Butler, 220(GL&L):Jan82-193
"The Oxford Senior Dictionary." (J.M. Hawkins, comp)
  R. Ilson, 617(TLS):4Jun82-605
"Oxford Slavonic Papers." (new ser, Vol 11)
  205(FMLS):Jan80-92
Oyama, T. - see "Shakespeare Translation"
Oyediran, O., ed. The Nigerian 1979 Elections.
  M. Crowder, 617(TLS):26Feb82-212
Oyler, J.E. and A.H. Schulze - see Gryphius, A.
Ozdoba, J. Heuristik der Fiktion.
  G. Bremner, 208(FS):Jul81-340
Özgüç, T. Excavations at Maşat Höyük and Investigations in its Vicinity.
  J. Yakar, 318(JAOS):Apr/Jun80-175
Ozick, C. Levitation.
  A. Alvarez, 453(NYRB):13May82-22
  L. Epstein, 441:14Feb82-11
  A. Mars-Jones, 617(TLS):23Apr82-456
  J. Mellors, 362:15Apr82-23
Ozment, S. The Age of Reform, 1250-1550.*
  C.J. Nederman, 539:Aug82-215

Paasivirta, J. Finland and Europe.
  K. Fitz Lyon, 617(TLS):7May82-518
Pacaly, J. Sartre au miroir.
  A.D. Ranwez, 207(FR):Feb82-421
Paccard, A. Traditional Islamic Craft in Moroccan Architecture.
  A. Hutt, 46:Oct81-259
Pacey, P. Hugh MacDiarmid and David Jones.
  R. Watson, 591(ScLJ):Summer80-122
Pacheco, J.E. "Don't Ask Me How the Time Goes By," Poems, 1964-1968.
  J.M. Labanyi, 447(N&Q):Dec80-574

Pachet, P. Nuits étroitement surveillées.
  L. Finas, 450(NRF):Feb81-118
Pachow, W. Chinese Buddhism.
  R.S.Y. Chi, 485(PE&W):Oct81-557
Pachter, M. - see Edel, L. and others
Paci, F. The Italians.
  R.W. Harvey, 102(CanL):Spring80-129
Pacifici, S. The Modern Italian Novel: From Pea to Moravia.*
  L. Kibler, 276:Winter81-326
Pacini, P. Gino Severini, disegni e incisione.
  J. Golding, 90:Feb81-107
Pack, J. Nelson's Blood.
  A. Ross, 617(TLS):12Nov82-1237
Packer, B.L. Emerson's Fall.
  R. Poirier, 441:20Jun82-14
Paczyńska, I. and A. Pilch, eds. Materiały do bibliografii dziejów emigracji oraz skupisk polonijnych w Ameryce Północnej i Południowej w XIX i XX wieku.
  W. Zalewski, 497(PolR):Vol26No1-114
Padfield, P. Tide of Empires. (Vol 2)
  J.S. Bromley, 617(TLS):26Nov82-1320
Padilla, H. Legacies: Selected Poems.
  E. Macklin, 472:Spring/Summer82-125
Padoan, G. Il Boccaccio, Le Muse, Il Parnaso e L'Arno.*
  L.G. Clubb, 545(RPh):Feb81(supp)-255
Padoan, G. Momenti del Rinascimento veneto.
  E. Bonora, 228(GSLI):Vol 158fasc501-112
Padoan, G. - see Beolco il Ruzante, A.
Padrón, J.R. - see under Rodríguez Padrón, J.
Paduano, G. Sui Persiani di Eschilo.
  J. Diggle, 123:Vol31No1-105
  A.F. Garvie, 303(JoHS):Vol 101-151
  S. Saïd, 555:Vol54fasc2-346
Page, N., ed. Dickens: "Hard Times," "Great Expectations," and "Our Mutual Friend."
  S. Monod, 189(EA):Jan-Mar81-98
Pagé, P. and R. Legris. Le Comique et l'humour à la radio québécoise.
  L.E. Doucette, 627(UTQ):Summer81-177
  J.M. Weiss, 102(CanL):Spring81-119
Pagé, P. and R. Legris. Répertoire des dramatiques québécoises à la télévision, 1952-1977.
  L.E. Doucette, 627(UTQ):Summer81-177
  D.M. Hayne, 102(CanL):Summer80-118
Pagé, P., R. Legris and L. Blouin. Répertoire des oeuvres de la littérature radiophonique québécoise, 1930-1970.
  L.E. Doucette, 627(UTQ):Summer81-177
Page, P.K., ed. To Say the Least.*
  D. Barbour, 648(WCR):Jun80-73
Pagels, E. The Gnostic Gospels.*
  F. Wisse, 529(QQ):Summer81-399
Pagels, H.R. The Cosmic Code.
  R.P. Geroch, 441:7Mar82-6
Pager, H. Ndedema.
  D. Brokensha, 2(AfrA):Feb81-78
Pagliai, M. - see Alfieri, V.
Pagnoulle, C. Malcolm Lowry.
  S.E. Grace, 102(CanL):Spring80-110
Pahlavi, M.R. Answer to History.
  W.L. Cleveland, 529(QQ):Summer81-273
Paige, K.E. and J.M. The Politics of Reproductive Ritual.
  P. Rivière, 617(TLS):16Apr82-444

Paine, J.H.E.   Theory and Criticism of the
   Novella.
      J. Pivato, 678(YCGL):No29-54
Paine, S., ed.   Six Children Draw.
      S. Dillon-Gibbons, 324:Feb82-161
Painter, N.   The Narrative of Hosea Hudson.
      H. Huntley, 9(AlaR):Jan81-62
      P. Le Blanc, 385(MQR):Summer82-486
Pais, A.   "Subtle is the Lord ... "
      T. Ferris, 441:28Nov82-9
Pais, D. - see "Gesta Hungarorum"
Pakenham, M. - see France, A.
Pakenham, T.   The Boer War.*
      A.J. Greenberger, 637(VS):Spring81-351
Palacios, E. - see Meléndez Valdés, J.
Palacios M.A.   The Mystical Philosophy of
   Ibn Masarra and His Followers.
      W. Gray, 485(PE&W):Jan81-110
Palagia, O.   Euphranor.
      R.R.R. Smith, 303(JoHS):Vol 101-212
      G.B. Waywell, 123:Vol31No2-261
Palais, J.B.   Politics and Policy in Tra-
   ditional Korea.
      V. Chandra, 293(JASt):Nov80-148
Palda, K.   The Science Council's Weakest
   Link.
      I.D. Chapman, 298:Summer81-119
Palisca, C.V., ed.   Hucbald, Guido, and
   John on Music.*
      D.S., 412:May80-142
Palladio, A.   I Quattro Libri dell'-
   Architettura.   (L. Magagnato and P.
   Marini, eds)
      B. Boucher, 617(TLS):19Mar82-317
Pallares Méndez, M.D.   El monasterio de
   Sobrado.
      K. Kennelly, 589:Oct81-897
Pallottino, M.   Saggi di antichità.
      D. Ridgway, 313:Vol71-234
Pallottino, M. and others, eds.   Popoli e
   civiltà dell' Italia antica.   (Vols 4
   and 5)
      D. Ridgway, 313:Vol71-208
Pallucchini, R.   La Pittura Veneziana del
   Seicento.
      H. Potterton, 39:Dec81-428
Palm, C.G. and D. Reed.   Guide to the
   Hoover Institution Archives.
      M.I. Elzy, 14:Winter81-53
Palmer, A.   The Penguin Dictionary of
   Twentieth Century History, 1900-1978.
      D. Kirby, 575(SEER):Jan81-110
Palmer, A.D.   Heinrich August Marschner
   1795-1861.
      J. Warrack, 617(TLS):22Jan82-85
Palmer, B.   "Man Over Money."
      639(VQR):Autumn81-120
Palmer, D.S.   Peru.
      M.C. Needler, 263(RIB):Vol31No2-280
Palmer, E.   The Growth of the African
   Novel.
      T.N. Hammond, 207(FR):Feb81-460
      P. Sabor, 49:Jul81-113
Palmer, F.R.   Modality and the English
   Modals.*
      T. Givón, 297(JL):Sep81-379
      L. Hermerén, 597(SN):Vol53No1-182
      P. Westney, 257(IRAL):Feb81-81
Palmer, I.   Matthew Arnold.
      C.A. Runcie, 637(VS):Autumn80-142
Palmer, J.   Thrillers.*
      E. Lauterbach, 395(MFS):Summer80-388
      T.A. Shippey, 447(N&Q):Jun80-278

Palmer, J.L. and I.V. Sawhill, eds.   The
   Reagan Experiment.
      A. Hacker, 441:24Oct82-12
Palmer, L.R.   The Greek Language.*
      J.H.W. Penney, 123:Vol31No2-227
Palmer, P.   The Lamp.
      R. Garfitt, 617(TLS):2Apr82-392
Palmer, R.   A Ballad History of England
   from 1588 to the Present Day.
      R. Wehse, 196:Band22Heft1/2-144
Palmer, R.C.   The County Courts of Medie-
   val England 1150-1350.
      M.T. Clanchy, 617(TLS):29Oct82-1199
Paloma, J.A., ed.   Romancer català.
      J-L. Marfany, 86(BHS):Jul81-277
Palomero Páramo, J.M.   Gerónimo Hernández.
      M. Estella, 48:Jul-Sep81-379
Pálsson, H. and P. Edwards - see "Göngu-
   Hrolfs Saga"
Paludan, A.   The Imperial Ming Tombs.
      W. Watson, 617(TLS):7May82-512
Paludan, P.S.   Victims.
      P.J. Parish, 617(TLS):4Jun82-603
"Pamyat' (Memory)."*   (No. 1-4) [entry in
   prev was No. 2]
      A. Nove, 617(TLS):3Sep82-950
Panagopoulos, B.K.   Cistercian and Mendi-
   cant Monasteries in Medieval Greece.*
      T.E. Gregory, 576:Dec81-328
      P. Hetherington, 90:Jan81-46
Pandit, S.   Indian Embroidery.
      R.L. Shep, 614:Fall81-17
Pane, R.   Il Rinascimento nell'Italia
   meridionale.
      C. Nichols, 576:Oct81-239
Panek, L.   Watteau's Shepherds.
      E. Lauterbach, 395(MFS):Summer80-388
Panfilov, V.Z., ed.   Filosofskie osnovy
   zarubežnych napravlenij v jazykoznanii.
      V. Žuravlev, 682(ZPSK):Band33Heft6-744
Pangle, T.L. - see Plato
Pani, M.   Tendenze politiche della succes-
   sione al principato di Augusto.
      R. Seager, 313:Vol71-230
Panizza, O.   Journal d'un chien.
      J. Stéfan, 450(NRF):Oct81-165
Pannick, D.   Judicial Review of the Death
   Penalty.
      G. Marshall, 617(TLS):20Aug82-899
      M. Warnock, 362:10Jun82-24
Panskaya, L., with D.D. Leslie.   Introduc-
   tion to Palladii's Chinese Literature of
   the Muslims.
      J.N. Lipman, 318(JAOS):Jan/Mar80-91
Panzer, B.   Der genetische Aufbau des
   Russischen.*
      H. Leeming, 575(SEER):Apr81-315
Paoletti, M. and R. Steele.   Civilisation
   française quotidienne.
      S. Smith, 207(FR):Feb82-454
Papadimitriou, E.   Ethische und Psycho-
   logische Grundlagen der Aristotelischen
   Rhetorik.
      H-J. Schild, 480(P&R):Summer81-190
Papamichael, A.J.   Birth and Plant Symbol-
   ism.
      K.F. Turner, 292(JAF):Jul-Sep81-397
Pape, G.   Border Crossings.
      N. Sheridan, 584(SWR):Autumn81-427
"Papers of the Athens Historical Society."
   (Vol 2)
      D.T. Morgan, 9(AlaR):Apr81-149

269

Papert, S. Mindstorms.
J.D. Burnett, 529(QQ):Summer81-371
Papetti, V. Arlecchino a Londra.*
K. Richards, 611(TN):Vol135No3-135
Papineau, D. For Science in the Social
Sciences.
A. Manser, 393(Mind):Jan81-151
D-H. Ruben, 84:Jun81-210
T.S. Torrance, 518:Jan81-62
Papineau, D. Theory and Meaning.*
G. Currie, 63:Sep81-347
R. Fellows, 518:Jul81-179
T. Nickles, 486:Sep81-500
G. Priest, 479(PhQ):Jan81-77
Papp, F. and G. Szépe, eds. Papers in
Computational Linguistics.
G.F. Meier, 682(ZPSK):Band33Heft4-508
Pappas, G., ed. Justification and Knowl-
edge.
H. Kornblith, 482(PhR):Oct81-627
Pappas, L.S. International Fish Cookery.
W. and C. Cowen, 639(VQR):Autumn81-139
Paradis, J.G. T.H. Huxley.*
C.B. Jones, 506(PSt):Sep81-216
Paradis, S. Adrienne Choquette.
J. Viswanathan, 102(CanL):Spring81-108
Parain-Vial, J., ed. L'esthétique musi-
cale de Gabriel Marcel.
P. Somville, 542:Jan-Mar81-120
Páramo, J.M.P. - see under Palomero Páramo,
J.M.
Parant, J-L. Le Bout des Bordes.
J. Stéfan, 450(NRF):Feb81-103
Parássoglu, G.M., ed. The Archive of
Aurelius Sakaon.
R.P. Duncan-Jones, 303(JoHS):Vol 101-
203
Paratore, E. Virgilio, "Eneide."* (Vols
1 and 2) [shown in prev under Vergil]
R.E.H. Westendorp Boerma, 394:Vol134
fascl/2-175
Paratore, E. Virgilio, "Eneide." (Vol 3)
J. Perret, 555:Vol154fasc2-369
R.E.H. Westendorp Boerma, 394:Vol134
fascl/2-175
Paravicini Bagliani, A. I testamenti dei
cardinali del duecento.
R. Brentano, 589:Jul81-622
Parazzoli, F. Uccelli del paradiso.
A. Caesar, 617(TLS):17Dec82-1397
Pare, R. Photography and Architecture
1839-1939.
A. Grundberg, 441:5Dec82-58
Parent, M.N. and N.S. Steinhardt - see
Suzuki, K.
Paret, P. The Berlin Secession.*
D. Cottington, 90:Nov81-682
S.S. Prawer, 617(TLS):19Mar82-295
D. Sutton, 39:Feb81-73
Paretsky, S. Indemnity Only.
N. Callendar, 441:25Apr82-21
M. Laski, 362:29Jul82-27
Pareyson, L., ed. Schellingiana Rariora.*
X. Tilliette, 489(PJGG):Band88Heft1-
201
Parfitt, G. - see Tourneur, C.
Parimoo, R., ed. Proceedings of the Work-
shop on the Problems of Teaching and
Research in History of Art in Indian
Universities.
A. Topsfield, 90:Jan81-46
Parini, J. Anthracite Country.
A. Stevenson, 617(TLS):27Aug82-916

Paris, B.J. Character and Conflict in
Jane Austen's Novel.*
R. Folkenflik, 445(NCF):Jun81-95
S.O. Taylor, 173(ECS):Summer81-494
Paris, C. La princesse Karahman.
M. Coyaud, 98:Mar80-325
"Paris."
J-F. Brière, 207(FR):Oct80-210
Parise, G. Sillabario N.2.
I. Quigly, 617(TLS):17Dec82-1397
Parker, C. and S. Arnold, eds. When the
Drumbeat Changes.
J.E. Nnadi, 49:Jul81-131
Parker, E.S. and E.M., comps. Asian
Journalism.
L.L. Chu, 302:Vol 18-160
Parker, G. Philip II.
E. Spivakovsky, 551(RenQ):Summer80-253
Parker, G.T. The Writing on the Wall.
639(VQR):Winter81-24
Parker, J. Father of the House.
A. Howard, 362:22Jul82-21
Parker, J.C., ed. City, County, Town, and
Township Index to the 1850 Federal
Census Schedules. An Index to the Biog-
raphies in 19th Century California
County Histories.
K.B. Harder, 424:Mar80-94
Parker, K. Contemporary Quilts.
M.Z. Cowan, 614:Summer82-14
Parker, N.C., comp. Personal Name Index
to the 1856 City Directories of Cali-
fornia.
K.B. Harder, 424:Mar80-93
Parker, P.A. Inescapable Romance.*
G.T. Amis, 191(ELN):Sep80-68
G. Pedersen, 599:Fall81-458
D.H. Reiman, 340(KSJ):Vol30-201
R.M. Torrance, 131(CL):Winter81-97
Parker, R. and G. Pollock. Old Mistresses.
P-L. Adams, 61:May82-106
Parker, R.B. The Judas Goat.
T.J. Binyon, 617(TLS):6Aug82-865
Parkes, C.M. and J. Stevenson-Hinde - see
under Murray Parkes, C. and J. Stevenson-
Hinde
Parkes, M.B., comp. The Medieval Manu-
scripts of Keble College, Oxford.*
J. Backhouse, 382(MAE):1981/1-107
P. Verdier, 589:Oct81-934
Parkin, A. The Dramatic Imagination of
W.B. Yeats.
B. Dolan, 305(JIL):May81-131
Parkin, F. Marxism and Class Theory.
B. Cooper, 529(QQ):Spring81-183
R. Hudelson, 482(PhR):Oct81-619
Parkin, F. Max Weber.
Z. Bauman, 617(TLS):2Jul82-715
Parkinson, T. - see Crane, H. and Y.
Winters
Parr, J. Labouring Children.*
A.R. McCormack, 529(QQ):Summer81-362
Parr, S. and others. City of Portland
Records Manual.
S.E. Haller, 14:Fall80-495
Parrado del Olmo, J.M. Los escultores
seguidores de Berruguete en Ávila.
M. Estella, 48:Jul-Sep81-380
Parrinder, P. Science Fiction.*
J-P. Vernier, 189(EA):Apr-Jun81-209
205(FMLS):Oct81-378
Parris, L. The Pre-Raphaelites.
R. Mander, 39:Apr81-269

Patel, G. How Do You Withstand, Body?
J.P. Gemmill, 314:Summer-Fall81-207
Pateman, C. The Problem of Political
Obligation.*
S.W. Ball, 482(PhR):Jul81-475
R. Rogowski, 185:Jan81-296
R. Young, 63:Dec81-460
Pater, W. An Imaginative Sense of Fact.
(P. Dodd, ed)
J. Uglow, 617(TLS):26Feb82-231
Pater, W. The Renaissance.* (D.L. Hill,
ed)
P. Barolsky, 39:Mar81-200
529(QQ):Spring81-195
636(VP):Summer81-201
Patera, C. The Mola Pattern Book.
M.Z. Cowan, 614:Summer82-17
Patera, C. The Stained Glass Pattern Book
for Reverse Appliqué.
M.Z. Cowan, 614:Summer82-19
Paterson, A., ed. 15 Contemporary New
Zealand Poets.
J.B. Ringer, 368:Mar81-95
Paterson, T. On Every Front.
F.W. Neal, 550(RusR):Apr81-203
Paterson, T.W. Encyclopedia of Ghost
Towns and Mining Camps of British
Columbia.
G.W., 102(CanL):Spring80-152
Paton, A. Ah, But Your Land is Beautiful.*
P-L. Adams, 61:Apr82-110
C. Hope, 364:Dec81/Jan82-136
J. Romano, 441:4Apr82-7
Paton, R. Business Case Studies — French.
B. Braude, 207(FR):May82-918
Patout, P. Alfonso Reyes et la France
(1889-1959).*
B.G. Carter, 238:Mar81-163
Saint Patrick. Confession et lettre à
Coroticus. (R.P.C. Hanson, with C.
Blanc, eds and trans)
P. Flobert, 555:Vol54fasc1-191
Patrick, J.M. and R.H. Sundell, eds.
Milton and the Art of Sacred Song.*
T.W. Hayes, 125:Spring81-346
Patrides, C.A., ed. Approaches to Mar-
vell.*
R.M. Cummings, 402(MLR):Jul81-669
H. Kelliher, 447(N&Q):Oct80-440
E. Miner, 551(RenQ):Spring80-142
Patrides, C.A., ed. The Cambridge Platon-
ists.
W. Schultz, 480(P&R):Fall81-257
Patrides, C.A. and R.B. Waddington, eds.
The Age of Milton.*
C. Hill, 366:Autumn81-228
Patruno, N. Language in Giovanni Verga's
Early Novels.
G. Cecchetti, 276:Spring81-66
Patschovsky, A., ed. Quellen zur böhmis-
chen Inquisition im 14. Jahrhundert.
R. Kieckhefer, 589:Oct81-899
Patten, R.L. Charles Dickens and his
Publishers.*
J.D.F., 447(N&Q):Oct80-462
C. Kent, 125:Winter81-241
Patterson, A.M. Marvell and the Civic
Crown.
G. Bradshaw, 184(EIC):Oct80-357
Patterson, D.W. The Shaker Spiritual.
I. Lowens, 414(MusQ):Jan81-131

Patterson, F. Photography and The Art of
Seeing.
W.N., 102(CanL):Autumn80-inside back
cover
Patterson, F. and E. Linden. The Educa-
tion of Koko.
T.A. Sebeok, 617(TLS):10Sep82-976
Patterson, M. Peter Stein.
M. Butler, 617(TLS):17Sep82-1018
Patterson, M.C., ed. Author Newsletters
and Journals.*
A. Bell, 402(MLR):Apr81-420
Pattison, R. The Child Figure in English
Literature.*
L.A. Schoch, 637(VS):Winter81-240
Pattison, R. On Literacy.
W. Goodman, 441:19Sep82-18
Pattison, R. Tennyson and Tradition.*
G.L. Bruns, 191(ELN):Dec80-150
W. Hellstrom, 301(JEGP):Jan81-147
G. Joseph, 637(VS):Winter81-235
H. Kozicki, 405(MP):Nov81-210
Pattison, W.T. - see Galdós, B.P.
Patton, B. - see Fisher, R. and W. Ury
Patton, P.C. and R.A. Holoien. Computing
in the Humanities.
T.K. Bender, 365:Spring-Summer82-119
Pauken, E. Das Steinmetzbuch WG 1572 im
Städelschen Kunstinstitut zu Frankfurt
am Main.
W. Müller, 683:Band44Heft1-95
Paul, B. Your Eyelids Are Growing Heavy.
T.J. Binyon, 617(TLS):29Oct82-1196
M. Laski, 362:2Dec82-23
Paul, C.B. Science and Immortality.
J. Barchilon, 207(FR):May82-930
Paul, D.W. The Cultural Limits of Revolu-
tionary Politics.
K. Dawisha, 104(CASS):Winter81-633
Paul, D.Y., with F. Wilson. Women in
Buddhism.
K.C. Lang, 293(JASt):Aug81-833
Paul, F. August Strindberg.*
G. Benda, 221(GQ):Jan81-104
Paul, J. The Mouths of the Year.
H. Thomas, 385(MQR):Winter82-200
Paul, J., ed. Reading Nozick.
J. Waldron, 617(TLS):19Nov82-1277
Paul, N.A. Bibliographie Jacques Copeau.
J.B. Blessing, 612(ThS):May81-111
Paul, R. The Thomas Street Horror.
P-L. Adams, 61:Apr82-110
Paul, R.A. The Tibetan Symbolic World.
J.H. Crook, 617(TLS):12Nov82-1236
Paul, S. The Lost America of Love.
L.M., 617(TLS):26Mar82-363
Paul, S. Olson's Push.*
P. Yannella, 295(JML):Vol8No3/4-581
Pauley, B.F. Hitler and the Forgotten
Nazis.
F.L. Carsten, 617(TLS):15Jan82-59
Pauli, W. Wolfgang Pauli: Wissenschaft-
licher Briefwechsel mit Einstein, Bohr,
Heisenberg u.a. (Vol 1) (A. Hermann,
K.V. Meyenn and V.F. Weisskopf, eds)
J. Hendry, 84:Sep81-277
Paulin, T. The Book of Juniper.
N. Corcoran, 617(TLS):30Jul82-830
Paulin, T. The Strange Museum.*
A. Cluysenaar, 565:Vol22No2-62
S. O'Brien, 493:Jun81-60

Paulsen, W., ed. Die Frau als Heldin und
Autorin.*
  E.T. Beck, 400(MLN):Apr81-704
  W. Hoffmeister, 301(JEGP):Jul81-397
  E. Sagarra, 402(MLR):Jan81-243
  H.T. Tewarson, 222(GR):Fall81-162
  L.Z. Wittmann, 67:Nov81-262
Paulsen, W., ed. Österreichische Gegen-
wart.
  J. Strelka, 221(GQ):Nov81-530
Paulson, M.G., ed. The Fallen Crown.
  T. Scanlan, 207(FR):May82-904
Paulson, R. Popular and Polite Art in the
Age of Hogarth and Fielding.*
  C.E. Pierce, Jr., 191(ELN):Sep80-55
Paulston, C.B. Bilingual Education Theo-
ries and Issues.
  A.B. Gaarder, 399(MLJ):Summer81-205
  R.W. Newman, 207(FR):May81-883
Paulton, A. Sir William Walton: a Discog-
raphy.
  M. Walker, 415:Jun81-380
Paulus Venetus. Super primum Sententiarum
Johannis de Ripa lecturae abbreviatio,
Prologus. (F. Ruello, ed)
  G. Gál, 589:Oct81-901
Pavel, T. Le miroir persan.
  C. Rubinger, 102(CanL):Spring80-118
Pavis, P. Dictionnaire du théâtre.
  M. Hays, 494:Spring81-265
  J.L. Savona, 397(MD):Dec81-563
Pavlovskis, Z., ed and trans. The Story
of Apollonius, King of Tyre (Historia
Apollonii Regis Tyri).
  J.M. Hunt, 122:Oct81-340
Pawelczynska, A. Values and Violence in
Auschwitz.
  A.L., 185:Jan82-390
Payen, J-C. Le prince d'Aquitaine.
  F.R.P. Akehurst, 589:Oct81-903
Payen, J-C. La Rose et l'Utopie.
  A. Knapton, 545(RPh):Feb81(supp)-353
Payn, G. and S. Morley - see Coward, N.
Payne, A.J. Louisa May Alcott.
  C. Gay, 26(ALR):Spring81-153
Payne, F.A. Chaucer and Menippean Satire.
  V. Adams, 617(TLS):15Jan82-56
Payne, L. Take the Money and Run.
  T.J. Binyon, 617(TLS):31Dec82-1448
Payne, S.B., Jr. The Soviet Union and
SALT.
  639(VQR):Summer81-90
Payot, R. Jean-Jacques Rousseau ou la
gnose tronquée.
  M. Eigeldinger, 535(RHL):Jan-Feb81-140
Payzant, J. The Journal of the Reverend
John Payzant (1749-1834). (B.C. Cuth-
bertson, ed)
  T. Sinclair-Faulkner, 150(DR):Autumn81-
  587
Paz, O. A Draft of Shadows.* (E. Weinber-
ger, ed and trans)
  639(VQR):Winter81-27
Paz, O. D'un mot à l'autre.
  L. Ray, 450(NRF):Apr81-152
Paz, O. In/Mediaciones.
  J.D. Henderson, 37:Feb81-45
Paz, O. Selected Poems. (C. Tomlinson,
ed)
  R. Cardinal, 529(QQ):Spring81-19
Paz, O. and others. Renga.*
  R. Cardinal, 529(QQ):Spring81-19

Paz, O. and C. Tomlinson. Airborn/Hijos
del Aire.*
  D. Gioia, 249(HudR):Winter81/82-583
Pazzaglini, P.R. The Criminal Ban of the
Sienese Commune, 1225-1310.
  W.M. Bowsky, 589:Oct81-904
Peabody, B. The Winged Word.*
  W.J. Verdenius, 394:Vol34fasc3/4-412
Peace, R. The Enigma of Gogol.
  D. Fanger, 617(TLS):4Jun82-621
Peacock, M. And Live Apart.
  R. Phillips, 249(HudR):Autumn81-427
Peacocke, C. Holistic Explanation.
  S. Haack, 479(PhQ):Jul81-273
Pearce, R.D. The Turning Point in Africa.
  J.D. Hargreaves, 617(TLS):29Oct82-1184
Pearce, R.H. - see Hawthorne, N.
Pearce, T.M. - see Austin, M.
Pearsall, D. Old and Middle English
Poetry.*
  F.C. Robinson, 402(MLR):Jul81-651
Pearsall, D. - see Langland, W.
Pearse, P.H. The Letters of P.H. Pearse.*
(S. O'Buachalla, ed)
  R.G. Yeed, 305(JIL):Jan81-94
Pearson, A. and E. Early Churches of
Washington State.
  E.D. Layman, 576:Dec81-341
Pearson, J. The Kindness of Dr. Avicenna.
  T.J. Binyon, 617(TLS):10Sep82-982
  R. Freedman, 441:24Oct82-42
Pearson, J. The Sitwells.
  M. Goldstein, 569(SR):Spring81-287
Pearson, J. Tragedy and Tragicomedy in
the Plays of John Webster.*
  S.C. Putt, 175:Autumn81-291
Pearson, J. and J. No Time but Place.
  P. Lehmberg, 649(WAL):Spring81-70
  639(VQR):Winter81-29
Pearson, K. The History of Statistics in
the 17th and 18th Centuries against the
Changing Background of Intellectual,
Scientific and Religious Thought.
  I. Hacking, 84:Jun81-177
Pearson, K. and R. - see Kim, J-H.
Pearson, M.N. Coastal Western India.
  C.R. Boxer, 617(TLS):6Aug82-859
Pearson, N.H. and M. King - see H.D.
Pearson, P.D. and D.D. Johnson. Teaching
Reading Comprehension.
  L. Baten, 277(ITL):No47-72
Pechter, E. Dryden's Classical Theory of
Literature.
  A. Clayborough, 179(ES):Feb81-69
Peck, G.T. The Fool of God.
  R.H. Schmandt, 589:Jul81-641
Peck, R.A. Kingship and Common Profit in
Gower's "Confessio Amantis."*
  R.F. Yeager, 402(MLR):Jul81-654
Peck, W.H. and J. Ross. Drawings from
Ancient Egypt.
  T.G.H. James, 39:Oct81-270
Peckenpaugh, A. Letters from Lee's Army.
  W. Slesinger, 448:Vol 19No1/2-246
Peden, M.S. Emilio Carballido.
  S.M. Cypess, 238:Sep81-484
Pedersen, F.S. Late Roman Public Profes-
sionalism.
  E.J. Jonkers, 394:Vol34fasc1/2-192
Pedicord, H.W. and F.L. Bergmann - see
Garrick, D.
Pedretti, C. Leonardo Architetto.
  J.S. Ackerman, 576:Mar81-66

Pedretti, C. The Literary Works of
Leonardo da Vinci: Commentary.*
J. Wasserman, 90:Oct81-623
Pedron, F. Histoire d'Ambroise, chirur-
gien du roi. (O. Orban, ed)
A. Vermeirre, 539:Feb82-62
Peebles, M. Court and Village.
R.L. Shep, 614:Winter82-16
Peers, F.W. The Public Eye.*
G.W., 102(CanL):Spring80-150
Peierls, R. Surprises in Theoretical
Physics.
M. Redhead, 84:Sep81-309
Peignot, J. Du Calligramme.
D.W. Seaman, 207(FR):Oct80-156
Peil, D. Zur "angewandten Emblematik" in
protestantischen Erbauungsbüchern.
D. Sulzer, 196:Band22Heftl/2-146
Peirce, C.S. Contributions to "The
Nation."* (Pts 1-3) (K.L. Ketner
and J.E. Cook, eds)
M. Thompson, 482(PhR):Apr81-289
"Peirce Studies." (No 1) (K.L. Ketner and
J.M. Ransdell, eds)
J.J. Zeman, 567:Vol36No3/4-309
Pekarik, A.J. Japanese Lacquer, 1600-
1900.
R. Bushell, 407(MN):Summer81-219
Peled, M. Al-Uqṣūṣah al-Taymūriyyah fī
marḥalatayn.
I. Peters, 318(JAOS):Jan/Mar80-33
Pelikan, J. The Christian Tradition.
(Vol 3)
E. Webb, 648(WCR):Jun80-65
Pelinski, R., L. Suluk and L. Amarock.
Inuit Songs From Eskimo Point.
T. Johnston, 187:Jan82-162
Pélissier, R. Les guerres grises.*
H. Deschamps, 69:Vol50No2-223
Pellaprat, H.P. The Great Book of French
Cuisine. (R. Kramer and D. White, eds)
M. Sheraton, 441:5Dec82-67
Pelletier, A. Le Sanctuaire Métroaque de
Vienne (France).
R.M. Ogilvie, 123:Vol31No2-306
Pelletier, A. - see Josephus
Pelletier, F.J., ed. Mass Terms.*
M. Lockwood, 393(Mind):Jul81-454
R. Nolan, 518:Jan81-37
Pelletier, R.J. The Interrelationship Be-
tween Prominent Character Types in "Le
Diable boiteux," "Gil Blas" and "Le Théâ-
tre de la Foire" by Alain-René Lesage.
H. Klüppelholz, 535(RHL):Mar-Apr81-297
Pelletier, Y. Thèmes et Symboles dans
l'oeuvre romanesque de Louis Guilloux.
W.D. Redfern, 402(MLR):Jul81-712
Pellew, J. The Home Office 1848-1914.
R.T. Shannon, 617(TLS):30Jul82-829
Pelling, M. Cholera, Fever and English
Medicine 1825-1865.*
S.E.D. Shortt, 529(QQ):Spring81-130
Pelous, J-M. Amour précieux, amour galant
(1654-1675).
J.F. Gaines, 207(FR):Apr81-734
Pempel, T.J., ed. Policymaking in Contem-
porary Japan.
R. Benjamin, 293(JASt):Nov80-69
Pena, J. Usos anómalos de los sustantivos
verbales en el español actual.
M. Torreblanca, 545(RPh):Feb81-343

Peñalosa, F. Chicano Sociolinguistics.
E. Martínez, 399(MLJ):Winter81-445
J.M. Sharp, 238:Dec81-650
Penkert, S., ed. Emblem und Emblematik-
rezeption.
F.L. Borchardt, 406:Winter81-453
Penman, S.K. The Sunne in Splendour.
P-L. Adams, 61:Dec82-107
M. Simpson, 441:19Dec82-13
Pennington, A.E. - see Kotošixin, G.
Pennington, D. and K. Thomas, eds. Puri-
tans and Revolutionaries.
J.A. Sharpe, 161(DUJ):Dec80-93
Pennock, J.R. Democratic Political Theory.
D. Johnston, 185:Jan82-356
Pennycock, A. The Book of Card Games.
M. Amory, 617(TLS):4Jun82-617
Penrose, R. and J. Golding, eds. Picasso
in Retrospect.
L. Cooke, 59:Jun81-231
"Pensée hispanique et phisosophie fran-
çaise des lumières."
H. Wagner, 53(AGP):Band63Heft3-350
Pentikäinen, J. Oral Repertoire and
World View.*
R. Wehse, 196:Band21Heft3/4-331
Peñuelas, M.C. Cultura hispánica en
Estados Unidos: Los chicanos.* (2nd ed)
E. Martínez, 399(MLJ):Spring81-101
Pepper, S. Aesthetic Quality.
P. Kivy, 290(JAAC):Winter81-201
Peppercorn, D. Bordeaux.
J. Robinson, 617(TLS):27Aug82-929
A. Watkins, 362:10Jun82-27
Percas de Ponseti, H. Cervantes y su
concepto del arte.
E.H. Friedman, 552(REH):May81-306
C. Iranzo, 241:May81-69
Percy, W. The Second Coming.*
G. Johnson, 461:Spring-Summer81-92
R.H. King, 639(VQR):Spring81-341
W. Koon, 580(SCR):Spring81-109
W. Prunty, 219(GaR):Spring81-160
N. Schmitz, 473(PR):4/1981-629
Perec, G. La Clôture et autres poèmes.
M. Bishop, 207(FR):Feb82-441
Pereira, T.A. Mas entramos en la noche.
J. Roy, 552(REH):May81-299
Pereira Leite, C.C. and R.C.P. Silveira,
eds. A gramática portuguesa na pesquisa
e no ensino, I.
B. Comrie, 350:Mar82-246
Perelló, J. The History of International
Association of Logopedics and Phonia-
trics.
H. Ulbrich, 682(ZPSK):Band33Heft2-265
Perelman, C. Introduction historique à la
philosophie morale.*
V.J.B., 543:Mar81-616
Perelman, C. Justice, Law, and Argument.
R.H., 185:Oct81-185
Perelman, C. Logique juridique, Nouvelle
rhétorique.
H.W. Johnstone, Jr., 480(P&R):Winter81-
64
Perel'muter, I.A. Obščeindoevropejskij i
grečeskij glagol.
P. Trost, 260(IF):Band85-328
Pereña, L. and C. Baciero, with others -
see Pérez de Mesa, D.
Perényi, E. Green Thoughts.*
C. Lloyd, 617(TLS):26Nov82-1321

Peres, S. From These Men.
  M. Louvish, 287:May81-19
Peretti, A. Il Periplo di Scilace.
  E.W. Gray, 123:Vol31No2-273
Pérez, G.J. Formalist Elements in the
  Novels of Juan Goytisolo.
  J.W. Kronik, 400(MLN):Mar81-462
  L.G. Levine, 238:Mar81-158
  E.W. Nelson, 399(MLJ):Spring81-96
Pérez de Mesa, D. Política o razón de
  estado. (L. Pereña and C. Baciero, with
  others, eds)
  A. Reix, 542:Jul-Sep81-362
Pérez Rivera, F. and M. Hurtado. Introduc-
  ción a la literatura española.
  G.M. Bearse, 241:Sep81-92
Pérez Rojas, J. Casinos de la región
  murciana.
  E. Casado, 48:Jan-Mar81-104
Periñán, B. Poeta ludens.
  A. Soons, 86(BHS):Jan81-81
Perkins, D. and others. Rural Small Scale
  Industry in the People's Republic of
  China.
  V.F.S. Sit, 302:Vol 18-146
Perkins, D.N. The Mind's Best Work.
  M. Gardner, 441:3Jan82-6
Perkins, L.L. and H. Garey, eds. The
  Mellon Chansonnier.*
  A.W. Atlas, 317:Spring81-132
  M. Picker, 551(RenQ):Winter80-771
Perl, W.R. The Four-Front War.*
  B.W. Varon, 390:Jun/Jul81-46
Perle, G. The Operas of Alban Berg.
  (Vol 1)
  P. Griffiths, 415:Sep81-604
  M.M. Hyde, 317:Fall81-573
Perlin, G. The Tory Syndrome.
  J. English, 529(QQ):Spring81-165
Perlmutter, A. Modern Authoritarianism.
  P.G.B., 185:Jul82 776
Perlmutter, D.M. and S. Soames. Syntactic
  Argumentation and the Structure of
  English.*
  J. Casagrande, 215(GL):Winter81-286
  M.S. Dryer, 361:Sep81-97
Perlmutter, N. and R.A. The Real Anti-
  Semitism in America.
  E. Willis, 441:3Oct82-15
Perloff, M. The Poetics of Indeterminacy.
  B. Hatlen, 468:Winter81-655
"Permissiveness and Control."
  L.P.F., 185:Oct81-183
Pernoud, R. La Femme au temps des cathé-
  dreles.
  J.D. Bragger, 207(FR):Apr82-696
Perosa, A. and J. Sparrow, eds. Renais-
  sance Latin Verse.*
  C. Fantazzi, 487:Spring81-101
  W. Ludwig, 551(RenQ):Summer80-238
  J.E. Ziolkowski, 124:Sep-Oct81-58
Pérouse, G-A. and others, eds. Le Paran-
  gon de nouvelles.
  J.L. Allaire, 207(FR):Oct80-159
  R. Godenne, 535(RHL):May-Jun81-454
  K.M. Hall, 208(FS):Jul81-321
  A. Saunders, 402(MLR):Jan81-183
Perriam, W. Bourbon for Breakfast.
  639(VQR):Autumn81-136
Perrie, W. By Moon and Sun.
  C. Craig, 571(ScLJ):Winter81-140
Perrier, A. Le Livre d'Ophélie.
  J. Devaud, 207(FR):Dec80-368

Perrois, L. Arts du Gabon.
  L. Siroto, 2(AfrA):Nov80-76
Perrone, C. - see Graf, A.
Perry, G. Snow in Summer.
  F. Adcock, 617(TLS):29Jan82-114
Perry, H.S. Psychiatrist of America.
  R. Coles, 441:7Mar82-7
Perry, J. Jack London.
  442(NY):15Feb82-140
Perry, J. - see London, J.
Perry, L. and M. Fellman, eds. Anti-
  slavery Reconsidered.*
  D.L. Lightner, 106:Fall81-225
Perry, R. Denizens.*
  R. Tillinghast, 569(SR):Spring81-265
Perry, T. The Butcher's Boy.
  J. Casey, 441:22Aug82-10
  442(NY):20Sep82-156
Perry, T.A., ed. Evidence and Argumenta-
  tion in Linguistics.
  G. Sampson, 84:Mar81-98
Perse, S-J. Amitié du Prince. (A. Henry,
  ed)
  R. Little, 208(FS):Oct81-474
  M. Parent, 535(RHL):Mar-Apr81-333
Persico, J.E. The Imperial Rockefeller.
  M. Carroll, 441:14Mar82-7
Persius. The Satires of Persius.* (W.S.
  Merwin, trans)
  W. Hutchings, 148:Summer81-95
Persson, I. Das System der kausativen
  Funktionsverbgefüge.
  A. Lötscher, 685(ZDL):1/1981-72
Peschel, E.R., ed. Medicine and Litera-
  ture.
  B. Haley, 651(WHR):Summer81-181
  A.H. Jones, 446(NCFS):Fall-Winter81/82-
  184
  J.P. Plottel, 210(FrF):May81-187
  G.S. Rousseau, 579(SAQ):Autumn81-481
  T. Ziolkowski, 569(SR):Fall81-652
Peschel, G-D. Prolog-Programm und Frag-
  ment-Schluss in Gotfrits Tristanroman.
  H. Heinen, 680(ZDP):Band99Heft1-130
Peschken, G. - see Schinkel, K.F.
Pesotsky, B. Stories Up to a Point.
  D. Montrose, 617(TLS):10Sep82-965
  D. Quammen, 441:14Feb82-11
  442(NY):1Mar82-128
Peskett, W. Survivors.
  L. Sail, 565:Vol122No1-66
Pesot, J. Silence, on parle.*
  M. Grimaud, 207(FR):Mar82-587
Pessin, A. and H-S. Torgue. Villes imagi-
  naires.
  P. Sansot, 98:Jan81-92
Petch, S. Sight Unseen.
  A. Ravel, 102(CanL):Summer81-158
Petech, L. The Kingdom of Ladakh, c. 950-
  1842 A.D.*
  J.C. Huntington, 318(JAOS):Jul/Sep80-
  325
Peter of Ailly. Concepts and Insolubles.
  (P.V. Spade, ed and trans)
  W.J. Courtenay, 589:Jul81-675
Peter, J. Vallor.
  A. Bukoski, 102(CanL):Autumn80-111
Peter, K. Friedrich Schlegel.*
  E. Behler, 680(ZDP):Band100Heft4-604
Peter, K. Stadien der Aufklärung.
  E.E. Reed, 221(GQ):May81-348
Peterlongo, P. The Violin.
  M. Parikian, 415:Jan81-32

Peters, E. The Leper of St. Giles.*
  N. Callendar, 441:26Sep82-41
Peters, E. The Magician, the Witch, and
  the Law.*
  B.P. Copenhaver, 319:Oct81-502
Peters, F.G. Robert Musil.*
  M.S. Fries, 395(MFS):Summer80-362
  K. Hasselbach, 435:Winter81-112
Peters, H. - see Donne, J.
Peters, J., ed. Collectible Books.*
  D.J. Hall, 503:Winter81-173
Peters, J.R.T.M. God's Created Speech.
  J.M. Pessagno, 318(JAOS):Jul/Sep80-332
Peters, L. Selected Poetry.
  A. Delius, 617(TLS):14May82-541
Peters, M. Pitt and Popularity.*
  M.M. Goldsmith, 83:Autumn81-235
Peters, M. Shaw and the Actresses.*
  T. Stephenson, 572:Vol 1-249
Peters, S. The Park is Mine.
  D. Profumo, 617(TLS):5Feb82-147
Peters, T.J. and R.H. Waterman, Jr. In
  Search of Excellence.
  J. Fallows, 61:Dec82-99
Petersen, C. On the Track of the Dixie
  Limited.
  T.L. McHaney, 395(MFS):Winter80/81-655
Petersen, G.B. The Moon in the Water.
  S. Goldstein, 295(JML):Vol8No3/4-380
  K. Tsuruta, 293(JASt):Feb81-393
Petersen, J.H. Max Frisch.*
  I.M. Goessl, 221(GQ):Jan81-112
Petersen, W. Malthus.
  A. Brundage, 637(VS):Spring81-364
Petersmann, G. Themenführung und Motiventer-
  faltung in der Monobiblos des Properz.
  J.C. McKeown, 123:Vol31No2-291
Peterson, C. Peter the Great's Administra-
  tive and Judicial Reforms.*
  L.R. Lewitter, 575(SEER):Jul81-439
Peterson, J.E. Curs'd Example.
  F. Lagarde, 189(EA):Jul-Sep81-339
Peterson, R. Leaving Taos.* (C. Kizer,
  ed)
  P. Stitt, 219(GaR):Fall81-647
  V. Young, 472:Fall/Winter81-155
Peterson, R.F. Mary Lavin.*
  M. Rohrberger, 395(MFS):Winter80/81-
  692
Peterson, R.T. and V.M. Audubon's Birds
  of America.
  D. Snow, 617(TLS):4Jun82-615
Peterson, T.H. Agricultural Exports, Farm
  Income, and the Eisenhower Administra-
  tion.
  T.F. Soapes, 14:Fall80-496
Peterson, W.J. Bitter Gourd.
  L. Struve, 293(JASt):Nov80-117
Peterson, W.S. - see Browning, R. and F.J.
  Furnivall
Peterson, W.S. - see "Browning Institute
  Studies"
Petesch, N.L.M. Duncan's Colony.
  B. Morton, 617(TLS):15Oct82-1142
Pethick, D. The Nootka Connection.
  W.N., 102(CanL):Spring81-173
  P. Roy, 298:Fall-Winter81-205
Petit, F. Introduction à la psychosociolo-
  gie des organisations.
  J-M. Gabaude, 542:Jan-Mar81-131
Petit, J. - see Barbey d'Aurevilly, J-A.

"Petit Larousse en couleurs 1980."* (C.
  Dubois, ed-in-chief)
  S. Haig, 207(FR):Oct80-200
Petitfils, P. Verlaine.*
  P-J. Founau, 450(NRF):Sep81-121
Petrarch. Petrarca, Obras. (Vol 1) (P.M.
  Cátedra, J.M. Tatjer and C. Yarza, eds)
  A. Scaglione, 545(RPh):Feb81-352
Petrarch. Petrarch in England. (J.
  D'Amico, ed)
  T.M. Greene, 677(YES):Vol 11-231
  A. Scaglione, 545(RPh):Feb81-352
  A.W. Vivarelli, 400(MLN):Jan81-159
  J.K. Wikeley, 276:Summer81-119
Petrarch. Petrarch's "Bucolicum Carmen."
  (T.G. Bergin, trans)
  A.S. Bernardo, 276:Summer81-116
Petrarch. Petrarch's Lyric Poems. (R.M.
  Durling, ed and trans)
  J. Ahern, 472:Spring/Summer82-231
  S. Bermann, 276:Summer81-117
Petrarch. Selected Poems. (A. Mortimer,
  trans)
  S. Bermann, 276:Summer81-117
Petrarch. Songs and Sonnets from Laura's
  Lifetime. (N. Kilmer, trans)
  J. Ahern, 472:Spring/Summer82-231
Petrella, R. La Renaissance des cultures
  régionales en Europe.
  A. Valdman, 207(FR):Oct81-165
Petrey, S. History in the Text.
  R.B. Grant, 446(NCFS):Fall-Winter81/82-
  144
Petrie, D.W. Ultimately Fiction.
  P.R. Broughton, 284:Spring82-203
  27(AL):Jan82-758
Petrie, G. Seahorse.*
  E. Friedman, 461:Fall-Winter81/82-93
Petrini, M. Le commedie popolari del
  Goldoni.
  G. Nuvoli, 228(GSLI):Vol 156fasc495-
  469
Petrounias, E. Funktion und Thematik der
  Bilder bei Aischylos.
  M.S. Silk, 303(JoHS):Vol 101-150
  W.J. Verdenius, 394:Vol134fasc1/2-151
Petrov, A. and others. Architekturdenk-
  mäler Leningrads.
  V. Antonov, 43:Band11Heft2-196
Petrovska, M. Victor Hugo.
  P.L. Horn, 446(NCFS):Spring-Summer82-
  374
Petry, C.F. The Civilian Elite of Cairo
  in the Later Middle Ages.
  P.J. Vatikiotis, 617(TLS):10Sep82-979
Petsalis-Diomidis, N. Greece at the Paris
  Peace Conference, 1919.
  D. Kitsikis, 104(CASS):Winter81-623
Petsopoulos, Y. Kilims.*
  M.H. Beattie, 463:Spring81-92
Petsopoulos, Y., ed. Tulips, Arabesques
  and Turbans.
  R. Cormack, 617(TLS):2Jul82-722
Pettas, W.A. The Giunti of Florence.*
  P. Needham, 517(PBSA):Jul-Sep81-357
  D.E. Rhodes, 354:Mar81-70
Petti, A.G. English Literary Hands from
  Chaucer to Dryden.*
  J. Gerritsen, 179(ES):Feb81-92
Pettigrew, J., with T.J. Collins - see
  Browning, R.

Pettit, A.G. Images of the Mexican American in Fiction and Film. (D.E. Showalter, ed)
  W.A. Bloodworth, Jr., 649(WAL): Winter82-323
Pettit, P. Judging Justice.
  B.B., 185:Jul82-775
  D. Browne, 63:Jun81-257
  T.D. Campbell, 479(PhQ):Oct81-377
  D.L.S., 543:Dec80-393
  F.F. Schauer, 518:Oct81-239
Pettman, R., ed. Moral Claims in World Affairs.
  C.R. Beitz, 185:Oct80-151
Pétursson, M. Isländisch.*
  S. Eliasson, 260(IF):Band85-364
Petzoldt, L., ed. Deutsche Schwänke.
  E. Moser-Rath, 196:Band22Heft1/2-147
Petzoldt, L., ed. Deutsche Volkssagen. (2nd ed)
  G. Petschel, 196:Band21Heft1/2-140
Peukert, D. Die KPD im Widerstand.
  T. Mason, 617(TLS):7May82-513
Peyre, H. What Is Symbolism?
  A.L. Amprimoz, 446(NCFS):Fall-Winter81/82-161
Peyrefitte, A. The Trouble with France.*
  442(NY):11Jan82-96
Peyrol, M. L'Oeil du chat.
  M.G. Hydak, 207(FR):Apr81-768
Peytard, J. Voix et traces narratives chez Stendhal.
  M-T. Ligot, 209(FM):Oct81-370
Pfarrer, D. Neverlight.
  A. Cheuse, 441:19Sep82-31
Pfeiffer, R. History of Classical Scholarship from 1300 to 1850.*
  E.C. Kopff, 122:Oct81-314
Pfister, F. Kleine Schriften zum Alexanderroman.
  C. Minis, 684(ZDA):Band110Heft3-113
Pfister, M. Einführung in die romanische Etymologie.
  V. Väänänen, 439(NM):1981/2-217
Pfister, M. LEI: Lessico etimologico italiano. (Vol 1, fasc 1)
  H.D. Bork, 72:Band217Heft2-447
Pflanz, H.M. Die lateinischen Textgrundlagen des St. Galler Passionsspieles in der mittelalterlichen Liturgie.
  U. Mehler, 684(ZDA):Band109Heft3-120
Pfohl, R. Racine's "Iphigénie."
  A.G. Engstrom, 207(FR):May82-903
Pheifer, J.D., ed. Old English Glosses in the Épinal-Erfurt Glossary.*
  H. Schabram, 260(IF):Band85-373
Phelan, J. Worlds from Words.
  27(AL):Jan82-758
Phelan, J.L. The People and the King.*
  S. Ramírez-Horton, 37:Sep81-26
Phelps, A. La Bélière caraibe.
  A. Moorhead, 207(FR):May81-900
Phelps, L.R., with A.T. Alt, eds. Creative Encounter.
  C. Walk, 52:Band15Heft1-56
Phelps, R. Belles Saisons.
  J.H. Stewart, 207(FR):Oct80-173
Philbrick, S. No Goodbye.
  R. Phillips, 249(HudR):Autumn81-420
Philby, H.S. The Queen of Sheba.
  P. Crone, 617(TLS):12Feb82-155

Philip, P. British Residents at the Cape 1795-1819.
  A. Delius, 617(TLS):23Apr82-468
Philipp, G. Einführung ins Frühneuhochdeutsche.
  H. Penzl, 350:Dec82-948
Philipp, K. Zeugung als Denkform in Platons geschriebener Lehre.
  A. Sheppard, 123:Vol31No2-300
Philippe de Thaon. Le Livre de Sibile. (H. Shields, ed)
  W.G. van Emden, 402(MLR):Oct81-955
  B. Merrilees, 382(MAE):1981/1-134
Philippe, R. Political Graphics.
  442(NY):4Oct82-152
Philippi, D.L., ed and trans. Songs of Gods, Songs of Humans.*
  M. Heller, 472:Spring/Summer81-269
Philippoff, E. Kurt Tucholskys Frankreichbild.
  H. Müssener, 406:Fall81-362
Philips, C.H. - see Bentinck, W.C.
Philips, R. - see Colette
Phillipps, K.C. The Language of Thackeray.*
  F. Austin, 179(ES):Aug81-391
Phillips, A., ed. A Newnham Anthology.
  J.S. Pedersen, 637(VS):Autumn80-126
Phillips, A.A. Responses.*
  M. Macleod, 381:Apr81-77
Phillips, C.D. Sentencing Councils in the Federal Courts.
  R.P.A., 185:Jan82-385
Phillips, D. The Coconut Kiss.
  P. Craig, 617(TLS):12Feb82-170
  A. Huth, 362:21Jan82-25
Phillips, D.L. Equality, Justice and Rectification.
  B.B., 185:Jan81-344
Phillips, E. Edgar Allan Poe.
  T.C. Carlson, 392:Spring81-148
  P.F. Quinn, 445(NCF):Jun80-88
Phillips, G.M. Help for Shy People and Anyone Else Who Ever Felt Ill at Ease on Entering a Room Full of Strangers.
  H.L. Goodall, Jr., 583:Spring82-348
Phillips, H. The Theatre and its Critics in Seventeenth-Century France.*
  H.T. Barnwell, 208(FS):Oct81-441
  M. Gutwirth, 612(ThS):May81-108
  J.L. Pallister, 568(SCN):Summer-Fall81-56
  M.G. Paulson, 207(FR):Dec81-266
Phillips, J.A. Black Tickets.*
  W. Cummins, 363(LitR):Spring82-462
  K. Cushman, 573(SSF):Winter81-92
Phillips, J.K., ed. Building on Experience — Building for Success.
  B. Ebling, 207(FR):Feb81-512
Phillips, J.K., ed. The New Imperative.*
  B. Ebling 2d, 207(FR):Mar81-611
Phillips, K. and J. Locke - see Rilke, R.M.
Phillips, M. Francesco Guicciardini.*
  R. Fubini, 551(RenQ):Winter80-744
Phillips, M., ed. Interpreting Blake.*
  J. Beer, 402(MLR):Jul81-676
  E. Larrissy, 447(N&Q):Oct80-450
Phillips, M.M. Erasmus and the Northern Renaissance.
  P. Gwyn, 617(TLS):16Apr82-445
Phillips, N. Sijobang.
  R.H. Barnes, 617(TLS):19Mar82-327

277

Phillips, R. Family Breakdown in Late
Eighteenth-Century France.*
    J. Lough, 83:Autumn81-226
Phillips, R. Mushrooms and Other Fungi of
Great Britain and Europe.
    R. O'Hanlon, 617(TLS):5Nov82-1216
Phillips, R. - see Schwartz, D.
Phillips, T. A Humument.*
    J.R.B., 148:Spring81-94
    A. Woods, 97(CQ):Vol 10No3-255
Philo of Alexandria. Les oeuvres de
Philon d'Alexandrie. (Vol 34A) (C.
Mercier, ed and trans)
    É. Des Places, 555:Vol54fasc1-170
Philonenko, A. - see Kant, I.
Physick, J. The Victoria and Albert
Museum.
    D. Watkin, 617(TLS):10Dec82-1379
"The Physics of Music."
    J.B., 412:Feb80-76
Phythian-Adams, C. Desolation of a City.*
    J.T. Rosenthal, 589:Jul81-643
Pi, W. - see under Wang Pi
Pia, P. - see Brantôme
Piatelli-Palmarini, M., ed. Language and
Learning.* (French title: Théories du
langage, Théories de l'apprentissage.)
[shown in prev under Piaget, J. and N.
Chomsky]
    W. Hare, 185:Apr82-574
    J.H. Hill, 350:Dec81-948
Piazza, P. Christopher Isherwood.*
    A. Wilde, 677(YES):Vol 11-360
Picard, G.C. and others. Recherches arché-
ologiques franco-tunisiennes à Maktar.*
(Vol 1, Pt 1)
    R.J.A. Wilson, 313:Vol71-173
Picard, H.R. Autobiographie im zeitgenös-
sischen Frankreich.*
    C. Miething, 72:Band217Heft1-233
"Picaresque espagnole." "Picaresque euro-
péenne."
    H.G. Hall, 208(FS):Apr81-202
Piccarreta, F. Astura.
    M.H. Crawford, 313:Vol71-153
Piccigallo, P.R. The Japanese on Trial.
    R.H. Minear, 293(JASt):Nov80-138
Piccinato, S. Testo e contesto della
poesia di Langston Hughes.
    R. Asselineau, 189(EA):Oct-Dec81-494
    R. Di Cuonzo, 27(AL):Mar81-146
Piccolpasso, C. Arte del Vasaio. (R.
Lightbown and A. Caiger-Smith, eds and
trans)
    135:Dec81-251
Piccolpasso, C. I tre libri dell'arte del
vasaio: The Three Books of the Potter's
Art.
    G. Wills, 39:Jan81-59
Pichette, J-P. Le Guide raisonné des
jurons.
    T.R. Wooldridge, 627(UTQ):Summer81-195
Pichois, C. Le Romantisme II, 1843-1869.
    G. Cesbron, 356(LR):Nov81-353
    G. Cesbron, 446(NCFS):Fall-Winter80/81-
    124
    J. Gaulmier, 535(RHL):Jan-Feb81-151
    J.S. Patty, 207(FR):Feb81-469
le Pichon, Y. The World of Henri Rousseau.
    P-L. Adams, 61:Dec82-105
Pick, C., ed. What's What in the 1980s.
    J. Vaizey, 362:8Apr82-21

Pickar, G.B. and K.E. Webb, eds. Expres-
sionism Reconsidered.
    G.P. Knapp, 400(MLN):Apr81-705
    L. Martens, 221(GQ):Mar81-237
    R.C. Reimer, 406:Winter81-477
    J.M. Ritchie, 402(MLR):Jul81-758
Pickard, O. Chalcis et la Confédération
eubéenne.
    F.W. Walbank, 303(JoHS):Vol 101-202
Picken, L., ed. Musica Asiatica.* (Vol 1)
    W.F. Malm, 318(JAOS):Jan/Mar80-95
Picken, L., ed. Musica Asiatica. (Vol 3)
    D.A. Lentz, 187:Sep82-480
Pickens, R.T., ed. The Songs of Jaufré
Rudel.*
    F.M. Chambers, 545(RPh):Feb81(supp)-
    222
Pickens, R.T. The Welsh Knight.*
    D.J. Shirt, 208(FS):Apr81-183
Pickering, F.P. Essays on Medieval German
Literature and Iconography.*
    J.A.W.B., 382(MAE):1981/1-156
Pickering, S.F. John Locke and Children's
Books in Eighteenth-Century England.
    P. Rogers, 617(TLS):7May82-500
Pickford, C.E., ed. Mélanges de littéra-
ture française moderne offerts à Garnet
Rees.
    H. Peyre, 207(FR):Feb82-415
Pickford, C.E. - see "Meliadus de Leonnoys,
1532"
Pickles, D. Problems of Contemporary
French Politics.
    S. Hoffmann, 453(NYRB):12Aug82-37
Piclin, M. Les philosophies de la triade
ou l'histoire de la structure ternaire.
    A. Reix, 542:Apr-Jun81-246
Picoche, J. Précis de morphologie histor-
ique du français.
    S.N. Rosenberg, 207(FR):Oct81-164
Picon-Vallin, B. - see Meyerhold, V.
Picton, J. and J. Mack. African Textiles.
    K.P. Kent, 2(AfrA):Feb81-81
Piercy, M. Braided Lives.
    K. Pollitt, 441:7Feb82-7
    R. Scruton, 617(TLS):23Jul82-807
    442(NY):22Feb82-128
Piercy, M. Circles on the Water.
    M. Atwood, 441:8Aug82-10
Piercy, M. Vida.*
    S.D. Lavine, 385(MQR):Winter82-189
Pierini, R.D. Studi su Accio.
    H.D. Jocelyn, 123:Vol131No2-198
Pierre, A.J. The Global Politics of Arms
Sales.
    J. Miller, 441:21Feb82-15
Pierrot, J. The Decadent Imagination.
    V. Brombert, 617(TLS):16Jul82-769
Pierson, J.D. Tokutomi Sohō 1863-1957.*
    Haruhara Akihiko, 285(JapQ):Jan-Mar81-
    107
    J.L. Huffman, 407(MN):Summer81-208
Pierssens, M. The Power of Babel.
    C.S. Brown, 131(CL):Fall81-372
Pietsch, H. Georg Forsters "Ansichten vom
Niederrhein."
    C. Träger, 654(WB):10/1981-171
Pifer, E. Nabokov and the Novel.*
    B.L. Clark, 659(ConL):Winter82-120
    E. Sampson, 574(SEEJ):Winter81-97
Piffard, G. - see "The Song of Roland"
Pignatti, T. Veronese: L'Opera completa.
    D. Rosand, 54:Mar81-163

Piirainen, I.T. Frühneuhochdeutsche
Bibliographie.
W.J. Jones, 402(MLR):Oct81-985
R.K. Seymour, 215(GL):Fall81-226
K-P. Wegera, 680(ZDP):Band100Heft1-
146
Pike, B. The Image of the City in Modern
Literature.*
L.M., 617(TLS):26Mar82-363
445(NCF):Dec81-378
Pike, C., ed. The Futurists, the Formal-
ists, and the Marxist Critique.
J. Graffy, 575(SEER):Apr81-294
Pike, D. German Writers in Soviet Exile,
1933-1945.
R. Conquest, 617(TLS):17Dec82-1385
S. Karlinsky, 441:14Mar82-10
Pike, F., ed. Ah! Mischief.
P. Lennon, 362:19Aug82-20
Pilcer, S. Maiden Rites.
L. Marcus, 617(TLS):17Sep82-992
T. Walton, 441:25Apr82-12
Pilch, H. and H. Tristram. Altenglische
Literatur.
S.B. Greenfield, 38:Band99Heft3/4-487
Pilkington, A.E. Bergson and His Influ-
ence.
A. Montefiore, 447(N&Q):Oct80-467
Pilkington, W. - see Kirkland, S.
Pilkington, W.T., ed. Critical Essays on
the Western American Novel.
D.A. Short, 268(IFR):Summer82-154
Pilling, G. Marx's "Capital."
A.L., 185:Jan82-392
Pillinger, R. Die Tituli Historiarum oder
das sogenannte Dittochaeon des Pruden-
tius.
P.B.T. Bilaniuk, 589:Apr81-461
Pilz, K.D. Phraseologie.
W. Mieder, 196:Band21Heft1/2-141
Pim, L.R. Invisible Additives.
M.L. Drache, 99:Feb82-44
Pimpaneau, J. Chanteurs, conteurs, bate-
leurs.
V. Alleton, 98:Mar80-217
du Pin, P.D. - see under de la Tour du Pin,
P.
Pincher, C. The Private World of St. John
Terrapin.
J. Symons, 617(TLS):7May82-502
Pindar. L'inno a Pan di Pindaro. (L.
Lehnus, ed)
M.M. Willcock, 303(JoHS):Vol 101-152
Pindar. Pindar's Victory Songs.* (F.J.
Nisetich, trans)
C.R. Beye, 472:Spring/Summer81-199
M.C. Howatson, 123:Vol31No2-162
Pineau, J. Le Mouvement rythmique en
français.
F. Corblin, 209(FM):Jan81-88
Pineaux, J. - see Désiré, A.
Piñero Green, E. Perfect Fools.
N. Callendar, 441:24Oct82-28
Pines, B.Y. Back to Basics.
A. Brinkley, 441:15Aug82-9
Ping, L.P. - see under Lee Poh Ping
Pinget, R. The Inquisitory.
617(TLS):19Feb82-198
Pinget, R. L'Aprocryphe.*
P. Dulac, 450(NRF):Apr81-123
R. Henkels, 207(FR):May82-926
J-C. Vareille, 98:Apr81-406

Pinget, R. The Libera me Domine. Passa-
caglia.
J-C. Liéber, 98:Apr81-418
Pinget, R. Monsieur Songe.
J. Sturrock, 617(TLS):7May82-502
Pinion, F.B. A George Eliot Companion.
445(NCF):Dec81-379
Pinion, F.B. A D.H. Lawrence Companion.*
D. Hewitt, 447(N&Q):Jun80-263
H.T. Moore, 402(MLR):Oct81-941
Pinner, D. The Potsdam Quartet.
D. Devlin, 157:2ndQtr81-55
Piñon, N. O Calor das Coisas.
M. Silverman, 399(MLJ):Autumn81-344
Pinsker, S. Between Two Worlds.
J.J. Waldmeir, 395(MFS):Winter80/81-
675
Pinsker, S., ed. Critical Essays on
Philip Roth.
N. Guild, 268(IFR):Summer82-148
Pinsker, S. The Languages of Joseph
Conrad.*
C. Watts, 447(N&Q):Dec80-560
Pinsky, R. An Explanation of America.*
C. Molesworth, 473(PR):2/1981-315
R.T. Smith, 577(SHR):Spring81-176
Pintacuda, M. La musica nella tragedia
greca.*
J. Solomon, 121(CJ):Dec81/Jan82-184
Pintner, W.M. and D.K. Rowney, eds. Rus-
sian Officialdom.
W.B. Lincoln, 550(RusR):Jul81-340
P. Longworth, 575(SEER):Jul81-441
Pio, N. Nicola Pio: Le vite di pittori
scultori et architetti.* (C. and R.
Enggass, eds)
C. Gould, 39:Sep81-205
Piotte, J-M. Un Parti pris politique.
S.R. Schulman, 207(FR):Mar81-627
R. Sutherland, 102(CanL):Spring81-92
Pipa, A. Hieronymus De Rada.
L.M. Ferrari, 276:Spring81-64
Piper, D. Artists' London.
C. Fox, 617(TLS):12Nov82-1253
Pipes, R.E. Struve: Liberal on the Right,
1905-1944.*
J. Keep, 575(SEER):Oct81 615
S.V. Utechin, 550(RusR):Apr81-158
Pippin, R.B. Kant's Theory of Form.
R.C.S. Walker, 617(TLS):26Nov82-1322
Pires-Ferreira, J. Cavalaria em cordel.
P. Zumthor, 98:Mar80-228
Pirie, D.B. William Wordsworth.
C. Watts, 617(TLS):24Sep82-1046
Pirouet, M.L. Black Evangelists.
T. Linden, 69:Vol50No2-210
de Pisan, C. - see under Christine
de Pisan
"Camille Pissarro 1830-1903."
R. Hobbs, 59:Mar81-121
Pitcher, G. Berkeley.*
C. Macdonald, 323:Jan81-91
Pitcher, H. Chekhov's Leading Lady.*
G. McVay, 575(SEER):Jan81-85
Archbishop Pitirim of Volokolamsk, ed.
The Orthodox Church in Russia.
K. Fitz Lyon, 617(TLS):24Dec82-1408
Pitkänen, A.J. Binominala genitiviska
hypotagmer i yngre nysvenska.
K. Nilsson, 563(SS):Winter81-93
Pitt, B. The Crucible of War.
S. Bidwell, 617(TLS):31Dec82-1450

Pittock, M. Ernst Toller.
  N.A. Furness, 402(MLR):Jul81-759
"I Pittori Bergamaschi dal XIII al XIX
Secolo." (Vol 3)
  J. Meyer zur Capellen, 471:Jul/Aug/
  Sep81-290
"La Pittura metafisica."
  S. Fauchereau, 98:Dec80-1164
Pivčević, E., ed. Phenomenology and Philo-
sophical Understanding.
  D.W. Smith, 449:Sep81-398
Piven, F.F. and R.A. Cloward. The New
Class War.
  B. Kuttner, 441:27Jun82-11
Pizer, D. Twentieth-Century American
Literary Naturalism.
  L. Mackinnon, 617(TLS):30Jul82-838
Pizzorusso, A. Prospettive seconde studi
francesi.*
  R. Francillon, 535(RHL):Nov-Dec81-1031
Plá, J. El Espejo y el Canasto.
  F.E. Feito, 37:Oct81-27
Placzek, B.R. - see Reich, W. and A.S.
Neill
Plaidy, J. Uneasy Lies the Head.
  S. Altinel, 617(TLS):17Dec82-1398
Plain, B. Eden Burning.
  M. Watkins, 441:22Aug82-12
"Plain and Elegant, Rich and Common."
  C. Robertson, 658:Spring81-92
Plamondon, A.L. Whitehead's Organic
Philosophy of Science.
  T.E. Burke, 518:Apr81-123
Planche, A. Charles d'Orléans ou la
recherche d'un langage.
  A. Iker-Gittleman, 545(RPh):May81-566
Plank, F., ed. Ergativity.
  N.E. Collinge, 603:Vol5No1-141
  R.M.W. Dixon, 297(JL):Sep81-368
  J. Heath, 353:Vol 18No9/10-877
  W.R. Schmalstieg, 215(GL):Spring81-31
Plann, S. Relative Clauses in Spanish
Without Overt Antecedents and Related
Constructions.
  J.M. Lipski, 238:Dec81-652
  G. Mallinson, 350:Sep82-694
Plant, R., H. Lesser and P. Taylor-Gooby.
Political Philosophy and Social Welfare.
  B.B., 185:Oct81-181
Plante, D. The Woods.
  R. Belben, 617(TLS):29Jan82-105
  E. Milton, 441:15Aug82-11
  K.C. O'Brien, 362:28Jan82-24
  R. Towers, 453(NYRB):16Dec82-38
  442(NY):20Sep82-152
Plantinga, A. Does God Have a Nature?
  T.K., 543:Jun81-798
  W.E. Mann, 484(PPR):Jun82-625
Plantos, T. The Universe Ends at Sher-
bourne and Queen.*
  J. Robinson, 102(CanL):Spring80-127
Plate, B. Heinrich Wittenwiler.
  H-J. Behr, 680(ZDP):Band99Heft1-139
Plater, W.M. The Grim Phoenix.*
  D. Tallack, 541(RES):Feb81-109
Plath, D.W. Long Engagements.
  C.W. Kiefer, 293(JASt):Feb81-394
  F. Moos, 407(MN):Summer81-223
Plath, O. Folklore Chileno.
  E.A. Echevarria, 292(JAF):Jul-Sep81-
  394

Plath, S. Collected Poems.* (T. Hughes,
ed)
  A. Brownjohn, 617(TLS):12Feb82-165
  I. Ehrenpreis, 453(NYRB):4Feb82-22
  D. Smith, 29:Jan/Feb82-36
  H. Vendler, 442(NY):15Feb82-124
Plath, S. The Journals of Sylvia Plath.
(T. Hughes and F. McCullough, eds)
  N. Milford, 441:2May82-1
  K. Pollitt, 61:May82-102
Plato. Gorgias. (T. Irwin, ed and trans)
  D.S. Hutchinson, 123:Vol31No1-56
  Q. Lauer, 124:Jan-Feb82-192
  S.U., 543:Dec80-395
Plato. The Laws of Plato. (T.L. Pangle,
ed and trans)
  S. Rosen, 480(P&R):Spring81-112
Plato. Platon, "Apologie des Sokrates."
(2nd ed) (F.J. Weber, ed)
  R.W., 555:Vol54fasc1-163
Plato. Platon, l'"Alcibiade" majeur.
(P-J. About, ed and trans)
  P. Somville, 542:Apr-Jun81-262
Plato. Symposium. (K. Dover, ed)
  F.H. Sandbach, 123:Vol31No1-126
Platonov, A. V Prekrasnom i Jarostnom
Mire.
  D. Milivojević, 558(RLJ):Spring-Fall81-
  289
Platt, C. The Atlas of Medieval Man.
  639(VQR):Spring81-50
Platt, C. The Parish Churches of Medieval
England.*
  A.J.S., 148:Autumn81-89
Platt, D.C.M., ed. Business Imperialism,
1840-1930.
  R.B. St. John, 37:Apr81-26
Plattner, M.F. Rousseau's State of Nature.
  E.J.E., 543:Sep80-155
Platts, M., ed. Reference, Truth and
Reality.
  L. Humberstone, 63:Dec81-464
Platts, M. Ways of Meaning.*
  A. Manser, 307:Apr81-48
Pleket, H.W. and R.S. Stroud, eds. In-
scriptiones Graecae: Supplementum epi-
graphicum Graecum.* (Vol 26)
  P.M. Fraser, 123:Vol31No1-142
  M.F. McGregor, 303(JoHS):Vol 101-227
Plenzdorf, U. The New Sufferings of Young
W.*
  J. Neubauer, 221(GQ):Jan81-125
Plesset, I.R. Noguchi and His Patrons.
  J.R. Bartholomew, 293(JASt):May81-610
  M. Lock, 407(MN):Summer81-227
Plessner, H. Gesammelte Schriften. (Vols
1, 3, 4 and 5)
  D. Johnson, 617(TLS):15Jan82-59
Plessner, H. Gesammelte Schriften. (Vol
2)
  D. Johnson, 617(TLS):1Oct82-1070
Plett, H.F., ed. Rhetorik.*
  E.H. Rehermann, 196:Band21Heft1/2-143
Plett, H.F. Textwissenschaft und Text-
analyse.*
  J.H. Petersen, 680(ZDP):Band99Heft4-
  597
Pliatzky, L. Getting and Spending.
  B. Trend, 617(TLS):16Jul82-755
Plimpton, G. - see Stein, J.
Pljušč, N.P. Intonacija vstavnosti v
ukraïns'kij movi.
  M. Nidecki, 682(ZPSK):Band33Heft5-610

Plommer, H. The Ugciad.
  P-G.B., 189(EA):Apr-Jun81-237
Plotinus. Plotin: "Traité sur les Nombres"
  (Ennéades VI [34]). (J. Bertier and
  others, eds and trans)
  Y. Lafrance, 154:Dec81-808
Plotinus. Plotini Opera. (Vol 2:
  Enneades IV-V.) (P. Henry and H-R.
  Schwyzer, eds)
  L.G. Westerink, 394:Vol134fasc1/2-166
Plott, J.C., with others. Global History
  of Philosophy. (Vol 2)
  W. Gray, 485(PE&W):Oct81-555
Ploude, R. and M. Taylor, eds. Fiddlehead
  Greens.
  A.A. MacKinnon, 102(CanL):Spring81-152
Plumb, J.H. Georgian Delights.
  T. Atkins, 566:Autumn81-51
"Pluralities 1980."
  W.N., 102(CanL):Spring81-173
Plutarch. Plutarchi "De Herodoti maligni-
  tae." (P.A. Hansen, ed)
  B. Hillyard, 123:Vol131No1-112
Plutarch. Plutarque, "Oeuvres morales."*
  (Vol 9, Pt 2) (F. Fuhrmann, ed and trans)
  R.W., 555:Vol54fasc1-167
Plutarch. Plutarque: "Vies."* (Vols 13-
  15) (R. Flacelière and É. Chambry, eds
  and trans)
  A.J. Gossage, 303(JoHS):Vol 101-162
Pluvier, J. South-East Asia from Colonial-
  ism to Independence.
  D.K. Emmerson, 293(JASt):Nov80-43
Pochat, G. Figur und Landschaft.
  A.R. Turner, 54:Mar81-140
Pocock, G. Boileau and the Nature of Neo-
  Classicism.*
  H.T. Barnwell, 208(FS):Apr81-199
  D.C. Potts, 402(MLR):Oct81-964
  G. Strickland, 97(CQ):Vol 10No2-179
  J.E. White, Jr., 207(FR):May81-866
    205(FMLS):Apr81-199
Pocock, J.G.A., ed. Three British Revolu-
  tions.*
  J.J. Hecht, 432(NEQ):Dec81-597
  G. Rudé, 656(WMQ):Oct81-735
Podgórecki, A. and M. Łoś. Multi-Dimen-
  sional Sociology.
  R.T. Peterson, 484(PPR):Dec81-301
Podhoretz, N. The Present Danger.
  R. Saidel, 390:Feb81-56
Podhoretz, N. Why We Were in Vietnam.
  J. Fallows, 441:28Mar82-7
  M. Howard, 617(TLS):24Sep82-1030
  A. Schlesinger, Jr., 231:Mar82-71
de Podio, G. Ars musicorum, libri VI et
  VIII. (A. Seay, ed)
  H.W. Kaufmann, 551(RenQ):Spring80-91
Podol, P.L. Fernando Arrabal.*
  C.J. Murphy, 207(FR):Oct80-177
Podro, M. The Critical Historians of Art.
  D. Thomas, 362:23and30Dec82-44
Poesse, W. - see Williamsen, V.G.
Pohl, R.J.A. Die Metamorphosen des nega-
  tiven Helden.*
  A. Mingelgrün, 535(RHL):Nov-Dec81-1026
Poinard, M. Le Retour des travailleurs
  portugais.
  B. Petit, 207(FR):Mar82-581
Pointer, L. and D. Goddard. Harry Jackson.
  A.B., 55:Nov81-42

Pointon, M. William Dyce 1806-1864.*
  D. Cherry, 59:Sep81-335
  P. Conner, 89(BJA):Winter81-79
  W. Vaughan, 90:May81-315
le Poirier, M. - see under Mahieu le
  Poirier
Poirot-Delpech, B. Feuilletons 1972-1982.
  Le Couloir du Dancing.
  S. Romer, 617(TLS):24Dec82-1427
Poirot-Delpech, B. La Légende du siècle.
  F. de Martinoir, 450(NRF):May81-120
Polakoff, C. Into Indigo.
  P. Bach, 614:Winter81-20
  K.P. Kent, 2(AfrA):Nov80-28
"Poland Today."
  L. Schapiro, 453(NYRB):4Feb82-3
Polansky, A. and B. Drukier, eds. The
  Beginnings of Communist Rule in Poland
  (December 1943-June 1945).
  W.W. Kulski, 497(PolR):Vol26No2-79
Polara, G. - see Virgilius Maro gram-
  maticus
Polhemus, R.M. The Changing World of
  Anthony Trollope.
  J. Roubaud, 98:Feb-Mar81-166
Polhemus, R.M. Comic Faith.*
  R.B. Henkle, 141:Fall81-364
  R.D. McMaster, 445(NCF):Dec81-352
  R.K. Simon, 594:Fall81-322
Polikarov, A. Probleme der wissenschaft-
  lichen Erkenntnis vom methodologischen
  Gesichtspunkt aus.
  C. Dontschev, 679:Band11Heft2-393
Poliziano, A. The "Stanze" of Angelo
  Poliziano. (D. Quint, trans)
  F. Day, 580(SCR):Fall80-106
Polk, N. Faulkner's "Requiem for a Nun."
  P. Kemp, 617(TLS):22Jan82-82
Polk, N.E. and J.R. Scafidel, eds. An
  Anthology of Mississippi Writers.
  G. Hendrick, 573(SSF):Winter81-96
Pollak, M. Mandarins, Jews and Mission-
  aries.*
  D.D. Leslie, 244(HJAS):Dec81-669
Pollard, A. Anthony Trollope.*
  J. Carlisle, 639(VQR):Winter81-176
  M. Harris, 72:Band217Heft2-430
Pollard, S. The Wasting of the British
  Economy.
  D. Coombes, 362:19Aug82-24
Pollidori, O.C. - see under Castellani
  Pollidori, O.
Pollin, B.R. Poe. (rev)
  K.B. Harder, 424:Sep81-253
Pollitt, K. Antarctic Traveller.
  B. Bennett, 441:14Mar82-12
  M. Kinzie, 29:Sep/Oct82-37
Pollock, G. Mary Cassatt.
  J.V. Turano, 16:Spring81-93
Pollock, J.L. Subjunctive Reasoning.*
  T. McCarthy, 316:Mar81-170
  D. Nute, 449:May81-212
Pollock, S.I. Aspects of Versification in
  Sanskrit Love Poetry.
  R. Gombrich, 259(IIJ):Jan81-51
Polmar, N. and T.B. Allen. Rickover.
  J. Fallows, 453(NYRB):1Apr82-15
  J.W. Finney, 441:31Jan82-6
    442(NY):18Jan82-130
Polverini, L. - see de Sanctis, G.
Polzin, R.M. Biblical Structuralism.
  H.C. White, 599:Winter81-68

Pomfret, R. The Economic Development of Canada.
H.V. Nelles, 529(QQ):Autumn81-556
Pomper, P. Sergei Nechaev.*
C.A. Ruud, 104(CASS):Winter81-582
Pompidou, G. Pour rétablir une vérité.
D. Johnson, 617(TLS):3Sep82-937
Pompili, B. - see Borel, P.
Pondrom, C.N. The Road from Paris.
I. Higgins, 208(FS):Jan81-111
Ponge, F. Comment une figue de paroles et pourquoi.
J-P. Richard, 98:Jun-Jul80-551
Ponge, F. Le Parti pris des choses.* (I. Higgins, ed)
B. Beugnot, 535(RHL):Mar-Apr81-332
F. Caro, 67:May81-119
M.R. Sorrell, 402(MLR):Apr81-481
205(FMLS):Oct80-376
Pongolini, F.P. I cento anni di Giuseppe Prezzolini.
F. Donini, 617(TLS):6Aug82-852
Poniatowski, M. L'avenir n'est écrit nulle part.
C. Rosset, 98:Jan80-87
Ponomareff, C. The Silenced Vision.
J.D. Simons, 104(CASS):Winter81-569
de Ponseti, H.P. - see under Percas de Ponseti, H.
Pontalis, J-B. - see "Le Temps de la réflexion"
Pontaut, A. La sainte alliance.
C. Rubinger, 102(CanL):Spring80-118
Pontiero, G. - see Nocciori, G.
Ponting, K.G. Discovering Textile History and Design.
R.L. Shep, 614:Spring82-13
da Pontormo, J. Journal. (J-C. Lebensztejn, with A. Parronchi, eds and trans)
D. Trento, 98:Jan81-13
Pontus de Tyard. Solitaire second. (C.M. Yandell, ed)
H. Sonneville, 356(LR):Aug81-250
Poole, R. Words Before Midnight.
A. Stevenson, 617(TLS):7May82-515
de Poorter, N. Corpus Rubenianum Ludwig Burchard.* (Pt 2) [filed in prev under De]
E. McGrath, 59:Dec81-474
C. White, 39:Feb81-130
Poortinga, Y. De foet fan de reinbôge.
H.L. Cox, 196:Band22Heft1/2-148
Poortinga, Y. De held en de draek.
H.L. Cox, 196:Band21Heft1/2-145
Pope, D. Admiral.
S. Altinel, 617(TLS):20Aug82-910
Pope, D. Ramage's Devil.
S. Altinel, 617(TLS):17Dec82-1398
Pope, I. and M. Kanazawa, eds. The Musical Manuscript Montecassino 871.*
L. Lockwood, 551(RenQ):Winter80-774
Pope, M.H., ed and trans. Song of Songs.
C.H. Gordon, 318(JAOS):Jul/Sep80-354
Pope, N. Dickens and Charity.*
A. Fleishman, 445(NCF):Jun80-105
Pope-Hennessy, J. A Lonely Business.* (P. Quennell, ed)
A. Ross, 364:Jul81-92
Pope-Hennessy, J. Luca della Robbia.*
F. Ames-Lewis, 59:Sep81-339
L.D. Ettlinger, 54:Sep81-510
N. Rubinstein, 90:Jan81-36

Pope-Hennessy, J. The Study and Criticism of Italian Sculpture.
F. Ames-Lewis, 617(TLS):16Apr82-443
Popkin, R.H. The High Road to Pyrrhonism.* (R.A. Watson and J.E. Force, eds)
A. Baier, 185:Jan82-346
G.B.H., 543:Dec80-396
Popkin, S.L. The Rational Peasant.*
L. Wright, 302:Vol 18-174
Popko, R. The Book of Basic Sewing.
P. Bach, 614:Winter82-14
Poppe, N. Mongolische Epen. (Vols 1, 2, 3 and 9)
E. Rosner, 196:Band22Heft3/4-364
Poppe, N. Mongolische Epen. (Vols 5 and 6)
W. Eberhard, 318(JAOS):Jul/Sep80-390
Poppe, N. Tsongol Folklore.
L. Bese, 318(JAOS):Apr/Jun80-214
Poppeliers, J. - see Bassett, W.B.
Popper, K. La Société ouverte et ses ennemis.
A. Compagnon, 98:Oct80-925
Popper, K. and J. Eccles. The Self and Its Brain.
D.O. Hebb, 488:Sep80-309
F. Jackson, 488:Sep80-316
K.H. Pribram, 488:Sep80-295
Popper, K.R. The Open Universe. Quantum Theory and the Schism in Physics. (W.W. Bartley 3d, ed of both)
L.J. Cohen, 617(TLS):3Dec82-1333
J. Lieberson, 453(NYRB):18Nov82-67 and cont in 2Dec82-51
Popper, K.R. Realism and the Aim of Science. (W.W. Bartley 3d, ed)
J. Lieberson, 453(NYRB):18Nov82-67 and cont in 2Dec82-51
Porcella, Y. Pieced Clothing.
R.L. Shep, 614:Winter81-20
Porcella, Y. Pieced Clothing Variations.
R.L. Shep, 614:Spring82-15
Porcher, L., ed. La Scolarisation des enfants étrangers en France.
A.J. Singerman, 207(FR):Apr82-694
Pörnbacher, H., comp. Bayerische Bibliothek. (Vol 1)
B.D. Haage, 680(ZDP):Band100Heft1-122
Porphyrios, D. Sources of Modern Eclecticism.
A. Saint, 617(TLS):8Oct82-1095
Porqueras-Mayo, A., S. Baldwin and J. Martí-Olivella, eds. Estudis de llengua, literatura i cultura catalanes.
L.L. Cofresí, 238:Sep81-479
J.M. Sobré, 240(HR):Autumn81-517
Porras Muñoz, G. La frontera con los indios de Nueva Vizcaya, en el siglo XVII.
E. de la Torre Villar, 263(RIB): Vol31No2-282
Porte, J. Representative Man.*
T.D. Eisele, 396(ModA):Winter81-88
J.S. Martin, 106:Fall81-209
Porte, J. - see Emerson, R.W.
Portelli, A. Il Re Nascoto.
R. Asselineau, 189(EA):Oct-Dec81-493
Porter, A.N. The Origins of the South African War.
A.J. Greenberger, 637(VS):Spring81-351
Porter, C. Seeing and Being.
L. Mackinnon, 617(TLS):18Jun82-678

Porter, C.A. Chateaubriand.*
P.J. Whyte, 402(MLR):Oct81-969
Porter, D. Dickinson.
M.L. Rosenthal, 617(TLS):26Mar82-357
Porter, D. Emerson and Literary Change.*
J.S. Martin, 106:Fall81-209
Porter, D. The Pursuit of Crime.
P. Craig, 617(TLS):9Apr82-403
Porter, F. Art in its Own Terms.* (R.
Downes, ed)
D. Sutton, 39:Aug81-74
Porter, G., ed. Vietnam.
D.P. Chandler, 293(JASt):Nov80-77
Porter, H.C. The Inconstant Savage.
F.P. Prucha, 432(NEQ):Mar81-131
Porter, J. The Measure of Canadian Soci-
ety.*
G.W., 102(CanL):Winter80-160
Porter, J.A. The Drama of Speech Acts.*
T. Hawkes, 541(RES):Aug81-320
Porter, J.R. and W.M.S. Russell, eds.
Animals in Folklore.*
G.E. Warshaver, 292(JAF):Jan-Mar81-96
Porter, L.M. The Literary Dream in French
Romanticism.
F. Carmignani-Dupont, 535(RHL):Jul-
Oct81-796
J.A. Hiddleston, 210(FrF):Sep81-279
J.P. Houston, 207(FR):Dec80-343
B. Knapp, 446(NCFS):Fall-Winter80/81-
152
Porter, L.M. The Renaissance of the Lyric
in French Romanticism.*
L. Le Guillou, 535(RHL):Mar-Apr81-305
B. Seaton, 546(RR):Mar81-244
205(FMLS):Jan80-93
Porter, M. The Paper Bridge.
G. Mikes, 617(TLS):4Jun82-623
Porter, P. English Subtitles.*
H. Lomas, 364:Jun81-73
Porter, R. English Society in the Eigh-
teenth Century.
W.A. Speck, 617(TLS):28May82-581
Porter, R.B. Presidential Decision Making:
The Economic Policy Board.
639(VQR):Winter81-24
Porterfield, N. Jimmie Rodgers.
G.T. Meade, 292(JAF):Apr-Jun81-260
de la Portilla, M. and B. Varela. Mejora
tu español.
M.I. Duke dos Santos, 238:Dec81-650
Portillo, J.L., D. Sodi and F. Diaz
Infante - see under López Portillo, J.,
D. Sodi and F. Diaz Infante
Portnoy, S.A. - see Medem, V.
Portuondo, A.A. Diez comedias atribuidas
a Lope de Vega.
V. Dixon, 86(BHS):Jul81-266
Porzio, D. and M. Valsecchi, eds. Picasso.
L. Cooke, 59:Jun81-231
Posener, J. Berlin auf dem Wege zu einer
neuen Architektur.
R. Pommer, 576:May81-162
Post, K.D. Günter Eich.
L. Marx, 406:Summer81-244
van der Post, L. Yet Being Someone Other.
J. Vaizey, 362:18Nov82-26
Postgate, J.N. Taxation and Conscription
in the Assyrian Empire.
R.A. Henshaw, 318(JAOS):Jan/Mar80-62
Postman, N. The Disappearance of Child-
hood.
P-L. Adams, 61:Oct82-106

Potash, R.A. The Army and Politics in
Argentina, 1945-1962.
T.H. Donghi, 263(RIB):Vol31No1-94
Potok, C. The Book of Lights.*
M. Haltrecht, 617(TLS):28May82-594
Potter, B. Beatrix Potter's Americans.
(J.C. Morse, ed)
442(NY):26Apr82-142
Potter, E. The Cooking School Murders.
N. Callendar, 441:26Sep82-41
Potter, J.H. Five Frames for the "Decam-
eron."
P. Shaw, 617(TLS):24Dec82-1425
Potter, J.H. Elio Vittorini.
T. De Lauretis, 276:Autumn81-219
Potter, J.L. Robert Frost Handbook.*
S.K. Hoffman, 27(AL):May81-325
Potter, K.H., ed. Indian Metaphysics and
Epistemology.*
W. Halbfass, 318(JAOS):Jan/Mar80-45
Potter, L., general ed. The "Revels" His-
tory of Drama in English. (Vol 4)
T.R. Griffiths, 617(TLS):19Nov82-1279
Potter, S. and L. Sargent. Pedigree.
M. Faraci, 35(AS):Spring-Summer77-154
Potter, T.W. The Changing Landscape of
South Etruria.
M.H. Crawford, 313:Vol71-153
P. Garnsey, 123:Vol31No2-244
Pottle, F.A. Pride and Negligence.
P-L. Adams, 61:Feb82-86
442(NY):5Apr82-199
Potts, T.C. Conscience in Medieval Philos-
ophy.*
V.J. Bourke, 589:Oct81-935
Potts, W., ed. Portraits of the Artist in
Exile.*
M. Beja, 395(MFS):Summer80-276
R. Boyle, 577(SHR):Winter81-86
Potulicki, E.B. La moderité de la pensée
de Diderot dans les oeuvres philoso-
phiques.
P.H. Meyer, 207(FR):Feb82-409
R. Niklaus, 83:Autumn81-224
Poulat, E. Une église ébranlée.
F. Busi, 207(FR):Feb82-455
Poulenc, F. Emmanuel Chabrier.
D. Puffett, 617(TLS):30Apr82-488
Poulet, G. Entre Moi et Moi.
G. Cesbron, 356(LR):Aug81-255
Poulin, J. The Jimmy Trilogy.*
P. Merivale, 102(CanL):Spring81-127
Pouliot, G. and others. Par Mille Chemins;
Un Ami sur la route; Le Temps d'une
rencontre.
W.N., 102(CanL):Winter80-159
Poulton, A., comp. The Recorded Works of
Sir William Walton.
L. Foreman, 607:Jun81-45
Pound, E. Collected Early Poems of Ezra
Pound.* (M.J. King, ed)
N. Shrimpton, 447(N&Q):Jun80-270
Pound, E. Ezra Pound and the Visual Arts.*
(H. Zinnes, ed)
E. Kreizman, 400(MLN):Dec81-1239
Pound, E. "Ezra Pound Speaking."* (L.W.
Doob, ed)
R. Reid, 29:Jan/Feb82-10
Pound, E. and F.M. Ford. Pound/Ford.
(B. Lindberg-Seyersted, ed)
H. Kenner, 441:14Nov82-13

Pound, O.S. and P. Grover. Wyndham Lewis.*
  D. Parker, 447(N&Q):Dec80-568
  J.H. Winterkorn, 78(BC):Spring81-112
Poupart, J-M. Le Champion de cinq heures
  moins dix.
  D.F. Rogers, 102(CanL):Summer81-148
Poupart, J-M. Ruches.
  G. Marcotte, 102(CanL):Autumn80-93
Pouradier Duteil, F. Trois suffixes
  nominalisateurs.
  W.J. Ashby, 207(FR):Dec80-385
  G. Gross, 209(FM):Jan81-84
Pourvoyeur, R. Offenbach Idillio e Paro-
  dia.
  H. MacDonald, 415:Jul81-479
Powell, A. Faces in My Time.*
  M. Gorra, 249(HudR):Winter81/82-595
Powell, A. Infants of the Spring. Messen-
  gers of the Day.
  M. Gorra, 249(HudR):Winter81/82-595
Powell, A. The Rise of Islam.
  H.A. Ali, 273(IC):Jul80-193
Powell, A. The Strangers All are Gone.
  J. Bayley, 362:13May82-23
  A. Bell, 617(TLS):4Jun82-604
Powell, C. Rehearsal for Dancers.
  D. Headon, 102(CanL):Autumn80-115
Powell, J.N. The Tao of Symbols.
  M. Peters, 441:21Nov82-20
Powell, L.E. A History of Spanish Piano
  Music.
  L. Salter, 415:Nov81-749
Powell, L.N. New Masters.*
  L. Cox, 9(AlaR):Apr81-136
  J.B. Kirby, 579(SAQ):Spring81-235
Powell, N. A Season of Calm Weather.
  D. Davis, 362:16Dec82-23
Powell, R. Shakespeare and the Critics'
  Debate.*
  M.W. Ferguson, 676(YR):Spring82-414
Powell, R.C. - see Vittorini, E.
Powers, D. Creating Environments for
  Troubled Children.
  L.C. Boag, 529(QQ):Winter81-761
Powers, J.F. Prince of Darkness and Other
  Stories. Morte d'Urban.
  M. Gordon, 453(NYRB):27May82-29
Powers, L.H. Faulkner's Yoknapatawpha
  Comedy.*
  J. Ditsky, 628(UWR):Fall-Winter81-125
  F. Lyra, 27(AL):May81-334
  L. Paddock, 150(DR):Summer81-379
  L.P. Simpson, 385(MQR):Spring82-365
Powicke, M. - see Daniel, W.
Powledge, F. Journeys Through the South.*
  A. Cheney, 392:Winter80/81-74
Powledge, F. Water.
  442(NY):13Sep82-173
Pozdneyev, A.M. Religion and Ritual in
  Society. (J.R. Krueger, ed)
  H. Serruys, 318(JAOS):Jul/Sep80-392
Pozzi, L. Le Consequentiae nella Logica
  Medievale.
  W. Risse, 53(AGP):Band63Heft1-86
Pozzi, M., ed. Trattatisti del Cinque-
  cento.
  M. Chiesa, 228(GSLI):Vol 157fasc498-
  296
da Pozzo, G. - see Foscolo, U.
"Práce z dějin slavistiky VII."
  D. Short, 575(SEER):Jul81-475
Prados, J. The Soviet Estimate.
  T. Powers, 61:Apr82-106

Praetorius, N. Subject and Object.
  L.B. Code, 488:Mar81-105
Pramoedya Ananta Toer. This Earth of Man-
  kind.
  J. Crace, 617(TLS):10Sep82-981
  D. May, 362:28Oct82-25
Prange, G.W., with D.M. Goldstein and K.V.
  Dillon. At Dawn We Slept.*
  N. Bliven, 442(NY):29Mar82-139
  D. Kahn, 453(NYRB):27May82-36
  C. Thorne, 617(TLS):4Jun82-603
Prasad, B., ed. India's Foreign Policy.
  N.D. Palmer, 293(JASt):Aug81-835
Prasad, M. Language of the Nirukta.
  R. Rocher, 318(JAOS):Jul/Sep80-321
Prati, A. Voci di gerganti, vagabondi e
  malviventi studiate nell'origine e nella
  storia.* (new ed rev by T. Bolelli)
  E.F. Tuttle, 545(RPh):Feb81(supp)-180
Prato, C. and D. Micalella - see Julian
Pratt, J.C. and V.A. Neufeldt - see Eliot,
  G.
Pratt, M.L. Toward a Speech Act Theory of
  Literary Discourse.*
  A. Schwarz, 196:Band22Heft1/2-150
Pratt, V. The Philosophy of the Social
  Sciences.*
  P. Pettit, 393(Mind):Jan81-149
Prauss, G. Einführung in die Erkenntnis-
  theorie.
  P. Rohs, 342:Band72Heft3-360
Prawer, S.S. Caligari's Children.*
  R.S. Langley, Jr., 577(SHR):Fall81-375
Prawer, S.S. Karl Marx and World Litera-
  ture.
  G.W. Most, 72:Band217Heft2-394
Praz, M. The House of Life. (Italian
  title: La casa della vita.)
  P. Mauriès, 98:Jan81-60
Préaux, C. Le monde hellénistique.
  É. Will, 555:Vol154fasc1-139
Preda, M. Cel mai iubit dintre pămînteni.
  V. Nemoianu, 617(TLS):19Feb82-198
Predmore, R.L. Lorca's New York Poetry.
  D. Harris, 86(BHS):Jul81-271
  F.L. Yudin, 405(MP):Nov81-224
Prescott, A.L. French Poets and the
  English Renaissance.*
  K. Brownlee, 131(CL):Spring81-186
  D. Crane, 161(DUJ):Dec80-109
  N. Mann, 447(N&Q):Feb80-91
  J.L. Pallister, 568(SCN):Spring81-15
"Preservation of Paper and Textiles of His-
  toric and Artistic Value II."
  R.L. Shep, 614:Summer81-21
Press, M.L. Chemehuevi.
  D.L. Shaul, 350:Mar81-246
Pressly, W.L. The Life and Art of James
  Barry.*
  D.G.C. Allan, 324:Dec81-60
  135:Nov81-174
Prest, J. The Garden of Eden.
  M. Girouard, 362:11Feb82-21
Preston, D.A., ed. Environment, Society,
  and Rural Change in Latin America.
  T.D. Anderson, 263(RIB):Vol31No2-281
Preston, H.L. Automobile Age Atlanta.
  M.E. Reed, 9(AlaR):Apr81-144
Prete, S. - see "Res Publica Litterarum"
Pretzer, L.A. Geschichts- und sozialkrit-
  ische Dimensionen in Paul Celans Werk.
  E. Petuchowski, 221(GQ):Nov81-532

Prévert, J. Soleil de nuit.
  D. Leuwers, 450(NRF):Mar81-119
Prévost, A. - see More, T.
Prévot, J. Cyrano de Bergerac romancier.
  M. Gaume, 535(RHL):Mar-Apr81-285
Prévot, J. - see de Cyrano de Bergerac, S.
du Prey, P.D. John Soane: The Making of
an Architect.
  D. Stroud, 617(TLS):10Dec82-1379
Preziosi, D. Architecture, Language, and
Meaning.*
  W.C. Watt, 576:Mar81-82
Prezzolini, G. Diario 1942-1968.
  F. Donini, 617(TLS):6Aug82-852
Price, A. The Old Vengeful.
  T.J. Binyon, 617(TLS):31Dec82-1448
Price, A. Soldier No More.*
  T.J. Binyon, 617(TLS):8Jan82-35
Price, D.C. Patrons and Musicians of the
English Renaissance.*
  D. Stevens, 414(MusQ):Oct81-592
Price, E. Inn of that Journey.
  H. Kosok, 447(N&Q):Oct80-474
Price, J. - see Jonson, B.
Price, J.L. Cadres, Commanders and Commis-
sars.
  D. Deal, 302:Vol 18-143
Price, R., ed. Maroon Societies.
  R. Rathbone, 69:Vol50No2-239
Price, R. Masters, Unions and Men.*
  W.H. Fraser, 637(VS):Spring81-361
Price, S. and R. Afro-American Arts of
the Suriname Rain Forest.
  P.J.C. Dark, 617(TLS):15Jan82-58
Prickett, S. Victorian Fantasy.*
  G. Ford, 445(NCF):Mar81-540
  J. Gattégno, 189(EA):Jul-Sep81-348
  R. Jackson, 677(YES):Vol 11-293
  J.R. Reed, 637(VS):Autumn80-123
Pride, J.B., ed. Sociolinguistic Aspects
of Language Learning and Teaching.
  B.C. Johnson, 350:Sep81-780
Prideaux, G.D., ed. Perspectives in
Experimental Linguistics.
  D.G. MacKay and T. Konishi, 350:Sep81-
751
Prideaux, G.D., B.L. Derwing and W.J.
Baker, eds. Experimental Linguistics.
  J.J. Jaeger and R.D. Van Valin, Jr.,
350:Mar82-233
  J.F. Kess, 320(CJL):Fall81-227
Priebsch, R. and E. von Steinmeyer. Rob-
ert Priebsch — Elias von Steinmeyer:
Briefwechsel. (A. Closs, ed)
  H. Oppel, 72:Band217Heft1-184
  H. Penzl, 350:Mar81-229
  M.O. Walshe, 402(MLR):Jul81-755
Priessnitz, H. Das englische "radio play"
seit 1945.
  H. Groene, 38:Band99Heft3/4-537
Priest, R. The Visible Man.*
  R. Billings, 628(UWR):Fall-Winter81-
111
Priestley, F.E.L. Language and Structure
in Tennyson's Poetry.
  J.R. Bennett, 599:Fall81-453
Priestley, M., comp. Comprehensive Guide
to the Manuscripts Collection and to the
Personal Papers in the University
Archives.
  C.G. Palm, 14:Summer81-244
Prieur, J. Nuits blanches.
  J. Laurans, 450(NRF):Mar81-147

Prigogine, I. and I. Stengers. La
Nouvelle Alliance.*
  Y. Gauthier, 154:Mar81-132
Primeau, R. Beyond "Spoon River."
  H. Beaver, 617(TLS):22Jan82-82
"Princely Magnificence."
  I. Himmelheber, 683:Band44Heft2-190
Pring, J.T. The Oxford Dictionary of
Modern Greek.
  M. Alexiou, 617(TLS):3Sep82-953
Pringle, P. and J. Spigelman. The Nuclear
Barons.*
  P. Johnson, 362:18Feb82-23
  J.N. Wilford, 441:31Jan82-6
Prinz, F. Gründungsmythen und Sagen-
chronologie.
  G. Huxley, 123:Vol31No2-225
Prior, M. Fisher Row.
  H. Carpenter, 617(TLS):14May82-535
Pritchard, W.H. Lives of the Modern
Poets.*
  D. Davie, 569(SR):Winter81-110
  D. Pope, 579(SAQ):Autumn81-489
Pritchard, W.H. Seeing Through Every-
thing.*
  C. Butler, 184(EIC):Jan81-69
Pritchett, F.W. Urdu Literature.
  C. Coppola, 314:Summer-Fall81-217
Pritchett, V.S. Collected Stories.
  W. Abrahams, 231:Aug82-74
  V. Cunningham, 617(TLS):25Jun82-687
  R. Kiely, 441:30May82-5
  J. Raban, 453(NYRB):24Jun82-8
  C. Sigal, 362:5Aug82-22
Pritchett, V.S. On the Edge of the Cliff.*
The Tale Bearers.* The Myth Makers.
  G. Core, 569(SR):Spring81-xxxviii
Pritchett, V.S. and R. Stone. The Turn
of the Years.
  J. Raban, 453(NYRB):24Jun82-8
  442(NY):28Jun82-119
Pritchett, W.K. The Greek State at War.
(Pt 3)
  N.G.L. Hammond, 123:Vol131No2-238
  N.J. Richardson, 303(JoHS):Vol 101-185
Probyn, C.T., ed. Jonathan Swift.*
  R.D. Hume, 568(SCN):Winter81-89
Probyn, H. Ted Hughes' "Gaudete."
  M. Perloff, 447(N&Q):Dec80-573
Prochnik, L. Endings.
  H. Ashmore, 436(NewL):Winter81/82-123
Proclus. Trois études sur la Providence.
(Vol 2) (D. Isaac, ed and trans)
  É. des Places, 555:Vol154fasc2-363
Procter, E.S. Curia and Cortes in León
and Castile 1072-1295.*
  D.W. Lomax, 86(BHS):Jul81-254
Procter, P., ed-in-chief. Dictionary of
Contemporary English.
  G. Core, 249(HudR):Autumn81-475
  H. Ulherr, 38:Band99Heft1/2-193
Procter, P., ed. Longman New Universal
Dictionary.
  R.R.K. Hartmann, 617(TLS):3Sep82-953
Proctor, G.A. Canadian Music of the
Twentieth Century.
  P. Griffiths, 415:Jun81-387
  C. Morey, 627(UTQ):Summer81-202
  B.W. Pennycook, 529(QQ):Winter81-781
Profeti, M.G. - see Vélez de Guevara, L.
Proffer, E. Tsvetaeva.*
  A.M. Kroth, 574(SEEJ):Spring81-105

Pronay, N. and D.W. Spring, eds. Propaganda, Politics and Film, 1918-45.
P. Smith, 617(TLS):1Oct82-1054
Pronay, N. and J. Taylor, eds. Parliamentary Texts of the Later Middle Ages.
G.P. Cuttino, 589:Jan81-188
J.R. Maddicott, 382(MAE):1981/2-323
Pronko, L.C. Eugène Labiche and Georges Feydeau.
N. de Jongh, 617(TLS):3Dec82-1347
Prontera, A. and F. Fiorentino - see Leroux, P.
Pronzini, B. Labyrinth.
T.J. Binyon, 617(TLS):26Mar82-339
Pronzini, B. Scattershot.
N. Callendar, 441:17Oct82-41
Propertius. Sesto Properzio: Il primo libro delle "Elegie." (P. Fedeli, ed)
J.A. Richmond, 123:Vol31No2-202
Propertius. Sex. Propertii "Elegiarum" Libri IV. (R. Hanslik, ed)
E.J. Kenney, 123:Vol31No2-200
Prost, A. Petite Histoire de la France au XXe siècle.
E. Morot-Sir, 207(FR):Oct81-171
Prou, S. Les Dimanches.
R. Kuhn, 207(FR):Oct80-197
Prou, S. Le Voyage aux Seychelles.
D.C. Cooper, 207(FR):May82-927
Proudfit, C.L. - see Landor, W.S.
Proust, J., ed. Recherches nouvelles sur quelques écrivains des lumières.* (Vol 2)
M. Delon, 535(RHL):Mar-Apr81-299
Proust, M. Les avant-textes de l'épisode de la madeleine dans les cahiers de brouillon. (L. Keller, ed)
B. Brun, 535(RHL):Mar-Apr81-327
Proust, M. Correspondance de Marcel Proust.* (Vol 5) (P. Kolb, ed)
D.W. Alden, 210(FrF):May81-182
W.C. Carter, 207(FR):Apr82-687
J. Cruickshank, 402(MLR):Apr81-475
Proust, M. Correspondance de Marcel Proust.* (Vol 6) (P. Kolb, ed)
W.C. Carter, 207(FR):Apr82-687
Proust, M. Correspondance de Marcel Proust. (Vol 8) (P. Kolb, ed)
J.M. Cocking, 617(TLS):21May82-548
Proust, M. Remembrance of Things Past.* (C.K. Scott Moncrieff, T. Kilmartin and A. Mayor, trans)
G. Brée, 659(ConL):Summer82-365
S. Tapscott, 676(YR):Summer82-612
Provine, D.M. Case Selection in the United States Supreme Court.
A.D.H., 185:Jul82-781
Proxenus a Sudetis, S. Commentarii de Itinere Francogallico. (D. Martínková, ed)
F.X. Hartigan, 104(CASS):Winter81-607
H. Leeming, 575(SEER):Jan81-71
Pruessen, R.W. John Foster Dulles: The Road to Power.
J.L. Gaddis, 441:16May82-10
R. Steel, 453(NYRB):21Oct82-42
Pruitt, I. Old Madam Yin.
K. Biggerstaff, 293(JASt):Nov80-118
de Prunes, M.I.S.C. - see under Santa Cruz de Prunes, M.I.
Pruslin, S., ed. Peter Maxwell Davies.
P.J.P., 412:May80-153

Pryce-Jones, D. Paris in the Third Reich.*
G. Steiner, 442(NY):25Jan82-96
Pryke, K.G. Nova Scotia and Confederation 1864-74.
R. MacLean, 529(QQ):Summer81-364
Pryor, R.J., ed. Migration and Development in South-East Asia.
L. Manderson, 293(JASt):Nov80-201
Pryse, M. The Mark and the Knowledge.*
H. Hill, 395(MFS):Summer80-320
D. Minter, 445(NCF):Jun80-85
R.A. Paredes, 594:Fall81-341
Psaar, W. and M. Klein. Wer hat Angst vor der bösen Geiss?
H. Lixfeld, 196:Band21Heft1/2-147
Pseudo Hyginus. De metatione castrorum.*
(A. Grillone, ed)
M. Lenoir, 555:Vol54fasc1-179
Pseudo Hyginus. Pseudo-Hygin, "Des fortifications du camp." (M. Lenoir, ed and trans)
J-C. Richard, 555:Vol54fasc2-373
"P'soch Li Shimcha." (rev)
E.D. Lawson, 424:Mar81-88
Pucciani, O.F. and J. Hamel. Langue et langage. (3rd ed)
N.A. Poulin, 207(FR):Mar81-612
J.W. Zdenek, 399(MLJ):Spring81-90
Puccini, D. La palabra poética de Vicente Aleixandre.
M.R. Coke, 402(MLR):Apr81-491
205(FMLS):Oct81-379
Puech, J-B. La bibliothèque d'un amateur.
R. Millet, 98:Jun-Jul80-668
Puel, G. Terre-plein.
D.L., 450(NRF):May81-149
Pugsley, A., ed. The Works of Isambard Kingdom Brunel.
C. Harvie, 637(VS):Spring81-387
Puhvel, M. "Beowulf" and Celtic Tradition.
G.W. Dunleavy, 301(JEGP):Jul81-402
D.N. Klausner, 627(UTQ):Summer81-103
A.H. Olsen, 191(ELN):Mar81-209
J. Simpson, 203:Vol191No2-250
Puig, J.C. Doctrinas internacionales y autonomía lationamericana.
J.D. Martz, 263(RIB):Vol31No3-416
Puig, M. Eternal Curse on the Reader of These Pages.
A. Josephs, 441:4Jul82-9
442(NY):26Jul82-95
Pujol, C. Leer a Saint-Simon.
H. Himelfarb, 535(RHL):Mar-Apr81-294
Pula, J.S. and M.N. An Index to Polish American Studies 1944-1973.
S.A. Blejwas, 497(PolR):Vol26No3-109
Pulgram, E. Latin-Romance Phonology.*
G. Ineichen, 260(IF):Band85-359
T. Janson, 545(RPh):Feb81(supp)-323
Pulido y Pulido, T. Datos para la historia artística cacereña.
M. Estella, 48:Oct-Dec81-460
Pullar, P. The Shortest Journey.
V. Glendinning, 362:14Jan82-22
Pullin, F., ed. New Perspectives on Melville.*
H. Cohen, 677(YES):Vol 11-326
Puntel, L.B. Wahrheitstheorien in der neueren Philosophie.
W. Franzen, 489(PJGG):Band88Heft1-220
Punter, D. The Literature of Terror.*
C.A. Howells, 175:Summer81-185
D. Jarrett, 366:Autumn81-260

Puppi, L. and others. Architettura e
utopia nella Venezia del cinquecento.
C. Elam, 59:Sep81-350
Puppo, M. Poesia e verità.
A. Ferraris, 228(GSLI):Vol 157fasc497-
151
Purcell, E.T. The Realizations of Serbo-
Croatian Accents in Sentence Environ-
ments.
G.F. Meier, 682(ZPSK):Band32Heft2-232
Purdy, A. No Other Country.
A. Globe, 102(CanL):Spring80-96
Purdy, A.T. Needle-Punching.
P. Bach, 614:Fall81-19
Purdy, R.L. and M. Millgate - see Hardy, T.
Pürschel, H. Pause und Kadenz.
A. Wollmann, 38:Band99Heft1/2-185
Purtill, R. Murdercon.
N. Callendar, 441:12Sep82-36
Pushkin, A.S. The Bronze Horseman. (D.M.
Thomas, trans)
S. Karlinsky, 441:26Sep82-11
Pushkin, A.S. Eugene Onegin.* (C. John-
ston, trans)
A. Pyman, 161(DUJ):Dec80-120
Puškin, A.S. Épigrammy.
S. Senderovich, 558(RLJ):Winter81-225
Puškin, A.S. Mednyj Vsadnik. (N.V. Izmaj-
lov, ed.
S. Ketchian, 574(SEEJ):Spring81-98
Putnam, H. Meaning and the Moral
Sciences.*
M. Thompson, 185:Apr81-511
Putnam, H. Reason, Truth and History.
D.H. Mellor, 617(TLS):16Jul82-774
Putnam, M.C.J. Essays on Latin Lyric,
Elegy, and Epic.
R. Stoneman, 617(TLS):11Jun82-634
Putnam, M.C.J. Virgil's Poem of the
Earth.*
G.K. Galinsky, 122:Oct81-329
J. Griffin, 123:Vol31No1-23
Putt, S.G. The Golden Age of English
Drama.
R. Warren, 617(TLS):9Apr82-419
Pütz, M. The Story of Identity.*
J. Klinkowitz, 594:Winter81-468
J.J. Waldmeir, 395(MFS):Winter80/81-
675
Puyo, J. and P. Van Eersel. Sacrés Fran-
çais, ou Les Nouveaux Cahiers de dolé-
ances.
J-M. Guieu, 207(FR):Oct81-170
Py, A. - see de Ronsard, P.
Pybus, R. The Loveless Letters.*
I. Hughes, 493:Sep81-78
Pye, M. The King over the Water.*
A. Dickins, 364:Aug-Sep81-142
Pyke, E.J. A Biographical Dictionary of
Wax Modellers. (Supp)
F.J.B. Watson, 617(TLS):14May82-542
Pyles, T. Selected Essays on English
Usage.* (J. Algeo, ed)
K.B. Harder, 424:Jun80-155
Pym, B. A Few Green Leaves.*
639(VQR):Spring81-59
Pym, B. Less Than Angels.
D. Kubal, 249(HudR):Autumn81-462
Pym, B. An Unsuitable Attachment.
A. Duchêne, 617(TLS):26Feb82-214
P. Kemp, 362:18Feb82-24
E. Milton, 441:20Jun82-11
442(NY):24May82-133

Pym, D. The Religious Thought of Samuel
Taylor Coleridge.
S. Prickett, 677(YES):Vol 11-303
Pyman, A. The Life of Aleksandr Blok.*
(Vol 1)
S. Karlinsky, 441:9May82-8
R. Kemball, 550(RusR):Jul81-354
C. Morgan, 565:Vol122No2-16
Pyman, A. The Life of Aleksandr Blok.*
(Vol 2)
D.L. Burgin, 574(SEEJ):Summer81-93
G. Donchin, 402(MLR):Apr81-511
S. Karlinsky, 441:9May82-8
R. Kemball, 550(RusR):Jul81-354
C. Morgan, 565:Vol122No2-16
639(VQR):Winter81-10
Pyne, S.J. Fire in America.
M. Abley, 617(TLS):5Nov82-1215
D. Smith, 441:15Aug82-3
Pyne, S.J. Grove Karl Gilbert.
C. Albritton, 584(SWR):Spring81-225
Pynsent, R., ed. Czech Prose and Verse.*
K. Brušák, 575(SEER):Jul81-419
205(FMLS):Jan80-83
Pythian, B.A., ed. A Concise Dictionary
of Correct English.
G. Core, 249(HudR):Autumn81-475
Pytlík, R. and H. Hrzalová, eds. Vztahy a
cíle socialistických literatur.
R.B. Pynsent, 575(SEER):Apr81-298

Qafisheh, H.A. Gulf Arabic: Intermediate
Level.
F.J. Cadora, 399(MLJ):Autumn81-334
A.S. Kaye, 320(CJL):Fall81-238
Qidwai, A.S. Ruhul-Qur'an.
A.W. Bukhari, 273(IC):Jul80-189
Quainton, M.D. Ronsard's Ordered Chaos.*
M.C. Smith, 208(FS):Jul81-320
205(FMLS):Oct80-381
Quandt, W.B. Saudi Arabia in the 1980s.
J. Hoagland, 453(NYRB):1Apr82-23
de Quehen, H. - see Butler, S.
de Queiroz, E. - see under Eça de Queiroz
Queneau, R. Exercises in Style.* We
Always Treat Women Too Well.*
J.D. O'Hara, 434:Summer82-603
Queneau, R. - see Kojève, A.
Quennell, P. Customs and Characters.
R. Blythe, 362:11Nov82-23
V. Glendinning, 617(TLS):26Nov82-1293
Quennell, P., ed. Vladimir Nabokov.*
M.T. Naumann, 558(RLJ):Spring-Fall81-
293
C.S. Ross, 395(MFS):Winter80/81-671
Quennell, P. - see Pope-Hennessy, J.
Quesada, M.A.L. - see under Ladero Quesada,
M.A.
Quesada, M.S. - see under Sáenz Quesada, M.
Queval, J. - see "Beowulf"
de Quevedo, F. El Buscón. (D. Ynduráin,
ed)
A. Carreño, 238:Dec81-637
Quigly, I. The Heirs of Tom Brown.
H. Carpenter, 617(TLS):23Jul82-787
J. Rae, 362:1Jul82-22
Quignard, P. Carus.*
G. Quinsat, 98:Jun-Jul80-571
Quilici, L. and S. Quilici Gigli. Antem-
nae.*
M.H. Crawford, 313:Vol71-153

Quilligan, M. The Language of Allegory.*
J.A. Burrow, 447(N&Q):Dec80-544
C.A.H., 604:Spring-Summer81-37
D. Haskin, 613:Jun81-226
T. Heller, 50(ArQ):Autumn81-282
"Quilting — Patchwork and Appliqué."
P. Bach, 614:Spring82-16
Quinault, P. Astrate. (E.J. Campion, ed)
A. Gable, 208(FS):Oct81-440
W. Leiner, 475:No14Pt1-190
Quine, W.V. Le mot et la chose. Roots of
Reference.
C. Imbert, 98:Apr80-393
Quine, W.V. Theories and Things.
P. Geach, 617(TLS):19Feb82-193
Quiney, A. John Loughborough Pearson.*
J. Bassin, 637(VS):Winter81-239
D.B. Brownlee, 576:Mar81-62
Quinn, A. The Confidence of British Phi-
losophers.
R.H. Popkin, 319:Jan81-127
Quinn, D.B., ed. Early Maryland in a
Wider World.
N. Canny, 617(TLS):12Nov82-1249
Quinn, D.B., with A.M. Quinn and S.
Hillier, eds. New American World.*
M.E. Miller, 551(RenQ):Summer80-274
Quinn, E. Picasso.
P. Hodges, 62:Feb81-71
Quinn, E.C. The Penitence of Adam.
G.J. Brault, 207(FR):Mar82-540
Quinn, J. American Tongue and Cheek.*
G. Core, 249(HudR):Autumn81-475
639(VQR):Summer81-85
Quinn, K. Texts and Contexts.*
J. Henderson, 627(UTQ):Summer81-97
P.G. Walsh, 487:Fall81-278
T.P. Wiseman, 125:Spring81-340
Quinnell, A.J. The Mahdi.*
E. Jakab, 441:7Feb82-13
Quinnell, A.J. Snap Shot.
T.J. Binyon, 617(TLS):31Dec82-1448
Quintana, R. Two Augustans.*
P. Danchin, 677(YES):Vol 11-272
Quintanilla Raso, M.C. Nobleza y señorios
en el reino de Córdoba.
P. Freedman, 589:Oct81-936
Quintilian. Quintilien, "Institution
Oratoire." (Vol 3, Bks 4 and 5) (J.
Cousin, ed)
F. Ahlheid, 394:Vol34fasc3/4-442
Quinton, A. Thoughts and Thinkers.
A.C. Danto, 617(TLS):9Jul82-736
M. Warnock, 362:18Feb82-22
Quirk, L.J. The Films of Myrna Loy.
D. McClelland, 200:Mar81-178
Quraishi, S.D. and U. Sims-Williams.
Catalogue of the Urdu Manuscripts in the
India Office Library.
R.K. Barz, 259(IIJ):Jan81-71
Quraishi, Z.M. Political Thought.
A. Moazzam, 273(IC):Oct81-291
Qureshi, A.H. "Edinburgh Review" and
Poetic Truth.
D.A. Low, 447(N&Q):Oct80-460
Qureshi, M.A. Marriage and Matrimonial
Remedies.
M. Imam, 273(IC):Apr81-131

Raabe, H., ed. Trends in kontrastiver
Linguistik. (2nd ed) (Vol 1)
L. Siegrist, 257(IRAL):Aug81-258

Rabain, J. L'enfant du lignage.
A. Adams, 69:Vol50No2-225
Raban, J. Old Glory.*
J.L. Hopkins, 364:Dec81/Jan82-121
Rabassa, C.C. Demetrio Aguilera-Malta and
Social Justice.
C.H. Monsanto, 238:Sep81-483
Rabbitt, T. The Booth Interstate.
R. Phillips, 249(HudR):Autumn81-422
639(VQR):Autumn81-131
Rabelais, F. Gargantua e Pantagruele.
(A. Frassineti, trans)
C. Dédéyan, 535(RHL):Nov-Dec81-978
Rabil, A., Jr. Laura Cereta Quattrocento
Humanist.
L.V.R., 568(SCN):Winter81-108
Rabineau, P. Feather Arts.
A.L. Kaeppler, 2(AfrA):May81-84
Rabinow, P. and W.M. Sullivan, eds. Inter-
pretive Social Science.
J. Skorupski, 518:Jul81-154
Rabinowicz, W. Universalizability.
J.L.M., 185:Jan82-395
Rabinowitz, S.J. Sologub's Literary
Children.
M.G. Barker, 558(RLJ):Spring-Fall81-
287
E. Bristol, 550(RusR):Apr81-223
Rabkin, N. Shakespeare and the Problem of
Meaning.
M.W. Ferguson, 676(YR):Spring82-414
A. Kirsch, 405(MP):May82-426
Raby, P. Fair Ophelia.
A. Brookner, 617(TLS):17Dec82-1395
Rachline, M. Tendre banlieu.
R. Henkels, Jr., 207(FR):Mar81-623
Racine, J. Andromache. (R. Wilbur, trans)
F. Steegmuller, 441:26Dec82-6
Racine, J. Four Greek Plays. (R.C.
Knight, ed)
J.H. Mason, 617(TLS):17Sep82-1018
Racine, J. Théâtre complet. (J. Morel
and A. Viala, eds)
P. France, 208(FS):Oct81-441
Racot, A. - see France, A.
Raddatz, F.J. - see Marx, K. and F. Engels
Rademacher, F. Die Gustorfer Chorschran-
ken.
P. Bloch, 683:Band44Heft1-92
Rader, M. Marx's Interpretation of
History.*
L. Baxandall, 290(JAAC):Spring82-338
R.R. Bhaskar, 518:Jul81-137
G.A. Cohen, 125:Winter81-219
W.L. McBride, 185:Jan82-316
Rader, M. and B. Jessup. Art and Human
Values.
A. Shields, 289:Apr81-113
Radhakrishnan, R. The Nancowry Word.
D. Sherwood, 350:Dec82-950
Radin, G. Virginia Woolf's "The Years."
D. Doner, 268(IFR):Summer82-156
Rädle, F., ed. Lateinische Ordensdramen
des XVI. Jahrhunderts.
U. Herzog, 684(ZDA):Band110Heft1-49
Radley, S. A Talent for Destruction.
M. Laski, 362:2Dec82-23
Radnitzky, G. and G. Andersson, eds. Pro-
gress and Rationality in Science.* (Ger-
man title: Fortschritt und Rationalität
der Wissenschaft.)
M. Schmid, 679:Band11Heft2-397

Radnóti, M. The Complete Poetry.* (E. George, ed and trans)
H. Thomas, 385(MQR):Winter82-200
Radt, S. - see Sophocles
Radu, M., ed. Eastern Europe and the Third World.
E.K. Valkenier, 550(RusR):Oct81-470
Radzinowicz, M.A. Toward "Samson Agonistes."*
G. Campbell, 677(YES):Vol 11-256
C.D. Murphy, 396(ModA):Winter81-104
J.H. Sims, 568(SCN):Winter81-81
Raevskii, N. and M. Gabinskii, eds. Scurt dicţionar etimologic al limbii moldoveneşti.
A. Lombard, 545(RPh):May81-467
Rafroidi, P. Irish Literature in English: The Romantic Period (1789-1850).*
R. Tracy, 445(NCF):Dec81-355
Rafroidi, P. and T. Brown, eds. The Irish Short Story.
R.F. Peterson, 573(SSF):Winter81-108
R. Wall, 49:Jan81-101
Ragsdale, H. Détente in the Napoleonic Era.
N.V. Riasanovsky, 550(RusR):Apr81-186
Ragsdale, H., ed. Paul I.
D. Christian, 550(RusR):Jan81-61
von Ragué, B. A History of Japanese Lacquerwork.
D.F. McCallum, 318(JAOS):Jul/Sep80-384
Ragusa, I. and R.B. Green, eds. "Meditations on the Life of Christ."
T. Barolini, 545(RPh):Feb81-355
Ragusa, O. Narrative and Drama.
J.H. Potter, 276:Winter81-324
M. Trovato, 546(RR):Mar81-250
Ragusa, O. Pirandello.
J.B. Rey, 397(MD):Dec81-568
Raguscio, M. The Subterfuge of Art.*
S.M. Tave, 677(YES):Vol 11-290
Rahman, M. Emergence of a New Nation in a Multi-polar World: Bangladesh.
H. Blair, 293(JASt):Nov80-175
ur-Rahman, T. Islamization of Pakistan Law.
A. Moazzam, 273(IC):Jan81-67
Rahn, J. Basic Atonal Theory.
P. Griffiths, 415:Nov81-751
Rahn, S. Children's Literature.
S.H. Goodacre, 283:Spring81-46
Rahner, K. Foundations of Christian Faith.
J. Pappin 3d, 396(ModA):Spring81-196
T. Sheehan, 453(NYRB):4Feb82-13
Rahner, K. Theological Investigations. (Vol 17)
J.L. Houlden, 617(TLS):3Sep82-954
Rahner, K. Theological Investigations. (Vol 20)
T. Sheehan, 453(NYRB):4Feb82-13
Rai, L. Sarmad.
S.A. Akbarabadi, 273(IC):Jan81-63
Railton, S. Fenimore Cooper.*
G. Dekker, 677(YES):Vol 11-307
Raimes, A. Problems and Teaching Strategies in ESL Composition.
M.P. Leamon and F.L. Jenks, 399(MLJ): Autumn81-326
Raimo, J.W., ed. A Guide to Manuscripts Relating to America in Great Britain and Ireland.
D.J. Martz, Jr., 14:Spring80-218

Raina, P. Independent Social Movements in Poland.
A. Brumberg, 617(TLS):11Jun82-640
Rainbolt, W.R. The History of Underground Communication in Russia Since the Seventeenth Century.
C.A. Ruud, 550(RusR):Apr81-184
Raine, C. A Free Translation.
D. Davis, 362:7Jan82-22
Raine, K. Blake and Antiquity.
V.A. De Luca, 627(UTQ):Winter80/81-238
L.M. Findlay, 447(N&Q):Jun80-251
J-J. Mayoux, 189(EA):Jul-Sep81-346
Raine, K. Blake and the New Age.
C. Gallant, 661(WC):Summer81-164
Raine, K. The Human Face of God.
R. Lister, 324:Aug82-595
M. Mason, 617(TLS):16Apr82-432
Raine, K. The Inner Journey of the Poet.
I. McGilchrist, 617(TLS):22Oct82-1148
Raine, K. David Jones and the Actually Loved and Known.
W.J. Keith, 627(UTQ):Spring81-330
Raitt, A. - see Flaubert, G.
Raitt, A.W. The Life of Villiers de l'Isle-Adam.*
M.G. Rose, 446(NCFS):Spring-Summer82-385
Rajan, B., ed. The Presence of Milton.
J. Carey, 541(RES):Feb81-79
Rajan, T. Dark Interpreter.*
G. Durrant, 627(UTQ):Summer81-117
H.R. Elam, 661(WC):Summer81-197
D. Wagenknecht, 591(SIR):Winter81-525
Räkel, H-H.S. Die musikalische Erscheinungsform der Trouvèrepoesie.*
J. Beck, 545(RPh):Nov80-250
Rakove, J.N. The Beginnings of National Politics.*
E.J. Ferguson, 656(WMQ):Jan81-125
Raley, H. La visión responsable.
J.B. Jelinski, 552(REH):Jan81-133
Ralph, B. Phonological Differentiation.
B. Kress, 682(ZPSK):Band33Heft2-277
Ramage, E.S., ed. Atlantis.*
R.W., 555:Vol54fasc1-163
Rambaux, C. Tertullien face aux morales des trois premiers siècles.
R.M. Ogilvie, 123:Vol31No1-121
Ramírez, J.A. Cinco lecciones sobre arquitectura y utopía.
F. Marías, 48:Apr-Jun81-226
Ramírez Molas, P. Tiempo y narración.*
E. Picón Garfield, 240(HR):Winter81-134
Ramke, B. White Monkeys.
639(VQR):Autumn81-130
Ramoneda, A.M. - see de Berceo, G.
Ramos Rosa, A. A palavra e o lugar. As marcas no deserto. Círculo aberto. A poesia moderna e a interrogação do real.
R. Bréchon, 98:Jan81-22
Ramsay, A. The Works of Allan Ramsay.* (Vols 1-6) (B. Martin and J.W. Oliver, eds)
G.R.R., 588(SSL):Vol 16-261
Ramsay, A. and R. Fergusson. Poems by Allan Ramsay and Robert Fergusson. (A.M. Kinghorn and A. Law, eds)
G.R.R., 588(SSL):Vol 16-261
Ramsden, H. - see Lorca, F.G.

289

Ramsey, P. The Fickle Glass.*
  J. Fuzier, 189(EA):Apr-Jun81-215
  C. Hoy, 405(MP):Feb82-316
Ranawake, S. Höfische Strophenkunst.*
  F.V. Spechtler, 680(ZDP):Band99Heft3-446
Rand, H. Arshile Gorky.*
  90:Nov81-712
Randall, G. Church Furnishing and Decoration in England and Wales.
  G. Darley, 135:Feb81-165
Randall, J.H., Jr. Philosophy after Darwin.* (B.J. Singer, ed)
  E.J. Machle, 319:Apr81-274
Randall, L.M.C. - see Lucas, G.A.
Ranelagh, E.L. The Past We Share.
  K.M. Briggs, 203:Vol91No2-250
Rang, B. - see Husserl, E.
Rangel-Guerrero, D. - see Vicente, G.
Ranger, R. Arms and Politics 1958-1978.
  P. Buteux, 529(QQ):Summer81-368
Ranke, K. Die Welt der Einfachen Formen.
  L. Degh, 678(YCGL):No29-43
Ranke, K. and others, eds. Enzyklopädie des Märchens.* (Vol 1)
  A. Gier, 72:Band217Heft1-173
Ranke, K. and others, eds. Enzyklopädie des Märchens. (Vol 2, Pts 1-4)
  E. Ettlinger, 203:Vol91No1-119
  M. Zender, 196:Band21Heft3/4-308
Ranke, K. and others, eds. Enzyklopädie des Märchens. (Vol 2, Pt 5)
  M. Zender, 196:Band21Heft3/4-308
Rannit, A. Invention and Tradition.*
  S. Hollerbach, 574(SEEJ):Winter81-87
Ransanus, P. Epithoma rerum hungararum. (P. Kulcsár, ed)
  A. Lengyel, 551(RenQ):Spring80-74
Ransel, D.L., ed. The Family in Imperial Russia.*
  R.K. Debo, 529(QQ):Spring81-115
Ransford, O. David Livingstone.*
  E. Halladay, 161(DUJ):Dec80-100
Rao, S.K.R. Tibetan Meditation.
  T.V. Wylie, 293(JASt):Feb81-370
Raoul, V. The French Fictional Journal.
  C. Britton, 208(FS):Oct81-484
  R. Le Huenen, 627(UTQ):Summer81-146
  P. Merivale, 102(CanL):Autumn81-166
Raper, J.R. From the Sunken Garden.*
  N. Baym, 301(JEGP):Jul81-464
  D. Scura, 392:Fall81-485
Raphael, C. Encounters with the Jewish People.
  H. Maccoby, 390:Jan81-53
Raphael, D.D. Hobbes: Morals and Politics.*
  N.O.K., 185:Oct80-175
Raphael, D.D. Justice and Liberty.*
  B.B., 185:Jul82-776
Raphael, D.D. Moral Philosophy.
  O. O'Neill, 617(TLS):12Mar82-285
Raphael, F. Byron.
  D. Davis, 617(TLS):26Nov82-1315
Raphael, F. and K. McLeish. The List of Books.*
  C.B. Cox, 148:Winter81-83
Raphael, M. Proudhon, Marx, Picasso.*
  R.A., 185:Oct81-180
  L. Cooke, 59:Jun81-231
Raphael, S. and others. Of Oxfordshire Gardens.
  J. Buxton, 617(TLS):30Jul82-823

Rapoport, J. Winter Flowers.
  D. Barbour, 648(WCR):Vol 15No3-43
Rapoport, N. Preparing for Sabbath.
  A.B. Carb, 287:Oct81-19
Rapp, F. Analytische Technikphilosophie.
  W. Strombach, 489(PJGG):Band88Heft1-194
Rappard, H.V. Psychology as Self-Knowledge.
  R. Smith, 518:Apr81-97
Rasberry, R.W. The "Technique" of Political Lying.
  D.A. Thomas, 583:Spring82-342
Rasch, W. Goethes "Iphigenie auf Tauris" als Drama der Autonomie.*
  D. Borchmeyer, 490:Band12Heft1-126
  H. Reiss, 133:Band14Heft1-75
Rashid, H.E. Geography of Bangladesh.
  B.L. Bhatt, 293(JASt):Nov80-177
Rashley, R.E. Rock Painter.*
  D. Barbour, 648(WCR):Jun80-78
Rasjidi, H.M., ed and trans. Documents pour servir à l'histoire de l'Islam à Java.
  T. Michel, 318(JAOS):Jan/Mar80-26
Raskin, V. and D. Segal - see "Slavica Hierosolymitana"
Rasky, F. The North Pole or Bust.
  T.D. MacLulich, 102(CanL):Spring80-90
Rasmussen, R.K. Migrant Kingdom.
  A. Barnard, 69:Vol50No2-224
Raso, M.C.Q. - see under Quintanilla Raso, M.C.
Rassias, J.A. and J. de la Chapelle-Skubly. Le Français.
  J.M. Goldman, 207(FR):Feb81-513
Rast, N. and T.S. Westoll - see Nalivkin, D.V.
Rastell, J. Three Rastell Plays. (R. Axton, ed)
  D. Bevington, 130:Summer81-176
Rataboul, L.J. Le Pasteur anglican dans le roman victorien.
  G.B. Tennyson, 445(NCF):Jun80-117
Ratcliff, C. John Singer Sargent.
  J. Russell, 441:5Dec82-66
Rather, L.J. The Dream of Self-Destruction.*
  G. Gillespie, 678(YCGL):No29-44
  R. Nicholls, 131(CL):Summer81-294
  H.R. Vaget, 221(GQ):Mar81-202
  M.A. Weiner, 406:Winter81-472
Rathmann, B. Der Einfluss Boileaus auf die Rezeption der Lyrik des frühen 17. Jahrhunderts in Frankreich.
  C. Abraham, 210(FrF):Jan81-88
  V. Kapp, 535(RHL):Jul-Oct81-766
  J. Marmier, 475:No13Pt1-152
Rathmayr, R. Die perfektive Präsensform im Russischen.*
  R-D. Keil, 688(ZSP):Band42Heft1-219
Raths, D., comp. Register of the Frederick Philip Grove Collection.
  W.J. Keith, 627(UTQ):Summer81-155
Rauch, I. and G.F. Carr, eds. The Grammar of Language and Experience.
  M.S. Kirch, 399(MLJ):Winter81-419
Rauch, I. and G.F. Carr, eds. Linguistic Method.
  A. Bammesberger, 38:Band99Heft3/4-406
  205(FMLS):Jan80-90

Rauh, G. Linguistische Beschrebung deiktischer Komplexität in narrativen Texten.
J.H. Shaw, 494:Winter81-211
Rausch, H-H. Methoden und Bedeutung naturkundlicher Rezeption und Kompilation im "Jüngeren Titurel."
K. Nyholm, 439(NM):1981/1-92
Rauschning, H. Hitler m'a dit. (A. Somogy, ed)
Y. Michaud, 98:Nov80-1044
Rauschning, H. La Révolution du nihilisme.
H. Cronel, 450(NRF):May81-134
Y. Michaud, 98:Nov80-1044
A. Reix, 542:Jul-Sep81-377
Rautenberg, H-W. Der polnische Aufstand von 1863 und die Europäische Politik im Spiegel der deutschen Diplomatie und der öffentlichen Meinung.
R.F. Leslie, 575(SEER):Apr81-307
Rautenberg, W. Klassische und nichtklassische Aussagenlogik.
W. Büttemeyer, 679:Band11Heft2-405
Raven, J. The Folklore of Staffordshire.
D. Froome, 203:Vol92No2-251
Raven, S. Shadows on the Grass.
D.A.N. Jones, 362:13May82-25
A. Ross, 617(TLS):30Apr82-478
Ravenhill, P.L. Baule Statuary Art.
D.M. Warren, 2(AfrA):Feb81-80
Ravera, R.M. Cuestiones de estética.
M. Nadin, 290(JAAC):Summer82-443
de Ravinel, H. Les Enfants du bout de la vie.
R. Hodgson, 102(CanL):Spring81-96
Raw, B.C. The Art and Background of Old English Poetry.*
P. Gradon, 677(YES):Vol 11-221
Rawlings, H.R. 3d. The Structure of Thucydides' History.
S. Hornblower, 617(TLS):12Feb82-157
Rawls, J. A Theory of Justice.
G. Kortian, 98:Jan81-3
Rawlyk, G. and K. Quinn. The Redeemed of the Lord Say So.
R.T. Handy, 529(QQ):Summer81-359
Rawski, T.G. China's Republican Economy.
S.M. Jones, 293(JASt):May81-539
Rawson, J. Ancient China: Art and Archaeology.
E. Capon, 463:Summer81-204
M. Medley, 39:Sep81-207
Ray, L. Le Corps obscur.
D.L., 450(NRF):Sep81-117
Ray, R.K. Industrialization in India.
T. Timburg, 293(JASt):Nov80-178
Ray, S. The Blyton Phenomenon.
N. Tucker, 617(TLS):23Jul82-798
Raychaudhuri, T. and I. Habib, eds. The Cambridge Economic History of India. (Vol 1)
V.G. Kiernan, 617(TLS):6Aug82-859
Raymond, J.C. and I.W. Russell, eds. James B. McMillan: Essays in Linguistics by his Friends and Colleagues.
B. Davis, 355(LSoc):Apr81-132
Raymond, M. Romantisme et rêverie.*
A.J. Steele, 208(FS):Jul81-349
Raynor, D.R., ed. Sister Peg.
D. Forbes, 617(TLS):23Jul82-806
Raynor, H. Music in England.*
N. Temperley, 415:May81-314

Raz, J. The Authority of Law.*
T. Morawetz, 185:Apr81-516
L.C. Ten, 393(Mind):Jul81-441
Razi, Z. Life, Marriage and Death in a Medieval Parish.*
M.K. McIntosh, 589:Oct81-906
"Razrushennye i oskvernennye khramy."
D.B. Miller, 550(RusR):Oct81-457
Rea, J.R. and P.J. Sijpesteijn. Griechische Texte. (Vol 2)
H. Hauben, 394:Vol34fasc1/2-183
Read, B. Victorian Sculpture.
J.M. Crook, 617(TLS):30Jul82-818
D.A.N. Jones, 362:12Aug82-22
J. Russell, 441:26Sep82-9
Read, C. Religion, Revolution and the Russian Intelligentsia, 1900-1912.*
E. Lampert, 575(SEER):Jul81-458
Read, F. '76: One World and "The Cantos" of Ezra Pound.
J.F. Knapp, 27(AL):Jan82-746
B.W. Richman, 468:Winter81-651
Read, J. The New Conquistadors.
A.M.R., 617(TLS):26Mar82-363
Read, M.K. Juan Huarte de San Juan.
M.L. Cozad, 304(JHP):Spring81-232
Read, P.P. The Villa Golitsyn.*
P-L. Adams, 61:Feb82-87
J. Mellors, 364:Feb82-93
442(NY):22Feb82-128
Reader, M., ed. Atom's Eye.
R.G., 185:Jul81-699
T.C. Holyoke, 42(AR):Winter81-129
Reader, W.J. Bowater.
T.C. Barker, 617(TLS):16Apr82-430
C. Carter, 324:May82-364
Reading, P. Tom o'Bedlam's Beauties.
G. Lindop, 617(TLS):18Jun82-662
Reagan, C.E., ed. Studies in the Philosophy of Paul Ricoeur.
M.J. Harney, 63:Sep81-358
Real, H.J. - see Swift, J.
Real, O.G. - see under González Real, O.
Reale, G. The Concept of First Philosophy and the Unity of the Metaphysics of Aristotle.
R.L. Enos, 480(P&R):Spring81-117
Reale, G. Storia della filosofia antica.
H. Wagner, 53(AGP):Band63Heft2-221
"Really Bad News."
P. Lennon, 362:19Aug82-20
Reaney, J. Apple Butter. Names and Nick-names. Geography Match. Ignoramus.
S. Stone-Blackburn, 102(CanL):Summer80-107
Reaney, J. The Dismissal.
J. Wasserman, 102(CanL):Summer80-104
Reaney, P.H. A Dictionary of British Surnames. (2nd ed rev by R.M. Wilson)
K.B. Harder, 424:Jun80-156
Reaney, P.H. The Origin of English Surnames.
K.B. Harder, 424:Sep80-215
Reavis, S.A. August Wilhelm Schlegels Auffassung der Tragödie im Zusammenhang mit seiner Poetik und ästhetischen Theorien seiner Zeit.
K. Peter, 221(GQ):Nov81-514
Rebholz, R.A. - see Wyatt, T.
Rebhorn, W.A. Courtly Performances.*
I. Fenlon, 131(CL):Summer81-286
Reboul, O. Langage et idéologie.
M. Adam, 542:Apr-Jun81-247

Reboussin, M. Drieu la Rochelle et le
 mirage de la politique.
   J.C. McLaren, 207(FR):May82-910
Recanati, F. Les Enoncés Performatifs.
   L.J. Cohen, 617(TLS):8Oct82-1115
Récanati, F. La transparence et l'énoncia-
 tion.*
   M. van Montfrans, 361:Jun/Jul81-267
"Recherches sur les Artes à Rome."
   A. Reix, 542:Jul-Sep81-331
Rechung Rinpoche Jampal Kunzang, ed and
 trans. Tibetan Medicine.
   T.V. Wylie, 293(JASt):Feb81-371
"Recipient Characteristics Study: Aid to
 Families with Dependent Children."
   A. Hacker, 453(NYRB):12Aug82-15
Réda, J. L'Improviste.
   J. Laurans, 450(NRF):Mar81-162
Redard, F. Vivre en Suisse romande.
   J. Laroche, 207(FR):May81-909
Rédei, K. Zyrian Folklore Texts.
   B. Schulze, 682(ZPSK):Band33Heft6-780
Redenbarger, W.J. Articulator Features
 and Portuguese Vowel Height.
   A.M. Zwicky, 350:Sep82-729
Redenius, C. The American Ideal of Equal-
 ity.
   J.L.H., 185:Jul82-782
Redfern, W.D. Queneau: "Zazie dans le
 métro."
   J. Cruickshank, 208(FS):Oct81-483
   G. Prince, 207(FR):Mar82-559
Redgrove, P. The Apple-Broadcast.
   P. Bland, 364:Feb82-79
   R. Garfitt, 617(TLS):12Mar82-278
Redgrove, P. The Facilitators.
   G. Lindop, 617(TLS):15Oct82-1141
Redmond, J. - see "Themes in Drama"
Redmond, J.R. "Viking" Hoaxes in North
 America.
   C.W. Thompson, 563(SS):Winter81-82
Redondo, A., ed. XIXe Colloque Interna-
 tional d'Études Humanistes, Tours, 5-17
 juillet 1976: L'Humanisme dans les
 lettres espagnoles.
   G.A. Davies, 86(BHS):Apr81-141
Redwood, D. Flecker and Delius — The Mak-
 ing of "Hassan."
   E.D. Mackerness, 447(N&Q):Dec80-563
Reed, A.W. Aboriginal Stories of Austra-
 lia.
   S. Gingell-Beckmann, 529(QQ):Winter81-
    789
Reed, A.W. Supplement to Place Names of
 New Zealand.
   L.H. Coltharp, 424:Sep80-222
Reed, I. The Terrible Twos.
   I. Gold, 441:18Jul82-9
   R. Towers, 453(NYRB):12Aug82-35
Reed, J. A Man Afraid.
   D. Davis, 362:16Dec82-23
   L. MacKinnon, 617(TLS):12Nov82-1251
Reed, J. Schubert.
   L.D., 412:May80-144
Reed, J. Sir Walter Scott: Landscape and
 Locality.*
   K. Sutherland, 148:Winter81-84
   A. Welsh, 445(NCF):Dec81-358
Reed, J.R. The Natural History of H.G.
 Wells.
   P. Kemp, 617(TLS):20Aug82-909

Reed, T.J. The Classical Centre.*
   M. Carlson, 612(ThS):Nov81-243
   M.K. Flavell, 402(MLR):Oct81-986
   R.R. Heitner, 221(GQ):Jan81-95
   D.F. Mahoney, 222(GR):Spring81-77
   C.E. Schweitzer, 301(JEGP):Jan81-93
Reed, V. When the Dogs Bark at Night.*
 (J. Beaver, ed)
   D. Barbour, 648(WCR):Jun80-75
Reed, W.L. An Exemplary History of the
 Novel.*
   R.M. Adams, 445(NCF):Dec81-348
   C.S. Brown, 569(SR):Fall81-cix
   L. Nelson, Jr., 676(YR):Winter82-285
Rees, D.M. Yorkshire Craftsmen at Work.
   R.W. Grant, 324:Oct82-753
Rees, J. The Poetry of Dante Gabriel
 Rossetti.
   D.M.R. Bentley, 401(MLQ):Dec81-398
Rees, J. Shakespeare and the Story.*
   A.R. Dutton, 179(ES):Feb81-59
Rees, M.A. Espronceda.
   D.T. Gies, 86(BHS):Jul81-270
   D.L. Shaw, 402(MLR):Jan81-224
Reese, W.L. Dictionary of Philosophy and
 Religion.
   J.A. Hutchison, 485(PE&W):Oct81-549
   R.W.L., 185:Jan81-349
Reeser, E. - see Mahler, G.
Reeves, R. American Journey.
   T.R. Edwards, 453(NYRB):15Jul82-28
   A. Hacker, 441:13Jun83-7
Reeves, T.C. The Life and Times of Joe
 McCarthy.
   E.F. Goldman, 441:11Apr82-9
Regan, D.H. Utilitarianism and Co-opera-
 tion.*
   D.W. Haslett, 518:Oct81-252
   W. Nelson, 185:Jul82-751
Regan, T., ed. Matters of Life and Death.
   B.B., 185:Jan81-342
Reggiani, R. I proemi degli Annales di
 Ennio.
   H.D. Jocelyn, 123:Vol31No1-16
Regnaut, M. - see Rilke, R.M.
Regosin, R.L. The Matter of My Book.*
   M.M. McGowan, 208(FS):Jan81-69
Rehbein, J. Albert Camus.
   J. Jurt, 224(GRM):Band31Heft2-256
Rehbein, J. Komplexes Handeln.
   K. Meng, 682(ZPSK):Band33Heft5-615
Reich, W. and A.S. Neill. Record of a
 Friendship. (B.R. Placzek, ed)
   P. Sedgwick, 617(TLS):12Feb82-163
Reich, W.T., ed-in-chief. Encyclopedia of
 Bioethics.
   L.E. Goodman, 485(PE&W):Apr81-225
Reich-Ranicki, M. Entgegnung.
   R. Crowley, 221(GQ):May81-387
Reichart, W.A. and L. Schlissel - see
 Irving, W.
Reichel-Dolmatoff, G. Beyond the Milky
 Way.
   M.D. de Rios, 37:Aug81-39
Reichenbach, H. Hans Reichenbach, Select-
 ed Writings, 1909-1953.* (M. Reichen-
 bach and R.S. Cohen, eds)
   D. Zittlau, 679:Band11Heft2-407
Reichenberger, K. and R. Bibliographis-
 ches Handbuch der Calderón-Forschung/
 Manual bibliográfico calderoniano.*
 (Vol 1)
   D.W. Cruickshank, 402(MLR):Apr81-489

Reichl, K. "Tractatus de Grammatica."
    P.O. Lewry, 72:Band217Heft1-156
Reid, C. Arcadia.*
    639(VQR):Winter81-26
Reid, C. Pea Soup.
    G. Grigson, 362:25Nov82-25
    M. Imlah, 617(TLS):10Dec82-1376
Reid, D. Notre patrie le Canada/Our Own
Country Canada.*
    L. Lacroix, 627(UTQ):Summer81-200
    W.N., 102(CanL):Winter80-160
Reid, E. Envoy to Nehru.*
    F.R. Frankel, 99:Mar82-31
Reid, I. Fiction and the Great Depres-
sion.*
    J.F. Burrows, 402(MLR):Oct81-952
Reid, I. The Short Story.*
    M. Rohrberger, 395(MFS):Winter80/81-
    692
Reid, J.G. Acadia, Maine, and New England.
    D.F. Chard, 150(DR):Winter81/82-772
Reid, P. Burke's and Savills Guide to
Country Houses. (Vol 2)
    A. Clifton-Taylor, 135:May81-74
Reille, J-F. Proust.
    W.L. Hodson, 402(MLR):Jan81-199
Reilly, B.F. The Kingdom of León-Castilla
under Queen Urraca, 1109-1126.
    R.A. Fletcher, 617(TLS):17Sep82-1014
Reilly, C.W., ed. Scars Upon My Heart.*
    R. Fuller, 364:Mar82-89
Reilly, J.H. Jean Giraudoux.
    M.G. Rose, 130:Spring81-94
    A.J. Singerman, 207(FR):Apr81-746
Reilly, P. Jonathan Swift.
    F.S.L. Lyons, 617(TLS):15Oct82-1135
Reilly, R. and G. Savage. The Dictionary
of Wedgwood.
    J.K. des Fontaines, 135:Jan81-83
Reiman, D.H., ed. English Romantic Poetry,
1800 1835.*
    C.W. Hagelman, Jr., 340(KSJ):Vol30-216
Reindl, P. Loy Hering.
    C. Lowenthal, 551(RenQ):Spring80-94
Reingold, N., ed. The Sciences in the
American Context.
    S. Bernstein, 42(AR):Fall81-511
Reinhold, H. Der englische Roman des 19.
Jahrhunderts.
    H. Foltinek, 224(GRM):Band30Heft2-250
Reiniche, M-L. Les dieux et les hommes.
    A. Hiltebeitel, 293(JASt):Aug81-837
Reininger, R. Kant, seine Anhänger und
seine Gegner.
    R. Malter, 342:Band71Heft2-274
Reinitzer, H. - see Frey, H.H.
"Reinke de Vos, Lübeck 1498." (T. Sodmann,
ed)
    H. Tervooren, 680(ZDP):Band100Heft3-
    450
Reis, M. Präsuppositionen und Syntax.
    G. Kolde, 260(IF):Band85-315
Reisinger, P. Idealismus als Bildtheorie.
    F. Wagner, 489(PJGG):Band88Heft2-414
Reiss, E. William Dunbar.
    J. Kinsley, 382(MAE):1981/1-176
Reiss, H. Kants politisches Denken.
    E.C. Sandberg, 342:Band71Heft4-510
Reiss, H. The Writer's Task from Nietz-
sche to Brecht.*
    D.G. Daviau, 221(GQ):Jan81-122
Reiss, T.J. Tragedy and Truth.
    S. Zebouni, 188(ECr):Fall81-95

Reiterman, T., with J. Jacobs. Raven.
    B. Bright, 441:26Dec82-9
Reliquet, P. Gilles de Rais, Maréchal,
Monstre et Martyr.
    J. Kirkup, 617(TLS):6Aug82-858
"Relire 'Les Destinées' d'Alfred de Vigny."
    M. Petrovska, 446(NCFS):Fall-Win-
    ter81/82-156
Remington, F. The Uncollected Writings of
Frederic Remington. (P. and H. Samuels,
eds)
    R.M. Quinn, 50(ArQ):Summer81-181
Remini, R.V. Andrew Jackson and the
Course of American Freedom, 1822-1832.*
    P. Marshall, 617(TLS):23Apr82-466
Remnant, P. and J. Bennett - see Leibniz,
G.W.
de Rémusat, C. L'Habitation de Saint-
Domingue ou l'insurrection. (J-R.
Derré, ed)
    B. Rigby, 208(FS):Apr81-214
Rena, S. A Painless Death.*
    M. Laski, 362:29Apr82-27
"Renaissance Drama." (new ser, No. 10)
(L. Barkan, ed)
    R. Soellner, 130:Fall81-286
Renard, J. Poil de Carotte. (A. Fermi-
gier, ed) L'Ecornifleur. (J-M. Gardair,
ed)
    N. Thatcher, 208(FS):Apr81-218
    R.E. Ziegler, 207(FR):May81-874
Renard, J-C. Selected Poems.* (G.D.
Martin, ed)
    N. Rinsler, 208(FS):Apr81-232
Renardy, C. Le monde des maîtres universi-
taires du diocèse de Liège, 1140-1350.
    K. Jensen, 589:Apr81-420
Renaud, T. Une mémoire déchirée.
    M. Recurt, 102(CanL):Spring80-115
Renault, M. Funeral Games.*
    P-L. Adams, 61:Jan82-87
    P. Green, 453(NYRB):18Mar82-35
    O. Murray, 617(TLS):1Jan82-12
    C. Ricks, 441:17Jan82-7
Renault, M. Le Singulier.*
    C. Troisfontaines, 154:Jun81-376
Rendell, R. The Fever Tree and Other
Stories.
    T.J. Binyon, 617(TLS):10Dec82-1378
Rendell, R. Master of the Moor.
    T.J. Binyon, 617(TLS):23Jul82-807
    M. Laski, 362:29Jul82-27
Render, S.L. Charles W. Chesnutt.
    J. Vassilowitch, Jr., 26(ALR):Autumn81-
    310
Rendra, W.S. The Struggle of the Naga
Tribe.
    B.R.O. Anderson, 293(JASt):Feb81-428
René d'Anjou. Le Livre de cuer d'amours
espris. (S. Wharton, ed)
    R. Morse, 402(MLR):Oct81-960
Renehan, R. Greek Lexicographical Notes.
    C. Dobias-Lalou, 555:Vol54fasc1-152
Renfrew, C. and M. Wagstaff, eds. An
Island Polity.
    A.M. Snodgrass, 617(TLS):2Jul82-721
Renn, L. Anstösse in meinem Leben.
    I. Hiebel, 654(WB):5/1981-149
Renoir, J. Geneviève.
    J. Laurans, 450(NRF):Feb81-108

Renouvier, C. Manuel républicain de
l'homme et du citoyen, 1848.* (M. Agul-
hon, ed)
 A. Reix, 542:Oct-Dec81-494
Renvoize, J. Incest.
 A. Clare, 362:29Apr82-22
Renwick, F. Noost.
 J.B. Caird, 571(ScLJ):Summer80-132
Renwick, J. - see Marmontel, J-F.
Renwick, R.D. English Folk Poetry.*
 639(VQR):Summer81-95
Renzi, L. Einführung in die romanische
Sprachwissenschaft. (G. Ineichen, ed)
 G. Price, 208(FS):Jul81-375
Renzi, L. Introduzione alla filologia
romanza.
 G. Lepschy, 545(RPh):Nov80-238
de Reparaz, G. Reparaz's Guide to Peru.
(3rd ed)
 37:Mar81-47
Reppert, C.P. - see Bishop, M.
Reps, J.W. Cities of the American West.*
 J.A. Jakle, 576:May81-171
 J.M. Neil, 658:Summer/Autumn81-225
Reps, J.W. The Making of Urban America.
Monumental Washington. Town Planning
in Frontier America. Tidewater Towns.
Cities on Stone.
 J.M. Neil, 658:Summer/Autumn81-225
"Res Publica Litterarum." (Vol 1) (S.
Prete, ed)
 I. Thomson, 551(RenQ):Summer80-236
Resch, G. Die Weinbauterminologie des
Burgenlandes.
 Y. Malkiel, 350:Mar81-232
Rescher, N. Cognitive Systematization.*
 H. Kornblith, 482(PhR):Jan81-144
 G.G.L. Stock, 518:Jul81-188
Rescher, N. Leibniz.*
 G.M. Ross, 518:Jan81-14
Rescher, N. Peirce's Philosophy of
Science.*
 B. Altshuler, 482(PhR):Jan81-138
 R. Fellows, 518:Jan81-17
 T.A. Goudge, 154:Jun81-357
 M.G. Murphey, 53(AGP):Band63Heft1-94
Rescher, N. Scepticism.
 J. Kekes, 84:Dec81-411
 B.M., 185:Apr82-592
 D-H. Ruben, 518:Jul81-190
Rescher, N. Scientific Progress.
 M. Ruse, 449:Sep81-418
Rescher, N. and R. Brandom. The Logic of
Inconsistency.
 C. Mortensen, 479(PhQ):Jul81-275
Ressel, G. Syntaktische Struktur und
semantische Eigenschaften russischer
Sätze.
 W. Birkenmaier, 257(IRAL):Aug81-253
Resta, G. - see Marrasii, J.
Rétat, P., ed. Études sur la presse au
XVIIIe siècle.
 J. Lough, 208(FS):Jan81-76
Rétat, P. and J. Sgard, eds. Presse et
Histoire au XVIIIe siècle: l'Annee 1734.
 R. Birn, 173(ECS):Fall80-94
 J. Lough, 208(FS):Oct81-456
Reulecke, J. and W. Weber, eds. Fabrik —
Familie — Feierabend.
 I. Dietrich, 654(WB):5/1981-186
Reus, G. Oktoberrevolution und Sowjetruss-
land auf dem deutschen Theater.
 W.F. Schwarz, 52:Band15Heft2-220

Revard, S.P. The War in Heaven.
 D.J. Enright, 617(TLS):25Jun82-699
 W.B. Hunter, Jr., 301(JEGP):Apr81-250
 H. MacCallum, 627(UTQ):Spring81-314
 W. Myers, 569(SR):Fall81-622
Revel, J-F. Culture and Cuisine.
 G. Grigson, 453(NYRB):18Nov82-65
Revel, J-F. Un Festin en paroles.
 B. Cap, 207(FR):Feb81-487
Revell, J. Teaching Techniques for Com-
municative English.
 K. Perkins, 399(MLJ):Autumn81-330
Revell, P. Quest in Modern American
Poetry.
 S. Ellis, 617(TLS):28May82-592
Reverdy, P. Au Soleil du plafond et
autres poèmes.
 M. Bishop, 207(FR):Apr82-711
"Review." (Vols 1 and 2) (J.O. Hoge and
J.L.W. West 3d, eds)
 D. Traister, 517(PBSA):Oct-Dec81-493
"Revista Nueva: 1899." (J.C. Mainer, ed)
 J. Butt, 86(BHS):Oct81-352
 L. Litvak, 240(HR):Autumn81-512
Rex, B. Ugly Girl.
 P-L. Adams, 61:Jul82-95
Rex, C. Comfort Clothes.
 P. Bach, 614:Winter82-15
Rexroth, K. The Morning Star.
 T. Enslin, 472:Spring/Summer81-301
Rexroth, K. and Ling Chung, eds and trans.
The Orchid Boat.
 T. Enslin, 472:Spring/Summer81-301
Rexroth, K. and Ling Chung - see Li Ch'ing-
chao
del Rey, L. The World of Science Fiction:
1926-1976.
 D.M. Miller, 395(MFS):Winter80/81-731
Rey, M.B. and K. Maloof. Deutsch macht
Spass.
 J.L. Cox, 399(MLJ):Winter81-432
Rey, P-L. L'Amorce.
 F. de Martinoir, 450(NRF):Oct81-144
Rey, W.H. Poesie der Antipoesie.*
 R.E. Lorbe, 301(JEGP):Jan81-109
Rey-Debove, J. and G. Gagnon. Diction-
naire des Anglicismes.
 G.E. Saunders, 207(FR):Feb82-428
Rey-Flaud, H. Pour une dramaturgie du
Moyen Age.
 S.M. Taylor, 207(FR):Dec81-260
Reynes, R. The Commonplace Book of Robert
Reynes of Acle. (C. Louis, ed)
 L.E. Voigts, 589:Oct81-909
Reynolds, C.J. - see Prince Vajiranana
Reynolds, D. The Creation of the Anglo-
American Alliance 1937-41.
 P. Kennedy, 617(TLS):25Jun82-684
Reynolds, D.K. The Quiet Therapies.
 C.W. Kiefer, 407(MN):Spring81-110
 C. Lewis, 293(JASt):Aug81-794
Reynolds, D.S. Faith in Fiction.
 S. Fender, 617(TLS):22Jan82-82
 A.S. Lang, 165(EAL):Spring82-91
Reynolds, G. Wallace Collection, Cata-
logue of Miniatures.
 B. Scott, 39:Oct81-274
Reynolds, G. - see Constable, J.
Reynolds, J.H. Letters from Lambeth.
(J. Richardson, ed)
 A. Bell, 617(TLS):12Feb82-168

Richardson, F.L. Andrea Schiavone.*
R. Cocke, 59:Sep81-352
J. Fletcher, 90:Aug81-491
E. Langmuir, 89(BJA):Winter81-76
Richardson, H.H. The Fortunes of Richard Mahony.
K. McLeod, 617(TLS):4Jun82-608
Richardson, J. Thomas Hardy.
V.L. Tollers, 295(JML):Vol18No3/4-516
Richardson, J. Zola.
F.S. Heck, 446(NCFS):Spring-Summer81-281
295(JML):Vol18No3/4-650
Richardson, J. - see Reynolds, J.H.
Richardson, R.D., Jr. Myth and Literature in the American Renaissance.*
D. Minter, 445(NCF):Jun80-85
Riché, P. Ecoles et Enseignement dans le Haut Moyen Age.
M. Larès, 189(EA):Oct-Dec81-461
Riché, P. Le écoles et l'enseignement dans l'Occident chrétien da la fin du Ve siècle au milieu du XIe siècle.
J.J. Contreni, 589:Jan81-189
Richer, J. Aspects ésotériques de l'oeuvre littéraire.
P. Somville, 542:Jan-Mar81-124
Richert, H-G. Wege und Formen der Passionalüberlieferung.
W. Williams-Krapp, 684(ZDA):Band109-Heft3-116
Riches, P.M., comp. An Analytical Bibliography of Universal Collected Biography.
M. Slackman, 77:Winter81-89
Richler, M. Joshua Then and Now.*
M.S. Dyment, 526:Winter81-82
D.L. Jeffrey, 102(CanL):Summer81-123
639(VQR):Winter81-20
Richmond, H.M. Puritans and Libertines.
C. Hill, 617(TLS):26Feb82-226
Richmond, I.M. Héroïsme et Galanterie.
S. Bayne, 475:No14Pt1-146
Richter, D. Art, Economics and Change.
P.L. Ravenhill, 2(AfrA):Feb81-22
Richter, F. Die zerschlagene Wirklichkeit.
G.W. Cunliffe, 406:Summer81-247
Richter, M., ed. Political Theory and Political Education.*
B.B., 185:Apr82-580
J.A.W. Gunn, 529(QQ):Winter81-794
Richter, M. The Political Theory of Montesquieu.
M.H. Waddicor, 208(FS):Jul81-332
Richter, M. Sprache und Gesellschaft im Mittelalter.
I. Short, 589:Jul81-650
Richter, P. and I. Ricardo. Voltaire.
V.W. Topazio, 207(FR):Feb82-410
Richter, W. Gegenständliches Denken, archaisches Ordnen.
R. Goujard, 555:Vol54fasc2-375
Rickard, P. Chrestomathie de la langue française au XVe siècle.
J.L. Grigsby, 545(RPh):Feb81(supp)-64
Rickard, P. and T.G.S. Combe - see Harmer, L.C.
Ricken, U. Grammaire et philosophie au siècle des lumières.
D.F. Essar, 173(ECS):Summer81-479
Rickman, G. The Corn Supply of Ancient Rome.
N. Purcell, 313:Vol71-197
D. Stockton, 123:Vol31No1-91

Rickman, H.P. Wilhelm Dilthey.*
E. Paczkowska-Łagowska, 484(PPR):Mar82-454
R.B.S., 185:Oct81-179
Rickman, H.P. - see Dilthey, W.
Rickword, E. Behind the Eyes.
L. Coupe, 565:Vol122No3-38
Rickword, E. Edgell Rickword: Literature in Society.* Edgell Rickword: Essays and Opinions 1921-1931. (A. Young, ed of both)
B. Bergonzi, 506(PSt):May81-110
L. Coupe, 565:Vol122No3-38
Rico, F., ed. Lazarillo de Tormes.
C. Stern, 545(RPh):Feb81-303
Rico, F. Nebrija frente a los bárbaros.*
G.J. MacDonald, 240(HR):Autumn81-496
de Rico, U. The Ring of the Nibelung.
R. Anderson, 415:May81-310
Ricoeur, P. Hermeneutics and the Human Sciences. (J.B. Thompson, ed and trans)
A. Giddens, 617(TLS):5Mar82-240
Ricoeur, P. Main Trends in Philosophy.*
D.A.H., 543:Sep80-157
R.B. Hunter, 484(PPR):Jun82-621
G. Stack, 321:Vol 15No4-329
Ricoeur, P. The Rule of Metaphor.*
(French title: La métaphore vive.)
D.H. Hirsch, 569(SR):Winter81-95
H.R. Pollio, 353:Vol 18No1/2-159
M.J. Valdés, 107(CRCL):Winter81-99
Ricoeur, P. and D. Tiffeneau. La Sémantique de l'action.
H.A.D., 543:Dec80-398
Ride, E. BAAG: Hong Kong Resistance 1942-1945.
P. Warner, 617(TLS):15Oct82-1134
Ridenour, R.C. Nationalism, Modernism, and Personal Rivalry in Nineteenth-Century Russian Music.
G. Abraham, 451:Spring82-242
Rider, R.W., with D. Paulsen. Sixshooters and Sagebrush.
K.I. Periman, 650(WF):Oct81-351
C.S. Peterson, 649(WAL):Spring81-59
Ridgway, B.S. The Archaic Style in Greek Sculpture.*
N. Leipen, 487:Spring81-92
Ridgway, B.S. Fifth Century Styles in Greek Sculpture.
R. Brilliant, 124:May-Jun82-320
M. Robertson, 617(TLS):23Apr82-459
Riding, L. Progress of Stories.
V. Cunningham, 617(TLS):1Oct82-1075
H. Mathews, 453(NYRB):29Apr82-37
Riding, L. - see also under Jackson, L. (Riding)
Ridley, J. The Statesman and the Fanatic.
J.A. Guy, 617(TLS):19Nov82-1264
Rieber, R.W., ed. Applied Psycholinguistics and Mental Health.
J.M. Noon, 353:Vol 18No11/12-1119
Rieber, R.W., ed. Psychology of Language and Thought.
R. Goodwin, 353:Vol 18No11/12-1164
Riede, D.G. Swinburne.*
J. Baird, 541(RES):Feb81-93
Riedel, N. Uwe Johnson Bibliographie 1959-1977. (Vol 2)
W.G. Cunliffe, 406:Spring81-117
J. Fletcher, 133:Band14Heft3-277

Riedel, V. Lessing und die römische Literatur.*
  M. Brück, 72:Band217Heft1-165
Riedinger, R. Lateinische Übersetzungen griechischer Häretikertexte des siebenten Jahrhunderts.
  P. Courcelle, 555:Vol54fasc2-382
Riegel, L. Guerre et littérature.*
  J. Cruickshank, 208(FS):Oct81-481
Rieger, D. Gattungen und Gattungsbezeichnungen der Trobadorlyrik.*
  W.D. Paden, Jr., 545(RPh):May81-508
Riemann, H. - see under Mickelsen, W.C.
Riemer, A.P. Antic Fables.
  D.R.C. Marsh, 67:Nov81-241
Riepe, D. Indian Philosophy Since Independence.
  W. Ruben and H. Rüstau, 484(PPR):Dec81-303
Riesz, J. Beat Ludwig von Muralts "Lettres sur les Anglais et les Français et sur les Voyages" und ihre Rezeption.*
  G.C. Roscioni, 52:Band15Heft3-332
  J. Voisine, 535(RHL):Nov-Dec81-992
Rieuneau, M. - see Martin du Gard, R.
Rieux, J. and B.E. Rollin - see Arnauld, A. and C. Lancelot
Riffaterre, H., ed. The Occult in Language and Literature.
  B.T. Lupack, 497(PolR):Vol26No3-96
Riffaterre, M. Essais de stylistique structurale.
  M.E. Blanchard, 153:Fall81-13
  P. de Man, 153:Winter81-17
Riffaterre, M. La production du texte.*
  G. Antoine, 209(FM):Jan81-52
  M.E. Blanchard, 153:Fall81-13
  P. de Man, 153:Winter81-17
Riffaterre, M. Semiotics of Poetry.*
  M.E. Blanchard, 153:Fall81-13
  J. Erickson, 207(FR):Oct81-129
  M. Grimaud, 131(CL):Winter81-74
  P. de Man, 153:Winter81-17
  L. Shumway, 567:Vol133No3/4-307
  P.M. Wetherill, 599:Winter81-72
Riftin, B.L., M. Chasanov and I. Jusupov, eds. Dunganski narodnye skazki i predanija.
  H-J. Uther, 196:Band22Heft3/4-365
Riga, F.P. and C.A. Prance. Index to "The London Magazine."*
  L. Madden, 447(N&Q):Oct80-461
Rigby, T.H., A. Brown and P. Reddaway, eds. Authority, Power and Policy in the USSR.*
  P. Kenez, 550(RusR):Jul81-347
Riggan, W. Picaros, Madmen, Naïfs, and Clowns.
  I. Salusinszky, 617(TLS):20Aug82-909
Riggio, T.P., J.L.W. West 3d and N.M. Westlake - see Dreiser, T.
Riggs, J. Blue Mountain Buckskin. (2nd ed)
  P. Bach, 614:Fall81-15
Rigney, B.H. Madness and Sexual Politics in the Feminist Novel.*
  P. Boumelha, 541(RES):Feb81-111
  E.B. Tenenbaum, 395(MFS):Summer80-290
Riha, K. Moritat, Bänkelsong, Protestballade. (2nd ed)
  L. Petzoldt, 196:Band22Heft1/2-153

Riiho, T. "Por" y "para."
  O. Välikangas, 439(NM):1981/1-89
  R. Wright, 86(BHS):Jan81-73
Riikonen, H. Die Antike im historischen Roman des 19. Jahrhunderts.
  E.J. Kenney, 123:Vol31No2-280
Riis, T. Les institutions politiques centrales du Danemark, 1100-1332.
  C.T. Wood, 589:Jan81-191
Rijlaarsdam, J.C. Platon über die Sprach.*
  G.B. Kerferd, 303(JoHS):Vol 101-155
  P. Louis, 555:Vol54fasc1-162
Riley, H.M.K. Ludwig Achim von Arnims Jugend- und Reisejahre.*
  B. Duncan, 680(ZDP):Band99Heft2-309
Riley, H.M.K. Idee und Gestaltung.
  R. Hoermann, 221(GQ):Jan81-99
Riley, J. The Collected Works.* (T. Longville, ed)
  R. Caddel, 493:Jun81-46
  J. Hooker, 493:Jun81-52
  Y. Lovelock, 493:Jun81-50
  D. McDuff, 493:Jun81-57
Riley, M.W. The History of the Viola.
  A.M. Woodward, 415:Nov81-750
Riley, P.W.J. King William and the Scottish Politicians.
  F.D. Dow, 447(N&Q):Aug80-371
  L.K.J. Glassey, 566:Autumn80-44
Riley, P.W.J. The Union of England and Scotland.
  F.D. Dow, 447(N&Q):Aug80-371
  G.M. Straka, 173(ECS):Fall80-103
Rilke, R.M. Nine Plays.* (K. Phillips and J. Locke, eds and trans)
  G.C. Schoolfield, 301(JEGP):Apr81-301
Rilke, R.M. La Princesse blanche. (M. Regnaut, ed and trans)
  J.S., 450(NRF):Sep81-156
Rilke, R.M. An Unofficial Rilke. (M. Hamburger, trans)
  R.J. Hollingdale, 617(TLS):30Apr82-476
Rilke, R.M. and A. Forrer. Rainer Maria Rilke/Anita Forrer Briefwechsel. (M. Kerényi, ed)
  I. Frowen, 617(TLS):8Oct82-1114
Rimer, J.T. Modern Japanese Fiction and Its Traditions.*
  M.G. Ryan, 293(JASt):Nov80-140
Rimmon, S. The Concept of Ambiguity.*
  C. Brooke-Rose, 494:Autumn79-397
Rinaldi, A. La Dernière Fête de l'Empire.*
  M. Whiting, 207(FR):Mar82-572
"Il Rinascimento."
  R. Belladonna, 539:Feb82-55
Rincé, D., R. Horville and A. Pagès, eds. Textes français et histoire littéraire: XIXe siècle.
  R.T. Denommé, 207(FR):Dec81-284
Ringle, M.D., ed. Philosophical Perspectives in Artificial Intelligence.
  N. Hornstein, 311(JP):Jul81-408
Riordan, M., ed. The Day After Midnight.
  E. Zuckerman, 441:31Oct82-9
Riordan, M.M. Lillian Hellman.
  J.H. Adler, 392:Fall81-463
  K. Lederer, 397(MD):Sep81-385
Ripley, J. "Julius Caesar" on Stage in England and America, 1599-1973.*
  J.H. Astington, 627(UTQ):Summer81-106
  F. Berry, 611(TN):Vol135No3-141
  R. Berry, 529(QQ):Autumn81-536
[continued]

Ripley, J. "Julius Caesar" on Stage in England and America, 1599-1973. [continuing]
  D. Peak, 67:May81-108
  H.M. Richmond, 570(SQ):Autumn81-410
  G.J. Williams, 405(MP):May82-423
Ripp, V. Turgenev's Russia.
  N.V. Riasanovsky, 550(RusR):Oct81-472
  639(VQR):Summer81-83
Risch, E. and H. Mulhenstein, eds. Colloquium Mycenaeum.
  L. Dubois, 555:Vol54fasc2-336
Risco, A. El demiurgo y su mundo.
  M. Lentzen, 72:Band217Heft1-231
Rissin, D. Offenbach ou le rire en musique.
  C. Rosset, 98:Apr81-390
Rist, A. - see Theocritus
Rist, J.M. On the Independence of Matthew and Mark.
  T.R.W. Longstaff, 487:Summer81-190
Rist, J.M., ed. The Stoics.*
  J.B. Gould, 319:Apr81-245
Ritchie, C.I.A. Rock Art of Africa.
  D. Brokensha, 2(AfrA):Feb81-78
Ritchie, D. Spacewar.
  H.S.F. Cooper, Jr., 441:17Oct82-7
Ritchie, D.A. James M. Landis.*
  639(VQR):Summer81-99
Ritchie, L.A. Modern British Shipbuilding.
  R. Storey, 325:Oct81-510
Ritsos, Y. Graganda, [suivi de] La Cloche [et de] Vue aérienne.
  J. Ancet, 450(NRF):Sep81-151
Ritsos, Y. Ritsos in Parentheses.*
  R. Hadas, 472:Spring/Summer81-342
  H. Thomson, 303(JoHS):Vol 101-235
Ritsos, Y. Scripture of the Blind.
  R. Hadas, 472:Spring/Summer81-342
Ritsos, Y. Subterranean Horses.*
  639(VQR):Spring81-66
Ritter, A. Anarchism.
  J.P.C., 185:Jul82-777
Ritter, A., ed. J.G. Müller von Itzehoe und die deutsche Spätaufklärung.
  S.L. Cocalis, 221(GQ):Jan81-91
Ritter, A., ed. Zeitgestaltung in der Erzählkunst.
  R. Kloepfer, 196:Band21Heft3/4-333
  J.H. Petersen, 52:Band15Heft2-190
  M. Wynn, 684(ZDA):Band109Heft4-152
Ritter, G.A., ed. Arbeiterkultur.
  I. Dietrich, 654(WB):11/1981-185
Ritter, G.A., ed. Die II. Internationale 1918/1919.
  F.L. Carsten, 575(SEER):Oct81-617
Ritter-Santini, L. Lesebilder.*
  H. Hinterhäuser, 52:Band15Heft2-183
Ritter-Santini, L. and E. Raimondi, eds. Retorica e critica letteraria.*
  U. Schulz-Buschhaus, 72:Band217Heft2-387
Ritzel, W. - see Vorländer, K.
Ritzmann, A. Winter und Untergang.
  J.M. Grandin, 406:Spring81-97
Rivais, Y. Les demoiselles d'A.
  C. Minière, 98:May80-523
Rival, N. Les Amours perverties.
  D. Coward, 617(TLS):8Oct82-1106
Rivard, Y. L'Imaginaire et le quotidien.
  J. Onimus, 535(RHL):Mar-Apr81-328

Rivarola Matto, J.B. Karai Rei Oha' ä Ramo Guare Tuka' ë Kañy.
  F.E. Feito, 37:Oct81-25
Rivaz, A. Jette ton pain.
  J. Devaud, 207(FR):Oct80-198
Rivera, B.V. German Music Theory in the Early Seventeenth Century.
  L. Hanna, 308:Fall81-326
Rivera, E. Family Installments.
  P. Lopate, 441:5Sep82-5
Rivera, F.P. and M. Hurtado - see under Pérez Rivera, F. and M. Hurtado
Rivers, I., ed. Books and their Readers in Eighteenth-Century England.
  H. Erskine-Hill, 617(TLS):10Dec82-1370
Rivers, I. Classical and Christian Ideas in English Renaissance Poetry.*
  C.D. Eckhardt, 568(SCN):Spring81-16
  D. Norbrook, 447(N&Q):Apr80-191
  L.V. Ryan, 551(RenQ):Winter80-803
Rivers, J.E. Proust and the Art of Love.*
  F.C. St. Aubyn, 207(FR):May82-909
  S. Tapscott, 676(YR):Summer82-612
Rivers, P. Cuaderno de español práctico comercial.
  M. Agosin, 238:Sep81-492
Rivers, W.M. Teaching Foreign-Language Skills. (2nd ed)
  A.T. Harrison, 207(FR):Apr82-717
  J. Yalden, 350:Sep82-738
Rivet, A. and C. Sarrau. Correspondance intégrale. (Vol 1) (H. Bots and P. Leroy, with J. Wijnhoven, eds)
  R. Zuber, 535(RHL):Jan-Feb81-128
Rivet, A.L.F. and C. Smith. The Place-Names of Roman Britain.
  W.F.H. Nicolaisen, 424:Dec80-299
Rivière, J-C. - see Jacques de Cambrai
Rivière, P. La Nef des Folz. (E. Du Bruck, ed)
  C.J. Brown, 207(FR):Oct81-131
Rix, M. The Art of the Botanist.
  A. Huxley, 617(TLS):12Mar82-288
Rizal, J. N'y touchez pas!
  J-L. Gautier, 450(NRF):Sep81-154
Rizzo, S. La Tradizione manoscritta della "pro Cluentio" di Cicerone.
  M. Winterbottom, 123:Vol31No1-120
Roach, W., ed. The Continuations of the Old French "Perceval" of Chrétien de Troyes. (Vols 1-4)
  H. Klüppelholz, 356(LR):Aug81-247
Roback, A.A. A Dictionary of International Slurs (Ethnophaulisms).
  U. Kutter, 196:Band22Heft3/4-366
Robb, J.D. Hispanic Folk Music of New Mexico and the Southwest.
  P. Sonnichsen, 650(WF):Oct81-345
  J. Vincent, 187:May82-326
Robb, J.W. El estilo de Alfonso Reyes (Imagen y estructura). (2nd ed)
  B.B. Aponte, 593:Fall80-270
Robbe-Grillet, A. Djinn.*
  A. Clerval, 450(NRF):Sep81-127
  S.E. Gray, 207(FR):Mar82-573
  C. Rullier, 98:Aug-Sep81-857
Robbe-Grillet, A. and Y. Lenard. Le Rendez-vous.
  R. Danner, 207(FR):Dec81-285
Robbins, H. Spellbinder.
  E. Hunter, 441:5Sep82-8
Robbins, R. - see Browne, T.

Robbins, T. Still Life with Woodpecker.*
  D.R. Hettinga, 114(ChiR):Autumn80-123
Robbins, W. The Arnoldian Principle of
  Flexibility.
  C.A. Runcie, 637(VS):Autumn80-142
Robe, S.L. Azuela and the Mexican Under-
  dogs.
  K.L. Levy, 238:Sep81-485
Robert, M. Franz Kafka's Loneliness.
  A. Storr, 617(TLS):31Dec82-1437
Roberts, B. The Mad Bad Line.*
  442(NY):9Aug82-95
Roberts, D. Paternalism in Early Victo-
  rian England.*
  D.C. Moore, 637(VS):Autumn80-144
Roberts, J., ed. The Guthlac Poems of the
  Exeter Book.
  J.C. Pope, 589:Apr81-422
Roberts, J.A. Shakespeare's English
  Comedy.*
  G.K. Paster, 570(SQ):Autumn81-411
Roberts, K. Deep Line.*
  B. Whiteman, 102(CanL):Summer80-141
Roberts, L. and C.B. Agey, eds. In the
  Pine.
  R.D. Morse, 650(WF):Jul81-277
Roberts, M. British Diplomacy and Swedish
  Politics, 1758-1773.*
  H.A. Barton, 563(SS):Summer81-352
  J. Black, 83:Autumn81-237
Roberts, P.B. - see Langton, S.
ap Roberts, R. The Moral Trollope.
  J. Roubaud, 98:Feb-Mar81-166
Roberts, W. Jane Austen and the French
  Revolution.
  T. Lockwood, 445(NCF):Jun81-99
"William Roberts."
  J. Beckett, 59:Dec81-461
Robertson, D.A. Sir Charles Eastlake and
  the Victorian Art World.*
  D. Cherry, 59:Sep81-335
Robertson, E.A. Four Frightened People.
  P. Craig, 617(TLS):13Aug82-888
Robertson, E.A. Ordinary Families.
  P. Craig, 617(TLS):22Oct82-1175
Robertson, J. Lizard Island.
  A. Chisholm, 617(TLS):30Jul82-832
Robertson, J.O. American Myth, American
  Reality.
  639(VQR):Spring81-54
Robertson, M. Greek Painting.
  R. Higgins, 39:Mar81-203
Robertson, M. A Shorter History of Greek
  Art.
  B.S. Ridgway, 124:May-Jun82-311
Robertson, M.E. After Freud.*
  C. Petroski, 502(PrS):Winter81/82-93
  S. Pinsker, 219(GaR):Winter81-888
Robertson, M.E. The Clearing.
  K. Crossley-Holland, 617(TLS):15Oct82-
  1142
  442(NY):25Oct82-171
Robertson, P. Movie Facts and Feats.
  A. Slide, 200:Oct81-508
Robertson, P.J.M. The Leavises on Fiction.
  C.J. Rawson, 617(TLS):16Apr82-440
Robertson, T. Plays by Tom Robertson. (W.
  Tydeman, ed)
  J. Hankey, 617(TLS):20Aug82-901
Robin, A. L'Homme sans nouvelle.
  J. Laurans, 450(NRF):Jun81-121

Robinett, B.W. Teaching English to
  Speakers of Other Languages.*
  F. Dubin, 350:Mar81-222
Robinson, A. George Meany and His Times.
  R. Sherrill, 441:3Jan82-3
Robinson, B.W. Persian Paintings in the
  John Rylands Library.
  B. Gray, 39:Jun81-410
  S.H. Safrani, 60:Jul-Aug81-142
Robinson, C. Lucian and his Influence in
  Europe.
  M.D. MacLeod, 123:Vol31No1-14
Robinson, D. Systems of Modern Psychology.
  D.J. Steinberg, 186(ETC.):Spring81-91
Robinson, D. and S. Wildman. Morris and
  Company in Cambridge.
  R. Mander, 39:Apr81-269
Robinson, D.J., ed. Studying Latin
  America.
  C.W. Minkel, 263(RIB):Vol31No3-417
Robinson, D.N. The Enlightened Machine.
  D. Joravsky, 453(NYRB):21Oct82-44
Robinson, F.J.G. and others. Eighteenth-
  Century British Books.* (Vols 1-3)
  T. Hofmann, 78(BC):Autumn81-413
Robinson, F.M. The Comedy of Language.
  R.K. Simon, 594:Fall81-322
  R.M. Torrance, 579(SAQ):Autumn81-479
Robinson, H. Somerville and Ross.
  B. Dolan, 305(JIL):May81-131
  M. Harmon, 637(VS):Summer81-515
Robinson, J. Dr. Rocksinger and the Age
  of Longing.
  M. Cantwell, 441:18Jul82-12
  442(NY):23Aug82-92
Robinson, J. Duty and Hypocrisy in
  Hegel's "Phenomenology of Mind."
  D.C. Hoy, 154:Mar81-84
Robinson, J.M. The Wyatts.*
  F. Fergusson, 576:Mar81-61
Robinson, J.S. H.D.
  D. Donoghue, 441:14Feb82-3
Robinson, K. A Critical Study of Chu
  Tsai-yü's Contribution to the Theory
  of Equal Temperament in Chinese Music.
  B. Yung, 293(JASt):Aug81-775
Robinson, L. Walk on Glass.
  M. Watkins, 441:22Aug82-12
Robinson, M. Housekeeping.*
  P. Craig, 617(TLS):13Aug82-888
  D. Kubal, 249(HudR):Autumn81-465
  T. Le Clair, 659(ConL):Winter82-83
Robinson, P. - see Stokes, A.
Robinson, R. Landscape with Dead Dons.
  M. Laski, 362:2Dec82-23
Robinson, R.A.H. Contemporary Portugal.
  N.J. Lamb, 86(BHS):Apr81-153
Robinson, S. Mindkiller.
  G. Jonas, 441:29Aug82-10
Robinson, S.K. Life Imitates Architecture.
  J.W. Rudd, 576:Dec81-347
Robinson, W.B. Gone from Texas.
  E.A. Connally, 576:Dec81-346
  L. Milazzo, 584(SWR):Autumn81-414
Robson, J.M. - see Mill, J.S.
Robson, J.M. and J. Stillinger - see Mill,
  J.S.
Rocchi, P. Un épisode de la bataille du
  Decadentismo.
  P. de Montéra, 549(RLC):Jul-Dec81-505

Roche, D. Dépôts de savoir et de technique.*
  M. Bishop, 207(FR):Feb82-442
  C. Minière, 98:May80-523
Roche, D. Le Siècle des Lumières en province.
  J.M. Goulemot, 98:Jun-Jul80-603
Roche, M. Macabré, ou Triumphe de Haulte Intelligence. Maladie Mélodie.
  C. Grivel, 98:Jun-Jul81-715
Roche, P. With Duncan Grant in Southern Turkey.
  F. Spalding, 617(TLS):12Nov82-1253
Roche, T.P., Jr., with C.P. O'Donnell, Jr. - see Spenser, E.
la Rochelle, P.D. - see under Drieu la Rochelle, P.
Rocher, D. Thomasin von Zerklaere: Der "Wälsche Gast" (1215-1216).
  C. Cormeau, 684(ZDA):Band110Heft4-152
de Rocher, G. Rabelais's Laughers and Joubert's "Traité du Ris."
  M. Tetel, 188(ECr):Spring81-105
Lord Rochester. The Letters of John Wilmot, Earl of Rochester.* (J. Treglown, ed)
  W. Chernaik, 175:Spring81-73
  L. Goldstein, 385(MQR):Summer82-528
  A.W., 148:Spring81-92
Rochet, B.L. The Formation and Evolution of the French Nasal Vowels.
  W. Oesterreicher, 685(ZDL):1/1981-109
Rochon, A., ed. Ville et campagne dans la littérature italienne de la Renaissance. (Vol 2)
  O. Büdel, 551(RenQ):Winter80-786
Rock, H.B. Artisans of the New Republic.
  W.B. Wheeler, 656(WMQ):Jan81-143
Rock, P. Circles of Time.
  D. Montrose, 617(TLS):26Mar82-361
Rockmore, T. Fichte, Marx, and the German Philosophical Tradition.
  C.G., 543:Jun81-801
  J.A. Settanni, 396(ModA):Fall81-441
Röd, W. Die Philosophie der Neuzeit 1.
  R. Margreiter, 489(PJGG):Band88Heft1-211
Rodack, M.T. - see Bandelier, A.F.
Rodd, L.R. - see Nichiren
Rodee, M.E. Old Navajo Rugs.
  P. Bach, 614:Fall81-19
  L. Milazzo, 584(SWR):Autumn81-414
Rödel, U. Königliche Gerichtsbarkeit und Streitfälle der Fürsten und Grafen im Südwesten des Reiches, 1250-1313.
  M.B. Dick, 589:Apr81-424
Roden, D.T. Schooldays in Imperial Japan.*
  Usui Masahisa, 285(JapQ):Jul-Sep81-435
  A. Waswo, 407(MN):Autumn81-349
Rodger, I. Radio Drama.
  D.A.N. Jones, 362:17Jun82-23
Rodgers, A.T. The Universal Drum.*
  C.K. Walker, 301(JEGP):Apr81-277
Rodgers, B.F., Jr. Philip Roth.*
  J. Krouchi, 189(EA):Apr-Jun81-235
Rodgers, W. The Politics of Change.
  C. Hitchens, 617(TLS):25Jun82-690
  P. Whitehead, 362:25Mar82-26
Rodinis, G.T. - see under Toso Rodinis, G.
Rodinson, M. The Arabs.
  385(MQR):Spring82-375
Rodis-Lewis, G., with G. Malbreil - see Malebranche, N.

Roditi, E. Thrice Chosen.
  P. Ramsey, 472:Spring/Summer82-172
Roditi, G. L'Esprit de perfection.
  P. Mahillon, 450(NRF):Feb81-125
Rodmell, G.E. - see de Malesherbes, C.G.D.
Rodney, J. Crystals.
  T. Olson, 436(NewL):Winter81/82-108
Rodney, W. A History of the Guyanese Working People, 1881-1905.
  S. Mintz, 441:17Jan82-9
Rodríguez, A. Estudios sobre la novela de Galdós.
  G. Gullón, 240(HR):Summer81-368
  M. Hemingway, 86(BHS):Oct81-351
Rodríguez, C. Lencinas y Cantoni.
  R.C. Newton, 263(RIB):Vol31No1-96
Rodriguez, J. Mudcrab at Gambaro's.
  G. Bitcon, 581:Dec81-469
  G. Catalano, 381:Apr81-114
Rodríguez, P.S. - see under Sainz Rodríguez, P.
Rodriguez, R. Hunger of Memory.
  P-L. Adams, 61:Mar82-88
  P. Zweig, 441:28Feb82-1
  442(NY):5Apr82-199
Rodríguez de Almela, D. Cartas. (D. Mackenzie, ed)
  J.N.H. Lawrance, 382(MAE):1981/2-334
  D.W. Lomax, 86(BHS):Oct81-349
  205(FMLS):Oct81-379
Rodríguez de Lena, P. El passo honroso de Suero de Quiñones.* (A. Labandeira Fernández, ed)
  F. Márquez-Villanueva, 545(RPh):Feb81-375
Rodríguez M. Montalvo, S. - see Alfonso X el Sabio
Rodríguez Monegal, E. Jorge Luis Borges.*
  M.G. Berg, 395(MFS):Summer80-382
  N.M. Valis, 396(ModA):Spring81-215
Rodríguez Monegal, E. and A. Reid - see Borges, J.L.
Rodríguez-Moñino, A. Los Pliegos Poéticos de la Biblioteca Colombina (siglo XVI).
  G. Di Stefano, 545(RPh):Aug80-78
Rodríguez Moñino, A.R. Los poetas extremeños del siglo XVI.
  D.L. Garrison, 238:Dec81-636
Rodríguez Padrón, J. - see Mihura, M.
Roe, D.A. The Lower and Middle Palaeolithic Periods in Britain.
  J.J. Wymer, 617(TLS):29Jan82-102
Roe, S. Estella: Her Expectations.
  R. Jackson, 617(TLS):11Jun82-643
  J. Mellors, 362:8Jul82-23
Roe, S.A. Matter, Life, and Generation.
  M. Pollock, 617(TLS):11Jun82-629
Roebuck, P. Slices of Cricket.
  T.D. Smith, 617(TLS):27Aug82-929
Roesdahl, E. Viking Age Denmark.
  G. Jones, 617(TLS):27Aug82-926
Roethel, H.K. and J. Hahl-Koch - see Kandinsky, V.
Roethlisberger, M. Bartholomeus Breenbergh: The Paintings.
  M. Waddingham, 90:Jul81-426
Roff, W.R. - see Majid bin Zainuddin, A.
Roffman, P. and J. Purdy. The Hollywood Social Problem Film.*
  T. Cripps, 18:Jul-Aug81-64
Rogers, C.R. A Way of Being.
  C.W. Kneupper, 583:Fall81-90

Rogers, E. A Funny Old Quist.
    S.P. Dance, 617(TLS):7May82-503
Rogers, E.R. The Perilous Hunt.
    J.G. Cummins, 402(MLR):Oct81-981
Rogers, F.M. Atlantic Islanders of the
Azores and Madeiras.*
    R.W. Sousa, 238:May81-316
Rogers, J. Alternate Endings.*
    L. Ricou, 102(CanL):Spring81-142
Rogers, K.H., ed. Lacock Abbey Charters.
    D.E. Greenway, 325:Apr81-430
Rogers, K.M., ed. Before Their Time.*
    F.M. Link, 566:Autumn80-46
Rogers, L.M. Te Wiremu.
    R. Grover, 368:Sep73-254
Rogers, P., ed. The Context of English
Literature: The Eighteenth Century.
    J.A. Downie, 83:Autumn81-197
    A. Varney, 447(N&Q):Feb80-94
    205(FMLS):Jan80-84
Rogers, P. Henry Fielding.*
    W.B. Coley, 402(MLR):Jul81-675
    M. Irwin, 541(RES):May81-223
Rogers, P. "Robinson Crusoe."*
    M.E. Bruce, 566:Autumn81-42
    D. Oakleaf, 49:Apr81-100
Rogers, P.P. and F.A. Lapuente. Diccion-
ario de seudónimos literarios españoles,
con algunas iniciales.
    J. Snow, 545(RPh):Feb81-372
Rogers, R. Metaphor.
    M. Grimaud, 599:Winter81-80
Rogers, T.D. - see Madden, F.
"Roget's Thesaurus of English Words and
Phrases." (S.M. Lloyd, comp)
    A. Quinton, 617(TLS):4Jun82-605
Roggiano, A., ed. Octavio Paz.
    E.J. Mullen, 238:Sep81-484
Rogledi Manni, T. La tipografia a Milano
nel XV secolo.
    D.E. Rhodes, 354:Sep81-250
Rognet, R. Petits poèmes en fraude.
    R.R. Hubert, 207(FR):Apr82-712
    D. Leuwers, 450(NRF):Feb81-99
Rogosin, E. The Dance Makers.
    B. Kohn, 42(AR):Winter81-125
Rogozinski, J. Power, Caste, and Law.
    M. Vale, 617(TLS):10Sep82-983
Röhl, J.C.G. and N. Sombart, eds. Kaiser
Wilhelm II.
    M. Balfour, 617(TLS):18Jun82-668
Rohlfs, G. Estudios sobre el léxico
románico. (M. Alvar, ed)
    I. Macpherson, 86(BHS):Jul81-275
Rohlfs, G. Le Gascon. (3rd ed)
    L. Wolf, 685(ZDL):1/1981-88
Röhrich, L. Der Witz.*
    E. Moser-Rath, 196:Band21Heft3/4-335
Rohwedder, E. Deutsch-spanisches Konversa-
tionsbuch.
    H. Isenberg, 682(ZPSK):Band33Heft2-267
Ro'i, Y. Soviet Decision Making in
Practice.
    A. Krammer, 550(RusR):Apr81-205
Rojas, F.D.M. - see under de Borja Medina
Rojas, F.
Rojas, J.P. - see under Pérez Rojas, J.
Roland, A., ed. Psychoanalysis, Creativ-
ity and Literature.
    J. Forrester, 208(FS):Apr81-170
Roland, A. Underwater Warfare in the Age
of Sail.
    F.J. Anderson, 70:Sep80-14

Röll, W. Vom Hof zur Singschule.*
    J. Rettelbach, 680(ZDP):Band99Heft1-
    121
Rolland, B., E. O'Connor and M.D. Meyer.
La Français. (2nd ed)
    N.A. Poulin, 207(FR):Dec80-357
Rölleke, H., ed. Märchen aus dem Nachlass
der Brüder Grimm. (2nd ed)
    K. Ranke, 196:Band21Heft3/4-337
Rölleke, H. - see Brentano, C.
Rölleke, H. - see Grimm, J. and W.
Roller, D.C. and R.W. Twyman, eds. The
Encyclopedia of Southern History.
    R.G. Gunderson, 583:Fall80-83
    R.L. Watson, Jr., 579(SAQ):Winter81-
    117
Röllig, W. and others. Altorientalische
Literaturen.
    W.L. Moran, 318(JAOS):Apr/Jun80-189
Rollin, B. Am I Getting Paid For This?
    T. Schwartz, 441:7Nov82-15
Rollin, B.E. Animal Rights and Human
Morality.
    L.W. Sumner, 617(TLS):5Feb82-126
Rollin, R.B. and J.M. Patrick, eds.
"Trust to Good Verses."*
    P. Palmer, 677(YES):Vol 11-253
Rollins, R.G. Sean O'Casey's Drama.*
    E. Durbach, 397(MD):Jun81-234
Rollins, R.M. The Long Journey of Noah
Webster.
    B. Granger, 27(AL):Mar81-147
    E.N. Harbert, 432(NEQ):Dec81-600
    S.J. Novak, 656(WMQ):Apr81-328
Rollins, Y.B. Baudelaire et le Grotesque.*
    D.J. Mossop, 208(FS):Jul81-348
Rollinson, P. Classical Theories of
Allegory and Christian Culture.
    604:Fall81-59
Roloff, H-G., ed. Die deutsche Literatur.
(Ser 2, Section B, Pts 1-3)
    G. von Wilpert, 67:May81-121
Rolshoven, J. Automatische Transkription
französischer Texte.
    O. Välikangas, 439(NM):1981/2-218
Romani, M.A. and A. Quondam, eds. Le
corti farnesiane di Parma e Piacenza
(1545-1622).
    T.C.P. Zimmermann, 551(RenQ):Winter80-
    780
Romano, E. Struttura degli "Astronomica"
di Manilio.*
    J. Soubiran, 555:Vol54fasc1-189
Romano, F. Porfirio di Tiro.
    G. Fowden, 313:Vol71-178
Romano, J. Dickens and Reality.*
    C.P. Havely, 447(N&Q):Oct80-461
Romeiser, J.B. Critical Reception of
André Malraux's "L'Espoir" in the French
Press.
    R. Robe, 207(FR):May81-877
Romer, J. Valley of the Kings.
    K. Kitchen, 617(TLS):27Aug82-926
Romeralo, A.S. - see under Sánchez
Romeralo, A.
Romeralo, A.S. and A. Valenciano - see
under Sánchez Romeralo, A. and A.
Valenciano
Romero, L. Por qué y cómo mataron a Calvo
Sotelo.
    H. Southworth, 617(TLS):8Oct82-1107

Rosen, G. Madness in Society.
   T. Brown, 529(QQ):Autumn81-588
Rosén, H. and H.B. On Moods and Tenses of
   the Latin Verb.
   L. Stephens, 350:Dec82-905
Rosen, L. Top of the City.
   P. Goldberger, 441:12Dec82-22
Rosen, N. At the Center.
   R. Miner, 441:21Feb82-12
Rosen, R.C. John Dos Passos.
   B. Foley, 268(IFR):Summer82-129
Rosen, S. The Limits of Analysis.
   R.B. Pippin, 480(P&R):Fall81-253
Rosenau, H. Vision of the Temple.*
   F. Simpson, 46:Feb81-127
Rosenbaum, A.S., ed. The Philosophy of
   Human Rights.
   C.R.B., 185:Apr82-582
Rosenbaum, J. Moving Places.
   M. Wood, 18:Oct80-84
Rosenberg, C. - see Meiselas, S.
Rosenberg, C.E. No Other Gods.
   F.E. Matthews, 488:Mar81-91
Rosenberg, D. Chosen Days.
   P. Ramsey, 472:Spring/Summer82-172
Rosenberg, D. and B. The Music Makers.
   L.D., 412:Aug80-239
Rosenberg, D.A., ed. Marcos and Martial
   Law in the Philippines.
   J.E. Rocamora, 293(JASt):Feb81-430
Rosenberg, I. The Collected Works of
   Isaac Rosenberg.* (I. Parsons, ed)
   G. Davenport, 569(SR):Winter81-xi
   J. Stallworthy, 541(RES):Nov81-483
Rosenberg, J.D. - see Ruskin, J.
Rosenberg, J.F. Linguistic Representation.
   P. Butchvarov, 449:Mar81-81
Rosenberg, M. The Masks of "Macbeth."*
   J. Kerrigan, 541(RES):Feb81-78
Rosenberg, R. Beyond Separate Spheres.
   F. Randall, 441:10Oct82-16
Rosenberg, W.G. and M.B. Young. Transform-
   ing Russia and China.
   C.D. May, 441:16May82-14
Rosenberry, E.H. Melville.*
   R. Mason, 447(N&Q):Jun80-267
   T. Philbrick, 445(NCF):Sep80-241
Rosenblatt, L.M. The Reader, the Text,
   the Poem.
   B.W. Long, 480(P&R):Winter81-54
   A. Stevenson, 402(MLR):Oct81-923
   205(FMLS):Jan80-93
Rosenfeld, A.H. A Double Dying.
   I. Abrahamson, 390:Apr81-58
   S. Cohen, 577(SHR):Fall81-347
Rosenfeld, H. Raoul Wallenberg.
   H. Schwartz, 441:14Nov82-16
Rosenfeld, H-F. and H. Deutsche Kultur im
   Spätmittelalter, 1250-1500.*
   W. Störmer, 684(ZDA):Band109Heft3-104
Rosenfeld, M.N. - see Serlio, S.
Rosenfeld, S. Georgian Scene Painters.
   135:Nov81-175
Rosenfeld, S. - see Nicoll, A.
Rosenfeldt, N.E. Knowledge and Power.*
   M. McCauley, 575(SEER):Jan81-120
Rosenfield, A. and I. Greenburg, eds. Con-
   fronting the Holocaust.
   S. Cohen, 577(SHR):Fall81-354
Rosenfield, J.M. and E. ten Grotenhuis.
   Journey of the Three Jewels.
   Egami Yasushi, 407(MN):Autumn81-358

Rosengarten, H. and M. Smith - see Brontë,
   C.
Rosengren, I. Ein Frequenzwörterbuch der
   deutschen Zeitungssprache.
   W.H. Veith, 685(ZDL):1/1981-105
Rosengren, I., ed. Sprache und Pragmatik.*
   E.C. Traugott, 350:Sep82-741
Rosenkrantz, R.D. Inference, Method and
   Decision.*
   S. Spielman, 311(JP):Jun81-356
Rosenmeier, H. - see Kierkegaard, S.
Rosenstiel, L. Nadia Boulanger.
   R. Craft, 453(NYRB):27May82-8
   N. Rorem, 441:23May82-1
   442(NY):4Oct82-151
Rosenthal, B. City of Nature.
   L. Buell, 445(NCF):Sep81-212
   C.W. Scruggs, 27(AL):Mar81-136
   A.J. Weitzman, 587(SAF):Spring81-128
   R.A. Yoder, 591(SIR):Fall81-387
Rosenthal, B., ed. Critical Essays on
   Charles Brockden Brown.
   R.S. Levine, 165(EAL):Spring82-92
Rosenthal, H. My Mad World of Opera.
   S. Pickles, 617(TLS):3Dec82-1335
Rosenthal, H. and J. Warrack. The Concise
   Oxford Dictionary of Opera. (2nd ed)
   L.D., 412:Feb80-62
Rosenthal, M. Virginia Woolf.*
   N. Bradbury, 541(RES):May81-237
   E.C. Bufkin, 219(GaR):Spring81-190
   J. Halperin, 579(SAQ):Winter81-113
   A.L. McLaughlin, 395(MFS):Summer80-282
   V. Shaw, 402(MLR):Jul81-686
Rosenthal, M.L. Sailing into the Unknown.
   K. Watson, 447(N&Q):Jun80-288
Rosenzweig, F. Der Mensch und sein Werk.
   (R. Rosenzweig and E. Rosenzweig-Schein-
   mann, eds)
   H-J. Görtz, 489(PJGG):Band88Heft1-205
Rosic, G. - see Miller, H.
Roskill, S. Admiral of the Fleet Earl
   Beatty.*
   D.M. Schurman, 529(QQ):Autumn81-584
Roskina, N. Chetyre glavy; iz literatur-
   nykh vospominanii.*
   A. Olcott, 550(RusR):Jan81-87
Rösler, W. Dichter und Gruppe.
   M.R. Lefkowitz, 124:May-Jun82-307
   R.C.T. Parker, 123:Vol31No2-159
Ross, C. Richard III.
   G.R. Elton, 617(TLS):22Jan82-70
   442(NY):8Feb82-128
Ross, C.L. The Composition of "The Rain-
   bow" and "Women in Love."
   N. Clausson, 395(MFS):Winter80/81-687
Ross, D. Military Uniforms from the New
   Brunswick Museum.
   R.L. Shep, 614:Summer81-20
Ross, I.S. William Dunbar.
   V. Adams, 617(TLS):19Feb82-185
Ross, J. Dark Blue and Dangerous.
   N. Callendar, 441:10Jan82-29
Ross, J. Death's Head.
   T.J. Binyon, 617(TLS):31Dec82-1448
Ross, M., ed. The Arts and Personal
   Growth.
   A. Simpson, 89(BJA):Autumn81-371
Ross, M. The Creative Arts.
   P. Meeson, 89(BJA):Spring81-182
Ross, M.H. and B.K. Walker. "On Another
   Day ... "*
   D.P. Biebuyck, 292(JAF):Apr-Jun81-237

Rosset, C. L'objet singulier.* Le réel, traité de l'idiotie. Le réel et son double. L'anti-nature. Logique du pire.
  P. Mengue, 98:Jun-Jul81-595
Rossetti, G. - see Calderón de la Barca, P.
Rossi, E.E. and J.C. Plano. The Latin American Political Dictionary.
  S.C. Ropp, 263(RIB):Vol31No3-419
de Rossi, G.M. Bovillae.
  M.H. Crawford, 313:Vol71-153
Rossing, N. and B. Rønne. Apocryphal — Not Apocryphal?
  H.F. Graham, 550(RusR):Oct81-444
Rosso, C. Mythe de l'égalité et rayonnement des Lumières.
  C. Roquin, 207(FR):Apr82-680
Rossum, R.A. Reverse Discrimination.
  B.R.G., 185:Jan82-387
Rossvaer, V. Kant.
  L. Aagaard-Mogensen, 342:Band71Heft2-271
Rossvaer, V. Kant's Moral Philosophy.
  D.L.L., 543:Sep80-158
  T. Mautner, 63:Jun81-258
Rosten, N. Selected Poems.
  H. Thomas, 385(MQR):Winter82-200
Roster, P.J., Jr. La ironía como método de análisis literario.*
  P.R. Beardsell, 86(BHS):Jan81-91
Roston, M. Milton and the Baroque.*
  J. Blondel, 189(EA):Oct-Dec81-467
  W.E. Cain, 400(MLN):Dec81-1121
  M. Chan, 67:Nov81-245
  W. Myers, 569(SR):Fall81-622
Rotelli, G.G. - see under Giani Rotelli, G.
Rotermund, H.O. - see Mujû, I.
Roters, E., with others. Berlin 1910-1933.
  J. Russell, 441:5Dec82-66
Roth, G. and W. Schluchter. Max Weber's Vision of History.*
  B. Fay, 185:Oct80-162
Roth, J. Weights and Measures.
  M. Hofmann, 617(TLS):5Feb82-131
  A. Huth, 362:21Jan82-25
Roth, K. Ehebruchschwänke in Liedform.*
  T. Habel, 38:Band99Heft3/4-517
Roth, K-H. "Deutsch."*
  O. Ehrismann, 680(ZDP):Band100Heft3-458
  H. Schmidt, 682(ZPSK):Band33Heft2-279
Roth, L.M. A Concise History of American Architecture.*
  C.V. Brown, 658:Spring81-89
Roth, M-L. Robert Musil: Les Oeuvres préposthumes.
  J. Strelka, 680(ZDP):Band100Heft4-618
Roth, P. Le Grand Roman américain.
  C. Jordis, 450(NRF):Jan81-156
Roth, P. Zuckerman Unbound.*
  W. Boyd, 364:Nov81-83
  G. Perez, 249(HudR):Winter81/82-618
  S. Pinsker, 390:Dec81-53
Rothberg, A. The Four Corners of the House.
  B. Allen, 434:Spring82-478
Rothchild, D. and R.L. Curry, Jr. Scarcity, Choice and Public Policy in Middle Africa.
  S. Malumo, 69:Vol50No2-235
Rothe, W. Tänzer und Täter.
  J.M. Ritchie, 402(MLR):Jul81-756

Rothenberg, J., ed. Technicians of the Sacred.
  M. Heller, 472:Spring/Summer81-269
Rothenberg, J. Vienna Blood and Other Poems.
  J.W. Saucerman, 649(WAL):Winter81-315
Rothenberg, J., with H. Lenowitz and C. Doria, eds. A Big Jewish Book.
  M. Heller, 472:Spring/Summer81-269
Rothermund, D. Government, Landlord and Peasant in India.
  A.A. Yang, 293(JASt):Nov80-179
Rothermund, D. and D.C. Wahdwa, eds. Zamindars, Mines and Peasants.
  J.R. Hagen, 293(JASt):Nov80-181
Rothman, W. Hitchcock — The Murderous Gaze.
  P. French, 617(TLS):8Oct82-1103
Rothstein, E. Restoration and Eighteenth-Century Poetry, 1660-1780.
  J. Engell, 405(MP):May82-438
  A.T. McKenzie, 566:Spring82-120
  K. Walker, 617(TLS):1Jan82-4
Rothstein, R.L. Global Bargaining.
  G.K. Lewis, 185:Jul81-687
Rothwell, V. Britain and the Cold War 1941-1947.
  W. Laqueur, 617(TLS):5Mar82-243
Rothwell, W. and others, eds. Studies in Medieval Literature and Language in Memory of Frederick Whitehead.*
  E. Rozgonyi-Szilagy, 549(RLC):Jul-Dec81-500
Rotrou, J. Les Sosies. (D. Charron, ed)
  R. Guichemerre, 535(RHL):Nov-Dec81-984
  H.C. Knutson, 402(MLR):Jul81-698
Rotter, P., ed. Last Night's Stranger.
  H.R., 231:Aug82-77
Rötzer, H.G. Traditionalität und Modernität in der europäischen Literatur.
  E. Geisler, 196:Band22Heft1/2-154
Roubaud, J. Dors.
  R. Buss, 617(TLS):16Apr82-442
Roubiczek, P. Across the Abyss.
  442(NY):13Sep82-175
Rouche, M. L'Aquitaine des Wisigoths aux Arabes, 418-781.
  W. Goffart, 589:Jul81-652
Roudaut, J. Ce qui nous revient.
  S. Canadas, 98:Aug-Sep81-836
  P.W. Lasowski, 450(NRF):Apr81-119
Roudiez, L.S. - see Kristeva, J.
Rouché, B. Special Places.
  R. Lingeman, 441:25Jul82-8
Rouger, G., ed and trans. Fabliaux.*
  [shown in prev under title]
  D.D.R. Owen, 208(FS):Jul81-315
Rountree, B. Bonaventure d'Argonne.
  Q.M. Hope, 207(FR):Feb82-407
Rouquette, Y. - see under Roqueta, I.
Rouse, R.H. and M.A. Preachers, Florilegia, and Sermons.
  M.W. Bloomfield, 589:Jan81-220
Rousseas, S. Capitalism and Catastrophe.
  J. Oppenheimer, 185:Jan82-373
Rousseau, A.M. Shopping Bag Ladies.
  A. Hacker, 453(NYRB):12Aug82-15
Rousseau, G.S. and R. Porter, eds. The Ferment of Knowledge.
  W. Coleman, 617(TLS):22Jan82-84
  J.F. Sena, 566:Spring82-130

Rousseau, J-J. Correspondance complète de Jean-Jacques Rousseau.* (Vols 26-32) (R.A. Leigh, ed)
  G. May, 546(RR):Mar81-246
Rousseau, J-J. Correspondance complète de Jean-Jacques Rousseau. (Vols 33-36) (R.A. Leigh, ed)
  G. May, 546(RR):Mar81-246
  J.S. Spink, 208(FS):Jul81-334
Rousseau, J-J. Émile, or On Education. (A. Bloom, ed and trans)
  C.E.B., 543:Jun81-804
  A. Rosenberg, 627(UTQ):Spring81-339
Rousseau, J-J. The Reveries of the Solitary Walker. (C.E. Butterworth, ed and trans)
  T.E.M., 543:Sep80-159
Rousseau, N. Le Déluge blanc.
  P.R. Côté, 207(FR):Apr82-713
Rousseau, P. Ascetics, Authority and the Church in the Age of Jerome and Cassian.
  E.D. Hunt, 313:Vol71-193
"Rousseau selon Jean-Jacques."
  C. Rosso, 535(RHL):Nov-Dec81-1004
Roussel, D. Tribu et cité.
  N.R.E. Fisher, 303(JoHS):Vol 101-189
Roussel, H. and F. Suard, eds. Alain de Lille, Gautier de Châtillon, Jakemart Giélée et leur temps.
  T. Hunt, 402(MLR):Jul81-690
Rousset, D. The Legacy of the Bolshevik Revolution.
  K. Fitz Lyon, 617(TLS):19Nov82-1277
Rousset, J. Le Mythe de Don Juan.*
  W.D. Howarth, 208(FS):Oct81-495
Roux, G. Delphes.
  H. Damisch, 98:Feb80-95
Roux, G. L'amphictionie, Delphes et le temple d'Apollon au IVe siècle.
  D.E.W. Wormell, 303(JoHS):Vol 101-182
Roux, L. - see Hobbes, T.
Roux, L. and H. Gilibert. Le Vocabulaire, la Phrase, et le Paragraphe du "Leviathan" de Thomas Hobbes.
  T.W. Hayes, 568(SCN):Summer-Fall81-65
Rowan, B. Scholars' Guide to Washington, D.C.: Film and Video Collections.
  A. South, 14:Spring81-162
Rowan, E., ed. Art in Wales 2000 B.C. - A.D. 1850.
  H. Richardson, 112:Vol 14-166
Rowan, R.H. Music Through Sources and Documents.
  I. Fenlon, 415:Jun81-386
Rowe, A.E. The Enchanted Country.*
  A. Cheney, 392:Winter80/81-74
Rowe, A.P. A Century of Change in Guatemalan Textiles.
  R.L. Shep, 614:Summer82-13
Rowe, A.P., E.P. Benson and A-L. Schaffer, eds. The Junius B. Bird Pre-Columbian Textile Conference.
  M. Graham, 2(AfrA):May81-87
Rowe, D.J., ed. Northern Business Histories.
  R. Storey, 325:Apr81-439
Rowe, G.E., Jr. Thomas Middleton and the New Comedy Tradition.*
  J.A. Bryant, Jr., 569(SR):Winter81-viii
  R. McDonald, 568(SCN):Summer-Fall81-44
Rowe, J. Inyo-Sierra Passage.
  P.T. Bryant, 649(WAL):Winter81-311

Rowe, W. Mito e ideología en la obra de José María Arguedas.*
  A. McDermott, 402(MLR):Apr81-493
  A.J. Vetrano, 238:Sep81-486
Rowe, W.W. Nabokov and Others.*
  J.D. Clayton, 104(CASS):Winter81-568
  K. Cunningham, 594:Fall81-343
  C.S. Ross, 395(MFS):Winter80/81-671
Rowe, W.W. Nabokov's Spectral Dimension.*
  A. Olcott, 550(RusR):Oct81-477
Rowell, G. Theatre in the Age of Irving.
  C.H. Shattuck, 612(ThS):Nov81-248
Rowell, G. - see Gilbert, W.S.
Rowell, M. The Planar Dimension.
  A. Elsen, 127:Fall/Winter80-413
Rowland, B. Birds with Human Souls.*
  C. Wood, 178:Spring81-104
Rowland, B., ed. Medieval Woman's Guide to Health.
  T.A. Shippey, 617(TLS):29Jan82-97
Rowland, J.R.R. The Clock Inside.
  C. Pollnitz, 581:Jun81-221
Rowlands, J. Hercules Segers.
  90:Mar81-192
Rowley, N., comp. Law and Order in Essex.
  V. Sand, 14:Fall81-364
Rowse, A.L. A Cornish Childhood.
  C. Causley, 617(TLS):28May82-576
Rowse, A.L. A Life.
  A. Stevenson, 617(TLS):8Jan82-38
Roy, C. Les Chercheurs de dieux.*
  M.F. Maurice, 450(NRF):May81-129
Roy, C. La Traversée du Pont des Arts.
  J. Hollenbeck, 207(FR):Dec80-369
Roy, G. Children of My Heart.*
  C. Gerson, 102(CanL):Spring81-124
Roy, J., ed. Narrativa y crítica de nuestro América.*
  R. Scott, 552(REH):May81-315
Roy, N. Art of Manipur.
  R.L. Shep, 614:Summer81-16
Roy-Hewitson, L. Harmonies d'un songe.
  D.E. Rivas, 207(FR):Apr81-769
Roy-Hewitson, L. L'Impasse.
  P.G. Lewis, 207(FR):Oct81-163
Royko, M. Sez Who? Sez Me.
  D.S.B., 231:Nov82-76
Royle, T. Death Before Dishonour.
  D. Judd, 617(TLS):3Dec82-1426
Royster, C. A Revolutionary People at War.*
  G.A. Billias, 432(NEQ):Mar81-127
  R. Buel, Jr., 656(WMQ):Jan81-121
  I. Mugridge, 106:Fall81-199
  S.F. Scott, 173(ECS):Winter80/81-218
Rozenthal, R. The Kibbutz in the Age of Doubt. [in Hebrew]
  R. Feldman, 287:Nov81-17
Różewicz, T. Conversation with the Prince.
  D. Davis, 362:6May82-26
  M. Irwin, 617(TLS):24Dec82-1426
Różewicz, T. "The Survivor" and Other Poems.
  J. Aaron, 472:Spring/Summer81-110
"Tadeusz Różewicz Vorbereitungen zur Dichterlesung."
  R. Stone, 574(SEEJ):Spring81-122
Ruane, K. The Polish Challenge.
  A. Ryan, 362:17Jun82-21
Ruark, G. Reeds.*
  R.T. Smith, 577(SHR):Spring81-176

Rubattel, C. Fonctions sémantiques et
fonctions grammaticales dans la théorie
transformationnelle.
   B.K. Barnes, 207(FR):Mar81-635
Ruben, D-H. Marxism and Materialism.*
   J. Rée, 98:Aug-Sep80-802
Rubens, B. Birds of Passage.*
   J. Mellors, 364:Nov81-88
   E. Milton, 441:20Jun82-11
   442(NY):9Aug82-94
Rubens, B. Madame Sousatzka.
   L. Taylor, 617(TLS):23Jul82-807
   442(NY):30Aug82-90
Rubens, G. - see Lethaby, W.R.
Rubenstein, C. and P. Shaver. In Search
of Intimacy.
   M. Bayles, 441:7Nov82-16
Rubenstein, J. Soviet Dissidents: Their
Struggle for Human Rights.*
   639(VQR):Winter81-24
Rubenstein, R. The Novelistic Vision of
Doris Lessing.*
   M.M. Rowe, 395(MFS):Spring80-163
   R.D. Sell, 541(RES):Nov81-494
Rubenstein, R.L. The Cunning of History.
   J.S. Himelright and M.S. Clinton,
   396(ModA):Spring81-218
   S. Kosmicki, 497(PolR):Vol26No3-118
Ruberg, U. Beredtes Schweigen in lehrhaf-
ter und erzählender deutscher Literatur
des Mittelalters.*
   E.S. Firchow, 221(GQ):Jan81-83
   H. Homann, 589:Jan81-193
   F. Wagner, 196:Band21Heft1/2-148
Rubert de Ventós, X. Heresies of Modern
Art.*
   42(AR):Winter81-131
Rubin, A. J.S. Bach.
   P.F.W., 412:May80-143
Rubin, B. Paved with Good Intentions.*
   W.L. Cleveland, 529(QQ):Summer81-273
   R.O. Freedman, 287:Apr81-24
   B.R. Kuniholm, 579(SAQ):Summer81-360
Rubin, B., R. Carlton and A. Rubin. L.A.
in Installments: Forest Lawn.
   D.A. Smith, 658:Winter81-362
Rubin, D.L. The Knot of Artifice.*
   T. Cave, 617(TLS):26Feb82-226
Rubin, J.S. Constance Rourke and American
Culture.
   S.I. Bellman, 584(SWR):Summer81-325
   P.J. Eakin, 569(SR):Winter81-xiii
   H.H. Kolb, Jr., 27(AL):Mar81-133
   D. Watson, 366:Autumn81-247
   S.J. Whitfield, 579(SAQ):Summer81-371
Rubin, L.D. Surfaces of a Diamond.
   A. Mars-Jones, 617(TLS):8Jan82-35
Rubin, L.D., Jr., ed. The American South.
   B. Clayton, 579(SAQ):Spring81-240
   R. Coles, 639(VQR):Winter81-141
Rubin, L.D., Jr. The Wary Fugitives.
   A. Massa, 447(N&Q):Jun80-271
Rubin, W.S., ed. Pablo Picasso: A Retro-
spective.*
   L. Cooke, 59:Jun81-231
Rubinstein, N. - see de' Medici, L.
von Rüden, P., with others, eds. Beiträge
zur Kulturgeschichte der deutschen Arbei-
terbewegung 1848-1918.
   H. Groschopp, 654(WB):7/1981-189
Rudenstine, A.Z., ed. Russian Avant-Garde
Art.*
   C. Douglas, 62:Summer82-78

Rudin, N.G. Pavlovsky Shawls.
   R.L. Shep, 614:Fall81-20
Rudner, J. and I. The Hunter and His Art.
   D. Brokensha, 2(AfrA):Feb81-78
Rudnitsky, K. Meyerhold the Director. (S.
Schultze, ed)
   J. Russell, 453(NYRB):15Jul82-3
Rudolf, M. The Grammar of Conducting.*
   N. Del Mar, 415:Dec81-823
Rudolph, E. Skepsis bei Kant.
   P. Rohs, 342:Band71Heft3-369
Rudrum, A. Henry Vaughan.
   R. Selden, 617(TLS):3Dec82-1332
Rudy, S. and M. Taylor - see Jakobson, R.
Ruelland, J. Bibliographie des oeuvres de
Gaston Bachelard, ainsi que des divers
ouvrages que sa pensée et sa personne
ont inspirés.
   N. Lacharité, 154:Jun81-382
Ruello, F. - see Paulus Venetus
Ruesch, J. Semiotic Approaches to Human
Relations.
   G.F. Meier, 682(ZPSK):Band32Heft2-233
Rueschemeyer, M. Professional Work and
Marriage.
   J. Uglow, 617(TLS):5Feb82-129
Ruf, U. Franz Kafka.
   B. Goldstein, 406:Spring81-67
Ruggeri, U. Francesco Capella.*
   A. Binion, 54:Mar81-168
Ruggeri, U. Carlo Ceresa.
   E. Waterhouse, 90:Feb81-105
Ruh, K. and others - see Stammler, W. and
K. Langosch
Ruhe, E., with B. Beck and S. Lippert -
see Benedeit
Ruiz, J. The Book of the Archpriest of
Hita ("Libro de Buen Amor"). (M. Single-
ton trans) The Book of Good Love. (R.
Mignani and M.A. Di Cesare, trans)
   L.V. Fainberg, 545(RPh):May81-536
Ruiz de Alarcón, J. Tres comedias de
enredo. (J. de Entrambasaguas, ed)
   M.D. McGaha, 552(REH):Jan81-156
Ruiz Nestosa, J. El Contador de Cuentos.
   F.E. Feito, 37:Oct81-25
Rule, J. Contract With the World.
   L. Ricou, 529(QQ):Winter81-793
   C. Ross, 102(CanL):Summer81-121
Rule, J. The Young in One Another's Arms.
   S. Scott-Fleming, 436(NewL):Fall81-124
Rule, M. The Mary Rose.
   D. Thomas, 362:14Oct82-29
"Rumanian Studies." (Vol 4)
   D. Deletant, 575(SEER):Jul81-450
Rumens, C. Unplayed Music.*
   P. Bland, 364:Jul81-72
Rumford, B.T., ed. American Folk Por-
traits.
   L.S. Ferber, 55:Nov81-48
   J.V. Turano, 16:Autumn81-90
Rumold, R. Sprachliches Experiment und
literarische Tradition.
   W. Hoffmeister, 406:Summer81-248
Rumphius, G.E. The Poison Tree. (E.M.
Beekman, ed and trans)
   C.R. Boxer, 617(TLS):19Nov82-1274
Runciman, S. The First Crusade.
   42(AR):Spring81-266
Rundle, B. Grammar in Philosophy.
   J.B., 543:Dec80-399
   B. Harrison, 479(PhQ):Oct81-369
   A.R. White, 518:Jan81-42

306

Runeberg, F. Fru Catharina Boije och hennes döttrar.
  G.C. Schoolfield, 563(SS):Spring81-247
Runte, A. National Parks.
  J.R. Leo, 649(WAL):Winter81-340
Runte, R. - see "Studies in Eighteenth-Century Culture"
Ruoff-Väänänen, E. Studies on the Italian Fora.*
  M.H. Crawford, 313:Vol71-153
Rupen, R. How Mongolia is Really Ruled.
  P. Hyer, 293(JASt):Nov80-128
Rüping, K. Philologische Untersuchungen zu den Brahmasūtra-Kommentaren des Śaṅkara und des Bhāskara. (Pt 1)
  E.R. Boose, 259(IIJ):Jan81-54
Rupp, R. Beyond Existentialism and Zen.
  A. Malhotra, 485(PE&W):Jan81-109
Rupp, H. and C.L. Lang, eds. Deutsches Literatur-Lexikon. (3rd ed) (Vol 7)
  P.M. Mitchell, 301(JEGP):Jan81-78
Rupp, L.J. Mobilizing Women for War.
  A.G. Marquis, 161(DUJ):Dec80-105
Ruppelt, G. Schiller im nationalsozialistischen Deutschland.*
  H. Henning, 406:Winter81-480
Ruryk, N.R., ed. Ukrainian Embroidery Designs and Stitches.
  N.K. Grobman, 292(JAF):Jan-Mar81-105
Ruscha, E. Guacamole Airlines and other Drawings.
  P. Hodges, 62:Jan81-64
Ruschenbusch, E. Athenische Innenpolitik im 5. Jahrhundert v. Chr.
  H.D. Westlake, 303(JoHS):Vol 101-195
Ruse, M. The Darwinian Revolution.*
  F.B. Churchill, 637(VS):Winter81-255
  P.R. Sloan, 486:Dec81-623
Ruse, M. Sociobiology.
  J. Beatty, 529(QQ):Winter81-607
  R.L. Simon, 185:Jan82-327
Rush, B., with L. Wittman. The Complete Book of Seminole Patchwork.
  M.Z. Cowan, 614:Spring82-11
Rushdie, S. Midnight's Children.*
  T. Hyman, 364:Dec81/Jan82-134
Rushton, G. Echoes of the Whistle.
  P. Roy, 298:Fall-Winter81-205
Rushton, J., ed. W.A. Mozart "Don Giovanni."
  H. Cole, 362:4Feb82-25
  M. Tanner, 617(TLS):8Jan82-25
Ruskin, J. The Genius of John Ruskin. (J.D. Rosenberg, ed)
  529(QQ):Summer81-402
Ruskin, J. John Ruskin: Letters from the Continent, 1858. (J. Hayman, ed)
  T. Hilton, 617(TLS):22Oct82-1153
Ruskin, J. The Stones of Venice.* (J. Morris, ed)
  J.G. Links, 324:Feb82-163
  135:Oct81-93
Russ, C.A.H. - see Andersch, A.
Russ, C.V.J. Historical German Phonology and Morphology.*
  K-P. Wegera, 680(ZDP):Band100Heft3-455
Russel, N. Poets by Appointment.
  C.H. Sisson, 617(TLS):1Jan82-4
Russell, A. The Clerical Profession.
  J. Bentley, 637(VS):Spring81-368

Russell, C.S., ed. Collective Decision Making.
  J. Aldrich, 185:Oct81-164
Russell, D.A. Criticism in Antiquity.
  F. Cairns, 617(TLS):3Sep82-942
  G.A. Kennedy, 124:May-Jun82-317
Russell, F.D. Picasso's Guernica.*
  L. Cooke, 59:Jun81-231
Russell, G.W. [AE] Selections from the Contributions to "The Irish Homestead" by G.W. Russell — AE. (H. Summerfield, ed)
  R.A. Cave, 541(RES):May81-235
  P.L. Marcus, 677(YES):Vol 11-345
Russell, H.S. Indian New England Before the Mayflower.
  K.O. Kupperman, 432(NEQ):Sep81-429
  B. Salwen, 656(WMQ):Jul81-517
Russell, J. The Acquisition of Knowledge.
  W. Mays, 518:Jul81-143
Russell, J. The Meanings of Modern Art.*
  S. Bayley, 362:14Jan82-23
  T. Hilton, 617(TLS):19Mar82-315
  I. Jeffrey, 364:Feb82-82
Russell, J. Style in Modern British Fiction.*
  N.E. Enkvist, 599:Winter81-50
  H.T. Moore, 402(MLR):Oct81-941
Russell, J.B. A History of Witchcraft.
  J. Simpson, 203:Vol192No1-120
Russell, J.B. Satan.
  J. Fenton, 362:1Apr82-22
Russell, K. The 3000 Ton Press.
  C. Pollnitz, 581:Jun81-221
Russell, L.A. Robert Challe.
  O.A. Haac, 546(RR):May81-357
  J. Popin, 535(RHL):Jul-Oct81-772
  S.J. Webb, 207(FR):Apr81-735
Russell, M. Land of Enchantment.
  L. Milazzo, 584(SWR):Summer81-v
Russell, M. Rainblast.
  T.J. Binyon, 617(TLS):12Mar82-276
Russell, P.E. Temas de "La Celestina" y otros estudios del Cid al Quijote.*
  R.V. Brown, 238:Mar81-151
Russell, R. Estudios Panos IV.
  K.M. Kensinger, 269(IJAL):Jan81-68
Russell, W. Educating Rita.
  D. Devlin, 157:Autumn81-51
Russi, A. Teanum Apulum.
  M.H. Crawford, 313:Vol71-153
"Russkij jazyk." (F.P. Filin, ed)
  L. Djurović, 559:Dec80-194
  Z. Dolgopolova, 558(RLJ):Spring-Fall181-280
  S. Lubensky, 574(SEEJ):Summer81-104
Russo, V. The Celluloid Closet.*
  S. Farber, 18:Sep81-72
  R. Wood, 99:Feb82-35
Rust, R.D. - see Cooper, J.F.
Rustin, J. Le Vice à la mode.
  S.F. Davies, 402(MLR):Jul81-702
  G. Décote, 535(RHL):Nov-Dec81-988
  L.W. Lynch, 207(FR):Apr81-736
  F. Showalter, Jr., 210(FrF):Sep81-278
Rüstow, A. Freedom and Domination. (D. Rustow, ed)
  G. Poggi, 676(YR):Spring82-409
  639(VQR):Summer81-92
Rutebeuf. I Fabliaux. (A. Limentani, ed and trans)
  E. Baumgartner, 545(RPh):Feb81-363

Ruth, C. and others, eds. The Woman's
Part.
V.W. Callies, 405(MP):Feb82-318
"Ruth." (J.M. Sasson, trans)
J. Fontenrose, 292(JAF):Jul-Sep81-389
Rutherford, A. The Literature of War.*
B. Gasser, 447(N&Q):Jun80-276
J. Stallworthy, 541(RES):Nov81-483
Ruthven, K.K. Critical Assumptions.*
J.M. Cocking, 208(FS):Apr81-241
T. Eagleton, 541(RES):Nov81-498
H. Ormsby-Lennon, 402(MLR):Jan81-139
D. Watson, 366:Spring81-127
205(FMLS):Jul81-288
Rutland, E.D. The Cranberry Tree.
D. Livesay, 102(CanL):Winter80-122
Rutland, R.A. The Democrats.
W.C. Havard, 639(VQR):Spring81-351
Rutland, R.A. James Madison and the
Search for Nationhood.
442(NY):12Apr82-155
Rutsala, V. Walking Home from the Ice-
house.
R. Phillips, 249(HudR):Autumn81-426
639(VQR):Autumn81-132
Ruzante, A.B. - see under Beolco il
Ruzante, A.
Ryan, A., ed. The Idea of Freedom.
B.R.B., 185:Jul81-694
Ryan, D.S. Looking for Kathmandu.
M. Trend, 617(TLS):18Jun82-676
Ryan, E.B. and W.J. Eakins. The Lord
Peter Wimsey Cookbook.
L. Duguid, 617(TLS):22Jan82-91
Ryan, J. Panel by Panel.
B. Andrews, 71(ALS):May81-133
Ryan, M. In Winter.*
P. Stitt, 219(GaR):Fall81-647
V. Young, 472:Fall/Winter81-155
Ryan, M-L. Rituel et poésie.*
L.C. Breunig, 546(RR):Mar81-248
Ryan, W. and D. Guinness. The White House.
E. Verheyen, 576:May81-149
Rybicki, M., ed. Sejm Ustawodawczy
Rzeczypospolitej Polskiej 1947-1952.
P.J. Best, 104(CASS):Winter81-629
Rydén, M. An Introduction to the Histori-
cal Study of English Syntax.
G.B., 189(EA):Oct-Dec81-497
B. Löfstedt, 350:Jun81-499
M. Rissanen, 439(NM):1980/4-446
K. Sørensen, 179(ES):Oct81-488
Rydjord, J. Kansas Place-Names.
K.B. Harder, 424:Sep81-253
du Ryer, P. Clitophon, Tragi-comédie. (L.
Zilli, ed)
R. Horville, 535(RHL):Mar-Apr81-287
Ryga, G. Beyond the Crimson Morning.
G.W., 102(CanL):Autumn80-inside back
cover
Ryga, G. Ploughmen of the Glacier. Seven
Hours to Sundown.
J. Wasserman, 102(CanL):Summer80-104
Rykwert, J. The First Moderns.*
E.G. Grossman, 505:Jul81-143
J. Kenworthy-Browne, 39:Jun81-414
J. Lubbock, 59:Jun81-233
J. Masheck, 62:Jan81-64
J. Summerson, 46:Jan81-63
D. Watkin, 576:Mar81-79
Rykwert, J. The Necessity of Artifice.
A. Saint, 617(TLS):8Oct82-1095

Ryle, G. On Thinking.* (K. Kolenda, ed)
A.P. Griffiths, 483:Jul81-424
G.B. Matthews, 482(PhR):Jul81-443
R.B.S., 185:Jul82-796
Rzhevsky, L.D. Solzhenitsyn.*
V.D. Mihailovich, 577(SHR):Spring81-
186

El Saadawi, N. The Hidden Face of Eve.
(S. Hetata, ed and trans)
V. Gornick, 441:14Mar82-3
Saalman, H. Filippo Brunelleschi: The
Cupola of Santa Maria del Fiore.
R. Mainstone, 46:Aug81-128
Saarinen, E., ed. Game-Theoretical Seman-
tics.*
D.E. Over, 393(Mind):Apr81-309
S. Read, 518:Jan81-40
Saarnio, U. and H. Enders. Die Wahrheits-
theorie der deskriptiven Sätze.
K. Albrecht, 682(ZPSK):Band33Heft5-617
Saavedra, M.D. - see under de Cervantes
Saavedra, M.
Saba, G. - see Théophile de Viau
Saba, U. Il Canzoniere, 1921. (G. Castel-
lani, ed)
F. Donini, 617(TLS):22Jan82-88
Saba, U. Lettere a un amico vescovo. (G.
Fallani, ed)
E. Favretti, 228(GSLI):Vol 158fasc502-
307
Saba, U. Thirty-one Poems.
J. Saunders, 565:Vol22No3-62
Sabar, Y. PěSAT WAYěHI BěSALLAH.
B. Grossfeld, 318(JAOS):Jan/Mar80-64
Sábato, E. Apologías y Rechazos.
A. Blasi, 238:Sep81-481
J.D. Henderson, 37:Feb81-45
Sábato, E. On Heroes and Tombs.*
J. Butt, 617(TLS):13Aug82-875
Sabino, F. O Grande Mentecapto.
M. Silverman, 399(MLJ):Summer81-209
el Sabio, A. - see under Alfonso X el
Sabio
Sabloff, J.A., ed. Handbook of Middle
American Indians. (supp Vol 1, Archae-
ology)
N. Hammond, 617(TLS):26Nov82-1323
Sabol, A.J., ed. Four Hundred Songs and
Dances from the Stuart Masque.*
F.W. Sternfeld, 551(RenQ):Spring80-131
Sabom, M.B. Recollections of Death.
J.F. Watkins, 617(TLS):26Mar82-360
Sachs, H. Toscanini.
M.K., 412:Feb80-74
Sachsse, H. Anthropologie der Technik.
W. Strombach, 489(PJGG):Band88Heft1-
194
Sachsse, H. Kausalität — Gesetzlichkeit —
Wahrscheinlichkeit.*
M. Stöckler, 167:Mar81-161
Sacken, C.V. - see under von der Osten
Sacken, C.
Sacks, E. Shakespeare's Images of Preg-
nancy.*
M.B., 214:Vol 10No37-121
Sacks, S., ed. On Metaphor.
J.B. Dilworth, 290(JAAC):Fall81-99
D.H. Hirsch, 569(SR):Winter81-95

Sackville, C. The Poems of Charles Sack-
ville Sixth Earl of Dorset. (B. Harris,
ed)
  R.D. Hume, 402(MLR):Apr81-444
Sacré, J. Un sang maniériste.*
  A. Scholar, 208(FS):Oct81-436
de Sacy, S.S. - see de Balzac, H.
Sadai, Y. Harmony in its Systematic and
Phenomenological Aspects.
  W. Drabkin, 415:Jun81-386
Saddlemyer, A., ed. Theatre Business.
  K. Worth, 617(TLS):22Oct82-1158
Sadie, S., ed. The New Grove Dictionary
of Music and Musicians.* (Vols 1-20)
  J. Barzun, 451:Spring82-253
  L.D. Berman, 451:Spring82-256
  R. Evidon, 451:Fall81-155
  J. Kerman, 451:Fall81-168
  J. Kerman, 451:Spring82-265
  B. Newhouse, 451:Fall81-157
  G.H. Phipps, 451:Fall81-167
  J.H. Roberts, 451:Fall81-161
  M. Solomon, 451:Spring82-262
  N. Temperley, 451:Fall81-164
  R. Trotter, 451:Fall81-166
  W. Weber, 451:Fall81-158
  S. Winklhofer, 451:Spring82-257
Sadie, S., ed. The New Grove Dictionary
of Music and Musicians.* (Vols 1 and 11)
  A.V. Jones, 415:Mar81-171
Sadie, S., ed. The New Grove Dictionary
of Music and Musicians.* (Vols 2 and 13)
  J. Smith, 415:May81-304
Sadie, S., ed. The New Grove Dictionary
of Music and Musicians.* (Vols 3 and 12)
  J.E. Gardiner, 415:Jun81-375
Sadie, S., ed. The New Grove Dictionary
of Music and Musicians.* (Vols 4 and 9)
  R. Orr, 415:Mar81-173
Sadie, S., ed. The New Grove Dictionary
of Music and Musicians.* (Vols 5 and 19)
  C. Hogwood, 415:Apr81-241
Sadie, S., ed. The New Grove Dictionary
of Music and Musicians.* (Vols 6 and 15)
  E. Boyle, 415:May81-307
Sadie, S., ed. The New Grove Dictionary
of Music and Musicians.* (Vols 7 and 17)
  B. Bujic, 415:Jun81-377
Sadie, S., ed. The New Grove Dictionary
of Music and Musicians.* (Vols 8 and 16)
  I. Keys, 415:May81-305
Sadie, S., ed. The New Grove Dictionary
of Music and Musicians.* (Vols 10 and
14)
  M. Greenhalgh, 415:Mar81-174
Sadie, S., ed. The New Grove Dictionary
of Music and Musicians.* (Vols 18 and
20)
  D. Puffett, 415:Apr81-242
Sadler, L. Thomas Carew.
  R. Messenger, 568(SCN):Spring81-10
Sadler, L.V. John Bunyan.
  E. Bourcier, 189(EA):Jan-Mar81-92
Saeger, U. Nöhr.
  K. Kändler, 654(WB):9/1981-155
Sáenz Quesada, M. Los estancieros.
  D. Balmori, 263(RIB):Vol31No1-97
Safarik, A. The Heart Is Altered.
  D. Precosky, 102(CanL):Winter80-142
Safarik, A. The Naked Machine Rides On.*
  H. Hoy, 102(CanL):Autumn81-153
  L. Mathews, 628(UWR):Fall-Winter81-119

Saffer, T.H. and O.E. Kelly. Countdown
Zero.
  B.W. Cook, 441:1Aug82-3
Safire, W. On Language
  G. Core, 249(HudR):Autumn81-475
Sagan, C. Cosmos.* Broca's Brain.
  M. Green, 128(CE):Oct81-569
Sagar, K. D.H. Lawrence: A Calendar of
His Works.
  M. Squires, 594:Fall81-345
Sagar, K. The Life of D.H. Lawrence.
  N. Clausson, 395(MFS):Winter80/81-687
  H. Lachtman, 77:Winter81-88
  295(JML):Vol8No3/4-549
Sagaster, K. Die weisse Geschichte.
  L. Kwanten, 318(JAOS):Jul/Sep80-387
Saha, S., ed. An Anthology of Indo-
English Love Poetry.
  A.L. Weir, 314:Summer-Fall81-226
Sahlberg, O. Gottfried Benns Phantasie-
welt.
  C. Pietzcker, 224(GRM):Band31Heft4-474
Sahlins, M. Au coeur des sociétés.
  L. Arénilla, 450(NRF):Feb81-129
Sahni, J. Classic Indian Cooking.
  W. and C. Cowen, 639(VQR):Autumn81-138
Said, E.W. Covering Islam.*
  C. Geertz, 453(NYRB):27May82-25
  F. Gerson, 99:Nov81-38
Said, E.W. Orientalism.*
  M.D. Biddiss, 208(FS):Jul81-372
  P. Gran, 318(JAOS):Jul/Sep80-328
  R. Luckett, 97(CQ):Vol 10No3-271
  D. O'Hara, 81:Spring80-259
Saïd, S. La Faute tragique.*
  F. Jouan, 555:Vol54fasc2-343
Saikaku, I. Tales of Samurai Honor. (C.A.
Callahan, trans)
  J. Kirkup, 617(TLS):20Aug82-906
Saikal, A. The Rise and Fall of the Shah.
  W.L. Cleveland, 529(QQ):Summer81-273
Sail, L. The Kingdom of Atlas.*
  D. Graham, 565:Vol22No4-62
Sainsbury, R.M. Russell.*
  P.R. Bell, 483:Apr81-271
  S. Haack, 393(Mind):Jan81-136
  G. Priest, 63:Sep81-346
de Saint-Amant, G. Oeuvres. (Vols 1-4)
(J. Bailbé and J. Lagny, eds)
  C. Rolfe, 208(FS):Oct81-437
de Saint-Amant, G. Oeuvres. (Vol 5) (J.
Bailbé and J. Lagny, eds)
  B. Nicholas, 402(MLR):Oct81-962
  B. Norman, 207(FR):Mar82-548
  A. Rathé, 535(RHL):Mar-Apr81-284
  C. Rolfe, 208(FS):Oct81-437
de Saint-Denys, H. Dreams and How to
Guide Them. (M. Schatzman, ed)
  C. Rycroft, 617(TLS):17Dec82-1387
de Saint-Évremond, C. Les Opéra.* (R.
Finch and E. Joliat, eds)
  D.C. Potts, 208(FS):Apr81-193
  205(FMLS):Jan80-93
de Saint-Évremond, C. Sir Politick Would-
be.* (R. Finch and E. Joliat, eds)
  205(FMLS):Jan80-93
St. James, B. The Seven Dreamers.
  N. Callendar, 441:16May82-26
St. John, C. A Scottish Naturalist. (A.
Atha, ed)
  B. Urquhart, 617(TLS):18Jun82-654

St. John, D. The Shore.*
   J.F. Cotter, 249(HudR):Summer81-286
   S. Yenser, 676(YR):Autumn81-97
St. John-Stevas, N. Pope John Paul II.
   D. Crane, 617(TLS):5Nov82-1227
   C.C. O'Brien, 362:27May82-20
St. Martin, G.L. and J.K. Voorhies.
   Écrits louisianais du dix-neuvième
   siècle.
   L-F. Hoffmann, 535(RHL):May-Jun81-495
Saint-Pierre, A. Le rideau se lève au
   Manitoba.
   L.E. Doucette, 108:Spring81-127
   L.E. Doucette, 627(UTQ):Summer81-177
Saint-Pol-Roux. La Rose et les épines du
   chemin. (Vol 1)
   R. Blin, 450(NRF):Jan81-117
de Saint-Sorlin, J. - see under Desmarests
   de Saint-Sorlin, J.
de Ste. Croix, G.E.M. The Class Struggle
   in the Ancient Greek World.
   E. Badian, 453(NYRB):2Dec82-47
Sáinz de Medrano, L. - see Hernández, J.
Sainz Rodríguez, P. Testimonio y Recuer-
   dos.
   A. Alted Vigil, 552(REH):Jan81-153
Saisselin, R.G. The Literary Enterprise
   in Eighteenth-Century France.*
   P. Baggio-Huerre, 207(FR):Oct81-138
Sajavaara, K. Imagery in Lawrence
   Durrell's Prose.
   M. Manzalaoui, 677(YES):Vol 11-364
Sakalis, D.T. Ē gnēsiotēta toy "Pseydoso-
   phistē" toy Loykianoy.
   M.D. MacLeod, 123:Vol31No1-113
Sakalis, D.T. Iōniko Lektiko ston Platōna,
   Meros a, Syntaxē.
   K.J. Dover, 123:Vol31No2-288
   P. Louis, 555:Vol54fasc1-163
Sakanishi, H., ed. Ecce homo.
   I. Lammel, 654(WB):1/1981-185
Sakharov, V. and U. Tosi. High Treason.
   V. Krasnov, 550(RusR):Oct81-458
Sakoian, F. and B. Caulifield. Astrologi-
   cal Patterns.
   42(AR):Winter81-133
Sala, J. Spaz Attack.
   P. Schjeldahl, 472:Spring/Summer81-284
Sala-Molins, L. Le Dictionnaire des
   Inquisiteurs.
   M. and B. Gazier, 450(NRF):Oct81-152
Salas, A.I.S. - see under Sotelo Salas,
   A.I.
de la Sale, A. Le Reconfort de Madame de
   Fresne. (I. Hill, ed)
   R. Morse, 402(MLR):Oct81-959
Sale, R. Fairy Tales and After.*
   H. Ashmore, 436(NewL):Winter81/82-121
Sale, R. On Not Being Good Enough.*
   H. Wirth-Nesher, 395(MFS):Summer80-385
Sale, W. Existentialism and Euripides.*
   W.J. Verdenius, 394:Vol34fasc3/4-424
Salem, L. Die Frau in den Liedern des
   "Hohen Minnesangs."
   V. Ziegler, 589:Jul81-676
Salerno, N.F. and R.M. Vanderburgh. Sha-
   man's Daughter.*
   D.R. Bartlett, 102(CanL):Summer81-157
   E. Fowke, 99:Nov81-35
Sales, H. Armado Cavaleiro o Audaz Moto-
   queiro.
   M. Silverman, 238:Dec81-646

Salgádo, G. English Drama.
   D.R., 214:Vol 10No37-133
Salgado, M.A. Rafael Arévalo Martínez.
   B. Miller, 238:May81-319
   D.R. Reedy, 399(MLJ):Spring81-100
Saliba, D.R. A Psychology of Fear.
   J.W. Gargano, 495(PoeS):Jun81-14
   H. Kerr, 573(SSF):Fall81-473
Salih, T. The Wedding of Zein.
   C.E.G. Berkley, 294:Vol 11-105
Salinger, P. America Held Hostage.*
   A. Holden, 617(TLS):30Jul82-837
Salinger, W. Folly River.*
   R. Tillinghast, 569(SR):Spring81-265
Salisbury, R. Close the Door Behind You.
   L. Taylor, 617(TLS):10Sep82-982
Sallenave, D. Les Portes de Gubbio.
   C. Coustou, 450(NRF):Jan81-133
Saller, R.P. Personal Patronage under the
   Early Empire.
   P.A. Brunt, 617(TLS):19Nov82-1276
Sallis, J. Being and Logos.
   D.F. Krell, 323:Jan81-93
Sallis, J. and K. Maly, eds. Heraclitean
   Fragments.
   M.R. Wright, 123:Vol31No2-297
Salmi, M. La Pittura di Piero della
   Francesca.
   R. Salvini, 683:Band43Heft4-426
Salminen, R. Marguerite de Navarre: "Le
   miroir de l'âme pécheresse."
   L. Löfstedt, 439(NM):1980/2-221
Salmon, N.U. Reference and Essence.
   C. Peacocke, 617(TLS):8Oct82-1115
Salmon, V. The Study of Language in
   Seventeenth Century England.
   I. Michael, 260(IF):Band85-304
Salmon, W.C., ed. Hans Reichenbach, Logi-
   cal Empiricist.*
   G. Joseph, 482(PhR):Jul81-448
   D. Zittlau, 679:Band11Heft2-407
Salomon, C. Charlotte.* (J. Herzberg,
   ed)
   T. Phillips, 617(TLS):26Mar82-356
   D. Ugoretz, 287:Nov81-20
Salstad, M.L. The Presentation of Women
   in Spanish Golden Age Literature.
   N.K. Mayberry, 304(JHP):Winter82-165
Salter, J.R., Jr. Jackson, Mississippi.
   E.N. Akin, 392:Spring81-135
Salter, M. Humour in the Works of Proust.
   N.M. Leov, 67:Nov81-260
Saltonstall, C. and H. A New Catalogue of
   Music for Small Orchestra.
   R. Andrewes, 415:Oct81-675
Saltonstall, W.G. Lewis Perry of Exeter.*
   639(VQR):Spring81-47
Saltykov-Shchedrin, M.E. The History of a
   Town. (S.C. Brownsberger, ed and trans)
   G.A. Hosking, 617(TLS):9Jul82-750
Saltykov-Shchedrin, M.E. The History of a
   Town. (I.P. Foote, trans)
   K. Armes, 574(SEEJ):Fall81-111
Salu, M., ed. Essays on Troilus and
   Criseyde.
   L.W. Patterson, 589:Oct81-912
Salu, M. and R.T. Farrell, eds. J.R.R.
   Tolkien, Scholar and Storyteller.*
   A. Crépin, 189(EA):Jan-Mar81-109
   M. Godden, 541(RES):Nov81-488
   C.E. Lloyd, 569(SR):Spring81-281

Salutin, R., with K. Dryden. Les Canadiens.
   J. Ripley, 102(CanL):Summer80-113
Salvador, M.L. Yer Dailege!
   F.H. Pettit, 37:May81-26
Salvatore, A. Scienza e poesia in Roma.
   P. Flobert, 555:Vol54fasc1-186
Salzman, L.F. Building in England Down to 1540.
   P. Draper, 576:May81-157
Samaran, C. Enfance et Jeunesse d'un Centenaire.
   N. Barker, 617(TLS):23Apr82-471
Sammons, J.L. Heinrich Heine.*
   R.C. Figge, 301(JEGP):Jul81-388
   N. Reeves, 402(MLR):Oct81-994
Sammons, J.L. Literary Sociology and Practical Criticism.*
   H.S. Daemmrich, 222(GR):Spring81-79
   H.D. Osterle, 406:Fall81-335
Sammut, A. Unfredo duca di Gloucester e gli umanisti italiani.
   C. Fahy, 617(TLS):2Jul82-726
Sampaio, M.L.P. Estudo Diacrônico dos Verbos "Ter" e "Haver."
   F. Cota Fagundes, 552(REH):Jan81-155
Sampson, A. The Changing Anatomy of Britain.
   P. Johnson, 617(TLS):8Oct82-1093
   A. Watkins, 362:23Sep82-22
Sampson, A. The Money Lenders.*
   R. Lekachman, 441:3Jan82-1
Sampson, E.D. Nilolay Gumilev.*
   E. Rusinko, 574(SEEJ):Spring81-103
   R.D.B. Thomson, 575(SEER):Apr81-293
Sampson, G. Liberty and Language.*
   H.M. Bracken, 154:Dec81-771
   D. Lightfoot, 297(JL):Mar81-160
   J.A. Mason, 307:Apr81-57
   P.H. Matthews, 84:Dec81-416
Sampson, G. Schools of Linguistics.
   D.C. Walker, 350:Mar82-240
Sampson, G.R. Making Sense.*
   J.R. Hurford, 350:Dec81-912
   T.P. Waldron, 402(MLR):Jan81-155
Sampson, R., ed. Early Romance Texts.
   N.B. Smith, 589:Apr81-427
   205(FMLS):Oct80-374
Sams, F. Run with the Horsemen.
   R. Miner, 441:28Nov82-27
Samsaris, D.K. Historikē geōgraphia tēs Anatolikēs Makedonias kata tēn archaiotēta.
   N.G.L. Hammond, 303(JoHS):Vol 101-201
Samson, J. The Music of Szymanowski.
   P.P. Nash, 607:Mar81-39
Samson, L. and K-S. Rehberg - see Gehlen, A.
Samuel, R., ed. People's History and Socialist Theory.
   A.L., 185:Jan82-393
Samuels, E. Bernard Berenson.*
   M. Goldstein, 569(SR):Spring81-287
   P. Mauriès, 98:Jun-Jul80-580
   W.M. Owen, 90:May81-317
Samuels, P. and H. Frederic Remington.
   M. Kammen, 441:13Jun83-9
Samuels, P. and H. - see Remington, F.
San, H., A. Pino and L. Epstein - see under Huang San, A. Pino and L. Epstein
Sanches, M. and B.G. Blount, eds. Sociocultural Dimensions of Language Use.
   J.T. Irvine, 355(LSoc):Apr81-97

Sánchez, L.R. Macho Camacho's Beat.*
   G. Kearns, 249(HudR):Summer81-306
   J.D. O'Hara, 434:Summer82-603
Sánchez, V. and C.S. Fuertes, eds.· España en Extremo Oriente.
   C.R. Boxer, 302:Vol 18-176
   K. Whinnom, 86(BHS):Jul81-278
Sánchez-Albornoz, C. El régimen de la tierra en el reino Asturleonés hace mil años.
   T.N. Bisson, 589:Jan81-221
Sánchez-Boudy, J. Diccionario de cubanismos más usuales.
   G.J. Fernández, 238:May81-324
Sánchez-Lafuente Gemar, R. Orfebrería del Museo de Málaga.
   A. López-Yarto, 48:Oct-Dec81-462
Sánchez Romeralo, A. - see Jiménez, J.R.
Sánchez Romeralo, A. and A. Valenciano, eds. Romancero rústico.
   J.G. Cummins, 86(BHS):Apr81-136
   S.H. Petersen, 238:May81-310
Sancho, M.P.C. - see under Cuartero Sancho, M.P.
de Sanctis, G. La guerra sociale.* (L. Polverini, ed)
   M.H. Crawford, 313:Vol71-153
Sand, G. Correspondance. (Vols 12 and 13) (G. Lubin, ed)
   L.J. Austin, 208(FS):Jan81-81
Sand, G. Correspondance. (Vol 14) (G. Lubin, ed)
   L.J. Austin, 208(FS):Jan81-81
   J. Gaulmier, 535(RHL):Mar-Apr81-309
Sand, G. Les Maîtres Sonneurs. (M-C. Bancquart, éd)
   M. Naudin, 207(FR):Feb82-415
Sand, G. My Life.* (D. Hofstadter, ed and trans)
   H. Ashmore, 436(NewL):Winter81/82-122
Sand, G. La Ville noire. (J. Courrier, ed)
   A. Buisine, 535(RHL):Jan-Feb81-153
"George Sand Papers: Conference Proceedings, 1976."
   J.M. Vest, 210(FrF):Sep81-280
Sandberg, B. Die neutrale -(e)n-Ableitung der deutschen Gegenwartssprache.
   P. Suchsland, 682(ZPSK):Band32Heft2-243
Sandell, R. Linguistic Style and Persuasion.
   R. Gläser, 682(ZPSK):Band32Heft2-217
Sander, A. August Sander: Menschen des 20. Jahrhunderts.
   J. Masheck, 62:Feb81-71
Sanders, A. The Victorian Historical Novel, 1840-1880.*
   R.L. Caserio, 445(NCF):Sep80-229
Sanders, C.R. Carlyle's Friendships and Other Studies.*
   P. Morgan, 179(ES):Feb81-84
Sanders, C.R. and K.J. Fielding - see Carlyle, T. and J.W.
Sanders, L. The Case of Lucy Bending.
   M. Watkins, 441:22Aug82-12
Sanders, N. and others. The Revels History of Drama in English.* (Vol 2)
   M.L. Ranald, 612(ThS):Nov81-229
Sanders, W. Linguistische Stilistik.*
   J.M. Ellis, 599:Winter81-31

Sanderson, M.H.B. Scottish Rural Society in the 16th Century.
T.C. Smout, 617(TLS):2Apr82-389
Sandig, B. Stilistik.*
S. Wichter, 490:Band12Heft3/4-512
Sandler, L.F. The Peterborough Psalter in Brussels and Other Fenland Manuscripts.
A. Stones, 683:Band43Heft2-211
Sandmel, S. Philo of Alexandria.
L.H. Feldman, 318(JAOS):Apr/Jun80-197
Sandoval, M.G. and G.L. Alonso. El mundo de la juventud.
B.S. Davis, 238:Sep81-491
J. Sager, 399(MLJ):Autumn81-336
Sandoz, M. Louis-Jacques Durameau, 1733-1796. Jean-Simon Berthélemy, 1743-1811.
P. Conisbee, 90:Jun81-369
B. Scott, 39:Jan81-61
Sandrieu, D. Cinq Cents Lettres pour tous les jours.
W. Wrage, 207(FR):Dec80-358
Sands, M. Robson of the Olympic.
M.R. Booth, 611(TN):Vol35No1-44
Sandt, L. Mythos und Symbolik im Zuberberg von Thomas Mann.*
U. Wolff, 680(ZDP):Band100Heft2-312
Sandys, E. Love and War.
S. Altinel, 617(TLS):16Jul82-775
Saner, R. So This Is the Map.
M. Kinzie, 29:Mar/Apr82-13
P. Stitt, 219(GaR):Fall81-647
Sanford, J. A Man Without Shoes.
M. Dickstein, 441:4Jul82-5
Sáṅkara. A Thousand Teachings. (S. Mayeda, ed and trans)
W. Halbfass, 318(JAOS):Jan/Mar80-43
J. Koller, 485(PE&W):Jul81-386
Sankoff, D., ed. Linguistic Variation.*
J. Milroy, 355(LSoc):Apr81-104
Sankovitch, T. Jodelle et la Création du Masque.
E.J. Campion, 475:No15Pt1-176
G. Crouse, 207(FR):Dec80-338
de San Pedro, D. Prison of Love. (K. Whinnom, ed and trans)
205(FMLS):Apr80-191
"Sanskrit Love Poetry."* (W.S. Merwin and J.M. Masson, trans)
L. Sternbach, 318(JAOS):Jul/Sep80-314
Sansone, D. Aeschylean Metaphors for Intellectual Activity.
M.S. Silk, 303(JoHS):Vol 101-150
Santa Cruz de Prunes, M.I. La genèse du monde sensible dans la philosophie de Plotin.
H.J. Blumenthal, 303(JoHS):Vol 101-164
A. Reix, 542:Jul-Sep81-329
Santagata, M. La lirica aragonese.
A. Tissoni Benvenuti, 228(GSLI): Vol 157fasc500-614
Santagata, M. Dal Sonetto al Canzoniere.
M. Marti, 228(GSLI):Vol 158fasc503-444
Santas, G.X. Socrates.*
S.M. Cohen, 482(PhR):Jan81-153
T.H. Irwin, 311(JP):May81-272
R. Kraut, 185:Jul81-651
Santerre, R. Anthologie de la littérature franco-américaine de la Nouvelle-Angleterre.
A.B. Chartier, 207(FR):Dec81-308
Marqués de Santillana. Poesías completas. (Vols 1 and 2) (M. Durán, ed)
K. Whinnom, 86(BHS):Apr81-140

Santinello, G. - see Nicholas of Cusa
Santini, G. Università e società nel XII secolo.
N.G. Siraisi, 589:Apr81-428
Santōka Taneda. Mountain Tasting.
J. Abrams, 407(MN):Summer81-232
Santoro, M. Fortuna, Ragione e Prudenza nella civiltà letteraria del Cinquecento.*
M. Olsen, 462(OL):Vol35No1-88
Santos, J.F. - see under Fernández Santos, J.
Santosuosso, A. Vita di Giovanni Della Casa. The Bibliography of Giovanni Della Casa.
E. Saccone, 400(MLN):Jan81-172
Sapergia, B. Dirt Hills Mirage.
B.K. Filson, 526:Spring81-72
Saperstein, A. Camp.
R.P. Brickner, 441:10Oct82-14
T.G., 231:Oct82-75
Sapir, J.D. and J.C. Crocker, eds. The Social Use of Metaphor.*
D. Ben-Amos, 355(LSoc):Apr81-111
Sapora, R.W., Jr. A Theory of Middle English Alliterative Meter with Critical Applications.*
E. Standop, 38:Band99Heft1/2-229
Sapp, A. A Cree Life.
F.E. Hoxie, 42(AR):Winter81-123
Sappler, P. and E. Strassner, eds. Maschinelle Verarbeitung altdeutscher Texte.
R.W. Dunbar, 589:Apr81-430
Šaradzenidze, T. Enisa da met'qvelebis urtiertobis p'roblema.
G.F. Meier, 682(ZPSK):Band33Heft6-759
Serafin, D. Christmas Rising.
T.J. Binyon, 617(TLS):31Dec82-1448
Sarano, J. L'homme double.
M. Adam, 542:Apr-Jun81-248
Saraydar, A. Proust disciple de Stendhal.
D. Backus, 446(NCFS):Spring-Summer82-368
Sarde, M. Colette.*
P. Grosskurth, 617(TLS):29Jan82-112
Sardesai, D.R. Southeast Asia.
D.J. Duncanson, 617(TLS):12Nov82-1238
Sareil, J. Voltaire et les grands.*
J.H. Brumfitt, 208(FS):Oct81-445
Sareil, J. and A. Bergens. Les Joies de la lecture.
R. Danner, 207(FR):May81-884
Sargeant, W. - see "The Bhagavad Gītā"
Sargent, L.T. British and American Utopian Literature 1516-1975.
K.M. Roemer, 26(ALR):Spring81-122
Sarna, L. Letters of State.*
B. Whiteman, 102(CanL):Summer80-141
Saroyan, A. Last Rites.
P-L. Adams, 61:Sep82-95
M. Harris, 441:1Aug82-7
Sarraute, N. Collected Plays.
D. Devlin, 157:Autumn81-51
Sarraute, N. L'Usage de la parole.*
G.R. Besser, 207(FR):Mar81-625
Sarraute, N. Pour un oui ou pour un non.
B. Wright, 617(TLS):30Jul82-835
Sartain, E.M. Jalāl al-dīn al-Suyūṭī.
W.M. Brinner, 318(JAOS):Apr/Jun80-135
Sarton, M. Anger.
S. Ballantyne, 441:17Oct82-14

Sartre, J-P. The Family Idiot.* (Vol 1)
    J. Bayley, 362:4Feb82-22
    V. Brombert, 617(TLS):29Jan82-98
    F. Brown, 453(NYRB):4Feb82-28
    442(NY):8Mar82-142
Sartre, J-P. Der Idiot der Familie.
    R. Neudeck, 489(PJGG):Band88Heft1-225
Saso, M. and D. Chappell, eds. Buddhist
    and Taoist Studies I.
    D.L. Overmyer, 318(JAOS):Jan/Mar80-89
Sass, H-M. - see Kapp, E.
Sassi, M.M. Le teorie della percezione in
    Democrito.
    N. Gulley, 303(JoHS):Vol 101-178
Sasso, G. Benedetto Croce.
    M.A.F., 543:Sep80-162
Sasson, J.M. - see "Ruth"
Sassoon, D. The Strategy of the Italian
    Communist Party.
    W. Kendall, 617(TLS):25Jun82-690
Sassoon, G. and R. Dale. The Manna
    Machine.
    R.N. Bracewell, 529(QQ):Autumn81-571
Sassoon, S. Siegfried Sassoon Diaries,
    1920-1922.* (R. Hart-Davis, ed)
    J. Stallworthy, 617(TLS):9Jul82-733
    F. Tuohy, 364:Feb82-84
Sato, H. - see Takamura Kōtarō
Sato, H. and B. Watson, eds and trans.
    From the County of Eight Islands.*
    639(VQR):Autumn81 132
Sato, K., ed. Industry and Business in
    Japan.
    L. Hollerman, 293(JASt):Aug81-735
    Shimizu Yoshiharu, 285(JapQ):Jul-Sep81-
    432
Satow, M. and R. Desmond. Railways of the
    Raj.*
    639(VQR):Autumn81-137
Satterfield, A. The Home Front.
    C. Kaiser, 441.21Feb82 20
Sauer, H., ed and trans. Theodulfi Capi-
    tula in England.*
    P. Bierbaumer, 38:Band99Heft1/2-221
Sauer, K. Anna Seghers.
    H.M.K. Riley, 133:Band14Heft3-273
Sauer, W., ed. The Metrical Life of
    Christ.*
    D. Pearsall, 72:Band217Heft1-190
Sauerland, K. Einführung in die Ästhetik
    Adornos.
    M.T. Jones, 221(GQ):May81-385
    P. Somville, 542:Jan-Mar81-125
Saul, N. Knights and Esquires.
    E. Miller, 617(TLS):22Jan82-70
Saumont, A. Dieu regarde et se tait.
    P.H. Solomon, 207(FR):May81-902
Saunders, A.C.D.M. A Social History of
    Black Slaves and Freedmen in Portugal
    1441-1555.
    C.R. Boxer, 617(TLS):15Oct82-1137
Saunders, P. Edward Jenner.
    D. Cannadine, 617(TLS):31Dec82-1439
Savage, C.W., ed. Perception and Cogni-
    tion.*
    G. Langford, 393(Mind):Jul81-471
Savage, E. Two if by Sea.
    N. Callendar, 441:12Sep82-38
Savage, P. Lorimer and the Edinburgh
    Craft Designers.*
    P. Davey, 46:Oct81-258

Savard, P. Aspects du catholicisme cana-
    dien-français au XIXe siècle.
    W.N., 102(CanL):Winter80-150
Savater, F. Childhood Regained.
    W.R. Katz, 150(DR):Winter81/82-754
von Savigny, E. Argumentation in der
    Literaturwissenschaft.
    D. Firmenich, 679:Band11Heft2-385
    H. Göttner, 494:Winter80/81-171
Savinio, A. Achille énamouré.
    S. Fáuchereau, 98:Dec80-1164
Savitch, J. Anchorwoman.
    T. Schwartz, 441:7Nov82-15
Savitzkaya, E. La traversée de l'Afrique.*
    L'empire. Mentir. Un jeune homme trop
    gros.
    C. Grivel, 98:May80-491
Saward, M. and D. Wilson, eds. Hymns for
    Today's Church.
    M. Trend, 617(TLS):26Nov82-1296
Sawin, M. Wolf Kahn.
    R. Bass, 55:Dec81-29
Sawyer, P. The New Theatre in Lincoln's
    Inn Fields.
    R. Leacroft, 611(TN):Vol135No2-93
    566:Autumn81-48
Sawyer, P.H., ed. Anglo-Saxon Charters II:
    Charters of Burton Abbey.
    J.L. Nelson, 325:Apr81-428
Sax, R., with D. Ricketts. Cooking Great
    Meals Every Day.
    M. Sheraton, 441:5Dec82 12
Saxo Grammaticus. The History of the
    Danes. (P. Fisher, trans; H.E. Davidson,
    ed)
    N. Wagner, 684(ZDA):Band110Heft4-147
Šaxovskaja, Z. V poiskax Nabokova.*
    V. Terras, 574(SEEJ):Summer81-98
Sayre, N. Running Time.
    F. Randall, 441:15Aug82-13
    J. Simon, 61:Apr82-103
Sayre, R.F. Thoreau and the American
    Indians.
    R.J. Schneider, 183(ESQ):Vol27No1-57
al-Sayyid-Marsot, A.L., ed. Society and
    Sexes in Medieval Islam.
    G.H.A. Juynboll, 294:Vol 12-161
Sbarbaro, C. La trama delle lucciole.
    (D. Astengo and F. Contorbia, eds)
    G. Tesio, 228(GSLI):Vol 157fasc499-462
Scammell, G.V. The World Encompassed.
    J.H. Parry, 617(TLS):29Jan82-103
Scammell, W. A Second Life.
    D. Davis, 362:16Dec82-23
Scannell, V. New and Collected Poems
    1950-1980.*
    T. Eagleton, 565:Vol22No4-74
Scannell, V. Winterlude.
    D. Davis, 362:6May82-26
    G. Szirtes, 617(TLS):15Oct82-1139
Scarce, J. Middle Eastern Costume from
    the Tribes and Cities of Iran and Turkey.
    R.L. Shep, 614:Summer82-17
Scarlett, J.D. How to Weave Fine Cloth.
    P. Bach, 614:Fall81-16
"La scena del principe."
    M. Pieri, 400(MLN):Jan81-178
Scenna, M.Á. Los militares.
    A. Ciria, 263(RIB):Vol31No2-284
Schaap, J.C. Sign of a Promise and Other
    Stories.*
    T.A. Lasansky, 649(WAL):Spring81-76

Schach, P., ed. Languages in Conflict.
S.G. Thomason, 350:Sep82-734
Schachten, W.H.J. Ordo salutis.
M. Müller, 489(PJGG):Band88Heft2-398
Schachter, F.F. Everyday Mother Talk to
Toddlers.
A.D. Pellegrini, 351(LL):Dec81-513
Schachtman, T. The Phony War.
D.J.R. Bruckner, 441:22Aug82-14
Schackne, R. The Parachuting Man.
G. Bitcon, 581:Dec81-469
Schade, R.E. and J. Glenn - see "Lessing
Yearbook 10"
Schaefer, A. Die Schopenhauer-Welt.
D. Johnson, 617(TLS):8Oct82-1115
Schaefer, J. The Canyon.
W. Gard, 584(SWR):Winter81-vii
Schaeffer, N. The Art of Laughter.
L. Mackinnon, 617(TLS):4Jun82-619
Schäfer, E. Deutscher Horaz.
G. Petersmann, 52:Band15Heft1-76
Schäfer, J. Documentation in the "O.E.D."
H. Käsmann, 38:Band99Heft3/4-463
Schäfer, W. Wirtschaftswörterbuch.
(Vol 1)
M. Burkhard, 301(JEGP):Jan81-80
Schakel, P.J. The Poetry of Jonathan
Swift.*
C. Perri, 599:Winter81-40
Schakel, P.J. Reading with the Heart.
J.J. Riley, 395(MFS):Winter80/81-698
Schalk, D.L. The Spectrum of Political
Engagement.*
S.R. Suleiman, 546(RR):Jan81-121
Schaller, M. The United States and China
in the Twentieth Century.
T.E. Lautz, 293(JASt):Nov80-119
Schank, R.C. and C.K. Riesbeck, eds. In-
side Computer Understanding.
J. Scancarelli, 350:Jun82-494
Schanz, G. Kommunikation im Unterricht.
H. Harnisch, 682(ZPSK):Band33Heft6-760
Schaper, E. Studies in Kant's Aesthetics.*
P. Guyer, 482(PhR):Jul81-429
M.A. McCloskey, 483:Apr81-262
D. Novitz, 63:Jun81-244
A. Savile, 89(BJA):Autumn81-363
Schäpers, R., R. Luscher and M. Glück.
Grundkurs Deutsch Lehrbuch.
G.G. Pfister, 399(MLJ):Autumn81-353
Schapiro, L. Turgenev.*
E. Kagan-Kans, 550(RusR):Apr81-219
Schapiro, L. and J. Godson, eds. The
Soviet Worker.
A. Pravda, 617(TLS):7May82-518
Schapiro, M. Late Antique, Early
Christian and Medieval Art.*
D. Buckton, 39:May81-340
G. Henderson, 90:Mar81-169
Schaps, D.M. Economic Rights of Women in
Ancient Greece.*
N.R.E. Fisher, 123:Vol31No1-72
D.M. MacDowell, 303(JoHS):Vol 101-188
Scharfstein, B-A. The Philosophers.
B.L., 185:Jul82-789
M. Midgley, 437:Spring81-251
483:Apr81-278
Scharfstein, B-A., and others. Philosophy
East/Philosophy West.*
M. Kroy, 63:Mar81-115
Scharnhorst, G. Horatio Alger, Jr.
F. Shuffelton, 26(ALR):Spring81-148
Schatzman, M. - see de Saint-Denys, H.

Schaub, T.H. Pynchon: The Voice of Ambi-
guity.
C. Ingraham, 400(MLN):Dec81-1254
P. Kemp, 617(TLS):26Feb82-220
Schecker, M. and P. Wunderli, eds. Text-
grammatik.
L. Lipka, 38:Band99Heft3/4-412
Scheer, R., with N. Zacchino and C. Mat-
thiessen. With Enough Shovels.
J. Klein, 441:28Nov82-7
S. Zuckerman, 453(NYRB):16Dec82-19
Schefer, J-L. L'homme ordinaire du
cinéma.
E. Michaud, 98:Dec81-1294
J. Prieur, 450(NRF):Feb81-150
Scheffler, I. Beyond the Letter.
G. Baker, 479(PhQ):Oct81-372
L.J. Cohen, 84:Mar81-95
S.R. Levin, 599:Fall81-492
C. Norris, 393(Mind):Jul81-448
G. Nunberg, 482(PhR):Jul81-467
R.A. Sharpe, 89(BJA):Spring81-183
Scheffler, S. The Rejection of Consequen-
tialism.
P. Foot, 617(TLS):5Nov82-1230
Scheffler, W. Goldschmiede Mittel- und
Nordostdeutschlands von Wernigerode bis
Lauenburg in Pommern.
G. Schiedlausky, 471:Jan/Feb/Mar81-95
Scheiber, A. - see Goldziher, I.
Scheicher, E. Die Kunst — und Wunder-
kammer der Habsburger.
J. Hayward, 90:Jun81-369
Scheick, W.J. The Half-Blood.*
J.L. Idol, Jr., 580(SCR):Fall80-102
A.L.B. Ruoff, 587(SAF):Spring81-130
Scheick, W.J. The Slender Human Word.*
J.S. Martin, 106:Fall81-209
E. Wagenknecht, 677(YES):Vol 11-318
Scheid, J. "Enfant terrible" of Contempor-
ary East German Drama.
R-E.B. Joeres, 400(MLN):Apr81-706
D. Sevin, 133:Band14Heft3-262
Scheier, C-A. Analytischer Kommentar zu
Hegels Phänomenologie des Geistes.
C.C., 227(GCFI):May-Aug81-268
Schein, S.L. The Iambic Trimeter in
Aeschylus and Sophocles.
T. Fleming, 121(CJ):Oct/Nov81-73
R. Seaford, 123:Vol31No1-108
Scheler, M. Problems of a Sociology of
Knowledge. (K.W. Stikkers, ed)
F. Dunlop, 323:Oct81-286
D.J. Levy, 396(ModA):Fall81-432
Schell, J. The Fate of the Earth.
T. Draper, 453(NYRB):15Jul82-35
K. Erikson, 441:11Apr82-3
M. Mason, 617(TLS):16Jul82-757
A. Ryan, 362:1Jul82-23
Schellekens, O., ed. Stendhal, le saint-
simonisme et les industriels.
Y. Ansel, 535(RHL):May-Jun81-468
J-J. Hamm, 446(NCFS):Fall-Winter81/82-
135
Schelling, F.W.J. Oeuvres métaphysiques
(1805-1821). (J-F. Courtine and E. Mar-
tineau, eds and trans)
J-M. Gabaude, 542:Oct-Dec81-495
J-M. Monnoyer, 450(NRF):Feb81-110
Schelling, F.W.J. The Unconditional in
Human Knowledge. (F. Marti, ed and
trans)
W. Schwarz, 484(PPR):Dec81-297

Schenker, H. Free Composition.* (E.
Oster, ed and trans)
   W.E. Benjamin, 308:Spring81-155
   D. Epstein, 308:Spring81-143
   R. Evans, 607:Mar81-37
   R. Kamien, 414(MusQ):Jan81-113
   C.E. Schachter, 308:Spring81-115
Schenker, W. Sprachliche Manieren.
   G. Lerchner, 682(ZPSK):Band33Heft6-762
Schenkowitz, G. Der Inhalt sowjetrussis-
cher Vorlesestoffe für Vorschulkinder.
   R. Alsheimer, 196:Band21Heft1/2-149
Scheper-Hughes, N. Saints, Scholars, and
Schizophrenics.
   D.H. Akenson, 529(QQ):Autumn81-490
Scherer, K.R. and H. Giles, eds. Social
Markers in Speech.
   E.B. Ryan and J.T. Cacioppo, 355(LSoc):
   Dec81-443
Schesaeus, C. Opera quae supersunt omnia.
(F. Csonka, ed)
   M.D. Birnbaum, 551(RenQ):Autumn80-422
Scheurer, P. Révolutions de la science et
permanence du réel.
   Y. Gauthier, 154:Dec81-815
Schiavone de Cruz-Sáenz, M. The Life of
Saint Mary of Egypt.
   B. Cazelles, 207(FR):May81-863
   B. Dutton, 589:Jul81-667
Schickel, R. Singled Out.*
   A. Hacker, 453(NYRB):18Mar82-37
Schiddel, E. Bad Boy.
   R. Miner, 441:8Aug82-13
Schiffhorst, G.J., ed. The Triumph of
Patience.ʌ
   W.A. McQueen, 577(SHR):Winter81-74
   J. Mulryan, 551(RenQ):Spring80-133
   C. von Nolcken, 541(RES):Aug81-312
Schiffman, H. A Grammar of Spoken Tamil.
   D.W. McAlpin, 293(JASt):Nov80-183
Schifko, P. Bedeutungstheorie — Einfüh-
rung in die linguistische Semantik.
   C.F. Meier, 682(ZPSK):Band33Heft5-619
Schild, U., ed and trans. Märchen aus
Papua-Neuguinea.
   E. Ettlinger, 203:Vol191No2-247
Schildkrout, E. People of the Zongo.
   J. Eades, 69:Vol150No4-447
Schildt, J., ed. Erbe — Vermächtnis und
Verpflichtung.
   K. Welke, 682(ZPSK):Band33Heft5-595
Schildt, J., ed. Zum Einfluss vom Marx
und Engels auf die deutsche Literatur-
sprache.
   H. Langner, 682(ZPSK):Band33Heft6-772
Schiller, F. Mary Stuart. (S. Spender,
ed and trans)
   V.A. Rudowski, 580(SCR):Fall81-130
Schiller, F. The Robbers; Wallenstein.
(F.J. Lamport, trans)
   H. Lederer, 399(MLJ):Summer81-234
Schilling, M. Imagines Mundi.
   K. Haberkamm, 684(ZDA):Band110Heft1-51
   D. Sulzer, 196:Band22Heft1/2-155
Schilling, R. Rites, cultes, dieux de
Rome.*
   P. Jal, 555:Vol54fasc1-192
Schilpp, P.A., ed. The Philosophy of
Brand Blanshard.
   W.W., 185:Jul82-804
Schimmel, A. As Through a Veil.
   P. Avery, 617(TLS):10Sep82-964

Schings, H-J. Der mitleidigste Mensch ist
der beste Mensch.
   S.D. Martinson, 221(GQ):May81-345
Schinkel, K.F. Lebenswerk: Das Architek-
tonische Lehrbuch. (G. Peschken, ed)
   E. Forssman, 683:Band43Heft3-340
Schirmacher, W. Ereignis Technik.
   W. Strombach, 489(PJGG):Band88Heft1-
   194
Schirmer, L. Avantgardistische und tradi-
tionelle Aspekte im Theater von Eugène
Ionesco.
   A. Meech, 610:Winter80/81-79
Schirmer, W. - see Valdenaire, A.
Schlack, B.A. Continuing Presences.*
   J. Gindin, 301(JEGP):Jan81-151
   E.B. Tenenbaum, 395(MFS):Summer80-290
Schlant, E. Hermann Broch.*
   P.M. Lützeler, 406:Winter81-479
Schlegel, L. Arans.
   P. Bach, 614:Winter81-21
Schlegel, S.A. Tiruray Subsistence.*
   R.D. Hill, 302:Vol 18-182
Schleifer, J.T. The Making of Tocque-
ville's "Democracy in America."*
   H.A. Tulloch, 366:Autumn81-244
Schleifer, R., ed. The Genres of the
Irish Literary Revival.*
   R. Boyle, 329(JJQ):Winter81-209
Schlenker, W. Das kulturelle Erbe in der
DDR.
   W. Karger, 654(WB):1/1981-152
Schlenstedt, D. Wirkungsästhetische Ana-
lysen.
   J. Pischel, 654(WB):3/1981-167
Schlereth, T. The Cosmopolitan Ideal in
Enlightenment Thought.*
   H.C. Payne, 173(ECS):Spring81-357
Schlesinger, S. and S. Kinzer. Bitter
Fruit.
   L. Bushkoff, 617(TLS):17Dec82-1391
   W. Hoge, 441:7Mar82-3
   442(NY):3May82-168
Schleucher, K. Das Leben der Amalia
Schoppe und Johanna Schopenhauer.
   I.C. Taylor, 221(GQ):Mar81-226
Schlosser, K. Die Bantubibel des Blitz-
zauberers Laduma Madela.
   T.O. Beidelman, 69:Vol150No1-104
Schluck, M. Die Vita Heinrici IV.
   K.F. Morrison, 589:Apr81-462
Schlütter, H-J., R. Borgmeier and H.W.
Wittschier. Sonett.
   W.E. Yates, 402(MLR):Jan81-237
Schmalstieg, W.R. Indo-European Linguis-
tics.
   W.P. Lehmann, 215(GL):Fall81-220
Schmalstieg, W.R. An Old Prussian Grammar.
Studies in Old Prussian.
   W.P. Schmid, 260(IF):Band85-385
Schmalstieg, W.R. and T.F. Magner, eds.
Sociolinguistic Problems in Czechoslo-
vakia, Hungary, Romania and Yugoslavia.
   H. Birnbaum, 350:Mar81-240
Schmeisky, G. Die Lyrik-Handschriften
m (Berlin, MS. germ. qu. 795) und n
(Leipzig, Rep. II fol. 70a).
   O. Sayce, 402(MLR):Apr81-500
Schmeling, G.L. Xenophon of Ephesus.
   A.M. Scarcella, 24:Winter81-450
Schmid, A. Die romanischen Orts- und
Flurnamen im Raume Landeck.
   E. Kühebacher, 685(ZDL):1/1981-111

Schmid, C.C.E. Wörterbuch zum leichtern
Gebrauch der Kantischen Schriften. (N.
Hinske, ed)
   R. Malter, 342:Band71Heft4-508
Schmid, K. and others, eds. Die Kloster-
gemeinschaft von Fulda im früheren
Mittelalter. (Vols 1-3)
   P.J. Geary, 589:Apr81-432
Schmidgall, G. Shakespeare and the
Courtly Aesthetic.
   P. Taylor, 617(TLS):5Mar82-266
Schmidlin, Y. - see Bürgin, H. and H-O.
Mayer
Schmidt, A.V.C. - see Langland, W.
Schmidt, A.V.C. and N. Jacobs, eds. Medie-
val English Romances.*
   P.M. Kean, 382(MAE):1981/2-342
Schmidt, C. Marcel Proust.
   H. Mehnert, 72:Band217Heft2-478
Schmidt, G. England in der Krise.
   P. Kennedy, 617(TLS):28May82-585
Schmidt, H. Heinrich von Kleist.
   M.M. Tatar, 406:Winter81-461
Schmidt, H.M. Der Meister des Marien-
lebens und sein Kreis.
   G. Goldberg, 471:Jan/Feb/Mar81-93
Schmidt, J. Hölderlins später Widerruf in
den Oden "Chiron," "Blödigkeit" und
"Ganymed."*
   B. Bjorklund, 406:Fall81-353
Schmidt, L. Das alte Volksschauspiel des
Burgenlandes. Zunftzeichen.
   E. Ettlinger, 203:Vol92No2-256
Schmidt, L., ed. Wortfeldforschung.
   M. Gorlach, 72:Band217Heft1-151
Schmidt, M. Green Island.
   442(NY):4Oct82-146
Schmidt, M. A Reader's Guide to Fifty
British Poets 1300-1900.
   636(VP):Summer81-203
Schmidt, M. - see Sisson, C.H.
Schmidt, P., ed. Meyerhold at Work.*
   H. Robinson, 574(SEEJ):Winter81-99
   J. Russell, 453(NYRB):15Jul82-3
Schmidt, S.J. Literaturwissenschaft als
argumentierende Wissenschaft.
   H. Göttner, 494:Winter80/81-171
Schmidt, W. and F.A. Schmidt-Künsemüller,
eds. Johannes Gutenbergs zweiundvierzig-
zeilige Bibel. [Kommentarband]
   J.E. Walsh, 517(PBSA):Jan-Mar81-107
Schmidt-Dengler, W. Genius.*
   L.E. Kurth-Voigt, 400(MLN):Apr81-708
Schmidt-Schweda, D. Werden und Wirken des
Kunstwerks.
   G. Merks-Leinen, 53(AGP):Band62Heft1-
113
Schmithausen, L. - see Hacker, P.
Schmitt, J-C. Le Saint lévrier.*
   R. Schenda, 196:Band21Heft1/2-152
Schmölders, C., ed. Die Kunst des
Gesprachs.
   R. Zeller, 52:Band15Heft3-315
Schmoller, H. - see Mardersteig, G.
Schnack, A. Animaux et paysages dans la
description des personnages romanesques
(1800-1845).
   M.E. Birkett, 466(NCFS):Spring-Sum-
mer81-259
Schnapper, A. David — Témoin de son temps.
   F. Haskell, 90:Dec81-749

Schneewind, J.B. Sidgwick's Ethics and
Victorian Moral Philosophy.*
   D.F. Koch, 319:Apr81-266
Schneider, B.R., Jr., comp. Index to The
London Stage, 1660-1800.*
   E.A. Langhans, 173(ECS):Fall80-72
Schneider, F. Momentaufnahme.
   K. Mehner, 654(WB):11/1981-156
Schneider, G. Geometrische Bauornamente
der Seldschuken in Kleinasien.
   C. Ewert, 43:Band11Heft2-183
Schneider, J.M. Clown at the Altar.*
   S.J. Collier, 208(FS):Jul81-358
Schneider, M. Blessures de mémoire.*
   J. le Hardi, 450(NRF):Jan81-144
Schneider, N. The Woman Who Lived in a
Prologue.*
   S. Scott-Fleming, 436(NewL):Fall81-124
Schneider, P. Der Mauerspringer.
   C. Russ, 617(TLS):30Jul82-814
Schnell, R. Zum Verhältnis von hoch- und
spätmittelalterlicher Literatur.*
   S.L. Wailes, 589:Jan81-221
Schnitzler, A. Berthe Garlan.
   L. Arénilla, 450(NRF):Oct81-163
Schnitzler, A. The Letters of Arthur
Schnitzler to Hermann Bahr. (D.G.
Daviau, ed)
   W. Schmitz, 72:Band217Heft1-182
Schnitzler, A. Tagebuch 1909-1912. (W.
Welzig and others, eds)
   E. Timms, 617(TLS):30Apr82-475
Schnitzler, A. and O. Brahm. Der Brief-
wechsel Arthur Schnitzler-Otto Brahm.
(O. Seidlin, ed)
   W. Schmitz, 72:Band217Heft1-182
Schnitzler, H., C. Brandstatter and R.
Urbach, eds. Arthur Schnitzler.
   E. Timms, 617(TLS):30Apr82-475
Schnyder, A., ed. Biterolf und Dietleib.
   R.H. Firestone, 133:Band14Heft4-357
Schnyder, H. Die Gründung des Klosters
Luzern.
   J.M. McCulloh, 589:Apr81-435
Schobinger, J-P. Kommentar zu Pascals
Reflexionen über Geometrie im Allge-
meinen
   J. Bernhardt, 542:Jul-Sep81-355
Schobinger, J-P. Variationen zu Walter
Benjamins Sprachmeditationen.
   P. Missac, 98:Apr80-370
Schöck, I. Hexenglaube in der Gegenwart.
   E. Tucker, 292(JAF):Jan-Mar81-99
Schoenbaum, S. William Shakespeare:
Records and Images.*
   D. Bevington, 405(MP):May82-429
Schoenbaum, S. Shakespeare: The Globe and
the World.
   W. Blissett, 551(RenQ):Winter80-807
   M. Grivelet, 189(EA):Jul-Sep81-336
Schoenberg, A. Theory of Harmony.*
   R.W. Wason, 308:Fall81-307
Schoenbrun, D. Soldiers of the Night.
   F. Russell, 396(ModA):Fall81-420
Schoendoerffer, P. Là-Haut.
   P.A. Mankin, 207(FR):May82-928
Schofield, M. An Essay on Anaxagoras.
   D. Babut, 542:Apr-Jun81-259
   S.U., 543:Jun81-806
   M.R. Wright, 123:Vol31No1-55
Schofield, M., M. Burnyeat and J. Barnes,
eds. Doubt and Dogmatism.
   W. Charlton, 483:Apr81-275

Scholberg, K.R. Algunos aspectos de la
sátira en el siglo XVI.
J. Lihani, 238:Mar81-154
Scholberg, K.R. and D.E. Aquí Mismo.
D.N. Flemming, 399(MLJ):Autumn81-342
Scholder, K. Die Kirchen und das Dritte
Reich. (Vol 1)
W.R. Ward, 161(DUJ):Dec80-104
Scholem, G. Walter Benjamin.*
A.A. Cohen, 441:16May82-12
Schöler-Beinhauer, M., ed and trans. Le
Roman d'Eneas.
R. Blumenfeld-Kosinski, 545(RPh):
Feb81(supp)-291
Scholes, R. Fabulation and Metafiction.*
M. Groden, 395(MFS):Summer80-377
S. Trombley, 541(RES):Aug81-365
Scholes, R. Semiotics and Interpretation.
T. Hawkes, 617(TLS):15Oct82-1140
Scholl, S.J., A.E. Bianco and D. Vigo-Glod.
A Quattr'occhi.*
G. Jackson, 399(MLJ):Autumn81-346
Schonberg, H. Facing the Music.
W. Bolcom, 385(MQR):Summer82-511
Schöndörffer, O. - see Kant, I.
Schöne, A. Götterzeichen, Liebeszauber,
Satanskult.
S.S. Prawer, 617(TLS):5Nov82-1221
Schöne, A., ed. Stadt — Schule — Univer-
sität — Buchwesen und die deutsche Lit-
eratur im 17. Jahrhundert.*
D. Peil, 224(GRM):Band30Heft3-358
Schoolfield, G. Janus Secundus.
L.V.R., 568(SCN):Summer-Fall81-80
Schoonhoven, H. Elegiae in Maecenatem.
M.D. Reeve, 123:Vol31No2-204
Schoonover, H.S. The Humorous and Gro-
tesque Elements in Döblin's Berlin Alex-
anderplatz.
M.S. Fries, 221(GQ):Jan81-108
Schopenhauer, A. Gesammelte Briefe. (A.
Hübscher, ed)
H. Oberer, 53(AGP):Band62Heft3-344
Schor, N. Zola's Crowds.*
W.J. Berg, 125:Winter81-226
F.P. Bowman, 399(MLJ):Spring81-94
R.T. Denommé, 400(MLN):Dec81-1264
C.B. Jennings, 627(UTQ):Spring81-323
Schorske, C.E. Fin-de-Siècle Vienna.*
J.B. Berlin, 221(GQ):May81-369
A. Comini, 54:Sep81-521
R. Harper, 396(ModA):Fall81-422
L. Kramer, 451:Summer81-76
P. Loewenberg, 473(PR):3/1981-463
P-Y. Petillon, 98:Nov80-1017
Schott, M. Up Where I Used to Live.
P. Lewis, 565:Vol22No1-60
Schouls, P.A. The Imposition of Method.*
D. Judovitz, 400(MLN):May81-916
E. Matthews, 518:Apr81-91
Schrag, C.O. Radical Reflection and the
Origin of the Human Sciences.
J.B., 543:Mar81-618
S. Glynn, 323:Oct81-285
J.D. Moon, 185:Jan82-351
Schramm, E. and L. Schmidt. Übungen zur
deutschen Aussprache.
U. Stötzer, 682(ZPSK):Band33Heft2-280
Schramm, P.E. and H. Fillitz. Denkmale
der deutschen Könige und Kaiser. (Vol 2)
G. Schmidt, 683:Band43Heft4-408

Schreiber, W. Zwischen Schwaben und
Schweiz.
T. Steiner, 685(ZDL):1/1981-82
Schreiner, O. From Man to Man.
P. Craig, 617(TLS):26Nov82-1318
Schrier, A. and J. Story - see Lakier, A.B.
"Schriften der Theodor-Storm-Gesellschaft."
(Vol 28) (K-E. Laage and V. Hand, eds)
A.T. Alt, 221(GQ):Mar81-234
Schröder, W. Die Exzerpte aus Wolframs
"Willehalm" in sekundärer Überlieferung.
H. Kratz, 133:Band14Heft4-355
Schröder, W. Der tragische Roman von
Willehalm und Gyburg.
S.M. Johnson, 406:Winter81-448
J.W. Thomas, 133:Band14Heft4-356
Schröder, W. - see Wolfram von Eschenbach
Schröder, W. - see "Wolfram-Studien V"
Schröder, W.H. Arbeitergeschichte und
Arbeiterbewegung.
I. Dietrich, 654(WB):7/1981-184
Schröter, K. Alfred Döblin in Selbstzeug-
nissen und Bilddokumenten dargestellt.
M.S. Fries, 406:Summer81-242
Schubel, F. Probleme der Beowulf-
Forschung.
K. Ostheeren, 196:Band21Heft3/4-340
Schubert, F. Sprachstruktur und Rechts-
funktion.
E. Schrader-Gentry, 406:Summer81-229
Schubiger, M. Einführung in die Phonetik.
(2nd ed)
B. Carstensen, 685(ZDL):1/1981-96
A. Liberman, 353:Vol 18No7/8-737
Schuchardt, H. The Ethnography of Varia-
tion. (T.L. Markey, ed and trans)
M.R. Key, 350:Sep81-777
E. Woolford, 355(LSoc):Apr81-128
Schuchardt, H. Pidgin and Creole Lan-
guages. (G.G. Gilbert, ed and trans)
M.R. Key, 350:Sep81-777
Schueler, D.G. Incident at Eagle Ranch.
P.T. Bryant, 649(WAL):Summer81-150
Schug, C. The Romantic Genesis of the
Modern Novel.*
K. Cushman, 594:Fall81-337
L. Thornton, 395(MF3):Winter80/81-722
Schuh, W. Richard Strauss: A Chronicle of
the Early Years.
H. Cole, 362:11Nov82-25
Schuhmacher, K. "Weil es geschehen ist."
I.M. Goessl, 221(GQ):Mar81-242
W. Schmitz, 72:Band217Heft1-187
Schulberg, B. Moving Pictures.*
J. Beaver, 200:Dec81-635
Schull, J. Ontario Since 1867.
G.W., 102(CanL):Spring80-150
Schuller, T. and J. Megarry, eds. Recur-
rent Education and Lifelong Learning.
B. Luckham, 437:Winter80/81-142
Schulman, G. and A.M. de Zavala - see
Cuadra, P.A.
Schultheis, R. The Hidden West.
J. Haskins, 441:13Jun82-16
442(NY):12Jul82-104
Schultz, D. Hero of Bataan.
D.J.R. Bruckner, 441:24Jan82-14
Schultz, K. and S. Kohler, eds. Richard
Strauss: "Feuersnot."
J.B. Robinson, 415:Feb81-109
Schultz, P. Like Wings.
K. Warren, 577(SHR):Summer81-269

Schultz, T.W., ed. Distortions of Agri-
cultural Incentives.
  B. Ward, 293(JASt):Feb81-335
Schultze, S. - see Rudnitsky, K.
Schulz, G. and U. - see Lessing, G.E.
Schulz, G-M. Negativität in der Dichtung
Paul Celans.
  M.J. Meyerhofer, 406:Summer81-245
Schulz-Behrend, G. - see Opitz, M.
Schumacher, J.N., ed. Readings in Philip-
pine Church History.
  D.R. Sturtevant, 293(JASt):Feb81-432
Schumacher, R. Untersuchungen zum
Absolutiv im modernen Hindi.
  M.H. Klaiman, 361:May81-87
Schuman, S. Vladimir Nabokov.*
  P. Tammi, 439(NM):1981/4-479
Schumann, O. and B. Bischoff - see "Latein-
isches Hexameter-Lexikon"
Schunck, F. Joseph Conrad.
  R. Davis, 395(MFS):Summer80-299
Schupp, V. Studien zu Williram von Ebers-
berg.*
  P. Godman, 382(MAE):1981/1-113
Schur, N.W. English, English.* (2nd ed)
  K.B. Harder, 424:Sep81-252
Schurhammer, G. Francis Xavier. (Vol 4)
(M.J. Costelloe, ed and trans)
  C.R. Boxer, 617(TLS):1Oct82-1081
Schurman, D.M. Julian S. Corbett 1854-
1922.
  B. Ranft, 617(TLS):16Apr82-428
Schurr, G. Le guidargus de la peinture.
  J.P., 98:Oct80-1014
Schutz, A. Life Forms and Meaning Struc-
ture. (H.R. Wagner, ed and trans)
  Z. Bauman, 617(TLS):19Nov82-1283
Schütz, H. Gesprochenes und geschriebenes
Französisch.
  R.E. Wood, 207(FR):Mar81-638
Schütz, H. Julia oder Erziehung zum Chor-
gesang.
  C. Berger, 654(WB):10/1981-144
Schütz-Güth, G. and H. Schütz. Typen des
britischen Arbeiterromans.
  H.G. Klaus, 224(GRM):Band31Heft1-121
Schütze, F. Sprache soziologisch gesehen.
Interaktionsfreiheit und Zwangskommunika-
tion.
  E.W.B. Hess-Lüttich, 680(ZDP):Band100
Heft3-468
Schützeichel, R., ed. Studien zur deuts-
chen Literatur des Mittelalters.
  H. Kratz, 133:Band14Heft4-352
Schuurman, E. Technology and the Future.
  M.A.K., 185:Jan82-389
Schüwer, H. Wortgeographische und etymol-
ogische Untersuchungen zur Terminologie
des Ackerwagens.
  D. Stellmacher, 260(IF):Band85-383
Schuyler, J. The Morning of the Poem.*
  R. von Hallberg, 659(ConL):Spring82-
225
Schwab, P. Haile Selassie I.
  R. Pankhurst, 69:Vol50No2-214
Schwartz, A., ed. When I Grew Up Long Ago.
  C.E. Martin, 292(JAF):Jan-Mar81-123
Schwartz, B. Vertical Classification.
  K.S., 185:Jul82-800
Schwartz, D. Last and Lost Poems of Del-
more Schwartz. (R. Phillips, ed)
  R. Dana, 436(NewL):Fall81-116

Schwartz, J. and others. Papyrus grecs de
la Bibliothèque nationale et universi-
taire de Strasbourg, nos. 681-700.
  R. Coles, 123:Vol31No1-143
Schwartz, L.S. Balancing Acts.
  M. Hofmann, 617(TLS):12Mar82-277
Schwartz, M. Realities.
  A. Hopkin, 617(TLS):18Jun82-676
Schwartz, N. Hamlet i klasskampen.
  M. Setterwall, 563(SS):Winter81-122
Schwartz, N.L., with S. Schwartz. The
Hollywood Writers' War.
  J.A. Lukas, 441:14Feb82-12
Schwartz, R. Nomads, Exiles, and Emigres.
  J. Hancock, 238:Dec81-644
Schwartz, R. - see Weimann, R.
Schwartz, R.B. Boswell's Johnson.*
  R. Folkenflik, 677(YES):Vol 11-284
  A. Pailler, 189(EA):Jan-Mar81-94
Schwartz, S. The Art Presence.
  442(NY):8Nov82-172
Schwartz, S., ed. Language and Cognition
in Schizophrenia.
  R.T. Lakoff, 567:Vol34No3/4-355
Schwartzberg, J.E., with others, eds. A
Historical Atlas of South Asia.
  N.G. Barrier, 293(JASt):May81-535
  R.J. Cohen, 293(JASt):May81-532
  F.F. Conlon, 293(JASt):May81-525
  M.D. Morris, 293(JASt):May81-536
  R. Murphey, 293(JASt):May81-528
  G.L. Possehl, 293(JASt):May81-530
  J.F. Richards, 293(JASt):May81-533
Schwarz, A. From Büchner to Beckett.
  S. Williams, 107(CRCL):Winter81-134
Schwarz, C. Der nicht-nominale ment-
Ausdruck im Französischen.
  L. Bauer, 209(FM):Jan81-77
Schwarz, D.R. Conrad: "Almayer's Folly"
to "Under Western Eyes."*
  S. Raval, 594:Winter81-439
  R. Roussel, 445(NCF):Sep81-249
  295(JML):Vol18No3/4-470
Schwarz, D.R. Disraeli's Fiction.*
  445(NCF):Dec81-381
Schwarz, H. Johann Nestroy im Bild. (J.
Hüttner and O.G. Schindler, eds)
  A. Obermayer, 67:Nov81-269
Schwarzbach, F.S. Dickens and the City.*
  A. Fleishman, 445(NCF):Jun80-105
Schwarzkopf, E. On and Off the Record.
  D. Hamilton, 453(NYRB):13May82-37
  442(NY):28Jun82-119
Schwedhelm, K., ed. John Henry Mackay.
  D. Barnouw, 221(GQ):Nov81-518
  E. Mornin, 133:Band14Heft3-283
Schwertheim, E., ed. Die Inschriften von
Kyzikos und Umgebung. (Pt 1)
  J.H. Oliver, 24:Spring81-113
Schwinzer, E. Schwebende Gruppen in der
pompejanischen Wandmalerei.
  R. Ling, 313:Vol71-212
Schwob, A. Historische Realität und
literarische Umsetzung.
  J. Goheen, 133:Band14Heft4-359
  G.F. Jones, 589:Jan81-195
  W. Röll, 684(ZDA):Band109Heft4-164
Schwob, M. Chroniques. (J.A. Green, ed)
The King in the Golden Mask and Other
Writings. (I. White, ed)
  P. Fawcett, 617(TLS):8Oct82-1096

Schwoerer, L.G. The Declaration of Rights, 1689.
K.H.D. Haley, 617(TLS):30Apr82-480
Schyfter, S.E. The Jew in the Novels of Benito Pérez Galdós.*
V.A. Chamberlin, 240(HR):Spring81-247
E. Rodgers, 402(MLR):Jan81-225
Sciascia, L. Candido.
K.C. O'Brien, 362:25Mar82-27
"Scientific and Technological Innovations."
I.D. Chapman, 298:Summer81-119
Scobbie, I., ed. Essays on Swedish Literature.
S.P. Sondrup, 563(SS):Autumn81-501
E. Törnqvist, 562(Scan):Nov81-230
Scobey, J., ed. The Michael Field Egg Cookbook.
W. and C. Cowen, 639(VQR):Spring81-72
Scobie, S. Leonard Cohen.*
L. McMullen, 102(CanL):Winter80-118
Scodel, R. The Trojan Trilogy of Euripides.
J. Diggle, 123:Vol31No1-106
Scofield, M. The Ghosts of "Hamlet."
M. Dodsworth, 617(TLS):1Jan82-10
G.F. Parker, 184(EIC):Oct81-346
Scollon, R. Conversations With a One Year Old.
B. Kraft, 682(ZPSK):Band33Heft6-780
Scoones, S. Les noms de quelques officiers féodaux.
U. Ricken, 682(ZPSK):Band33Heft2-281
Scorza, T.J. In the Time Before Steamships.*
T. Philbrick, 445(NCF):Sep80-241
Scott, A., ed. Modern Scots Verse 1922-1977.
R. Watson, 571(ScLJ):Summer80-122
Scott, C. French Verse-Art.*
R. Buss, 402(MLR):Oct81-953
M. Cranston, 207(FR):Oct81-130
I. Higgins, 205(FMLS):Oct81-361
Scott, D.H. Chinese Popular Literature and the Child.
P. Link, 293(JASt):May81-590
Scott, E. Background in Tennessee.
P. Bach, 435:Summer81-209
Scott, F.R. The Collected Poems of F.R. Scott.
F.W. Watt, 99:Mar82-32
Scott, G. The Architecture of Humanism.
J. Lees-Milne, 39:Apr81-267
Scott, H. Operation 10.
J. Astor, 362:8Apr82-23
K. Jeffery, 617(TLS):16Apr82-446
Scott, J.A. Dante Magnanimo.
A. Scaglione, 545(RPh):Feb81(supp)-32
Scott, J.S. An Uprush of Mayhem.
N. Callendar, 441:10Oct82-22
Scott, K.W. Zane Grey.
G. Topping, 649(WAL):Summer81-145
Scott, M. Late Gothic Europe, 1400-1500.
J. Gardner, 39:Jul81-65
Scott, M. John Marston's Plays.*
W.D. Lehrman, 568(SCN):Summer-Fall81-47
M.R. Woodhead, 447(N&Q):Oct80-438
Scott, M. Mauriac.
J. Forbes, 208(FS):Jul81-359
Scott, M. Renaissance Drama and a Modern Audience.
I. Salusinszky, 617(TLS):3Dec82-1347

Scott, P.H. Walter Scott and Scotland.
C. Lamont, 617(TLS):13Aug82-890
Scott, P.H. 1707: The Union of Scotland and England.*
R. Mitchison, 571(ScLJ):Summer80-93
Scott, P.H. and A.C. Davis, eds. The Age of MacDiarmid.*
R. Huff, 134(CP):Spring81-102
Scott, P.J.M. Reality and Comic Confidence in Charles Dickens.*
S. Monod, 402(MLR):Jan81-171
Scott, R.B. Cancer.
E.A. Clarke, 529(QQ):Summer81-376
Scott, R.I. - see Jeffers, R.
Scott, R.M. Robert the Bruce.
C. Bingham, 617(TLS):17Sep82-1015
Scott, W. The Prefaces to the Waverley Novels.* (M.A. Weinstein, ed)
P.H. Sosnoski, 125:Winter81-228
G.A.M. Wood, 447(N&Q):Oct80-454
Scott, W. Waverley. (C. Lamont, ed)
A. Welsh, 445(NCF):Dec81-358
Scovell, B. Ken Barrington.
T.D. Smith, 617(TLS):27Aug82-929
Scovell, E.J. The Space Between.
D. Davis, 362:16Dec82-23
P. Scupham, 617(TLS):29Oct82-1200
Scranton, R., J.W. Shaw and L. Ibrahim. Kenchreai.* (Vol 1)
E.K. Gazda, 54:Jun81-316
Screech, M.A. Rabelais.*
D.G. Coleman, 208(FS):Jan81-67
J.C. Nash, 188(ECr):Spring81-106
S. Rendall, 400(MLN):May81-921
J-C. Seigneuret, 399(MLJ):Winter81-426
Scrimgeour, G.J. A Woman of Her Times.
J. Moody, 617(TLS):9Apr82-422
Scrimgeour, J.R. Sean O'Casey.
M.G. Rose, 130:Spring81-94
Scruton, R. The Aesthetics of Architecture.*
A. Gomme, 437:Spring81 254
A. Jackson, 529(QQ):Spring81-155
M. McMordie, 576:Mar81-85
C.F. Otto, 127:Fall/Winter80-423
Scruton, R. From Descartes to Wittgenstein.
J. Passmore, 617(TLS):19Feb82-182
Scruton, R. Kant.
A. Ryan, 362:18Mar82-21
Scruton, R. The Meaning of Conservatism.*
D. Wells, 63:Dec81-459
Scull, A., ed. Madhouses, Mad-Doctors and Madmen.
R. Brown, 617(TLS):8Jan82-23
L. Stone, 453(NYRB):16Dec82-28
Scullard, H.H. A History of the Roman World 753 to 146 B.C. (4th ed)
D.L. Stockton, 123:Vol31No2-312
Scullard, H.H. - see MacDowell, D.M.
Scully, J. May Day.
P. Schjeldahl, 472:Spring/Summer81-284
Scully, T. - see Mahieu le Poirier
Scully, V. The Earth, The Temple, and the Gods. (rev)
J.P. Hodin, 89(BJA):Winter81-90
Scupham, P. Summer Palaces.
V. Young, 249(HudR):Spring81-142
Scura, D.M. Henry James 1960-1974.*
A.W. Bellringer, 677(YES):Vol 11-339

Seaborg, G.T., with B.S. Loeb. Kennedy,
Khrushchev and the Test Ban.
  K. Kyle, 362:24Jun82-23
  J.S. Nye, Jr., 441:28Feb82-11
Seabrook, J. Unemployment.
  P. Willmott, 617(TLS):28May82-576
Seabrook, J. Working Class Childhood.
  N. Roberts, 617(TLS):12Nov82-1240
Seager, R. Pompey.*
  A.J. Marshall, 487:Fall81-281
Seale, W. The Tasteful Interlude. (rev)
  R.L. Shep, 614:Summer81-22
Sealts, M.M., Jr. Pursuing Melville
1940-1980.
  H. Beaver, 617(TLS):17Sep82-1013
Searle, E., ed and trans. The Chronicle
of Battle Abbey.
  M. Brett, 382(MAE):1981/2-319
Searle, J.R. Expression and Meaning.*
  N. Fotion, 355(LSoc):Apr81-114
  J. Heal, 483:Apr81-270
Searle, M.V. John Ireland.
  C. Palmer, 415:May81-314
Sears, J.N. The First One Hundred Years
of Town Planning in Georgia.
  F.D. Nichols, 656(WMQ):Oct81-746
Seay, A. - see de Podio, G.
Seay, A. - see "Tractatus de discantu (Con-
cerning Discant)"
Sebastián, S. Iconografía e iconología en
el arte de Aragón.
  D. Angulo Íñiguez, 48:Jul-Sep81-374
Sebold, R.P. - see de Iriarte, T.
Secrest, M. Being Bernard Berenson.*
  M. Goldstein, 569(SR):Spring81-287
  P. Mauriès, 98:Jun-Jul80-580
  W.M. Owen, 90:May81-317
Sedgwick, J. Night Vision.
  E. Hunter, 441:7Nov82-14
Sedgwick, P. Psycho Politics.
  C. Gordon, 617(TLS):16Jul82-773
Sedlar, J.W. India and the Greek World.
  E.W. Gray, 123:Vol31No2-233
See, C. Rhine Maidens.*
  H.S. Arnow, 385(MQR):Fall82-674
von See, K., ed. Europäische Heldendich-
tung.*
  M. Bošković-Stulli, 196:Band21Heft1/2-
154
  J. Heinzle, 684(ZDA):Band109Heft1-1
von See, K. Skaldendichtung.
  K. Düwel, 196:Band22Heft3/4-368
Seebohm, C. The Man Who Was Vogue.
  P-L. Adams, 61:Jul82-96
  C. Curtis, 441:20Jun82-3
  N. von Hoffman, 617(TLS):1Oct82-1056
  C. Sigal, 362:9Sep82-23
  442(NY):31May82-107
Seeck, G.A., ed. Die Naturphilosophie des
Aristoteles.
  A. Preus, 53(AGP):Band63Heft1-83
Seelbach, D. Transformationsregeln im
Französischen aus der Sicht der histor-
ischen und romanischen Syntax.
  N.C.W. Spence, 208(FS):Oct81-500
Seelig, S.C. The Shadow of Eternity.
  R. Selden, 617(TLS):19Mar82-324
Seelig, W. Wille, Vorstellung und Wirk-
lichkeit.
  R. Kroczek, 679:Band12Heft2-403
Segal, C. Poetry and Myth in Ancient
Pastoral.
  J. Griffin, 617(TLS):2Apr82-374

Segal, C. Tragedy and Civilization.
  P.E. Easterling, 617(TLS):2Apr82-374
  J.E. Rexine, 124:May-Jun82-307
Segel, H.B. Twentieth-Century Russian
Drama.*
  J.T. Baer, 579(SAQ):Winter81-110
  E.J. Czerwinski, 130:Spring81-90
  D. Gerould, 397(MD):Jun81-242
  A. Smith, 574(SEEJ):Fall81-132
  Z. Yurieff, 550(RusR):Jan81-83
Segerstrom, J. Look Like Yourself and
Love It!
  P. Bach, 614:Spring81-20
Segert, S. A Grammar of Phoenician and
Punic.*
  P. Swiggers, 660(Word):Aug80-217
dei Segni, L. (Pope Innocent III) De
Miseria Condicionis Humane.* (R.E.
Lewis, ed and trans)
  P. Brown, 354:Sep81-246
  V. Gillespie, 382(MAE):1981/2-309
  A.V.C. Schmidt, 541(RES):May81-200
Segre, C. Semiotica, storia e cultura.
Semiotica filologica.
  M. Pozzi, 228(GSLI):Vol 157fasc498-307
Segre, C. Structures and Time.*
  J.J. White, 402(MLR):Apr81-429
Seguín, C.A., ed. Psiquiatría Folklórica.
  M.D. Altschule, 37:Sep81-25
Seguin, J-P. Diderot, le discours et les
choses.*
  A. Becq, 535(RHL):Jan-Feb81-136
  P. France, 208(FS):Jul81-337
Seguin, P. Caliban.
  M. Dorsinville, 102(CanL):Spring80-84
Seibert, J. Die politischen Flüchtlinge
und Verbannten in der griechischen
Geschichte.
  D.M. Lewis, 123:Vol31No1-132
Seidel, F. Sunrise.*
  F. Garber, 29:May/Jun82-44
Seidel, L. Songs of Glory.
  A. Borg, 617(TLS):26Mar82-336
Seidel, M. Satiric Inheritance.*
  J.M. Aden, 569(SR):Summer81-441
  E.A. and L.D. Bloom, 566:Autumn80-42
  W.B. Carnochan, 301(JEGP):Jan81-141
  K. Tölölyan, 400(MLN):May81-932
Seidenfeld, T. Philosophical Problems of
Statistical Inference.
  L. Sklar, 482(PhR):Apr81-295
Seidensticker, P. and others. Didaktik
der Grundsprache.
  W. Schmidt, 682(ZPSK):Band33Heft2-269
Seidl, T. Texte und Einheiten in Jeremia
27-29. (Pt 1)
  W.L. Holladay, 318(JAOS):Jan/Mar80-67
Seidler, H. Grundfragen einer Wissen-
schaft von der Sprachkunst.*
  H. Penzl, 350:Mar82-255
Seidler, H. Österreichischer Vormärz und
Goethezeit.
  D. Johnson, 617(TLS):9Jul82-748
Seidlin, O. Von erwachendem Bewusstsein
und vom Sündenfall.
  E. Schwarz, 221(GQ):Jan81-119
  J. Strelka, 400(MLN):Apr81-710
Seidlin, O. - see Schnitzler, A. and O.
Brahm
Seifert, A. Logik zwischen Scholastik und
Humanismus.
  E.J. Ashworth, 319:Apr81-249
  W. Risse, 53(AGP):Band62Heft2-213

Seifert, J. The Plague Column.
  D. Graham, 565:Vol22No1-73
Seiffert, H. Sprache heute.
  U. Schröter, 682(ZPSK):Band33Heft5-636
Seiler, R.M. Walter Pater: The Critical
  Heritage.
  P. Mauriès, 98:Apr81-376
Seiler-Baldinger, A. Classification of
  Textile Techniques.
  R.L. Shep, 614:Winter82-15
Sekaninová, E. Sémantická analýza pred-
  ponového slovesa v ruštine a slovenčine.
  H. Galton, 574(SEEJ):Winter81-103
Sekora, J. Luxury.*
  P.D. McGlynn, 577(SHR):Winter81-77
Selbourne, D. Through the Indian Looking-
  Glass.
  T.J. Byres, 617(TLS):6Aug82-851
Selden, R. English Verse Satire: 1590-
  1765.*
  W.B. Carnochan, 677(YES):Vol 11-275
  G.S. Rousseau, 173(ECS):Winter80/81-
  181
Seligman, P. Being and Not-Being.
  A.A. Krentz, 154:Jun81-391
Seligson, M.A. Peasants of Costa Rica and
  the Development of Agrarian Capitalism.
  H.A. Landsberger, 263(RIB):Vol31No1-98
Selimović, M. La Forteresse.
  L. Kovacs, 450(NRF):Jul-Aug81-219
de Selincourt, E. - see Wordsworth, W. and
  D.
Seling, H. Die Kunst der Augsburger Gold-
  schmiede 1529-1868.
  C. Blair, 617(TLS):9Jul82-749
  C. Hernmarck, 341:Vol50No2-102
Seliščev, A.M. Slavjanskoe naselenie v
  Albanii.
  A.E. Pennington, 575(SEER):Jul81-414
Selkirk, E.O. The Phrase Phonology of
  English and French.
  G.K. Pullum, 350:Dec82-947
Sellars, W. Pure Pragmatics and Possible
  Worlds. (J.F. Sicha, ed) Naturalism
  and Ontology.
  A. Reix, 542:Apr-Jun81-249
Sellers, M., with S. and V. Sellers. P.S.
  I Love You.*
  W. Lawson, 441:4Apr82-11
Seltén, B. The Anglo-Saxon Heritage in
  Middle English Personal Names: East
  Anglia 1100-1399. (Vol 2)
  C. Clark, 179(ES):Oct81-473
  G.F. Jensen, 447(N&Q):Dec80-546
  E.C. Smith, 424:Jun80-158
Selzer, M. Deliverance Day.
  J.W. Bendersky, 390:Jan81-59
Selzer, R. Confessions of a Knife.
  T. Ziolkowski, 569(SR):Fall81-652
Selzer, R. Letters to a Young Doctor.
  F. Mullan, 441:29Aug82-8
Semanov, V.I. Lu Hsün and His Predeces-
  sors. (C.J. Alber, ed and trans)
  L.O-F. Lee, 293(JASt):May81-592
Sembdner, H., ed. Heinrich von Kleists
  Lebensspuren.* (2nd ed)
  D. Grathoff, 224(GRM):Band30Heft1-109
Sen, A. Poverty and Famines.
  K.J. Arrow, 453(NYRB):15Jul82-24
  M. Lipton, 617(TLS):5Mar82-265
Sen, A. and B. Williams, eds. Utilitari-
  anism and Beyond.
  P. Singer, 617(TLS):27Aug82-925

de Sena, J. The Poetry of Jorge de Sena.
  (F.G. Williams, ed) Sobre Esta Praia.
  In Crete, With the Minotaur, and Other
  Poems.
  K. Oderman, 435:Fall81-312
Sena Chiesa, G. Gemme di Luni.*
  R. Winkes, 54:Mar81-138
Sender, R.J. Ensayos sobre el infrigi-
  miento cristiano.
  L. Lorenzo-Rivero, 552(REH):Jan81-159
Seneca. Agamemnon.* (R.J. Tarrant, ed)
  G. Williams, 122:Jan81-75
Seneyiratne, H.L. Rituals of the Kandyan
  State.
  S. Arasaratnam, 302:Vol 18-186
Seng, P.J., ed. Tudor Songs and Ballads
  from MS. Cotton Vespasian A-25.
  P.J. Croft, 447(N&Q):Apr80-187
Senger, V. No. 12 Kaiserhofstrasse.
  A.H. Rosenfeld, 390:Nov81-49
Senghor, L.S. Selected Poems of Léopold
  Sédar Senghor.* (A. Irele, ed)
  G. Moore, 447(N&Q):Jun80-266
Sengle, F. Biedermeierzeit. (Vols 1 and
  2)
  V. Nemoianu, 591(SIR):Winter81-532
Sengle, F. Biedermeierzeit.* (Vol 3)
  V. Nemoianu, 591(SIR):Winter81-532
  J.L. Sammons, 221(GQ):May81-359
Sen Gupta, S.C. Aspects of Shakespearian
  Tragedy. A Shakespeare Manual.
  D. Lindley, 447(N&Q):Oct80-431
Senn, A.E. Jonas Basanavičius.
  V. Kavolis, 550(RusR):Apr81-191
  J.L. Press, 575(SEER):Oct81-613
Senner, W.M. and G.B. Schuback. Geschich-
  ten zur Unterhaltung.
  W. Blomster, 399(MLJ):Autumn81-357
Sennett, R. The Frog Who Dared to Croak.
  R.M. Adams, 453(NYRB):12Aug82-11
  C. Mikes, 617(TLS):29Oct82-1203
  K.C. O'Brien, 362:11Nov82-27
  M. Wood, 441:27Jun82-3
Sennett, T. Hollywood Musicals.*
  A. Croce, 442(NY):18Jan82-128
  D. McClelland, 200:Dec81-637
Senofonte, C. Pierre Bayle dal Calvinismo
  all'Illuminismo.
  P. Rétat, 535(RHL):Jan-Feb81-130
Seppälä, R. "Poika."
  M. Rintala, 563(SS):Autumn81-473
Sequoia, A. (née Schneider) The Official
  J.A.P. Handbook.
  M. Lefkowitz, 617(TLS):24Dec82-1429
Serafin, D. Madrid Underground.
  T.J.B., 617(TLS):16Jul82-775
Sergeev, F.P. Formirovanie russkogo dip-
  lomatičeskogo jazyka XI-XVII vv.
  P.B. Brown, 550(RusR):Oct81-445
  Z. Lenkevič, 559:Aug81-324
Sergooris, G. Peter Handke und die
  Sprache.
  C.C. Zorach, 221(GQ):Mar81-245
Serlio, S. Sebastiano Serlio, "On Domes-
  tic Architecture."* (M.N. Rosenfeld, ed)
  D.R. Coffin, 551(RenQ):Spring80-102
  H. Lorenz, 43:Band10Heft2-186
  D. Thomson, 90:Mar81-174
Serres, M. Hermes. (J.V. Harari and D.F.
  Bell, eds)
  M. Tiles, 617(TLS):31Dec82-1449
Serres, M. Le Parasite.
  D.F. Bell, 400(MLN):May81-884

Shakespeare, W. Shakespeare's Sonnets.*
(S. Booth, ed)
J. Fuzier, 189(EA):Apr-Jun81-215
Shakespeare, W. Shakespeare's Sonnets.
(S.C. Campbell, ed)
J. Fuzier, 189(EA):Apr-Jun81-215
Shakespeare, W. The Taming of the Shrew.
(B. Morris, ed)
D. Daniell, 617(TLS):5Mar82-266
"Shakespeare Translation." (Vols 1-6) (T.
Oyama, ed)
A.K. France, 570(SQ):Autumn81-407
Shalamov, V. Graphite.*
G.A. Hosking, 617(TLS):10ct82-1064
Shalamov, V. Kolyma Tales.*
J. Haig, 573(SSF):Fall81-476
Shales, T. On the Air!
J. Powers, 231:Dec82-62
Shalhope, R.E. John Taylor of Caroline.
C.F. Hobson, 656(WMQ):Jul81-537
Shamosh, A. My Sister the Bride.
N. Wachtel, 390:Mar81-58
el-Shamy, H.M. Folktales of Egypt.*
N. Salem, 196:Band22Heft3/4-330
Shange, N. Sassafrass, Cypress and Indigo.
S. Isaacs, 441:12Sep82-12
Shank, T. American Alternative Theatre.
N. de Jongh, 617(TLS):3Dec82-1347
Shanks, B. Love is Not Enough.
N. Johnson, 441:11Jul82-14
Shannon, R. Gladstone. (Vol 1)
S. Koss, 617(TLS):22Oct82-1151
Shapira, M. - see James, H.
Shapiro, A. After the Digging.
R. von Hallberg, 659(ConL):Fall82-550
Shapiro, F.C. Radwaste.*
C. Kaiser, 441:21Feb82-16
Shapiro, L. The History of ORT.
A. Kagedan, 287:Oct81-19
Shapiro, M. Asymmetry.*
S. Fleischman, 545(RPh):Feb81-329
Shapiro, M. Children of The Revels.*
R.W. Ingram, 677(YES):Vol 11-237
Shapiro, M. Courts.
C.S., 185:Jul82-797
Shapley, F.R. Catalogue of Italian Paint-
ings.* (National Gallery of Art)
E.W. Rowlands, 39:Nov81-352
Shapo, M.S. A Nation of Guinea Pigs.
S.A. Lakoff, 185:Oct80-100
Sharif, M.M. Islamic and Educational
Studies.
H.A. Ali, 273(IC):Jan80-55
Sharkey, M. Barbarians.
G. Bitcon, 581:Dec81-469
Sharma, D.D. A Study of Loan Words in
Central Pahari.
H.C. Patyal, 261:Jun80-122
Sharma, J.N. The International Fiction of
Henry James.
D.J. Schneider, 395(MFS):Winter80/81-
646
Sharma, V. Studies in Victorian Verse
Drama.
T. Otten, 637(VS):Autumn80-136
Sharma, V. Vākyapadīya-sambandhasamuddeśa.
J.D. Singh, 261:Sep/Dec80-200
Sharp, D. - see Muthesius, H.
Sharp, F.M. The Poet's Madness.
42(AR):Summer81-392
Sharp, G. Gandhi as a Political Strate-
gist.
G. Ostergaard, 185:Oct81-140

Sharp, G. Social Power and Political Free-
dom.
N.C.F., 185:Jul81-696
Sharp, R.A. Keats, Skepticism, and the
Religion of Beauty.*
S. Hall, 577(SHR):Summer81-266
D.H. Reiman, 340(KSJ):Vol30-201
R.M. Ryan, 301(JEGP):Apr81-259
S.M. Sperry, 591(SIR):Spring81-126
L. Waldoff, 191(ELN):Mar81-217
Sharpe, K. Sir Robert Cotton, 1586-1631.
N. Ball, 161(DUJ):Jun81-242
D.R. Butler, 568(SCN):Summer-Fall81-65
R.B. Manning, 125:Spring81-332
A.G. Watson, 447(N&Q):Aug80-360
G. Williams, 354:Jun81-164
Sharpe, K., ed. Faction and Parliament.
G.E. Aylmer, 161(DUJ):Dec80-92
Sharpe, L. Schiller and the Historical
Character.
H.W. O'Kelly, 617(TLS):8Oct82-1114
Sharpe, T. Vintage Stuff.
J. Mellors, 362:18Nov82-28
S. Sutherland, 617(TLS):12Nov82-1243
Sharratt, B. Reading Relations.
D. Lodge, 617(TLS):23Apr82-458
Sharrer, H.L., ed. The Legendary History
of Britain in Lope García de Salazar's
"Libro de las bienandanzas e fortunas."
J.B. Avalle-Arce, 240(HR):Autumn81-494
Sharrock, J.T.R., ed. The Frontiers of
Bird Identification.
R. O'Hanlon, 617(TLS):20Aug82-905
Sharrock, R. and J.F. Forrest - see Bunyan,
J.
Châotrî, U.P. and N. Menant, eds and trans.
Hymnes à la Déesse.
G. Barrière, 450(NRF):Jul-Aug81-204
Shatto, S. and M. Shaw - see Tennyson, A.
Shattock, J. and M. Wolff, eds. The Victo-
rian Periodical Press.
P. Keating, 617(TLS):25Jun82-700
Shattuck, R. The Forbidden Experiment.*
A.J. Singerman, 207(FR):May81-905
Shattuck, R. and S.W. Taylor - see Jarry,
A.
Shaver, C.L. and A.C., comps. Words-
worth's Library.
J.A. Butler, 191(ELN):Jun81-301
Shaw, B. A Better Mantrap.
W. Logan, 617(TLS):12Mar82-276
Shaw, B.D. and R.P. Saller - see Finley,
M.I.
Shaw, C.M. Richard Brome.
J.S. Nania, 568(SCN):Summer-Fall81-48
J.C. Thompson, 610:Autumn81-219
Shaw, G.B. The Collected Screenplays of
Bernard Shaw. (B.F. Dukore, ed)
A. Ganz, 130:Fall81-268
S. Weintraub, 572:Vol2-195
Shaw, G.B. Heartbreak House. (S. Wein-
traub and A. Wright, eds)
R. Chapman, 572:Vol2-201
Shaw, G.B. Shaw and Ibsen.* (J.L. Wisen-
thal, ed)
N. Jenckes, 397(MD):Mar81-108
D. Rubin, 108:Fall80-151
J.P. Smith, 627(UTQ):Summer81-128
Shaw, G.B. Bernard Shaw: Early Texts.
(D.H. Laurence, general ed)
N. Grene, 617(TLS):16Jul82-768

Shaw, G.B. Shaw's Music.* (D.H. Laurence, ed)
 R. Anderson, 415:Nov81-747
 E. Rothstein, 453(NYRB):1Apr82-27
Shaw, G.B. and A. Douglas. Bernard Shaw and Alfred Douglas: A Correspondence. (M. Hyde, ed)
 R. Ellmann, 441:14Nov82-12
 J. Gross, 453(NYRB):16Dec82-11
 M. Holroyd, 617(TLS):31Dec82-1438
 N. Shrimpton, 362:2Dec82-19
Shaw, H. Death of a Don.
 N. Callendar, 441:14Feb82-22
Shaw, I. Acceptable Losses.
 J.J. Osborn, Jr., 441:3Oct82-13
Shaw, M.F. Folksongs and Folklore of South Uist.* (2nd ed)
 V. Blankenhorn, 112:Vol 14-164
Shaw, P. American Patriots and the Rituals of Revolution.*
 D. Leverenz, 165(EAL):Winter81/82-285
 639(VQR):Summer81-88
Shaw, W.D. Tennyson's Style.*
 J.R. Bennett, 599:Fall81-453
Shaw, W.H. Marx's Theory of History.
 R.R. Bhaskar, 518:Jul81-137
Shawcross, J.T. With Mortal Voice.
 L. Mackinnon, 617(TLS):3Dec82-1332
Shawcross, W. Sideshow.
 D.P. Chandler, 293(JASt):Nov80-77
Shchutskii, I.K. Researches on the "I Ching."*
 J. Hoodock, 485(PE&W):Oct81-551
She, L. - see under Lao She
Shea, M. Tomorrow's Men.
 K. Jeffery, 617(TLS):26Nov82-1318
Shea, P. Voices and the Sound of Drums.*
 J. Keegan, 617(TLS):29Oct82-1186
Shear, T.L., Jr. Kallias of Sphettos and the Revolt of Athens in 286 B.C.*
 É. Will, 555:Vol54fasc2-356
Sheard, W.S. Antiquity in the Renaissance.
 M.S. Young, 39:Aug81-138
Sheard, W.S. and J.T. Paoletti, eds. Collaboration in Italian Renaissance Art.*
 M.T. Rajam, 551(RenQ):Spring80-97
Sheed, W. Clare Boothe Luce.
 M. Cantwell, 441:21Feb82-3
 F.D. Gray, 453(NYRB):1Apr82-12
 N. von Hoffman, 617(TLS):1Oct82-1056
Sheehan, B.W. Savagism and Civility.*
 D.B. Quinn, 656(WMQ):Jul81-506
Sheehan, S. Is There No Place On Earth for Me?
 M. Scarf, 441:2May82-14
Shefton, B.B. Die "rhodischen" Bronzekannen.
 A. Johnston, 303(JoHS):Vol 101-217
Shek, B-Z. Social Realism in the French-Canadian Novel.
 J. Pivato, 296(JCF):No31/32-231
Shelby, L.R. Gothic Design Techniques.
 W. Müller, 683:Band44Heft1-95
Sheldon, D. Victim of Love.
 L. Taylor, 617(TLS):17Sep82-992
Sheldon, S. Master of the Game.
 R. Lekachman, 441:29Aug82-11
Sheldrake, R. A New Science of Life.
 S. Clark, 617(TLS):12Mar82-279
Shell, M. The Economy of Literature.*
 C.R. Beye, 131(CL):Summer81-280
 M. Clark, 494:Autumn79-419
 T.J. Reiss, 567:Vol34No1/2-177

Shell, O.A. Estudios Panos III.
 K.M. Kensinger, 269(IJAL):Jan81-68
Shell, S.M. The Rights of Reason.
 E.M. Pybus, 518:Oct81-203
 H.P. Rickman, 483:Jan81-128
Shelley, M.W. The Letters of Mary Wollstonecraft Shelley.* (Vol 1) (B.T. Bennett, ed)
 E.W. Marrs, Jr., 340(KSJ):Vol30-203
 H.S. Spatt, 651(WHR):Summer81-188
Shelnutt, E. The Love Child.
 W.V. Davis, 573(SSF):Spring81-200
Shenker, I. In the Footsteps of Johnson and Boswell.
 J. Morris, 441:21Mar82-6
 442(NY):26Apr82-143
Shennan, J.H. Philippe, Duke of Orléans, Regent of France 1715-1723.
 R. Waller, 83:Spring81-103
Shenton, G. The Fictions of the Self.
 F. Busi, 207(FR):May81-876
Shep, R.L. Textile, Costume, and Doll Collections.
 R.L. Shep, 614:Fall81-21
Shepard, S. Angel City and Other Plays.
 A. Messenger, 102(CanL):Autumn80-89
Shepard, S. Four Two-Act Plays.
 D. Devlin, 157:Autumn81-51
Shepherd, J. A Fistful of Fig Newtons.
 M.A. Jackson, 441:28Feb82-12
Shepherd, J. and others. Whose Music?
 H.B.R., 412:Aug80-240
Shepherd, S. Amazons and Warrior Women.
 L. Lerner, 617(TLS):4Jun82-619
Sheppard, A.D.R. Studies on the 5th and 6th Essays of Proclus' Commentary on the "Republic."
 A. Smith, 303(JoHS):Vol 101-166
Sheppard, L. and H.R. Axelrod. Paganini.
 R. Anderson, 415:Feb81-107
Sheppard, M. Taman Budiman.
 P.H. Kratoska, 293(JASt):Aug81-851
Sheppard, R., ed. Dada.
 R. Cardinal, 529(QQ):Spring81-19
 M. Perloff, 402(MLR):Jan81-152
Sherburne, J. Death's Clenched Fist.
 N. Callendar, 441:30May82-15
Sherburne, J. Death's Gray Angel.*
 N. Callendar, 441:14Feb82-22
Shergold, N.D. and J.E. Varey. Teatros y comedias en Madrid: 1687-1699.
 K.C. Gregg, 593:Summer81-183
 I.L. McClelland, 610:Spring81-149
Sheridan, A. Michel Foucault.*
 G.P. Bennington, 208(FS):Jul81-369
Sherman, D. Dynasty of Spies.
 639(VQR):Spring81-60
Sherman, M. and G. Hawkins. Imprisonment in America.
 G. Hughes, 453(NYRB):1Apr82-39
Sherrill, R.A. The Prophetic Melville.*
 E.A. Dryden, 50(ArQ):Winter81-371
 D. Leverenz, 445(NCF):Sep81-238
 N. Wright, 580(SCR):Fall80-101
Sherry, C. Wordsworth's Poetry of the Imagination.*
 F. Ferguson, 661(WC):Summer81-149
 S. Wolfson, 400(MLN):Dec81-1221
Sherwin-White, S.M. Ancient Cos.*
 J.M. Fossey, 487:Summer81-172
Sherwood, J. A Shot in the Arm.
 T.J. Binyon, 617(TLS):29Oct82-1196

Sherwood, R. Modern Housing Prototypes.
G. Anselevicius, 576:May81-166
Shevelov, G.Y. A Historical Phonology of
The Ukrainian Language.
G.A. Perfecky, 574(SEEJ):Spring81-134
Shewell, C. and V. Dean, eds. A Way with
Words.
C. Brown, 617(TLS):24Dec82-1431
Shi, D.E. Matthew Josephson, Bourgeois
Historian.*
W. Sypher, 569(SR):Fall81-648
A. Wald, 385(MQR):Summer82-525
27(AL):Nov81-567
639(VQR):Autumn81-122
Shi Nai-an and Luo Guan-zhong. Au bord de
l'eau. (J. Dars, ed and trans)
P-E. Will, 98:Aug-Sep81-771
Shichor, Y. The Middle East in China's
Foreign Policy, 1949-1977.
M. Gurtov, 293(JASt):Aug81-776
Shields, C. Happenstance.*
J.M. Kertzer, 529(QQ):Winter81-791
Shields, H. - see Philippe de Thaon
Shigeyoshi, M. - see under Murakami
Shigeyoshi
Shikes, R.E. and P. Harper. Pissarro.*
R.R. Brettell, 127:Fall81-271
R. Hobbs, 59:Mar81-121
Shillony, H. Le Roman contradictoire, une
lecture du "Noeud de Vipères" de Mauriac.
A. Séailles, 535(RHL):Nov-Dec81-1024
Shiloah, A., ed. The Theory of Music in
Arabic Writings (c. 900-1900).
D.M. Randel, 187:Sep82-478
Shils, E. Center and Periphery.
C.A. Woodward, 488:Sep80-333
Shils, E. Tradition.
P.L. Berger, 441:14Feb82-9
D.A. Martin, 617(TLS):23Jul82-801
K.S., 185:Jul82-800
Shimanoff, S.B. Communication Rules.
H.L. Goodall, Jr., 480(P&R):Summer81-
194
Shimer, D.B. Bhabani Bhattacharya.
S. Sinha, 314:Summer-Fall81-218
Shimi, S.F. Portrait d'un espion du dix-
septième siècle.
E.M. Tilton, 207(FR):Mar82-547
Shimoni, G. Jews and Zionism.*
C.S. Liebman, 390:Nov81-60
Shindler, C. Hollywood Goes to War.
R. Robertson, 658:Spring81-125
G. Weales, 219(GaR):Spring81-166
Shiner, R.A. Knowledge and Reality in
Plato's "Philebus."
H.G. Zekl, 53(AGP):Band62Heft1-80
Shingleton, R.G. John Taylor Wood.
R.E. Johnson, 9(AlaR):Apr81-135
Shinn, T. L'Ecole polytechnique, 1794-
1914.
A. Douglas, 207(FR):Apr81-752
Shinran. Letters of Shinran. (Yoshifumi
Ueda, ed)
T.P. Kasulis, 485(PE&W):Apr81-246
Shinran. Notes on Once-calling and Many-
calling.
P.O. Ingram, 407(MN):Winter81-484
Shiokawa, T. Pascal et les Miracles.*
B. Rathmann, 475:No13Pt1-155
Shipman, D. The Story of Cinema.
G. Kaufman, 362:23and30Dec82-42

Shipp, G.P. Modern Greek Evidence for the
Ancient Greek Vocabulary.
M.G. Carroll, 67:May81-132
P. Colaclides, 350:Dec81-967
A.C. Moorhouse, 123:Vol31No2-307
Shippey, T.A. The Road to Middle-Earth.
G. Watson, 617(TLS):8Oct82-1098
Shire, H.M. - see Fraser, O.
Shirer, R.K. Kulturelle Begegnungen.
G.L. Ervin, 399(MLJ):Spring81-118
Shirer, W.L. Gandhi.
G.O., 185:Jul81-696
Shirk, S.L. Competitive Comrades.
M. Bayles, 441:20Jun82-17
J.K. Fairbank, 453(NYRB):2Dec82-13
Shirley, F.A. Swearing and Perjury in
Shakespeare's Plays.
S.P. Zitner, 551(RenQ):Autumn80-472
Shloss, C. Flannery O'Connor's Dark Come-
dies.
J. Cunningham, 573(SSF):Summer81-332
639(VQR):Spring81-54
Shneidman, N.N. Soviet Literature in the
1970s.*
D. Brown, 574(SEEJ):Summer81-98
H. Eagle, 627(UTQ):Summer81-152
Shochat, Y. Recruitment and the Programme
of Tiberius Gracchus.
A.E. Astin, 313:Vol71-188
Shoemaker, W.H. La crítica literaria de
Galdós.
L.J. Hoar, Jr., 238:May81-314
Shoemaker, W.H. The Novelistic Art of
Galdós.
R.M. Fedorchek, 238:Dec81-638
Shoesmith, D.J. and T.J. Smiley. Multiple-
Conclusion Logic.*
R. Harrop, 316:Mar81-161
Shogren, L. The Quilt Pattern Index.
T. Cowan, 614:Fall81-20
Shone, R. The Post-Impressionists.
R.R. Brettell, 127:Fall/Winter80-409
Shopsin, W.C. and others. The Villard
Houses.
A. Saint, 46:Jul81-65
Shor, I. Critical Teaching and Everyday
Life.
H. Brent, 128(CE):Dec81-824
Shore, S. Uncommon Places.
A. Grundberg, 441:5Dec82-59
Short, I. and B. Merrilees - see Benedeit
Short, P. The Dragon and the Bear.
E. de Mauny, 617(TLS):20Aug82-908
Shorter, E. A History of Women's Bodies.
T.G., 231:Nov82-75
Shortt, S.E.D., ed. Medicine in Canadian
Society.*
C. Howell, 150(DR):Summer81-368
Shostak, M. Nisa.*
J. Clifford, 617(TLS):17Sep82-994
J. Olney, 676(YR):Summer82-591
Shostakovich, D. Testimony.* (S. Volkov,
ed)
M. Ellmann, 569(SR):Summer81-454
R. Jordan, 648(WCR):Jun80-43
Shouldice, L., ed and trans. Contemporary
Quebec Criticism.*
C.F. Coates, 207(FR):Dec81-260
P. Merivale, 102(CanL):Spring81-127
D.W. Russell, 529(QQ):Spring81-181
Shoup, P.S. The East European and Soviet
Data Handbook.
639(VQR):Autumn81-133

Showalter, D.E. - see Pettit, A.G.
Showalter, E., ed. These Modern Women.*
   A. Woodlief, 577(SHR):Winter81-94
Showalter, E., Jr. Madame de Graffigny
and Rousseau.*
   R. Grimsley, 208(FS):Jan81-74
Shrader-Frechette, K.S., ed. Environ-
mental Ethics.
   R.G., 185:Apr82-585
Shrader-Frechette, K.S. Nuclear Power and
Public Policy.
   R.E.G., 185:Jan81-345
Shrubsall, D. - see Hudson, W.H., with M.
Beaven
Shu-Huan, L. - see under Li Shu-Huan
Shuffelton, F. Thomas Hooker, 1586-1647.
   R. Morton, 106:Fall81-191
Shukman, A. Literature and Semiotics.*
   P. Galloway, 599:Winter81-55
Shulman, D.D. Tamil Temple Myths.
   F.W. Clothey, 314:Summer-Fall81-245
   E. Leach, 617(TLS):24Sep82-1042
Shumaker, W., ed and trans. John Dee on
Astronomy.
   M.E. Bowden, 551(RenQ):Summer80-271
Shumaker, W. The Occult Sciences in the
Renaissance.
   N.A. Greco, 568(SCN):Winter81-96
Shute, M.N. - see Winthrop, J.
Shuttle, P. The Orchard Upstairs.*
   E. Boland, 493:Sep81-71
Sibley, W.F. The Shiga Hero.
   P. Anderer, 293(JASt):Aug81-795
   J.T. Rimer, 395(MFS):Summer80-380
Siccardo, F. "Police." "Intégriste" e
"intégrisme."
   G. Gorcy, 209(FM):Apr81-167
Sicha, J.F. - see Sellars, W.
Siciliano, E. Pasolini.* (Italian title:
Vita di Pasolini.)
   N.S. Thompson, 617(TLS):8Oct82-1105
   E. White, 441:27Jun82-8
Sicker, P. Love and the Quest for
Identity in the Fiction of Henry James.*
   P.J. Eakin, 27(AL):Mar81-153
   A.H., 148:Spring81-93
   P. Horne, 184(EIC):Apr81-149
   J.L. Idol, Jr., 573(SSF):Winter81-102
   M. Jacobson, 301(JEGP):Apr81-272
   D.J. Schneider, 395(MFS):Winter80/81-
   646
   W. Veeder, 405(MP):Aug81-104
   M.R. Winchell, 577(SHR):Fall81-367
   W.F. Wright, 284:Fall81-72
   295(JML):Vol8No3/4-530
Siculus - see under Diodorus Siculus
Sidane, V. Le printemps de Pékin:
novembre 1978-mars 1980.
   V. Alleton, 98:Aug-Sep81-762
Siddayao, C.M. The Off-Shore Petroleum
Resources of South-East Asia.
   J.J. MacDougall, 293(JASt):Feb81-434
Sidorova, A.A. and S.P. Luppova, eds.
Kniga v Rossii do serediny XIX veka.
   R.H. Burger, 574(SEEJ):Spring81-119
Sidorsky, D., with S. Liskofsky and J.J.
Shestack, eds. Essays on Human Rights.
   D.G. Dalin, 390:Jan81-57
Sieben, H.J. Die Konzilsidee der alten
Kirche.
   E. Ferguson, 589:Apr81-437

Sieber, H. Language and Society in "La
vida de Lazarillo de Tormes."*
   J. Herrero, 405(MP):Aug81-75
   D. McGrady, 593:Summer80-178
   C. Stern, 545(RPh):Feb81-303
Sieber, R. African Furniture and House-
hold Objects.
   J. Masheck, 62:Feb81-72
   E.L.R. Meyerowitz, 39:Aug81-134
   A. Rubin, 2(AfrA):Nov80-22
Siebert Klein, M. The Challenge of Commu-
nist Education.
   M. McCauley, 575(SEER):Oct81-633
Sieburth, R. Instigations.
   D. Perkins, 131(CL):Spring81-205
Siefken, H. Thomas Mann Goethe — "Ideal
der Deutschheit."
   U. Wolff, 680(ZDP):Band100Heft4-613
Siegchrist, M. Rough in Brutal Print.
   D. Karlin, 617(TLS):18Jun82-678
Siegel, L. Sacred and Profane Dimensions
of Love in Indian Traditions as Exempli-
fied in the "Gītagovinda" of Jayadeva.*
   N.E. Falk, 314:Winter-Spring81-223
Siegel, M. Tom Robbins.
   A. Frietzsche, 649(WAL):Fall81-231
Siegel, P. Revolution and the 20th Cen-
tury Novel.
   E. Echevarria, 659(ConL):Winter82-123
Siegel, R. and C. Rheins, eds. The Jewish
Almanac.
   S. Bronznick, 287:May81-20
Siegel, S.W. - see Strauss, H.A.
Siegert, R. Aufklärung und Volkslektüre.
   R. Schenda, 196:Band21Heft3/4-342
Siegman, A. and S. Feldstein, eds. Of
Speech and Time.
   K. Kaye, 355(LSoc):Aug81-317
   B. McLane, 399(MLJ):Spring81-109
Siegmeister, E., ed. The Music Lover's
Handbook.
   G. Poole, 415:Mar81-179
Siegrist, C. - see Lavater, J.K.
Siemieniuk, L. Almost a Ritual.
   D. Barbour, 648(WCR):Jun80-76
   J. Giltrow, 102(CanL):Spring81-145
Siems, H. Studien zur Lex Frisionum.
   K.F. Drew, 589:Jul81-656
Sienaert, E. Les "lais" de Marie de
France.*
   J.L. Grigsby, 545(RPh):Feb81(supp)-73
   W. Rothwell, 208(FS):Jan81-60
Siep, L. Anerkennung als Prinzip der
praktischen Philosophie.
   M.G., 543:Sep80-164
Siepe, H.T. Der Leser des Surrealismus.*
   J. Schultz, 535(RHL):May-Jun81-478
Sifford, D. Father and Son.
   G. Wolff, 441:21Nov82-15
Magister Siguinus. Ars lectoria. (C.H.
Kneepkens and H.F. Reijnders, eds)
   B.M. Marti, 589:Jan81-196
Siikala, A-L. The Rite Technique of the
Siberian Shaman.
   U. Kutter, 196:Band21Heft3/4-343
Siilivask, K., ed. Revolutsioon, kodusôda
ja välisriikide interventsioon Eestis
(1917-1920). (Vol 1)
   D. Kirby, 575(SEER):Apr81-272
Sijpesteijn, P.J. and K.A. Worp, eds.
Zwei Landlisten aus dem Hermupolites.
   R.P. Duncan-Jones, 313:Vol71-198

326

Simons, M.A. Sémiotisme de Stendhal.
W.J. Berg, 446(NCFS):Fall-Winter81/82-133
G. Strickland, 402(MLR):Oct81-970
205(FMLS):Oct80-371
Simons, W.B., ed. The Constitutions of the Communist World.
H. Hanak, 575(SEER):Oct81-626
Simonsuuri, K. Homer's Original Genius.*
F. Blessington, 566:Autumn80-41
D.W. Hopkins, 402(MLR):Jul81-650
P. Rogers, 541(RES):May81-221
N. Suckling, 208(FS):Apr81-210
205(FMLS):Jan80-93
Simov, P., ed and trans. Frenska Poesia.
N. Dontchev, 535(RHL):Jan-Feb81-160
Simpson, C.R. SoHo.
B. Wolner, 55:Nov81-50
42(AR):Summer81-391
Simpson, D. Irony and Authority in Romantic Poetry.*
M. Brown, 191(ELN):Dec80-148
M. Butler, 447(N&Q):Dec80-552
W. Keach, 591(SIR):Winter81-539
A.K. Mellor, 661(WC):Summer81-196
E.B. Murray, 541(RES):Nov81-459
Simpson, D. Six Feet Under.
T.J. Binyon, 617(TLS):28May82-594
Simpson, D. Wordsworth and the Figurings of the Real.
E. Neill, 617(TLS):3Dec82-1340
Simpson, E. Poets in Their Youth.
J. Atlas, 441:2May82-1
P. Kemp, 362:30Sep82-25
B. Morrison, 617(TLS):29Oct82-1181
H. Moss, 453(NYRB):15Jul82-8
W. Sheed, 61:Jun82-90
442(NY):15Nov82-204
Simpson, E. Reason Over Passion.*
D.A., 543:Mar81-619
S.L. Mendus, 518:Oct81-246
J.D. Rabb, 154:Sep81-627
Simpson, G.G. Splendid Isolation.*
R.P. Thompson, 529(QQ):Spring81-186
Simpson, H.N. Invisible Armies.
J.C. Burnham, 658:Winter81-369
Simpson, J. Matthew Arnold and Goethe.*
C.A. Runcie, 637(VS):Autumn80-142
Simpson, L. Caviare at the Funeral.*
P. Bland, 364:Feb82-79
C.B. Cox, 148:Autumn81-2
D. Davis, 362:7Jan82-22
G.E. Murray, 249(HudR):Spring81-155
R.B. Shaw, 491:Dec81-171
P. Stitt, 219(GaR):Spring81-182
Simpson, L. Kowalski's Last Chance.*
L. Rogers, 102(CanL):Summer81-141
Simpson, L.P. The Brazen Face of History.
M. O'Brien, 385(MQR):Summer82-515
Simpson, M.R. The Novels of Hermann Broch.*
205(FMLS):Oct80-381
Simpson, R. Carl Nielsen: Symphonist. (2nd ed)
W.H. Reynolds, 415:Nov81-749
Simpson, R. Richard Simpson as Critic. (D. Carroll, ed)
J. Shattock, 402(MLR):Apr81-448
Simpson, R.A., ed. Poems from "The Age," 1967-79.
C. Pollnitz, 581:Jun81-221
Simpson, R.H. Mycenaean Greece.
J. Rutter, 124:May-Jun82-313

Simpson, R.H. and O.T.P.K. Dickinson. A Gazetteer of Aegean Civilisation in the Bronze Age. (Vol 1)
V. Hankey, 303(JoHS):Vol 101-207
Simpson, V., ed. Women's Attire/Les Vêtements féminins.
R.L. Shep, 614:Fall81-22
Sims, G. The Keys of Death.
T.J. Binyon, 617(TLS):16Apr82-446
Sims, W.D. and S.B. Hammond, eds. Award-Winning Foreign Language Programs.
R.M. Valette, 399(MLJ):Winter81-411
Sinclair, A. The Other Victoria.
G. Battiscombe, 617(TLS):26Mar82-362
E.S. Turner, 362:21Jan82-23
Sinclair, C. Bed Bugs.
T. Sutcliffe, 617(TLS):28May82-579
Sinclair, C. Hearts of Gold.*
P. Lewis, 565:Vol22No1-60
Sinclair, J.L. New Mexico.
L. Milazzo, 584(SWR):Spring81-v
Sinclair, K. - see Bodell, J.
Sinclair, K.V. Prières en ancien français.*
W. Rothwell, 208(FS):Jul81-314
Sinden, D. A Touch of the Memoirs.
N. de Jongh, 617(TLS):7May82-517
Sinding-Larsen, S. Christ in the Council Hall.
M. Muraro, 54:Mar81-157
Sindler, A.P. Bakke, De Funis, and Minority Admissions.
I. Thalberg, 185:Oct80-138
Sinfield, A. Dramatic Monologue.*
J. Utz, 72:Band217Heft1-169
Sinfield, A. The Language of Tennyson's "In Memoriam."
J.R. Bennett, 599:Fall81-453
Singal, D.J. The War Within.
D.H. Donald, 441:31Oct82-13
Singer, B.J. - see Randall, J.H., Jr.
Singer, D.G., J.L. Singer and D.M. Zuckerman. Teaching Television.
B. Weeks, 18:Mar81-72
Singer, I.B. The Collected Stories of Isaac Bashevis Singer.
C. Ozick, 441:21Mar82-1
C. Sinclair, 617(TLS):16Jul82-761
Singer, P. The Expanding Circle.*
J. Beatty, 529(QQ):Winter81-607
D. Locke, 617(TLS):15Jan82-46
Singer, P. Practical Ethics.
J. Annas, 479(PhQ):Apr81-180
D. Browne, 63:Mar81-121
M. Ebell, 111:5Dec80-45
J. Fishkin, 185:Jul81-665
J. Harris, 518:Oct81-193
C.K., 543:Jun81-808
E.M. Pybus, 483:Apr81-267
Singh, C. Textiles and Costume from the Maharaja Sawai Man Singh II Museum, Jaipur.
J. Housego, 463:Summer81-204
Singh, G. - see Leavis, F.R.
Singh, K. and C. Sahay. ādhunika bhāṣāvijñāna.
A. Jha, 261:Dec79-322
Singh, R., with J. Lelyveld. Rajasthan.*
M. Kozloff, 62:Nov81-76
A. Ross, 364:Jun81-10
Singh, S.N. My India.
H. Tinker, 617(TLS):6Aug82-850

Sinha, P. Calcutta in Urban History.
C. Furedy, 293(JASt):Nov80-184
Sinistri, C. and C. Perini. Verona nelle
antiche stampe.
W. Krönig, 683:Band43Heft1-110
Sinjavskij, A. - see under Tertz, A.
Sinopoulos, T. Stones.
J. Saunders, 565:Vol22No3-62
Sinor, D., ed. Modern Hungary.*
I. Volgyes, 104(CASS):Winter81-615
Šipova, E.N. Slovar' tjurkizmov v russkom
jazyke.
K.H. Menges, 688(ZSP):Band41Heft2-421
Sipović, C., ed. The Pontifical Liturgy
of Saint John Chrysostom.
H. Leeming, 575(SEER):Apr81-281
Sipper, R. - see Macdonald, R.
Sirc, L. The Yugoslav Economy under Self-
Management.
D. McGlue, 575(SEER):Jul81-469
Širjaev, A.F. Sinxronnyj perevod.
H. Salevsky, 75:3/1980-180
Sissman, L.E. Hello, Darkness.* (P. Davi-
son, ed) Innocent Bystander.
D.E. Richardson, 569(SR):Winter81-134
Sisson, C.H. The Avoidance of Literature.
(M. Schmidt, ed)
C.R. Beye, 472:Spring/Summer82-75
Sisson, C.H. Exactions.*
T. Eagleton, 565:Vol22No4-74
Sisson, C.H. Selected Poems. English
Poetry, 1900-1950.
S. Medcalf, 617(TLS):23Apr82-457
Sisson, C.H. - see Hardy, T.
Sisson, C.H. - see Swift, J.
Sito Alba, M. Montherlant et l'Espagne.*
A. Blanc, 535(RHL):Mar-Apr81-330
Sitta, H., ed. Ansätze zu einer pragmat-
ischen Sprachgeschichte.
H. Penzl, 350:Mar81-230
Sivachev, N.V. and N.N. Yakovlev. Russia
and the United States.
H. Hanak, 575(SEER):Oct81-610
B. Steinberg, 104(CASS):Winter81-589
Sizer, S.S. Gospel Hymns and Social
Religion.*
J. and U. Rempel, 106:Winter81-331
D. Yoder, 658:Spring81-98
Sjögren, M. Rep utan knutar.
H.H. Borland, 563(SS):Winter81-117
Skagestad, P. The Road of Inquiry.
J.M.I., 185:Jul82-786
Skelhorn, N. Public Prosecutor.
D. Pannick, 362:28Jan82-21
Skelton, J. Magnificence. (P. Neuss, ed)
R.B. Bond, 49:Jan81-97
J.W. Robinson, 610:Autumn81-218
V.J. Scattergood, 184(EIC):Apr81-145
Skelton, R. Landmarks.
D. Barbour, 648(WCR):Vol 15No3-45
A.J. Harding, 102(CanL):Spring81-138
R. Hornsey, 461:Fall-Winter81/82-101
Skelton, R., ed. Six Poets of British
Columbia.
S.H. Nelson, 526:Autumn81-156
Skendi, S. Balkan Cultural Studies.
V.A. Friedman, 574(SEEJ):Winter81-105
Skey, M., ed. Dizionario Inglese Italiano
Italiano Inglese.
G.C. Lepschy, 617(TLS):3Sep82-951
Skiles, D. Miss America.
W. Logan, 617(TLS):6Aug82-865

Skilling, H.G. Charter 77 and Human
Rights in Czechoslovakia.
G. Theiner, 617(TLS):19Feb82-180
Skillings, R.D. P-Town Stories or The
Meatrack.
D. Kirby, 448:Vol 19No3-178
Skilton, D. - see Hardy, T.
Skinner, A.S. A System of Social Science.
W.J. Samuels, 185:Jul81-689
Skinner, G.W. - see Freedman, M.
Skinner, M.B. Catullus' "Passer."
P.Y. Forsyth, 124:May-Jun82-321
Skinner, Q. The Foundations of Modern
Political Thought.* (Vols 1 and 2)
R. Ashcraft, 319:Jul81-388
J. Coleman, 111:5Dec80-50
R.E. Giesey, 551(RenQ):Spring80-60
N. Tarcov, 185:Jul82-692
Sklar, K.K. - see Stowe, H.B.
Sklar, R. Prime-time America.
M. Church, 617(TLS):26Feb82-204
Skocpol, T. States and Social Revolu-
tions.*
J. Dunn, 185:Jan82-299
Skowronski, H. and S. Tacker. Doup Leno.
P. Bach, 614:Spring81-18
Skrine, P.N. The Baroque.*
G. Gillespie, 131(CL):Spring81-202
G. Müller-Schwefe, 551(RenQ):Autumn80-
484
Skrubbeltrang, F. Den danske Landbosam-
fund 1500-1800.
S. Oakley, 562(Scan):Nov81-224
Skura, M.A. The Literary Use of the
Psychoanalytic Process.
D.J. Gordon, 676(YR):Winter82-288
H. Skulsky, 290(JAAC):Winter81-210
Sky, G. Appaloosa Rising.
J.H. Maguire, 649(WAL):Spring81-77
Skyrms, B. Causal Necessity.
J.H. Fetzer, 486:Jun81-329
L.J. O'Neill, 63:Jun81-226
Slaate, H.A. Time and Its End.
A.W. Munk, 484(PPR):Dec81-296
Slater, C. Defeatists and Their Enemies.
E. Weber, 617(TLS):19Feb82-184
Slater, M. Humour in the Works of Proust.
R. Gibson, 535(RHL):Jul-Oct81-830
C. Lang, 400(MLN):May81-906
Slater, M. - see Dickens, C.
Slatkes, L.J. Vermeer and His Contempor-
aries.
J. Nash, 617(TLS):14May82-542
Slaughter, C. Heart of the River.
J. Crace, 617(TLS):17Dec82-1398
Slaughter, C. Marxism, Ideology and Lit-
erature.
F. Shor, 478:Spring81-119
"Slavica Hierosolymitana."* (Vol 2) (V.
Raskin and D. Segal, eds)
H. Jachnow, 688(ZSP):Band42Heft2-408
Slavitt, D.R. Dozens.
V. Young, 472:Spring/Summer82-241
Slawson, J. Unequal Americans.
T.A. Sullivan, 185:Oct80-160
Slide, A. and E. Wagenknecht. Fifty Great
American Silent Films 1912-1920.
C.P.R., 200:Aug-Sep81-445
Slights, C.W. The Casuistical Tradition
in Shakespeare, Donne, Herbert, and
Milton.*
J.R. Knott, Jr., 401(MLQ):Sep81-292

Sloman, A. The Computer Revolution in
Philosophy.*
    S.P. Stich, 482(PhR):Apr81-300
Slotkin, R. The Crater.*
    639(VQR):Autumn81-136
Slotkin, R. and J.K. Folsom, eds. So
Dreadfull a Judgment.
    R. Morton, 106:Fall81-191
Sluga, H. Gottlob Frege.
    G. Currie, 84:Jun81-200
Smakov, G. Baryshnikov.*
    R. Philp, 151:Sep81-98
Small, A., ed. Monte Irsi, Southern Italy:
the Canadian Excavations in the Iron Age
and Roman Sites, 1971-72.
    M.H. Crawford, 313:Vol71-153
Small, D. Almost Famous.
    R. Miner, 441:28Nov82-27
Small, I. - see Wilde, O.
Smalley, B. Studies in Medieval Thought
and Learning.
    M. Chibnall, 617(TLS):17Sep82-1014
Smallwood, R.L. and S. Wells - see
Dekker, T.
Smart, C. The Poetical Works of Christo-
pher Smart.* (Vol 1) (K. Williamson, ed)
    C. Rawson, 83:Autumn81-198
    639(VQR):Summer81-95
Smart, N. Beyond Ideology.
    G. Parrinder, 617(TLS):28May82-589
de Smedt, R. - see under De Smedt, R.
Smelser, N.J. and R. Content. The Chang-
ing Academic Marketplace.
    J.H. Fisher, 128(CE):Dec81-838
Smelser, R.M. The Sudeten Problem, 1933-
1938.
    M. Hauner, 575(SEER):Jan81-125
Smethurst, C. Émile Zola: "Germinal."
    V. Minogue, 208(FS):Jul81-349
Smethurst, C. - see de Balzac, H.
Smets, M. L'Avènement de la Cité-Jardin
en Belgique.
    A. Tzonis and L. Lefaivre, 576:Dec81-
    337
Smiley, L. A Nice Clean Plate.
    T. Fitton, 617(TLS):19Feb82-192
Smith, A., ed. The Art of Malcolm Lowry.
    R. Binns, 102(CanL):Spring80-108
    L. Blanchard, 395(MFS):Summer80-295
Smith, A., ed. George Eliot.*
    445(NCF):Dec81-379
Smith, A., ed. Newspapers and Democracy.
    639(VQR):Spring81-62
Smith, A., ed. The Novels of Thomas
Hardy.*
    J.L. Bradley, 677(YES):Vol 11-330
    J. Halperin, 395(MFS):Summer80-302
    M. Millgate, 445(NCF):Sep80-216
Smith, A. Paper Money.*
    639(VQR):Summer81-92
Smith, A.D. The Ethnic Revival.
    M. Banton, 617(TLS):29Jan82-95
Smith, A.G. The Analysis of Motives.*
    C.L. Anderson, 27(AL):Jan82-740
Smith, B. Place, Taste and Tradition.
    U. Hoff, 39:Feb81-128
Smith, B.F. The Road to Nuremberg.
    J.M. Blum, 676(YR):Autumn81-141
    R. Dallek, 453(NYRB):18Feb82-30
Smith, B.H. On the Margins of Discourse.*
    D. Lodge, 599:Fall81-451
    M. Peckham, 494:Autumn80-191
    M.E. Workman, 292(JAF):Jan-Mar81-90

Smith, B.L. O'Casey's Satiric Vision.*
    E. Durbach, 397(MD):Jun81-234
    D. Kiberd, 541(RES):May81-240
Smith, C. Forget Harry.
    S.D. Lavine, 385(MQR):Winter82-189
Smith, C.B. - see under Babington Smith, C.
Smith, C.H. - see Krotkov, Y.
Smith, C.R. Supermannerism.
    R. Peters, 576:Mar81-84
Smith, C.S. A Search for Structure.*
    C. Wert, 290(JAAC):Summer82-441
Smith, D. Conflict and Compromise.
    H. Perkin, 617(TLS):25Jun82-686
Smith, D. Dream Flights.
    R. Phillips, 249(HudR):Autumn81-433
    T. Swiss, 434:Spring82-489
Smith, D. Goshawk, Antelope.*
    S. Yenser, 29:Jan/Feb82-32
Smith, D. Homage to Edgar Allan Poe.
    J. Ditsky, 628(UWR):Spring-Summer82-
    105
    R. Phillips, 249(HudR):Autumn81-433
Smith, D. Onliness.*
    J. Ditsky, 628(UWR):Spring-Summer82-
    105
Smith, D., ed. The Pure Clear Word.
    E. Hirsch, 441:18Apr82-15
Smith, D. Scarecrow.*
    E. Popham, 102(CanL):Autumn81-157
Smith, D. Socialist Propaganda in the
Twentieth-Century British Novel.*
    H.G. Klaus, 224(GRM):Band31Heft1-121
Smith, D.B. Inside the Great House.*
    D.C. Skaggs, 579(SAQ):Autumn81-494
    639(VQR):Spring81-54
Smith, D.M., ed. English Episcopal Acta,
1.
    F.L. Cheyette, 589:Jan81-222
    D.E. Greenway, 325:Oct81-502
Smith, D.M. - see under Mack Smith, D.
Smith, E. By Mourning Tongues.*
    W. Franke, 38:Band99Heft3/4-520
Smith, E. Pianos.
    C. Ehrlich, 415:May81-315
Smith, E. A Woman with a Purpose. (V.
Strong-Boag, ed)
    M. Fowler, 102(CanL):Autumn81-138
Smith, E.H.F. St. Peter's.
    D.A. Sykes, 447(N&Q):Oct80-426
Smith, F.B. Florence Nightingale.
    R. Shannon, 617(TLS):28May82-571
Smith, F.B. The People's Health, 1830-
1910.
    R.J. Morris, 637(VS):Autumn80-131
Smith, F.J. First Prelude.
    P. Ramsey, 472:Spring/Summer82-172
Smith, F.J. The Experiencing of Musical
Sound.
    D. Ihde, 290(JAAC):Winter81-224
Smith, F.N. Language and Reality in
Swift's "A Tale of a Tub."
    A.C. Kelly, 566:Spring82-116
Smith, G.M. - see Meddāh, Y-I.
Smith, G.V. The Dutch in Seventeenth-
Century Thailand.
    D.R. Sar Desai, 293(JASt):Feb81-436
Smith, H., ed. Learning from Shōgun.*
    M. Cooper, 407(MN):Spring81-111
Smith, H. The Tension of the Lyre.
    A. Ferry, 401(MLQ):Dec81-389
    J. Stachniewski, 617(TLS):30Jul82-838
Smith, H., ed. X-1.
    R.J. Stout, 435:Winter81-100

Smith, H.A. The Compleat Practical Joker.
529(QQ):Summer81-402
Smith, H.D. Preaching in the Spanish
Golden Age.*
H. Sieber, 551(RenQ):Spring80-124
Smith, H.D. The Smith Āgama Collection.
W.G. Neevel, Jr., 293(JASt):Aug81-840
Smith, H.F. The Popular American Novel,
1865-1920.
H.N. Smith, 445(NCF):Sep81-193
Smith, H.N. Democracy and the Novel.*
H. Hill, 395(MFS):Summer80-320
Smith, H.R. David Garrick 1717-1779.*
H.W. Pedicord, 611(TN):Vol35No2-90
Smith, I.C. - see under Crichton Smith, I.
Smith, J. The Arts Betrayed.*
M.G. Perloff, 677(YES):Vol 11-347
Smith, J. Jack Smith's L.A.
J. Trimbur, 649(WAL):Spring81-81
Smith, J.H., ed. Kierkegaard's Truth.
R. Poole, 617(TLS):5Mar82-260
Smith, J.H., ed. The Literary Freud.*
J. Forrester, 208(FS):Apr81-170
G.S. Rousseau, 579(SAQ):Summer81-362
Smith, J.L. An Annotated Bibliography Of
and About Ernesto Cardenal.
J. Higgins, 86(BHS):Apr81-165
Smith, J.S. Elsie de Wolfe.
C. Curtis, 441:20Jun82-3
442(NY):14Jun82-135
Smith, K. When A Girl Looks Down.
D. Cooper-Clark, 102(CanL):Autumn80-
108
Smith, K.E. The Dialect Muse.
K.C. Phillipps, 571(ScLJ):Winter81-135
Smith, L.R. Some Grammatical Aspects of
Labrador Inuttut (Eskimo).
A.C. Woodbury, 269(IJAL):Jan81-75
Smith, M. - see de Ronsard, P.
Smith, M.C. Gorky Park.*
639(VQR):Summer81-99
Smith, M.G. The Affairs of Daura.
G. Nicolas, 69:Vol50No4-442
Smith, M.M. When the Emperor Dies.
T.J. Binyon, 617(TLS):29Jan82-104
Smith, M.R. Harpers Ferry Armory and the
New Technology.
A.P. McDonald, 9(AlaR):Apr81-148
Smith, M.S. Aspects of Future Reference
in a Pedagogical Grammar of English.
D. Nehls, 38:Band99Heft3/4-449
Smith, N. and D. Wilson. Modern Linguis-
tics.
R.I. Binnick, 350:Mar81-182
R.P. Ebert, 399(MLJ):Winter81-420
R. Salkie, 353:Vol 18No3/4-311
Smith, N.B. and J.T. Snow, eds. The Expan-
sion and Transformations of Courtly Lit-
erature.
D. Kelly, 589:Apr81-440
Smith, N.R. and M.B. Franklin, eds. Sym-
bolic Functioning in Childhood.
M.J. Parsons, 290(JAAC):Fall81-107
T.M. Reed, 289:Apr81-109
Smith, O. Recollections of O. Smith:
Comedian.* (W.W. Appleton, ed)
G. Speaight, 610:Spring81-150
Smith, P. Nursling of Mortality.
R. Janko, 123:Vol31No2-285
Smith, P. Realism and the Progress of
Science.
M. McGinn, 617(TLS):25Jun82-697

Smith, P. The Shaping of America.
M. Cunliffe, 656(WMQ):Jul81-514
Smith, P. Trial by Fire.
W. Goodman, 441:31Oct82-16
Smith, P. and C. Daniel. The Chicken Book.
D.J. Enright, 617(TLS):16Jul82-772
Smith, P.F. The Syntax of Cities.
J. Rykwert, 576:May81-172
Smith, P.M. - see Estienne, H.
Smith, R. The Red Smith Reader. (D.
Anderson, ed)
P-L. Adams, 61:Aug82-94
D. Hall, 441:18Jul82-3
W. Sheed, 453(NYRB):23Sep82-45
442(NY):16Aug82-92
Smith, R. To Absent Friends from Red
Smith.
P-L. Adams, 61:Aug82-94
D. Hall, 441:18Jul82-3
W. Sheed, 453(NYRB):23Sep82-45
442(NY):16Aug82-93
Smith, R. and others, comps. Southeast
Asia.
D.K. Emmerson, 293(JASt):Nov80-43
Smith, R.E. Type-Index and Motif-Index of
the Roman de Renard.
F. Wagner, 196:Band22Heft3/4-370
Smith, R.K. Jane's House.
C. Duchen, 617(TLS):17Dec82-1398
Smith, R.N. Thomas E. Dewey and His Times.
G.C. Ward, 441:22Aug82-1
442(NY):4Oct82-150
Smith, R.S. The Lagos Consulate 1851-1861.
A.J. Greenberger, 637(VS):Spring81-351
Smith, R.T. Good Water.
P. Shirley, 577(SHR):Winter81-89
Smith, S. Me Again.* (J. Barbera and W.
McBrien, eds)
P-L. Adams, 61:Jul82-95
W. Pritchard, 441:16May82-7
442(NY):2Aug82-87
Smith, S. Novel on Yellow Paper. Over
the Frontier. The Holiday.
J.C. Oates, 441:30Oct82-11
J.S., 231:Nov82-76
Smith, S.B. and H.C. Owsley - see Jackson,
A.
Smith, S.M. The Other Nation.*
T.C. Barker, 366:Autumn81-264
P. Brantlinger, 445(NCF):Sep81-218
L. Lerner, 89(BJA):Summer81-281
I. Nadel, 141:Summer81-273
S. Pickering, 569(SR):Spring81-306
638(VQR):Summer81-84
Smith, T. Literary and Linguistic Works.
(Pt 2) (B. Danielsson, ed)
205(FMLS):Jan80-93
Smith, T., ed. The Macmillan Guide to
Family Health.
J.F. Watkins, 617(TLS):4Jun82-618
Smith, T. The Pattern of Imperialism.
J. Keegan, 453(NYRB):23Sep82-27
Smith, T.C., with R.Y. Eng and R.T. Lundy.
Nakahara.*
W.B. Hauser, 318(JAOS):Apr/Jun80-211
Smith, W.C. On Understanding Islam.
C. Geertz, 453(NYRB):27May82-25
Smith, W.D. The German Colonial Empire.
H.P. von Strandmann, 161(DUJ):Jun81-
246
Smith, W.J. Army Brat.
R. Phillips, 461:Spring-Summer81-103
639(VQR):Spring81-48

Smither, E. Casanova's Ankle.
    F. Adcock, 617(TLS):17Dec82-1399
Smither, E. The Legend of Marcello
  Mastoianni's Wife.
    C. Rumens, 617(TLS):12Feb82-166
Smithers, A.J. Dornford Yates.
    T.J. Binyon, 617(TLS):19Mar82-307
    E.S. Turner, 362:4Mar82-21
Smithers, D.W. Jane Austen in Kent.
    B. Southam, 617(TLS):23Apr82-470
Smithies, E. Crime in Wartime.
    V. Bailey, 617(TLS):9Apr82-417
Smollett, T. The Adventures of Roderick
  Random.* (P-G. Boucé, ed)
    M. Irwin, 541(RES):Nov81-454
    I. Jack, 189(EA):Apr-Jun81-223
    F. McCombie, 447(N&Q):Dec80-550
    D.T. Siebert, Jr., 588(SSL):Vol 16-278
Smollett, T. Travels through France and
  Italy.* (F. Felsenstein, ed)
    P-G. Boucé, 189(EA):Jul-Sep81-343
    M. Irwin, 541(RES):Nov81-454
Smoodin, R. Presto!
    F. Levine, 441:22Aug82-11
    442(NY):27Sep82-145
Smoodin, R. Ursus Major.*
    K.M. Morsberger, 649(WAL):Summer81-171
Smuda, M. Der Gegenstand in der bildenden
  Kunst und Literatur.
    M. Kesting, 490:Band12Heft3/4-532
Smyer, R.I. Primal Dream and Primal
  Crime.*
    J.V. Knapp, 395(MFS):Winter80/81-701
    205(FMLS):Apr81-200
Sneddon, J.N. Proto-Minahasan.
    R.A. Blust, 350:Dec82-921
Snell, B. and H. Erbse. Lexicon des Fruh-
  griechischen Epos. (Pt 9)
    P. Monteil, 555:Vol54fasc1-155
Snell, B.M., ed. Translating and the
  Computer.
    W. Wilss, 603:Vol5No3-424
Snell, D.C. Workbook of Cuneiform Signs.
    D.A. Foxvog, 350:Mar81-226
Snell, R. Théophile Gautier.
    N. Bryson, 617(TLS):2Jul82-722
Snellgrove, D. and H. Richardson. A Cul-
  tural History of Tibet.
    R.A. Miller, 293(JASt):May81-596
Sniderman, P. A Question of Loyalty.
    J.L.H., 185:Jul82-783
Snipes, K. Robert Graves.*
    L. Blanchard, 395(MFS):Summer80-295
Snow, E.A. A Study of Vermeer.
    B. Wind, 568(SCN):Summer-Fall81-59
Snow, E.R. Sea Disasters and Island Catas-
  trophes.
    639(VQR):Autumn81-137
Snow, K. Wonders.*
    D. Smith, 29:Jan/Feb82-36
Snow, P. Stranger and Brother.
    R. Fuller, 362:28Oct82-19
Snow, P., comp. The United States: A
  Guide to Library Holdings in the UK.
    D.W. Bryant, 617(TLS):7May82-519
Snow, R.J. The Extant Music of Rodrigo de
  Ceballos and its Sources.
    L. Salter, 415:Dec81-824
Snowden, R. and G.D. Mitchell. The Arti-
  ficial Family.
    T.M.R., 185:Apr82-599
Snyder, B. Encuentros Culturales.
    G.L. Ervin, 399(MLJ):Spring81-118

Snyder, G. The Real Work.* (S. McLean,
  ed)
    B. Almon, 649(WAL):Spring81-55
Snyder, G.A.S. Minoische und mykenische
  Kunst.
    S. Hood, 303(JoHS):Vol 101-220
Snyder, S. The Comic Matrix of Shake-
  speare's Tragedies.*
    T.W. Craik, 161(DUJ):Jun81-251
    W. Habicht, 570(SQ):Autumn81-413
    W.A. Rebhorn, 551(RenQ):Autumn80-474
Snyder, S. - see Du Bartas, S.
Soames, S. and D.M. Perlmutter. Syntactic
  Argumentation and the Structure of
  English.*
    J.K. Gundel, 300:Mar81-36
Sobejano, G., ed. Francisco de Quevedo.*
    L.S. Lerner, 240(HR):Spring81-233
    F. Schalk, 72:Band217Heft2-471
Soble, A. Philosophy of Sex.
    J.K., 185:Oct81-188
Soder, M. Hausarbeit und Stammtischsozial-
  ismus.
    D. Mühlberg and A. Neef, 654(WB):
      11/1981-182
Sodmann, T. - see "Dat narren schyp,
  Lübeck 1497"
Sodmann, T. - see "Reinke de Vos, Lübeck
  1498"
Soebadio, H. and C.A.D. Sarvaas, eds. The
  Dynamics of Indonesian History.
    J. Taylor, 293(JASt):Aug81-852
Soellner, R., with G.J. Williams. "Timon
  of Athens."*
    J.C. Bulman, 402(MLR):Apr81-441
    L.S. Champion, 551(RenQ):Summer80-293
    E.A.J. Honigmann, 447(N&Q):Oct80-435
    G. Taylor, 541(RES):Feb81-76
Soghoian, R.J. The Ethics of G.E. Moore
  and David Hume.
    J.M. Orenduff, 185:Oct80-165
Sokolov, R. Fading Feast.
    F. Randall, 441:28Feb82-16
Sokolov, R. Wayward Reporter.
    639(VQR):Spring81-47
Sol, H.B., ed. La Vie du pape saint
  Grégoire.*
    U. Mölk, 224(GRM):Band31Heft1-115
Sola-Solé, J.M. Los sonetos "al itálico
  modo" del marqués de Santillana.
    K. Whinnom, 86(BHS):Apr81-140
Solà-Solé, J.M., S.G. Armistead and J.H.
  Silverman, eds. Hispania Judaica.
  (Vol 1)
    R.B. Tate, 86(BHS):Jul81-256
Solé-Leris, A. The Spanish Pastoral
  Novel.*
    D.H. Darst, 238:Dec81-637
Soleri, P. Fragments.
    J. Jordan, 42(AR):Summer81-388
Solignac, P. The Christian Neurosis.
    J. Dominian, 617(TLS):9Apr82-406
Söll, L. Gesprochenes und geschriebenes
  Französisch.
    H. and R. Kahane, 545(RPh):Feb81(supp)-
      15
Sollertinsky, D. and L. Pages from the
  Life of Dmitri Shostakovich.*
    C. Bennett, 607:Dec81-49
    J. Ronsheim, 42(AR):Fall81-514
Solodow, J.B. The Latin Particle
  "Quidem."*
    H.C. Gotoff, 122:Apr81-159

Sorrentino, G. Aberration of Starlight.*
D. Flower, 249(HudR):Spring81-106
J. Morse, 114(ChiR):Autumn80-112
Sorrentino, G. Mulligan Stew.*
M. Kirby, 435:Winter81-111
W. Templeton, 648(WCR):Jun80-54
Sorrentino, G. Selected Poems 1958-1980.*
H. McNeil, 617(TLS):29Jan82-113
Sosa, E., ed. The Philosophy of Nicholas
Rescher.
R. Haack, 479(PhQ):Apr81-172
Sotelo Salas, A.I. - see Garcilaso de la
Vega
Sötemann, A.L. Op het voetspoor van de
dichter.
P. de Vroomen, 204(FdL):Jun81-213
Sötér, I. and I. Neupokoyeva, eds. Euro-
pean Romanticism.
M. Szegedy-Maszák, 549(RLC):Jul-Dec81-
480
Soubeille, G. - see Macrin, J.S.
Souchal, F. French Sculptors of the 17th
and 18th Centuries: The Reign of Louis
XIV.* (Vol 1)
F. Haskell, 453(NYRB):15Apr82-32
Souchal, F. French Sculptors of the 17th
and 18th Centuries: The Reign of Louis
XIV. (Vol 2)
F. Haskell, 453(NYRB):15Apr82-32
M. Levey, 90:Dec81-751
F. Watson, 324:Mar82-229
Souchal, F. Les Frères Coustou.
P. Fusco, 39:Sep81-204
Součková, M. Baroque in Bohemia.
H.R. Cooper, Jr., 574(SEEJ):Winter81-
102
R.B. Pynsent, 402(MLR):Jul81-767
Soucy, R. Fascist Intellectual: Drieu la
Rochelle.
J. Birkett, 208(FS):Jan81-95
R. Veasey, 402(MLR):Jan81-201
Souleïmenov, O. Transformation du feu.
L. Ray, 450(NRF):Dec81-125
Soulié, H. A cloche-pied.
M.B. Kline, 207(FR):Mar81-626
Soulier, J-P. Lautréamont, génie ou
maladie mentale?
A-M. Roux, 535(RHL):Mar-Apr81-316
Soupault, P. Last Nights of Paris.
R. Cardinal, 617(TLS):6Aug82-846
Sourvinou-Inwood, C. Theseus as Son and
Stepson.
E. Simon, 123:Vol31No1-64
Soussouev, P.O. - see under Oster Sous-
souev, P.
Souster, R. Collected Poems of Raymond
Souster.
T. Marshall, 529(QQ):Spring81-184
Souster, R. Hanging In.*
L. Daniel, 102(CanL):Winter80-128
Soutet, O. La Littérature française de la
Renaissance.
M. Tetel, 207(FR):Feb82-403
Southam, B. Mixed Singles.
A. Paterson, 368:Dec81-471
Southam, B. - see Austen, J.
Southerland-Holmes, N. Creative Christmas.
R.L. Shep, 614:Fall81-16
Southwell, S.B. Quest for Eros.
E. Cook, 637(VS):Summer81-523
J.A. Dupras, 85(SBHC):Fall81-96
C.D. Ryals, 301(JEGP):Jul81-429

Southwick, M. The Night Won't Save Anyone.
J.F. Cotter, 249(HudR):Summer81-282
Souza, M. The Emperor of the Amazon.*
(Brazilian title: Galvez, o Imperador do
Acre.) Mad Maria.
C.F. Moisés, 37:May81-25
Sow, A.I., ed. Langues et politiques de
langues en Afrique Noire.
S. Brauner, 682(ZPSK):Band33Heft4-511
Sowell, T. Knowledge and Decisions.
L.W. Dunbar, 639(VQR):Spring81-366
Sowell, T. Markets and Minorities.
K. Schott, 617(TLS):26Mar82-358
Sowers, R. The Language of Stained Glass.
R. Kehlmann, 139:Dec81/Jan82-42
Soyez, B. Byblos et la fête des Adonies.
R.A. Oden, Jr., 318(JAOS):Jul/Sep80-
372
Soyinka, W. Aké, the Years of Childhood.*
P-L. Adams, 61:Sep82-95
D. Duerden, 617(TLS):26Feb82-228
N. Gordimer, 453(NYRB):21Oct82-3
J. Olney, 441:10Oct82-7
Spackman, W.M. A Presence with Secrets.
639(VQR):Summer81-102
Spacks, P.M. The Adolescent Idea.*
L. Mackinnon, 617(TLS):15Oct82-1140
Spade, P.V. - see Heytesbury, W.
Spade, P.V. - see Peter of Ailly
Spahn, P. Mittelschicht und Polisbildung.
N.R.E. Fisher, 303(JoHS):Vol 101-189
Spahn, P. Unterhaltung im Sozialismus.
C. Ziermann, 654(WB):11/1981-179
Spalding, F. Roger Fry.*
M. Goldstein, 569(SR):Spring81-287
D. Mannings, 89(BJA):Summer81-276
B. Wolmer, 55:Feb81-36
Spalek, J.M., with A. Ash and S.H. Hawryl-
chak. Guide to the Archival Materials
of the German-Speaking Emigration to the
United States After 1933.
W.D. Elfe, 406:Summer81-225
J.L. Heilbron, 486:Mar81-161
Spalek, J.M. and W. Frühwald - see Toller,
E.
Spann, E.K. The New Metropolis.*
J. Potter, 617(TLS):19Mar82-325
Spann, M. Franz Kafka.
B. Goldstein, 406:Spring81-67
Spanos, W.V., ed. Martin Heidegger and
the Question of Literature.*
S.A. Erickson, 478:Spring81-108
Spark, M. Loitering with Intent.*
M. Dodsworth, 175:Autumn81-309
W. Scammell, 364:Oct81-96
Sparke, P. - see Banham, R.
Sparrow, J. Words on the Air.*
N. Annan, 453(NYRB):4Feb82-35
Sparshott, F. The Naming Of The Beasts.*
P. Stevens, 102(CanL):Spring81-155
Sparshott, F. The Rainy Hills.
M. Darling, 102(CanL):Summer81-135
Spate, V. Orphism.*
W.A. Camfield, 127:Fall81-267
N. Lynton, 89(BJA):Summer81-275
M. Sheringham, 208(FS):Jul81-366
Spater, G. William Cobbett.
R. Blythe, 453(NYRB):10Jun82-29
J.F.C. Harrison, 617(TLS):25Jun82-685
W. Safire, 441:6Jun82-14
442(NY):24May82-136
Spaulding, F. Roger Fry.
B.R. Tilghman, 289:Jul81-117

Spaziani, M. Don Giovanni dagli scenari
    dell'arte alla "Foire."
    W.D. Howarth, 208(FS):Oct81-495
Speake, G. Anglo-Saxon Animal Art and its
    Germanic Background.*
    B.C. Raw, 382(MAE):1981/2-327
Spear, F.A. Bibliographie de Diderot.
    O. Fellows, 546(RR):Jan81-110
    A. Strugnell, 402(MLR):Jul81-704
    R.P. Thomas, 207(FR):Mar81-596
Spear, R. Silks.*
    R. Tillinghast, 569(SR):Spring81-265
Speck, J., ed. Philosophie der Neuzeit I.
    R. Margreiter, 489(PJGG):Band88Heft1-
    211
Speck, W.A. The Butcher.
    A. Hetherington, 362:14Jan82-24
    R. Mitchison, 617(TLS):2Apr82-390
Speck, W.A. Stability and Strife.
    A.N. Newman, 366:Autumn81-254
Spector, M. Concepts of Reduction in
    Physical Science.
    R. Yoshida, 84:Dec81-400
Spector, R.D. Arthur Murphy.
    W.H. Pedicord, 610:Autumn81-220
Speer, A. Infiltration.*
    M. Ebon, 390:Dec81-59
    N. Stone, 453(NYRB):13May82-24
Speidel, M.P. Mithras-Orion.
    R.M. Ogilvie, 123:Vol31No2-305
Speidel, W. A Complete Contextual Concor-
    dance to Franz Kafka "Der Prozess."
    A.P. Foulkes, 301(JEGP):Apr81-305
Speiss, K. Peripherie Sowjetwirtschaft.
    N.W. Balabkins, 550(RusR):Apr81-198
Spence, C.C. The Rainmakers.
    W. Gard, 584(SWR):Summer81-324
Spence, J. Search for Justice.
    M.P. Petracca, 185:Jul81-673
Spence, J.D. The Gate of Heavenly Peace.*
    R. Blythe, 362:18Feb82-20
    J.B. Grieder, 676(YR):Summer82-584
    B. Raffel, 385(MQR):Spring82-361
    F. Wakeman, Jr., 453(NYRB):18Feb82-37
Spence, J.D. and J.E. Wills, Jr., eds.
    From Ming to Ch'ing.*
    L.D. Kessler, 293(JASt):Nov80-120
    A.Y.C. Lui, 302:Vol 18-139
Spencer, B. Collected Poems. (R. Bowen,
    ed)
    G. Ewart, 364:Nov81-80
    A. Thwaite, 617(TLS):1Jan82-7
Spencer, E. The Stories of Elizabeth
    Spencer.*
    C.C. Park, 249(HudR):Winter81/82-601
Spencer, H., ed. American Art.
    J.V. Turano, 16:Spring81-93
Spender, D. Man Made Language.
    N.H., 185:Jan82-389
    S. Trömel-Plötz, 603:Vol5No3-432
Spender, D. Women of Ideas and What Men
    Have Done to Them.
    P. Willmott, 617(TLS):24Dec82-1410
Spender, S. Letters to Christopher.* (L.
    Bartlett, ed)
    S. Corey, 219(GaR):Summer81-431
Spender, S. - see Schiller, F.
Spender, S. and D. Hockney. China Diary.
    P. Fussell, 617(TLS):26Nov82-1294
Spengemann, W.C. The Forms of Autobiogra-
    phy.*
    G.W. Allen, 219(GaR):Summer81-411
                                    [continued]

[continuing]
    J.H. Buckley, 445(NCF):Jun81-79
    C.T. Holly, 405(MP):Nov81-230
    J.N. Morris, 191(ELN):Mar81-229
    J. Olney, 579(SAQ):Summer81-369
    D.H. Reiman, 301(JEGP):Jan81-130
    T.R. Smith, 249(HudR):Summer81-290
Spenser, E. The Faerie Queene.* (A.C.
    Hamilton, ed)
    W.C. Johnson, 179(ES):Apr81-171
    T.P. Roche, 402(MLR):Jul81-660
Spenser, E. The Faerie Queene.* (T.P.
    Roche, Jr., with C.P. O'Donnell, Jr.,
    eds)
    H. Dubrow, 161(DUJ):Jun81-250
Spenser, E. The Illustrated "Faerie
    Queene." (D. Hill, ed)
    W.F.M. 604:Winter81-1
"Spenser Studies." (Vol 2) (P. Cullen and
    T.P. Roche, eds)
    H. Woudhuysen, 617(TLS):18Jun82-678
Sperlich, N. and E.K. Guatemalan Back-
    strap Weaving.*
    F.H. Pettit, 37:May81-26
Sperling, D. and G. Mingay. Mrs. Hurst
    Dancing, and Other Scenes from Regency
    Life, 1812-23.*
    135:Dec81-251
Speroni, C. and C.L. Golino. Panorama
    Italiano. (4th ed)
    A. Seldis, 399(MLJ):Winter81-437
Sperry, K.P., ed. Index to Genealogical
    Periodical Literature, 1960-77.
    K.B. Harder, 424:Mar80-94
    K.B. Harder, 424:Sep80-219
Speyer, J.S. Vedische und Sanskrit-Syntax.
    W. Morgenroth, 682(ZPSK):Band33Heft2-
    281
Sphrantzes, G. The Fall of the Byzantine
    Empire. (M. Philippides, trans)
    R. Browning, 123:Vol31No2-331
    D.M. Nicol, 382(MAE):1981/2-318
Spicer, J. One Night Stand and Other
    Poems. (D. Allen, ed)
    J. Trimbur, 649(WAL):Fall81-226
Spicker, S.F., ed. Organism, Medicine,
    and Metaphysics.
    J.C. Moskop, 185:Jan82-381
Spicker, S.F. and H.T. Engelhardt, Jr.,
    eds. Philosophical Medical Ethics.*
    Philosophical Dimensions of the Neuro-
    Medical Sciences.
    J.C. Moskop, 185:Jan82-381
Spike, J.T. Italian Baroque Paintings
    from New York Private Collections.
    R. Kultzen, 471:Jan/Feb/Mar81-94
Spilka, M. Virginia Woolf's Quarrel with
    Grieving.*
    H.M. Daleski, 454:Winter82-188
Spiller, R.E. Late Harvest.
    27(AL):Nov81-573
Spiller, R.E. and J.F. Beard - see Cooper,
    J.F.
Spilling, H. Handschriftenkataloge der
    Staats- und Stadtbibliothek Augsburg.
    (Vol 2)
    H. Thurn, 684(ZDA):Band110Heft1-7
Spinelli, D.C., ed. A Concordance to Mari-
    vaux's Comedies in Prose.
    W. Wrage, 399(MLJ):Summer81-211
Spinelli, E. English Grammar for Students
    of Spanish.
    M.A. Marks, 399(MLJ):Autumn81-341

335

Spinner, H.F. Begründung, Kritik und
Rationalität.* (Vol 1)
G. Wolters, 53(AGP):Band63Heft2-216
Spinosa, N. Velázquez.
T. Crombie, 39:Jun81-415
Spinosa, N. and others. Civiltà del '700
a Napoli, 1734-1799. (Vol 1)
R. Enggass, 54:Jun81-340
de Spinoza, B. Briefwisseling. (F. Akker-
man, H.G. Hubbeling and A.G. Westerbrink,
eds and trans) Ethica. (N. van Such-
telen, ed and trans)
M. Walther, 53(AGP):Band63Heft2-196
de Spinoza, B. Sämtliche Werke. (Vols 2
and 4-7) (C. Gebhardt, ed)
H.P. Rickman, 53(AGP):Band62Heft2-215
Spinoza, B. Traité politique. (P.F.
Moreau, ed and trans)
G. Brykman, 542:Jul-Sep81-357
Spires, E. Globe.
B. Bennett, 441:14Mar82-12
Spitz, D. The Real World of Liberalism.
G. Sampson, 617(TLS):19Nov82-1277
Spitz, R.S. Barefoot in Babylon.
J.P. Hammersmith, 577(SHR):Summer81-
257
Spitzer, L. and J. Brody. Approches tex-
tuelles des "Mémoires" de Saint-Simon.
D. Bellos, 208(FS):Jul81-329
J. Dubu, 475:No15Pt1-179
Spivey, T.R. The Journey Beyond Tragedy.
J.L. Abbott, 573(SSF):Fall81-468
Splett, J. Samanunga-Studien.
P.F. Ganz, 402(MLR):Jan81-229
Spliet, H. Russland von der Autokratie
der Zaren zur imperialen Grossmacht.
M.S. Anderson, 575(SEER):Jul81-437
J. Keep, 550(RusR):Apr81-182
Spoehr, A. Protein from the Sea.
M.K. Orbach, 293(JASt):Aug81-854
de Sponde, J. Oeuvres littéraires.* (A.
Boase, ed)
J. Pineaux, 535(RHL):Mar-Apr81-283
205(FMLS):Jan80-95
"Spotlight on Drama."
R. Stuart, 108:Fall81-116
Spragens, T.A. The Irony of Liberal
Reason.
A. Ryan, 617(TLS):10Dec82-1354
Sprague, E. Metaphysical Thinking.*
H.P.K., 543:Sep80-166
Sprague, P.E. The Drawings of Louis Henry
Sullivan.*
R.C. Twombly, 658:Spring81-109
L.S. Weingarden, 54:Dec81-690
J. Zukowsky, 576:Oct81-251
Sprague, R.K. Plato's Philosopher-King.*
R.A. Hornsby, 121(CJ):Oct/Nov81-68
Sprengel, K. A Study in Word-Formation.*
E. Burgschmidt, 38:Band99Heft1/2-167
E. Pennanen, 179(ES):Apr81-187
Sprengel, P., ed. Jean Paul im Urteil
seiner Kritiker.
W. Koepke, 221(GQ):Nov81-510
R-R. Wuthenow, 133:Band14Heft4-371
Springborg, R. Family Power and Politics
in Egypt.
P.J. Vatikiotis, 617(TLS):10Sep82-979
"Sprog i Norden 1980." (E. Bojsen and
others, eds)
C. Henriksen, 563(SS):Autunn81-469

Sprung, M. Lucid Exposition of the Middle
Way.
J.W. de Jong, 259(IIJ):Jul81-227
Squadrito, K.M. Locke's Theory of Sensi-
tive Knowledge.
K.G. Van Leeuwen, 319:Apr81-254
Squarotti, G.B. - see under Bàrberi
Squarotti, G.
Squibb, G.D. Precedence in England and
Wales.
A. Wagner, 617(TLS):5Mar82-259
Squier, C.L. Sir John Suckling.
J. Buxton, 677(YES):Vol 11-257
Squires, G. XXI Poems.
S. O'Brien, 493:Jun81-60
Squires, R. Gardens of the World.*
D. Gioia, 249(HudR):Winter81/82-579
J.R. Reed, 385(MQR):Fall82-680
Srabian de Fabry, A. Etudes autour de "La
Nouvelle Héloïse."
R.J. Howells, 208(FS):Apr81-206
M.B. Therrien, 207(FR):Oct80-163
Srinivas, M.N., A.M. Shah and E.A. Ramas-
wamy, eds. The Fieldworker and the
Field.
P.M. Gardner, 293(JASt):Feb81-412
Staar, R.F. - see "Yearbook on Interna-
tional Communist Affairs, 1980"
Stabler, A.P., general ed. Four French
Renaissance Plays.
N. Aronson, 399(MLJ):Spring81-95
C.E. Campbell, 207(FR):Feb82-405
G. Jondorf, 208(FS):Oct81-435
Stachura, P.D. The German Youth Movement
1900-1945.
W. Laqueur, 617(TLS):15Jan82-59
Stack, G.J. Kierkegaard's Existential
Ethics.
J.C. Morrison, 319:Jan81-123
von Stackelberg, J. Themen der Aufklärung.
R. Mercier, 535(RHL):May-Jun81-461
von Staden, W. Darkness Over the Valley.
H. Demetz, 676(YR):Autumn81-138
Stadler, U. Die theuren Dinge.
D.F. Mahoney, 221(GQ):May81-344
Stadter, P.A. Arrian of Nicomedia.*
S. Hornblower, 123:Vol131No1-12
Staehelin, M. Die Messen Heinrich Isaacs.
R. Sherr, 317:Spring81-144
Madame de Staël. Des Circonstances actuel-
les qui peuvent terminer la Révolution
et des principes qui doivent fonder la
République en France. (L. Omacini, ed)
J. Gaulmier, 535(RHL):Jan-Feb81-141
M. Gutwirth, 207(FR):Dec81-274
N. King, 402(MLR):Jan81-190
Madame de Staël. Correspondance générale.*
(Vol 4, Pt 2) (B.W. Jasinski, ed)
N. King, 402(MLR):Jan81-190
J. Kitchin, 208(FS):Oct81-454
Stafford, B.M. Symbol and Myth.*
G. Collier, 289:Apr81-124
M.S. Kinsey, 446(NCFS):Fall-Win-
ter81/82-171
F.D. Martin, 290(JAAC):Winter81-233
Stafford, D. Britain and European Resist-
ance 1940-1945.
G.F.G. Stanley, 529(QQ):Spring81-175
Stafford, D.E. In the Classic Mode.
639(VQR):Spring81-66

Starr, C.G. The Roman Empire 27 B.C. -
A.D. 476.
  W. Goodman, 441:19Sep82-16
States, B.O. The Shape of Paradox.*
  L.S. Butler, 447(N&Q):Dec80-572
Statius. Opere di Publio Papinio Stazio.
  (A. Traglia and G. Aricò, eds and trans)
  D.E. Hill, 123:Vol31No2-207
Stavenhagen, K. Absolute Stellungnahmen.
  F. Dunlop, 323:Jan81-98
Staves, S. Players' Scepters.*
  J. Milhous, 173(ECS):Summer81-486
Stavola, T.J. Scott Fitzgerald.
  K. Carabine, 402(MLR):Oct81-947
  S. Donaldson, 395(MFS):Summer80-332
Stead, C. Divine Substance.*
  K. Bärthlein, 53(AGP):Band63Heft1-80
Stead, C.K. Five for the Symbol.
  C. Bates, 368:Dec81-466
  J. Mellors, 364:Aug-Sep81-139
Stead, C.K. - see Duggan, M.
Steadman, J.M. Nature into Myth.
  J. Norton-Smith, 541(RES):Aug81-314
Steadman, P. The Evolution of Designs.*
  J. Mascheck, 62:Jan81-64
Stebbins, S. Studien zur Tradition und
Rezeption der Bildlichkeit in der
"Eneide" Heinrichs von Veldeke.
  L. Okken, 680(ZDP):Band99Heft1-125
Steblin-Kamenskij, M.I. Drevneskandinav-
skaja literatura.
  A. Liberman, 563(SS):Summer81-344
Stedje, A. Deutsch gestern und heute.
  K. Nyholm, 439(NM):1981/3-354
Steegmuller, F. - see Flaubert, G.
Steel, B. Translation from Spanish.
  J.J. Deveny, Jr., 399(MLJ):Spring81-
  102
  T.D. Terrell, 238:May81-323
Steel, C.G. The Changing Self.*
  S. Gersh, 53(AGP):Band63Heft2-189
Steel, D. Crossings.
  E.R. Lipson, 441:3Oct82-13
Steel, G.H. Chronology and Time in "A la
recherche du temps perdu."
  W.C. Carter, 207(FR):Dec81-278
  E. Dezon-Jones, 535(RHL):Nov-Dec81-
  1021
Steel, R. Walter Lippmann and the Ameri-
can Century.*
  T.J. Hamilton, 219(GaR):Summer81-441
Steele, E.J. Somatic Selection and Adap-
tive Evolution.*
  J.C. Semple, 529(QQ):Winter81-767
Steele, H. McCandy.
  C. Hawtree, 364:Oct81-99
Steele, R.S. Freud and Jung.
  A. Storr, 617(TLS):1Oct82-1080
Steele, T. Uncertainties and Rest.*
  M. Kinzie, 29:Mar/Apr82-13
  R.T. Smith, 577(SHR):Spring81-176
van Steenberghen, F. Thomas Aquinas and
Radical Aristotelianism.
  S.F. Brown, 589:Jan81-224
van Steenberghen, F. Le problème de
l'existence de Dieu dans les écrits de S.
Thomas d'Aquin.
  B.M. Bonansea, 258:Dec81-461
Steensma, R.C. Dr. John Arbuthnot.*
  C.J. Rawson, 677(YES):Vol 11-271

Steer, A.G., Jr. Goethe's Science in the
Structure of the "Wanderjahre."*
  A.P. Cottrell, 301(JEGP):Jan81-97
  G-L. Fink, 133:Band14Heft1-78
  D.F. Mahoney, 222(GR):Summer81-119
  H.M.K. Riley, 406:Fall81-349
Steer, J. Alvise Vivarini.
  C. Hope, 617(TLS):18Jun82-675
Steer, K.A. and J.W.M. Bannerman, with G.H.
Collins. Late Medieval Monumental
Sculpture in the West Highlands.
  A.V.B. Norman, 39:Aug81-134
  H. Richardson, 112:Vol 14-166
Steermann-Imre, G. Untersuchung des
Königswahlmotivs in der indischen
Märchenliteratur.
  G. von Simson, 196:Band21Heft1/2-156
Stefanis, I.E. Ho Doylos stis Kōmōdies
toy Aristophanē.
  J.D. Smart, 123:Vol31No2-286
di Stefano, G. Monumenti della Sicilia
normanna. (2nd ed) (W. Krönig, ed)
  R.P. Bergman, 576:Oct81-237
Steffan, J. Darstellung und Wahrnehmung
der Wirklichkeit in Franz Kafkas Romanen.
  B. Goldstein, 406:Spring81-67
Steffens, H.J. The Development of Newtoni-
an Optics in England.*
  S.J. Dundon, 319:Jan81-116
Steffens, K., ed. Die Historia de preliis
Alexandri Magni.
  C. Minis, 684(ZDA):Band110Heft3-113
Stegeman, J. Aspekte der kontrastiven
Syntax am Beispiel des Niederländischen
und Deutschen.
  B. Comrie, 353:Vol 18No9/10-950
Stegemann, H. Studien zu Alfred Döblins
Bildlichkeit.
  M.S. Fries, 221(GQ):Jan81-107
Stegner, W. One Way to Spell Man.
  V. Bourjaily, 441:30May82-19
Steig, M. Dickens and Phiz.*
  S. Monod, 402(MLR):Jan81-171
  P. Preston, 447(N&Q):Dec80-557
Stein, A. The Art of Presence.
  R.H. Sundell, 568(SCN):Spring81-3
Stein, A., ed and trans. Four German
Poets.*
  G. Stern, 133:Band14Heft3-286
Stein, B. 'Ludes.
  C. Crowe, 441:4Jul82-6
Stein, B.L. - see Twain, M.
Stein, D. Der Beginn des byzantinischen
Bilderstreites und seine Entwicklung bis
in die 40er Jahre des 8. Jahrhunderts.
  S. Gero, 589:Jan81-223
Stein, D.L. City Boys.
  A. Schroeder, 102(CanL):Summer80-144
Stein, D.L. The Hearing.
  J. Wasserman, 102(CanL):Summer80-104
Stein, G. Studies in the Function of the
Passive.
  C. Beedham, 297(JL):Mar81-148
  A. Davison, 603:Vol5No3-438
Stein, G. The Yale Gertrude Stein, Selec-
tions.* (R. Kostelanetz, ed)
  S.P. Edelman, 584(SWR):Winter81-103
  L. Wagner, 573(SSF):Spring81-193
  639(VQR):Spring81-54
Stein, H. Zur Herkunft und Altersbestim-
mung einer Novellenballade (DV1dr Nr. 76
[continued]

338

[continuing]
und Nr. 77).
  J. Dittmar, 196:Band22Heft1/2-156
  E. Ettlinger, 203:Vol91No2-248
Stein, J. Edie. (G. Plimpton, ed)
  J. Atlas, 61:Jul82-92
  F. Taliaferro, 231:Jul82-70
  J. Wolcott, 453(NYRB):15Jul82-17
  G. Wolff, 441:4Jul82-3
  442(NY):19Jul82-99
Stein, P.K. Literaturgeschichte — Rezep-
  tionsforschung — "Produktive Rezeption."
  U. Wyss, 602:Vol 12No1-266
Stein, R.L. The French Slave Trade in the
  Eighteenth Century.
  J-F. Brière, 207(FR):Apr81-750
Stein, S. Populism in Peru.
  S.M. Gorman, 263(RIB):Vol31No3-421
Steinberg, D.J., ed. In Search of South-
  east Asia.
  D.K. Emmerson, 293(JASt):Nov80-43
Steinberg, J. Locke, Rousseau, and the
  Idea of Consent.
  W. Euchner, 53(AGP):Band63Heft2-193
  C. Pateman, 185:Apr81-513
Steinberg, J. Why Switzerland?
  M. Hobson, 208(FS):Oct81-498
Steinbock, B., ed. Killing and Letting
  Die.*
  B. Barry, 185:Apr82-555
Steinecke, H. Romantheorie und Roman-
  kritik in Deutschland.
  I. Wegner, 654(WB):9/1981-188
Steiner, C. Martin Heidegger.*
  H. Eiland, 81:Spring80-309
  S.A. Erickson, 478:Spring81-108
  M.C. Gelven, 154:Sep81-566
  A. Janik, 319:Jul81-403
  R.S.N., 185:Jul82-790
  W.T. Stevenson, 396(ModA):Winter81-95
Steiner, G. On Difficulty.*
  K. Kolenda, 478:Fall81-236
  C. Norris, 402(MLR):Jan81-138
  205(FMLS):Jan80-95
Steiner, G. The Portage to San Cristobal
  of A.H.*
  R.M. Adams, 453(NYRB):12Aug82-11
  M. Dickstein, 441:2May82-13
  P. Lewis, 565:Vol122No4-69
  J. Mellors, 364:Oct81-93
Steiner, G.Y. The Futility of Family Pol-
  icy.*
  A. Hacker, 453(NYRB):18Mar82-37
Steiner, K., E.S. Krauss and S.C. Flanagan,
  eds. Political Opposition and Local
  Politics.
  Funaba Masatomi, 285(JapQ):Oct-Dec81-
  564
Steiner, R. La philosophie de Thomas
  d'Aquin.
  A. Reix, 542:Jul-Sep81-339
Steiner, S. The Ranchers.*
  J.F. Hoy, 649(WAL):Fall81-225
Steiner, W. Exact Resemblance to Exact
  Resemblance.*
  P.M.S. Dawson, 541(RES):Feb81-99
  B. Landon, 481(PQ):Winter80-117
  M.G. Perloff, 677(YES):Vol 11-347
Steiner, W., ed. The Sign in Music and
  Literature.
  W. Coker, 290(JAAC):Spring82-340

Steiner, Z., ed. The Times Survey of
  Foreign Ministries of the World.
  D.C. Watt, 617(TLS):12Nov82-1238
Steinfels, P. The Neoconservatives.
  M. Shefter, 185:Jan82-380
  D.H. Wrong, 473(PR):1/1981-96
Steinhagen, H. Wirklichkeit und Handeln
  im barocken Drama.*
  M. Schilling, 224(GRM):Band31Heft1-109
Steinhart, E.I. Conflict and Collabora-
  tion.
  R.G. Abrahams, 69:Vol150No2-220
Steinhaussen, U. Über Entstehungsprobleme
  sozialistischer Gegenwartsliteratur.
  M. Krumrey, 654(WB):11/1981-175
Steinkraus, W.E. and K.L. Schmitz, eds.
  Art and Logic in Hegel's Philosophy.*
  A. Rapaczynski, 185:Jan82-362
  E. Schaper, 89(BJA):Spring81-173
Steinle, G. Hartmann von Aue.
  D.H. Green, 402(MLR):Jul81-735
Steinmann, M., ed. CIAM-International
  Kongresse für Neues Bauen/Congrès
  Internationaux d'Architecture Moderne,
  Dokumente 1928-1939.
  W. Nerdinger, 576:Dec81-338
Steinmetz, D.C. Luther and Staupitz.
  G. Rupp, 617(TLS):16Apr82-447
Steinmetz, H. Galloromanische Bezeich-
  nungen für "betrunken/sich betrinken,"
  "Trunkenheit," "Trunkenhold."*
  K.A. Goddard, 208(FS):Jul81-316
Steinmetz, H., ed. Gotthold Ephraim Less-
  ings "Minna von Barnhelm."
  R.R. Heitner, 221(GQ):May81-342
Steinmetz, H. Suspensive Interpretation.
  B. Goldstein, 406:Spring81-67
Steinmeyer, G. Historische Aspekte des
  Français avancé.
  G. Kleiber, 209(FM):Jan81-70
Steite, S. Les porteurs de feu. L'eau
  froide gardée. Fragments: poème. Ob-
  scure lampe de cela. Ur en poésie.
  Inversion de l'arbre et du silence.
  R. Micha, 98:Jun-Jul81-685
Steklis, H.D. and M.J. Raleigh, eds.
  Neurobiology of Social Communication
  in Primates.
  R.D. Buhr, 350:Mar81-249
Stella, L.A. Tradizione micenea e poesia
  dell'Iliade.
  J.T. Hooker, 303(JoHS):Vol 101-149
Stelzer, S., ed. Probleme des "Lexikons"
  in der Transformationsgrammatik.
  G.F. Meier, 682(ZPSK):Band32Heft2-236
Stempel, J.D. Inside the Iranian Revolu-
  tion.*
  H. Enayat, 617(TLS):21May82-553
Stempel, U. Realität des Phantastischen.
  U. Schulz-Buschhaus, 72:Band217Heft1-
  237
Stempel, W-D. Gestalt, Ganzheit, Struktur.
  W. Neumann, 682(ZPSK):Band33Heft2-271
Stendhal. Chroniques pour l'Angleterre.
  (K.G. McWatters, ed)
  G. Strickland, 208(FS):Jul81-345
Stenson, M. Class, Race and Colonialism
  in West Malaysia.
  C. Hirschman, 293(JASt):Feb81-437
Stent, A. From Embargo to Ostpolitik.
  C.D. May, 441:16May82-14

Stent, G.S., ed. Morality as a Biological
Phenomenon.
  R.J.P., 185:Apr82-596
Stenwall, Å. Den frivilligt ödmjuka
kvinnan.*
  G.C. Schoolfield, 563(SS):Spring81-247
"A Step to Kimono and Kumihimo."
  R.L. Shep, 614:Fall82-20
Stepan, N. The Idea of Race in Science.
  J. Lewis, 617(TLS):19Nov82-1274
Stephan, A. Die deutsche Exilliteratur
1933-1945.
  T.S. Hansen, 221(GQ):Jan81-101
  S. Schlenstedt, 654(WB):4/1981-158
  J.J. White, 402(MLR):Jul81-761
Stephan, W.G. and J.R. Feagin, eds.
School Desegregation.
  C.N.S., 185:Jul81-699
Stephen, L. Leslie Stephen: Selected Writ-
ings in British Intellectual History.
  (N. Annan, ed)
  E.B. Greenwood, 506(PSt):Sep81-222
  K.M. Hewitt, 447(N&Q):Jun80-256
Stephens, E.H. The Politics of Workers'
Participation.
  D.S. Palmer, 263(RIB):Vol31No4-561
Stephens, J.R. The Censorship of English
Drama 1824-1901.
  J.W. Lambert, 157:Autumn81-48
Stephenson, H. Claret and Chips.
  D. Steel, 362:16Sep82-24
Stephenson, J. The Nazi Organization of
Women.*
  I.V. Hull, 221(GQ):Nov81-535
Stepto, R.B. From Behind the Veil.*
  M. Fabre, 189(EA):Jul-Sep81-360
  J. Olney, 579(SAQ):Autumn81-483
  J.O. Perry, 219(GaR):Spring81-170
  C. Werner, 301(JEGP):Apr81-286
Sterba, J. Justice.
  J.L.H., 185:Oct81-187
Sterba, J.P. The Demands of Justice.
  D.P.L., 185:Jul81-693
Sterba, R.F. Reminiscences of a Viennese
Psychoanalyst.
  P. Sedgwick, 617(TLS):5Nov82-1209
Sterk, H. Bilder österreichischer Land-
schaft.
  90:Nov81-711
Sterling, C. The Terror Network.*
  L. Raditsa, 390:Dec81-42
Stern, G. The Red Coal.*
  S. Pinsker, 434:Spring82-494
  P. Stitt, 219(GaR):Winter81-874
Stern, J.P. A Study of Nietzsche.*
  J. Grundy, 393(Mind):Oct81-610
  T.B. Strong, 185:Jan81-324
  C.S. Taylor, 518:Apr81-114
  J.D.W., 543:Sep80-166
  205(FMLS):Jan80-95
Stern, R. The Invention of the Real.
  M. Bayles, 441:2May82-18
Stern, R. Packages.*
  D. Kubal, 249(HudR):Autumn81-458
Stern, V.F. Gabriel Harvey.*
  P.J. Croft, 541(RES):Nov81-442
  S.K. Heninger, Jr., 551(RenQ):Winter80-
805
  D. McKitterick, 354:Dec81-348
  R.J. Schoeck, 191(ELN):Jun81-295
  W. Tydeman, 506(PSt):Dec81-340

Sternbach, L. Mahāsubhāṣitasaṃgraha.
  (Vol 3) (S.B. Nair, ed)
  P. Bandyopadhyay, 318(JAOS):Jan/Mar80-
42
Sternbach, L. Unknown Verses Attributed
to Kṣemendra.
  J.W. de Jong, 259(IIJ):Apr81-161
Sternberg, M. Expositional Modes and
Temporal Ordering in Fiction.*
  N. Friedman, 599:Winter81-42
Sternberger, D. Schriften III-VI.*
  D. Johnson, 617(TLS):17Dec82-1385
Sternburg, J., ed. The Writer on Her
Work.*
  F.W. Kaye, 502(PrS):Winter81/82-94
  M. McQuade, 114(ChiR):Spring81-128
Sterne, M. The Passionate Eye.
  H.W. Morgan, 658:Summer/Autumn81-233
Sternfeld, R. and H. Zyskind. Plato's
"Meno."
  R.G. Turnbull, 319:Oct81-497
Sternhell, Z. La Droite révolutionnaire
1885-1914.
  P.A. Ouston, 208(FS):Jan81-87
Steunou, J. and L. Knapp. Bibliografía de
los cancioneros castellanos del siglo XV
y repertorio de sus géneros poéticos.
  (Vol 2)
  D.C. Clarke, 545(RPh):Feb81(supp)-376
Stevens, A. Archetype.
  A. Storr, 617(TLS):7May82-511
Stevens, C. and J. Aurbach, eds. Theatre
Byways.
  W. Gourd, 583:Spring81-314
Stevens, D. - see Monteverdi, C.
Stevens, P.S. Handbook of Regular
Patterns.
  J. Jordan, 42(AR):Summer81-388
Stevenson, A. Minute by Glass Minute.
  D. Davis, 362:16Dec82-23
Stevenson, A. Turkish Rondo.
  S. Altinel, 617(TLS):12Feb82-170
Stevenson, D. Scottish Covenanters and
Irish Confederates.
  T.C. Barnard, 617(TLS):12Feb82-171
Stevenson, J. Popular Disturbances in
England, 1700-1870.
  H.T. Dickinson, 566:Spring81-122
  J. Epstein, 637(VS):Spring81-380
Stevenson, R.L. An Old Song and Edifying
Letters of the Rutherford Family. (R.G.
Swearingen, ed)
  442(NY):23Aug82-92
Stevenson, R.L. Selected Short Stories of
R.L. Stevenson.*
  J. Calder, 571(ScLJ):Winter81-117
Stevick, E.W. Memory Meaning and Method.
  E. Slater, 447(N&Q):Feb80-88
Stevick, E.W. Teaching Languages.*
  J.N. Davis, 351(LL):Dec81-509
  E. Hocking, 207(FR):Apr82-718
  T.D. Terrell, 350:Sep81-782
Stevick, P. Alternative Pleasures.
  L. Mackinnon, 617(TLS):21May82-567
  27(AL):Jan82-758
Steward, M.A. - see Boyle, R.
Stewart, A. Attika.
  C.E. Vafopoulou-Richardson, 123:Vol131
No2-315
  S. Walker, 313:Vol71-211
Stewart, A.G. Unequal Lovers.
  E. Fleurbaay, 600:Vol 12No2/3-162

340

Stewart, A.M., ed. The Complaynt of Scot-
land.
P. Morère, 189(EA):Apr-Jun81-214
Stewart, B. and M. Cutten. The Shayer
Family of Painters.
J. Gage, 617(TLS):19Mar82-320
Stewart, C.D. - see Gilbert, A.T.
Stewart, D. The Foreigner.
H. Carpenter, 617(TLS):9Apr82-408
Stewart, D. The Palestinians.
P. Mansfield, 362:21Oct82-23
Stewart, E. For Richer, For Poorer.
A. Bold, 617(TLS):30Apr82-493
Stewart, G. A New Mythos.
J. Grumman, 395(MFS):Winter80/81-731
Stewart, G.M. The Literary Contributions
of Christoph Daniel Ebeling.
H. Gronemeyer, 133:Band14Heft2-191
Stewart, H. Looking at Indian Art of the
Northwest Coast.
R. Ridington, 292(JAF):Apr-Jun81-250
G.W., 102(CanL):Spring80-151
Stewart, J. So the Night World Spins.*
A. Munton, 150(DR):Autumn81-569
Stewart, J.H. - see Riccoboni, M-J.
Stewart, J.I.M. A Villa in France.
A. Bell, 617(TLS):26Nov82-1318
J. Mellors, 362:16Dec82-24
Stewart, R. Sam Steele.
G.W., 102(CanL):Spring81-175
Stewart, S. Nonsense.*
D.H., 355(LSoc):Aug81-318
P. Strachan, 89(BJA):Winter81-92
Stewart, S. Yellow Stars and Ice.
H. McNeil, 617(TLS):29Jan82-113
D. Smith, 29:Jan/Feb82-36
Stewart, W., ed. Canadian Newspapers.
G.W., 102(CanL):Summer81-171
Stewart, W.K. Time Structure in Drama.
J. Neubauer, 173(ECS):Spring81-331
H. Rowland, 221(GQ):Jan81-94
Stewart, W.T., A.F. McClure and K.D. Jones.
International Film Necrology.
A. Slide, 200:Apr81-241
Stibbe, C.M. and others. Lapis Satricanus.
R.M. Ogilvie, 313:Vol71-207
Stich, K.P., ed. The Duncan Campbell
Scott Symposium.*
D.M.R. Bentley, 627(UTQ):Summer81-163
"Sticks, Shingles and Stones."
E.R. McKinstry, 576:Dec81-344
Stieber, J.W. Pope Eugenius IV, the Coun-
cil of Basel and the Secular and Ecclesi-
astical Authorities in the Empire.
F. Oakley, 589:Apr81-441
Stieber, W.J.C.E. The Chancellor's Spy.*
639(VQR):Autumn81-124
Stieber, Z. A Historical Phonology of the
Polish Language.
H. Birnbaum, 279:Vol23-181
"Alfred Stieglitz: Photographs and Writ-
ings." (S. Greenough and J. Hamilton,
comps)
H. Kramer, 441:19Dec82-1
Stikkers, K.W. - see Scheler, M.
Stilgoe, J.R. Common Landscape of America,
1580 to 1845.
C. Bridenbaugh, 617(TLS):8Oct82-1112
442(NY):23Aug82-93
Stillman, L.R. La Théâtralité dans
l'oeuvre d'Alfred Jarry.
K.J. Brady, 446(NCFS):Fall-Winter81/82-
166   [continued]

[continuing]
B.L. Knapp, 207(FR):May81-872
N. Perry, 208(FS):Jul81-357
Stillwell, A. The Technique of Teneriffe
Lace.
P. Bach, 614:Winter81-22
Stimpson, B. - see Colette
Stirling, R. The Weather of Britain.
O.M. Ashford, 617(TLS):4Jun82-616
Stites, R. - see Miliukov, P.N.
Stock, D., ed. Khmer Ceramics — 9th-14th
Century.
S. Markbreiter, 60:May-Jun81-155
Stock, R.D. The Holy and the Daemonic
from Sir Thomas Browne to William Blake.
R. Robbins, 617(TLS):24Sep82-1046
Stockanes, A.E. Ladies Who Knit for a
Living.
L.K. Abbott, Jr., 580(SCR):Spring82-
133
B. Allen, 434:Spring82-478
Stockton, D. The Gracchi.
A.E. Astin, 313:Vol71-188
A. Lintott, 123:Vol31No1-134
Stockwell, J. Red Sunset.
S. Brook, 617(TLS):4Jun82-622
Stockwood, M. Chanctonbury Ring.
G. Priestland, 362:30Sep82-21
Stoehr, T. Hawthorne's Mad Scientists.*
J.E. Becker, 125:Fall80-115
M.J. Colacurcio, 183(ESQ):Vol27No2-108
G. Guffey, 445(NCF):Mar81-567
Stoever, W.K.B. "A Faire and Easie Way
to Heaven."*
E.B. Lowrie, 568(SCN):Summer-Fall81-67
R. Morton, 106:Fall81-191
Stojanović, S. In Search of Democracy in
Socialism.
J.L.H., 185:Jul82-783
Stoker, B. Shades of Dracula. (P. Hain-
ing, ed)
E.S. Turner, 617(TLS):22Oct82-1174
Stokes, A. With All the Views. (P. Robin-
son, ed)
D. Davie, 617(TLS):30Apr82-483
Stokes, G., ed. The Village Voice Anthol-
ogy (1956-1980).
N. Perrin, 441:18Jul82-6
Stoler, J.A. and R.D. Fulton. Henry
Fielding.
J.C. Beasley, 365:Winter82-39
J.A. Downie, 566:Autumn81-43
Stoljar, S. Moral and Legal Reasoning.
D.A.J. Richards, 185:Jul82-757
Stoll, M. and G. Ibeji.
R.P. Armstrong, 2(AfrA):Feb81-23
Stollmann, R. Ästhetisierung der Politik.
E. Bahr, 221(GQ):May81-384
Stolojan, S. Duiliu Zamfirescu.
D. Deletant, 402(MLR):Oct81-1008
G. Price, 575(SEER):Jul81-421
Stoltzfus, B. Gide and Hemingway.*
D.H. Walker, 208(FS):Jul81-356
Stone, D., Jr. - see de Larivey, P.
Stone, D.D. The Romantic Impulse in Vic-
torian Fiction.*
A.M. Duckworth, 445(NCF):Mar82-475
A.L. Harris, 268(IFR):Summer82-149
R. Kiely, 661(WC):Summer81-190
J.H. Maddox, Jr., 454:Spring82-263
Stone, G. An Introduction to Polish.
205(FMLS):Oct80-381

341

Stone, G.W., Jr. and G.M. Kahrl. David Garrick.
  M.S. Auburn, 405(MP):May82-441
  L. Bertelsen, 301(JEGP):Oct81-575
  F. Blessington, 566:Autumn80-40
  E.A. Langhans, 173(ECS):Spring81-334
  H.W. Pedicord, 611(TN):Vol135No1-41
  G. Weales, 569(SR):Summer81-448
Stone, H. Dickens and the Invisible World.
  K.J. Fielding, 637(VS):Spring81-360
  G. Ford, 445(NCF):Mar81-540
  S. Prickett, 155:Spring81-43
  G. Wing, 49:Jan81-95
Stone, I. The Origin.*
  R. Colp, Jr., 77:Summer81-275
Stone, L. The Past and the Present.*
  G. Himmelfarb, 441:10Jan82-9
  K. Thomas, 617(TLS):30Apr82-479
Stone, P. Oriental Rug Repair.
  P. Bach, 614:Fall82-19
Stone, P. Portuguese Needlework Rugs.
  P. Bach, 614:Winter82-19
Stone, P.W.K. The Textual History of "King Lear."*
  J. Reibetanz, 539:Nov82-294
Stone, R. A Flag for Sunrise.*
  442(NY):4Jan82-89
Stonum, G.L. Faulkner's Career.*
  T.L. Heller, 50(ArQ):Summer81-173
  A.F. Kinney, 395(MFS):Summer80-336
  B. Lawson-Peebles, 541(RES):Nov81-493
  295(JML):Vol18No3/4-492
Stopp, H. Schreibsprachwandel.
  H. Moser, 680(ZDP):Band99Heft1-153
Stopp, H. - see Michels, V.
Stoppard, M. Everywoman's Life-Guide.
  M. Warnock, 617(TLS):4Jun82-618
Storch, G. Semantische Untersuchungen zu den inchoativen Verben im Deutschen.
  U. Schröter, 682(ZPSK):Band33Heft2-282
Storer, M.B., ed. Humanist Ethics.
  V.C. Aldrich, 651(WHR):Spring81-86
  J. Donnelly, 258:Jun81-218
  D.P.L., 185:Oct81-189
Storey, D. Early Days/Sisters/Life Class.
  D. Devlin, 157:2ndQtr81-55
Storey, D. A Prodigal Child.
  D.J. Enright, 362:1Jul82-27
  P. Kemp, 617(TLS):2Jul82-710
Storey, G. A Preface to Hopkins.
  R.B., 617(TLS):26Mar82-363
Storey, G. and K.J. Fielding - see Dickens, C.
Storey, J. The Thames and Hudson Manual of Dyes and Fabrics.
  P. Bach, 614:Summer82-19
Storey, R.F. Pierrot.*
  P. Baggio-Huerre, 399(MLJ):Spring81-93
  B.C. Bowen, 131(CL):Summer81-288
  O.G. Brockett, 402(MLR):Jul81-649
Storing, H.J., with M. Dry, eds. The Complete Anti-Federalist.
  L.W. Levy, 441:21Feb82-9
Storing, H.J., with M. Dry. What the Anti-Federalists Were For.
  L.W. Levy, 441:21Feb82-9
Stork, H. Einführung in die Philosophie der Technik.
  W. Strombach, 489(PJGG):Band88Heft1-194

Storm, T. and E. Esmarch. Theodor Storm — Ernst Esmarch, Briefwechsel. (A.T. Alt, ed)
  W.A. Coupe, 402(MLR):Jan81-246
Storrs, M. God's Galloping Girl.* (W.L. Morton, ed)
  V. Strong-Boag, 298:Fall-Winter81-217
Story, R. The Forging of an Aristocracy.*
  D.L. Miller, 432(NEQ):Jun81-280
Story, W.L. Cemeteries are for Dying.
  N. Callendar, 441:5Sep82-20
Stovin, C. Journals of a Methodist Farmer 1871-1875. (J. Stovin, ed)
  R. Blythe, 617(TLS):12Mar82-287
Stow, R. To the Islands.
  C. Hope, 617(TLS):12Mar82-277
Stow, R. Visitants.* The Girl Green as Elderflower.
  B. King, 569(SR):Summer81-461
Stowe, H.B. Uncle Tom's Cabin; The Minister's Wooing; Oldtown Folks. (K.K. Sklar, ed)
  M. Cowley, 441:25Apr82-3
Stowell, H.P. Literary Impressionism, James and Chekhov.*
  T.K. Bender, 191(ELN):Sep80-70
  E.K. Hay, 301(JEGP):Oct81-603
  M.E. Kronegger, 587(SAF):Spring81-135
  D. Maxwell, 574(SEEJ):Fall81-113
  J. Nagel, 27(AL):May81-328
  E. Nettels, 445(NCF):Jun81-123
  D.J. Schneider, 395(MFS):Winter80/81-646
  M.R. Winchell, 577(SHR):Fall81-367
van Straaten, Z., ed. Philosophical Subjects.
  D. Papineau, 617(TLS):19Feb82-193
  M. Thompson, 185:Jul82-760
Strabo. Strabon, "Géographie." (Vol 5) (R. Baladié, ed and trans)
  P. Pédech, 555:Vol54fasc2-359
Strachey, B. Remarkable Relations.
  P. Maier, 441:12Dec82-9
Strachey, L. The Shorter Strachey. (M. Holroyd and P. Levy, eds)
  J.D. Cushman, 569(SR):Spring81-xlvi
Strachey, R. A Strachey Boy.* A Strachey Child.
  P.S. Guptara, 77:Spring81-175
Stradling, R.A. Europe and the Decline of Spain.
  H. Kamen, 617(TLS):1Jan82-17
Straka, G. Les sons et les mots.*
  V. Kallioinen, 439(NM):1981/3-353
  O. Soutet, 209(FM):Apr81-173
  B. Tranel, 350:Sep81-773
Straková, V. Ruský přízvuk v přehledech a komentářích.
  W. Lehfeldt, 559:Dec80-191
  C.E. Townsend, 574(SEEJ):Spring81-138
Strand, M. Selected Poems.*
  L. Gregerson, 472:Fall/Winter81-90
  R.B. Shaw, 491:Dec81-171
  P. Stitt, 219(GaR):Winter81-874
  V. Young, 249(HudR):Spring81-147
von Strassburg, G. - see under Gottfried von Strassburg
Strasser, S. Never Done.
  N. Bliven, 442(NY):6Sep82-104
  F. Randall, 441:12Dec82-16
Strassfeld, S. and M., eds. The Third Jewish Catalog.
  S. Berrin, 287:Nov81-24

Strassner, E. Graphemsystem und Wortkon-
stituenz.
  N.R. Wolf, 684(ZDA):Band109Heft2-73
Stratford, J. Catalogue of the Jackson
Collection.
  J. Backhouse, 617(TLS):17Sep82-1019
Stratton, D. The Last New Wave.
  M. Magill, 200:Dec81-635
Stratton, J.L. Pioneer Women.*
  D. Quantic, 649(WAL):Winter82-325
  639(VQR):Summer81-88
Straus, D. Under the Canopy.
  F. Taliaferro, 441:29Aug82-12
Strauss, D. Menace in the West.
  J. McDermott, 106:Spring81-101
  B. Petit, 207(FR):Dec80-376
Strauss, G. Luther's House of Learning.*
  T. Tentler, 551(RenQ):Autumn80-427
Strauss, H.A., ed. Jewish Immigrants of
the Nazi Period in the U.S.A. (Vol 1
comp by S.W. Siegel)
  R.W. Marcus, 14:Spring80-219
Strauss, W.L. The Complete Drawings of
Albrecht Dürer.
  F. Winzinger, 471:Oct/Nov/Dec81-372
Strauss, W.L., ed. Hendrik Goltzius 1558-
1617: The Complete Engravings and Wood-
cuts.*
  N. Bialler, 54:Jun81-337
Strauss, W.L. - see Sumowski, W.
Stravinsky, L. Stravinsky: Selected Cor-
respondence. (Vol 1) (R. Craft, ed)
  G. Josipovici, 617(TLS):29Oct82-1201
  R. Shattuck, 441:23May82-1
  D. Shawe-Taylor, 442(NY):11Oct82-174
Strawson, J. El Alamein.
  B. Montgomery, 617(TLS):29Jan82-118
Strelcyn, S. Catalogue of Ethiopic Manu-
scripts in the John Rylands University
Library of Manchester.
  W. Leslau, 318(JAOS):Apr/Jun80-146
Strelka, J. Auf der Suche nach dem ver-
lorenen Selbst.*
  K. Weissenberger, 133:Band14Heft2-189
Strelka, J., ed. Broch heute.*
  B. Mitchell, 133:Band14Heft3-280
Strelka, J. Methodologie der Literatur-
wissenschaft.*
  F. Claudon, 535(RHL):May-Jun81-492
  K. Weissenberger, 221(CQ):Mar81-250
  U. Weisstein, 131(CL):Fall81-376
Strelka, J.P., R.F. Bell and E. Dobson,
eds. Protest — Form — Tradition.
  M.S. Fries, 395(MFS):Summer80-362
Streller, S., with others - see von
Kleist, H.
Strelow, M., ed. An Anthology of North-
west Writing 1900-1950.
  M. Lewis, 649(WAL):Winter81-297
Strenio, A.J., Jr. The Testing Trap.*
  J.L.H., 185:Apr82-588
Strevens, P. New Orientations in the
Teaching of English.
  R.J. Alexander, 257(IRAL):May81-165
Stricker, G. Stilistische und verbalsyn-
taktische Untersuchungen zum moskovi-
tischen Prunkstil des 16. Jahrhunderts.
  H. Leeming, 575(SEER):Apr81-316
Strickland, G. Structuralism or Criti-
cism.*
  D. Holbrook, 437:Autumn81-507
Strickland, M. Angela Thirkell.
  M. Roe, 381:Apr81-131

Striker, C.L. The Myrelaion (Bodrum Camii)
in Istanbul.
  C. Mango, 617(TLS):24Sep82-1039
"Strindberg i offentligheten." (Vols 1-3)
  W. Johnson, 563(SS):Spring81-237
Strobach, H. Deutsches Volkslied in
Geschichte und Gegenwart.
  K. Thomas, 654(WB):11/1981-166
Strobel, G. and W. Wolf - see Wagner, R.
Stroh, G.W. American Ethical Thought.
  L.T., 185:Jul81-692
Stroh, W. Taxis und Taktik.*
  D.C. Innes, 123:Vol31No1-121
Strolz, M.K. - see Newman, J.H.
Ström, G.W. Development and Dependence in
Lesotho, the Enclave of South Africa.
  C. Murray, 69:Vol50No1-103
Stronach, D. Pasargadae.*
  L.D. Levine, 318(JAOS):Jan/Mar80-68
Strong, E. Flesh ... the Greatest Sin.
  R.H., 305(JIL):Jan81-93
Strong, G.T. The Diary of George Temple-
ton Strong. (A. Nevins and M.H. Thomas,
eds)
  B. Raffel, 77:Fall81-360
Strong-Boag, V. - see Smith, E.
Strosetzki, C. Konversation.
  R. Behrens, 224(GRM):Band30Heft2-239
Stroud, M.D. - see Calderón de la Barca, P.
Strouse, J. Alice James.*
  L.Y. Gossett, 569(SR):Fall81-641
  J.V. Gunn, 27(AL):Jan82-730
  R.E. Long, 26(ALR):Spring81-139
  A. Phillips, 364:Jul81-93
  C. Strout, 284:Fall81-59
Strozier, C.B. Lincoln's Quest for Union.
  G.M. Fredrickson, 453(NYRB):15Jul82-13
Strugatsky, A. and B. Escape Attempt.
  G. Jonas, 441:19Dec82-13
Struk, D.H. - see under Husar Struk, D.
Struve, N. Ossip Mandelstam.
  H. Gifford, 617(TLS):24Sep82-1044
Struve, T. Die Entwicklung der organolog-
ischen Staatsauffassung im Mittelalter.
  V. Honemann, 684(ZDA):Band109Heft4-145
Stuart, D. Dear Duchess.
  V. Glendinning, 617(TLS):5Mar82-259
Stuart, F. The High Consistory.*
  A. Ross, 364:Apr/May81-12
Stubblebine, J.H. Duccio di Buoninsegna
and His School.
  J. Cannon, 90:Mar81-168
  E. Fahy, 39:Aug81-130
Stubbs, J. The Vivian Inheritance.
  S. Altinel, 617(TLS):17Dec82-1398
Stubbs, P. Women and Fiction.*
  P. Brown, 148:Spring81-90
  A. Coombes, 366:Autumn81-261
  S. Roxman, 172(Edda):1981/1-61
  M. Vicinus, 445(NCF):Mar82-496
Stüben, P.E. Die Struktur und Funktion
transzendentaler Argumentationsfiguren.
  K-H. Brendgen, 679:Band12Heft2-404
Stückrath, J. Historische Rezeptionsfor-
schung.
  D. Barnouw, 406:Spring81-106
Stucky, S. Lutoslawski and his Music.
  J. Casken, 415:Dec81-822
Studd, S. Herbert Chapman: Football
Emperor.
  P. Smith, 617(TLS):5Feb82-125
Studdert-Kennedy, G. Dog-Collar Democracy.
  K. Leech, 617(TLS):24Dec82-1422

"Studi danteschi." (Vol 51)
  M. Marti, 228(GSLI):Vol 156fasc495-447
"Studies in Eighteenth-Century Culture."
  (Vol 7) (R. Runte, ed)
  J. Lough, 208(FS):Jul81-344
  J.V. Price, 402(MLR):Apr81-425
"Studies in Eighteenth-Century Culture."
  (Vol 8) (R. Runte, ed)
  M. Delon, 535(RHL):Mar-Apr81-298
  E.J.H. Greene, 107(CRCL):Winter81-125
  P. Rogers, 541(RES):Nov81-450
"Studies in Eighteenth-Century Culture."
  (Vol 9) (R. Runte, ed)
  P. Rogers, 506(PSt):May81-99
  W. Wrage, 399(MLJ):Spring81-111
Studing, R. and E. Kruz, comps. Mannerism
  in Art, Literature, and Music.
  J. Haar, 551(RenQ):Winter80-766
  205(FMLS):Oct80-379
Stuip, R.E.V., ed. Langue et littérature
  françaises du moyen âge.
  W. Rothwell, 208(FS):Apr81-185
  C. Thiry, 356(LR):Feb-May81-154
Sturgeon, M.C. Corinth.* (Vol 9, Pt 2)
  E. Alföldi-Rosenbaum, 487:Spring81-95
Sturm, J.L. and J. Chotas. Stained Glass
  From Medieval Times to the Present.
  P. Goldberger, 441:26Dec82-3
Sturrock, J. Paper Tigers.*
  M.G. Berg, 395(MFS):Summer80-382
Sturrock, J., ed. Structuralism and Since.
  M. Green, 363(LitR):Spring82-431
  M.J. Harney, 63:Sep81-358
  R. Jones, 402(MLR):Jul81-714
Styan, J.L. The Shakespeare Revolution.*
  T.W. Craik, 161(DUJ):Jun81-251
Stynen, H. Urbanisme et Société.
  J.J. Read, 46:Apr81-255
Styron, W. Sophie's Choice.* (French
  title: Le choix de Sophie.)
  P. Dulac, 450(NRF):Jul-Aug81-209
  A. Suied, 98:Dec81-1334
Styron, W. This Quiet Dust and Other
  Writings.
  T.R. Edwards, 441:21Nov82-9
Su, J. and Luo Lun - see under Jing Su and
  Luo Lun
Suard, F. Guillaume d'Orange.*
  T. Scully, 546(RR):Mar81-243
Suarès, A. Caprices.* (Y-A. Favre, ed)
  H. Godin, 208(FS):Apr81-221
  M. Maurin, 535(RHL):Mar-Apr81-327
Suarès, A. 2: Suarès et l'Allemagne.
  (Y-A. Favre, ed)
  H. Godin, 208(FS):Apr81-221
Suarez, F. De juramento fidelitatis.
  J-L. Gardies, 542:Jul-Sep81-348
Subirà, E.J. - see under Junyent i Subirà,
  E.
Suchoff, B. - see Bartók, B.
Suchomski, J., ed. Lateinische Comoediae
  des 12. Jahrhunderts.
  P. Stotz, 684(ZDA):Band110Heft1-13
van Suchtelen, N. - see de Spinoza, B.
Sucksmith, H.P. - see Dickens, C.
Sudetis, S.P. - see under Proxenus a
  Sudetis, S.
Suelflow, A.R. Religious Archives.
  P. Barr, 14:Winter81-52
Suerbaum, U., U. Broich and R. Borgmeier.
  Science Fiction.
  M. Hadley, 268(IFR):Winter82-65

Suetonius. The Twelve Caesars. (R.
  Graves, trans; rev by M. Grant)
  H.E. Moritz, 399(MLJ):Summer81-228
Sugar, M. The Ford Hunger March.
  A. Wald, 385(MQR):Summer82-526
Sugg, R. Motherteacher.
  M.S. Littleford, 577(SHR):Winter81-67
Sugg, R.P. Hart Crane's "The Bridge."
  P.R. Yannella, 295(JML):Vol8No3/4-473
Sugg, R.S., Jr., ed. Walter Anderson's
  Illustrations of Epic and Voyage.
  R.N. Scott, 392:Winter80/81-84
Sührig, H. Die Entwicklung der niedersäch-
  sischen Kalender im 17. Jahrhundert.
  E. Moser-Rath, 196:Band22Heft3/4-371
Sukenick, R. Long Talking Bad Condition
  Blues.
  P. Quartermain, 114(ChiR):Autumn80-65
Suknaski, A. East of Myloona.*
  L. Ricou, 102(CanL):Spring81-142
Suknaski, A. The Ghosts Call You Poor.
  L. Ricou, 102(CanL):Autumn80-128
Suleiman, S. and I. Crosman, eds. The
  Reader in the Text.
  R. Amossy, 546(RR):Mar81-226
  D. Bellos, 208(FS):Oct81-485
  H.O. Brown, 141:Fall81-335
  K. Elam, 617(TLS):8Jan82-34
  M. Fischer, 478:Fall81-233
  C. Norris, 402(MLR):Oct81-906
  S.L. Pucci, 188(ECr):Summer81-102
Sullivan, J. Quelque temps de la vie de
  Jude et Cie.
  R.J. Sealy, 207(FR):Dec81-310
Sullivan, D.H. Wind Sun Stone and Ice.
  B. Whiteman, 102(CanL):Summer80-141
Sullivan, E.B. Collecting Political Ameri-
  cana.
  R.A. Fischer, 658:Winter80-337
Sullivan, E.J. and N.A. Mallory. Painting
  in Spain 1650-1700 from North American
  Collections.
  E. Harris, 617(TLS):22Oct82-1168
Sullivan, F. Spy Wednesday's Kind.
  P. Ramsey, 472:Spring/Summer82-172
  R.J. Stout, 584(SWR):Winter81-110
Sullivan, J. Elegant Nightmares.*
  G.R. Thompson, 395(MFS):Winter80/81-
  714
Sullivan, J. and C.L. Drage, eds. An Un-
  published Religious Song-Book of Mid-
  Eighteenth-Century Russia.*
  L. Hughes, 402(MLR):Jan81-253
Sullivan, M. The Arts of China. (rev)
  J.W. Best, 318(JAOS):Jan/Mar80-97
Sullivan, M. Chinese Landscape Painting
  in the Sui and T'ang Dynasties.
  E. Capon, 463:Autumn81-324
  A.C. Soper, 54:Dec81-693
  A.C. Soper, 57:Vol142No2/3-223
  J. Sweetman, 90:Jul81-427
Sullivan, M. Symbols of Eternity.
  R.A. Rorex, 293(JASt):Feb81-365
  A.C. Soper, 54:Dec81-693
  A.C. Soper, 57:Vol142No2/3-223
  J. Sweetman, 90:Jul81-427
  M. Tregear, 324:Jun82-436
Sullivan, R.E. John Toland and the Deist
  Controversy.
  D. Cupitt, 617(TLS):26Nov82-1296

Sulloway, F.J. Freud, Biologist of the
Mind.*
  D. Duncalfe, 529(QQ):Spring81-159
  M. Pierssens, 98:Apr80-422
Sulser, W. and H. Claussen. Sankt Stephan
in Chur. Frühchristliche Grabkammer und
Friedhofskirche.
  A. Reinle, 683:Band44Heft4-445
Sulzberger, C.L. How I Committed Suicide.
  F. Taliaferro, 441:18Apr82-16
Sumerkin, A. - see Tsvetaeva, M.
Sumiya, M. and K. Taira, eds. An Outline
of Japanese Economic History 1603-1940.
  B.K. Marshall, 293(JASt):Nov80-142
Summerfield, H. An Introductory Guide to
"The Anathemata" and the "Sleeping Lord"
Sequence of David Jones.*
  W. Blissett, 178:Fall81-370
  N. Jacobs, 541(RES):May81-241
Summerfield, H. - see Russell, G.W. [AE]
Summers, C.J. and T-L. Pebworth. Ben
Jonson.*
  J.A. Bryant, Jr., 301(JEGP):Jul81-407
  J.M. Patrick, 568(SCN):Summer-Fall81-
  42
Summers, D. Michelangelo and the Language
of Art.*
  C. Gould, 39:Nov81-352
  T. Puttfarken, 617(TLS):19Mar82-318
Summers, M. The Galanty Show.
  J.R. Taylor, 157:Oct80-70
Summerson, J. The Life and Work of Sir
John Nash, Architect.*
  J.S. Curl, 324:Mar82-230
  M. Whiffen, 576:Dec81-334
Sumner, L.W. Abortion and Moral Theory.*
  S. Sherwin, 150(DR):Autumn81-591
Sumner, L.W., J.G. Slater and F. Wilson,
eds. Pragmatism and Purpose.
  G,W,T-S., 185:Jul82-802
Sumowski, W. Drawings of the Rembrandt
School. (W.L. Strauss, ed and trans)
  K. Renger, 471:Oct/Nov/Dec81-374
Sundquist, E.J. Home as Found.*
  J.P. McWilliams, Jr., 432(NEQ):Mar81-
  146
  D. Minter, 445(NCF):Jun80-85
Suomela-Härmä, E. Les structures narra-
tives dans le "Roman de Renart."
  L. Löfstedt, 439(NM):1981/4-475
Super, R.H. - see Arnold, M.
Suppe, F., ed. The Structure of Scien-
tific Theories. (2nd ed)
  P. Skagestad, 449:May81-234
"A Supplement to the Oxford English Dictio-
nary." (Vol 3) (R.W. Burchfield, ed)
  R. Harris, 617(TLS):3Sep82-935
  D.A.N. Jones, 362:16Sep82-27
Surdučki, M. Srpskohrvatski i engleski u
kontaktu.
  D. Jutronić-Tihomirović, 574(SEEJ):
  Winter81-110
Surette, L. A Light from Eleusis.*
  H.M. Dennis, 402(MLR):Oct81-945
  E. Greene, 529(QQ):Winter81-774
  A.J. Kappel, 295(JML):Vol8No3/4-594
  P. Stevens, 106:Winter81-355
Suri, S. Politics and Society in India.
  B.W. Coyer, 293(JASt):May81-643
Surkov, A.A. - see "Kratkaja literaturnaja
Enciklopedija"
"Le Surnaturalisme français."*
  D.Y. Kadish, 207(FR):Apr81-741

Surtees, R.S. Mr. Sponge's Sporting Tour.
(V. Blain, ed) Mr. Sponge's Sporting
Tour. [Surtees Society]
  R. Carr, 617(TLS):7May82-503
Surtees, V. - see Brown, F.M.
Suryadinata, L., ed. Political Thinking
of the Indonesian Chinese 1900-1977.
  K. Kane, 293(JASt):Nov80-204
Suryadinata, L. Pribumi Indonesians, the
Chinese Minority and China. The Chinese
Minority in Indonesia. Eminent Indo-
nesian Chinese.
  K. Kane, 293(JASt):Nov80-204
Sussex, R.T. Home and the Homeland Novel.
  I.H. Smith, 67:Nov81-253
Sussman, H. Franz Kafka.
  K.J. Fickert, 395(MFS):Summer80-359
  R. Karst, 400(MLN):Apr81-712
Sussman, H.L. Fact into Figure.*
  M. Baumgarten, 651(WHR):Summer81-175
  F.S. Boos, 637(VS):Spring81-375
  K. Garlick, 447(N&Q):Oct80-464
  L. Ormond, 39:Apr81-272
Sussman, L. Spode/Copeland Transfer-
Printed Patterns Found at Twenty
Hudson's Bay Company Sites.
  A.R. Pilling, 658:Spring81-97
Sussman, L.A. The Elder Seneca.*
  M.E. Welsh, 487:Summer81-181
Süssmilch, J.P. L'ordre divin, aux ori-
gines de la démographie. (J. Hecht, ed
and trans)
  A. Reix, 542:Jul-Sep81-379
Suszynski, O.C. The Hagiographic-Thauma-
turgic Art of Gonzalo de Berceo "Vida de
Santo Domingo de Silos."
  L.S. Lefkowitz, 545(RPh):May81-533
  L.N. de Villavicencio, 241:Sep81-93
Suter, K.D. and K. Stearman. Aboriginal
Australians.
  R. Blow, 617(TLS):15Oct82-1123
Sutherland, H. The Making of a Bureau-
cratic Elite.
  C. Trocki, 293(JASt):Aug81-855
Sutherland, J. Bestsellers.*
  C. Hawtree, 364:Jun81-96
Sutherland, J. Offensive Literature.
  J. Symons, 617(TLS):3Dec82-1330
Sutherland, Z. Children in Libraries.
  N. Tucker, 617(TLS):26Mar82-342
Sutherland-Smith, J. A Singer from
Sabiya.*
  J. Mole, 493:Sep81-76
Sutton, D. Absences and Celebrations.
  D. Davis, 362:6May82-26
  J. Mole, 617(TLS):16Jul82-770
Sutton, D. Robert Langton Douglas.
  J. Byam Shaw, 90:Feb81-109
Sutton, J.L. The King's Honor and the
King's Cardinal.
  M.S. Anderson, 575(SEER):Jul81-445
  639(VQR):Spring81-49
Sutton, S.B. - see Olmsted, F.L.
Suvin, D. Metamorphoses of Science Fic-
tion.*
  S. Gresham, 577(SHR):Spring81-189
  E.S. Rabkin, 295(JML):Vol8No3/4-415
  K.M. Roemer, 26(ALR):Spring81-122
  G. Slusser, 445(NCF):Jun80-73
  S. Stone-Blackburn, 529(QQ):Summer81-
  387
  J-P. Vernier, 189(EA):Jul-Sep81-331

Symons, J. The Detling Murders.
    T.J. Binyon, 617(TLS):25Jun82-702
Symons, J. The Great Detectives.
    T.J. Binyon, 617(TLS):12Feb82-170
Synge, J.M. Les Iles d'Aran.*
    C. Jordis, 450(NRF):Dec81-126
Synge, J.M. In Wicklow, West Kerry and
    Connemara.
    C. Kaltenborn, 305(JIL):Jan81-96
Syrkis, A. Os Carbonários.
    G. Rabassa, 399(MLJ):Winter81-435
"Systèmes de signes."
    A. Gottlieb, 69:Vol50No4-430
Szabó, Á. The Beginnings of Greek Mathe-
    matics.*
    A.G. Molland, 84:Sep81-306
Szabó, A. L'accueil critique de Paul
    Valéry en Hongrie.
    H. Laurenti, 535(RHL):Mar-Apr81-318
Szabo, T. The Unification and Differentia-
    tion in Socialist Criminal Justice.
    G.B. Smith, 104(CASS):Winter81-616
Szabolcsi, M., L. Illés and J. Farkas, eds.
    "Wir kämpften treu für die Revolution."*
    G. Lück, 654(WB):4/1981-178
Szajkowski, B., ed. Marxist Governments.
    A. Brown, 617(TLS):23Apr82-464
Szalavary, A. Hungarian Folk Designs.
    P. Bach, 614:Spring81-19
Szarkowski, J. and M.M. Hombourg. The
    Work of Atget. (Vol 2)
    A. Grundberg, 441:5Dec82-59
Szarmach, P.E. and B.F. Huppé, eds. The
    Old English Homily and its Backgrounds.*
    D.G. Scragg, 677(YES):Vol 11-220
Szarota, E.M. Das Jesuitendrama im deuts-
    chen Sprachgebiet. (Vol 1, Pts 1 and 2)
    R. Aulich, 133:Band14Heft3-267
Szasz, T. The Theology of Medicine.
    R.E. Vatz and L.S. Weinberg, 480(P&R):
    Winter81-60
Szatmary, D.P. Shays' Rebellion.*
    R.D. Brown, 432(NEQ):Jun81-277
    V.B. Hall, 656(WMQ):Jul81-533
Szczypiorski, A. The Polish Ordeal.
    A. Brumberg, 617(TLS):11Jun82-640
    A. Ryan, 362:17Jun82-21
Székely, J. Franziska Gräfin zu Revent-
    low.*
    D.C.G. Lorenz, 221(GQ):Mar81-236
Szemerényi, O. Studies in the Kinship
    Terminology of the Indo-European Lan-
    guages.*
    P. Considine, 303(JoHS):Vol 101-174
Sziklai, L. Zur Geschichte des Marxismus
    und der Kunst.
    G.H.R. Parkinson, 518:Apr81-109
Szirtes, G. November and May.
    D. Davis, 362:7Jan82-22
    T. Dooley, 617(TLS):2Jul82-720
Szlezák, T.A. Platon und Aristoteles in
    der Nuslehre Plotins.
    M.J. Atkinson, 123:Vol31No2-302
    H.J. Blumenthal, 303(JoHS):Vol 101-164
    É. des Places, 555:Vol54fasc2-362
Szokolay, S.V. World Solar Architecture.
    D. Michaelis, 46:Mar81-192
Szuchman, M.D. Mobility and Integration
    in Urban Argentina.
    D. Rock, 263(RIB):Vol31No4-562
Szulc, T. Diplomatic Immunity.*
    T.O. Treadwell, 617(TLS):30Apr82-493

Szymborska, W. Sounds, Feelings, Thoughts.
    J. Anders, 453(NYRB):21Oct82-47
Szymborska, W. Vokabeln. (J. Janke, ed)
    H. Olschowsky, 654(WB):10/1981-152

Tabarelli, G.M. Palazzi pubblici d'Italia.
    J. Paul, 576:Oct81-238
Tabatabai, S.M.H., ed. A Shi'ite Anthol-
    ogy.
    S. Kazim, 273(IC):Jul81-212
Tachau, M.K.B. Federal Courts in the
    Early Republic: Kentucky, 1789-1816.
    J.E. Crowley, 106:Spring81-67
    H.A. Johnson, 173(ECS):Winter80/81-217
    D.R. Kepley, 14:Winter80-85
Tacitus. The "Annals" of Tacitus, Books
    1-6. (Vol 1) (F.R.D. Goodyear, ed)
    P. McGushin, 394:Vol134fasc1/2-181
Tacitus. The "Annals" of Tacitus, Books
    1-6. (Vol 2) (F.R.D. Goodyear, ed)
    M. Grant, 617(TLS):29Jan82-117
Tadashi, F. - see under Fukutake Tadashi
Tadgell, C. Ange-Jacques Gabriel.*
    A. Braham, 90:Mar81-175
Tadié, J-Y. Le Récit poétique.*
    Y-A. Favre, 535(RHL):May-Jun81-488
Taëni, R. Rolf Hochhuth.
    M. Krueger, 406:Summer81-246
Tafuri, M. Theory and History of Architec-
    ture.
    B. Paczowski, 46:Nov81-319
    A.D. Rifkin, 59:Sep81-349
Tafuri, M. and F. dal Co. Modern Architec-
    ture.
    W. Curtis, 576:May81-168
    C.F. Otto, 127:Fall/Winter80-423
    B. Paczowski, 46:Nov81-319
Taggard, G. To the Natural World.*
    J.W. Saucerman, 649(WAL):Winter81-315
Taggart, J. Peace on Earth.
    C. Watson, 448:Vol 19No3-29
Tahara, M.M., ed and trans. Tales of
    Yamato: A Tenth-Century Poem-Tale.*
    E. Miner, 407(MN):Spring81-85
Tait, A.A. The Landscape Garden in Scot-
    land, 1735-1835.*
    D. Irwin, 83:Spring81-115
Tait, W.J. A Day Between Weathers.
    J.B. Caird, 571(ScLJ):Winter81-148
Takamura Kōtarō. Chieko and Other Poems
    of Takamura Kōtarō. (H. Sato, ed and
    trans)
    C. van den Heuvel, 472:Spring/Summer81-
    357
    D. Keene, 407(MN):Spring81-95
Takamura Kōtarō. Cheiko's Sky. (S.
    Furuta, trans)
    C. van den Heuvel, 472:Spring/Summer81-
    357
Takatori Masao, Akai Tatsurō and Fujii
    Manabu, eds. Zusetsu Nihon Bukkyōshi.
    C. Blacker, 617(TLS):19Feb82-199
Talbot, E., ed. La Critique stendhalienne
    de Balzac à Zola.
    D. Bellos, 535(RHL):Jul-Oct81-797
    J.T. Day, 207(FR):Mar82-553
    C. Smethurst, 402(MLR):Jul81-706
Talbot, M. Vivaldi.* [BBC Music Guides]
    Vivaldi. [Master Musicians series]
    J.B., 412:Aug80-238
Talbott, S. Endgame.
    P. Buteux, 529(QQ):Summer81-368

Taylor, A. Laurence Oliphant 1829-1888.
J. Burrow, 617(TLS):23Jul82-780
J. Grigg, 362:8Jul82-21
Taylor, A.H. Travail and Triumph.
J. Mason, 392:Fall81-472
Taylor, B. The Green Avenue.*
J. Cronin, 174(Éire):Winter81-125
T.H. Kelly, 174(Éire):Winter81-156
R.G. Yeed, 305(JIL):May81-131
Taylor, B. The Moorstone Sickness.
N. Callendar, 441:18Apr82-20
Taylor, C. Hegel and Modern Society.*
N. Gerth, 482(PhR):Jul81-436
S.B. Smith, 185:Jul82-764
Taylor, D. The Exorcism.
D. Devlin, 157:Autumn81-51
Taylor, D. Hardy's Poetry, 1860-1928.*
J. Halperin, 401(MLQ):Mar81-104
Taylor, D. and M. Yapp, eds. Political
Identity in South Asia.
B.R. Joshi, 293(JASt):Aug81-843
Taylor, D.S. Thomas Chatterton's Art.*
D. Fairer, 541(RES):May81-225
Taylor, E. The Sleeping Beauty. Mrs.
Palfrey at the Claremont.
P. Craig, 617(TLS):9Jul82-751
Taylor, E.R. Marcel Proust and His Con-
texts.
C.D. Rifelj, 446(NCFS):Spring-Summer82-
386
Taylor, F.K. The Concepts of Illness,
Disease and Morbus.
J.P. Wright, 518:Apr81-89
Taylor, G. Henry Irving at the Lyceum.
J. McDonald, 610:Autumn81-223
Taylor, G. - see under Wells, S.
Taylor, H.M. Anglo-Saxon Architecture.*
(Vol 3)
G. Zarnecki, 39:Jun81-412
Taylor, I. - see Holden, E.
Taylor, J. Five Months with Solidarity.
A. Brumberg, 617(TLS):11Jun82-640
Taylor, J.C. The Fine Arts in America.*
R.L. Wilson, 658:Spring81-87
Taylor, J.H.M., ed. Le Roman de Perce-
forest.* (Pt 1)
C.E. Pickford, 382(MAE):1981/2-330
M.J. Routledge, 402(MLR):Jul81-692
Taylor, J.R. Hitch.*
D.R. Noble, 577(SHR):Summer81-272
Taylor, L.K. Not for Break Alone. (3rd
ed)
C. Handy, 324:Jan82-105
Taylor, M. Kierkegaard's Pseudonymous
Authorship.
P. Bové, 81:Fall80-233
Taylor, M.C. Journeys to Selfhood.
R. Poole, 617(TLS):5Mar82-260
Taylor, P. Collected Stories.
Z. Leader, 617(TLS):22Jan82-75
Taylor, P. In the Miro District and Other
Stories.
P. Lewis, 565:Vol22No1-60
Taylor, R. Beyond Art.
D.C. Barrett, 290(JAAC):Summer82-436
Taylor, R. China's Intellectual Dilemma.
J.K. Fairbank, 453(NYRB):2Dec82-13
Taylor, R. The Drama of W.B. Yeats.*
E. Mackenzie, 447(N&Q):Oct80-471
Taylor, R. Evidence for an Autobiography.
S. Ellis, 617(TLS):2Apr82-393

Taylor, R. The Politics of the Soviet
Cinema, 1917-1929.*
J.E. Bowlt, 575(SEER):Jan81-98
Taylor, R. Robert Schumann.
A. Fitz Lyon, 617(TLS):17Dec82-1396
Taylor, R. Richard Wagner.*
R.L.J., 412:Feb80-67
M.A. Roth, 610:Winter80/81-76
H.R. Vaget, 221(GQ):Mar81-202
Taylor, R.H. Certain Small Works.
354:Mar81-84
Taylor, R.H. - see Hardy, T.
Taylor, R.J. Colonial Connecticut.*
J. Sainsbury, 106:Spring81-57
Taylor, S.K., ed. The Musician's Piano
Atlas.
C. Ehrlich, 415:Nov81-749
Taylor, S.S.B., ed. The Theatre of the
French and German Enlightenment.
W. Wrage, 207(FR):Dec80-341
Taylor, T.J. Linguistic Theory and
Structural Stylistics.
D. Hymes, 350:Dec82-953
"Teaching Modern Languages in Secondary
Schools."
205(FMLS):Jan80-80
"The Teaching of Ethics in Higher Educa-
tion."
J.M. Giarelli, 185:Apr82-549
Teague, M. Mrs. L.*
A. Forbes, 617(TLS):12Mar82-283
Teague, S.J. The City University.
J.S. Hurt, 324:Mar82-228
Tebbel, J. A History of Book Publishing
in the United States. (Vol 3)
S.O. Thompson, 517(PBSA):Apr-Jun81-230
Tefs, W. - see Ammeter, A.E.
Teichman, J. The Meaning of Illegitimacy.*
K.V. Wilkes, 482(PhR):Apr81-310
Teichmann, F. Der Mensch und seine Tempel:
Griechenland.
R. Elvin, 46:Nov81-320
Teika, F. Fujiwara Teika's Hundred-Poem
Sequence of the Shōji Era, 1200. (R.H.
Brower, trans)
R. Bowring, 318(JAOS):Apr/Jun80-208
Tekavčić, P. Grammatica storica dell'-
italiano. (2nd ed)
P.A. Gaeng, 276:Autumn81-216
Telfer, E. Happiness.*
B. Cohen, 479(PhQ):Oct81-381
J.C.B. Gosling, 518:Oct81-248
Tellenbach, H. La mélancolie.
A. Reix, 542:Jan-Mar81-135
Teller, V. and S.J. White, eds. Studies
in Child Language and Multilingualism.
L. Löfstedt, 350:Dec81-977
"Sergio Telles; Paintings, Etchings, Litho-
graphs."
T. Crombie, 39:Oct81-273
Temperley, N., ed. The Athlone History of
Music in Britain. (Vol 5)
R. Fairman, 617(TLS):30Apr82-488
Temperley, N. The Music of the English
Parish Church.*
R.F. French, 317:Summer81-345
Temple, N. John Nash and the Village
Picturesque.*
M. Whiffen, 576:Dec81-334
Templeman, I. Poems.*
C. Pollnitz, 581:Jun81-221

349

Templeton, K.S., Jr., ed. The Politiciza-
tion of Society.
  H. Belz, 396(ModA):Winter81-83
"Le Temps de la réflexion." (Vol 1) (J-B.
Pontalis, ed)
  G.S. Kirk, 208(FS):Oct81-491
"The Ten Thousand Leaves." (Vol 1) (I.H.
Levy, trans)
  J. Kirkup, 617(TLS):9Apr82-423
  R.A. Miller, 676(YR):Spring82-453
Tengström, E. A Study of Juvenal's Tenth
Satire.
  R.A. La Fleur, 121(CJ):Apr/May82-372
Tennant, E. Queen of Stones.
  A. Mars-Jones, 617(TLS):19Nov82-1268
  J. Mellors, 362:16Dec82-24
Tennant, N. Natural Logic.
  H.A. Lewis, 479(PhQ):Oct81-376
Tennant, R. Joseph Conrad.*
  L. Mackinnon, 617(TLS):5Mar82-236
Tennenbaum, S. Yesterday's Streets.*
  J. Chernaik, 617(TLS):9Apr82-422
Tennyson, A. The Letters of Alfred Lord
Tennyson. (Vol 1) (C.Y. Lang and E.F.
Shannon, Jr., eds)
  J. Bayley, 362:17Jun82-20
  D.J.R. Bruckner, 441:18Apr82-14
  L. Mackinnon, 617(TLS):14May82-530
  442(NY):15Mar82-144
Tennyson, A. Tennyson: "In Memoriam."
(S. Shatto and M. Shaw, eds)
  M. Mason, 617(TLS):14May82-528
Tennyson, G.B. Victorian Devotional
Poetry.*
  W.V. Harris, 401(MLQ):Jun81-196
Tennyson, H., ed. Studies in Tennyson.
  P. Conrad, 617(TLS):14May82-529
"Lady Tennyson's Journal." (J.O. Hoge, ed)
  C. Tomalin, 617(TLS):14May82-527
Teodorsson, S-T. The Phonemic System of
the Attic Dialect, 400-340 B.C.*
  A.M. Davies, 303(JoHS):Vol 101-176
Teodorsson, S-T. The Phonology of
Ptolemaic Koine.
  A.M. Davies, 303(JoHS):Vol 101-176
  H. Schmoll, 260(IF):Band85-355
Te Paske, J.J., general ed. Research
Guide to Andean History.
  P.J. Sehlinger, 263(RIB):Vol31No3-422
Tepe, P. Transzendentaler Materialismus.
  W. Hogrebe, 342:Band72Heft1-110
Teply, K. Türkische Sagen und Legenden um
die Kaiserstadt Wien.
  L. Schmidt, 196:Band22Heft3/4-373
de Terán, L.S. Keepers of the House.
  H. Eley, 617(TLS):9Jul82-739
  J. Mellors, 362:5Aug82-22
Terdiman, R. The Dialectics of Isolation.
  R.J. Niess, 207(FR):Oct80-171
Terence. Adelphoe.* (R.H. Martin, ed)
  H.A. Oude Essink, 394:Vol34fasc3/4-433
Terhune, A.M. and A.B. - see Fitz Gerald,
E.
Terkel, S. American Dreams.*
  639(VQR):Spring81-63
Terracini, L. Lingua come problema nella
letteratura spagnola del Cinquecento
(con una frangia cervantina).
  E.L. Rivers, 400(MLN):Mar81-448
Terras, V., ed. American Contributions to
the Eighth International Congress of
Slavists.* (Vol 2)
  M.T. Naumann, 558(RLJ):Spring-Fall81-
  317
Terreaux, L., ed. Culture et pouvoir au
temps de l'Humanisme et de la Renais-
sance.*
  F.M. Higman, 402(MLR):Jul81-693
Terrell, C.F. A Companion to "The Cantos"
of Ezra Pound. (Vol 1)
  639(VQR):Summer81-84
Terrell, C.F., ed. Louis Zukofsky.*
  P. Smith, 150(DR):Summer81-356
Terrell, P. and others, eds. Collins Ger-
man-English, English-German Dictionary.*
  B.J. Koekkoek, 221(GQ):Nov81-533
Terrell, T.D. and M. Salgués de Cargill.
Lingüística aplicada a la enseñanza del
español a anglohablantes.
  G.D. Keller, 238:May81-325
  W.H. Klemme, 399(MLJ):Autumn81-340
Terrill, R. Mao.*
  D.E. Waterfall, 529(QQ):Summer81-279
Terry, R.C. Anthony Trollope.*
  J. Carlisle, 639(VQR):Winter81-176
Tertulian, N. Georges Lukács.
  S.Z. Levine, 290(JAAC):Spring82-334
Tertullian. Tertullien, "La Résurrection
des morts." (J-P. Mahé, ed; M. Moreau,
trans)
  G. Sartoris, 450(NRF):Apr81-139
Tertz, A. [A. Sinjavskij] Progulki s Puš-
kinym.
  J. Woll, 558(RLJ):Winter81-233
Tesich, S. Summer Crossing.
  D. Wakefield, 441:31Oct82-15
Tetel, M., ed. Symbolism and Modern Lit-
erature.*
  J. Cruickshank, 208(FS):Jul81-365
Teunissen, J.J. and E.J. Hinz - see
Williams, R.
"Texas County Records Manual."
  D.J. Kraska, 14:Winter80-86
Thackeray, W.M. Vanity Fair. (A.O.J.
Cockshut, ed)
  D. Hawes, 541(RES):Nov81-462
  S. Monod, 189(EA):Apr-Jun81-229
Thak Chaloemtiarana, ed. Thai Politics.
(Vol 1)
  C.A. Trocki, 293(JASt):Nov80-191
Thak Chaloemtiarana. Thailand.
  D. Morell, 293(JASt):Aug81-857
Thakore, D. The Eccentricity Factor.
  H.R.F. Keating, 617(TLS):6Aug82-863
van Thal, H. Eliza Lynn Linton.
  M. Vicinus, 637(VS):Spring81-369
Thalberg, I. Perception, Emotion and
Action.
  M. Bratman, 449:Mar81-84
Thalmann, W.G. Dramatic Art in Aeschy-
lus's "Seven Against Thebes."*
  E.M. Jenkinson, 161(DUJ):Jun81-238
  A.J. Podlecki, 487:Spring81-78
  S. Saïd, 555:Vol54fasc2-346
de Thaon, P. - see under Philippe de Thaon
Thatcher, A. The Ontology of Paul Tillich.
  P. Helm, 449:May81-209
Theatre Passe Muraille. The Farm Show.
  C. Johnson, 102(CanL):Summer80-131
"Thematisches Sonderheft zur germanistis-
chen Linguistik."
  G. Hänse, 682(ZPSK):Band33Heft4-512

"Themes in Drama 1." (J. Redmond, ed)
G. Bas, 189(EA):Jul-Sep81-329
205(FMLS):Jan80-84
"Themes in Drama 4." (J. Redmond, ed)
A. Brissenden, 617(TLS):17Sep82-1018
Theocritus. The Poems of Theocritus.* (A. Rist, ed and trans)
E. Jenkinson, 161(DUJ):Dec80-87
Théophile de Viau. Oeuvres complètes.* (Vol 2) (G. Saba, ed)
G. Castor, 208(FS):Jan81-71
Théophile de Viau. Oeuvres complètes.* (Vol 3) (G. Saba, ed)
H. Lafay, 535(RHL):Jul-Oct81-761
Thériault, M-J. The Ceremony!
A. Moorhead, 526:Winter81-86
Thériault, S.A. La Quête d'équilibre dans l'oeuvre romanesque d'Anne Hébert.
P. Perron, 627(UTQ):Summer81-190
Thériault, S.A. and R. Juéry. Approches structurales des textes.
P. Perron, 627(UTQ):Summer81-190
Thernstrom, S., A. Orlov and O. Handlin, eds. Harvard Encyclopedia of American Ethnic Groups.ᴬ
R. Polchaninov, 550(RusR):Oct81-462
Theroux, A. Darconville's Cat.*
T. Le Clair, 659(ConL):Winter82-83
Theroux, P. The London Embassy.
J. Mellors, 362:21Oct82-23
F. Tuohy, 617(TLS):80ct82-1090
Theroux, P. The Mosquito Coast.*
T.R. Edwards, 441:14Feb82-1
J.L. Hopkins, 364:Mar82-84
F. Taliaferro, 231:Apr82-104
R. Towers, 453(NYRB):15Apr82-37
Theroux, P. The Old Patagonian Express.*
R. Johnstone, 364:Aug-Sep81-121
Theroux, P. World's End and Other Stories.*
W. Cummins, 363(LitR):Spring82-462
G. Locklin, 573(SSF):Winter81-87
639(VQR):Summer81-100
Thesen, S. Artemis Hates Romance.
R. Brown, 99:Feb82-37
Theunissen, M. Sein und Schein.*
U. Richli, 53(AGP):Band63Heft1-61
Thibau, J. La France colonisée.
J-F. Brière, 207(FR):Feb82-451
Thibault, P., ed. Le français parlé.
W.J. Ashby, 350:Sep81-744
Thibaut de Blaison. Les Poésies de Thibaut de Blaison. (T.H. Newcombe, ed)
F.R.P. Akehurst, 207(FR):Feb82-401
T.D. Hemming, 208(FS):Jan81-62
H.S. Kay, 545(RPh):May81-552
Thickett, D. Estienne Pasquier (1529-1615).
S. Bisarello, 356(LR):Nov81-357
P. Sharratt, 402(MLR):Apr81-464
Thiele, W., ed. Vetus Latina. (Pt 3)
P. Courcelle, 555:Vol54fasc2-380
Thiergen, P. Wilhelm Heinrich Riehl in Russland (1856-1866).
D. La Belle, 104(CASS):Winter81-585
Thierry, A. Récits des temps mérovingiens.
J-P. Guinle, 450(NRF):Sep81-131
Thiher, A. The Cinematic Muse.*
D.T. Stephens, 207(FR):Dec80-372
Thilo, T. Klassische chinesische Baukunst.
N.S. Steinhardt, 576:May81-144
wa Thiong'o, N. - see under Ngugi wa Thiong'o

Thiry, C., ed. Le "Jeu de l'étoile" du manuscrit de Cornillon (Liège).*
H. Arden, 589:Jul81-678
Thoburn, J.T. Primary Commodity Exports and Economic Development.
M-H. Lim, 293(JASt):Nov80-188
Thody, P. Roland Barthes.*
S. Tiefenbrun, 567:Vol34No1/2-143
Thom, M. Immanuel Kant.
R.M., 342:Band71Heft4-510
Thom, M. - see Kant, I.
Thom, R. Parabole e Catastrofi.* (G. Giorello and S. Morini, eds)
J. Largeault, 98:Nov80-1055
Thomas, A. The Phototropic Woman.
L.K. Abbott, 460(OhR):No28-133
B. Allen, 434:Spring82-478
Thomas, A.R. The Linguistic Geography of Wales.
H. Pilch, 685(ZDL):1/1981-108
Thomas Aquinas - see under Aquinas, T.
Thomas, C. Jade Tiger.
T.J. Binyon, 617(TLS):10Sep82-982
Thomas, D. Naturalism and Social Science.*
D-H. Ruben, 84:Jun81-210
Thomas, D. Swinburne.*
R. Beum, 569(SR):Spring81-xliii
R.A. Greenberg, 637(VS):Autumn80-125
Thomas, D.M. Dreaming in Bronze.
D. Davis, 362:7Jan82-22
T. Dooley, 617(TLS):22Jan82-90
Thomas, D.M. The White Hotel.*
J. Mellors, 364:Jun81-93
639(VQR):Summer81-99
Thomas, E. The Collected Poems of Edward Thomas.* (R.G. Thomas, ed) Edward Thomas on the Countryside. (R. Gant, ed)
J. Adlard, 72:Band217Heft2-439
Thomas, E. Voix d'en Bas.
P. Brochon, 535(RHL):Jul-Oct81-801
Thomas, E.J. The Solitary Place.
R. Garfitt, 617(TLS):2Apr82-392
Thomas, G. and M. Morgan-Witts. Trauma.
T. Mangold, 362:7Jan82-21
Thomas, H. Time and Again.* (M. Thomas, ed)
J. Adlard, 72:Band217Heft2-439
Thomas, J.W. - see "Eilhart von Oberge's 'Tristrant'"
Thomas, J.W. and C. Dussère - see "The Legend of Duke Ernst"
Thomas, L. The Lives of a Cell.
M. Green, 128(CE):Oct81-569
Thomas, M. Louis-Ferdinand Céline.*
S.L. Luce, 207(FR):Dec80-351
D. Schier, 569(SR):Fall81-cxiii
M. Tilby, 208(FS):Jul81-361
Thomas, M. One of These Fine Days.
A. Motion, 617(TLS):16Jul82-760
Thomas, M.M. Someone Else's Money.
R. Lekachman, 441:29Aug82-11
Thomas, P. Robert Kroetsch.
R.H. Ramsey, 99:Nov81-34
Thomas, P. Karl Marx and the Anarchists.
R.A., 185:Oct81-178
Thomas, P.J. Songs of the Pacific Northwest.
W.H.N., 102(CanL):Spring80-149
Thomas, R.N. and J.M. Hunter, eds. Internal Migration Systems in the Developing World.
E.A. Wagner, 263(RIB):Vol31No2-286

351

Thomas, R.S.   Between Here and Now.
    D. Davis, 362:6May82-26
    A. Stevenson, 617(TLS):7May82-515
Thomas, S.N.   The Formal Mechanics of Mind.
    G. Harman, 185:Jan82-350
    E. Wilson, 518:Jul81-170
Thomas, T.   Film Score.
    P. Cook, 200:May81-307
Thomas, T.   The Films of Ronald Reagan.
    D. McClelland, 200:Jan81-59
Thomas, W.   The Philosophical Radicals.
    B.B., 185:Jan81-343
    K. Britton, 483:Jan81-124
Thomas, W.K.   The Crafting of "Absalom
and Achitophel."*
    D. Hopkins, 677(YES):Vol 11-260
    S.N. Zwicker, 566:Autumn80-36
Thomas, W.K.   The Fizz Inside.
    J.M. Robson, 627(UTQ):Summer81-99
Thomason, B.C.   Making Sense of Reifica-
tion.
    Z. Bauman, 617(TLS):19Nov82-1283
Thomasset, C.A., ed.   Placides et Timéo ou
Li secrés philosophes.
    N. Mann, 208(FS):Oct81-425
Thomi, P.   Cūḍālā.
    J.W. de Jong, 259(IIJ):Jul81-221
Thomke, H. - see Wetter, J.
Thompson, A.   Russia/U.S.S.R.
    G. Walker, 575(SEER):Jan81-158
Thompson, A.   Shakespeare's Chaucer.*
    G.C. Britton, 447(N&Q):Apr80-184
    E.T. Donaldson, 551(RenQ):Summer80-284
    T. McAlindon, 301(JEGP):Apr81-241
Thompson, B.R. and J.K. Walsh, eds.   "La
Vida de santa María Egipçiaca."
    P.F. Dembowski, 545(RPh):Feb81-374
Thompson, C.R. - see Erasmus
Thompson, D., ed.   Change and Tradition in
Rural England.
    S. Marshall, 437:Autumn81-505
Thompson, D., ed.   Distant Voices.*
    D. Graham, 565:Vol22No1-73
Thompson, D.   Cesare Pavese.
    D. Robey, 617(TLS):6Aug82-852
Thompson, D.   The Uses of Poetry.*
    P. Faulkner, 161(DUJ):Dec80-127
Thompson, D.F.   John Stuart Mill and
Representative Government.
    C.D. MacNiven, 488:Sep80-328
Thompson, D.M.   A History of Harmonic
Theory in the United States.
    P.S. Hesselink, 308:Fall81-316
Thompson, E.M.   Witold Gombrowicz.*
    R. Grol-Prokopczyk, 497(PolR):Vol26No3-
    82
    P. Hultberg, 402(MLR):Jan81-255
Thompson, E.P.   Beyond the Cold War.
    R.J. Barnet, 441:14Nov82-7
    442(NY):22Nov82-197
Thompson, E.P.   William Morris.*   (rev)
    J. Gattégno, 98:Feb-Mar81-300
Thompson, E.P.   Zero Option.
    C.M. Woodhouse, 617(TLS):24Sep82-1030
Thompson, E.P. and others.   Exterminism
and Cold War.
    C.M. Woodhouse, 617(TLS):24Sep82-1030
Thompson, I.   Dilemmas of Dying.
    N. Abrams, 185:Oct81-146
Thompson, J.   At the Edge of the Chopping
there are no Secrets.   Stilt Jack.
    P.K. Smith, 102(CanL):Summer80-136

Thompson, J.   The Gasoline Wars.*
    D. Edmonds, 573(SSF):Spring81-198
    P. Lewis, 565:Vol22No1-60
Thompson, J.   Shadow of a Doubt.
    T.J. Binyon, 617(TLS):22Jan82-77
Thompson, J., with M.F. Beaufort and J.
Horne.   The Peasant in French Nineteenth-
Century Art.
    N. McWilliam, 59:Dec81-466
Thompson, J.B. - see Ricoeur, P.
Thompson, J.B. and D. Held, eds.   Habermas.
    Q. Skinner, 453(NYRB):7Oct82-35
Thompson, J.C.   Rolling Thunder.
    639(VQR):Winter81-25
Thompson, K.   Morality and Foreign Policy.
    J.A.S., 185:Apr82-605
Thompson, K.   Shacking Up.*
    D.R. Bartlett, 628(UWR):Fall-Winter81-
    116
    T. Marshall, 102(CanL):Summer81-120
Thompson, K.   Shotgun And Other Stories.*
    M. Hurley, 102(CanL):Winter80-144
Thompson, K.W.   Cold War Theories.   (Vol 1)
    W. Laqueur, 617(TLS):5Mar82-243
Thompson, K.W.   Ethics, Functionalism, and
Power in International Politics.
    C.R. Beitz, 185:Oct80-151
Thompson, L. and A. Prior.   South African
Politics.
    S.C. Nolutshungu, 617(TLS):27Aug82-928
Thompson, M.   Rubbish Theory.
    R.E. Goodin, 185:Jul81-681
Thompson, N.D. and R.C. Anderson, eds.   A
Tribute to John Insley Coddington.
    K.B. Harder, 424:Jun81-165
Thompson, P.   La Religion de Benjamin
Constant.
    F.P. Bowman, 535(RHL):Jan-Feb81-142
Thompson, P.   The Voice of the Past.
    W.W. Moss, 14:Winter80-84
Thompson, P. and G. Harkell.   The Edward-
ians from Photographs.
    H.L. Malchow, 637(VS):Spring81-373
Thompson, R.   Unfit for Modest Ears.*
    L. Oliver, 568(SCN):Summer-Fall81-67
    K.E. Robinson, 677(YES):Vol 11-267
    M. Shinagel, 566:Autumn80-42
Thompson, T.   Celebrity.
    M. Watkins, 441:9May82-14
Thompson, V. and R. Adloff.   Conflict in
Chad.
    M. Crowder, 617(TLS):5Mar82-261
Thompson, W.I.   The Time Falling Bodies
Take to Light.*
    G. Krist, 186(ETC.):Fall81-319
    639(VQR):Summer81-104
Thomsen, R.   King Servius Tullius.
    R.M. Ogilvie, 123:Vol31No2-245
Thomson, D.   A Descriptive Catalogue of
Middle English Grammatical Texts.*
    A.G. Watson, 447(N&Q):Jun80-249
Thomson, D.F.S. - see "Catullus, A Criti-
cal Edition"
Thomson, E.P.   Tapestry.
    M. Rogoyska, 46:Oct81-260
Thomson, J.   New Zealand Literature to
1977.
    354:Dec81-371
Thomson, J.   The Plays of James Thomson.*
    (P.G. Adams, ed)
    J.C. Greene, 517(PBSA):Oct-Dec81-487
    A.J. Sambrook, 354:Sep81-257

Thomson, J. To Make a Killing.
    T.J. Binyon, 617(TLS):31Dec82-1448
Thomson, J.J. Acts and Other Events.*
    M. Brand, 488:Dec81-485
    J.R. Cameron, 479(PhQ):Jan81-75
    J. Hornsby, 311(JP):Apr81-234
    B.F. Scarlett, 63:Mar81-136
Thomson, P. George Sand and the Victo-
rians.*
    P. Morgan, 179(ES):Apr81-182
Thomson, V. A Virgil Thomson Reader.*
    R. Craft, 453(NYRB):4Feb82-8
    442(NY):8Feb82-131
Thomson Davis, M. The Making of a Novel-
ist.
    C. Rumens, 617(TLS):17Sep82-996
Thon, N. Ikone und Liturgie.
    H. Röhling, 688(ZSP):Band42Heft1-184
Thông, H.S., ed and trans. The Heritage
of Vietnamese Poetry.
    J. Spragens, Jr., 293(JASt):Nov80-208
Thorburn, D. and H. Eiland, eds. John
Updike.
    G.F. Waller, 106:Winter81-413
Thormählen, M. The Waste Land.*
    M. Lojkine-Morelec, 189(EA):Jul-Sep81-
354
Thorne, H. Tuesday at Nine.
    D. Hamilton, 271:Winter81-157
Thorne, T. A Nickle in My Mouth.*
    G. Pollnitz, 561:Jun81-221
Thornton, A. The Living Universe.
    J.R. Fears, 122:Jul81-241
Thornton, P. and M. Tomlin. The Furnish-
ing and Decoration of Ham House.*
    G. Wills, 39:Jun81-413
Thornton, R. The Temple of Flora.
    J. Buxton, 617(TLS):12Mar82-288
Thornton, W. J.M. Synge and the Western
Mind.*
    D. Kiberd, 541(RES):Aug81-358
Thorold, A. Artists, Writers, Politics.
    R. Hobbs, 59:Mar81-121
Thorp, J. Free Will.*
    R. Young, 518:Jul81-172
Thorp, R. and C. Bertram. Peru, 1890-1977.
    R.B. St. John, 37:Apr81-26
Thorpe, M. Doris Lessing's Africa.
    M.M. Rowe, 395(MFS):Spring80-163
    R. Smith, 178:Summer81-252
Thorson, J.L., ed. Yugoslav Perspectives
on American Literature.
    S. Trachtenberg, 27(AL):Nov81-561
Threatte, L. The Grammar of Attic Inscrip-
tions. (Vol 1)
    S. Levin, 215(GL):Winter81-264
    J.W. Poultney, 24:Winter81-453
Thrower, N.J.W., ed. The Compleat Platt-
maker.
    W.J. Scheick, 568(SCN):Summer-Fall81-
69
    W.E. Washburn, 551(RenQ):Summer80-306
Thrower, N.J.W., ed. The Three Voyages of
Edmond Halley in the Paramore 1698-1701.
    O.M. Ashford, 617(TLS):23Jul82-805
Thuente, M.H. W.B. Yeats and Irish Folk-
lore.*
    G. Davenport, 569(SR):Summer81-469
    M. Fuchs, 174(Éire):Winter81-141
    C.H., 128:Spring81-94
Thulstrup, N. Kierkegaard's Relation to
Hegel.
    H.P.K., 543:Mar81-620

Thunecke, J. and E. Sagarra, eds. Formen
realistischer Erzählkunst.
    H.B. Garland, 402(MLR):Jul81-752
Thurber, J. Selected Letters of James
Thurber.* (H. Thurber and E. Weeks, eds)
    A. Coren, 617(TLS):29Jan82-101
    C. Sigal, 362:28Jan82-20
    442(NY):4Jan82-90
Thurley, G. The American Moment.*
    S. Fender, 677(YES):Vol 11-365
Thurman, J. Isak Dinesen.
    M. Drabble, 441:14Nov82-1
Thurnher, E. and others - see "Hugo von
Montfort"
Thurow, L.C. The Zero-Sum Society.
    R.B. Du Boff, 473(PR):2/1981-298
    J. Oppenheimer, 185:Jan82-373
    D. Usher, 529(QQ):Winter81-651
Thwaite, A., ed. Larkin at Sixty.
    D. May, 362:3Jun82-22
Thwaite, A. Victorian Voices.*
    H. Lomas, 364:Jun81-77
Thwaite, A. and R. Hayman, eds. My Oxford,
My Cambridge.
    S. Pickering, 569(SR):Winter81-xxiii
Thweatt, V. La Rochefoucauld and the
Seventeenth-Century Concept of the Self.
    M.S. Koppisch, 207(FR):Feb82-408
Tibbetts, G.R. A Study of the Arabic
Texts Containing Material on South-East
Asia.
    K.R. Hall, 293(JASt):Feb81-439
Tichá, Z., ed. Spisování slavného
frejíře.
    R.B. Pynsent, 575(SEER):Jan81-81
Tichi, C. New World, New Earth.*
    R. Asselineau, 189(EA):Jul-Sep81-355
    C. Bush, 677(YES):Vol 11-263
    D. Schuyler, 432(NEQ):Jun81-295
    D. Tallack, 541(RES):May81-219
    R.A. Yoder, 591(SIR):Fall81-387
von Tiedemann, R. Fabels Reich.*
    M. von Albrecht, 52:Band15Heft1-98
Tieder, I. Michelet et Luther.*
    M-M. Münch, 549(RLC):Jul-Dec81-503
Tiefenbrun, S.W. Signs of the Hidden.
    C. Britton, 402(MLR):Oct81-965
Tiempo, E. His Native Coast.
    N. Rosca, 293(JASt):Aug81-859
Tierney, B. Religion, Law, and the Growth
of Constitutional Thought, 1150-1650.
    J. Morrall, 617(TLS):29Oct82-1199
Tierney, B. and P. Linehan, eds. Author-
ity and Power.*
    J.H. Burns, 111:1Jun81-228
Tiger, P. and M. Babcock. The Life and
Art of Jerome Tiger.
    L. Milazzo, 584(SWR):Spring81-v
Tigerman, S. Versus.
    P. Goldberger, 441:8Aug82-9
Tigerman, S. and S. Cohen. Chicago Tri-
bune Tower Competition and Late Entries
to the Chicago Tribune Tower Competi-
tion.*
    R. Banham, 576:Oct81-257
Tikkanen, H. A Winter's Day.
    Y.L. Sandstroem, 563(SS):Summer81-371
    639(VQR):Winter81-9
Tillett, G. The Elder Brother.
    A. Calder-Marshall, 617(TLS):9Jul82-
732
Tillinac, D. Le Rêveur d'Amériques.
    L.K. Penrod, 207(FR):Mar82-574

Tillinghast, R. The Knife and other
Poems.*
   J.F. Cotter, 249(HudR):Summer81-283
   C.B. Cox, 148:Autumn81-2
   A. Williamson, 472:Fall/Winter81-247
Tillmann, H.G., with P. Mansell. Phonetik.
   T.F. Shannon, 350:Sep81-769
Tillotson, G. A View of Victorian Litera-
ture.*
   A. Easson, 677(YES):Vol 11-309
   P. Goetsch, 38:Band99Heft3/4-526
Tillotson, K., with N. Burgis - see Dick-
ens, C.
Tilton, H. Deutsch mit Emil.
   J.L. Cox, 399(MLJ):Winter81-432
Timerman, J. The Longest War.
   A. Elon, 441:12Dec82-1
Timerman, J. Prisoner Without a Name,
Cell Without a Number.*
   B.W. Varon, 390:Aug/Sep81-36
Timko, M., F. Kaplan and E. Guiliano - see
"Dickens Studies Annual"
Tindall, G. City of Gold.
   J. Grigg, 362:11Mar82-22
   A. Motion, 617(TLS):16Apr82-429
Tine, R. Uneasy Lies the Head.
   N. Callendar, 441:14Feb82-22
Ting, N-T. The Type Index of Chinese Folk-
tales in the Oral Tradition and Major
Works of Non-Religious Chinese Litera-
ture.
   C.H. Wang, 293(JASt):Feb81-367
Ting Wang. Chairman Hua.
   D.E. Waterfall, 529(QQ):Summer81-279
Tingyi, G. - see under Guo Tingyi
Tinker, H., ed. A Message from the Falk-
lands.
   J. Keegan, 617(TLS):12Nov82-1237
Tinkle, L. An American Original.*
   B. Singer, 77:Summer81-278
Tinniswood, P. Collected Tales from a
Long Room.
   A. Ross, 617(TLS):22Oct82-1174
Tippett, M. Emily Carr.*
   M.K. Westra, 73:Sep/Oct80-23
   G. Woodcock, 102(CanL):Spring80-105
Tippett, M. Music of the Angels.* (M.
Bowen, ed)
   N. Goodwin, 415:Feb81-108
   R. Warren, 437:Spring81-260
Tipton, S.M. Getting Saved from the
Sixties.
   M. Bayles, 441:31Jan82-12
Tirmizi, S.A.I. Edicts from the Mughal
Harem.
   M.A. Nayeem, 273(IC):Oct81-294
Tirso de Molina. El bandolero. (A.
Nougué, ed)
   G.E. Wade, 238:May81-312
Tischler, H., ed. The Montpellier Codex.
   H. van der Werf, 589:Jan81-200
Tismar, J. Kunstmärchen.
   V. Bosley, 107(CRCL):Winter81-124
Tison-Braun, M. Poétique de paysage.
   B.L. Knapp, 446(NCFS):Fall-Winter81/82-
163
Titzmann, M. Strukturwandel der philoso-
phischen Ästhetik 1800-1880.
   H.S. Daemmrich, 222(GR):Summer81-120
Tiusanen, T. Dürrenmatt.
   J. Sandford, 161(DUJ):Jun81-264

Tiwari, J.N. Disposal of the Dead in the
Mahābhārata.
   I.M. Proudfoot, 259(IIJ):Oct81-300
Tixonov, A.N. Škol'nyj slovoobrazovatel'-
nyj slovar' russkogo jazyka.
   P.M. Mitchell, 399(MLJ):Spring81-84
Tkachuk, M., M. Kishchuk and A. Nicholai-
chuk. Pysanka.
   N.R. Grobman, 292(JAF):Jan-Mar81-105
Tobias, A. The Invisible Bankers.
   P. Passell, 441:14Mar82-9
Tobin, P.D. Time and the Novel.*
   H. Foltinek, 402(MLR):Jul81-643
   L. Hutcheon, 107(CRCL):Winter81-119
   S. Soupel, 189(EA):Apr-Jun81-207
Tobin, T. James Bridie.
   D. Hutchison, 571(ScLJ):Winter81-128
Tocanne, B. L'Idée de nature en France
dans la seconde moitié du XVIIe siècle.*
   M-O. Sweetser, 475:No13Pt1-157
Todd, C. Bibliographie des oeuvres de
Jean-François de La Harpe.
   A. Jovicevich, 207(FR):May81-868
   R. Landy, 535(RHL):Jul-Oct81-792
   J. Lough, 208(FS):Apr81-209
   J. Renwick, 402(MLR):Jul81-704
Todd, J.M. Luther.
   R.M. Brown, 441:26Dec82-1
   R. Scribner, 617(TLS):28May82-587
Todd, J.M. Women's Friendship in Litera-
ture.*
   M. Butler, 184(EIC):Jul81-246
   N.K. Miller, 546(RR):Jan81-118
   S. Rava, 207(FR):May82-896
   S. Roxman, 172(Edda):1981/1-61
   M. Schonhorn, 566:Autumn81-47
Todd, L. Some Day Been Dey.
   M.F., 189(EA):Apr-Jun81-241
Todd, O. Un fils rebelle.*
   A. Clerval, 450(NRF):May81-127
Todd, W.M. The Familiar Letter as a Lit-
erary Genre in the Age of Pushkin.
   G. Scheidegger, 688(ZSP):Band41Heft2-
429
Todorov, T. La Conquête de l'Amerique.
   A. Pagden, 617(TLS):1Oct82-1081
Todorov, T. Les Genres du discours.
   G. Cesbron, 356(LR):Aug81-260
   A. Jefferson, 494:Autumn80-231
   T.G. Pavel, 107(CRCL):Winter81-104
Todorov, T. The Poetics of Prose.
   J.M. Cocking, 208(FS):Jan81-101
Todorov, T. Symbolisme et interprétation.
   A. Jefferson, 494:Autumn80-231
   T.G. Pavel, 107(CRCL):Winter81-104
Todorov, T. Théories du symbole.*
   A. Jefferson, 494:Autumn80-231
Toer, P.A. - see under Pramoedya Ananta
Toer
Toffler, A. The Third Wave.* (French
title: La 3me vague.)
   B. Elson, 529(QQ):Spring81-168
   J.P., 98:Apr81-439
Tőkés, R.L., ed. Opposition in Eastern
Europe.
   G. Kolankiewicz, 575(SEER):Jan81-136
Toland, J. Infamy.
   D.J.R. Bruckner, 441:22Aug82-12
   D. Kahn, 453(NYRB):27May82-36
Toland, J. No Man's Land.*
   639(VQR):Winter81-8
de Toledano, R. Devil Take Him.
   N. Weyl, 396(ModA):Spring81-206

de Toledo, A.M. - see under Martínez de Toledo, A.

Tolkien, J.R.R. Das Silmarillion.
M. Verch, 196:Band21Heft1/2-157

Tolkien, J.R.R. Unfinished Tales of Numenor and Middle-Earth. (C. Tolkien, ed)
C.E. Lloyd, 569(SR):Spring81-281

Toller, E. Gesammelte Werke. (J.M. Spalek and W. Frühwald, eds)
H.L. Cafferty, 221(GQ):Jan81-103

Tolles, B.F., Jr., with C.K. Tolles. New Hampshire Architecture.*
J. Quinan, 658:Winter81-356

de Tolnay, C. Corpus dei disegni di Michelangelo.
P. Joannides, 54:Dec81-679

Toloudis, C. Jacques Audiberti.
A. Cismaru, 207(FR):Feb81-476

Tolson, M.B. A Gallery of Harlem Portraits. (R.M. Farnsworth, ed)
205(FMLS):Oct80-381

Tolstoi, A.N., comp. Märchen aus Russland.
I. Köhler-Zülch, 196:Band3Heft3/4-347

Tolstoy, A. Out of the Past.
P-L. Adams, 61:Jan82-87
W.G. Jones, 617(TLS):4Jun82-621
442(NY):18Jan82-130

Tolstoy, I. James Clerk Maxwell.
R. O'Hanlon, 617(TLS):22Jan82-83

Tolstoy, N. Stalin's Secret War.*
K. Fitz Lyon, 617(TLS):22Jan82-89
M.D. Shulman, 441:9May82-8

Tomalin, R. W.H. Hudson.
N. Shakespeare, 617(TLS):26Nov82-1292

Tombs, R. The War Against Paris 1871.
E. Schulkind, 617(TLS):11Jun82-646

Tomlinson, C. The Flood.*
H. Beaver, 472:Spring/Summer82-117
D. Gioia, 249(HudR):Winter81/82-582
H. Lomas, 364:Nov81-70

Tomlinson, C., ed. The Oxford Book of Verse in English Translation.*
J. Saunders, 565:Vol22No3-62

Tomlinson, C. Some Americans.*
H. Beaver, 472:Spring/Summer82-117
M. Hennessy, 659(ConL):Spring82-254
C. Wilmer, 617(TLS):5Feb82-141
639(VQR):Summer81-97

Tomlinson, C. - see Paz, O.

Tomory, W.M. Frank O'Connor.
T.A. Gullason, 573(SSF):Summer81-333

Tompkins, J.P. Reader-Response Criticism.*
H.O. Brown, 141:Fall81-335
L.D. Kritzman, 188(ECr):Winter81-116
S. Mailloux, 400(MLN):Dec81-1149

Tompson, B. Benjamin Tompson, Colonial Bard. (P. White, ed)
E.S. Fussell, 27(AL):Jan82-743
R.C. Simmons, 617(TLS):1Jan82-14

Tønnessen, J.N. and A.O. Johnsen. The History of Modern Whaling.
S. Mills, 617(TLS):30Apr82-490
W.M. Stern, 324:Sep82-676

Toohey, R.E. Liberty and Empire.
B. Peach, 656(WMQ):Jul81-529

Tool, M.R. The Discretionary Economy.
C.W. Anderson, 185:Jul81-675

Toole, J.K. A Confederacy of Dunces.*
C.M. Saunders, 585(SoQ):Winter81-89

van den Toorn, M.C. Dietsch en volksch.
R.E. Wood, 660(Word):Dec80-329

Topham, J. and others. Traditional Crafts of Saudi Arabia.
R.L. Shep, 614:Fall82-21

Toporišič, J. Glasoslovna in naglasna podoba slovenskega jezika.
J. Paternost, 215(GL):Fall81-198

Topsfield, L.T. Chrétien de Troyes.*
H.F. Williams, 207(FR):Feb82-401

Topsfield, L.T. Troubadours and Love.
F.M. Chambers, 545(RPh):Feb81-348

Torgovnick, M. Closure in the Novel.*
D.P. Deneau, 268(IFR):Winter82-66

Tornay, S., ed. Voir et nommer les couleurs.
J.M.V. Marrelli, 297(JL):Sep81-353

Torrance, R.M. The Comic Hero.*
L. Nelson, Jr., 131(CL):Summer81-274

de la Torre, A.V. Jorge Mañach, maestro del ensayo.*
O. Olivera, 238:Mar81-162

de la Torre, F. Institución de un rey christiano (Antwerp, 1556).* (R.W. Truman, ed)
205(FMLS):Apr80-187

Torreblanca Espinosa, M. Estudio del habla de Villena y su comarca.
M. Garcia Pinto, 238:Mar81-166

Torres, A. Carta ao Bispo.
M. Silverman, 238:Mar81-160

Torretti, R. Philosophy of Geometry from Riemann to Poincaré.*
N. Griffin, 479(PhQ):Oct81-374

Tortel, J. Instants qualifiés. Des corps attaqués.
M. Broda, 98:Jan81-31

Tosches, N. Hellfire.
M. Bayles, 441:20Jun82-16

Tošev, K. Struškiot govor.*
V. Friedman, 350:Mar81-241

Toso Rodinis, G., ed. "Le Rose del deserto."*
A. Bonn Gualino and C. Bonn, 535(RIIL):Jan-Feb81-158

Totman, C. The Collapse of the Tokugawa Bakufu, 1862-1868.*
H. Bolitho, 244(HJAS):Dec81-629
M.D. Jansen, 293(JAS):Nov80-143

Touhill, B.M. William Smith O'Brien and his Irish Revolutionary Companions in Penal Exile.
R. Foster, 617(TLS):5Mar82-238

Toulet, P-J. Les Contrerimes.* (M. Décaudin, ed)
P.W.M. Cogman, 208(FS):Apr81-220

Toulouse, G. Crystal Palace.
M. Cagnon, 207(FR):Feb82-443

de la Tour du Pin, P. Une somme de poésie. (Vol 1)
I. Bell, 617(TLS):2Apr82-386

Tourneur, C. The Plays of Cyril Tourneur.* (G. Parfitt, ed)
P. Hollindale, 677(YES):Vol 11-245
G.B. Shand, 539:Feb82-60

Tourney, L.D. Joseph Hall.*
D.L. Russell, 568(SCN):Spring81-14

Tournier, M. The Four Wise Men.
P-L. Adams, 61:Oct82-105
J. Baumbach, 441:24Oct82-14

Tournier, M. Gaspard, Melchior et Balthazar.*
M.A. Daly, 400(MLN):May81-949
L. Kovacs, 450(NRF):Apr81-131

[continued]

355

Tournier, M. Gaspard, Melchior et Baltha-
zar. [continuing]
  S. Smith, 207(FR):Dec81-311
  G. Strickland, 97(CQ):Vol 10No3-238
Tournoux, R. Pétain et la France.*
  A. Douglas, 207(FR):Mar82-579
Tournoux, R. Le Royaume d'Otto.
  D. Pryce-Jones, 617(TLS):10ct82-1057
de Tourtier-Bonazzi, C. - see Napoleon I
Toury, G. In Search of a Theory of Trans-
lation.
  R. Vanderauwera, 204(FdL):Dec81-342
Tovar Martín, V. Los cinco gremios
mayores de Madrid.
  I. Mateo Gómez, 48:Jul-Sep81-376
Tovell, R.L. Reflections in a Quiet Pool.*
  F.K. Smith, 529(QQ):Winter81-751
Toweett, T. A Study of Kalenjin Linguis-
tics.
  D. Odden, 350:Sep82-731
Toynbee, A. The Greeks and Their Heri-
tages.*
  R. Jenkyns, 441:3Jan82-6
  D.A.N. Jones, 362:7Jan82-24
Tozzi, P. La rivolta ionica.*
  F.D. Harvey, 303(JoHS):Vol 101-192
Trachsler, E. Der Weg im mittelhoch-
deutschen Artusroman.
  I. Henderson, 133:Band14Heft4-356
"Tractatus de discantu (Concerning
Discant)." (A. Seay, ed and trans)
  H.W. Kaufmann, 551(RenQ):Spring80-90
Tracy, A. The Gothic Novel 1790-1830.
  I.S., 617(TLS):20Aug82-909
Tracy, B.B., with M. Black. Federal Furni-
ture and Decorative Arts at Boscobel.
  J.V. Turano, 16:Autumn81-92
Tracy, D. The Analogical Imagination.
  J.L. Houlden, 617(TLS):30Jul82-836
Tracy, J.D. The Politics of Erasmus.
  J.K. Sowards, 551(RenQ):Spring80-86
Tracy, L. Amateur Passions.*
  J. Mellors, 364:Aug-Sep81-139
Tracy, P.J. Jonathan Edwards, Pastor.
  J.M. Lovejoy, 165(EAL):Winter81/82-290
Tracy, R. Trollope's Later Novels.*
  J. Carlisle, 639(VQR):Winter81-176
  V. Shaw, 677(YES):Vol 11-322
Traeger, J. Mittelalterliche Architektur-
fiktion.
  W. Haas, 43:Band11Heft2-186
  F. Oswald, 471:Jul/Aug/Sep81-292
Traer, J.F. Marriage and the Family in
Eighteenth-Century France.
  R. Forster, 400(MLN):May81-928
  T.M. Scanlan, 207(FR):Apr81-750
Tragesser, R.S. Phenomenology and Logic.
  D.W. Smith, 316:Mar81-166
Traglia, A. and G. Aricò - see Statius
"La traite des noirs par l'Atlantique."
  H.J. Fisher, 69:Vol50No2-238
Trambaiolo, S. and N. Newbigin - see
"Altro Polo"
Tran, Q-P. William Faulkner and the
French New Novelists.
  R.A. Champagne, 207(FR):Feb81-479
Tranter, J., ed. The New Australian
Poetry.*
  V. Brady, 368:Mar81-110
Trapido, B. Brother of the More Famous
Jack.
  B.S. Altinel, 617(TLS):21May82-566
  442(NY):20Dec82-138

Trapp, J.B. - see More, T.
Traubel, H. With Walt Whitman in Camden.
(Vol 6) (G. Traubel and W. White, eds)
  R. Christiansen, 617(TLS):10Dec82-1377
Traugott, E.C. and M.L. Pratt. Linguis-
tics for Students of Literature.
  H. Penzl, 350:Sep81-782
  G. Prince, 599:Fall81-490
Trautmann, T.R. Dravidian Kinship.
  C.J. Fuller, 617(TLS):24Sep82-1042
Traversa, V. Parola e Pensiero. (3rd ed)
  G. Jackson, 399(MLJ):Winter81-436
Traves, T. The State and Enterprise.*
  D. McCalla, 298:Fall-Winter81-212
Travis, C. The True and the False.
  E.A. Edwards, 350:Sep82-742
Traxel, D. An American Saga.
  A. Berman, 55:Feb81-40
"Treasures of Indian Textiles: Calico
Museum."
  R.L. Shep, 614:Summer81-23
Tregear, M. Chinese Art.
  M. Medley, 39:Feb81-130
  62:Feb81-71
Tregear, T.R. China.
  L.J.C. Ma, 293(JASt):Aug81-778
Treglown, J. - see Lord Rochester
Tremain, R. The Animals' Who's Who.
  S.D. Smith, 441:5Dec82-65
de Trémaudin, A.H. Histoire de la Nation
métisse dans l'Ouest-canadien.
  D. Morton, 627(UTQ):Summer81-204
Tremblay, M. La grosse femme d'à côté est
enceinte.*
  G. Marcotte, 102(CanL):Autumn80-93
Tremblay, M. Thérèse et Pierrette à
l'école des Saints-Anges.
  E-M. Kroller, 102(CanL):Spring81-118
  P.G. Lewis, 207(FR):Feb82-444
Treneer, A. School House in the Wind.
  C. Causley, 617(TLS):28May82-576
Trenhaile, J. Kyril.
  M. Laski, 362:29Apr82-27
"Trent Study."
  T. Cantell, 324:Dec81-63
"Trésor de la langue française." (Vol 7)
(P. Imbs, ed)
  V. Väänänen, 439(NM):1980/1-84
Treuherz, J. Pre-Raphaelite Paintings
from the Manchester City Art Gallery.
  J. Christian, 39:Apr81-271
Trevelyan, R. Rome '44.*
  N. Lewis, 441:21Feb82-14
  C. Seton-Watson, 617(TLS):12Feb82-158
Trevor, W. Beyond the Pale.*
  D.A. Callard, 364:Nov81-90
  T. Solotaroff, 441:21Feb82-7
Trevor, W. Other People's Worlds.*
  639(VQR):Summer81-102
Trevor-Roper, H. Princes and Artists.
  T.D. Kaufmann, 576:Mar81-70
Trewin, J.C. Going to Shakespeare.
  H.S. Weil, Jr., 570(SQ):Summer81-278
Trewin, J.C., ed. Plays of the Year.
(Vol 48)
  B.A. Young, 157:Winter81-49
Trewin, J.C. Up From The Lizard.
  C. Causley, 617(TLS):28May82-576
Trewin, W. All on Stage.*
  M.B., 214:Vol 10No37-122
  B.A. Young, 157:1stQtr81-52

Trexler, R.C. Public Life in Renaissance
Florence.
F. Gilbert, 453(NYRB):21Jan82-62
"Tribal and Ethnic Art."
J.B. Donne, 617(TLS):3Sep82-955
Tribble, E. - see Wilson, W. and E.B. Galt
Tricotel, C. Comme deux troubadours.
G. Lubin, 535(RHL):Mar-Apr81-311
Triefenbach, P. Der Lebenslauf des Simpli-
cius Simplicissimus.
H.G. Rötzer, 224(GRM):Band31Heft3-375
Trifonov, J.V. Povesti.
D. Milivojević, 558(RLJ):Spring-Fall81-
298
Trifonov, Y. The Long Goodbye.
M.K. Frank, 399(MLJ):Spring81-82
Trigg, R. Reality at Risk.
S.P.S., 185:Oct81-196
Trillin, C. Uncivil Liberties.
J. Leonard, 441:4Jul82-2
442(NY):14Jun82-135
Trilling, D. Mrs. Harris.*
J. Cindin, 385(MQR):Spring82-353
A. Holden, 617(TLS):17May82-526
P. Whitehead, 362:6May82-23
Trilling, L. The Last Decade.* (D.
Trilling, ed)
R.B. Hovey, 396(ModA):Summer81-318
Trilling, L. Of This Time, Of That Place,
and Other Stories.* (D. Trilling, ed)
S. Lainoff, 390:Dec81-54
Trilling, L. Speaking of Literature and
Society. (D. Trilling, ed)
W.H. Pritchard, 249(HudR):Spring81-117
Trilse, C. Das Werk des Peter Hacks.
D. Leistner, 654(WB):7/1981-143
Trinkaus, C. The Poet as Philosopher.*
O. Büdel, 405(MP):Nov81-188
J.H. Whitfield, 382(MAE):1981/1-163
Tripathi, P.D. The Doctrinal English
Novel (Later Eighteenth Century).
M. Butler, 447(N&Q):Aug80-377
Tripet, A. La Rêverie littéraire.
R.L. Frautschi, 210(FrF):May81-176
J.F. Hamilton, 207(FR):May81-869
Triska, J. and C. Gati, eds. Blue-Collar
Workers in Eastern Europe.
A. Brown, 617(TLS):8Oct82-1111
Tristan, F. The London Journal of Flora
Tristan, 1842. (J. Hawkes, trans)
R. Scott, 362:28Jan82-23
Troendle, Y. Journey to the Sun.
J.K. Kealy, 102(CanL):Spring80-113
Troiani, L. and others. Richerche di
storiografia greca di età romana.
T.E.J. Wiedemann, 313:Vol71-201
Troisi, J. Tribal Religion.
L.A. Babb, 293(JASt):Nov80-185
Troll, C.W. Sayyid Ahmad Khan.*
K.A. Faruqi, 273(IC):Jul80-191
Trollope, A. Anthony Trollope: The Com-
plete Short Stories.* (Vols 1 and 2)
(B.J. Bryer, ed)
529(QQ):Spring81-195
Trombley, S. "All that Summer She was
Mad."
G. Strawson, 617(TLS):1Jan82-15
F. Taliaferro, 441:29Aug82-12
Trompf, G.W. The Idea of Historical Recur-
rence in Western Thought.
H.C.M., Jr., 543:Dec80-400
D.J. Wilcox, 551(RenQ):Autumn80-417

Trost, K. Untersuchungen zur Übersetzungs-
theorie und -praxis des späteren Kirchen-
slavischen.*
D. Huntley, 104(CASS):Winter81-554
Trousdale, M. Shakespeare and the Rhetori-
cians.
B. Vickers, 617(TLS):8Oct82-1110
Trousson, R. Le Thème de Prométhée dans
la litterature européenne. (2nd ed)
J.R. Loy, 207(FR):Oct80-158
Trousson, R., ed. Thèmes et figures du
siècle des lumières.
M. Delon, 535(RHL):Nov-Dec81-1009
H. Mason, 83:Autumn81-221
E. Showalter, Jr., 207(FR):Apr82-678
Trousson, R. Voyages aux pays de nulle
part.* (2nd ed)
A. Rosenberg, 627(UTQ):Spring81-336
Trower, P. Ragged Horizons.
J. Ferns, 102(CanL):Spring80-126
Troyat, H. Catherine the Great.
639(VQR):Spring81-47
Troyat, H. Grandeur nature. (N. Hewitt,
ed)
205(FMLS):Oct81-380
Trubetzkoy, N.S. N.S. Trubetzkoy's
Letters and Notes. (R. Jacobson, with
others, eds)
A. Liberman, 353:Vol 18No5/6-543
Trueba, H.T. and C. Barnett-Mizrahi, eds.
Bilingual Multicultural Education and
the Professional.
C. Stansfield, 238:Mar81-167
Trullinger, J.W., Jr. Village at War.
W.S. Turley, 293(JASt):May81-654
Truman, H.S. Off the Record.* (R.H. Fer-
rell, ed)
639(VQR):Spring81-69
Truman, M. Murder in the Supreme Court.
N. Callendar, 441:7Nov82-39
Truman, R.W. - see de la Torre, F.
Trunz, E. - see Meyfart, J.M.
Trypanis, C.A. Greek Poetry.
P. Sherrard, 617(TLS):21May82-555
Tsagarakis, O. Nature and Background of
Major Concepts of Divine Power in Homer.
O. Taplin, 123:Vol31No1-103
H. Vos, 394:Vol34fasc1/2-146
Tschilingirov, A. Die Kunst des christ-
lichen Mittelalters in Bulgarien, 4.
bis 18. Jahrhundert.
K. Wessel, 471:Oct/Nov/Dec81-375
Tschulik, N. Franz Schmidt.
D. Puffett, 415:May81-313
Tsigakou, F-M. The Rediscovery of
Greece.*
J. Ferguson, 324:Jul82-503
D.A.N. Jones, 362:7Jan82-24
H. Lloyd-Jones, 617(TLS):12Feb82-157
Tson-kha-pa. Calming the Mind and Discern-
ing the Real.* (A. Wayman, trans)
R. Kritzer, 485(PE&W):Jul81-380
Tsuchida, S. Reconstruction of Proto-
Tsouic Phonology.
R.A. Blust, 350:Mar81-205
Tsuda, M. A Preliminary Study of Japanese-
Filipino Joint Ventures.
G.K. Goodman, 293(JASt):May81-656
Tsuge Hideomi. Tōa kenkyūjo to Watakushi.
D.R. Reynolds, 293(JASt):Nov80-129
Tsuji, N. Comparative Phonology of
Guangxi Yue Dialects.
M. Hammond, 350:Mar81-243

Tsuji, S. Japanese Cooking.
T. Whittaker, 529(QQ):Autumn81-573
Tsurumi, Y. Japanese Business.
B.K. Marshall, 293(JASt):Nov80-142
Tsurutani, T. Political Change in Japan.
R. Benjamin, 293(JASt):Nov80-69
Tsvetaeva, M. A Captive Spirit.* (J.M.
King, ed and trans)
A.M. Kroth, 574(SEEJ):Spring81-105
Tsvetaeva, M. The Demesne of the Swans.
(R. Kemball, ed and trans)
A.M. Kroth, 574(SEEJ):Spring81-105
Tsvetaeva, M. Izbrannaja proza v dvux
tomax, 1917-1937.* (A. Sumerkin, ed)
J.M. King, 399(MLJ):Autumn81-351
Tsvetayeva, M. Selected Poems. (E.
Feinstein, trans)
H. Gifford, 617(TLS):8Jan82-39
D. McDuff, 453(NYRB):15Apr82-6
Tual, D. Le temps dévoré.
J. Piel, 98:Apr81-435
Tucci, G. The Religions of Tibet.
B.N. Aziz, 293(JASt):Feb81-373
Tuck, R. Natural Rights Theories.
G.B.H., 543:Jun81-810
A. Reeve, 185:Oct81-159
Tucker, D.F.B. Marxism and Individualism.*
K.S., 185:Jan82-401
Tucker, H.F., Jr. Browning's Beginnings.
W.H. Pritchard, 249(HudR):Autumn81-416
Tucker, P.H. Monet at Argenteuil.
S. Gardiner, 362:24Jun82-24
J. House, 617(TLS):29Oct82-1180
J. Russell, 441:5Dec82-13
D. Thomas, 324:Nov82-827
Tucker, P.L. Time and History in Valle-
Inclán's Historical Novels and "Tirano
Banderas."
R. Lima, 238:Dec81-639
G. Minter, 86(BHS):Apr81-148
Tucker, W. Progress and Privilege.
S.C. Florman, 441:8Aug82-8
Tuckey, J.S. - see Twain, M.
Tuckman, D. The Grapevine.
P. Bach, 614:Summer82-16
Tufte, V. and B. Myerhoff, eds. Changing
Images of the Family.
G.R. Lowe, 529(QQ):Spring81-13
Tugendhat, E. Vorlesungen zur Einführung
in die sprachanalytische Philosophie.
(2nd ed) Selbstbewusstsein und Selbst-
bestimmung.
V. Descombes, 98:Apr81-351
Tugwell, R.G. To the Lesser Heights of
Morningside.
W. Goodman, 441:30May82-10
den Tuinder, B.A. Ivory Coast.
M. Haswell, 69:Vol50No4-437
Tulard, J. - see de Maistre, J.
Tulloch, G. The Language of Sir Walter
Scott.*
J.H. Raleigh, 599:Fall81-461
Tulloch, J. Chekhov.*
G. Cox, 399(MLJ):Autumn81-350
P.D. Rayfield, 575(SEER):Oct81-636
M. Senderovich, 550(RusR):Jul81-353
Tullock, G. Trials on Trial.
R.P.A., 185:Apr82-579
Tully, G.F. Solar Heating Systems.
505:Apr81-103
Tully, J. A Discourse on Property.
L.C. Becker, 185:Jan82-361

Tumanjan, E.G. Struktura indoevropejskikh
imën v armjanskom jazyke.
J.A.C. Greppin, 318(JAOS):Apr/Jun80-
220
K.H. Schmidt, 260(IF):Band85-326
Tuomioja, E. K.H. Wiik.
J.H. Hodgson, 563(SS):Autumn81-472
Turel, A. - see Bachofen, J.K.
Turk, E-B. Baroque Fiction-Making.*
M. Cuénin, 535(RHL):Jan-Feb81-126
Turnbull, P. Dead Knock.
T.J. Binyon, 617(TLS):2Jul82-725
M. Laski, 362:2Dec82-23
Turnbull, P. Deep and Crisp and Even.
N. Callendar, 441:9May82-33
Turnbull, P. Dordogne.
H.L. Butler, 207(FR):Oct80-211
Turner, A., ed. Critical Essays on George
W. Cable.
L.J. Budd, 587(SAF):Spring81-127
K. King, 392:Fall81-488
639(VQR):Winter81-14
Turner, A. Nathaniel Hawthorne.*
K. Bales, 651(WHR):Summer81-183
N. Baym, 445(NCF):Jun81-102
B.B. Cohen, 301(JEGP):Oct81-601
M.J. Colacurcio, 183(ESQ):Vol27No2-108
J.L. Idol, Jr., 580(SCR):Spring81-112
Turner, E.G. Greek Papyri. (2nd ed)
A.K. Bowman, 123:Vol31No2-325
Turner, E.H. - see Compton, C.
Turner, F. Beyond Geography.
J. Nice, 649(WAL):Summer81-142
C.L. Sanford, 656(WMQ):Jul81-509
Turner, G. No Country for White Men.*
D. Barbour, 648(WCR):Jun80-77
E. Popham, 102(CanL):Autumn81-157
Turner, J. The Politics of Landscape.*
K.S. Datta, 551(RenQ):Autumn80-482
J.F.S. Post, 405(MP):Aug81-77
Turner, J. Reckoning with the Beast.*
B. Harrison, 617(TLS):29Jan82-116
Turner, J.M.W. Collected Correspondence
of J.M.W. Turner, with an Early Diary
and a Memoir by George Jones.* (J.
Gage, ed)
M. Pointon, 89(BJA):Winter81-77
A. Wilton, 39:Jan81-56
Turner, K. The Legacy of the Great Wheel.
P. Bach, 614:Fall81-17
Turner, L. Lana.
W. Lawson, 441:5Sep82-7
Turner, M. Things That Fly.*
K. MacLean, 134(CP):Spring81-61
Turner, N. Italian Baroque Drawings.*
A. Blunt, 90:Jun81-364
D. Scrase, 39:Jan81-61
Turville-Petre, E.O.G. Scaldic Poetry.
D.A.H. Evans, 597(SN):Vol53No2-388
Turville-Petre, T. The Alliterative
Revival.*
W.R.J. Barron, 179(ES):Feb81-56
A.T.E. Matonis, 382(MAE):1981/1-169
Tutorow, N.E. Texas Annexation and the
Mexican War.*
R. Acuña, 579(SAQ):Summer81-375
Tuttle, A. - see Bihaly, A.
Tutuola, A. The Witch-Herbalist of the
Remote Town.
D.A.N. Jones, 617(TLS):26Feb82-224
C.R. Larson, 441:4Jul82-8
Tuwhare, H. Selected Poems.
R. Healey, 368:Sep81-324

Uluxanov, I.S. Slovoobrazovatel'naja
semantika v russkom jazyke i principy
ee opisanija.
H. Jachnow, 559:Aug81-315
Unali, L. Descrizione di sè.
R. Asselineau, 189(EA):Oct-Dec81-493
Undank, J. Diderot.*
J. Creech, 173(ECS):Summer81-474
P. O'Donnell, 599:Fall81-471
D. O'Hara, 81:Spring80-259
W.E. Rex, 207(FR):Feb81-466
Underwood, M. The Hand of Fate.
N. Callendar, 441:9May82-33
Undhagen, L. "Morale" et les autres
lexèmes formés sur le radical "moral-"
étudiés dans des dictionnaires et dans
des textes littéraires français de la
seconde moitié du XVIIIe siècle.
S. Ettinger, 685(ZDL):1/1981-89
Ungaretti, G. Notes pour une poésie.
B. Chambaz, 450(NRF):Jan81-114
Unger, I. and D. The Vulnerable Years.
G. Adams, Jr., 106:Fall81-245
Unger, J. Education Under Mao.
J.K. Fairbank, 453(NYRB):2Dec82-13
Unger-Hamilton, C., ed. The Entertainers.
M.B., 214:Vol 10No37-116
M. Norgate, 157:2ndQtr81-54
Unseld, S. The Author and His Publisher.*
E. Schwarz, 221(GQ):Mar81-255
Unsworth, W. Everest.
J. Bernstein, 442(NY):7Jun82-136
R. Faux, 617(TLS):1Jan82-19
Unwin, D. Fifty Years with Father.
N. Cross, 617(TLS):21May82-552
Updike, J. Bech is Back.
J. Atlas, 61:Oct82-103
E. Hoagland, 441:17Oct82-1
J. Rubins, 453(NYRB):18Nov82-17
442(NY):29Nov82-174
Updike, J. Problems and Other Stories.*
The Coup.
P. Lewis, 565:Vol22No1-60
Updike, J. Rabbit is Rich.*
R. Davies, 362:14Jan82-21
C. Rumens, 617(TLS):15Jan82-48
Updike, J. La vie littéraire.
J-C. Liéber, 98:Apr81-418
Uphaus, R.W. Beyond Tragedy.
B. Vickers, 617(TLS):22Oct82-1158
Uphaus, R.W. The Impossible Observer.*
A.M. Duckworth, 579(SAQ):Spring81-237
P. Rogers, 566:Autumn80-34
Uppal, J.S., ed. India's Economic Prob-
lems. (2nd ed)
A. Bhargava, 293(JASt):Aug81-844
Uppendahl, K. - see Calderón de la Barca,
P.
Upton, A.F. The Finnish Revolution, 1917-
1918.*
639(VQR):Summer81-88
Upton, L.F.S. Micmacs and Colonists.*
C. Devens, 656(WMQ):Jul81-523
G.W., 102(CanL):Summer80-179
Urban, R. Die sorbische Volksgruppe in
der Lausitz, 1949-1977.
G. Stone, 575(SEER):Jul81-467
Urban, R. Wachstum und Krise des achäis-
chen Bundes.*
J. Briscoe, 123:Vol31No1-89
Urbanski, M.M.O. Margaret Fuller's "Woman
in the Nineteenth Century."*
F. Turner, 432(NEQ):Mar81-144

Urdang, C. The Lone Woman and Others.
J.F. Cotter, 249(HudR):Summer81-281
639(VQR):Spring81-66
Urdang, L. and C. Hoequist, Jr. -OLOGIES
and -ISMS. (2nd ed)
K.B. Harder, 424:Dec81-314
Urdang, L. and N. La Roche, eds. Pictur-
esque Expressions.
K.B. Harder, 424:Mar81-93
Ureland, P.S., ed. Sprachvariation und
Sprachwandel.
J-C. Muller, 350:Jun82-481
Ureland, P.S., ed. Standardsprache und
Dialekte in mehrsprachigen Gebieten
Europas.
Y. Malkiel, 350:Mar81-228
Urey, D.F. Galdós and the Irony of Lan-
guage.
A. Terry, 617(TLS):4Jun82-601
Urkowitz, S. Shakespeare's Revision of
"King Lear."*
R. Berry, 529(QQ):Autumn81-536
R. Knowles, 405(MP):Nov81-197
J. Reibetanz, 539:Nov82-294
Urmson, J.O. Berkeley.
A. Ryan, 362:18Mar82-21
Ury, M., ed and trans. Tales of Times Now
Past.*
S. Matisoff, 293(JASt):Aug81-797
D.E. Mills, 244(HJAS):Jun81-291
Usener, H. Glossarium Epicureum. (M.
Gigante and W. Schmid, eds)
A.A. Long, 303(JoHS):Vol 101-158

Vachon, G-A. Esthétique pour Patricia,
[suivi d'un] Ecrit de Patricia B.
J. Michon, 627(UTQ):Summer81-174
Vachon, G-A. Rabelais tel quel.
P. Somville, 102(CanL):Spring81-114
Vacuro, V.È. "Severnye cvety."
W. Busch, 688(ZSP):Band42Heft2-428
Vadée, M. and others. Science et Dialec-
tique chez Hegel et Marx.
J-M. Gabaude, 542:Oct-Dec81-496
Vaerst, C. Dichtungs- und Sprachreflexion
im Werk von Nelly Sachs.
R. Dinesen, 462(OL):Vol135No4-373
Vagianos, S.C. Paul Claudel and "La Nou-
velle Revue Française" (1909-1918).*
R.J. Nelson, 207(FR):Mar82-556
Vago, R.M. The Sound Pattern of Hungarian.
J.T. Jensen, 350:Mar82-218
Vaillancourt, S. Perspectives françaises
1.
P. Siegel, 207(FR):May81-887
Vaillant, A. Grammaire comparée des
langues slaves. (Vol 4)
H. Birnbaum, 279:Vol24-166
Vaillant, A. La Langue de Dominko
Zlatarić, poète ragusain de la fin du
XVIe siècle. (Vol 3)
M. Samilov, 575(SEER):Jul81-475
Vaillant, J. "Der Ruf."
H. Lehnert, 221(GQ):Jan81-111
U. Reinhold, 654(WB):1/1981-172
Vainstein, S. Nomads of South Siberia.
A.E. Dien, 550(RusR):Oct81-461
Vaïs, M. L'Écrivain scénique.
D.I. Grossvogel, 107(CRCL):Winter81-
139

Prince Vajiranana. Autobiography. (C.J. Reynolds, ed and trans)
C.A. Trocki, 293(JASt):Nov80-212
Valadier, P. Jésus-Christ ou Dionysos.
E. Blondel, 542:Oct-Dec81-497
Valcke, L. - see Ockham, William of
Valdenaire, A. Friedrich Weinbrenner. (3rd ed) (W. Schirmer, ed)
R. Dorn, 43:Band11Heft1-83
de Valdés, A. Diálogo de las cosas ocur-ridas en Roma. (J.L. Abellán, ed)
J.F. Cirre, 552(REH):Jan81-147
Valdés, J.M. - see under Meléndez Valdés, J.
Valdés, M.J. and O.J. Miller, eds. Inter-pretation of Narrative.*
D. Jackel, 178:Dec81-507
A. Kramer, 102(CanL):Autumn80-100
A. Reed, 478:Spring81-123
Valdés, S.C. - see under Claro Valdés, S.
Valdivieso, L.T. España.*
J. Almeida, 238:Mar81-157
J. Ferrán, 593:Summer81-182
Valdman, A. Le Créole.*
R. Morgan, Jr., 207(FR):Dec81-296
Valdman, A. Introduction to French Phonol-ogy and Morphology.
N.L. Corbett, 545(RPh):Feb81-293
Valdman, A., with R. Chaudenson and G. Manessy, eds. Le Français hors de France.
J-M. Klinkenberg, 209(FM):Jan81-64
Valdman, A. and A. Highfield, eds. Theo-retical Orientations in Creole Studies.
M.R. Miller, 399(MLJ):Winter81-418
Vale, M., ed. Poland — The State of the Republic.
A. Brumberg, 617(TLS):11Jun82-640
Valencia, P. and F. Merlonghi. En con-tacto.
M.J. Cousino, 399(MLJ):Autumn81-341
Valency, M. The End of the World.
L.C. Pronko, 397(MD):Mar81-115
G. Wellwarth, 141:Winter81-100
Valenstein, E.S., ed. The Psychosurgery Debate.
J.C.M., 185:Apr82-594
Valentin, J-M. Le théâtre des Jesuites dans les pays de langue allemande (1554-1680).*
J.A. Parente, Jr., 568(SCN):Spring81-30
Valentiner, T. - see Kant, I.
"Paul Valéry 2."* (H. Laurenti, ed)
C.A. Hackett, 535(RHL):Jul-Oct81-844
Valette, J-P., G.S. Kupferschmid and R. Valette. Con mucho gusto.
D.A. Klein, 238:May81-328
Valette, J-P. and R. Contacts. (2nd ed)
M. Maione, 207(FR):Oct81-177
Valette, R.D. - see Éluard, P.
"Les Valeurs chez les mémorialistes fran-çais du XVIIe siècle avant la Fronde."
J. Brighelli, 535(RHL):May-Jun81-458
Valgardson, W.D. Gentle Sinners.*
P. Klovan, 102(CanL):Spring81-136
Valgardson, W.D. Red Dust.*
J. Reid, 102(CanL):Autumn80-123
Valin, J. Dead Letter.
T.J. Binyon, 617(TLS):29Oct82-1196
N. Callendar, 441:17Jan82-29

Valkhoff, M.F., ed. Miscelänea Luso-Africana.
A.S. Kaye, 545(RPh):Feb81(supp)-342
Valla, L. Antidotum primum. (A. Wessel-ing, ed)
C. Trinkaus, 551(RenQ):Spring80-67
P. Viti, 228(GSLI):Vol 156fasc495-455
Valla, L. On Pleasure: De Voluptate. (A.K. Hieatt and M. Lorch, eds and trans)
L.V.R., 568(SCN):Spring81-33
del Valle, J.C. José del Valle: Antología. (R. Oquelí, ed)
E. Paz Barnica, 263(RIB):Vol31No3-415
Valle, J.E. Rocks and Shoals.
C. McKee, 656(WMQ):Apr81-325
Valli, D., ed. Catalogo della Biblioteca "Siciliani" di Galatina.
D.E. Rhodes, 354:Jun81-161
Vallin, G. Voie de gnose et voie d'amour.
M. Adam, 542:Apr-Jun81-249
Vallois, R. L'architecture hellénique et hellénistique à Délos jusqu'a l'eviction des Déliens (166 av. J.-C.). (Vol 2)
H. Plommer, 303(JoHS):Vol 101-208
Vallverdú, F. Aproximació crítica a la sociolingüística catalana.
M.M. Azevedo, 350:Jun81-516
Van Binsbergen, W.M.J. Religious Change in Zambia.
L. Mair, 617(TLS):28May82-589
Vandenabeele, F. and J-P. Olivier. Les idéogrammes archéologiques du Linéaire B.
J.T. Hooker, 303(JoHS):Vol 101-223
Van den Berghe, C.L. La Phonostylistique du français.
N.L. Corbett, 545(RPh):Feb81(supp)-208
Vander Kam, J.C. Textual and Historical Studies in the Book of Jubilees.
G.W.E. Nickelsburg, 318(JAOS):Jan/Mar80-83
Vander Molen, R. Along the River.
M. Thalman, 436(NewL):Fall81-123
Vander Veer, G.L. Philosophical Skepti-cism and Ordinary-Language Analysis.*
S.C. Brown, 518:Jan81-48
Vandervell, A. and C. Coles. Game and the English Landscape.*
T. Crombie, 39:Mar81-202
Van de Vate, D., Jr. Romantic Love.
J.F.M.H., 185:Jul82-786
Van de Water, F.F. Rudyard Kipling's Vermont Feud.
442(NY):25Jan82-104
Van Duyn, M. Letters from a Father.
M. Kinzie, 29:Sep/Oct82-37
Van Fossen, R.W. - see Chapman, G., B. Jonson and J. Marston
Vanger, M.I. The Model Country.
P.B. Taylor, Jr., 263(RIB):Vol31No3-423
Van Horn, D. Carved in Wood.*
R.L. Welsch, 292(JAF):Jul-Sep81-380
Van Inwagen, P., ed. Time and Cause.
G. Nerlich, 63:Sep81-350
Van Kirk, S. "Many Tender Ties."
V. Strong-Boag, 298:Fall-Winter81-217
Van Laan, T.F. Role-Playing in Shake-speare.*
M. Mack, Jr., 131(CL):Spring81-192
R.S. White, 447(N&Q):Oct80-432
Vann, J.D. and R.T. Van Arsdel, eds. Vic-torian Periodicals.*
L. Brake, 447(N&Q):Dec80-556

[continued]

361

Vann, J.D. and R.T. Van Arsdel, eds. Vic-
torian Periodicals. [continuing]
    M. Harris, 72:Band217Heft2-432
    J.M. Robson, 637(VS):Winter81-243
Vannebo, K.I. Tempus og tidsreferense.
    B. Comrie, 350:Mar81-234
    T.L. Markey, 562(Scan):Nov81-213
Van Nostrand, J. The First Hundred Years
of Painting in California, 1775-1875.
    B. Hanson, 70:Nov/Dec80-67
Vannoy, R. Sex Without Love.
    B. Hendley, 529(QQ):Winter81-809
Vanossi, L. Dante e il "Roman de la Rose."
    M. Picone, 545(RPh):Feb81(supp)-360
Van Parijs, P. Evolutionary Explanation
in the Social Sciences.
    R.H., 185:Jul82-780
Van Royen, R.A. and B.H. Isaac. The
Arrival of the Greeks.
    S. Hood, 123:Vol31No2-314
Van Santen, J.P. L'Essence du mal dans
l'oeuvre de Bernanos.
    A. Noël, 356(LR):Nov81-369
Vansina, J. The Children of Woot.
    D.P. Biebuyck, 69:Vol50No2-222
Vansittart, P. The Death of Robin Hood.*
    D. Durrant, 364:Jul81-86
Vansittart, P. Voices from the Great War.*
    A. Dickins, 364:Dec81/Jan82-132
Van Steen, E., ed. O Papel do Amor/Love
Stories.
    R. Catz, 399(MLJ):Autumn81-343
Van Walleghen, M. More Trouble With the
Obvious.
    D. Gioia, 249(HudR):Winter81/82-589
    W. Scammell, 617(TLS):28May82-592
    S. Yenser, 676(YR):Autumn81-97
Van Windekens, A.J. Le tokharien con-
fronté avec les autres langues indo-
européennes. (Vol 1)
    W. Winter, 350:Dec81-935
Van Young, E. Hacienda and Market in
Eighteenth-Century Mexico.
    G.P.C. Thomson, 617(TLS):3Dec82-1341
Varbanets, N.V. Ĭokbann Gutenberg i
nachalo knigopechataniya v Evrope.
    354:Sep81-267
Vardin, P.A. and I.N. Brody, eds. Chil-
dren's Rights.
    N.O.K., 185:Oct80-175
Varela, B. Lo chino en el habla cubana.
    D. Wogan, 263(RIB):Vol31No3-424
Vargas Llosa, M. Aunt Julia and the
Scriptwriter.* (Spanish title: La tia
Julia y el escribidor.)
    W. Kennedy, 441:1Aug82-1
Vargas Llosa, M. Die ewige Orgie.
    T. Degering, 224(GRM):Band31Heft4-479
Vargas Llosa, M. L'Orgie perpétuelle.
    C. Gothot-Mersch, 535(RHL):Mar-Apr81-
312
Varro. Varron, "Satires Ménippées." (Vol
5) (J-P. Cèbe, ed and trans)
    R. Astbury, 123:Vol31No2-294
Vasco, G.M. Diderot and Goethe.*
    M.K. Flavell, 402(MLR):Jan81-240
    A. Miller, 406:Spring81-110
    R.F. O'Reilly, 593:Summer81-181
de Vasconcellos, S. Vida e obra de
Antonio Francisco Lisboa, o Aleijadinho.
    N.W. Guilherme Ortega, 37:Aug81-38
van der Vat, D. The Grand Scuttle.
    B. Ranft, 617(TLS):24Sep82-1043

Vatnikova-Prizel, Z. O russkoj memuarnoj
literature.
    C.N. Lee, 574(SEEJ):Spring81-113
Vatuk, V.P. Studies in Indian Folklore
Traditions.
    J.L. Erdman, 293(JASt):Nov80-187
Vaughan, A. Born to Please.
    R. Findlater, 611(TN):Vol35No2-95
Vaughan, E.C. Some Desperate Glory.
    B.M., 617(TLS):26Mar82-363
Vaughan, W. German Romantic Painting.
    J. Whiteley, 59:Jun81-228
Vaughan, W. German Romanticism and
English Art.*
    D. Cherry, 59:Sep81-335
    E. Mai, 471:Apr/May/Jun81-188
    A. Sanders, 637(VS):Winter81-247
Vaughan, W. Romantic Art.
    L. Eitner, 90:Jun81-368
Vaughn, K.I. John Locke.
    E.J. Hundert, 518:Oct81-201
    W.A. Speck, 83:Autumn81-214
    S.W., 185:Jul82-803
Vauthier, J. L'"Othello" de Shakespeare.
    J. Guérin, 450(NRF):Jun81-131
de Vaux, R. and J.T. Milik. Qumran Grotte
4, II. (Pts 1 and 2)
    L.H. Schiffman, 318(JAOS):Apr/Jun80-
170
Vax, L. Les Chefs-d'oeuvre de la littérature fantastique.
    D. Bellos, 402(MLR):Apr81-426
    G. Crichfield, 207(FR):Mar81-585
Veatch, R.M. A Theory of Medical Ethics.
    H.J. Geiger, 441:31Jan82-10
de la Vega, G. - see under Garcilaso de la
Vega
de Vega Carpio, L. Lírica. (J.M. Blecua,
ed)
    T.E. Case, 304(JHP):Spring81-239
de Vega Carpio, L. El perro del hortelano.
(V. Dixon, ed)
    L.C. Pérez, 304(JHP):Spring81-237
Veilhan, J-C. The Rules of Musical Inter-
pretation in the Baroque Era.
    H. Schott, 415:Mar81-178
Veit, V. Mongolische Epen. (Vol 7)
    W. Eberhard, 318(JAOS):Jul/Sep80-390
Veitch, D.W. Lawrence, Greene and Lowry.*
    R.H. Costa, 395(MFS):Summer80-293
    S.S. Pearson, 295(JML):Vol8No3/4-416
    R. Seamon, 178:Summer81-248
van der Vekene, E., with P. Hamanová and
H.M. Nixon. Les Reliures aux Armoiries
de Pierre Ernest de Mansfeld.
    M.M. Foot, 78(BC):Spring81-116
Vélez de Guevera, L. El amor en vizcaíno.
(M.G. Profeti, ed)
    C.G. Peale, 240(HR):Winter81-123
Velie, A.R., ed. American Indian Litera-
ture.*
    U. Kutter, 196:Band22Heft1/2-158
    R.T. Smith, 577(SHR):Spring81-179
    R. Vanderbeets, 573(SSF):Fall81-477
    P.G. Zolbrod, 292(JAF):Apr-Jun81-251
Véliz, C. The Centralist Tradition of
Latin America.*
    H.E. Davis, 37:Feb81-46
Vella, W.F., with D. Vella. Chaiyo!
    C.A. Trocki, 293(JASt):Nov80-212
Velli, G. Petrarca e Boccaccio.
    A. Tissoni Benvenuti, 228(GSLI):
    Vol 157fasc500-611

van Velthoven, T. Gottesschau und mensch-
liche Kreativität.
    K. Bormann, 53(AGP):Band62Heft2-208
Veltroni, W., ed. Il Sogno degli anni '60.
    P. McCarthy, 617(TLS):22Jan82-88
Vendler, H. Part of Nature, Part of Us.*
    D. Davie, 569(SR):Winter81-110
    A. Gelpi, 27(AL):May81-314
    W. Spiegelman, 560:Spring-Summer81-200
Venesoen, C., ed. Racine.
    J. Dubu, 535(RHL):Mar-Apr81-289
Venetus, P. - see under Paulus Venetus
de Ventós, X.R. - see under Rubert de
Ventós, X.
Venturi, G. Le scene dell'Eden.
    M. Pieri, 400(MLN):Jan81-178
Vera, L.C. - see under Cervera Vera, L.
"The Verb 'be' and its Synonyms." (Pt 5)
    G.F. Meier, 682(ZPSK):Band32Heft2-238
Verde, A.F. Lo Studio fiorentino, 1473-
1503. (Vol 3)
    M. Pozzi, 228(GSLI):Vol 157fasc498-293
Verdier, Y. Façons de dire, Façons de
faire.
    D. Fabre, 98:Nov80-1075
Verdu, A. Dialectical Aspects in Buddhist
Thought.
    R.A.F. Thurman and T.F. Cleary,
    318(JAOS):Jul/Sep80-375
Verdu, A. Early Buddhist Philosophy in
the Light of the Four Noble Truths.
    G.D. Bond, 293(JASt):Aug81-846
Verdugo, I.H. - see Asturias, M.Á.
Verene, D.P., ed. Hegel's Social and
Political Thought.
    A. Rapaczynski, 185:Jan82-362
Verene, D.P. Vico's Science of Imagina-
tion.
    R.S.N., 185:Jul82-792
Verene, D.P. - see Cassirer, E.
Verga, G. Tutte le novelle. (C. Riccardi,
ed)
    B.T. Sozzi, 228(GSLI):Vol 158fasc503-
    465
Vergé, R. Cuisine of the South of France.
    W. and C. Cowen, 639(VQR):Spring81-70
Vergil. The Georgics. (R. Wells, trans)
The Georgics. (L.P. Wilkinson, trans)
    C. Martindale, 617(TLS):17Dec82-1386
Vergil. P. Vergili Maronis "Aeneidos"
Libri vii-viii.* (C.J. Fordyce, ed)
    J. den Boeft, 394:Vol34fasc1/2-179
Vergil. Virgil's "Eclogues."* (G. Lee,
trans)
    R.G.M. Nisbet, 123:Vol31No2-290
Vergil. Virgil's "Georgics" with Dry-
den's Translation. (A. Elliott, ed)
    E. Miner, 566:Spring82-126
Vergil - see also under Paratore, E.
Verhoeff, H. Les Comédies de Corneille.*
    J. Emelina, 535(RHL):Mar-Apr81-287
    H.C. Knutson, 546(RR):Jan81-106
    M.R. Margitić, 475:No15Pt1-186
Verhuyck, P.E.R., ed. La Bible de Macé de
la Charité. (Vol 2)
    B. Cazelles, 545(RPh):Feb81-359
Verkamp, B.J. The Indifferent Mean.
    J.K. Yost, 551(RenQ):Winter80-793
Verlaine, P. Femmes/Hombres: Women/Men.*
    (A. Elliot, trans) Femmes/Hombres. (W.
    Packard and J.D. Mitchell, trans)
    C. Chadwick, 208(FS):Apr81-216

Verleun, J.A. The Stone Horse.
    D. Hewitt, 541(RES):Aug81-353
Verma, M.K. and T.N. Sharma. Intermediate
Nepali Structure. Intermediate Nepali
Reader.
    J. Forman, 314:Summer-Fall81-250
Verma, S.P. Art and Material Culture in
the Paintings of Akbar's Court.
    F. Lehmann, 293(JASt):Feb81-414
    R. Shyam, 273(IC):Apr80-130
Verma, S.P. Devnagari lipi.
    K.K. Goswami, 261:Jun79-123
Vermeule, C.C. 3d. Greek Sculpture and
Roman Taste.
    H.P. Laubscher, 54:Sep81-506
Vermeule, E. Aspects of Death in Early
Greek Art and Poetry.*
    J.W. Day, 24:Spring81-110
    N.J. Richardson, 123:Vol31No1-124
    M. Robertson, 90:Mar81-168
Vermeule, E.T. Götterkult.
    J.M. Hemelrijk, 394:Vol34fasc3/4-413
Vermigli, P.M. The Political Thought of
Peter Martyr Vermigli. (R.M. Kingdon,
ed)
    K.R. Bartlett, 539:Aug82-223
Vernant, J-P. The Origins of Greek
Thought.
    M. Schofield, 617(TLS):29Oct82-1183
Vernant, J-P. and others. Divination et
rationalité.
    H. Damisch, 98:Feb80-95
Vernet, J. La cultura hispanoárabe en
Oriente y Occidente.
    M.R. Menocal, 240(HR):Spring81-229
Vernon, B.D. Ellen Wilkinson.
    K.O. Morgan, 617(TLS):5Feb82-125
    D.R. Thorpe, 362:28Jan82-23
Vernon, F. Privileged Children.
    J. Astor, 362:23Sep82-23
    J. Uglow, 617(TLS):24Sep82-1032
"Vernunft, Erkenntnis, Sittlichkeit."
    K. Mainzer, 679:Band12Heft1-180
Veroff, J., E. Douvan and R. Kulka. The
Inner American.*
    A. Hacker, 453(NYRB):18Mar82-37
Verschueren, J. On Speech Act Verbs.
    J. Mey, 350:Dec82-930
    B. Stross, 355(LSoc):Dec81-456
Verschueren, J. Pragmatics.
    D.A. Good, 353:Vol 18No1/2-163
Versini, L. Le Roman épistolaire.
    H. Coulet, 535(RHL):May-Jun81-488
    E. Showalter, Jr., 207(FR):Dec80-333
Versini, L. - see de Laclos, C.
Verstappen, P. The Book of Surnames.
    E.C. Smith, 424:Mar81-93
Verzea, I. Byron și byronismul în litera-
tura română.
    J. Amsler, 549(RLC):Jul-Dec81-499
Vescovini, G.F. Astrologia e scienza.
    W.A. Wallace, 589:Oct81-918
Vesey, G., ed. Communication and Under-
standing.
    J.S.M., 543:Jun81-811
Vet, C. Temps, aspects et adverbes de
temps en français contemporain.
    B. Comrie, 350:Mar82-245
Vetterling-Braggin, M., ed. Sexist Lan-
guage.
    R. Scruton, 617(TLS):1Jan82-6

Viorst, M. Fire in the Streets.*
    E.S. Shapiro, 390:Dec81-56
Virgil - see under Vergil
Virgilius Maro grammaticus. Epitomi ed
    epistole. (G. Polara, ed; L. Caruso and
    G. Polara, trans)
    B. Löfstedt, 589:Jan81-205
Virgo, S. Deathwatch on Skidegate Narrows
    and Other Poems.*
    D.W. West, 102(CanL):Winter80-112
Virgo, S. White Lies and other Fictions.*
    E. Crawley, 529(QQ):Autumn81-561
Virkkunen, S. Relander.
    M. Rintala, 563(SS):Winter81-100
Virmaux, A. and O. Roger Gilbert-Lecomte
    et le Grand Jeu.
    J. Stéfan, 450(NRF):Dec81-110
Visconti, G. I canzonieri per Beatrice
    d'Este e per Bianca Maria Sforza. (P.
    Bongrani, ed)
    M. Pozzi, 228(GSLI):Vol 158fasc503-446
Visson, L. Sergei Esenin.
    G. McVay, 575(SEER):Jul81-477
    M.T. Naumann, 558(RLJ):Spring-Fall81-
    290
    R.D.B. Thomson, 574(SEEJ):Summer81-97
Viswanathan, S. The Shakespeare Play as
    Poem.*
    J.C. Trewin, 157:2ndQtr81-53
Vitalis, O. - see under Orderic Vitalis
Vittorini, E. Conversazione in Sicilia.*
    (R.C. Powell, ed)
    205(FMLS):Jan80-96
Vivante, A. Run to the Waterfall.*
    G.W. Jarecke, 577(SHR):Spring81-176
Vivas, E. Two Roads to Ignorance.*
    A. Levine, 185:Oct80-167
Vivas, R.L. - see under Leiva Vivas, R.
Vives, J.L. Against the Pseudodialecti-
    cians. (R. Guerlac, ed and trans) In
    Pseudodialecticos. (C. Fantazzi, ed and
    trans)
    E.J. Ashworth, 551(RenQ):Winter80-742
    C.B. Schmitt, 319:Jan81-111
Vlach, J.M. The Afro-American Tradition
    in Decorative Arts.
    C. Camp, 292(JAF):Jan-Mar81-100
Vladiv, S.B. Narrative Principles in
    Dostoevskij's Besy.
    M. Futrell, 104(CASS):Winter81-563
Vliet, R.G. Water and Stone.*
    J.W. Saucerman, 649(WAL):Winter81-315
    A. Williamson, 472:Fall/Winter81-247
Vogel, C. Indian Lexicography.
    J.W. de Jong, 259(IIJ):Jul81-220
Vogel, M.E. Schnitzler in Schweden.
    D.G. Daviau, 406:Winter81-474
Vogel, M.J. The Invention of the Modern
    Hospital.
    S. Bernstein, 42(AR):Winter81-128
    S.E.D. Shortt, 529(QQ):Summer81-374
Vogel, S., ed. For Spirits and Kings.
    J.B. Donne, 617(TLS):26Feb82-227
Vogel, S.M. Beauty in the Eyes of the
    Baule.
    D.M. Warren, 2(AfrA):Feb81-80
von der Vogelweide, W. - see under Walther
    von der Vogelweide
Vogely, M.A. A Proust Dictionary.
    F.C. St. Aubyn, 207(FR):Oct81-145
Vogler, R.A., ed. Graphic Works of George
    Cruikshank.
    R.L. Patten, 445(NCF):Sep81-226

Vogt, A.M., U.J-S. Strathaus and B. Reich-
    lin. Architektur 1940-1980.
    H-W. Kruft, 471:Apr/May/Jun81-186
Vogt, E.Z. and R. Hyman. Water Witching
    U.S.A.
    J.C. Beck, 650(WF):Jul81-282
Voidy, J. Les contes de la source perdue.
    K. Mezei, 102(CanL):Autumn80-119
"Les Voies de la Création Théâtrale."
    (Vol 8)
    B. Beckerman, 546(RR):Nov81-495
Voigt, J.H. Indien im zweiten Weltkrieg.
    F. Wilhelm, 318(JAOS):Apr/Jun80-163
Vojnović, V.N. Pretendent na prestol.
    D.M. Fiene, 399(MLJ):Winter81-439
Volbach, W.F. Elfenbeinarbeiten der
    Spätantike und des frühen Mittelalters.
    (3rd ed)
    D.H. Wright, 54:Dec81-675
Vold, J.E. Det norske syndromet.
    J. Mawby, 562(Scan):Nov81-234
Volkoff, V. Les Humeurs de la mer.
    J. Blot, 450(NRF):Mar81-127
Volkoff, V. Vers une métrique française.
    G. Chesters, 402(MLR):Jul81-689
    J. Fox, 208(FS):Jan81-112
Volkov, S. - see Shostakovich, D.
Volle, N. Jean-Simon Berthélemy, 1743-
    1811.*
    P. Conisbee, 90:Jun81-369
Volney, C-F. La loi naturelle. (J. Gaul-
    mier, ed)
    A. Reix, 542:Jul-Sep81-377
Vol'pert, L.I. Puškin i Psixologičeskaja
    Tradicija Vo Francuzskoj Literature.
    T. Seifrid, 558(RLJ):Winter81-227
Volpi, F. Heidegger e Brentano.
    R. Schaeffler, 489(PJGG):Band88Heft1-
    217
Volponi, M. Lo sfondo italico della lotta
    triumvirale.
    M.H. Crawford, 313:Vol71-153
Volponi, P. Ich, der Unterzeichnete.
    H. Heintze, 654(WB):1/1981-128
de Voltaire, F.M.A. Correspondance. (Vol
    5) (T. Besterman, ed)
    J.H. Brumfitt, 208(FS):Apr81-205
de Voltaire, F.M.A. Thérèse: A Fragment.
    (D. Flower, ed)
    N. Barker, 617(TLS):17Dec82-1403
"Voltaire and the English."*
    A. Gunny, 535(RHL):Jul-Oct81-780
    O.R. Taylor, 402(MLR):Jan81-186
"Voltaire: un homme, un siècle."
    H. Mason, 402(MLR):Jan81-188
Vonnegut, K. Deadeye Dick.
    B. De Mott, 441:17Oct82-1
    442(NY):8Nov82-170
Vonnegut, K. Jailbird.*
    J. Mills, 529(QQ):Spring81-145
Vonnegut, K. Palm Sunday.*
    W. Boyd, 364:Jul81-84
    639(VQR):Summer81-98
Vorländer, K. Immanuel Kant. (2nd ed rev
    by W. Ritzel)
    R. Cadenbach, 53(AGP):Band62Heft1-96
    M. Kleinschneider, 342:Band72Heft4-518
Vorländer, K. - see Kant, I.
Vos, N. The Great Pendulum of Becoming.
    T.F. Marshall, 27(AL):Nov81-539
    J. Schlueter, 397(MD):Mar81-113
Vose, R.H. Glass.*
    A. Polak, 135:Feb81-166

Wakin, M.M., ed. War, Morality, and the
Military Profession.
C.R.B., 185:Apr82-581
"Waking Up Dormant Land."
T. Cantell, 324:Aug82-598
Walbank, F.W. The Hellenistic World.
P. Green, 617(TLS):26Feb82-206
Walbank, F.W. A Historical Commentary on
Polybius.* (Vol 3)
P. Pédech, 555:Vol54fasc2-358
Walbank, M.B. Athenian Proxenies of the
Fifth Century B.C.
D. Whitehead, 123:Vol131No1-87
Walbruck, H.A. Spannende Geschichten.
D.C. Hausman, 399(MLJ):Summer81-237
Walbruck, H.A. and A. Henschel. Lustige
Geschichten.
D.C. Hausman, 399(MLJ):Summer81-237
Walcot, P. Envy and the Greeks.
H.W. Stubbs, 303(JoHS):Vol 101-180
Walcott, D. The Fortunate Traveller.
C. Bedient, 472:Fall/Winter81-31
D. Davis, 362:6May82-26
D. Donoghue, 441:3Jan82-5
R. Garfitt, 617(TLS):24Sep82-1041
H. Vendler, 453(NYRB):4Mar82-23
Walcott, D. Rembrance [and] Pantomine.
D. Devlin, 157:1stQtr81-54
Walcott, D. The Star-Apple Kingdom.*
J. Figueroa, 364:Apr/May81-115
Waldeck, P.B. The Split Self from Goethe
to Broch.*
N. Ritter, 133:Band14Heft2-175
Walder, D. Dickens and Religion.
A.O.J. Cockshut, 617(TLS):15Jan82-57
Waldman, D. Anthony Caro.
T. Hilton, 617(TLS):4Jun82-599
Waldmann, G. Kommunikationsästhetik I.
J.H. Petersen, 680(ZDP):Band99Heft4-
597
Waldmeir, J.J., ed. Critical Essays on
John Barth.
H. Ziegler, 268(IFR):Winter82-71
Waldo, D. The Enterprise of Public Admin-
istration.
S. Postbrief, 185:Apr82-573
Waldron, E.E. Walter White and the Harlem
Renaissance.*
M. Fabre, 677(YES):Vol 11-356
Waldrop, K. Windfall Losses.
H. Thomas, 385(MQR):Winter82-200
Waldrop, R. When They Have Senses.
H. Thomas, 385(MQR):Winter82-200
Waldschmidt, E. and R.L. Miniatures of
Musical Inspiration in the Collection of
the Berlin Museum of Indian Art. (Pt 2)
H. Powers, 318(JAOS):Oct/Dec80-473
Walens, S. Feasting with Cannibals.
K.O.L. Burridge, 617(TLS):2Jul82-724
Waley, A. A Half of Two Lives.
H. Lee, 617(TLS):15Oct82-1120
F. Watson, 362:16Sep82-26
Walford, D. - see Cooper, A.A.
Walicki, A. A History of Russian Thought.*
The Slavophile Controversy.
I. Berlin, 575(SEER):Oct81-572
Walk, C. Hofmannsthals Grosses Welt-
theater.
H.J. Meyer-Wendt, 221(GQ):Nov81-525
Walker, A. The Color Purple.
R. Towers, 453(NYRB):12Aug82-35
M. Watkins, 441:25Jul82-7
442(NY):6Sep82-106

Walker, A. Peter Sellers.*
W. Lawson, 441:4Apr82-11
Walker, A. You Can't Keep a Good Woman
Down.* Meridian.
C. Rumens, 617(TLS):18Jun82-676
Walker, B.K. and W.S., eds. Nigerian Folk
Tales. (2nd ed)
P. Stevens, Jr., 2(AfrA):Feb81-83
Walker, D. The Architecture and Planning
of Milton Keynes.
S. Gardiner, 362:28Jan82-22
Walker, D.M. The Oxford Companion to Law.
B.W., 543:Jun81-812
Walker, D.P. Unclean Spirits.
L. Stone, 453(NYRB):16Dec82-28
Walker, E., ed. Explorations in the Biol-
ogy of Language.
D. Bekerian, 297(JL):Mar81-137
H. Birnbaum, 350:Mar81-248
Walker, G. The Hamelin Incident.
O. Wymark, 157:Oct80-73
Walker, G.F. Zastrozzi.
A. Messenger, 102(CanL):Autumn80-89
Walker, J. - see Cunninghame Graham, R.B.
Walker, J.A. The Japanese Novel of the
Meiji Period and the Ideal of Individual-
ism.*
J.T. Rimer, 395(MFS):Summer80-380
Walker, J.M. Nailing Up the Home Sweet
Home.
R. Phillips, 249(HudR):Autumn81-428
D. Smith, 29:Jan/Feb82-36
Walker, K.L. La Cohésion Poétique de
L'oeuvre Césairienne.
J. Ngate, 188(ECr):Spring81-108
E. Sellin, 207(FR):Oct81-148
Walker, K.S. - see under Sorley Walker, K.
Walker, M., ed. Canadian Confederation at
the Crossroads.
V. Lyon, 298:Summer81-122
Walker, M. Powers of the Press.
M. Davie, 617(TLS):10Oct82-1076
Walker, M. Robert Penn Warren.*
N. Nakadate, 594:Fall81-346
G. Rotella, 587(SAF):Autumn81-279
W.J. Stuckey, 395(MFS):Winter80/81-662
295(JML):Vol18No3/4-632
639(VQR):Winter81-14
Walker, N. Punishment, Danger and Stigma.
J.G. Cottingham, 518:Oct81-243
Walker, R. Rachmaninoff.
G. Norris, 415:May81-311
Walker, R.G. Eighteenth-Century Arguments
for Immortality and Johnson's "Rasse-
las."*
P.D. McGlynn, 577(SHR):Winter81-78
Walker, R.G. Infernal Paradise.*
H.T. Moore, 402(MLR):Oct81-941
S.S. Pearson, 295(JML):Vol18No3/4-416
Walker, S. Popular Justice.
M.P.P., 185:Jul81-695
Walker, S.F. Theocritus.
J. Clack, 124:Sep-Oct81-61
Walker, W.S. Plots and Characters in the
Fiction of James Fenimore Cooper.
R.A., 189(EA):Oct-Dec81-498
Walkley, C. The Ghost in the Looking
Glass.*
P. Bach, 614:Fall81-16
Walkley, C. and V. Foster. Crinolines and
Crimping Irons.
P. Bach, 614:Spring81-17

Walkowitz, J.R. Prostitution and Victorian Society.
  J.A. Banks, 637(VS):Summer81-513
Wall, K. L'inversion dans la subordonnée en français contemporain.*
  J.M. Julien, 350:Mar81-237
  L. Löfstedt, 439(NM):1981/2-222
Wall, M. Hermitage.
  C. Hawtree, 617(TLS):5Nov82-1231
Wall, R. Einführung in die Logik und Mathematik für Linguisten II.
  G.F. Meier, 682(ZPSK):Band33Heft6-781
Walla, F. - see Nestroy, J.
Wallace, A.F.C. The Social Context of Innovation.
  T. Kidder, 441:19Sep82-14
Wallace, B. - see under di Michele, M.
Wallace, D.R. Idle Weeds.
  S. Kremp, 649(WAL):Summer81-151
Wallace, I. The Almighty.
  H. Raucher, 441:31Oct82-15
Wallace, I. Birdwatching in the Seventies.
  R. O'Hanlon, 617(TLS):20Aug82-905
Wallace, J. Blowing Dust Off the Lens.
  D. Barbour, 648(WCR):Jun80-76
Wallace, J.D. Virtues and Vices.*
  R. Gaita, 393(Mind):Jan81-139
Wallace, M. British Government in Northern Ireland: From Devolution to Direct Rule.
  P. Arthur, 617(TLS):9Jul82-747
Wallace, R. The Last Laugh.*
  R.G. Collins, 106:Winter81-375
  R.B. Hauck, 395(MFS):Summer82-349
Wallace, R. Plums, Stones, Kisses and Hooks.
  H. Thomas, 385(MQR):Winter82-200
Wallace, R.W. The Etchings of Salvator Rosa.*
  E. Cropper, 551(RenQ):Winter80-769
Wallace-Crabbe, C., ed. The Golden Apples of the Sun.*
  G. Catalano, 381:Apr81-114
Wallace-Crabbe, C. Splinters.
  A. Hollinghurst, 617(TLS):5Feb82-147
Wallace-Crabbe, C. Toil and Spin.
  M. Macleod, 381:Apr81-77
Wallach, J. Working Wardrobe.
  614:Spring82-17
Wallack, F.B. The Epochal Nature of Process in Whitehead's Metaphysics.*
  L.S. Ford, 484(PPR):Sep81-133
Waller, B. Vallée suspendue.
  F. de Martinoir, 450(NRF):Nov81-126
Waller, G.F. Dreaming America.*
  W. MacNaughton, 102(CanL):Winter80-116
Waller, M. Democratic Centralism.
  W. Kendall, 617(TLS):3Sep82-950
Waller, M.R. Petrarch's Poetics and Literary History.
  F. Chiappelli, 589:Jul81-658
  A. di Tommaso, 141:Summer81-263
Walliser, S. That Nature is a Heraclitean Fire and of the Comfort of the Resurrection.*
  H-W. Ludwig, 72:Band217Heft1-198
Wallner, B., ed. The Middle English Translation of Guy de Chauliac's Treatise on Wounds. (Pt 1)
  C. Lindberg, 597(SN):Vol53No2-387

Wallner, B., ed. The Middle English Translation of Guy de Chauliac's Treatise on Wounds. (Pt 2)
  C. Lindberg, 597(SN):Vol53No2-387
  M.S. Ogden, 541(RES):Feb81-70
Walser, M. The Swan Villa.
  E. Pawel, 441:10Oct82-11
Walser, M. Travail d'âme.
  L. Kovacs, 450(NRF):Dec81-135
Walser, R. L'Institut Benjamenta.
  G. Quinsat, 450(NRF):Jul-Aug81-207
Walser, R. Selected Stories.
  R. De Feo, 441:24Oct82-14
  I. Parry, 617(TLS):19Nov82-1268
Walsh, B. Cheat.
  T.J. Binyon, 617(TLS):26Mar82-339
Walsh, C. Hang Me Up My Begging Bowl.
  W. Scammell, 617(TLS):28May82-592
Walsh, C. The Literary Legacy of C.S. Lewis.
  C.E. Lloyd, 569(SR):Spring81-281
  H.H. Watts, 395(MFS):Summer80-315
Walsh, D. Seasonal Bravery.*
  A. Munton, 150(DR):Autumn81-569
Walsh, D.D. - see Cardenal, E.
Walsh, J.E. Plumes in the Dust.*
  D.A. Daiker, 573(SSF):Summer81-342
  P.F. Quinn, 27(AL):Nov81-516
Walsh, T.J. Second Empire Opera.*
  H. Cole, 362:4Feb82-25
Walsh, W. Introduction to Keats.
  M. Casserley, 617(TLS):5Mar82-248
Walsh, W. F.R. Leavis.*
  W.E. Cain, 579(SAQ):Summer81-367
  R.G. Cox, 569(SR):Winter81-118
  T. Mallon, 659(ConL):Summer82-395
Walsh, W.H. Kant's Criticism of Metaphysics.
  V. Gerhardt, 53(AGP):Band62Heft3-339
Walter, H-A. Deutsche Exilliteratur 1933-1950. (Vol 4)
  R. Kieser, 406:Winter81-482
Walther von der Vogelweide. Frau Welt ich hab von Dir Getrunken. (2nd ed) (H. Witt, ed and trans)
  G.F. Jones, 221(GQ):May81-335
Walther, B.E. Hermann Broch.
  S. Dahl, 680(ZDP):Band100Heft4-622
  E. Schlant, 221(GQ):Nov81-519
Walther, H. Franz Kafka.
  B. Goldstein, 406:Spring81-67
  R.S. Struc, 133:Band14Heft3-278
Walther, W. Woman in Islam.
  A. Soueif, 617(TLS):10Sep82-977
Waltner-Toews, D. The Earth Is One Body.
  D. Barbour, 648(WCR):Jun80-77
  D. Precosky, 102(CanL):Winter80-142
Walton, D.N. On Defining Death.*
  N. Abrams, 185:Oct81-148
  N. Davis, 482(PhR):Jul81-489
  E-H.W. Kluge, 154:Sep81-616
Walton, E. Die Vier Zweige des Mabinogi.
  K.H. Schmidt, 196:Band22Heft1/2-161
Walton, G.M., ed. Regulatory Change in an Atmosphere of Crisis.
  R.H., 185:Apr81-536
Walton, G.M. and J.F. Shepherd. The Economic Rise of Early America.
  J.A. Ernst, 656(WMQ):Apr81-314
Walz, J. The Early Acquisition of a Second Language Phonology.
  J. Ludwig, 399(MLJ):Spring81-88
  H. Neidzielski, 207(FR):Feb81-483

368

Walzer, M. Just and Unjust Wars.
D. Lackey, 185:Apr82-533
B. Paskins, 479(PhQ):Jul81-285
Walzer, M. Radical Principles.*
B. Barry, 185:Jan82-369
Wan, G. and W. Johnson, with others.
Advanced Reader in Chinese History.
E.B. Brooks, 318(JAOS):Apr/Jun80-206
Wandor, M., ed. Strike While the Iron's
Hot; Care and Control; My Mother Says I
Never Should.
D. Devlin, 157:2ndQtr81-55
Wandruszka, M. Die Mehrsprachigkeit des
Menschen.
K. Reiss, 72:Band217Heft2-384
Wandruszka, U. Probleme der neuifranzö-
sischen Wortbildung.
H. and R. Kahane, 545(RPh):Feb81(supp)-
2
Wands, J.M. - see Hall, J.
Wandycz, P.S. The United States and
Poland.
R.C. Lukas, 497(PolR):Vol26No1-120
Wang Pi. Commentary on the Lao Tzu by
Wáng Pì. (A. Rump, with W-T. Chan,
trans)
D. Hall, 485(PE&W):Jan81-97
Wang, S-W. The Organization of Chinese
Emigration, 1848-1888.
L.E. Armentrout-Ma, 293(JASt):Feb81-
368
Wang, T. - see under Ting Wang
Wang, W.S-Y., ed. The Lexicon in Phono-
logical Change.*
M.J. Hashimoto, 350:Mar81-183
Wansbrough, J. Quranic Studies.
W.A. Graham, 318(JAOS):Apr/Jun80-137
Ward, A. and P. The Small Publisher.
M. Tims, 437:Spring81-172
Ward, B. The Conservative Economic World
View. The Liberal Economic World View.
The Radical Economic World View.
C.W. Anderson, 185:Jul81-675
Ward, C.A. Next Time You Go to Russia.
M. Chamot, 39:May81-341
Ward, D. Border Country.*
J. Cassidy, 493:Sep81-81
Ward, D. Sing a Rainbow.
P. Standford, 415:Apr81-244
Ward, J. A Late Harvest.
G. Szirtes, 617(TLS):15Oct82-1139
Ward, J. The Social and Religious Plays
of Strindberg.
W. Johnson, 563(SS):Spring81-236
M. Kaufman, 130:Summer81-173
295(JML):Vol18No3/4-623
Ward, J.P. To Get Clear.
A. Stevenson, 617(TLS):7May82-515
Ward, K. Rational Theology and the Crea-
tivity of God.
R.G. Swinburne, 617(TLS):3Sep82-954
Ward, P. Joseph Joubert and the Critical
Tradition.
M.E. Birkett, 446(NCFS):Fall-Win-
ter81/82-145
Ward, P., ed. The Oxford Companion to
Spanish Literature.
R. Keightley, 67:May81-129
G. Ribbans, 86(BHS):Jul81-252
205(FMLS):Jan80-92
Ward, R.E. Japan's Political System.
(2nd ed)
R. Benjamin, 293(JASt):Nov80-69

Ward Jouve, N. Baudelaire.
E.K. Kaplan, 207(FR):May81-871
Warde, A. Consensus and Beyond.
B. Pimlott, 617(TLS):15Oct82-1143
Wardle, R.M. - see Wollstonecraft, M.
Wardman, H.W. Renan.
D.C.J. Lee, 402(MLR):Jan81-197
L. Rétat, 535(RHL):Jul-Oct81-821
Wardropper, B.W. La comedia española del
Siglo de Oro.
E.N. Sims, 552(REH):May81-319
Wardropper, B.W. - see under Olson, E.
Wardwell, A. Objects of Bright Pride.*
W.N., 102(CanL):Winter80-159
Ware, A. The Logic of Party Democracy.
M.P. Fiorina, 185:Jul81-679
Ware, W.P. and T.C. Lockard, Jr. P.T.
Barnum Presents Jenny Lind.
H.M.K. Riley, 563(SS):Spring81-227
Warhol, A. and P. Hackett. POPism.*
P. Hodges, 62:Feb81-71
Waridel, B., comp. Bibliographie analyt-
ique des écrits sur Benjamin Constant
(1796-1978).
P. Deguise, 207(FR):Apr82-682
Warming, W. and M. Gaworski. The World of
Indonesian Textiles.
P. Bach, 614:Summer81-23
Warncke, C-P. Die ornamentale Groteske in
Deutschland 1500-1650.
E. Forssman, 683:Band44Heft3-313
C. Unverfehrt, 471:Oct/Nov/Dec81-374
Warner, A. - see Hewitt, J.
Warner, F. Requiem.
M.B., 214:Vol 10No37-119
Warner, I.R. and A.G. de Sousa, eds. An
Anthology of Modern Portuguese and
Brazilian Prose.*
205(FMLS):Jan80-80
Warner, M. Death in Time.
N. Callendar, 441:26Sep82-41
Warner, M. The Skating Party.
J. Astor, 362:8Apr82-23
R. Jackson, 617(TLS):30Apr82-481
Warner, M. Queen Victoria's Sketch Book.
F. Hardie, 637(VS):Spring81-357
Warner, P. Auchinleck.*
M. Carver, 617(TLS):29Jan82-118
Warner, P. The D-Day Landings.
A.M.R., 617(TLS):26Mar82-363
Warner, R. The Aerodrome.
J. Symons, 617(TLS):6Aug82-846
Warner, S.T. Letters: Sylvia Townsend
Warner. (W. Maxwell, ed) Collected
Poems. (C. Harman, ed)
P. Beer, 362:23and30Dec82-41
Warner, S.T. Scenes of Childhood.*
J. Gies, 441:17Jan82-10
M. Howard, 61:Mar82-83
Warner, W.B. Reading "Clarissa."*
P.R. Crabtree, 401(MLQ):Mar81-96
I. Grundy, 566:Spring81-108
J. Harris, 173(ECS):Fall80-85
J. Traugott, 454:Winter82-163
Warnock, R.G. and A. Zumkeller - see Hein-
rich von Freimar
Warren, B. Semantic Patterns of Noun-noun
Compounds.*
N. Davis, 541(RES):May81-198
Warren, M.A. The Nature of Woman.
M.U. Coyne, 258:Mar81-117
Warren, P. Irish Glass.
T. Hughes, 324:Oct82-752

                        [continued]

[continuing]
J. Kertzer, 49:Jan81-81
C.R. La Bossière, 268(IFR):Summer82-158
J. Lothe, 172(Edda):1981/1-73
S. Pinsker, 573(SSF):Spring81-191
M. Ray, 148:Autumn81-80
D.R. Schwarz, 136:Vol 13No1-73
L. Simpson, 454:Spring82-257
L.M. Whitehead, 150(DR):Winter81/82-743
639(VQR):Summer81-98
Wattenmaker, B.S. and V. Wilson. A Guidebook for Teaching English as a Second Language.
K.A. Mullen, 399(MLJ):Autumn81-333
Wattenmaker, B.S. and V. Wilson. A Guidebook for Teaching Foreign Language.
J.M. Purcell, 399(MLJ):Winter81-414
Watts, C. Conrad's "Heart of Darkness."*
M. Ray, 148:Autumn81-80
Watts, C. - see Cunninghame Graham, R.B.
Watts, C. and L. Davies. Cunninghame Graham.*
N. Curme, 571(ScLJ):Winter81-125
J. Walker, 541(RES):Feb81-95
Watts, D.A. Cardinal de Retz.
J.H. Broome, 402(MLR):Apr81-466
F.E. Sutcliffe, 208(FS):Apr81-194
Watts, D.A. - see Corneille, T.
Watts, I.N. A Chain of Words.
P. Nodelman, 102(CanL):Summer80-109
Watts, R.J. Lokative Präpositionen im Deutschen, Englischen und Zürichdeutschen.*
A. Lötscher, 685(ZDL):1/1981-81
Waugh, D.C. The Great Turkes Defiance.*
A.W. Fisher, 104(CASS):Winter81-572
W.F. Ryan, 575(SEER):Apr81-279
D.S. Worth, 550(RusR):Jan81-56
Waugh, E. Charles Ryder's Schooldays and Other Stories.
F. Donaldson, 441:14Nov82-25
442(NY):27Dec82-78
Waugh, E. The Letters of Evelyn Waugh.*
(M. Amory, ed)
C.H. Moore, 111:5Dec80-61
42(AR):Spring81-265
Waugh, E. PRB.
Q. Bell, 617(TLS):12Nov82-1253
D. Thomas, 362:9Dec82-27
Way, B. F. Scott Fitzgerald and the Art of Social Fiction.
G.M. Spangler, 27(AL):Nov81-521
Way, B. Herman Melville: "Moby Dick."
N. Schwenk, 447(N&Q):Oct80-468
Wayman, T. Free Time.
S. Dragland, 102(CanL):Spring80-124
Wayman, T., ed. Going for Coffee.
F.C. Sim, 526:Spring81-63
Wayman, T. Introducing Tom Wayman.*
J.F. Cotter, 249(HudR):Summer81-279
Wayman, T. Living on the Ground.*
T. Goldie, 526:Spring81-69
W. Keitner, 102(CanL):Autumn81-149
P. Stevens, 529(QQ):Autumn81-504
Wayman, T. A Planet Mostly Sea.*
E. Popham, 102(CanL):Autumn81-157
Weaver, G. Getting Serious.*
J.L. Halio, 573(SSF):Summer81-340
Weaver, L. Houses and Gardens by E.L. Lutyens.*
P. Davey, 46:Oct81-258

Weaver, R., ed. Canadian Short Stories. (3rd ser)
A.J. Harding, 102(CanL):Summer80-149
Weaver, W. The Golden Century of Italian Opera from Rossini to Puccini.
J. Budden, 415:Mar81-177
Webb, B. The Diary of Beatrice Webb.* (Vol 1) (N. and J. MacKenzie, eds)
M. Drabble, 362:14Oct82-26
J. Harris, 617(TLS):15Oct82-1119
J. Marcus, 441:12Dec82-9
Webb, C. The Wilderness Effect.
M. Abley, 617(TLS):29Jan82-104
K.C. O'Brien, 362:28Jan82-24
Webb, E. Eric Voegelin.
R.S.N., 185:Jul82-792
Webb, I. From Custom to Capital.
R. Brown, 617(TLS):18Jun82-660
Webb, J. Mechanism, Mentalism, and Metamathematics.
M. Detlefesen, 449:Nov81-559
Webb, M. Gone to Earth. Precious Bane.
S. Newell, 441:24Oct82-30
Webb, M. Seven For a Secret.
P. Craig, 617(TLS):26Nov82-1318
Webb, T. The Violet in the Crucible.*
R. Breuer, 38:Band99Heft1/2 253
Webb, V. A Little Ladykilling.
N. Callendar, 441:10Oct82-22
Webber, J.M. Milton and his Epic Tradition.*
D. Haskin, 613:Jun81-226
C.A. Patrides, 125:Fall80-101
I. Rivers, 551(RenQ):Autumn80 488
Weber, D., ed. New Spain's Far Northern Frontier.
D.C. Betts, 584(SWR):Winter81-102
Weber, E. Friedrich Dürrenmatt und die Frage nach Gott.
G.P. Knapp, 221(GQ):May81-378
Weber, F.J. - see Plato
Weber, H.B., ed. The Modern Encyclopedia of Russian and Soviet Literature.* (Vols 1-3)
R. Freeborn, 575(SEER):Jan81-80
Weber, M. Roscher and Knies. Critique of Stammler.
T.E. Huff, 488:Dec81-461
Weber, R. The Literature of Fact.*
S. Brown, 569(SR):Summer81-431
Weber, S. Unwrapping Balzac.
D. Bellos, 402(MLR):Jan81-196
M. Kanes, 210(FrF):Sep81-281
M.S. McCarthy, 207(FR):Feb81-470
205(FMLS):Oct80-382
Weber, V-F. Ko-Ji Hō-Ten.
S.E. Thompson, 70:Nov/Dec80-62
Weber, W. Geld, Glaube, Gesellschaft.
G. Merk, 489(PJGG):Band88Heft2-420
Webster, C., ed. Biology, Medicine and Society 1840-1940.
J. Lewis, 617(TLS):19Mar82-300
Webster, C., ed. Health, Medicine and Mortality in the Sixteenth Century.
L. Stone, 453(NYRB):16Dec82-28
Webster, G. Boudica.
J.R. Fears, 122:Jul81-243
Webster, G. The Republic of Letters.*
T.H. Adamowski, 529(QQ):Autumn81-442
M. Bucco, 649(WAL):Winter82-309
M. Le Fanu, 97(CQ):Vol 10No3-250
S. Paul, 301(JEGP):Apr81-273
[continued]

Webster, G.   The Republic of Letters.
  [continuing]
    D.H. Richter, 349:Summer81-232
    J.P. Riquelme, 125:Spring81-342
Webster, G.   The Roman Imperial Army of
  the First and Second Centuries A.D.*
  (2nd ed)
    C.M. Wells, 24:Winter81-465
Webster, G.   Rome Against Caratacus.
    B. Cunliffe, 617(TLS):23Apr82-467
Webster, J.   Due South.
    P. Craig, 617(TLS):5Mar82-246
Webster, M.   Hogarth.
    N. Llewellyn, 89(BJA):Winter81-80
Webster, N.   A Problem in Prague.
    N. Callendar, 441:30ct82-16
Wechsberg, J.   The Vienna I Knew.
    M. Ellmann, 569(SR):Summer81-454
Wechsler, J.   A Human Comedy.
    M. Neve, 617(TLS):17Sep82-991
Weckermann, H-J.   Verständigungsprobleme
  in Shakespeares Dramen.
    D. Mehl, 551(RenQ):Summer80-286
Weckherlin, G.R.   Stuttgarter Hoffeste.
  Esaias van Hulsen/Matthäus Merian, "Rep-
  raesentatio Der fürstlichen Aufzug und
  Ritterspil." (L. Krapf and C. Wagen-
  knecht, eds of both)
    J. Leighton, 402(MLR):Jul81-739
Wedderburn, R.   The Complaynt of Scotland
  (c. 1550) by Mr. Robert Wedderburn.
    P. Bawcutt, 571(ScLJ):Summer80-86
Wedekind, F.   Spring Awakening.
    D.R., 214:Vol 10No37-112
Wedgwood, B. and H.   The Wedgwood Circle
  1730-1897.
    T.A. Lockett, 135:Jan81-82
Weedon, G. and R. Ward.   Fairground Art.
    C. Raine, 617(TLS):19Mar82-302
Weeks, E.   Writers and Friends.
    M. Bayles, 441:21Mar82-12
van der Weele, S.J.   The Critical Reputa-
  tion of Restoration Comedy in Modern
  Times up to 1950.
    A.H. Scouten, 677(YES):Vol 11-262
"Weggefährten-Zeitgenossen."
    H. Möbius, 654(WB):3/1981-182
Wehrli, F., ed.   Sotion; Supplementband II.
    R.W., 555:Vol54fasc1-166
Wehrli-Johns, M.   Geschichte des Züricher
  Predigerkonvents (1230-1524).
    P. Dinzelbacher, 684(ZDA):Band110Heft4-
    178
Wehse, R.   Schwanklied und Flugblatt in
  Grossbritannien.
    V.E. Neuburg, 196:Band21Heft1/2-159
Weider, B. and D. Hapgood.   The Murder of
  Napoleon.
    P-L. Adams, 61:Mar82-89
    E.S. Turner, 362:29Apr82-23
    442(NY):12Apr82-155
Weidhorn, M.   Sir Winston Churchill.
    I.B. Holley, Jr., 579(SAQ):Winter81-
    118
Weiermair, P.   Photographie als Kunst,
  1879-1979. Kunst als Photographie, 1949-
  1979.
    R.A. Sobieszek, 127:Spring81-79
Weiers, M., ed.   Tungusica.
    N. Poppe, 318(JAOS):Jul/Sep80-394
Weigel, S.   Flugschriftenliteratur 1848 in
  Berlin.
    R-E.B. Joeres, 221(GQ):Nov81-516

Weiger, J.G.   Cristóbal de Virués.*
    J.G. Fucilla, 551(RenQ):Spring80-116
Weiger, J.G.   The Individuated Self.
    M.D. McGaha, 238:Mar81-152
    L.C. Pérez, 568(SCN):Winter81-94
    R.L. Predmore, 551(RenQ):Spring80-120
Weigl, B.   A Romance.*
    R.T. Smith, 577(SHR):Spring81-176
Weijnen, A. - see "Atlas Linguarum Europae
  (ALE)"
Weil, F.   Jean Bouhier et sa correspon-
  dance.
    J. Schlobach, 535(RHL):Nov-Dec81-991
Weil, H.   The Order of Words in the
  Ancient Languages Compared with that
  of the Modern Languages. (new ed)
    M.A. Covington, 350:Jun82-482
    C.F. Justus, 545(RPh):May81-442
Weil, J.   Christopher Marlowe.
    G.D. Aggeler, 179(ES):Apr81-173
Weiler, I.   Der Sport bei den Völkern der
  Alten Welt.
    W.E. Sweet, 124:Jul-Aug82-379
Weiler, I. - see Hampl, F.
Weills, C. and S. Satterlee.   The Goodfel-
  low Catalog of Wonderful Things #3.
    P. Bach, 614:Summer82-16
Weimann, R.   Shakespeare and the Popular
  Tradition in the Theatre.* (R. Schwartz,
  ed and trans)
    B. Vickers, 570(SQ):Spring81-107
Weimar, K.   Enzyklopädie der Literatur-
  wissenschaft.
    L. Orr, 599:Fall81-501
Weinberg, G.L.   The Foreign Policy of Hit-
  ler's Germany: Starting World War II,
  1937-1939.*
    639(VQR):Spring81-52
Weinberg, H.G.   Saint Cinema.
    M. Elliot, 200:Feb81-117
Weinberger, E. - see Aridjis, H.
Weinberger, E. - see Paz, O.
Weinbrenner, F.   Ausgeführte und Pro-
  jectirte Gebäude. (Pts 1-3 and 7)
    R. Dorn, 43:Band11Heft1-83
Weinbrot, H.D.   Augustus Caesar in
  "Augustan" England.*
    J. Mezciems, 161(DUJ):Dec80-113
    J. Richetti, 125:Fall80-98
Weiner, A.D.   Sir Philip Sidney and the
  Poetics of Protestantism.*
    J. van Dorsten, 551(RenQ):Autumn80-467
    N. Lindheim, 568(SCN):Spring81-5
    W.W. Wooden, 125:Fall80-96
Weiner, M.   Sons of the Soil.
    S.P. Cohen, 293(JASt):Feb81-415
Weiner, S.L.   Ajaṇṭā.*
    D. Srinivasan, 576:May81-143
Weinheber, J.   Sämtliche Werke. (Vol 1,
  Pt 1; Vol 2 [3rd ed]; Vol 4 [2nd ed];
  Vol 5 [2nd ed]) (F. Jenaczek, ed)
    A. Berger, 602:Vol 12No2-393
Weinreich, M.   History of the Yiddish
  Language.
    J.A. Howard, 301(JEGP):Oct81-606
    G. Jochnowitz, 350:Sep81-741
Weinreich, U.   On Semantics. (W. Labov
  and B.S. Weinreich, eds)
    K. Allan, 350:Dec81-941
    S.R. Levin, 494:Autumn80-196
Weinrich, H.   Sprache in Texten.
    R. de Beaugrande, 599:Winter81-86

372

Weinstein, A. Fictions of the Self: 1550-1800.
  H.M. Klein, 268(IFR):Summer82-145
  K. Tölölyan, 400(MLN):Dec81-1208
  J. Wilson, 617(TLS):15Jan82-57
Weinstein, M.A. Structure of Human Life.
  J.D. Moon, 185:Jan82-351
Weinstein, M.A. - see Scott, W.
Weinstein, W., ed. Chinese and Soviet Aid to Africa.
  A.H. Smith, 575(SEER):Jul81-474
  E.K. Valkenier, 550(RusR):Jan81-79
Weinstock, J., ed. The Nordic Languages and Modern Linguistics/3.
  O. Holzapfel, 196:Band21Heftl/2-161
Weintraub, K.J. The Value of the Individual.*
  J.F. Jones, Jr., 207(FR):Mar82-538
Weintraub, S. The London Yankees.
  P.J. Ferlazzo, 395(MFS):Summer80-324
Weintraub, S. and A. Wright - see Shaw, G.B.
Weinzweig, H. Basic Black With Pearls.*
  E. Crawley, 529(QQ):Autumn81-561
  P. Klovan, 102(CanL):Spring81-136
Weir, J.E. - see Baxter, J.K.
Weir, R.F., ed. Death in Literature.
  529(QQ):Summer81-402
Weisberg, G.P. François Bonvin (1817-1887).*
  P. Fitzgerald, 90:Dec81-753
Weisberg, G.P. The Realistic Tradition.
  N. McWilliam, 59:Dec81-466
  C. Rosen and H. Zerner, 453(NYRB):18Feb82-21
  C. Rosen and H. Zerner, 453(NYRB):4Mar82-29
Weisberg, G.P., with W.S. Talbot. Chardin and the Still-Life Tradition in France.
  M.S. Kinsey, 446(NCFS):Fall-Winter80/81-147
Weisbrod, C. The Boundaries of Utopia.
  D.H. Meyer, 658:Spring81-101
Weiss, C.H. and M.J. Bucuvalas. Social Science Research and Decision-making.
  W.H.P., 185:Apr82-595
Weiss, P. Kandinsky in Munich.*
  J. Masheck, 62:Jan81-66
  S. Ringbom, 54:Sep81-523
Weiss, P. You, I, and the Others.
  R. Neville, 258:Jun81-211
Weiss, T. Recoveries. The Man from Porlock.
  W.H. Pritchard, 441:17Oct82-25
Weissenberger, K. Zwischen Stein und Stern.
  A. von Bormann, 406:Winter81-483
Weissert, G. Ballade.
  W. Ruttkowski, 221(GQ):Nov81-490
Weissman, F.S. Du monologue intérieur à la sous-conversation.
  P.M. Wetherill, 402(MLR):Apr81-428
Weissman, S. and H. Krosney. The Islamic Bomb.
  C. May, 441:7Mar82-22
Weissmann, J.S. Goffredo Petrassi. (2nd ed)
  C. Bennett, 607:Dec81-47
  J.C.G. Waterhouse, 415:Oct81-674
Weisz, J. Das deutsche Epigramm des 17. Jahrhunderts.
  M. Beetz, 680(ZDP):Band100Heft2-288

Weithase, I. Sprachwerke-Sprechhandlungen.
  J. Müller, 680(ZDP):Band100Heft4-627
Weitzmann, K., ed. Age of Spirituality.*
  J. Trilling, 59:Sep81-344
Weitzmann, K. Byzantine Book Illumination and Ivories.*
  A. Cutler, 589:Apr81-444
Weitzmann, K. Late Antique and Early Christian Book Illumination.*
  78(BC):Spring81-14
Weitzmann, K. The Miniatures of the Sacra Parallela; Parisinus graecus 923.
  R. Cormack, 90:Mar81-170
  H.L. Kessler, 589:Jan81-208
  J. Mitchell, 59:Jun81-235
Weizman, E. The Battle for Peace.*
  D.M. Szonyi, 287:Nov81-14
Welch, A.T. and P. Cachia, eds. Islam.
  J. Renard, 377:Mar81-56
Welch, B. and G. Vecsey. Five O'Clock Comes Early.
  C. Kaiser, 441:21Feb82-16
Welch, H. and A. Seidel, eds. Facets of Taoism.*
  E. Chen, 485(PE&W):Oct81-545
  Y-H. Jan, 293(JASt):Aug81-778
Welch, L. and C. Address.
  D.M. Betz, 207(FR):Apr82-685
  M.M. Brewer, 478:Spring81-121
  P. Collier, 402(MLR):Apr81-474
  L.S. Roudiez, 535(RHL):Jul-Oct81-827
Welch, R. Irish Poetry from Moore to Yeats.
  M. Harmon, 637(VS):Summer81-515
Welch, W. The Art of Political Thinking.
  A.N., 185:Jul82-793
Welchman, G. The Hut Six Story.
  J. Moore, 617(TLS):15Oct82-1134
Welcome, J. The Sporting World of R.S. Surtees.
  T.J. Binyon, 617(TLS):22Oct82-1150
Weldon, F. Action Replay.
  D. Devlin, 157:2ndQtr81-55
Weldon, F. The President's Child.
  P. Craig, 617(TLS):24Sep82-1031
  K.C. O'Brien, 362:30Sep82-27
Weldon, F. Watching Me, Watching You.*
  J. Mellors, 364:Aug-Sep81-139
Welish, M. Handwritten.
  P. Schjeldahl, 472:Spring/Summer81-284
Welland, D. Mark Twain in England.*
  H. Cohen, 677(YES):Vol 11-329
Wellek, R. The Attack on Literature and Other Essays.
  C. Rawson, 617(TLS):10Dec82-1371
Wellek, R. and A. Ribeiro, eds. Evidence in Literary Scholarship.*
  P. Rogers, 83:Spring81-89
Wellington, H. - see Delacroix, E.
Wellington, M.A. and M. O'Nan, eds. Romance Literary Studies.
  M.I. Lichtblau, 238:May81-318
Welliver, W., ed and trans. Dante in Hell.
  N. Vincent, 402(MLR):Oct81-977
Wells, D.F. The Ghosts of Rowan Oak.
  C.S. Brown, 392:Summer81-367
Wells, J.C. Accents of English.
  R. Burchfield, 617(TLS):20Aug82-900
Wells, S. Modernizing Shakespeare's Spelling [together with] Taylor, G. Three Studies in the Text of "Henry V."
  T.L. Berger, 354:Jun81-162

Welsh, A. Reflections on the Hero as
  Quixote.
    L. Nelson, Jr., 676(YR):Winter82-285
Welsh, A. Roots of Lyric.*
    C. Lindahl, 292(JAF):Jan-Mar81-88
Welslau, E. Imitation und Plagiat in der
  französischen Literatur von der Renais-
  sance bis zur Revolution.
    W. Helmich, 224(GRM):Band30Heft1-117
    C. Strosetzki, 475:No14Pt1-194
Welte, W. Negationslinguistik.*
    E. König, 297(JL):Sep81-380
Welty, E. The Collected Stories of Eudora
  Welty.*
    J.L. Idol, Jr., 573(SSF):Spring81-187
    J. Uglow, 617(TLS):8Jan82-26
Welty, E. Losing Battles.
    P. Bailey, 617(TLS):4Jun82-608
Welty, E. The Robber Bridegroom. Delta
  Wedding.
    P. Craig, 617(TLS):13Aug82-888
Welwood, J., ed. The Meeting of the Ways.
    G. Parkes, 485(PE&W):Oct81-543
Welzig, W. and others - see Schnitzler, A.
Wemple, S.F. Atto di Vercelli.
    D.H. Miller, 589:Oct81-919
Wendell, C. - see al-Bannā, H.
Wender, D. The Last Scenes of the "Odys-
  sey."*
    F.M. Combellack, 122:Apr81-145
"Wim Wenders."
    J. Laurans, 450(NRF):Jun81-129
Wendland, V. Ostermärchen und Ostergeläch-
  ter.
    E. Moser-Rath, 196:Band22Heft3/4-379
Wendler, W., ed. Carl Sternheim: Material-
  ienbuch.
    R.W. Williams, 402(MLR):Oct81-999
Wendorf, R. William Collins and Eigh-
  teenth-Century English Poetry.
    I. Salusinszky, 617(TLS):23Apr82-470
Wendorf, R. and C. Ryskamp - see Collins,
  W.
Wendt, A., ed. Lali.
    T. James, 368:Sep81-287
Weng, W-G. and Y. Boda. The Palace
  Museum: Peking.
    J. Russell, 441:5Dec82-13
Wenham, B., ed. The Third Age of Broad-
  casting.
    P. Fox, 362:30Sep82-23
Wenisch, F. Spezifisch anglisches Wortgut
  in der nordhumbrischen Interlinearglos-
  sierungen des Lukasevangeliums.
    H. Sauer, 38:Band99Heft3/4-420
Wennrich, P. Anglo-American and German
  Abbreviations in Environmental Protec-
  tion.
    K.B. Harder, 424:Dec80-296
Went-Daoust, Y. Le Symbolisme des objets
  et l'espace mythique dans le théâtre de
  Jean Genet.
    A. Callen, 402(MLR):Oct81-976
    H. Stewart, 207(FR):Dec81-280
Wentworth, D. The Alden Family in the
  Alden House.
    L. Pizer, 432(NEQ):Sep81-431
Wentzel, L-C. Kurdische Märchen.
    H-J. Uther, 196:Band22Heft3/4-381
Wenzel, P. Die Lear-Kritik im 20. Jahr-
  hundert.
    E. Auberlen, 189(EA):Oct-Dec81-464

Wenzel, S. Verses in Sermons.
    J.B. Allen, 589:Jul81-660
    J.A. Burrow, 402(MLR):Apr81-433
    A.J. Fletcher, 382(MAE):1981/2-310
    M. Rigby, 541(RES):Nov81-439
Werbell, F.E. and T. Clarke. Lost Hero.
    W. Goodman, 441:7Feb82-16
Werenfels, S. A Dissertation concerning
  Meteors of Stiles, or False Sublimity.
    566:Spring81-123
Werkmeister, W.H., ed. Facets of Plato's
  Philosophy.
    R. Hahn, 319:Apr81-242
Werkmeister, W.H. Kant.
    R.B.P., 543:Jun81-813
Werkmeister, W.H., ed. Reflections on
  Kant's Philosophy.
    R. Malter, 342:Band72Heft3-377
Wermser, R. Statistische Studien zur Ent-
  wicklung des englischen Wortschatzes.*
    K. Hansen, 682(ZPSK):Band33Heft5-628
Werner, F. Die Vergeudete moderne.
    R. Elvin, 46:Oct81-260
Werner, J., ed. Lady, Wilt Thou Love Me?
    A. Seabrook, 572:Vol2-200
Wernigg, F. Bibliographie österreichis-
  cher Drucke während der "erweiterten
  Pressfreiheit" (1781-1795).
    P.R. Frank, 173(ECS):Fall80-82
Wertheim, A.F. The New York Little Renais-
  sance.
    J. Bochner, 106:Winter81-345
Wertheimer, J. Dialogisches Sprechen im
  Werk Stefan Georges.
    K. Weissenberger, 221(GQ):Mar81-238
Wertmüller, L. The Head of Alvise.
    442(NY):16Aug82-90
Wertsman, V., ed. The Romanians in
  America and Canada.
    K.B. Harder, 424:Sep80-219
Weschler, L. Seeing Is Forgetting the
  Name of the Thing One Sees.
    P. Schjeldahl, 441:18Apr82-3
Weschler, L. Solidarity.
    R.M. Watt, 441:25Apr82-11
"Adriaen van Wesel, een Utrechtse beeld-
  houwer uit de late middeleeuwen."
    J.W.M. de Jong, 600:Vol 12No1-85
Wesker, A. The Journalists/The Merchant/
  The Wedding Feast.
    D. Devlin, 157:2ndQtr81-55
Wesley, J. The Works of John Wesley.*
  (Vol 25) (F. Baker, ed)
    F.W. Bradbrook, 83:Autumn81-191
Wesley, J. The Works of John Wesley.
  (Vol 26) (F. Baker, ed)
    B. Drewery, 617(TLS):3Sep82-954
Wesling, D. The Chances of Rhyme.*
    C. Altieri, 301(JEGP):Jul81-431
    H. Gross, 131(CL):Summer81-298
    A. Helms, 569(SR):Winter81-xvii
Wesseling, A. - see Valla, L.
Wessell, L.P., Jr. Karl Marx, Romantic
  Irony, and the Proletariat.
    D. Cottom, 478:Spring81-125
West, D. Franklin and McClintock.
    J. Giltrow, 102(CanL):Winter80-136
West, D.M. Mandelstam: "The Egyptian
  Stamp."*
    C.J.G. Turner, 574(SEEJ):Summer81-95
West, D.S. Poems and Elegies 1972-1977.
    B. Whiteman, 102(CanL):Summer80-141

West, G.D. An Index of Proper Names in
French Arthurian Prose Romances.*
  A.H. Diverres, 208(FS):Jan81-63
  M.D. Legge, 382(MAE):1981/1-156
West, J.L.W. 3d, ed. Gyascutus.*
  M.A. Wimsatt, 392:Spring81-123
West, J.L.W. 3d and others - see Dreiser,
  T.
West, M.L. - see Hesiod
West, P. The Very Rich Hours of Count von
  Stauffenberg.*
  639(VQR):Winter81-22
West, R. An English Journey.*
  C. Brown, 617(TLS):12Mar82-284
  P. Vansittart, 364:Feb82-91
West, R. Harriet Hume.
  R. Dinnage, 453(NYRB):12Aug82-12
West, R. 1900.
  P-L. Adams, 61:May82-106
  R. Dinnage, 453(NYRB):12Aug82-12
  V. Glendinning, 362:25Feb82-23
  P. Keating, 617(TLS):5Mar82-247
  V.S. Pritchett, 442(NY):19Jul82-95
West, R. The Return of the Soldier.
  P. Craig, 617(TLS):22Oct82-1175
  R. Dinnage, 453(NYRB):12Aug82-12
West, R. The Young Rebecca. (J. Marcus,
  ed)
  P-L. Adams, 61:May82-106
  R. Dinnage, 453(NYRB):12Aug82-12
West, T.G. Plato's "Apology of Socrates."*
  M. Volpe, 480(P&R):Summer81-192
Westbrook, M. Country Boy.
  J.W. Saucerman, 649(WAL):Winter81-315
Westbrook, P.D. William Bradford.
  N.S. Grabo, 568(SCN):Spring81-21
Westbook, P.D. Free Will and Determinism
  in American Literature.*
  J.B. Colvert, 587(SAF):Autumn81-277
Westbrook, W.W. Wall Street in the Amer-
  ican Novel.
  J.F. Light, 27(AL):Nov81-556
Western, J. Outcast Cape Town.
  J. Lelyveld, 441:24Jan82-9
von Westernhagen, C. Wagner.*
  J. Deathridge, 451:Summer81-81
Westfall, R.S. Never at Rest.*
  T. Ferris, 441:26Sep82-16
Westlake, D.E. Kahawa.
  R. Hogan, 441:16May82-19
  442(NY):17May82-142
Westman, R.S. and J.E. McGuire. Hermeti-
  cism and the Scientific Revolution.*
  P.M. Rattansi, 319:Jul81-392
Westphal, M. History and Truth in Hegel's
  "Phenomenology."*
  C.G., 543:Sep80-168
  M.H. Miller, Jr., 125:Summer81-423
Westphal-Schmidt, C. Studien zum "Renne-
  wart" Ulrichs von Türheim.
  D.H. Green, 402(MLR):Oct81-983
Wetlesen, J. The Sage and The Way.
  E. Alexander, 485(PE&W):Jan81-101
Wetter, J. Karl von Burgund. (H. Thomke,
  ed)
  R.E. Schade, 133:Band14Heft4-367
Wetzel, H.H. Die romanische Novelle bis
  Cervantes.
  H.P. Clive, 107(CRCL):Winter81-123
Wexler, J.P. Laura Riding's Pursuit of
  Truth.
  J. Marcus, 473(PR):4/1981-643

Wexler, K. and P.W. Culicover. Formal
  Principles of Language Acquisition.
  C.L. Baker, 350:Jun82-413
Weyergans, F. Les Figurants.
  A. Clerval, 450(NRF):Jan81-138
  P.H. Solomon, 207(FR):Feb82-445
Weyl, N. Karl Marx: Racist.
  J.A. Settanni, 396(ModA):Fall81-441
Whalen, P. Enough Said.*
  J. Trimbur, 649(WAL):Fall81-226
Whalley, G. - see Christian, E.
Whalley, G. - see Coleridge, S.T.
Whalley, P. Post Mortem.
  T.J. Binyon, 617(TLS):29Oct82-1196
Wharton, D.P. In the Trough of the Sea.
  R.C. Davis, 106:Winter81-301
Wharton, D.P. Richard Steere.
  W.J. Scheick, 568(SCN):Spring81-23
Wharton, E. Chez les heureux du monde.
  C. Jordis, 450(NRF):Jun81-137
Wharton, S. - see René d'Anjou
Wharton, W. Dad.*
  D. Durrant, 364:Nov81-85
Wharton, W. A Midnight Clear.
  P-L. Adams, 61:Oct82-105
  J. Astor, 362:28Oct82-28
  T.R. Edwards, 441:12Sep82-13
  P. Kemp, 617(TLS):29Oct82-1189
  R. Towers, 453(NYRB):16Dec82-38
Whatley, C.A., ed. John Galt: 1779-1979.
  H. Gibault, 571(ScLJ):Winter81-113
Wheatcroft, A. The Tennyson Album.
  J.H. Buckley, 637(VS):Summer81-511
Wheaton, P.D. Razzmatazz.
  639(VQR):Summer81-100
Wheeler, M. The Art of Allusion in Victor-
  ian Fiction.*
  N. Auerbach, 445(NCF):Mar81-555
  P.K. Garrett, 637(VS):Winter81-251
  C. Perri, 599:Fall81-463
  B. Richards, 402(MLR):Apr81-450
Wheeler, M.C. Britain and the War for
  Yugoslavia, 1940-1943.
  E. Barker, 575(SEER):Jul81-466
Wheelock, A.K. Jan Vermeer.
  J. Nash, 617(TLS):14May82-542
Whelan, J.G. Soviet Diplomacy and Negoti-
  ating Behaviour.
  H. Neubroch, 575(SEER):Jan81-138
Whetmore, E.J. Mediamerica.
  D.L. Eason, 658:Spring81-126
Whinnom, K., ed. Dos opúsculos isabeli-
  nos.*
  N.G. Round, 382(MAE):1981/2-332
  205(FMLS):Jan80-84
Whinnom, K. - see de San Pedro, D.
Whitaker, H. and H.A., eds. Studies in
  Neurolinguistics. (Vol 4)
  J.C. Marshall, 353:Vol 18No3/4-362
Whitby, T.J. and T. Lorković. Introduc-
  tion to Soviet National Bibliography.*
  J.S.G. Simmons, 575(SEER):Jan81-153
White, A. Frost in May.* The Lost Travel-
  er. The Sugar House. Beyond the Glass.
  J.B., 231:Dec82-72
White, A. Names and Nomenclature in
  Goethe's "Faust."
  E. Boa, 402(MLR):Oct81-990
  A.P. Cottrell, 221(GQ):Nov81-509
White, A.D. Bertolt Brecht's Great Plays.*
  K.H. Schoeps, 400(MLN):Apr81-715
White, C.S.J. - see Harivaṃś, Ś.H.

Wickham, G. Early English Stages: 1300 to
1600.* (Vol 3)
   D. Buck, 157:Winter81-50
   M.L. Ranald, 612(ThS):Nov81-229
Wicks, C.B. The Parisian Stage. (Pt 5)
   J. Decock, 207(FR):Apr82-686
Wicks, L. The Vanguard Sleeps In.
   G. Bitcon, 581:Dec81-469
Widdess, D.R. and R.F. Wolpert, eds.
   Music and Tradition.
   W.P. Malm, 187:Sep82-482
   W. Mellers, 415:May81-314
Widdowson, H.G. Explorations in Applied
   Linguistics.*
   S. Belasco, 399(MLJ):Summer81-231
Widdowson, P., ed. Re-Reading English.
   C. Rawson, 617(TLS):10Dec82-1371
Wideman, J.E. Damballah.* Hiding Place.*
   M. Watkins, 441:11Apr82-6
Widener, A. - see Le Bon, G.
Widenor, W.C. Henry Cabot Lodge and the
   Search for an American Foreign Policy.*
   R.E. Welch, Jr., 432(NEQ):Sep81-451
Widmann, J. Die Grundstruktur des trans-
   zendentalen Wissens.
   C. Kumamoto, 53(AGP):Band62Heft2-222
Widmer, K. Edges of Extremity.
   C. Baxter, 141:Winter81-97
Wiebe, R. The Mad Trapper.*
   D. Carpenter, 102(CanL):Summer81-129
Wiebe, R. and others. A Voice in the Land.
   (W.J. Keith, ed)
   T. Marshall, 99:Mar82-30
Wiebe, R. and Theatre Passe Muraille. Far
   as the Eye Can See.
   R.J. Merrett, 102(CanL):Summer80-126
   A. Messenger, 102(CanL):Autumn80-89
Wied, A. Bruegel.
   K. Baetjer, 39:Jul81-66
Wiedemann, K. Arbeit und Bürgertum.
   D. Smith, 221(GQ):May81-341
Wiener, M.J. English Culture and the
   Decline of the Industrial Spirit, 1850-
   1980.*
   P. Gorb, 324:Nov82-825
Wienpahl, P. The Radical Spinoza.*
   E. Alexander, 485(PE&W):Jan81-101
Wier, D. The 8-Step Grapevine.
   639(VQR):Summer81-94
Wierzbicka, A. The Case for Surface Case.
   D. Kilby, 402(MLR):Jul81-764
   J. Nichols, 350:Sep82-696
Wierzbicka, A. Lingua mentalis.
   R.M.W. Dixon, 361:Oct/Nov81-265
von Wiese, B. Perspektiven II.
   J. Müller, 680(ZDP):Band99Heft4-630
von Wiese, S. Max Beckmanns zeichner-
   isches Werk 1903-1925.
   P. Selz, 54:Mar81-170
Wiesel, E. The Testament.* (French title:
   Le Testament d'un poète juif assassiné.)
   A.B. Carb, 287:Nov81-25
   R.C. Lamont, 207(FR):Apr81-770
Wiesel, E. The Trial of God.
   W. Kluback, 390:Aug/Sep81-51
Wiesenfarth, J. George Eliot's Mythmaking.
   W. Baker, 179(ES):Dec81-569
   P. Preston, 447(N&Q):Dec80-558
Wiesenfeld, J. Spratt.*
   J. Wasserman, 102(CanL):Autumn80-88
Wiessman, F.S. Du monologue intérieur à
   la sous-conversation.
   G. Idt, 535(RHL):May-Jun81-496

Wiethölter, W. Witzige Illumination.
   W. Koepke, 221(GQ):Nov81-512
Wigger, M. Tempora in Chrétien's "Yvain."
   M. Sandmann, 72:Band217Heft1-204
Wiggins, D. Sameness and Substance.*
   P.B., 543:Mar81-623
   H. Noonan, 479(PhQ):Jul81-260
   L.J. Splitter, 63:Jun81-229
   P.F. Strawson, 393(Mind):Oct81-603
Wigginton, E. - see "Foxfire 6"
Wiik, K.H. Karl H. Wiiks Dagbok från stor-
   strejken till upproret 1917-1918. (S.
   Lindman, ed)
   J.H. Hodgson, 563(SS):Autumn81-472
Wiingaard, J., ed. Henrik Ibsen i scenisk
   belysning.
   D. Thomas, 562(Scan):May81-99
Wijk-Andersson, E. En svensk minigram-
   matik.
   A.L. Rice, 563(SS):Summer81-374
Wikan, U. Behind the Veil in Arabia.
   A. Soueif, 617(TLS):10Sep82-977
von Wilamowitz-Moellendorff, U. History
   of Classical Scholarship. (H. Lloyd-
   Jones, ed)
   B. Knox, 453(NYRB):23Sep82-57
Wilcockson, C. - see Jones, D.
Wilcox, C. Stalking Horse.
   N. Callendar, 441:16May82-26
Wilcoxon, G.D. Athens Ascendant.
   H.C. Avery, 122:Jul81-232
Wilczynski, J. An Encyclopedic Dictionary
   of Marxism, Socialism and Communism.
   R. Scruton, 617(TLS):9Jul82-747
Wild, D. Nicolas Poussin.
   E.M. Vetter, 4/1:Jul/Aug/Sep81-286
Wild, I. Zur Überlieferung und Rezeption
   des "Kudrun"-Epos.
   W. Hoffmann, 684(ZDA):Band110Heft1-30
Wildavsky, A. How to Limit Government
   Spending.
   J.A., 185:Jul81-700
Wilde, A. Horizons of Assent.*
   P.A. Bové, 659(ConL):Spring82-244
Wilde, J. Michelangelo.* (M. Hirst and J.
   Shearman, eds)
   P. Joannides, 90:Oct81-620
   A.H. Mayor, 551(RenQ):Autumn80-448
Wilde, O. The Complete Shorter Fiction of
   Oscar Wilde. (I. Murray, ed)
   D. Kramer, 573(SSF):Summer81-331
Wilde, O. The Importance of Being Earnest.
   (R. Jackson, ed)
   S. Rusinko, 397(MD):Jun81-236
Wilde, O. Lady Windermere's Fan. (I.
   Small, ed)
   G. Rowell, 610:Autumn81-227
Wilde, W.H. and T.I. Moore - see Gilmore,
   M.
Wilde-Stockmeyer, M. Sklaverei auf Island.
   M. Cormack, 563(SS):Spring81-213
Wilden, A. System and Structure.*
   W. Rewar, 567:Vol33No3/4-337
Wilden, T. The Imaginary Canadian.
   S. Kane, 627(UTQ):Summer81-162
van den Wildenberg-de Kroon, C.E.C.M. Das
   Weltleben und die Bekehrung der Maria
   Magdalena im deutschen religiösen Drama
   und in der Bildenden Kunst des Mittel-
   alters.
   G.F. Jones, 406:Winter81-451
   K. Kunze, 684(ZDA):Band109Heft1-36

Wilder, A.N. Thornton Wilder and His
Public.
E.E. Ericson, Jr., 396(ModA):Summer81-
323
Wilders, J. The Lost Garden.*
M. Charney, 125:Winter81-234
R.A. Foakes, 402(MLR):Apr81-440
Wilding, M. Political Fictions.*
P. Parrinder, 366:Autumn81-238
Wiles, D. The Early Plays of Robin Hood.
J.A. Burrow, 617(TLS):1Jan82-9
Wiles, M. Faith and the Mystery of God.
D.M. MacKinnon, 617(TLS):28May82-588
Wiles, T.J. The Theatre Event.
M.B., 214:Vol 10No37-118
Wiley, B.I., ed. Slaves No More.
P.D. Escott, 9(AlaR):Jul81-229
H. Johnson, 577(SHR):Fall81-360
R.L. Watson, 579(SAQ):Autumn81-496
Wilford, J.N. The Mapmakers.*
639(VQR):Autumn81-119
Wilhelm, F. and J.L. Panglung, comps.
Tibetische Handschriften und Blockdrucke.
(Pt 7)
J.W. de Jong, 259(IIJ):Jul81-232
M.L. Walter, 318(JAOS):Apr/Jun80-219
Wilhelm, H. Heaven, Earth, and Man in the
Book of Changes.*
J. Hart, 318(JAOS):Jul/Sep80-379
Wilhelm, R. Lectures on the I Ching.
K. Smith, 293(JASt):Aug81-783
Wilhoit, G.C. and H. de Bock - see "Mass
Communication Review Yearbook"
Wilke, J. Literarische Zeitschriften des
18. Jahrhunderts (1688-1789).
M.K. Torbruegge, 406:Spring81-109
Wilkes, G.A. The Stockyard and the Cro-
quet Lawn.
R. Brain, 617(TLS):15Oct82-1123
Wilkes, L. John Dobson.*
T. Faulkner, 83:Autumn81-253
Wilkie, B. and M.L. Johnson. Blake's
"Four Zoas."*
J. Beer, 402(MLR):Jul81-676
V.A. De Luca, 627(UTQ):Winter80/81-238
Wilkin, D. - see de Magny, O.
Wilkins, N. Music in the Age of Chaucer.*
B.R. Hanning, 414(MusQ):Apr81-285
Wilkins, R. A Man's Life.
J. Dreyfuss, 441:20Jun82-8
Wilkins, R., with T. Mathews. Standing
Fast.
P-L. Adams, 61:Aug82-96
R. Kluger, 441:1Aug82-10
Wilkinson, A. Midnights.
P. Benchley, 441:22Aug82-6
T.G., 231:Aug82-77
442(NY):9Aug82-94
Wilkinson, G. A History of Britain's
Trees.
S. Leathart, 617(TLS):2Jul82-727
Wilkinson, J.D. The Intellectual Resist-
ance in Europe.
R. Boyers, 617(TLS):15Jan82-45
Wilkinson, S. Bone of My Bones.
D. Quammen, 441:21Feb82-13
Wilks, C.W. The Magic Box.
J.C. Oates, 461:Spring-Summer81-106
Will, G.F. The Pursuit of Virtue and
Other Tory Notions.
N. Johnston, 441:28Mar82-16

Will, P.E. Bureaucratie et famine en
Chine au XVIIIe siècle.
S.L. Kaplan, 98:Jun-Jul81-660
L.M. Li, 293(JASt):May81-594
J. Spence, 453(NYRB):1Apr82-45
Willard, N. A Visit to William Blake's
Inn.
385(MQR):Winter82-220
Wille, G. Einführung in das Römische
Musikleben.
J-P. Cèbe, 555:Vol54fasc1-193
Willemyns, R. Het niet-literaire Middel-
nederlands.*
A. Berteloot, 685(ZDL):1/1981-115
Willenbrink, G.A. The Dossier of Flau-
bert's "Un Coeur Simple."
R. Debray-Genette, 535(RHL):Jul-Oct81-
804
Willett, J. and R. Manheim, with E. Fried
- see Brecht, B.
Willetts, R.F. The Civilization of
Ancient Crete.
G. Cadogan, 303(JoHS):Vol 101-199
M.H. Jameson, 122:Apr81-141
E. Vermeule, 24:Spring81-109
Willey, T.E. Back to Kant.
J.B., 543:Dec80-402
M. Jay, 473(PR):1/1981-143
Williams, A.L. An Approach to Congreve.*
H. Hawkins, 541(RES):Feb81-80
A. Kaufman, 301(JEGP):Jan81-135
J.S. Malek, 141:Winter81-85
K. Muir, 677(YES):Vol 11-274
M.E. Novak, 566:Autumn80-32
P.E. Parnell, 568(SCN):Summer-Fall81-
50
Williams, B. Descartes.*
R.J. Delahunty, 161(DUJ):Dec80-129
J. Harrison, 393(Mind):Jan81-122
Williams, B. Moral Luck.
T. Nagel, 617(TLS):7May82-501
M. Warnock, 362:18Feb82-22
Williams, B.B. A Literary History of
Alabama: The Nineteenth Century.
O.B. Emerson, 577(SHR):Summer81-275
L.P. Simpson, 9(AlaR):Jan81-59
Williams, C.H., ed. National Separatism.
R. Mitchison, 617(TLS):19Nov82-1281
Williams, C.J.F. What is Existence?
T. Baldwin, 617(TLS):9Jul82-736
Williams, D. Copper, Gold and Treasure.
N. Callendar, 441:12Sep82-36
Williams, D. Genesis and Exodus.
M.J. Peterson, 637(VS):Autumn80-135
295(JML):Vol18No3/4-351
Williams, D. President and Power in
Nigeria.
A.H.M. Kirk-Greene, 617(TLS):3Dec82-
1346
Williams, D. A World of His Own.
M. Mason, 617(TLS):10Dec82-1353
Williams, D.A., ed. The Monster in the
Mirror.*
G. Hainsworth, 208(FS):Oct81-465
205(FMLS):Jan80-91
Williams, F. Callimachus: "Hymn to
Apollo."*
A. Griffiths, 303(JoHS):Vol 101-159
Williams, F.G. - see de Sena, J.
Williams, G. Figures of Thought in Roman
Poetry.*
R.O.A.M. Lyne, 123:Vol31No2-218

Wills, G. Explaining America.*
639(VQR):Autumn81-119
Wills, G. The Kennedy Imprisonment.
J.G. Dunne, 453(NYRB):15Apr82-10
J. McGinniss, 441:14Mar82-7
Willson, R.F., Jr. Landmarks of Shake-
speare Criticism.
A.W. Bellringer, 447(N&Q):Oct80-430
Wilmerding, J., ed. American Light.
B.J. Wolf, 219(GaR):Spring81-195
Wilmerding, J. American Masterpieces from
the National Gallery of Art.
A. Berman, 55:Sep81-29
M.S. Young, 39:May81-338
Wilmet, M. Études de morpho-syntaxe ver-
bale.*
N.L. Corbett, 545(RPh):May81-474
Wilmet, M., ed. Sémantique lexicale et
sémantique grammaticale en moyen fran-
çais.
P. Rickard, 208(FS):Oct81-428
S.N. Rosenberg, 207(FR):Oct80-202
Wilmeth, D.B. American and English Popu-
lar Entertainment.*
G. Speaight, 611(TN):Vol35No3-136
Wilmeth, D.B. George Frederick Cooke.
E. Brown, 610:Autumn81-221
J.C. Trewin, 157:1stQtr81-50
Wilmot, J. - see under Lord Rochester
Wilmut, R. From Fringe to Flying Circus.*
M.B., 214:Vol 10No37-117
von Wilpert, G. Sachwörterbuch der
Literatur. (6th ed)
V.A. Dedas, 133:Band14Heft2-175
von Wilpert, G. Der verlorene Schatten.
F. Voit, 67:May81-124
Wilson, A. Setting the World on Fire.*
D. Flower, 249(HudR):Spring81-114
I. Malin, 639(VQR):Summer81-566
S. Monod, 189(EA):Oct-Dec81-488
Wilson, A.N. The Laird of Abbotsford.*
K. Curry, 661(WC):Summer81-174
K. Sutherland, 148:Winter81-84
A. Welsh, 445(NCF):Dec81-358
639(VQR):Spring81-58
Wilson, A.N. Who Was Oswald Fish?*
J. Mellors, 364:Feb82-93
Wilson, A.N. Wise Virgin.
J. Astor, 362:28Oct82-28
P. Rogers, 617(TLS):5Nov82-1211
Wilson, B. Religion in Sociological Per-
spective.
R. Towler, 617(TLS):24Sep82-1045
Wilson, C. Treasures on Earth.
T.O. Treadwell, 617(TLS):12Mar82-289
Wilson, C.N. - see Calhoun, J.C.
Wilson, D. Bear Rampant.
L. Duguid, 617(TLS):1Jan82-12
Wilson, D. Tito's Yugoslavia.
P. Auty, 575(SEER):Jan81-130
Wilson, D. When Tigers Fight.
W. Goodman, 441:18Jul82-22
W. Mendl, 617(TLS):20Aug82-906
Wilson, D.S. In the Presence of Nature.
H.P. Simonson, 173(ECS):Summer81-477
J. Woodcock, 125:Fall80-117
Wilson, E. The Mental as Physical.*
D. Garrett, 311(JP):Jul81-416
T.E. Wilkerson, 518:Jan81-55
M. Williams, 185:Apr81-519
Wilson, E. The Thirties.* (L. Edel, ed)
J. Chernaik, 364:Jun81-84
W.H. Pritchard, 249(HudR):Spring81-117

Wilson, E.M. Spanish and English Litera-
ture of the Sixteenth and Seventeenth
Centuries.*
T.R.H., 131(CL):Fall81-383
F. Pierce, 86(BHS):Jul81-260
205(FMLS):Apr81-200
Wilson, E.O. On Human Nature.*
J. Beatty, 529(QQ):Winter81-607
R.L. Simon, 185:Jan82-327
Wilson, G.K. Interest Groups in the
United States.
E. Wright, 617(TLS):26Feb82-225
Wilson, G.M. Alexander McDonald.
J. Hunter, 617(TLS):15Oct82-1133
Wilson, H. The Chariot of Israel.*
T. Clarke, 441:13Jun82-12
Wilson, H.S. The Imperial Experience in
Sub-Saharan Africa since 1870.
J.D. Fage, 69:Vol50No4-433
Wilson, H.W. and D.L. Hoeveler. English
Prose and Criticism in the Nineteenth
Century.*
P.G. Scott, 506(PSt):May81-106
J. Shattock, 402(MLR):Apr81-448
Wilson, I. Mind Out of Time?
K. McCulloch, 617(TLS):26Mar82-360
Wilson, I.C., ed. Hollywood in the 1940s.
D. McClelland, 200:Feb81-117
Wilson, J. Entertainments for Elizabeth I.
C.E. McGee, 539:May82-144
R. Strong, 617(TLS):9Apr82-419
Wilson, J. Octavio Paz.*
R. Cardinal, 529(QQ):Spring81-19
C. Cosgrove, 86(BHS):Apr81-160
205(FMLS):Apr80-192
Wilson, J. Preface to the Philosophy of
Education.
E. Telfer, 393(Mind):Oct81-618
Wilson, J., ed. Texas and Germany: Cross-
currents.*
K. Kehr, 685(ZDL):1/1981-84
Wilson, J.B. Pylos 425 B.C.
G.L. Cawkwell, 123:Vol31No1-132
J.D. Smart, 303(JoHS):Vol 101-197
Wilson, J.F. Public Religion in American
Culture.
C.H. Lippy, 658:Spring81-128
J.S. Rubin, 106:Spring81-79
Wilson, J.M. I was an English Poet.
B. Bergonzi, 617(TLS):23Jul82-782
Wilson, J.V.K. - see under Kinnier Wilson,
J.V.
Wilson, K. A History of Textiles.*
P. Bach, 614:Summer81-18
Wilson, K.J. - see Elyot, T.
Wilson, M.D. Descartes.*
T.M. Lennon, 319:Apr81-250
R. Montague, 393(Mind):Apr81-304
Wilson, M.I. Organ Cases of Western
Europe.*
J.G. Morris, 576:Mar81-72
Wilson, N. Bernard-Lazare.*
205(FMLS):Jan80-96
Wilson, P.J. Man, the Promising Primate.*
R.J.P., 185:Apr82-596
639(VQR):Spring81-68
Wilson, R.A. Modern Book Collecting.*
T.A. Goldwasser, 517(PBSA):Jul-Sep81-
363
S. Wright, 569(SR):Winter81-xxvii
Wilson, R.A. and B. Hosokawa. East to
America.
C.D. Lummis, 285(JapQ):Jul-Sep81-430

Wiredu, K. Philosophy and an African
Culture.
  D. Emmet, 483:Apr81-269
  K. Nielsen, 49:Jul81-127
Wirth, J. La Jeune Fille et La Mort.
  C.D. Cuttler, 551(RenQ):Autumn80-452
Wirzberger, K-H. Von Cooper bis O'Neill.
  U. Riese, 654(WB):1/1981-175
"Wisden's Cricketers' Almanack 1982." (J.
  Woodcock, ed)
  T.D. Smith, 617(TLS):4Jun82-607
Wiseman, C. Beyond the Labyrinth.*
  W. Blissett, 178:Fall81-370
  P. Butter, 571(ScLJ):Summer80-118
Wiseman, C. The Upper Hand.
  R. Garfitt, 617(TLS):2Apr82-392
Wiseman, J. The Land of the Ancient Corin-
thians.*
  P. Roesch, 555:Vol54fasc1-156
Wiseman, T.P. Clio's Cosmetics.
  J. Briscoe, 123:Vol31No1-49
Wisenthal, J.L. - see Shaw, G.B.
Wisse, R.R. The Schlemiel as Modern Hero.
  J.S. Winkler, 573(SSF):Winter81-101
Wistrand, E. Caesar and Contemporary
Roman Society.*
  F. Hinard, 555:Vol54fasc2-385
Wistrand, M. Cicero Imperator.*
  J-L. Ferrary, 555:Vol54fasc2-376
  D.R. Shackleton Bailey, 122:Oct81-327
Wistrich, R. Leon Trotsky.
  D.M. Szonyi, 287:May81-23
de Wit, W. Auke Komter/architect.
  H. Searing, 576:May81-159
Witemeyer, H. George Eliot and the
Visual Arts.*
  D.P. Deneau, 577(SHR):Winter81-81
  A.S., 155:Summer81-112
  R.L. Stein, 131(CL):Summer81-292
Witheford, H. A Possible Order.
  C. Dunsford, 368:Sep81-364
Withey, L. Dearest Friend.*
  D. Mitchell, 617(TLS):23Apr82-454
Witt, H. - see Walther von der Vogelweide
Witt, J. William Henry Hunt (1790-1864).
  G. Reynolds, 617(TLS):25Jun82-688
Witt, P.N. and J.S. Rovner, eds. Spider
Communication.
  J. Cloudsley-Thompson, 617(TLS):
    11Jun82-630
Witte, J.F. Democracy, Authority, and
Alienation in Work.
  E.S., 185:Apr82-600
Wittenberg, J.B. Faulkner.*
  T.L. McHaney, 395(MFS):Winter80/81-654
  L.W. Wagner, 454:Fall81-90
Wittgenstein, L. Culture and Value. (G.H.
  von Wright, with H. Nyman, eds)
  R.L. Arrington, 569(SR):Fall81-cviii
  R.H., 185:Oct81-185
Wittgenstein, L. The Essential Wittgen-
stein. (G. Brand, ed)
  R.C-S., 543:Mar81-598
  M.U. Coyne, 258:Jun81-226
Wittgenstein, L. Grammaire philosophique.*
  (M-A. Lescourret, ed and trans)
  J. Bouveresse, 98:Dec80-1156
Wittgenstein, L. Remarks on Colour.*
  (G.E.M. Anscombe, ed)
  M. Yudkin, 482(PhR):Jan81-118

Wittgenstein, L. Remarks on the Philoso-
phy of Psychology.* (Vol 1 ed by G.E.M.
Anscombe and G.H. von Wright; Vol 2 ed
by G.H. von Wright and H. Nyman)
  I. Hacking, 453(NYRB):1Apr82-42
Wittig, S. Stylistic and Narrative Struc-
tures in the Middle English Romances.*
  J.M. Stitt, 292(JAF):Jan-Mar81-94
Wittkower, R. Idea and Image.
  P. Joannides, 90:Oct81-620
  S. Lang, 576:Mar81-63
Wittkowski, W. Georg Büchner.
  L.F. Helbig, 221(GQ):May81-352
Wittkowski, W. Henrich von Kleists
"Amphitryon."*
  M. Gelus, 406:Fall81-356
Wittlin, C. - see Eiximenis, F.
Wittner, L.S. American Intervention in
Greece, 1943-1949.
  C.M. Woodhouse, 617(TLS):20Aug82-908
Wittreich, J.A., Jr. Visionary Poetics.*
  A. Burnett, 447(N&Q):Aug80-368
  G. Campbell, 677(YES):Vol 11-255
  M. Evans, 541(RES):Aug81-329
  D. Haskin, 613:Jun81-226
  F.L. Huntley, 551(RenQ):Autumn80-490
  H. MacCallum, 627(UTQ):Spring81-314
Wittschier, H.W. Die italienische
Literatur.
  G. Costa, 545(RPh):Feb81-350
Wlosok, A., ed. Römischer Kaiserkult.
  J-C. Richard, 555:Vol54fasc1-195
Wobbe, R.A. Graham Greene.
  A.R. Redway, 78(BC):Spring81-108
  J.J. Riley, 395(MFS):Winter80/81-698
Wode, H. Learning a Second Language.
  C. Abdul-Ghani, 350:Dec82-951
Wodehouse, P.G. The Eighteen-Carat Kid
and Other Stories. (D.A. Jasen, ed)
  S. Pickering, 219(GaR):Fall81-678
Wodehouse, P.G. Wodehouse on Wodehouse.*
  D. Durrant, 364:Apr/May81-124
Woehr, R., F. Vergara and B. Mujica. Pasa-
porte.
  L.S. Sikka, 238:Sep81-492
  E.C. Torbert, 399(MLJ):Winter81-453
Wohl, H. The Paintings of Domenico Vene-
ziano, ca. 1410-1461.*
  F. Ames-Lewis, 59:Sep81-339
  K. Christiansen, 39:Jul81-66
  A.M. Schulz, 54:Jun81-334
Wohl, R. The Generation of 1914.
  A. Douglas, 639(VQR):Summer81-558
  E. Glass, 221(GQ):Mar81-239
  D. Latimer, 577(SHR):Spring81-185
Wohlfeil, R. Einführung in die Geschichte
der deutschen Reformation.
  R. Scribner, 617(TLS):28May82-587
Wohlgelernter, M. Frank O'Connor.*
  J. Kelly, 447(N&Q):Dec80-565
Wohmann, G. Einsamkeit.
  C. Russ, 617(TLS):4Jun82-622
Woiwode, L. Poppa John.*
  B. Buford, 617(TLS):29Oct82-1188
  K.C. O'Brien, 362:11Nov82-27
Wojahn, D. Icehouse Lights.
  A. Williamson, 441:100ct82-30
Wojowasito, S. A Kawi Lexicon. (R.F.
Mills, ed)
  J.M. Echols, 293(JASt):May81-657
Wojtyła, K. [Pope John Paul II] Collected
Poems.
  D. Crane, 617(TLS):5Nov82-1227

Woodbridge, S. and R. Montgomery. A Guide
to Architecture in Washington State.
    M.L. Peckham, 576:Dec81-342
Woodcock, G. The Canadians.
    W.N., 102(CanL):Summer80-180
Woodcock, G. The Mountain Road.
    L. Mathews, 628(UWR):Fall-Winter81-119
Woodcock, G. 100 Great Canadians.
    A. Lucas, 102(CanL):Autumn81-143
Woodcock, G. The World of Canadian Writ-
ing.
    W. Cude, 296(JCF):No31/32-218
    W.J. Keith, 627(UTQ):Summer81-157
    L. Shouldice, 102(CanL):Summer81-162
Woodcock, G. - see Hardy, T.
Woodcock, J. - see "Wisden's Cricketers'
    Almanack 1982"
Woodfield, A., ed. Thought and Object.
    J. McDowell, 617(TLS):16Jul82-774
Woodhouse, C.M. Something Ventured.
    P.L. Fermor, 617(TLS):27Aug82-918
Woodhouse, J.R. Baldesar Castiglione: A
Reassessment of "The Courtier."
    J. Bryce, 402(MLR):Jan81-211
    E. Saccone, 551(RenQ):Winter80-754
        205(FMLS):Oct80-382
Woodman, R. A King's Cutter.
    S. Altinel, 617(TLS):20Aug82-910
Woodruff, J., with K. Maxa. "This is Judy
Woodruff at the White House."
    T. Schwartz, 441:7Nov82-15
Woods, E.R. "Aye d'Avignon."*
    T.D. Hemming, 208(FS):Apr81-182
Woods, R.D. Reference Materials on Latin
America in English: The Humanities.
    M.H. Sable, 263(RIB):Vol31No2-287
    B.A. Shaw, 238:Dec81-645
Woods, R.D. and G. Alvarez-Altman. Span-
ish Surnames in the Southwestern United
States.*
    M.C. Peñuelas, 238:May81-326
Woods, S. Enter a Gentlewoman.
    N. Callendar, 441:10Oct82-22
Woods, S.M. Samuel Williams of Te Aute.
    J. Owens, 368:Sep81-372
Woodsmall, A. Contemporary Appliqued
Beadwork.
    R.L. Shep, 614:Winter81-23
Woodson, L. A Handbook of Modern Rhetori-
cal Terms.
    S. Watson, 599:Fall81-465
Woodward, A. Ezra Pound and "The Pisan
Cantos."*
    R. Bush, 141:Winter81-77
    B. Quinn, 27(AL):Nov81-552
    P. Smith, 150(DR):Summer81-356
Woodward, C.V. - see Chesnut, M.
Woodward, J.B. Ivan Bunin.*
    R. Bowie, 550(RusR):Apr81-225
    J.W. Connolly, 574(SEEJ):Spring81-101
    D.J. Richards, 402(MLR):Jul81-765
Woodward, J.B. Gogol's "Dead Souls."*
    K. Lantz, 104(CASS):Winter81-557
Woodward, K. At Last, The Real Distin-
guished Thing.*
    G.F. Butterick, 27(AL):Jan82-748
Woodward, K., ed. The Myths of Informa-
tion.
    T.J. Knight, 385(MQR):Fall82-688
Woolf, C. and J.M. Wilson, eds. Authors
Take Sides on the Falklands.
    A. Ryan, 362:9Sep82-22

Woolf, D. The Concept of the Text.
    M. Hollington, 67:May81-104
Woolf, H., ed. Some Strangeness in the
Proportion.
    T. Ferris, 441:26Sep82-18
Woolf, L. The Wise Virgins.
    E.C. Bufkin, 219(GaR):Spring81-190
Woolf, V. The Diary of Virginia Woolf.*
(Vol 2) (A.O. Bell, with A. McNeillie,
eds)
    J. Giltrow, 648(WCR):Jun80-50
Woolf, V. The Diary of Virginia Woolf.*
(Vol 3) (A.O. Bell, with A. McNeillie,
eds)
    S. Disbrow, 502(PrS):Spring-Summer81-
        313
    S. Hynes, 569(SR):Winter81-125
    G. Johnson, 584(SWR):Winter81-107
Woolf, V. The Diary of Virginia Woolf.
(Vol 4) (A.O. Bell, with A. McNeillie,
eds)
    P-L. Adams, 61:Aug82-94
    M. Drabble, 362:11Mar82-20
    R. Kiely, 441:11Jul82-3
    P. Levy, 617(TLS):25Jun82-701
        442(NY):6Sep82-107
Woolf, V. The Letters of Virginia Woolf.*
(Vol 4) (N. Nicolson and J. Trautmann,
eds)
    J. Giltrow, 648(WCR):Jun80-50
Woolf, V. The Letters of Virginia Woolf.*
(Vol 5) (British title: The Sickle Side
of the Moon.) (N. Nicolson and J. Traut-
mann, eds)
    S. Hynes, 569(SR):Winter81-125
Woolf, V. The London Scene.
    P.N. Furbank, 362:11Mar82-21
Woolf, V. Virginia Woolf's "Melymbrosia."
(L.A. De Salvo, ed)
    J. Haule, 659(ConL):Winter82-100
Woollcott, A. The Dramatic Criticism of
Alexander Woollcott. (M.U. Burns, ed)
    M.B., 214:Vol 10No37-119
Woolley, P., ed. The Wild and Woolley
Comix Book.
    B. Andrews, 71(ALS):May81-133
Woolrich, C. The Black Curtain. The
Black Angel. The Black Path of Fear.
    N. Callendar, 441:28Nov82-20
Woolrych, A. Commonwealth to Protectorate.
    B. Worden, 617(TLS):30Apr82-480
Wooster, R.A. and R.A. Calvert, eds.
Texas Vistas.
    W. Gard, 584(SWR):Winter81-vi
Woozley, A.D. Law and Obedience.*
    R. Kraut, 185:Jul81-651
    C.C.W. Taylor, 393(Mind):Oct81-608
    T.G.W., 543:Dec80-403
Worcester, D. The Chisholm Trail.
    L. Milazzo, 584(SWR):Autumn81-413
Worcester, D.E. The Apaches.*
    S. Steiner, 649(WAL):Summer81-164
Wordsworth, W. Benjamin the Waggoner.
(P.F. Betz, ed)
    R. Ashton, 617(TLS):15Jan82-57
    L. Goldstein, 385(MQR):Summer82-527
Wordsworth, W. Home at Grasmere.* (B.
Darlington, ed)
    R. Sharrock, 402(MLR):Jan81-167
Wordsworth, W. and D. The Letters of Wil-
liam and Dorothy Wordsworth. (2nd ed)
(Vol 5, Pt 2) (E. de Selincourt, ed)
    B. Darlington, 661(WC):Summer81-146

Wyatt, T. Sir Thomas Wyatt: The Complete
Poems.* (R.A. Rebholz, ed)
    H. Dubrow, 161(DUJ):Dec80-110
    H.A. Mason, 97(CQ):Vol 10No3-219
Wyatt, W. The Secret of the Sierra Madre.
    R.B. Olafson, 649(WAL):Summer81-153
Wyatt-Brown, B. Southern Honor.
    J.B., 231:Aug82-76
    C.V. Woodward, 453(NYRB):18Nov82-26
Wycherley, W. The Plays of William Wycher-
ley.* (A. Friedman, ed)
    W. Myers, 541(RES):Aug81-332
Wymer, J. The Palaeolithic Age.
    A.M. Ap Simon, 617(TLS):26Nov82-1323
Wynand, D. One Cook, Once Dreaming.
    C. MacCulloch, 526:Autumn81-165
Wynar, L.R. and L. Buttlar. Guide to
Ethnic Museums, Libraries, and Archives
in the United States.*
    R.L. Welsch, 292(JAF):Jan-Mar81-126
Wynne, J. Crime Wave.
    J. Uglow, 617(TLS):4Jun82-622
Wyse, L. The Granddaughter.
    C. See, 441:14Feb82-14
Wyss, U. Die wilde Philologie.
    S. Clausing, 406:Winter81-460
    O. Ehrismann, 680(ZDP):Band100Heft3-
    451
    U-K. Ketelsen, 221(GQ):May81-355
    L. Zgusta, 301(JEGP):Jan81-98
Wytrwal, J.A. Behold! the Polish Ameri-
cans.
    F. Renkiewicz, 497(PolR):Vol26No3-104
Wytwycky, B. The Other Holocaust.
    A. Rosenberg and A. Bardosh, 497(PolR):
    Vol26No3-88

Xénophon. Cyropédie. (Vol 3) (É. Delebecque, ed)
    R.W., 555:Vol54fasc1-161
Xénophon. De l'Art équestre. (É. Delebecque, ed and trans)
    P. Louis, 555:Vol54fasc1-161

"Y a rien là!"
    A. Wagner, 108:Spring81-124
Yacopino, F. Threadlines Pakistan.
    R.L. Shep, 614:Fall81-21
Yadav, C.S. Land Use in Big Cities.
    A.D. King, 293(JASt):Feb81-417
Yagi, K. A Japanese Touch for Your Home.
    R.L. Shep, 614:Fall82-18
Yaguello, M. Alice au pays du langage.
    A. Compagnon, 208(FS):Oct81-501
Yandell, C.M. - see Pontus de Tyard
Yanov, A. The Origins of Autocracy.
    A.B. Ulam, 617(TLS):8Oct82-1111
Yanowitch, M., ed. Soviet Work Attitudes.
    M. Matthews, 575(SEER):Jan81-142
Yapp, B. Birds in Medieval Manuscripts.
    R. O'Hanlon, 617(TLS):21May82-564
Yashpal. Amita.*
    R. Jha, 314:Summer-Fall81-219
Yates, D. Bureaucratic Democracy.
    J. Brademas, 441:28Nov82-10
Yates, D.A., ed. Espejos.
    R.H. Gilmore, 399(MLJ):Spring81-103
    T. Murad, 238:Sep81-490
Yates, F.A. Lull and Bruno.
    R. Briggs, 617(TLS):27Aug82-931

Yates, F.A. The Occult Philosophy in the
Elizabethan Age.
    R.D., 543:Mar81-626
    L.B. Smith, 570(SQ):Spring81-106
    R.B. Waddington, 551(RenQ):Winter80-
    796
Yau, J. The Sleepless Night of Eugene
Delacroix.
    P. Schjeldahl, 472:Spring/Summer81-284
"The Yearbook of English Studies."* (Vol
8) (G.K. Hunter and C.J. Rawson, eds)
    J.R. Watson, 161(DUJ):Jun81-259
"The Yearbook of English Studies."* (Vol
9) (G.K. Hunter and C.J. Rawson, eds)
    G. Bas, 189(EA):Apr-Jun81-208
    P. Thomson, 402(MLR):Apr81-455
    J.R. Watson, 161(DUJ):Jun81-259
"Yearbook on International Communist
Affairs, 1980." (R.F. Staar, ed)
    R.E. Kanet, 550(RusR):Jan81-76
Yeats, W.B., ed. Representative Irish
Tales.*
    R.A. Cave, 541(RES):Nov81-501
Yeats, W.B. Uncollected Prose by W.B.
Yeats. (Vol 2) (J.P. Frayne and C.
Johnson, eds)
    E. Mackenzie, 447(N&Q):Oct80-471
Yeats, W.B. The Writing of "The Player
Queen."* (C.B. Bradford, ed)
    V.B. Rohan, 130:Spring81-76
Yeazell, R.B. - see James, A.
Yehoshua, A.B. Between Right and Right.
    J. Shatzmiller, 287:Nov81-15
Yeni-Komshian, G.H., J.F. Kavanagh and C.A.
Ferguson, eds. Child Phonology.
    P.A. Keating, 350:Sep82-719
Yergin, D. and M. Hillenbrand, eds.
Global Insecurity.
    K.E. Meyer, 441:15Aug82-8
Yerkes, D. Two Versions of Waerferth's
Translation of Gregory's Dialogues.*
    E.A. Ebbinghaus, 215(GL):Spring81-30
Yerkes, J. The Christology of Hegel.
    R.F. Brown, 258:Mar81-99
    M. Westphal, 125:Summer81-425
Yevtushenko, Y. Invisible Threads.*
    A. Ross, 364:Feb82-101
Yndurάin, D. - see de Quevedo, F.
Yoccoz, D. - see Stanislavski, C.
Yochelson, E.L., ed. The Scientific Ideas
of G.K. Gilbert.
    C. Albritton, 584(SWR):Spring81-225
Yoder, R.A. Emerson and the Orphic Poet
in America.*
    J.S. Martin, 106:Fall81-209
Yoffee, N. The Economic Role of the Crown
in the Old Babylonian Period.
    D. Charpin, 318(JAOS):Oct/Dec80-461
York, A. In This House There Are No
Lizards.
    G. McWhirter, 102(CanL):Autumn81-160
Yorke, M. Devil's Work.
    T.J. Binyon, 617(TLS):23Jul82-807
Yorke, M. Eric Gill.*
    B. Crutchley, 324:Nov82-826
    A. Ross, 364:Mar82-9
Yoshifumi Ueda - see Shinran
Young, A. William Cumin.
    M.R. Foster, 161(DUJ):Dec80-90
Young, A. Dada and After.
    B. Bergonzi, 617(TLS):19Feb82-190
Young, A. The Surgeon's Knot.
    S. Altinel, 617(TLS):25Jun82-702

Zamparelli, T.L. The Theater of Claude Billard.*
  C.N. Smith, 208(FS):Jul81-327
Zangrando, R.L. The NAACP Crusade Against Lynching, 1909-1950.
  W.D. Smith, 9(AlaR):Jul81-238
de Zapata, C.C. and L. Johnson. Detrás de la reja.
  S. Menton, 238:Dec81-643
Zapién, T.H. - see under Herrera Zapién, T.
Zaranka, W., ed. The Brand-X Anthology of Poetry.
  P-L. Adams, 61:Feb82-87
Zaranka, W. A Mirror Driven Through Nature.
  C. Inez, 472:Fall/Winter81-231
Zarbaugh, J.R. Jerry's Two Needle Pyramid.
  R.L. Shep, 614:Winter82-18
Zarnecki, G. Studies in Romanesque Sculpture.
  G. Henderson, 90:Mar81-169
Zatočnik, D. Slovo [e] Molenie. (M. Colucci and A. Danti, eds)
  G. Brogi-Bercoff, 688(ZSP):Band42Heft1-187
Zavarzadeh, M. The Mythopoeic Reality.*
  R. Vanderauwera, 494:Spring80-187
Zayas-Bazán, E. and M.L. Suárez. De aquí y de allá.
  J.E. Keller, 238:May81-327
Zdenek, J.W., ed. The World of Nature in the Works of Federico García Lorca.
  D. Harris, 86(BHS):Jul81-271
van der Zee, H. The Hunger Winter.
  G. Best, 617(TLS):15Oct82-1134
Zehetner, L.G. Bairisch.*
  H. Fischer, 680(ZDP):Band99Heft3-467
Zeidler, H. Das "français fondamental (1er degré Entstehung)," linguistische analyse und fremdsprachendidaktischer standort.
  C. Muller, 209(FM):Jul81-266
El-Zein, A.H. The Sacred Meadows.
  P. Caplan, 69:Vol50No2-216
Zeisel, J. Inquiry by Design.
  G. Hack, 505:Aug81-110
Zeitlin, S.J., A.J. Kotkin and H.C. Baker, eds. A Celebration of American Family Folklore.
  K. Simon, 441:19Dec82-10
"Zeitschrift für celtische Philologie." (Band 35-37)
  B. Ó Cuív, 112:Vol 14-178
Zelazny, R. Eye of Cat.
  G. Jonas, 441:19Dec82-13
Zeldin, J. Nikolai Gogol's Quest for Beauty.
  J.E. Falen, 399(MLJ):Winter81-444
  K. Lantz, 104(CASS):Winter81-557
Zeldin, T. France 1848-1945: Taste and Corruption.
  M.D. Biddiss, 208(FS):Oct81-498
Zelinsky, B., ed. Der russische Roman.*
  A. McMillin, 575(SEER):Jan81-156
Zelinzer, V.R. Morals and Markets.
  T.R.M., 185:Apr81-535
Zell, G. Information und Wirtschaftslenkung in der USSR.
  P. Jonas, 550(RusR):Oct81-454
Zell, H. - see "African Books in Print"
Zelver, P. A Man of Middle Age and Twelve Stories.*
  S. Pinsker, 573(SSF):Summer81-338

Zelvin, E. I am the Daughter.
  C. Inez, 472:Fall/Winter81-231
Zeman, H., ed. Die Österreichische Literatur.
  J. Strelka, 680(ZDP):Band100Heft2-291
Zemskaja, E.A. Russkaja razgovornaja reč'.
  S. Lubensky, 574(SEEJ):Winter81-101
Zenk, G.K. Project SEARCH.
  W.W. Pflug, 14:Spring80-213
von Zesen, P. Sämtliche Werke. (Vol 1, Pt 1) (F. van Ingen, ed)
  E.A. Philippson, 301(JEGP):Oct81-608
Zetterberg, S. Suomi ja Viro: 1917-1919, Poliittiset suhteet syksystä 1917 reunavaltiopolitiikan alkuun.
  D. Kirby, 575(SEER):Apr81-272
Zettersten, A., ed. Waldere.*
  G. Cubbin, 382(MAE):1981/1-195
  T.A. Shippey, 161(DUJ):Jun81-248
Zettler, H.G., ed. -Ologies & -Isms.*
  M. Dilkes, 35(AS):Summer81-141
Zetzel, J.E.G. Latin Textual Criticism in Antiquity.
  W.S. Anderson, 124:May-Jun82-319
Zevi, B. The Modern Language of Architecture.
  C. Jameson, 576:Mar81-80
Zgusta, L., ed. Theory and Method in Lexicography.
  Y. Malkiel, 350:Mar81-251
Zguta, R. Russian Minstrels.*
  T.A. Greenan, 402(MLR):Jan81-252
  N.K. Moyle, 292(JAF):Jan-Mar81-117
Zhang Jing and Zhang Zhi-gong. A New Grammar of Contemporary Chinese. [in Chinese]
  Wu Qi-zhu, 361:Feb-Mar81-255
Zhang Mingtao and others. The Roof of the World.
  D.J.R. Bruckner, 441:12Dec82-13
Zhuravlev, A.P. Foneticheskoe znachenie.
  I.T. Molnár and G. Székely, 567:Vol134No3/4-375
Zicàri, M. Scritti Catulliani.* (P. Parroni, ed)
  D. Konstan, 122:Oct81-323
Ziegler, P. Diana Cooper.*
  M. Panter-Downes, 442(NY):27Sep82-138
  F. Taliaferro, 441:18Apr82-16
Ziff, L. Literary Democracy.*
  V. Shetley, 249(HudR):Winter81/82-622
  H.N. Smith, 445(NCF):Mar82-484
Zijderveld, A.C. On Clichés.
  C. Slater, 541(RES):Nov81-499
Zikmund, H., ed and trans. Die russische Sprache in der heutigen Welt.
  C. Fleckenstein, 682(ZPSK):Band33Heft2-274
Zilli, L. - see du Ryer, P.
Zilliacus, C. Beckett and Broadcasting.*
  A.P. Frank, 38:Band99Heft1/2-266
Zilliacus, H. and others, eds. Corpus Papyrorum Raineri. (Vol 7)
  J.D. Thomas, 123:Vol131No2-265
Zilyns'kyj, I. A Phonetic Description of the Ukrainian Language.* (W.T. Zyla and W.M. Aycock, eds and trans)
  M.S. Flier, 350:Sep81-775
Zima, P.V. Literatuur en maatschappij.
  J. den Ouden, 204(FdL):Dec81-347
Ziman, J. Puzzles, Problems and Enigmas.
  J. Agassi, 617(TLS):25Jun82-697

388

Zweig, S. The Royal Game and other
  Stories.*
    S. Rushdie, 441:24Jan82-7
    S. Spender, 453(NYRB):18Mar82-7
Zwerenz, G. Kurt Tucholsky.
    H. Mörchen, 680(ZDP):Band99Heft2-298
Zwettler, M.J. The Oral Tradition of
  Arabic Poetry.
    I. Shahid, 318(JAOS):Jan/Mar80-31
Zwilgmeyer, F. Stufen der Bewusstseinser-
  weiterung bei Goethe.
    K.J. Fink, 133:Band14Heft1-81

Zydatiss, W. Tempus und Aspekt im Englis-
  chunterricht.
    B. Hansen, 682(ZPSK):Band33Heft6-774
Zyla, W.T., ed. Tvorčist' Jara Slavutyča/
  The Poetry of Yar Slavutych.
    J. Sirka, 688(ZSP):Band42Heft2-433
Zyla, W.T. and W.M. Aycock - see Zilyns'-
  kyj, I.
Zytaruk, G.J. and J.T. Boulton - see Law-
  rence, D.H.

WITHDRAWAL